3 —

Fourth Edition

# Mathematics for Management and Finance

Stephen P. Shao, Ph. D.

Professor of Management Information Systems
Old Dominion University

M33

*Published by*

**SOUTH-WESTERN PUBLISHING CO.**

CINCINNATI    WEST CHICAGO, ILL.    DALLAS    PELHAM MANOR, N.Y.    PALO ALTO, CALIF.

ISBN: 0–538–13330–9

Library of Congress  Catalog
Card Number: 78–60115




2345678D7654321
Printed in the United States of America

# Preface

The fourth edition of *Mathematics for Management and Finance* has been updated and reorganized. Many illustrations and problems have been added. New material, such as higher interest rates in the Appendix and the metric system, makes this book more flexible than the former in meeting various curricular demands.

This fourth edition, like the three previous editions, is designed for the first course in mathematics for students of business administration. Students who have had little or perhaps no algebra in high school, but who have determination in learning, will find that this text is suitable to their capacities. Those who have a strong background in algebra will find challenging material throughout the text. After the completion of this course, the student should be prepared to continue with more advanced work in subjects involving quantitative analysis, such as accounting, statistics, investments, and insurance. This leads the author to believe that for a student of business administration, this text is more adequate and practical than a one-year course in mathematical analysis or college algebra. The latter courses traditionally emphasize theoretical mathematics, which is less pertinent to the foreseeable needs of a business student.

This edition is divided into four parts. Part One discusses basic and modern mathematics. It presents fundamental arithmetic and algebraic operations, beginning with elementary concepts. Students who have not had sufficient mathematics in high school will thus have an opportunity to strengthen their background. Furthermore, sufficient material has been provided for those students who may have had mathematics some time ago but now need a review in beginning a study of the subject of mathematics for management and finance.

Part Two discusses mathematics in business management. The topics included in this part represent problem areas found in almost every type of business enterprise. These topics are fundamental statistical methods, common percentage problems, simple interest, and bank discount. Part Three discusses the basic topics of the mathematics of long-term investment—compound interest and annuities. Part Four discusses the applications of the mathematics of compound interest and annuity to debt extinction, bonds, depreciation, depletion, perpetuity, capitalization, life annuities, and life insurance.

Experience shows that when students readily know the principles involved in each type of calculation, they usually become better prepared for problem solving and for more advanced work. Throughout this text, the basic principle for each topic in financial problems is illustrated in detail. Special terms are clearly defined and explained before they are applied. Diagrams are frequently employed as aids to illustrate the more complex examples. After the principles have been illustrated, formulas are often used to facilitate computation. However, the number of formulas has been kept to a minimum, and the formulas are presented in a simple manner. (A list of the basic formulas is provided on page 777.) Proofs for the more complicated formulas are given in footnotes to the text where they are presented.

Enough number problems (drills) are placed at the beginning of each exercise so that students can quickly learn the mechanics of the new symbols and terms in each new process. In the statement problems that follow, students have the opportunity to exercise their reasoning ability. In addition, ample review problems are provided at the end of certain chapters to give students an opportunity to solve problems independently without referring to the illustrations in the individual sections of the text.

The problems in each exercise are arranged so that either all odd-numbered or all even-numbered problems can be assigned by the instructor without fear of omitting the material that has been illustrated in the examples. Answers to the odd-numbered problems are placed at the end of the book. Detailed solutions to the odd-numbered and even-numbered problems are given in the instructor's manual.

The material presented in this text is sufficient for a one-year course, offered either in two semesters or in three quarters. However, if there is not sufficient time to cover all material, those sections and problems which have been starred may be omitted without interrupting the continuity of the text organization. The text may also be used as a one-semester course under either of the following suggestions:

1. To emphasize general management and financial problems—Chapters 6 through 13 and Chapters 15 and 16.
2. To emphasize investment problems—Chapters 9 through 13 and Chapters 15 through 19.

Each of the two suggestions may easily be adjusted for either a one-quarter or a two-quarter course. More detailed assignment suggestions are given in the instructor's manual.

The tables included in the Appendix have been designed primarily for this textbook. However, coverage in the tables is complete enough for most practical business problems involving logarithms, compound interest, annuities, and life insurance. The tables of logarithms include six-place and seven-place mantissas.

The compound interest and annuity tables include the forty most commonly used periodic interest rates on the investment market today. The insurance mortality table is the latest, the Commissioners 1958 Standard Ordinary Table of Mortality. Other special features of the tables are summarized in the preface to the tables.

I am indebted to my colleagues of the School of Business Administration and the Department of Mathematical and Computing Sciences of Old Dominion University for their encouragement and for their suggestions made from reading and teaching the first three editions of this book. Above all, I am deeply grateful to my late wife, Betty Outen Shao, for her expert services in editing the manuscript of the first edition of this book.

Stephen Pinyee Shao
Virginia Beach, Va.

# Contents

**Part Four     MATHEMATICS IN INVESTMENT—APPLICATIONS**

**Appendix A   TABLES**

## Appendix B  FORMULAS

# Part One

**BASIC AND MODERN MATHEMATICS**

# Chapter 1

# Fundamental Arithmetic Operations

Arithmetic operations are basic to the study of mathematics for management and finance. This text thus begins with the discussion of fundamental arithmetic operations. There are four fundamental operations in arithmetic: *addition, subtraction, multiplication,* and *division.* In general, students not only should know how to perform these operations rapidly but also should learn how to check the accuracy of the results of the operations.

This chapter reviews the fundamental operations concerning whole numbers (integers), decimal numbers, and fractions. However, emphasis is placed on the topic of fractions. Fractional operations are relatively more complicated in calculation and thus require more attention in illustrations. Also, commonly used methods of checking answers are included in this chapter.

## 1.1 BASIC ASPECTS OF COMMON FRACTIONS

## A. Terminology

A fraction has two *terms:* the *numerator,* which is written above a line, and the *denominator,* which is written below the line. Thus, $\frac{2}{5}$ is a fraction; 2 is the numerator and 5 is the denominator. The numbers 2 and 5 are the terms of the fraction. The denominator 5 represents the number of equal parts into which the whole of a thing has been divided. The numerator shows the number of equal parts that have been taken out of the whole. If the whole is an apple, $\frac{2}{5}$ of the apple is 2 parts of the apple which has been divided into 5 equal parts.

The three types of common fraction are:

*Proper Fraction*  The numerator is less than the denominator, such as $\frac{1}{3}$ and $\frac{15}{21}$.

*Improper Fraction*    The numerator is equal to or greater than the denominator, such as $\frac{7}{7}$, $\frac{5}{3}$, and $\frac{17}{6}$.

*Complex Fraction*    One or more fractions are found in either the numerator or denominator, or in both. The line which separates the numerator from the denominator is usually longer than the lines which are in the numerator or the denominator, such as

$$\frac{\frac{3}{5}}{11}, \quad \frac{9}{\frac{2}{5}}, \quad \frac{\frac{2}{3}}{\frac{15}{21}}.$$

A complex fraction may be converted to a simple form by dividing the numerator by the denominator. For example, $\dfrac{\frac{3}{5}}{11}$ may be written as $\frac{3}{5} \div 11$. When the division is complete, the answer is $\frac{3}{55}$, a proper fraction. (See Example 8, Section 1.5.)

When a number consists of a whole number and a fraction, it is called a *mixed number*. Thus, a mixed number is the sum of a whole number and a fraction, such as the sum of 3 and $\frac{1}{4}$ being written as $3\frac{1}{4}$. A mixed number may be expressed as an improper fraction, such as $3\frac{1}{4}$ being written as $\frac{13}{4}$ because

$$3\frac{1}{4} = \frac{(3 \times 4) + 1}{4} = \frac{13}{4}.$$

An improper fraction, such as $\frac{17}{6}$, may be expressed as a mixed number by writing it as $2\frac{5}{6}$.

## B. Reducing (or Converting) Fractions to Higher and Lower Terms

The terms of a fraction may be converted to either higher or lower terms without changing the value of the fraction. The process of converting a fraction in this manner is called *reduction*. Thus, the word "reduction" (or reduce) as used in this sense does not mean to reduce a fraction to a smaller or a lower value. In division, multiplying or dividing both the dividend and divisor by the *same number* does not affect the quotient. For example, $6 \div 3 = 2$ and $(6 \times 10) \div (3 \times 10) = 2$; or $(6 \div 3) \div (3 \div 3) = 2$. The principle that multiplying or dividing both the numerator and the denominator by the same number, other than zero, does not affect the value of the fraction is shown in the following examples.

**Example 1**    Reduce (or convert) $\frac{2}{3}$ to higher terms.

$$\frac{2}{3} = \frac{2 \times 4}{3 \times 4} = \frac{8}{12}; \qquad\qquad \frac{8}{12} = \frac{8 \times 3}{12 \times 3} = \frac{24}{36}$$

There is an unlimited number of higher terms of $\frac{2}{3}$.

**Example 2**     Reduce $\frac{84}{315}$ to lower terms.

$$\frac{84}{315} = \frac{84 \div 3}{315 \div 3} = \frac{28}{105}; \qquad \frac{28}{105} = \frac{28 \div 7}{105 \div 7} = \frac{4}{15}$$

In Example 2, 3 is the common divisor of 84 and 315; 7 is the common divisor of 28 and 105; and there is no common divisor for the terms of the fraction $\frac{4}{15}$. When the numerator and the denominator have no common divisor, the fraction has been reduced to its *simplest form,* also called *lowest terms.* The best way to reduce a fraction to its *lowest terms* is to divide both the numerator and the denominator by their *greatest common divisor.* In Example 2, the product of the two common divisors (3 and 7) equals 21, which is the greatest common divisor of 84 and 315; that is,

$$\frac{84}{315} = \frac{84 \div 21}{315 \div 21} = \frac{4}{15}.$$

# C. Method of Finding the Greatest Common Divisor (G.C.D.)

When the *greatest common divisor* (g.c.d.), also called the *highest common factor,* of the numerator and denominator is not apparent, the following procedure is recommended to find the desirable divisor:

**Step (1)**     Divide the larger number by the smaller number.

**Step (2)**     If there is a remainder in Step (1), divide the smaller number by the remainder.

**Step (3)**     If there is a remainder in Step (2), divide the remainder in Step (1) by the remainder in Step (2).

**Step (4)**     Continue dividing each remainder by its succeeding remainder until there is no remainder (0). The last divisor is the greatest common divisor.

**Example 3**     Find the g.c.d. of 84 and 315.

Here 315 is larger than 84. Thus,

$$\begin{array}{r} 3 \\ 84\overline{)315} \end{array} \ \dots\dots\dots\dots\dots \text{ Step (1)}$$
$$\begin{array}{r} 252 \\ \hline 63 \end{array} \ \begin{array}{r} 1 \\ \overline{)84} \end{array} \ \dots\dots\dots\dots \text{ Step (2)}$$
$$\begin{array}{r} 63 \\ \hline 21 \end{array} \ \begin{array}{r} 3 \\ \overline{)63} \end{array} \ \dots\dots\dots \text{ Steps (3) and (4)}$$

Last divisor — The g.c.d. is 21.     $\dfrac{63}{0}$ (Remainder)

**Example 4**     Find the g.c.d. of 170 and 9.

$$
\begin{array}{r}
18 \\
9\overline{)170} \\
9 \\
\hline
80 \\
72 \\
\hline
8
\end{array}
\quad
\begin{array}{r}
1 \\
8\overline{)9} \\
8 \\
\hline
1
\end{array}
$$

Last divisor     $1\overline{)8}$
The g.c.d. is 1.     $\dfrac{8}{0}$

In general, the g.c.d of two or more numbers is the product of all the prime factors *common* to these numbers. A *prime factor* is a number consisting of no other factors but itself and 1, such as 1, 2, 3, 5, 7, and 11. All other integers (whole numbers), called *composite numbers,* may consist of two or more prime factors. Thus, the product of all the prime factors of a number is the number itself. For example, the prime factors of the composite number 6 are 2 and 3, and the product of 2 and 3 is 6.

**Example 5**    Find the g.c.d. of 4, 16, 24, 28, 36.

Since 4 consists of two prime factors, 2 and 2, it may be written: $4 = 2 \times 2$. Hence, the numbers above may be written by their respective prime factors as follows:

$4 = 2 \times 2$
$16 = 2 \times 2 \times 2 \times 2$
$24 = 2 \times 2 \times 2 \times 3$
$28 = 2 \times 2 \times 7$
$36 = 2 \times 2 \times 3 \times 3$

The prime factors common to all of the five numbers are 2 and 2; therefore, the g.c.d. is $2 \times 2 = 4$.

The work is usually done by division and can be conveniently arranged as follows:

$$
\begin{array}{r}
2\overline{)4,\ 16,\ 24,\ 28,\ 36} \\
2\overline{)2,\ \ \ 8,\ 12,\ 14,\ 18} \\
\hline
1,\ \ \ 4,\ \ \ 6,\ \ \ 7,\ \ \ 9
\end{array}
$$

The common divisors of the five numbers are 2 and 2; thus, the g.c.d. is $2 \times 2 = 4$.

Note that the method of finding a g.c.d. of more than two numbers is useful in reducing the terms of a ratio to the lowest terms, such as the ratio having five terms $4:16:24:28:36 = \frac{4}{4}:\frac{16}{4}:\frac{24}{4}:\frac{28}{4}:\frac{36}{4} = 1:4:6:7:9$. A more complete discussion on the subject of ratios is presented in Chapter 7.

# D. Method of Finding the Least Common Multiple (L.C.M.)

A multiple of a given number is the product of that number and any multiplier. For example, 18 is a multiple of the given number 6 since 18 is the product of 6 and the multiplier 3. Also, 6 and 12 are multiples of 6 since

$$6 \times 1 = 6$$
$$6 \times 2 = 12$$

A common multiple of a group of numbers is a number which is a multiple of each of the numbers in the group. For example, 18 is a common multiple of 18, 9, 6, 3, 2, and 1 since

$$18 \times 1 = 18$$
$$9 \times 2 = 18$$
$$6 \times 3 = 18$$

Every integer is a multiple of 1, such as $6 \times 1 = 6$ and $18 \times 1 = 18$ as illustrated above.

The following methods may be used to find the least common multiple (l.c.m.) of a group of numbers:

**Method A**    When there is no common factor in a group of numbers, the product of the numbers in the group is the l.c.m. Thus,

6 is the l.c.m. of 2 and 3, since $2 \times 3 = 6$
33 is the l.c.m. of 3 and 11, since $3 \times 11 = 33$
70 is the l.c.m. of 2, 5, and 7, since $2 \times 5 \times 7 = 70$

There is no common factor in the group of numbers 2 and 3, or 3 and 11, or 2, 5, and 7.

**Method B**    When there are common factors in a group of numbers, the l.c.m. can be determined by division as shown below. In each step of the division, at least *two* of the numbers are divided by their common *prime* factor. The product of the common prime factors and the final quotients is the l.c.m.

**Example 6**    Find the l.c.m. of 12, 30, and 56.

$$
\begin{array}{r}
2\overline{)12,\ 30,\ 56} \\
2\overline{)\ \ 6,\ 15,\ 28} \\
3\overline{)\ \ 3,\ 15,\ 14} \\
\hline
\ \ 1,\ \ 5,\ 14
\end{array}
$$

The l.c.m. is $2 \times 2 \times 3 \times 1 \times 5 \times 14 = 840$

**Note:**    The first divisor 2 is the common prime factor to all numbers. However, the second divisor 2 is the common prime factor to 6 and 28 only; the number 15 is not divisible by 2 and remains unchanged. The divisor 3 is the prime factor to 3 and 15 only; the number 14 is not divisible by 3 and remains unchanged.

If a divisor is not a common prime factor, there is danger of obtaining a common multiple which is not the *least* common multiple, such as the result in the following division:

$$6)\underline{12, \ 30, \ 56}$$
$$2)\underline{\ 2, \ \ 5, \ 56}$$
$$\ \ 1, \ \ 5, \ 28$$

$6 \times 2 \times 1 \times 5 \times 28 = 1,680$, which is not the l.c.m. Here, the divisor 6 is not a prime factor since $6 = 2 \times 3$.

When the l.c.m. of a set of numbers is to be found, any number which is a factor of others in the set may be omitted in the computation. For example, the l.c.m. of numbers 6, 12, 30, and 56 should be the same as the l.c.m. of numbers 12, 30, and 56, because number 6 is a factor of 12 and 30. Thus, the l.c.m. of 6, 12, 30, and 56 is also 840.

Note carefully the distinction between the method used in finding the g.c.d. and the method for finding the l.c.m. when the division method is used. The g.c.d. for a group of numbers is found by multiplying the prime factors which are divisible into *all* of the numbers in the group; whereas, the l.c.m. is found by multiplying the prime factors, which are divisible into at least two of the numbers in each step, *and* the quotients of the division. In the preceding example, 2 (the first divisor common to *all* three numbers) is the g.c.d. of the group of numbers 12, 30, and 56; whereas, the l.c.m. is 840. The g.c.d. is generally used for reducing a fraction to its lowest terms, whereas the l.c.m. is used for finding the lowest common denominator for a group of fractions.

## E. Method of Finding the Lowest Common Denominator (L.C.D.)

In order to compare one fraction with other fractions, there is a need to find a *common denominator* for all of the fractions.

**Example 7**  Compare the fractions $\frac{2}{3}$ and $\frac{7}{11}$. Which is larger?

By visual inspection, it is difficult to know which one of the two fractions is larger. However, when the two fractions are reduced to the point that they have a common denominator, the comparison becomes a simple operation.

$$\frac{2}{3} = \frac{2 \times 11}{3 \times 11} = \frac{22}{33} \qquad\qquad \frac{7}{11} = \frac{7 \times 3}{11 \times 3} = \frac{21}{33}$$

Since $\frac{22}{33}$ is larger than $\frac{21}{33}$, the fraction $\frac{2}{3}$ is found to be the larger one.

However, in the above example, there are an unlimited number of common denominators of the fractions $\frac{2}{3}$ and $\frac{7}{11}$, such as 33, $33 \times 2$ or 66, and $33 \times 3$ or 99; but 33 is the lowest and the simplest one. In adding and subtracting fractions, the work is greatly simplified if the *lowest common denominator* is used.

The lowest common denominator (l.c.d.) of a group of fractions is the *least common multiple* (l.c.m.) of the denominators of the fractions.

**Example 8**    Reduce the fractions $\frac{5}{12}$, $\frac{13}{30}$, and $\frac{23}{56}$ to fractions with a l.c.d. Then arrange them in order beginning with the largest.

The l.c.m. of the *denominators* of the three fractions is 840 (see Example 6), or the l.c.d. of the three *fractions* is 840. When the denominator of a fraction is multiplied by a number, the numerator must also be multiplied by the same number if the value of the fraction is to stay unchanged.

$$\text{Since} \quad 840 \div 12 = 70, \quad \text{then} \quad \frac{5}{12} = \frac{5 \times 70}{12 \times 70} = \frac{350}{840}$$

$$840 \div 30 = 28, \qquad \frac{13}{30} = \frac{13 \times 28}{30 \times 28} = \frac{364}{840}$$

$$840 \div 56 = 15, \qquad \frac{23}{56} = \frac{23 \times 15}{56 \times 15} = \frac{345}{840}$$

The order of the three fractions is as follows:

$$\frac{13}{30}, \frac{5}{12}, \frac{23}{56}.$$

## EXERCISE 1–1

### Reference: Section 1.1

**A.** *Change the following mixed numbers to improper fractions:*

**1.** $1\frac{1}{3}$    **4.** $6\frac{4}{15}$    **7.** $9\frac{3}{5}$    **10.** $15\frac{23}{81}$

**2.** $4\frac{2}{5}$    **5.** $2\frac{11}{12}$    **8.** $20\frac{6}{25}$    **11.** $124\frac{12}{325}$

**3.** $11\frac{3}{8}$    **6.** $8\frac{5}{7}$    **9.** $26\frac{5}{6}$    **12.** $453\frac{235}{311}$

**B.** *Change the following improper fractions to mixed numbers:*

**13.** $\frac{5}{4}$    **16.** $\frac{17}{4}$    **19.** $\frac{42}{5}$    **22.** $\frac{233}{46}$

**14.** $\frac{7}{3}$    **17.** $\frac{27}{8}$    **20.** $\frac{31}{6}$    **23.** $\frac{4,617}{124}$

**15.** $\frac{11}{8}$    **18.** $\frac{33}{5}$    **21.** $\frac{156}{31}$    **24.** $\frac{3,263}{216}$

**C.** *Find the g.c.d. of the numerator and the denominator in each of the following and then reduce the fraction to its lowest terms:*

**25.** $\frac{4}{8}$    **28.** $\frac{16}{64}$    **31.** $\frac{847}{1,331}$    **34.** $\frac{114}{171}$

**26.** $\frac{3}{12}$    **29.** $\frac{15}{40}$    **32.** $\frac{215}{258}$    **35.** $\frac{308}{374}$

**27.** $\frac{10}{15}$    **30.** $\frac{25}{10}$    **33.** $\frac{69}{184}$    **36.** $\frac{2,231}{4,559}$

**D.** *Arrange the fractions in each group in order beginning with the largest:*

**37.** $\frac{3}{8}, \frac{1}{3}$    **40.** $\frac{14}{15}, \frac{22}{25}$    **43.** $\frac{1}{2}, \frac{2}{7}, \frac{3}{5}$    **46.** $\frac{12}{15}, \frac{2}{3}, \frac{3}{5}, \frac{12}{5}, \frac{1}{3}$

**38.** $\frac{4}{9}, \frac{3}{5}$    **41.** $\frac{3}{4}, \frac{5}{6}, \frac{2}{5}$    **44.** $\frac{7}{8}, \frac{3}{4}, \frac{1}{2}, \frac{2}{3}$    **47.** $\frac{25}{48}, \frac{21}{32}, \frac{19}{30}, \frac{23}{40}$

**39.** $\frac{5}{12}, \frac{6}{14}$    **42.** $\frac{2}{3}, \frac{8}{9}, \frac{1}{4}$    **45.** $\frac{3}{8}, \frac{3}{6}, \frac{3}{7}, \frac{3}{4}, \frac{3}{5}$    **48.** $\frac{11}{9}, \frac{9}{7}, \frac{5}{3}, \frac{13}{11}$

## 1.2 ADDITION

## A. Addition of Whole and Decimal Numbers

A common way to check an answer in addition is to use the *reverse order adding method.* In using this method, addition is performed by adding each column from the *top to the bottom.* The *checking operation* is then performed from the *bottom to the top.*

**Example 1**    Add 5,674, 3,922, 6,137, and 2,308.

*Add:*                                        *Check:*

| | | | |
|---|---|---|---|
| Addend | 5,674 | | 5,674 |
| Addend | 3,922 | | 3,922 |
| Addend | 6,137 | | 6,137 |
| Addend | 2,308 | | 2,308 |

$$21 = 4 + 2 + 7 + 8 \qquad 21 = 8 + 7 + 2 + 4$$
$$12 = 7 + 2 + 3 + 0 \qquad 12 = 0 + 3 + 2 + 7$$
$$19 = 6 + 9 + 1 + 3 \qquad 19 = 3 + 1 + 9 + 6$$
$$16 = 5 + 3 + 6 + 2 \qquad 16 = 2 + 6 + 3 + 5$$

Total    18,041                          18,041

When addends include decimal numbers, it is important to place the decimal points in one column so that each column represents a definite unit. When this arrangement is used, it is easy to add tenths to tenths, hundredths to hundredths, and so on.

**Example 2**    Find the sum of 2.54, .123, and 579.

| 2.54 | | 2.540 |
|---|---|---|
| .123 | or | 0.123 |
| +579 | | +579.000 |
| 581.663 | | 581.663 |

Because zeros do not change the value of a number when placed on the left side of a whole number or on the right side of a decimal fraction, they may be supplied for ease in addition. In the example above, the addition at the right is an illustration of this rule. However, if a zero is *annexed* to the right of an *integer* (a whole number), the value of the number is changed. For example, 579 is not equal to 579,000, but 579 is equal to 579.000.

## B. Addition of Fractions

When fractions are added, all addends should be reduced to fractions having a lowest common denominator. The sum of the numerators of all addends is the numerator of the required sum; the common denominator is unchanged and is the denominator of the required sum. The required sum will be a proper or an improper fraction. If the sum is an improper fraction, it should be reduced to a mixed number. When mixed numbers are added, it is unnecessary to reduce the numbers to improper fractions. It is much easier to add the integers and the fractions separately. The fractional part of an answer should always be reduced to its lowest terms.

**Example 3**   Add $\frac{2}{3}, \frac{3}{8}, \frac{1}{2}$.

Here the least common multiple (l.c.m.) of the denominators 3, 8, and 2 is 24. The three fractions are reduced to fractions with the l.c.m. as the common denominator:

$$\frac{2}{3} = \frac{2 \times 8}{3 \times 8} = \frac{16}{24}; \qquad \frac{3}{8} = \frac{3 \times 3}{8 \times 3} = \frac{9}{24}; \qquad \frac{1}{2} = \frac{1 \times 12}{2 \times 12} = \frac{12}{24}$$

Thus, $\dfrac{2}{3} + \dfrac{3}{8} + \dfrac{1}{2} = \dfrac{16}{24} + \dfrac{9}{24} + \dfrac{12}{24} = \dfrac{16 + 9 + 12}{24} = \dfrac{37}{24} = 1\dfrac{13}{24}$

**Example 4**   Add $5\frac{6}{7}, \frac{16}{3}, \frac{232}{21}, 29\frac{3}{7}$.

The l.c.m. of the denominators 7, 3, 21, and 7 is 21.

$5\frac{6}{7} = 5\frac{18}{21};$ $\qquad\qquad$ $\frac{232}{21} = 11\frac{1}{21};$

$\frac{16}{3} = 5\frac{1}{3} = 5\frac{7}{21};$ $\qquad$ $29\frac{3}{7} = 29\frac{9}{21}$

Thus, $5\frac{6}{7} + \frac{16}{3} + \frac{232}{21} + 29\frac{3}{7} = 5\frac{18}{21} + 5\frac{7}{21} + 11\frac{1}{21} + 29\frac{9}{21}$

$$= 5 + 5 + 11 + 29 + \frac{18 + 7 + 1 + 9}{21}$$

$$= 50 + \tfrac{35}{21} = 51\tfrac{14}{21} = 51\tfrac{2}{3}$$

# 1.3 SUBTRACTION

## A. Subtraction of Whole and Decimal Numbers

To check an answer in subtraction, a simple and effective method is to add the remainder to the subtrahend; the sum should be equal to the minuend.

**Example 1**   *Subtract:* $\qquad\qquad\qquad$ *Check:*

2,761 (Minuend) $\qquad\qquad$ 2,215 (Remainder)
$-\ \ 546$ (Subtrahend) $\qquad\ $ $+\ \ 546$ (Subtrahend)
$\overline{2,215}$ (Remainder) $\qquad\ \ \ \overline{2,761}$ (Minuend)

From the example above, it is easy to see that *subtraction is the reverse operation of addition.*

When subtraction involves decimals, the rule used in addition also applies; that is, place the decimal points of the minuend and the subtrahend in the same vertical column (if the subtraction is computed in a columnar form).

**Example 2**   Subtract 169.564 from 295.4562.

295.4562
$-169.5640$
$\overline{125.8922}$

## B. Subtraction of Fractions

When fractions are subtracted, both the minuend and the subtrahend should be reduced to fractions with a lowest common denominator. The difference between the numerators of the minuend and the subtrahend is the numerator of the required remainder; the common denominator is unchanged and is the denominator of the required remainder. Mixed numbers do not need to be reduced to improper fractions before the subtraction is performed unless the fractional part of the minuend is smaller than the fractional part of the subtrahend.

**Example 3**   Subtract $\frac{2}{7}$ from $\frac{3}{5}$.

Here the l.c.m. of the denominators 7 and 5 is 35.

$$\frac{3}{5} - \frac{2}{7} = \frac{21}{35} - \frac{10}{35} = \frac{11}{35}$$

**Example 4**   Subtract $\frac{2}{7}$ from $2\frac{3}{5}$.

$$2\frac{3}{5} - \frac{2}{7} = 2\frac{21}{35} - \frac{10}{35} = 2\frac{11}{35}$$

**Example 5**   Subtract $\frac{4}{9}$ from 3.

$$3 - \frac{4}{9} = 2\frac{9}{9} - \frac{4}{9} = 2\frac{5}{9}$$

**Example 6**   Subtract $\frac{4}{9}$ from $3\frac{1}{3}$.

$$3\frac{1}{3} - \frac{4}{9} = 3\frac{3}{9} - \frac{4}{9} = 2\frac{9+3}{9} - \frac{4}{9} = 2\frac{12}{9} - \frac{4}{9} = 2\frac{8}{9}$$

## 1.4 MULTIPLICATION

## A. Multiplication of Whole and Decimal Numbers

When an answer in multiplication must be checked precisely, either one of the following two methods may be used.

**INTERCHANGING MULTIPLICAND AND MULTIPLIER**

**Example 1**   *Multiply:*                          *Check:*

```
  463 (Multiplicand)         72 (Multiplier)
 ×72 (Multiplier)          ×463 (Multiplicand)
  926                       216
32 41                       4 32
33,336 (Product)           28 8
                           33,336 (Product)
```

**DIVIDING THE PRODUCT BY ONE OF THE FACTORS**

The multiplicand and the multiplier are also called *factors* of the product. By dividing the product by one of the factors, the quotient thus obtained must be equal to the other factor. The product in Example 1 may be checked as follows:

$$
\begin{array}{r}
72 \text{ (Quotient, the other factor) or,} \\
\text{(Factor) } 463\,\overline{)33{,}336} \text{ (Product)} \\
32\ 41 \\
\hline
926 \\
926 \\
\hline
\end{array}
\qquad
\begin{array}{r}
463 \text{ (Factor)} \\
\text{(Factor) } 72\,\overline{)33{,}336} \text{ (Product)} \\
28\ 8 \\
\hline
4\ 53 \\
4\ 32 \\
\hline
216 \\
216 \\
\hline
\end{array}
$$

An answer in multiplication can be checked mentally by estimating the product after the multiplicand and the multiplier have been rounded to simple numbers. For instance, the multiplicand 4,363 and the multiplier 184 may be rounded to 4,000 and 200 respectively. The product of the two round numbers can thus be found mentally and used as a guide in checking the answer. Since the product of 4,000 and 200 is 800,000, the answer 802,792 (4,363 × 184 = 802,792) is considered reasonable. If the answer had been calculated to be near 500,000, it would be considered unreasonable since it is apparently greatly different from the estimation. However, when the answer in multiplication must be checked precisely, one of the two above-mentioned methods should be used.

When there are decimals in multiplication, the number of decimal places in the product should equal the total number of decimal places in the factors.

**Example 2**    Find the product of factors 4.23 and 1.1052.

Since 4.23 times 1.1052 equals 1.1052 times 4.23, the shorter factor is usually used as the multiplier.

$$
\begin{array}{r}
1.1052 \\
\times 4.23 \\
\hline
3\ 3156 \\
22\ 104 \\
442\ 08 \\
\hline
4.67\ 4996 \text{ (Product)}
\end{array}
$$

Since there are 4 decimal places in the multiplicand and 2 in the multiplier, there should be 6 decimal places in the product. The answer thus is 4.674996.

## B. Multiplication of Fractions

When multiplying fractions, there is no need to find a common denominator of the fractions. The product of the numerators is the numerator of the required product, and the product of the denominators is the denominator of the required product.

**Example 3**    Multiply $\frac{6}{11}$ by $\frac{2}{9}$.

$$
\frac{6}{11} \times \frac{2}{9} = \frac{6 \times 2}{11 \times 9} = \frac{12}{99} = \frac{4}{33}
$$

Since the product of 6 × 2 is the same as the product of 2 × 6, the above computation may be written as follows:

$$\frac{6}{11} \times \frac{2}{9} = \frac{2}{11} \times \frac{6}{9} = \frac{2}{11} \times \frac{6 \div 3}{9 \div 3} = \frac{2}{11} \times \frac{2}{3} = \frac{4}{33}$$

For convenience, $\frac{6 \div 3}{9 \div 3} = \frac{2}{3}$ is usually written as $\dfrac{\overset{2}{\cancel{6}}}{\underset{3}{\cancel{9}}}$. The method of simplifying

the fractions should be used in multiplication whenever possible. Thus, multiplication for the above example may be simplified in the following manner:

$$\frac{\overset{2}{\cancel{6}}}{11} \times \frac{2}{\underset{3}{\cancel{9}}} = \frac{4}{33}$$

In *multiplication involving mixed numbers* a simple method is to reduce each mixed number to an improper fraction before multiplying.

**Example 4**   Multiply $\frac{3}{5}$ by $3\frac{3}{4}$.

$$\frac{3}{5} \times 3\frac{3}{4} = \frac{3}{5} \times \frac{(3 \times 4) + 3}{4} = \frac{3}{\underset{1}{\cancel{5}}} \times \frac{\overset{3}{\cancel{15}}}{4} = \frac{9}{4} = 2\frac{1}{4}$$

**Example 5**   Multiply $5\frac{3}{5}$ by $3\frac{3}{4}$.

$$5\frac{3}{5} \times 3\frac{3}{4} = \frac{\overset{7}{\cancel{28}}}{\underset{1}{\cancel{5}}} \times \frac{\overset{3}{\cancel{15}}}{\underset{1}{\cancel{4}}} = 21$$

# EXERCISE 1–2

## Reference: Sections 1.2 to 1.4

**A.** *Add the following (check answers for Problems 1 to 6):*

| **1.** | **2.** | **3.** |
|---|---|---|
| 50,742 | 5,639 | 2,842.31 |
| 68,201 | 35,904 | 19,086.02 |
| 56,174 | 678,510 | 57,382.47 |
| 56,473 | 56,783 | 56,732.13 |
| 24,182 | 478,341 | 87,531.56 |
| 53,218 | 57,832 | 6,793.48 |
|  |  | 58,410.29 |

| **4.** | **5.** | **6.** |
|---|---|---|
| 5,421.562 | 7,459.23 | 3,420.62 |
| 57,342.43 | 3,972.12 | 7,604.245 |
| 489,263.72 | 21,057.45 | 2,058.47 |
| 175,625.813 | 44,958.67 | 24,157.52 |
| 907,256.93 | 35,784.81 | 22,553.324 |
| 61,432.247 | 55,687.95 | 3,468.761 |
| 36,721.65 | 4,679.24 | 357.32 |
|  | 356.16 | 11,467.46 |
|  | 45,673.28 | 4,568.58 |

**7.** $\frac{1}{3} + \frac{1}{3}$

**8.** $\frac{1}{4} + \frac{1}{2}$

**9.** $\frac{1}{5} + \frac{4}{5}$

**10.** $\frac{7}{8} + \frac{3}{4}$

**11.** $8 + \frac{2}{3}$

**12.** $\frac{3}{4} + \frac{1}{2}$

**13.** $\frac{2}{3} + 5\frac{3}{4}$

**14.** $2\frac{3}{5} + \frac{1}{2}$

**15.** $2\frac{2}{5} + \frac{1}{8}$

**16.** $1\frac{3}{7} + 3\frac{2}{5}$

**17.** $5\frac{1}{4} + 11\frac{7}{8}$

**18.** $8\frac{1}{12} + 21\frac{4}{5}$

**19.** $\frac{3}{7} + \frac{1}{3} + \frac{1}{7}$

**20.** $\frac{5}{12} + \frac{5}{6} + \frac{1}{5}$

**21.** $\frac{7}{16} + \frac{3}{8} + \frac{3}{4}$

**22.** $\frac{5}{21} + \frac{2}{3} + \frac{4}{7}$

**23.** $\frac{7}{20} + \frac{3}{25} + \frac{7}{10}$

**24.** $5\frac{1}{6} + 4\frac{2}{3} + 1\frac{5}{12}$

**25.** $\frac{3}{5} + 2\frac{7}{6} + \frac{19}{3} + \frac{4}{3}$

**26.** $\frac{3}{2} + 2\frac{1}{4} + \frac{16}{9} + \frac{24}{5}$

**27.** $\frac{65}{11} + 7\frac{14}{33} + \frac{137}{22} + 3\frac{1}{66}$

**28.** $3\frac{5}{8} + 4\frac{5}{6} + \frac{7}{12} + \frac{211}{12}$

**29.** $\frac{17}{4} + \frac{130}{3} + \frac{82}{5} + \frac{19}{6}$

**30.** $64\frac{1}{2} + 15\frac{1}{3} + 11\frac{1}{6} + 8\frac{2}{5}$

**B.** *Perform each subtraction (check each answer for Problems 31 to 36):*

**31.**   568,432
  $-390,681$

**32.**   910,432
  $- 56,143$

**33.**   563,214
  $- 24,861$

**34.**   176,513
  $- 96,852$

**35.**   90,183.052
  $-56,732.199$

**36.**   458,732.146
  $- 65,321.405$

**37.** $\frac{3}{4} - \frac{1}{4}$

**38.** $\frac{3}{8} - \frac{1}{4}$

**39.** $\frac{4}{5} - \frac{1}{3}$

**40.** $\frac{9}{11} - \frac{2}{7}$

**41.** $\frac{33}{100} - \frac{87}{300}$

**42.** $\frac{8}{15} - \frac{29}{60}$

**43.** $1 - \frac{4}{7}$

**44.** $3\frac{5}{8} - \frac{3}{8}$

**45.** $4\frac{5}{9} - 2\frac{2}{9}$

**46.** $9\frac{13}{15} - \frac{4}{5}$

**47.** $8\frac{1}{3} - \frac{2}{3}$

**48.** $7\frac{1}{5} - \frac{5}{7}$

**49.** $15\frac{2}{3} - 7\frac{8}{9}$

**50.** $23\frac{1}{3} - 5\frac{1}{2}$

**51.** $6\frac{7}{11} - \frac{8}{9}$

**52.** $6 - \frac{7}{9}$

**53.** $4 - 1\frac{3}{4}$

**54.** $10\frac{11}{13} - 4\frac{11}{12}$

**55.** $7\frac{11}{12} - 7\frac{3}{4}$

**56.** $4\frac{3}{5} - \frac{6}{7}$

**57.** $\frac{12}{5} - \frac{9}{4}$

**58.** $212\frac{1}{4} - \frac{460}{11}$

**59.** $\frac{436}{45} - 2\frac{4}{9}$

**60.** $\frac{543}{20} - \frac{104}{15}$

**C.** *Multiply (check each answer for Problems 61 to 72 by the following methods: (a) interchanging multiplicand and multiplier and (b) dividing the product by one of the factors):*

**61.** $79 \times 56$

**62.** $21 \times 93$

**63.** $234 \times 63$

**64.** $673 \times 52$

**65.** $54,291 \times 4,734$

**66.** $98,013 \times 3,627$

**67.** $45.7 \times 34.2$

**68.** $37.83 \times 56.42$

**69.** $346.72 \times 41$

**70.** $574.01 \times 32.1$

**71.** $1.452 \times 23.4$

**72.** $4.671 \times 54.7$

**73.** $\frac{1}{4} \times \frac{1}{3}$

**74.** $\frac{3}{5} \times \frac{6}{7}$

**75.** $\frac{8}{9} \times \frac{7}{16}$

**76.** $\frac{5}{12} \times \frac{6}{11}$

**77.** $\frac{39}{40} \times \frac{20}{39}$

**78.** $\frac{21}{23} \times \frac{1}{7}$

**79.** $\frac{5}{13} \times \frac{5}{12}$

**80.** $\frac{16}{19} \times \frac{3}{7}$

**81.** $\frac{14}{25} \times \frac{7}{18}$

**82.** $\frac{11}{12} \times \frac{4}{3}$

**83.** $\frac{17}{22} \times \frac{9}{2}$

**84.** $\frac{124}{17} \times \frac{5}{44}$

**85.** $\frac{4}{7} \times \frac{14}{19} \times \frac{5}{36}$

**86.** $\frac{25}{42} \times \frac{3}{5} \times \frac{4}{15}$

**87.** $\frac{6}{7} \times \frac{2}{3} \times \frac{7}{8} \times \frac{4}{9}$

**88.** $\frac{13}{25} \times \frac{3}{14} \times \frac{5}{78} \times \frac{2}{27}$

**89.** $2\frac{1}{5} \times 3\frac{2}{3}$

**90.** $4\frac{6}{7} \times 7\frac{4}{5}$

**91.** $11\frac{1}{2} \times 13\frac{2}{7}$

**92.** $39\frac{5}{9} \times 20\frac{7}{8}$

**93.** $211\frac{4}{5} \times 16\frac{3}{8}$

**94.** $250\frac{7}{16} \times 16$

**95.** $362\frac{1}{7} \times 2\frac{2}{3}$

**96.** $156\frac{1}{4} \times 111\frac{1}{5}$

## 1.5 DIVISION

## A. Division of Whole and Decimal Numbers

In the previous section, it can be seen that the process of division may be thought of as the process of finding an unknown factor in multiplication when one factor and the product are known.

In checking an answer in division, first find the product of the divisor and the quotient; then add the product to the remainder, if there is one. The result must be equal to the dividend. This method is based on the basic relationship in division:

$$Divisor \times Quotient + Remainder\ of\ Division = Dividend$$

**Example 1**    *Divide:*

```
                          31  (Quotient)          Check:
        (Divisor)  108)3,375  (Dividend)            108  (Divisor)
                   3 24                            × 31  (Quotient)
                   ────                            ────
                    135                             108
                    108                             324
                    ────                           ─────
                     27  (Remainder)              3,348  (Product)
                                               +     27  (Remainder)
                                                  ─────
                                                  3,375  (Dividend)
        Complete quotient = 31 27/108
```

When the product of the divisor and the quotient is not the same amount as the dividend, there will be a remainder in division. The remainder may be expressed as a part of the quotient in two ways: (1) as a common fraction with the remainder as the numerator and the divisor as the denominator, such as the complete quotient $31\frac{27}{108}$ in the example above, or (2) as a decimal fraction. The division in Example 1 may be carried further by annexing zeros to the dividend until there is no remainder or until the number of decimal places in the quotient is as many as desired.

```
              31.25   Notice that the decimal      Check:
    108)3,375.00      point in the quotient is al-         108  (Divisor)
        3 24          ways placed right above           ×31.25  (Quotient)
        ────          the decimal point in the          ──────
         135          dividend.                           5 40
         108                                              21 6
         ────                                             108
         27 0                                             3 24
         21 6        Complete quotient = 31.25          ──────
         ────                                          3,375.00  (Dividend)
          5 40
          5 40
```

When only the dividend contains decimal places, the decimal point in the quotient is placed directly above the decimal point in the dividend. Example 2 is used to illustrate this method.

When both the dividend and the divisor contain decimal places, the decimal point in the divisor is usually eliminated and the divisor becomes a whole number. The decimal point in the dividend is moved to the right the same number of places as the number of decimal places in the divisor. The decimal point in the quotient is placed directly above the new decimal point in the dividend. Example 3 is used to illustrate this method. Since there are only two digits after the original decimal point in the dividend of the example, annexing one zero is necessary in order to make the three places.

**Example 2**    Divide 2,547.62 by 174.

$$
\begin{array}{r}
14.64 \\
\text{(Divisor) } 174\overline{)2,547.62} \text{ (Dividend)} \\
1\,74 \\
\hline
807 \\
696 \\
\hline
111\,6 \\
104\,4 \\
\hline
7\,22 \\
6\,96 \\
\hline
.26
\end{array}
$$

The complete quotient is $14.64\frac{26}{174}$.

Here, the remainder 26 has an actual value of .26.

*Check:*
$(174 \times 14.64) + .26 = 2,547.62$

**Example 3**    Divide 2,547.62 by .174.

$$
\begin{array}{r}
14\,641. \\
\text{(Divisor) } .174\overline{)2,547.620.} \text{ (Dividend)} \\
1\,74 \\
\hline
807 \\
696 \\
\hline
111\,6 \\
104\,4 \\
\hline
7\,22 \\
6\,96 \\
\hline
260 \\
174 \\
\hline
.086
\end{array}
$$

The complete quotient is $14,641\frac{86}{174}$.

The remainder 86 has an actual value of .086. Note that the original decimal point indicates the location of the decimal point of the remainder.

*Check:*
$(.174 \times 14,641) + .086 = 2,547.62$

## B. Rounding Decimal Places

There are various methods of rounding decimal places to a desired number of places for meeting different needs. For example, the rounding method for an engineer is different from the rounding method for a statistician. However, the following rounding method, which is used in this text, does meet most purposes in business.

To round a given number to a desired number of decimal places, the general rule is that *if the portion to be dropped begins with the figure 5* (which is one half of the unit of the last figure retained) *or above, add 1 to the last figure retained; if the portion to be dropped is less than 5, discard it.*

**Example 4**    The numbers in the left-hand column below have been rounded to two decimal places:

| | |
|---|---|
| 1.376 | 1.38 |
| 51.2454 | 51.25 |
| $ 2.983 | $ 2.98 (rounded to the nearest cent) |
| $32.72451 | $32.72 (rounded to the nearest cent) |

*Note:* Refer to the number 1.376. Since 6 (thousandths) is more than 5 (or one half of the unit of the last figure retained, 7 (hundredths)), 1 is added to 7 and the answer is 1.38. Now refer to the number $32.72451. Since the thousandth digit is 4, the places consisting of 4 and thereafter are discarded.

## C. Division of Fractions

Generally, the following three methods are used in division of fractions. Although the first method is relatively popular, it is not superior in every case. Students should be familiar with all the methods in order to perform the division efficiently.

**Method A**    *Multiply the dividend by the reciprocal of the divisor.* The method may be expressed as follows:

$$\text{Dividend} \div \text{Fraction} = \text{Dividend} \times \text{Reciprocal of the Fraction}$$

The reciprocal of a fraction is the fraction inverted. The product of a fraction and its reciprocal is always equal to 1. Thus, the reciprocal of the fraction $\frac{5}{7}$ is $\frac{7}{5}$ and their product is 1; that is, $\frac{5}{7} \times \frac{7}{5} = 1$. The following example is used to illustrate the method.

**Example 5**    Divide 20 by $\frac{3}{4}$.

$$20 \div \tfrac{3}{4} = 20 \times \tfrac{4}{3} = \tfrac{80}{3} = 26\tfrac{2}{3}$$

The above method is derived from the definition of division which gives the following equation:

$$\text{Dividend} \div \text{Divisor} = \text{Quotient, or}$$
$$\text{Quotient} \times \text{Divisor} = \text{Dividend}$$

Let the dividend be 20 and the divisor be $\frac{3}{4}$; the above equations become

$$20 \div \tfrac{3}{4} = \text{Quotient, or}$$
$$\text{Quotient} \times \tfrac{3}{4} = 20$$

If the left side of the above equation is multiplied by $\frac{4}{3}$, the right side of the equation must be multiplied by the same quantity in order to keep both sides equal. Thus,

$$\text{Quotient} \times \tfrac{3}{4} \times \tfrac{4}{3} = 20 \times \tfrac{4}{3}; \quad \text{Quotient} = 20 \times \tfrac{4}{3}$$

Notice that $\frac{4}{3}$ is the reciprocal of the fraction $\frac{3}{4}$, which is the divisor. Thus, *when a number is to be divided by a fraction, invert the terms of the fraction and then multiply. The product obtained is the quotient of the division.* This method is further illustrated by the following examples:

**Common Fractions.**

**Example 6**     Divide $\frac{2}{3}$ by $\frac{5}{7}$.

$$\frac{2}{3} \div \frac{5}{7} = \frac{2}{3} \times \frac{7}{5} = \frac{14}{15}$$

**Example 7**     Divide 1 by $\frac{3}{8}$.

$$1 \div \frac{3}{8} = \frac{1}{1} \times \frac{8}{3} = \frac{8}{3} = 2\frac{2}{3}$$

***Note:***     $\frac{8}{3}$ is the reciprocal of $\frac{3}{8}$. When 1 is divided by a given number, the quotient is the reciprocal of the given number.

**Example 8**     Divide $\frac{3}{5}$ by 11.

$$\frac{3}{5} \div 11 = \frac{3}{5} \times \frac{1}{11} = \frac{3}{55}$$

**Example 9**     Simplify $\dfrac{\frac{10}{33}}{\frac{5}{11}}$.

This problem means the same as $\frac{10}{33}$ divided by $\frac{5}{11}$.

$$\frac{10}{33} \div \frac{5}{11} = \frac{\overset{2}{\cancel{10}}}{\underset{3}{\cancel{33}}} \times \frac{\overset{1}{\cancel{11}}}{\underset{1}{\cancel{5}}} = \frac{2}{3}$$

**Mixed Numbers.** A simple method is to reduce the mixed numbers to improper fractions; then divide.

**Example 10**   Divide $26\frac{1}{4}$ by $2\frac{2}{5}$.

$$26\frac{1}{4} \div 2\frac{2}{5} = \frac{105}{4} \div \frac{12}{5} = \frac{\overset{35}{\cancel{105}}}{4} \times \frac{5}{\underset{4}{\cancel{12}}} = \frac{175}{16} = 10\frac{15}{16}$$

**Example 11**   Divide $27\frac{3}{4}$ by 6.

$$27\frac{3}{4} \div 6 = \frac{111}{4} \div \frac{6}{1} = \frac{\overset{37}{\cancel{111}}}{4} \times \frac{1}{\underset{2}{\cancel{6}}} = \frac{37}{8} = 4\frac{5}{8}$$

**Method B**     *After reducing both the dividend and the divisor to fractions having the lowest common denominator, cancel the common denominators and divide. This method is recommended when the fractions have a common denominator, such as in Example 13.*

**Example 12**   Divide $\frac{2}{3}$ by $\frac{5}{7}$.

The l.c.m. of the denominators 3 and 7 is 21. This division may be written as a complex fraction and divided as follows:

$$\frac{\frac{2}{3}}{\frac{5}{7}} = \frac{\frac{14}{21}}{\frac{15}{21}} = \frac{\frac{14}{21} \times 21}{\frac{15}{21} \times 21} = \frac{14}{15}, \text{ or it may be written}$$

$$\frac{2}{3} \div \frac{5}{7} = \frac{14}{21} \div \frac{15}{21} = 14 \div 15 = \frac{14}{15}$$

**Example 13**  Divide $2\frac{7}{30}$ by $\frac{11}{30}$.

Here the common denominator is 30.

$$2\frac{7}{30} \div \frac{11}{30} = \frac{67}{30} \div \frac{11}{30} = \frac{67}{11} = 6\frac{1}{11}$$

**Method C**  *Divide after reducing both the dividend and the divisor to integers.* The reduction may be accomplished by multiplying the dividend and the divisor by the l.c.m. of their denominators. This method is useful when the denominator of one fraction is a factor of the denominator of the other fraction, such as in Example 15.

**Example 14**  Divide $\frac{2}{3}$ by $\frac{5}{7}$.

The l.c.m. of the denominators 3 and 7 is 21.

$$\frac{2}{3} \div \frac{5}{7} = \frac{\frac{2}{3}}{\frac{5}{7}} = \frac{\frac{2}{3} \times \overset{7}{21}}{\frac{5}{7} \times \underset{3}{21}} = \frac{14}{15}, \text{ or it may be written}$$

$$\frac{2}{3} \div \frac{5}{7} = \left(\frac{2}{3} \times \overset{7}{21}\right) \div \left(\frac{5}{7} \times \underset{3}{21}\right) = 14 \div 15 = \frac{14}{15}$$

**Example 15**  Divide $6\frac{1}{20}$ by $2\frac{2}{5}$.

Here 5 is a factor of 20 since $5 \times 4 = 20$.

$$6\frac{1}{20} \div 2\frac{2}{5} = \frac{121}{20} \div \frac{12}{5} = \left(\frac{121}{20} \times 20\right) \div \left(\frac{12}{5} \times \overset{4}{20}\right) = \frac{121}{48} = 2\frac{25}{48}$$

# EXERCISE 1–3

## Reference: Section 1.5

**A.** *Find the quotient and the actual value of the remainder in each division problem below. Check each answer.*

1. $356 \div 23$
2. $651 \div 57$
3. $452 \div 65$
4. $135 \div 24$
5. $5,632 \div 165$
6. $8,720 \div 163$

7. $5,673 \div 542$
8. $6,512 \div 901$
9. $567.12 \div 34$
10. $482.23 \div 23$
11. $23.518 \div 53$

12. $56.09 \div 15$
13. $347.23 \div 18.36$
14. $231.45 \div .43$
15. $75.43 \div 1.067$
16. $24.154 \div .6301$

**B.** *Divide each of the following and express the remainder as a part of the quotient in two ways: (a) as a common fraction, and (b) as a decimal fraction (round to hundredths).*

**17.** $35 \div 6$

**18.** $57 \div 7$

**19.** $463 \div 12$

**20.** $873 \div 23$

**21.** $4,587 \div 361$

**22.** $7,632 \div 719$

**23.** $568.341 \div 23.106$

**24.** $9,017.34 \div 51.2461$

**C.** *Round the following numbers to two decimal places:*

**25.** 12.7541

**26.** 468.6552

**27.** 132.437

**28.** 63.763

**29.** 0.5825

**30.** 0.7345

**31.** 7,362.0564

**32.** 8,319.0486

**33.** 1.3712

**34.** 5.4998

**35.** 21.0051

**36.** 57.0349

Reduce all answers to lowest terms for the following problems.

**D.** *Write the reciprocal of each number:*

**37.** $\frac{2}{7}$

**38.** 6

**39.** $\frac{4}{5}$

**40.** $\frac{4}{9}$

**41.** $\frac{17}{19}$

**42.** $1\frac{10}{13}$

**43.** $3\frac{9}{110}$

**44.** $2\frac{26}{43}$

**E.** *Divide by using the reciprocal:*

**45.** $\frac{3}{7} \div \frac{1}{7}$

**46.** $\frac{3}{5} \div \frac{2}{15}$

**47.** $\frac{4}{9} \div \frac{16}{17}$

**48.** $10 \div 2\frac{1}{2}$

**49.** $25 \div 3\frac{2}{7}$

**50.** $32 \div \frac{4}{5}$

**51.** $\frac{8}{9} \div 1\frac{1}{7}$

**52.** $\frac{11}{12} \div 3\frac{5}{12}$

**53.** $\frac{6}{13} \div 2$

**54.** $\frac{12}{17} \div \frac{16}{31}$

**55.** $\frac{15}{2} \div \frac{9}{4}$

**56.** $\frac{27}{4} \div \frac{13}{8}$

**57.** $\frac{108}{25} \div \frac{54}{205}$

**58.** $18\frac{2}{3} \div 6\frac{2}{5}$

**59.** $22\frac{6}{7} \div 3\frac{5}{9}$

**60.** $104\frac{3}{8} \div 28\frac{7}{11}$

**F.** *Divide after reducing to fractions having a common denominator:*

**61.** $\frac{2}{3} \div \frac{1}{4}$

**62.** $\frac{3}{7} \div \frac{2}{21}$

**63.** $\frac{5}{6} \div \frac{5}{9}$

**64.** $\frac{11}{12} \div \frac{7}{15}$

**65.** $\frac{14}{15} \div 3$

**66.** $\frac{7}{42} \div 2$

**67.** $\frac{25}{33} \div \frac{14}{11}$

**68.** $\frac{98}{99} \div \frac{22}{9}$

**69.** $32\frac{4}{5} \div 6\frac{1}{5}$

**70.** $42\frac{11}{12} \div 7\frac{13}{15}$

**71.** $\frac{5}{12} \div 3\frac{1}{3}$

**72.** $12\frac{6}{7} \div 11\frac{5}{14}$

**G.** *Divide after reducing both the dividend and the divisor to integers:*

**73.** $\frac{3}{4} \div \frac{1}{2}$

**74.** $\frac{7}{9} \div \frac{2}{3}$

**75.** $\frac{4}{5} \div \frac{6}{7}$

**76.** $\frac{13}{14} \div \frac{7}{8}$

**77.** $\frac{15}{16} \div 2$

**78.** $\frac{8}{60} \div 3$

**79.** $\frac{24}{33} \div \frac{15}{22}$

**80.** $\frac{69}{88} \div \frac{15}{8}$

**81.** $46\frac{5}{7} \div 5\frac{2}{7}$

**82.** $32\frac{12}{17} \div 5\frac{2}{3}$

**83.** $8\frac{4}{9} \div 11\frac{1}{3}$

**84.** $12\frac{7}{9} \div 11\frac{5}{6}$

# 1.6 DECIMAL FRACTIONS, ALIQUOT PARTS, AND REPETENDS

## A. Decimal Fractions

Common fractions whose denominators are 10 or some power of 10 (that is, the product of 10's, such as 100, 1,000 and 10,000) can be written in a special way by using a decimal point as follows:

$$\frac{1}{10} = .1, \quad \frac{3}{100} = .03, \quad \frac{57}{1,000} = .057$$

The above equivalents of the common fractions are called *decimal fractions, decimal numbers,* or simply decimals. In fact, any common fraction can be written in a decimal fraction form. To change a common fraction to a decimal fraction form, simply divide the numerator by the denominator in the given common fraction.

**Example 1**   $\frac{9}{20} = 9 \div 20 = .45$

**Example 2**   $5\frac{3}{15} = 5 + \frac{3}{15} = 5 + .2 = 5.2$

**Example 3**   $12\frac{6}{19} = 12 + \frac{6}{19} = 12.315\frac{15}{19}$

> **Note:**   When the result in Example 3 is rounded to 3 decimal places, the answer is 12.316 since $\frac{15}{19}$ is more than one half of the unit of the last figure retained.

When a decimal fraction is written in a common fraction form, the figures are used as the numerator, and 1 with as many zeros annexed as there are decimal places is used as the denominator. The common fraction is then simplified or reduced to its lowest terms.

**Example 4**   $.0195 = \frac{195}{10,000} = \frac{39}{2,000}$

**Example 5**   $6.52 = 6\frac{52}{100} = 6\frac{13}{25}$

**Example 6**   $14.641\frac{2}{7} = 14\frac{641\frac{2}{7}}{1,000} = 14\frac{\frac{4,489}{7}}{\frac{1,000}{1}} = 14\frac{4,489}{7,000}$

> **Note:**   In Example 6, there are only three decimal places since $\frac{2}{7}$ is a fraction of the thousandth unit.

# B. Aliquot Parts

An *aliquot part* is the part of a number by which the number may be divided leaving no remainder. For example, $1\frac{1}{2}$, 2, and 3 are aliquot parts of 6, because $6 \div 1\frac{1}{2} = 4$, $6 \div 2 = 3$, and $6 \div 3 = 2$. Numbers 50, $33\frac{1}{3}$, and 20 are aliquot parts of 100, because $100 \div 50 = 2$, $100 \div 33\frac{1}{3} = 3$, and $100 \div 20 = 5$. Since percentage (% or $\frac{1}{100}$) problems frequently occur in business computations, the aliquot parts of 100 are of particular interest. In many cases, computation in multiplication and division is greatly simplified when percents with aliquot parts of 100, such as $33\frac{1}{3}$% in Example 7, are converted to common fractions before the computation. Of course, if there is to be any practical value to students, they should memorize the aliquot parts of the numbers that they use frequently. The most important aliquot parts of 100 as expressed in hundredths ($\frac{1}{100}$ or %) and their equivalent values in the lowest common fraction form are given in Table 1–1.

**Table 1–1    COMMON ALIQUOT PARTS OF 100, AS EXPRESSED IN HUNDREDTHS (1/100 OR %) AND THEIR EQUIVALENT VALUES IN THE LOWEST COMMON FRACTION FORM**

| Denominator of Common Fraction | Numerator of Common Fraction | | | | | | | | | | | | |
|---|---|---|---|---|---|---|---|---|---|---|---|---|---|
| | 1 | 2 | 3 | 4 | 5 | 6 | 7 | 8 | 9 | 10 | 11 | 12 | 13 |
| | Unit: $\frac{1}{100}$ or % | | | | | | | | | | | | |
| 2 | 50 | | | | | | | | | | | | |
| 3 | $33\frac{1}{3}$ | $66\frac{2}{3}$ | | | | | | | | | | | |
| 4 | 25 | | 75 | | | | | | | | | | |
| 5 | 20 | 40 | 60 | 80 | | | | | | | | | |
| 6 | $16\frac{2}{3}$ | | | | $83\frac{1}{3}$ | | | | | | | | |
| 7 | $14\frac{2}{7}$ | $28\frac{4}{7}$ | $42\frac{6}{7}$ | $57\frac{1}{7}$ | $71\frac{3}{7}$ | $85\frac{5}{7}$ | | | | | | | |
| 8 | $12\frac{1}{2}$ | | $37\frac{1}{2}$ | | $62\frac{1}{2}$ | | $87\frac{1}{2}$ | | | | | | |
| 9 | $11\frac{1}{9}$ | $22\frac{2}{9}$ | | $44\frac{4}{9}$ | $55\frac{5}{9}$ | | $77\frac{7}{9}$ | $88\frac{8}{9}$ | | | | | |
| 10 | 10 | | 30 | | | | 70 | | 90 | | | | |
| 11 | $9\frac{1}{11}$ | $18\frac{2}{11}$ | $27\frac{3}{11}$ | $36\frac{4}{11}$ | $45\frac{5}{11}$ | $54\frac{6}{11}$ | $63\frac{7}{11}$ | $72\frac{8}{11}$ | $81\frac{9}{11}$ | $90\frac{10}{11}$ | | | |
| 12 | $8\frac{1}{3}$ | | | | $41\frac{2}{3}$ | | $58\frac{1}{3}$ | | | | $91\frac{2}{3}$ | | |
| 13 | $7\frac{9}{13}$ | $15\frac{5}{13}$ | $23\frac{1}{13}$ | $30\frac{10}{13}$ | $38\frac{6}{13}$ | $46\frac{2}{13}$ | $53\frac{11}{13}$ | $61\frac{7}{13}$ | $69\frac{3}{13}$ | $76\frac{12}{13}$ | $84\frac{8}{13}$ | $92\frac{4}{13}$ | |
| 14 | $7\frac{1}{7}$ | | $21\frac{3}{7}$ | | $35\frac{5}{7}$ | | | | $64\frac{2}{7}$ | | $78\frac{4}{7}$ | | $92\frac{6}{7}$ |
| 15 | $6\frac{2}{3}$ | $13\frac{1}{3}$ | | $26\frac{2}{3}$ | | | $46\frac{2}{3}$ | $53\frac{1}{3}$ | | | $73\frac{1}{3}$ | | $86\frac{2}{3}$ |
| 16 | $6\frac{1}{4}$ | | $18\frac{3}{4}$ | | $31\frac{1}{4}$ | | $43\frac{3}{4}$ | | $56\frac{1}{4}$ | | $68\frac{3}{4}$ | | $81\frac{1}{4}$ |
| 20 | 5 | | 15 | | | | 35 | | 45 | | 55 | | 65 |
| 25 | 4 | 8 | 12 | 16 | | 24 | 28 | 32 | 36 | | 44 | 48 | 52 |
| 30 | $3\frac{1}{3}$ | | | $13\frac{1}{3}$ | | | $23\frac{1}{3}$ | | 30 | | $36\frac{2}{3}$ | | $43\frac{1}{3}$ |
| 40 | $2\frac{1}{2}$ | | $7\frac{1}{2}$ | | | | $17\frac{1}{2}$ | | $22\frac{1}{2}$ | | $27\frac{1}{2}$ | | $32\frac{1}{2}$ |
| 50 | 2 | | 6 | | | | 14 | | 18 | | 22 | | 26 |

For example: $\frac{1}{2} = 50\%$; $\frac{2}{6} = \frac{1}{3} = 33\frac{1}{3}\%$; $\frac{4}{10} = \frac{2}{5} = 40\%$; $\frac{12}{14} = \frac{6}{7} = 85\frac{5}{7}\%$; $\frac{8}{40} = \frac{4}{20} = \frac{2}{10} = \frac{1}{5} = 20\%$.

The following examples illustrate the use of Table 1–1 in multiplication and division.

**Example 7**    Multiply 21 by $33\frac{1}{3}\%$.

The table shows that $33\frac{1}{3}\% = \frac{1}{3}$. Thus,

$$21 \times 33\frac{1}{3}\% = \overset{7}{\cancel{21}} \times \frac{1}{\cancel{3}} = 7$$

**Example 8**   Multiply 21 by $33\frac{1}{3}$.

$33\frac{1}{3} = 33\frac{1}{3}\% \times 100 = \frac{1}{3} \times 100$. Thus,

$$21 \times 33\frac{1}{3} = \overset{7}{\cancel{21}} \times \frac{1}{\cancel{3}} \times 100 = 700$$

**Example 9**   Divide 140 by $58\frac{1}{3}\%$.

The table shows that $58\frac{1}{3}\% = \frac{7}{12}$. Thus,

$$140 \div 58\frac{1}{3}\% = 140 \div \frac{7}{12} = \overset{20}{\cancel{140}} \times \frac{12}{\cancel{7}} = 240$$

**Example 10**   Divide by 140 by $58\frac{1}{3}$.

$58\frac{1}{3} = 58\frac{1}{3}\% \times 100 = \frac{7}{12} \times 100 = \frac{700}{12}$. Thus,

$$140 \div 58\frac{1}{3} = 140 \div \frac{700}{12} = \cancel{140} \times \frac{12}{\underset{5}{\cancel{700}}} = \frac{12}{5} = 2\frac{2}{5} \text{ or } 2.40$$

# ★C. Repetends

When some common fractions are reduced to decimals, it may be found that the remainders do not terminate and the decimals continue repeating. For example, when the fraction $\frac{1}{3}$ is reduced to a decimal, the result is .3333. . . . Decimals that continue to repeat infinitely are called *repetends*. They are also known as *circulating* or *periodic decimals*. A repetend may be expressed by placing a dot (˙) or dots above the figure or figures that do the repeating.

When any common fraction is expressed in its lowest terms, it may be reduced to a *finite decimal* if its denominator contains only the prime factors 2's and/or 5's. If the denominator contains other prime factors as well as 2's and/or 5's, the reduced decimal is a mixed one; it is partly finite and partly repeating. If the denominator contains neither 2 nor 5 as a factor, the reduced decimal is a purely repeating one.

Thus, $\frac{1}{4}$ and $\frac{1}{20}$ may be reduced to finite decimals.

$\frac{1}{4} = .25$; the denominator 4 contains the prime factors 2 and 2.

$\frac{1}{20} = .05$; the denominator 20 contains the prime factors 2, 2, and 5.

$\frac{1}{12}$ and $\frac{1}{70}$ may be reduced to partly finite and partly repeating decimals.

$\frac{1}{12} = .083333 . . . = .08\dot{3}$; the denominator 12 contains the prime factors 2, 2, and 3.

$\frac{1}{70} = .0\ 142857\ 142857\ 142857\ . . . . . . . . . . . . = .0\dot{1}4285\dot{7}$; the denominator 70 contains the prime factors 2, 5, and 7.

$\frac{2}{3}$ and $\frac{1}{21}$ may be reduced to purely repeating decimals.

$$\frac{2}{3} = .666666 \ldots \ldots = .\dot{6}$$

$$\frac{1}{21} = .047619 \ 047619 \ 047619 \ \ldots \ldots \ldots \ldots = .\dot{0}4761\dot{9}; \text{ the}$$
denominator 21 contains the prime factors 3 and 7.

A repetend may be reduced to a fraction. Use the repeating figures as the numerator and write as many 9's as the number of repeating figures to form the denominator.

**Example 11**   $.\dot{6} = \frac{6}{9} = \frac{2}{3}$

**Example 12**   $.\dot{9} = \dfrac{9}{9} = 1$   (Thus, .9999 . . . . = 1.) [1]

**Example 13**   $.08\dot{3} = .08\dfrac{3}{9} = \dfrac{8\frac{3}{9}}{100} = \dfrac{\frac{75}{9}}{100} = \dfrac{75}{900} = \dfrac{1}{12}$

**Example 14**   $.4\dot{1}2\dot{3} = .4\dfrac{123}{999} = \dfrac{4\frac{41}{333}}{10} = \dfrac{1,373}{3,330}$

**Example 15**   $5.8\dot{7} = 5.8\dfrac{7}{9} = 5\dfrac{8\frac{7}{9}}{10} = 5\dfrac{79}{90}$

A partly finite and partly repeating decimal may be directly reduced to a fraction as follows:

**Step (1)**   Subtract the finite figures from the over-all figures; the remainder is the numerator.

**Step (2)**   Write as many 9's as there are places in the repeating figures and annex as many zeros as there are finite decimal places to form the denominator.

**Example 16**   $.08\dot{3} = \dfrac{83-8}{900} = \dfrac{75}{900} = \dfrac{1}{12}$

**Example 17**   $.4\dot{1}2\dot{3} = \dfrac{4,123-4}{9,990} = \dfrac{4,119}{9,990} = \dfrac{1,373}{3,330}$

**Example 18**   $5.8\dot{7} = 5\dfrac{87-8}{90} = 5\dfrac{79}{90}$

---

[1] This relationship, .9999. . . . = 1, can further be illustrated as follows:

$$\text{Let } 10x = 9.99999 \ \ldots \ldots \ldots \ldots (1)$$
$$x = \ .99999 \ \ldots \ldots \ldots \ldots (2)$$

---

$$9x = 9.00000 \ \ldots \ldots \ldots \ldots (1) - (2)$$
$$x = \frac{9}{9} = 1$$

## EXERCISE 1–4

**Reference: Section 1.6**

**A.** *Reduce the following common fractions to decimal fractions (round to 3 decimal places):*

1. $\frac{3}{4}$      5. $\frac{12}{13}$      9. $\frac{40}{13}$      13. $3\frac{7}{20}$
2. $\frac{5}{6}$      6. $\frac{15}{22}$      10. $\frac{56}{11}$      14. $12\frac{8}{9}$
3. $\frac{4}{15}$      7. $\frac{23}{40}$      11. $\frac{72}{15}$      15. $42\frac{7}{16}$
4. $\frac{6}{21}$      8. $\frac{32}{47}$      12. $\frac{103}{25}$      16. $32\frac{71}{80}$

**B.** *Reduce the following decimals to common fractions in lowest terms:*

17. .5      21. .076      25. 3.002      29. $4.35\frac{1}{2}$
18. .35      22. $.085\frac{1}{3}$      26. 1.254      30. $10.42\frac{2}{3}$
19. .44      23. 1.75      27. 11.035      31. $2.875\frac{1}{4}$
20. .62      24. 5.042      28. 15.005      32. $4.305\frac{2}{5}$

**C.** *Perform the following indicated operations by the aliquot parts method:*

33. $36 \times 66\frac{2}{3}\%$    46. $40 \times 2\frac{1}{2}$    59. $48 \times 12\frac{1}{2}\%$    72. $85 \div 31\frac{1}{4}$
34. $28 \times 42\frac{6}{7}\%$    47. $20 \times 17\frac{1}{2}$    60. $80 \times 17\frac{1}{2}\%$    73. $99 \div 56\frac{1}{4}\%$
35. $36 \times 44\frac{4}{9}\%$    48. $27 \times 33\frac{1}{3}$    61. $26 \times 38\frac{6}{13}$    74. $121 \div 68\frac{3}{4}\%$
36. $55 \times 27\frac{3}{11}\%$    49. $36 \times 83\frac{1}{3}\%$    62. $33 \times 66\frac{2}{3}$    75. $210 \div 23\frac{1}{3}\%$
37. $72 \times 55\frac{5}{9}$    50. $42 \times 16\frac{2}{3}\%$    63. $21 \times 42\frac{6}{7}$    76. $49.7 \div 53\frac{11}{13}\%$
38. $56 \times 71\frac{3}{7}$    51. $77 \times 57\frac{1}{7}\%$    64. $48 \times 43\frac{3}{4}$    77. $42 \div 33\frac{1}{3}$
39. $39 \times 46\frac{2}{13}$    52. $63 \times 28\frac{4}{7}\%$    65. $52 \div 33\frac{1}{3}\%$    78. $30 \div 16\frac{2}{3}$
40. $60 \times 46\frac{2}{3}$    53. $16 \times 37\frac{1}{2}$    66. $56.6 \div 28\frac{4}{7}\%$    79. $500 \div 71\frac{3}{7}$
41. $160 \times 43\frac{3}{4}\%$    54. $56 \times 12\frac{1}{2}$    67. $360 \div 27\frac{3}{11}\%$    80. $600 \div 42\frac{6}{7}$
42. $75 \times 53\frac{1}{3}\%$    55. $18 \times 11\frac{1}{9}$    68. $55 \div 83\frac{1}{3}\%$    81. $1,500 \div 55\frac{5}{9}\%$
43. $480 \times 27\frac{1}{2}\%$    56. $66 \times 36\frac{4}{11}$    69. $74 \div 22\frac{2}{9}$    82. $55 \div 45\frac{5}{11}\%$
44. $270 \times 43\frac{1}{3}\%$    57. $60 \times 8\frac{1}{3}\%$    70. $78.3 \div 23\frac{1}{13}$    83. $72 \div 46\frac{2}{13}\%$
45. $30 \times 3\frac{1}{3}$    58. $42 \times 35\frac{5}{7}\%$    71. $44 \div 26\frac{2}{3}$    84. $84 \div 46\frac{2}{3}\%$

**★D.** *Reduce the following common fractions to decimal fractions and indicate the repetends by placing a dot or dots above the repeating figures:*

85. $\frac{1}{6}$      88. $\frac{7}{30}$      91. $\frac{14}{27}$      94. $\frac{25}{42}$
86. $\frac{5}{7}$      89. $\frac{23}{60}$      92. $\frac{17}{90}$      95. $\frac{17}{150}$
87. $\frac{4}{35}$      90. $\frac{11}{45}$      93. $\frac{13}{15}$      96. $\frac{41}{270}$

**★E.** *Reduce the following to common fractions or mixed numbers:*

97. $.\dot{4}$      101. $.\dot{2}\dot{3}$      105. $4.3\dot{8}$      108. $5.3\dot{1}2\dot{6}$
98. $.\dot{7}$      102. $.\dot{3}\dot{1}$      106. $3.5\dot{7}$      109. $8.42\dot{1}3\dot{6}$
99. $.1\dot{1}$      103. $.04\dot{3}$      107. $1.4\dot{5}6\dot{7}$      110. $7.3823\dot{4}$
100. $.1\dot{6}$      104. $.05\dot{6}$

# Chapter 2

## Basic Algebraic
## Operations and Equations

This chapter introduces two important areas of ordinary algebra. The first area includes the basic algebraic operations (Sections 2.1 to 2.7). The second area deals with the operations of equations (Sections 2.8 to 2.11). The basic algebraic operations included in this chapter are essential in performing the equation operations. The knowledge of equations, in turn, is essential in deriving some simple formulas and in solving algebraically the problems in the following chapters. Mathematical operations for a large portion of the problems in this text usually can be simplified greatly when algebraic methods are used.

## 2.1 INTRODUCTION

Arithmetic operations and algebraic operations are closely related. In fact, the basic principles of the four fundamental operations of algebra—addition, subtraction, multiplication, and division—are the same as those of arithmetic operations. However, algebra is characterized by the use of letters as symbols for numbers and by the relationships among numbers being expressed in the form of equations.

## A. Basic Arithmetic Rules as Applied to Algebra

Let $a$, $b$, $c$, and $d$ represent numbers.

If $a = b$ and $c = b$, then $a = c$;
if $a = b$ and $c = d$, then $a + c = b + d$;
if $a = b$ and $c = d$, then $a - c = b - d$;
if $a = b$ and $c = d$, then $a \times c = b \times d$; and
if $a = b$ and $c = d$, then $a/c = b/d$, provided $c$ is a number other than zero.

Other important arithmetic rules which are accepted for algebra are as follows:

$a + b = b + a$. *Check:* Let $a$ and $b$ represent any two numbers. For example, let $a = 9$ and $b = 7$. Thus, $9 + 7 = 7 + 9 = 16$.

$a + b + c = (a + b) + c = a + (b + c)$. *Check:* Let $a = 9$, $b = 7$, $c = 4$. Thus, $9 + 7 + 4 = (9 + 7) + 4 = 9 + (7 + 4) = 20$.

$a \times b = b \times a$. *Check:* Let $a = 5$, $b = 3$. Thus, $5 \times 3 = 3 \times 5 = 15$.

$a \times b \times c = (a \times b) \times c = a \times (b \times c)$. *Check:* Let $a = 5$, $b = 3$, $c = 2$. Thus, $5 \times 3 \times 2 = (5 \times 3) \times 2 = 5 \times (3 \times 2) = 30$.

Other signs instead of "$\times$" are frequently used in multiplication in algebra. For example, the product of $a$ and $c$ may be written $a \cdot c$, $(a)(c)$, or simply $ac$. Thus, the two equations above may be written as $ab = ba$, and $abc = (ab)c = a(bc)$, respectively.

Division should be done in the order indicated. Thus,

$$a \div b \div c = (a \div b) \div c, \text{ or } \frac{\frac{a}{b}}{c} = \frac{a}{b} \cdot \frac{1}{c} = \frac{a}{bc},$$

$$not = a \div (b \div c), \text{ or } \frac{a}{\frac{b}{c}} = a \cdot \frac{c}{b} = \frac{ac}{b}$$

$$48 \div 6 \div 2 = (48 \div 6) \div 2 = 8 \div 2 = 4,$$
$$not = 48 \div (6 \div 2) = 48 \div 3 = 16$$

However, the following order is also permissible:

$$a \div b \div c = (a \div c) \div b, \text{ or } = \frac{\frac{a}{c}}{b} = \frac{a}{c} \cdot \frac{1}{b} = \frac{a}{bc}$$

$$48 \div 6 \div 2 = (48 \div 2) \div 6 = 24 \div 6 = 4$$

Note that in the above division, $a$ is the dividend, and $b$ and $c$ are divisors. The order of divisors may be changed in division.

## B. Terminology in Algebra

### ALGEBRAIC EXPRESSION

An *algebraic expression,* or simply an *expression,* is any symbol or combination of symbols that represents a number. When an expression consists of several parts that are connected by plus (+) and minus (−) signs, each of the parts, together with the sign preceding it, is called a *term.* If there is no sign expressed preceding a term, the sign is understood to be plus. An expression consisting of one term is called a *monomial,* whereas an expression having more than one term is called a *multinomial,* or a *polynomial.* An expression of two terms is also called a *binomial,* whereas one of three terms is a *trinomial.* For example, $+4ax$ or $4ax$ is an expression and is a *monomial;* $4ax + 7$ is also an expression but has two terms and is a binomial; and the expression $ax^2 + 4x + 5$ is a trinomial.

## FACTOR AND COEFFICIENT

If two or more numbers are multiplied together, each number or the product of any of the numbers is called a *factor.* Any factor of a term is called the *coefficient* of the remaining factors. When a factor is an explicit number, it is called the *numerical coefficient* of the term; other factors are called *literal coefficients.* As an illustration let us examine the term $6xy.$ Each number and symbol—6, $x,$ and $y$—or the product of any of these—$6x,$ $6y,$ and $xy$—is called a factor. The coefficient of $6x$ is $y;$ $y$ is the literal coefficient. The coefficient of $xy$ is 6; 6 is the numerical coefficient. If no numerical coefficient is indicated in a term, it is understood that the numerical coefficient is one.

## POWER

The product of equal factors is called a *power* of the factor. Thus, $a \cdot a \cdot a$ is the third power of $a$ and is written $a^3;$ $2 \cdot 2 \cdot 2 \cdot 2$ $(= 16)$ is the fourth power of 2 and is written $2^4.$ The symbol $a$ is called the *base,* and the number 3, which indicates the number of equal factors, is the *exponent.* The expression of an indicated power of a given symbol or number is called an *exponential,* such as $a^3.$ The exponent for the first power of a base is 1, which is understood and usually is not written; that is, $a^1 = a.$ A second power is called a *square,* whereas a third power is a *cube.*

## + AND − SIGNS

The plus and minus signs which were used exclusively to indicate addition and subtraction in arithmetic are now also used as the indicators of positive numbers and negative numbers. When the concept of positive or negative numbers is disregarded, the value of any number is then called its *absolute value* and is denoted by the sign $\|.$ When no sign is written, the number is understood to be a positive one. For example, $+3$ or $3$ is a positive number, whereas $-3$ is a negative number; $|+3|$ and $|-3|$ indicate the absolute value of 3; that is, $|+3| = |-3| = |3|.$

# C. Operations with 0 and 1

The numbers zero and one have certain properties which are explained as follows:

1. When zero is added to a number, the sum is the number unchanged. Thus, $3 + 0 = 3$; $a + 0 = a$; $0 + 0 = 0$.
2. When zero is subtracted from a number, the remainder is the number unchanged. Thus, $3 - 0 = 3$; $a - 0 = a$; $0 - 0 = 0$. However, when a number is subtracted from zero, the remainder is the absolute value of the number with its sign changed. Thus $0 - 3$ or $0 - (+3) = -3$; $0 - (-3) = +3$ or $3$; $0 - a = -a$; $0 - (-a) = a$.
3. When zero is multiplied by a number, or a number is multiplied by zero, the product is zero. Thus, $3 \times 0 = 0$; $0 \times 3 = 0$; $0 \times 0 = 0$; $a \times 0 = 0$.
4. When zero is divided by any number except zero, the quotient is zero. Thus, $0 \div 3$ or $\dfrac{0}{3} = 0$; $\dfrac{0}{a} = 0$.
5. Division by zero has no meaning because there is no answer. For example, if $\dfrac{7}{0} = c$, then by multiplying both sides of the equation by 0, we have $\dfrac{7}{\cancel{0}} \times \cancel{0} = c0$, or $7 = c0 = 0$. We know that $7 \neq 0$, or 7 is not equal to 0. When $\frac{0}{0}$, the quotient is meaningless. (Note that the symbol $\neq$ is read "is not equal to.")
6. When a number is multiplied by one, the product is the number unchanged. Thus, $6 \times 1 = 6$; $a \times 1 = a$.
7. When a number is divided by one, the quotient is the number unchanged. Thus, $\dfrac{6}{1} = 6$; $\dfrac{a}{1} = a$.

## 2.2 ADDITION

## A. Addition of Signed Numbers

### ADDITION OF NUMBERS HAVING THE SAME SIGNS

When adding numbers that have the same signs, first find the sum of their absolute values. Second, prefix the common sign to this sum.

**Example 1**    Add $(-5)$, $(-6)$, and $(-3)$.

The sum of the absolute values is $5 + 6 + 3 = 14$.
The common sign is negative. Thus,

$$(-5) + (-6) + (-3) = -14$$

**Example 2**    $(+4) + (+2.16) + (+7.59) = +13.75$

### ADDITION OF NUMBERS HAVING UNLIKE SIGNS

When adding numbers that have unlike signs, first subtract the smaller absolute value from the larger. Second, prefix the sign of the larger to the remainder.

**Example 3**    Add $(-9)$ and $(+3)$.

The difference between the two absolute values is $9 - 3 = 6$.
The sign of the larger number, 9, is negative. Thus,

$$(-9) + (+3) = -6$$

To obtain the sum of three or more numbers having unlike signs, we may first add two of the numbers; then add the sum to the third number, and so on.

**Example 4**    $(+14) + (-15) + (+.8179) = (-1) + (+.8179) = -.1821$.

Or, first add numbers having the same sign, then combine:

$$(+14) + (-15) + (+.8179) = (+14.8179) + (-15) = -.1821.$$

## B. Addition of Algebraic Expressions

### ADDITION OF MONOMIALS

Terms whose literal factors are the same are called *like terms*. To add like terms, add the numerical coefficients. The sum thus obtained is the coefficient of the common literal factors.

**Example 5**    Add $5ax$, $9ax$, and $(-20ax)$.

The sum of the numerical coefficients is
$5 + 9 + (-20) = -6$. Thus,

$$5ax + 9ax + (-20ax) = -6ax$$

The numerical coefficients of *unlike terms*, such as $5a$ and $6b$, cannot be combined; their sum is simply indicated by signs and is written as a polynomial, $5a + 6b$.

**Example 6**    Add $6xy$, $(-5x)$, $(-3xy)$, and $(-4x)$.

$6xy + (-3xy) = 3xy$
$(-5x) + (-4x) = -9x$. Thus,

$$6xy + (-5x) + (-3xy) + (-4x) = 3xy + (-9x) = 3xy - 9x$$

The process of finding the algebraic sum of like terms and unlike terms is sometimes called *collecting terms*.

### ADDITION OF POLYNOMIALS

Like terms should be combined when two or more polynomials are added. Each set of like terms may be arranged in a vertical column before adding.

**Example 7**    Add $(3a + 4b + 6)$, $(-4a - 6b - 3)$, and $(7a + 4b - 9)$.

$$
\begin{array}{r}
3a + 4b + 6 \\
-4a - 6b - 3 \\
7a + 4b - 9 \\
\hline
6a + 2b - 6
\end{array}
$$

## 2.3 SUBTRACTION

## A. Subtraction of Signed Numbers

When subtracting signed numbers, first change the sign of the subtrahend (the number to be subtracted). Second, add.

**Example 1**  Subtract $(-17)$ from $(-8)$.

$$(-8) - (-17) = (-8) + (+17) = 9$$

**Example 2**  Subtract $(-16)$ from $(+19)$.

$$(+19) - (-16) = 19 + (+16) = 35$$

**Example 3**  Subtract $(+17.436)$ from $(+12)$

$$(+12) - (+17.436) = 12 + (-17.436) = -5.436$$

## B. Subtraction of Algebraic Expressions

### SUBTRACTION OF MONOMIALS

To subtract like terms, subtract the numerical coefficient of the subtrahend from that of the minuend. The remainder thus obtained is the coefficient of the common literal factors.

**Example 4**  Subtract $5xy$ from $18xy$.

$18xy - 5xy = 13xy$, or
$(18 - 5)xy = 13xy$

**Example 5**  Subtract $-7ab$ from $11ab$.

$11ab - (-7ab) = 11ab + 7ab = 18ab$, or
$[11 - (-7)]ab = 18ab$

### SUBTRACTION OF POLYNOMIALS

When one polynomial is subtracted from another, change the sign of each term in the subtrahend and then add.

**Example 6**  Subtract:

$$
\begin{array}{ll}
\phantom{xxxxxxxxxx} 5a - 2b + 9 & \text{(Minuend)} \\
\phantom{xxxxxxxxxx} -2a + 9b - 4 & \text{(Subtrahend)}
\end{array}
$$

| | | |
|---|---|---|
| Minuend | $5a - 2b + 9$ | (with the same signs) |
| Subtrahend | $2a - 9b + 4$ | (signs are changed) |
| | $7a - 11b + 13$ | (add) |

Or, written in horizontal form,

$(5a - 2b + 9) - (-2a + 9b - 4)$
$= 5a - 2b + 9 + 2a - 9b + 4$
$= 7a - 11b + 13$

**Example 7**   Subtract $(-3a + 4b - 5)$ from $(5a - 8 + 6b)$.

$(5a - 8 + 6b) - (-3a + 4b - 5)$
$= 5a - 8 + 6b + 3a - 4b + 5$
$= 8a + 2b - 3$

## EXERCISE 2–1

### Reference: Sections 2.2 and 2.3

**A.** *Addition of Signed Numbers:*

**1.** $(-4) + (-5)$        **17.** $(+35) + (-46.23)$
**2.** $(-7) + (-6)$        **18.** $(+29) + (-60.15)$
**3.** $(-16) + (-18)$      **19.** $(+56) + (-80.37)$
**4.** $(-13) + (-17)$      **20.** $(+48) + (-54.49)$
**5.** $(-14) + (-24)$      **21.** $(-17.264) + (+30)$
**6.** $(-19) + (-2)$       **22.** $(-42.317) + (+46)$
**7.** $(-21) + (-16)$      **23.** $(-40.943) + (+64)$
**8.** $(-42) + (-9)$       **24.** $(-39.174) + (+50)$
**9.** $(+15) + (+7)$       **25.** $(-7) + (-4) + (-12)$
**10.** $(+51) + (+16)$     **26.** $(-18) + (+20) + (+6)$
**11.** $(+18) + (+13)$     **27.** $(+4) + (-8) + (+11)$
**12.** $(+57) + (+41)$     **28.** $(+10) + (-42) + (-41)$
**13.** $(+46) + (-30)$     **29.** $(+6) + (-4) + (-12) + (-17)$
**14.** $(+26) + (-15)$     **30.** $(-2) + (+4) + (-21) + (+6)$
**15.** $(+24) + (-13)$     **31.** $(+4) + (+19) + (+42) + (-63)$
**16.** $(+36) + (-15)$     **32.** $(-41) + (-36) + (-42) + (-7)$

**B.** *Addition of Algebraic Terms:*

**33.** $20a + (-16a)$              **43.** $24w + (-3w) + (7w)$
**34.** $29bc + (-12bc)$            **44.** $(-36q) + 3q + (-16q)$
**35.** $(-30c) + 5c$               **45.** $8cd + (-6c) + 4c + (-6cd)$
**36.** $(-16t) + (-2t)$            **46.** $6xy + 3x + (-15xy) + (-2x)$
**37.** $(-32et) + 7et$             **47.** $4ab + (-a) + 7ab + (-2ab)$
**38.** $(-42d) + 3d$               **48.** $7tb + 5t + 16tb + (-3t)$
**39.** $(-45f) + (-32f)$           **49.** $(3a + 7b + 4) + (2a + 5b - 2) + (5a - 2b + 1)$
**40.** $(-46g) + 5g$               **50.** $(6x + 4y + 3) + (3x - 7y - 2) + (5x + 2y - 6)$
**41.** $28h + 46h + (-17h)$        **51.** $(4xy + 33x + 11y + 1) + (3xy - 5x - 4y - 1)$
**42.** $43v + 13v + 40v$           **52.** $(6abc + 4ab - 3bc + 6) + (3abc - 2ab + bc - 2)$

**C.** *Subtraction of Signed Numbers:*

**53.** $(+10) - (-4)$        **56.** $(+36) - (-5)$
**54.** $(+15) - (-6)$        **57.** $(-6) - (-8)$
**55.** $(+42) - (-7)$        **58.** $(-16) - (-17)$

**59.** $(-40) - (-12)$

**60.** $(-19) - (-6)$

**61.** $(-6.24) - (+11.1278)$

**62.** $(+3.19) - (-12.4654)$

**63.** $(-6.145) - (+25.216)$

**64.** $(+8.627) - (-17.354)$

**65.** $(+5) - (-6) - (+4.21)$

**66.** $(+9) - (+6) - (-15.46)$

**67.** $(-10) - (-11) - (-13.83)$

**68.** $(-16) - (+7) - (+2.59)$

**69.** $(-32) + (-4) - (+6) - (-10)$

**70.** $(+46) - (-3) + (-4) - (-10)$

**71.** $(-43) + (+7) - (-63) - (+4)$

**72.** $(+39) + (-30) - (+7) + (-4)$

**D.** *Subtraction of Algebraic Terms:*

**73.** $16xy - 6xy$

**74.** $31x - (-7x)$

**75.** $46ab - 6ab$

**76.** $36t - 2t$

**77.** $(-9bc) - (-4bc)$

**78.** $(-6cd) - 7cd$

**79.** $(-4b) - (-2b)$

**80.** $(-12ct) - 5ct$

**81.** $4a - (2a + 7a - 6d)$

**82.** $(-8t) - (-4t + 3t - 6t)$

**83.** $(23f - 4f) - (5f + 2f)$

**84.** $(17g + 4g) - (7g - 3g)$

**85.** $(14h + 2h) - (3h + 4h)$

**86.** $(17tb + 2tb) - (-4tb - 7tb)$

**87.** $(5a + 2b + 7) - (4a + 3b + 6)$

**88.** $(4xy + 2x + 6) - (2xy - 6x + 4)$

**89.** $(-72b + 6a - 9) - (-3ab + 4b + 5)$

**90.** $(-6xy - 5x + 4) - (2xy - 7y - 3)$

## 2.4 MULTIPLICATION

## A. Multiplication of Signed Numbers

When multiplying two numbers having unlike signs, multiply the numerical values and prefix a negative sign to the product.

**Example 1**    $(+6) \times (-9) = -54$; and $(-6) \times (+3) = -18$

If the two numbers have like signs, prefix a positive sign to the product.

**Example 2**    $(-4) \times (-5) = +20$, and $(+4) \times (+5) = +20$

## B. Multiplication of Algebraic Expressions

### MULTIPLICATION OF EXPONENTIALS

When multiplication involves exponentials, the following laws apply. When exponentials have the same base:

**Law (1)**    $a^m \cdot a^n = a^{m+n}$

*Illustration:*

$$a^m \cdot a^n = \overbrace{(a \cdot a \cdot a \cdot a \ldots)}^{m \text{ factors}} \overbrace{(a \cdot a \cdot a \cdot a \ldots)}^{n \text{ factors}} = a^{m+n}$$

**Example 3**    $2^3 \cdot 2^2 = (2 \cdot 2 \cdot 2)(2 \cdot 2) = 2^5$; or $2^3 \cdot 2^2 = 2^{3+2} = 2^5 = 32$

**Example 4**    $x^3 \cdot x^4 = (x \cdot x \cdot x)(x \cdot x \cdot x \cdot x) = x^7$; or $x^3 \cdot x^4 = x^{3+4} = x^7$

The above law gives the following definitions:

$$\text{I. } a^0 = 1 \quad (a \neq 0)$$

***Note:***     "$\neq$" means "not equal to."

*Illustration:*     $a^m \cdot a^0 = a^{m+0} = a^m$

$$a^0 = \frac{a^m}{a^m} = 1$$

Thus, $4^0 = 1$;    $5^0 = 1$;    $126^0 = 1$

$$\text{II. } a^{-m} = \frac{1}{a^m}$$

*Illustration:*     $a^m \cdot a^{-m} = a^{m+(-m)} = a^0 = 1$

$$a^{-m} = \frac{1}{a^m}$$

Thus, $4^{-1} = \frac{1}{4}$;   $5^{-2} = \frac{1}{5^2} = \frac{1}{25}$;   $2^{-4} = \frac{1}{2^4} = \frac{1}{16}$

When exponentials have different bases but have the same exponent:

**Law (2)**     $a^m \cdot b^m = (ab)^m$

*Illustration:*

$$a^m \cdot b^m = \overbrace{(a \cdot a \cdot a \cdot a \ \ldots\ldots\ldots)}^{m \text{ factors}}\overbrace{(b \cdot b \cdot b \cdot b \ldots\ldots\ldots)}^{m \text{ factors}}$$

$$= \overbrace{ab \cdot ab \cdot ab \cdot ab \ldots\ldots\ldots\ldots}^{m \text{ products}}$$

$$= (ab)^m$$

**Example 5**     $5^2 \cdot 4^2 = 5 \cdot 5 \cdot 4 \cdot 4 = (5 \cdot 4)(5 \cdot 4) = 20^2 = 400$;

or $5^2 \cdot 4^2 = (5 \cdot 4)^2 = 20^2 = 400$

**Example 6**     $x^3 \cdot y^3 = (x \cdot x \cdot x)(y \cdot y \cdot y) = (xy)(xy)(xy) = (xy)^3$; or $x^3 y^3 = (xy)^3$

When the base is an exponential:

**Law (3)**     $(a^m)^n = a^{mn}$, or $(a^{\frac{1}{m}})^n = a^{\frac{n}{m}}$

*Illustration:*     $(a^m)^n = \overbrace{a^m \cdot a^m \cdot a^m \cdot a^m \ldots\ldots\ldots\ldots}^{n \text{ exponentials}}$

$$= a^{\overbrace{m+m+m+m \ \cdot\ \cdot\ \cdot\ \cdot\ \cdot\ \cdot\ \cdot}^{n \text{ times}}}$$

$$= a^{mn}$$

**Example 7**     $(3^2)^3 = (3 \cdot 3)(3 \cdot 3)(3 \cdot 3) = 3^6 = 729$, or

$(3^2)^3 = 3^{2 \cdot 3} = 3^6 = 729$

**Example 8**   $(x^3)^2 = (x \cdot x \cdot x)(x \cdot x \cdot x) = x^6$; or $(x^3)^2 = x^{3 \cdot 2} = x^6$

**Example 9**   $(3^{\frac{1}{2}})^4 = (3^{\frac{1}{2}})(3^{\frac{1}{2}})(3^{\frac{1}{2}})(3^{\frac{1}{2}}) = 3^{\frac{1}{2}+\frac{1}{2}+\frac{1}{2}+\frac{1}{2}} = 3^2 = 9$; or

$(3^{\frac{1}{2}})^4 = 3^{\frac{4}{2}} = 3^2 = 9$

**Example 10**   $(x^{\frac{1}{3}})^2 = (x^{\frac{1}{3}})(x^{\frac{1}{3}}) = x^{\frac{1}{3}+\frac{1}{3}} = x^{\frac{2}{3}}$; or $(x^{\frac{1}{3}})^2 = x^{\frac{2}{3}}$

## MULTIPLICATION OF MONOMIALS

The product of two or more monomials is equal to the product of their numerical coefficients multiplied by the product of their literal factors.

**Example 11**   $5ab \cdot 4c = 20abc$

**Example 12**   $3x^2 \cdot 4x^3y \cdot 5y^2 = (3 \cdot 4 \cdot 5)x^{2+3}y^{1+2} = 60x^5y^3$

## MULTIPLYING A POLYNOMIAL BY A MONOMIAL

Multiply each term of the polynomial by the monomial. The algebraic sum of the partial products is the product of the multiplication.

**Example 13**   Multiply $(4a + 7b)$ by $3c$.

$$\begin{array}{r} 4a + 7b \\ 3c \\ \hline \end{array}$$

$12ac + 21bc$, or, as written:

$(4a + 7b)3c = (4a \times 3c) + (7b \times 3c) = 12ac + 21bc$

## MULTIPLYING A POLYNOMIAL BY ANOTHER POLYNOMIAL

Multiply each term of the multiplicand by each term of the multiplier. The algebraic sum of the partial products is the product of the multiplication.

**Example 14**   Multiply $(4a + 7b)$ by $(3c + 5d)$.

$$\begin{array}{l} 4a + 7b \\ 3c + 5d \\ \hline 12ac + 21bc \\ \phantom{12ac + 21bc} + 20ad + 35bd \\ \hline 12ac + 21bc + 20ad + 35bd, \text{ or, as written:} \end{array}$$

$(4a + 7b)(3c + 5d) = 12ac + 21bc + 20ad + 35bd$

Notice that $12ac = (4a)(3c)$; $21bc = (7b)(3c)$; $20ad = (4a)(5d)$; and $35bd = (7b)(5d)$.

The following examples are used to illustrate the multiplication of polynomials involving exponentials:

**Example 15**   Multiply: $(3a - 2)(2a + 5)$.

$$\begin{array}{r} 3a - 2 \\ 2a + 5 \\ \hline 6a^2 - 4a \\ + 15a - 10 \\ \hline 6a^2 + 11a - 10, \text{ or} \end{array}$$

$$(3a-2)(2a+5) = 6a^2 - 4a + 15a - 10 = 6a^2 + 11a - 10.$$

Notice that $6a^2 = (3a)(2a)$; $-4a = (-2)(2a)$; $+15a = (3a)(5)$; and $-10 = (-2)(5)$.

**Example 16**    Multiply: $(4bx - 3y)(3b^2 + 2y)$.

$$4bx - 3y$$
$$3b^2 + 2y$$
$$\overline{12b^3x - 9b^2y}$$
$$\phantom{12b^3x - 9b^2y}\ + 8bxy - 6y^2$$
$$\overline{12b^3x - 9b^2y + 8bxy - 6y^2,}\ \text{or}$$

$$(4bx - 3y)(3b^2 + 2y) = 12b^3x - 9b^2y + 8bxy - 6y^2$$

# EXERCISE 2–2

## Reference: Section 2.4

**A.** *Multiply the following signed numbers:*

1. $(-5)(-6)$
2. $(+4)(+7)$
3. $(-6)(-10)$
4. $(+5)(+9)$
5. $(-6)(-3)$
6. $(+9)(+4)$

7. $(+5)(+7)$
8. $(-3)(-8)$
9. $(-6)(+4)$
10. $(+5)(-7)$
11. $(-8)(+9)$

12. $(-12)(+11)$
13. $(-7)(+2)$
14. $(+10)(-5)$
15. $(+34)(-62)$
16. $(+14)(-45)$

**B.** *Simplify the following:*

17. $2^5 \cdot 2^2$
18. $4^2 \cdot 4^0$
19. $5^3 \cdot 5^4$
20. $6^2 \cdot 6^2$
21. $a^6 \cdot a^2$
22. $b^3 \cdot b^{-5}$
23. $c^4 \cdot c^0$
24. $d^5 \cdot d^2$
25. $3^2 \cdot 4^2$

26. $2^3 \cdot 5^3$
27. $x^3 \cdot y^3$
28. $a^4 \cdot b^4 \cdot c^4$
29. $m^a n^a$
30. $t^7 r p^7 r$
31. $(5^2)^3$
32. $(4^3)^2$
33. $(p^5)^2$

34. $(x^4)^3$
35. $(y^a)^b$
36. $(ab^2)^3$
37. $(b^{\frac{1}{x}})^y$
38. $(d^{\frac{1}{p}})^q$
39. $(4^{\frac{1}{2}})^6$
40. $(16^{\frac{1}{2}})^4$

**C.** *Multiply the following algebraic expressions:*

41. $(9x)(-3y)$
42. $5ab \cdot 7c$
43. $4xy \cdot 5y$
44. $(-7ab) \cdot 2b$
45. $4x^2 \cdot 2xy \cdot 3y$
46. $6t \cdot (-3t) \cdot (-4tp)$
47. $(-5pq) \cdot 3pq^2 \cdot p^3$
48. $(-8bc) \cdot (-4bcd) \cdot 3b$

49. $2(4a + 3)$
50. $3(2b + 7)$
51. $5(4c - 3)$
52. $-4(3d - b)$
53. $4t(a + b)$
54. $-5c(-4c + 5)$
55. $7b(-3e + 2b)$
56. $3t(-3t - 2p)$

57. $(a + b)(a - b)$
58. $(a + b)(a + b)$
59. $(a - b)(a - b)$
60. $(3m + 2)(4m - 3)$
61. $(-4y + 2)(y - 3)$
62. $(3ab + 2c)(a + 3c)$
63. $(3t^2 - 3a)(2t^3 + 4)$
64. $(-5d^2 + e)(3c^2 - e)$

## 2.5 DIVISION

## A. Division of Signed Numbers

When dividing one number by another with unlike signs, divide the numerical values and prefix a negative sign to the quotient.

**Example 1**     $10 \div (-2) = -5; (-18) \div (+3) = -6$

If two numbers have like signs, the quotient is positive.

**Example 2**     $10 \div 2 = 5; (-18) \div (-3) = 6$

## B. Division of Algebraic Expressions

### DIVISION INVOLVING EXPONENTIALS

When division involves exponentials, the following laws apply:

When exponentials have the same base:

**Law (1)**     $a^m \div a^n = \dfrac{a^m}{a^n} = a^{m-n}$

**Example 3**     $2^5 \div 2^3 = \dfrac{2 \cdot 2 \cdot 2 \cdot 2 \cdot 2}{2 \cdot 2 \cdot 2} = 2^2 = 4$, or

$2^5 \div 2^3 = \dfrac{2^5}{2^3} = 2^{5-3} = 2^2 = 4$

**Example 4**     $2^3 \div 2^5 = \dfrac{2 \cdot 2 \cdot 2}{2 \cdot 2 \cdot 2 \cdot 2 \cdot 2} = \dfrac{1}{2 \cdot 2} = \dfrac{1}{2^2} = \dfrac{1}{4}$, or

$2^3 \div 2^5 = \dfrac{2^3}{2^5} = 2^{3-5} = 2^{-2} = \dfrac{1}{2^2} = \dfrac{1}{4}$

**Note:**     See Law (1), definition II on page 34.

**Example 5**     $x^4 \div x^2 = \dfrac{x^4}{x^2} = \dfrac{x \cdot x \cdot x \cdot x}{x \cdot x} = x \cdot x = x^2$, or

$\dfrac{x^4}{x^2} = x^{4-2} = x^2$

Similarly,

$a^m \div a^n = \dfrac{a^m}{a^n} = a^{m-n}$, if $m > n$;

$\dfrac{a^m}{a^n} = a^{m-n} = a^{-(n-m)} = \dfrac{1}{a^{n-m}}$, if $m < n$;

$\dfrac{a^m}{a^n} = a^{m-n} = a^0 = 1$,   if $m = n$

***Note:*** The sign ">" means greater than; "$m > n$" means $m$ is greater than $n$. The sign "<" means smaller than; "$m < n$" means $m$ is smaller than $n$.

$a^m \div a^n = a^{m-n}$ may be proved in the following manner:

$$\frac{a^m}{a^n} = a^m \cdot \frac{1}{a^n}$$
$$= a^m \cdot a^{-n}$$
$$= a^{m-n}$$

When exponentials have different bases but have the same exponent:

**Law (2)**    $\dfrac{a^m}{b^m} = \left(\dfrac{a}{b}\right)^m$

*Illustration:*    $\dfrac{a^m}{b^m} = \dfrac{a \cdot a \cdot a \cdot a \dots\dots (m \text{ factors})}{b \cdot b \cdot b \cdot b \dots\dots (m \text{ factors})}$

$$= \frac{a}{b} \cdot \frac{a}{b} \cdot \frac{a}{b} \cdot \frac{a}{b} \dots\dots (m \text{ factors}) = \left(\frac{a}{b}\right)^m$$

**Example 6**    $\dfrac{6^2}{3^2} = \dfrac{6 \cdot 6}{3 \cdot 3} = \dfrac{6}{3} \cdot \dfrac{6}{3} = \left(\dfrac{6}{3}\right)^2 = 2^2 = 4$, or

$$\frac{6^2}{3^2} = \left(\frac{6}{3}\right)^2 = 2^2 = 4$$

**Example 7**    $x^3 \cdot y^{-3} = \dfrac{x^3}{y^3} = \left(\dfrac{x}{y}\right)^3$

## DIVISION INVOLVING MONOMIALS

When dividing a monomial by another monomial, the quotient of the division is found by multiplying the quotient of the numerical coefficients by the quotient of the literal coefficients.

**Example 8**    Divide $-45x^3$ by $5x$.

$$\frac{-45x^3}{5x} = \frac{-45}{5} \cdot \frac{x^3}{x} = -9x^2$$

**Example 9**    Divide $36x^5y^2z^4$ by $9ax^2y^3$.

$$\frac{36x^5y^2z^4}{9ax^2y^3} = \frac{36}{9} \cdot \frac{1}{a} \cdot \frac{x^5}{x^2} \cdot \frac{y^2}{y^3} \cdot \frac{z^4}{1} = \frac{4x^3z^4}{ay}$$

## DIVIDING A POLYNOMIAL BY A MONOMIAL

Divide each term of the polynomial by the monomial. The algebraic sum of the partial quotients is the quotient of the division.

**Example 10**    Divide $28a^2b^3 - 7a^3b + 3ab^3$ by $7a^2b^2$.

$$\frac{28a^2b^3}{7a^2b^2} = 4b; \quad \frac{-7a^3b}{7a^2b^2} = -\frac{a}{b}; \quad \frac{3ab^3}{7a^2b^2} = \frac{3b}{7a}. \quad \text{Thus,}$$

$$\frac{28a^2b^3 - 7a^3b + 3ab^3}{7a^2b^2} = 4b - \frac{a}{b} + \frac{3b}{7a}$$

## DIVIDING A POLYNOMIAL BY ANOTHER POLYNOMIAL

The procedure of dividing one polynomial by another is illustrated in the following example:

**Example 11** 　Divide $(15x^3 - 3 + 2x^2)$ by $(3x^2 + 5 - 2x)$.

The division is arranged as follows:

(Dividend)
$$\begin{array}{r|l} 15x^3 + \phantom{0}2x^2 \phantom{+25x} - 3 & 3x^2 - 2x + 5 \quad \text{(Divisor)} \\ \underline{15x^3 - 10x^2 + 25x} & 5x + 4 \qquad\quad \text{(Quotient)} \\ 12x^2 - 25x - \phantom{0}3 \\ \underline{12x^2 - \phantom{0}8x + 20} \\ - 17x - 23 \quad \text{(Remainder)} \end{array}$$

The division may also be written in the following form:

(Divisor)
$$\begin{array}{r} 5x + \phantom{0}4 \quad \text{(Quotient)} \\ 3x^2 - 2x + 5 \overline{)\phantom{0}15x^3 + \phantom{0}2x^2 \phantom{+25x} - 3} \quad \text{(Dividend)} \\ \underline{15x^3 - 10x^2 + 25x} \\ 12x^2 - 25x - \phantom{0}3 \\ \underline{12x^2 - \phantom{0}8x + 20} \\ - 17x - 23 \quad \text{(Remainder)} \end{array}$$

Thus, the solution equation is

$$(15x^3 + 2x^2 - 3) \div (3x^2 - 2x + 5) = (5x + 4) + \frac{-17x - 23}{3x^2 - 2x + 5}$$

The steps in the division above are summarized below:

**Step (1)** 　Arrange the terms of both the dividend and the divisor in descending (or ascending) powers of the same letter.

Dividend: $15x^3 - 3 + 2x^2 = 15x^3 + 2x^2 - 3$
Divisor: 　$3x^2 + 5 - 2x \phantom{0}= \phantom{0}3x^2 - 2x \phantom{0}+ 5$

**Step (2)** 　Divide the first term of the dividend by the first term of the divisor to obtain the first term of the quotient.

$$15x^3 \div 3x^2 = 5x$$

**Step (3)** 　Multiply the divisor by the quotient term of Step (2).

$$(3x^2 - 2x + 5)(5x) = 15x^3 - 10x^2 + 25x$$

**Step (4)** 　Subtract the product of Step (3) from the dividend to obtain a remainder. If the remainder is not zero or is not a lower power than the divisor, continue dividing it by the procedure used in Steps (2), (3), and (4).

*Check:*          **Method A**  Let $x = 2$ (or any number except 0 or 1.)

Substitute the value in the solution equation.

Left side $= [15(2)^3 + 2(2)^2 - 3] \div [3(2)^2 - 2(2) + 5]$
$= (120 + 8 - 3) \div (12 - 4 + 5)$
$= 125 \div 13 = 9\frac{8}{13}$

Right side $= [5(2) + 4] + \dfrac{-17(2) - 23}{3(2)^2 - 2(2) + 5} = 14 + \dfrac{-57}{13}$

$= 14 - 4\frac{5}{13} = 9\frac{8}{13}$

★**Method B**   $\dfrac{\text{Dividend}}{\text{Divisor}} = \text{Quotient} + \dfrac{\text{Remainder}}{\text{Divisor}}$, or

Dividend $=$ Quotient $\times$ Divisor $+$ Remainder

Thus,          Dividend $= (5x + 4)(3x^2 - 2x + 5) + (-17x - 23)$
$= 5x(3x^2 - 2x + 5) + 4(3x^2 - 2x + 5) + (-17x - 23)$
$= 15x^3 - 10x^2 + 25x + 12x^2 - 8x + 20 - 17x - 23$
$= 15x^3 + 2x^2 - 3$, which is correct.

## EXERCISE 2–3

**Reference: Section 2.5**

**A.** *Divide:*

1. $12 \div (-3)$
2. $10 \div (-2)$
3. $16 \div (-4)$
4. $20 \div (-5)$
5. $(-18) \div 2$
6. $(-36) \div 9$
7. $(-81) \div 3$
8. $(-121) \div 11$
9. $(-42) \div (-2)$
10. $(-55) \div (-11)$
11. $(-76) \div (-4)$
12. $(-36) \div (-12)$
13. $72 \div 3$
14. $136 \div 4$
15. $\dfrac{72}{-8}$
16. $\dfrac{-48}{12}$
17. $\dfrac{-55}{-5}$

18. $\dfrac{27}{(-3)(-3)}$
19. $\dfrac{(-4)(-5)}{-2}$
20. $\dfrac{-32}{(-4)(2)}$
21. $2^5 \div 2^3$
22. $4^5 \div 4^2$
23. $6^3 \div 6^5$
24. $7^4 \div 7^6$
25. $a^5 \div a^2$
26. $b^9 \div b^8$
27. $x^5 \div x^9$
28. $t^3 \div t^7$
29. $15^2 \div 3^2$
30. $4^2 \div 2^2$
31. $8^3 \div 2^3$
32. $26^3 \div 13^3$
33. $a^3 \div b^3$
34. $x^5 \div y^5$

**35.** $(ab)^4 \div c^4$

**36.** $(x^2y^2) \div y^2$

**37.** $52x^2 \div 2x$

**38.** $36x^3 \div (-2x^2)$

**39.** $42a^2 \div 2a$

**40.** $34b^2c \div 17bc$

**41.** $7ab \div 4a^2b$

**42.** $(-5x) \div 4x^3$

**43.** $(-6x) \div 2x^4$

**44.** $4t^3 \div 12t^5$

**45.** $(2b^4 - 18b^2) \div 3b$

**46.** $(4n^3 + 5n^2t) \div 2n^2$

**47.** $(8a^5 - ab^2) \div (-2a)$

**48.** $(14t^7 - 4t^3q) \div 2t^2$

**49.** $(-18m^3n - 4m^2n^8 - 6mn) \div 2mn$

**50.** $(14p^2q^3 - 21pq^3 - 7q^6) \div (-7q^4)$

**51.** $(-18a^2b + 8ab - 8b^2) \div 8b$

**52.** $(2b^3 - 3b^2 + 10b^5cx) \div (-6b^4)$

**B.** *Divide the following and check (let* x $=2$):

**53.** $(12x^2 + 5x - 25) \div (4x - 5)$

**54.** $(21x^2 - 5x + 23) \div (7x + 3)$

**55.** $(24x^3 - x^2 - 2x + 42) \div (8x + 5)$

**56.** $(36x^3 + 2x^2 + x + 4) \div (9x - 4)$

**57.** $(25x^3 + 5x^2 + 3x - 2) \div (5x^2 - 2x + 3)$

**58.** $(20x^3 + 3x^2 - 4x + 5) \div (4x^2 + 3x - 7)$

**59.** $(28x^3 + 2x + 4) \div (7x^2 - 3)$

**60.** $(30x^3 + 22x^2 - 6) \div (15x^2 - 4x + 3)$

## 2.6 SYMBOLS OF GROUPING

Frequently in mathematical problems one has to do a sequence of algebraic operations. In such cases, grouping symbols should be used to indicate the groups of the terms in an expression. The most common grouping symbols are parentheses ( ). The terms inside the symbol ( ) are treated as a single number. When a symbol of grouping is required within another symbol of grouping, different symbols, such as brackets [ ], braces { }, and the vinculum—in addition to parentheses are often used in order to avoid confusion. To carry out the indicated operations in an expression including several symbols of grouping, it is often convenient to remove the inside symbol first. When this is being done, the following rules should be observed:

1. When a symbol of grouping is preceded by a plus (+) sign, the symbol may be removed without changing the signs of the terms inside the symbol.

**Example 1**   $24 + [17 + (8 + 3)] = 24 + [17 + 8 + 3] = 24 + 17 + 8 + 3 = 52$, or
$$= 24 + [17 + (11)] = 24 + [28] = 52$$

**Example 2**   $20 + [42 + (5 - 30)] = 20 + [42 + 5 - 30] = 20 + [17] = 37$, or
$$= 20 + [42 + (-25)] = 20 + [17] = 37$$

**Example 3**   $x + [y + 2(a - b)] = x + [y + (2a - 2b)] = x + [y + 2a - 2b]$
$$= x + y + 2a - 2b$$

2. When a symbol of grouping is preceded by a minus $(-)$ sign, the symbol may be removed only if the signs of the terms inside the symbol are changed; that is, $(+)$ to $(-)$, and $(-)$ to $(+)$.

**Example 4**     $7 - [23 - (9 + 4)] = 7 - [23 - 9 - 4] = 7 - [10] = -3$, or
$$= 7 - [23 - 13] = 7 - [10] = -3$$

**Example 5**     $x - [y - 3(2a - b)] = x - [y - (6a - 3b)] = x - [y - 6a + 3b]$
$$= x - y + 6a - 3b$$

The following examples illustrate expressions which include three symbols of grouping:

**Example 6**     $10\{4 + 3[5 - \frac{2}{3}(8 - 2) + 7] - 9\} = 10\{4 + 3[5 - 4 + 7] - 9\}$
$$= 10\{4 + 3[8] - 9\}$$
$$= 10\{19\}$$
$$= 190$$

**Example 7**     $9x - \{4x + 2[(3x + y) - \frac{1}{4}(4x + 12)] - 5y\} + 7$
$$= 9x - \{4x + 2[3x + y - x - 3] - 5y\} + 7$$
$$= 9x - \{4x + 2[2x + y - 3] - 5y\} + 7$$
$$= 9x - \{4x + 4x + 2y - 6 - 5y\} + 7$$
$$= 9x - \{8x - 3y - 6\} + 7$$
$$= 9x - 8x + 3y + 6 + 7$$
$$= x + 3y + 13$$

# EXERCISE 2–4

**Reference: Section 2.6**

*Perform the indicated operations in each of the following expressions:*

| | |
|---|---|
| **1.** $(35 \div 5) \times 2$ | **17.** $44 - [29 - (6 + 5)]$ |
| **2.** $(88 \div 11) \times 2$ | **18.** $68 - [31 - (22 + 10)]$ |
| **3.** $276.5 \div (7.9 \times 5)$ | **19.** $82 - [40 - (30 - 7)]$ |
| **4.** $120.4 \div (4 \times 7)$ | **20.** $120 - [67 - (48 - 36)]$ |
| **5.** $(84 \div 3) \div 4$ | **21.** $3\{942 - 5[32 + 17(5 + 3)] + 6\} - 15$ |
| **6.** $(126 \div 6) \div 7$ | **22.** $40\{87 - 4[45 - 2(8 + 5)] - 9\} - 83$ |
| **7.** $480 \div (5 \div 12)$ | **23.** $32 - \{45 + [18 - 6(7 - 2)] + \frac{1}{3}(24 - 3)\}$ |
| **8.** $252 \div (9 \div 14)$ | **24.** $86 - \{52 + [47 - 12(10 - 4)] + \frac{2}{5}(80 - 5)\}$ |
| **9.** $(5 + 4) \times 2$ | **25.** $2x + [3x - \frac{1}{2}(4x + 6)]$ |
| **10.** $(17 - 88) \div 4$ | **26.** $8y + [4y - \frac{1}{6}(6y + 18)]$ |
| **11.** $(192 \div 8) \times (4 - 5)$ | **27.** $4x - [2x - (5x - 4)]$ |
| **12.** $(252 \div 7) \times (3 + 5)$ | **28.** $10y - [11y - (8y - 3)]$ |
| **13.** $62 + [41 + (10 + 5)]$ | **29.** $14x - [20x + 9(4x - y)]$ |
| **14.** $37 + [30 + (7 + 12)]$ | **30.** $11y - [16y + 7(5x - 2y)]$ |
| **15.** $15 + [18 + (9 - 3)]$ | **31.** $2x - \{5y + 4x + [7y - 3(2x - y)] - 2x\}$ |
| **16.** $42 + [20 + (8 - 15)]$ | **32.** $16y - \{7x + 3y - [4x + 5(x + y - z) - 3y] + 4z\}$ |

## 2.7 FACTORING

In arithmetic, the operations of multiplication and division can be greatly simplified when the products of every two of the basic figures from 0 to 9 are memorized. For example, although $5 \times 9$ means to repeat five 9 times, it does not actually have to be repeated. A student should readily know that the product of 5 and 9 is 45. Also, when one is able to recognize the factors of a number, such as the factors of 45 being 5 and 9, or 5, 3, and 3, a great amount of computation in arithmetic is facilitated. Similarly, if one knows certain algebraic expressions and their factors that frequently occur, much work in algebraic operations is reduced. The process of finding the factors in a given expression is called *factoring*. The most common types of factoring are illustrated below.

### A. Monomial Factor

Frequently, each term in an expression contains the same or *common* factor which can easily be detected by inspection. When this occurs, the given expression may be written as the product of the common monomial factor and another factor. The other factor is obtained by dividing the given expression by the common factor. In general, the factors can be expressed as follows:

$$ax + ay = a(x + y).$$

Factor $(x + y)$ is obtained by dividing $(ax + ay)$ by $a$; $a$ is the common factor. The left side of the equation is the expanded form, and the right side is the factor form.

**Example 1**    Factor $7x + 7y$

$7x + 7y = 7(x + y)$

**Example 2**    Factor $5x - 5y$

$5x - 5y = 5(x - y)$

**Example 3**    Factor $12ax - 18ay + 6az$

$12ax - 18ay + 6az = 6a(2x - 3y + z)$

### B. Common Binomial Factors

In general, this type of factor form is expressed as follows:

$$a(x + y) + b(x + y) = (a + b)(x + y)$$

Factor $(a + b)$ on the right side is obtained by dividing $a(x + y) + b(x + y)$ by the common factor $(x + y)$.

**Example 4**    Factor $3ax - ay + 6cx - 2cy$

$3ax - ay + 6cx - 2cy = a(3x - y) + 2c(3x - y) = (a + 2c)(3x - y)$

## C. Difference of Two Squares

This type of factor form is generally expressed:

$$x^2 - y^2 = (x + y)(x - y)$$

The above equation is obtained by multiplying the factors on the right side:

$$
\begin{array}{r}
x + y \\
(\times)\ \ x - y \\
\hline
x^2 + xy \\
-\,xy - y^2 \\
\hline
x^2 \qquad -\,y^2
\end{array}
$$

**Example 5**    Factor $25x^2 - 9y^2$

$$25x^2 - 9y^2 = (5x)^2 - (3y)^2 = (5x + 3y)(5x - 3y)$$

## D. Trinomials—Perfect Squares

The general forms of this type are written below:

$$x^2 + 2xy + y^2 = (x + y)^2$$
$$\text{and}\quad x^2 - 2xy + y^2 = (x - y)^2$$

The above two equations may also be obtained by multiplying the factors on the right side of each equation.

**Example 6**    Factor $9a^2 + 12ab + 4b^2$

$$9a^2 + 12ab + 4b^2 = (3a)^2 + 2(3a)(2b) + (2b)^2$$
$$= (3a + 2b)^2$$

**Example 7**    Factor $16a^2 - 24ab + 9b^2$

$$16a^2 - 24ab + 9b^2 = (4a)^2 - 2(4a)(3b) + (3b)^2$$
$$= (4a - 3b)^2$$

## E. Trinomial—General Case

The general form of this type is written below:

$$acx^2 + (ad + bc)x + bd = (ax + b)(cx + d)$$

Because,

$$
\begin{array}{r}
ax + b \\
(\times)\ \ \ cx + d \\
\hline
acx^2 + bcx \\
+\,adx \qquad +\,bd \\
\hline
acx^2 + (ad + bc)x + bd
\end{array}
$$

The numerical coefficients of each term in a factor form thus may be determined by the trial-and-error method as illustrated in the following examples. This method may be conveniently carried out when the required numbers are arranged in columnar form as shown at the left so that $(1) = ac$, $(2) = bd$, and $(3) = ad + bc$.

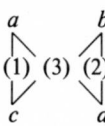

**Example 8**    Factor $6x^2 + 23x + 7$.

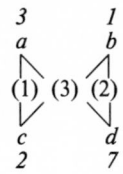

**Step (1)**    Find a pair of numbers ($a$ and $c$) whose product is 6. The factors of 6 are 2 and 3 and also 1 and 6.

**Step (2)**    Find a pair of numbers ($b$ and $d$), whose product is 7. The factors of 7 are 1 and 7.

**Step (3)**    Place the 2 pairs of numbers ($a$, $c$; $b$, $d$) in appropriate positions; that is, the algebraic sum of the products *(ad)* and *(bc)* must equal 23.

According to the trial-and-error method, the result is that $a = 3$, $b = 1$, $c = 2$, and $d = 7$. Thus, the desired factors are:

$$6x^2 + 23x + 7 = (3x + 1)(2x + 7)$$

**Example 9**    Factor $10x^2 - 21 + 29x$.

The trinomial should be arranged in the order of descending powers of $x$. The expression thus obtained is shown below.

$$10x^2 + 29x - 21$$

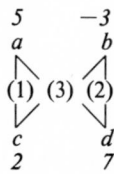

**Step (1)**    Find a pair of numbers ($a$ and $c$) whose product is 10. (Factors of 10 are 1 and 10; 2 and 5.)

**Step (2)**    Find a pair of numbers ($b$ and $d$) whose product is ($-21$). (Factors of 21 are 1 and 21; 3 and 7.)

**Step (3)**    Place the 2 pairs of numbers ($a$, $c$; $b$, $d$) in proper positions; that is, the algebraic sum of the products *(ad)* and *(bc)* must equal 29.

According to the trial-and-error method, the result is that $a = 5$; $b = (-3)$; $c = 2$; $d = 7$. Thus,

$$10x^2 + 29x - 21 = (5x - 3)(2x + 7)$$

★The following procedure may also be used to factor a trinomial:

**Step (1)**    Multiply the coefficient of $x^2$ by the term not containing $x$.

**Step (2)**    Find two numbers whose algebraic sum is the coefficient of $x$ and whose product is equal to the one obtained in Step (1).

**Step (3)**    Use the two numbers to replace the coefficient of $x$ in the trinomial and factor the new expression by grouping the terms.

**Example 10**   Factor $6x^2 + 23x + 7$.

         **Step (1)**    $(6)(7) = 42$

         **Step (2)**    According to the trial-and-error method, $21 + 2 = 23$ and $(21)(2) = 42$

         **Step (3)**    $6x^2 + (21 + 2)x + 7 = 6x^2 + 21x + 2x + 7$
$$= 3x(2x + 7) + (2x + 7)$$
$$= (3x + 1)(2x + 7)$$

**Example 11**   Factor $10x^2 + 29x - 21$.

         **Step (1)**    $(10)(-21) = -210$

         **Step (2)**    According to the trial-and-error method, $35 + (-6) = 29$ and $(35)(-6) = -210$

         **Step (3)**    $10x^2 + (35 - 6)x - 21 = 10x^2 + 35x - 6x - 21$
$$= 5x(2x + 7) - 3(2x + 7)$$
$$= (5x - 3)(2x + 7)$$

## EXERCISE 2–5

**Reference: Section 2.7**

*Factor the following:*

| | | |
|---|---|---|
| **1.** $15a + 5b$ | **13.** $9x^2 - y^4$ | **25.** $9a^2 + 24ab + 16b^2$ |
| **2.** $8a - 4b$ | **14.** $x^2 - 1$ | **26.** $25t^2 - 30ts + 9s^2$ |
| **3.** $3x + 6$ | **15.** $25x^2 - 16y^2$ | **27.** $x^2 + 3x + 2$ |
| **4.** $20t - 5$ | **16.** $a^2b^2 - 64c^2$ | **28.** $x^2 - 3x + 2$ |
| **5.** $-18x + 6y - 6z$ | **17.** $x^4 - 49$ | **29.** $2y^2 + 5y + 3$ |
| **6.** $24ab + 9ac - 3az$ | **18.** $36x^4 - 81y^2$ | **30.** $3y^2 + 5y - 2$ |
| **7.** $3ax - ay + 6cx - 2cy$ | **19.** $x^2 + 6x + 9$ | **31.** $2a^2 - a - 3$ |
| **8.** $ax + ay + bx + by$ | **20.** $x^2 + 8x + 16$ | **32.** $12x^2 + 10x + 2$ |
| **9.** $ax + ay - bx - by$ | **21.** $4x^2 + 24x + 36$ | **33.** $7x^2 + 20x - 3$ |
| **10.** $ax - ay - bx + by$ | **22.** $9x^2 - 18x + 9$ | **34.** $20x^2 + 9x - 18$ |
| **11.** $28ac + 14bc - 4ad - 2bd$ | **23.** $36y^2 - 60y + 25$ | **35.** $21b^2 + 13b - 20$ |
| **12.** $6am - 9an + 4bm - 6bn$ | **24.** $16a^2 - 16a + 4$ | **36.** $-15x^2 + 28x - 12$ |

# 2.8 LINEAR EQUATIONS IN ONE UNKNOWN

## A. Concept of an Equation

An *equation* is a statement which indicates that two algebraic expressions are equal. The two expressions are called the *sides* or *members* of the equation. There are two types of equations: the identical equation, and the conditional equation.

When the two sides of an equation are equal for any value that may be substituted for the letter or letters involved, the equation is called an *identical equation,* or simply an *identity.* For example, $2x + x = 3x$ is an identity because the two sides are equal when $x$ represents any value. Thus, when $x = 1$, the left side becomes $2(1) + 1 = 3$, and the right side becomes $3(1) = 3$.

When the sides of an equation are equal for only definite values of the letters involved, the equation is called a *conditional equation,* or simply an *equation.* For example, $2x + 1 = 7$ is a conditional equation, because only when $x$ represents 3 are the two sides equal to each other. The value, 3, which satisfies the equation is called the *solution* or the *root.* The letter or letters whose value is desired is called the *unknown.* When only one letter occurs in an equation, the root is a number; and when letters other than the unknown are included, the root is usually expressed in terms of those letters.

The number of powers of the single unknown value in an equation indicates the *degree* of an equation. Equations of the *first power* are called *linear equations.* Thus, $2x + 1 = 7$ is a linear equation because $x = x^1$.

## B. Solution of Equations

In solving a linear equation in one unknown, the operations are based on the axiom that if the *same* number is added to, subtracted from, multiplied by, or divided into both sides of an equation, the two sides are still equal; that is, the equality of the equation is not destroyed. By applying this axiom, if an equation is obtained in such a way that the unknown is alone on one side, the other side is the desired solution. The procedure for finding the solution of an equation in one unknown is shown below.

**Step (1)**   Add (or subtract) the same numbers to (or from) both sides so that the resulting equation will have the term which has the unknown on one side and all other terms on the other.

**Step (2)**   Divide both sides of the new equation by the coefficient of the unknown to obtain the solution.

**Example 1**   Solve $4x + 3 = 6x - 15$.

**Step (1)**   Subtract $6x$ from both sides to remove $6x$ at the right:
$4x + 3 - 6x = 6x - 15 - 6x$

Collect the like terms on both sides:
$-2x + 3 = -15$

Subtract 3 from both sides to remove 3 at the left:
$-2x + 3 - 3 = -15 - 3$

Collect the like terms on both sides:
$-2x = -18$

**Step (2)**   Divide both sides by $(-2)$:
$x = 9$

The operations listed above may be simplified by moving the terms from one side of the equation to the other side after changing their signs, *i.e.,* from $+$ to $-$, $-$ to $+$, $\times$ to $\div$, and $\div$ to $\times$. Usually, all the terms containing the unknown are moved to the left side and all other terms are moved to the right side until the unknown remains alone on the left side. The above example thus may be simplified as follows:

$$4x + 3 = 6x - 15 \qquad\qquad \textit{Check:}\ 4(9) + 3 = 6(9) - 15$$
$$4x - 6x = -15 - 3 \qquad\qquad\qquad 36 + 3 = 54 - 15$$
$$-2x = -18,\ x = \frac{-18}{-2} \qquad\qquad\qquad 39 = 39$$
$$x = 9$$

**Example 2**   Solve $4x - 8 = 2x$.

$$4x - 2x = 8 \qquad\qquad \textit{Check:}\ 4(4) - 8 = 2(4)$$
$$2x = 8 \qquad\qquad\qquad\qquad 16 - 8 = 8$$
$$x = 4 \qquad\qquad\qquad\qquad\quad 8 = 8$$

**Example 3**   Solve $5(x - 2) = x + 18$.

$$5x - 10 = x + 18 \qquad\qquad \textit{Check:}\ 5[(7) - 2] = (7) + 18$$
$$5x - x = 10 + 18 \qquad\qquad\qquad\quad 5[5] = 7 + 18$$
$$4x = 28 \qquad\qquad\qquad\qquad\qquad 25 = 25$$
$$x = 7$$

**Example 4**   Solve $2ax + b = 3c$ for $x$.

$$2ax = 3c - b$$
$$x = \frac{3c - b}{2a} \qquad\qquad \textit{Check:}\ \ 2a\left(\frac{3c - b}{2a}\right) + b = 3c$$
$$3c - b + b = 3c$$
$$3c = 3c$$

# C. Solution of Statement Problems Involving One Unknown

A *statement* or *word problem* may conveniently be solved by the use of a linear equation in one unknown. The steps are:

**Step (1)**   Represent one of the unknown quantities by a letter, usually $x$; and express other unknown quantities, if there are any, in terms of the same letter.

**Step (2)**   Translate the quantities from the statement of the problem into algebraic expressions and set up an equation.

**Step (3)**   Solve the equation for the unknown that is represented by the letter, and find the other unknowns from the solution.

**Step (4)**   Check the findings according to the statement in the problem.

**Example 5**   If $4 is added to 3 times an amount, and the sum is $19, what is the amount?

**Step (1)**    Let $x =$ the unknown amount.

**Step (2)**    Then $4 + 3x = 19$.

**Step (3)**    Solve the equation: $3x = 19 - 4$
$$3x = 15$$
$$x = 5$$

**Step (4)**    Check the statement of the problem.

If 4 is added to 3 times 5, the answer is $4 + 3 \cdot 5 = 19$. Thus, the answer is correct.

**Example 6**    A typewriter is sold for \$140. The gross profit is computed as $\frac{3}{4}$ of the cost. Assume that the selling price is equal to the gross profit added to the cost. What are the cost and the gross profit?

**Step (1)**    Let $x =$ cost. Then, gross profit $= (\frac{3}{4})x$.

**Step (2)**    According to the statement, gross profit $+$ cost $=$ selling price; then $(\frac{3}{4})x + x = 140$.

**Step (3)**    Solve the equation in Step (2).
$$(1\tfrac{3}{4})x = 140, \quad \frac{7x}{4} = 140, \quad 7x = 140(4) = 560,$$
$$x = \$80 \ \text{(cost)}$$
Gross profit $= (\frac{3}{4})x = (\frac{3}{4})(80) = \$60$

**Step (4)**    *Check:* Gross profit $+$ Cost $=$ Selling price
$$60 + 80 = \$140.$$

Or, the problem may be solved as follows:

**Step (1)**    Let $x =$ gross profit. Then, $(\frac{3}{4})$ cost $= x$, or cost $= (\frac{4}{3})x$.

**Step (2)**    $x + (\frac{4}{3})x = 140$

**Step (3)**    Solve the equation: $(1\tfrac{4}{3})x = 140 \qquad (\frac{7}{3})x = 140$
$$x = 140 \cdot \tfrac{3}{7} = \$60 \ \text{(gross profit)}$$
$$\text{Cost} = (\tfrac{4}{3})x = (\tfrac{4}{3})(60) = \$80$$

# EXERCISE 2–6

## Reference: Section 2.8

**A.** *Solve the following equations for* x:

1. $3x - 7 = 0$
2. $4x + 6 = 22$
3. $5x - 7 = 8$
4. $2x - 9 = 5x$
5. $4x - 13 = 7$
6. $7 - 5x = -18$
7. $6x + 3 = 3x + 12$
8. $5x - 4 = 2x + 32$
9. $3(x - 1) = 2x + 9$
10. $5x - 2(2x - 5) = 15$
11. $0.48 + x = 0.26 + 3x$
12. $3x - 0.33 = 0.44 - 4x$
13. $4x = 8a$
14. $4a - 3x = -2a$

**15.** $2x + 7d = 11d$         **18.** $4y + 2x = 7y$

**16.** $7b + 3x = 16b + 6$         **19.** $5(3a - x) - 4(2a - 7x) = -3x$

**17.** $3cx + d = 5n$         **20.** $3(x - 6g) = 5(9x - 2g) - 9g$

**B.** *Statement Problems:*

**21.** If an amount is added to 2 times the amount, the sum is $66. Find the amount.

**22.** If $5 is subtracted from 3 times an amount, the remainder is $40. Find the amount.

**23.** Ten years ago John's firm was twice as old as Mary's firm. Now the sum of the years in business of the two firms is 38. How many years has John been in business today?

**24.** Divide $99 into two parts. The difference between the two parts should be $7.

**25.** The difference between two amounts is $98 and their sum is $260. What are the amounts?

**26.** The sum of three amounts is $85. The largest is $15 more than the middle one and the smallest is one half of the largest one. What are the amounts?

**27.** Betty and Joan together have $1,496. If Betty has $452 more than Joan, how much does Betty have?

**28.** A man is 4 times as old as his daughter. The difference between their ages is 27 years. What is the man's age?

**29.** Rita would like to change a $10 bill into dimes and quarters. She wants to have 12 more quarters than dimes. How many of each should she receive?

**30.** The sum of three numbers is 86. The second number is five times the first, and the third is 9 more than the first. What are the three numbers?

**31.** The sum of the digits of a two digit number is 10. If the digits are reversed, the number is decreased by 18. What is the number?

**32.** A service station has two kinds of gasoline, one selling for 63.5¢ a gallon and the other for 59¢ a gallon. How many gallons of each must be used to make 90 gallons of a mixture that can be sold for 62¢ a gallon?

**33.** A bus which averages 50 miles per hour leaves a station 30 minutes before another bus which averages 60 miles per hour. If both buses take the same route, how long will it take for the second bus to catch up with the first and how far will the buses have traveled?

**34.** Two planes leave an airport for the East Coast and West Coast respectively. The westbound plane travels 20 miles per hour faster than the other. At the end of 3 hours they are 900 miles apart. What is the average speed of each plane?

**35.** A car which travels 45 miles an hour left a city 15 minutes after a truck, and was passing it in 2 hours. What was the average speed of the truck?

**36.** Two cars left a place at the same time and headed in the same direction. The average hourly speed of one car is $1\frac{1}{4}$ times the speed of the other. At the end of 2 hours they are 26 miles apart. Find the average speed of each car.

37. A washing machine was sold for $168. The gross profit is computed as $\frac{2}{5}$ of the cost. Assume that the selling price is equal to the gross profit plus the cost. What is the cost?
38. Jack and Peter made $1,400 net profit from their partnership at the end of the year. By agreement, Jack's share is $\frac{2}{5}$ as much as Peter's. How much does Jack receive?
39. In a mathematics of finance class, there are 30 students. The number of boys is 4 times the number of girls. How many girls are there?
40. A student made A grades on $\frac{1}{3}$ of a semester's assignments and B grades on $\frac{3}{7}$ of the assignments. The remaining 5 assignments were not handed in. What was the total number of the assignments in the semester?
41. Bill has three times as many dimes as quarters and twice as many half-dollars as dimes. The total value of his money amounts to $10.65. How many coins of each kind does he have?
42. Maria has 48 dimes and quarters totaling $7.05. How many of each does she have?

## 2.9 SYSTEMS OF LINEAR EQUATIONS

### A. Concept of a System of Equations

A *system* of equations is a group of two or more equations. A linear equation in *one* unknown has only *one* solution, but a linear equation in *two* unknowns has an *unlimited number* of solutions. For example, $x + 2y = 11$ is satisfied by unlimited pairs of numbers such as $x = 1$, $y = 5$; $x = 3$, $y = 4$; and $x = 7$, $y = 2$. If $x$ is equal to any particular numerical value, there is a solution for $y$ in the equation. However, in general, if there are two linear equations in two unknowns, there is only one solution for each unknown that satisfies both equations. The two equations are called *independent simultaneous equations,* or simply *independent equations.* If two equations can be reduced to the same form, they are said to be *dependent.* Thus, $x + y = 2$ and $2x + 2y = 4$ are dependent equations because the latter can be reduced to the form of the previous one by dividing by 2; hence there are unlimited pairs of numbers which satisfy the equation. If there is no common solution for two linear equations in two unknowns, they are called *inconsistent equations.* Thus, $x + y = 5$ and $x + y = 7$ are inconsistent equations.

### B. Solution by Elimination

To solve two independent linear equations simultaneously, first eliminate one of the two unknowns from the two equations and solve the resulting equation in one unknown. The eliminated unknown is then found by substituting the value obtained in either one of the given equations or their derived equivalents.

Two methods of elimination are illustrated by the following example. Method A is the simpler method.

**Example 1**     Solve     $3x + y = 5$   (1)
$\phantom{Solve\quad}6x - y = 6$   (2)

**Method A**     *Elimination by Addition or Subtraction:*

| *Eliminate* y *by Addition* | *Eliminate* x *by Subtraction* | |
|---|---|---|
| Add equations (1) and (2) | Multiply equation (1) by 2 | $6x + 2y = 10$   (3) |
| $3x + 6x = 5 + 6$ | Rewrite (2) | $6x - \phantom{2}y = \phantom{1}6$   (4) |
| $9x = 11,\ x = \frac{11}{9}$ | Subtraction: (3) $-$ (4) | $3y = \phantom{1}4$   (5) |
| | | |
| Substitute $x = \frac{11}{9}$ in (1) | Solve (5) for $y$ | $y = \frac{4}{3}$ |
| $3(\frac{11}{9}) + y = 5$ | Substitute $y = \frac{4}{3}$ in (2) | $6x - \frac{4}{3} = 6$   (6) |
| $\frac{11}{3} + y = 5$ | | |
| $y = 5 - \frac{11}{3} = \frac{4}{3}$ | Solve (6) for $x$ | $6x = 6 + \frac{4}{3}$ |
| | | $x = \frac{11}{9}$ |

*Check:*     Substitute $x = \frac{11}{9}$, and $y = \frac{4}{3}$ in (1) and (2).

In (1):     $3(\frac{11}{9}) + \frac{4}{3} = 5,\ \frac{11}{3} + \frac{4}{3} = 5,\ \frac{15}{3} = 5,\ 5 = 5$

In (2):     $6(\frac{11}{9}) - \frac{4}{3} = 6,\ \frac{22}{3} - \frac{4}{3} = 6,\ \frac{18}{3} = 6,\ 6 = 6$

**Method B**     *Elimination by Substitution:*

Solve (2) for $y$ in terms of $x$.     $y = 6x - 6$     (7)
Substitute (7) in (1). (Note: Do not substitute in (2) since (7) is derived from (2).)     $3x + (6x - 6) = 5$     (8)
Solve (8) for $x$.     $3x + 6x - 6 = 5,\ 9x = 11,\ x = \frac{11}{9}$
Solve for $y$ as in Method A when $x$ is found first. Thus, $y = \frac{4}{3}$.

*Check:*     As in Method A.

When there are *three* linear equations in *three* unknowns, a solution that satisfies the three equations may be obtained. However, it must be an independent system. The method of solving a system of three linear equations in three unknowns is an extension of the methods used in solving two equations in two unknowns. Similarly, the methods may be extended to $n$ number of linear equations in $n$ number of unknowns.

# C. Solution of Statement Problems Involving Two Unknowns

The four steps discussed in Section 2.8C are also applicable in solving statement problems involving two unknowns. However, two letters and two independent equations are set up instead of one letter and one equation.

**Example 2**     The cost of three dozen eggs and two dozen oranges is $5.16. The cost of two dozen eggs and one dozen oranges is $2.88. What is the cost per dozen of each item?

**Step (1)**     Let $x =$ cost in dollars of one dozen eggs
$y =$ cost in dollars of one dozen oranges

**Step (2)**     Then $3x + 2y = 5.16$   (1)
$2x + y = 2.88$   (2)

**Step (3)**     Solve the above two equations simultaneously by eliminating $x$:

Multiply (1) by 2     $6x + 4y = 10.32$   (3)
Multiply (2) by 3     $6x + 3y = 8.64$   (4)
(3) − (4)                     $y = 1.68$

Note that 6, the coefficient of $x$ in (3) and (4), is the *lowest common multiple* of 3 and 2, which are the coefficients of $x$ in (1) and (2) respectively.

Substitute $y = 1.68$ in (1). $3x + 2(1.68) = 5.16$
$$3x + 3.36 = 5.16$$
$$3x = 5.16 - 3.36 = 1.80,$$
$$x = \frac{1.80}{3} = .60.$$

The cost of one dozen eggs is $ .60.
The cost of one dozen oranges is $1.68.

**Step (4)**     According to the statement of the problem, the answer gives the following:

The cost of three dozen eggs and two dozen oranges is $3(.60) + 2(1.68) = 1.80 + 3.36 = \$5.16$.
The cost of two dozen eggs and one dozen oranges is $2(.60) + 1.68 = 1.20 + 1.68 = \$2.88$.

**Example 3**     John and Jimmy divided $500. If John had received $70 more and Jimmy had spent $30 of his money, they would have had equal amounts. How much did each receive?

Let $x =$ John's share in dollars
$y =$ Jimmy's share in dollars

Then $x + y = 500$
$x + 70 = y - 30$

Solve the two equations:

$x = 200$                              *Answer:*   John received $200.
$y = 300$                                            Jimmy received $300.

*Check:*     If John had received $70 more, he would have had ($200 + $70) or $270. If Jimmy had spent $30 of his money, he would have had ($300 − $30) or $270. Their shares are $200 and $300; the sum is ($200 + $300) or $500.

**Example 4**     A typewriter is sold for $140. The gross profit is computed as $\frac{3}{4}$ of the cost. Assume that the selling price is equal to the gross profit added to the cost. What are the cost and the gross profit? (This problem is the same as that of Example 6, Section 2.8.)

Let $x =$ cost, and $y =$ gross profit.
Then, $x + y = 140$
$$y = (\tfrac{3}{4})x$$

Solve the two equations:
$x = \$80$ (cost)         $y = \$60$ (gross profit)

*Check:*       Selling price $= 80 + 60 = \$140$.
Gross profit $= \tfrac{3}{4}(80) = \$60$.

## EXERCISE 2–7

### Reference: Section 2.9

**A.** *Solve for* x *and* y *(elimination by addition or subtraction):*

1. $x + y = 8$
$x - 2y = 14$

2. $x + y = 8$
$2x - y = 7$

3. $3x - y = 5$
$x + 4y = 19$

4. $2x + 3y = 23$
$3x - 2y = 28$

5. $5x + 4y = 29$
$7x + 6y = 41$

6. $3x - 4y = 26$
$5x - 8y = 46$

7. $x + 2y = -4$
$2x + y = 1$

8. $2x + 3y = 11$
$x + 4y = 8$

9. $2x - y = 4$
$2x + y = 16$

10. $3x - 2y = 1$
$2x + y = -4$

11. $4x + 2y = -12$
$x - y = -6$

12. $5x + y = -7$
$x + 4y = 10$

13. $2x - y = 15$
$3x + 2y = 40$

14. $3x - 2y = 23$
$x + 3y = 4$

15. $x + 2y = 19$
$4x + y = -8$

16. $2x + y = 5$
$x - 2y = 10$

17. $4x + 3y = 3$
$2x - 6y = -1$

18. $8x + 3y = 8$
$4x - 3y = 1$

**B.** *Solve for* x *and* y *(elimination by substitution):*

19. $x + y = 5$
$5x - 2y = 4$

20. $3x - 2y = 7$
$x + 3y = 6$

21. $x + 2y = 3$
$4x - 3y = -10$

22. $2x - y = 11$
$4x + y = 13$

23. $2x + y = -7$
$3x + 2y = -12$

24. $5x - y = 1$
$4x - 2y = -4$

25. $5x + 2y = 11$
$2x + y = 5$

26. $3x - 5y = -26$
$x + y = 2$

27. $x + 2y = 1$
$3x + 2y = -5$

28. $3x + 2y = 13$
$x - y = 1$

29. $x + 5y = -1$
$3x + y = 11$

30. $2x + 6y = -2$
$6x + 4y = 1$

31. $4x - y = 13$
$2x - 3y = 19$

32. $2x + y = 1$
$5x + 2y = 4$

33. $3x - y = 15$
$x + y = 1$

34. $2x + 5y = 5$
$3x + 2y = -9$

35. $2x + 3y = 4$
$3x + 2y = 11$

36. $3x + 5y = -1$
$6x + 15y = -5$

**C.** *State whether each of the following is a dependent or an inconsistent system of equations:*

**37.** $3x + 4y = 11$
$\phantom{}6x + 8y = 22$

**38.** $5x - 4y = 20$
$\phantom{}10x - 8y = 40$

**39.** $4x + y = 6$
$\phantom{}4x + y = 16$

**40.** $8x - 17y = 15$
$\phantom{}8x - 17y = 19$

**41.** $2x + 5y = 19$
$\phantom{}6x + 15y = 57$

**42.** $3x + y = 7$
$\phantom{}15x + 5y = 35$

**43.** $6x + 4y = 22$
$\phantom{}3x + 2y = 10$

**44.** $7x + 2y = 14$
$\phantom{}21x + 6y = 9$

**D.** *Statement Problems:*

**45.** The cost of a hat and a coat is $64.00, and the cost of 3 hats and 2 coats is $143.50. Find the cost of the hat and the cost of the coat.

**46.** The sum of $A$ and $B$ is 575. The sum of $A$ times $\frac{1}{25}$ and $B$ times $\frac{3}{50}$ is 30. What is the value of $A$? of $B$?

**47.** The sum of two amounts is $12 and their difference is $2. What are the amounts?

**48.** Two students made a total of 185 points in a game. One student made 15 points more than the other student. How many points did each student make?

**49.** A theater sold 40 tickets amounting to $128.75 in one evening. The tickets were sold to adults for $3.50 and to children for $1.25. How many of each were sold?

**50.** A druggist wishes to prepare 100 gallons of 45% alcohol. She has two kinds of alcohol solution in stock; one is 55% pure and the other is 30% pure. How many gallons of each kind must be used for the mixture?

**51.** The sum of the ages of a girl and her brother is 20. Four years ago her age was 3 times the age of her brother then. Find the girl's age and her brother's age.

**52.** Two cars start at the same place and the same time but travel in opposite directions. After 6 hours, they are 540 miles apart. If one car travels 10 miles per hour slower than the other, what are their speeds per hour?

**53.** The sum of the digits of a two-digit number is 17. The tens' digit is greater than the units' digit by 1. Find the number.

**54.** Work out Problem 31 of Exercise 2–6 by a system of two equations.

**55.** A grocer wishes to make 50 pounds of coffee by mixing two grades of coffee worth $2.70 and $3.00 a pound respectively. If the mixed coffee will be sold at $2.79 a pound, how many pounds of each grade of coffee should the grocer use?

**56.** Work out Problem 32 of Exercise 2–6 by a system of two equations.

## 2.10 FRACTIONS AND FRACTIONAL EQUATIONS

### A. General Statements

The rules for computing algebraic fractions are the same as those for computing fractions in arithmetic. However, algebraic fractions are more involved because symbols, as well as numbers, are employed in computation. The principle which indicates that multiplying or dividing both the numerator and the denominator by the same number, other than zero, does not affect the value of the fraction is also important to algebraic fractions. Thus, $\frac{2}{5}$ may be reduced to $\frac{2 \times 7}{5 \times 7} = \frac{14}{35}$; likewise, $\frac{a}{b}$ may be reduced to $\frac{ac}{bc}$. Furthermore, if the numerator and the denominator of a fraction can be factored and divided by any common factor, it is possible to reduce the fraction to a simpler form. If the numerator and the denominator have no common factors, the fraction is in its simplest form. Thus,

$$\frac{x^2 - 9}{x^2 - 8x + 15} = \frac{(x+3)(x-3)}{(x-5)(x-3)} = \frac{x+3}{x-5}, \text{ and } \frac{x+3}{x-5} \text{ is the simplest form.}$$

When a fraction is reduced to its simplest form, the numerator and the denominator in the final answer are usually retained in factored form, as shown in the answer in Example 3 below.

### B. Addition and Subtraction of Algebraic Fractions

Algebraic fractions should have a common denominator if the fractions are to be added or subtracted. If the given fractions do not have the same denominator, it is necessary to reduce them to equivalent fractions with the lowest common denominator (l.c.d.) before adding or subtracting. The algebraic sum of the numerators is the numerator of the resulting fraction, and the l.c.d. is its denominator.

**Example 1**    Combine and simplify: $\frac{2x}{3} + \frac{x}{5}$

Here the l.c.d. is $3 \times 5 = 15$

$$\frac{2x}{3} + \frac{x}{5} = \frac{2x \cdot 5}{3 \cdot 5} + \frac{x \cdot 3}{5 \cdot 3} = \frac{10x + 3x}{15} = \frac{13x}{15}$$

**Example 2**    Combine and simplify: $\frac{2}{a} + \frac{5}{b}$

Here the l.c.d. is $ab$.

$$\frac{2}{a} + \frac{5}{b} = \frac{2b}{ab} + \frac{5a}{ab} = \frac{2b + 5a}{ab}$$

**Example 3**   Combine and simplify: $\dfrac{10}{a^2 - b^2} + \dfrac{3}{a - b}$

Here the l.c.d. is $a^2 - b^2 = (a + b)(a - b)$

$$\frac{10}{a^2 - b^2} = \frac{10}{(a + b)(a - b)}; \quad \frac{3}{(a - b)} = \frac{3(a + b)}{(a + b)(a - b)}$$

Thus:   $\dfrac{10}{a^2 - b^2} + \dfrac{3}{a - b} = \dfrac{10}{(a + b)(a - b)} + \dfrac{3(a + b)}{(a + b)(a - b)} = \dfrac{10 + 3(a + b)}{(a + b)(a - b)}$

**Example 4**   Combine and simplify: $\dfrac{a}{a - b} - \dfrac{b}{a + b}$

Here the l.c.d. is $(a - b)(a + b)$

$$\frac{a}{a - b} - \frac{b}{a + b} = \frac{a(a + b)}{(a - b)(a + b)} - \frac{b(a - b)}{(a + b)(a - b)}$$

$$= \frac{a(a + b) - b(a - b)}{(a + b)(a - b)} = \frac{a^2 + ab - ab + b^2}{(a + b)(a - b)}$$

$$= \frac{a^2 + b^2}{(a + b)(a - b)}$$

**Example 5**   Combine and simplify: $\dfrac{2}{x + 1} + \dfrac{3x + 1}{2x^2 + 5x + 3}$

Here the l.c.d. is $(x + 1)(2x + 3)$ or $2x^2 + 5x + 3$

$$\frac{2}{x + 1} + \frac{3x + 1}{2x^2 + 5x + 3} = \frac{2(2x + 3)}{(x + 1)(2x + 3)} + \frac{3x + 1}{(x + 1)(2x + 3)}$$

$$= \frac{4x + 6 + 3x + 1}{(x + 1)(2x + 3)} = \frac{7x + 7}{(x + 1)(2x + 3)} = \frac{7(\cancel{x + 1})}{(\cancel{x + 1})(2x + 3)} = \frac{7}{2x + 3}$$

## C. Multiplication and Division of Algebraic Fractions

The rules of multiplication and division used in arithmetic also apply in calculations involving algebraic fractions. In some cases, however, the numerators and the denominators of the given fractions may be factored before multiplying.

**Example 6**   Multiply: $\dfrac{10x}{6y}$ by $\dfrac{3y}{15x}$

$$\frac{10x}{6y} \cdot \frac{3y}{15x} = \frac{30xy}{90xy} = \frac{1}{3}$$

**Example 7**   Multiply: $\dfrac{x^2 - y^2}{2x^2}$ by $\dfrac{3y}{x + y}$

$$\frac{x^2 - y^2}{2x^2} \cdot \frac{3y}{x + y} = \frac{(\cancel{x + y})(x - y)}{2x^2} \cdot \frac{3y}{\cancel{x + y}} = \frac{3y(x - y)}{2x^2}$$

**Example 8**  Simplify: $\dfrac{\dfrac{x-1}{x+y}}{\dfrac{3x+y}{3(x+y)}}$

The problem can be simplified by various methods as shown below.

**Method A**  Multiply the dividend by the reciprocal of the divisor. This complex fraction may be written as follows:

$$\frac{x-1}{x+y} \div \frac{3x+y}{3(x+y)} = \frac{x-1}{\cancel{x+y}} \cdot \frac{3(\cancel{x+y})}{3x+y} = \frac{3(x-1)}{3x+y}$$

**★Method B**  After reducing both of the simple fractions (the numerator and the denominator of the complex fraction) to have the lowest common denominator (l.c.d.), cancel the l.c.d. and then divide. Here the l.c.d. is $3(x+y)$.

$$\frac{\dfrac{x-1}{x+y}}{\dfrac{3x+y}{3(x+y)}} = \frac{\dfrac{3(x-1)}{\cancel{3(x+y)}}}{\dfrac{3x+y}{\cancel{3(x+y)}}} = \frac{3(x-1)}{3x+y}$$

**★Method C**  Multiply the numerator and the denominator of the complex fraction by the l.c.d. of the simple fractions. Here the l.c.d. also is $3(x+y)$.

$$\frac{\dfrac{x-1}{x+y}}{\dfrac{3x+y}{3(x+y)}} = \frac{\dfrac{x-1}{\cancel{x+y}} \cdot 3(\cancel{x+y})}{\dfrac{3x+y}{\cancel{3(x+y)}} \cdot \cancel{3(x+y)}} = \frac{3(x-1)}{3x+y}$$

**Example 9**  Divide: $\dfrac{5x+10}{9x-9}$ by $\dfrac{5}{3x-3}$

Method A is used for this illustration.

$$\frac{5x+10}{9x-9} \div \frac{5}{3x-3} = \frac{5x+10}{9x-9} \cdot \frac{3x-3}{5} = \frac{\cancel{5}(x+2)}{\underset{3}{\cancel{9}(\cancel{x-1})}} \cdot \frac{3(\cancel{x-1})}{\cancel{5}}$$

$$= \frac{x+2}{3}$$

# D. Operations of Fractional Equations

When solving an equation involving fractions, first multiply both sides by the lowest common denominator to derive an equation that will contain no fractions. This step is called *clearing* an equation of fractions. Next, solve the derived equation for the unknown, as discussed in Section 2.8.

When a fractional equation is being cleared, multiplying by a denominator other than the lowest common denominator may introduce solutions which are not solutions of the original equations. These extra solutions are called *extraneous roots.* When both sides of an equation are multiplied by the same expression containing the unknown, or when both sides of the equation are raised to the same integral power, the resulting equation may also have more solutions than the original equation possessed. The extraneous roots are discarded in solving statement problems. However, when both sides of an equation are divided by an expression containing the unknown, the new equation may have fewer roots than the original equation had. Furthermore, division or multiplication by zero should be excluded.

**Example 10**    Solve $\dfrac{x}{x-6} = 4$.

Clear the equation.

$$\frac{x}{\cancel{x-6}}\,(\cancel{x-6}) = 4(x-6)$$
$$x = 4(x-6)$$

Solve the derived equation.

$$x = 4x - 24$$
$$x - 4x = -24$$
$$-3x = -24$$
$$x = 8$$

*Check:*    $\dfrac{x}{x-6} = \dfrac{8}{8-6} = \dfrac{8}{2} = 4$

**Example 11**    Solve $\dfrac{7}{x+2} = \dfrac{3}{x-6}$.

Here the l.c.d. is $(x+2)(x-6)$.

Clear the equation.

$$\frac{7}{\cancel{x+2}}\cdot(\cancel{x+2})(x-6) = \frac{3}{\cancel{x-6}}\cdot(x+2)(\cancel{x-6}),$$
$$7(x-6) = 3(x+2)$$

Solve the derived equation.

$$7x - 42 = 3x + 6$$
$$7x - 3x = 42 + 6$$
$$4x = 48$$
$$x = 12$$

*Check:*    Substitute the $x$ value in the original equation:

$$\text{Left side} = \frac{7}{x+2} = \frac{7}{12+2} = \frac{7}{14} = \frac{1}{2}$$

$$\text{Right side} = \frac{3}{x-6} = \frac{3}{12-6} = \frac{3}{6} = \frac{1}{2}$$

**Example 12**    A gasoline tank can be filled by one pipe in 2 hours, and drained by another pipe in 5 hours. How long will it take to fill the tank if the drain is left open?

Let $x =$ the number of hours needed to fill the tank if the drain is left open.

The one pipe can fill $\frac{1}{2}x$ of the tank in $x$ hours because it can fill $\frac{1}{2}$ of the tank each hour (or it can fill the entire tank in 2 hours).

The other pipe can drain $\frac{1}{5}x$ of the tank in $x$ hours because it can drain $\frac{1}{5}$ of the tank each hour (or it can drain the entire tank in 5 hours).

Thus, $\frac{1}{2}x - \frac{1}{5}x = 1$ (the capacity of the tank).

Solve the above equation. Here the l.c.d. is $(2)(5) = 10$.

$$\frac{x}{2} - \frac{x}{5} = 1, \qquad\qquad 10\left(\frac{x}{2} - \frac{x}{5}\right) = 10(1)$$

$$5x - 2x = 10, \qquad\qquad 3x = 10,$$

$$x = \frac{10}{3} = 3\frac{1}{3} \text{ hours}$$

*Check:*      One pipe will fill $(\frac{1}{2})(3\frac{1}{3})$ tanks of gasoline in $3\frac{1}{3}$ hours, and the other pipe will drain $(\frac{1}{5})(3\frac{1}{3})$ tanks of gasoline in $3\frac{1}{3}$ hours. Thus the amount which remains in the tank is the difference, or $(\frac{1}{2})(3\frac{1}{3}) - (\frac{1}{5})(3\frac{1}{3}) = \frac{10}{6} - \frac{10}{15} = \frac{50}{30} - \frac{20}{30} = 1$, or one tank full of gasoline.

# EXERCISE 2–8

**Reference: Section 2.10**

**A.** *Simplify the following fractions to their lowest terms:*

1. $\dfrac{24}{36}$

5. $\dfrac{x+y}{ax+ay+bx+by}$

9. $\dfrac{4x^2+28}{x^4-49}$

2. $\dfrac{121}{110}$

6. $\dfrac{x^2-4}{(x+2)(x+1)}$

10. $\dfrac{12x-12}{9x^2-18x+9}$

3. $\dfrac{4}{4a-4b}$

7. $\dfrac{3x+y^2}{9x^2-y^4}$

11. $\dfrac{4x+12}{x^2+6x+9}$

4. $\dfrac{a+b}{5a+5b}$

8. $\dfrac{2ab-16c}{a^2b^2-64c^2}$

12. $\dfrac{6a+8b}{9a^2+24ab+16b^2}$

**B.** *Perform the following indicated operations and simplify:*

13. $\dfrac{3x}{4} + \dfrac{x}{5}$

16. $\dfrac{3}{7y} + \dfrac{5}{4xy}$

14. $\dfrac{5y}{7} + \dfrac{2y}{3}$

17. $1 + \dfrac{a}{a+b}$

15. $\dfrac{5}{3x} + \dfrac{2}{4x}$

18. $\dfrac{4}{x+2} + \dfrac{7}{x^2+3x+2}$

**19.** $\dfrac{3}{4x+2} + \dfrac{3x}{12x^2 + 10x + 2}$

**20.** $\dfrac{4x}{2-x} + \dfrac{2}{3x-4}$

**21.** $\dfrac{2x}{5} - \dfrac{x}{3}$

**22.** $\dfrac{5y}{4} - \dfrac{3y}{7}$

**23.** $\dfrac{3}{4x} - \dfrac{8}{6x}$

**24.** $\dfrac{4}{9y} - \dfrac{5}{3xy}$

**25.** $1 - \dfrac{a}{a+c}$

**26.** $\dfrac{15}{4x-3} - \dfrac{3x}{20x^2 + 9x - 18}$

**27.** $\dfrac{-4}{5x-6} - \dfrac{-9x}{-15x^2 + 28x - 12}$

**28.** $\dfrac{7}{6x^2 + x - 1} - \dfrac{3}{4x^2 - 1}$

**29.** $\dfrac{2a^3 b^4}{3x^2 y^4} \cdot \dfrac{9x^3 y^2}{8ab}$

**30.** $\dfrac{6x^2}{7y^2} \cdot \dfrac{5y}{4z} \cdot \dfrac{2z^2}{3x^3}$

**31.** $\dfrac{24\,m^2 n^3}{36\,x^2 y^3} \cdot \dfrac{12\,x^2 y^2}{6\,m^4 n}$

**32.** $\dfrac{9}{3x-12} \cdot \dfrac{x-4}{3}$

**33.** $\dfrac{x^2 y^3}{x^2 + 2xy + y^2} \cdot \dfrac{x+y}{x^3 y^4}$

**34.** $\dfrac{x^2 - y^2}{y^4} \cdot \dfrac{4y^2}{x-y}$

**35.** $\dfrac{6x^2 - 18x}{4x^2 - 1} \cdot \dfrac{4x^2 + 8x + 3}{12x^2 - 30x - 18}$

**36.** $\dfrac{2x-8}{x^2 - 16} \cdot \dfrac{x^2 + x - 12}{x-3}$

**37.** $\dfrac{4x-10}{8x-12} \div \dfrac{2x-5}{2x-3}$

**38.** $\dfrac{5x^2 y^3}{6x^3 y^4} \div \dfrac{4xy}{3xy^3}$

**39.** $\dfrac{6x^2 + 6xy}{2x-y} \div \dfrac{3x^2 - 3y^2}{6x^2 - y^2}$

**40.** $\dfrac{4x+8}{8x-8} \div \dfrac{8x+16}{4x-4}$

**41.** $\dfrac{10x^2 - 9x + 2}{15x - 6} \div \dfrac{5x^2 + 23x - 10}{3x + 15}$

**42.** $\dfrac{4 - x^2}{x^2 - 9} \div \dfrac{12 + 6x}{x^2 - 6x + 9}$

**43.** $\dfrac{x + \dfrac{2}{y^2}}{\dfrac{2+x}{y^2}}$

**44.** $1 - \dfrac{1}{3 - \dfrac{1}{2 - \frac{1}{3}}}$

**C.** *Solve for* x:

**45.** $\dfrac{x}{3} + \dfrac{x}{6} = 24$

**46.** $\dfrac{x}{2} + \dfrac{2x}{5} = 9$

**47.** $\dfrac{2x}{x-8} = 6$

**48.** $\dfrac{x}{x+5} = \dfrac{2}{3}$

**49.** $\dfrac{x}{x-8} = 5$

**50.** $\dfrac{4}{3+x} = \dfrac{5}{8+x}$

**51.** $\dfrac{6x+3}{3} = \dfrac{7x-2}{4}$

**52.** $\dfrac{x+6}{x} = \dfrac{x-9}{x-6}$

**53.** $\dfrac{x+1}{x+3} = \dfrac{4}{3}$

**54.** $\dfrac{x^2}{x-4} = x-2$

**55.** $\dfrac{x-2}{x+3} = \dfrac{x-1}{x+5}$

**56.** $\dfrac{x+3}{x+12} = \dfrac{x-5}{x-4}$

**57.** $\dfrac{x+10}{x-2} = \dfrac{x-1}{x-3}$

**58.** $S = x(1 + in)$

**59.** $\dfrac{a-b}{x} = \dfrac{b-c}{a+b}$

**60.** $\dfrac{4}{3x-3a} = \dfrac{a}{x^2-a^2}$

**D.** *Statement Problems:*

**61.** The sum of two amounts is $80, and one amount is $\frac{7}{9}$ of the other. Find the amounts.

**62.** If $\frac{1}{5}$ of an amount is added to $\frac{2}{3}$ of the amount, the sum is $26. What is the amount?

**63.** If a swimming pool can be filled by one pipe in 10 hours and drained by another pipe in 14 hours, how long will it take to fill the pool if the drain is left open?

**64.** Steve and Dale together can paint a house in 10 hours. If Dale can paint it by himself in 30 hours, how long would it take Steve to paint it alone?

**65.** A toy store purchased a shipment of toy guns at $4.20 a dozen. The store sold $\frac{5}{8}$ of the shipment at 48¢ each and the remainder at 3 for $1. The total profit was $9.00. How many of the toy guns were in this shipment?

**66.** A student answered correctly 80% of the problems in a test. Thirty-seven correct answers were made in the first 41 problems. Five out of every 8 answers were correct in the remaining problems. How many problems were in the test?

**67.** A bus driver estimated that his gasoline supply would last 10 hours, but it lasted only 8 hours. The actual consumption per hour was $\frac{1}{4}$ gallon more than he had estimated. How many gallons of gasoline did he have?

**68.** Doris beat Jean by 10 miles and Anna by 20 miles in a 1,000-mile car race. If Jean and Anna kept their respective speeds until Jean finished, by how many miles did Jean beat Anna?

## 2.11 GRAPHS AND ALGEBRAIC EQUATIONS

The method of graphic presentation of quantitative data is used frequently in analyzing business and economic activities. Details of the method are presented in Chapter 6, which describes statistical methods. In this section the discussion concerning graphs emphasizes their use in solving a system of equations.

## A. Rectangular Coordinates

A graph is constructed according to the system of rectangular coordinates. *Rectangular coordinates* are based on two straight reference lines perpendicular to each other in a plane, as shown in Figure 2–1. The horizontal line is usually referred to as the *X-axis,* or the *abscissa.* The vertical line is referred to as the *Y-axis,* or the *ordinate.* The two lines divide the plane into four parts called *quadrants,* which are numbered I, II, III, and IV, as indicated in the chart. The point of intersection of the two lines is called the *origin,* which is usually regarded as the zero point. Scales, which begin at the point of origin, are placed along the horizontal and vertical axes. The scale is not necessarily the same for both axes, although use of the same scale is customarily preferred. The abscissas to the *right* of the origin are conventionally designated as *positive,* whereas those to the *left* of the origin are *negative.* The ordinates *above* the origin are *positive* and those *below* the origin are *negative.*

In the plane it is possible to describe the location of any point which refers to two variables. One is called the *dependent* variable and the other, the *independent* variable. The dependent variable is so called because its location depends upon the value of the independent variable; that is, once the value of the independent variable is fixed, the corresponding value of the dependent variable is determined from it according to an equation. The independent variable

## Figure 2–1  RECTANGULAR COORDINATES

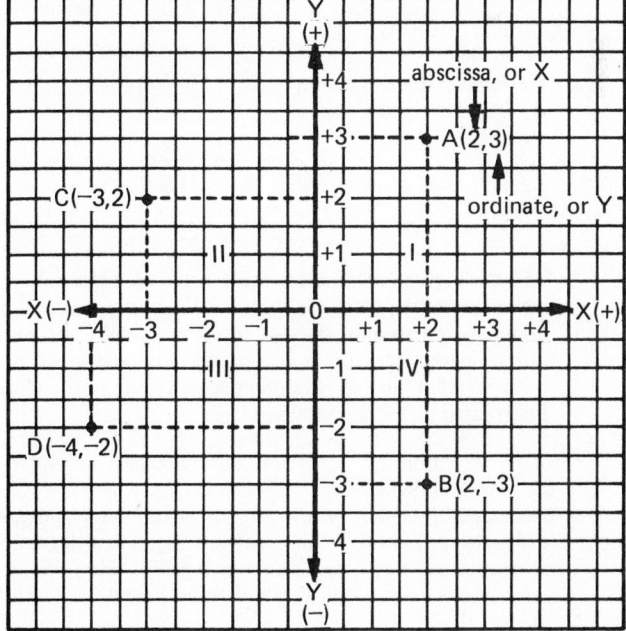

is usually placed on the *X*-axis and thus is also called the *X*-variable (or *x*). The dependent variable is usually placed on the *Y*-axis and is called the *Y*-variable (or *y*).

In placing a point on the plane for a set of corresponding *X* and *Y* values, first draw a line parallel to the *Y*-axis, starting at a distance equal to the *X*-value (abscissa). Second, draw a line parallel to the *X*-axis, starting at the *Y*-axis at a distance equal to the *Y*-value (ordinate), until it intersects the first line. The point of intersection is the desired answer. The abscissa and the ordinate of the point of intersection are called the *coordinates* of the point.

For example, in Quadrant I of Figure 2–1 the abscissa of point A is 2, while the ordinate of A is 3. The values of 2 and 3 constitute the coordinates of A. It is customary to write the coordinates in parentheses and to separate them by a comma; the abscissa is written before the ordinate. Thus, (2,3) means that 2 is the abscissa and 3 is the ordinate of point A. Notice that the coordinates of B, C, and D, are also written in the same manner as those of A.

## B. Drawing the Graph of an Equation

The following example is used to illustrate the method of drawing the graph of an equation.

**Example 1**    Draw a graph for each of the following two equations:

     (a) $x + y = 4$              (b) $2x - y = 14$

     (a) In the equation $x + y = 4$, there are unlimited answers for *x* and *y*. For example, when $x = 1$, the equation becomes $1 + y = 4$, $y = 4 - 1 = 3$.

Here, only three pairs of the answers are arranged at the right side.

| $x$ | $y$ |
|-----|-----|
| 1   | 3   |
| −8  | 12  |
| 10  | −6  |

The three pairs of answers are plotted in Figure 2–2. Notice that when the three points are connected, straight line A is formed. Any point on the straight line, in turn, will satisfy the equation. Thus, a first-degree equation in one or two unknowns can be represented by a straight line. A first-degree equation is therefore frequently referred to as a linear equation.

     (b) In the equation $2x - y = 14$, there are also unlimited answers for the two unknowns, *x* and *y*. For example, when $x = 10$, the equation becomes $2(10) - y = 14$, $y = 20 - 14 = 6$. Theoretically, as illustrated in (a) above, a straight line representing a first-degree equation can be determined by knowing only two points. However, as a checking point, three pairs of answers are listed below.

The three points give the straight line B in Figure 2–2.

| $x$ | $y$ |
|-----|-----|
| 10 | 6 |
| 8 | 2 |
| 1 | −12 |

**Figure 2–2  GRAPHIC SOLUTION OF TWO LINEAR EQUATIONS (Example 1, Section 2.11)**

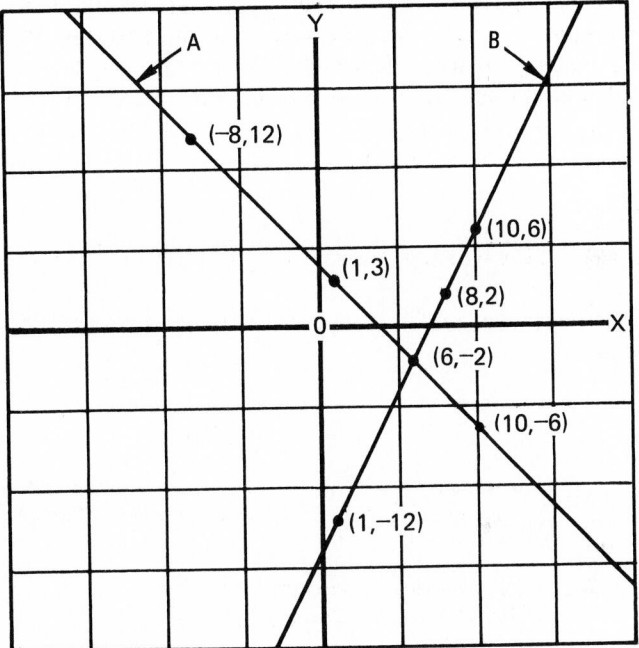

## C. Graphic Solution

Observe that in Figure 2–2 lines A and B intersect at the point $(6,-2)$. The values, $x=6$ and $y=-2$, thus satisfy both Equations (a) and (b). Therefore, the graphic method can be used to solve the problem of a pair of simultaneous linear equations in two unknowns. The graphic solution of the two equations above is checked as follows:

Substitute $x=6$ and $y=-2$ in Equations (a) and (b).

Equation (a): $x+y=4$, $6+(-2)=4$, $4=4$
Equation (b): $2x-y=14$, $2(6)-(-2)=14$, $14=14$

## EXERCISE 2–9

**Reference: Section 2.11**

*Solve for* x *and* y *graphically:*

**1.**   $x + y = 8$
      $2x - y = 10$

**2.**   $x - 2y = 9$
      $x + y = 3$

**3.** $2x + 3y = 17$
      $3x - 2y = 19$

**4.** $3x - y = 5$
      $x + 4y = 19$

**5.**   $x + 2y = -6$
      $2x - y = 8$

**6.**   $x - y = 1$
      $x + 2y = 13$

**7.** $3x + y = 6$
      $5x - y = 2$

**8.** $2x + 3y = 5$
      $4x - y = 17$

**9.** $2x - y = 4$
      $3x + y = 11$

**10.**   $x + y = 10$
      $x - 3y = -6$

**11.**   $x + y = -5$
      $2x - 3y = 5$

**12.**   $x - 2y = 2$
      $3x + 2y = -18$

# Chapter 3

# *Supplemental Algebraic Operations

The topics included in this chapter are: radicals, quadratic equations, progressions, the binomial theorem, and logarithms. Those selected topics are useful in proving certain complicated formulas (proofs of which are placed in footnotes) in this text and in preparing for advanced studies in the fields of business and economics.

## 3.1 RADICALS

## A. Introduction

In the previous chapter, Section 2.1B, it was stated that the product of equal factors can be expressed in an exponential form, such as $a \cdot a \cdot a \cdot a = a^4$. One of the equal factors of a quantity is called a *root* of the quantity. Thus, if $a^4 = b$, the base $a$ is the 4th root of $b$.

A root is usually indicated by the sign $\sqrt{\phantom{x}}$, and is then called a *radical*. The number written at the upper left of the sign is the *index* of the radical, and the quantity under the sign is called the *radicand*. Thus, the expression "$a$ is the 4th root of $b$" may be written $\sqrt[4]{b} = a$. In the radical $\sqrt[4]{b}$, $b$ is the radicand and 4 is the index; the radical indicates the 4th root of $b$. When the index is 2, it is usually omitted and is understood to be the square root. Thus, $\sqrt[2]{9} = \sqrt{9}$.

When the index is an *even* integer, a *positive* radicand has two numerically equal roots; one is positive and the other is negative, such as

9 has two square roots, $\pm 3$
since $(+3)(+3) = 9$, and $(-3)(-3) = 9$;
16 also has two 4th roots, $\pm 2$
since $(+2)(+2)(+2)(+2) = 16$, and $(-2)(-2)(-2)(-2) = 16$.

However, the radical sign $\sqrt{\phantom{x}}$ is restricted to represent only the positive root, called the *principal root*. The restriction is necessary since mathematicians always like to have an operation lead to a unique result. Thus

$$\sqrt{9} = +3, \text{ not } -3; \sqrt[4]{16} = +2, \text{ not } -2.$$

To indicate a negative root, we place a minus sign before the radical, such as

$$-\sqrt{9} = -3, \text{ and } - \sqrt[4]{16} = -2.$$

When the index is an *odd* integer, a *positive* radicand has only a *positive* root, and a *negative* radicand has only a *negative* root, such as

$$\sqrt[3]{27} = +3 \text{ since } (+3)(+3)(+3) = 27$$
$$\sqrt[3]{-27} = -3 \text{ since } (-3)(-3)(-3) = -27$$
$$\sqrt[5]{-32} = -2 \text{ since } (-2)(-2)(-2)(-2)(-2) = -32, \text{ but}$$
$$(+2)(+2)(+2)(+2)(+2) = +32, \textit{ not } -32$$

When the index is an *even* integer, a radical with a *negative* radicand represents an imaginary number, such as

$$\sqrt{-9} \text{ since neither } +3 \text{ nor } -3 \text{ qualifies as a square root of the radicand } -9.$$

Since imaginary numbers are rarely used in business and economics, they are excluded in the following discussion.

## B. Fractional Exponents

When an exponential has a fractional exponent, the exponential may be changed to the form of a radical according to the following definition:

$$a^{\frac{n}{m}} = (\sqrt[m]{a})^n = \sqrt[m]{a^n}$$

The definition is illustrated as follows:

Let $n = 1$ and $m = 2$. $a^{\frac{n}{m}} = a^{\frac{1}{2}}$. When $a^{\frac{1}{2}}$ is raised to its second power
$$a^{\frac{1}{2}} \cdot a^{\frac{1}{2}} = a^{\frac{1}{2}+\frac{1}{2}} = a^1 = a$$

Since $a^{\frac{1}{2}}$ is one of the two equal factors whose product is $a$, the square root of $a$ should be $a^{\frac{1}{2}}$, or as it is written, $\sqrt{a} = a^{\frac{1}{2}}$.

Similarly, let $n = 4$ and $m = 3$. $a^{\frac{n}{m}} = a^{\frac{4}{3}}$

When $a^{\frac{4}{3}}$ is raised to its third power,
$$a^{\frac{4}{3}} \cdot a^{\frac{4}{3}} \cdot a^{\frac{4}{3}} = (a^{\frac{4}{3}})^3 = a^{\frac{4}{3}\cdot 3} = a^4$$

Thus, $a^{\frac{4}{3}}$ is the third root of $a^4$, or $a^{\frac{4}{3}} = \sqrt[3]{a^4}$

According to the illustrations above, the following occurs:
$$a^{\frac{n}{m}} = \sqrt[m]{a^n}; \text{ and } a^{\frac{1}{m}} = \sqrt[m]{a}$$

But, $a^{\frac{n}{m}} = (a^{\frac{1}{m}})^n = (\sqrt[m]{a})^n$ (See Section 2.4, Law (3).)

Thus, $a^{\frac{n}{m}} = \sqrt[m]{a^n} = (\sqrt[m]{a})^n$

From the above definition, it may be seen that an exponential with a fractional exponent can be changed to its equivalent value in the form of a radical. However, the change must be made in conformity with the laws of exponents, as presented on pages 33 and 34.

**Example 1**     Express the exponentials in their radical forms.

$$64^{\frac{1}{3}} = \sqrt[3]{64} \qquad\qquad k^{\frac{1}{2}} = \sqrt[2]{k} = \sqrt{k}$$

$$84^{\frac{3}{4}} = \sqrt[4]{84^3} \text{ or } (\sqrt[4]{84})^3 \qquad\qquad x^{\frac{2}{5}} = \sqrt[5]{x^2} \text{ or } (\sqrt[5]{x})^2$$

**Example 2**     Express the radicals in their exponential forms.

$$\sqrt{81} = 81^{\frac{1}{2}} \qquad\qquad\qquad \sqrt[3]{x} = x^{\frac{1}{3}}$$

$$\sqrt[4]{25^5} = 25^{\frac{5}{4}} \qquad\qquad\qquad \sqrt[7]{y^4} = y^{\frac{4}{7}}$$

**Example 3**     Express the coefficients of the radicals as part of their respective radicands.

$$a\sqrt{b} = a^{\frac{2}{2}}b^{\frac{1}{2}} = (a^2b^1)^{\frac{1}{2}} = \sqrt{a^2b}$$

$$x \cdot \sqrt[3]{y} = x^{\frac{3}{3}}y^{\frac{1}{3}} = (x^3y^1)^{\frac{1}{3}} = \sqrt[3]{x^3y}$$

$$x^3 \cdot \sqrt{y} = x^{\frac{6}{2}}y^{\frac{1}{2}} = (x^6y^1)^{\frac{1}{2}} = \sqrt{x^6y}$$

In general, the calculations in Example 3 may be made by following two steps:

**Step (1)**     Raise the coefficient to the power of the index of the radical.

**Step (2)**     Write the result obtained in Step (1) as a factor of the radicand.

Thus, the illustrations in Example 3 may be simplified as follows:

$$a\sqrt{b} = \sqrt{a^2b}, \text{ since the index of the radical is 2}$$
$$x \cdot \sqrt[3]{y} = \sqrt[3]{x^3y}, \text{ since the index of the radical is 3}$$
$$x^3 \cdot \sqrt{y} = \sqrt{x^6y}, \text{ here } x^6 \text{ is obtained by raising } x^3$$
$$\text{to the second power, or } (x^3)^2 = x^6$$

The following example further illustrates the applications of the two steps above.

**Example 4**     Express the coefficients of the radicals as part of their respective radicands.

$$3\sqrt{2} = \sqrt{3^2 \cdot 2} = \sqrt{18}$$
$$2 \cdot \sqrt[4]{3} = \sqrt[4]{2^4 \cdot 3} = \sqrt[4]{48}$$
$$3^2 \cdot \sqrt{2} = \sqrt{3^{2 \cdot 2} \cdot 2} = \sqrt{3^4 \cdot 2} = \sqrt{162}$$

# C. Computation of Radicals

## ADDITION AND SUBTRACTION

Radicals whose indexes and radicands are the same are called *like radicals.* To add (or to subtract) numbers with like radicals, first add (or subtract) the numerical coefficients. The sum (or remainder) thus obtained is the coefficient of the common radical.

**Example 5**   Combine $7\sqrt{3} + 4\sqrt{3} - 5\sqrt{3}$.

$$7\sqrt{3} + 4\sqrt{3} - 5\sqrt{3} = (7 + 4 - 5)\sqrt{3} = 6\sqrt{3}$$

**Example 6**   Combine $\sqrt{18} - \sqrt{32} + \sqrt{50}$.

Here the three terms have unlike radicals. However, they can be changed to like radicals as follows:

$$\sqrt{18} = \sqrt{3^2 \cdot 2} = 3\sqrt{2}; \ \sqrt{32} = \sqrt{4^2 \cdot 2} = 4\sqrt{2}$$
$$\sqrt{50} = \sqrt{5^2 \cdot 2} = 5\sqrt{2}$$

(Notice that the procedure for changing a factor of each radicand to the coefficient of the radical is the reverse of the procedure employed in Examples 3 and 4.)

Thus, $\sqrt{18} - \sqrt{32} + \sqrt{50} = 3\sqrt{2} - 4\sqrt{2} + 5\sqrt{2}$
$$= (3 - 4 + 5)\sqrt{2} = 4\sqrt{2}$$

## MULTIPLICATION OF RADICALS

In multiplying radicals, when the indexes are the same, observe the following rule:

$$\sqrt[n]{a} \cdot \sqrt[n]{b} = \sqrt[n]{ab}, \text{ where } a \text{ and } b \text{ are greater than zero.}$$

*Illustration:*   $\sqrt[n]{a} \cdot \sqrt[n]{b} = a^{\frac{1}{n}} \cdot b^{\frac{1}{n}} = (ab)^{\frac{1}{n}} = \sqrt[n]{ab}$

**Example 7**   Multiply $(4\sqrt{3})$ by $(2\sqrt{5})$.

$$(4\sqrt{3})(2\sqrt{5}) = (4)(2)(\sqrt{3})(\sqrt{5}) = 8\sqrt{(3)(5)} = 8\sqrt{15}$$

When the indexes are different, follow the laws of exponents.

**Example 8**   Multiply $\sqrt[3]{2}$ by $\sqrt{5}$.

$$\sqrt[3]{2} \cdot \sqrt{5} = 2^{\frac{1}{3}} \cdot 5^{\frac{1}{2}} = 2^{\frac{2}{6}} \cdot 5^{\frac{3}{6}} = (2^2 \cdot 5^3)^{\frac{1}{6}} = \sqrt[6]{500}$$

Note that the fractional exponents $\frac{1}{3}$ and $\frac{1}{2}$ above have been reduced to fractions having the lowest common denominator 6.

## DIVISION OF RADICALS

In dividing radicals, when the indexes are the same, observe the following rule:

$$\frac{\sqrt[n]{a}}{\sqrt[n]{b}} = \sqrt[n]{\frac{a}{b}}, \text{ where } a \text{ and } b \text{ are greater than zero.}$$

*Illustration:*   $\dfrac{\sqrt[n]{a}}{\sqrt[n]{b}} = \dfrac{a^{\frac{1}{n}}}{b^{\frac{1}{n}}} = \left(\dfrac{a}{b}\right)^{\frac{1}{n}} = \sqrt[n]{\dfrac{a}{b}}$

**Example 9**   Divide $\sqrt{20}$ by $\sqrt{5}$.

$$\sqrt{20} \div \sqrt{5} = \frac{\sqrt{20}}{\sqrt{5}} = \sqrt{\frac{20}{5}} = \sqrt{4} = 2$$

The quotient secured from the division of radicals is frequently expressed in fractional form. Fractions involving radicals are considered to be in their simplest form when the denominators include no radicals.

**Example 10**   Divide $\sqrt{3}$ by $\sqrt{5}$.

$$\frac{\sqrt{3}}{\sqrt{5}} = \frac{\sqrt{3}}{\sqrt{5}} \cdot \frac{\sqrt{5}}{\sqrt{5}} = \frac{\sqrt{15}}{5}$$

When the indexes are different, follow the laws of exponents.

**Example 11**   Divide $\sqrt{3}$ by $\sqrt[3]{2}$.

$$\frac{\sqrt{3}}{\sqrt[3]{2}} = \frac{3^{\frac{1}{2}}}{2^{\frac{1}{3}}} = \frac{3^{\frac{3}{6}}}{2^{\frac{2}{6}}} = \frac{3^{\frac{3}{6}}}{2^{\frac{2}{6}}} \cdot \frac{2^{\frac{4}{6}}}{2^{\frac{4}{6}}} = \frac{(3^3 \cdot 2^4)^{\frac{1}{6}}}{2^{\frac{6}{6}}} = \frac{(432)^{\frac{1}{6}}}{2} = \frac{\sqrt[6]{432}}{2}$$

Note that the fractional exponents of both numerator and denominator in the third fraction have been reduced to have a lowest common denominator 6.

# D. Finding the Square Root

The radicals which occur most frequently in business and economic studies are the square roots. The method of finding the square root of a radicand is illustrated by the following examples.

**Example 12**   Find $\sqrt{1,049.76}$

The steps for finding the square root of 1,049.76 are:

1. The radicand 1,049.76 is divided into groups of two digits each, starting at the decimal point and moving in both directions, or

$$\sqrt{10\,\overline{49.76}}$$

Each group will have one digit in the final answer. The three groups will provide a three-digit answer.
2. Beginning with the first group at the left, 10, find the largest square that is less than or equal to 10. The square found is 9, which has a square root of 3. The square root of 9, or 3, is the first digit of the answer and is positioned on the answer line directly above the 10.
3. Subtract the square 9 from 10; then bring down the next pair of digits, 49, to form the first remainder, 149.

$$\begin{array}{r} 3 \quad\quad\quad \text{(Answer line)} \\ \hline \sqrt{10 \quad \overline{49.76}} \end{array}$$

$$3^2 \text{-----------------} \underline{9(-)\downarrow}$$
$$1 \quad 49$$

4. The next step involves operating on the first remainder, 149. To begin this step the value of the answer line, 3, must be doubled (or $3 \times 2 = 6$) and placed in a position to the left of 149. This is shown below:

$$
\begin{array}{r}
3 \quad \text{(Answer line)} \\
\sqrt{10\ \overline{49}.\ \overline{76}} \\
\underline{9(-)} \\
1\ 49
\end{array}
$$

$3 \times 2$ ------------- $6\underline{\phantom{0}}$

The 6 is placed to the left of 149. Note that a blank space has been placed to the right of the 6; its use will be described below.

The 149 is operated on by attempting to find a particular (from the 10 possible) single-digit integer (from digits 0 to 9). The integer when placed in the blank space will form a number between 60 and 69. Multiplying the number by the integer should produce the largest product that is less than or equal to 149. If 0 is tried, the result will be: $60 \times 0 = 0$, which is less than 149. Use of 1 yields: $61 \times 1 = 61$, which is also less than 149 but nearer to it. When 2 is tried, the result is: $62 \times 2 = 124$, which again is less than 149 but nearer yet. The integer 3 yields: $63 \times 3 = 189$, which exceeds 149. Hence the sought integer is 2, since it yields a product which is as near to 149 as possible without exceeding it.

Having located the particular integer, place it both in the blank space and on the answer line directly above the 49. The 62 is multiplied by the 2 on the answer line and the product, 124, is subtracted from 149. The next pair of digits is brought down and the next remainder of 2,576 is formed.

$$
\begin{array}{r}
3 \quad 2 \quad \text{(Answer line)} \\
\sqrt{10\ \overline{49}.\quad \overline{76}} \\
\underline{9(-)} \\
1\ 49 \\
1\ 24(-) \\
\overline{25 \qquad 76}
\end{array}
$$

$62 \times 2$ ------------------- $6\,\underline{2}$

5. The same procedure established in step 4 is used to operate on the 2,576 remainder. The numbers on the answer line are doubled (or $32 \times 2 = 64$) and placed along with a blank to the left of 2,576.

$$
\begin{array}{r}
3 \quad 2 \quad \text{(Answer line)} \\
\sqrt{10\ \overline{49}.\quad \overline{76}} \\
\underline{9(-)} \\
1\ 49 \\
1\ 24(-) \\
\overline{25 \qquad 76}
\end{array}
$$

$6\,\underline{2}$

$32 \times 2$ ------------ $64\underline{\phantom{0}}$

Now an attempt is made to find the integer for the blank space to form a number which, when multiplied by the integer, will result in the largest product that is less than or equal to 2,576. When 4 is tried, the result is $644 \times 4 = 2,576$, which is exactly equal to the remainder being operated on. Hence, 4 is the sought integer. It is written in the blank space and on the answer line above the 76. The 644 is multiplied by the 4 on the answer line and the product, 2,576, is subtracted from 2,576. The 0 remainder indicates that the computation has been completed. Finally, a decimal point is located on the answer line at a position directly above the decimal point in the radicand. The answer, 32.4, is read directly from the answer line.

$$
\begin{array}{r}
3 \quad 2. \quad 4 \\
\sqrt{10 \ \overline{49}. \ \overline{76}} \\
\end{array}
$$

```
              3  2. 4
        √ 10 49. 76
                 9(−)
       6 2 |   1 49
           |   1 24(−)
       64 4|    25 76
644 × 4 ----------|----25 76(−)
           |      00 00
```

6. Check: $32.4^2 = 32.4 \times 32.4 = 1{,}049.76$

**Example 13**  Find $\sqrt{104.976}$ to two decimal places.

The steps for finding the square root of 104.976 are basically the same as those used in Example 12. However, there are a few exceptions as noted below:

1. The radicand 104.976 is divided into groups of two digits each, or

$\overline{1} \ \overline{04}. \ \overline{97} \ \overline{60} \ \overline{00}$

Observe that zeros are annexed in the radicand in obtaining decimal places in the answer. For each additional decimal place in the answer, two zeros are annexed.

```
                            1  0.  2   4   5     which is rounded
                      √ 1  04.97 60 00          to two decimal
          1² -------------1(−)|                  places, 10.25 (answer)
      1 × 2 -------2 0|    0 04|
      20 × 0 -----------|---0 00|(−)
      10 × 2 -------20 2|    0 04|97
      202 × 2 ----------|------ 4|04(−)
      102 × 2 -------204 4|       |93 60
      2044 × 4 ------------|-------|81 76(−)
      1024 × 2 -------2048 5|      |11 84 00
      20485 × 5 -----------|-------|10 24 25(−)
                           |       |01 59 75      (remainder)
```

2. The last remainder, 15975, has an actual value of .015975. (The decimal point of the remainder is located at the same column as the decimal point in the given radicand.) This remainder can be used for further computation and for checking the final answer.
3. *Check:* $10.245^2 = 10.245 \times 10.245 = 104.960025$

$$
\begin{array}{r}
104.960025 \\
+ \ .015975 \\
\hline
104.976000
\end{array}
$$

**Example 14**　Find $\sqrt{256}$.

$$
\begin{array}{r}
1\ \ 6.\ \ \ \ \ \ \ \ \\
\hline
\sqrt{2\ \ 56.}\ \ \ \ \ \ \ \ \\
\end{array}
$$

$$1^2 \text{---------------------} 1(-)$$
$$1 \times 2 \text{--------------} 2\,\underline{6}\ \ 1\ 56$$
$$26 \times 6 \text{----------------------} \underline{1\ 56}\,(-)$$
$$0\ 00$$

*Check:* $16^2 = 16 \times 16 = 256.$

## EXERCISE 3–1

**Reference: Section 3.1**

**A.** *Express the following in radical forms:*

1. $m^{\frac{1}{4}}$　　　　5. $x^{\frac{1}{4}}$　　　　9. $127^{\frac{3}{4}}$

2. $(pq)^{\frac{3}{4}}$　　　6. $n^{\frac{2}{5}}$　　　　10. $108^{\frac{2}{7}}$

3. $35^{\frac{1}{3}}$　　　　7. $x^{\frac{5}{3}}$　　　　11. $a^{\frac{3}{5}}$

4. $26^{\frac{1}{2}}$　　　　8. $y^{\frac{3}{7}}$　　　　12. $b^{\frac{4}{3}}$

**B.** *Express the following in exponential forms:*

13. $\sqrt[5]{a^3}$　　　17. $\sqrt{45^3}$　　　21. $\sqrt[3]{28}$
14. $\sqrt[4]{y^2}$　　　18. $\sqrt{62^5}$　　　22. $\sqrt[3]{46}$
15. $\sqrt{19}$　　　　19. $\sqrt[3]{x^5}$　　　23. $\sqrt[6]{b^2}$
16. $\sqrt[3]{26}$　　　20. $\sqrt[4]{u^3}$　　　24. $\sqrt[8]{t^4}$

**C.** *Express the coefficient of the following radicals as part of the radicand:*

25. $x\sqrt{y^4}$　　　　29. $c \cdot \sqrt[3]{d^2}$　　　33. $3^2 \cdot \sqrt{2t}$
26. $3\sqrt{7}$　　　　30. $4 \cdot \sqrt[3]{5}$　　　34. $2^3 \cdot \sqrt{4y}$
27. $5^2 \cdot \sqrt{x}$　　　31. $5^3 \cdot \sqrt{3}$　　　35. $a^2 \cdot \sqrt{ab}$
28. $6^2 \cdot \sqrt{u}$　　　32. $2^4 \cdot \sqrt{5}$　　　36. $n^3 \cdot \sqrt{7mn}$

**D.** *Compute the following:*

37. $16\sqrt{2} + 4\sqrt{2} - 3\sqrt{2}$　　　　45. $(2\sqrt{5})(4\sqrt{7})(3\sqrt{2})$
38. $13\sqrt{5} - 7\sqrt{5} + 12\sqrt{5}$　　　　46. $(12\sqrt{22})(4\sqrt{9})(3\sqrt{21})$
39. $3\sqrt{48} + \sqrt{12} - \sqrt{3}$　　　　47. $\sqrt{64} \div \sqrt{16}$
40. $7\sqrt{20} - \sqrt{45} + \sqrt{125}$　　　48. $\sqrt{52} \div \sqrt{4}$
41. $\sqrt{112} - \sqrt{28} + \sqrt{63}$　　　　49. $\sqrt{5} \div \sqrt{8}$
42. $\sqrt{150} + \sqrt{96} - \sqrt{54}$　　　　50. $\sqrt{144} \div \sqrt{7}$
43. $(3\sqrt{4})(5\sqrt{6})$　　　　　　51. $\sqrt{2} \div \sqrt[3]{3}$
44. $(6\sqrt{3})(9\sqrt{2})$　　　　　　52. $\sqrt{5} \div \sqrt[4]{4}$

**E.** *Find the square root of each of the following:*

**53.** $\sqrt{361}$

**54.** $\sqrt{729}$

**55.** $\sqrt{21,025}$

**56.** $\sqrt{45,369}$

**57.** $\sqrt{1,024}$

**58.** $\sqrt{2,601}$

**59.** $\sqrt{4,542.76}$

**60.** $\sqrt{1,459.24}$

**61.** $\sqrt{454.276}$ (to two decimal places)

**62.** $\sqrt{145.924}$ (to two decimal places)

**63.** $\sqrt{1.024}$ (to three decimal places)

**64.** $\sqrt{260.1}$ (to three decimal places)

## 3.2 QUADRATIC EQUATIONS

A *quadratic equation* in one unknown is an equation which contains up to the second power of the unknown. The standard form of the quadratic equation in $x$, which represents the unknown, is written as follows:

$$ax^2 + bx + c = 0.$$

The left side of the equation is arranged in order of descending powers of the unknown $x$, and $a$, $b$, and $c$ are constants. The letter $a$ may have any value other than zero, and the letters $b$ and $c$ may have any values including zero. If $a = 0$, the equation will reduce to the form $bx + c = 0$, which is not quadratic, but linear. A quadratic equation in one unknown has only two roots. Any of the following three methods may be used to solve a quadratic equation.

## A. Solution by Factoring

When the left side of a quadratic equation is readily factored, the roots can be obtained by applying the principle which indicates that if a product equals zero, one or more factors of the product equals zero.

**Example 1**  Solve $x^2 - x = 6$.

Transpose: $x^2 - x - 6 = 0$

Factor:  $(x - 3)(x + 2) = 0$

Equate each factor to zero and solve for $x$:

When $x - 3 = 0$,   $x = 3$

When $x + 2 = 0$,   $x = -2$

*Check:*  Substitute separately each root in the original equation.

When $x = 3$,    $3^2 - 3 = 6$;   $9 - 3 = 6$;   $6 = 6$

When $x = -2$,    $(-2)^2 - (-2) = 6$;   $4 + 2 = 6$;   $6 = 6$

**Example 2**    Solve $49x^2 = 81$

$49x^2 = 81$ may be written as $(7x)^2 = 9^2$

Transpose: $(7x)^2 - 9^2 = 0$

Factor    $(7x + 9)(7x - 9) = 0$

Equate each factor to zero and solve for $x$:

When $7x + 9 = 0$,    $x = \dfrac{-9}{7}$

When $7x - 9 = 0$,    $x = \dfrac{9}{7}$

*Check:*    Substitute separately each root in the original equation.

When $x = \dfrac{-9}{7}$,    $49\left(\dfrac{-9}{7}\right)^2 = 81$    $81 = 81$

When $x = \dfrac{9}{7}$,    $49\left(\dfrac{9}{7}\right)^2 = 81$    $81 = 81$

# B. Solution by Completing the Squares

This method of solving a quadratic equation applies to all quadratic equations whether or not a solution can be found by the factoring method illustrated above.

**Example 3**    Solve for $x$. $ax^2 + bx + c = 0$

Subtract $c$ from both sides of equation $ax^2 + bx + c = 0$.

$$ax^2 + bx = -c$$

Divide each side by $a$.    $x^2 + \dfrac{b}{a}x = -\dfrac{c}{a}$

Add the square of half the coefficient of $x$ to both sides to make the left side a perfect square.

$$x^2 + \frac{b}{a}x + \left(\frac{b}{2a}\right)^2 = -\frac{c}{a} + \left(\frac{b}{2a}\right)^2; \text{ the right side} = \frac{b^2}{4a^2} - \frac{c}{a} = \frac{b^2 - 4ac}{4a^2}$$

Thus, $\left(x + \dfrac{b}{2a}\right)^2 = \dfrac{b^2 - 4ac}{4a^2}$

Extract the square root of each side.

$$x + \frac{b}{2a} = \pm\frac{\sqrt{b^2 - 4ac}}{2a}$$

Solve for $x$.    $x = \dfrac{-b \pm \sqrt{b^2 - 4ac}}{2a}$

## C. Solution by the Quadratic Formula

A formula is a general fact, rule, or principle expressed in algebraic symbols. According to the above example, when

$$ax^2 + bx + c = 0,$$

$$x = \frac{-b \pm \sqrt{b^2 - 4ac}}{2a}$$

The fact thus expressed is a formula and can be used to find the roots of any quadratic equation. When the left side of any quadratic equation is written in the order of descending powers of the unknown and the right side of the equation is a zero, only the values of $a$, $b$, and $c$ need to be substituted in the formula. Here $a$ equals the coefficient of the unknown square $(x^2)$, $b$ equals the coefficient of the unknown $(x)$, and $c$ is the constant number.

**Example 4**    Solve $x^2 - x = 6$ by formula.

Transpose. $x^2 - x - 6 = 0$

Hence: $a = 1$, $b = -1$, $c = -6$

Substituting in the formula,

$$x = \frac{-(-1) \pm \sqrt{(-1)^2 - 4(1)(-6)}}{2 \cdot 1} = \frac{1 \pm \sqrt{1 + 24}}{2}$$

$$= \frac{1 \pm \sqrt{25}}{2} = \frac{1 \pm 5}{2}$$

$$x = \frac{1 + 5}{2} = 3$$

$$x = \frac{1 - 5}{2} = -2$$

*Check:*    Substitute the answers in the given equation.

When $x = 3$,        $3^2 - 3 = 6$,        $6 = 6$

When $x = -2$,      $(-2)^2 - (-2) = 6$,      $6 = 6$

## EXERCISE 3–2

### Reference: Section 3.2

**A.** *Solve the following by factoring:*

1. $4x^2 = 9$
2. $9x^2 = 25$
3. $16x^2 - 36 = 0$
4. $25x^2 - 4 = 0$

5. $15x^2 + 14x - 8 = 0$
6. $6x^2 + 7x + 2 = 0$
7. $8x^2 + 3 = 14x$
8. $8y^2 + 6y = 9$

**9.** $3y^2 + 17y - 28 = 0$

**10.** $12y^2 + 3y = 42$

**11.** $12y^2 + 5 = -23y$

**12.** $41x - 10 = 21x^2$

**13.** $x^2 - 5x = -6$

**14.** $9x^2 - 1 = 0$

**15.** $3x^2 - 13x + 4 = 0$

**16.** $15x^2 - x - 2 = 0$

**B.** *Solve the following by the quadratic formula:*

**17.** $6x^2 - 11x + 4 = 0$

**18.** $10x^2 + 13x - 3 = 0$

**19.** $4x^2 - 31x + 21 = 0$

**20.** $x^2 - 64 = 0$

**21.** $18x^2 - 14 = 9x$

**22.** $14x^2 - 11x = 15$

**23.** $9x^2 - 49 = 0$

**24.** $20x^2 - 76x + 72 = 0$

**25.** $7m^2 - 19m - 6 = 0$

**26.** $35y^2 - y - 12 = 0$

**27.** $24n^2 - 41n + 12 = 0$

**28.** $4x^2 + 12x - 40 = 0$

**29.** $35x^2 - 57x = -18$

**30.** $18x^2 + 25x = 3$

**31.** $12x^2 - 9 = -23x$

**32.** $35x^2 - 32 = 36x$

# 3.3 PROGRESSIONS

## A. Definition and Terminology

When a set of numbers is arranged in such a manner that there is a first number, a second number, a third number, and so on, the set of numbers is called a *sequence* of numbers. The successive numbers are called the *terms* of the sequence. The terms of a sequence are generally increased (or decreased) in one of two patterns: the arithmetic progression or the geometric progression.

## B. Arithmetic Progression

An *arithmetic progression* (abbreviated A. P.) is a sequence of numbers in which each term following the first one is obtained by adding the preceding term to a fixed number called the *common difference*. Thus, 1, 3, 5, 7, 9 is an arithmetic progression with a common difference of 2.

### THE $n$TH TERM OF AN ARITHMETIC PROGRESSION

According to the above definition of an arithmetic progression, if the first number of a sequence of numbers is 1 and the common difference is 2, the sequence is obtained as follows:

$$
\begin{aligned}
\text{The first term} \;&= 1 \\
\text{The second term} &= 1 + 2 = 3 \\
\text{The third term} \;&= 1 + (2 \cdot 2) = 5 \\
\text{The fourth term} &= 1 + (3 \cdot 2) = 7 \quad \text{or } 1 + (4 - 1) \cdot 2 = 7 \\
\text{The fifth term} \;&= 1 + (4 \cdot 2) = 9 \quad \text{or } 1 + (5 - 1) \cdot 2 = 9
\end{aligned}
$$

If the number of the terms is $n$, then

the $n$th term $= 1 + (n - 1)2$

Furthermore, if the first term of an A. P. is $a$, the common difference is $d$, and the $n$th term is $L$, then:

The first term   $= a$
The second term $= a + d$
The third term   $= a + 2d$
The fourth term $= a + 3d$   or $a + (4 - 1)d$
The fifth term    $= a + 4d$   or $a + (5 - 1)d$

The $n$th term $L = a + (n - 1)d$

## THE SUM OF AN ARITHMETIC PROGRESSION

Let $S_n$ denote the sum of the first $n$ terms of an arithmetic progression. The sum may be written in both direct and reverse order as follows:

$$S_n = a + (a + d) + (a + 2d) + (a + 3d) + \ldots\ldots\ldots L$$
$$S_n = L + (L - d) + (L - 2d) + (L - 3d) + \ldots\ldots\ldots a$$

Add the two equations, then

$$2S_n = (a + L) + (a + L) + (a + L) + (a + L) \ldots\ldots (a + L)$$
$$= n(a + L)$$

Thus,

$$S_n = \frac{n}{2}(a + L)$$

According to the two formulas above, if any three of the five quantities $a$, $d$, $n$, $L$, and $S_n$ are given, the other two may be found.

**Example 1**   Find the 25th term and the sum of A. P. 1, 3, 5, 7, $\ldots\ldots$ to 25 terms

$n = 25$, $a = 1$, $d = 3 - 1 = 2$
$L = a + (n - 1)d = 1 + (25 - 1)2 = 49$

$$S_n = \frac{n}{2}(a + L) = \frac{25}{2}(1 + 49) = \frac{25}{2} \cdot 50 = 625$$

**Example 2**   Given $S_n = 100$, $L = 19$, $n = 10$. Find $a$ and $d$.

$$S_n = \frac{n}{2}(a + L), \quad 100 = \frac{10}{2}(a + 19), \quad 100 \cdot \frac{2}{10} = a + 19$$

$20 = a + 19$,   $a = 1$
$L = a + (n - 1)d$,   $19 = 1 + (10 - 1)d$,   $18 = 9d$

$$d = \frac{18}{9}, \quad d = 2$$

*Check:*       According to the answer, the A. P. is 1, 3, 5, 7, 9, 11, 13, 15, 17, 19 $(= L)$. The sum is $1 + 3 + 5 + 7 + 9 + 11 + 13 + 15 + 17 + 19 =$ 100.

## ARITHMETIC MEANS

In an A. P., the terms between any two given terms are called the *arithmetic means.* To insert a given number of arithmetic means between two terms, apply the following formula: $L = a + (n - 1)d$, where $n =$ the number of terms to be inserted plus 2.

**Example 3**    Insert five arithmetic means between 4 and 16.

$a = 4$, $L = 16$, $n = 5 + 2 = 7$

Apply the formula:

$16 = 4 + (7 - 1)d$
$16 = 4 + 6d$,    $12 = 6d$
$d = 2$

Thus, the required means are

$4 + 2 = 6$
$6 + 2 = 8$
$8 + 2 = 10$
$10 + 2 = 12$
$12 + 2 = 14$

*Check:*          The A. P. is 4, 6, 8, 10, 12, 14, 16.

# C. Geometric Progression

A *geometric progression* (abbreviated G. P.) is a sequence of numbers in which each term following the first one is obtained by multiplying the preceding term by a constant factor, called the *common ratio.* Thus, 1, 2, 4, 8, 16, is a geometric progression with a common ratio of 2.

## THE $n$TH TERM OF A GEOMETRIC PROGRESSION

According to the above definition of a geometric progression, if the first number of a sequence of numbers is 1 and the common ratio is 2, the sequence is obtained as follows:

The first term     $= 1$
The second term $= 1 \cdot 2$
The third term     $= 1 \cdot 2^2 = 4$
The fourth term  $= 1 \cdot 2^3 = 8$     or $1 \cdot 2^{4-1}$
The fifth term      $= 1 \cdot 2^4 = 16$   or $1 \cdot 2^{5-1}$

The $n$th term     $= 1 \cdot 2^{n-1}$

Furthermore, if the first term of a G. P. is $a$, the common ratio is $r$, the number of terms is $n$, and the $n$th term is $L$, then,

The first term     $= a$
The second term $= ar$
The third term     $= ar^2$

$$\text{The fourth term} = ar^3 \quad \text{or} \quad ar^{4-1}$$
$$\text{The fifth term} \ = ar^4 \quad \text{or} \quad ar^{5-1}$$

Thus,        The $n$th term $L = ar^{n-1}$

## THE SUM OF A GEOMETRIC PROGRESSION

Let $S_n$ denote the sum of the first $n$ terms of a G. P. To derive a formula for the sum, first write the sum as indicated in (1) below, and then multiply (1) by $r$ as indicated in (2).

(1)    $S_n = a + ar + ar^2 + ar^3 + \ldots\ldots ar^{n-2} + ar^{n-1}$
(2)    $rS_n = ar + ar^2 + ar^3 + \ldots\ldots ar^{n-2} + ar^{n-1} + ar^n$

Subtract (2) from (1). The answer is

$S_n - rS_n = a - ar^n$. Factor,
$S_n(1 - r) = a(1 - r^n)$. Solve for $S_n$,

$$S_n = \frac{a(1 - r^n)}{1 - r}$$

According to the two formulas above, if any three of the five quantities $a, r, n, L,$ and $S_n$ are given, the other two may be found.

**Example 4**    Find $L$ and $S_n$ for G. P. 2, 6, 18, . . . to 8 terms.

Here $a = 2$, $r = \dfrac{6}{2} = 3$, $n = 8$

$$L = ar^{n-1} = 2 \cdot 3^{8-1} = 2 \cdot 3^7 = 2 \cdot 2{,}187 = 4{,}374$$

$$S_n = \frac{a(1 - r^n)}{1 - r} = \frac{2(1 - 3^8)}{1 - 3} = \frac{2(1 - 6{,}561)}{-2}$$

$$= \frac{2(-6{,}560)}{-2} = 6{,}560$$

**Example 5**    Given: $a = 2$, $L = -128$, $S_n = -102$. Find $r$ and $n$.

$L = ar^{n-1}$,        $-128 = 2r^{n-1}$,        $r^{n-1} = -64$        (1)

$S_n = \dfrac{a(1 - r^n)}{1 - r}$,        $-102 = \dfrac{2(1 - r^n)}{1 - r}$    (2)

Simplifying (2)        $-102(1 - r) = 2(1 - r^n)$
$-102 + 102r = 2 - 2r^n$
$2r^n + 102r = 2 + 102$        (3)

Factoring (3)        $r(2r^{n-1} + 102) = 104$        (4)

Substituting (1) or $r^{n-1} = -64$ in (4)

$$r[2(-64) + 102] = 104$$
$$-26r = 104$$
$$r = -4$$

Substituting $r = -4$ in (1)    $(-4)^{n-1} = -64$,    or    $(-4)^{n-1} = (-4)^3$

Since both sides of the equation above have the same base, $(-4)$, their exponents must be equal, or, $n - 1 = 3$

$$n = 3 + 1 = 4$$

*Check:*          According to the answer, the G. P. is 2, $-8$, 32, $-128$ $(=L)$.
The sum of the G. P. is $2 + (-8) + 32 + (-128) = -102$ $(S_n)$.

## GEOMETRIC MEANS

In a G. P., the terms between any two given terms are called the *geometric means.* To insert a given number of geometric means between two terms, apply the following formula: $L = ar^{n-1}$, where $n =$ the number of terms to be inserted plus 2.

**Example 6**     Insert five geometric means between 3 and 192.

$a = 3$, $L = 192$, $n = 5 + 2 = 7$

Apply the formula:

$$192 = 3r^{7-1}$$

$$\frac{192}{3} = r^6, \quad 64 = r^6, \quad 2^6 = r^6$$

$$r = 2$$

Thus, the required geometric means are

$$3 \cdot 2 = 6$$
$$6 \cdot 2 = 12$$
$$12 \cdot 2 = 24$$
$$24 \cdot 2 = 48$$
$$48 \cdot 2 = 96$$

*Check:*          The answer gives a G. P. as follows:

3, 6, 12, 24, 48, 96, 192 $(=L)$

## EXERCISE 3–3

### Reference: Section 3.3

**A.** *Find* L *and* $S_n$ *for each of the following A. P.s:*

**1.** 4, 7, 10,  . . . . . . to 7 terms          **5.** 0.2, 0.6, 1.0,  . . . . to 9 terms
**2.** 10, 7, 4,  . . . . . . to 6 terms          **6.** 1, 2, 3,  . . . . . . . to 25 terms
**3.** 2, 4, 6,  . . . . . . . to 8 terms          **7.** $-2$, $-4$, $-6$,  . . . . to 8 terms
**4.** $\frac{1}{6}, \frac{1}{4}, \frac{1}{3}$,  . . . . . . . to 10 terms          **8.** $(a + d)$, $a$, $(a - d)$,  to $n$ terms

**B.** *Three of the five elements,* a, d, n, L, *and* $S_n$ *of an A. P. are given in each of the following problems. Find the remaining elements for each.*

9. $L = -11$, $d = -4$, $n = 7$

10. $d = -3$, $L = -12$, $S_n = -21$

11. $a = 1$, $n = 8$, $S_n = 92$

12. $n = 14$, $L = -23$, $S_n = -49$

13. $d = \frac{1}{6}$, $n = 5$, $S_n = 3\frac{1}{3}$

14. $a = 14$, $d = -4$, $S_n = 24$

15. $a = 5$, $d = -3$, $S_n = -44$

16. $a = -16$, $n = 10$, $S_n = 20$

**C.** *Find* L *and* $S_n$ *for each of the following G. P.s:*

17. 3, 6, 12, . . . . . . to 12 terms

18. 1, 2, 4, . . . . . . . to 25 terms

19. 1, 3, 9, . . . . . . . to 7 terms

20. 54, 18, 6, . . . . . . to 8 terms

21. 2, 6, 18, . . . . . . to 7 terms

22. $\frac{1}{3}$, $-\frac{1}{9}$, $\frac{1}{27}$, . . . . . . to 6 terms

23. 18, 0.18, 0.0018, . . to 4 terms

24. .2, .04, .008, . . . . to 6 terms

**D.** *Three of the five elements* a, r, n, L, *and* $S_n$ *of a G. P. are given below for each problem. Find the remaining elements for each.*

25. $a = -3$, $n = 3$, $S_n = -93$

26. $a = 4$, $L = 324$, $n = 5$

27. $a = -1$, $r = -3$, $S_n = 182$

28. $a = \frac{1}{3}$, $r = 3$, $S_n = 364\frac{1}{3}$

29. $a = 2$, $n = 5$, $L = 32$

30. $a = 32$, $L = 1$, $S_n = 63$

31. $r = 2$, $L = 96$, $S_n = 189$

32. $a = 12$, $r = \frac{1}{2}$, $L = \frac{3}{8}$

**E.** *Insert A. P. means and G. P. means between the two given terms.*

33. Insert 4 arithmetic means between 2 and $14\frac{1}{2}$.

34. Insert 5 arithmetic means between 2 and 5.

35. Insert 6 arithmetic means between 1 and 15.

36. Insert 3 arithmetic means between 3 and 31.

37. Insert 4 geometric means between 2 and 64.

38. Insert 5 geometric means between 128 and 2.

39. Insert 6 geometric means between 1 and 128.

40. Insert 3 geometric means between 3 and 1,875.

**F.** *Statement Problems:*

41. If a student saves $10 in the first week, $12 in the second week, and continues to increase her savings $2 each week, what will be the total of her savings at the end of 52 weeks?

42. The Smiths plan to give a total of $2,700 to their 6 children. Beginning with the oldest, they will give each younger child $20 less than the one preceding. How much will each child receive?

43. Baxter deposits $10 at the end of January of this year. Thereafter at the end of every following month, she deposits 20% more than the preceding deposit. Find the sum of her total deposits at the end of December of this year.

44. A married couple has 3 sons. Each son has a wife and 3 boys. Each grandson also has a wife and 3 boys who are married. How many people are in the family?

## 3.4 THE BINOMIAL THEOREM

Any power of a binomial $(a + b)$ may be expanded by multiplication as follows:

$$(a+b)^1 = a+b$$
$$(a+b)^2 = a^2 + 2ab + b^2$$
$$(a+b)^3 = a^3 + 3a^2b + 3ab^2 + b^3$$
$$(a+b)^4 = a^4 + 4a^3b + 6a^2b^2 + 4ab^3 + b^4$$
$$(a+b)^5 = a^5 + 5a^4b + 10a^3b^2 + 10a^2b^3 + 5ab^4 + b^5$$

If $n$ represents the exponent of $(a + b)$ in any of the preceding expansions, the following properties may be indicated:

1.  The first term is $a^n$, and the second term is $na^{n-1}b$.
2.  In each succeeding term, the exponents of $a$ decrease by 1, and those of $b$ increase by 1. The sum of the exponents of $a$ and $b$ in each term is $n$.
3.  If the coefficient of any term is multiplied by the exponent of $a$ and divided by the exponent of $b$ increased by 1, the result is the coefficient of the next term. The exponent of $b$ increased by 1 equals the number of the term.
4.  The total number of terms in the expansion is $(n + 1)$.
5.  The coefficients of terms equally distant from the ends of the expansion are the same. For example, in the expansion of $(a + b)^5$, the coefficient of the first and the last term is one; the coefficient of the second and next to the last term is 5.

The above properties give us the following formula which is known as the *binomial theorem:*[1]

$$(a+b)^n = a^n + na^{n-1}b + \frac{n(n-1)}{2} a^{n-2}b^2$$
$$+ \frac{n(n-1)(n-2)}{2 \cdot 3} a^{n-3}b^3 + \cdots + b^n$$

This formula applies for any positive integral value of $n$. When $n$ is negative or fractional, the binomial theorem is also valid if $\frac{b}{a}$ is numerically less than one; that is, if the absolute value of $a$ is greater than the absolute value of $b$. However, when $n$ is negative (see Example 4) or fractional (see Example 5), the resulting expansion does not have a last term. Nevertheless, a very close value of $(a + b)^n$ can be approximated if a sufficient number of terms of the expansion are included in the computation.

---

[1] The binomial theorem may also be written with the combination notations: (See footnote on page 123.)

$$(a+b)^n = {_nC_0}a^n + {_nC_1}a^{n-1}b + {_nC_2}a^{n-2}b^2 + \cdots + {_nC_{n-1}}ab^{n-1} + {_nC_n}b^n$$

**Example 1**   Expand $(3x + y)^4$

$a = 3x$, $b = y$, $n = 4$. Substituting the values in the binomial formula,

$$(3x + y)^4 = (3x)^4 + 4(3x)^3y + \frac{4 \cdot 3}{2}(3x)^2y^2 + \frac{4 \cdot 3 \cdot 2}{2 \cdot 3}(3x)y^3$$

$$+ \frac{4 \cdot 3 \cdot 2 \cdot 1}{2 \cdot 3 \cdot 4}y^4$$

$$= 81x^4 + 108x^3y + 54x^2y^2 + 12xy^3 + y^4$$

Examples 2 to 5 will be useful in solving problems relating to compound interest and annuities (Chapters 11 to 14) when the interest rates are not given in the tables in the text.

**Example 2**   Expand $(1 + i)^5$

$a = 1$, $b = i$, $n = 5$. Substituting the values in the binomial formula

$$(1 + i)^5 = 1^5 + 5 \cdot 1^4i + \frac{5 \cdot 4}{2}1^3i^2 + \frac{5 \cdot 4 \cdot 3}{2 \cdot 3}1^2i^3 + \frac{5 \cdot 4 \cdot 3 \cdot 2}{2 \cdot 3 \cdot 4}1 \cdot i^4$$

$$+ \frac{5 \cdot 4 \cdot 3 \cdot 2 \cdot 1}{2 \cdot 3 \cdot 4 \cdot 5}i^5$$

$$= 1 + 5i + 10i^2 + 10i^3 + 5i^4 + i^5$$

**Example 3**   Find the value of $(1 + 2\%)^6$

$a = 1$, $b = .02$, $n = 6$. Substituting the values in the binomial formula,

$$(1 + 2\%)^6 = 1^6 + 6(1)^5(.02) + \frac{6 \cdot 5}{2}(1)^4(.02)^2 + \frac{6 \cdot 5 \cdot 4}{2 \cdot 3}(1)^3(.02)^3$$

$$+ \frac{6 \cdot 5 \cdot 4 \cdot 3}{2 \cdot 3 \cdot 4}(1)^2(.02)^4 + \frac{6 \cdot 5 \cdot 4 \cdot 3 \cdot 2}{2 \cdot 3 \cdot 4 \cdot 5}(1)(.02)^5$$

$$+ \frac{6 \cdot 5 \cdot 4 \cdot 3 \cdot 2 \cdot 1}{2 \cdot 3 \cdot 4 \cdot 5 \cdot 6}(.02)^6$$

$$= 1 + .12 + (15 \times .0004) + (20 \times .000008)$$
$$+ (15 \times .00000016) + (6 \times .0000000032)$$
$$+ .000000000064$$
$$= 1.126162419264$$

*Note:*   If only 8 decimal places are required, the last term may be disregarded in computation. Also, see Table 5 in the Appendix:

$$(1 + 2\%)^6 = 1.12616242.$$

**Example 4**   Evaluate $(1 + .02)^{-3}$ to 3 decimal places.

$a = 1$, $b = .02$, $n = -3$. Substituting the values in the binomial formula,

$$(1 + .02)^{-3} = 1^{(-3)} + (-3)(1)^{-4}(.02) + \frac{(-3)(-4)}{2}(1)^{-5}(.02)^2$$

$$+ \frac{(-3)(-4)(-5)}{2 \cdot 3}(1)^{-6}(.02)^3 + \quad \cdot \quad \cdot \quad \cdot \quad \cdot \quad \cdot \quad \cdot \quad \cdot \quad \cdot$$

$$= 1 + (-.06) + 6(.0004) + (-10)(.000008) + \cdots \cdots$$
$$= 1 - .06 + .0024 - .00008 + \cdots \cdots \cdots$$
$$= .94232, \text{ rounded to 3 decimal places,}$$
$$= .942$$

**Note:**   Since only 3 decimal places are desired, only those terms having values in the first 4 decimal places need be retained in computation. Here, the 4th term $(-10)(.000008)$ or $(-.00008)$ may be omitted in adding. Also, see Table 6 in the Appendix:

$$(1 + 2\%)^{-3} = .94232233.$$

**Example 5**   Expand $(1 + .02)^{\frac{1}{4}}$ to 4 terms and simplify.

$a = 1$, $b = .02$, $n = \frac{1}{4}$. Substituting the values in the binomial formula,

$$(1 + .02)^{\frac{1}{4}} = 1^{\frac{1}{4}} + \frac{1}{4}(1)^{\frac{1}{4}-1}(.02) + \frac{(\frac{1}{4})(\frac{1}{4}-1)}{2}(1)^{\frac{1}{4}-2}(.02)^2$$

$$+ \frac{(\frac{1}{4})(\frac{1}{4}-1)(\frac{1}{4}-2)}{2 \cdot 3}(1)^{\frac{1}{4}-3}(.02)^3 + \cdots \cdots$$

$$= 1 + \frac{1}{4}(.02) + (-\frac{3}{32})(.0004) + \frac{7}{128}(.000008) + \cdots \cdots$$
$$= 1 + .005 - .0000375 + .0000004375 + \cdots \cdots$$
$$= 1.0049629375$$

**Note:**   When $(1 + .02)^{\frac{1}{4}}$ is expanded to 5 terms, the result is 1.00496293149. Round the result to 8 decimal places, $(1 + .02)^{\frac{1}{4}} = 1.00496293$. Also, see Table 5A in the Appendix: $(1 + 2\%)^{\frac{1}{4}} = 1.00496293$.

Another simple way to learn the binomial coefficients of the terms in the binomial expansion of $(a + b)^n$ is to arrange the coefficients in a triangular array. Such an array, as illustrated below, is known as Pascal's triangle.

| Binomial | Coefficients of the terms in the binomial expansion, according to the order of terms |
|----------|-------------------------------------------------------------------------------------|
| $(a+b)^0$ | 1 |
| $(a+b)^1$ | 1   1 |
| $(a+b)^2$ | 1   2   1 |
| $(a+b)^3$ | 1   3   3   1 |
| $(a+b)^4$ | 1   4   6   4   1 |
| $(a+b)^5$ | 1   5   10   10   5   1 |
| $(a+b)^6$ | 1   6   15   20   15   6   1 |
| $(a+b)^7$ | 1   7   21   35   35   21   7   1 |
| . . . . | . . . . . . . . . . . . . . . . . |

Excluding the 1's at the corners of the base of the triangle, each numerical coefficient in the table is the sum of the two numbers in the row above the coefficient. For example, in the fifth row, $4 = 1 + 3$, $6 = 3 + 3$, and $4 = 3 + 1$. Thus,

$$(a + b)^4 = a^4 + 4a^3b + 6a^2b^2 + 4ab^3 + b^4$$

## EXERCISE 3–4

**Reference: Section 3.4**

**A.** *Expand each of the following by the binomial formula and simplify:*

| | | | |
|---|---|---|---|
| **1.** $(x + y)^6$ | **4.** $(5x + 2y)^3$ | **7.** $(x - 2y)^6$ | **10.** $(1 + 0.025)^4$ |
| **2.** $(2x + 3y)^5$ | **5.** $(1 + i)^7$ | **8.** $(m - n)^5$ | **11.** $(1 + 2\%)^5$ |
| **3.** $(x + 4y)^4$ | **6.** $(1 - i)^3$ | **9.** $(1 + 0.02)^3$ | **12.** $(1 + 3\%)^6$ |

**B.** *Find the numerical value of each of the following problems by expanding to 4 terms only (round the answers to 7 decimal places):*

| | | | |
|---|---|---|---|
| **13.** $(1 + 1\frac{1}{4}\%)^{10}$ | **17.** $(1 + 2\%)^{-5}$ | **21.** $(1 + 4\%)^{\frac{1}{12}}$ | **23.** $(1 + 7\%)^{\frac{1}{4}}$ |
| **14.** $(1 + 5\%)^{40}$ | **18.** $(1 + 2\frac{1}{2}\%)^{-6}$ | **22.** $(1 + 3\%)^{\frac{1}{6}}$ | **24.** $(1 + 2\frac{1}{4}\%)^{\frac{1}{3}}$ |
| **15.** $(1 + 1\frac{1}{2}\%)^{36}$ | **19.** $(1 + 4\%)^{-10}$ | | |
| **16.** $(1 + 2\frac{1}{2}\%)^{50}$ | **20.** $(1 + 3\%)^{-20}$ | | |

# 3.5 LOGARITHMS—BASIC ASPECTS

## A. General Statement

Logarithms can be used to simplify the operations of multiplication, division, raising to powers, and extracting roots. In mathematics of finance, logarithms are especially useful in solving problems that involve compound interest and annuities when interest rates are not given in the available tables.

## B. Meaning of Logarithm

A *logarithm* is an exponent. In an exponential form, if $b^x = N$, the exponent $x$ is the logarithm of the number $N$ to the base $b$. Likewise, since

$2^3 = 8$, the exponent 3 is the logarithm of the number 8 to the base 2
$5^2 = 25$, the exponent 2 is the logarithm of the number 25 to the base 5
$10^3 = 1{,}000$, the exponent 3 is the logarithm of the number 1,000 to the base 10

The above relationship can be written in simpler form as follows:

Since   $b^x = N$,      then $\log_b N = x$,
where *log* represents *the logarithm of.*
Since   $2^3 = 8$.        then $\log_2 8 = 3$
Since   $5^2 = 25$,      then $\log_5 25 = 2$
Since $10^3 = 1{,}000$, then $\log_{10} 1{,}000 = 3$

Among various bases, 10 is the most convenient base for logarithmic computation since 10 is also the base in our decimal number system. When the base 10 is used, it is customary to omit the subscript that indicates the base; thus, $\log_{10} 1{,}000$ can be written as $\log 1{,}000$. The logarithms based on 10 are called the *common or Briggsian* (Henry Briggs, 1560–1631) system of logarithms. In this system, the following corresponding forms may be written:

| *Logarithmic Form* | *Exponential Form* |
|---|---|
| $\log 100{,}000 = 5$ | $10^5 = 100{,}000$ |
| $\log 10{,}000 = 4$ | $10^4 = 10{,}000$ |
| $\log 1{,}000 = 3$ | $10^3 = 1{,}000$ |
| $\log 100 = 2$ | $10^2 = 100$ |
| $\log 10 = 1$ | $10^1 = 10$ |
| $\log 1 = 0$ | $10^0 = 1$ |
| $\log .1 = -1$ | $10^{-1} = \frac{1}{10} = .1$ |
| $\log .01 = -2$ | $10^{-2} = \frac{1}{10^2} = \frac{1}{100} = .01$ |
| $\log .001 = -3$ | $10^{-3} = \frac{1}{10^3} = \frac{1}{1{,}000} = .001$ |

In general.    $\log N = x$        $10^x = N$

Note that all numbers *(N)* indicated above have *positive values.*

From the above explanation, it may be seen that as the number becomes greater, the logarithm of the number also becomes greater. Thus, if $N$ and $M$ are two positive numbers and $N$ is larger than $M$, then $\log N$ is also larger than $\log M$. This concept is important in finding the logarithm of a number which is not an exact power of 10. For example, if the number is 249, which is larger than 100 (or $10^2$), the logarithm of 249 is larger than the logarithm of 100. Further, since the number 249 is smaller than 1,000 (or $10^3$), the logarithm of 249 is smaller than the logarithm of 1,000. The relationships may be written as follows:

$$\log 100 < \log 249 < \log 1{,}000$$
or,        $2 < \log 249 < 3$
since      $\log 100 = 2$ and $\log 1{,}000 = 3$

Thus, $\log 249 = 2 +$ a decimal (since $2 + 1 = 3$), or in exponential form, $10^{2 + \text{a decimal}} = 249$.

Similarly, we may find the logarithm of a positive number which is less than 1, such as .0045.

Since        $.001 < .0045 < .01$
or,          $10^{-3} < .0045 < 10^{-2}$
then,      $\log .001 < \log .0045 < \log .01$
or,          $-3 < \log .0045 < -2$

Thus, $\log .0045 = (-3) +$ a decimal (since $(-3) + 1 = (-2)$), or in exponential form, $10^{-3 + \text{a decimal}} = .0045$.

In general, when a number is not an exact power of 10, the logarithm of the number consists of a whole-number part and a decimal part. The whole-number part is called the *characteristic* of the logarithm, and the decimal part is called the *mantissa* of the logarithm.

Logarithm of a positive number = Characteristic + Mantissa

Examples of the characteristics of the selected numbers are tabulated below:

| Number | Digits in Whole-Number Part (1 and Above) ==or== Zeros Between Decimal Point and First Nonzero Digit (Less than 1) | Characteristic |
|---|---|---|
| 10,000 to 99,999.99 . (but less than 100,000) | 5 | 4 |
| 1,000 to 9,999.99 .. (but less than 10,000) | 4 | 3 |
| 100 to 999.99 ... (but less than 1,000) | 3 | 2 |
| 10 to 99.99 .... (but less than 100) | 2 | 1 |
| 1 to 9.99 ..... (but less than 10) | 1 | 0 |
| .1 to .99 ...... (but less than 1) | none | −1 |
| .01 to .099 ..... (but less than .1) | 1 | −2 |
| .001 to .0099 .... (but less than .01) | 2 | −3 |
| .0001 to .00099 ... (but less than .001) | 3 | −4 |
| etc. | | |

This table shows that the characteristic of the logarithm of a number depends only on the position of the decimal point, regardless of the value of the individual digits in the number. The following rules may be used in determining characteristics.

*Rule 1:* If a number is greater than or equal to 1, the characteristic of its logarithm is positive and is 1 less than the number of digits to the left of the decimal point.

*Rule 2:* If a number is less than 1, the characteristic of its logarithm is negative and is 1 more than the number of zeros between the decimal point and the first nonzero digit.

Unlike the characteristic, the mantissa of the logarithm of a number is independent of the position of the decimal point in the number. The mantissa is always positive and is determined by the significant digits of the number. The logarithms of numbers which have the same significant digits arranged in the same order thus have the same mantissas. Here the significant digits in a number are the digits which do not include the zeros at the left of the first nonzero digit, such as in a decimal, or the zeros at the right of the last nonzero digit, such as in a whole number. Thus, the significant digits of the numbers 3,408,000, 34,080, 34.08, and .003408 are 3,4,0,8, and the logarithms of the numbers have the same mantissas, although not the same characteristics.

## C. Tables of Mantissas

Tables of mantissas are also called tables of logarithms. The mantissas of the logarithms of most numbers are unending decimal fractions, but they can be computed to any required number of decimal places. Methods of computing most values of mantissas are developed in advanced algebra. Because they are beyond the scope of this text, those methods are not introduced here. However, for practical uses, various tables of mantissas are available; they are known as six-place tables, seven-place tables, etc., according to the number of digits in the mantissas. It should be noted that while mantissas are decimal fractions, they are usually given in tables without decimal points. Therefore, a decimal point should always be placed before the first digit in the mantissa when it is used. In this text, a six-place table, which gives the mantissas of numbers from 1 to 9,999, and a seven-place table, which gives the mantissas of numbers from 10,000 to 11,009, are used for computing logarithmic problems.[2] The uses of these two tables are described below.

### HOW TO DETERMINE THE LOGARITHM OF A GIVEN NUMBER

In general, three operations are required to determine the logarithm of a given number:

1. Determine the characteristic by the rules given above.
2. In the table find the mantissa corresponding to the significant digits of the given number. Two steps are necessary when this is done:

   **Step (A)** In Column $N$ find the first three significant digits of the given number. The mantissa required is in the row horizontal with these digits.

   **Step (B)** In this row locate the required mantissa in the column headed by the fourth significant digit of the given number.

3. Place a decimal point before the first digit of the mantissa, and add the mantissa to the characteristic. The sum is the required logarithm of the given number.

**Example 1**     Find log 82.46.

> 1. The characteristic is +1 since there are two digits to the left of the decimal point.

---

[2] See Tables 2 and 3 in the Appendix.

2. **Step (A)** The first three significant digits 824 are found in Column $N$ of Table 2 of the Appendix.

**Step (B)** Opposite the finding in Step (A), the required mantissa is found in the column which has 6 at the top. The mantissa is 916243.[3]

3. The logarithm of 82.46 is $1 + .916243 = 1.916243$, or

    log 82.46 = 1.916243.

    In exponential form, the logarithm is written as

    $10^{1.916243} = 82.46.$

**Example 2** Find log 0.008246.

1. The characteristic is $-3$ since there are two zeros between the decimal point and the first nonzero digit 8.
2. The mantissa is 916243 because the significant digits of the given number are the same as those in the preceding example.
3. The logarithm of 0.008246 is $-3 + .916243 = -2.083757$.

    Thus,   log 0.008246 = $-3 + .916243$, or

       log 0.008246 = $-2.083757$.

    In exponential form, the logarithm is written as

    $10^{-3+.916243} = 0.008246$, or

    $10^{-2.083757} = 0.008246.$

When a characteristic is negative, there are other ways to write the logarithm of a number. It can be written by placing the negative sign above the characteristic. Thus, the logarithm in Example 2 may be written as

   log 0.008246 = $\bar{3}.916243$

Or, it may be written in a more convenient way by using an equivalent form, such as

   log 0.008246 = 7.916243 − 10,

because $7 - 10 = -3$. In exponential form the logarithm now is written:

   $10^{7.916243-10} = 0.008246.$

---

[3] The first two digits of each mantissa are not printed in every column in the tables of mantissas. They are printed only in the columns which have 0 at the top. However, when the mantissas have the same first two digits, only the digits for the line having the smallest mantissa and the line having the largest mantissa of the group are printed in the 0 column. In order to secure a six-place mantissa, the first two digits must be prefixed to each entry on the same line and the lines below it until the two digits change. The first two digits of an entry marked by * are located on the line below the entry in the 0 column. Thus, in Example 1, Step (B), the first two digits 91 are prefixed to 6243, or written as 916243. On the same page in the tables, the first two digits 92 must be prefixed to entry *0019, or written as 920019.

*Additional illustrations:*   (Use Table 2 for the first five illustrations.)

> log 8246 = 3.916243
> log 1.175 = 0.070038
> log 0.0004269 = −4 + .630326 = −3.369674,
>
> > or = $\overline{4}$.630326 = 6.630326 − 10
>
> log 732.4 = 2.864748
> log 0.7901 = −1 + .897682 = −.102318,
>
> > or = $\overline{1}$.897682 = 9.897682 − 10
>
> log 10,742 = 4.0310851 (Use Table 3)

## HOW TO DETERMINE THE NUMBER FROM A GIVEN LOGARITHM (FINDING THE ANTILOGARITHM)

In general, the process of determining the number from a given logarithm is the inverse of the process used in determining the logarithm of a number. The number found is called the *antilogarithm* (abbreviated *antilog*) of the given logarithm. The steps in this process follow:

1. Find the given mantissa in the table.
2. Determine the significant digits from the location of the mantissa.
3. The required number is determined by placing a decimal point in the significant digits according to the given characteristic.

**Example 3**    If log $N$ = 2.072617, find $N$.

1. In Table 2 of the Appendix, find the mantissa 072617.
2. The significant digits are 1182.
3. The required number, $N$, is 118.2 because the characteristic is 2. The solution may be written:

$N$ = Antilog 2.072617 = 118.2

**Example 4**    If log $N$ = −1.9609033, find $N$.

Since the mantissas in the tables are all positive, first convert the given negative value of the log $N$ to its equivalent form having the positive mantissa 0390967. The conversion may be done by adding 10 to, and subtracting 10 from, the given value as follows:

−1.9609033 = −1.9609033 + 10 − 10
          = 10 − 1.9609033 − 10
          = 8.0390967 − 10.

Thus,

log $N$ = −1.9609033 = 8.0390967 − 10

Then proceed with the usual process:

1. In Table 3 of the Appendix, find the mantissa 0390967.
2. The significant digits are 10942.
3. The required number, $N$, is 0.010942 because the characteristic is 8 − 10 = −2.

$N$ = Antilog (8.0390967 − 10) = 0.010942

## EXERCISE 3–5

**Reference: Sections 3.5 B and C**

**A.** *Write the following in logarithmic form:*

1. $4 = 10^{0.602060}$
2. $49 = 10^{1.690196}$
3. $0.00325 = 10^{7.511883-10}$
4. $0.02513 = 10^{8.400192-10}$
5. $0.2759 = 10^{9.440752-10}$

6. $5,683 = 10^{3.754578}$
7. $136 = 10^{2.133539}$
8. $10,253 = 10^{4.0108510}$
9. $0.010492 = 10^{8.0208583-10}$
10. $0.000395 = 10^{6.596597-10}$

**B.** *Write the following in exponential form:*

11. $\log 10.6 = 1.025306$
12. $\log 147 = 2.167317$
13. $\log 2,452 = 3.389520$
14. $\log 2.603 = 0.415474$
15. $\log 58 = 1.763428$

16. $\log .003559 = 7.551328 - 10$
17. $\log .0634 = 8.802089 - 10$
18. $\log 10,356 = 4.0151920$
19. $\log 104.23 = 2.0179927$
20. $\log 5,684 = 3.754654$

**C.** *From Tables 2 and 3, determine the logarithm of each number:*

21. 285
22. 0.00285
23. 3.823

24. 43.25
25. 4,328
26. 624

27. 0.0003952
28. 0.687
29. 2,374

30. 453.6
31. 10.452
32. 102,830

**D.** *Find* N *if log* N *is:*

33. 2.201670
34. 3.176959
35. 0.445604

36. 8.431685 − 10
37. 7.600428 − 10
38. 9.799478 − 10

39. 4.691081
40. 1.700184
41. 0.162564

42. 6.202761 − 10
43. 5.446537 − 10
44. 4.596047 − 10

## D. Interpolation Method

Since tables of mantissas provide only a limited number of digits, a mantissa for a number containing more than the provided significant digits cannot be found directly in the tables. The mantissa for such a number thus is approximated by using the interpolation method. When this method is used, it is assumed, although it is not necessarily so, that the differences between numbers and the differences between corresponding mantissas of the numbers in the tables are proportional.

**Example 5**  Find log 584.36.

In Table 2 the *nearest number larger* than and the *nearest number smaller* than the given number 584.36 are 584.40 and 584.30 respectively. The mantissa of 584.40 is 766710 and that of 584.30 is 766636. When the decimal points in the numbers are disregarded, they may be arranged in the following manner:

|                      | Number | Mantissa |     |
|----------------------|--------|----------|-----|
|                      | 58440  | 766710   | (1) |
|                      | 58436  | $x$      | (2) |
|                      | 58430  | 766636   | (3) |

Subtract line (3) from (2)   $\dfrac{6}{10}$ $=$ $\dfrac{x-766636}{74}$   (4)
Subtract line (3) from (1)                        (5)

The differences between the numbers are assumed to be proportional to the differences between the corresponding mantissas, *i.e.*, 6 is to $(x-766636)$ as 10 is to 74.

Solve for $x$ from the proportion formed by the differences on lines (4) and (5).

$$x-766636 = 74 \cdot \tfrac{6}{10} \qquad x-766636 = 44.4, \text{ or } 44$$
$$x = 766636 + 44 = 766680$$

The characteristic of log 584.36 is 2. Thus,

$$\log 584.36 = 2.766680$$

**Note:**  In the above arrangement, the larger number and mantissa are placed on the top line in order to facilitate subtraction. Although there are many other ways of interpolation, the method introduced above is a convenient one. A reader who is familiar with the arrangement can immediately write the value of $x$ as follows:

$$x = 766636 + 74 \left(\frac{6}{10}\right) = 766636 + 44.4 = 766680.4$$

The difference, 74, can be derived from the D column of Table 2. (Also see the footnote to Table 2 in defining the values in the D column.)

The interpolation method may also be used in finding the number of a given logarithm when the mantissa is not listed in the tables.

**Example 6**  If log $N = 3.642682$, find $N$ to five significant digits.

The mantissa 642682 can not be found in Table 2. Thus, it must be approximated by the interpolation method. The nearest mantissa larger than and that smaller than the given mantissa are 642761 and 642662, which correspond to numbers 43930 and 43920 respectively. The decimal point is disregarded in computing the value of $N$ at first. The numbers and the corresponding mantissas may be arranged as follows:

|           | Number | Mantissa |     |
|-----------|--------|----------|-----|
|           | 43930  | 642761   | (1) |
|           | $x$    | 642682   | (2) |
|           | 43920  | 642662   | (3) |

(2) − (3)   $\dfrac{x-43920}{10}$ $=$ $\dfrac{20}{99}$   (4)
(1) − (3)                        (5)

Solve for $x$ from the proportion formed by the differences on lines (4) and (5).

$x - 43920 = 10 \cdot \frac{20}{99} = 2.02$, or 2
$x = 43920 + 2 = 43922$

Since the characteristic is 3, $N = 4{,}392.2$.

**Note:**   If six significant digits are required, two zeros may be added to the numbers 4392 and 4393; that is, the required number is between 439200 and 439300. When six-place tables are used, there is usually no need to compute seven or more significant digits since the values obtained from the interpolation method are approximations. However, when seven-place tables are used, we may interpolate to seven, or sometimes to eight, significant digits to obtain close approximations. See note 4 to Example 6 of Section 11.3 for an example.

## EXERCISE 3–6

### Reference: Section 3.5 D

**A.** *Using the interpolation method, determine the logarithm of each number:*

| | | | |
|---|---|---|---|
| **1.** 0.0032468 | **4.** 1.3784 | **7.** 0.78614 | **10.** 371,256 |
| **2.** 0.32465 | **5.** 0.026584 | **8.** 531.13 | **11.** 82.564 |
| **3.** 6,523.5 | **6.** 45.375 | **9.** 386.24 | **12.** 503,723 |

**B.** *Using the interpolation method, find N if log N is: (Problems 13–20, find N to 5 significant digits; Problems 21–24, find N to 6 significant digits. Use Table 3 for Problems 23 and 24.)*

| | | | |
|---|---|---|---|
| **13.** 0.536274 | **16.** 1.760141 | **19.** 4.447211 | **22.** 1.663084 |
| **14.** 3.740654 | **17.** 7.536274 − 10 | **20.** 2.944895 | **23.** 8.0184568 − 10 |
| **15.** 2.568254 | **18.** 9.929455 − 10 | **21.** 3.462894 | **24.** 0.0283795 |

## 3.6 LOGARITHMS—COMPUTATION

The operations of multiplication, division, raising to powers, and extracting roots by using logarithms are presented in this section. Although logarithms can be used to simplify such operations, there is a disadvantage in their use; except for a few numbers, the results of the operations computed by means of logarithms are approximations. In general, the results in logarithmic computations will be more accurate if the mantissa parts have more places included. Unless otherwise specified, the interpolation process is omitted for simplifying the following illustrations. The nearest value in the tables of mantissas is used in finding an antilog of a computed logarithm.

## A. Law for Multiplication

*The logarithm of the product of two or more factors equals the sum of their logarithms.*

The general form is  **log** $MN=$ **log** $M+$ **log** $N$.[4]

The above law may be used to simplify computation in multiplication as shown in the following examples:

**Example 1**    If $MN = (1.67)(.055)$, find the product.

First, take logarithms of both sides of the equation.

log $(MN) =$ log $[(1.67)(.055)]$, or

log $MN =$ log $1.67 +$ log $.055$.

$$\begin{array}{r} \log 1.67 = 0.222716 \\ (+)\ \log .055 = 8.740363 - 10 \\ \hline \log MN = 8.963079 - 10 \end{array}$$

Find the antilog,
$MN = 0.09185$

**Example 2**    Compute $(-1.67)(.055)$.

First, change the negative factor $(-1.67)$ to a positive factor as follows:

$(-1.67)(.055) = -[(1.67)(.055)]$

Then, find the value of $(1.67)(.055)$ by logarithms. In Example 1, $(1.67)(.055) = .09185$. Thus, $(-1.67)(.055) = -.09185$

**Example 3**    If $MN = (23.57)(5.598)$, find the product.

log $MN =$ log $23.57 +$ log $5.598$.

$$\begin{array}{r} \log 23.57 = 1.372360 \\ (+)\ \log 5.598 = 0.748033 \\ \hline \log MN = 2.120393 \end{array}$$

Find the antilog,
$MN = 131.9$ (approximately)

**Note:**    The nearest value to the computed mantissa 120393 in the six-place table (Table 2) is 120245, where the number is 1319.

For a more accurate result, further significant digits in Example 3 may be obtained by the interpolation method. The interpolation shown below is computed to six significant digits.

| | | *Number* | | *Mantissa* | |
|---|---|---|---|---|---|
| | | 132000 | | 120574 | (1) |
| | | $x$ | | 120393 | (2) |
| | | 131900 | | 120245 | (3) |
| (2) − (3) | | $\dfrac{x - 131900}{100}$ | $=$ | $\dfrac{148}{329}$ | (4) |
| (1) − (3) | | | | | (5) |

---

[4] *Proof:*    Let $x =$ log $M$, or $M = 10^x$
$\phantom{Let\ } y =$ log $N$, or $N = 10^y$

Then, $MN = 10^x \cdot 10^y = 10^{x+y}$; and
log $MN = x + y =$ log $M +$ log $N$

Solve for $x$ from the proportion formed by the differences on lines (4) and (5):

$x - 131900 = 100 \cdot \frac{148}{329} = 44.98$ or 45
$x = 131900 + 45 = 131945$

Thus $MN = 131.945$ (approximately)

**Note:**      The actual product is $(23.57)(5.598) = 131.94486$

## B. Law for Division

*The logarithm of a quotient equals the logarithm of the dividend (numerator) minus the logarithm of the divisor (denominator).*

The general form is     $\log \dfrac{M}{N} = \log M - \log N.$[5]

The above law may be used to simplify computation in division as shown in the following example:

**Example 4**      If $\dfrac{M}{N} = \dfrac{0.1071}{2.38}$, find the quotient.

First, take logarithms of both sides of the equation.

$$\log \left( \frac{M}{N} \right) = \log \left( \frac{0.1071}{2.38} \right), \text{ or}$$

$$\log \frac{M}{N} = \log 0.1071 - \log 2.38$$

$$\begin{array}{l} \log 0.1071 = 9.029789 - 10 \\ (-) \log 2.38 \quad = 0.376577 \\ \hline \qquad \log \dfrac{M}{N} = 8.653212 - 10 \end{array}$$

Find the antilog,      $\dfrac{M}{N} = 0.045$

## C. Law for Powers and Roots

*The logarithm of an exponential equals the exponent times the logarithm of its base.*

---

[5] *Proof:*  Let $x = \log M$, or $M = 10^x$
$\qquad\qquad y = \log N$, or $N = 10^y$

Then, $\dfrac{M}{N} = \dfrac{10^x}{10^y} = 10^{x-y}$; and $\log \dfrac{M}{N} = x - y = \log M - \log N$

The general form is   $\log M^p = p(\log M).$[6]

If the exponent is a fraction, the general form may be written as:

$$\log M^{\frac{1}{q}} = \frac{1}{q}(\log M), \text{ or}$$

$$\log \sqrt[q]{M} = \frac{1}{q}(\log M)$$

Applications of the above law are illustrated below:

**Example 5**   Compute $(17)^3$.

Let $N = (17)^3$. Then,
$\log N = \log (17)^3 = 3 \log 17$
$\qquad\qquad = 3(1.230449) = 3.691347$

$N = \text{antilog } 3.691347 = 4{,}913, \text{ or } (17)^3 = 4{,}913$

**Example 6**   Compute $(-17)^3$.

$(-17)^3 = [(-1)(17)]^3 = (-1)^3(17)^3 = (-1)(17)^3$

Find the value of $(17)^3$ by logarithms. (See Example 5.)

$(-17)^3 = (-1)(17)^3 = (-1)(4{,}913) = -4{,}913.$

**Example 7**   Compute $(1.045)^{32}$.

Let $N = (1.045)^{32}$. Then,
$\log N = \log (1.045)^{32} = 32 \log 1.045$
$\qquad\qquad\qquad = 32(0.019116) = 0.611712$

$N = \text{antilog } (0.611712) = 4.09, \text{ or}$
$(1.045)^{32} = 4.09$

***Note:***   1. The multiplication, $32(0.019116) = 0.611712$, is carried out by the conventional method. It may also be done by using logarithms as illustrated in Example 1.
2. The nearest value to the computed mantissa 611712 in the six-place table is 611723, where $N = 4{,}090$.
3. The answer may be checked by using Table 5, where $i = 4\frac{1}{2}\%$, $n = 32$, and $(1 + i)^n = (1 + 4\frac{1}{2}\%)^{32} = 4.08998104$.

**Example 8**   Find $N$ if $N = \sqrt[7]{2{,}187}$.

Let $N = \sqrt[7]{2{,}187} = 2{,}187^{\frac{1}{7}}$. Then,

$\log N = \log (2{,}187)^{\frac{1}{7}} = \frac{1}{7} \log 2{,}187 = \frac{1}{7}(3.339849) = 0.477121, \text{ or}$

---

[6] *Proof:*   Let $x = \log M$, or $M = 10^x$. When both sides of the equation are raised to the $p$th power, the following results:

$$M^p = (10^x)^p = 10^{px}, \text{ and}$$
$$\log M^p = px = p(\log M)$$

$$\log N = 0.477121$$
$$N = \text{antilog } 0.477121 = 3.000, \text{ or } 3$$

*Check:*        $3^7 = 2,187$

**Example 9**   Compute $\sqrt{0.6576}$.

Let $N = \sqrt{0.6576} = (0.6576)^{\frac{1}{2}}$. Then,
$$\log N = \tfrac{1}{2}\log 0.6576 = \tfrac{1}{2}(-1 + .817962)$$
$$= \tfrac{1}{2}(-.182038) = -.091019$$

There are only positive mantissas in the tables of logarithms. The negative result therefore must be converted to its equivalent form having a positive mantissa before using the table to find the antilog.

Since $-.091019 = -.091019 + 10 - 10 = 10 - .091019 - 10$
$$= 9.908981 - 10,$$
$\log N = -.091019 = 9.908981 - 10, \text{ or } -1 + .908981$
$N = \text{antilog}(-1 + .908981) = .8109, \text{ or } \sqrt{0.6576} = .8109$

*Note:*   The nearest value to the computed mantissa 908981 in the six-place table is 908967, where $N = 8,109$.

## EXERCISE 3–7

### Reference: Section 3.6 A, B, and C

Perform each of the following indicated operations by use of logarithms. Compute Problems 1, 2, 3, and 4 to six significant digits. Omit interpolation in the remaining problems.

**A.** *Multiplication:*

**1.** $2.35 \times 0.453$    **4.** $5,684 \times 39$    **7.** $(-4.25) \times 728.6$
**2.** $46.25 \times 3.42$    **5.** $0.03452 \times 236$    **8.** $56.73 \times (-68.54)$
**3.** $743 \times 235$    **6.** $431.6 \times 35.47$

**B.** *Division:*

**9.** $0.2346 \div 1.46$    **12.** $4.768 \div 2.167$    **15.** $6.543 \div 7,428$
**10.** $4,326 \div 26.4$    **13.** $74.26 \div 2.75$    **16.** $3.427 \div 0.01648$
**11.** $375.6 \div 0.134$    **14.** $88 \div 22$

**C.** *Powers and roots:*

**17.** $(1.015)^{27}$    **21.** $(-45)^2$    **25.** $\sqrt[3]{4,913}$    **29.** $\sqrt[6]{583}$
**18.** $(1.025)^{46}$    **22.** $(-26)^2$    **26.** $\sqrt[3]{2,744}$    **30.** $\sqrt[8]{642}$
**19.** $(3.752)^{12}$    **23.** $(-33.64)^3$    **27.** $\sqrt{15.21}$    **31.** $\sqrt[4]{0.4243}$
**20.** $(23.4)^5$    **24.** $(-12.2)^3$    **28.** $\sqrt{84.64}$    **32.** $\sqrt[5]{0.8736}$

## D. Solving Equations

To solve an equation by using logarithms, first equate the logarithms of both sides of the equation; then solve the unknown from the new logarithmic equation.

**Example 10**   If $(1 + i)^{69} = 2.794$, find $i$.

First, equate the logarithms of both sides.

$$\log (1 + i)^{69} = \log 2.794$$

$$69 \log (1 + i) = 0.446226$$

$$\log (1 + i) = \frac{0.446226}{69} = 0.006467$$

$$1 + i = \text{antilog } 0.006467 = 1.015$$

$$i = 1.015 - 1 = 0.015, \text{ or } 1\tfrac{1}{2}\%$$

**Note:**   1. The nearest value to the computed mantissa 006467 in the six-place table is 006466, where $N = 1,015$.
2. The answer may be checked by using Table 5, where $i = 1\tfrac{1}{2}\%$, $n = 69$, and $(1 + i)^n = (1 + 1\tfrac{1}{2}\%)^{69} = 2.79355300$.

**Example 11**   If $(1 + i)^{-46} = 0.2871$, find $i$.

First, equate the logarithms of both sides.

$$\log (1 + i)^{-46} = \log 0.2871$$

$$(-46) \log (1 + i) = -1 + .458033 = -.541967$$

$$\log (1 + i) = \frac{-.541967}{-46} = 0.0117819$$

$$1 + i = \text{antilog } 0.0117819 = 1.0275$$

$$i = 1.0275 - 1 = 0.0275 \text{ or } 2\tfrac{3}{4}\%$$

**Note:**   1. The nearest value to the computed mantissa 0117819 in the seven-place table is 0117818, where $N = 10,275$.
2. The answer may be checked by using Table 6, where $i = 2\tfrac{3}{4}\%$, $n = 46$, and $(1 + i)^{-n} = (1 + 2\tfrac{3}{4}\%)^{-46} = 0.28710172$.

**Example 12**   If $(1 + 2\tfrac{1}{2}\%)^n = 2.15$, find $n$.

First, equate the logarithms of both sides.

$$\log (1 + 2\tfrac{1}{2}\%)^n = \log 2.15$$

$$n(\log 1.025) = \log 2.15$$

$$n = \frac{\log 2.15}{\log 1.025} = \frac{0.332438}{0.010724} = 31$$

**Note:**   1. The division, $0.332438/0.010724 = 31$, is carried out by the conventional method. It may also be done by using logarithms as illustrated in Example 4.

2. The answer may also be checked by using Table 5, where $i = 2\frac{1}{2}\%$, $n = 31$, and $(1 + i)^n = (1 + 2\frac{1}{2}\%)^{31} = 2.15000677$.

## EXERCISE 3–8

### Reference: Section 3.6 D

*Solving equations: (Omit interpolation.)*

1. If $(1 + i)^{46} = 1.771$, find $i$.
2. If $(1 + i)^{25} = 1.45$, find $i$.
3. If $(1 + i)^{\frac{2}{5}} = 1.008$, find $i$.
4. If $(1 + i)^{\frac{1}{6}} = 1.0049$, find $i$.
   (Hint: Use 7-place table.)
5. If $(1 + i)^{-20} = .3118$, find $i$.
6. If $(1 + i)^{-4} = .8548$, find $i$.

7. If $(1 + i)^{-\frac{1}{4}} = .9951$, find $i$.
8. If $(1 + i)^{-\frac{1}{2}} = .9713$, find $i$.
9. If $(1 + 1\frac{1}{2}\%)^n = 4.432$, find $n$.
10. If $(1 + 4\%)^n = 1.9479$, find $n$.
11. If $(1 + 4\frac{1}{2}\%)^{-n} = .267$, find $n$.
12. If $(1 + 5\%)^{-n} = .0107$, find $n$.

# Chapter 4

# Basic Modern Algebra

Decision-making techniques have been developed rapidly in recent years for solving many types of business and economic problems. The topics included in Chapters 4 and 5 are important to the study of such techniques. This chapter will present the basic topics, including sets and subsets, counting procedures, and probabilities. The concept of sets and subsets is basic in modern mathematics. The fundamental theories of many branches of mathematics are now commonly expressed in the language of sets. Probability theory introduced in Section 4.3 is one of the branches based on set theory. Probabilities are fundamental to statistical decision theory applicable to business problems. The counting procedures are included in this chapter since they are useful in computing probabilities.

## 4.1 SETS AND SUBSETS

This section introduces the concept of sets, the ways of specifying sets, and the operations with sets. The algebra of sets is frequently referred to as *Boolean Algebra,* in honor of the English mathematician George Boole (1815–64).

## A. The Concept of Sets

We often use the word *set* to represent a group of things having some common property, such as a set of books, a set of tools, and a set of golf clubs. Similarly, in mathematics a set is used to represent a *well-defined* collection of objects, things, numbers, or symbols. A member of a set is called an *element* of the set. Each element of a set must be well-defined; that is, we must be able to tell without any doubt whether or not a given object belongs to that set. For example, a set may consist of the three numbers (or elements) 5, 7, and 9.

A set may be *finite* or *infinite*. If the number of elements in a set is limited, or it can be expressed by a positive number, the set is finite. If the number of elements in a set is unlimited, the set is infinite.

**Example 1**    The following collections are regarded as finite sets:

1. The members of a fraternity (such as 20 members).
2. The students in a mathematics class (such as 30 students).
3. The integers above 1 but less than 5 (or 2, 3, and 4).
4. The even numbers larger than 4 but smaller than 12 (or 6, 8, and 10).

**Example 2**    The following collections are regarded as infinite sets:

1. The stars in the universe  (unlimited stars).
2. The people in the past, present, and future  (unlimited people).
3. The integers above 1 (or 2, 3, 4, . . .).
4. The numbers below 1 (or .1, .01, .001, . . .).

A set which has no elements is called an *empty* set or a *null* set, and is denoted by the symbol φ (the Greek letter phi, pronounced fī). The role of the empty set in the algebra of sets is similar to that of zero in the decimal number system.

**Example 3**    The following collections are regarded as empty sets:

1. The trees over 50 miles tall.
2. The students over 1,000 years old now attending college.
3. The even integers above 4 but below 6.
4. The odd integers above 1 but below 3.

There are also *universal set* and *subsets*. The universal set, usually denoted by *U,* is the total collection of all elements under consideration in a given problem. A universal set may have many *subsets*. The relationship between a universal set and its subsets may clearly be shown by a diagram, called a *Venn diagram,* in honor of the English logician John Venn (1834–83).

**Example 4**    Let *U* = the set of all students in a college,
    *A* = the set of all freshmen in the college, and
    *B* = the set of all sophomores in the college.

The Venn diagram is shown below:

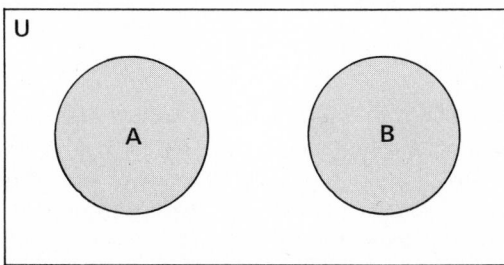

If every element of a set is also an element of another set, we then say that the former is a subset of the latter. Observe the diagram in the above example. The total area of the rectangle represents the set of all students in the college, or the universal set. Since every element of set $A$ (a freshman) is also an element of set $U$ (a student in the college), set $A$ is a subset of the universal set $U$. Also, $B$ is a subset of $U$. Similarly, we may reason that a set is a subset of itself, such as $U$ is a subset of $U$. In addition, the empty set $\phi$ is a subset of every set.

## B. Ways of Specifying Sets

It is customary to use a capital letter to indicate a set and to specify all elements within braces. There are two basic ways of specifying the elements of a set:

1. *List* the names of all elements of the set. This method is convenient when the number of elements of the set is not too large.
2. *Describe* a rule by which all elements of the set can be determined.

**Example 5**    The grades of the five students in Professor Minton's class are expressed as set $A$ by the listing method below:

$A = \{80, 85, 88, 90, 95\}$

**Example 6**    The integers above 3 but less than 6,150 are expressed as set $B$ by the description method as follows:

$B = \{x \mid x \text{ is an integer and } 3 < x < 6,150\}$

The above expression may be read: "$B$ is the set of all elements $x$ such that $x$ is an integer and $x$ is larger than 3 but less than 6,150."

## C. Operations with Sets

There are three basic operations with sets: *union, intersection,* and the *complement.* The operations with sets may be performed or reasoned in a manner similar to the basic operations (addition, subtraction, multiplication, and division) in ordinary algebra. Let $A$ and $B$ represent two subsets of the universal set $U$. The three basic operations may be conveniently illustrated by using a Venn diagram of the subsets and the universal set.

### (1) UNION

The union of sets $A$ and $B$ is denoted by the set $A \cup B$ (read: $A$ union $B$, or $A$ cup $B$), which contains all elements of $U$ that belong either to $A$ or to $B$ or to both. The set $A \cup B$ is also called the *sum* of sets $A$ and $B$ and written $A + B$. The sum is indicated by the shaded area in each of the Venn diagrams below. We shall use the symbol $\cup$ in this text.

Case (a)                    Case (b)                    Case (c)

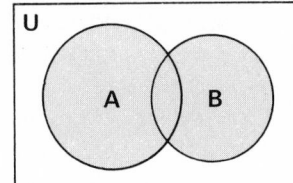 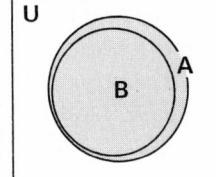 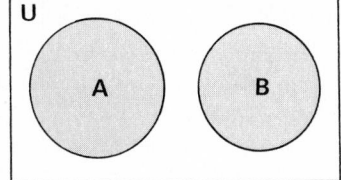

Observe that every element of $A$ belongs to $A \cup B$; also, every element of $B$ belongs to $A \cup B$.

**Example 7**    Let all (8) students in a classroom be the universal set, or

$$U = \left\{ \begin{array}{l} \text{Alan, Dale, Larry, Stevie, Peter,} \\ \text{Betty, Nancy, Mary} \end{array} \right\}$$

Also, let all (6) students in the classroom who are majoring in English be set $A$, or

$A = \{\text{Alan, Dale, Larry, Stevie, Betty, Nancy}\};$

and all (3) girls in the classroom be set $B$, or

$B = \{\text{Betty, Nancy, Mary}\}.$

Then,
$$A \cup B = \left\{ \begin{array}{l} \text{Alan, Dale, Larry, Stevie, Betty,} \\ \text{Nancy, Mary} \end{array} \right\}$$

$A \cup B$ represents the set of all (7) students in the classroom who are either majoring in English or girls. Note that Betty and Nancy are not listed twice in the set $A \cup B$ and that Peter does not fit in either set $A$ or $B$. See Case (a) in the diagram at the top of this page.

**Example 8**    Let $U = \{x \mid x \text{ is an integer and } 5 < x < 20\}$
$A = \{6, 8, 9, 12, 18, 19\}$
$B = \{7, 11\}$

Then,
$A \cup B = \{6, 7, 8, 9, 11, 12, 18, 19\}.$

(See Case (c) in the diagram at the top of this page.)

Similarly, for any set $A$, we have $A \cup \phi = A$.

## (2) INTERSECTION

The intersection of sets $A$ and $B$ is denoted by the set $A \cap B$ (read: $A$ intersect $B$, or $A$ cap $B$), which contains all elements of $U$ that belong to both $A$ and $B$. The set $A \cap B$ is also called the *product* of sets $A$ and $B$ and written $A \cdot B$. The product is indicated by the shaded area in each of the Venn diagrams below. We shall use the symbol $\cap$ in this text.

Case (a)                    Case (b)                    Case (c)

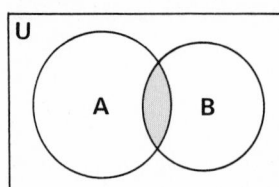  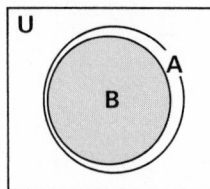  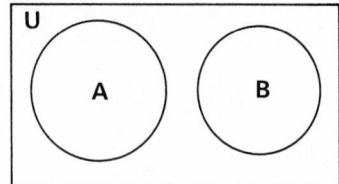

Observe that every element which belongs to both $A$ and $B$ belongs to $A \cap B$. Note that $A \cap B$ is an empty set in Case (c) above since there are no elements that belong to both $A$ and $B$. Sets $A$ and $B$ in Case (c) are said to be *disjoint* or *mutually exclusive*.

**Example 9**   Refer to Example 7. Find the set $A \cap B$.

$A \cap B = \{$Betty, Nancy$\}$ (See Case (a) in the diagram above.)

$A \cap B$ represents the set of all (2) students in the classroom who are majoring in English and are girls.

**Example 10**   Refer to Example 8. Find the set $A \cap B$.

$A \cap B = \phi$ (the empty set) (See Case (c) in the diagram above.)

$A$ and $B$ are disjoint since their intersection is the empty set. Note that neither 7 nor 11 (elements of set $B$) is an element of set $A$.

Similarly, for any set $A$, we have $A \cap \phi = \phi$.

## (3) COMPLEMENT

The complement of set $A$ is denoted by the set $A'$ (read $A$ prime or written $\bar{A}$, $\sim A$, or $\check{A}$), which contains all elements of $U$ that do not belong to $A$. Set $A'$ is indicated by the shaded area in the diagram below:

Complement of $A$ ($=A'$)

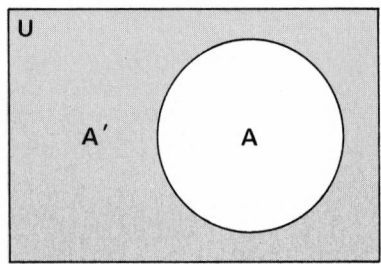

**Example 11**   Refer to Example 7. Find (a) set $A'$, and (b) set $B'$.

(a) $A' = \{$Peter, Mary$\}$
The set $A'$ represents all students in the classroom not majoring in English.

(b) $B' = \{$Alan, Dale, Larry, Stevie, Peter$\}$
The set $B'$ represents all students in the classroom who are not girls.

## ★(4) OTHER OPERATIONS WITH SETS

**Operations of Difference (or Subtraction).** A set may also be subtracted from another set. In a universal set $U$, to subtract $B$ from $A$, denoted by the set $A - B$, is to find the difference between $A$ and $B$. The difference is obtained by taking all elements that belong both to $B$ and to $A$ away from $A$. The set $A - B$ is shown by the shaded area in each of the diagrams following. Note the difference between Case (b) and Case (d).

Case (a)

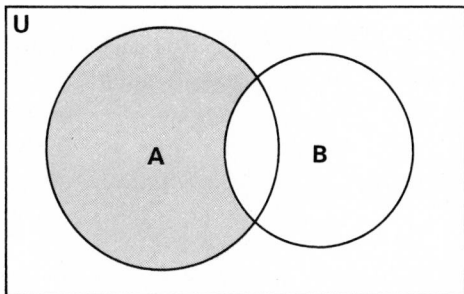

Case (b)

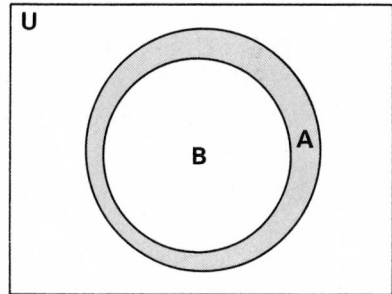

Case (c)

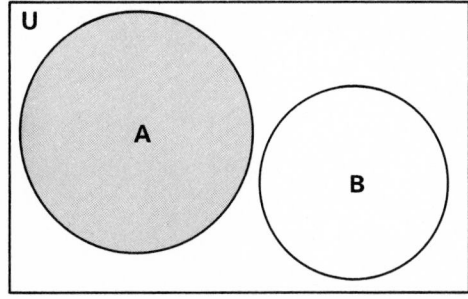

Case (d) $A - B = \phi$

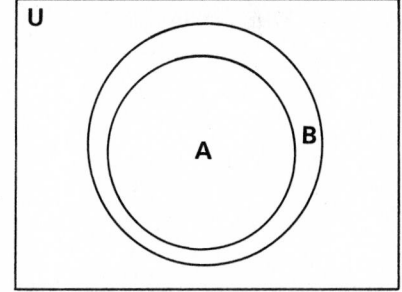

Observe that every element that belongs to $A - B$ belongs to both $A$ and $B'$. In other words,

$$\text{set } A - B = \text{set } A \cap B'.$$

Since the subtraction operation $(A - B)$ may be replaced by the combined operations of intersection and complement $(A \cap B')$, it is generally not regarded as a basic operation in the algebra of sets.

**Example 12**   Let $U = \{1, 2, 3, 4, 5, 6, 7, 8, 9, 10\}$
            $A = \{1, 2, 4, 5\}$
            $B = \{2, 3, 5, 6\}$

         Find (a) $A - B$, and (b) $B - A$.

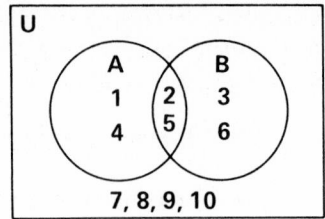

(a) $A - B = \{1, 4\}$, or
     $A - B = A \cap B' = \{1, 4\}$, where $B' = \{1, 4, 7, 8, 9, 10\}$

(b) $B - A = \{3, 6\}$, or
     $B - A = B \cap A' = \{3, 6\}$, where $A' = \{3, 6, 7, 8, 9, 10\}$

**Operations with Three or More Subsets.** The operations with sets or subsets presented above may be expanded for three or more sets or subsets. Observe the diagram below. We may find:

**Set A ∩ B ∩ C′**          **Set A ∩ B ∩ C**

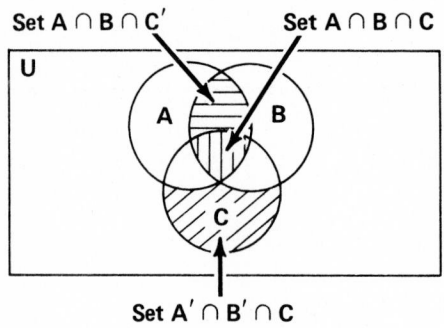

**Set A′ ∩ B′ ∩ C**

1. The shaded area with vertical lines represents set $A \cap B \cap C$.
2. The shaded area with horizontal lines represents set $A \cap B \cap C'$.
3. The shaded area with diagonal lines represents set $A' \cap B' \cap C$.

**Example 13**    Let $U = \{1, 2, 3, 4, 5, 6, 7, 8, 9, 10\}$

              $A = \{1, 2, 4, 5\}$
              $B = \{2, 3, 5, 6\}$
              $C = \{4, 5, 6, 7, 8\}$

Find the following sets:

(a) $A \cup B \cup C$,   (b) $A \cap B \cap C$,   (c) $A \cap B \cap C'$,   and
(d) $A' \cap B' \cap C$

The elements of each set are written on the diagram below:

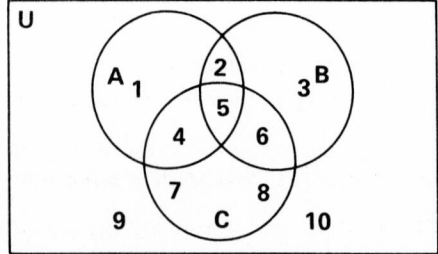

(a) $A \cup B \cup C = \{1, 2, 3, 4, 5, 6, 7, 8\}$
(b) $A \cap B \cap C = \{5\}$
(c) $A \cap B \cap C' = \{2\}$, where $C' = \{1, 2, 3, 9, 10\}$
(d) $A' \cap B' \cap C = \{7, 8\}$, where $A' = \{3, 6, 7, 8, 9, 10\}$ and $B' = \{1, 4, 7, 8, 9, 10\}$

**Operations by Postulates.** The operations with sets may be performed according to postulates instead of diagrams as illustrated above. Many of the postulates for sets are the same as those for ordinary algebra. Examples are listed below:

(a) The commutative laws: $A \cup B = B \cup A.$
$\qquad\qquad\qquad\qquad\quad A \cap B = B \cap A.$

(b) The associative laws: $(A \cup B) \cup C = A \cup (B \cup C).$
$\qquad\qquad\qquad\qquad\;\; (A \cap B) \cap C = A \cap (B \cap C).$

(c) The distributive law: $A \cap (B \cup C) = (A \cap B) \cup (A \cap C).$

**Example 14** Refer to Example 13. Find the set $A \cap (B \cup C)$ by the distributive law.

Since $A \cap B = \{2, 5\}$ and $A \cap C = \{4, 5\},$

Then $A \cap (B \cup C) = (A \cap B) \cup (A \cap C) = \{2, 5\} \cup \{4, 5\} = \{2, 4, 5\}.$

This answer may be checked by observing the diagram in Example 13.

## EXERCISE 4–1

### Reference: Section 4.1

1. Determine each of the following collections: a finite set? an infinite set? or an empty set?

   (a) The living members of your immediate family.
   (b) The points on a straight line.
   (c) The cats in New York City weighing more than two tons.
   (d) The integers above 2 but below 120.

2. Determine each of the following collections: a finite set? an infinite set? or an empty set?

   (a) The chairs in a classroom.
   (b) The integers above 10.
   (c) The even integers lying between 10 and 12.
   (d) The numbers between 7 and 9.

3. Use both the listing method and the description method to specify the sets given below:

   (a) The first eight letters of the alphabet.
   (b) The integers from 2 to 9, inclusive.

4. Use either the listing method or the description method to specify each set given below. State your reason for selecting the method in each case.

   (a) The integers above 40.
   (b) The students whose names are Adams, Clark, Fink, Jones, and Shaw.

5. Draw a Venn diagram to show the universal set $U$ and the subsets $A$ and $B$:

$U = \{x \mid x \text{ is an integer and } 4 < x < 15\}$
$A = \{7, 8, 10, 11, 14\}$
$B = \{5, 6, 12\}$

6. From the information given in Problem 5 above, find sets:

   (a) $A \cup B$     (b) $A \cap B$     (c) $B'$     ★(d) $U - B$

7. From the information given in Problem 5 above, find sets:

   (a) $A \cup B'$     (b) $A \cap B'$     (c) $A'$     ★(d) $B - A$

8. Draw a Venn diagram to show the universal set $U$ and the subsets $A$ and $B$:

   $U = \{a, b, c, d, e, f, g, h, i, j, k\}$
   $A = \{a, c, e, g, h, i\}$
   $B = \{a, b, d, e, f\}$

9. From the information given in Problem 8 above, find sets:

   (a) $A \cup B$ (b) $A \cap B$ (c) $A'$ (d) $A \cup A'$ ★(e) $A - B$

10. From the information given in Problem 8 above, find sets:

    (a) $A \cup U$ (b) $A \cap U$ (c) $B'$ (d) $A \cap A'$ ★(e) $B - A$

★11. Let $U = \{1, 2, 3, 4, 5, 6, 7, 8, 9, 10, 11, 12\}$
     $A = \{1, 2, 3, 5, 6\}$
     $B = \{3, 4, 6, 7\}$
     $C = \{5, 6, 7, 8, 9, 10\}$

   List the elements of each of the sets:

   (a) $A \cup B$ (c) $A \cap B$ (e) $A \cap B \cap C$   (g) $A' \cap B' \cap C$
   (b) $A - C$ (d) $B \cap C$ (f) $(A \cup B) \cap C$ (h) $A \cap B \cap C'$

★12. From the information given in Problem 11, list the elements of each of the sets:

   (a) $A \cup C$  (c) $A \cap C$     (e) $(B \cup C) \cap A$ (g) $A \cap B' \cap C'$
   (b) $A - B$ (d) $A \cup B \cup C$ (f) $(A \cup C) \cap B$   (h) $A' \cap B' \cap C'$

★13. Let the area inside the circle be set $A$; inside the square, set $B$; and inside the triangle, set $C$. Shade the area that represents each of the following sets by the type of lines indicated in the parentheses:

   (a) $(A \cap B') \cup C$  (////)
   (b) $(A - B) - C$  (\\\\\\)
   (c) $(B - C) \cap A'$  (≡)

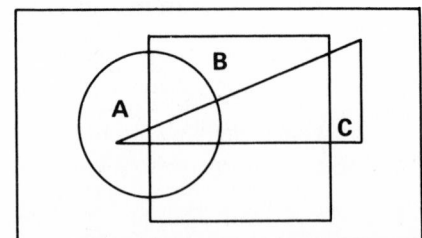

★**14.** Let the area inside the square be set $X$; inside the circle, set $Y$; and inside the triangle, set $Z$. Shade the area that represents each of the following sets by the type of lines indicated in the parentheses:

(a) $X \cup Y \cup Z$  (////)
(b) $(Y \cup Z) \cap X$  (\\\\)
(c) $(Z - Y) \cap X'$  (≡)

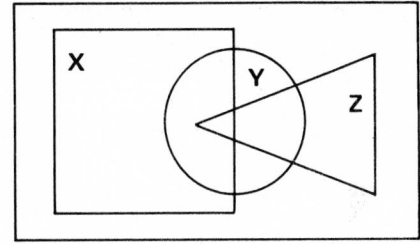

## 4.2 COUNTING PROCEDURES

This section presents the procedures for counting the number of possible arrangements of the elements (or objects) in a set or sets. The counting procedures may be performed in four ways: the tree diagram, the multiplication principle, permutation, and combination.

## A. Tree Diagram

When the number of elements included in a set or sets is small, we can list all the possible arrangements of the elements in a form of tree, called a *tree diagram,* as shown in the example below.

**Example 1**   A vacationing student wishes to go to Boston from Chicago with a stop in New York City. Assume that he has the choice of methods of traveling as follows:

Chicago to New York, represented by set $A = \{$plane, train, bus$\}$

New York to Boston, represented by set $B = \{$plane, bus$\}$

How many possible ways can the trip be made by the student?

There are six possible ways to make the trip as shown in the following tree diagram:

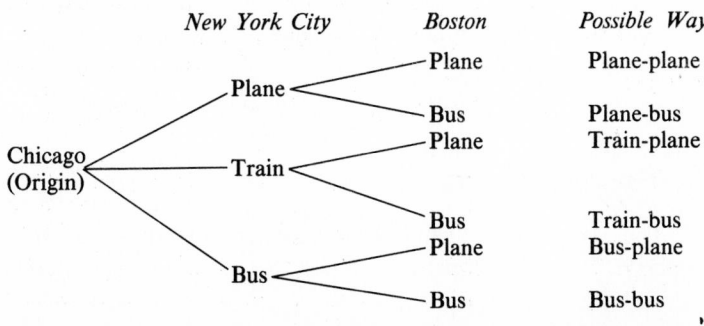

## B. The Multiplication Principle

When the number of elements in a set or sets is large, the tree-diagram method is not convenient. In such a case, the multiplication principle, which is based on the reasoning method illustrated in the tree-diagram example, may be used to compute the number of possible arrangements:

> *The multiplication principle—If one thing can be performed in* a *ways, a second thing in* b *ways, a third thing in* c *ways, and so on for* n *things, then the* n *things can be performed together in*
>
> **a × b × c × . . . (n** *factors) ways.*

Example 1 is now computed by the use of the multiplication principle as follows:

> 3 (ways from Chicago to New York) × 2 (ways from New York to Boston) = 6 (ways from Chicago to Boston)

**Example 2**     Let $U = \{a, b, c\}$. What is the total number of possible subsets of *U*?

According to the multiplication principle, we may use *a* in 2 ways (*include* it or *do not include* it in the subset); after *a* we may use *b* in 2 ways; and after *b* we may use *c* in 2 ways. Then, we may use the three letters together into

$$2 \times 2 \times 2 = 2^3 = 8 \text{ subsets.}$$

The 8 subsets may also be obtained by the use of a tree diagram:

| First Letter | Second Letter | Third Letter | Possible Subsets |
|---|---|---|---|
| | | *c* | *a, b, c* ( = universal set) |
| | *b* | 0 | *a, b* |
| *a* | | *c* | *a, c* |
| | 0 | 0 | *a* |
| Origin | | *c* | *b, c* |
| | *b* | 0 | *b* |
| 0 | | *c* | *c* |
| | 0 | 0 | no element (empty set) |

0 represents "do not include the letter in the subset."

## C. Permutations

The procedures illustrated in the tree diagram and the multiplication principle provide a general method for counting the number of possible arrangements of elements of a single set or several sets. The formulas developed for permutations and combinations, however, give more convenient counting procedures for the elements of a *single* set.

A permutation is an arrangement of all or part of the elements of a set in a *definite order*. The formulas for computing the total number of permutations of the elements of a set are presented below.

## (1) PERMUTATIONS OF DIFFERENT ELEMENTS TAKEN ALL AT A TIME

Let $n =$ the number of elements in a given set, and

$_nP_n =$ the total number of permutations of $n$ elements taken $n$ at a time. (It may also be written as $P(n, n)$.)

Then,

$$_nP_n = n(n-1)(n-2)(n-3) \ldots (2)(1),$$

or simply written

$$_nP_n = n! \text{ (Read } n \text{ factorial or factorial } n.)$$

**Note:** When $n = 0$, by definition $0! = 1$.

**Example 3** What is the total number of permutations of the set of the three letters *a,b,c,* taken all at a time?

$$n = 3,$$
$$_nP_n = {}_3P_3 = (3)(2)(1) = 6.$$

This answer may be checked by the tree diagram as follows:

| | Order of Arrangements | | Permutations (Possible Orderly Arrangements) |
|---|---|---|---|
| First | Second | Third | |

| | | | Permutations |
|---|---|---|---|
| | b ——— c | | abc |
| a | c ——— b | | acb |
| | a ——— c | | bac |
| Origin — b | c ——— a | | bca |
| | a ——— b | | cab |
| c | b ——— a | | cba |

The order of each letter in the sequence is important in a permutation. For example, the arrangement *abc* is different from *acb*.

The 6 permutations may also be obtained by the use of the multiplication principle as follows:

3 (possibilities for the first position) × 2 (possibilities for the second position) × 1 (possibility for the third position) = 6 possible orderly arrangements.

**Example 4**   *Additional illustrations.*

$_2P_2 = 2! = 2 \times 1 = 2.$        $_4P_4 = 4! = 4 \times 3 \times 2 \times 1 = 24.$
$_6P_6 = 6! = 6 \times 5 \times 4 \times 3 \times 2 \times 1 = 720.$

## (2) PERMUTATIONS OF DIFFERENT ELEMENTS TAKEN A PART AT A TIME

Let $n$ = the number of elements in a given set,
  $r$ = the number of elements taken at a time for each permutation, and
  $_nP_r$ = the total number of permutations of $n$ elements taken $r$ at a time. (It may also be written as $P(n,r)$.)

Then,

$$_nP_r = n(n-1)(n-2)(n-3) \ldots (n-r+1) \text{ for } r \text{ factors,}$$

or simply written

$$_nP_r = \frac{n!}{(n-r)!}$$

**Example 5**   What is the total number of permutations of the set of the three letters $a,b,c,$ taken two at a time?

Here $n = 3$, and $r = 2$.

$_nP_r = {_3P_2} = (3)(2) = 6$, or

$$_nP_r = \frac{n!}{(n-r)!} = \frac{3!}{(3-2)!} = \frac{3 \times 2 \times 1}{1} = 3 \times 2 = 6.$$

Also, see the tree diagram in Example 7.

**Example 6**   Three persons enter a car containing five seats. In how many ways can they be seated?

The total number of seating arrangements for five seats taken three at a time is

$_nP_r = {_5P_3} = (5)(4)(3) = 60$, or

$$= \frac{5!}{(5-3)!} = \frac{5 \times 4 \times 3 \times 2 \times 1}{2 \times 1} = 5 \times 4 \times 3 = 60.$$

Note that when the multiplication principle is used, this example can be computed in the following manner:

5 (seats available for the first person) $\times$ 4 (seats available for the second person) $\times$ 3 (seats available for the third person) = 60 seating arrangements.

# D. Combinations

A combination is a collection of all or part of the elements of a single set *without regard to the order* of the elements. The possible arrangements from the set of letters $a$ and $b$ are $ab$ and $ba$. The arrangements $ab$ and $ba$ are considered as two different permutations; but they are considered as only one combination. Thus, the total number of possible combinations of a set of elements taken all at a time is always 1.

The total number of possible combinations of a set of $n$ different elements taken $r$ (part of $n$) at a time, denoted by $_nC_r$, may be obtained:

$$_nC_r = \frac{_nP_r}{r!}$$

$$= \frac{n(n-1)(n-2) \ldots \text{ for } r \text{ factors}}{r(r-1)(r-2) \ldots 1}, \text{ or written}$$

$$_nC_r = \frac{n!}{r!(n-r)!},$$

where $r!$ represents the total number of permutations with the same $r$ elements. The $r!$ permutations are considered as one combination.

Note that the symbol $_nC_r$ is sometimes written as $C(n,r)$ or $\binom{n}{r}$.

**Example 7**     What is the total number of possible combinations of the set of the three letters $a,b,c$, taken two at a time?

Here $n = 3$, and $r = 2$.

$$_nC_r = {_3C_2} = \frac{_3P_2}{2!} = \frac{3 \times 2}{2 \times 1} = 3. \text{ Or,}$$

$$_nC_r = \frac{n!}{r!(n-r)!} = \frac{3!}{2!(3-2)!} = \frac{3 \times 2 \times 1}{2 \times 1 \times 1} = 3.$$

Example 7 is diagrammed below for aiding the understanding of the combination formula:

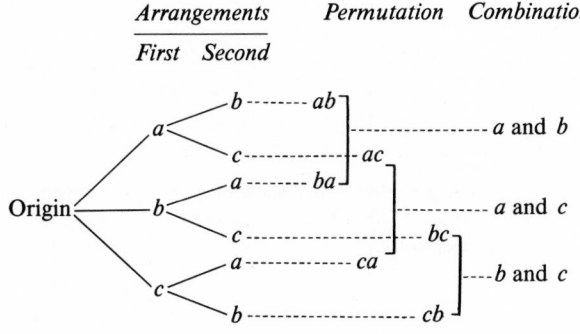

|  | Order of Arrangements | Permutation | Combination |
|---|---|---|---|
|  | First   Second |  |  |

Observe that the total number of permutations of 3 letters taken 2 letters at a time is

$$_3P_2 = 3 \times 2 = 6.$$

The total number of permutations of the *same* 2 letters taken all at a time is

$$_2P_2 = 2! = 2 \times 1 = 2,$$

such as *ab* and *ba* from letters *a* and *b*. Permutations with the same letters are considered as only one combination. Therefore, the total number of combinations is

$$\frac{_3P_2}{2!} = \frac{6}{2} = 3.$$

**Example 8**  A club has 15 members. (a) Three members are to be chosen to fill the positions of manager, assistant manager, and treasurer. In how many ways can the positions be filled? (b) Three members are to be chosen to form a committee. In how many ways can the committee be formed?

(a) The order of arrangement is taken into consideration in this case. For example, the set of manager A, assistant manager B, and treasurer C is different from the set of manager C, assistant manager A, and treasurer B. Thus, this is a permutation problem.

$$_{15}P_3 = 15 \times 14 \times 13 = 2{,}730 \text{ ways.}$$

(b) The order of arrangement is disregarded in this case. For example, the set of committee members Adams, Brown, and Clark is the same as the set of committee members Clark, Adams, and Brown. Thus, this is a combination problem.

$$_{15}C_3 = \frac{15 \times 14 \times 13}{3 \times 2 \times 1} = \frac{2{,}730}{6} = 455 \text{ ways.}$$

When *r* is larger than $n - r$, we may use the following expression to simplify the computation for a combination:

$$_nC_r = {_nC_{n-r}}$$

**Example 9**  Compute (a) $_3C_2$, and (b) $_{50}C_{47}$.

(a) $_3C_2 = {_3C_{3-2}} = {_3C_1} = \dfrac{3}{1} = 3$ (Also see the answer of Example 7).

(b) $_{50}C_{47} = {_{50}C_{50-47}} = {_{50}C_3} = \dfrac{50 \times 49 \times 48}{3 \times 2 \times 1} = 19{,}600.$

## EXERCISE 4–2

### Reference: Section 4.2

1. Calculate:  (a) $_8P_5$    (b) $_6P_3$    (c) $_5P_4$    (d) $_8P_8$
   (e) $_4C_4$    (f) $_6C_3$    (g) $_7C_0$    (h) $_{120}C_{117}$
2. Calculate:  (a) $_5P_5$    (b) $_7P_2$    (c) $_9P_3$    (d) $_6P_0$
   (e) $_9C_4$    (f) $_8C_8$    (g) $_8C_0$    (h) $_{100}C_{96}$
3. Let the universal set $U = \{p, r, s, t\}$. Find the total number of possible subsets of $U$.
4. Let the universal set $U = \{f, g, h, i, j\}$. Find the total number of possible subsets of $U$.

5. A traveling salesperson in city $W$ plans to go to city $Z$ with stops in cities $X$ and $Y$. There are 3 highways from $W$ to $X$, 4 highways from $X$ to $Y$, and 2 highways from $Y$ to $Z$. In how many ways can the trip be made?

6. How many unique automobile license plates can be produced if two different letters of the alphabet are printed on each plate, followed by a 3-digit number from 100 through 999?

7. Find the total number of possible permutations from the set of letters $a$, $b$, $c$, and $d$ taken (a) all at a time, and (b) two at a time.

8. Find (a) the number of 3-letter groups and (b) the number of 4-letter groups that can be formed from the letters of the word *special*.

9. In how many ways can three different books be placed on a shelf?

10. In how many ways can 5 students be seated in a classroom with 10 chairs?

11. A car containing six seats is being used by six persons for a trip. In how many ways can the persons be seated if only three of them can drive?

12. Find how many 3-digit numbers can be formed from the digits 1, 2, 3, and 4 (a) if no digits may be repeated in the numbers, and (b) if the digits may be repeated in the numbers.

13. In how many ways can we take a sample of the ages of 5 students from a group of 30 students?

14. A bureau of business research wishes to know the average family income in a city of 1,000 families. If a sample of three families is required, how many possible samples can be taken from the families in the city?

15. Find the total number of combinations of the set of letters $a$, $b$, $c$, and $d$ taken (a) all at a time, (b) 3 at a time, and (c) 0 at a time.

16. What is the total number of combinations of the 26 letters of the alphabet taken (a) all at a time, (b) 2 at a time, and (c) 24 at a time?

17. An association was organized by 12 persons. (a) In how many ways can the offices of president, vice-president, and secretary be filled by the 12 persons? (b) In how many ways can a committee of 4 members be formed by the 12 persons?

18. A restaurant offers mayonnaise, tomato, lettuce, cheese, and pickle as toppings for the ham sandwich. How many different ways can a ham sandwich be made by the restaurant?

19. In how many ways can a coach select a team of 5 from a group of 12 players if (a) two certain players must be included in the team, and (b) no restrictions are made on the selection?

20. A bridge deck of 52 cards has 13 different kinds of 4 cards each. In how many ways can we select 5 cards from the deck if (a) 4 of the 5 cards must be of one kind, and (b) there are no restrictions on the selection?

## 4.3 PROBABILITY

The idea of probability was originated in gambling games during the 17th century in France. However, the theory of probability has now become one of the most important topics in modern mathematics and statistical decision theory.

The subject of probability deals with the chance of success or failure from a trial or experiment. Let

> $P=$ the probability of,
> $A=$ the event of success from a trial,
> $A'$ (or not $A$) = the event of a failure,
> $n=$ the number of possible outcomes from the trial,
> $h=$ the number of successful outcomes, and
> $n-h=$ the number of unsuccessful (or failure) outcomes.

The probabilities of success and failure can be expressed in ratio forms as follows:

$$\text{Probability of success} = P(A) = \frac{h}{n}$$

$$\text{Probability of failure} = P(A') = \frac{n-h}{n} = 1 - \frac{h}{n} = 1 - P(A)$$

The sum of the probability of success and the probability of failure is always equal to 1, or

$$P(A) + P(A') = \mathbf{1}.$$

Probabilities can be computed under two conditions: (1) We can assume that all the possible outcomes from a trial will occur on an *equally likely* basis. The probability computed under this condition is called *theoretical* or *mathematical* probability. (2) We cannot assume, or we are in doubt, that all the possible outcomes will happen on an equally likely basis. The computation of the probability of the event under such a condition thus must be based on our experiences, experiments, or statistical data of what has happened on similar occasions in the past. This type of probability is called *empirical* or *statistical probability.*

## A. Computing Theoretical Probability

In a trial, we may wish to compute the probability of a single event or that of two or more events occurring. Also, we may perform repeated trials of a single event. The methods of computing the various theoretical probabilities are presented below.

### (1) PROBABILITY OF ONE EVENT OCCURRING

Probabilities may be conveniently computed by the use of the theory of sets.

**Example 1**   One ball is drawn at random from a bag containing 4 red balls and 5 white balls. Compute the probability that it is (a) red, (b) not red, (c) white, and (d) black.

Let the possible outcomes from the trial be the universal set *U.* The universal set has 4 (red balls) + 5 (white balls) = 9 elements, or

$$U = \{R,\ R,\ R,\ R,\ W,\ W,\ W,\ W,\ W\}$$
and      $n = 9$.

(a) Let $A =$ the event of drawing a red ball. The successful outcomes are the 4 red balls, or set

$$A = \{R,\ R,\ R,\ R,\} \quad (A \text{ is a subset of } U.)$$
and      $h = 4$.

$$P(A) = \frac{h}{n} = \frac{4}{9}.$$

(b) Let $A' =$ the event of not drawing a red ball. Then,

$$A' = \{W,\ W,\ W,\ W,\ W\}, \text{ and}$$
$$n - h = 9 - 4 = 5.$$

$$P(A') = \frac{n - h}{n} = \frac{5}{9}, \text{ or}$$

$$P(A') = 1 - P(A) = 1 - \frac{4}{9} = \frac{5}{9}.$$

(c) Let $B =$ the event of drawing a white ball. The successful outcomes are the 5 white balls, or set

$$B = \{W,\ W,\ W,\ W,\ W\}$$

$$P(B) = \frac{h}{n} = \frac{5}{9}$$

(d) Let $C =$ the event of drawing a black ball. Since there are no black balls in the bag, this set is an empty set. Thus, set

$$C = \phi, \text{ or } h = 0. \qquad P(C) = \frac{0}{9} = 0.$$

## (2) PROBABILITY OF TWO OR MORE EVENTS

Two or more events may be (a) mutually exclusive (disjoint), (b) intersected, (c) independent, or (d) dependent.

**Mutually Exclusive (or Disjoint) Events.** Two or more events are mutually exclusive if the events cannot occur together. In other words, the occurrence of any one of the events precludes the occurrences of the others.

Let $A$ and $B$ be mutually exclusive events as shown in the Venn diagram below:

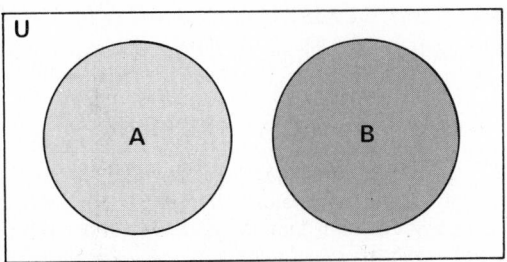

Then, the probability of event $A$ or $B$ is the sum of the probability of $A$ and that of $B$, or

$$P(A \text{ or } B) = P(A) + P(B).$$

Observe that events $A$ and $B$ are subsets of the universal set $U$. The two subsets have no elements in common. Thus they are *disjoint* subsets.

**Example 2**   What is the probability that one throw of a die will yield either 2 or 4?

Let $A =$ the event yielding 2, and
$\quad B =$ the event yielding 4.

The two events are mutually exclusive since *one* throw of a die cannot yield *both* 2 and 4 on the top.

$\quad U = \{1, 2, 3, 4, 5, 6\}$, or $n = 6$ (sides of a die, or 6 possible outcomes or elements)
$\quad A = \{2\}$, or $h = 1$ (successful outcome or 1 element),
$P(A) = h/n = \frac{1}{6}$;
$\quad B = \{4\}$, or $h = 1$ (element),
$P(B) = h/n = \frac{1}{6}$.

Thus, $P(A \text{ or } B) = P(A) + P(B) = \frac{1}{6} + \frac{1}{6} = \frac{2}{6} = \frac{1}{3}$.

**Intersected Events.** Two or more events are intersected if the events have some elements in common. Let $A$ and $B$ be intersected events as shown in the Venn diagram below:

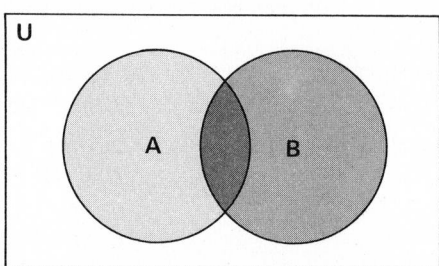

Observe that the area with the darkest shading represents the elements in the intersection of subsets $A$ and $B$. The probability of the events occurring for the common elements is denoted by $P(A \text{ and } B)$. Since it belongs to $P(A)$ and also to $P(B)$, one $P(A \text{ and } B)$ must be subtracted from the sum of $P(A)$ and $P(B)$ to avoid counting it twice. The probability of the intersected events $A$ *or* $B$ thus is:

$$P(A \text{ or } B) = P(A) + P(B) - P(A \text{ and } B)$$

**Example 3**   In a group of 15 students, 7 are boys and 8 are girls; 3 of the boys and 2 of the girls are taking algebra. If one student is selected from the group at random, find the probability that the student is a boy or is taking algebra.

This example is diagrammed below:

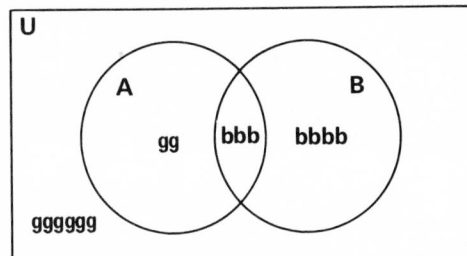

Let $U = \{b, b, b, b, b, b, b, g, g, g,$ $g, g, g, g, g\}$, or 15 elements,
$A =$ the event of taking algebra, and
set $A = \{b, b, b, g, g\}$, or 5 elements,
$B =$ the event of selecting a boy, and
set $B = \{b, b, b, b, b, b, b\}$, or 7 elements.

Observe that 3 elements (boys) belong to set $A$ and also belong to set $B$. The intersection of sets $A$ and $B$, denoted by the set $A \cap B$, or set "$A$ and $B$," is

$A$ and $B = \{b, b, b\}$.

Thus,

$$P(A \text{ or } B) = P(A) + P(B) - P(A \text{ and } B) = \frac{5}{15} + \frac{7}{15} - \frac{3}{15} = \frac{9}{15} = \frac{3}{5}.$$

**Independent Events.** Two or more events are independent if the happenings of the events in no way affect each other. Thus, if $A$ and $B$ are independent events, the occurrence of event $A$ has no effect on the occurrence of event $B$. The probability that both independent events $A$ and $B$ will occur is based on the multiplication principle as follows:

$$P(A \text{ and } B) = P(A) \cdot P(B)$$

**Example 4**   One ball is drawn at random from a bag containing 4 red balls and 5 white balls. A second ball is drawn after the first is replaced into the bag. What is the probability that both balls drawn will be red?

Since the second ball is drawn after the first ball is replaced, the result of the first drawing obviously has nothing to do with the second drawing. Therefore, the two drawings are independent events.

Here, $U = \{R, R, R, R, W, W, W, W, W\}$, or 9 elements.
Let $A =$ the event of the first drawing that will yield a red ball.
Set $A = \{R, R, R, R\}$, or 4 elements.
Let $B =$ the event of the second drawing that will yield a red ball.
Then,
set $B = \{R, R, R, R\}$, or 4 elements.

$$P(A \text{ and } B) = P(A) \cdot P(B) = \frac{4}{9} \cdot \frac{4}{9} = \frac{16}{81}$$

**Dependent Events.** If the occurrence of a second event depends on the occurrence of the first event, the two events are called dependent. Thus, $A$ and $B$ are dependent events when the occurrence of $B$ depends on the occurrence of $A$. The probability of event $B$ depending on the occurrence of event $A$ is called *conditional probability,* which is written:

$P(B|A)$ or $P_A(B)$. (Read: The probability of $B$, given $A$.)

The probability that both the dependent events $A$ and $B$ will occur is based on the multiplication principle as follows:

$$P(A \text{ and } B) = P(A) \cdot P(B|A)$$

**Example 5**　　Refer to Example 4. Assume that the first ball is not replaced in the bag before the second ball is drawn. What is the probability that in the two drawings both balls are red?

Since the first ball is not replaced for the second draw, the result of the first drawing affects the result of the second drawing. Thus, the two drawings are dependent events.

In the first drawing,
set $U = \{R, R, R, R, W, W, W, W, W\}$, or 9 elements.
Let $A = $ the event of the first drawing that will yield a red ball.
Set $A = \{R, R, R, R\}$, or 4 elements.

$$P(A) = \frac{4}{9}$$

In the second drawing,
set $U = \{R, R, R, W, W, W, W, W\}$, or 8 elements, since the first ball, which is red, is not replaced.
Let $B = $ the event of the second drawing that will yield a red ball, and set $B = \{R, R, R\}$, or 3 elements.

$$P(B|A) = \frac{3}{8}$$

The probability that both balls of the two drawings are red is

$$P(A \text{ and } B) = P(A) \cdot P(B|A) = \frac{4}{9} \times \frac{3}{8} = \frac{12}{72} = \frac{1}{6}.$$

***Note:***　　The above solution may also be obtained by the use of the combination formula as follows:

The number of successful outcomes from 4 red balls taken 2 at a time is

$$_4C_2 = \frac{4!}{2!(4-2)!} = \frac{4 \times 3}{2 \times 1} = 6.$$

The number of possible outcomes from 9 balls taken 2 at a time is

$$_9C_2 = \frac{9 \times 8}{2 \times 1} = 36.$$

$$P(A \text{ and } B) = \frac{_4C_2}{_9C_2} = \frac{6}{36} = \frac{1}{6}.$$

## ★(3) REPEATED TRIALS

Let $p = P(A)$, the probability that event $A$ will happen in a single trial, and
$q = P(A')$, the probability that event $A$ will *not* happen in the single trial, or
$q = 1 - p.$

Then, the probability that event $A$ will happen exactly $r$ times in $n$ repeated trials is [1]

$$P(\textbf{exactly } r \textbf{ times}) = {}_nC_r \cdot p^r \cdot q^{n-r}.$$

Note that the outcome of a trial referred to here is not affected by that of any other trial; that is, the *events are independent.*

**Example 6**   A bag contains 4 red balls and 5 white balls. One ball is drawn and is replaced after each drawing. In two repeated drawings find the probability that the drawings will yield (a) exactly 2 red balls, (b) exactly 1 red ball, and (c) no red ball.

Let $A =$ the event of drawing a red ball in each drawing, and
$A' =$ the event of not drawing a red ball in each drawing.

Then,
$$P(A) = p = \frac{4}{9},$$

and
$$P(A') = q = 1 - p = 1 - \frac{4}{9} = \frac{5}{9};$$

$$n = 2 \text{ (repeated drawings)}$$

(a) The probability that event $A$ will occur twice (or $r = 2$ red balls) in the 2 repeated drawings is

$$P(2 \text{ red}) = {}_2C_2 \cdot \left(\frac{4}{9}\right)^2 \cdot \left(\frac{5}{9}\right)^0 = 1 \cdot \left(\frac{16}{81}\right) \cdot 1 = \frac{16}{81}. \quad \text{(Same as Example 4.)}$$

Note that ${}_2C_2 = 1$ represents the number of combinations from 2 (repeated trials) taken 2 (red balls) at a time; that is,

$R, R$ (or the first is red and the second is red.)

(b) The probability that event $A$ will occur once (or $r = 1$ red ball) in the 2 repeated drawings is

$$P(1 \text{ red}) = {}_2C_1 \cdot \left(\frac{4}{9}\right)^1 \cdot \left(\frac{5}{9}\right)^1 = 2\left(\frac{20}{81}\right) = \frac{40}{81}.$$

Note that ${}_2C_1 = 2$ represents the number of combinations from 2 (repeated trials) taken 1 (red ball) at a time; that is, there are two ways:

$R, W$ (the first is red and the second is white);
$W, R$ (the first is white and the second is red).

(c) The probability that event $A$ will not occur either time, or $r = 0$ (red ball) in the 2 repeated drawings is

$$P(0 \text{ red}) = {}_2C_0 \cdot \left(\frac{4}{9}\right)^0 \cdot \left(\frac{5}{9}\right)^2 = 1 \cdot 1 \cdot \frac{25}{81} = \frac{25}{81}.$$

$W, W$ (the first is white, or not red, and the second is also white.)

---

[1] This is the general expression of the $(r + 1)$th term of the binomial theorem. See footnote on page 84.

The sum of the probabilities of all possible happenings (2, 1, and 0 red balls) in the 2 repeated trials must be 1.

*Check:*      $P(2 \text{ red}) + P(1 \text{ red}) + P(0 \text{ red}) = \dfrac{16}{81} + \dfrac{40}{81} + \dfrac{25}{81} = \dfrac{81}{81} = 1.$

# ★B. Computing Empirical Probability

The computation of the empirical probability based on the results of experiments or experiences is illustrated in the following examples.

**Example 7**      A coin is tossed 1,000 times. The results are 497 heads and 503 tails. What is the probability that one toss of the given coin will turn up a head?

Based on the record, the probability that one toss of the coin will turn up a head is

$$P(\text{head}) = \frac{497}{497 + 503} = \frac{497}{1,000} = .497.$$

The probability based on the theory that the two possible outcomes, head and tail, will occur equally likely is

$$P(\text{head}) = \frac{1}{2} = .5.$$

The empirical probability (.497) is very close to the theoretical probability (.5) in this example. In practice, experiments are often used to check the results obtained by theoretical computations.

**Example 8**      Find the probability that a man who is now 30 years old will (a) be alive at age 31, or (b) die before reaching age 31.

In the present case, although we can count exactly the different conditions in which the man will be at age 31, dead or alive, we cannot assume that the two occurrences are *equally likely.* The record concerning similar statistics in the past thus must be used as a basis to compute the probability of a given event.

According to the Commissioners 1958 Standard Ordinary Mortality Table, based on the experience of life insurance companies for the years from 1950 to 1954 (Table 14 in the Appendix), 9,460,165 out of 9,480,358 men now aged 30 will be alive at age 31. Thus,

(a)   $P(\text{the man will be alive at age 31}) = \dfrac{9,460,165}{9,480,358} = .99787$

(b)   $P(\text{the man will die before age 31}) = \dfrac{9,480,358 - 9,460,165}{9,480,358}$

$$= \frac{20,193}{9,480,358} = .00213$$

*Check:*      (a) + (b) = .99787 + .00213 = 1.

The death rate per 1,000 men is .00213 × 1,000 = 2.13 men. The rate is shown in the 4th column of Table 14 in the Appendix.

Note that the empirical probability is usually based on a large number of occurrences or trials in an experiment.

## EXERCISE 4–3

**Reference: Section 4.3**

1. A box contains 6 black chips and 17 yellow chips. One chip is drawn at random from the box. Find the probability that it is (a) black, (b) not black, (c) yellow, (d) black or yellow, and (e) red.

2. A group consists of 10 boys and 11 girls. One person is selected at random from the group. Find the probability that the person is (a) a boy, (b) not a boy, (c) a girl, (d) a boy or a girl, and (e) an adult.

3. A group of 432 students contains 120 students who read the *New York Times* and 75 students who read the *Wall Street Journal.* Among the readers, 30 students read both the *New York Times* and the *Wall Street Journal.* A student is chosen at random from the group. Find the probability that the student reads either the *New York Times* or the *Wall Street Journal.*

4. A college has 120 teachers. There are 58 teachers who can speak French, 40 who can speak German, and 33 who can speak both French and German. A teacher is chosen at random from the college. What is the probability that the teacher can speak either French or German?

5. In a group of 35 employees, 6 of the 23 women and 7 of the 12 men are working in the business office. If one employee is selected at random from the group, what is the probability that the employee is (a) a woman? (b) a man? (c) working in the business office? (d) a man or a woman? (e) a man or working in the business office?

6. One card is drawn at random from a bridge deck of 52 cards. (The deck has 13 different values—2, 3, 4, 5, 6, 7, 8, 9, 10, jack, queen, king, and ace—and each value has 4 suits—spade, heart, diamond, and club.) Find the probability of drawing (a) a spade, (b) a diamond, (c) a face card (face cards are jacks, queens, and kings), (d) a spade or a diamond, and (e) a spade or a face card.

7. A bag contains 6 black balls and 10 red balls. One ball is drawn at random from the bag. A second ball is drawn after the first is replaced. What is the probability that (a) both balls in the two drawings are black? (b) first a black ball is drawn and then a red ball? (c) one ball is black and one is red? (d) both are red? Also, find the sum of the probabilities found in (a), (c), and (d). Is the sum equal to 1? Explain.

8. Two dice, one white and the other red, are tossed. Find the probability that (a) both dice are 2 or less, (b) the white die is 2 or less and the red die is more than 2, (c) one is 2 or less and the other is more than 2, (d) both dice are more than 2. Also, find the sum of the probabilities found in (a), (c), and (d). Is the sum equal to 1? Explain.

9. Refer to Problem 7. Suppose that the first ball is not replaced before the second ball is drawn. What is the probability that (a) both balls in the two drawings are black and (b) the first ball is black and the second one is red?

10. One card is drawn at random from a bridge deck of 52 cards. A second card is drawn but the first card is not replaced for the second drawing. Find the probability that (a) both cards are hearts and (b) the first card is a heart and the second card is a spade. (See Problem 6 for the description of the deck of cards.)

★11. A box contains 7 red chips and 3 white chips. One chip is drawn at random and is replaced into the box for the next drawing. In three repeated drawings, find the probability that the drawings will yield (a) 3 red chips, (b) 2 red chips, (c) 1 red chip, and (d) 0 red chip. Is the sum of the probabilities equal to 1?

★12. There are 2 girls and 18 boys in a classroom. One student is selected at random and is asked to return to the classroom after each selection. In 5 repeated selections, find the probability that the selections will have (a) exactly 5 girls, (b) exactly 3 girls, and (c) exactly 2 girls.

★13. 125 heads and 875 tails occurred when a coin was tossed 1,000 times. According to the results, find the probability that one toss of the given coin yields a head. Is it a well-balanced coin?

★14. A die is tossed 900 times, of which 150 throws show 4 dots on the top of the die. What is the probability that one toss of the given die will have a 4 based on the above results? Do you think that it is an honest die (that is, the occurrences of the six sides of the die are equally likely)?

★15. What is the probability that a person who is now 20 years old will (a) be alive at age 21, and (b) die before reaching age 21?

★16. Find the probability that a person who is now 40 years old will (a) be alive at age 41, and (b) die before reaching age 41.

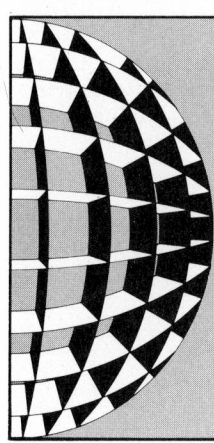

# Chapter 5

# *Supplemental Modern Algebra

The topics included in this chapter are matrix algebra, linear programming, and the binary number system. Matrix algebra covers the operations of vectors, matrices, determinants, the inverse of a square matrix, and solving linear equations. Linear programming uses inequalities and equations to find optimum solutions for many types of business problems, such as maximizing profits and minimizing costs. The binary number system can be used to represent data within electronic computers. Those topics have become increasingly important in recent years since they are very useful in solving many complicated problems by the utilization of modern high-speed electronic computers.

## 5.1 VECTORS

A vector is an ordered collection of numbers. The numbers may be arranged either in a row or in a column and enclosed in brackets [ ] or in boldfaced parentheses ( ). In general vectors are represented by lower-case letters, such as $a$, $b$, $c$, and so on.

For example, vectors $a$ and $b$ are *row vectors:*

$$a = [1, 7] \qquad b = [6, 4]$$

and $c$ and $d$ are *column vectors:*

$$c = \begin{bmatrix} 2 \\ 5 \\ 9 \end{bmatrix} \qquad d = \begin{bmatrix} 3 \\ 8 \\ 4 \end{bmatrix}$$

The above vectors may be applied to a practical problem as follows:

Company $R$ has two plants: #1 and #2. Each plant manufactures products $X$ and $Y$. The production of the products during a given period

**127**

by each plant is shown in Table 5–1. (See vectors *a* and *b*.) Each product is made of three different types of raw material, M-1, M-2, and M-3. The material required by each product is shown in Table 5–2. (See vectors *c* and *d*.)

**Table 5–1 COMPANY R PRODUCTION BY PLANTS**

(**Row vectors *a* and *b***)

| Product | Plant | |
|---------|-------|-------|
|         | #1    | #2    |
| X       | 1 unit | 7 units |
| Y       | 6     | 4     |
| Total   | 7     | 11    |

**Table 5–2 COMPANY R MATERIAL REQUIREMENTS BY PRODUCTS**

(**Column vectors *c* and *d***)

| Type of Material | Product | | Total |
|------------------|---------|-------|-------|
|                  | X       | Y     |       |
| M-1              | 2 lbs   | 3 lbs | 5 lbs |
| M-2              | 5       | 8     | 13    |
| M-3              | 9       | 4     | 13    |

The numbers in the rows or columns are also known as the *components* of the vectors. Thus, *a* and *b* are two-component row vectors, and *c* and *d* are three-component column vectors. The concept of components is important in the basic vector operations: addition, subtraction, and multiplication.

## A. Addition

Vectors with the same number of components and the same arrangement may be added. The corresponding components of the vectors are added to obtain the components of the sum of the addition. The sum is also a vector with the same arrangement as the given vectors.

**Example 1**     (a) Add the two-component row vectors *a* and *b*:

$$a + b = [1, 7] + [6, 4] = [1 + 6, \quad 7 + 4] = [7, 11]$$ (See the total row of Table 5–1.)

(b) Add the three-component column vectors *c* and *d*:

$$c + d = \begin{bmatrix} 2 \\ 5 \\ 9 \end{bmatrix} + \begin{bmatrix} 3 \\ 8 \\ 4 \end{bmatrix} = \begin{bmatrix} 2 + 3 \\ 5 + 8 \\ 9 + 4 \end{bmatrix} = \begin{bmatrix} 5 \\ 13 \\ 13 \end{bmatrix}$$ (See the total column of Table 5–2.)

## B. Subtraction

Vectors with the same number of components and the same arrangement may be subtracted. The corresponding components of the vectors are subtracted to obtain the components of the remainder of the subtraction. The remainder is also a vector with the same arrangement as the given vectors.

**Example 2**   (a) Subtract vector $b$ from vector $a$:

$$a - b = [1, 7] - [6, 4] = [1 - 6, \quad 7 - 4] = [-5, 3]$$

(b) Subtract vector $d$ from vector $c$:

$$c - d = \begin{bmatrix} 2 \\ 5 \\ 9 \end{bmatrix} - \begin{bmatrix} 3 \\ 8 \\ 4 \end{bmatrix} = \begin{bmatrix} 2 - 3 \\ 5 - 8 \\ 9 - 4 \end{bmatrix} = \begin{bmatrix} -1 \\ -3 \\ 5 \end{bmatrix}$$

## C. Multiplication

Multiplication involving vectors is presented under two different cases below.

### CASE I. SCALAR MULTIPLICATION

Any real number, called a *scalar* (as opposed to an imaginary number), may be multiplied by a vector. The number must be multiplied by each component of the vector to obtain the components of the product. The product thus is also a vector with the same number of components and the same arrangement as the vector multiplied.

**Example 3**   (a) Multiply 7 by vector $e = \begin{bmatrix} 3 \\ 5 \end{bmatrix}$.

$$7 \cdot e = 7 \begin{bmatrix} 3 \\ 5 \end{bmatrix} = \begin{bmatrix} 7 \times 3 \\ 7 \times 5 \end{bmatrix} = \begin{bmatrix} 21 \\ 35 \end{bmatrix}$$

(b) Multiply 2 by vector $f = [1, 3, 7]$.

$$2 \cdot f = 2[1, 3, 7] = [2 \times 1, 2 \times 3, 2 \times 7 = [2, 6, 14]$$

### CASE II. MULTIPLICATION OF TWO VECTORS

In multiplying two vectors, a row vector is multiplied by a column vector with the same number of components. Each component of the row vector is multiplied by the corresponding component of the column vector to obtain the partial product. The sum of all partial products, called the *inner product,* or *dot product,* of the two vectors multiplied, is a *number,* not a vector.

**Example 4**   (a) Multiply the row vector $a$ by the column vector $e$.

$$a \cdot e = [1, 7] \begin{bmatrix} 3 \\ 5 \end{bmatrix} = (1 \times 3) + (7 \times 5) = 38.$$

(b) Multiply the row vector $f$ by the column vector $c$.

$$f \cdot c = [1, 3, 7] \begin{bmatrix} 2 \\ 5 \\ 9 \end{bmatrix} = (1 \times 2) + (3 \times 5) + (7 \times 9) \\ = 2 + 15 + 63 = 80.$$

Note that the row vector is always written first and the column vector second.

Vectors may be shown graphically. A two-component vector, such as $a = [1, 7]$ or its *transposed* column vector $a' = \begin{bmatrix} 1 \\ 7 \end{bmatrix}$, may be represented by a point $(X = 1, \ Y = 7)$ in a 2-dimensional space based on the system of rectangular coordinates. Figure 5–1, for example, shows the points representing vectors $a$, $b$, and $a + b$ on a 2-dimensional space. Likewise, a three-component vector, such as $c = \begin{bmatrix} 2 \\ 5 \\ 9 \end{bmatrix}$ or its transposed row vector $c' = [2, 5, 9]$ may be represented by a point $(2, 5, 9)$ in a 3-dimensional space.

**Figure 5–1    TWO-COMPONENT VECTORS $a$, $b$, AND $a + b$ AS SHOWN IN A TWO-DIMENSIONAL SPACE**

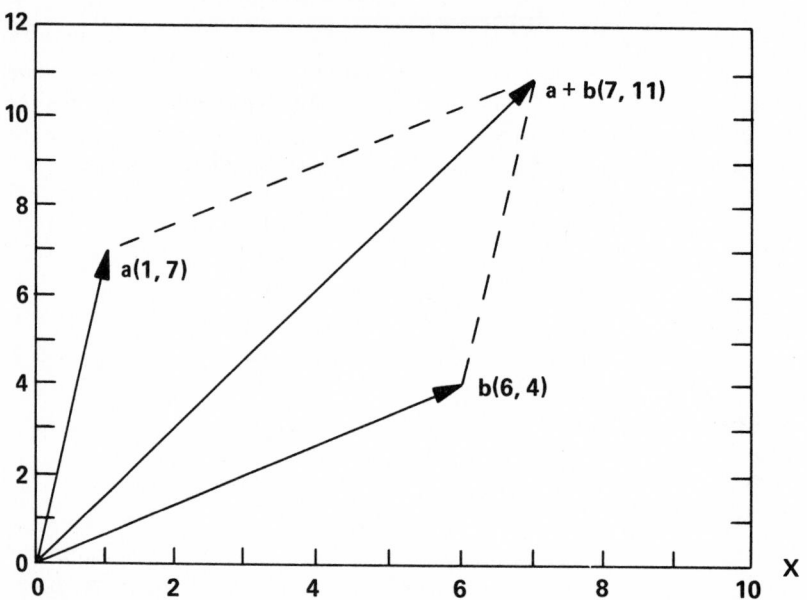

The lines drawn from the origin (0) to the three points ($a$, $b$, and $a + b$) show the geometric interpretation of vectors. Vectors may be interpreted as lines representing direction and length.

Note that two vectors are said to be equal if, and only if, both vectors are arranged in the same form (both in rows or both in columns) and their corresponding components are equal. Thus, row vector $a$ is not equal to column vector $a'$, although they are represented by the same point on a graph. This concept is consistent with matrices presented in the next sections.

*Additional illustration:* $a = [1, 7]$, $a' = \begin{bmatrix} 1 \\ 7 \end{bmatrix}$,

$$g = [7, 1], \ h = [1, 7]$$

We have, $a = h$, $a \neq a'$, $a \neq g$, $g \neq h$, $a' \neq h$ and $a' \neq g$. ($\neq$ represents "is not equal to.")

## 5.2 MATRICES

A matrix is a rectangular array of numbers enclosed in brackets or in boldfaced parentheses. In general, matrices are represented by capital letters, such as *A, B, C,* and *D* as shown below:

$$A = \begin{bmatrix} 1 & 7 \\ 6 & 4 \end{bmatrix}, \quad B = \begin{bmatrix} 3 & 2 \\ 5 & 8 \end{bmatrix}, \quad C = \begin{bmatrix} 2 & 3 \\ 5 & 8 \\ 9 & 4 \end{bmatrix}, \quad D = \begin{bmatrix} 6 & 1 \\ 4 & 2 \\ 9 & 7 \end{bmatrix}$$

A matrix is usually described first by its number of rows and then by its number of columns. This type of description is referred to as the *order* of a matrix. In the above illustrations, the order of matrices *A* and *B* is 2 by 2, or written 2 × 2, and that of matrices *C* and *D* is 3 by 2, or written 3 × 2. In general, let *m* represent the number of rows and *n* represent the number of columns of a matrix. Then, the order of a matrix is *m* × *n* and we may call it an *m* × *n* matrix. When *m* = *n*, it is called a *square matrix.* Thus, *A* and *B* are also called square matrices of order 2.

Operations with matrices are basically the same as those with vectors. When a matrix has only one row or only one column, it is identical to a row or a column vector. Thus, in performing the basic operations—addition, subtraction, and multiplication—with matrices, it is convenient to consider a matrix as a collection of vectors of the same number of components.

However, the numbers in the brackets of a matrix are called *elements.* Note that two matrices are equal if, and only if, they are of the same order and they consist of equal elements in corresponding positions. Thus, matrix $\begin{bmatrix} 1 & 7 \\ 6 & 4 \end{bmatrix}$ is not equal to matrix $\begin{bmatrix} 6 & 4 \\ 1 & 7 \end{bmatrix}$, since the corresponding elements are not equal although the two matrices are of the same order, but $\begin{bmatrix} 1 & 7 \\ 6 & 4 \end{bmatrix} = \begin{bmatrix} 3-2 & 8-1 \\ 6 \times 1 & 2+2 \end{bmatrix}$.

## A. Addition

The corresponding elements of two matrices with the same order (the same number of rows and the same number of columns) may be added. The sum is a matrix with the same order as the given matrices.

**Example 5**  (a) Add the 2 × 2 matrices *A* and *B.*

$$A + B = \begin{bmatrix} 1 & 7 \\ 6 & 4 \end{bmatrix} + \begin{bmatrix} 3 & 2 \\ 5 & 8 \end{bmatrix} = \begin{bmatrix} 1+3 & 7+2 \\ 6+5 & 4+8 \end{bmatrix} = \begin{bmatrix} 4 & 9 \\ 11 & 12 \end{bmatrix}$$

(b) Add the 3 × 2 matrices *C* and *D.*

$$C + D = \begin{bmatrix} 2 & 3 \\ 5 & 8 \\ 9 & 4 \end{bmatrix} + \begin{bmatrix} 6 & 1 \\ 4 & 2 \\ 9 & 7 \end{bmatrix} = \begin{bmatrix} 2+6 & 3+1 \\ 5+4 & 8+2 \\ 9+9 & 4+7 \end{bmatrix} = \begin{bmatrix} 8 & 4 \\ 9 & 10 \\ 18 & 11 \end{bmatrix}$$

# B. Subtraction

Like addition, the corresponding elements of two matrices of the same order may be subtracted. The remainder is a matrix with the same order as the given matrices.

**Example 6**     (a) Subtract matrix $B$ from matrix $A$.

$$A - B = \begin{bmatrix} 1 & 7 \\ 6 & 4 \end{bmatrix} - \begin{bmatrix} 3 & 2 \\ 5 & 8 \end{bmatrix} = \begin{bmatrix} 1-3 & 7-2 \\ 6-5 & 4-8 \end{bmatrix} = \begin{bmatrix} -2 & 5 \\ 1 & -4 \end{bmatrix}$$

(b) Subtract matrix $D$ from matrix $C$.

$$C - D = \begin{bmatrix} 2 & 3 \\ 5 & 8 \\ 9 & 4 \end{bmatrix} - \begin{bmatrix} 6 & 1 \\ 4 & 2 \\ 9 & 7 \end{bmatrix} = \begin{bmatrix} 2-6 & 3-1 \\ 5-4 & 8-2 \\ 9-9 & 4-7 \end{bmatrix} = \begin{bmatrix} -4 & 2 \\ 1 & 6 \\ 0 & -3 \end{bmatrix}$$

# C. Multiplication

Multiplication involving matrices is also presented under two different cases below:

### CASE I. SCALAR MULTIPLICATION

When a real number (scalar) is multiplied by a matrix, the number must be multiplied by each element of the matrix. The product thus is also a matrix with the same order of the matrix multiplied.

**Example 7**     (a) Multiply 4 by the $2 \times 3$ matrix $E = \begin{bmatrix} 1 & 3 & 6 \\ 2 & 5 & 7 \end{bmatrix}$

$$4 \cdot E = 4 \begin{bmatrix} 1 & 3 & 6 \\ 2 & 5 & 7 \end{bmatrix} = \begin{bmatrix} 4\times1 & 4\times3 & 4\times6 \\ 4\times2 & 4\times5 & 4\times7 \end{bmatrix} = \begin{bmatrix} 4 & 12 & 24 \\ 8 & 20 & 28 \end{bmatrix}$$

(b) Multiply $\frac{1}{2}$ by the $2 \times 2$ matrix $A$.

$$\frac{1}{2} \cdot A = \frac{1}{2} \begin{bmatrix} 1 & 7 \\ 6 & 4 \end{bmatrix} = \begin{bmatrix} \frac{1}{2}\times1 & \frac{1}{2}\times7 \\ \frac{1}{2}\times6 & \frac{1}{2}\times4 \end{bmatrix} = \begin{bmatrix} \frac{1}{2} & 3\frac{1}{2} \\ 3 & 2 \end{bmatrix}$$

### CASE II. MULTIPLICATION OF TWO MATRICES

A matrix may be multiplied by another matrix if, and only if, the number of columns in the first matrix is equal to the number of rows in the second matrix. Thus, an $m \times n$ matrix may be multiplied by an $n \times p$ matrix. The product of the two matrices is an $m \times p$ matrix.

## Multiplication of Two Matrices

| First matrix | | Second matrix | |
|---|---|---|---|
| Rows | Columns | Rows | Columns |
| $m$ | $\times$ $n$ | $n$ | $\times$ $p$ |

$m \times p$ matrix
(product)

Let $A$ be the first matrix and $B$ be the second matrix. Each row vector of $A$ is multiplied by each column vector of $B$ to obtain the corresponding element of the product matrix $A \cdot B$. Or, more generally, the element in the $i$th row and $j$th column in the product is obtained by multiplying the $i$th row vector in the first matrix by the $j$th column vector in the second matrix.

**Example 8**    (a) Multiply matrix $A$ by matrix $B$. The order of each matrix is written directly under the matrix for checking the answer. Since $A$ and $B$ are $2 \times 2$ matrices, the product $A \cdot B$ should be a $2 \times 2$ matrix also.

$$A \cdot B = \underset{2 \times 2}{\begin{bmatrix} 1 & 7 \\ 6 & 4 \end{bmatrix}} \cdot \underset{2 \times 2}{\begin{bmatrix} 3 & 2 \\ 5 & 8 \end{bmatrix}} = \begin{bmatrix} [1 \; 7]\begin{bmatrix} 3 \\ 5 \end{bmatrix} & [1 \; 7]\begin{bmatrix} 2 \\ 8 \end{bmatrix} \\ [6 \; 4]\begin{bmatrix} 3 \\ 5 \end{bmatrix} & [6 \; 4]\begin{bmatrix} 2 \\ 8 \end{bmatrix} \end{bmatrix}$$

$$= \begin{bmatrix} (1 \times 3) + (7 \times 5) & (1 \times 2) + (7 \times 8) \\ (6 \times 3) + (4 \times 5) & (6 \times 2) + (4 \times 8) \end{bmatrix} = \underset{2 \times 2}{\begin{bmatrix} 38 & 58 \\ 38 & 44 \end{bmatrix}}$$

**Note:**    It can easily be verified that $A \cdot B \neq B \cdot A$.

(b) Multiply matrix $C$ by matrix $A$.

Since $C$ is a $3 \times 2$ matrix and $A$ is a $2 \times 2$ matrix, the product $C \cdot A$ will be a $3 \times 2$ matrix.

$$C \cdot A = \underset{3 \times 2}{\begin{bmatrix} 2 & 3 \\ 5 & 8 \\ 9 & 4 \end{bmatrix}} \cdot \underset{2 \times 2}{\begin{bmatrix} 1 & 7 \\ 6 & 4 \end{bmatrix}} = \begin{bmatrix} [2 \; 3]\begin{bmatrix} 1 \\ 6 \end{bmatrix} & [2 \; 3]\begin{bmatrix} 7 \\ 4 \end{bmatrix} \\ [5 \; 8]\begin{bmatrix} 1 \\ 6 \end{bmatrix} & [5 \; 8]\begin{bmatrix} 7 \\ 4 \end{bmatrix} \\ [9 \; 4]\begin{bmatrix} 1 \\ 6 \end{bmatrix} & [9 \; 4]\begin{bmatrix} 7 \\ 4 \end{bmatrix} \end{bmatrix}$$

$$= \begin{bmatrix} (2 \times 1) + (3 \times 6) & (2 \times 7) + (3 \times 4) \\ (5 \times 1) + (8 \times 6) & (5 \times 7) + (8 \times 4) \\ (9 \times 1) + (4 \times 6) & (9 \times 7) + (4 \times 4) \end{bmatrix} = \underset{3 \times 2}{\begin{bmatrix} 20 & 26 \\ 53 & 67 \\ 33 & 79 \end{bmatrix}}$$

Note that since the number of columns in $A$ (2 columns) is not equal to the number of rows in $C$ (3 rows), we could not multiply $A$ by $C$

(or $A \cdot C$). Also, Example 8 may be written in a practical problem as shown in Table 5–3. This table is constructed from the information given in Section 5.1 (Tables 5–1 and 5–2). It shows the total amount of each type of raw material required by each plant. The totals shown in the table are the same as the elements in the product matrix $C \cdot A$.

**Table 5–3     COMPANY R—MATERIAL REQUIREMENTS BY PLANTS**

| Material | Plant #1 | | | | | | | Plant #2 | | | | | | |
| | Product X | | | Product Y | | | Total | Product X | | | Product Y | | | Total |
| | For each unit | Units of X | Sub-total | For each unit | Units of Y | Sub-total | | For each unit | Units of X | Sub-total | For each unit | Units of Y | Sub-total | |
|---|---|---|---|---|---|---|---|---|---|---|---|---|---|---|
| M-1 | 2 lbs | 1 | 2 lbs | 3 lbs | 6 | 18 lbs | 20 lbs | 2 lbs | 7 | 14 lbs | 3 lbs | 4 | 12 lbs | 26 lbs |
| M-2 | 5 | 1 | 5 | 8 | 6 | 48 | 53 | 5 | 7 | 35 | 8 | 4 | 32 | 67 |
| M-3 | 9 | 1 | 9 | 4 | 6 | 24 | 33 | 9 | 7 | 63 | 4 | 4 | 16 | 79 |

First column vector— of matrix $C \cdot A$                Second column vector— of matrix $C \cdot A$

Source: Computed from Tables 5–1 and 5–2. See Example 8(b) for matrix $C \cdot A$.

## EXERCISE 5–1

### Reference: Sections 5.1 and 5.2

**A.** *Operations with vectors.*

Let $u = [6, \quad 2]$; $\quad v = [4, \quad 5]$; $\quad v' = \begin{bmatrix} 4 \\ 5 \end{bmatrix}$; $\quad w = \begin{bmatrix} 3 \\ 7 \end{bmatrix}$;

$x = \begin{bmatrix} 1 \\ 6 \\ 5 \end{bmatrix}$; $\quad y = \begin{bmatrix} 2 \\ 3 \\ 7 \end{bmatrix}$; and $z = [4, \quad 8, \quad 9]$.

*Perform the indicated operations in each of the following expressions:*

| | | | |
|---|---|---|---|
| **1.** $u - v$ | **6.** $x + y$ | **11.** $2v'$ | **16.** $v \cdot v'$ |
| **2.** $u + v$ | **7.** $x - y$ | **12.** $3w$ | **17.** $u \cdot w$ |
| **3.** $v' + w$ | **8.** $y - x$ | **13.** $6z$ | **18.** $v \cdot w$ |
| **4.** $w - v'$ | **9.** $5u$ | **14.** $4x$ | **19.** $z \cdot x$ |
| **5.** $v - u$ | **10.** $\frac{3}{4}v$ | **15.** $\frac{1}{5}y$ | **20.** $z \cdot y$ |

**B.** *Operations with matrices.*

Let $A = \begin{bmatrix} 3 & 9 \\ 2 & 4 \end{bmatrix}$; $B = \begin{bmatrix} 5 & 6 \\ 1 & 7 \end{bmatrix}$; $C = \begin{bmatrix} 1 & 2 \\ 3 & 9 \\ 8 & 4 \end{bmatrix}$; $D = \begin{bmatrix} 5 & 1 \\ 2 & 7 \\ 3 & 6 \end{bmatrix}$;

$$E = \begin{bmatrix} 4 & 6 & 3 \\ 1 & 5 & 8 \end{bmatrix}; \text{ and } F = \begin{bmatrix} 2 & 4 & 7 \\ 5 & 3 & 1 \end{bmatrix}$$

*Perform the indicated operations in each of the following expressions:*

| | | | |
|---|---|---|---|
| **21.** $A + B$ | **27.** $\frac{1}{4}C$ | **33.** $A \cdot F$ | **39.** $F \cdot C$ |
| **22.** $C + D$ | **28.** $\frac{1}{3}E$ | **34.** $B \cdot E$ | **40.** $E \cdot D$ |
| **23.** $C - D$ | **29.** $A \cdot B$ | **35.** $E \cdot C$ | **41.** $C \cdot E$ |
| **24.** $A - B$ | **30.** $B \cdot A$ | **36.** $F \cdot D$ | **42.** $D \cdot F$ |
| **25.** $3A$ | **31.** $A \cdot E$ | **37.** $C \cdot A$ | **43.** $C \cdot F$ |
| **26.** $2B$ | **32.** $B \cdot F$ | **38.** $D \cdot B$ | **44.** $D \cdot E$ |

## 5.3 DETERMINANTS

A determinant is a number which determines whether or not there is an *inverse* of a square matrix. The details concerning the inverse of a square matrix are presented in the next section. This section introduces the basic operations with determinants.

A determinant is written in a manner similar to its associated square matrix except that two vertical lines instead of brackets are used. For example, if the $2 \times 2$ square matrix

$$A = \begin{bmatrix} 2 & 5 \\ 1 & 3 \end{bmatrix}, \text{ the determinant of } A, \text{ denoted by } |A|, \text{ is}$$

$$|A| = \begin{vmatrix} 2 & 5 \\ 1 & 3 \end{vmatrix}, \text{ which is also called a determinant of order 2.}$$

The value of a determinant may be computed in two ways: (1) by cross multiplying the elements, and (2) by finding the minors. Each of these methods is discussed in more detail below.

## A. Evaluating Determinants by Cross Multiplication

We shall evaluate only the determinants of orders 2 and 3 by this method. If the $2 \times 2$ square matrix

$$A = \begin{bmatrix} a_{11} & a_{12} \\ a_{21} & a_{22} \end{bmatrix}, \text{ then the determinant of } A \text{ is}$$

$$|A| = \begin{vmatrix} a_{11} & a_{12} \\ a_{21} & a_{22} \end{vmatrix} = a_{11}a_{22} - a_{12}a_{21}.$$

secondary    primary
diagonal     diagonal

Observe that the letter $a$ represents the elements of the matrix $A$, with the first subscript indicating the location of the row and the second subscript indicating the location of the column. The positive product $(+a_{11}a_{22})$ consists of the elements on the primary diagonal and the negative product $(-a_{12}a_{21})$ consists of the elements on the secondary diagonal of the determinant; also, each product has only one element from each row and each column.

**Example 1**　　Evaluate the determinant of the matrix $A$ if

(a) $A = \begin{bmatrix} 2 & 5 \\ 1 & 3 \end{bmatrix}$, and (b) $A = \begin{bmatrix} 3 & 1 \\ 6 & -1 \end{bmatrix}$.

(a) $|A| = \begin{vmatrix} 2 & 5 \\ 1 & 3 \end{vmatrix} = (2 \times 3) - (5 \times 1) = 6 - 5 = 1$.

(b) $|A| = \begin{vmatrix} 3 & 1 \\ 6 & -1 \end{vmatrix} = (3 \times (-1)) - (1 \times 6) = -3 - 6 = -9$.

Likewise, the determinant of order 3 is associated with a $3 \times 3$ matrix, or written

$$|A| = \begin{vmatrix} a_{11} & a_{12} & a_{13} \\ a_{21} & a_{22} & a_{23} \\ a_{31} & a_{32} & a_{33} \end{vmatrix} = a_{11}a_{22}a_{33} + a_{12}a_{23}a_{31} + a_{13}a_{21}a_{32}$$
$$- a_{13}a_{22}a_{31} - a_{12}a_{21}a_{33} - a_{11}a_{23}a_{32}$$

The three positive products are obtained from the primary diagonals as shown below:

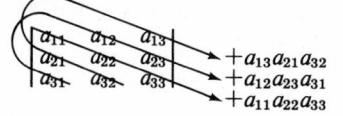

The three negative products are obtained from the secondary diagonals as shown below:

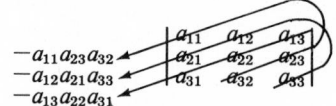

Note that the cross multiplication method as shown above does not work for determinants of order higher than 3. Determinants of higher order should be evaluated by the minors, as shown below.

**Example 2**　　Evaluate the determinant $|A|$.

$$|A| = \begin{vmatrix} 2 & -3 & 4 \\ 1 & 5 & -2 \\ 4 & 2 & 6 \end{vmatrix} = (2 \times 5 \times 6) + [(-3) \times (-2) \times 4]$$
$$+ (4 \times 1 \times 2) - (4 \times 5 \times 4)$$
$$- [(-3) \times 1 \times 6] - [2 \times (-2) \times 2]$$
$$= 60 + 24 + 8 - (80) - (-18) - (-8) = 38.$$

The positive and negative products may be computed in the following manner. Note that the first two columns of the determinant are written as the 4th and the 5th columns respectively to facilitate the computation.

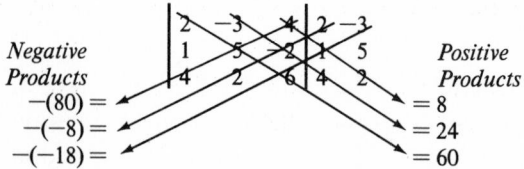

Negative Products
$-(80) =$
$-(-8) =$
$-(-18) =$

Positive Products
$= 8$
$= 24$
$= 60$

# B. Evaluating Determinants by Minors

A minor is a determinant of order $(n - 1)$ obtained from a determinant of order $n$. Thus, in a $3 \times 3$ determinant, we may have $2 \times 2$ minors. A minor is specified by an element. The minor of the element $a_{ij}$, located in the $i$th row and the $j$th column in a determinant, is denoted by $A_{ij}$. Minor $A_{ij}$ is obtained by deleting both the $i$th row and $j$th column of the determinant. Thus, in the $2 \times 2$ determinant

$$|A| = \begin{vmatrix} a_{11} & a_{12} \\ a_{21} & a_{22} \end{vmatrix}, \text{ minor } A_{11} = \begin{vmatrix} a_{11} & a_{12} \\ a_{21} & a_{22} \end{vmatrix} = |a_{22}|,$$

and in the $3 \times 3$ determinant

$$|A| = \begin{vmatrix} a_{11} & a_{12} & a_{13} \\ a_{21} & a_{22} & a_{23} \\ a_{31} & a_{32} & a_{33} \end{vmatrix}, \text{ minor } A_{21} = \begin{vmatrix} a_{11} & a_{12} & a_{13} \\ a_{21} & a_{22} & a_{23} \\ a_{31} & a_{32} & a_{33} \end{vmatrix} = \begin{vmatrix} a_{12} & a_{13} \\ a_{32} & a_{33} \end{vmatrix}$$

(The element $a_{ij}$ ($a_{11}$ and $a_{21}$) is circled in each illustration.)

A minor should be prefixed by a sign when it is used for evaluating a determinant. When $i + j$ is an even number, the sign of the minor is positive, or $+A_{ij}$. When $i + j$ is an odd number, the sign is negative, or $-A_{ij}$.

*Illustrations:*    The minor of element $a_{11}$ is $+A_{11}$ since it appears in the first row and first column and $1 + 1 = 2$, an even number.

$$\text{If } |A| = \begin{vmatrix} 2 & 5 \\ 1 & 3 \end{vmatrix}, a_{11} = 2 \text{ and } +A_{11} = \begin{vmatrix} 2 & 5 \\ 1 & 3 \end{vmatrix} = +|3|.$$

The minor of element $a_{21}$ is $-A_{21}$ since it appears in the second row and first column and $2 + 1 = 3$, an odd number.

$$\text{If } |A| = \begin{vmatrix} 2 & -3 & 4 \\ 1 & 5 & -2 \\ 4 & 2 & 6 \end{vmatrix}, a_{21} = 1 \text{ and } -A_{21} = -\begin{vmatrix} 2 & -3 & 4 \\ 1 & 5 & -2 \\ 4 & 2 & 6 \end{vmatrix}$$

$$= -\begin{vmatrix} -3 & 4 \\ 2 & 6 \end{vmatrix}.$$

**Note:**    A signed minor is also called a *cofactor* of the element $a_{ij}$.

A determinant may be evaluated by signed minors as follows:

**Step (1)**    Multiply each element of *any* column (or any row) by its signed minor.

**Step (2)**    Add the $n$ products obtained above. The sum is the value of the determinant.

Thus, for a $2 \times 2$ determinant $|A|$, we may express the value in terms of the elements of the *first column* and their signed minors:

$$|A| = a_{11}A_{11} - a_{21}A_{21}.$$

**Example 3**    Evaluate the determinants in Example 1 by minors.

(a) $|A| = \begin{vmatrix} 2 & 5 \\ 1 & 3 \end{vmatrix} = 2\begin{vmatrix} 2 & 5 \\ 1 & 3 \end{vmatrix} - 1\begin{vmatrix} 2 & 5 \\ 1 & 3 \end{vmatrix} = 2|3| - 1|5|$
$= 6 - 5 = 1.$

(b) $|A| = \begin{vmatrix} 3 & 1 \\ 6 & -1 \end{vmatrix} = 3\begin{vmatrix} 3 & 1 \\ 6 & -1 \end{vmatrix} - 6\begin{vmatrix} 3 & 1 \\ 6 & -1 \end{vmatrix} = 3|-1| - 6|1|$
$= (-3) - 6 = -9.$

For a $3 \times 3$ determinant $|A|$, we may also express the value in terms of the elements of the *first column* and their signed minors:

$$|A| = a_{11}A_{11} - a_{21}A_{21} + a_{31}A_{31}.$$

**Example 4**    Evaluate the determinant in Example 2 by minors.

$$|A| = \begin{vmatrix} 2 & -3 & 4 \\ 1 & 5 & -2 \\ 4 & 2 & 6 \end{vmatrix} = 2\begin{vmatrix} 2 & -3 & 4 \\ 1 & 5 & -2 \\ 4 & 2 & 6 \end{vmatrix} - 1\begin{vmatrix} 2 & -3 & 4 \\ 1 & 5 & -2 \\ 4 & 2 & 6 \end{vmatrix} + 4\begin{vmatrix} 2 & -3 & 4 \\ 1 & 5 & -2 \\ 4 & 2 & 6 \end{vmatrix}$$

$$= 2\begin{vmatrix} 5 & -2 \\ 2 & 6 \end{vmatrix} - 1\begin{vmatrix} -3 & 4 \\ 2 & 6 \end{vmatrix} + 4\begin{vmatrix} -3 & 4 \\ 5 & -2 \end{vmatrix}$$

$$= 2[30 - (-4)] - 1[(-18) - 8] + 4(6 - 20)$$
$$= 68 + 26 - 56 = 38.$$

Determinants of higher order may be evaluated by repeating the process of finding the products of the elements of the first column and their signed minors as illustrated in Example 4. For instance, a $4 \times 4$ determinant may be evaluated from its $3 \times 3$ signed minors. Each of the $3 \times 3$ signed minors is then evaluated from its $2 \times 2$ signed minors.

## EXERCISE 5–2

### Reference: Section 5.3

**A.** *Evaluate each of the following determinants by (a) the cross multiplication method, and (b) finding the signed minors of the first column elements:*

**1.** $\begin{vmatrix} 2 & 7 \\ 3 & 5 \end{vmatrix}$     **3.** $\begin{vmatrix} -2 & 8 \\ 4 & -9 \end{vmatrix}$     **5.** $\begin{vmatrix} 1 & -2 & 3 \\ 4 & 5 & -6 \\ 7 & 8 & 9 \end{vmatrix}$     **7.** $\begin{vmatrix} 1 & 2 & 0 \\ -1 & 1 & 2 \\ 2 & 1 & 0 \end{vmatrix}$

**2.** $\begin{vmatrix} 4 & -5 \\ 7 & 3 \end{vmatrix}$     **4.** $\begin{vmatrix} -3 & 12 \\ -7 & 8 \end{vmatrix}$

**6.** $\begin{vmatrix} 3 & 5 & -1 \\ 2 & -7 & 8 \\ 4 & 1 & 6 \end{vmatrix}$     **8.** $\begin{vmatrix} 1 & 3 & 2 \\ 2 & -1 & 0 \\ 3 & 2 & 1 \end{vmatrix}$

**B.** *Evaluate each determinant by the signed minors of the elements of the row or column indicated:*

**9.** The determinant given in Problem 1—Use the elements in the first row.
**10.** The determinant given in Problem 2—Use the elements in the first row.
**11.** The determinant given in Problem 5—Use the elements in the 2nd row.
**12.** The determinant given in Problem 6—Use the elements in the 2nd column.

## 5.4 THE INVERSE OF A SQUARE MATRIX

In algebra, the *inverse* or *reciprocal* of the number $a$ is $a^{-1}$ (or $\frac{1}{a}$); the product of the number and its inverse is always equal to 1, or $a \cdot a^{-1} = 1$. A similar relationship between a matrix and its inverse may be expressed.

Let $A = $ a square matrix, and
$A^{-1} = $ the inverse of $A$.

Then, $A^{-1} \cdot A = A \cdot A^{-1} = I$,
where $I = $ an identity matrix of the same order as $A$ and $A^{-1}$.

An *identity matrix* or *unit matrix* is a square matrix with all elements on its *principal diagonal* (the line from the upper left corner to the lower right corner) equal to 1 and all other elements 0, such as

$$\text{the } 2 \times 2 \text{ identity matrix } I = \begin{bmatrix} 1 & 0 \\ 0 & 1 \end{bmatrix}, \text{ and}$$

$$\text{the } 3 \times 3 \text{ identity matrix } I = \begin{bmatrix} 1 & 0 & 0 \\ 0 & 1 & 0 \\ 0 & 0 & 1 \end{bmatrix}.$$

An identity matrix acts in matrix algebra in the same way as 1 in the ordinary algebra concerning multiplication. Thus, the expression

$$A \cdot I = I \cdot A = A \text{ is true for all matrices } A.$$

**Example 1**   Let the $2 \times 2$ matrix $A = \begin{bmatrix} 2 & 5 \\ 1 & 3 \end{bmatrix}$ and $I = \begin{bmatrix} 1 & 0 \\ 0 & 1 \end{bmatrix}$.

$$A \cdot I = \begin{bmatrix} 2 & 5 \\ 1 & 3 \end{bmatrix} \cdot \begin{bmatrix} 1 & 0 \\ 0 & 1 \end{bmatrix} = \begin{bmatrix} (2 \times 1) + (5 \times 0) & (2 \times 0) + (5 \times 1) \\ (1 \times 1) + (3 \times 0) & (1 \times 0) + (3 \times 1) \end{bmatrix}$$

$$= \begin{bmatrix} 2 & 5 \\ 1 & 3 \end{bmatrix} = A.$$

$$I \cdot A = \begin{bmatrix} 1 & 0 \\ 0 & 1 \end{bmatrix} \cdot \begin{bmatrix} 2 & 5 \\ 1 & 3 \end{bmatrix} = \begin{bmatrix} (1 \times 2) + (0 \times 1) & (1 \times 5) + (0 \times 3) \\ (0 \times 2) + (1 \times 1) & (0 \times 5) + (1 \times 3) \end{bmatrix}$$

$$= \begin{bmatrix} 2 & 5 \\ 1 & 3 \end{bmatrix} = A.$$

There are various methods of finding the inverse of a square matrix. We shall introduce two methods: (A) the basic method, and (B) the short method by using determinants.

## A. Basic Method

This method is illustrated by the example below.

**Example 2**   Find the inverse of the square matrix $A = \begin{bmatrix} 2 & 5 \\ 1 & 3 \end{bmatrix}$. Let $I = \begin{bmatrix} 1 & 0 \\ 0 & 1 \end{bmatrix}$.

If $A^{-1}$, the inverse of $A$, exists, then we may write $A \cdot A^{-1} = I$ as

$$\begin{bmatrix} 2 & 5 \\ 1 & 3 \end{bmatrix} \cdot A^{-1} = \begin{bmatrix} 1 & 0 \\ 0 & 1 \end{bmatrix}$$

Since $A$ is a $2 \times 2$ square matrix and the product $I$ is a $2 \times 2$ square matrix, the unknown matrix $A^{-1}$ must also be a $2 \times 2$ square matrix. Let $b$ represent the elements of the matrix $A^{-1}$, with the first and second subscripts indicating the locations of rows and columns in the matrix respectively, or

$$A^{-1} = \begin{bmatrix} b_{11} & b_{12} \\ b_{21} & b_{22} \end{bmatrix}$$

We then have

$$\begin{bmatrix} 2 & 5 \\ 1 & 3 \end{bmatrix} \cdot \begin{bmatrix} b_{11} & b_{12} \\ b_{21} & b_{22} \end{bmatrix} = \begin{bmatrix} 1 & 0 \\ 0 & 1 \end{bmatrix}$$

Multiply the left side,

$$\begin{bmatrix} (2b_{11} + 5b_{21}) & (2b_{12} + 5b_{22}) \\ (1b_{11} + 3b_{21}) & (1b_{12} + 3b_{22}) \end{bmatrix} = \begin{bmatrix} 1 & 0 \\ 0 & 1 \end{bmatrix}$$

Equate corresponding elements of the matrices on both sides. We have a system of four equations:

$$\begin{cases} 2b_{11} + 5b_{21} = 1 & (1) \\ 1b_{11} + 3b_{21} = 0 & (2) \end{cases} \qquad \begin{cases} 2b_{12} + 5b_{22} = 0 & (3) \\ 1b_{12} + 3b_{22} = 1 & (4) \end{cases}$$

Solve equations (1) and (2) for $b_{11}$ and $b_{21}$:

| | | |
|---|---|---|
| $(2) \times 2$ | $2b_{11} + 6b_{21} = 0$ | $(2)'$ |
| $(2)' - (1)$ | $b_{21} = -1$ | |

Substitute $b_{21} = -1$ in (2),
$$b_{11} + 3(-1) = 0,$$
$$b_{11} = 3.$$

Solve equations (3) and (4) for $b_{12}$ and $b_{22}$:

| | | |
|---|---|---|
| $(4) \times 2$ | $2b_{12} + 6b_{22} = 2$ | $(4)'$ |
| $(4)' - (3)$ | $b_{22} = 2$ | |

Substitute $b_{22} = 2$ in (4),
$$b_{12} + 3(2) = 1,$$
$$b_{12} = -5.$$

Thus,

$$A^{-1} = \begin{bmatrix} b_{11} & b_{12} \\ b_{21} & b_{22} \end{bmatrix} = \begin{bmatrix} 3 & -5 \\ -1 & 2 \end{bmatrix}$$

*Check:*

$$A \cdot A^{-1} = \begin{bmatrix} 2 & 5 \\ 1 & 3 \end{bmatrix} \cdot \begin{bmatrix} 3 & -5 \\ -1 & 2 \end{bmatrix} = \begin{bmatrix} 6 + (-5) & (-10) + (10) \\ 3 + (-3) & (-5) + 6 \end{bmatrix}$$

$$= \begin{bmatrix} 1 & 0 \\ 0 & 1 \end{bmatrix} = I$$

Also, $A^{-1} \cdot A = \begin{bmatrix} 3 & -5 \\ -1 & 2 \end{bmatrix} \cdot \begin{bmatrix} 2 & 5 \\ 1 & 3 \end{bmatrix} = \begin{bmatrix} 6 + (-5) & 15 + (-15) \\ (-2) + 2 & (-5) + 6 \end{bmatrix}$

$$= \begin{bmatrix} 1 & 0 \\ 0 & 1 \end{bmatrix} = I.$$

The results from the checking show that $A^{-1} \cdot A = A \cdot A^{-1} = I$.

## B. Short Method

The process of finding the inverse of a square matrix can be simplifed when determinants are used. Observe the procedures illustrated in Example 2. Let the $2 \times 2$ square matrix $A$ be written in a general form, or

$$A = \begin{bmatrix} a_{11} & a_{12} \\ a_{21} & a_{22} \end{bmatrix}. \text{ If } A^{-1} \text{ exists, we may write } A \cdot A^{-1} = I \text{ as}$$

$$\begin{bmatrix} a_{11} & a_{12} \\ a_{21} & a_{22} \end{bmatrix} \cdot \begin{bmatrix} b_{11} & b_{12} \\ b_{21} & b_{22} \end{bmatrix} = \begin{bmatrix} 1 & 0 \\ 0 & 1 \end{bmatrix}$$

After multiplying the matrices on the left side of the above equation, equating corresponding elements to obtain the four equations, and solving the four equations, we have [1]

$$b_{11} = \frac{a_{22}}{|A|}, \quad b_{12} = \frac{-a_{12}}{|A|},$$

---

[1] Multiply the left side:

$$\begin{bmatrix} a_{11}b_{11} + a_{12}b_{21} & a_{11}b_{12} + a_{12}b_{22} \\ a_{21}b_{11} + a_{22}b_{21} & a_{21}b_{12} + a_{22}b_{22} \end{bmatrix} = \begin{bmatrix} 1 & 0 \\ 0 & 1 \end{bmatrix}$$

Equate corresponding elements:

$$\begin{cases} a_{11}b_{11} + a_{12}b_{21} = 1 & \dots (1) \\ a_{21}b_{11} + a_{22}b_{21} = 0 & \dots (2) \end{cases} \quad \begin{cases} a_{11}b_{12} + a_{12}b_{22} = 0 & \dots (3) \\ a_{12}b_{12} + a_{22}b_{22} = 1 & \dots (4) \end{cases}$$

Solve Equations (1) and (2) for $b_{11}$ and $b_{21}$:

$$\begin{array}{ll} (1) \times a_{21} & a_{21}a_{11}b_{11} + a_{21}a_{12}b_{21} = a_{21} \quad \dots \dots (1)' \\ (2) \times a_{11} & a_{11}a_{21}b_{11} + a_{11}a_{22}b_{21} = 0 \quad \dots \dots (2)' \\ (1)' - (2)' & \overline{\quad a_{21}a_{12}b_{21} - a_{11}a_{22}b_{21} = a_{21}} \end{array}$$

$$b_{21}(a_{21}a_{12} - a_{11}a_{22}) = a_{21}$$

$$b_{21} = \frac{a_{21}}{a_{21}a_{12} - a_{11}a_{22}}$$

$$= \frac{a_{21}}{-(a_{11}a_{22} - a_{21}a_{12})} = \frac{-a_{21}}{|A|}$$

Substitute $b_{21}$ value in (2):

$$a_{21}b_{11} + a_{22}\left( \frac{a_{21}}{a_{21}a_{12} - a_{11}a_{22}} \right) = 0$$

$$b_{11} = -\frac{a_{22}a_{21}}{a_{21}a_{12} - a_{11}a_{22}} \cdot \frac{1}{a_{21}} = \frac{a_{22}}{|A|}$$

We may solve equations (3) and (4) in a similar manner to obtain the values of $b_{12}$ and $b_{22}$.

$$b_{21} = \frac{-a_{21}}{|A|}, \quad b_{22} = \frac{a_{11}}{|A|};$$

and
$$A^{-1} = \begin{bmatrix} b_{11} & b_{12} \\ b_{21} & b_{22} \end{bmatrix} = \begin{bmatrix} \dfrac{a_{22}}{|A|} & \dfrac{-a_{12}}{|A|} \\ \dfrac{-a_{21}}{|A|} & \dfrac{a_{11}}{|A|} \end{bmatrix} = \frac{1}{|A|}\begin{bmatrix} a_{22} & -a_{12} \\ -a_{21} & a_{11} \end{bmatrix}.$$

where
$$|A| = \begin{vmatrix} a_{11} & a_{12} \\ a_{21} & a_{22} \end{vmatrix} = a_{11}a_{22} - a_{12}a_{21} \neq 0.$$

Thus, the determinant $|A|$ determines the existence of the inverse of a square matrix $A$. If, and only if, $|A| \neq 0$, the inverse $A^{-1}$ exists.

Example 2 now may be solved by the short method as follows:

$$A = \begin{bmatrix} a_{11} & a_{12} \\ a_{21} & a_{22} \end{bmatrix} = \begin{bmatrix} 2 & 5 \\ 1 & 3 \end{bmatrix} \quad |A| = \begin{vmatrix} 2 & 5 \\ 1 & 3 \end{vmatrix} = (2 \times 3) - (5 \times 1) = 1.$$

Since $|A| \neq 0$, $A$ has an inverse.

$$A^{-1} = \frac{1}{|A|}\begin{bmatrix} a_{22} & -a_{12} \\ -a_{21} & a_{11} \end{bmatrix} = \frac{1}{1}\begin{bmatrix} 3 & -5 \\ -1 & 2 \end{bmatrix} = \begin{bmatrix} 3 & -5 \\ -1 & 2 \end{bmatrix}$$

In summary, to write the inverse of a $2 \times 2$ square matrix $A$ for which $|A| \neq 0$, we may interchange the elements on the principal diagonal, prefix each of the other two elements with a negative sign, and multiply the resulted matrix by $1/|A|$.

The inverse of a $2 \times 2$ square matrix may also be written in terms of signed minors as follows:

$$A^{-1} = \frac{1}{|A|}\begin{bmatrix} A_{11} & -A_{21} \\ -A_{12} & A_{22} \end{bmatrix}, \text{ since } \begin{cases} A_{11} = a_{22}, & -A_{21} = -a_{12}, \\ -A_{12} = -a_{21}, & A_{22} = a_{11}. \end{cases}$$

Observe that the signed minors in the above matrix are in *transposed order*. For example, the subscripts 21 in element $a_{21}$ indicate that the element is in the second *row* and the first *column*. Now, the subscripts 21 in the signed minor $-A_{21}$ indicate the location of the minor being in the second *column* and the first *row*.

Similarly, the inverse of a $3 \times 3$ square matrix may be written in terms of signed minors:

$$A^{-1} = \frac{1}{|A|}\begin{bmatrix} A_{11} & -A_{21} & A_{31} \\ -A_{12} & A_{22} & -A_{32} \\ A_{13} & -A_{23} & A_{33} \end{bmatrix}$$

Again observe the transposed subscripts, such as 31 in the signed minor $A_{31}$ indicating the location of the minor in the third column and the first row. Note that the minor of element $a_{31}$ is $+A_{31}$ (a positive determinant) since the sum of the subscripts $3 + 1 = 4$ is an even number. The minors $A_{12}, A_{21}, A_{23},$ and $A_{32}$ have negative signs since the sums of their subscripts are odd numbers, such as $1 + 2 = 3$, and $2 + 3 = 5$.

**Example 3**    Find the inverse of the $3 \times 3$ square matrix $A = \begin{bmatrix} 2 & -3 & 4 \\ 1 & 5 & -2 \\ 4 & 2 & 6 \end{bmatrix}$.

$$|A| = \begin{vmatrix} 2 & -3 & 4 \\ 1 & 5 & -2 \\ 4 & 2 & 6 \end{vmatrix} = 38. \text{ (See Example 4, page 138.)}$$

Since $|A| \neq 0$, $A^{-1}$ or the inverse of $A$ exists. Use the $A^{-1}$ formula above; we have

$$A_{11} = \begin{vmatrix} 5 & -2 \\ 2 & 6 \end{vmatrix}, \quad -A_{21} = -\begin{vmatrix} -3 & 4 \\ 2 & 6 \end{vmatrix}, \text{ and so on.}$$

Thus,

$$A^{-1} = \frac{1}{38} \begin{bmatrix} \begin{vmatrix} 5 & -2 \\ 2 & 6 \end{vmatrix} & -\begin{vmatrix} -3 & 4 \\ 2 & 6 \end{vmatrix} & \begin{vmatrix} -3 & 4 \\ 5 & -2 \end{vmatrix} \\ -\begin{vmatrix} 1 & -2 \\ 4 & 6 \end{vmatrix} & \begin{vmatrix} 2 & 4 \\ 4 & 6 \end{vmatrix} & -\begin{vmatrix} 2 & 4 \\ 1 & -2 \end{vmatrix} \\ \begin{vmatrix} 1 & 5 \\ 4 & 2 \end{vmatrix} & -\begin{vmatrix} 2 & -3 \\ 4 & 2 \end{vmatrix} & \begin{vmatrix} 2 & -3 \\ 1 & 5 \end{vmatrix} \end{bmatrix}$$

$$= \frac{1}{38} \begin{bmatrix} 34 & 26 & -14 \\ -14 & -4 & 8 \\ -18 & -16 & 13 \end{bmatrix}.$$

*Check:*      $A^{-1} \cdot A = \dfrac{1}{38} \begin{bmatrix} 34 & 26 & -14 \\ -14 & -4 & 8 \\ -18 & -16 & 13 \end{bmatrix} \cdot \begin{bmatrix} 2 & -3 & 4 \\ 1 & 5 & -2 \\ 4 & 2 & 6 \end{bmatrix} = \begin{bmatrix} 1 & 0 & 0 \\ 0 & 1 & 0 \\ 0 & 0 & 1 \end{bmatrix}.$

# EXERCISE 5–3

**Reference: Section 5.4**

**A.** *Let* $A = \begin{bmatrix} 1 & -3 \\ 4 & 7 \end{bmatrix}$, $B = \begin{bmatrix} 3 & 4 \\ 2 & 6 \end{bmatrix}$, *and* $I = \begin{bmatrix} 1 & 0 \\ 0 & 1 \end{bmatrix}$.

**1.** Show that $A \cdot I = A$ and $I \cdot A = A$.
**2.** Show that $B \cdot I = B$ and $I \cdot B = B$.

**B.** *Find the inverse of each matrix* A *if the inverse exists by (a) the basic method, and (b) the short method. Also, check your answers by the relationship* A $\cdot$ A$^{-1}$ = I.

**3.** $A = \begin{bmatrix} 2 & 2 \\ 7 & 7 \end{bmatrix}$      **4.** $A = \begin{bmatrix} -4 & 2 \\ -1 & \frac{1}{2} \end{bmatrix}$      **5.** $A = \begin{bmatrix} 4 & 5 \\ 9 & 7 \end{bmatrix}$      **6.** $A = \begin{bmatrix} 1 & -6 \\ 2 & 3 \end{bmatrix}$

**C.** *Find the inverse of each matrix* A *if the inverse exists by the short method. Also, check your answers by the relationship* A · A$^{-1}$ = I.

**7.** $A = \begin{bmatrix} 1 & -2 & 3 \\ 4 & 5 & -6 \\ 7 & 8 & 9 \end{bmatrix}$, $|A| = 240$.      **8.** $A = \begin{bmatrix} 3 & 5 & -1 \\ 2 & -7 & 8 \\ 4 & 1 & 6 \end{bmatrix}$, $|A| = -80$.

## 5.5 SOLVING LINEAR EQUATIONS BY MATRIX ALGEBRA

A system of linear equations may be solved by the usual algebraic operations as presented in Chapter 2. However, the work of solving a system of three or more linear equations becomes increasingly difficult by the ordinary method. Matrix algebra offers a simplified and systematic method of solving the equations. The systematic steps may also be conveniently programmed for electronic computers to speed the calculations.

There are various methods of solving a system of *n* linear equations in *n* unknowns by matrix algebra. We shall introduce two methods below: (A) by using the inverse of a square matrix, and (B) by using determinants.

## A. Using Inverse of a Square Matrix in Solving Equations

This method is illustrated by Example 1. Example 1 uses only 2 equations, although this method is applicable to a system of more than 2 linear equations.

**Example 1**     Solve the following equations simultaneously:

$$\begin{cases} 3x + y = 5 \\ 6x - y = 6. \end{cases}$$

The two equations can be written in matrix form as follows:

$$\begin{bmatrix} 3 & 1 \\ 6 & -1 \end{bmatrix} \cdot \begin{bmatrix} x \\ y \end{bmatrix} = \begin{bmatrix} 5 \\ 6 \end{bmatrix}$$

The first matrix on the left side is formed by the coefficients of unknowns *x* and *y*, the second matrix by the unknowns, and the matrix on the right side by the constants.

Let *A* be the coefficient matrix, or $A = \begin{bmatrix} 3 & 1 \\ 6 & -1 \end{bmatrix}$. Then,

$$A \cdot \begin{bmatrix} x \\ y \end{bmatrix} = \begin{bmatrix} 5 \\ 6 \end{bmatrix}.$$

Multiply both sides by $A^{-1}$, the inverse of the 2 × 2 square matrix *A*,

$$A^{-1} \cdot A \cdot \begin{bmatrix} x \\ y \end{bmatrix} = A^{-1} \cdot \begin{bmatrix} 5 \\ 6 \end{bmatrix}.$$

Since $A^{-1} \cdot A = I$ and $I \cdot \begin{bmatrix} x \\ y \end{bmatrix} = \begin{bmatrix} x \\ y \end{bmatrix}$, we obtain

$$\begin{bmatrix} x \\ y \end{bmatrix} = A^{-1} \cdot \begin{bmatrix} 5 \\ 6 \end{bmatrix}$$

Thus, the problem of solving a system of linear equations now becomes a problem of finding the inverse of the coefficient matrix, $A^{-1}$. The value of $A^{-1}$ is computed first:

$$|A| = \begin{vmatrix} 3 & 1 \\ 6 & -1 \end{vmatrix} = (3 \times (-1)) - (1 \times 6) = -9.$$

Since $|A| \neq 0$, $A$ has an inverse.

$$A^{-1} = \frac{1}{-9} \begin{bmatrix} -1 & -1 \\ -6 & 3 \end{bmatrix}.$$

Substitute the value of $A^{-1}$ in the above obtained equation,

$$\begin{bmatrix} x \\ y \end{bmatrix} = \frac{1}{-9} \begin{bmatrix} -1 & -1 \\ -6 & 3 \end{bmatrix} \cdot \begin{bmatrix} 5 \\ 6 \end{bmatrix} = \frac{1}{-9} \begin{bmatrix} (-5) + (-6) \\ (-30) + 18 \end{bmatrix}$$

$$= \begin{bmatrix} -11/-9 \\ -12/-9 \end{bmatrix} = \begin{bmatrix} 11/9 \\ 4/3 \end{bmatrix}.$$

Thus, $x = \dfrac{11}{9} = 1\dfrac{2}{9}$

$$y = \dfrac{4}{3} = 1\dfrac{1}{3}$$

# B. Cramer's Rule: Using Determinants in Solving Equations

Let $|A| =$ the determinant formed by coefficients of unknowns in a system of linear equations. The following rule, called *Cramer's Rule* in honor of Gabriel Cramer of Geneva (1704–1752), has been established:

> A system of $n$ linear equations in $n$ unknowns has a single solution if, and only if, the determinant formed by the coefficients of the unknowns is not equal to zero; that is, $|A| \neq 0$. Each unknown is equal to the product of $1/|A|$ and the determinant obtained from $|A|$ by replacing the column of coefficients of this unknown by the column of constants.

The application of this rule is illustrated in the examples below.

**Example 2**    Solve: $\begin{cases} 3x + y = 5, \\ 6x - y = 6. \end{cases}$ (Same as Example 1.)

Let $|A| =$ the determinant of the coefficients of the unknowns in the two equations, or

$$|A| = \begin{vmatrix} 3 & 1 \\ 6 & -1 \end{vmatrix} = -9.$$

The coefficients of $x$ in $|A|$ are replaced by the constants.

$$x = \frac{1}{|A|}\begin{vmatrix} 5 & 1 \\ 6 & -1 \end{vmatrix} = \frac{1}{-9}[5(-1) - 1(6)] = \frac{11}{9} = 1\frac{2}{9}.$$

The coefficients of $y$ in $|A|$ are replaced by the constants.

$$y = \frac{1}{|A|}\begin{vmatrix} 3 & 5 \\ 6 & 6 \end{vmatrix} = \frac{1}{-9}[3(6) - 5(6)] = \frac{12}{9} = \frac{4}{3} = 1\frac{1}{3}.$$

**Example 3**    Solve: $\begin{cases} 2x - 3y + 4z = -4, \\ x + 5y - 2z = 15, \\ 4x + 2y + 6z = 10. \end{cases}$

Let $|A| =$ the determinant of the coefficients of the unknowns in the three equations, or

$$|A| = \begin{vmatrix} 2 & -3 & 4 \\ 1 & 5 & -2 \\ 4 & 2 & 6 \end{vmatrix} = 38. \text{ (See Example 4, page 138.)}$$

The coefficients of $x$ in $|A|$ are replaced by the constants.

$$x = \frac{1}{|A|}\begin{vmatrix} -4 & -3 & 4 \\ 15 & 5 & -2 \\ 10 & 2 & 6 \end{vmatrix} = \frac{1}{38}\left(-4\begin{vmatrix} 5 & -2 \\ 2 & 6 \end{vmatrix}\right.$$

$$\left. -15\begin{vmatrix} -3 & 4 \\ 2 & 6 \end{vmatrix} + 10\begin{vmatrix} -3 & 4 \\ 5 & -2 \end{vmatrix}\right) = \frac{1}{38}(114) = 3.$$

The coefficients of $y$ in $|A|$ are replaced by the constants.

$$y = \frac{1}{|A|}\begin{vmatrix} 2 & -4 & 4 \\ 1 & 15 & -2 \\ 4 & 10 & 6 \end{vmatrix} = \frac{1}{38}\left(2\begin{vmatrix} 15 & -2 \\ 10 & 6 \end{vmatrix}\right.$$

$$\left. -1\begin{vmatrix} -4 & 4 \\ 10 & 6 \end{vmatrix} + 4\begin{vmatrix} -4 & 4 \\ 15 & -2 \end{vmatrix}\right) = \frac{1}{38}(76) = 2.$$

The coefficients of $z$ in $|A|$ are replaced by the constants.

$$z = \frac{1}{|A|}\begin{vmatrix} 2 & -3 & -4 \\ 1 & 5 & 15 \\ 4 & 2 & 10 \end{vmatrix} = \frac{1}{38}\left(2\begin{vmatrix} 5 & 15 \\ 2 & 10 \end{vmatrix}\right.$$

$$\left. -1\begin{vmatrix} -3 & -4 \\ 2 & 10 \end{vmatrix} + 4\begin{vmatrix} -3 & -4 \\ 5 & 15 \end{vmatrix}\right) = \frac{1}{38}(-38) = -1.$$

*Check:*          Substitute $x = 3$, $y = 2$, and $z = -1$ in the given equations:

$$2x - 3y + 4z = 2(3) - 3(2) + 4(-1) = -4,$$
$$x + 5y - 2z = (3) + 5(2) - 2(-1) = 15,$$
$$4x + 2y + 6z = 4(3) + 2(2) + 6(-1) = 10.$$

*Note:*     1. If there are 3 unknowns, we must have 3 equations in order to have a single solution. If one of the 3 given equations includes only 2 unknowns, we may change it to an equation with 3 unknowns by adding the third unknown with a zero coefficient, such as $3x + 4y = 17$ is equal to $3x + 4y + 0z = 17$. This addition of a zero coefficient is necessary if we wish to have a square determinant $|A|$.

2. If $|A| = 0$ and $1/|A| = 1/0$ for a system of linear equations, there will be no single solution. That is, the system either has an infinitely large number of solutions, such as for dependent equations

$$\begin{cases} x + y = 2 \\ 2x + 2y = 4, \end{cases} |A| = \begin{vmatrix} 1 & 1 \\ 2 & 2 \end{vmatrix} = 0, \text{ or has no solution, such as for}$$

inconsistent equations $\begin{cases} x + y = 5 \\ x + y = 7, \end{cases} |A| = \begin{vmatrix} 1 & 1 \\ 1 & 1 \end{vmatrix} = 0.$

3. The symbol $|A|$ used in Cramer's Rule above is sometimes written as $\Delta$ (delta).

## EXERCISE 5–4

### Reference: Section 5.5

**A.** *Solve each of the following systems of equations by (a) using the inverse of a square matrix, and (b) using determinants:*

**1.** $\quad x + y = 8$          **3.** $\quad x + 2y = -4$
$\quad\quad 2x - y = 10$          $\quad\quad\ 2x + y = 1$
**2.** $3x - y = 5$          **4.** $5x + y = -7$
$\quad\quad x + 4y = 19$          $\quad\quad x + 4y = 10$

**B.** *Solve each of the following systems of equations by using determinants:*

**5.** $3x + y + z = 4$          **7.** $2x + y + 2z = 3$
$\quad\ 2x + 2y + 3z = 1$          $\quad\ x - 2y - 3z = 1$
$\quad\ 3x - y - 2z = 7$          $\quad\ 3x + 2y + 4z = 5$
**6.** $3x + 2y - z = 1$          **8.** $\quad x - 3y + 3z = -2$
$\quad\ 2x \quad\quad + z = 13$          $\quad\ 2x + y - 2z = 3$
$\quad\ x + y + 2z = 11$          $\quad\ 3x - y + z = 2$

## 5.6 INEQUALITIES AND LINEAR PROGRAMMING

This section introduces the basic concepts of inequalities and linear programming. We shall first present the concept of inequalities since it is needed in the illustrations of linear programming problems.

## A. Inequalities

An inequality is a statement which indicates that one algebraic expression is *greater than* ($>$) or *less than* ($<$) another. Let $a$, $b$, and $c$ be real numbers. Then, the statement *"a is greater than b"* or written symbolically

$$a > b$$

is an inequality. Also, the statement *"a is less than c"* or

$$a < c$$

is an inequality. The rules for dealing with inequality operations are as follows:

1. If the same number is added to, or subtracted from, both sides of an inequality, the same inequality sign is used for the new inequality. Thus, let

$$15 > 2. \text{ Then, } 15 + 8 > 2 + 8, \text{ or } 23 > 10.$$
$$\text{Also, } 15 < 25. \text{ Then, } 15 - 8 < 25 - 8, \text{ or } 7 < 17.$$

2. If both sides of an inequality are multiplied or divided by the *same positive number,* the same inequality sign is used for the new inequality. Thus, let

$$6 < 12. \text{ Then, } 6 \times 3 < 12 \times 3, \text{ or } 18 < 36,$$
$$\text{and } 6 \div 3 < 12 \div 3, \text{ or } 2 < 4.$$

3. If both sides of an inequality are multiplied or divided by the *same negative number,* the reversed inequality sign is used for the new inequality. Thus, let

$$8 > 3. \text{ Then, } 8(-4) < 3(-4), \text{ or } -32 < -12,$$
$$\text{and } 8 \div (-2) < 3 \div (-2), \text{ or } -4 < -1\tfrac{1}{2}.$$

The signs representing equality ($=$) and inequality ($>$ or $<$) may also be written together. The sign $\geq$ represents "is equal to or greater than," and the sign $\leq$ represents "is equal to or less than." Thus,

$$X \geq 20 \text{ means that } X \text{ is equal to 20 or is greater than 20, and}$$
$$Y \leq 30 \text{ means that } Y \text{ is equal to 30 or is less than 30.}$$

Note that the $=$ part of a combined sign indicates the limit of the inequality, such as 20 being the lower limit of the inequality $X \geq 20$ and 30 being the upper limit of the inequality $Y \leq 30$.

Inequalities may be presented graphically according to the system of rectangular coordinates.

**Example 1**     Graph each of the following statements:

(a) $X \geq 0$,          (b) $Y \geq 0$,          (c) $3X + Y \leq 15$, and
(d) $2X + 4Y \leq 20$.

The four graphs are shown in Figure 5–2. Note the following:

(a) The graph of $X=0$ is the set of points on the $Y$-axis. The graph of $X>0$ is the set of points on the right side of the $Y$-axis. The graph of $X = 0$ and $X > 0$, or $X \geq 0$ is shown by the shaded area on graph (a) of the chart. *Check:* Point $K$ (in the shaded area) has $X = 3$ and $X > 0$.

(b) The graph of $Y = 0$ is the set of points on the $X$-axis. The graph of $Y > 0$ is the set of points above the $X$-axis. The graph of $Y = 0$ and $Y > 0$, or $Y \geq 0$ is shown by the shaded area on graph (b). *Check:* Point $K$ has $Y = 2$ and $Y > 0$.

(c) The graph of equation $3X + Y = 15$ is determined by the points representing the following three pairs of $X$ and $Y$ values:

| X | Y |
|---|---|
| 0 | 15 |
| 5 | 0 |
| 2 | 9 |

The three points are on a straight line as shown on graph (c). The two points representing ($X = 0$, $Y = 15$) and ($X = 5$, $Y = 0$) are called *terminal points*.

The graph of the inequality $3X + Y < 15$ is the set of the points below the straight line as indicated by the shaded area on graph (c). *Check:* Point $K$ on the graph has $X = 2$ and $Y = 4$. $3X + Y = 3(2) + 4 = 10$, which is smaller than 15.

**Figure 5–2**                    **(Example 1)**

(a) $X \geq 0$

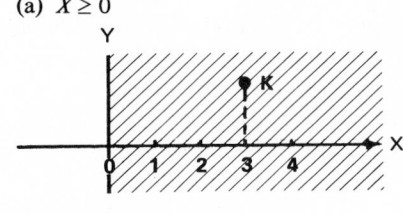

(b) $Y \geq 0$

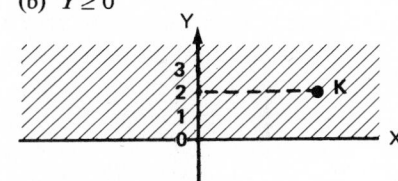

(c) $3X + Y \leq 15$

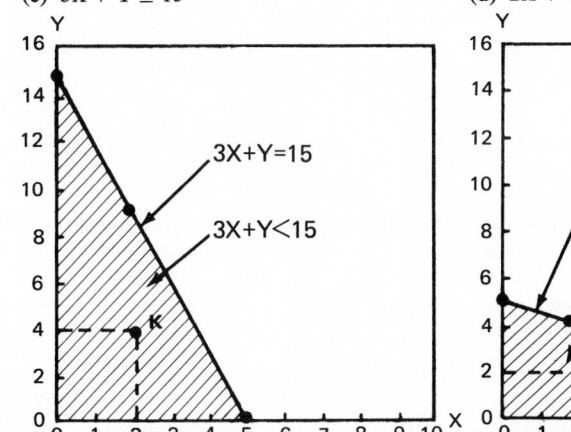

(d) $2X + 4Y \leq 20$

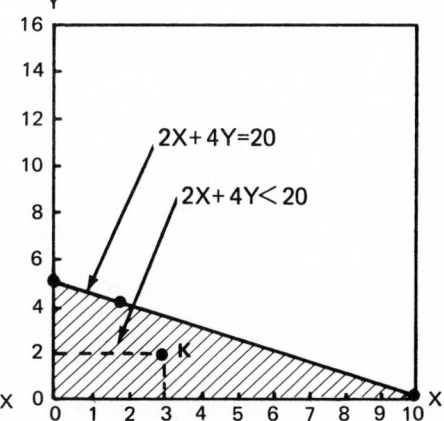

(d) The graph of equation $2X + 4Y = 20$ is determined by the points representing the following three pairs of $X$ and $Y$ values:

| $X$ | $Y$ |
|---|---|
| 0 | 5 |
| 10 | 0 |
| 2 | 4 |

The three points are on a straight line as shown on the graph (d). The two terminal points represent ($X = 0$, $Y = 5$) and ($X = 10$, $Y = 0$). The graph of the inequality $2X + 4Y < 20$ is the set of the points below the straight line as indicated by the shaded area on graph (d). *Check:* Point $K$ in the graph has $X = 3$ and $Y = 2$. $2X + 4Y = 2(3) + 4(2) = 14$, which is smaller than 20.

# B. Linear Programming

Linear programming is a mathematical technique for finding the best or *optimum* solution from a set of possible solutions to a given problem. It can be used to solve various complicated business problems, such as maximizing profits and minimizing costs. The basic steps for solving a problem by the linear programming technique are:

1. Derive a group of linear equations and inequalities under certain restraining conditions given by the problem.
2. Solve the group of linear equations and inequalities for an optimum solution.

There are various methods for solving a group of linear equations and inequalities in linear programming. The simplex method, which is derived by the use of matrix algebra, is commonly used. The chief advantage of the simplex method is that its systematic steps in computation can be programmed conveniently on an electronic computer to solve very complicated problems. To illustrate the detailed steps of the simplex method is beyond the scope of this text. We shall use only the graphic method in introducing the basic concept of linear programming techniques.

Note that the example illustrated below involves only two variables ($X$ and $Y$). Two variables can easily be shown on a two-dimensional space (Figure 5–3). Drawing a three-dimensional space is more difficult but is occasionally used with the graphic method. However, the graphic method becomes impracticable when a linear programming problem involves more than three variables.

**Example 2**    A toy factory is planning to produce two types of toys: boats and cars. Each boat requires 3 hours on machine I and 2 hours on machine II. Each car requires 1 hour on machine I and 4 hours on machine II. Machine I has a maximum of 15 hours available. Machine II has a maximum of 20 hours available.

The profit on each boat is $7. The profit on each car is $9.
Determine the best combination of boats and cars that should be produced in order to maximize profit.

**Figure 5–3**                    **(Example 2)**

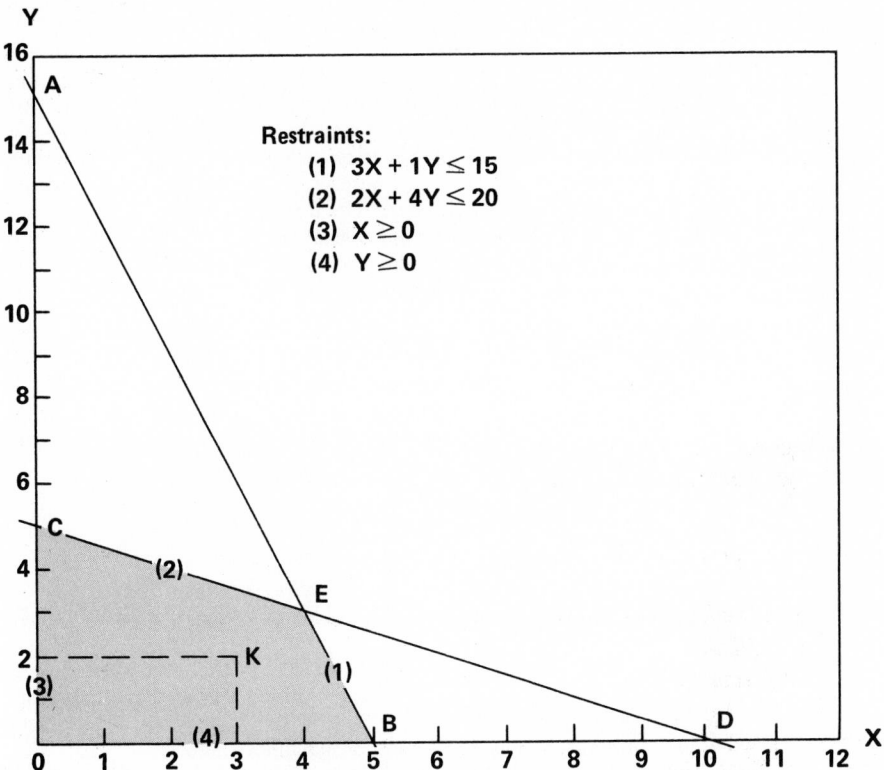

Restraints:
(1) $3X + 1Y \leq 15$
(2) $2X + 4Y \leq 20$
(3) $X \geq 0$
(4) $Y \geq 0$

Let $X$ = the number of boats to be produced, and
$Y$ = the number of cars to be produced.

Then, the equation representing the objective of our study, called the *objective function,* is:

Maximize the profit: Profit = $7X + $9Y.
                    ($X$ boats at $7 each and $Y$ cars at $9 each)

The inequalities based on the restraining conditions, called *restraints,* are:

Restraint on machine I—

(1) $3X + 1Y \leq 15$   (Each boat requires 3 hours on the machine and each car requires 1 hour on the machine. The total number of hours on the machine should be equal to or less than 15 hours.

Restraint on machine II—

(2) $2X + 4Y \leq 20$   (Each boat requires 2 hours on the machine and each car requires 4 hours on the machine. The total number of hours on the machine should be equal to or less than 20 hours.)

Other restraints—

(3) $X \geq 0$, and        (The values of $X$ and $Y$ must be positive. We cannot
(4) $Y \geq 0$.            produce a negative number of boats or cars.)

The four straight lines, (1) $AB$, (2) $CD$, (3) $Y$-axis, and (4) $X$-axis, representing the four equations of the above restraints respectively are plotted in Figure 5–3. Lines $AB$ and $CD$ may be determined by finding the two terminal points for each equation represented. Details concerning the construction of the four lines were presented in Example 1. Observe the four straight lines on the chart. The lines form a four-sided polygon, *OCEB*, the shaded area. The polygon also represents the four inequalities stated above. Any point within the polygon will satisfy the four restraints and thus is a possible solution.

However, our problem is to maximize the objective function, the profit. Thus, we should select a point in the shaded area that will give the highest profit. This point must be located on an extreme far position of the polygon. There are four extreme points on the polygon: *O, C, E,* and *B*. The profits based on the four points are computed from the profit equation as follows:

Objective function:   Profit $= \$7X + \$9Y$.
Point *O*—$X = 0$ and $Y = 0$:   Profit $= \$7(0) + \$9(0) = \$\ 0$.
Point *C*—$X = 0$ and $Y = 5$:   Profit $= \$7(0) + \$9(5) = \$45$.
Point *E*—$X = 4$ and $Y = 3$:   Profit $= \$7(4) + \$9(3) = \$55$.
Point *B*—$X = 5$ and $Y = 0$:   Profit $= \$7(5) + \$9(0) = \$35$.

Point *E*, which gives the highest profit ($55), is the optimum solution, or the best solution from all possible solutions indicated by the points in the shaded area. Thus, the toy factory should produce 4 boats and 3 cars by using the available hours of machines I and II.

*Check:*     The four restraints are satisfied by the optimum solution $X = 4$ and $Y = 3$ since

(1) $3X + Y = 3(4) + 1(3) = 15$    (hours available on machine I).
(2) $2X + 4Y = 2(4) + 4(3) = 20$    (hours available on machine II).
(3) $X = 4$, which is larger than 0.
(4) $Y = 3$, which is larger than 0.

Also,
select any point in the shaded area, say point *K*, which has $X = 3$ and $Y = 2$. Substitute the $X$ and $Y$ values in the profit equation:

Profit $= \$7(3) + \$9(2) = \$39$, which is smaller than the profit based on the optimum solution.

It is possible to have more than one optimum solution. This fact is illustrated in the example below.

**Example 3**    Refer to Example 2. Find the answer if the profit of each boat is $18 and that of each car is $6.

Here, the objective function is to maximize: Profit $= \$18X + \$6Y$.

The profits based on the four points in Figure 5–3 are computed from the new profit equation as follows:

$$\begin{array}{ll}
\text{Objective function:} & \text{Profit} = \$18X + \$6Y. \\
\text{Point } O\text{---}X = 0 \text{ and } Y = 0: & \text{Profit} = \$18(0) + \$6(0) = \$0. \\
\text{Point } C\text{---}X = 0 \text{ and } Y = 5: & \text{Profit} = \$18(0) + \$6(5) = \$30. \\
\text{Point } E\text{---}X = 4 \text{ and } Y = 3: & \text{Profit} = \$18(4) + \$6(3) = \$90. \\
\hline
\text{Point } B\text{---}X = 5 \text{ and } Y = 0: & \text{Profit} = \$18(5) + \$6(0) = \$90.
\end{array}$$

Thus, the toy factory may produce either 4 boats and 3 cars (indicated by point $E$) or 5 boats and 0 cars (indicated by point $B$) to realize the highest profit, $90.

Note that when two points give the same maximized profit, the line formed by the two points is the optimum solution. That is, any point on line $EB$ indicates a combination of the number of boats and the number of cars that may be produced to obtain the maximized profit of $90 under the conditions given in Example 3.

# EXERCISE 5–5

## Reference: Section 5.6

**1.** Graph each of the following statements: (Shade areas representing the statements.)

(a) $X \geq 4$, (b) $Y \geq 5$, (c) $4Y + 3X \leq 12$, (d) $5Y + 2X \leq 10$.

**2.** Graph each of the following statements: (Shade areas representing the statements.)

(a) $X \leq 2$, (b) $Y \leq 6$, (c) $4Y + 5X \geq 20$, (d) $2Y + X \geq 6$.

**3.** Restraints:

$$\begin{aligned}
X + Y &\leq 7, \\
2X + 5Y &\leq 20, \\
X &\geq 0, \\
Y &\geq 0.
\end{aligned}$$

Use the graphic method to find the values of $X$ and $Y$ which maximize the objective function $F$:

(a) $F = 3X + 8Y$, and
(b) $F = 3X + 4Y$.

**4.** Refer to Problem 3. Find the answers if (a) $F = 10X + 8Y$, and
(b) $F = 7X + 7Y$.

**5.** Restraints:

$$\begin{aligned}
X + \tfrac{1}{2}Y &\leq 6, \\
2X + 3Y &\leq 24, \\
X &\geq 0, \\
Y &\geq 0.
\end{aligned}$$

Use the graphic method to find the values of $X$ and $Y$ which maximize the objective function $F$:

(a) $F = 8X + 7Y$, and
(b) $F = 16X + 6Y$.

**6.** Refer to Problem 5. Find the answers if (a) $F = 8X + 16Y$, and
(b) $F = 8X + 4Y$.

**7.** Smith Company makes chairs and tables among other products. The company can realize a profit of $5 on each chair and $10 on each table. Each chair requires 1 hour on the machine and 2 hours of skilled labor. Each table requires 3 hours on the machine and 1 hour of skilled labor. The company has a maximum of 9 hours on the machine available and a maximum of 8 hours of skilled labor available. Determine the units of chairs and tables that should be produced in order to maximize profit. Use the graphic method.

**8.** Find the answer to Problem 7 if the company can realize a profit of

(a) $5 on each chair and $15 on each table, and

(b) $5 on each chair and $20 on each table.

## 5.7  BINARY NUMBER SYSTEM

The number systems discussed in this section concern the methods of expressing numbers. A number system usually has a *base*. The base may consist of any fixed number of symbols, such as two *(binary system)*, ten *(decimal system)*, and twelve *(duodecimal system)*.

The decimal system is by far the most popular one among the various number systems. Perhaps the popularity is mainly due to the fact that human beings have ten fingers. It is rather convenient for a person to count by tens. The ten symbols used in the decimal system are Arabic figures or digits 0, 1, 2, 3, 4, 5, 6, 7, 8, and 9. The decimal system was used in the previous sections and also will be used in illustrations of later chapters throughout this text.

Among other number systems, the binary system is more frequently mentioned in many areas during the recent years. The binary system uses the two symbols 0 and 1. This system can be used conveniently to represent data within modern high-speed electronic computers, although other number systems may also be used. Data within a computer are indicated by electronic signals in two possible conditions, *on* (or the presence of the electrical pulse) and *off* (or the absence of the electrical pulse). This is the same principle as turning an electric light bulb on or off. We may assign the symbol 1 to indicate *on* and the symbol 0 to indicate *off.*

After a base is selected for a system, the principle of place value is usually employed in expressing numbers larger and smaller than the values of basic symbols. The *principle of place value* is that the value of a symbol varies according to its location in a number. In the decimal system, the value of any digit is *ten* times the value of a *like* digit placed in a position immediately to its right. For example, the value of 9 in the three-digit number 900 is ten times the value of 9 in the two-digit number 90.

Table 5–4 further illustrates the place values of basic symbols in the decimal system.

Note that whole numbers are separated from decimal fractions by a decimal point. For convenience in reading large numbers, the digits are usually divided by commas or by extra spaces into groups of three to the left of the decimal point. The number 8,267,943.21 should be read as "eight million, two hundred sixty-seven thousand, nine hundred forty-three, *and* twenty-one hundredths."

**Table 5–4    ILLUSTRATION OF PLACE VALUE IN DECIMAL SYSTEM (BASE 10)**

| Place Value | $10^6 =$ 1,000,000 | $10^5 =$ 100,000 | $10^4 =$ 10,000 | $10^3 =$ 1,000 | $10^2 =$ 100 | $10^1 =$ 10 | $10^0 =$ 1 * | $\frac{1}{10} =$ .1 | $\frac{1}{100} =$ .01 |
|---|---|---|---|---|---|---|---|---|---|
| Value of Each Digit | millions | hundred thousands | ten thousands | thousands | hundreds | tens | ones | tenths | hundredths |
| | 8, | 2 | 6 | 7, | 9 | 4 | 3 . | 2 | 1 |

* By definition any number raised to zero power is equal to 1 (see page 34).

In the binary system the principle of place value means that the value of the digit 1 is *two* times the value of the like digit placed in a position immediately to its right. For example, the value of 1 in the three-digit number 100 (equivalent to $1 \times 2^2 + 0 \times 2^1 + 0 \times 2^0 = 4$ with base 10) is two times the value of 1 in the two-digit number 10 (equivalent to $1 \times 2^1 + 0 \times 2^0 = 2$ with base 10). With the understanding of the principle of place value, a binary number can easily be changed to its equivalent decimal number, and vice versa. Also the fundamental arithmetic operations for binary numbers can be performed in a manner similar to those for decimal numbers.

# A. Changing a Binary Number to Its Equivalent Decimal Number

A number with base 2 (a binary number) may be changed to its equivalent number with base 10 (a decimal number) by adding the place values of individual digits of the binary number. The steps of the change are illustrated in Example 1 below.

**Example 1**    Change the number 1010111.11 with base 2 to its equivalent number with base 10.

The place value of each digit of the given binary number is listed in Table 5–5:

**Table 5–5    ILLUSTRATION OF PLACE VALUE IN BINARY SYSTEM (BASE 2)**

| Place Value | $2^6 =$ 64 | $2^5 =$ 32 | $2^4 =$ 16 | $2^3 =$ 8 | $2^2 =$ 4 | $2^1 =$ 2 | $2^0 =$ 1 | $2^{-1} =$ $\frac{1}{2} = .5$ | $2^{-2} =$ $\frac{1}{2^2} = .25$ |
|---|---|---|---|---|---|---|---|---|---|
| Binary Digit | 1 | 0 | 1 | 0 | 1 | 1 | 1 . | 1 | 1 |
| Value of Each Digit | 64 | 0 | 16 | 0 | 4 | 2 | 1 | .5 | .25 |

Since $64 + 0 + 16 + 0 + 4 + 2 + 1 + .5 + .25 = 87.75$, the number 1010111.11 with base 2 is equivalent to the number 87.75 with base 10.

# B. Changing a Decimal Number to Its Equivalent Binary Number

A number with base 10 may be changed to its equivalent number with base 2 by reversing the steps illustrated in Example 1 above.

**Example 2**    Change the number 53 with base 10 to its equivalent number with base 2.

First, subtract successively the place values as listed in the first row of the table in Example 1 from the given number 53 until the remainder is zero:

$$
\begin{array}{r}
53 \\
-32 \\
\hline
21 \\
-16 \\
\hline
5 \\
-\ 4 \\
\hline
1 \\
-\ 1 \\
\hline
0
\end{array}
$$

Observe that the first place value 32 in the subtraction is the largest number that is smaller than the given number 53. Also, since the remainder after subtracting 16 is only 5 and that after subtracting 4 is only 1, the place values 8 and 2 are omitted respectively in the successive subtractions.

Next, write 1's under the place values used in the subtractions and 0's under the place values omitted as follows:

| Place value  | 32 | 16 | 8 | 4 | 2 | 1 |
|--------------|----|----|---|---|---|---|
| Binary figure | 1  | 1  | 0 | 1 | 0 | 1 |

Thus, the number 53 with base 10 is equivalent to the number 110101 with base 2.

Table 5–6 shows 0 to 16 with base 10 and their equivalent numbers with base 2 for the purpose of further comparison of the two systems:

**Table 5–6**    **DECIMAL NUMBERS 0 TO 16 AS COMPARED TO EQUIVALENT BINARY NUMBERS**

| Decimal Numbers (Base 10) | Binary Numbers (Base 2) | Decimal Numbers (Base 10) | Binary Numbers (Base 2) |
|---------------------------|-------------------------|---------------------------|-------------------------|
| 0                         | 0                       | 9                         | 1001                    |
| 1                         | 1                       | 10                        | 1010                    |
| $2\,(=2^1)$               | $10\,(=10^1)$           | 11                        | 1011                    |
| 3                         | 11                      | 12                        | 1100                    |
| $4\,(=2^2)$               | $100\,(=10^2)$          | 13                        | 1101                    |
| 5                         | 101                     | 14                        | 1110                    |
| 6                         | 110                     | 15                        | 1111                    |
| 7                         | 111                     | $16\,(=2^4)$              | $10000\,(=10^4)$        |
| $8\,(=2^3)$               | $1000\,(=10^3)$         |                           |                         |

# C. Performing Fundamental Arithmetic Operations

The methods of performing the four fundamental operations—addition, subtraction, multiplication, and division—in the binary system are basically the same as those in the decimal system. However, we should remember that the binary system has only two digits, 0 and 1. Keep the place value of the binary digits in mind as you look at the examples below.

**Example 3**   Addition.

(a) $\underline{\text{Base 2}}$ $\qquad$ $\underline{\text{Base 10}}$

$$\begin{array}{r} 1 \\ +\ 1 \\ \hline 10 \end{array} = \begin{array}{r} 1 \\ +1 \\ \hline 2 \end{array}$$

(b) $\underline{\text{Base 2}}$ $\qquad$ $\underline{\text{Base 10}}$

$$\begin{array}{r} 1011 = \\ +\ \ 110 = \\ \hline 10001 = \end{array} \begin{array}{r} 8+0+2+1 = 11 \\ 4+2+0 = \ \ 6 \\ \hline 16+0+0+0+1 = 17 \end{array}$$

Detailed steps for the addition with base 2 of (b), adding columns from right to left, are:

$$\begin{array}{r} 1011 \\ +\ \ 110 \end{array}$$

$$\begin{array}{ll} 1 = 1+0 & \text{(add 1st column)} \\ 10\ = 1+1 & \text{(add 2nd column)} \\ 1\ = 0+1 & \text{(add 3rd column)} \\ 1\ = 1 & \text{(add 4th column)} \\ \hline 01 \\ 10 \\ 1 \\ \hline 10001 \end{array}$$

**Example 4**   Subtraction.

(a) $\underline{\text{Base 2}}$ $\qquad$ $\underline{\text{Base 10}}$

$$\begin{array}{r} 1000 = \\ -\ \ 11 = \\ \hline 101 = \end{array} \begin{array}{r} 8+0+0+0 = 8 \\ 2+1 = 3 \\ \hline 4+0+1 = 5 \end{array}$$

(b) $\underline{\text{Base 2}}$ $\qquad\qquad$ $\underline{\text{Base 10}}$

$$\begin{array}{r} 110111 = \\ -\ \ 1101 = \\ \hline 101010 = \end{array} \begin{array}{r} 32+16+0+4+2+1 = 55 \\ 8+4+0+1 = 13 \\ \hline 32+\ \ 0+8+0+2+0 = 42 \end{array}$$

Detailed steps for each subtraction with base 2 may be illustrated in two ways:

(1) *Borrowing Method.* This method may be used when 1 is subtracted from 0 in a column. Since 0 is smaller than 1, the value in a higher place-value column must be borrowed for the subtraction. The borrowing process can be done in two steps:

First, move to the left of the given 0 in the minuend until finding a 1.

Second, change the found 1 to 0, each 0 (if any) between the found 1 and the given 0 to 1, and the given 0 to 10 (two).

The detailed steps for (a) and (b) are thus as follows:

(a) $\quad$ 0 1 1 10

$$\begin{array}{r} \not{1}\,\not{0}\,\not{0}\,\not{0} \quad \text{(Minuend)} \\ -\qquad 1\ 1 \quad \text{(Subtrahend)} \\ \hline 1\ 0\ 1 \quad \text{(Remainder)} \end{array}$$

(b) $\quad$ 0 10

$$\begin{array}{r} 1\,\not{1}\,\not{0}\,1\ 1\ 1 \quad \text{(Minuend)} \\ -\qquad 1\ 1\ 0\ 1 \quad \text{(Subtrahend)} \\ \hline 1\ 0\ \ 1\ 0\ 1\ 0 \quad \text{(Remainder)} \end{array}$$

(2) *Complementing Method.* The complement of a binary number is obtained by replacing each 0 by 1 and each 1 by 0 in the number. Subtraction by the complementing method involves three steps:

First, add zeros to the left of the subtrahend until there are the same number of digits as there are in the minuend and find the complement of the new subtrahend.

Second, add the minuend, the complement of the new subtrahend, and 1.

Third, cancel the 1 in the far-left position of the sum obtained in the second step.

The detailed steps for (a) and (b) by the complementing method are presented below.

(a)    1000 (Minuend)                (b)    110111 (Minuend)
    +  1100 (Complement of                  110010 (Complement of
    _____ subtrahend 0011)               _____ subtrahend 001101)
       10100                                1101001
    +      1                                +      1
    _____                                _____
    $\chi$0101 (Answer: 101)                $\chi$101010 (Answer: 101010)

**Note:**  1. There are 4 digits in the minuend 1000 of (a). The subtrahend 11 is therefore prefixed by two zeros to obtain the 4 digit binary number 0011. There are 6 digits in the minuend 110111 of (b). The subtrahend 1101 is written as the 6 digit binary number 001101.

2. The complementing method is based on the fact that the sum of a binary number, its complement, and 1 is always equal to 1 with as many zeros annexed as there are digits in the binary number, such as

    0011 (a binary number)
 +  1100 (complement of 0011)
    _____
    1111
 +     1
    _____
    10000 (1 with 4 zeros)

Subtraction (a) in Example 4 thus may be written in a more complicated form as shown below:

$$\left.\begin{matrix}1000\\-\ \ 11\end{matrix}\right\} = \left\{\begin{matrix}+\ 1000 & \text{(Minuend)}\\-\ 0011 & \text{(Subtrahend)}\\ & \\ +\ 0011 & \text{(Same as the subtrahend)}\\+\ 1100 & \text{(Complement of 0011)}\\+\quad 1 & \\-10000 & \\ \hline \chi 0101 & \end{matrix}\right.\ \left.\begin{matrix} \\ \\ \end{matrix}\right\} = 0$$

The sum of the two subtrahends ($-0011$ and $+0011$) is zero. Thus, the complicated form may be simplified as the arrangement presented in the complementing method above.

**Example 5**    Multiplication.

The multiplication with base 2 may be arranged for ease in addition as follows:

| Base 2 | Base 10 | |
|---|---|---|
| $1101 =$ | $8+4+0+1=13$ | 1101 |
| $\times\ 111 =$ | $4+2+1=\ \ 7$ | $\times\ 111$ |
| 1101 | 21 | 1101 |
| 1101 | 7 | $+\ 1101$ |
| 1101 | | 100111 |
| $1011011 = 64+0+16+8+0+2+1=\overline{91}$ | | $+\ 1101$ |
| | | 1011011 |

**Example 6**   Division.

(a)

| Base 2 | Base 10 |
|---|---|
| $101 = 4+0+1 = 5$ | |
| $110\overline{)11110}$ | $6\overline{)30}$ |
| $\underline{110}$ | $\underline{30}$ |
| $110$ | |
| $\underline{110}$ | |

(b)

| Base 2 | Base 10 |
|---|---|
| $1101$ | $= 13$ |
| $111\overline{)1011011}$ | $7\overline{)91}$ |
| $\underline{111}$ | $\underline{7}$ |
| $1000$ | $21$ |
| $\underline{111}$ | $\underline{21}$ |
| $111$ | |
| $\underline{111}$ | |

*Check:*

|  | Base 2 | Base 10 |
|---|---|---|
| Dividend | $11110 =$ | $16+8+4+2+0 = 30$ |
| Divisor | $110 =$ | $4+2+0 = 6$ |
| Quotient | $101 =$ | $4+0+1 = 5$ |

*Check:* See Example 5.

# EXERCISE 5–6

## Reference: Section 5.7

**A.** *Convert each of the following numbers with base 2 to its equivalent number with base 10:*

| | | | |
|---|---|---|---|
| **1.** 111 | **4.** 1011 | **7.** 111101 | **10.** 1101101 |
| **2.** 101 | **5.** 10111 | **8.** 101111 | **11.** 11101111 |
| **3.** 1100 | **6.** 11011 | **9.** 1111101 | **12.** 11101110 |

**B.** *Convert each of the following numbers with base 10 to its equivalent number with base 2:*

| | | | |
|---|---|---|---|
| **13.** 12 | **16.** 30 | **19.** 49 | **22.** 263 |
| **14.** 19 | **17.** 42 | **20.** 38 | **23.** 336 |
| **15.** 26 | **18.** 57 | **21.** 125 | **24.** 448 |

**C.** *The following numbers are expressed with base 2. Perform each indicated operation for the numbers (a) with base 2, and (b) after converting them to base 10:*

*Addition*

| | | | |
|---|---|---|---|
| **25.**  10<br>+11 | **27.**  101<br>+100 | **29.**  1110<br>+1011 | **31.**  11001<br>+100111 |
| **26.**  11<br>+ 1 | **28.**  110<br>+111 | **30.**  1101<br>+1011 | **32.** 1101110<br>+110101 |

*Subtraction—Use the borrowing method to compute and the complementing method to check your answers for the numbers with base 2.*

| | | | |
|---|---|---|---|
| **33.**  1001<br>− 11 | **34.**  110<br>−100 | **35.**  1110<br>− 101 | **36.**  1100<br>− 111 |

| | | | |
|---|---|---|---|
| **37.**    111110 <br>    − 10010 | **38.**    101101 <br>    − 11011 | **39.**    1100011 <br>    −1011101 | **40.**    1100000 <br>    − 100010 |

*Multiplication*

| | | | |
|---|---|---|---|
| **41.**    111 <br>    ×110 | **43.**    1100 <br>    ×1010 | **45.**    10100 <br>    × 1010 | **47.**    11111 <br>    × 1100 |
| **42.**    101 <br>    ×101 | **44.**    1101 <br>    ×1001 | **46.**    11011 <br>    × 1101 | **48.**    11111 <br>    × 1001 |

*Division*

**49.** $10\overline{)110}$      **52.** $101\overline{)1111}$      **55.** $110\overline{)111100}$      **57.** $101\overline{)1100100}$

**50.** $11\overline{)110}$      **53.** $111\overline{)100011}$      **56.** $111\overline{)1000110}$      **58.** $10100\overline{)1111000}$

**51.** $11\overline{)1100}$      **54.** $1001\overline{)110110}$

# Part Two

## MATHEMATICS IN BUSINESS MANAGEMENT

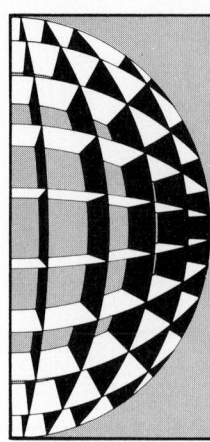

# Chapter 6

# Fundamental Statistical Methods

## 6.1 STATISTICAL DATA AND STATISTICAL METHODS

Numerous quantitative information (or numerical data) can be found in our daily activities. Statistics is developed to deal with the abundant quantitative information. The word *statistics* thus has been broadly referred to as either the information itself or the methods of dealing with the information. However, statisticians prefer to call the quantitative information *statistical data* and the methods of dealing with the information, *statistical methods*. Statistical methods include the techniques used in collecting, organizing, presenting, analyzing, and interpreting statistical data. The techniques not only can be used in business and economic studies but may also be applied in such fields as education, psychology, agriculture, and biology. In this chapter, we shall introduce the following fundamental statistical topics since they are particularly useful in solving business management problems:

1. Presentation of data—Presenting the statistical data tabularly and graphically.

2. Averages—Finding a single value that can be used as a representative value of a series of data.

3. Dispersion—Measuring the deviation from an average of a given series of data.

4. Frequency distribution—Organizing the data into groups in order to facilitate statistical analysis and interpretation.

## 6.2 PRESENTATION OF DATA

The first step in statistical work is to collect data. Not all quantitative information is regarded as statistical data. Statistical data are the numbers that represent some measurable or countable things and show significant relationships. The so-called "statistics" of *a* customer as measured by a tailor are not statistical data since the individual measurements, such as his height, weight, and waist, show no significant relationship to each other. However, information regarding the heights of all the tailor's customers within a certain period of time is statistical since the measurements can be compared, analyzed, and interpreted according to their relationships.

Statistical data may be obtained from various sources, such as government units, corporations, magazines, books or other publications, and firsthand collections. Data collected from sources other than firsthand collections may be in organized or unorganized form. Firsthand collections in the original form usually need organization. The process of a complete organization involves the work of editing, classifying, and tabulating the collected data. Although statistical data can be presented in paragraphs without formal organization, an organized presentation is usually appreciated by most readers. A formal statistical presentation may be in the form of tables or graphs.

## A. Tables

When statistical data are presented in tabulated form, the data are systematically arranged in columns and rows. The major parts of a table are as follows:

1. Title—The title is a description of the contents of the table. It should be compact and complete. When more than one table is presented, each table should be numbered.

2. Headnote—The headnote usually concerns the whole body of the table. It is written below the title.

3. Captions—Captions are the headings of the columns.

4. Stubs—Stubs are the descriptions of the rows.

5. Body—The body is the content of the statistical data.

6. Footnotes—Footnotes are used to clarify certain items or some part of the table. They are placed below the stubs.

7. Source—The source is the place from which the data were obtained. It is usually written below the footnotes. If the data were not collected originally by the one who presents them, the source should be stated to enable the reader to check the data or to obtain additional information from the source.

Table 6–1 is presented as an illustration:

TITLE——→

HEADNOTE————————————→

CAPTIONS

STUBS——→

| Table 6–1 | **SALES OF RETAIL STORES BY KINDS OF BUSINESS, 1970 AND 1977** |
|---|---|

(Billions of Dollars)

| Kinds of Business | Year | |
|---|---|---|
| | 1970 | 1977 * |
| Automotive group................ | 65.0 | 143.9 |
| Furniture and appliance group ..... | 17.8 | 31.8 |
| Lumber, building, hardware group .. | 15.3 | 31.9 |
| Apparel group................... | 19.8 | 28.9 |
| Drug and proprietary stores ....... | 13.4 | 21.6 |
| Eating and drinking places ........ | 29.7 | 58.2 |
| Food group .................... | 86.1 | 152.8 |
| Gasoline service stations ......... | 28.0 | 53.1 |
| General merchandise group ........ | 61.3 | 110.7 |
| Liquor stores ................... | 8.0 | 11.7 |
| All retail stores ** .............. | 375.5 | 710.8 |

}BODY

FOOTNOTE→

*Estimated sales based on the seasonally adjusted sales of June, 1977.
**Total includes lines of trade not shown separately.

SOURCE——→   **Source:** United States Department of Commerce, *Survey of Current Business,* November, 1972, and July, 1977, issues.

# B. Graphs

A *graph* or a *chart* is a pictorial device for presenting certain statistical data or for showing the relationships among several classes of quantities. It is a visual aid to management, policy makers, researchers, and other readers. A person using graphs can acquire certain types of information much more quickly than by studying the figures in tabulated form or reading the same information in paragraph form.

Nearly all types of quantitative data may be expressed in the form of graphs. A graph should be presented in an interesting and effective manner. A well-organized and vivid graphical presentation can help readers acquire much knowledge in a short period of time. However, a graph gives a reader only an approximate value of the facts. If an exact amount is desired, the tabulated figures or the original source of the graph should be consulted.

Generally, graphs are drawn according to a coordinate system (see Section 2.11, page 63). The types of graphs that are most commonly used by statisticians are the line chart, the bar chart, and the component-part chart.

## LINE CHART

A chart that consists of lines or broken lines is called a *line chart*. To construct a line chart, first plot the data by points according to the scales on the two reference lines. Then connect the points by straight lines. The scales used on the two reference lines may or may not be equal. They may be arithmetic or logarithmic. When one line is arithmetic and the other is logarithmic, the chart is called a *semilogarithmic* chart or a *ratio* chart. The logarithmic scale is usually placed on the vertical line in a semilogarithmic chart. A logarithmic scale is rarely used for both reference lines.

On an arithmetic scale, equal distances represent equal amounts. On a logarithmic scale, the distance between two numbers represents the difference between the logarithms of the two numbers; it does not represent the difference between the actual numbers. In other words, equal distances on a logarithmic scale represent the equal ratios of the numbers. Therefore, a logarithmic scale cannot have zero as the origin.

**Example 1**    The amount of the annual net income of the Walton Hardware Store from 1972 to 1980 is listed in Table 6–2. Using these data, construct (a) an arithmetic line chart and (b) a semilogarithmic line chart.

**Table 6–2     NET INCOME OF WALTON HARDWARE STORE, 1972–1980**

| Year | Net Income | Year | Net Income |
|------|-----------|------|-----------|
| 1972 .......... | $ 300 | 1977 .......... | $ 6,800 |
| 1973 .......... | 600 | 1978 .......... | 8,800 |
| 1974 .......... | 1,200 | 1979 .......... | 10,800 |
| 1975 .......... | 2,400 | 1980 .......... | 12,800 |
| 1976 .......... | 4,800 | | |

**Source:**    Hypothetical.
**Solution:**    (a) See Figure 6–1.
             (b) See Figure 6–2.

A semilogarithmic chart can be constructed either by plotting the numbers in a series on a logarithmic scale or by plotting the logarithms of the numbers in a series on an arithmetic scale. The former method is usually preferred since it does not require finding the logarithms, and plotting the numbers on a logarithmic scale is as easy as plotting the numbers on an arithmetic scale. This method has been used in constructing Figure 6–2.

On printed semilogarithmic paper, the value at the top of a cycle on the logarithmic scale is always ten times the value at the bottom of the cycle. Notice the logarithmic scale in Figure 6–2. The value at the top of the first cycle is 2,000 (200 × 10 = 2,000) and the value at the top of the second cycle is 20,000 (2,000 × 10 = 20,000). When the ratio of two numbers is equal to the ratio of two other numbers, the distances between the points representing the numbers are the same. For example, the ratio of 600 to 300 (=2) is the same as the ratio of 1,200 to 600 (=2). Thus, the distance between 600 and 300 is the same as the distance between 1,200 and 600. Further, when the ratio is constant, the points are on a straight line. For example, all the ratios of 4,800 to 2,400, 2,400 to 1,200, 1,200 to 600, and 600 to 300 are 2. Thus, the points representing the net income for the years from 1972 to 1976 are on a straight line when the logarithmic scale is used. This is not true in Figure 6–1 where the arithmetic scale is used.

**Figure 6–1     ARITHMETIC LINE CHART**
**NET INCOME OF WALTON**
**HARDWARE STORE, 1972–1980**

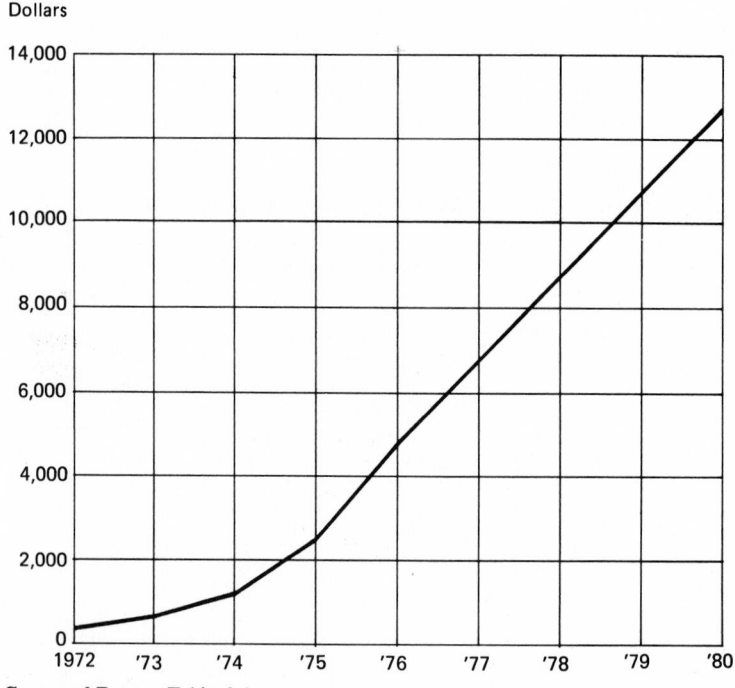

Source of Data:    Table 6–2.

***Note:***    Time is always regarded as the independent variable in time series and is placed on the horizontal reference line.

However, the points for the years 1976, 1977, 1978, 1979, and 1980 are not on a straight line in Figure 6–2, but are on a straight line in Figure 6–1. When a series of numbers increases by a constant *amount* ($2,000 each year from 1976 to 1980 in the present case), the points representing the numbers are on a straight line on an arithmetic scale, such as in Figure 6–1.

**Figure 6–2** **SEMILOGARITHMIC LINE CHART**
**NET INCOME OF WALTON HARDWARE**
**STORE, 1972–1980**

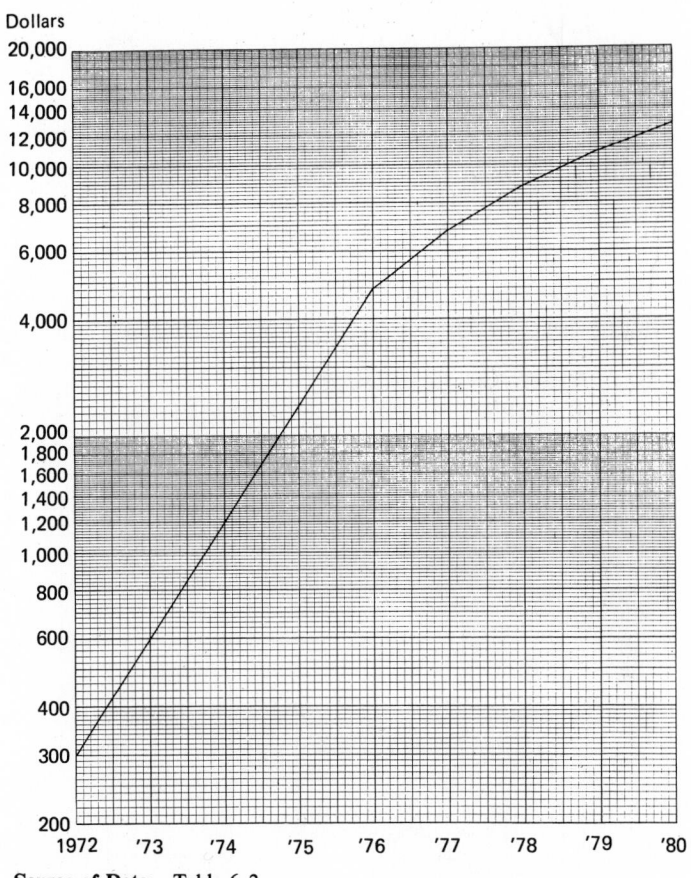

**Source of Data:** Table 6–2.

## BAR CHART

A *bar chart* is a graph that consists of a number of rectangular bars which may be arranged in vertical or horizontal manner. The width of the bars is usually equal. The length of each bar shows the data represented.

**Example 2** The number of houses constructed by Wells Company during each year from 1968 to 1980 is given in Table 6–3. Use the information to draw a vertical bar chart.

Table 6–3    NUMBER OF HOUSES
             CONSTRUCTED BY WELLS
             COMPANY 1968–1980

| Year | Number of Houses |
|------|------------------|
| 1968 ........................... | 250 |
| 1969 ........................... | 266 |
| 1970 ........................... | 278 |
| 1971 ........................... | 288 |
| 1972 ........................... | 290 |
| 1973 ........................... | 298 |
| 1974 ........................... | 308 |
| 1975 ........................... | 316 |
| 1976 ........................... | 323 |
| 1977 ........................... | 334 |
| 1978 ........................... | 346 |
| 1979 ........................... | 359 |
| 1980 ........................... | 372 |

Source:    Hypothetical.
Solution:  See Figure 6–3.

Figure 6–3    VERTICAL BAR CHART
              NUMBER OF HOUSES CONSTRUCTED
              BY WELLS COMPANY 1968–1980

Number
(Millions)

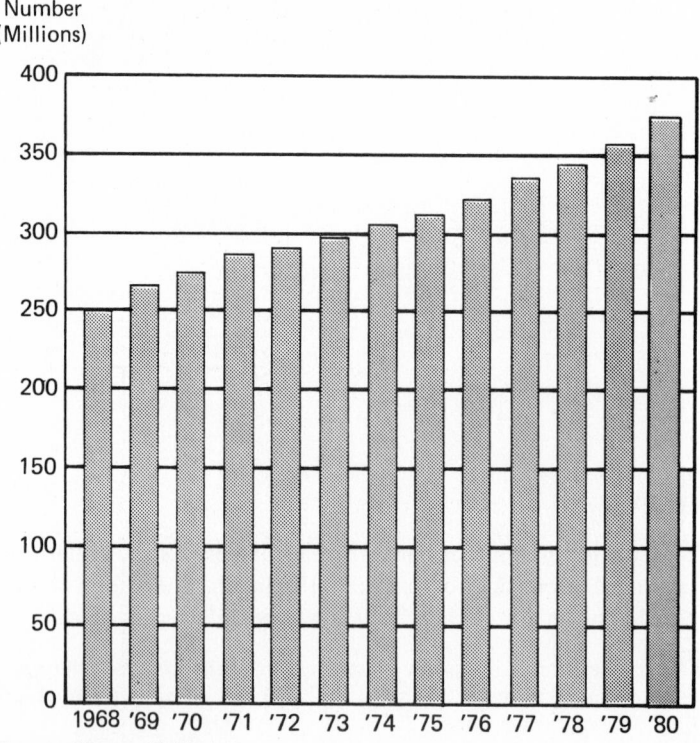

Source of Data:  Table 6–3.

**Example 3**    Use the facts in the following table to draw a horizontal bar chart.

Table 6–4     DENOMINATIONS OF
            CURRENCY IN CIRCULATION,
            OCTOBER 31, 1972

| Denomination | Dollars (Millions) |
|---|---|
| Coin | 7,172 |
| $1 | 2,378 |
| $2 | 135 |
| $5 | 3,209 |
| $10 | 9,334 |
| $20 | 20,857 |
| $50 | 5,570 |
| $100 | 14,503 |
| $500 | 194 |
| $1,000 | 226 |
| $5,000 | 2 |
| $10,000 | 4 |
| Total | 63,584 |

**Source:**    Board of Governors of the Federal Reserve System, *Federal Reserve Bulletin,* December, 1972, p. A-16. (Note: The October, 1978, issue of the *Bulletin* stated that the total currency in circulation is $108 billion. The distribution of the denominations of the total, however, is not available.)

**Solution:**    See Figure 6–4.

Figure 6–4     HORIZONTAL BAR CHART
            DENOMINATIONS OF CURRENCY IN
            CIRCULATION, OCTOBER 31, 1972

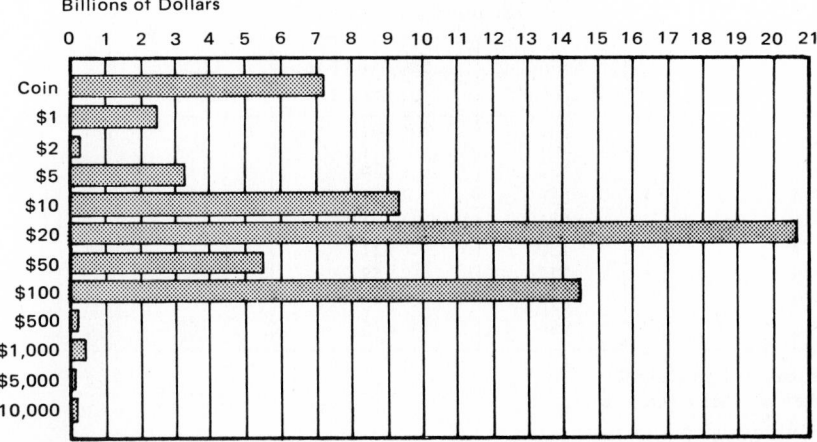

**Source of Data:**    Table 6–4.

## COMPONENT-PART CHART

A *component-part chart* is used to show the relationships among the individual items of a total or of a series of totals. It is frequently constructed by using bars, lines, or segments of a circle (pie diagram). The following three examples illustrate the various ways to construct component-part charts.

**Example 4**    Use the information in Table 6–5 to construct a component-part bar chart showing the number of employees in each educational group for each year.

**Table 6–5    EMPLOYEES IN WAXEN COMPANY BY EDUCATION, 1975 AND 1980**

| Education | Number of Employees | |
|---|---|---|
| | 1975 | 1980 |
| 3 years high school or less..................... | 1,570 | 2,804 |
| 4 years high school.......................... | 2,750 | 3,130 |
| 1 to 3 years college......................... | 1,540 | 2,587 |
| 4 years college or more ...................... | 2,420 | 3,566 |
| Not classified by education ................... | 350 | 403 |
| Total .................................. | 8,630 | 12,490 |

Source:    Hypothetical.
Solution:    See Figure 6–5.

**Example 5**    Use the facts in Table 6–6 to construct a component-part line chart.

**Table 6–6    SELLING, ADMINISTRATIVE, AND OTHER EXPENSES PAID BY JACKSTON COMPANY, 1973–1980**
(Thousands of Dollars)

| Year | Selling Expenses | Administrative Expenses | Other Expenses | Total |
|---|---|---|---|---|
| 1973 ............. | 600 | 252 | 106 | 958 |
| 1974 ............. | 532 | 270 | 118 | 920 |
| 1975 ............. | 589 | 309 | 128 | 1,026 |
| 1976 ............. | 641 | 301 | 141 | 1,083 |
| 1977 ............. | 730 | 321 | 141 | 1,192 |
| 1978 ............. | 773 | 358 | 150 | 1,281 |
| 1979 ............. | 818 | 396 | 161 | 1,375 |
| 1980 ............. | 986 | 416 | 168 | 1,570 |

Source:    Hypothetical.
Solution:    See Figure 6–6.

In Figure 6–5, the length of each part of a bar is made according to the size of each educational group. For example, the part representing 4-year high school employees in 1975 is placed on the scale between 1,570 and 4,320 since 1,570 + 2,750 = 4,320. The individual parts are shaded in different ways to show distinctively the number represented.

**Figure 6–5      COMPONENT-PART BAR CHART
EMPLOYEES IN WAXEN COMPANY
BY EDUCATION, 1975 AND 1980**

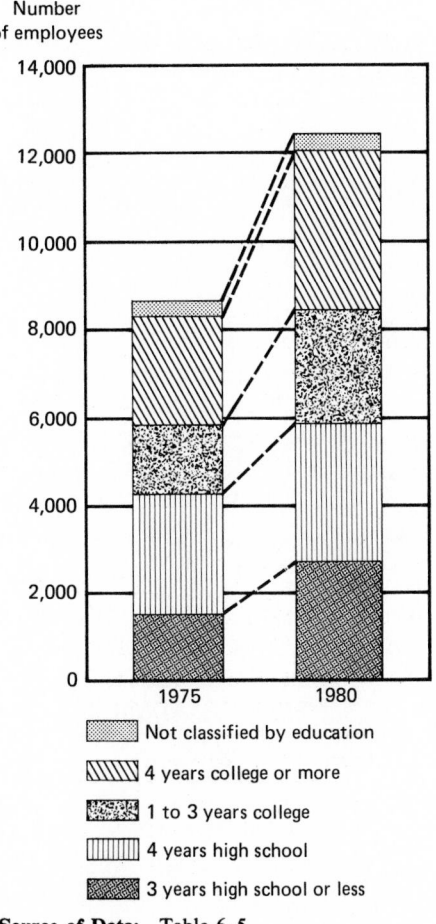

Source of Data: Table 6–5.

Note that in Figure 6–6 the changes in the component parts are again shown by different shades. Figures 6–5 and 6–6 show the actual numbers of each distribution. However, the two types of component-part charts may also be used in showing percent distributions. A total is usually expressed as 100% when a percent distribution is shown.

**Figure 6–6     COMPONENT-PART LINE CHART**
**SELLING, ADMINISTRATIVE, AND OTHER EXPENSES**
**PAID BY JACKSTON COMPANY, 1973–1980**

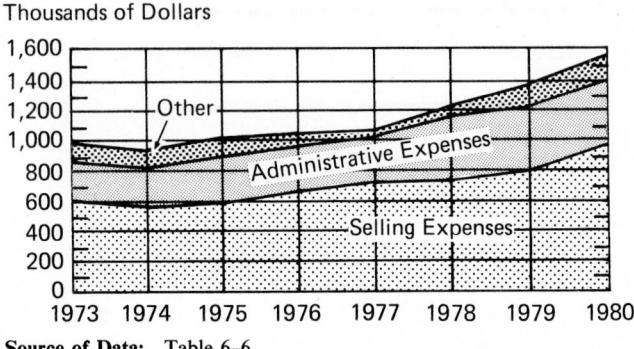

Source of Data:   Table 6–6.

A percent distribution may also be shown by means of a pie chart. A *pie chart* is a circle divided proportionally into component parts according to the sizes of the individual items that make up the total. The circle may be conveniently divided into either 360 degrees or 100 equal parts by means of a printed form or a protractor. However, if a 360-degree protractor is used, the percent distribution should be multiplied by 3.6 before the data are plotted.

**Example 6**     Use the data provided in Table 6–7 to construct a pie chart for the year 1980.

**Table 6–7     PERCENT DISTRIBUTION OF**
**SELLING, ADMINISTRATIVE,**
**AND OTHER EXPENSES PAID**
**BY JACKSTON COMPANY, 1980**

| Types of Payment | 1980 |
|---|---|
| Selling Expenses . . . . . . . . . . . . . . . . . . . . . . . . . . . . . | 62.8% |
| Administrative Expenses . . . . . . . . . . . . . . . . . . . . . . . | 26.5% |
| Other Expenses . . . . . . . . . . . . . . . . . . . . . . . . . . . . . . | 10.7% |
| Total . . . . . . . . . . . . . . . . . . . . . . . . . . . . . . . . . . . | 100.0% |

Source:     Computed from Example 5. For example, 986 ÷ 1,570 = 62.8%, the first figure of the 1980 column.
Solution:   See Figure 6–7.

**Figure 6–7** **PIE CHART**
**PERCENT DISTRIBUTION OF SELLING,**
**ADMINISTRATIVE, AND OTHER EXPENSES**
**PAID BY JACKSTON COMPANY, 1980**

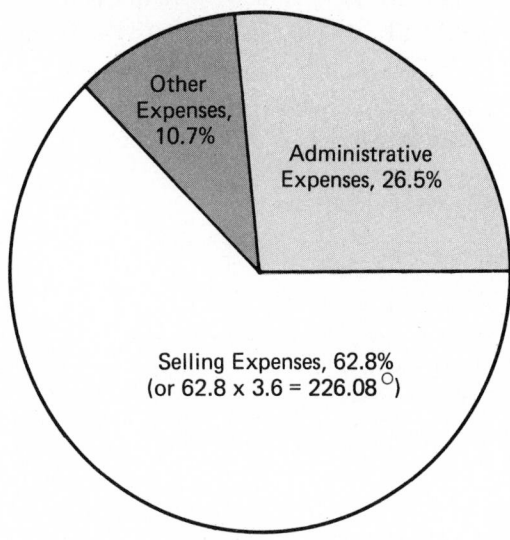

Other
Expenses,
10.7%

Administrative
Expenses, 26.5%

Selling Expenses, 62.8%
(or 62.8 x 3.6 = 226.08°)

**Source of Data:** Table 6–7.

# EXERCISE 6–1

**Reference: Section 6.2**

1. The *Survey of Current Business,* issued by the United States Department of Commerce, contains in the July, 1977, issue the following information concerning national income:

   Compensation of employees amounted to $1,109.9 billion in 1977, $73.6 billion more than the compensation in 1976; proprietors' income rose to $95.1 billion in 1977, $7.1 billion more than the income in 1976; rental income of persons showed $24.5 billion in 1977, $1.2 billion higher than the rent in 1976; corporate profits and inventory valuation adjustment totaled $125.4 billion in 1977, $2.7 billion below the figure of 1976; and net interest advanced to $95.3 billion, up $6.9 billion from the 1976 interest.

   Construct a table showing the above information and the totals of the national income for 1976 and 1977.

2. The *Federal Reserve Bulletin,* issued by the Board of Governors of the Federal Reserve System, has the following facts in the July, 1977, issue concerning personal consumption expenditures:

The total of personal consumption expenditures in the United States was $192.0 billion in 1950, and $1,193.0 billion in 1977. The 1977 total includes the expenditures for durable goods in the amount of $179.1 billion, which is $148.3 billion more than the expenditures in 1950; nondurable goods, $475.3 billion, which is $377.1 billion above the figure in 1950; and services, $538.6 billion, which is $475.6 billion higher than the expenditures for services in 1950.

Construct a table showing the above facts.

3. The number of units shipped by Fox Distributors from 1970 to 1979 are given below. Construct (a) an arithmetic line chart and (b) a semilogarithmic line chart depicting this time series.

| Year | No. of Units | Year | No. of Units |
|------|------|------|------|
| 1970 ......... 3,500 | | 1975 ......... 8,000 | |
| 1971 ......... 4,400 | | 1976 ......... 8,900 | |
| 1972 ......... 5,300 | | 1977 ......... 8,600 | |
| 1973 ......... 6,200 | | 1978 ......... 8,300 | |
| 1974 ......... 7,100 | | 1979 ......... 8,000 | |

4. The total deposits of a bank from 1973 to 1980 are listed in the following table. Construct (a) an arithmetic line chart and (b) a semilogarithmic line chart showing the total deposits for each year.

| Year | Total Deposits | Year | Total Deposits |
|------|------|------|------|
| 1973 ............. | $ 3,600 | 1977 ............. | $20,500 |
| 1974 ............. | 5,800 | 1978 ............. | 12,400 |
| 1975 ............. | 8,200 | 1979 ............. | 9,300 |
| 1976 ............. | 10,900 | 1980 ............. | 18,000 |

5. Use the data in Problem 3 to draw a vertical bar chart.
6. The total number of transactions during a month for each of the four branches of a company is listed below. Draw a horizontal bar chart illustrating these data.

| Branch | Total Transactions |
|------|------|
| East .................... | 2,300 |
| South ................. | 1,900 |
| West ................. | 2,700 |
| North ................. | 1,600 |

7. Use the data given in the following table to construct a component-part bar chart showing the actual amount of stocks of each type for the years 1974 and 1980:

### TYPES OF COMMON STOCKS OWNED BY BAGGE INVESTMENT COMPANY

(Thousands of Dollars)

| Type | 1974 | 1980 |
|------|------|------|
| Railroad ..................... | 39 | 49 |
| Public Utility .................. | 815 | 1,217 |
| Industrial and Miscellaneous ...... | 2,329 | 4,666 |
| Total | 3,183 | 5,932 |

Source:    Hypothetical.

8. Use the information in the following table to construct a component-part line chart showing the actual income of each item for 1974 to 1980.

### GROSS INCOME OF GRIFFIN DEPARTMENT STORE, 1974–1980

(Thousands of Dollars)

| Year | Income from Clothing Department | Income from Shoes Department | Income from Other Department | Total Income |
|------|------|------|------|------|
| 1974 | 324 | 50 | 84 | 458 |
| 1975 | 341 | 51 | 90 | 482 |
| 1976 | 366 | 52 | 100 | 518 |
| 1977 | 394 | 57 | 111 | 562 |
| 1978 | 436 | 59 | 122 | 617 |
| 1979 | 470 | 58 | 122 | 650 |
| 1980 | 498 | 60 | 128 | 686 |

Source:    Hypothetical.

9. Use the data provided in Problem 7 to construct a pie chart for 1980.
10. Refer to the data provided in Problem 8. Compute the percent of total income for each item, and construct: (a) a component-part bar chart showing the percents for the years 1974, 1976, 1978, and 1980; (b) a component-part line chart showing the percents for the years from 1974 to 1980; and (c) a pie chart for the year 1980.

## 6.3 AVERAGES

Since statistical data usually include a large number of items, it is rather difficult for a person to describe simultaneously the characteristics of all items included in the data or to compare one group of data with another. However, if a single value which can be used as the representative value of the given data can be determined, the task of description or comparison becomes simpler.

Statisticians have developed various methods of finding the representative value, called the *average*. Each type of average has its particular characteristics, which should be understood thoroughly before being used under various circumstances. The three types of averages that are most commonly used by statisticians are described in this section. They are: (1) the arithmetic mean, (2) the median, and (3) the mode.

## A. Arithmetic Mean

Of all types of averages, the *arithmetic mean*, generally referred to as the *mean*, has been used most frequently by both statisticians and nonstatisticians. The arithmetic mean of a group of values is obtained by dividing the sum of the values by the number of items in the group, or as expressed:

$$\text{Mean} = \frac{\text{Sum of values}}{\text{Number of items}}$$

**Example 1**   Find the arithmetic mean of the values 3, 4, 8, 2, 5, 8, and 12.

Sum of the values $= 3 + 4 + 8 + 2 + 5 + 8 + 12 = 42$
Number of items $= 7$
Arithmetic mean $= \dfrac{42}{7} = 6$

The chief characteristics of an arithmetic mean are:

1. The mean is rigidly defined by the above expression and it can be treated algebraically. Thus, if any two of the three elements in the expression (mean, sum of values, and number of items) are known, the third one can be determined. For example, if the mean is 6 and the number of items is 7, the sum of the values in the series of data can be determined, or $6 \times 7 = 42$.
2. Every value in the series is taken into consideration in computing the mean. The mean thus obtained lies at the point at which the deviations of the individual values from the mean are in balance. In other words, the sum of the positive deviations is equal to the sum of the negative deviations. The algebraic sum of the deviations is equal to zero.

| Values | Deviations (Values from the Mean 6) |
|:------:|:------:|
| 2 | −4 ⎫ |
| 3 | −3 ⎬ = −10 |
| 4 | −2 |
| 5 | −1 ⎭ |
| 8 | +2 ⎫ |
| 8 | +2 ⎬ = +10 |
| 12 | +6 ⎭ |
| Total | 0 |

**Note:** The deviations are computed as follows:

$2 - 6 = -4$
$3 - 6 = -3$
and so on. (See Example 1)

3. The arithmetic mean is sensitive to the extreme values since the value of each item in the series affects the mean. Thus, the mean becomes less representative of the group of data when the group includes extreme values. For example, the mean of the values 2, 2, 3, 4, and 89 is 20, or $(2 + 2 + 3 + 4 + 89)/5 = 20$. It is obvious that the mean does not represent very well any one of the five values.

## B. Median

The *median* of a group of values is the middle item when the values are arranged according to their magnitude. The number of items above the median is the same as the number of items below the median. If there is an even number of items, the median is the mid-point of the two central items.

**Example 2**    Find the median of the values 3, 4, 8, 2, 5, 8, and 12.

The values in the series are first arranged in order according to their magnitudes.

2
3
4
5 (median) The median is 5 since it is the middle item in the orderly
8            arrangement. There are three items (2, 3, 4) above 5 and
8            three items (8, 8, 12) below 5.
12

**Example 3**    Find the median of the values 3, 4, 6, 8, 9, and 10.

The given values are already in the proper order. The median is the mid-point of the two central items 6 and 8, or

$$\text{Median} = \frac{6 + 8}{2} = 7$$

The chief characteristics of a median are:

1. The median is determined according to position. It is not defined algebraically as is the arithmetic mean. For example, if the median is 5 and the number of items is 7, the sum of the values in the series is not necessarily 35 (or $5 \times 7$). Note that the sum of the values in Example 2 is 42.
2. The median is not affected by the values of other items. However, since the median is centrally located, the absolute sum (disregarding positive and negative signs) of the deviations of the individual values from the median is at a minimum. For example, the absolute sum of the deviations

from median 5 in Example 2 is 19 (see below), whereas the absolute sum of the deviations from mean 6 in Example 1 is 20 (= 10 + 10).

| Values | Deviations (Values from the Median 5) |
|--------|--------------------------------------|
| 2 | 3 (= 2 − 5) |
| 3 | 2 |
| 4 | 1 |
| 5 | 0 |
| 8 | 3 |
| 8 | 3 |
| 12 | 7 |
| Total | 19 (absolute sum, disregarding signs) |

3. Unlike the mean, the median is not sensitive to the extreme values since the median is not computed from all values. For example, the median of the values 2, 2, 3, 4, and 89 is 3. Here the median is more representative of the group of data than the mean, 20.

## C. Mode

The *mode* of a group of values is obtained by finding the value which occurs most frequently in the series. It is the value of greatest density in a given set of data.

**Example 4**    Find the mode of the values 2, 3, 4, 5, 8, 8, and 12.

The mode is 8 since it occurs two times; the other numbers occur only once.

The chief characteristics of a mode are:

1. The mode is determined according to the frequencies of the values in the series. Unlike the mean, it is not defined algebraically. For example, if the mode is 8 and the number of items is 7, the sum of the values in the series is not necessarily 56 (or 7 × 8). Note that the sum of the values in Example 4 is 42.
2. The mode is generally regarded as the most typical value in a series. If an item is selected at random, a modal item is the most likely item to be selected since the modal item occurs more times than any other item. However, frequently, a mode is not determinable. For example, there is no mode in the values 2, 3, 4, and 7 since each value appears only once. On the other hand, in some cases there is more than one mode, such as a series of values 2, 2, 3, 3, 6, and 8, which has two modes.

The arithmetic mean and the median can easily be determined under such circumstances.

3. The mode, unlike the mean, is not sensitive to extreme values since the mode is not computed from all values. For example, the mode of the values 2, 2, 3, 4, and 89 is 2. Here the mode is more representative for the group of data than the mean, 20. However, in this case, the mode is inferior to the median according to the absolute sums of the deviations from the averages as follows:

| Values | Deviations | | |
|:------:|:------:|:------:|:------:|
| | **From Mean (20)** | **From Median (3)** | **From Mode (2)** |
| 2 | 18 | 1 | 0 |
| 2 | 18 | 1 | 0 |
| 3 | 17 | 0 | 1 |
| 4 | 16 | 1 | 2 |
| 89 | 69 | 86 | 87 |
| Absolute Sum | 138 | 89 (smallest) | 90 |

# EXERCISE 6–2

**Reference: Section 6.3**

1. Find (a) the arithmetic mean, (b) the median, and (c) the mode of the following values, which represent the consumption of cigarettes for a group of 9 workers during one week:

   10, 2, 3, 8, 4, 7, 11, 5, 4 (packages)

   Which one of the averages may be regarded as the most representative figure for the given data?

2. What are (a) the arithmetic mean, (b) the median, and (c) the mode of the following values, which represent numbers of visits to a doctor by a group of five families during one month:

   1, 2, 4, 8, 16

   Which one of the averages may be regarded as the most typical number of visits for the group of families?

3. Find (a) the median and (b) the mode of the following values:

   1, 7, 20, 22, 22, 22.

4. What are (a) the median, and (b) the mode of the following values:

   1, 18, 12, 12, 12, 24, 24, 24.

## 6.4 DISPERSION

An average alone cannot give a complete description of the characteristics of the items included in a group of data. More measures are needed for a complete description. For example, the mean of numbers 1, 10, and 19 is 10 or $[(1 + 10 + 19)/3 = 10]$, and the mean of numbers 9, 10, and 11 is also 10 or $[(9 + 10 + 11)/3 = 10]$. Since 10 is not as close to values 1 and 19 as to values 9 and 11, the mean is less representative in the first group of numbers than in the latter group. A very common method for supplementing the usefulness of averages is to find a *measure of dispersion,* which indicates how the items included in the data disperse (deviate or scatter) from the average. When the value of the measure of dispersion is high, the average thus becomes of little or no significance. On the other hand, if the value of the measure is low, the value of the average becomes increasingly significant; that is, the average is a highly representative figure.

A measure of dispersion is commonly expressed in absolute numbers as follows: (1) range, (2) quartile deviation, (3) average deviation, and (4) standard deviation. Although the range and the quartile deviation are not based on an average, they are discussed here because they may also be used as measures of dispersion.

## A. Range

The *range* of a group of data is the difference between the lowest and the highest values. It is easy to compute. Although the range is the simplest measure of dispersion, it has the disadvantage of being based on only two items. Thus, the manner of dispersion of the other items about the central value is ignored.

**Example 1**    Find the range of the following data:   3, 4, 5, 10, and 13.

The highest value is 13, and the lowest value is 3. The range is

$$13 - 3 = 10$$

Notice that the items with values between 3 and 13 have no effect on the range.

## B. Quartile Deviation

To find the *quartile deviation* of a group of data, first divide the items into 4 equal parts according to their values. The first quartile $(Q_1)$ is the point on the scale of value below which there are $\frac{1}{4}$ of the items. The second quartile $(Q_2)$ is the point below or above which there are $\frac{1}{2}$ of the items. Thus, $Q_2$ corresponds to the median. The third quartile $(Q_3)$ is the point below which there are $\frac{3}{4}$ of the items. The distance between the first quartile and the third quartile is called the *interquartile range*. When this distance is divided by 2, the quotient is the quartile deviation *(QD)*, or

$$QD = \frac{Q_3 - Q_1}{2}$$

**Example 2**   Find (a) $Q_1$, (b) $Q_2$, (c) $Q_3$, and (d) $QD$ of the following data:

2, 5, 4, 8, 7, 18, 13, and 11

First, arrange the data in ascending order according to the values.

2
4
$(Q_1) = (4 + 5)/2 = 4.5$
5
7
$(Q_2) = (7 + 8)/2 = 7.5$
8
11
$(Q_3) = (11 + 13)/2 = 12$
13
18

(a) $Q_1$ is defined as the point on the scale of values below which $\frac{1}{4}$ of the items lie. There are 8 items in the group. One fourth of the 8 items is 2 items. The point must be above values 2 and 4 but below 5. Thus, $Q_1$ is determined to be 4.5, the halfway point between 4 and 5.

(b) $Q_2$ = the median, above or below which there must be $\frac{1}{2}$ (or 50%) of the items ($8 \times \frac{1}{2} = 4$). Thus, the value of $Q_2$ must be between the two central values 7 and 8. The halfway point between the two values is 7.5.

(c) $Q_3$ = the point below which there are $\frac{3}{4}$ of the items ($8 \times \frac{3}{4} = 6$). The point must be between the 6th and 7th items, or between values 11 and 13. Thus, $Q_3$ is determined to be 12, the halfway point between 11 and 13.

(d) $QD = \dfrac{Q_3 - Q_1}{2} = \dfrac{12 - 4.5}{2} = 3.75$

Frequently the number of items in a series is not divisible by 4. In such cases, the following rules are generally used in finding the *approximate* values of $Q_1$ and $Q_3$:

1. If the number of items in a series is even, such as 10 or 14 items, $Q_1$ is the median obtained from the lower 50% of the values.
2. If the number of items in a given series is odd, such as 7 items or 9 items, disregard the middle item *($Q_2$)*; then locate $Q_1$ as in rule 1.

The method of locating the value of $Q_3$ is the same as that of $Q_1$ except that the higher 50% of the values in the series is used.

**Example 3**   Find the $QD$ of values in each of the following groups:

(a) 3, 7, 8, 10, 13, 17, 19, 20, 25, and 30;
(b) 1, 3, 4, 6, 8, 11, and 13.

(a) The group has 10 items.

Use rule 1:

$$\text{Lower}\atop{50\%\atop\text{values}}\left\{\begin{matrix}3\\7\\8\text{---}Q_1\\10\\13\end{matrix}\right.$$

$$\text{Upper}\atop{50\%\atop\text{values}}\left\{\begin{matrix}17\\19\\20\text{---}Q_3\\25\\30\end{matrix}\right.$$

$$QD=\frac{20-8}{2}=6.$$

(b) The group has 7 items.

Use rule 2:

$$\text{Lower}\atop{50\%\atop\text{values}}\left\{\begin{matrix}1\\3\text{---}Q_1\\4\end{matrix}\right.$$

Disregarded in →6—$Q_2$
locating $Q_1$ and $Q_3$

$$\text{Upper}\atop{50\%\atop\text{values}}\left\{\begin{matrix}8\\11\text{---}Q_3\\13\end{matrix}\right.$$

$$QD=\frac{11-3}{2}=4.$$

Extending this idea further, a series of data may be divided into 10 groups, thus obtaining a decile; or into 100 groups, thus obtaining a percentile.

## C. Average Deviation

When statisticians wish to consider the effects of all items in measuring the dispersion around the average, they generally use two methods—the average deviation and the standard deviation.

The *average deviation (AD)* is the arithmetic mean of the deviations of the individual items from the average of the given data. The average which is frequently used is either the median or the arithmetic mean. However, only the arithmetic mean will be used here for illustration purposes. In computing the average deviation, the absolute values of the deviations are used; that is, the positive or negative signs of the deviations are ignored.

**Example 4**     Compute the average deviation of each group:

(a) 3, 4, 5, 10, 13.   (b) 1, 2, 4, 13, 15.

(a) The *AD* is 3.6. The following procedure should be used for the computation:

| (1) Items | (2) Deviations (1) − Mean, 7 | (3) Absolute Values of Deviations |
|---|---|---|
| 3 | −4 | 4 |
| 4 | −3 | 3 |
| 5 | −2 | 2 |
| 10 | 3 | 3 |
| 13 | 6 | 6 |
| Total   35 | 0 | 18 |

Mean $=\frac{35}{5}=7$                  $AD=\frac{18}{5}=3.6$

(b) The *AD* is 5.6. It is computed in the following table:

| (1) Items | (2) Deviations, (1) − Mean, 7 (Absolute Values) |
|:---:|:---:|
| 1 | 6 |
| 2 | 5 |
| 4 | 3 |
| 13 | 6 |
| 15 | 8 |
| Total   35 | 28 |

Mean $= \frac{35}{5} = 7$       $AD = \frac{28}{5} = 5.6$

# D. Standard Deviation

The *standard deviation* (commonly represented by the small Greek letter sigma, $\sigma$) is computed in the same manner as the average deviation, except that the signs (either positive or negative) of the individual deviations from the mean are considered. Each type of deviation is squared, and thus all become positive. All the squared numbers are added; then the sum is divided by the number of items included. The standard deviation is then found by taking the square root of that quotient. The standard deviation has a mathematical advantage over the average deviation, although its calculation requires considerably more work than that of the average deviation. The standard deviation is widely used for further statistical analysis. (See the last paragraph in Section 6.5 for an example of the use of a standard deviation.)

**Example 5**   Refer to Example 4. Compute the standard deviation of each group.

(a) The standard deviation is 3.85. It is computed as follows:

| (1) Items | (2) Deviations (1) − Mean, 7 | (3) Squares of (2) |
|:---:|:---:|:---:|
| 3 | −4 | 16 |
| 4 | −3 | 9 |
| 5 | −2 | 4 |
| 10 | 3 | 9 |
| 13 | 6 | 36 |
| Total   35 | 0 | 74 |

Mean $= \frac{35}{5} = 7$    Standard deviation $= \sqrt{\frac{74}{5}} = \sqrt{14.8}$
$= 3.85$

(b) The standard deviation is 5.83. It is computed as follows:

| (1) Items | (2) Deviations (1) − Mean, 7 | (3) Squares of (2) |
|:---:|:---:|:---:|
| 1 | −6 | 36 |
| 2 | −5 | 25 |
| 4 | −3 | 9 |
| 13 | 6 | 36 |
| 15 | 8 | 64 |
| Total    35 | 0 | 170 |

$$\text{Mean} = \tfrac{35}{5} = 7 \qquad \text{Standard deviation} = \sqrt{\tfrac{170}{5}} = \sqrt{34}$$
$$= 5.83$$

Note that the measures of dispersion about the mean are smaller in group (a) than those in group (b) in both Examples 4 and 5, although the means of the two groups (7) are the same. Thus, the mean is regarded as a more representative figure for group (a) than for group (b).

## EXERCISE 6–3

**Reference: Section 6.4**

1. The following numbers are the years of employment for a group of eight drivers at the K. W. Boston Taxicab Co. Find (a) the range and (b) the quartile deviation.

   9, 7, 13, 3, 19, 17, 16, 20.

2. The weight in pounds for eight soldiers is listed below. What are (a) the range and (b) the quartile deviation?

   140, 174, 176, 146, 184, 130, 180, 230.

3. The weekly earnings of a group of nine workers in a manufacturing company are given below. Find the quartile deviation.

   $170, $190, $180, $193, $182, $195, $189, $210, $200.

4. The grade points of 14 students in an English class are as follows:

   75, 78, 74, 80, 73, 84, 60, 85, 65, 90, 62, 92, 100, 70.

   What is the quartile deviation?

5. Refer to Problem 1. Compute (a) the average deviation and (b) the standard deviation.

6. Refer to Problem 2. Compute (a) the average deviation and (b) the standard deviation.

## 6.5 FREQUENCY DISTRIBUTION

When statistical data include a large number of items, the values of the items should be organized in order to facilitate statistical analysis. The values are usually arranged according to ascending order. The data so arranged are called an *array*. Thus, the values 12, 6, 3, 12, 8, 3, 6, 8, 8, and 11 may be arranged as an array: 3, 3, 6, 6, 8, 8, 8, 11, 12, 12. However, in many cases, there are repeating values in an array. If the number of times that a certain value repeats in an array is indicated, the arrangement of the data is shortened by such an indication. This arrangement is known as a *frequency array,* and the number indicating the times a value is repeated is called the *frequency.* Thus, the above illustration may be arranged as a frequency array:

| Value | Frequency |
|:-----:|:---------:|
| 3 | 2 |
| 6 | 2 |
| 8 | 3 |
| 11 | 1 |
| 12 | 2 |
| Total | 10 (items) |

When the values are grouped into several classes and the number of values within each class is indicated in the arrangement, a more compact presentation is provided than otherwise. Such an arrangement showing grouped data is called a *frequency distribution.* The size of the class, called the *class interval,* is preferred to be the same for each class. The number of classes depends upon the number of items to be grouped and the type of information that the arranger wishes to have. Thus, the above illustration may be further grouped into the following frequency distribution:

| Class Interval | Frequency |
|:--------------:|:---------:|
| 1–4 | 2 |
| 5–8 | 5 |
| 9–12 | 3 |
| Total | 10 (items) |

Basically, the procedures of various statistical methods applied to grouped data are the same as those applied to ungrouped data in Sections 6.3 and 6.4.

However, certain details are involved in applying these methods to grouped data. The following example is used to illustrate the methods involved in a frequency distribution in finding the arithmetic mean and two types of deviation from the mean—the average deviation and the standard deviation.

**Example 1**  The hourly wages of 18 workers in a construction company are classified below.

| Wages (Class Interval) | Number of Workers (Frequency) |
|---|---|
| $ 1–3 | 1 |
| 4–6 | 2 |
| 7–9 | 3 |
| 10–12 | 8 |
| 13–15 | 4 |

Find (a) the arithmetic mean, (b) the average deviation, and (c) the standard deviation.

(a) The following table is arranged to find the mean:

| (1) Wages (Class Interval) | (2) Average Wages (Mid-point) | (3) Number of Workers (Class Frequency) | (4) Total Wages (2) × (3) |
|---|---|---|---|
| $ 1–$ 3 | $ 2 | 1 | 2 |
| 4– 6 | 5 | 2 | 10 |
| 7– 9 | 8 | 3 | 24 |
| 10– 12 | 11 | 8 | 88 |
| 13– 15 | 14 | 4 | 56 |
| Total | . . . | 18 | 180 |

$$\text{Mean} = \frac{\text{Total wages}}{\text{Number of workers}} = \frac{180}{18} = \$10$$

The mid-point value of each class is obtained by dividing the sum of the lower limit and the upper limit in the class by 2. The mid-point of each class is assumed to be the average value of the items included in the class and is used as a base for computing the value of the class. For example, in the class $7–$9, the lower limit is $7, the upper limit is $9, and the mid-point is $8 (or $(7 + 9)/2 = 8$). The total wages for the class are $24 (or $8 × 3). The actual values included in the class may vary from $7 to $9. Thus, each of the actual values may lose its identity in a frequency distribution.

(b) The following table is arranged to find the average deviation:

| (1) Wages (Class Interval) | (2) Average Wages (Mid-point) | (3) Number of Workers (Class Frequency) | (4) Deviations from Mean, (2) − 10 | (5) Total Deviations (3) × (4) (Disregard Signs) |
|---|---|---|---|---|
| $ 1–$ 3 | $ 2 | 1 | −8 | 8 |
| 4– 6 | 5 | 2 | −5 | 10 |
| 7– 9 | 8 | 3 | −2 | 6 |
| 10– 12 | 11 | 8 | 1 | 8 |
| 13– 15 | 14 | 4 | 4 | 16 |
| Total | . . . | 18 | . . . | 48 |

$$\text{Average deviation} = \frac{48}{18} = 2.67$$

Again the mid-point of each class is used to represent the value of the class. First, deviation of each mid-point from the mean is found (column (4)). Next, each deviation is multiplied by the class frequency (column (5)). The sum of the products, regardless of positive or negative signs, is then divided by the total number of workers.

(c) The following table is arranged to find the standard deviation:

| (1) Wages (Class Interval) | (2) Average Wages (Mid-point) | (3) Number of Workers (Class Frequency) | (4) Deviations from Mean (2) − 10 | (5) Squares of Deviations (4)$^2$ | (6) Total Squared Deviations (3) × (5) |
|---|---|---|---|---|---|
| $ 1–$ 3 | $ 2 | 1 | −8 | 64 | 64 |
| 4– 6 | 5 | 2 | −5 | 25 | 50 |
| 7– 9 | 8 | 3 | −2 | 4 | 12 |
| 10– 12 | 11 | 8 | 1 | 1 | 8 |
| 13– 15 | 14 | 4 | 4 | 16 | 64 |
| Total | . . . | 18 | . . . | . . . | 198 |

$$\text{Standard deviation} = \sqrt{\frac{198}{18}} = \sqrt{11} = 3.32$$

The method for computing the standard deviation involving a frequency distribution is the same as that used for ungrouped data except that each of the deviations is squared and is multiplied by the class frequency to obtain the total squared deviation for each class (see column (6)). Notice that the first 4 columns above are the same as the first 4 columns in solution (b) for the average deviation. In computing the standard deviation, however, the sign for each deviation is considered.

*Note:*  There are various short-cut methods for computing the arithmetic mean, the average deviation, and the standard deviation. Students may consult any standard statistics textbook for further study.

When the values in a large set are *normally distributed,* the values in the set are expected theoretically to fall within the ranges as follows:

68.268% of the values will be within the mean ± one standard deviation

95.45% of the values will be within the mean ± two standard deviations

99.73% of the values will be within the mean ± three standard deviations

Observe the values in the frequency distribution of Example 1 above that fall within one standard deviation. There are 11 or more items (3 in the class $7–$9, 8 in the class $10–$12, and an undetermined number of items in the class $13–$15) out of the total of 18 items, or 61% (= 11/18) or more of the values in the distribution, within the range:

$10 ± $3.32 = $6.68 to $13.32.

There are 17 items (except the 1 item in the class $1–$3) out of the total of 18 items, or 94% (= 17/18) of the values in the distribution, within the range:

$10 ± 2($3.32) = $3.36 to $16.64.

All of the 18 items, or 100% of the values, are within the range:

$10 ± 3($3.32) = $0.04 to $19.96.

Thus, the values in the set of Example 1 are close to a normal distribution.

# EXERCISE 6–4

**Reference: Section 6.5**

1. From the following frequency distribution table, compute: (a) the arithmetic mean, (b) the average deviation, and (c) the standard deviation.

| Class Interval | Class Frequency |
|:---:|:---:|
| 2–4 | 2 |
| 5–7 | 3 |
| 8–10 | 4 |
| 11–13 | 10 |
| 14–16 | 2 |

2. From the following frequency distribution table, find: (a) the arithmetic mean, (b) the average deviation, and (c) the standard deviation.

| Class Interval | Class Frequency |
|:---:|:---:|
| 1–5 | 1 |
| 6–10 | 3 |
| 11–15 | 5 |
| 16–20 | 5 |
| 21–25 | 3 |
| 26–30 | 1 |

**3.** The amount of sales for 32 transactions in a retail store is given below. What are (a) the average deviation and (b) the standard deviation?

| Sales | Number of Transactions |
|:---:|:---:|
| $2 and under $4 | 1 |
| $4 and under $6 | 4 |
| $6 and under $8 | 6 |
| $8 and under $10 | 9 |
| $10 and under $12 | 8 |
| $12 and under $14 | 3 |
| $14 and under $16 | 1 |
| | 32 |

**4.** The grades of twenty students in a mathematics of finance class are given below:

38  41  45  51  53  57  58  59  61  62
63  65  67  69  70  73  75  81  85  95

(a) Use the following class intervals to construct a frequency distribution table, and compute the standard deviation.

*Class Interval*
*(Grades)*
26–40
41–55
56–70
71–85
86–100

(b) Indicate the number of grades that fall within the range:

(1) the mean ± one standard deviation
(2) the mean ± two standard deviations
(3) the mean ± three standard deviations

What percent of the total number of grades is within each range?

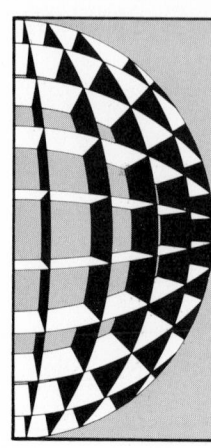

# Chapter 7

## Ratio, Proportion, and Percent

Ratio, proportion, and percent are closely related topics. Those topics are basic for mathematical operations in the numerous types of business problem to be presented in this and the subsequent chapters. Performing the metric system conversion (Section 7.3), for example, requires knowledge of ratio and proportion. Many problems, such as discounts, commissions, taxes, interests, annuities, and insurance premiums, frequently involve percentage operations.

## 7.1 RATIO

### A. Meaning of Ratio

Numbers may be compared in various ways. One convenient way is to express the comparison according to the relative values of the things being compared instead of stating the actual values. For example, in one city there are 220,000 women and 110,000 men. Since $\frac{220,000 \text{ women}}{110,000 \text{ men}} = \frac{2 \text{ women}}{1 \text{ man}}$, it is more convenient to state that the number of women compared with the number of men is 2 to 1, which are relative values, instead of saying 220,000 to 110,000, which are actual values. *Ratio* is a way of expressing the relative values of various things. Thus, the comparison above may also be indicated as: "the ratio of the number of women to the number of men in the city is 2 to 1," which may be written 2 : 1.

Generally, when two numbers are expressed in ratio form, the ratio is the quotient of the two numbers. When a number, called the *first term,* is divided by another number, called the *second term,* the quotient is the ratio of the first term to the second term. This relationship may be written as follows:

Ratio of the first term to the second term = The first term : The second term

$$= \frac{\text{The first term}}{\text{The second term}}.$$

Thus, the ratio of $a$ to $b$ is expressed as $a : b$, or $\frac{a}{b}$, or $a \div b$. The ratio of $b$ to $a$ is expressed as $b : a$, or $\frac{b}{a}$, or $b \div a$. The ratio of 2 to 10 is 2 : 10 or $\frac{2}{10}$; whereas, the ratio of 10 to 2 is 10 : 2, or $\frac{10}{2}$.

Since a ratio may be expressed as a fraction, the rules applying to fractions likewise apply to ratios. For convenience, the fraction may be reduced to its lowest terms. Thus, $\frac{2}{10}$ may be reduced to $\frac{1}{5}$, and the ratio of 2 to 10 is equal to the ratio of 1 to 5, or 2 : 10 = 1 : 5. The quotient of the fraction is sometimes reduced to a decimal or a whole number. The quotient then represents the value of the first term, and the value of the second term is always considered to be 1. In the above examples, the ratio of 2 to 10 may be expressed as .2, which has the same meaning as the ratio of .2 to 1; and the ratio of 10 to 2 may be expressed as 5, which has the same meaning as the ratio of 5 to 1. A ratio of an improper fraction in its lowest terms is usually not reduced to a mixed number.

When more than two relative values are expressed in ratio form, the ratios of the values may be written in separate form or in combined form. For example, assume that the relative values of three things, $A$, $B$, and $C$ are 2, 3, and 4 respectively. If $A = 2$, then $B = 3$, and $C = 4$; if one of them is doubled, then the others are also doubled; if one of them is tripled, then the others are also tripled; and so on. Thus, if $A = 4$ (or $2 \times 2$), then $B = 6$ (or $3 \times 2$), and $C = 8$ (or $4 \times 2$). The relationships may be expressed individually as $A : B = 2 : 3$, $B : C = 3 : 4$, $A : C = 2 : 4$, or written in combined form as follows: $A : B : C = 2 : 3 : 4$, where

$$2 : 3 : 4 = (2 \times 2) : (3 \times 2) : (4 \times 2)$$
$$= (2 \times 3) : (3 \times 3) : (4 \times 3) \text{ and so on, or}$$
$$A : B : C = 2 : 3 : 4 = 4 : 6 : 8 = 6 : 9 : 12 \text{ and so on.}$$

In other words, if each term of the ratio in combined form is multiplied (or divided) by the same number, other than zero, the value of the ratio does not change.

Ratios are important in measurement, for basically every measurement is a ratio. For example, the statement that the length of a desk is 3 yards means that the ratio of the length of the desk to the unit of length used, a yard, is $3 : 1 = \frac{3}{1} = 3$. Here, the answer means that 3 yards are 3 times 1 yard. However, if the unit of length used is a foot, since 3 yards equal 9 feet, the ratio thus is $9 : 1 = \frac{9}{1} = 9$, in which case the length of the desk becomes 9 feet and is 9 times the unit of length used.

To determine the ratio of the length of this desk to a book shelf 18 inches in length, their measurements must be expressed in the *same* unit when dividing.

If the unit of measurement is an inch, the ratio is obtained as follows:

108 (inches) ∶ 18 (inches) = $\frac{108}{18}$ = 6, since 9 feet (the length of the desk) equals 108 inches (or 9 × 12).

If the unit of measurement is a foot, the same answer may be obtained by computing as follows:

9 (feet) ∶ $1\frac{1}{2}$ (feet) = $\dfrac{9}{1\frac{1}{2}}$ = (9)($\frac{2}{3}$) = 6, since 18 inches (the length of the book shelf) equals $1\frac{1}{2}$ feet (or $\frac{18}{12}$ = $1\frac{1}{2}$).

The answer indicates that the length of the desk is 6 times the length of the book shelf. In these examples, the quantities compared are of the same kind, the length. When numbers of the same kind are compared, the ratio is always abstract.

There are also ratios of different kinds of quantities. For example, if a carpenter makes 10 chairs in 5 days, the ratio of the chairs produced to the time consumed is expressed as 10 chairs ∶ 5 days, which may be written $\dfrac{10 \text{ chairs}}{5 \text{ days}}$ = $\dfrac{2 \text{ chairs}}{1 \text{ day}}$ = 2 chairs/day, or simply 2. However, when the number 2 is written, it is understood that the ratio indicates the carpenter's average speed; that is, he can make 2 chairs each day during that time.

# B. Allocation of a Number According to Ratio

To allocate or divide a number into parts according to a ratio, consider the sum of the terms of the ratio as a unit for dividing. For example, if a number is to be divided into parts $A$ and $B$ according to a ratio of 2 ∶ 3 respectively, consider the sum of the terms of the ratio, 5 (or 2 + 3), as a unit for dividing. From each unit, $A$ gets 2 shares and $B$ gets 3 shares. In other words, $A$ gets 2 out of every 5 and $B$ gets 3 out of every 5. If the number to be divided is 100, the value of $A$ is computed as follows:

100 ÷ 5 = 20 (units); 20 × 2 = 40; or it may be written as

100 × $\frac{2}{5}$ = 40.

The value of $B$ is computed as follows:

100 ÷ 5 = 20 (units); 20 × 3 = 60; or it may be written as

100 × $\frac{3}{5}$ = 60.

The value of $B$ may also be computed by subtracting the value of $A$ from the number to be divided; thus, $100 - A = 100 - 40 = 60$. The answer may be checked as follows:

$A ∶ B = 40 ∶ 60 = \frac{40}{60} = \frac{2}{3} = 2 ∶ 3$
$A + B = 40 + 60 = 100$

In general, to allocate or divide a number into parts according to ratio, use the following procedure: To obtain the first part, multiply the number by the fraction whose denominator is the sum of the terms of the ratio and whose numerator is the first term of the ratio. To obtain the second part, use the second term of the ratio as the numerator of the fraction. The following examples further illustrate the problems involved in dividing a number according to ratio.

**Example 1**   Divide 45 into three parts in the ratio 2 : 3 : 4.

$$2 + 3 + 4 = 9$$
$$45 \times \tfrac{2}{9} = 10$$
$$45 \times \tfrac{3}{9} = 15$$
$$45 \times \tfrac{4}{9} = 20$$

The three parts are 10, 15, and 20.

*Check:*   $10 + 15 + 20 = 45$
$10 : 15 : 20 = \tfrac{10}{5} : \tfrac{15}{5} : \tfrac{20}{5} = 2 : 3 : 4$

**Example 2**   \$510 is to be divided among A, B, and C in the ratio of $\tfrac{1}{2}$, $\tfrac{2}{3}$, and $\tfrac{1}{4}$ respectively. How much should each receive?

First, reduce each term of the given ratio to have a common denominator. Here the l.c.d. is 12. If each term of the reduced ratio is multiplied by 12, the value of the ratio does not change. Thus,

$$\tfrac{1}{2} : \tfrac{2}{3} : \tfrac{1}{4} = \tfrac{6}{12} : \tfrac{8}{12} : \tfrac{3}{12} = 6 : 8 : 3$$

According to the ratio 6 : 8 : 3, the amount is divided as follows:

$$6 + 8 + 3 = 17$$
A's share $= 510 \times \tfrac{6}{17} = \$180$
B's share $= 510 \times \tfrac{8}{17} = \$240$
C's share $= 510 \times \tfrac{3}{17} = \$\ 90$

*Check:*   $180 + 240 + 90 = 510$
$180 : 240 : 90 = \tfrac{180}{30} : \tfrac{240}{30} : \tfrac{90}{30} = 6 : 8 : 3$

Thus, to allocate a number in fractional ratio (such as $\tfrac{1}{2} : \tfrac{2}{3} : \tfrac{1}{4}$), reduce the given fractions to fractions with their lowest common denominator ($\tfrac{6}{12} : \tfrac{8}{12} : \tfrac{3}{12}$); then use the numerators (6 : 8 : 3) as the ratio in allocating the number.

## EXERCISE 7–1

### Reference: Section 7.1

**A.** *Express the ratios of the following in fractional form and reduce them to their lowest terms:*

1. 25 to 5
2. 7 to 28
3. 13 to 32
4. 47 to 14

5. $8\tfrac{2}{3}$ to $5\tfrac{1}{4}$
6. $6\tfrac{5}{12}$ to $12\tfrac{5}{6}$
7. 2.45 to 9.13
8. 6.5 to 2.5

9. 80 miles to 4 hours
10. 32 minutes to 8 hours
11. 20 dollars to 5 days
12. 8 ounces to 1 pound

**B.** *Statement Problems:*

13. Company A has current assets of $26,000 and current liabilities of $16,000. Company B has current assets of $40,000 and current liabilities of $30,000. What is the ratio of the current assets to the current liabilities of Company A? of Company B? Which of the two ratios is higher?

14. Last year George's income was $12,000. There were 6 persons in his family. John's income was $16,000. There were 10 persons in his family. (a) Find the ratios of their respective annual income to the size of their families. (b) According to the size of the families, whose income per person was larger?

15. A retail store sold an article for $40. The cost of the article sold is $25, the total amount of other expenses is $5, and the remaining part is the profit. Find the ratios of (a) the cost to the selling price, (b) the total amount of other expenses to the selling price, and (c) the profit to the selling price.

16. Refer to Problem 15. Find the ratios of the following: (a) the total of other expenses to the cost and (b) the profit to the cost.

17. Divide 240 into two numbers in the ratio 1 : 3.

18. Divide 300 into two numbers in the ratio 3 : 5.

19. Divide 648 into three numbers in the ratio 2 : 3 : 7.

20. Divide 680 into three numbers in the ratio 4 : 5 : 8.

21. Divide 1,020 into four numbers in the ratio 2 : 3 : 5 : 7.

22. Divide 720 into four numbers in the ratio 1 : 4 : 5 : 8.

23. Divide 7,688 into three numbers in the ratio $2\frac{3}{4} : \frac{5}{7} : 3\frac{2}{5}$.

24. Divide 2,040 into three numbers in the ratio $\frac{2}{7} : \frac{3}{8} : \frac{1}{4}$.

25. Eleanor divides her estate of $46,200 among her four daughters in the ratio $\frac{1}{2} : \frac{1}{3} : \frac{1}{4} : \frac{1}{5}$. How much does each daughter receive?

26. Four partners, *A, B, C,* and *D,* agree to share profits in the ratio of $\frac{1}{2}$, $\frac{2}{3}$, $\frac{1}{4}$, and $\frac{2}{5}$ respectively. This year the partnership has a profit of $4,360. How much does each partner receive?

## 7.2 PROPORTION

A *proportion* is a statement of the equality of two ratios. For example, $2 : 10 = 1 : 5$, or $\frac{2}{10} = \frac{1}{5}$, is a proportion. Thus, $a : b = c : d$, or $a/b = c/d$, is also a proportion. It is read *"a is to b as c is to d,"* or "the ratio of a to b is equal to the ratio of c to d." The letters *a, b, c,* and *d* are the *terms* of the proportion; *a* and *d* are the *extremes;* *b* and *c* are the *means.*

Since proportions are equations, the rules and operations of equations also apply to proportions. For example, if both sides of the proportion $\frac{a}{b} = \frac{c}{d}$ are multiplied by *bd,* the common denominator, the answer is $\frac{a}{b} \cdot bd = \frac{c}{d} \cdot bd$, or $ad = bc$. The answer indicates that by cross multiplication of the terms in the proportion, the two products are equal. The answer is diagrammed as follows:

$$\frac{a}{b} = \frac{c}{d}; \qquad ad = bc$$

Since the proportion may be written in the form $a : b = c : d$, the answer also indicates that the product of the extremes $(ad)$ equals the product of the means $(bc)$. When any three of the four terms in a proportion are given, the other unknown term can always be found by this relationship. Proportion thus may be used in solving many types of problems in business and is referred to frequently in the forthcoming chapters. The following examples illustrate some uses of proportion in various types of problems.

**Example 1**     Solve for $x$. $13 : 4 = 52 : x$

Multiply the extremes and the means, $13 : 4 = 52 : x$

$$13x = 4 \cdot 52 = 208; \qquad\qquad x = \frac{208}{13} = 16$$

**Example 2**     Solve for $x$. $\dfrac{28}{7} = \dfrac{x}{5}$

Use cross multiplication

$$\frac{28}{7} = \frac{x}{5}; \quad 7x = 28 \cdot 5 = 140; \quad x = \frac{140}{7} = 20$$

**Example 3**     Solve for $x$. $x : \frac{3}{4} = \frac{1}{5} : \frac{9}{11}$

$$\tfrac{9}{11}x = (\tfrac{3}{4})(\tfrac{1}{5}); \quad x = \frac{(\tfrac{3}{4})(\tfrac{1}{5})}{\tfrac{9}{11}} = \frac{\tfrac{3}{20}}{\tfrac{9}{11}}$$

$$= (\tfrac{3}{20})(\tfrac{11}{9}) = \tfrac{11}{60}$$

**Example 4**     A grocery store charges $2.80 for 5 dozen eggs. How much will it charge for 18 dozen eggs?

Let $y$ be the price of 18 dozen eggs. Thus, the problem may be stated in proportional language as follows:

$2.80 is to 5 dozen as $y$ is to 18 dozen eggs, which may be written

$$\frac{2.80}{5 \text{ dozen}} = \frac{y}{18 \text{ dozen}}, \quad \text{or simply,} \quad \frac{2.80}{5} = \frac{y}{18}; \quad 5y = (2.80)(18)$$

$$y = \frac{(2.80)(18)}{5} = \$10.08$$

**Example 5**     When a tree casts a shadow 24 feet long, the shadow of a boy $5\frac{1}{2}$ feet tall is 8 feet long. How high is the tree?

The ratio of the boy's height to his shadow equals the ratio of the tree's height to its shadow. Let $x =$ the height of the tree. Thus,

$$\underset{\text{boy}}{\frac{5\frac{1}{2}}{8}} = \underset{\text{tree}}{\frac{x}{24}}; \quad 8x = (5\frac{1}{2})(24); \quad x = \frac{(5\frac{1}{2})(24)}{8} = 16\frac{1}{2} \text{ (feet)}$$

***Note:***    Two things are frequently related in quantitative variation. When the quantity of one thing varies *as* the quantity of another thing changes, the variation is direct. In *direct variation,* the ratio of one thing to another is constant and their changes are proportional to each other. Examples 4 and 5 are direct variation problems. In Example 4, for instance, the total price for a certain number of dozen of eggs varies with the number of dozen of eggs sold. The total price increases as the number of dozens of eggs increases. However, the ratio of the total price to the corresponding number of dozen of eggs sold is constant:

$$\frac{\$2.80}{5 \text{ dozen}} = \frac{\$10.08}{18 \text{ dozen}} = \$.56 \text{ per dozen}$$

## EXERCISE 7–2

### Reference: Section 7.2

**A.** *Solve for* x *in each of the following proportions:*

**1.** $\dfrac{x}{6} = \dfrac{5}{12}$

**2.** $\dfrac{52}{x} = \dfrac{2}{3}$

**3.** $\dfrac{x}{8} = \dfrac{7}{12}$

**4.** $\dfrac{2}{7} = \dfrac{x}{15}$

**5.** $\dfrac{30}{x} = \dfrac{3}{25}$

**6.** $\dfrac{14.04}{27} = \dfrac{x}{5}$

**7.** $\dfrac{21.35}{21} = \dfrac{30.5}{x}$

**8.** $\dfrac{60}{73} = \dfrac{45}{x}$

**9.** $4 : 14 = x : 7$

**10.** $15 : x = 8 : 32$

**11.** $3 : 15 = x : 32$

**12.** $x : 6 = 9 : 21$

**13.** $19 : x = 30 : 65$

**14.** $\dfrac{5}{4} : \dfrac{6}{7} = \dfrac{5}{6} : x$

**15.** $x : \dfrac{3}{7} = \dfrac{2}{3} : \dfrac{6}{7}$

**16.** $15 : 5 = 9 : x$

**B.** *Solve for* x *in each of the following problems:*

**17.** A car runs 58 miles on 3 gallons of gasoline. How far will it run on 5 gallons?

**18.** A man can plow 15 acres in 4 days. How much time is needed to plow 74 acres?

**19.** If 7 yards of cloth cost $25, what will 21 yards cost?

**20.** If 130 bushels of corn cost $275, what will 220 bushels cost?

**21.** When a building casts a shadow 45 feet long, the shadow of a man 6 feet tall is $3\frac{1}{2}$ feet. Find the height of the building.

**22.** The scale of a map is $1\frac{1}{4}$ inches for 300 miles. How many miles are represented by 5 inches?

**23.** If a seamstress is paid at the rate of $9.00 per dress completed, how much does she receive after completing 12 dresses?

24. The B. B. Candy Store bought 560 boxes of candy at 90¢ a box. How much is the total cost?
25. If a plane travels 20 miles in 16 minutes, how long will it take to travel 125 miles?
26. If a field containing 35 acres yields 1,071 bushels of wheat, how much will a field containing 100 acres yield?
27. If 25 men can build 1,000 cubic feet of brick wall in one day, how many men will be needed to build 2,560 cubic feet of brick wall in one day?
28. If a pile of wood containing 344 cubic feet costs $160, how much will a pile containing 4,730 cubic feet cost?

## ★7.3 THE METRIC SYSTEM

The metric system is a decimal system of weights and measures. A distinct advantage of the metric system over the United States system used today is its simplicity. This advantage plus its popular usage now by most nations leads us to believe that it is only a matter of time before the United States joins the world in using the metric system.

Under the metric system, the name of each unit has a prefix which indicates the value of the unit based on 10. Thus, it is easy to convert between units. Some of the prefixes and their meanings are listed in Table 7–1.

**Table 7–1**　　**SELECTED PREFIXES AND THEIR MEANINGS USED IN THE METRIC SYSTEM**

| Prefix | Meaning |
|---|---|
| Micro | $10^{-6} = \dfrac{1}{1,000,000} = .000001$, one millionth |
| Milli | $10^{-3} = \dfrac{1}{1,000} = .001$, one thousandth |
| Centi | $10^{-2} = \dfrac{1}{100} = .01$, one hundredth |
| Deci | $10^{-1} = \dfrac{1}{10} = .1$, one tenth |
| — | $10^{0} = 1$, the basic unit |
| Deca | $10^{1} = 10$, ten times |
| Hecto | $10^{2} = 100$, one hundred times |
| Kilo | $10^{3} = 1,000$, one thousand times |
| Mega | $10^{6} = 1,000,000$, one million times |

The basic unit of weight is the *gram,* which is equivalent to 0.0353 ounce. Thus, a centigram is 0.01 gram, a decagram is 10 grams, a hectogram is 100 grams, a kilogram is 1,000 grams, and so on. Notice that the ratio of a larger unit to its smaller unit is always 10 to 1.

The same prefixes are used for length, area, volume, and capacity. The basic unit of length is the *meter (m)*. One meter is equivalent to 3.2808 feet (or 39.3701 inches) approximately.

The basic unit of area is the *square meter (m²)*. One square meter is equivalent to 10.7639 square feet. However, in measuring land, the basic unit of the metric system is the *are*. One *are* (= 100 square meters) is equivalent to 0.0247 acre.

The basic unit of volume is the *cubic meter (m³)*. One cubic meter is equivalent to 35.3147 cubic feet.

The *liter (L)* is the basic unit of capacity. A liter is equal to 1,000 cubic centimeters, or a volume with each side being 10 centimeters since $10^3 = 1,000$. Converting to U.S. units, one liter is equivalent to 0.9081 quart for dry capacity, or 1.0567 quart for liquid capacity.

More conversion factors between selected metric units and their corresponding U.S. units are given in Table 7–2. Mathematical operations based on Tables 7–1 and 7–2 are presented below.

## A. Conversion Between Metric Units

To convert one metric unit to another metric unit, first find the relationship between the two units as defined in Table 1. Next, use either the proportional method or move the decimal point to find the answer. In converting a larger unit to a smaller unit, move the decimal point to the right. Conversely, in converting a smaller unit to a larger unit, move the decimal point to the left.

**Example 1**      Convert (a) 2.46 kilograms to grams and (b) 736.5 centimeters to meters.

    (a) 1 kilogram = 1,000 grams (Table 7–1)
        2.46 kilograms = 2.46(1,000)
                  = 2,460 grams, or
        2.46 kilograms = 2.460 grams.

    (b) 1 centimeter = .01 meter (Table 7–1)
        736.5 centimeters = 736.5(.01)
                   = 7.365 meters, or
        736.5 centimeters = 7.36.5 meters.

**Example 2**      Convert (a) 25 meters to millimeters and (b) 36 grams to hectograms.

    (a) 1 millimeter = .001 meter (Table 7–1)
        Thus,

        1 meter = 1,000 millimeters,
        25 meters = 25.000 or 25,000 millimeters.

        Or, let $x$ = unknown converted millimeters.
        Then, by proportional expression,

        $x$ is to 25 meters as 1 millimeter to .001 meter,

$$\frac{x}{1} = \frac{25}{.001}, \qquad x = \frac{25}{.001} = 25,000 \text{ millimeters.}$$

(b) 1 hectogram = 100 grams (Table 7–1)
Thus,

$$1 \text{ gram} = \frac{1}{100} = .01 \text{ hectogram,}$$

36 grams = ͜36, or .36 hectograms.

Or, let $x$ = unknown hectograms.
Then, by proportional expression,

$x$ is to 36 grams as 1 hectogram to 100 grams,

$$\frac{x}{1} = \frac{36}{100}, \qquad x = .36 \text{ hectograms.}$$

The above two examples illustrate the methods of converting a metric unit to its basic unit (Example 1) and the basic unit to a smaller or larger unit (Example 2). In the conversion between nonbasic units, it is usually convenient for a beginner to use a basic unit in the intermediate steps. This method is illustrated in Example 3 below.

**Example 3**   Convert (a) 41.76 hectograms to kilograms, (b) 238 decimeters to millimeters, and (c) 65 centimeters to decameters.

(a) 1 hectogram = 100 grams,
1 kilogram  = 1,000 grams,

$$\frac{1 \text{ hectogram}}{1 \text{ kilogram}} = \frac{100}{1,000} = .1,$$

1 hectogram = .1 kilogram.

Thus, 41.76 hectograms = 41.76(.1) = 4.176 kilograms.

(b) 1 decimeter  = .1 meter,
1 millimeter = .001 meter.

$$\frac{1 \text{ decimeter}}{1 \text{ millimeter}} = \frac{.1}{.001} = 100,$$

1 decimeter = 100 millimeters.

Thus, 238 decimeters = 238(100) = 23,800 millimeters.

(c) 1 centimeter = .01 meter,
1 decameter = 10 meters.

$$\frac{1 \text{ centimeter}}{1 \text{ decameter}} = \frac{.01}{10} = .001,$$

1 centimeter = .001 decameter.

Thus, 65 centimeters = 65(.001) = .065 decameter.

**Table 7–2     CONVERSION FACTORS BETWEEN METRIC UNITS AND U.S. UNITS**

| Metric Unit | Approximate U.S. Equivalent | U.S. Unit | Approximate Metric Equivalent |
|---|---|---|---|
| **Weight (Metric Basic Unit: Gram (g))** | | | |
| 1 decigram (0.1 g) | 1.5432 grains | 1 grain | 0.0648 gram |
| 1 gram (1 g) | 0.0353 ounce | 1 ounce | 28.3495 grams |
| 1 kilogram (1,000 g) | 2.2046 pounds | 1 pound | 453.5924 grams |
| 1 metric ton (1,000,000 g) | 1.1023 short tons | 1 short ton | 0.9072 metric ton |
| **Length (Metric Basic Unit: Meter (m))** | | | |
| 1 centimeter (0.01 m) | 0.3937 inch | 1 inch | 2.5400 centimeters |
| 1 meter (1 m) | 3.2808 feet | 1 foot | 0.3048 meter |
| 1 kilometer (1,000 m) | 0.6214 mile | 1 mile | 1.6093 kilometers |
| **Area (Metric Basic Unit: Square Meter (m$^2$))** | | | |
| 1 square centimeter = (.01 m)$^2$ = .0001 m$^2$ | 0.1550 square inch | 1 square inch | 6.4516 square centimeters |
| 1 square meter (1 m$^2$) | 10.7639 square feet | 1 square foot | 0.0929 square meter |

| 1 square decameter $= (10\ m)^2 = 100\ m^2$ $= 1$ are | 0.0247 acre | 1 acre | 4,046.8564 square meters $= 40.4686$ ares |
| 1 square kilometer $= (1,000\ m)^2$ $= 1,000,000\ m^2$ | 0.3861 square mile | 1 square mile | 2.5900 square kilometers |

**Volume (Metric Basic Unit: Cubic Meter ($m^3$))**

| 1 cubic meter (1 $m^3$) | 35.3147 cubic feet | 1 cubic foot | 0.0283 cubic meter |

**Capacity (Metric Basic Unit: Liter (L))**
**1 Liter = 1,000 Cubic Centimeters = .001 Cubic Meter**

*A. Dry*

| 1 deciliter (.1 L) | 0.1816 pint | 1 pint | 0.5506 liter |
| 1 liter (.001 $m^3$) | 0.9081 quart | 1 quart | 1.1012 liters |
| 1 hectoliter (100 L) | 2.8378 bushels | 1 bushel | 35.2381 liters |

*B. Liquid*

| 1 deciliter (.1 L) | 0.2113 pint | 1 pint | 0.4732 liter |
| 1 liter (.001 $m^3$) | 1.0567 quarts | 1 quart | 0.9463 liter |
| 1 decaliter (10 L) | 2.6418 gallons | 1 gallon | 3.7853 liters |

## B. Conversion from Metric Units to U.S. Units, and Vice Versa

The following illustrations are based on the conversion factors between metric units and U.S. units shown in Table 7–2.

**Example 4**   Convert (a) 7 meters to feet, (b) 4 square meters to square feet, and (c) 5 cubic meters to cubic feet.

   (a) 1 meter = 3.2808 feet
   7 meters = 3.2808(7) = 22.9656 feet.

   (b) 1 square meter = 10.7639 square feet
   4 square meters = 10.7639(4) = 40.0556 square feet.

   (c) 1 cubic meter = 35.3147 cubic feet
   5 cubic meters = 35.3147(5) = 176.5735 cubic feet.

**Example 5**   Convert (a) 10 pounds to kilograms, (b) 6 feet 2 inches to centimeters, and (c) 6 gallons to liters.

   (a) 1 pound = 453.5924 grams
   10 pounds = 453.5924(10) = 4,535.924 grams
                      = 4.535924 kilograms.

   (b) 1 inch = 2.54 centimeters
   6 feet 2 inches = 6(12) + 2 = 74 inches
                         = 74(2.54) = 187.96 centimeters.

   (c) 1 gallon = 3.7853 liters
   6 gallons = 3.7853(6) = 22.7118 liters.

## ★EXERCISE 7–3

**Reference: Section 7.3**

**A.** *Convert the following between metric units:*

1. Convert 85.2 meters to (a) millimeters, (b) decimeters, and (c) hectometers.
2. Convert 136.4 grams to (a) centigrams, (b) micrograms, and (c) decagrams.
3. Convert 14.3 decagrams to (a) decigrams, (b) centigrams, and (c) kilograms.
4. Convert 213.7 decimeters to (a) millimeters, (b) hectometers, and (c) megameters.
5. Convert 3.58 kilograms to (a) grams, (b) decigrams, and (c) decagrams.
6. Convert 1,254 centimeters to (a) meters, (b) millimeters, and (c) hectometers.
7. Convert 1 square meter to (a) square centimeters and (b) square decameters.
8. Convert 1 cubic meter to (a) cubic decimeters and (b) cubic hectometers.
9. Convert 5 liters to (a) deciliters and (b) kiloliters.
10. Convert 35 decaliters to (a) centiliters and (b) hectoliters.

**B.** *Convert the following from metric units to U.S. units, and vice versa: (Round your final answers to two decimal places.)*

**11.** Convert 15 meters to (a) feet and (b) yards (1 yard = 3 feet).
**12.** Convert 238 centimeters to (a) inches and (b) feet (1 foot = 12 inches).
**13.** Convert 20 kilometers to (a) miles, (b) yards, and (c) feet (1 mile = 1,760 yards = 5,280 feet).
**14.** Convert 600 grams to (a) ounces and (b) pounds (1 pound = 16 ounces).
**15.** Convert 500 decigrams to (a) grains and (b) ounces (1 ounce = 437.5 grains).
**16.** Convert 1,000 kilograms to (a) pounds and (b) short tons (1 short ton = 2,000 pounds).
**17.** Convert 10,000 square meters to (a) square feet and (b) acres (1 acre = 43,560 square feet).
**18.** Convert 10 square kilometers to (a) square miles and (b) acres (1 square mile = 640 acres).
**19.** Convert 10 cubic meters to (a) cubic feet and (b) cubic yards (1 cubic yard = 27 cubic feet).
**20.** Convert 10 dry liters to (a) quarts and (b) pints (1 quart = 2 pints).
**21.** Convert 5 dry hectoliters to (a) bushels, (b) pecks, and (c) quarts (1 bushel = 4 pecks, 1 peck = 8 quarts).
**22.** Convert 10 liquid liters to (a) quarts, (b) pints, (c) ounces, (d) gallons, and (e) barrels (1 quart = 2 pints, 1 pint = 16 ounces, 1 gallon = 4 quarts, and 1 barrel = 31.5 gallons).
**23.** Convert to dry liters from (a) 100 pints, (b) 200 quarts, and (c) 10 bushels.
**24.** Convert to liquid liters from (a) 500 pints, (b) 300 quarts, and (c) 100 gallons.
**25.** A company sold 3,000 pounds of sugar to a dealer in France. How many kilograms should the company put on the invoice for the sale?
**26.** An American wishes to purchase 100 feet of silk material in Taiwan. How many meters of the material is this?
**27.** The measurements of a room are 10 feet wide and 20 feet long. What is the room size in square meters?
**28.** Johnson Company plans to build a 20,000 cubic feet warehouse in its Italian branch. Express the size of the warehouse in cubic meters.
**29.** An American car averages 25 miles per gallon of gasoline. The average would be advertised as how many kilometers per liter of gasoline in the European market?
**30.** A company shipped 4,000 yards of clothing material to Japan. The shipping company charges 5¢ per meter of material. How much is the shipping cost?

# 7.4 PERCENT—BASIC CONCEPTS AND OPERATIONS

The word "percent" is derived from the Latin words *per* and *centum,* which indicate "in the hundred." The symbol for percent, %, means $\frac{1}{100}$ or .01 (one hundredth). Thus, percent is a form of fraction and is also a type of ratio. For example, 5% may be written as $\frac{5}{100}$, which is the ratio of 5 to 100.

Since percent (%) may be written as a fraction ($\frac{1}{100}$) or a decimal (.01), the following basic operations should be regarded as essential in solving problems involving percent.

## A. Reducing a Percent to a Decimal or a Whole Number

To reduce a percent to a decimal or a whole number, move the decimal point in the percent two places to the left and drop the percent sign (%).

**Example 1**   
$100\% = 1$         $4,700\% = 47$         $29\frac{1}{4}\% = .29\frac{1}{4}$
$126\% = 1.26$         $35.52\% = .3552$         $\frac{1}{2}\% = .00\frac{1}{2}$
$2.234\% = .02234$         $4\% = .04$

## B. Reducing a Percent to a Common Fraction

A general way to reduce a percent to a common fraction is first to drop the percent sign (%) and then use the number as the numerator and 100 as the denominator. Next, reduce the fraction to its lowest terms.

**Example 2**   
$5\% = \frac{5}{100} = \frac{1}{20}$         $239\% = \frac{239}{100} = 2\frac{39}{100}$
$71\% = \frac{71}{100}$         $.015\% = \frac{.015}{100} = \frac{15}{100,000} = \frac{3}{20,000}$
$6.3\% = \frac{6.3}{100} = \frac{63}{1,000}$         $.25\% = \frac{.25}{100} = \frac{25}{10,000} = \frac{1}{400}$

The reduction may also be done by changing the percent to a decimal and then changing the decimal to a common fraction in its lowest terms.

**Example 3**   
$25\% = .25 = \frac{25}{100} = \frac{1}{4}$         $1.25\% = .0125 = \frac{125}{10,000} = \frac{1}{80}$
$.065\% = .00065 = \frac{65}{100,000} = \frac{13}{20,000}$

To reduce a fractional percent to a common fraction, simply drop the percent sign (%) and then annex two zeros to the denominator.

**Example 4**   $\frac{3}{4}\% = \frac{3}{400}$         $\frac{10}{21}\% = \frac{10}{2100} = \frac{1}{210}$

## C. Reducing a Decimal or a Whole Number to a Percent

To reduce a decimal or a whole number to a percent, move the decimal point two places to the right and annex a percent sign (%).

**Example 5**   
$.15 = 15\%$         $.034 = 3.4\%$
$683 = 68,300\%$         $1.2 = 120\%$
$23.4 = 2,340\%$         $.0089 = .89\%$

## D. Reducing a Common Fraction to a Percent

To reduce a common fraction to a percent, reduce the fraction to a decimal and then reduce the decimal to a percent. Note that the decimals in the illustrations in Example 6 are carried to two places.

**Example 6**
$\frac{2}{5} = .4 = 40\%$

$\frac{7}{25} = .28 = 28\%$

$\frac{25}{4} = 6\frac{1}{4} = 6.25 = 625\%$

$\frac{2}{3} = .66\frac{2}{3} = 66\frac{2}{3}\%$, or rounded to 67% since $\frac{2}{3}\%$ is more than one half of the unit to be retained (% unit)

$\frac{31}{6} = 5\frac{1}{6} = 5.16\frac{2}{3}\%$, or rounded to 517%

$\frac{1}{14} = .07\frac{2}{14} = 7\frac{2}{14}\%$, or rounded to 7% since $\frac{2}{14}\% = \frac{1}{7}\%$, which is less than $\frac{1}{2}\%$

However, if the denominator of the fraction is an aliquot part of 100, the fraction may be reduced to a percent without first being changed to a decimal.

**Example 7**
$\frac{3}{10} = \frac{(3)(10)}{(10)(10)} = \frac{30}{100} = 30\%$

$\frac{2}{5} = \frac{(2)(20)}{(5)(20)} = \frac{40}{100} = 40\%$

$\frac{7}{20} = \frac{(7)(5)}{(20)(5)} = \frac{35}{100} = 35\%$

*Note:* At this point, a review of the method of reducing a common fraction to a decimal and vice versa, as given in Section 1.6, page 20, should be helpful. Also, it will be found that computations in multiplication and division are greatly simplified when percentage problems concerning aliquot parts of 100 are converted to common fractions before the computation. See the same section for a detailed discussion of aliquot parts of 100.

## EXERCISE 7–4

### Reference: Section 7.4

**A.** *Express each of the following as a decimal or a whole number:*

| | | | |
|---|---|---|---|
| **1.** .39% | **4.** 3.6% | **7.** 148% | **9.** 4,500% |
| **2.** .76% | **5.** 14% | **8.** 224% | **10.** 3,400% |
| **3.** 4.5% | **6.** 26% | | |

**B.** *Express each of the following as a common fraction in its lowest terms:*

| | | | |
|---|---|---|---|
| **11.** 6% | **14.** 6,025% | **17.** .024% | **19.** .0042% |
| **12.** 15% | **15.** 1.2% | **18.** .062% | **20.** .005% |
| **13.** 525% | **16.** 4.8% | | |

**C.** *Express each of the following as a percent: (In Problems 31 to 40, carry decimals to two places, then reduce the decimals to percents; round the fractional percents, if any.)*

| | | | |
|---|---|---|---|
| **21.** .29 | **27.** 72 | **33.** $3\frac{5}{7}$ | |
| **22.** .18 | **28.** 62 | **34.** $2\frac{3}{8}$ | **39.** $\dfrac{4.5}{8.25}$ |
| **23.** .022 | **29.** 1.46 | **35.** $\frac{12}{13}$ | |
| **24.** .043 | **30.** 2.84 | **36.** $\frac{22}{27}$ | **40.** $\dfrac{5.62}{6.48}$ |
| **25.** .0026 | **31.** $\frac{1}{50}$ | **37.** $16\frac{15}{32}$ | |
| **26.** .00057 | **32.** $\frac{2}{5}$ | **38.** $23\frac{71}{82}$ | |

# 7.5 PERCENT—COMPUTATION

## A. Finding the Percentage

The term *percentage* has a twofold meaning. It is the name used for calculations in which hundredths or percents are involved. It is also the product of the base and the rate.

The *base* is the number which is regarded as a whole and from which a certain number of hundredths (%) is expressed or taken. The number of hundredths (%) is called the *rate*. *A percent has no meaning if it does not have a base.* For example, 10% standing alone has no meaning, but 10% of 200 has meaning. To solve the problem of finding 10% of 200, regard 200 as a whole (base) or 100%. If 200 is 100%, what is 10%? To answer the question, first find the value of 1%: $\frac{200}{100} = 2$. Then find the value of 10%: $2 \times 10 = 20$. The entire computation may be written as follows:

$$\frac{200}{100} \times 10 = 20, \text{ or } 200 \times \frac{10}{100} = 200 \times 10\% = 20$$

Therefore, 20 is 10% of 200. In other words, 200 is the base, 10% is the rate, and 20 is the product which is called percentage. The relationship may be expressed as follows:

$$\textbf{Percentage} = \textbf{Base} \times \textbf{Rate}$$

From the above relationship, the following is derived:

$$\textbf{Rate} = \frac{\textbf{Percentage}}{\textbf{Base}} \qquad \textbf{Base} = \frac{\textbf{Percentage}}{\textbf{Rate}}$$

The following examples are presented to illustrate the uses of the expression Percentage = Base × Rate.

**Example 1**  What is 25% of $510?

25% is the rate, and $510 is the base from which 25% is taken. Thus,

Percentage $= 510 \times 25\% = 510 \times \frac{1}{4} = \$127.50$

*Check:* Since $510 is 100% (base), then 1% should be $\frac{\$510}{100} = \$5.10$, and 25% should be $\$5.10 \times 25 = \$127.50$.

**Example 2** Charles Taylor sold 10 dozen eggs for $7 for Robert Anderson. If his commission is 6% of the selling price and he paid $.80 as selling expense, how much should he remit to Anderson?

6% is the rate and $7 is the base from which 6% is taken. Thus, the amount of commission is the percentage.

$$7 \times 6\% = \frac{42}{100} = \$.42 \text{ (commission)}$$

$7 - \$.42 - \$.80 = \$5.78$ (amount he should remit to Anderson)

## EXERCISE 7–5

### Reference: Section 7.5 A

**A.** *Find the percentage in each of the following: (Note: Some of the problems may be solved by using the aliquot part method, as discussed in Section 1.6, page 21.)*

| Base | Rate | | Base | Rate |
|------|------|---|------|------|
| **1.** 525 | 25% | | **11.** 36 | $41\frac{2}{3}\%$ |
| **2.** 426 | 17% | | **12.** 49 | $14\frac{2}{7}\%$ |
| **3.** 24.52 | 75% | | **13.** 36.25 | 15% |
| **4.** 65.48 | $16\frac{2}{3}\%$ | | **14.** 13.50 | 22% |
| **5.** 43.20 | 72% | | **15.** 45 | $6\frac{2}{3}\%$ |
| **6.** 36.25 | 43% | | **16.** 60 | $37\frac{1}{2}\%$ |
| **7.** 56.8 | $62\frac{1}{2}\%$ | | **17.** 612 | 12% |
| **8.** 56 | $87\frac{1}{2}\%$ | | **18.** 835 | 35% |
| **9.** 67.32 | 16% | | **19.** 66.93 | $66\frac{2}{3}\%$ |
| **10.** 39.12 | 24% | | **20.** 24.60 | $83\frac{1}{3}\%$ |

**B.** *Statement Problems:*

**21.** What is 45% of $425?

**22.** What is 70% of $560?

**23.** Rose purchased a dress which was priced at $35. She made a down payment of 20% of the price. (a) How much was the down payment? (b) What percent of the price was the unpaid balance?

**24.** A retail store sold an article at 25% more than its cost. What was the selling price if the cost of the article was $60?

**25.** A man's take-home pay is $500 a month. His family expenses for each month are as follows: rent, $100; gas and electricity, $16; telephone, $6; food and clothing, 25% and 10% respectively of his monthly pay. Other incidental expenses amount to $1,200 a year. How much can he save in a year?

26. James Kelley and Howard Smith are co-owners of a service station. They have agreed that profits should be divided as follows: 55% to Kelley, 40% to Smith, and the remaining part to a local boys' camp. If the profits amount to $4,500 this year, how much will Kelley and Smith each receive? How much will the boys' camp receive? What percent of the profits will the camp receive?

## B. Finding the Rate

The following examples are presented to illustrate the uses of the expression $\text{Rate} = \dfrac{\text{Percentage}}{\text{Base}}$.

**Example 3**    What percent of $428 is $64.20?

$428 is the base from which the percent (rate) is taken, and the part taken is $64.20, which is the percentage. Thus,

$$\text{Rate} = \frac{64.20}{428} = .15 = 15\%$$

*Check:*    1% of $428 is $4.28. $64.20 contains 15 times $4.28 (or 64.20 ÷ 4.28 = 15). Hence, $64.20 is 15% of $428.

**Example 4**    In 1979 the total sales of a store were $28,000; in 1980 sales were $34,440. What was the percent of change in 1980?

(1) The amount of increase based on the sales of 1979 is

$34,440 − $28,000 = $6,440

The amount of the 1979 sales must also be the base from which the percent of increase is expressed. Thus, the percent of increase is

$$\frac{6,440}{28,000} = .23 = 23\%$$

The sales of 1980 were 23% more than the sales of 1979.

(2) This problem may be solved in a different way as follows:

First, the following question must be answered: What percent of $28,000 is $34,440? Here $28,000 is the base from which the percent is computed, and $34,440 is the percentage. Thus,

$$\frac{34,440}{28,000} = 1.23 = 123\%$$

Then, $34,440, the amount of the 1980 sales, is 123% of $28,000, the amount of the 1979 sales. Since a base is always equal to 100%, the percent of increase of 1980 sales over 1979 sales is 123% − 100% = 23%.

*Check:*    23% of 1979 sales is $6,440 (or 28,000 × 23%)
$28,000 + $6,440 = $34,440, the sales of 1980

## EXERCISE 7–6

**Reference: Section 7.5 B**

(Round all answers to the nearest tenth of one percent. *Example:* 2.34% is rounded to 2.3%.)

**A.** *Find the rate in percent (%) of each of the following:*

|      | Rate | Percentage | Base |      | Rate | Percentage | Base |
|------|------|-----------|------|------|------|-----------|------|
| 1.   | ?    | 9         | 36   | 6.   | ?    | 120       | 560  |
| 2.   | ?    | 20        | 20   | 7.   | ?    | 65        | 50   |
| 3.   | ?    | 62        | 31   | 8.   | ?    | 24        | 48   |
| 4.   | ?    | 35        | 175  | 9.   | ?    | 30        | 75   |
| 5.   | ?    | 56.4      | 400  | 10.  | ?    | 28.5      | 57   |

**B.** *Statement Problems:*

11. What percent of $120 is $9.60?
12. What percent of $45 is $16?
13. $7.50 is what percent of $45?
14. $16 is what percent of $84?
15. $13 is what percent more than $10?
16. $32 is what percent more than $24?
17. $45 is what percent less than $60?
18. $224 is what percent less than $320?
19. A radio bought for $24.50 is sold for $32. What percent of the cost is the profit?
20. In the above problem, what percent of the selling price is the profit?
21. Alice pays an employment agency a fee of $273.75 from her first month's salary of $750. What percent of the salary is the fee?
22. A boy gave $15 from his week's pay of $45 to his sister for her birthday party. What percent of his pay did he give?
23. The price of a pound of ground beef was $.96 in 1974 and $1.20 in 1975. What was the percent of change in 1975?
24. There were 600 freshmen last year and 800 this year in a small midwestern college. Find the percent of increase.
25. A girl sold her typewriter for 90% of its cost. (a) What percent did she lose? (b) If the cost was $145, how much did she lose?
26. A retailer has an investment of $5,000 in his store. His net income for last year was 55% of his investment. His net income for this year is $2,200. What is the percent of decrease or increase this year?

## C. Finding the Base

A base may be found in two ways: (A) directly by using the expression $\text{Base} = \dfrac{\text{Percentage}}{\text{Rate}}$, and (B) by letting $x =$ the base, and then solving for $x$ in the translated algebraic equation. Of the two methods, Method (A) is easier to compute if one understands the relationship between the percentage and the rate.

When Method (A) is applied in finding the base, it is vitally important to know that the base always corresponds to 100% and the percentage always corresponds to the rate. The expression has the same meaning as the proportion $\dfrac{\text{Base}}{100\%} = \dfrac{\text{Percentage}}{\text{Rate}}$, which states that "Base is to 100% as Percentage is to Rate." *The base is always 100% of itself.* The following examples are used to illustrate the problems in finding the base by the two methods.

**Example 5**    If 14% of a number is 112, what is the number?

**Method A**    The unknown number is the base, which is equivalent to 100%. Since 14% is equivalent to 112, the value of 100% is $\dfrac{112}{14\%} = 800$.

By examining the division $\dfrac{112}{14\%}$, the following method is derived:

*To find a number which is equivalent to 100% (the base), divide a given number (percentage) by its equivalent percent (rate).*

*Check:*    1% of the number is $\frac{112}{14} = 8$. 100% of the number is $8 \times 100 = 800$. Or, $800 \times 14\% = 112$.

**Method B**    Let $x =$ the number (base). Then,

$$x(14\%) = 112$$

$$x = \frac{112}{14\%} = 800$$

**Example 6**    Georgette had $3,348 at the end of last year after losing 7% of her investment. What was the amount of her investment?

**Method A**    The unknown amount is the base (100%) from which 7% has been lost. The remainder, 93% (or 100% − 7%), corresponds to the remaining amount, $3,348. In other words, 93% is equivalent to $3,348. Thus, the value of 100% is computed as follows:

$$\frac{3,348}{93\%} = \frac{3,348}{.93} = \$3,600$$

**Method B**    Let $x =$ the amount of investment. Then,

$$x - 7\%x = 3,348$$
$$x(1 - 7\%) = 3,348$$

$$x = \frac{3,348}{93\%} = \$3,600$$

*Check:*    $\$3,600 \times 7\% = \$252$
$\$3,600 - \$252 = \$3,348$

**Example 7**  A store manager priced his sugar at $9.01 per sack. The price was 6% more than the cost. What was the cost per sack?

**Method A**  The cost is the base (100%) from which 6% is computed. The price $9.01 is the percentage which corresponds to 106% (or 100% + 6%). In other words, $9.01 is to 106% as the unknown cost is to 100%.

Thus, the value of 100% is $\dfrac{9.01}{106\%} = \$8.50$ (cost)

**Method B**  Let $x =$ cost
Then,

$$x + 6\%x = 9.01$$

$$x(1 + 6\%) = 9.01$$

$$x = \frac{9.01}{106\%} = \$8.50$$

*Check:*  $\$8.50 \times 6\% = \$.51$
$\$8.50 + \$.51 = \$9.01$ (price)

**Example 8**  If a number decreased by 52% is 364.8, what is the number?

**Method A**  364.8 corresponds to 48% (or 100% − 52%). Thus, the value of 100%, the number (base), is

$$\frac{364.8}{48\%} = 760$$

**Method B**  Let $x =$ the number

$$x - x \cdot 52\% = 364.8$$
$$x(1 - 52\%) = 364.8$$

$$x = \frac{364.8}{48\%} = 760$$

*Check:*  $760 \cdot 52\% = 395.2$ $\qquad\qquad$ $760 - 395.2 = 364.8$

**Example 9**  What number increased by 12% of itself is 296.8?

**Method A**  296.8 corresponds to 112% (or 100% + 12%). Thus, the value of 100%, the number (base), is

$$\frac{296.8}{112\%} = 265$$

**Method B**  Let $x =$ the number

$$x + 12\%x = 296.8$$
$$112\%x = 296.8$$

$$x = \frac{296.8}{112\%} = 265$$

*Check:*  $265 \times 12\% = 31.8$
$265 + 31.8 = 296.8$

## EXERCISE 7–7

**Reference: Section 7.5 C**

**A.** *Find the base (or 100%) in each of the following:*

| | Base | Percentage | Rate | | | Base | Percentage | Rate |
|---|---|---|---|---|---|---|---|---|
| **1.** | ? | 184 | 46% | | **7.** | ? | 740 | 148% |
| **2.** | ? | 117 | 39% | | **8.** | ? | 1,470 | 245% |
| **3.** | ? | 625 | 12.5% | | **9.** | ? | 89.84 | 112.3% |
| **4.** | ? | 248 | 62% | | **10.** | ? | 17,304 | 432.6% |
| **5.** | ? | 5,264 | 75.2% | | **11.** | ? | 514.65 | 282% |
| **6.** | ? | 1,470 | 2.1% | | **12.** | ? | 247.39 | 71.5% |

**B.** *Statement Problems:*

**13.** If 29% of a number is 58, what is the number?
**14.** If 5% of a number is 7, what is the number?
**15.** 8.4 is 7% of what number?
**16.** 27 is 12% of what number?
**17.** What number decreased by 10% of itself is 193.50?
**18.** What number decreased by 30% of itself is 302.40?
**19.** What number increased by $5\frac{1}{2}$% of itself is 42.20?
**20.** What number increased by 9% of itself is 34.88?
**21.** James Kart received a dividend of $125, which is 5% of his investment. What is the size of the investment?
**22.** Linda West purchased a car and made a down payment of $270. After the payment, she owes 85% of the purchase price. What is the price of the car?
**23.** A piece of jewelry was sold for $5.60, which includes a federal tax of 10% and a state sales tax of 2%. What is the price excluding the taxes?
**24.** A man sold a washing machine for $123.50. His profit was 30% of his original purchase price. What was his purchase price?
**25.** A certain cloth will shrink 2% after washing. If 176.4 inches of the cloth are needed, how long should the piece be before washing?
**26.** A retailer sold an odd lot of ladies' dresses for $232.50, a loss of 7% on her purchase price. What was her purchase price?

## 7.6 ANALYZING RELATIONSHIPS AMONG INCOME STATEMENT ITEMS WITH PERCENTS

Buying and selling are basic business activities. A business person usually buys merchandise at a lower cost but sells it at a higher price. The difference between the *selling price* and *buying cost* is called *gross profit on sales.* From the gross profit, the *operating expenses,* such as store supplies and rents, are deducted to obtain the *net profit* or *net loss.*

*Illustration:*   If the selling price of an article is $125, the cost of the good is $100, and the operating expenses are $15, the gross profit and the net profit may be obtained as follows:

Selling price ................... $125
Cost .......................... − 100
   Gross profit ................. $ 25
Operating expenses ............ − 15
   Net profit .................. $ 10

The five items—selling price, cost, gross profit, operating expenses, and net profit—usually constitute the major parts of an *income statement.* The income statement reports in dollar amounts the periodic results of the business operation. It gives important information to the business concern in reviewing its operations during the period and thus assists management in making policies for the future. Detailed discussion concerning individual items of an income statement is presented in the next chapter. This section discusses the methods of analyzing the relationships among the major items with percents.

To express in percents the relationships among the items, a base (or 100%) must first be selected. Theoretically, any one of the items may be selected as the base. However, in most business concerns, either the cost or the selling price is used as the base. Many businesses, such as manufacturers, that keep inventory records at cost, usually find that the cost is a convenient figure to be used as a basis for computing selling price, gross profit, operating expenses, and net profit. On the other hand, some business concerns find that the selling price is the most convenient figure to be used as a basis for computing cost, gross profit, operating expenses, and net profit. In these firms, sales commissions and bonuses are often expressed as a certain percent of the selling price instead of the cost.

The relative values in percent form for the preceding illustration are computed as shown in the table below.

| | | Relative Values | |
|---|---|---|---|
| **Actual Values** | | **Selling Price as the Base** | **Cost as the Base** |
| Selling price ............$125 | | 100% (or $\frac{125}{125}$) | 125% (or $\frac{125}{100}$) |
| Cost | 100 | 80% (or $\frac{100}{125}$) | 100% (or $\frac{100}{100}$) |
| Gross profit ...........$ 25 | | 20% (or $\frac{25}{125}$) | 25% (or $\frac{25}{100}$) |
| Operating expenses ........ 15 | | 12% (or $\frac{15}{125}$) | 15% (or $\frac{15}{100}$) |
| Net profit ............$ 10 | | 8% (or $\frac{10}{125}$) | 10% (or $\frac{10}{100}$) |

The rates (in percent form) for the above computation are calculated from the formula Rate $= \dfrac{\text{Percentage}}{\text{Base}}$. The base is always 100% of itself. Thus, when the selling price is the base, the selling price is 100% of itself. The cost is

80% of the base, gross profit is 20%, operating expenses are 12%, and net profit is 8% of the base. These percentages may be proved as follows:

$$
\begin{aligned}
\text{Cost} &= 125(\text{selling price}) \times 80\% = \$100 \\
\text{Gross profit} &= 125 \times 20\% = \$25 \\
\text{Operating expenses} &= 125 \times 12\% = \$15 \\
\text{Net profit} &= 125 \times \ \ 8\% = \$10
\end{aligned}
$$

When the cost is the base, the cost is 100% of itself. The selling price is 125% of the base, gross profit is 25%, operating expenses are 15%, and net profit is 10% of the base. These percentages may be proved as follows:

$$
\begin{aligned}
\text{Selling price} &= 100(\text{cost}) \times 125\% = \$125 \\
\text{Gross profit} &= 100 \times 25\% = \$25 \\
\text{Operating expenses} &= 100 \times 15\% = \$15 \\
\text{Net profit} &= 100 \times 10\% = \$10
\end{aligned}
$$

When the dollar amounts are reduced to relative values, preferably in percent form, the relationships among the income statement items may easily be analyzed. Thus, the "reduced" statement may serve as a more powerful guide to management. For example, it should be an easier task in pricing various articles if the relative values, in percents, of the gross profit and the base cost are known. Also, management would be more alert if it were informed that operating expenses were 25% of the selling price this year and the rate was only 10% last year.

The following examples illustrate additional problems that involve the use of cost and selling price as the basis for computation.

# A. Finding the Selling Price from the Cost, and Vice Versa

### (1) THE VALUE OF A BASE IS GIVEN

The base may be the selling price or the cost. When the value of a base is given, the required item can easily be computed by the formula Percentage = Base × Rate.

**Example 1**    If the cost of an item is $14.25 and the gross profit is 15% of the cost, what is the selling price?

The cost is the base and is given at $14.25.

Gross profit = 14.25 × 15% = $2.1375, rounded to $2.14

$$
\left(
\begin{aligned}
\text{Selling price} &= \text{Cost} + \text{Gross profit} \\
&= 14.25 + 2.14 = \$16.39
\end{aligned}
\right)
$$

**Example 2**    The selling price of an item is $90, the operating expenses are 30% of the selling price, and the net profit is 10% of the selling price. What is the cost?

The selling price is the base and is given at $90.

Operating expenses $= 90 \times 30\% = \$27$
Net profit $\qquad = 90 \times 10\% = \$\ 9\ (+)$
Gross profit $= 90 \times 40\% = \$36$

$$\text{Cost} = \text{Selling price} - \text{Gross profit}$$
$$= 90 - 36 = \$54.$$

## (2) THE VALUE OF A BASE IS NOT GIVEN

Under this condition, the value of an item related to the base and the percent rate representing the item must be given or can be determined. When a given value and its percent rate are known, the base can be obtained by dividing the given value by its corresponding percent rate, or

$$\text{Base} = \frac{\text{Percentage}}{\text{Rate}} \qquad \text{(See Section 7.5C)}$$

**Example 3**   If the cost of an item is $13.75 and the gross profit is 45% of the selling price, what should the selling price be?

The selling price is the base (100%), from which the gross profit (45%) is computed. The given cost ($13.75) is not the base.

Cost $=$ Selling price $-$ Gross profit
$\qquad = 100\% - 45\% = 55\%$ (of selling price), or

Selling price $\times 55\% = $ Cost $= \$13.75$

Since $13.75 is 55% of the selling price, the selling price should be

$$\frac{13.75}{55\%} = \frac{13.75}{.55} = \$25$$

**Note:**   Example 3 may also be solved in either of the following two ways:

1. By proportional expression.

Let $x =$ the selling price. Then,

|  | $ Value | % of Selling Price |
|---|---|---|
| Selling price | $x$ | 100% |
| Gross profit | —— | 45% (−) |
| Cost | $13.75 | 55% |

Thus, $x$ is to 100% as $13.75 is to 55%, or

$$\frac{x}{13.75} = \frac{100\%}{55\%}.$$

By cross multiplication, $x(55\%) = 13.75(100\%)$,

$$x = \frac{13.75}{55\%} = \$25.$$

2. By using algebra.

Let $x =$ the selling price. Then,

$$x = 13.75 + 45\%x,$$
$$x - 45\%x = 13.75,$$
$$x(1 - 45\%) = 13.75,$$

$$x = \frac{13.75}{55\%} = \$25.$$

**Example 4**   The selling price of an item is $29.28 and the gross profit is 15% of the cost. What is the cost?

The cost is the base (100%), from which the gross profit (15%) is computed. The given selling price ($29.28) is not the base.

Selling price = Cost + Gross profit
      = 100% + 15% = 115% (of cost), or

Cost × 115% = Selling price = $29.28.

Since $29.28 is 115% of the cost, the cost should be

$$\frac{29.28}{115\%} = \$25.46.$$

*Check:*      25.46 × 15% = 3.82
       25.46 + 3.82 = $29.28 (selling price)

**Note:**   Example 4 may also be solved in either of the following two ways:

1. By proportional expression.

   Let $x$ = the cost. Then,

   |               | $ Value | % of Cost |
   |---------------|---------|-----------|
   | Cost          | $x$     | 100%      |
   | Gross profit  |         | 15% (+)   |
   | Selling price | $29.28  | 115%      |

   Thus, $x$ is to 100% as $29.28 is to 115%, or

   $$\frac{x}{29.28} = \frac{100\%}{115\%}.$$

   By cross multiplication, $x(115\%) = 29.28(100\%)$,

   $$x = \frac{29.28}{115\%} = \$25.46.$$

2. By using algebra.

   Let $x$ = cost. Then,

   $$x + 15\%x = 29.28$$
   $$x(1 + 15\%) = 29.28$$

   $$x = \frac{29.28}{115\%} = \$25.46$$

## EXERCISE 7-8

**Reference: Section 7.6 A**

**A.** *Find the selling price in each of the following problems:*

| | Cost | Gross Profit Based on Cost | | Cost | Gross Profit Based on Selling Price |
|---|---|---|---|---|---|
| **1.** | $16.00 | 10% | **7.** | $ 72.00 | 10% |
| **2.** | 8.50 | 12% | **8.** | 39.60 | 12% |
| **3.** | 7.40 | 7% | **9.** | 41.73 | 22% |
| **4.** | 52.00 | 15% | **10.** | 42.00 | 25% |
| **5.** | 13.25 | 6% | **11.** | 227.15 | 30% |
| **6.** | 63.75 | 8% | **12.** | 204.96 | 20% |

**B.** *Find the cost in each of the following problems:*

| | Selling Price | Gross Profit Based on Cost | | Selling Price | Gross Profit Based on Selling Price |
|---|---|---|---|---|---|
| **13.** | $ 19.88 | 42% | **19.** | $ 24.00 | 40% |
| **14.** | 27.72 | 26% | **20.** | 30.00 | 25% |
| **15.** | 287.76 | 32% | **21.** | 46.50 | 38% |
| **16.** | 524.40 | 52% | **22.** | 53.40 | 26% |
| **17.** | 331.16 | 36% | **23.** | 267.42 | 55% |
| **18.** | 2,461.69 | 15% | **24.** | 654.14 | 45% |

**C.** *Statement Problems:*

25. The gross profit of a furniture store as figured on cost is 45%. What is (a) the gross profit and (b) the selling price of a table that costs $18?

26. A jewelry store wishes to price a watch that costs $65 to yield a gross profit of 52% of the cost. What should the selling price be?

27. The cost of a mattress is $95, the operating expenses are 20% of the cost, and the net profit is 5% of the cost. What should be the selling price?

28. The cost of a comb and brush set is $1.30, the operating expenses are 15% of the cost, and the retailer wishes to gain 7% net profit of the cost. What should be the selling price of the set?

29. The gross profit of a shoe store is 35% based on the selling price. What are (a) the selling price and (b) the gross profit of a pair of shoes that costs $18.59?

30. A department store bought 250 scarves for $487.50. At what price should the store sell each scarf if it is to have a gross profit of 22% of the selling price?

31. A retail store owner purchased men's dress slacks at $22.75 per pair. He knows from past experience that the operating expenses are 20% of the selling price. If he wishes to gain 15% of the selling price as the net profit, what is the lowest price at which he should sell each pair of slacks?

32. The cost of a dozen pairs of socks is $18, the operating expenses are 18% of the selling price, and the net profit is 7% of the selling price. What is the selling price for each pair of socks?

33. The gross profit of a hardware store is 30% of cost. How much are (a) the cost and (b) the gross profit of a shovel that sells for $9.50?

34. A shop figures its gross profit at 45% of cost. What are (a) the cost and (b) the gross profit of a blouse that sells for $13.95?

35. The selling price of a watch is $75.60, the operating expenses are 20% of the cost, and the net profit is 15% of the cost. What is the cost?

36. The selling price of a fan is $49, the operating expenses are 28% of the cost, and the retailer wishes to have a net profit of 12% of the cost. What is the cost?

37. The gross profit of a women's apparel store is 45% of the selling price. What are (a) the gross profit and (b) the cost of a coat that sells for $49.98?

38. A garden store owner plans to buy garden hoses for a line that sells for $8.50 per hose. What is the highest price that she can afford to pay for this line if her gross profit must be 38% of the selling price?

39. A dealer needs a camera that sells for $96. He knows from past experience that the operating expenses are 35% of the selling price. If he wishes to gain 20% of the selling price as the net profit from the sale, what is the highest price that he can afford to pay for the purchase of the camera?

40. A clothier sells a dozen sweaters for $150. If her operating expenses are 32% of the selling price and her net profit is 16% of the selling price, what is the cost of each sweater?

# B. Finding the Gross Profit Rates from the Selling Price and the Cost, and Vice Versa

## (1) FINDING THE GROSS PROFIT RATES

Example 5 indicates how the gross profit rate based on the selling price (also called *margin rate*) and the gross profit rate based on cost (also called *markup rate*) are determined when the selling price and the cost are given.

**Example 5**     The selling price of an item is $90 and the cost is $54. What is the gross profit and its rate (a) based on the selling price and (b) based on the cost?

Gross profit = Selling price − Cost
         = 90 − 54 = $36

(a) Gross profit rate on selling price $= \dfrac{\text{Gross profit}}{\text{Selling price}} = \dfrac{36}{90} = \dfrac{2}{5} = 40\%$

(b) Gross profit rate on cost $= \dfrac{\text{Gross profit}}{\text{Cost}} = \dfrac{36}{54} = \dfrac{2}{3} = 66\tfrac{2}{3}\%$

## (2) FINDING THE SELLING PRICE AND THE COST

Examples 6 and 7 illustrate how the selling price and the cost are determined when the gross profit and its rate on the selling price and on the cost are given.

**Example 6**  The gross profit of an item is $35 and the gross profit rate is 7% of the selling price. What are the selling price and the cost?

The selling price is the base, 100%. Since $35 is equivalent to 7% of the selling price, or

the selling price $\times 7\% = 35$

the selling price $= \dfrac{35}{7\%} = \$500$

The cost $=$ the selling price $-$ the gross profit
$= 500 - 35 = \$465$

*Check:*  The cost $= 100\% - 7\% = 93\%$ (of the selling price)
The cost $= 500 \times 93\% = \$465$

**Example 7**  The gross profit of an item is $25 and the gross profit rate is 20% of the cost. What are the selling price and the cost?

The cost is the base, 100%. Since $25 is equivalent to 20% of the cost, or

the cost $\times 20\% = 25$

the cost $= \dfrac{25}{20\%} = \$125$

The selling price $=$ the cost $+$ the gross profit
$= 125 + 25 = \$150$

*Check:*  The selling price $= 100\% + 20\% = 120\%$ (of the cost)
The selling price $= 125 \times 120\% = \$150$

## EXERCISE 7–9

### Reference: Section 7.6 B

**A.** *In each of the following problems, find (a) the gross profit, (b) the gross profit rate on the selling price, and (c) the gross profit rate on the cost:*

| | Selling Price | Cost | | Selling Price | Cost |
|---|---|---|---|---|---|
| **1.** | $60.00 | $45.00 | **6.** | $ 8.25 | $ 6.00 |
| **2.** | 20.50 | 15.00 | **7.** | 88.20 | 65.10 |
| **3.** | 37.25 | 28.10 | **8.** | 76.24 | 55.40 |
| **4.** | 12.50 | 10.50 | **9.** | 128.50 | 86.20 |
| **5.** | 7.28 | 5.20 | **10.** | 456.46 | 384.72 |

**B.** *In each of the following problems, find (a) the selling price, and (b) the cost.*

| | Gross Profit | Gross Profit Rate on Cost | Gross Profit Rate on Selling Price |
|---|---|---|---|
| **11.** | $ 25.00 | 10% | |
| **12.** | 42.00 | | 15% |
| **13.** | 1.95 | | 5% |
| **14.** | 43.80 | 12% | |
| **15.** | 16.80 | 32% | |
| **16.** | 18.99 | | 45% |
| **17.** | 12.71 | | 50% |
| **18.** | 15.26 | 35% | |
| **19.** | 761.42 | 55% | |
| **20.** | 313.45 | | 25% |
| **21.** | 987.51 | | 30% |
| **22.** | 529.06 | 20% | |

**C.** *Statement Problems:*

**23.** A dealer bought a piano for $590.40 and sold it for $820. (a) What was the gross profit? (b) What was the gross profit rate on the cost? (c) What was the gross profit rate on the selling price?

**24.** A furniture store bought a chair for $48 less 15% and sold it for $52.80. (a) What was the gross profit? (b) What was the gross profit rate on the cost? (c) What was the gross profit rate on the selling price?

**25.** A jewelry store buys a dozen watches for $540 less 12%, and sells them at $52 each. What is the gross profit rate (a) on the cost? (b) on the selling price?

**26.** A grocery store sold 3 pounds of peaches for $1.80. The cost of the fruit was $20.00 per box containing 40 pounds. What was the gross profit rate (a) on the cost? (b) on the selling price?

**27.** The gross profit of a furniture store for last year was $5,600. The store manager figured the gross profit rate on all pieces of furniture at 40% of cost. What was (a) the total cost of sales? (b) the amount of the sales?

**28.** A department store made a gross profit of 32% of the selling price on all merchandise sold. The gross profit for last month was $39,580. What was (a) the total amount of the sales? (b) the cost of the sales?

**29.** On March 1, a shoe store had merchandise on hand worth $1,400 at cost. Merchandise worth $2,200 had been purchased during March. The net sales at selling price during the month amounted to $1,000. The gross profit was estimated to be 40% of the selling price. At the end of the month, the store was destroyed by fire. At the time of the fire, what was the value of the inventory at cost?

**30.** On June 1, a hardware store had merchandise worth $1,200 at cost. The selling price of the merchandise was $2,000. Later the store sold part of it for $750. What is the value of the remaining merchandise at cost?

## C. Converting One Base to Another Base

In converting the base on cost to the base on selling price or vice versa, first set up the Selling price–Cost–Gross profit relationship according to the base (100%) of the gross profit rate. Then find the desired answer from the relationship as illustrated in the examples below.

**Example 8**   The gross profit rate of an item is $66\frac{2}{3}\%$ of the cost. What is the gross profit rate based on the selling price?

Since the known rate is based on the cost, the cost is the original base and is 100% of itself. Thus,

| | |
|---|---|
| Cost | 100% of cost |
| Gross profit | (+) $66\frac{2}{3}\%$ of cost |
| Selling price | $166\frac{2}{3}\%$ of cost |

Since the gross profit rate on selling price $= \dfrac{\text{Gross profit (or Rate)}}{\text{Selling price (or Rate)}}$, the new converted gross profit rate on selling price is

$$\frac{66\frac{2}{3}\%}{166\frac{2}{3}\%} = \frac{66\frac{2}{3}}{166\frac{2}{3}} = 40\%$$

*Check:*   Let the cost be any amount, such as $300.
Then, the gross profit is $300 \times 66\frac{2}{3}\% = \$200$
The selling price is $300 + 200 = \$500$
When the gross profit rate on the selling price is 40%, the gross profit should be

$$500 \times 40\% = \$200$$

**Example 9**   The gross profit rate of an item is 20% of the selling price. What is the gross profit rate based on cost?

The selling price is the original base and is 100% of itself since the given rate is based on the selling price. Thus,

| | |
|---|---|
| Selling price | 100% of selling price |
| Gross profit | (−) 20% of selling price |
| Cost | 80% of selling price |

Gross profit rate on cost $= \dfrac{\text{Gross profit}}{\text{Cost}}$. Hence, the new converted gross profit rate on cost is $\dfrac{20\%}{80\%} = \dfrac{1}{4} = 25\%$.

*Check:*   Let the selling price be any amount, such as $200.

Then, the gross profit on selling price is $200 \times 20\% = \$40$

The cost is $200 - 40 = \$160$

The gross profit on the cost is $160 \times 25\% = \$40$

**Example 10**     The gross profit rate of an item is 10% of the selling price and the operating expenses are 7.2% of the selling price. What percent of the cost are the operating expenses?

The selling price is the original base and is 100% of itself since the given gross profit rate is based on the selling price. Thus,

Selling price         100% of selling price
Gross profit     (−) 10% of selling price
Cost                   90% of selling price
Operating expenses     7.2% of selling price

Since the operating expenses are also based on the selling price and the

operating expenses rate on cost $= \dfrac{\text{Operating expenses}}{\text{Cost}}$, the new converted

operating expenses rate on cost is $\dfrac{7.2\%}{90\%} = \dfrac{7.2}{90} = .08 = 8\%$.

*Check:*     Let the selling price be any amount, such as $200.

Then, the gross profit is $200 \times 10\% = \$20$

The cost is $200 - 20 = \$180$

The operating expenses based on the selling price are

$200 \times 7.2\% = \$14.40$

The operating expenses based on the cost are

$180 \times 8\% = \$14.40$

**Example 11**     What percent of the selling price is equal to 34% of the cost if the gross profit is 26% of the selling price?

The selling price is the base and is 100% of itself since the known profit rate is based on the selling price. Thus,

Selling price       100% of selling price
Gross profit   (−) 26% of selling price
Cost                 74% of selling price

34% of the cost $=$ 34% of 74% of selling price
                $=$ 34% $\times$ 74% of selling price
                $=$ 25.16% of selling price

*Check:*     Let the selling price be any amount, such as $200.

Then, the gross profit is $200 \times 26\% = \$52$

The cost is $200 - 52 = \$148$

The value of 34% of the cost is

$148 \times 34\% = \$50.32$

The value of 25.16% of the selling price is

$200 \times 25.16\% = \$50.32$

## EXERCISE 7–10

**Reference: Section 7.6 C**

**A.** *Convert each of the following gross profit rates based on cost to the rate based on selling price:*

| | | | |
|---|---|---|---|
| **1.** 22% | **4.** 30% | **7.** 65% | **10.** 140% |
| **2.** 35% | **5.** 45% | **8.** 70% | **11.** 150% |
| **3.** 45% | **6.** 50% | **9.** 80% | **12.** 200% |

**B.** *Convert each of the following gross profit rates based on selling price to the rate based on cost:*

| | | | |
|---|---|---|---|
| **13.** 14% | **16.** 40% | **19.** 75% | **22.** 45% |
| **14.** 25% | **17.** 56% | **20.** 85% | **23.** 10% |
| **15.** 36% | **18.** 62% | **21.** 90% | **24.** 50% |

**C.** *Statement Problems:*

**25.** If the gross profit rate on the sale of a watch is 26% of the cost, what is the gross profit rate based on the selling price?

**26.** If the gross profit rate on the sale of a radio is 28% of the selling price, what is the gross profit rate based on the cost?

**27.** The gross profit rate on the sale of a table is 55% of the selling price and the operating expenses are 15% of the selling price. What percent of the cost are the operating expenses?

**28.** For the sale of a typewriter, the operating expenses are 22% of the selling price and the gross profit is 40% of the selling price. What percent of the cost are the operating expenses?

**29.** If the gross profit rate is 65% of the selling price, what percent of the selling price is equal to 30% of the cost?

**30.** What percent of the selling price is equal to 38% of the cost if the gross profit is 48% of the cost?

**31.** When the gross profit is 65% of the selling price, what percent of the selling price is equal to 54% of the cost?

**32.** What percent of the selling price is equal to 36% of the cost if the gross profit rate based on cost is 25%?

**33.** If the gross profit is 75% of the cost, what percent of the cost is equal to 42% of the selling price?

**34.** What percent of the cost is equal to 26% of the selling price if the gross profit is 32% of the cost?

**35.** If the gross profit rate on the sale of a television set is 36% of the cost, what is the gross profit rate based on the selling price?

**36.** When the gross profit is 52% of the selling price, what percent of the cost is 35% of the selling price?

37. If the gross profit rate on the sale of a book is 45% of the selling price, what is the gross profit rate based on the cost?
38. The gross profit rate on the sale of a fan is 25% of the cost and the operating expenses are 12% of the cost. What percent of the selling price are the operating expenses?

## EXERCISE 7–11

### Review of Chapter 7

1. A field of 12 acres yields 368 bushels of wheat. How much should a field of 42 acres yield?
2. If it costs $28,375 to repair $3\frac{1}{2}$ miles of highway, how much will it cost to repair $\frac{4}{5}$ mile of the same type of highway?
3. If a car runs 315 miles on $20\frac{1}{2}$ gallons of gasoline, how many gallons of gasoline are needed for going 1,200 miles?
4. If 120 pounds of potatoes cost $9.60, what will 88 pounds cost?
5. Divide 76 into two parts in the ratio 3 : 5.
6. Divide 825 into two parts in the ratio 7 : 8.
7. Divide 686 into three parts in the ratio 2 : 5 : 7.
8. Divide 151.2 into three parts in the ratio 1 : 2 : 3.
9. How should Dean and Mesk divide $1,704 if Dean's share is to exceed Mesk's share by 40%?
10. In Problem 9, if Dean's share is to be 40% less than Mesk's, how much should each of them receive?
11. Convert 120 meters to (a) decimeters, (b) centimeters, (c) decameters, and (d) millimeters.
12. Convert 31.5 kilograms to (a) grams, (b) milligrams, (c) hectograms, and (d) decagrams.
13. Convert 42.6 meters to (a) feet, (b) inches, and (c) yards.
14. Convert 5,000 square meters to (a) square feet, (b) acres, and (c) square miles.
15. Find 5% of 100, of 200, of 450, of 620.
16. Find 10% of 13.7, of 42.5, of 63.58, of 65.45.
17. What is 7% of 425?
18. What percent of $260 is $150?
19. 50.60 is 11% of what number?
20. Find 15.5% of 76.
21. 25% of how many dollars is $30?
22. $180 is what percent of $750?
23. What percent of $28 is $42?
24. 180% of $65 is what?
25. How many dollars plus 15% is $414?
26. How many dollars less 20% is $360?

27. *A, B,* and *C* started a business as partners. *A* contributed $15,000; *B,* $24,000; and *C,* $32,000. In proportion to their investments, how much should each of the partners receive from a profit of $9,372?

28. In a partnership consisting of three persons, *X* contributed $23,000; *Y,* $21,000; and *Z,* $17,000. At the end of the first year the loss was $7,747. If the partners shared the loss in proportion to their contributions, how much loss did each bear?

29. Liza bought two cows for $525. She sold one cow at an 8% profit and the other at a 3% loss. Her net profit was $20. How much did she pay for each?

30. Nancy has an annual income of $111 from her investments. She invested $\frac{1}{6}$ of her total investments at 6%, $\frac{1}{10}$ at 5%, and the remainder at 3%. Find the amount of her total investments.

31. If unroasted coffee, which is purchased at 60¢ a pound, shrinks 10% in weight when roasted, what is the total cost of unroasted coffee needed to secure 15 pounds of roasted coffee?

32. If 85% of the weight of wheat is made into flour, how many pounds of wheat are needed to make $701\frac{1}{4}$ pounds of flour?

33. Based on his experience, a manufacturer found that the change in the quantity sold is approximately proportional to the change in price. His records show that when the price of television sets was $299.99 each, 1,000 were sold in a one-month period; but only 800 were sold when the price was $319.99. How many television sets should the manufacturer expect to sell in a one-month period when the price is $289.99?

34. A grocery store manager found that she could sell 1,200 pounds of apples a day at 25¢ per pound and 1,500 pounds a day when the price was 20¢. If the change in the quantity sold is approximately proportional to the change in price, how many pounds should she expect to sell in a day if the price is 22¢?

35. If the cost of an item is $25 and the gross profit is 20% of the cost, what is the selling price?

36. Carla bought a chair for $125. If she wishes to sell it and to realize a gross profit equal to 15% of the cost, what should the selling price be?

37. The cost of an electric drill is $18. If the operating expenses are 16% of the cost and the net profit is 12% of the cost, find the selling price.

38. The cost of a refrigerator is $350. The company wants to sell it so as to cover 28% of the cost as the operating expenses and to earn 15% of the cost as the net profit. What should the selling price be?

39. The cost of a table is $51.60 and the gross profit is 14% of the selling price. What is the selling price?

40. The cost of a radio is $35.20 and the gross profit is 12% of the selling price. What is the selling price?

41. The cost of a trailer is $385, the operating expenses are 35% of the selling price, and the net profit is 10% of the selling price. Find the selling price.

42. What is the selling price of a pair of shoes that costs $10.98 if the operating

expenses are 24% of the selling price and the net profit is 15% of the selling price?

43. The selling price of a pound of beef is $1.25 and the gross profit is 30% of the cost. What is the cost?

44. The selling price of a box of candy is $4.35 and the gross profit is 45% of the cost. Find the cost.

45. An electric sewing machine is sold for $65. The gross profit is 30% of the selling price. What is the cost of the machine?

46. A bottle of perfume sells at a price to give a gross profit of $2.50, which is also 33⅓% of cost. What is the selling price?

47. A shoe store manager figures that her operating expenses are 34% of cost and that she needs a net profit of 13% of cost. What is the cost of a pair of shoes that sells for $6?

48. An office equipment store manager buys some typewriters for $68 each. Her operating expenses are 33% of the selling price and her net profit is 22% of the selling price. At what price should she mark the typewriters?

49. The selling price of a bag of sugar is $7.37, the operating expenses are 14% of the cost, and the net profit is 20% of the cost. What is the cost of the bag of sugar?

50. In a retail store, the manager computed the operating expenses at 22% of the cost and the net profit at 15% of the cost. What is the cost of a handbag that sells for $6.85?

51. A pair of scissors sells for $5 and the gross profit is 40% of the selling price. What is the cost?

52. The selling price of an electric coffee maker is $18 and the gross profit is 45% of the selling price. What is the cost?

53. The selling price of a box of cookies is $1.60 and the cost is $1.20. What is the amount of gross profit and its rate (a) based on the selling price and (b) based on the cost?

54. The cost of a portable typewriter is $150 and it sells for $180. Find the amount of gross profit and the gross profit rate based on (a) the cost and (b) the selling price.

55. The gross profit on the sale of a clock is $6, which is 40% of the cost. What are (a) the cost and (b) the selling price?

56. A company computed its gross profit rate as 25% of cost. If the gross profit on the sale of a cabinet is $50, find (a) the cost and (b) the selling price of the cabinet.

57. The gross profit on the sale of a book is $4.20, which is 35% of the selling price. What are (a) the selling price and (b) the cost?

58. A company computed its gross profit as 42% of the selling price. Find (a) the cost and (b) the selling price of a boy's jacket if the gross profit on the sale of the jacket is $2.10.

59. The gross profit rate on the sale of a bag of potatoes is 35% of the cost. What is the gross profit rate based on the selling price?

60. The gross profit rate on the sale of a set of tools is 55% of the cost. What is the gross profit rate based on the selling price?
61. The gross profit rate on the sale of a machine is 30% of the cost and the operating expenses are 26% of the cost. What percent of the selling price are the operating expenses?
62. On the sale of a handsaw, the operating expenses are figured at 30% of the cost and the gross profit rate is 42% of the cost. What percent of the selling price are the operating expenses?
63. What percent of the selling price is 65% of the cost if the gross profit is 30% of the selling price?
64. What percent of the selling price is 52% of the cost if the gross profit is 35% of the selling price?
65. If the gross profit rate on the sale of an item is 38% of the selling price, what is the gross profit rate based on cost?
66. If the gross profit rate on the sale of a truck is 28% of the selling price, what is the gross profit rate based on the cost of the truck?
67. The gross profit rate on the sale of a mirror is 15% of the selling price and the operating expenses are 6% of the selling price. What percent of the cost are the operating expenses?
68. The operating expenses are 14% of the selling price for a desk and the gross profit rate is 24% of the selling price. Find the operating expense rate based on the cost.
69. What percent of the cost is 42% of the selling price if the gross profit is 35% of the cost?
70. What percent of the cost is 58% of the selling price if the gross profit is 30% of the cost?

# Chapter 8

# The Income Statement

## 8.1  INTRODUCTION

This chapter, as stated in Section 7.6, will present the detailed discussion concerning individual items of the income statement. The income statement, sometimes called the *profit and loss statement,* is one of the most important types of financial reports of a business. The profit or loss is obtained as a result of comparison between the revenue and the expenses listed in the statement for a designated period of operation. When the total revenue exceeds the total expenses, there is a profit; otherwise, there is a loss. The period of operation may be a month, a year, or any other unit of time, depending on the intention of the management or the accounting system of the business. Since the income statement shows the result of operation, the arrangement of the items listed in the statement provides a logical order in discussing the common percentage problems in business.

The income statement of a trading business, whose major activities are purchasing and selling merchandise, is given in Figure 8–1 as an illustrative example. In the income statement, the total of the revenue is the net sales of $10,000; and the total of the expenses is $9,000, which includes the cost of goods sold, $5,300, and the total operating expenses, $3,700. Thus, the net income from operations before income tax is $1,000. The income tax is not treated by an accountant as an operating expense but is considered to be a share of profit.

Because of their simplicity, not all of the income statement items need a detailed mathematical discussion. A brief explanation of the items and the plan for discussing them are presented below:

## A.  Sales (Selling Price)

In a trading business, the transactions which involve the delivery of merchandise in exchange for cash or promises to pay are called *sales*. The amount recorded by an accountant under this title is the actual selling price at which the seller agrees to sell and the buyer agrees to buy. Thus, the selling price is the buyer's purchase price.

**Figure 8–1    INCOME STATEMENT OF A TRADING BUSINESS**

W. R. Grace Furniture
Income Statement
For the Month Ended June 30, 19—

| | | |
|---|---|---|
| Revenue from sales: | | |
| Sales (or selling price) ......................................... | | $10,200 |
| Less: Sales discount (or cash discount) .............................. | | 200 |
| Net sales...................................................... | | $10,000 |
| Cost of goods sold (or cost) ....................................... | | 5,300 |
| Gross profit on sales (or gross profit) ............................... | | $ 4,700 |
| Operating expenses: | | |
| Delivery expenses ..................................... | $  400 | |
| Store supplies expenses .............................. | 200 | |
| Store rent expense ................................... | 450 | |
| Salespersons' salaries ................................ | 1,800 | |
| Sales commissions and fees ............................ | 400 | |
| Taxes expense (other than income tax) .................. | 300 | |
| Interest expense .................................... | 50 | |
| Depreciation expense—office furniture and equipment ....... | 100 | |
| Total operating expenses ......................................... | | 3,700 |
| Net income from operations (net profit) ............................. | | $ 1,000 |
| Estimated income tax ............................................ | | 250 |
| Net income after income tax ...................................... | | $   750 |

Sometimes, a trade discount may be involved in determining the selling price. In this case, the selling price is the amount remaining after the trade discount has been deducted from the list price (the price listed in the sales catalog). For example, a portion of the selling price in the above income statement may have been derived as follows:

List price ............... $100
Less: trade discount ...... 20 ( = 20% of the list price)
Selling price ............. $ 80

The detailed method of computing trade discounts is discussed in Section 8.2.

## B. Sales Discounts (or Cash Discounts)

*Sales discounts* are also called *cash discounts.* A cash discount is called a sales discount by the seller and a purchase discount by the buyer. Details concerning cash discounts are discussed in Section 8.3.

The difference between the selling price and the sales discount is the *net sales.* The seller collects the net sales as revenue.

## C. Cost of Goods Sold (or Cost)

The *cost of goods sold* is the total cost of purchase of the merchandise which has been sold. The cost of purchases includes not only the net purchase price but also the incidental costs relating to merchandise acquisition, preparation, and placement for sale. Examples of the incidental costs are transportation charges, duties, taxes, insurance, and storage.

## D. Gross Profit on Sales (or Gross Profit)

As shown in the income statement, the *gross profit on sales,* or *gross profit,* is the excess of the net sales over the cost of goods sold. It is called gross profit because the operating expenses of the business must be deducted from gross profit before the net income from operations is obtained.

## E. Operating Expenses

In a large business the various types of operating expenses may be classified into a number of groups. As shown in the income statement, Figure 8–1, however, only the common types of operating expenses are listed and these have been classified in a single group in order to simplify the discussion. The mathematical operations required to determine the delivery expenses, store supplies expenses, store rent and salespersons' salaries are not discussed because their calculation is relatively simple. Other operating expenses are discussed as follows:

*Sales commissions and fees* are discussed in Section 8.4.

Taxes expense (other than income tax) is discussed in Sections 8.5 through 8.8. Only the taxes that frequently affect every business are discussed in these sections. These taxes are: *sales taxes* (8.5), *excise taxes* (8.6), *property taxes* (8.7), and *payroll taxes* (8.8). If a tax is imposed upon the business, the tax payment is classified as an operating expense. However, if the business is required by law to collect the tax and to transfer the tax collected to a government agency at a later date, the amount is not listed as an income statement item.

The calculations necessary to determine *interest expense* require a detailed discussion. From Chapter 9 to the end of this text, almost all of the discussion is devoted to the mathematics of interest computation.

*Depreciation expense* can be computed in various ways. Some of the methods of computing depreciation expense require a knowledge of compound interest and annuity. For convenience and uniformity, the discussion of methods of computing depreciation expense is deferred until Chapter 17.

## F. Net Income from Operations (Net Profit)

As shown in the income statement, the excess of the gross profit on sales over the total operating expenses is the *net income from operations,* or, as it is commonly called, *net profit.*

## G. Estimated Income Tax

Income taxes are levied on a taxpayer's annual income by the federal government, by many states, and by some cities. Net income from business operations is subject to tax under income tax laws. The tax rate usually increases as the taxable income increases. In the above income statement, it is assumed that the net income from operations, $1,000, is a portion of the business owner's taxable income of the year and that the tax rate applied to the portion is 25%. The method of computing income taxes is discussed in Section 8.9.

## H. Net Income After Income Tax

The *net income after income tax* is the actual income that the owner of a business may use as he or she wishes.

The income statement items mentioned above, from *sales* through *net income after income tax,* give complete financial information about the business operations. However, if the information is further analyzed, the use of the statement can be increased and thus a more intelligent business policy may be achieved. An analysis of the relationships among the individual income statement items may be performed in a manner similar to that presented in Section 7.6.

## 8.2 TRADE DISCOUNT

## A. General Concept and Computation

Generally speaking, there are two types of merchants in the trading business: the wholesaler and the retailer. The *wholesale merchant* usually purchases goods from manufacturers and producers and sells them to retailers and large consumers. The *retail merchant* purchases goods from several sources including wholesalers, producers, manufacturers, and agent middlemen, such as brokers and manufacturer's agents. The retailer mainly sells the goods to ultimate consumers.

Wholesalers normally tend to buy in larger amounts than retailers, and retailers tend to buy in larger amounts than consumers. Manufacturers, wholesalers, or other types of sellers therefore frequently grant substantial reductions from the list price quoted in their catalogs to allow for price differentials among different classes of customers. Such reductions, usually based on list price, are called *trade discounts*. For example, a manufacturer may offer the following selling prices:

> *Type of Customer*                 *Selling Price*
> Ultimate consumer . . . . . . . .list (as quoted in catalog)
> Retailer . . . . . . . . . . . . . . . . .10% off list
> Wholesaler . . . . . . . . . . . . . . .10% and 5% off list

Trade discounts are sometimes used to make a revision in list prices without reprinting the catalog. As prices fluctuate, new schedules of trade discounts are issued. For example, as market prices decrease, a manufacturer may offer a 5% discount from all prices listed in the catalog for the purpose of establishing new prices for the consumer. When market prices increase, the discounts might be reduced or dropped. Other reasons for granting trade discounts are: the location of the customer, the size of the order, and the customer's credit rating.

If there are two or more trade discounts applying to a list price, the discounts are known as a *discount series* or as *chain discounts*. When chain discounts are allowed, each succeeding discount is deducted from the remainder of the preceding discount.

**Example 1**   The price of a typewriter listed in a catalog at $150 is subject to a discount of 10%. What are the trade discount and the selling price?

Trade discount = List price × Discount rate
= 150 × 10% = $15

Selling price = List price − Trade discount
= 150 − 15 = $135

**Example 2**   The list price of $400 for a television set is subject to discounts of 10%, 5%, and 2%. What is the selling price?

This problem may be computed in the following two ways:

|  | (a) |  | (b) |
|---|---|---|---|
| $400.00 | List price | $400.00 | |
| −40.00 | 10% of $400 | ×.90 | 100% − 10% = 90% |
| $360.00 | 1st remainder | $360.00 | |
| −18.00 | 5% of $360 | ×.95 | 100% − 5% = 95% |
| $342.00 | 2d remainder | $342.00 | |
| −6.84 | 2% of $342 | ×.98 | 100% − 2% = 98% |
| $335.16 | Selling price | $335.16 | |

Chain discounts may be converted to a single equivalent discount. In Example 2, the total amount of trade discounts is:

400.00 − 335.16 = $64.84

If the amount $64.84 is considered as a single trade discount, since

List price × Discount rate = Trade discount, then

400 × Discount rate = 64.84

$$\text{Discount rate} = \frac{64.84}{400} = .1621, \text{ or } 16.21\%$$

The answer indicates that the single discount rate 16.21% is equivalent to the discounts 10%, 5%, and 2%. The single discount rate is *not* equal to the sum of the chain discounts, since 10% + 5% + 2% = 17%. The result is used to check the answer in Example 2 as follows:

$$400 \times 16.21\% = \quad 64.84$$
$$400 - 64.84 \quad = \$335.16$$

## EXERCISE 8–1

### Reference: Section 8.2 A

**A.** *Find (a) the selling price, (b) the total amount of the trade discount, and (c) the single equivalent discount rate in Problems 1–10.*

| | List Price | Discount Rates | | | List Price | Discount Rates |
|---|---|---|---|---|---|---|
| 1. | $200 | 20%, 10%, 5% | | 6. | $2,500 | 15%, 30%, 20% |
| 2. | $450 | 12½%, 8%, 4% | | 7. | $30 | 40%, 40%, 40% |
| 3. | $150 | 10%, 12½%, 15% | | 8. | $80 | 50%, 50%, 50% |
| 4. | $800 | 5%, 10%, 20% | | 9. | $15.20 | 2%, 1% |
| 5. | $1,000 | 25%, 20%, 16⅔% | | 10. | $35.50 | 5%, 3% |

**B.** *Statement Problems:*

**11.** The list price of an electric clock is $8.50 and the trade discount rate is 26%. Find the net price (selling price).

**12.** If the list price of a chair is $25.40 and the trade discount is 5%, what is the selling price?

**13.** The list price of a fountain pen is $12, and the discount rate listed on the discount sheet for this item is 15%. Find the selling price.

**14.** If the list price of an electric fan is $45 and the discount rate is 12%, what is the selling price?

**15.** A wholesaler ordered a dozen kitchen ranges listed at $250 each less discounts of 10%, 5%, and 2%. What is the net price of the entire order?

**16.** What is the net price of a sewing machine listed at $340, less discounts of 20%, 12%, and 10%?

## B. Calculation by Formulas

The computation of the solution in Example 2 (b), page 232, may be written in the following manner:

$$\begin{aligned}
\text{Selling price} &= 400(100\% - 10\%)(100\% - 5\%)(100\% - 2\%) \\
&= 400(90\%)(95\%)(98\%) \\
&= 400 \times .8379 \\
&= \$335.16
\end{aligned}$$

According to this method, the following formula may be developed in computing chain discounts:

$$\begin{aligned}
\text{Selling price} = \text{List price } &(1 - \text{First discount rate})(1 - \text{Second discount} \\
&\text{rate})(1 - \text{Third discount rate})(\ldots\ldots)
\end{aligned}$$

**Note:**     $1 = 100\%$

| | |
|---|---|
| Let $S =$ Selling price | $r_2 = $ 2d discount rate |
| $L =$ List price | $r_3 = $ 3d discount rate |
| $r_1 = $ 1st discount rate | $r_n = $ $n$th discount rate |

The above formula can be simplified as follows:

$$S = L(1 - r_1)(1 - r_2)(1 - r_3) \ldots\ldots\ldots (1 - r_n) \qquad \textbf{(8–1)}$$

**Note:**     The order in which the individual discount rates in a chain are multiplied does not affect the results. For example, the result of $400(90\%)(95\%)(98\%)$ is the same as the result of $400\,(95\%)(98\%)(90\%)$, or $400(98\%)(90\%)(95\%)$. In other words, the result of any one of the calculations equals 335.16.

**Example 3**     The list price of $300 for a refrigerator is subject to discounts of $33\frac{1}{3}\%$, 25%, and 10%. Find (a) the selling price, and (b) the total amount of trade discount.

(a) $L = \$300$, $r_1 = 33\frac{1}{3}\%$, $r_2 = 25\%$, $r_3 = 10\%$

Substituting the values in formula (8–1):

$$\begin{aligned}
S &= 300(1 - 33\tfrac{1}{3}\%)(1 - 25\%)(1 - 10\%) \\
&= 300(1 - \tfrac{1}{3})(1 - \tfrac{1}{4})(1 - \tfrac{1}{10}) \\
&= 300(\tfrac{2}{3})(\tfrac{3}{4})(\tfrac{9}{10}) \\
&= \$135
\end{aligned}$$

(b) Trade discount $= 300 - 135 = \$165$.

**Note:**     In the above example, the percents that are aliquot parts of 100% are replaced by the common fractions for the purpose of simplifying the computation. The aliquot parts method is presented in Section 1.6, on page 21.

When the selling price and the trade discounts are known, the list price may be found by formula (8–1), as shown in the following example:

**Example 4**     The selling price of a suit is $27.36. At what price should the suit be listed if a series of discounts of 20%, 10%, and 5% is allowed?

$S = \$27.36$, $r_1 = 20\%$, $r_2 = 10\%$, $r_3 = 5\%$

Substituting the values in formula (8–1):

$$27.36 = L(1 - 20\%)(1 - 10\%)(1 - 5\%)$$
$$27.36 = L(.8)(.9)(.95) = L(.684)$$

$$L = \frac{27.36}{.684} = \$40$$

*Check:*

| | |
|---|---|
| $40.00 | |
| −8.00 | 20% of $40 |
| $32.00 | |
| −3.20 | 10% of $32 |
| $28.80 | |
| −1.44 | 5% of $28.80 |
| $27.36 | Selling price |

Or

$$S = 40(1 - 20\%)(1 - 10\%)(1 - 5\%)$$
$$= 40(.8)(.9)(.95) = 40(.684)$$
$$= \$27.36$$

Chain discounts may be converted to a single equivalent discount rate by formula (8–2), as shown below, without referring to the list price or the selling price.

Let $r =$ the single discount rate which is equivalent to a series of discounts, $r_1, r_2, r_3 \dots \dots$

Formula (8–1) becomes $S = L(1 - r)$

Equate the right sides of the above equation and formula (8–1). The following equation is obtained:

$$L(1 - r) = L(1 - r_1)(1 - r_2)(1 - r_3) \dots \dots (1 - r_n)$$

Divide both sides by $L$ and solve for $r$. Then

$$r = 1 - (1 - r_1)(1 - r_2)(1 - r_3) \dots \dots \dots (1 - r_n) \qquad \textbf{(8–2)}$$

**Example 5**  What is the single trade discount rate which is equivalent to chain discounts of 10%, 5%, and 2%?

$r_1 = 10\%, \ r_2 = 5\%, \ r_3 = 2\%$

Substituting the values in formula (8–2), the single equivalent discount rate $r$ is computed as follows:

$$r = 1 - (1 - 10\%)(1 - 5\%)(1 - 2\%)$$
$$= 1 - (90\%)(95\%)(98\%)$$
$$= 1 - (.9)(.95)(.98)$$
$$= 1 - .8379$$
$$= .1621, \text{ or } 16.21\%$$

The answer may be used to check the solution in Example 2, page 232, as shown below:

$$\text{Selling price, } S = L(1 - r) = 400(1 - 16.21\%) = 400 \times .8379$$
$$= \$335.16$$

# EXERCISE 8–2

**Reference: Section 8.2 B**

**A.** *Find (a) the selling price and (b) the total amount of trade discount in Problems 1–6:*

| List Price | Rates of Trade Discounts |
|---|---|
| **1.** $16 | 10%, 7%, 5% |
| **2.** $25 | 12%, 15%, 18% |
| **3.** $48 | 15%, 20%, 45% |
| **4.** $75 | 20%, 22%, 35% |
| **5.** $125.70 | $33\frac{1}{3}\%$, $37\frac{1}{2}\%$, $88\frac{8}{9}\%$ |
| **6.** $434 | $66\frac{2}{3}\%$, 75%, $28\frac{4}{7}\%$ |

**B.** *Find the list price in Problems 7–12:*

| Selling Price | Rates of Trade Discounts |
|---|---|
| **7.** $27.72 | 10%, 20%, 30% |
| **8.** $4,143.75 | 15%, 25%, 35% |
| **9.** $237.00 | 30%, 40%, 50%, 60% |
| **10.** $1,534.26 | 20%, 25%, 30%, 35% |
| **11.** $581.40 | 5%, 15% |
| **12.** $1,764.00 | 2%, 10% |

**C.** *Find the single equivalent rate of trade discount in Problems 13–18:*

| | |
|---|---|
| **13.** 20%, 10%, 2% | **16.** 10%, 12%, 15% |
| **14.** 25%, 20%, 10% | **17.** 25%, $28\frac{4}{7}\%$, $37\frac{1}{2}\%$ |
| **15.** 5%, 10%, 20% | **18.** $12\frac{1}{2}\%$, $18\frac{2}{11}\%$, $8\frac{1}{3}\%$ |

**D.** *Statement Problems:*

**19.** A dealer can buy a chair from manufacturer X for $20 less discounts of 15% and 10%, or from manufacturer Y for $25 less discounts of 20%, 5%, and 15%. (a) Which manufacturer has offered the lower price? (b) What is the difference between the two prices?

**20.** Company A offers a retailer trade discounts of $33\frac{1}{3}\%$, 25%, 5%, and 1%. Company B offers the retailer trade discounts of 30%, 20%, and 15%. Which company offers the lower price on an article if the list price is the same at both companies?

**21.** A manufacturer of hosiery offers to ship 500 pairs of ladies' hose to a retailer at $1.50 per pair less discounts of 10%, 5%, and 2%. If the 2% discount is later removed, by what amount will the retailer's cost be affected?

**22.** Two television manufacturers offer similar products at prices as follows: Manufacturer C offers a list price less 20%, 8%, and 2%. Manufacturer D offers a list price less 15%, 10%, and 5%. Which manufacturer has the lower net price on the item if the list price is the same for both manufacturers?

23. A refrigerator which sold for $581.40 net has been subject to discounts of 5%, 10%, and 15%. What is the list price?

24. A wholesaler paid $54 in cash for an electric sander which was bought at trade discounts of 20%, 25%, and 10%. What was the list price?

25. The selling price of a washing machine is $327.60. At what price should the machine be listed if a series of discounts 10%, 20%, and 30% is allowed?

26. The selling price of a car is $2,422.50. At what price should the car be listed if the list price is subject to discounts of 25%, 15%, and 5%?

27. A manufacturer can cover his expenses and make a fair profit if he sells his tape recorder for $136.89. What should the list price of the item be in his catalog so that his customers can be allowed a series of discounts of 35% and 22%?

28. An invoice shows that the net price of an electric saw is $106.19 after discounts of 30% and 18% have been taken. Find the list price.

29. The list price of an electric fan is $28.80 less a discount of 10%. The wholesaler later allowed an additional discount to make the selling price of $19.44. (a) What was the additional discount rate? (b) What single discount rate will give the same new selling price?

30. The list price of an electric coffee pot is $18.60 less discounts of 15% and 12%. Because of rising costs, the company changed the 12% discount to 10%. (a) What is the net change in the selling price? (b) What single discount rate will give the same new selling price?

## 8.3 CASH DISCOUNT

There is considerable variation in the methods of payment among different types of businesses. Some firms require immediate payment, but others allow their customers to pay their bills within a specified period of time known as the *credit period.* Many companies offer their customers a discount from the selling price called a *cash discount.* A cash discount is also called a *sales discount* by the seller, and a *purchase discount* by the buyer. Such a discount, which is usually stated on the invoice, is generally used to induce an early payment before the expiration of the credit period. For example, the seller may offer his debtor cash discount terms of "2/10, *n*/30." These terms mean that if payment is made within 10 days from the date of the invoice, a 2% cash discount is allowed, although the debtor is permitted a period of 30 days to pay the bill. However, if the bill is paid after the end of 10 days but on or before the end of the 30-day period, the *net amount* of the invoice must be paid. After 30 days, the bill will be considered overdue and may be subject to an interest charge.

When an invoice states credit terms in a form such as 2/10, 1/20, *n*/30, the number at the left in each term is the discount rate in percent; the number at the right is the allowed credit period in number of days; and *n* indicates the net amount in the invoice, or the selling price.

The amount of cash discount is determined as follows:

**Cash discount = Invoice amount (or selling price) ×
Cash discount rate (%)**

**Example 1**    An invoice $600 was dated May 1 with credit terms of 2/10, 1/20, *n*/30. What amount should the buyer pay if he pays in full on (a) May 8? (b) May 15? (c) May 31?

(a) It is 7 days from May 1 to May 8. Thus, 2% cash discount is allowed.

$600 \times 2\% = 12$
$600 - 12 = \$588$

(b) It is 14 days from May 1 to May 15. Thus, 1% cash discount is allowed.

$600 \times 1\% = 6$
$600 - 6 = \$594$

(c) It is 30 days from May 1 to May 31. Thus, no cash discount is allowed. The debtor must pay the entire bill of $600.

**Example 2**    An invoice dated April 6 states that the selling price for merchandise is $620.50; the freight charge is $12.60; and the terms are 2/10, *n*/30. Find the total payment if the bill is paid on (a) April 12, (b) April 20.

(a) It is 6 days from April 6 to April 12. Thus, a discount of 2% of the selling price is allowed. However, discount is not taken on the freight charges.

$620.50 \times 2\% = 12.41$
$620.50 - 12.41 + 12.60 = \$620.69$

(b) It is 14 days from April 6 to April 20. Thus, no cash discount is allowed. The total amount of the payment for the invoice is the selling price plus the freight charge.

$620.50 + 12.60 = \$633.10$

Although the credit period generally begins with the date of the invoice, it may begin on the day of receipt of goods *(ROG)*. The ROG dating is particularly useful when a considerable amount of time is required for transportation. Or, it may begin at the end of the month *(EOM)* following the date of the invoice, such as "2/10 EOM."

"2/10 EOM." means that if the invoice is paid during the first ten days following the end of the month of the invoice date, the buyer is entitled to a 2% cash discount. If the invoice is not paid during the cash discount period, an additional 20-day period is usually allowed to pay the net amount.

Sometimes the buyer makes a partial payment on the invoice. If the partial payment is made within the discount period, the purchaser is entitled to a discount on the portion of the amount paid.     ,

**Example 3**　　An invoice of $400 dated September 25 with credit terms of 2/10 EOM was issued to G. D. Miller. He paid $245 on the invoice on October 7. What is: (a) the amount credited to Miller's account by the seller? (b) the cash discount? (c) the balance due?

　　(a) The credit period begins at the end of September. It is 7 days from the end of September to October 7. Thus, Miller is entitled to a 2% cash discount on the amount he pays. Since $245 is equivalent to 98% (or 100% − 2%), the base (100%) must be

　　　　$245 \div 98\% = \$250$

　　The amount credited to Miller's account is $250, which is the partial payment before the 2% discount is taken.

　　(b) Cash discount is

　　　　$250 - 245 = \$5$　　　　*Check:*　$250 \times 2\% = \$5$

　　(c) Balance due is

　　　　$400 - 250 = \$150$

## EXERCISE 8–3

**Reference: Section 8.3**

**A.** *In each of the following cases find: (a) the amount of cash discount, and (b) the amount paid. Assume that the invoice date and the date of payment are for the same year.*

| Invoice Amount | Invoice Date | Terms | Payment Date |
|---|---|---|---|
| **1.** $550 | Jan. 6 | 2/10, *n*/30 | Jan. 16 |
| **2.** $478 | Feb. 2 | 2/10, *n*/30 | Feb. 12 |
| **3.** $456.20 | March 10 | 4/10, 2/30, *n*/60 | March 26 |
| **4.** $725.60 | April 7 | 4/10, 2/30, *n*/60 | April 20 |
| **5.** $65.16 | May 20 | 3/10, 2/20, *n*/30 | May 24 |
| **6.** $38.58 | June 3 | 3/10, 2/20, *n*/30 | June 9 |
| **7.** $24.30 | July 5 | 5/10, 2/30, *n*/60 | Aug. 10 |
| **8.** $15.50 | Aug. 4 | 5/10, 2/30, *n*/60 | Sept. 29 |
| **9.** $29.65 | Sept. 21 | 2/10 EOM | Oct. 8 |
| **10.** $62.28 | Oct. 26 | 3/10 EOM | Nov. 7 |

**B.** *Statement Problems:*

**11.** The Metro Company received a check from a customer who took the company's usual 2% cash discount on an invoice for $1,582. What was the amount received?

**12.** What is the amount of the check sent in payment of an invoice for $236.40; terms 3/10, *n*/30; dated November 16 and paid November 21?

13. An invoice for $850 was issued on September 10 with credit terms of 3/10, 2/20, *n*/30. What amount should a buyer pay if she makes the payment in full on: (a) September 15? (b) September 22? (c) October 6?

14. An invoice for $522.40 dated October 16 has the terms 2/10, 1/15, *n*/30. Find the amount of payment if the bill is paid on: (a) October 20, (b) October 28, and (c) November 10.

15. Billy Meyer, a wholesaler, made a sale of merchandise having a list price of $750 and a trade discount of 25%. He prepared the sales invoice on February 16 and included a freight charge of $16.50. The credit terms are 2/10, *n*/20. How much should the customer pay if the bill is paid on (a) February 24? (b) February 28?

16. Sue Parker, a retailer, received an invoice which gives the following information:

    Date of invoice—June 16, 19—
    Item 1—2 kitchen ranges; list price, $125 each, less trade discounts of 5% and 10%
    Item 2—12 radios; list price, $22 each, less trade discounts of 15% and 8%
    Freight charges—$25.20
    Credit terms—2/10 EOM

    Determine: (a) the last day on which the cash discount may be taken, and (b) the total amount of the payment for the bill if it is paid on that day.

17. An invoice for $500 dated June 2 with credit terms of 2/10, *n*/30 was received by George Sanders. He paid $196 on June 6 and $162 on June 15. (a) What was the total cash discount on the two payments? (b) What was the balance due after the payments were made?

18. On an invoice for $650 with credit terms of 5/10, 2/20, *n*/30, dated May 24, the partial payments were made as follows: $285 cash on June 1; $260 cash on June 5. Find: (a) the total cash discount on the two payments, and (b) the balance due after the payments were made.

## 8.4 COMMISSIONS AND FEES

Wholesalers and retailers are merchant middlemen who take title to the goods they handle and assume complete responsibility for the risks involved in their trade. Their profits, if any, are obtained by subtracting the cost of goods sold and the operating expenses from the net sales. However, there are other types of middlemen known as agents or agent middlemen, who do not actually buy, sell, or take title to goods themselves. They only negotiate or assist in purchasing or selling for people, called *principals,* who wish to buy or sell merchandise. Agent middlemen generally receive their remuneration in the form of commissions or fees. The most important types of agent middlemen are brokers, commission merchants, manufacturers' agents, sales agents, purchasing agents, auction companies, and resident buyers.

Commissions and fees are usually expressed as a certain percent of the selling price if the agents represent sellers. If the agents represent buyers, the commissions and fees are usually expressed as a certain percent of the purchase price, known as the *prime cost.* The prime cost includes the price paid to a seller but excludes the amount which is paid for other incidental costs of the purchase, such as the cost of assembling and shipping. As explained below, the computation of commissions and fees is the same as that of percentage problems.

**Commission for selling = Selling price × Commission rate**

**Commission for buying = Prime cost × Commission rate**

**Selling price − Commission − Expenses = Net proceeds** (the amount received by the principal from the agent who sells for the principal)

**Prime cost + Commission + Expenses = Net purchase cost** (the amount paid by the principal to the agent who buys for the principal)

**Example 1**     Betty Kramer, a farmer, shipped a carload of tomatoes to Harry Baum, a commission merchant. Baum sold the shipment for $350 and paid $15 for freight charges. If Baum charges 4% commission, how much will Kramer receive from the shipment?

Commission for the sale is

$350 \times 4\% = \$14$

Net proceeds that Kramer will receive are

350 (selling price) − 14 (commission) − 15 (expenses) = $321

**Example 2**     George Larson, a purchasing agent for Mary Rice, bought 200 crates of apples. He paid $2.45 per crate and $35 for shipping costs. If he charged 5% commission, how much should Larson receive from Rice?

Commission for the purchase is computed below:

$2.45 \times 200 = \$490$     (prime cost)
$490 \times 5\% = \$24.50$     (commission)

The total amount that Larson should receive from Rice is

490 (prime cost) + 24.50 (commission) + 35 (expenses) = $549.50

# EXERCISE 8–4

## Reference: Section 8.4

1. John Hanson, a commission merchant, received a shipment of 260 cases of bananas from Jane Todd. He stored the entire shipment in a warehouse

for 3 days at a cost of 2 cents a case per day. He then sold the shipment for $5.50 per case. If he charged 10% of the selling price as his commission, how much did Todd receive?

2. The Farmers' House, a sales agent, sold 50 cases of corned beef for $14.40 per case. The House paid freight charges of $6.50. If the commission was $6\frac{1}{2}\%$, how much did the principal receive?

3. Dee Kerr, a purchasing agent, purchased 460 pounds of margarine at 18 cents per pound. Kerr charged a 2% commission and paid $2.25 for shipping costs. How much did her principal pay?

4. Helen Berman purchased 250 dozen eggs at 55¢ per dozen and 460 dozen eggs at 52¢ per dozen for Be-Rite Super Market. The cost of crating and shipping was $12.50 for the two purchases. If Berman received a check for $426.87, what rate of percent was the commission?

5. The Food Market, a sales agent, received a shipment of 600 cases of eggs. Each case contained 30 dozen eggs, but some of them were broken. They were sorted and repacked at a cost of 7¢ per case. The remaining 575 cases and 2 dozen were sold at $.55 per dozen. If the commission charged was $2\frac{1}{2}\%$ of the selling price, what amount did the principal receive?

6. Cathy Winston, an auctioner, sold some goods amounting to $5,678.50 for R. G. Paddler and charged 12% commission. How much did Winston receive?

7. Edward Kent sent his agent a shipment of potatoes for sale. The shipment was sold for $55. If the commission was figured at $4\frac{1}{2}\%$ and Kent received $47, what was the amount of the other expenses?

8. A broker negotiated the sale of 540 cases of B-N baby food for $9.20 per case. His commission was 3% of the selling price. (a) What was the broker's fee? (b) What was the net amount received by the seller?

9. George Martin, a salesman in a shoe store, made sales as follows: $2,500 in January, $4,300 in February, and $3,650 in March. His monthly salary is $150 plus 6% commission on the amount of sales exceeding $2,000 each month. How much did he receive for each of the three months?

10. Alice Simons has asked a real estate agent to sell her home. She wishes to realize a net amount of $33,250. If the agent charges 5% commission, what should be the selling price of the house?

11. A collection agent remitted to her principal $522.50 after deducting her 5% fee. What was the amount collected by the agent?

12. A collection agent collected 85% of a debt of $700. If his commission was 8% of the amount collected, how much did he remit to his principal?

13. Dorothy Clinton sold a lot through a real estate agent who charged $4\frac{1}{2}\%$ commission. Clinton's net proceeds were $2,101 after she had paid the agent's commission. What was the selling price of the lot?

14. A sales agent receives a commission of 7% on his sales. In order to receive $507.50 commission in a month, what should be the amount of his sales in the month?

15. A sales agent receives a salary of $140 a month plus 6% commission on all sales. What must the amount of her sales be each month in order to have a total monthly income of $800?
16. A sales agent receives a salary of $150 a month plus 8% commission on all sales over $2,000 to $2,500 during the month. He also receives 10% commission on all sales over $2,500 during the month. What must be the amount of his sales each month in order to earn a total monthly income of $1,000?

## 8.5 SALES TAXES

Many states and cities look upon the sales tax as one of their main sources of revenue. Sales taxes are usually levied on retail sales, although in some states they may apply to general sales and other receipts. *Retail sales* are sales of tangible personal property at retail prices to the consumer. Retail sales also include the sales of specified services, such as amusements, restaurant meals, hotel rooms, and public utility services. *General sales* include both wholesale and retail sales of tangible personal property and, in some cases, specified services. The rate of retail sales taxes, which ranges from 2% to 7%, varies among states. The tax is calculated as follows:

**Sales tax = Selling price × Sales tax rate**

However, when the selling price is less than one dollar, or exceeds a whole number of dollars, the tax on the fraction of a dollar is usually based on a published list or guide.

**Example 1**  The sales tax schedule used in a certain state is shown below:

| *Amount of Sale* | *Amount of Tax* |
|---|---|
| 1¢ to 10¢ ............none | |
| 11¢ to 40¢ ............1¢ | |
| 41¢ to 70¢ ............2¢ | |
| 71¢ to $1 ............3¢ | |
| $1 and up ............3¢ on each dollar (whole dollars) | |

Find the amount of tax that a furniture store should charge on the sale of a chair priced at $10.50.

| Tax on $10 ....................30¢ | (10 × 3¢) |
|---|---|
| Tax on 50¢ .................... 2¢ | (per schedule, 41¢ to 70¢) |
| Tax on $10.50 .................32¢ | |

Generally the sales tax law levies the tax upon the purchaser but requires the seller to collect the tax. Some companies may not maintain a separate record of the sales tax on each sale. In such cases, the combined amount of the sale and the sales tax is recorded for each sale. At the end of each accounting period, the tax liability is then computed from the total amount of sales.

**Example 2**     During the month of June, a store collected $2,550, which includes sales and sales taxes. If the sales tax rate is 2%, (a) what is the amount of the sales? (b) the sales tax?

(a) The sales tax is 2% of the sales. Therefore, the sales are the base (100%). The amount $2,550 is equivalent to

$$100\% + 2\% = 102\% \text{ (of the sales)}$$

Thus, the amount of the sales during the month is

$$\$2,550 \div 102\% = \$2,500$$

(b) The tax is $2,550 - 2,500 = \$50$

*Check:*

|  | $2,500 | Sales |
|---|---|---|
| $2,500 × 2% = | $   50 | Tax |
|  | $2,550 | Total amount collected |

## 8.6 EXCISE TAXES

The term *excise tax* has been used broadly to refer to taxes which are levied upon the manufacture, sale, or consumption of commodities within this country, or are in the form of exactions for a license, for permission to practice or to conduct certain sports, trades, or occupations. Excise taxes have been most widely used by the federal government, although they have also been used by some state and local governments. The tax is calculated in a manner similar to that of sales tax, or

**Excise tax = Selling price × Excise tax rate**

The tax rates are frequently changed by the government. The following examples are selected for illustration purpose. The sale of the articles by a manufacturer, producer, or importer is subject to federal excise taxes.

### MANUFACTURERS EXCISE TAXES (BASED ON MANUFACTURERS' SELLING PRICE)

| Article | Tax Rate |
|---|---|
| Trucks, trailers, buses | 10% |
| Passenger automobiles | 7% |
| Fishing equipment | 10% |
| Pistols and revolvers | 10% |
| Shells and cartridges on firearms | 11% |
| Tires (highway vehicle type) (per pound) | 10¢ |
| Gasoline (per gallon) | 4¢ |

## EXERCISE 8–5

**Reference: Sections 8.5 and 8.6**

**A.** *Use the schedule in Section 8.5 to compute the amount of sales tax for each of the following sales:*

| | | | |
|---|---|---|---|
| **1.** $ .35 | **4.** $ .05 | **7.** $3.75 | **10.** $1.06 |
| **2.** $ .50 | **5.** $2.05 | **8.** $5.82 | **11.** $3.12 |
| **3.** $ .75 | **6.** $4.15 | **9.** $6.60 | **12.** $1.56 |

**13.** Bill Becker purchased the following articles at Gray's Department Store: A pair of socks for $2.50, a handkerchief for $1.10, and a sweatband for $1.78. (a) How much sales tax must he pay on the total amount? (b) What is the total cost of the purchase?

**14.** Mary Jennings bought a brush for $.78, a mirror for $1.20, and a comb for $.45. (a) How much is the sales tax? (b) What is the total amount that she had to pay?

**15.** A retail store received $14.42 in cash from a sale that included 3% sales tax. (a) What is the price of the article sold? (b) How much is the sales tax?

**16.** A department store received $25.50 in cash, which included a sales tax of 2%, from the sale of a dress. (a) What is the price of the dress? (b) How much is the sales tax?

**B.** *Find the amount of excise tax in each of the following cases. Use the rates given in Section 8.6.*

|             *Article* | *Price* |
|---|---|
| **17.** (a) Fishing rods and reels . . . . . . . . . . . . . .$ 35.20 (tax included) | |
| (b) Truck . . . . . . . . . . . . . . . . . . . . . . . . .$ 5,302 (tax included) | |
| **18.** (a) Passenger automobile . . . . . . . . . . . . . . .$ 4,626 (plus tax) | |
| (b) 16 gallons of gasoline . . . . . . . . . . . . . .$ 0.50 per gallon (plus tax) | |
| **19.** (a) Bus . . . . . . . . . . . . . . . . . . . . . . . . . . .$83,000 (plus tax) | |
| (b) Pistol . . . . . . . . . . . . . . . . . . . . . . . . . .$ 82.50 (plus tax) | |
| **20.** (a) Shells . . . . . . . . . . . . . . . . . . . . . . . . . .$ 32.19 (tax included) | |
| (b) Revolver . . . . . . . . . . . . . . . . . . . . . . . .$ 61.82 (tax included) | |

## ★8.7 PROPERTY TAXES

Property taxes are commonly looked upon as a chief source of revenue by local governmental units, such as the city, town, and county. Any object, tangible or intangible, capable of being reduced to exclusive possession is considered as *property.*

Generally, property is classified as either real or personal. *Real property,* also referred to as realty or real estate, includes land or anything permanently attached to the land, such as buildings. All other property is thought of as *personal property.* The value of real property which is subject to tax is usually determined by a tax assessor appointed by the governmental unit. The value determined by the assessor is called the *assessed value,* which is generally lower than the fair market value of the property. Personal property may also be appraised by an assessor, although in some cases the property owner may be required to declare the value of the property. The governmental unit determines the property tax rate by dividing the total revenue to be raised from the tax by the total taxable assessed value of the property within the jurisdiction of the governmental unit.

**Example 1**   If the estimated revenue of County X from the property tax amounts to $2,578,400 and the taxable property in the county has an assessed value of $100,000,000, what is the tax rate of the property if all of the assessed value is taxable?

$$\text{Tax rate} = \frac{\text{Estimated revenue from the tax}}{\text{Taxable assessed value}} = \frac{2,578,400}{100,000,000}$$

$$= .025784, \text{ or } \$.025784 \text{ per dollar of the assessed value}$$

The tax rate may also be expressed as 25.784 mills per dollar or 2.5784% of the assessed value of the property. ($1 = 1,000 mills.) Note that the tax rate is usually rounded to the next higher figure so that there is assurance of no shortage of revenue. The above tax rate may be rounded to 25.79 mills or 2.58% if only two decimal places are to be retained.

**Example 2**   In Example 1, if only 80% of the assessed value is taxable, what should the tax rate be? Assume that the same amount of revenue is to be raised from the property tax.

$$\text{Tax rate} = \frac{\text{Estimated revenue from the tax}}{\text{Taxable assessed value}} = \frac{2,578,400}{100,000,000 \times 80\%}$$

$$= .03223, \text{ or } \$.03223 \text{ per dollar of } 80\% \text{ of the assessed value}$$

The tax rate may also be expressed as 32.23 mills per dollar or 3.223% of 80% of the assessed value.

**Example 3**   If Cornelia has property assessed at $5,000 in County X, how much is her tax on the property?

According to the tax rate in Example 1,

$$\text{Tax} = \text{Taxable value} \times \text{Tax rate}$$
$$= 5,000 \times .025784 = \$128.92$$

According to the tax rate in Example 2,

$$\text{Tax} = 5,000 \times 80\% \times .03223 = \$128.92$$
The taxable value is $5,000 \times 80\%$, or $4,000

**Example 4**   Paul Hopkins has a house assessed at $15,000 in Johnson City. The property tax rate of the city is 85 mills per dollar on 60% of the assessed value. How much is his property tax for the year?

$$\text{Taxable value} = 15,000 \times 60\% = 9,000$$
$$\text{Tax} = 9,000 \times .085 = \$765$$

# EXERCISE 8–6

**Reference: Section 8.7**

**A.** *Find (a) the property tax rate in mills (to two decimal places) and (b) the tax on the property owned by an individual in Problems 1 through 8.*

|    | Revenue to Be Raised by the Tax | Total Assessed Value in a County | Assessed Value of an Individual's Property | Taxable Assessed Value |
|----|-------------|-------------|-------------|----------|
| 1. | $ 25,000    | $    800,000 | $   200    | 100%     |
| 2. | 150,000     | 5,000,000    | 650        | 80%      |
| 3. | 50,000      | 3,500,000    | 4,000      | 70%      |
| 4. | 76,000      | 4,800,000    | 700        | 100%     |
| 5. | 83,400      | 6,520,000    | 1,000      | 90%      |
| 6. | 12,000      | 600,000      | 300        | 60%      |
| 7. | 185,000     | 8,520,000    | 500        | 85%      |
| 8. | 450,000     | 10,000,000   | 1,800      | 65%      |

**B.** *Statement Problems:*

9. The required revenue of a city for the coming year is $258,520. Miscellaneous income is estimated at $42,620. The difference is to be raised by a property tax on the total assessed value of $12,000,000. What is the tax rate in mills (to two decimal places)?

10. The taxable property in a town is assessed at $50,000,000. The amount required to meet the expenses during the coming year is $3,750,000. The amount estimated for receipts from other sources is $250,000. The estimate of the surplus at the end of this year is $160,000. What is the tax rate in mills?

11. Sam Quine owns a house that has an assessed value of $19,000. If the property tax rate is 7.52 mills per dollar on 80% of the assessed value, what is his property tax for the year?

12. The real property in one county is assessed at $4,500,000, and the personal property is assessed at $850,000. The revenue to be raised from the property tax for the coming year is $250,000. The tax will be levied on 100% of the assessed value of the real property, but will be on only 80% of the personal property. What should be the tax rate in mills (to two decimal places) for the real property and the personal property?

13. The assessed value of taxable property of a school district is $9,000,000. The cost of maintaining the schools for the coming year is $150,000, of which $25,000 will be paid by the state and by tuition fees. (a) What should the tax rate be? (b) If a woman owns property having an assessed value of $5,000, how much is her property tax?

14. The assessed value of the taxable property in one county is $35,000,000. The county needs $320,000 for the coming year. However, 10% of the property tax must be turned over to the state government. (a) What should

the tax rate be in order for the county to meet its needs and to pay the state government its stated share? (b) If a person has $1,200 in property at its assessed value, how much property tax must he pay?

# ★8.8 PAYROLL TAXES

A *payroll* is a schedule which gives information regarding the earnings of employees for a certain period of time. When a payroll is made, payroll taxes are imposed upon either the employees or the employer or, in some instances, upon both the employees and the employer. In general, the payroll taxes imposed upon employees are those levied under the Federal Insurance Contributions Act and the federal income tax laws. The payroll taxes imposed upon employers are levied under the Federal Insurance Contributions Act, the Federal Unemployment Tax Act, and the state unemployment compensation laws.

## A. Employees' Payroll Taxes

### FICA TAX

The Federal Insurance Contributions Act, which was enacted in 1937 and amended in later years, provides a federal program of old-age and survivors' insurance. The tax levied under this program is frequently referred to as the FICA tax, or the Social Security tax. The program insures almost every kind of employment and self-employment against loss from earnings because of old age, death, or prolonged disability. Some occupations, such as farming and household workers, however, are covered only if certain conditions are met. Beginning July 1, 1966, millions of persons 65 and over became eligible for two kinds of health insurance protection: hospital insurance and medical insurance, often called "Medicare." The persons who are entitled to social security benefits are automatically eligible for hospital insurance. The medical insurance, on the other hand, is only for those who choose to take it.

The law requires an equal contribution of the FICA tax from both employees and employers. The tax rates are frequently changed by Congress. In this text we use the rate 6.05% of the first $17,700 paid to each employee during a calendar year. Self-employed persons, who do not have an employer to contribute an equal amount, are taxed at a higher rate than an employee, 8.10%.

The hospital insurance rate is the same for both the self-employed (under the Self-Employment Contributions Act) and the employer and employee (under the Federal Insurance Contributions Act) even though the social security tax rates under these two Acts are different.

The following table gives the hospital insurance rate, the social security rates under both Acts, and the combined rate:

| Calendar Year | Maximum Taxable Wage Base | For Hospital Insurance (a) | For Retirement, Survivors, and Disability Insurance (b) | Tax Rate Employee (Also Employer) (a) + (b) | Tax Rate Self-employed |
|---|---|---|---|---|---|
| 1978 | $17,700 | 1.00% | 5.05% | 6.05% | 8.10% |
| 1979 | 22,900 | 1.05 | 5.08 | 6.13 | 8.10 |
| 1980 | 25,900 | 1.05 | 5.08 | 6.13 | 8.10 |
| 1981 | 29,700 | 1.30 | 5.35 | 6.65 | 9.30 |
| 1982–1984 | Automatic | 1.30 | 5.40 | 6.70 | 9.35 |
| 1985 | cost-of- | 1.35 | 5.70 | 7.05 | 9.90 |
| 1986–1989 | living | 1.45 | 5.70 | 7.15 | 10.00 |
| 1990 and after | adjust- ments in wage base | 1.45 | 6.20 | 7.65 | 10.75 |

**Source:** U.S. Department of Health, Education, and Welfare, Social Security Administration.

The premiums for medical insurance payable by a subscriber were $8.70 a month beginning July 1, 1979, with the federal government matching this amount. During December of each calendar year the amount of the premium is adjusted (depending upon medical and other costs covered by this program), and the new rate will go into effect on July 1 of the following year.

The tax contributed by an employee is not paid directly by the employee to the federal tax collector but is paid through the employer, who withholds the tax from wages paid to its employees. The employer sends the withheld tax, with an equal amount as its own share of the contribution, to the District Director of the Internal Revenue Service. The contributions are used to pay the benefits and administrative expenses for the program and are administered by the Social Security Administration of the Department of Health, Education, and Welfare.

**Example 1**   The Webb Company prepares a monthly payroll. The total amount of wages earned by Alan Taylor, an employee, during August is $800. The record of the employee's earnings for the current year shows that Alan Taylor has cumulative earnings of $5,600 prior to August. How much FICA tax should the employer (The Webb Company) withhold from Taylor's August wages?

The sum of $5,600 and $800 is $6,400, which is less than the maximum taxable amount, $17,700. Thus, all of the $800 is taxable. The tax is $48.40, or

$$\$800 \times 6.05\% = \$48.40$$

**Example 2**   In Example 1, assume that Alan Taylor's total earnings of this year prior to August were $17,400. How much FICA tax should be withheld from his wages in August?

The amount of his wages subject to withholding tax in August is $300. The computation is as follows:

$17,700 − $17,400 = $300

$17,700 is the maximum taxable amount.

The other portion of his wages, $500 (= 800 − 300), is not taxable under the FICA tax law. The FICA withholding tax is $18.15, or

$300 × 6.05% = $18.15

## FEDERAL INCOME TAX

Since 1943, the federal income tax on individuals has been collected at the time the income is earned instead of during the following year. Under the "pay-as-you-go" plan as provided by law, employers are required to withhold income taxes from wages paid to their employees. The amount to be withheld may be determined either by reference to withholding tables provided by the government or by exact computation. Under both methods, the amount of tax to be withheld is based on the length of the payroll period, the amount of wages, the number of exemptions claimed by the employee, and the marital status of the employee.

Withholding tables are provided for weekly, biweekly, semimonthly, monthly, and daily or miscellaneous payroll periods. A portion of the income tax withholding table based on a monthly payroll period for married persons is presented on pages 252 and 253.

Exact computation of the income tax to be withheld is based on the percentage method. The method requires a set of tables with progressive tax rates. The tables can be obtained from the *Employer's Tax Guide,* issued by the Internal Revenue Service. Exact computation is required for quarterly, semiannual, or annual payroll periods although it is not required for the periods already provided on the withholding tables. The percentage method is not illustrated here since the method involves only simple mathematical operations.

**Example 3**    Refer to Example 1. The employee, Alan Taylor, is married. He claims four exemptions. How much income tax should be withheld from his wages by the employer?

The monthly income tax withholding table for married persons shows that $800 is in the $800–$840 bracket of the table. When the number of withholding exemptions claimed is 4, the amount of tax to be withheld as shown on the line of the bracket is $49.60.

# B. Employers' Payroll Taxes

## FICA TAX

The nature and requirements of the FICA tax upon an employer are the same as those for an employee. The law levies an equal amount of FICA tax upon employee and employer.

**Example 4**      Refer to Example 1. For what amount of FICA taxes is the employer liable to the government for Taylor's employment in August?

     (a) The employer must pay its share of the FICA tax, $48.40, the same as Taylor's tax.

     (b) The employer is liable to the government for its own tax and for the tax withheld from Taylor's wages. The total amount of the FICA taxes for which the employer is liable for the employment period is $96.80, or

$$\$48.40 + \$48.40 = \$96.80$$

## FUTA TAX

The Federal Unemployment Tax Act provides a state-federal program which is designed to protect wage earners and their families from wage losses through involuntary unemployment. Under the program, unemployed workers are referred to suitable jobs, but if no such jobs are available, weekly benefits are paid for a certain period of time.

Under the Act and its subsequent amendments, the federal government levies a tax of 3.4% on the first $6,000 paid by eligible employers to every employee during the calendar year. The provisions of the Act are applicable to those employers who (a) paid a certain amount of wages in any calendar quarter (the amount during 1978 was $1,500 or more), or (b) had one or more employees at any time in each of 20 calendar weeks of the year. No unemployment tax is levied on the employee by the federal government. The employer is allowed a specified credit (not in excess of 2.7% of the wages, $6,000) against the tax for contributions it makes to state unemployment compensation funds, including credits under merit rating plans of the state.

**Example 5**      Refer to Example 1. Assume that the employer's FUTA tax rate is .7% after it made the contribution to state unemployment funds. How much FUTA tax should the employer pay for Taylor's employment during August?

The wages subject to FUTA tax amount to $6,000 - 5,600 = \$400$

The tax is $400 \times .7\% = 400 \times .007 = \$2.80$

## STATE UNEMPLOYMENT TAX

Benefits paid to unemployed workers are financed by state taxes levied upon the employers under the state unemployment compensation laws. In most states only employers are required to pay the unemployment tax, but in a few states employees are also required to contribute. The tax rates are not the same in all states. The maximum rate that states may credit toward the federal unemployment tax is 90% of a 3% FUTA tax rate, or 2.7% (90% $\times$ 3% = 2.7%),

# INCOME TAX WITHHOLDING TABLE
## MONTHLY PAYROLL PERIOD—MARRIED PERSONS

| And the wages are— | | And the number of withholding exemptions claimed is— | | | | | | | | | | |
|---|---|---|---|---|---|---|---|---|---|---|---|---|
| At least | But less than | 0 | 1 | 2 | 3 | 4 | 5 | 6 | 7 | 8 | 9 | 10 or more |
| | | The amount of income tax to be withheld shall be— | | | | | | | | | | |
| $ 0 | $ 264 | $ 0 | $ 0 | $ 0 | $ 0 | $ 0 | $ 0 | $ 0 | $ 0 | $ 0 | $ 0 | $ 0 |
| 264 | 272 | .80 | 0 | 0 | 0 | 0 | 0 | 0 | 0 | 0 | 0 | 0 |
| 272 | 280 | 2.00 | 0 | 0 | 0 | 0 | 0 | 0 | 0 | 0 | 0 | 0 |
| 320 | 328 | 9.20 | 0 | 0 | 0 | 0 | 0 | 0 | 0 | 0 | 0 | 0 |
| 328 | 336 | 10.40 | 1.10 | 0 | 0 | 0 | 0 | 0 | 0 | 0 | 0 | 0 |
| 336 | 344 | 11.60 | 2.30 | 0 | 0 | 0 | 0 | 0 | 0 | 0 | 0 | 0 |
| 344 | 352 | 12.80 | 3.50 | 0 | 0 | 0 | 0 | 0 | 0 | 0 | 0 | 0 |
| 352 | 360 | 14.00 | 4.70 | 0 | 0 | 0 | 0 | 0 | 0 | 0 | 0 | 0 |
| 680 | 720 | 73.00 | 61.80 | 50.50 | 39.30 | 28.10 | 18.80 | 9.40 | 0 | 0 | 0 | 0 |
| 720 | 760 | 80.20 | 69.00 | 57.70 | 46.50 | 35.20 | 24.80 | 15.40 | 6.00 | 0 | 0 | 0 |
| 760 | 800 | 87.40 | 76.20 | 64.90 | 53.70 | 42.40 | 31.20 | 21.40 | 12.00 | 2.60 | 0 | 0 |
| 800 | 840 | 94.60 | 83.40 | 72.10 | 60.90 | 49.60 | 38.40 | 27.40 | 18.00 | 8.60 | 0 | 0 |
| 840 | 880 | 101.80 | 90.60 | 79.30 | 68.10 | 56.80 | 45.60 | 34.30 | 24.00 | 14.60 | 5.30 | 0 |

| At least | But less than | 0 | 1 | 2 | 3 | 4 | 5 | 6 | 7 | 8 | 9 | 10 |
|---|---|---|---|---|---|---|---|---|---|---|---|---|
| 880 | 920 | 109.00 | 97.80 | 86.50 | 75.30 | 64.00 | 52.80 | 41.50 | 30.30 | 20.60 | 11.30 | 1.90 |
| 920 | 960 | 116.20 | 105.00 | 93.70 | 82.50 | 71.20 | 60.00 | 48.70 | 37.50 | 26.60 | 17.30 | 7.90 |
| 960 | 1,000 | 124.00 | 112.20 | 100.90 | 89.70 | 78.40 | 67.20 | 55.90 | 44.70 | 33.40 | 23.30 | 13.90 |
| 1,000 | 1,040 | 132.80 | 119.40 | 108.10 | 96.90 | 85.60 | 74.40 | 63.10 | 51.90 | 40.60 | 29.40 | 19.90 |
| 1,040 | 1,080 | 141.60 | 127.90 | 115.30 | 104.10 | 92.80 | 81.60 | 70.30 | 59.10 | 47.80 | 36.60 | 25.90 |

| At least | But less than | 0 | 1 | 2 | 3 | 4 | 5 | 6 | 7 | 8 | 9 | 10 |
|---|---|---|---|---|---|---|---|---|---|---|---|---|
| 3,880 | 3,920 | 1,067.20 | 1,044.70 | 1,022.20 | 999.70 | 977.20 | 954.70 | 932.20 | 909.70 | 887.20 | 864.70 | 842.20 |
| 3,920 | 3,960 | 1,081.60 | 1,059.10 | 1,036.60 | 1,014.10 | 991.60 | 969.10 | 946.60 | 924.10 | 901.60 | 879.10 | 856.60 |
| 3,960 | 4,000 | 1,096.00 | 1,073.50 | 1,051.00 | 1,028.50 | 1,006.00 | 983.50 | 961.00 | 938.50 | 916.00 | 893.50 | 871.00 |
| 4,000 | 4,040 | 1,110.40 | 1,087.90 | 1,065.40 | 1,042.90 | 1,020.40 | 997.90 | 975.40 | 952.90 | 930.40 | 907.90 | 885.40 |
| 4,040 | 4,080 | 1,124.80 | 1,102.30 | 1,079.80 | 1,057.30 | 1,034.80 | 1,012.30 | 989.80 | 967.30 | 944.80 | 922.30 | 899.80 |
| $4,080 and over | 36-percent of the excess over $4,080 plus— | 1,132.00 | 1,109.50 | 1,087.00 | 1,064.50 | 1,042.00 | 1,019.50 | 997.00 | 974.50 | 952.00 | 929.50 | 907.00 |

of the first $6,000 of wages paid to each eligible employee.[1] A state may provide a merit rating plan under which employers who have stable employment records are taxed at lower rates. Savings under the state merit-rating plan are allowed as a credit in the calculation of the federal contribution made by the employers.

**Example 6**     Refer to Example 1. Compute the state unemployment tax for the employer. Assume that the state unemployment tax rate is (a) 2.7% and (b) 1.6%.

        (a) $400 \times 2.7\% = 400 \times .027 = \$10.80$ (See Example 5.)

        (b) $400 \times 1.6\% = 400 \times .016 = \$6.40$

The illustrations in Example 1 and the related examples, Examples 3, 4, 5, and 6(a), based on Alan Taylor's cumulative earnings of $5,600 prior to August, are summarized below:

    (a) The amount of Taylor's take-home pay:

| | | |
|---|---|---|
| Wages | | .$800.00 |
| Less: Withholding FICA tax | $48.40 | |
|        Withholding income tax | 49.60 | 98.00 |
|        Take-home pay | | .$702.00 |

    (b) The total cost to the Webb Company for the employment of Taylor during August:

| | | |
|---|---|---|
| Employee's wages | | .$800.00 |
| Add: Employer's payroll taxes— | | |
|     FICA tax | $48.40 | |
|     FUTA tax | 2.80 | |
|     State unemployment tax | 10.80 | 62.00 |
|     Total cost | | .$862.00 |

    (c) The distribution of the employer's cost:

| | | |
|---|---|---|
| Taylor's take-home pay | | .$702.00 |
| Liability to federal government— | | |
|     Withholding FICA tax | $48.40 | |
|     Withholding income tax | 49.60 | |
|     Employer's FICA tax | 48.40 | |
|     FUTA tax | 2.80 | 149.20 |
| Liability to state government | | 10.80 |
|     Total cost | | .$862.00 |

To summarize, under the 1978 laws and regulations, the payroll taxes in a calendar year for eligible employers and employees were as follows:

---

[1] Prior to 1961, the credit was equal to 90% of the 3% federal tax. The limit on the amount of credit allowable remains the same even though the federal tax after 1961 was increased to 3.4%. The credit will continue to be calculated as a percentage of a 3% tax rate.

| Payroll Tax | Imposed upon Employers | Imposed upon Employees |
|---|---|---|
| FICA | 6.05% of first $17,700 paid | Same as employers |
| FUTA | .7% of first $6,000 paid | None |
| State unemployment | Varies from state to state | Generally none |
| Federal income tax | None for the payroll | Based on earnings, payroll period, exemptions claimed, and marital status |

## ★EXERCISE 8–7

### Reference: Section 8.8

Assume that the following rates apply: FICA, 6.05% of first $17,700; FUTA, .7% of first $6,000; and state unemployment, 2.7% (or less if it is specified in a problem) of first $6,000 paid to each employee.

**A.** *In Problems 1 through 10, find:*

    (a) The employee's payroll taxes:
        (1) Federal income tax (if it is not given in the problem.)
        (2) FICA tax
    (b) The employee's take-home pay
    (c) The employer's payroll taxes:
        (1) FICA tax
        (2) FUTA tax
        (3) State unemployment tax
    (d) The total employer's cost for the employment during the current period
    (e) The distribution of the employer's cost

| Employee (Married or Single) | Earnings in the Current Period | Payroll Period | Cumulative Earnings Prior to Current Period | Number of Exemptions Claimed | Federal Income Tax[2] |
|---|---|---|---|---|---|
| 1. A($M$) | $ 700 | Monthly | $ 5,900 | 2 | $ ? |
| 2. B($M$) | 380 | Weekly | 7,000 | 3 | $ 56.00 |
| 3. C($S$) | 450 | Biweekly | 8,000 | 4 | 48.70 |
| 4. D($S$) | 650 | Semimonthly | 4,500 | 5 | 84.30 |
| 5. E($M$) | 5,375 | Quarterly | 500 | 2 | 878.37 |

---

[2] The given taxes are obtained from the 1977 *Employer's Tax Guide,* issued by the Internal Revenue Service.

| Employee (Married or Single) | Earnings in the Current Period | Payroll Period | Cumulative Earnings Prior to Current Period | Number of Exemptions Claimed | Federal Income Tax |
|---|---|---|---|---|---|
| 6. F(M) | $14,350 | Semiannually | $ 0 | 3 | $2,739.98 |
| 7. G(S) | 21,450 | Annually | 0 | 4 | 3,990.00 |
| 8. H(S) | 46 | Daily | 6,000 | 2 | 8.30 |
| 9. I(M) | 950 | Monthly | 17,500 | 3 | ? |
| 10. J(M) | 4,000 | Monthly | 7,000 | 5 | ? |

**B.** *Statement Problems:*

11. The total amount of J. D. Kener's wages for this year up to July 31 was $5,900. He earned $840 in August. Assume that the employer prepares the monthly payroll on August 31 and that Kener, married, claims 2 exemptions. How much FICA tax and federal income tax should the employer withhold from Kener's wages for the month of August?

12. Refer to Problem 11. For how much payroll tax is the employer subject? Assume that the tax rate for state unemployment is only 1.6% of the first $6,000 paid to the employee.

13. The earnings record for the current week shows that C. T. Olson worked 42 hours at the rate of $5.20 per hour for the first 40 hours and at $1\frac{1}{2}$ times $5.20 for all additional hours. His FICA tax withheld prior to the current week is $1,060. He is single and claims 4 exemptions. Find (a) Olson's earnings for the current week, (b) the FICA tax to be withheld, and (c) Olson's take-home pay. (His federal income tax withheld is $24.30.)

14. Refer to Problem 13. Find the payroll taxes imposed upon the employer. Assume that the tax rate for state unemployment is only 2.3% of first $6,000 paid to the employee.

15. The total salary and wage expense of a retail store for a year was $160,000. The payroll taxes imposed upon the store were FICA, $7,260.00; FUTA tax, $294.00; and state unemployment tax, $1,134.00. (a) How much of the total salary and wages was exempt from the FICA taxes? (b) from the state and federal unemployment taxes?

16. The November monthly payroll of Fuller's Department Store indicated that the total salary and wage expense was $20,000. During that month, $2,000 was exempt from the FICA tax and $6,000 was exempt from the state and federal unemployment taxes. Find the employer's payroll taxes in November. Assume that the tax rate for state unemployment is only 1.7%.

# ★8.9 INCOME TAXES

## A. Introduction

Income taxes are levied by the federal government, by most of the states, and by some cities. The states and cities generally follow the federal income tax pattern, although the income tax rates and the details of the methods of computing the tax vary from state to state and city to city. In order to illustrate the principles of income taxation, only the most important and representative tax system—the federal system—is discussed here.

The 16th Amendment to the Constitution of the United States gave Congress the power to lay and collect taxes on income. The first revenue act was passed in 1913 and since that date, revenue acts and other laws containing tax provisions have been enacted in almost every year. The methods of computing individual and corporation income taxes illustrated in the following material are based on the instructions for 1978 income tax returns issued by the Internal Revenue Service in 1979.

# B. Individual Income Tax Returns

Generally speaking, the method of computing an individual's income tax may be outlined in the following manner (see Examples 1 and 7(a)):

1. Gross income . . . . . . . . . . . . . . . . . . . . . . . . . . . . . . . . . . $20,000.00
2. Deductions I—For adjusted gross income . . . . . . . . . . . 500.00
3. Adjusted gross income . . . . . . . . . . . . . . . . . . . . . . . . . $19,500.00
4. Deductions from adjusted gross income:
   Deductions II—Itemized or standard
         (a) Itemized . . . . . . . . . . . . . $5,400.00
   Less:  (b) Standard . . . . . . . . . . . . 3,200.00
5. Excess itemized deductions . . . . . . . . . . . . . . . . . . . . . 2,200.00
6. Tax table income . . . . . . . . . . . . . . . . . . . . . . . . . . . . . $17,300.00
7. Tax:  Based on Tax Table B (Standard
         deduction $3,200 has been allowed) . . . . . . . . . . $1,712.00
8. Prepaid tax payments . . . . . . . . . . . . . . . . . . . . . . . . . . 2,000.00
9. Net tax payable to government (or refundable
   to taxpayer) . . . . . . . . . . . . . . . . . . . . . . . . . . . . . . . . . ($ 288.00)

**GROSS INCOME**

Gross income is the income that must be reported in an income tax return. The tax law states that all kinds of income, other than a return of capital, in whatever form received are subject to tax unless the income is specifically excluded by law and by the Constitution. The following examples are types of gross income which must be reported in tax returns: wages, salaries, bonuses, commissions, tips, profits from business, rents, royalties, taxpayer's share of partnership profits, estate or trust income, and contest awards and prizes.

The amount of a person's gross income is the decisive factor of whether or not a person must file an income tax return. For example, in 1978 a person was required to file a return if single and under 65 and gross income was $2,950 or more. A person with less income had to file a return to get a refund if tax was withheld by an employer.

## DEDUCTIONS I—FOR ADJUSTED GROSS INCOME

Deductions for adjusted gross income are generally of a business nature. Examples of such deductions are the ordinary and necessary expenses directly incurred by a taxpayer in carrying on a trade, profession, or business; the travel expenses of a taxpayer incurred while away from home in connection with an employer's business; the moving expenses of an employee in connection with employment; and the expenses incurred in performing services as an outside sales agent for the employer. Also, "sick pay" can be deducted if it is included in income.

## ADJUSTED GROSS INCOME

The amount of the adjusted gross income is computed because it is useful in determining the right to use a tax table compiled by the federal government for those who have an adjusted gross income of $20,000 or less ($40,000 or less if married filing joint return.) The adjusted gross income is also a base for computing certain itemized deductions as discussed below.

## DEDUCTIONS II—ITEMIZED OR STANDARD

Itemized deductions are generally personal expenses and are not deductible from the gross income in determining the adjusted gross income. If the total amount of the itemized deductions is more than the allowed standard deduction, it would be to the taxpayer's advantage to take the itemized deductions. Examples of deductible personal expenses are: charitable contributions, interest paid on personal loans, state and local income taxes, medical and dental expenses, union dues, casualty losses not covered by insurance, employment fees paid to agencies.

Instead of itemizing deductions, the taxpayer may take a standard deduction for personal expenses. A standard deduction is deductible from the adjusted gross income. However, the deduction is not performed by a taxpayer in tax computation since the 1978 tax tables and tax rate schedules do not tax the first:

1. $3,200 of income, if the taxpayer is married filing a joint return or a qualifying widow(er),
2. $2,200 of income, if the taxpayer is single or an unmarried head of household, or
3. $1,600 of income, if the taxpayer is married filing separately.

These standard deduction amounts are called *zero bracket amounts* in the *1978 United States Individual Income Tax Return Instructions,* issued by the Internal Revenue Service. Since these amounts are built into the tax tables and tax rate schedules, taxpayers who itemize deductions will need to make an adjustment.

## DEDUCTIONS III—PERSONAL EXEMPTIONS

A taxpayer is always entitled to at least one exemption. At the end of the taxable year, a taxpayer who is blind or is 65 years of age or over may count two exemptions. A taxpayer who is both blind and 65 or over may claim three exemptions. If husband and wife are filing a joint return, the wife's exemptions are determined under the same rules as the husband's. Thus, if both a taxpayer and spouse are blind and 65 or over, they may claim a total of 6 exemptions. The taxpayer can also claim one exemption for each qualified dependent. According to the 1978 law, each exemption is entitled to a $750 deduction. The deduction for a limited number of exemptions has been taken into account in figuring the tax shown in the 1978 tax tables.

## TAX TABLE INCOME

Tax table income is equal to the adjusted gross income for those who *do not itemize* deductions. For those who *do itemize* deductions,

Tax table income = Adjusted gross income − Excess itemized deductions, where
Excess itemized deductions = Itemized deductions − Zero bracket amount

This adjustment of subtracting the zero bracket amount is necessary because the amount is already built into the tax tables and the tax rate schedules. The tax table income is used in finding the tax from the tables and schedules. Thus, if the total amount of the itemized deductions is less than the zero bracket amount (or if the excess itemized deductions were negative), it would be to the taxpayer's advantage not to take the itemized deductions.

## TAXABLE INCOME

Taxable income is determined by subtracting the personal exemptions (Deductions III) from the tax table income. Taxable income is the base to which the tax rate schedules are applied in computing the tax.

## TAX COMPUTATION

Since income tax rates and regulations are subject to change by the federal government from year to year, the following illustrations are used to present principles rather than to be of practical use. The tax rates in the following examples represent those used in computing the 1978 federal income tax. It is important to consult the current tax regulations when computing taxes in any particular year.

Two tax computation methods are illustrated here:

(A) Using tax tables (Tables A, B, C, and D), illustrated in Examples 1 and 2.

(B) Using tax rate schedules (Schedules X, Y, and Z), illustrated in Examples 3 and 4.

## TAX TABLE A—For SINGLE persons with tax table income of $20,000 or less who claim fewer than 4 exemptions

(The $2,200 zero bracket amount, deduction for exemptions and the general tax credit have been taken into account in figuring the tax shown in this table.)

| If tax table income is: | | And the total number of exemptions claimed is: | | |
|---|---|---|---|---|
| Over | But not over | 1 | 2 | 3 |
| | | Your tax is: | | |
| (If $3,200 or less, your tax is $0) | | | | |
| $ 3,200 — | $ 3,250 | $ 4 | $ 0 | $ 0 |
| 3,250 — | 3,300 | 11 | 0 | 0 |
| 3,300 — | 3,350 | 18 | 0 | 0 |
| . . . . . . . . . . . | | | | |
| 9,850 — | 9,900 | 1,194 | 1,029 | 881 |
| 9,900 — | 9,950 | 1,205 | 1,040 | 890 |
| 9,950 — | 10,000 | 1,216 | 1,051 | 900 |
| . . . . . . . . . . . | | | | |
| 17,200 — | 17,250 | 3,115 | 2,892 | 2,675 |
| 17,250 — | 17,300 | 3,131 | 2,907 | 2,689 |
| 17,300 — | 17,350 | 3,146 | 2,921 | 2,704 |
| . . . . . . . . . . . | | | | |
| 19,850 — | 19,900 | 3,965 | 3,710 | 3,472 |
| 19,900 — | 19,950 | 3,982 | 3,727 | 3,487 |
| 19,950 — | 20,000 | 3,999 | 3,744 | 3,503 |

**TAX TABLE B—For MARRIED persons filing JOINT returns or QUALIFYING WIDOW(ER)S with tax table income of $40,000 or less who claim fewer than 10 exemptions**

(The $3,200 zero bracket amount, deduction for exemptions and the general tax credit have been taken into account in figuring the tax shown in this table.)

| If tax table income is: | | And the total number of exemptions claimed is: | | | | | | | |
|---|---|---|---|---|---|---|---|---|---|
| Over | But not over | 2 | 3 | 4 | 5 | 6 | 7 | 8 | 9 |
| | | | | | Your tax is: | | | | |
| (If $5,200 or less, your tax is $0) | | | | | | | | | |
| $ 5,200— | 5,250 | $ 4 | $ 0 | $ 0 | $ 0 | $ 0 | $ 0 | $ 0 | $ 0 |
| 5,250— | 5,300 | 11 | 0 | 0 | 0 | 0 | 0 | 0 | 0 |
| 5,300— | 5,350 | 18 | 0 | 0 | 0 | 0 | 0 | 0 | 0 |
| ······ | | | | | | | | | |
| 9,850— | 9,900 | 740 | 596 | 425 | 263 | 108 | 0 | 0 | 0 |
| 9,900— | 9,950 | 748 | 605 | 433 | 271 | 116 | 0 | 0 | 0 |
| 9,950— | 10,000 | 757 | 615 | 442 | 279 | 124 | 0 | 0 | 0 |
| ······ | | | | | | | | | |
| 17,250— | 17,300 | 2,224 | 2,042 | 1,877 | 1,712 | 1,517 | 1,317 | 1,117 | 937 |
| 17,300— | 17,350 | 2,236 | 2,053 | 1,888 | 1,723 | 1,528 | 1,328 | 1,128 | 946 |
| 17,350— | 17,400 | 2,249 | 2,064 | 1,899 | 1,734 | 1,539 | 1,339 | 1,139 | 956 |
| ······ | | | | | | | | | |
| 39,850— | 39,900 | 9,814 | 9,499 | 9,184 | 8,869 | 8,524 | 8,191 | 7,863 | 7,536 |
| 39,900— | 39,950 | 9,835 | 9,520 | 9,205 | 8,890 | 8,545 | 8,210 | 7,883 | 7,555 |
| 39,950— | 40,000 | 9,856 | 9,541 | 9,226 | 8,911 | 8,566 | 8,230 | 7,902 | 7,575 |

## TAX TABLE C—For MARRIED persons filing SEPARATE returns with tax table income of $20,000 or less who claim fewer than 4 exemptions

(The $1,600 zero bracket amount, deduction for exemptions and the general tax credit have been taken into account in figuring the tax shown in this table.)

| If tax table income is: | | And the total number of exemptions claimed is: | | |
|---|---|---|---|---|
| | | **1** | **2** | **3** |
| Over | But not over | Your tax is: | | |
| (If $2,600 or less, your tax is $0) | | | | |
| $ 2,600—$ 2,625 | | $   2 | $   0 | $   0 |
| 2,625—   2,650 | | 5 | 0 | 0 |
| 2,650—   2,675 | | 9 | 0 | 0 |
| . . . . . . . . . | | | | |
| 9,850—   9,900 | | 1,476 | 1,254 | 1,031 |
| 9,900—   9,950 | | 1,489 | 1,266 | 1,044 |
| 9,950—  10,000 | | 1,501 | 1,279 | 1,056 |
| . . . . . . . . . | | | | |
| 15,600—  15,650 | | 3,254 | 2,949 | 2,653 |
| 15,650—  15,700 | | 3,272 | 2,967 | 2,669 |
| 15,700—  15,750 | | 3,290 | 2,985 | 2,685 |
| . . . . . . . . . | | | | |
| 19,850—  19,900 | | 4,936 | 4,586 | 4,236 |
| 19,900—  19,950 | | 4,957 | 4,607 | 4,257 |
| 19,950—  20,000 | | 4,978 | 4,628 | 4,278 |

## TAX TABLE D—For unmarried or legally separated persons who qualify as HEADS OF HOUSEHOLD with tax table income of $20,000 or less who claim fewer than 9 exemptions

(The $2,200 zero bracket amount, deduction for exemptions and the general tax credit have been taken into account in figuring the tax shown in this table.)

| If tax table income is: | | And the total number of exemptions claimed is: | | | | | | | |
|---|---|---|---|---|---|---|---|---|---|
| Over | But not over | 1 | 2 | 3 | 4 | 5 | 6 | 7 | 8 |
| | | | | | Your tax is: | | | | |
| (If $3,200 or less, your tax is $0) | | | | | | | | | |
| $ 3,200— | 3,250 | $ 4 | $ 0 | $ 0 | $ 0 | $ 0 | $ 0 | $ 0 | $ 0 |
| 3,250— | 3,300 | 11 | 0 | 0 | 0 | 0 | 0 | 0 | 0 |
| 3,300— | 3,350 | 18 | 0 | 0 | 0 | 0 | 0 | 0 | 0 |
| . . . . . . . . | | | | | | | | | |
| 9,850— | 9,900 | 1,105 | 955 | 822 | 648 | 472 | 302 | 132 | 0 |
| 9,900— | 9,950 | 1,115 | 965 | 831 | 658 | 481 | 311 | 141 | 0 |
| 9,950— | 10,000 | 1,125 | 975 | 839 | 667 | 490 | 320 | 150 | 0 |
| . . . . . . . . | | | | | | | | | |
| 16,200— | 16,250 | 2,604 | 2,402 | 2,204 | 2,016 | 1,829 | 1,621 | 1,413 | 1,206 |
| 16,250— | 16,300 | 2,618 | 2,415 | 2,216 | 2,029 | 1,841 | 1,632 | 1,425 | 1,217 |
| 16,300— | 16,350 | 2,631 | 2,429 | 2,229 | 2,041 | 1,854 | 1,644 | 1,436 | 1,229 |
| . . . . . . . . | | | | | | | | | |
| 19,850— | 19,900 | 3,647 | 3,414 | 3,199 | 2,989 | 2,780 | 2,547 | 2,310 | 2,079 |
| 19,900— | 19,950 | 3,662 | 3,430 | 3,213 | 3,003 | 2,793 | 2,561 | 2,323 | 2,091 |
| 19,950— | 20,000 | 3,678 | 3,445 | 3,227 | 3,017 | 2,807 | 2,574 | 2,337 | 2,104 |

## METHOD A—USING TAX TABLES

For illustrative purposes, only selected amounts from the four tax tables (Tables A, B, C, and D) are given in this section.

**Example 1**   John Verson had a salary of $20,000 in 1978. His deductions for the adjusted gross income are $500. His itemized deductions are $5,400. He is married and claims 5 personal exemptions. How much is his tax for 1978 if he files a joint return with his wife?

First, find his tax table income, $17,300, as follows: (Also see item 6, page 257.)

Adjusted gross income = 20,000 − 500 = $19,500.

Excess itemized deductions = 5,400 − 3,200 = $2,200.

Tax table income = 19,500 − 2,200 = $17,300.

In computing the excess itemized deductions, we use $3,200 in the subtraction since it is the zero bracket amount for a joint return.

Next, find the appropriate tax table. Table B is provided for married persons filing joint returns. The computed tax table income $17,300 is on the line of "over $17,250 but not over $17,300." His tax on the line in column 5 (exemptions) is found to be $1,712.

**Example 2**   Assume that the facts are the same as in Example 1, except that Verson is unmarried and qualifies as head of household. His 5 personal exemptions include himself and his three brothers and one sister. How much is his tax?

His adjusted gross income is the same, $19,500. In computing the excess itemized deductions, we use $2,200 in the subtraction since it is the zero bracket amount for an unmarried head of household. Thus,

Excess itemized deductions = 5,400 − 2,200 = $3,200.

Tax table income = 19,500 − 3,200 = $16,300.

Table D is provided for unmarried heads of household. The computed tax table income $16,300 is on the line of "over $16,250 but not over $16,300." His tax on the line in column 5 (exemptions) is found to be $1,841.

## METHOD B—USING TAX RATE SCHEDULES

A taxpayer must use the tax rate schedules to figure the tax instead of using the tax tables if (a) the tax table income is more than $20,000 (more than $40,000 for married persons filing joint returns or qualifying widow(er)s), or (b) the number of exemptions is more than the coverage in the tax tables. For illustrative purposes, again only selected amounts from the four tax rate schedules (Schedules X, Y(1), Y(2), and Z) are given in this section.

In general, the tax rates are based on the taxable income in computing the tax, and

$$\text{Taxable income} = \text{Tax table income} - \left( \$750 \times \begin{array}{c} \text{Number of} \\ \text{exemptions} \end{array} \right)$$

**Example 3**     Assume that the facts are the same as in Example 1, except that Verson files a separate return (and still claims 5 personal exemptions). How much is his tax?

His adjusted gross income is the same, $19,500. In computing the excess itemized deductions, we use $1,600 in the subtraction since it is the zero bracket amount for a married person filing separately. Thus,

Excess itemized deductions = $5,400 − $1,600 = $3,800.

Tax table income = 19,500 − 3,800 = $15,700.

Then, observe Tax Table C, which is provided for married persons filing separate returns with tax table income of $20,000 or less who claim fewer than 4 exemptions. However, we have 5 exemptions in this problem. Thus, we must use a tax rate schedule to compute the tax. First, find the taxable income:

$$\begin{aligned} \text{Taxable income} &= \$15,700 - (\$750 \times 5) \\ &= \$15,700 - \$3,750 \\ &= \$11,950. \end{aligned}$$

Since he files a separate return, the rate in Schedule Y(2) must be applied. His taxable income is on the line of "over $11,600 but not over $13,600" and the tax rate is $2,190 plus 32% of the amount over $11,600.

$$\begin{aligned} \text{Income tax} &= 2,190 + (11,950 - 11,600)32\% \\ &= 2,190 + (350)32\% \\ &= \$2,302. \end{aligned}$$

## TAX RATE SCHEDULE X. SINGLE TAXPAYERS—Not qualifying for rates in Schedule Y or Z

| If the taxable income is: | The tax is: | of the amount |
|---|---|---|
| Not over $2,200 . . . . . . . . . . . . . . . . . . . . . . . . . . . . . . . .$0 | | over |
| **Over—   But not over** | | |
| $   2,200—$   2,700  . . . . . . . . . . . . . . . . . . . . . . . . .14% | | $   2,200 |
| $   2,700—$   3,200  . . . . . . . . . . . . . . . .$     70 + 15% | | $   2,700 |
| $   3,200—$   3,700  . . . . . . . . . . . . . . . .$   145 + 16% | | $   3,200 |
| . . . . . . . . | | |
| $ 12,200—$ 14,200  . . . . . . . . . . . . . . . .$ 2,090 + 27% | | $ 12,200 |
| $ 14,200—$ 16,200  . . . . . . . . . . . . . . . .$ 2,630 + 29% | | $ 14,200 |
| $ 16,200—$ 18,200  . . . . . . . . . . . . . . . .$ 3,210 + 31% | | $ 16,200 |
| $ 18,200—$ 20,200  . . . . . . . . . . . . . . . .$ 3,830 + 34% | | $ 18,200 |
| . . . . . . . . | | |
| $ 82,200—$ 92,200  . . . . . . . . . . . . . . . .$39,390 + 68% | | $ 82,200 |
| $ 92,200—$102,200  . . . . . . . . . . . . . . . .$46,190 + 69% | | $ 92,200 |
| $102,200—  . . . . . . . . . . . . . . . . . . . . . . . .$53,090 + 70% | | $102,200 |

## TAX RATE SCHEDULE Y(1). MARRIED TAXPAYERS filing joint returns and QUALIFYING WIDOWS and WIDOWERS*

| If the taxable income is: | The tax is: | of the amount over |
|---|---|---|
| Not over $3,200 . . . . . . . . . . . . . . . . . . . . . . . . . . . . . . . . $0 | | |
| Over—    But not over | | |
| $   3,200—$   4,200 . . . . . . . . . . . . . . . . . . . . . . . . . . . .14% | | $   3,200 |
| $   4,200—$   5,200 . . . . . . . . . . . . . . . .$      140 + 15% | | $   4,200 |
| $   5,200—$   6,200 . . . . . . . . . . . . . . . .$      290 + 16% | | $   5,200 |
| $ 15,200—$ 19,200 . . . . . . . . . . . . . . . .$   2,260 + 25% | | $ 15,200 |
| $ 19,200—$ 23,200 . . . . . . . . . . . . . . . .$   3,260 + 28% | | $ 19,200 |
| $ 23,200—$ 27,200 . . . . . . . . . . . . . . . .$   4,380 + 32% | | $ 23,200 |
| $ 27,200—$ 31,200 . . . . . . . . . . . . . . . .$   5,660 + 36% | | $ 27,200 |
| $163,200—$183,200 . . . . . . . . . . . . . . . .$ 83,580 + 68% | | $163,200 |
| $183,200—$203,200 . . . . . . . . . . . . . . . .$ 97,180 + 69% | | $183,200 |
| $203,200—    . . . . . . . . . . . . . . . . . . . . . .$110,980 + 70% | | $203,200 |

* Certain widows and widowers with dependent child may compute the tax as if a joint return had been filed for the first two taxable years after the taxable year in which his or her spouse dies.

## TAX RATE SCHEDULE Y(2). MARRIED TAXPAYERS filing separate returns

| If the taxable income is: | The tax is: | of the amount over |
|---|---|---|
| Not over $1,600 . . . . . . . . . . . . . . . . . . . . . . . . . . . . . . . $0 | | |
| Over—    But not over | | |
| $   1,600—$   2,100 . . . . . . . . . . . . . . . . . . . . . . . . .14% | | $   1,600 |
| $   2,100—$   2,600 . . . . . . . . . . . . . . . .$       70 + 15% | | $   2,100 |
| $   2,600—$   3,100 . . . . . . . . . . . . . . . .$      145 + 16% | | $   2,600 |
| $ 11,600—$ 13,600 . . . . . . . . . . . . . . . .$ 2,190 + 32% | | $ 11,600 |
| $ 13,600—$ 15,600 . . . . . . . . . . . . . . . .$ 2,830 + 36% | | $ 13,600 |
| $ 15,600—$ 17,600 . . . . . . . . . . . . . . . .$ 3,550 + 39% | | $ 15,600 |
| $ 17,600—$ 19,600 . . . . . . . . . . . . . . . .$ 4,330 + 42% | | $ 17,600 |
| $ 81,600—$ 91,600 . . . . . . . . . . . . . . . .$41,790 + 68% | | $ 81,600 |
| $ 91,600—$101,600 . . . . . . . . . . . . . . . .$48,590 + 69% | | $ 91,600 |
| $101,600—    . . . . . . . . . . . . . . . . . . . . . .$55,490 + 70% | | $101,600 |

**Example 4**     Assume that the facts are the same as in Example 1, except that Verson is single and claims 5 personal exemptions. How much is his tax?

His adjusted gross income is the same, $19,500. In computing the excess itemized deductions, we use $2,200 in the subtraction since it is the zero bracket amount for a single person. Thus,

Excess itemized deductions = 5,400 − 2,200 = $3,200.

## TAX RATE SCHEDULE Z. UNMARRIED (or legally separated) TAXPAYERS
### who qualify as HEADS OF HOUSEHOLD

| If the taxable income is: | The tax is: | of the amount |
|---|---|---|
| Not over $2,200 ................................$0 | | over |
| Over— But not over | | |
| $  2,200—$  3,200 ...........................14% | | $  2,200 |
| $  3,200—$  4,200 .................$    140 + 16% | | $  3,200 |
| $  4,200—$  6,200 .................$    300 + 18% | | $  4,200 |
| . . . . . . . . . | | |
| $ 14,200—$ 16,200 .................$  2,440 + 27% | | $ 14,200 |
| $ 16,200—$ 18,200 .................$  2,980 + 28% | | $ 16,200 |
| $ 18,200—$ 20,200 .................$  3,540 + 31% | | $ 18,200 |
| $ 20,200—$ 22,200 .................$  4,160 + 32% | | $ 20,200 |
| . . . . . . . . . | | |
| $142,200—$162,200 .................$ 75,720 + 68% | | $142,200 |
| $162,200—$182,200 .................$ 89,320 + 69% | | $162,200 |
| $182,200—  ......................$103,120 + 70% | | $182,200 |

Tax table income $= 19,500 - 3,200 = \$16,300$.

Then, observe Tax Table A, which is provided for single persons with tax table income of $20,000 or less who claim fewer than 4 exemptions. However, we have 5 exemptions in this problem. Thus, we must use a tax rate schedule to compute the tax. First, find the taxable income:

$$\text{Taxable income} = \$16,300 - (\$750 \times 5)$$
$$= \$16,300 - \$3,750$$
$$= \$12,550.$$

Since he files a single return, the rate in Schedule X must be applied. His taxable income is on the line of "over $12,200 but not over $14,200" and the tax rate is $2,090 plus 27% of the amount over $12,200.

$$\text{Income tax} = 2,090 + (12,550 - 12,200)27\%$$
$$= \$2,184.50.$$

## CREDITS AGAINST TAX

There are many kinds of credits that are allowed as deductions from the income tax of a taxpayer, such as credit for contributions to candidates for public office, credit for the elderly, and foreign tax credit. However, the kind that applies to every taxpayer for the 1978 tax return is the *general tax credit*. The general tax credit already has been taken into account in constructing the tax tables. For those who use the tax rate schedules in computing the income tax, the general tax is determined as follows:

(a) Married taxpayers filing separate returns will be limited to a credit based on $35 per exemption.

(b) Other taxpayers must select the larger of the amount found in (1) or the amount (not more than $180) computed in (2) below. The larger amount is the general tax credit.

(1) Credit = $35 × total number of exemptions claimed
(2) Credit = (Taxable income − Zero bracket amount) × 2%

Zero bracket amount:

$3,200 for a married person filing a joint return (or a qualifying widow(er));

$2,200 for a single (or an unmarried head of household).

**Example 5**   Refer to Example 3. Find (a) Verson's general tax credit, and (b) his final tax after the general tax credit is deducted.

(a) Since he files a separate return, his general tax credit is limited to the amount based on $35 per exemption, or

$35 × 5 (exemptions) = $175

(b) His final tax = $2,302 (see Example 3) − $175
          = $2,127.

**Example 6**   Refer to Example 4. Find (a) Verson's general tax credit, and (b) his final tax after the general tax credit is deducted.

(a) Since he files a single return, his general tax credit is limited to $180 and is derived as follows:

(1) Credit = $35 × 5 = $175
(2) Credit = ($12,550 − $2,200) × 2%
         = ($10,350) × 2%
         = $207 (limited to $180)

Select the larger of the amount in (1), $175, or the amount in (2), $180: $180 is the general tax credit for him.

(b) His final tax = $2,184.50 (see Example 4) − $180.00
          = $2,004.50.

## NET TAX PAYABLE TO GOVERNMENT (OR REFUNDABLE TO THE TAXPAYER)

There are amounts prepaid by taxpayers to the government before filing tax returns. The amounts that occur most frequently are the tax withheld from the taxpayer's wages by an employer and the taxpayer's prepayment of estimated tax. If the tax indicated on the return is larger than the prepaid payment, the difference must be paid to the government with the return. On the other hand, if the tax on the return is smaller than the prepaid payment, the difference will be refunded to the taxpayer at a later date.

**Example 7**   If the tax withheld from John Verson's salary for the taxable year were $2,000, what is the net tax payable or refundable in (a) Example 1? (b) Example 2? (c) Examples 3 and 5? (d) Examples 4 and 6?

(a) Example 1:
    Total tax in the return . . . . . . . . . . . . . . $1,712.00
    Less: tax withheld . . . . . . . . . . . . . . . . . 2,000.00
         Tax refundable                      ($ 288.00)

(b) Example 2:
    Total tax in the return . . . . . . . . . . . . . . 1,841.00
    Less: tax withheld . . . . . . . . . . . . . . . . . 2,000.00
         Tax refundable . . . . . . . . . . . . . . . . .($ 159.00)

(c) Examples 3 and 5:
    Total tax in the return . . . . . . . . . . . . . . $2,127.00
    Less: tax withheld . . . . . . . . . . . . . . . . . 2,000.00
         Tax payable . . . . . . . . . . . . . . . . . . $ 127.00

(d) Examples 4 and 6:
    Total tax in the return . . . . . . . . . . . . . . $2,004.50
    Less: tax withheld . . . . . . . . . . . . . . . . . 2,000.00
         Tax payable . . . . . . . . . . . . . . . . . . $    4.50

Notice that the joint return gives a lower amount of tax (Example 1, $1,712) than the separate return (Example 5, $2,127.)

# C. Corporation Taxes

As a general rule, the taxable income of a corporation is computed in much the same manner as that of an individual. However, the tax rates are different and there are a number of variations in terminology and deductions. The ordinary business corporation is subject to two taxes—a normal tax and a surtax.

Since there is no provision in the tax law for an adjusted gross income in the case of a corporation, there is no division of deductions between those for adjusted gross income and other itemized deductions. Corporations are generally entitled to the same itemized business deductions as individuals. Examples of the itemized deductions are salaries and wages, rent, repairs, interest, advertising, bad debts, and net operating loss. Deductions of a purely personal nature, such as medical expenses, alimony payments, the standard deduction, and deductions for personal exemptions, are excluded. However, corporations are entitled to special deductions not available to individuals. For example, corporations are allowed a deduction equal to 85% of dividends received from taxable domestic corporations.

Under 1978 tax regulations, the normal tax was 20% of the first $25,000 of taxable income plus 22% on taxable income in excess of $25,000, and the surtax was 26% of taxable income in excess of $50,000. The following pattern is an outline for computing the normal tax and the surtax of a corporation:

Gross income .......................................$180,000
Less: Itemized deductions ....................$76,000
       Special deductions ......................  4,000    80,000
       Taxable income ..................................$100,000

Normal tax:
First $25,000 taxable in-
     come ...........................$25,000 × 20% = $5,000
     Excess of $25,000 .........($100,000 − $25,000) × 22% = $16,500
                                     Sub-Total   $21,500

Surtax:
     Excess of $50,000 .........($100,000 − $50,000) × 26% = $13,000
     Total tax:                                     $34,500

The same result may be obtained by the following method:

Tax on the first amount:     $ 25,000 × 20%  = $ 5,000
Tax on the second amount:   $ 25,000 × 22%  = $ 5,500
Tax on the third amount:     $ 50,000 × 48%* = $24,000
     Total:                   $100,000         $34,500

*22% + 26% = 48%.

# ★EXERCISE 8–8

## Reference: Section 8.9

In each of the following problems involving individual tax returns, find the tax after the general tax credit is deducted.

**A.** *Compute the tax in Problems 1–8 for each type of return as indicated in the last column. The letters in the last column represent returns as follows:·* *(a) single, (b) joint, (c) head of household, and (d) married, filing separately. (Round to the nearest dollar figure.)*

| | Gross Income | Deductions for Adjusted Gross Income | Deductions— Itemized | Deductions— Number of Personal Exemptions | Type of Return |
|---|---|---|---|---|---|
| 1. | $ 14,000 | $1,300 | $ 5,000 | 3 | (a), (c) |
| 2. | 19,760 | 1,000 | 4,700 | 2 | (b), (d) |
| 3. | 21,950 | 2,000 | Not used | 2 | (a), (c), (d) |
| 4. | 10,400 | 400 | Not used | 3 | (a), (b), (c) |
| 5. | 12,000 | 2,100 | Not used | 1 | (a), (d) |
| 6. | 17,300 | None | Not used | 2 | (a), (b) |
| 7. | 26,000 | 3,000 | 6,000 | 5 | (b), (c) |
| 8. | 100,000 | 1,000 | 10,000 | 4 | (a), (d) |

**B.** *Statement Problems:*

9. A married couple who file a joint return had a gross income of $18,350 in 1978. The husband's travel expenses incurred while away from home in connection with his employment were $650. Their itemized deductions were $3,500, and they claimed three exemptions. The tax withheld from their wages for the year was $2,050. Find (a) the tax and (b) the net tax payable or refundable.

10. Refer to Problem 9. Suppose the couple file separate returns and the information concerning his tax is as follows: gross income, $18,000; travel expenses, $650; itemized deductions, $3,200; exemptions, 2. (a) What is his tax? (b) Compare the total amount of their taxes (her tax is $0) with the tax computed in Problem 9. Which amount is larger? (Note: If husband and wife (not legally separated) file separate returns and one itemizes deductions, the other must also itemize deductions).

11. Joe Hanson had a salary of $21,000 in 1978. His deductions for adjusted gross income were $420, and his itemized deductions were $960. He is single and claims one exemption for himself. (a) What is the amount of his tax for the year? (b) If the tax withheld was $4,000, what is the net tax payable or refundable?

12. In Problem 11, if Hanson were a married man and claimed 2 exemptions, what would be his tax on a joint return?

13. During the year a corporation has a gross income of $130,000, itemized deductions of $20,000, and special deductions of $350. The normal tax rate is 20% of the first $25,000 of taxable income plus 22% on taxable income in excess of $25,000, and the surtax rate is 26% on taxable income over $50,000. Find the tax.

14. In Problem 13, assume the corporation has a gross income of $1,000,000, itemized deductions of $540,000 and special deductions of $1,500. (a) How much is the tax? (b) If the income and the itemized deductions (excluding the special deductions) applied to married persons who claim two exemptions and file a joint return, how much would the tax be?

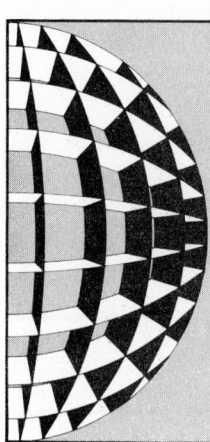

# Chapter 9

# Simple Interest
# and Simple Discount

This chapter discusses the concepts and operations of simple interest and simple discount. These discussions are essential in understanding the topics to be presented in the following chapters. Students should be very skillful with the illustrations and problems included in this chapter if they plan to study the areas related to bank discount, compound interest, annuities, and life insurance premiums.

## 9.1 SIMPLE INTEREST

## A. Basic Concept and Computation

A person who borrows money usually pays *interest* as a fee for the use of the money. The money borrowed is called the *principal*. The sum of the principal and the interest due is called the *amount*. The *rate of interest* is usually expressed as a percent of the principal for a specified period of time, which is generally one year. Interest paid only on the principal borrowed is called *simple interest*. When the interest for each period is added to the principal in computing the interest for the next period, it is called *compound interest*. Simple interest is usually charged for short-term borrowing, whereas compound interest is commonly employed in long-term obligations. In this chapter only simple interest is involved. Compound interest problems are discussed in Part 3.

The basic formula for computing simple interest is:

$$\text{Interest} = \text{Principal} \times \left(\begin{array}{c}\text{Interest rate} \\ \text{per period}\end{array}\right) \times \left(\begin{array}{c}\text{Number of interest} \\ \text{periods (or Time)}\end{array}\right)$$

The formula may be simply written:

$$I = Pin \tag{9-1}$$

The values of rate and time must correspond to each other. If the rate is an annual rate, the time must be expressed in years; whereas, if the rate is a quarterly rate, the time must be stated in quarters. Hereafter, unless otherwise specified, the annual interest rate will be used in computing simple interest problems. When the unit of time is one year, the formula is explained as follows:

$$I = Pin, \text{ where } I = \text{interest}$$
$$P = \text{principal}$$
$$i = \text{interest rate per year}$$
$$n = \text{number of } years, \text{ or a fraction of } one\ year$$

**Example 1**    What is the simple interest on $100 at 6% (a) for three years and (b) for two months?

(a) $P = 100$, $i = 6\%$ (per year), $n = 3$ (years).
Substituting the values in formula (9–1):

$$I = Pin = 100 \times 6\% \times 3 = \$18$$

(b) $n = \frac{2}{12}$, since 2 months $= \frac{2}{12}$ years.

$$I = Pin = 100 \times 6\% \times \frac{2}{12} = \$1$$

# B. Determining the Number of Days

Since time may be expressed in days, the number of days in a year must be determined before computing the interest. There are two methods used in determining the number of days in a year—the *exact method* and the *approximate method*. Under the exact method, as shown in Table 1 of the Appendix, each year has 365 days except leap years, which have 366 days. When the approximate method is used, it is assumed that each of the 12 months in a year has 30 days, and thus there are 360 days in a year. In finding the number of days between two given dates, count either the beginning date or the ending date, but not both. In this text, the practice of counting the ending date will be followed.

**Example 2**    Find (a) the exact time and (b) the approximate time from June 24, 1981, to September 27, 1981.

(a) The exact time:

| | |
|---|---|
| June ................. | 6 days (remainder, or $30 - 24 = 6$) |
| July ................. | 31 days |
| Aug ................. | 31 days |
| Sept. ................ | 27 days |
| | 95 days |

Or, according to Table 1, which shows the exact number of days, June 24 is the 175th day of the year and September 27 is the 270th day. $270 - 175 = 95$ days.

(b) The approximate time:

First, write the two given dates in the following form, arranging the months to the left of the days, and then subtract:

| *Month* | *Day* |
|---|---|
| 9 (Sept.) . . . . . . . . . . . . . . . . . | .27 |
| 6 (June) . . . . . . . . . . . . . . . . . | .24 |
| 3 months . . . . . . . . . . . . . . . . . | 3 days |

Since there are 30 days in each month by the approximate method, the number of days between the two given dates is $3 \times 30 + 3 = 93$ days.

**Example 3**     Find (a) the exact time and (b) the approximate time from November 14, 1980 to April 24, 1981.

(a) The exact time:

| 1980 | November . . . . . . . . | 16 days (remainder, or $30 - 14 = 16$) |
|---|---|---|
| | December . . . . . . . . | 31 days |
| 1981 | January . . . . . . . . . | 31 days |
| | February . . . . . . . . | 28 days |
| | March . . . . . . . . . . | 31 days |
| | April . . . . . . . . . . . | 24 days |
| | Total . . . . . . . . . | 161 days |

Or, according to Table 1 in the Appendix, which shows the exact number of days, November 14 is the 319th day of year 1980. The number of days remaining in 1980 is $366 - 319 = 47$ days. April 24 is the 114th day of year 1981. Thus, the total number of days between the two given dates is $47 + 114 = 161$ days. (1980 is a leap year.)

(b) The approximate time:

Arrange the two given dates in the following form by the order of year, month, and day, and then subtract:

| | *Year* | *Month* | *Day* |
|---|---|---|---|
| Ending date . . . . . . . | 198$\not{1}^{0}$ | $\not{4}^{16}$ | 24 |
| Beginning date . . . . . . | 1980 | 11 | 14 |
| | 0 | 5 | 10 |

In the month column, since 11 months are larger than 4 months, borrow 1 year or 12 months from the year column to make a total of 16 months before subtracting.

The approximate time $= 5 \times 30 + 10 = 160$ days.

Leap years are those years evenly divisible by 4, such as 1976, 1980, and 1984, in which the month of February has 29 days instead of 28 days as in other years. But the last year of any century, although it is divisible by 4, is not a leap year unless it is divisible by 400. Thus, 1700, 1800, and 1900 were not leap years, but 2000 will be a leap year.

**Example 4**     Find the exact time from January 22, 1980, to March 12, 1980.

| January . . . . . . . . . . . . . . | 9 days (remainder, or $31 - 22 = 9$) |
|---|---|
| February . . . . . . . . . . . . . | 29 days (leap year) |
| March . . . . . . . . . . . . . . | 12 days |
| | 50 days |

## EXERCISE 9–1

### Reference: Sections 9.1 A and B

**A.** *Find the simple interest in each of the following problems:*

|  | Principal | Interest Rate | Time |
|---|---|---|---|
| **1.** | $462.60 | 8% | 4 months |
| **2.** | 283.20 | 7% | 5 months |
| **3.** | 540.00 | 6% | 1 year |
| **4.** | 480.50 | 4% | $\frac{1}{2}$ year |
| **5.** | 126.60 | 9% | 6 months |
| **6.** | 235.20 | 10% | 3 months |
| **7.** | 35.00 | 12% | 18 months |
| **8.** | 78.00 | 18% | 15 months |
| **9.** | 268.80 | 15% | 1 year, 5 months |
| **10.** | 346.40 | 14% | 1 year, 7 months |

**B.** *Determine the number of days in each of the following problems by (a) the exact time method and (b) the approximate time method:*

**11.** April 30, 1980, to July 6, 1980.
**12.** May 16, 1980, to September 7, 1980.
**13.** July 5, 1981, to December 12, 1981.
**14.** August 13, 1981, to November 20, 1981.
**15.** September 19, 1982, to October 28, 1982.
**16.** June 16, 1982, to August 15, 1982.
**17.** January 6, 1984, to January 30, 1985.
**18.** February 17, 1984, to March 10, 1985.
**19.** December 16, 1985, to April 9, 1986.
**20.** October 10, 1985, to May 7, 1986.

## C. Ordinary and Exact Interest

The exact and approximate methods of determining the number of days provide four possible ways to express a number of days as a fraction of a year:

1. $\dfrac{\text{Exact time}}{360}$ (Banker's Rule) ⎫

2. $\dfrac{\text{Approximate time}}{360}$ ⎬ for computing ordinary interest

3. $\dfrac{\text{Exact time}}{365}$ ⎫

4. $\dfrac{\text{Approximate time}}{365}$ ⎬ for computing exact interest

The value of interest computed by using 360 as the divisor in the time factor is called *ordinary interest.* The first time fraction, which is used in the *Banker's Rule,* is much more commonly used in commercial practice than the second time fraction. Unless otherwise specified, hereafter the Banker's Rule will be used in this text in computing ordinary interest. Also, the unqualified term "simple interest" will mean "ordinary interest" when a number of days is given in a problem.

When 365 is used as the divisor, the result is called *exact interest.* The third time fraction is usually used in calculating interest payments on government obligations, in foreign trade, and in rediscounting notes for member banks by the Federal Reserve Banks. The fourth time fraction is seldom used. Hereafter, only the third time fraction will be used in illustrations and problems in this text for computing exact interest.

**Example 5**     Express the time from June 24, 1980, to September 27, 1980, in years for computing (a) ordinary interest, and (b) exact interest.

The exact time between the two dates is 95 days (see Example 2 on page 273). Thus,

(a) $\dfrac{95}{360}$ (b) $\dfrac{95}{365}$

## CALCULATING ORDINARY INTEREST

Ordinary interest may be calculated by formula or by the 6% for 60 days method.

**By Formula.** When the number of days is given, the days should be expressed as a fraction of a year. Let $t$ denote the exact number of days. In computing ordinary simple interest *(I)* by the Banker's Rule, formula (9–1) becomes

$$I = Pi\left(\frac{t}{360}\right) = \frac{Pit}{360} \tag{9–2}$$

**Example 6**     Find the ordinary interest on $450 at 5% for 30 days.

$P = 450$, $i = 5\%$, $t = 30$ (days). Substituting these values in formula (9–2):

$I = 450 \times 5\% \times \frac{30}{360} = 1.875$, or $1.88

**Example 7**     Find the ordinary interest on $1 at 6% $(= \frac{6}{100})$ for 60 days.

$I = 1 \times \frac{6}{100} \times \frac{60}{360} = \frac{1}{100} = \$.01$

**By 6% for 60 Days Method.** Example 7 indicates that the ordinary interest on $1 at 6% for 60 days is $.01. A short-cut method of computing ordinary simple interest can thus be derived: *The interest on any amount at 6% for 60 days is determined by moving the decimal point in the principal two places to the left.*

**Example 8**    Find the ordinary interest on $139.20 at 6% for 60 days.

The ordinary interest is $1.39,20 or $1.3920, rounded to $1.39.

When the above idea is extended, the ordinary interest on a principal at any rate and for any number of days may be found by the short-cut method. The following examples are used to illustrate how ordinary interest is computed for a certain period other than 60 days or at a rate other than 6%.

**Example 9**    Find the ordinary interest on $1,392 at 6% for 70 days.

Interest at 6% for 60 days . . . . .$13.92
(+) Interest at 6% for 10 days . . . . .   2.32 (= 13.92 × $\frac{1}{6}$, since 10 days is $\frac{1}{6}$ of 60 days)
_____
Interest at 6% for 70 days . . . . .$16.24

**Example 10**    Find the ordinary interest on $1,392 at 9% for 70 days.

Interest at 6% for 70 days . . . . .$16.24 (See Example 9)
(+) Interest at 3% for 70 days . . . . .   8.12 (= $16.24 × $\frac{1}{2}$, since 3% = $\frac{1}{2}$ of 6%)
_____
Interest at 9% for 70 days . . . . .$24.36

*Check:*        $1,392 \times 9\% \times \frac{70}{360} = 24.36$

**Example 11**    Find the ordinary interest on $324 at 5% for 40 days.

Interest at 6% for 60 days . . . . .$3.24
(−) Interest at 1% for 60 days . . . . .   .54 (= 3.24 × $\frac{1}{6}$, since 1% is $\frac{1}{6}$ of 6%)
_____
Interest at 5% for 60 days . . . . .$2.70
(−) Interest at 5% for 20 days . . . . .   .90 (= 2.70 × $\frac{1}{3}$, since 20 days is $\frac{1}{3}$ of 60 days)
_____
Interest at 5% for 40 days . . . . .$1.80

*Check:*        $324 \times 5\% \times \dfrac{40}{360} = \$1.80$

Note that the 6% for 60 days method may also be used in computing the simple interest when the time is given in a number of months. The interest on $1 at 6% for two months is also $.01 since $I = 1 \times 6\% \times \frac{2}{12} = \$.01$.

## CALCULATING EXACT INTEREST

Let $I_e$ denote the exact simple interest. When the number of days is given, formula (9–1) is written in the following manner:

$$I_e = Pi\left(\frac{t}{365}\right) = \frac{Pit}{365} \qquad\qquad \textbf{(9–3)}$$

**Example 12**    Find the exact interest on $450 at 5% for 30 days.

$450 \times \frac{5}{100} \times \frac{30}{365} = 1.849$, or $1.85

## ★THE RELATIONSHIP BETWEEN I AND I$_e$

Use of the ordinary interest method always gives a larger value of interest than the exact interest method. When the answer in Example 6 is compared with the answer in Example 12, the ordinary interest is found to be larger than the exact interest by $.03 (or $1.88 − $1.85). The relationship between $I$ and $I_e$ is expressed as follows:

$$\frac{I}{I_e} = \frac{73}{72}, \text{ which means that "the ratio of } I \text{ to } I_e \text{ is } \frac{73}{72}."\ {}^{[1]}$$

Or, $$\frac{I_e}{I} = \frac{72}{73}.$$

Using the method described above, the ordinary interest for Example 6 may be computed from the exact interest as follows:

Since $I_e = 1.849$ (Example 12),

$$\frac{I}{1.849} = \frac{73}{72}$$

$$I = 1.849(\tfrac{73}{72}) = 1.849(1 + \tfrac{1}{72})$$

$$= 1.849 + 1.849(\tfrac{1}{72}) = 1.849 + .026 = 1.875, \text{ or } 1.88$$

Thus, $I$ is $\tfrac{1}{72}$ more than $I_e$. Or $I = I_e + I_e(\tfrac{1}{72})$

The exact interest for Example 12 may be computed from the ordinary interest as shown below:

Since $I = 1.875$ (Example 6),

$$\frac{I_e}{1.875} = \frac{72}{73}$$

$$I_e = 1.875(\tfrac{72}{73}) = 1.875(1 - \tfrac{1}{73})$$
$$= 1.875 - 1.875(\tfrac{1}{73}) = 1.875 - .026 = 1.849, \text{ or } 1.85$$

Thus, $I_e$ is $\tfrac{1}{73}$ less than $I$. Or, $I_e = I - I(\tfrac{1}{73})$

# EXERCISE 9–2

## Reference: Section 9.1 C

**A.** *Express the time in years in each of the following problems for computing (a) ordinary interest, and (b) exact interest.*

1. June 6 to September 30.
2. July 10 to November 7.
3. May 21 to July 5.

4. April 15 to June 22.
5. January 4 to February 3.
6. August 17 to December 8.

---

[1] *Proof:*

$$\frac{I}{I_e} = \frac{\dfrac{Pit}{360}}{\dfrac{Pit}{365}} = \frac{Pit}{360} \times \frac{365}{Pit} = \frac{365}{360} = \frac{73}{72}$$

**B.** *In each of the following cases, find: (a) the ordinary interest by (1) the formula method, and (2) the 6% for 60 days method; (b) the exact interest.*

| Principal | *Interest Rate* | *Time* |
|-----------|-----------------|--------|
| **7.** $ 3,180 | 10% | 72 days |
| **8.** 4,080 | 18% | 15 days |
| **9.** 42,200 | 15% | 30 days |
| **10.** 14,400 | 12% | 70 days |
| **11.** 2,192 | 9% | 45 days |
| **12.** 2,970 | 8% | 80 days |
| **13.** 365 | 7% | 120 days |
| **14.** 216 | 6% | 36 days |
| **15.** 2,880 | $5\frac{1}{2}$% | 40 days |
| **16.** 360 | $4\frac{1}{2}$% | 66 days |

★**C.** *For each of the following exact interests ($I_e$), find the ordinary interest (I):*

**17.** $0.72          **19.** $5.04          **21.** $6.48
**18.** $2.52          **20.** $1.44          **22.** $4.32

★**D.** *For each of the following ordinary interests (I), find the exact interest ($I_e$):*

**23.** $0.73          **25.** $2.92          **27.** $3.65
**24.** $1.46          **26.** $2.19          **28.** $5.84

## 9.2  AMOUNT, RATE, AND TIME

## A. Finding the Amount

The *amount* is the sum of the principal and the interest. Let $S$ denote the amount. The formula below is based on this definition:

$S = P + I$, or
$S = P + Pin$, or factoring $P$,

$$S = P(1 + in) \tag{9-4}$$

**Example 1**     (a) What is the simple interest on $700 for 125 days at 10%?
(b) What is the amount? (Use the Banker's Rule.)

(a) Since the number of days is given in the problem, the simple interest is computed by formula (9–2) as follows:

$$I = Pi\left(\frac{t}{360}\right) = 700 \times 10\% \times \frac{125}{360} = \$24.31$$

(b) Substituting the interest and the principal in formula (9–4):

$$S = P + I$$
$$= 700 + 24.31 = \$724.31$$

**Example 2**    A man borrows $500 for four months at 9%. How much must he repay?

Since the number of months is given in the problem, the simple interest is computed by expressing four months as $\frac{4}{12}$ or $\frac{1}{3}$ of a year and by substituting the given values in formula (9–4) as follows:

$$I = 500 \times 9\% \times \tfrac{1}{3} = 15;$$
$$S = P + I = 500 + 15 = \$515, \text{ or}$$
$$S = P(1 + in) = 500(1 + 9\% \times \tfrac{1}{3}) = 500(1.03) = \$515$$

**Example 3**    On May 24, 1980, Joan Harrison borrowed $650 and agreed to repay the loan together with interest at 8% in 90 days. What amount must she repay? On what date?

$$I = 650 \times 8\% \times \tfrac{90}{360} = \$13.00$$
$$S = 650 + 13.00 = \$663.00$$

May . . . . . . . . . . . . . 7 days $(31 - 24 = 7)$
June . . . . . . . . . . . . . .30 days
July . . . . . . . . . . . . . .<u>31</u> days
                            68 days
August . . . . . . . . . .<u>22</u> days
                            90 days

The amount, $663.00, must be repaid on August 22, 1980.

# B. Finding the Rate

An *interest rate (i)* is obtained by dividing the interest by the product of the principal and the time. This is based on formula (9–1). When both sides of the formula $I = Pin$ are divided by $Pn$, the following result is obtained:

$$i = \frac{I}{Pn} = \frac{\text{Interest}}{\text{Principal} \times \text{Time}}$$

Note that the interest rate and the time must correspond to each other. In other words, when the given time is expressed in months, the interest rate found is expressed in a monthly rate; when the time is expressed in years, the rate found is a yearly rate. In computing simple interest, the time should be expressed in years since the rate is usually expressed in a yearly rate in such a problem.

**Example 4**    At what interest rate will $450 yield $236.25 in five years?

Substituting $P = 450$, $I = 236.25$, and $n = 5$ (years) in the formula $I = Pin$; then

$$236.25 = 450(i)(5)$$

Solving for *i:*

$$i = \frac{236.25}{(450)(5)} = \frac{236.25}{2,250} = .105 \text{ or } 10\tfrac{1}{2}\% \text{ (yearly)}$$

**Example 5**    A payment of $1,521.25 was made for discharging a four-month loan of $1,500. What was the interest rate charged?

When the principal and the amount are given, the interest should be found first. This is done by using formula (9–4): $I = S - P$, since $S = P + I$. Substituting the values $S = 1,521.25$ and $P = 1,500$ in the formula:

$$I = 1,521.25 - 1,500 = \$21.25$$

Substituting $I = 21.25$, $n = \tfrac{4}{12} = \tfrac{1}{3}$ (year), and $P = 1,500$:

$$i = \frac{I}{Pn} = \frac{21.25}{1,500(\tfrac{1}{3})} = \frac{21.25}{500} = .0425, \text{ or } 4.25\% = 4\tfrac{1}{4}\%$$

**Example 6**    A man who borrowed $1,350 paid $1,363.50 as the total amount at the end of 90 days. What was the interest rate he paid?

$$I = 1,363.50 - 1,350 = 13.50$$

$$i = \frac{13.50}{1,350 \times \tfrac{90}{360}} = \frac{13.50}{1,350 \times \tfrac{1}{4}} = \frac{1}{100 \times \tfrac{1}{4}} = \frac{4}{100}, \text{ or } 4\%$$

# C. Finding the Time

The *time (n)* of a loan is obtained by dividing the interest by the product of the principal and the interest rate. This is also based on formula (9–1). When both sides of the formula $I = Pin$ are divided by $Pi$, the following result is obtained:

$$n = \frac{I}{Pi} = \frac{\text{Interest}}{\text{Principal} \times \text{Rate}}$$

**Example 7**    How long will it take $1,000 to yield $100 interest at 8%?

Substituting $I = 100$, $P = 1,000$, and $i = 8\%$ in the formula $I = Pin$:

$$100 = 1,000(8\%)(n),$$

Solving for *n:*

$$n = \frac{100}{1,000 \times .08} = \frac{100}{80} = 1.25 \text{ (years)}$$

The answer may be converted to months as $1.25 \times 12 = 15$ (months). It may also be converted to days, if it is an exact time, as $1.25 \times 365 = 456.25$ days; or if it is an approximate time, as $1.25 \times 360 = 450$ days.

## EXERCISE 9–3

**Reference: Section 9.2**

**A.** *In each of the following cases, find the unknown values:*

| | Principal | Annual Interest Rate | Time | Interest | Amount |
|---|---|---|---|---|---|
| **1.** | $ 120 | 12% | 30 days | ? | ? |
| **2.** | 2,500 | ? | 45 days | ? | $2,512.50 |
| **3.** | 4,500 | 6% | ? days | $ 56.25 | ? |
| **4.** | 345 | ? | 120 days | 9.20 | ? |
| **5.** | 720 | 8% | ? months | ? | 739.20 |
| **6.** | 640 | ? | 6 months | 16.00 | ? |
| **7.** | 570 | ? | 4 months | ? | 577.60 |
| **8.** | 1,000 | 15% | ? months | 100.00 | ? |
| **9.** | 2,000 | 18% | ? years | 720.00 | ? |
| **10.** | 2,250 | ? | $2\frac{1}{2}$ years | ? | 2,587.50 |
| **11.** | 3,460 | ? | 3 years | 519.00 | ? |
| **12.** | 4,280 | 7% | ? years | ? | 4,729.40 |

**B.** *Statement Problems:*

**13.** (a) Find the simple interest on $72,400 at 7% for 45 days. (b) What is the amount?

**14.** (a) Find the simple interest on $325 at 5% for two years. (b) What is the amount?

**15.** A man borrowed $1,000 at 10% for five months. How much must he repay?

**16.** A man borrowed $500 at 12% for 66 days. How much must he repay?

**17.** If $540 is borrowed for three years at 8%, what is the amount due at the end of the third year?

**18.** If $820 is borrowed for eight months at 9%, what is the amount due at the end of the period?

**19.** On July 10, 1980, Jim Tedd borrowed $950 and agreed to repay it with interest at 15% in 120 days. (a) What amount must he repay and (b) on what date?

**20.** On May 21, 1981, Jane Herbert borrowed $1,200 at 9% interest for 45 days. (a) What amount must she repay and (b) when?

**21.** At what interest rate will $260 yield $1.30 interest in 60 days?

**22.** At what interest rate will $450 yield $4.50 interest in (a) three months? (b) one year?

**23.** A man borrowed $1,350 and paid $1,372.50 after four months. What was the interest rate charged for the debt?

**24.** A note for $2,400 was repaid after 120 days in the amount of $2,432. What was the interest rate on the note?

**25.** The Taylor Hardware Store received an invoice for the purchase of handsaws costing $500. The terms were 2/10, *n*/30. If the store were to borrow money to pay the bill in 10 days and repay the loan in 30 days from the date of invoice, what is the highest interest rate at which the store could afford to borrow?

26. The Moore Drug Store received an invoice of $250, terms 3/10, 1/20, n/30. If the store borrows money in 10 days to pay the bill and repays the loan in 20 days from the date of invoice, what is the highest interest rate at which the store can afford to borrow?

27. How many months are required for $260 to yield $3.90 interest at 6%?

28. How many years will be required for $55 to yield $11 interest at 10%?

29. How many days are necessary for $240 to yield $1.60 interest at 8%?

30. How many days are needed for $380 to (a) amount to $389.50 at 5%? (b) yield $1.90 interest at 3%?

31. A woman has part of her money invested at 4% and the remainder at 6%. Her annual income from the investment is $22.80. If she had received 1% less interest on both of her two investments, her income would have been $18.60 annually. How much did she invest at each interest rate?

32. A woman borrows $3,000 and agrees to pay $500 on the principal plus the simple interest at 4% on the principal outstanding at the end of each six-month period. Find the total amount that must be paid to discharge the debt.

# 9.3 PRINCIPAL, PRESENT VALUE, AND SIMPLE DISCOUNT

## A. Finding the Principal

The principal may be obtained in the following ways:

By formula, $I = Pin$:

When both sides of the formula $I = Pin$ are divided by $in$, the following result is obtained:

$$P = \frac{I}{in}$$

**Example 1**  A woman receives $300 interest in three months from an investment which pays 12% interest. What is the principal that she has invested?

Substituting $I = 300$, $i = 12\%$, $n = \frac{3}{12} = \frac{1}{4}$ (year), in $I = Pin$:

$300 = P(12\%)(\frac{1}{4})$

Solving for $P$:

$$P = \frac{300}{(12\% \times 1/4)} = \frac{300}{(\frac{12}{100} \times \frac{1}{4})} = 300 \times \frac{100}{3} = \$10,000$$

By formula, $S = P + I = P + Pin = P(1 + in)$:

**Example 2**  A man paid a debt with a $280 check which included $30 interest. Find the principal.

Substituting $S = 280$ and $I = 30$ in the formula $P = S - I$, since $S = P + I$:

$P = 280 - 30 = \$250$

When both sides of the formula $S = P(1 + in)$ are divided by $(1 + in)$, the following result is obtained:

$$P = \frac{S}{1 + in} = \frac{S}{\textbf{Amount of 1}}$$

The numerator, $S$, is the total amount, while the denominator is the amount of 1 unit; that is, when the principal is \$1 and is invested at $i$ for $n$ periods, the amount is $\$(1 + in)$.

**Example 3**     How much money must Jones invest today at 6% simple interest if he is to receive \$1,416, the amount, in three years?

Substituting $S = 1,416$, $i = 6\%$, and $n = 3$ (years) in the formula $S = P(1 + in)$:

$1,416 = P[1 + 6\%(3)]$

Solving for $P$:

$$P = \frac{1,416}{1 + 6\%(3)} = \frac{1,416}{1.18} = \$1,200$$

In the above example, 1.18 is the amount of a principal of 1 (dollar) plus its interest at 6% for three years.

# B. Present Value

*Present value* is the value at the time of investment, such as the principal, or at any time before the maturity date (due date). Example 3 indicates that if Jones invests \$1,200 today at 6% simple interest, he will get \$1,416 in three years. In other words, the present value of \$1,416 which is due in three years and includes 6% interest is \$1,200. Thus, the method of finding the present value of a given amount which is due in the future, is the same as the method used in Example 3 in finding the principal.

# C. Simple Discount

The process of finding the present value of a given amount which is due on a future date is called *discounting at simple interest,* or commonly, the *simple discount method.* In other words, to discount an amount by the simple interest process is to find its present value.

When interest is involved, the amount must be larger than its present value. The difference between the amount and its present value is called the *simple discount.* Thus, the simple discount on the amount is the same as the simple interest on the principal or the present value. There are numerous occasions in business when it becomes necessary to discount an amount which is due on a future date. The principle of simple discount is important to compound discount problems dealing with long-term investments (Part 3), although the bank discount method (Section 10.1) is used widely in discounting short-term loans.

## DISCOUNTING A NON-INTEREST-BEARING DEBT

The following examples are given to illustrate the discounting of a non-interest-bearing debt.

**Example 4**  What is the present value of $3,248 which is due at the end of two months if the interest rate is 9%? What is the simple discount?

$S = 3,248$, $i = 9\%$, and $n = \frac{2}{12}$ or $\frac{1}{6}$ (year), the discount period.

Substituting the values in

$$S = P(1 + in), \text{ or } P = \frac{S}{1 + in}:$$

$$P = \frac{3,248}{1 + (\frac{9}{100})(\frac{1}{6})} = \frac{3,248}{1 + .015} = \$3,200$$

$$I = 3,248 - 3,200 = \$48 \text{ (Simple discount)}$$

*Check:*   According to the answer, the amount due at the end of two months should be

$$S = P(1 + in) = 3,200[1 + (.09)(\tfrac{1}{6})] = 3,200(1.015) = \$3,248$$

**Note:**   The simple discount on the amount, $3,248, is the same as the simple interest on the present value, $3,200. In other words, $I$ has a twofold meaning: it is the simple interest on the principal or the present value; it is also the simple discount on the amount.

**Example 5**  Discount $3,248 for two months at the simple interest rate 9%. What is the present value and the simple discount?

The answer in this example is the same as that in Example 4, since the two examples have the same meaning.

**Example 6**  A debt of $875.50 is due in six months. If the debt is settled now and the simple interest rate of 6% is allowed, what is the present value and the simple discount?

Substituting $S = 875.50$, $n = \frac{6}{12} = \frac{1}{2}$, and $i = 6\%$ in

$$P = \frac{S}{1 + in}, \text{ then the present value is}$$

$$P = \frac{875.50}{1 + 6\%(\frac{1}{2})} = \frac{875.50}{1.03} = \$850$$

The simple discount is

$$I = S - P = 875.50 - 850.00 = \$25.50$$

*Check:*   $850 \times 6\% \times \frac{1}{2} = \$25.50$

## DISCOUNTING AN INTEREST-BEARING DEBT

To find the present value of an interest-bearing debt (or to discount the amount by the simple discount method), take the following steps:

**Step (1)**   Find the maturity value (the amount) according to the original interest rate and the time stipulated for the debt. Use the formula $S = P(1 + in)$, where $S$ is the maturity value and $P$ is the original debt.

**Step (2)**   Find the present value (the value on the date of discount) of the maturity value according to the interest rate for discounting and the discount period. The discount period is the period from the date of discount to the maturity date. Use the formula in the form, $P = \dfrac{S}{1 + in}$, where $P$ is the present value and $S$ is the maturity value. However, the values of $i$ and $n$ in this step are often different from the values of $i$ and $n$ in Step (1).

**Example 7**   A man borrowed $1,000 on May 1, 1980, and agreed to repay the money plus 8% interest in six months. Two months after the money was borrowed, the creditor agreed to settle the debt by discounting it at the simple interest rate of 9%. How much did the creditor receive when he discounted the debt?

**Step (1)**   Find the maturity value of the debt according to the original stipulation of the debt. $P = 1,000$, $i = 8\%$, $n = \frac{6}{12} = \frac{1}{2}$ (year).

Substituting these values in the formula:

$S = P(1 + in) = 1,000(1 + 8\% \times \frac{1}{2})$
$= 1,000(1.04) = \$1,040$ (amount on November 1, 1980)

**Step (2)**   Find the present value of the maturity value according to the discounting terms. $S = 1,040$, $i = 9\%$, $n = \frac{4}{12} = \frac{1}{3}$ (year), or $6 - 2 = 4$ (months).

Substituting these values in the formula:

$$P = \frac{S}{1 + in} = \frac{1,040}{1 + 9\%(\frac{1}{3})} = \frac{1,040}{1.030} = \$1,009.71 \text{ (value on July 1, 1980)}$$

The example may be diagrammed as follows:

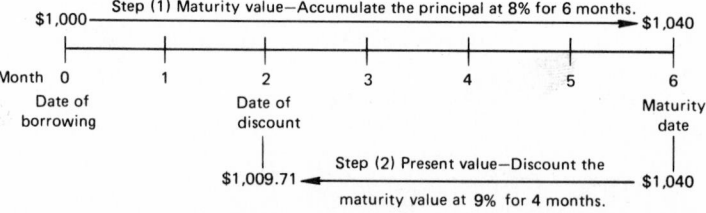

**Example 8**   In Example 7, assume that the simple interest rate for discounting is also 8%. How much would the creditor receive when discounting the debt?

**Step (1)**     The maturity value is the same, $1,040.

**Step (2)**     The present value of the maturity value is found as follows:

$S = 1,040$, $i = 8\%$, $n = \frac{1}{3}$ (year)

$$P = \frac{S}{1 + in} = \frac{1,040}{1 + 8\%(\frac{1}{3})} = \frac{1,040}{\frac{308}{300}} = \$1,012.99$$

***Note:***     1. The fraction $\frac{308}{300}$ in Example 8 is not changed to a decimal in computing

the final answer since it is a repetend, $\frac{308}{300} = 1.02666\ldots = 1.02\dot{6}$.

If the repetend is rounded to a decimal in the computation, the final answer might be different from the above obtained answer, such as

$$\frac{1,040}{1.0267} = 1,012.95, \text{ but } \frac{1,040 \times 300}{308} = 1,012.99$$

2. Even when the interest rate for computing the maturity value is the same as the interest rate for discounting, the two steps are still required. Refer to Example 8. The sum of the principal and the interest for two months (the period between the date of borrowing and the date of discounting) at a rate of 8% is

$$S = P + Pin = 1,000 + (1,000 \times 8\% \times \tfrac{2}{12}) = \$1,013.33$$

The sum is not the same as the present value $1,012.99 obtained by the method used in Example 8.

## EXERCISE 9–4

### Reference: Section 9.3

**A.** *In each of the following cases, find the principal:*

| | Interest Rate | Time | Interest | Amount |
|---|---|---|---|---|
| **1.** | ... | ... | $ 16.42 | $ 344.82 |
| **2.** | 10% | 2 years | 60.00 | ... |
| **3.** | 8% | 6 months | ... | 5,720.00 |
| **4.** | 12% | 4 months | 320.00 | ... |
| **5.** | 6% | $2\frac{1}{2}$ years | ... | 258.75 |
| **6.** | 8% | 120 days | ... | 3,542.00 |
| **7.** | 5% | 90 days | 42.50 | ... |
| **8.** | ... | ... | 24.38 | 487.00 |
| **9.** | 15% | 60 days | 75.00 | ... |
| **10.** | 18% | 90 days | ... | 4,180.00 |

**B.** *Statement Problems:*

**11.** What principal will yield $23.70 interest in two months at 9%?

**12.** What principal will yield (a) $67.20 in three years at 8%?, and (b) $14 in 180 days at 5%?

13. What principal will accumulate to $501.40 in two years at $4\frac{1}{2}\%$ simple interest?

14. What principal will amount to $839.70 in eight months at $5\frac{1}{2}\%$ simple interest?

15. How much money must J. D. Gooch invest at 8% interest for two years in order to receive $2,552 at the end of the second year?

16. B. C. Dodge will receive $543.60 on June 30. How much can he borrow at 9% on May 1, if he uses his receipts to repay the loan?

17. (a) What is the present value of $1,000 due in two years if the money is worth 7%? (b) How much is the simple discount?

18. (a) What is the present value of $640 due at the end of four months if the money is worth 8%? (b) What is the simple discount?

19. A debt of $1,800 is due in $1\frac{1}{2}$ years. If the debt is settled now and the simple interest rate of 8% is allowed, what are: (a) the present value and (b) the simple discount?

20. A debt of $2,500 is due eight months from now. (a) What is the present value of the debt if 9% simple interest is allowed? (b) What is the simple discount on the debt if it is settled now?

21. Mrs. J. A. Outen purchased a refrigerator and made a down payment of $120. She agreed to pay $100 after one month and $150 after two months. If the rate of interest is 6%, what is the cash price of the refrigerator?

22. Mrs. W. R. Wages plans to purchase a television set. She is offered the option of paying $100 down and $300 in four months, or of paying $200 down and $200 in five months. If the rate of interest is 6%, which option would be a better offer for her?

23. Mr. Green borrowed $500 on June 1 of this year and agreed to repay the principal plus 9% interest in four months. On July 1, he wishes to pay the loan by discounting it at the simple interest rate of 8%. How much should he pay according to the discount?

24. Refer to Problem 23. If the debt is discounted at the simple interest rate of 10%, how much should he pay?

25. On May 1, J. D. Taylor borrowed $1,000 from J. C. Bennett and agreed to pay the debt plus 6% simple interest in 90 days. If the debt is settled on May 31 at 8% simple interest, how much did J. C. Bennett receive?

26. In Problem 25, if the debt is settled at an interest rate of 12% how much did J. C. Bennett receive?

## 9.4 PARTIAL PAYMENTS

If partial payments are made on a debt before it is due, there should be an agreement between the creditor and the borrower regarding the interest on each partial payment. Some creditors may agree to reduce the interest when partial payments on the debt are made. In general, the two methods used by a creditor in reducing the interest are the Merchants' Rule and the United States Rule. The Merchants' Rule is simpler and is preferred by most business people, whereas use of the United States Rule results from a decision made by the United States Supreme Court.

## A. Merchants' Rule

Under the *Merchants' Rule,* the principal and all partial payments are treated as if they earn interest from the time they are made to the date of final settlement. The following steps may be employed:

**Step (1)**    Find the sum of the principal and its interest for the period from the date of borrowing to the date of final settlement.

**Step (2)**    Find the sum of the partial payments and the interest on each partial payment from the date of payment to the date of final settlement. This sum is the debtor's credit against the sum in Step (1).

**Step (3)**    Subtract the result in Step (2) from the result in Step (1). The difference is the balance to be discharged on the date of final settlement.

**Example 1**    On July 1, a man borrowed $2,000 at 6%. He paid $500 on August 30, and $600 on September 29. Find the balance on October 29 of the same year, by the Merchants' Rule:

*The Merchants' Rule:*

Original debt (7/1) ................................. .$2,000
Add: interest on $2,000 for 120 days (7/1–10/29) ...... 40
   Amount on 10/29 ............................. .$2,040

Deduct: partial payments and their interest

First payment (8/30) ...................$500
Add: Interest on $500 for 60 days
   (8/30–10/29)....................... 5    $505

Second payment (9/29) ...............$600
Add: interest on $600 for 30 days
   (9/29–10/29)....................... 3    603

Total partial payments and their interest ............. 1,108
   Balance on 10/29 ............................ .$ 932

The above method is diagrammed below:

### Merchants' Rule

Interest rate: 6%

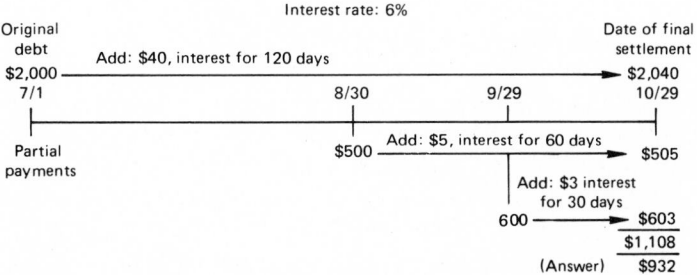

(Answer)    $932

# B. United States Rule

Under the *United States Rule,* each partial payment must first be applied to the accumulated interest up to the date of the payment. Any remainder is then credited as a deduction from the principal. Therefore, when the United States Rule is applied, the successive interest is computed from a declining balance each time a payment is made. A debtor may thus know the actual amount of unpaid balance immediately after each payment. The following steps may be employed:

**Step (1)**   Find the interest on the principal for the period from the date of borrowing to the date of the first partial payment.

**Step (2)**   Subtract the interest from the first payment. If there is a remainder, subtract the remainder from the principal to obtain the unpaid balance. If the partial payment is not sufficient to cover the interest due, the partial payment is then held and is included in the next payment.

**Step (3)**   If there are further partial payments, the processes in Steps (1) and (2) are repeated, but the interest is computed on the declining unpaid balance. Each payment must be first applied to the interest which has accumulated up to the date of each payment. The final balance is the sum of the unpaid principal and the accumulated interest up to the date of the final settlement.

**Example 2**   Refer to Example 1. Find the balance on October 29 by the United States Rule.

*The United States Rule:*

Original debt (7/1) . . . . . . . . . . . . . . . . . . . . . . . . . . . . . . . . . .$2,000.00

Deduct:
First payment (8/30) . . . . . . . . . . . . . . . . . . . . . . .$500.00
Deduct: interest on $2,000 for
60 days (7/1–8/30) . . . . . . . . . . . . . . . . . . . . . . .  20.00
Remainder applied to principal . . . . . . . . . . . . . . . . . . . . . . .  480.00
Balance on 8/30 . . . . . . . . . . . . . . . . . . . . . . . . . . . . . . . . . .$1,520.00

Deduct:
Second payment (9/29) . . . . . . . . . . . . . . . . . . . . . . .$600.00
Deduct: interest on $1,520 for
30 days (8/30–9/29) . . . . . . . . . . . . . . . . . . . . . . .  7.60
Remainder applied to principal . . . . . . . . . . . . . . . . . . . . . . .  592.40
Balance on 9/29 . . . . . . . . . . . . . . . . . . . . . . . . . . . . . . . .$  927.60

Add: interest on $927.60 for 30 days (9/29–10/29) . . . . . . . . . .  4.64
Balance on 10/29 . . . . . . . . . . . . . . . . . . . . . . . . . . . . . . . . . .$  932.24

The above method is diagrammed below:

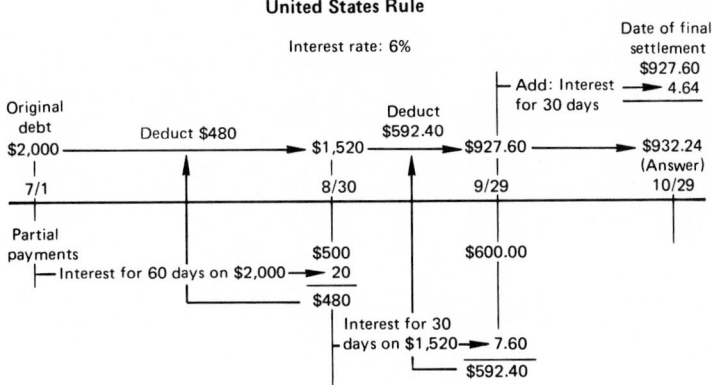

**United States Rule**

Interest rate: 6%

*Note:*  The balance on the date of final settlement as calculated by the United States Rule is slightly greater than that by the Merchants' Rule, because compound interest is involved in the United States Rule method. Hence, it is better for a debtor to use the Merchants' Rule in reducing a debt by partial payments.

**Example 3**  On July 1, a man borrowed $1,000 at 6%. He paid $300 on July 31, $6 on September 29, and $400 on October 14. Find the balance due November 13 of the same year by the United States Rule.

Original debt (7/1) ................................$1,000.00

Deduct:
  First payment (7/31) ........................$300.00
  Deduct: interest on $1,000.00 for 30 days
    (7/1–7/31) ..............................  5.00
  Remainder applied to principal .....................  295.00
  Balance on 7/31 .................................$  705.00

Deduct:
  Second payment (9/29) .....................$  6.00*
  Third payment (10/14) ......................  400.00
    Total payment as of 10/14 .................$406.00
  Deduct: interest on $705 for 75 days
    (7/31–10/14) ...........................  8.81
  Remainder applied to principal .....................  397.19
Balance on 10/14 .................................$  307.81

Add: interest on $307.81 for 30 days
  (10/14–11/13) ...............................  1.54
  Balance on 11/13 ...............................$  309.35

*Interest on $705 for 60 days (7/31–9/29) is $7.05, which is larger than the partial payment $6. Thus, the payment is held and is included in the third payment on 10/14.

## EXERCISE 9–5

**Reference: Section 9.4**

**A.** *In each of the following problems find the unpaid balance on the indicated date by (a) the Merchants' Rule and (b) the United States Rule:*

| Date of Loan | Principal | Rate of Interest | First Partial Payment Date | First Partial Payment Amount | Second Partial Payment Date | Second Partial Payment Amount | Date of Unpaid Balance |
|---|---|---|---|---|---|---|---|
| **1.** 4/1/80 | $1,000 | 4% | 5/1 | $ 300 | 6/30 | $ 500 | 7/30/80 |
| **2.** 6/10/80 | 2,500 | 8% | 8/9 | 500 | 10/8 | 800 | 12/7/80 |
| **3.** 1/19/81 | 560 | $4\frac{1}{2}$% | 2/8 | 200 | ... | ... | 3/20/81 |
| **4.** 9/24/81 | 840 | 7% | 11/3 | 300 | ... | ... | 12/23/81 |
| **5.** 8/15/81 | 1,600 | 6% | 9/14 | 200 | 11/13 | 1,000 | 1/12/82 |
| **6.** 7/6/82 | 2,800 | 10% | 7/21 | 1,000 | 8/20 | 1,200 | 9/19/82 |
| **7.** 11/15/82 | 4,200 | 5% | 1/14 | 3,000 | ... | ... | 4/4/83 |
| **8.** 10/2/82 | 3,500 | 9% | 12/1 | 2,000 | ... | ... | 1/10/83 |
| **9.** 3/25/83 | 3,700 | 12% | 6/23 | 1,000 | 8/22 | 2,000 | 10/21/83 |
| **10.** 5/6/83 | 4,800 | 18% | 6/5 | 2,400 | 11/2 | 1,800 | 1/31/84 |

**B.** *Statement Problems:*

**11.** On January 12, 1981, Jack Southerland purchases a lot for $5,000. He makes a partial payment of $1,000 once every 30 days, beginning February 11. On June 11 he plans to make the last payment plus the interest. If the rate of interest is 6%, what is the amount due? Use the Merchants' Rule.

**12.** A note for $6,000 with an interest rate of 8%, dated March 18, 1981, has the following partial payments: May 17, $2,000; July 1, $2,000, and September 14, $1,000. Find the balance due on December 13, 1981, by using the Merchants' Rule.

**13.** Find the amount due in Problem 11 by using the United States Rule.

**14.** Find the balance due in Problem 12 by using the United States Rule.

**15.** On April 25, 1982, Gloria South borrowed $4,000 at 4% interest. She paid $1,000 on June 24, $500 on July 24, $5 on August 23, and $2,000 on September 22. Find the balance due November 21, 1982, by the United States Rule.

**16.** Betty Farr borrowed $3,000 on May 7, 1983. Partial payments were made as follows: $500 on June 6, $15 on July 21, $1,000 on September 4, and $800 on November 3. On December 3, 1983, she wishes to settle her obligation. If the interest charged is 6%, what is the total amount due by the United States Method?

**17.** Find the balance due in Problem 15 by the Merchants' Rule.

**18.** Find the amount due in Problem 16 by the Merchants' Rule.

## 9.5 EQUIVALENT VALUES INVOLVING SIMPLE INTEREST

Occasionally there arises the need to replace a single debt or a set of debts by another single debt or another set of debts due at different times. In order to satisfy both the creditor and the debtor, the values of the new debts should be equivalent to the values of the original ones. For example, if a debt of $100 due now is to be replaced by a new debt due in one year and the money is worth 6%, the new debt is computed as follows:

$$S = P(1 + in) = 100(1 + 6\% \times 1) = \$106$$

The computation indicates that $100 due now is *equivalent* to $106 due in one year if the money is worth 6%. Thus, the creditor may allow the debtor to repay $100 now or $106 in a year. On the other hand, if a debt of $212 due in a year is to be replaced by a new debt due now, and the interest rate agreed by the creditor and the debtor is 6%, the new debt is computed as follows:

$$P = \frac{S}{1 + in} = \frac{212}{1 + 6\% \times 1} = 212 \div 1.06 = \$200$$

The computation indicates that $212 due in a year is equivalent to $200 due now if the rate of interest is 6%. Thus, the creditor and the debtor may agree to settle the debt now by the debtor's payment of only $200.

When interest is involved, a sum of money has different values at various times. For convenience, a *comparison date,* also called a *focal date,* should first be chosen in comparing the values of old debts with the values of new debts. An *equation of value,* which gives the equivalent values of original debts and new debts on the comparison date at the specified interest rate, should then be arranged for obtaining the required equivalent values. The answer for a required equivalent value may vary slightly in simple interest problems depending on the selection of the comparison date, but it does not vary in compound interest problems. The following examples are used to illustrate problems in equivalent values involving simple interest.

**Example 1**    A debt of $200 is due in six months. If the rate of interest is 6%, what is the value of the debt if it is paid (a) two months hence? (b) six months hence? (c) nine months hence?

According to the problem, $200 is the maturity value or the amount due at the end of six months, and the interest rate agreed upon by both creditor and debtor for settlement of the debt is 6%.

(a) If the $200 debt is paid two months hence, which is four months before the original due date, the required equivalent value is less than $200. Thus, the present value formula $P = S/(1 + in)$ should be used to compute the required value. In other words, the value is obtained by discounting the maturity value at a simple interest rate for the advance time of the payment.

$S = 200$, $i = 6\%$, $n = \frac{4}{12} = \frac{1}{3}$ (year). Substituting the values in the formula:

$$P = \frac{200}{1 + 6\% \times 1/3} = \frac{200}{1.02} = \$196.08$$

If the debt is paid two months hence, the payment is $196.08.

(b) If the debt is paid in six months, at which time the debt is due, the payment is $200 unchanged.

(c) If the debt of $200 is paid nine months from now, which is three months after the due date, the required equivalent value is more than $200. Thus, the amount formula $S = P(1 + in)$ should be used to compute the required value. In other words, the value is obtained by accumulating the original debt $200 for the extended time.

$P = 200$, $i = 6\%$, $n = \frac{3}{12} = \frac{1}{4}$ (year). Substituting the values in the formula:

$$S = 200(1 + 6\% \times \tfrac{1}{4}) = 200(\tfrac{203}{200}) = \$203$$

When the debt is paid at the end of nine months, the payment is $203.

The example may be diagrammed as follows:

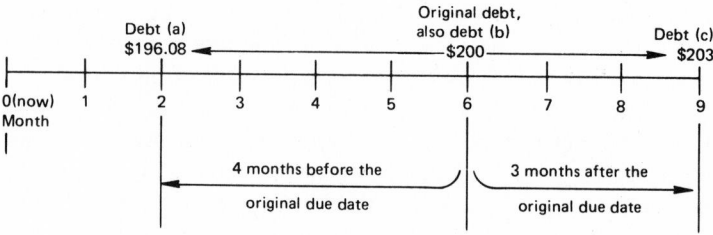

**Example 2**  A man owes (1) $100 due in two months and (2) $400 due in eight months. His creditor has agreed to settle the debts by 2 equal payments in four months and ten months, respectively. Find the size of each payment if the rate of interest is 6% and the comparison date is four months hence.

Let $x$ represent each equal payment. The values as of the comparison date are computed as follows:

(a) The value of the old debt of $100 becomes $101 on the comparison date. The value is computed as follows:

$P = 100$, $i = 6\%$, $n = \frac{2}{12} = \frac{1}{6}$ (year) since the comparison date is two months after the due date.

$$S = 100[1 + (6\%)(\tfrac{1}{6})] = 100(1.01) = \$101$$

(b) The value of the old debt of $400 becomes $392.16 on the comparison date. The value is computed as follows:

$S = 400$, $i = 6\%$, $n = \frac{4}{12} = \frac{1}{3}$ (year) since the comparison date is four months before the due date.

$$P = \frac{400}{1 + (6\%)(\tfrac{1}{3})} = \frac{400}{1.02} = \$392.16$$

(c) The value of the first new debt, which is due in four months, does not change and is $x$ since the comparison date is also in four months.

(d) The value of the second new debt, which is due in ten months, becomes $x/(1.03)$ on the comparison date. It is computed as follows:

$S = x$, $i = 6\%$, $n = \frac{6}{12} = \frac{1}{2}$ (year) since the comparison date is six months before the due date.

$$P = \frac{x}{1 + (6\%)(\frac{1}{2})} = \frac{x}{1.03}$$

The values are diagrammed in the following manner:

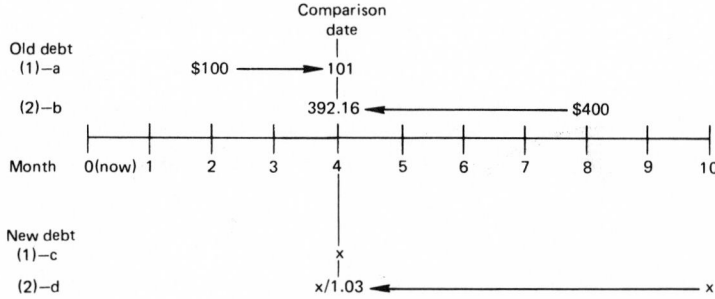

The equation of value based on the comparison date is given below:

$$\overbrace{\text{New Debts}}^{} \qquad \overbrace{\text{Old Debts}}^{}$$

$$\underbrace{(c) \qquad (d)}_{} \quad \underbrace{(a) \qquad (b)}_{}$$

$$x \quad + \quad \frac{x}{1.03} = 101 \quad + \quad 392.16$$

Solve for $x$:

$$x\left(1 + \frac{1}{1.03}\right) = 493.16,$$

$$x\left(\frac{1.03}{1.03} + \frac{1}{1.03}\right) = 493.16,$$

$$x\left(\frac{2.03}{1.03}\right) = 493.16$$

$$x = 493.16\left(\frac{1.03}{2.03}\right) = \$250.22$$

The two original debts may be discharged by paying $250.22 in four months and $250.22 in ten months.

*Check:* On the comparison date,

$$\text{New debts} = 250.22 + \frac{250.22}{1 + 6\%(\frac{1}{2})} = 250.22 + 242.94 = \$493.16$$

$$= \text{Old debts}$$

**Example 3**   In the above example, what is the size of each equal payment if the comparison date is set ten months hence?

Let $x$ represent each payment. The values as of the comparison date are computed as follows:

(a) The value of the old debt (1), $100, becomes

$S = 100[1 + (6\%)(8/12)] = 104$ (eight months after due date)

(b) The value of the old debt (2), $400 becomes

$S = 400[1 + (6\%)(2/12)] = 404$ (two months after due date)

(c) The value of the first new debt, which is due in four months, becomes

$S = x[1 + (6\%)(6/12)] = 1.03\, x$ (six months after due date)

(d) The value of the second new debt, which is due in ten months, does not change and is $x$ since the comparison date is also in ten months.

Example 3 is diagrammed in the following manner:

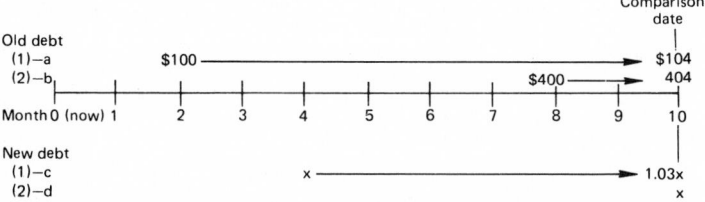

The equation of value based on the comparison date is given below:

New Debts     Old Debts

$$\overbrace{x + x(1.03)}^{} = \overbrace{404 + 104}^{}$$

Solve for $x$:

$x(1 + 1.03) = 508,$
$\qquad 2.03\, x = 508,$

$$x = \frac{508}{2.03} = \$250.25$$

This answer may be compared with that given on page 295. The difference is only $.03 (or $250.25 − $250.22), which is due to the selection of the comparison date.

**Note:**   When the due date of the last new debt is selected as the comparison date, division in the discounting process may be avoided.

**Example 4**   Donna owes (a) $500 due in six months and (b) $1,000 plus 8% interest due in three months. If money is worth 6%, what single payment nine months hence will be equivalent to the two original debts?

Let $x$ represent the unknown single payment. The comparison date is nine months hence. Since debt (b) is interest bearing, its maturity value, having an 8% interest rate for three months, should be computed first. The maturity value plus 6% interest for six months is the value of debt (b) on the comparison date.

The maturity value of debt (b) is

$$1,000[1 + (8\%)(3/12)] = 1,000(1.02) = \$1,020,$$

and its value on the comparison date becomes

$$1,020[1 + (6\%)(6/12)] = 1,020(1.03) = \$1,050.60$$

The value of debt (a) $500 becomes

$$S = 500[1 + 6\%(1/4)]$$

on the comparison date, which is three months (or $\frac{3}{12} = \frac{1}{4}$ year) after the due date.

The entire problem is diagrammed in the following manner:

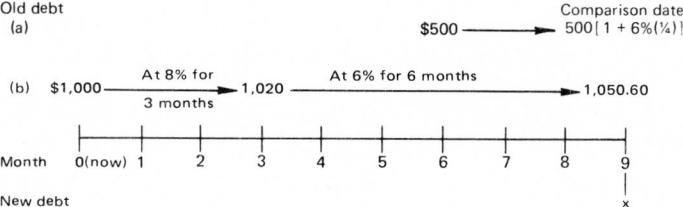

The equation of value based on the comparison date is written below:

$$\begin{aligned} x &= 1,050.60 + 500[1 + (6\%)(1/4)] \\ &= 1,050.60 + 507.50 \\ &= \$1,558.10 \end{aligned}$$

The single payment at the end of nine months is $1,558.10.

## EXERCISE 9–6

### Reference: Section 9.5

**A.** *Find the value of the new obligations in each of the following problems:*

| Original Debt | Worth of Money (%) | New Debt and Comparison Date |
|---|---|---|
| **1.** $2,000 due in 2 months | 6% | All in 5 months |
| **2.** $3,000 due in 3 months | 6% | All in 1 month |
| **3.** $3,040 due in 6 months | 9% | All in 2 months |
| **4.** $1,200 due in 4 months | 5% | All in 6 months |
| **5.** (a) $5,000 due in 4 months | 8% | All in 6 months |
| (b) $2,400 due in 1 month | | |

|  | Worth of | New Debt and |
| Original Debt | Money (%) | Comparison Date |

6. (a) $2,200 due in 1 month     10%     All in 4 months
   (b) $4,600 due in 9 months

7. (a) $1,000 in 5 months     6%     Two equal payments: one in 3
   (b) $1,800 in 8 months           months, the other in 10 months. Comparison date, 3 months hence.

8. (a) $1,000 in 5 months     6%     Same as Problem 7, except the
   (b) $1,800 in 8 months           comparison date in 10 months hence.

**B.** *Statement Problems:*

9. A debt of $1,000 is due in four months. If money is worth 8%, what is the value of the debt if it is paid (a) one month hence, (b) four months hence, and (c) six months hence?

10. A debt of $2,000 is due at the end of six months. If money is worth 9%, what is the value of the debt (a) at the end of five months, (b) at the end of six months, and (c) at the end of ten months?

11. A man owes (a) $1,000 due in three months and (b) $2,000 due in seven months. He and his creditor agree to settle the obligations by 2 equal payments, one in five months and the other in 11 months. Find the size of each payment if money is worth 6% and the comparison date is five months hence.

12. Answer the questions in Problem 11 if the comparison date is 11 months hence.

13. A debt of $2,400 due in two months is to be paid by 3 equal payments due three, five, and seven months hence. Money is worth 10%. What is the size of each payment? Let the comparison date be seven months hence.

14. Answer the questions in Problem 13 if the comparison date is two months hence.

15. A woman owes (a) $1,000 due in four months and (b) $3,000 plus interest at 5% due in six months. If money is worth 8%, what single payment ten months hence will be equivalent to the two original debts?

16. In Problem 15, if money is worth 8%, what single payment three months hence will be equivalent to the two original debts?

17. Jack Simpson owes Dale Peterson (a) $1,000 which is four months overdue, (b) $2,000 which is three months overdue, and (c) $1,500 which is due today. Simpson now wishes to sign a three-month non-interest-bearing note to cover all the debts. If a 6% interest rate is used to compute the obligations, what should be the face value of the note?

18. In Problem 17, assume that Simpson wishes to sign two non-interest-bearing notes of equal amounts with one note due in one month and the other due in two months. The 6% interest rate is used throughout. What should be the face value for each note if the comparison date is (a) now, and (b) two months hence?

# ★9.6 EQUIVALENT TIME

In the preceding section, the unknown in an equation of value is the value of each new debt. In this section the value of each new debt in the equation is known, but the equivalent time at which the new debt is due is unknown.

**Example 1**　　When will a single payment of $1,010 discharge the debts of (a) $400, (b) $500, and (c) $100 due in 30 days, 60 days, and 90 days, respectively? Assume that the rate of interest is 6%.

Let the last due date, which is 90 days from now, be the comparison date. The total value of the three original debts is $1,006.50 on the comparison date. The computation is shown below:

| Original Debts | Value on Comparison Date |
|---|---|
| (a) $ 400 | $400[1 + (\frac{60}{360})(6\%)] = \$$ 404.00 |
| (b) $ 500 | $500[1 + (\frac{30}{360})(6\%)] =$ 502.50 |
| (c) $ 100 | 100.00 |
| Total $1,000 | $1,006.50 |

Since the single payment of $1,010 is larger than the total value of $1,006.50, the single payment is considered as the amount $S$ and the total value as the principal $P$. The due date for the amount, denoted by $t$ (or $t$ days from now), must come later than 90 days from now. Thus, $1,010 is discounted to the value of $1,006.50 for $(t - 90)$ days.

The entire problem is diagrammed as shown below.

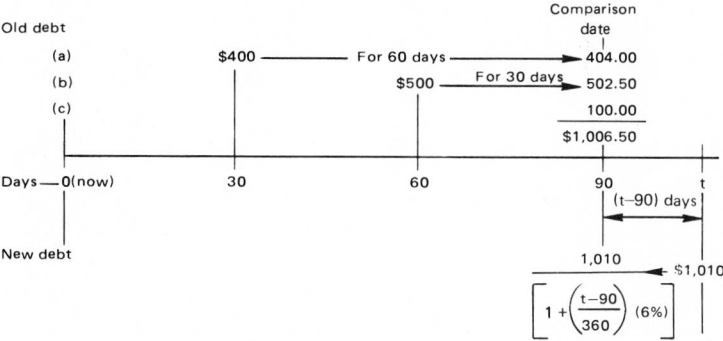

The equation of value based on the comparison date is shown below:

$$\frac{1,010}{1 + \left(\dfrac{t - 90}{360}\right)(6\%)} = 1,006.50$$

Solve for $t$:

$$\frac{1,010}{1,006.50} = 1 + \left(\frac{t - 90}{6,000}\right)$$

$$\frac{1,010}{1,006.5} - 1 = \frac{t - 90}{6,000}$$

$$\frac{3.5}{1,006.5}\left(6,000\right) = t - 90$$

$$20.86 = t - 90$$

$$t = 90 + 20.86 = 110.86, \text{ or } 111 \text{ days}$$

A single payment of $1,010 may be made in 111 days to discharge the three original debts.

**Note:**   When the comparison date is set on the last due date of the old debts, division, which is a necessary operation in a discounting process, may be avoided in finding the new value of each old debt. Here again note that the selection of a different comparison date does affect the answer slightly.

In the computation above, when a set of debts is discharged by a single payment or a new set of debts, the sum of the old debts may not be equal to the sum of the new debts. For example, in the above illustration, the old debts totaling $1,000 were discharged by the new debt of $1,010. In Example 4, page 296, the sum of the old debts is $1,520, whereas, the new single debt is $1,558.10. In the following examples, the single payment which discharges the old debts is assumed to be *equal* to the sum of the old debts. The date on which the single payment is made is called the *equated date* or the *average due date*. It is found by using the equation of value or a formula as derived below.

**Example 2**   When will a single payment of $1,000 discharge the debts in Example 1?

The single payment of $1,000 equals the three debts: $400, $500, and $100. Assume that the single payment is to be made in $t$ days. The number that $t$ represents must be less than 90, the last due date, because, if there are 90 or more days, the payment must include additional interest and thus be larger than $1,000.

The example is diagrammed as follows:

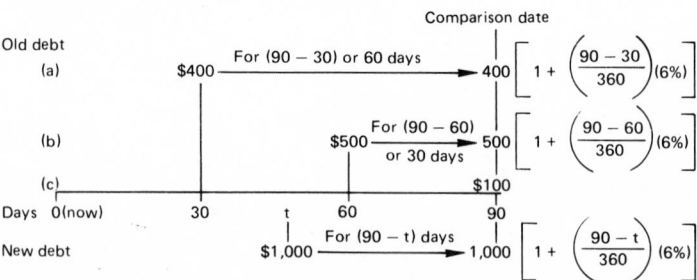

The equation of value based on the comparison date is written below:

$$1,000\left[1+\left(\frac{90-t}{360}\right)(6\%)\right]=400\left[1+\left(\frac{90-30}{360}\right)(6\%)\right]$$

$$+500\left[1+\left(\frac{90-60}{360}\right)(6\%)\right]+100=1,006.50. \text{ (See Example 1)}$$

Solve for $t$:

$t = 51$ days

A single payment of \$1,000 may be made in 51 days to discharge the three debts.

In Example 2, \$ 400 = the first debt due in 30 days
500 = the second debt due in 60 days
<u>100</u> = the third debt due in 90 days, and
\$1,000 = the sum of the three debts

In general, let $D_1$ = the first debt due in $t_1$ days
$D_2$ = the second debt due in $t_2$ days
$D_3$ = the third debt due in $t_3$ days
$D = D_1 + D_2 + D_3$, and $D$ will be due in $t$ days

The following formula[2] is obtained:

$$t=\frac{D_1 t_1 + D_2 t_2 + D_3 t_3}{D} \tag{9-5}$$

By applying this formula, Example 2 is computed as follows:

$$t=\frac{400 \cdot 30 + 500 \cdot 60 + 100 \cdot 90}{1,000}=51$$

In formula (9–5) $t$ is derived after the interest rate (which is not equal to zero) has been canceled. Thus, an interest rate need not be included in computing

---

[2] *Proof—Formula (9–5)*

Substitute the symbols in the equation of value in Example 2. Then,

$$D\left[1+\left(\frac{t_3-t}{360}\right)(6\%)\right]=D_1\left[1+\left(\frac{t_3-t_1}{360}\right)(6\%)\right]+D_2\left[1+\left(\frac{t_3-t_2}{360}\right)(6\%)\right]+D_3$$

Extend and subtract $D$ ( = $D_1 + D_2 + D_3$) from both sides, and then divide by 6% and multiply by 360:

$$D(t_3 - t) = D_1(t_3 - t_1) + D_2(t_3 - t_2)$$

Extend,

$$Dt_3 - Dt = D_1 t_3 - D_1 t_1 + D_2 t_3 - D_2 t_2$$
$$Dt = Dt_3 - D_1 t_3 + D_1 t_1 - D_2 t_3 + D_2 t_2 = (D - D_1 - D_2)t_3 + D_1 t_1 + D_2 t_2$$
$$= D_3 t_3 + D_1 t_1 + D_2 t_2. \text{ Thus,}$$

$$t=\frac{D_1 t_1 + D_2 t_2 + D_3 t_3}{D}$$

an equated date. Furthermore, the values of the $t$'s may also represent the number of months or years or other units of time. The equality of formula (9–5) does not change if both sides of the formula are divided by 30 or 360 or other numbers in order to convert the unit of time. However, the unit of time represented by $t$'s in the formula should be consistent throughout. The formula may be extended to include any number of $D$'s, and is written in the following manner:

$$t = \frac{D_1 t_1 + D_2 t_2 + D_3 t_3 + \cdots \cdots \cdots}{D}$$

where,

$D = D_1 + D_2 + D_3 + \cdots \cdots \cdots$ (that is, $D$ may equal any number of debts.)

**Example 3**   A store purchased merchandise in the following amounts: $200, due in three months; $500, due in four months; and $100, due in six months. When will the equated date be if a single payment of $800 discharges the three debts? Assume that the rate of interest is 5%.

Since the sum of the three debts is known, $200, $500, and $100 equal $800, formula (9–5) may be applied to compute the equated date. The interest rate need not be included in the computation.

$D_1 = \$200$, $t_1 = 3$ (months); $D_2 = \$500$, $t_2 = 4$ (months); $D_3 = \$100$, $t_3 = 6$ (months); and $D = \$800$.

$$t = \frac{200 \cdot 3 + 500 \cdot 4 + 100 \cdot 6}{800} = \frac{600 + 2,000 + 600}{800} = \frac{3,200}{800}$$

$= 4$ months, since the unit of time throughout this problem is one month.

***Note:***   If there is no interest ($i = 0$), the balance, $800, probably can be paid at any time; that is, there is no equated date.

**Example 4**   The debts $200, $300, and $500 are due in 11 days, 20 days, and 30 days, respectively. If the payment plans are changed to pay $100, $200, and $300 in 10 days, 20 days, and 30 days, when will a single payment of $400 discharge the balance?

According to formula (9–5), the equated date of the original debts is

$$t = \frac{200 \cdot 11 + 300 \cdot 20 + 500 \cdot 30}{1,000}$$

Assume that the new fourth payment of $400 is paid in $T_4$ days. According to formula (9–5), the equated date of the new payment is

$$t = \frac{100 \cdot 10 + 200 \cdot 20 + 300 \cdot 30 + 400 \cdot T_4}{1,000}$$

Equate the values of $t$, and solve for $T_4$. Then,

$$T_4 = \frac{200 \cdot 11 + 300 \cdot 20 + 500 \cdot 30 - (100 \cdot 10 + 200 \cdot 20 + 300 \cdot 30)}{400}$$

$$= 23 \text{ days}$$

*Check:* Let the comparison date be in 30 days, and 6% (or any rate other than zero) be the rate of interest. The values of the old debts on the comparison date are as follows:

(a) $200\left[1 + \left(\frac{30-11}{360}\right)(6\%)\right] = 200(1.00317) = 200.63$

(b) $300\left[1 + \left(\frac{30-20}{360}\right)(6\%)\right] = 300(1.00167) = 300.50$

(c) $500\left[1 + \left(\frac{30-30}{360}\right)(6\%)\right] = 500(1) \qquad = 500.00$

$\qquad\qquad\qquad\qquad\qquad\qquad\qquad\qquad\qquad\qquad \overline{\$1,001.13}$

The values of the new debts on the comparison date are computed as follows:

(a) $100\left[1 + \left(\frac{30-10}{360}\right)(6\%)\right] = 100(1.00333) = 100.33$

(b) $200\left[1 + \left(\frac{30-20}{360}\right)(6\%)\right] = 200(1.00167) = 200.33$

(c) $300\left[1 + \left(\frac{30-30}{360}\right)(6\%)\right] = 300(1) \qquad = 300.00$

(d) $400\left[1 + \left(\frac{30-23}{360}\right)(6\%)\right] = 400(1.00117) = 400.47$

$\qquad\qquad\qquad\qquad\qquad\qquad\qquad\qquad\qquad\qquad \overline{\$1,001.13}$

The total value of the old debts is equal to the total value of the new debts, $1,001.13, on the comparison date. Thus, the answer is correct. The single payment of $400 in 23 days will discharge the balance.

Let $D_1$, $D_2$, and $D_3$ be the original debts due in $t_1$, $t_2$, and $t_3$ days respectively, and $P_1$, $P_2$, $P_3$, and $P_4$ be the new payments to be made in $T_1$, $T_2$, $T_3$, and $T_4$ days respectively, where $D_1 + D_2 + D_3 = P_1 + P_2 + P_3 + P_4$. In a manner similar to that followed in determining the solution for Example 4, the following formula is derived in finding the value of $T_4$:

$$T_4 = \frac{D_1 t_1 + D_2 t_2 + D_3 t_3 - (P_1 T_1 + P_2 T_2 + P_3 T_3)}{P_4} \qquad (9\text{--}6)$$

Formula (9–6) may be extended to any number of $D$'s and $P$'s. Also, the values of $t$'s and $T$'s may represent the number of months, years, or other units of time.

**Example 5** A man made the following purchases at the Harrow Hardware Co.: September 25, $400; October 25, $300; December 4, $500. He made the following payments: October 19, $200; and November 5, $100. When is the equated date on which he may make a single payment of $900 to discharge the balance?

Let September 25 be the *present*. Then

$D_1 = \$400$, $t_1 = 0$ (due at present)
$D_2 = \$300$, $t_2 = 30$ days (from 9/25 to 10/25)
$D_3 = \$500$, $t_3 = 70$ days (from 9/25 to 12/4)
$P_1 = \$200$, $T_1 = 24$ days (from 9/25 to 10/19)
$P_2 = \$100$, $T_2 = 41$ days (from 9/25 to 11/5)
$D = 400 + 300 + 500 = \$1,200$
$P_3 = D - (P_1 + P_2) = 1,200 - (200 + 100) = 1,200 - 300 = \$900$,
which equals the single payment. Apply formula (9–6) by using the above values;

$$T_3 = \frac{(400 \cdot 0) + (300 \cdot 30) + (500 \cdot 70) - [(200 \cdot 24) + (100 \cdot 41)]}{900}$$

$$= \frac{0 + 9,000 + 35,000 - (4,800 + 4,100)}{900}$$

$$= \frac{35,100}{900} = 39 \text{ days from September 25, or on November 3.}$$

In such a case as the above, the debt is probably settled after December 4, the last purchase date. The final amount then will include the balance $900 and the interest on the balance for the period from November 3 to the date of settlement. For example, if the debt is paid on December 23 (or 50 days after November 3) and the interest rate is 6%, the amount due is

$$I = 900 \times \frac{50}{360} \times 6\% = 7.5$$

$$S = 900 + 7.5 = \$907.50$$

# ★EXERCISE 9–7

## Reference: Section 9.6

**A.** *In the following problems, assume that the interest rate is not equal to 0, or $i \neq 0$. Find the equated date* t *or* T *in each problem:*

|  | Original Debts | Payment Plan |
|---|---|---|
| **1.** | (a) $3,000 in 20 days | |
| | (b) $2,000 in 40 days | $10,000 in *t* days |
| | (c) $5,000 in 60 days | |
| **2.** | (a) $1,500 in 22 days | |
| | (b) $2,600 in 35 days | $5,000 in *t* days |
| | (c) $900 in 40 days | |

|                | *Original Debts*       | *Payment Plan*          |
| -------------- | ---------------------- | ----------------------- |

**3.** (a) $200 in 2 months
   (b) $400 in 3 months          $1,200 in $t$ months
   (c) $600 in 4 months

**4.** (a) $1,200 in 5 months
   (b) $2,500 in 6 months        $8,000 in $t$ months
   (c) $4,300 in 10 months

**5.** (a) $200 in 1 month
   (b) $200 in 2 months
   (c) $200 in 3 months          $800 in $t$ months
   (d) $200 in 4 months

**6.** (a) $500 in 90 days
   (b) $1,000 in 120 days        $1,500 in $t$ days

**7.** (a) $600 in 60 days       (a) $400 in 29 days
   (b) $800 in 90 days           (b) $700 in 77 days
   (c) $1,000 in 120 days        (c) $1,300 in $T$ days

**8.** (a) $1,000 in 2 months    (a) $500 in 3 months
   (b) $1,500 in 4 months        (b) $2,000 in 7 months
   (c) $3,000 in 6 months        (c) $3,000 in $T$ months

**9.** $4,000 in 6 months        (a) $400 in 2 months
                                 (b) $800 in 4 months
                                 (c) $1,000 in 11 months
                                 (d) $1,800 in $T$ months

**10.** $2,500 due now           (a) $800 in 20 days
                                 (b) $500 in 50 days
                                 (c) $200 in 70 days
                                 (d) $1,000 in $T$ days

**B.** *Statement Problems:*

**11.** When will a single payment of $2,200 discharge the debts of (a) $500 due in four months, (b) $1,000 due in six months, and (c) $650 due in eight months? Assume that money is worth 9%.

**12.** How many days are needed for a single payment of $1,702 to discharge the debts of (a) $300 due in 20 days, (b) $600 due in 40 days, and (c) $800 due in 60 days? Assume that money is worth 6%.

**13.** How many months are required for a single payment of $2,000 to discharge the debts of (a) $500 due in two months, (b) $1,200 due in six months, and (c) $300 due in eight months?

**14.** A retailer purchased merchandise for $300 due in 10 days, $600 due in 22 days, and $900 due in 30 days. How many days are needed for a single payment of $1,800 to discharge the three purchases?

15. If the three debts in Problem 13 were paid by partial payments of $400 in three months and $600 in seven months, when is the equated date on which a single payment of $1,000 will discharge the balance?

16. If the retailer in Problem 14 had made payments of $400 in 15 days and $200 in 25 days, when is the equated date on which a single payment of $1,200 will discharge the balance?

17. A shoe store purchased merchandise as follows: June 10, $560, terms n/20; July 20, $240, terms n/10; August 26, $400, terms n/15. Find the equated date on which a single payment of $1,200 will discharge the three debts. If the single payment is made on September 28, how much is the payment? Interest is charged at 6%.

18. A retailer bought merchandise from a wholesaler as follows: April 10, $600; May 13, $400; June 9, $800. What is the equated date on which a single payment of $1,800 will discharge the three debts? If the single payment is made on June 13, and money is worth 9%, how much should be paid?

## 9.7 SUMMARY OF SIMPLE INTEREST AND SIMPLE DISCOUNT FORMULAS

| Application | Formula | Formula Number | Reference Page |
|---|---|---|---|
| *Simple Interest* | | | |
| Computation in General | $I = Pin$ | (9–1) | 272 |
| Calculating Ordinary Interest (the Banker's Rule) | $I = Pi\left(\dfrac{t}{360}\right) = \dfrac{Pit}{360}$ | (9–2) | 276 |
| Calculating Exact Interest | $I_e = Pi\left(\dfrac{t}{365}\right) = \dfrac{Pit}{365}$ | (9–3) | 277 |
| *Amount, Rate, and Time* | | | |
| Finding the Amount | $S = P + I$  $= P(1 + in)$ | (9–4) | 279 |
| ★Finding the Equated Date | $t = \dfrac{D_1 t_1 + D_2 t_2 + D_3 t_3}{D}$ | (9–5) | 301 |
| | $T_4 = \dfrac{D_1 t_1 + D_2 t_2 + D_3 t_3 - (P_1 T_1 + P_2 T_2 + P_3 T_3)}{P_4}$ | (9–6) | 303 |

## EXERCISE 9–8

### Review of Chapter 9

1. What is the simple interest on $500 at 10% for (a) four years? (b) three months?

2. Find the simple interest on $650 at 12% for (a) two years, (b) five months.

3. What are (a) the exact time and (b) the approximate time from April 10 to July 24?

4. Find (a) the exact time and (b) the approximate time from August 2 to December 25.

5. Determine the number of days by (a) the exact time method and (b) the approximate time method from January 14, 1979, to June 10, 1980.

6. Find the number of days by (a) the exact time method and (b) the approximate time method from July 8, 1980, to February 15, 1981.

7. Find (a) the ordinary interest and (b) the exact interest on $2,000 at 8% for 45 days.

8. What are (a) the ordinary interest and (b) the exact interest on $3,500 at 6% for 60 days?

9. What are (a) the ordinary interest and (b) the exact interest on $145 at 9% for 120 days?

10. Find (a) the ordinary interest and (b) the exact interest on $396 at 7% for 78 days.

11. What is the amount of $440 loaned for nine months at 5%?

12. What is the amount of $600 invested for five months at 9%?

13. What is the amount if $630 is borrowed for 120 days at 7%?

14. Find the amount if $1,500 is invested for 95 days at 6%.

15. On June 30, 1980, Jack Horner borrowed $600 and agreed to repay the loan in 60 days. The interest rate is 12%. (a) What is the simple interest? (b) What amount must he repay? (c) On what date?

16. If $800 is borrowed at $5\frac{1}{2}$% simple interest for two years, what will be the amount due?

17. At what interest rate will $360 yield $27 in $2\frac{1}{2}$ years?

18. Mary borrowed $320 four years ago. She paid $384 today to discharge the loan. What was the interest rate charged?

19. Bill borrowed $240 sixty days ago. He has to pay $241.60 now to settle the debt. What is the interest rate?

20. A payment of $676 was made to discharge a six-month loan of $650. What was the interest rate?

21. How many months will it take $1,500 to yield $37.50 interest at 10% simple interest?

22. How many days are required for $2,000 to yield $20 interest at 8% simple interest?

23. How many days are needed for $420 to yield (a) $2.80 interest at 8%? (b) $1.40 interest at 6%?

24. How many months are necessary for $500 to yield $15 interest at 12% simple interest?

25. Cathy receives $50 every two months from an investment which pays 5% interest. What is the principal that she has invested?

26. Denton paid $650 for discharging a debt which includes $60 interest. What is the principal?

27. How much money should Eaton invest now at 14% simple interest if she is to receive $6,400 in two years?

28. What is the present value of $6,300 which is due at the end of ten months? The interest rate is 6%.

29. Discount $810 for three months at the simple interest rate of 5%. What are (a) the present value and (b) the simple discount?

30. Fred promised to pay Jack $750 nine months from now. (a) If the debt is settled now and the simple interest rate of 12% is allowed, how much should Fred pay now? (b) What is the simple discount?

31. Gray borrowed $800 and agreed to repay the loan plus 5% interest at the end of one year. Four months after the loan had been made, his creditor agreed to settle the debt by discounting it at the simple interest rate of 4%. (a) How much should Gray pay? (b) What is the simple discount?

32. On April 10, Hilda borrowed $1,200 and agreed to pay the loan plus 5% simple interest in 60 days. If the debt is settled on May 25 at 6% simple interest, how much should she pay?

33. Sherwood borrowed $4,500 on February 6, 1981, at 4%. He paid $600 on February 21, and $1,400 on March 23. Find the balance on April 22, 1981, by (a) the Merchants' Rule and (b) the United States Rule.

34. On May 2, 1980, Martha borrowed $2,400 at 6%. She paid $800 on June 1, $8 on July 1, and $1,000 on July 16. Find the balance due August 15, 1980, by (a) the Merchants' Rule and (b) the United States Rule.

35. A debt of $600 is due in eight months. If the rate of interest is 12%, what is the value of the debt if it is paid (a) three months hence? (b) eight months hence? (c) ten months hence?

36. A debt of $1,500 is due at the end of five months. If money is worth 6%, what will be the value of the debt if it is settled at the end of (a) three months, (b) five months, (c) nine months?

37. A man owes $600 due in three months and $900 due in nine months. His creditor has offered to settle the debts by two equal payments in five months and in 11 months respectively. If the man were to accept the offer, what would be the size of each payment, assuming the interest rate is 4% and the comparison date is five months from now?

38. Refer to Problem 37. If the comparison date were set 11 months from now, what would be the size of each payment?

39. Debbie owes $700 due in eight months and $1,200 plus 5% interest due in two months. If money is worth 7% now, what single payment ten months hence will be equivalent to the two original debts?

40. Eleanor owes $300 due in four months and $500 plus 7% interest due in six months. If money is worth 6% now, what single payment one year from now will be equivalent to the two original debts?

★41. When will a single payment of $2,410 discharge the debts of $600, $1,400, and $400 due in 30 days, 45 days, and 60 days respectively? Assume that the rate of interest is 3%.

★**42.** When will a single payment of $2,950 discharge the debts of $800, $1,000, and $1,120 due in 15 days, 30 days, and 90 days respectively? Assume that the rate of interest is 6%.

★**43.** Refer to Problem 41. When will a single payment of $2,400 discharge the three debts?

★**44.** Refer to Problem 42. When will a single payment of $2,920 discharge the three original debts?

★**45.** A store purchased merchandise for the following amounts: $300, due in two months; $40, due in five months; and $150, due in six months. When will the equated date be if a single payment of $490 can discharge the three debts? Assume that the rate of interest is 6%.

★**46.** Debts of $500, $100, and $60 are due in 15 days, 30 days, and 60 days respectively. If the payment plans are changed to have $200, $250, and $80 paid in 10 days, 25 days, and 45 days, when will a single payment of $130 discharge the balance?

★**47.** Robert made the following purchases at the Jenkin Hardware Store in 1980: April 10, $500; July 9, $600; October 7, $800. He made the following payments: June 9, $300; August 8, $250. When is the equated date on which he may make a single payment of $1,350 to discharge the balance?

★**48.** Taylor made the following purchases at the Kent Retail Store in 1980: March 16, $200; June 14, $700; August 23, $900. He made the following payments: April 15, $100; June 24, $500. When is the equated date on which he may make a single payment of $1,200 to discharge the balance?

# Chapter 10

# Bank Discount and Negotiable Instruments

## 10.1 BANK DISCOUNT—INTEREST DEDUCTED IN ADVANCE

### A. Introduction

When a bank loan is made, the interest is usually computed on the basis of the *maturity value*, the final amount of the loan on the due date. The interest rate used in computing the loan is called the *bank discount rate*, or simply the *discount rate*. The time used in computing is called the *period of discount*, which is the period from the date of discount to the maturity date. The interest thus computed is deducted immediately from the maturity value of the loan. This deduction is known as the *bank discount*, or *interest deducted in advance*. The value received by the borrower after the deduction is called the *proceeds*.

### B. General Computation

In general, bank discount and proceeds may be expressed as follows:

Bank discount = Maturity value × Discount rate × Period of discount
Proceeds = Maturity value − Bank discount

In computing bank discount, the rate and the time must correspond to each other. The discount rate is usually stated as a yearly rate. Since the bank discount method is generally used for short-term borrowing, the period of discount normally is a fraction of a year. When a fraction is expressed, the ordinary interest method, discussed on pages 275 and 276, is again followed. In other words, when the period is stated in days, the exact time is used as the numerator and 360 is used as the denominator. Also, when the period is given in months, the numerator is the number of months and the denominator is 12.

Let $P' = $ proceeds
$S = $ maturity value
$I' = $ bank discount or the interest in advance
$d = $ annual discount rate
$n = $ period of discount expressed in years

The above expressions may be written as follows:

$$I' = Sdn \qquad\qquad\qquad \textbf{(10-1)}$$

$P' = S - I'$, or
$\quad = S - Sdn$, or factoring $S$,
$\quad = S(1 - dn)$ $\qquad\qquad\qquad\qquad$ **(10-2)**

## FINDING THE VALUE OF BANK DISCOUNT AND PROCEEDS

To find the value of bank discount and proceeds, formulas (10–1) and (10–2) are used as illustrated in Examples 1 and 2 below:

**Example 1**   A woman promises to repay a bank loan of $450 at the end of 60 days.

(a) If the bank charges 8% interest in advance, what is the discount?
(b) How much does the woman receive?

(a) Substituting $S = 450$, $d = 8\%$, and $n = \frac{60}{360} = \frac{1}{6}$ (year) in formula (10–1):

$$I' = Sdn = 450 \times 8\% \times \tfrac{1}{6} = \$6 \text{ (bank discount)}$$

(b) Substituting $S = 450$ and $I' = 6$ in formula (10–2):

$$P' = S - I' = 450 - 6 = \$444 \text{ (proceeds received by the woman)}$$

**Example 2**   A man borrows $300 for three months from a bank that charges a discount rate of 6%. Find the proceeds.

Substituting $S = 300$, $d = 6\%$, and $n = \frac{3}{12} = \frac{1}{4}$ (year) in formula (10–2):

$P' = S(1 - dn) = 300(1 - .06 \times \tfrac{1}{4}) = 300(1 - .015)$
$\quad = 300 \times .985 = \$295.50$

## FINDING THE MATURITY VALUE

To find the maturity value, select either formula (10–1) or (10–2). Examples 3, 4, and 5 are used to illustrate this selection.

**Example 3**   What is the final amount of a loan if a bank charges $2 interest in advance for three months at 8%?

$$I' = 2, \ d = 8\%, \ n = \tfrac{3}{12} = \tfrac{1}{4} \text{ (year)}$$

Substituting the values in formula (10–1):

$I' = Sdn$
$2 = S(8\%)(\tfrac{1}{4})$

$$S = \frac{2}{(8\%)(\tfrac{1}{4})} = \frac{2}{(\tfrac{2}{100})} = \$100$$

**Example 4**     If a man received $98 from a bank as the proceeds and the discount was $2, what is the total amount of the loan?

$P' = 98, \ I' = 2$

Substituting the values in formula (10–2):

$P' = S - I'$
$98 = S - 2$

$S = 98 + 2 = \$100$

**Example 5**     Johnson wants $2,450 in cash as the proceeds of a 90-day loan from a bank which charges 6% discount. What is the loan that Johnson must pay on the maturity date?

$P' = 2,450, \ d = 6\%, \text{ and } n = \frac{90}{360} = \frac{1}{4} \text{ (year)}$

Substituting the values in formula (10–2):

$P' = S(1 - dn)$
$2,450 = S[1 - (6\%)(\frac{1}{4})] = S(\frac{197}{200})$

$S = 2,450(\frac{200}{197}) = \$2,487.31$

***Note:***     When both sides of the formula $P' = S(1 - dn)$ are divided by $(1 - dn)$, the following result is obtained:

$$S = \frac{P'}{1 - dn}$$

The above result may be used directly in finding the maturity value for Example 5.

## FINDING THE ANNUAL DISCOUNT RATE

To find the annual discount rate $d$, or the rate of interest charged in advance, divide the discount $I'$ by the product of the final amount $S$ and the discount period $n$. This is based on formula (10–1). When both sides of the formula $I' = Sdn$ are divided by $Sn$, the following result is obtained:

$$d = \frac{I'}{Sn}$$

**Example 6**     A man received a 60-day loan of $550 from a bank. The proceeds were $544.50. What is the discount rate?

$S = 550, \ P' = 544.50, \ n = 60/360 = 1/6 \text{ (year)}$
$I' = S - P' = 550 - 544.50 = \$5.50$

Substituting the values in formula (10–1):

$I' = Sdn$
$5.5 = 550(d)(1/6)$

$$d = \frac{5.5}{550(1/6)} = \frac{1}{100 \times 1/6} = \frac{6}{100} = 6\%$$

## FINDING THE PERIOD OF DISCOUNT

To find the period of discount $n$ (in years), divide the discount $I'$ by the product of the final amount $S$ and the discount rate $d$. This is also based on formula (10–1). When both sides of the formula $I' = Sdn$ are divided by $Sd$, the following result is obtained:

$$n = \frac{I'}{Sd}$$

**Example 7**    A man borrowed $800 from a bank which charged 6% interest in advance. He received $788 from the loan. When will the loan be due?

$S = 800,\ P' = 788,\ d = 6\%$
$I' = S - P' = 800 - 788 = 12$

Substituting the values in formula (10–1):

$I' = Sdn$
$12 = (800)(6\%)n$

$$n = \frac{12}{(800)(6\%)} = \frac{12}{48} = \frac{1}{4}\ \text{(year), or}$$

$\frac{1}{4} \times 360 = 90$ days after the date of borrowing.

## EXERCISE 10–1

### Reference: Section 10.1

**A.** *In each of the following cases, find the unknown values:*

| | Maturity Value (S) | Discount Rate (d) | Period of Discount (n) | Bank Discount (I') | Proceeds (P') |
|---|---|---|---|---|---|
| **1.** | $240,000 | 7% | 2 months | ? | ? |
| **2.** | 80,000 | 9% | ? months | $600.00 | ? |
| **3.** | ? | ? | 3 months | 12.00 | $ 788.00 |
| **4.** | 3,000 | ? | 60 days | 40.00 | ? |
| **5.** | 3,600 | 10% | ? days | ? | 3,555.00 |
| **6.** | ? | 12% | ? days | 120.00 | 3,880.00 |
| **7.** | 9,000 | ? | 75 days | 112.50 | ? |
| **8.** | 1,800 | ? | 4 months | ? | 1,773.00 |
| **9.** | ? | 10½% | 6 months | ? | 758.00 |
| **10.** | ? | 15% | ? days | 50.00 | 950.00 |

**B.** *Statement Problems:*

**11.** Brady Company borrowed $40,000 for 90 days from a bank which charged 9% interest in advance. What was the discount and how much did the company receive?

**12.** A bank loaned $420 to a man for 120 days. The charge was 10% in advance. How much did the bank charge? What were the proceeds?

13. On July 15, K. C. King received a loan from a bank and agreed to pay $3,500 for the loan on October 16. If the bank charged 6% interest in advance, find the proceeds.

14. On April 1, James Timer obtained a 60-day loan of $4,200 from a bank which charged 7% interest in advance. How much did Timer receive from the loan? On what date does he have to pay his loan?

15. Teresa needs $650 in cash for 45 days. If a bank lends her the money and charges 4% interest in advance, how much must Teresa pay after 45 days?

16. Tina desires $3,650 in cash as the proceeds of a 150-day loan from a bank which charges 8% discount. What is the loan that Tina must pay on the maturity date?

17. George Company borrowed $70,000 from a bank for four months. The proceeds were $67,900. What was the discount rate?

18. Shaw received $1,200 in cash as the proceeds from a bank for a 120-day loan of $1,224. What was the interest rate charged by the bank in advance?

19. A man borrowed $3,600 from a bank which charged $4\frac{1}{2}$% interest in advance. The proceeds were $3,546. In how many months after the borrowing must he pay the loan?

20. Jackie received $2,632 in cash as the proceeds from a bank for a loan of $2,800. The discount rate was 12%. Find the discount period in years.

## 10.2 NATURE OF NEGOTIABLE INSTRUMENTS

*Negotiable instruments* are written promises or orders to pay money. They are transferrable or salable by one person to another person or to a bank. Frequently, negotiable instruments are discounted by the bank discount method. Generally speaking, there are two types of negotiable instruments—*promissory notes* and *bills of exchange.*

Promissory notes, or simply notes, have two parties: the *maker,* who makes the promise to pay, and the *payee,* to whom the promise is made (see Figure 10–1).

### Figure 10–1 A PROMISSORY NOTE

| $ 500.00 | New York, New York, November 15, 19 80 |
|---|---|

_____ 90 days _____ AFTER DATE ___I___ PROMISE TO PAY TO

THE ORDER OF __Charles L. Benson__ **(Payee)**

PAYABLE AT *Merchants Bank*

Five hundred 00/100- - - - - - - - - - - - - - - - - - - - - - - - - - - - - - DOLLARS

VALUE RECEIVED WITH INTEREST AT __6%__

No.__16__ DUE __February 13, 1981__

*James Kent* **(Maker)**

The following information is found in this promissory note:

*Face Value:* $500
*Date of the Note:* November 15, 1980
*Term of the Note:* 90 days
*Interest Rate:* 6%
*Maturity Date:* 90 days after November 15, 1980, or February 13, 1981
*Maturity Value:* 500(6%)(90/360) = $7.50
                             500 + 7.50 = $507.50

A bill of exchange has three parties: the *drawer,* the person who draws the bill; the *drawee,* the person to whom the bill is addressed and who is ordered to pay the bill; and the *payee,* the person to whom the payment is made. The drawee is not bound to pay the bill unless he or she accepts the order of payment from the drawer. When the bill is accepted by the drawee, he or she immediately becomes the *acceptor* and is liable for the bill.

The most frequently used bills of exchange in commercial practice are *checks* and *drafts.* A check is always drawn upon a bank as the drawee and is always payable upon demand. Drafts are classified as *sight drafts* or *time drafts.* A draft which is payable at sight is called a sight draft. Checks and sight drafts are demand bills of exchange; that is, they are payable as soon as they are presented for payment. There is no need for a discount process in making payments with demand bills. A time draft, however, is payable at a future time, either within a certain number of days *after sight* (see Figure 10–2), *after date* (see Figure 10–3), or on a *specified date* (see Figure 10–4). The maturity date (or due date) of an after-sight draft is determined by counting the days after the date on which the drawee accepts the draft. The maturity date of an after-date draft is determined by counting the days after the date on which the draft is drawn. If the draft is negotiated or sold before the maturity date, a discount process is involved in determining the selling price.

## Figure 10–2 AN AFTER-SIGHT TIME DRAFT

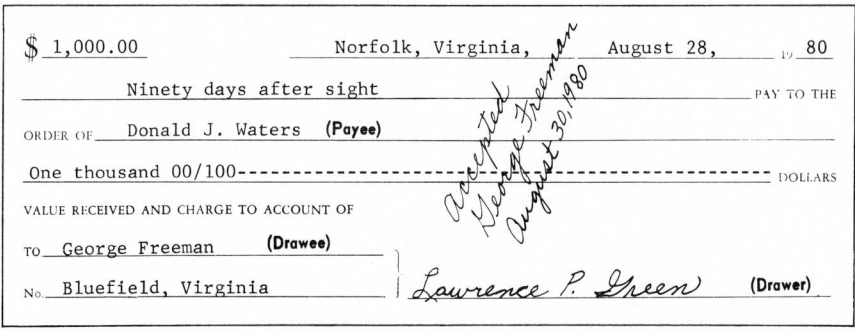

The following information is found in this after-sight time draft:

*Face Value:* $1,000
*Date of the Draft:* August 28, 1980

*Accepted Date:* August 30, 1980
*Term of the Draft:* 90 days after sight (accepted date)
*Interest Rate:* None
*Maturity Date:* 90 days after August 30, 1980, or November 28, 1980
*Maturity Value:* $1,000

**Figure 10–3 AN AFTER-DATE TIME DRAFT**

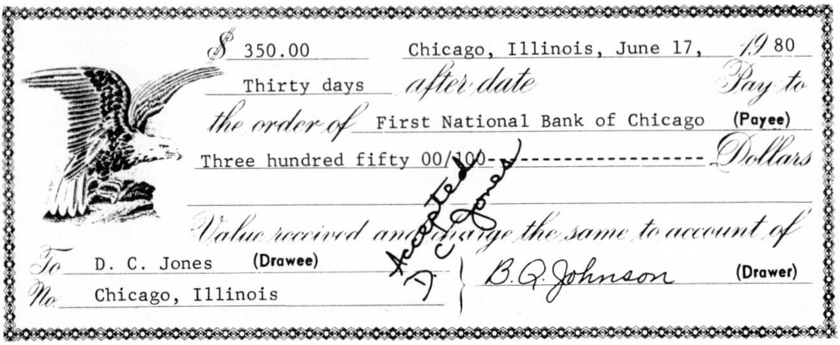

$ 350.00 Chicago, Illinois, June 17, 1980
Thirty days after date Pay to
the order of First National Bank of Chicago (Payee)
Three hundred fifty 00/100------------------ Dollars
Value received and charge the same to account of
To D. C. Jones (Drawee)
No. Chicago, Illinois
Accepted D. C. Jones
B. Q. Johnson (Drawer)

The following information is found in this after-date time draft:

*Face Value:* $350
*Date of the Draft:* June 17, 1980
*Term of the Draft:* 30 days after date
*Interest Rate:* None
*Maturity Date:* 30 days after June 17, 1980, or July 17, 1980
*Maturity Value:* $350

**Figure 10–4 A TRADE ACCEPTANCE (A TYPE OF DRAFT)**

TRADE ACCEPTANCE

No. 36 St. Louis October 12, 1980
To S. P. Simpson Dallas, Texas
On December 2, 1980 Pay to the order of Ourselves
Three hundred eighty 00/100------------------- Dollars, ($ 380.00)

The obligation of the acceptor hereof arises out of the purchase of goods from the drawer. The drawee may accept this bill payable at any bank, banker, or trust company in the United States which such drawee may designate.

Accepted at Dallas, Texas on Oct. 18, 1980
Payable at The First National Bank
Bank Location Dallas, Texas
Buyers Signature S. P. Simpson
By Agent or Officer

The Horton Co.
By G. C. Fort Manager

The following information is found in this trade acceptance:

*Face Value:* $380
*Date of Draft:* October 12, 1980
*Accepted Date:* October 18, 1980

*Term of the Draft:* 45 days (from October 18, 1980, to December 2, 1980)
*Interest Rate:* None
*Maturity Date:* December 2, 1980
*Maturity Value:* $380

A promissory note may or may not bear interest, but a draft generally bears none. If no interest is mentioned in the note, it is assumed to be non-interest-bearing, and the face value is the maturity value. However, the omission of a stated interest rate does not necessarily indicate that the original debt bears no interest. The interest, if any, might have been added to the original debt when the face value was determined.

## 10.3 DISCOUNTING NEGOTIABLE INSTRUMENTS

The basic principles of discounting a note or a draft at a bank are the same as those of obtaining a loan from a bank which deducts interest in advance. The following examples are used to illustrate the problems involved in discounting negotiable instruments by the bank discount method. Observe that when the term of a note or a draft is stated in *days,* the *exact time* is used in determining the maturity date and the period of discount (see Example 1 below). However, when the term is stated in *months,* the corresponding date in the due *month* is used in determining the maturity date although the exact time is still used in counting the period of discount (see Example 2).

## A. Discounting Non-Interest-Bearing Notes

**Example 1**     After D. C. Jones had accepted the draft for $350 (see Figure 10–3), B. Q. Johnson discounted the draft at the First National Bank of Chicago on June 17. How much did Johnson receive if the draft was discounted at 6%?

The maturity value of the note: $S = 350$. The discount rate: $d = 6\%$.

The period of discount: 30 days (from June 17, date of discount, to July 17, maturity date), or $n = 30/360 = 1/12$ (year).

Substituting these values in the formula $I' = Sdn$:

$$I' = 350 \times \frac{6}{100} \times \frac{1}{12} = \$1.75$$

Substituting the values of $S$ and $I'$ in the formula $P' = S - I'$:

$$P' = 350 - 1.75 = \$348.25$$

**Example 2**     A three-month, non-interest-bearing note dated on March 2, 1980, was discounted in a bank on April 3 at 6%. The proceeds were $1,485. Find the face value of the note.

The face value of the non-interest-bearing note is the maturity value $S$ on the due date. The due date is June 2, or on the corresponding date three months from March 2. The period of discount is 60 days, from April 3 to June 2.

$P' = 1,485,\ d = 6\%,\ n = 60/360 = 1/6$ (year). Thus,

$$S = \frac{P'}{1 - dn} = \frac{1,485}{1 - (6\%)(1/6)} = \frac{1,485}{1 - (1/100)}$$

$$= \frac{1,485}{99/100} = 1,485 \times \frac{100}{99} = \$1,500$$

# B. Discounting Interest-Bearing Notes

In Example 1, the discount is computed from the maturity value, which is given. However, the maturity value is usually not given on an interest-bearing note. Thus, in discounting an interest-bearing note, take the following two steps:

**Step (1)**  Find the maturity value:

Add the interest to the face value of the note. Compute the interest according to the rate and the time stipulated on the note. (Use the formula $S = P(1 + in)$, where $S$ is the maturity value and $P$ is the face value.)

**Step (2)**  Find the proceeds:

Discount the maturity value. Compute the interest in advance (or the discount) according to the discount rate charged by the buyer (or the bank) and the period of discount, which is from the date of discount to the maturity date. (Use the formula $P' = S - I' = S - Sdn$.)

**Example 3**  Charles L. Benson had a note for $500 with an interest rate of 6%. The note was dated November 15, 1980, and the maturity date was 90 days after date (see Figure 10–1). On November 30, 1980, he took the note to his bank, which discounted it at a discount rate of 7%. How much did he receive from the bank?

**Step (1)**  Find the maturity value according to the face value, the rate, and the time stipulated on the note.

$P = 500,\ i = 6\%,\ n = 90/360 = 1/4$ (year)

Substituting the values in the formula $S = P(1 + in)$:

$S = 500[1 + (6\%)(1/4)] = \$507.50$

**Step (2)**  Find the proceeds:

Discount the maturity value according to the discount rate and the period of discount.

$S = 507.50$ (the maturity value of the note)
$d = 7\%$ (the discount rate charged by the bank)

$n = 75$ days (from November 30, 1980, the date of discount, to February 13, 1981, the maturity date, which is 90 days after November 15, 1980.)

Substituting these values in the formula $I' = Sdn$:

$$I' = 507.50 \times .07 \times \frac{75}{360} = \$7.40$$

Substituting the values of $S$ and $I'$ in the formula $P' = S - I'$:

$$P' = 507.50 - 7.40 = \$500.10$$

This computation may be tabulated as follows:

| | |
|---|---:|
| Face value of note | $500.00 |
| Add: Interest on note (90 days at 6%) | 7.50 |
| Maturity value of note | $507.50 |
| Less: Discount on the maturity value | |
| (75 days at 7%) | 7.40 |
| Proceeds of note discounted | $500.10 |

Example 3 is diagrammed as follows:

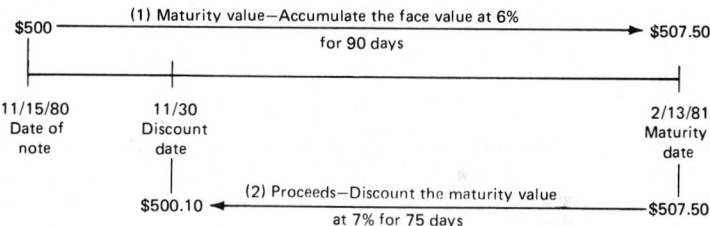

# EXERCISE 10–2

## Reference: Sections 10.2 and 10.3

**A.** *For each of the following promissory notes, find the (a) maturity date, (b) maturity value, (c) discount period, (d) discount, and (e) proceeds.*

| | | Interest | | | Bank |
|---|---|---|---|---|---|
| Date of Note | Face Value | Rate on Note | Term | Date of Discount | Discount Rate |
| **1.** 1/6/80 | $2,000 | 6% | 30 days | 1/16/80 | 10% |
| **2.** 2/10/81 | 1,200 | 5% | 45 days | 2/25/81 | 12% |
| **3.** 4/18/80 | 1,800 | None | 2 months | 4/29/80 | 6% |
| **4.** 6/14/81 | 570 | 8% | 120 days | 7/14/81 | 6% |
| **5.** 8/5/82 | 4,200 | 4½% | 90 days | 9/4/82 | 5% |
| **6.** 9/16/82 | 1,540 | 6% | 3 months | 11/16/82 | 8% |
| **7.** 10/1/83 | 2,500 | 9% | 2 months | 11/1/83 | 7% |

| Date of Note | Face Value | Interest Rate on Note | Term | Date of Discount | Bank Discount Rate |
|---|---|---|---|---|---|
| 8. 1/15/83 | 880 | 7% | 180 days | 5/15/83 | 6% |
| 9. 3/24/84 | 1,620 | 8% | 150 days | 6/7/84 | 9% |
| 10. 4/12/84 | 630 | None | 4 months | 7/2/84 | 10% |

**B.** *Statement Problems:*

11. Herbert signs a promissory note for $250 due in 90 days to a bank that charges 12% interest in advance. What is the discount? What should Herbert receive as the proceeds from the loan?

12. On September 29, 1980, the draft in Figure 10–2 was discounted at 8% by Donald J. Waters. What are the discount and the proceeds?

13. Johnson needs $4,387.50 in cash as the proceeds of a three-month, non-interest-bearing note from a bank that charges 10% discount. What should be the face value of the note?

14. A non-interest-bearing note is discounted at 7% at a bank 180 days before the date of maturity. The proceeds are $3,600. Find the face value of the note.

15. On November 2, 1980, the trade acceptance in Figure 10–4 was discounted by The Horton Co. at a local bank which charged a discount of 5%. What are the discount and the proceeds?

16. J. K. Osburn has a three-month, non-interest-bearing note for $2,800. When should she discount it at 7% so that she can receive $2,770.60 as the proceeds?

17. A. C. Tent received a 90-day, 5% note dated March 6 for $2,400 from B. F. Rice. Tent discounted the note at 4% at a bank on March 16. What are the (a) maturity date, (b) maturity value, (c) discount period, (d) discount, and (e) proceeds?

18. A four-month, 6% interest-bearing note of $1,500 is discounted at 8% one month before maturity. What are the (a) maturity value, (b) discount, and (c) proceeds?

19. A note for $2,100 at 6% for 180 days is discounted at 5% in a bank 120 days before maturity. What is the discount? What are the proceeds?

20. D. H. Horton has a 60-day note for $2,500 at 6% interest. The maturity date is May 6. If the note is discounted on March 17 at $4\frac{1}{2}\%$, how much will Horton receive?

21. A 120-day note bearing 6% interest is discounted at $4\frac{1}{2}\%$ 90 days before maturity. If the discount is $573.75, what is the face value?

22. Johnson signed a 60-day, non-interest-bearing note for $2,000 and discounted it at 9% at the First National Bank. If the note was immediately rediscounted by the bank at 7% at a Federal Reserve Bank, what is the profit of the First National Bank? (Note: Federal Reserve Banks use 365 days as a year in rediscounting notes for member banks. The previous discounts have no effect on the rediscount.)

## 10.4 RELATIONSHIP BETWEEN SIMPLE DISCOUNT AND BANK DISCOUNT

When the simple interest rate $(i)$ and the bank discount rate $(d)$ are the same, the discount computed by the bank discount method is greater than that computed by the simple discount method; that is,

when $i = d,$    $I' > I$

**Example 1**    Discount $1,000 for 60 days at 6% by using (a) the bank discount method and (b) the simple discount method. What are the discount and the proceeds by method (a)? What are the present value and the discount by method (b)? How much is the difference between the two types of discounts? Indicate which discount is larger.

(a) *Bank Discount Method:*

$$\text{Discount} = I' = Sdn = 1,000 \left(\frac{6}{100}\right)\left(\frac{60}{360}\right) = \$10$$

$$\text{Proceeds} = P' = S - I' = 1,000 - 10 = \$990$$

(b) *Simple Discount Method:*

$$\text{Present value} = P = \frac{S}{(1 + in)} = \frac{1,000}{1 + (6/100)(60/360)} = \frac{1,000}{1 + .01}$$

$$= \$990.10$$

$$\text{Discount} = I = S - P = 1,000 - 990.10 = \$9.90$$

The difference between the discounts by methods (a) and (b) is

$$I' - I = 10.00 - 9.90 = \$.10$$

The bank discount is larger than the discount calculated by the simple discount method.

When the simple discount $I$ and the bank discount $I'$ are the same, the interest rate computed by the simple discount method is greater than that computed by the bank discount method; that is,

when $I = I',$    $i > d$

**Example 2**    A man who borrowed $990 paid $1,000 at the end of 60 days. (a) Consider the difference as the interest deducted in advance from the maturity value, $1,000. What is the bank discount rate? (b) Consider the difference as the interest added to the borrowed principal, $990. What is the simple interest rate? Which rate is larger?

(a) $S = 1,000,$ $I' = 1,000 - 900 = \$10,$ $n = 60/360 = 1/6$ (year)

Substituting the values in $d = \dfrac{I'}{Sn}$:

$$d = \frac{10}{1,000(1/6)} = 6\% \text{ (bank discount rate)}$$

(b) $P = 990$, $I = 1,000 - 990 = 10$, $n = 1/6$ (year)

Substituting the values in $i = \dfrac{I}{Pn}$:

$$i = \frac{10}{990(1/6)} = \frac{\overset{2}{\cancel{10}}}{\underset{33}{\cancel{165}}} = 6.06\% \text{ (simple interest rate)}$$

The simple interest rate is larger than the bank discount rate by

$$6.06\% - 6\% = .06\%$$

From the above illustration, it may be seen that the bank discount rate of 6% is equivalent to the simple interest rate of 6.06% in the transaction. In general, if $P = P'$, the relationship between a simple interest rate and a bank discount rate may be expressed by the following formulas:

$$i = \frac{d}{1 - dn} \qquad\qquad\qquad (10\text{--}3)[1]$$

$$d = \frac{i}{1 + in} \qquad\qquad\qquad (10\text{--}4)[2]$$

By applying formulas (10–3) and (10–4), Example 2 is computed as follows:

(a) $i = 6.06\% = 2/33$ (see Solution (b) above), $n = 1/6$ (year)

Substituting the values in formula (10–4):

$$d = \frac{i}{1 + in} = \frac{2/33}{1 + (2/33)(1/6)} = \frac{6}{100} = 6\%$$

---

[1] *Proof—Formula (10–3)*

If $P = P'$, the formula $S = P(1 + in)$ may be written as

$S = P'(1 + in)$; but from formula (10–2), $S = P'/(1 - dn)$.

Thus, $P'(1 + in) = P'/(1 - dn)$; divide both sides by $P'$; $(1 + in) = 1/(1 - dn)$.

Subtract 1 from both sides and simplify as below:

$$in = \frac{1}{1 - dn} - 1 = \frac{1 - (1 - dn)}{1 - dn} = \frac{dn}{1 - dn}$$

Divide both sides by $n$, $\quad i = \dfrac{d}{1 - dn}$

[2] *Proof—Formula (10–4)*

Multiply both sides of formula (10–3) by $(1 - dn)$; then

$\quad i(1 - dn) = d$, and

$\quad i - idn = d$. Add $idn$ to both sides:

$\quad i = d + idn = d(1 + in)$

Divide both sides by $1 + in$:

$$d = \frac{i}{1 + in}$$

(b) $d = 6\%$ (see Solution (a) in Example 2), $n = 1/6$ (year)

Substituting the values in formula (10–3):

$$i = \frac{d}{1 - dn} = \frac{6\%}{1 - (6\%)(1/6)} = \frac{\frac{6}{\cancel{6}}^2}{\frac{99}{33}} = 6.06\%$$

The answers are the same as those in the original computation. Note that formulas (10–3) and (10–4) do not make use of the amount $S$ nor the proceeds $P'$. Therefore, in finding the simple interest rate which is equivalent to a bank discount rate, or vice versa, a knowledge of the amount and the proceeds is unnecessary.

**Example 3**  A bank discounts a 75-day note at 9%. What is the equivalent simple interest rate earned by the bank?

$d = 9\%$, $n = 75/360 = 5/24$ (year)

Substituting the values in formula (10–3):

$$i = \frac{9\%}{1 - (9\%)(5/24)} = \frac{9\%}{1 - 15/800} = \frac{9}{100} \cdot \frac{800}{785} = \frac{72}{785} = .0917197,$$

or rounded to 9.17%

**Example 4**  At what rate should a bank discount a 60-day note if the bank is to earn simple interest equivalent to 8%?

$i = 8\%$, $n = 60/360 = 1/6$ (year)

Substituting the values in formula (10–4):

$$d = \frac{8\%}{1 + (8\%)(1/6)} = \frac{8\%}{1 + 1/75} = \frac{8/100}{76/75} = \frac{3}{38} = .078947,$$

or rounded to 7.89%

# EXERCISE 10–3

## Reference: Section 10.4

**A.** *In each of the following problems, find the corresponding unknown rate:*

| Discount Period | Discount Rate | Simple Interest Rate |
|---|---|---|
| **1.** 3 months | ? | 9% |
| **2.** 4 months | ? | 10% |
| **3.** 120 days | ? | 7% |
| **4.** 150 days | ? | 8% |
| **5.** $\frac{1}{2}$ year | ? | 6% |
| **6.** 3 months | 9% | ? |
| **7.** 4 months | 10% | ? |

| Discount Period | Discount Rate | Simple Interest Rate |
|---|---|---|
| **8.** 120 days | 7% | ? |
| **9.** 150 days | 8% | ? |
| **10.** $\frac{1}{2}$ year | 6% | ? |

**B.** *Statement Problems:*

**11.** A bank discounts a 90-day note at 12%. What is the equivalent simple interest rate earned by the bank?

**12.** What is the corresponding simple interest rate earned by a bank if it discounts a four-month note at $7\frac{1}{2}$%?

**13.** If a bank's policy is to earn 5% simple interest, what discount rate should be charged on a 60-day note?

**14.** At what rate should a bank discount a 180-day note if the bank is to earn 7% simple interest?

**15.** A woman received a 90-day loan of $2,500 from a bank which charged 8% interest in advance. What are the proceeds? What is the simple interest rate of the advanced interest?

**16.** Johnson signs a three-month note for $1,200. The bank charges 6% interest in advance. How much does Johnson receive as the proceeds? If she borrows the proceeds at simple interest and repays $1,200 at the end of a three-month period, what is the simple interest rate that she must pay?

**17.** Jackson signs a 60-day note for $3,600 at a bank which deducts 5% interest in advance. What is the value that Jackson receives from the bank? At what simple interest rate is he paying the advanced interest?

**18.** A retailer received an invoice for $1,000 with the terms 2/10, $n$/30. In order to take advantage of the cash discount, he plans to borrow money. (a) How long should the loan period be? (b) What is the highest interest rate that he can afford to pay (1) if he pays the interest in advance and (2) if he pays the interest at the end of the period?

**19.** Frieda signs a 120-day note for $840. She receives $826 as the proceeds. (a) What is the bank discount rate? (b) What is the simple interest rate if the present value is $826?

**20.** Stevenson received $3,450 in cash from a bank on April 1 and agreed to pay $3,600 on August 29 for the loan. What is the bank discount? What is the equivalent simple interest rate?

# 10.5 SUMMARY OF BANK DISCOUNT FORMULAS

| Application | Formula | Formula Number | Reference Page |
|---|---|---|---|
| Finding the bank discount—interest deducted in advance | $I' = Sdn$ | (10–1) | 311 |
| Finding the proceeds | $P' = S(1 - dn)$ | (10–2) | 311 |

| Application | Formula | Formula Number | Reference Page |
|---|---|---|---|
| Finding the simple interest rate | $i = \dfrac{d}{1 - dn}$ | (10–3) | 322 |
| Finding the bank discount rate | $d = \dfrac{i}{1 + in}$ | (10–4) | 322 |

## EXERCISE 10–4

### Review of Chapter 10

1. Ivan promised to pay a bank $630 at the end of 30 days for a loan. If the bank charges 12% interest in advance (a) what is the discount? (b) how much does Ivan receive now?

2. Jimmy borrows $500 for four months from a bank that charges a discount rate of $4\frac{1}{2}$%. What are the proceeds?

3. Karl wishes to borrow money and will pay $700 at the end of eight months. Find (a) the proceeds if the creditor charges 6% interest in advance, (b) the present value if the creditor charges 6% simple interest.

4. Refer to Problem 1. What are the answers if the interest is charged at 12% simple interest?

5. What is the final amount of a loan if a bank charged $5 interest in advance for 120 days at 5%?

6. If a bank charged $12 interest in advance for a ten-month loan at 18%, find the total amount of the loan.

7. A man received a 90-day loan of $600 from a bank. The proceeds were $580. What is the discount rate?

8. Find the bank discount rate if the amount is $300, the discount is $2, and discount time is 60 days.

9. Lynn borrowed $1,000 from a bank which charged 5% interest in advance. He received $980 from the loan. For how long did he borrow the money?

10. Margaret received $671.50 in cash as the proceeds from a bank loan of $680. The discount rate was 5%. Find the discount period in months.

11. A non-interest-bearing note was discounted in a bank 45 days before maturity at 4%. The proceeds were $597. What was the face value of the note?

12. A non-interest-bearing note is discounted in a bank 90 days before maturity at 5%. Find the face value of the note if the proceeds are $197.50.

13. Nancy had a note for $800 with an interest rate of 5%. It was dated April 7, 1980, and the maturity date was 60 days after date. On April 22, 1980, the note was discounted at a discount rate of 6%. How much did Nancy receive as the proceeds from the discounting?

14. A 90-day note bearing 4% interest is discounted 30 days before it is due at 5%. If the discount is $8.20, what is the face value of the note? What are the proceeds?

15. Discount $2,000 for 90 days at 5% by using (a) the bank discount method, and (b) the simple interest method. What are the discount and the proceeds by method (a)? What are the present value and the discount by method (b)? How much is the difference between the two types of discounts?

16. Otis borrowed $800 in cash but paid $805 at the end of 45 days to the lender. (a) Consider the difference of $5 as the interest deducted in advance from the maturity value of $805. Find the bank discount rate. (b) Consider the $5 as the interest added to the principal of $800. Find the simple interest rate.

17. A bank discounts a 60-day note at 5%. What is the equivalent simple interest rate earned by the bank?

18. What is the corresponding simple interest rate earned by a bank if it discounts a two-month note at 6%?

19. At what rate should a bank discount a 75-day note if the bank is to earn a 5% simple interest equivalent?

20. If a bank desires to earn 12% simple interest, what discount rate should be charged by the bank on a 45-day note?

# Part Three
## MATHEMATICS IN INVESTMENT — BASIC TOPICS

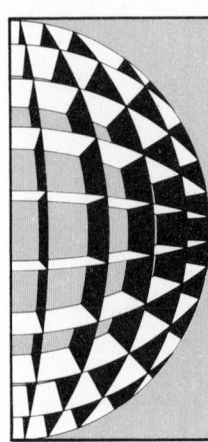

# Chapter 11

## Compound Interest— Computing Basic Values

## 11.1 INTRODUCTION

This chapter introduces the method of computing interest and related values based on the concept of *compounding* interest. The compound interest method is generally used in long-term borrowing. There is usually more than one period for computing interest during the borrowing time. The interest for each period is added (compounded or converted) to the principal before the interest for the next period is computed. The final sum at the end of the period of borrowing is called the *compound amount*.

The process of accumulating a principal to obtain a compound amount is called *compound accumulation. Compound interest* is the difference between the original principal and the compound amount. The period for computing interest, usually at regularly stated intervals such as annually, semiannually, quarterly, or monthly, is called the *conversion period,* or the *interest period.* The interest rate per conversion period is equal to the stated annual interest rate divided by the number of conversion periods in one year. The stated annual interest rate is called the *nominal annual rate,* or simply the *nominal rate.* Thus, if the nominal rate is 6%, the interest rate for the annual conversion period is also 6%; but, if the conversion period is semiannual, the interest rate for a period of six months is 6%/2, or 3%.

## 11.2 BASIC METHOD OF COMPUTING COMPOUND INTEREST

The basic method of computing compound interest for *each* conversion period is the same as the method of computing simple interest. Thus, if there is only one conversion period, compound interest is the same as simple interest. The following example illustrates the method of computing compound interest in general.

**Example 1**    What are the compound amount and the compound interest at the end of nine months if $10,000 is borrowed at 4% compounded quarterly?

The original principal is $10,000.

The conversion period is one quarter, or three months.

The number of conversion periods in nine months is $\dfrac{9 \text{ months}}{3 \text{ months}} = 3$.

The interest rate per conversion period is

$$\frac{\text{Annual interest rate}}{\text{Number of conversion periods in one year}} = \frac{4\%}{4} = 1\%$$

The computation is written as follows:

Original principal . . . . . . . . . . . . . . . . . . . .$10,000.00
Add: Interest for the 1st quarter . . . . . . . .      100.00 = $10,000 × 1%
Principal at the end of 1st quarter . . . . . .$10,100.00
Add: Interest for the 2d quarter  . . . . . . . .      101.00 = $10,100 × 1%
Principal at the end of 2d quarter . . . . . .$10,201.00
Add: Interest for the 3d quarter  . . . . . . . .      102.01 = $10,201 × 1%
Principal at the end of 3d quarter, or the
compound amount . . . . . . . . . . . . . . . . . . . .$10,303.01

Compound interest = Compound amount − Original principal
              = 10,303.01 − 10,000 = $303.01

The simple interest at 4% on $10,000 for nine months is:

$10,000 \times 4\% \times \frac{9}{12} = \$300$

In Example 1 the compound interest is greater than the simple interest by:

$303.01 − 300 = \$3.01$

## EXERCISE 11–1

**Reference: Section 11.2**

**A.** *Find the compound amount and the compound interest in each of the following problems:*

1. $6,000 for one year at 10% compounded semiannually.
2. $100 for two years at 6% compounded annually.
3. $3,000 for six months at 12% compounded quarterly.
4. $2,000 for two months at 6% compounded monthly.
5. $1,000 for three years at 5% compounded annually.
6. $5,000 for one year at 8% compounded quarterly.
7. $10,000 for three months at 12% compounded monthly.
8. $8,000 for $1\frac{1}{2}$ years at 8% compounded semiannually.

**B.** *Statement Problems:*

9. (a) Find the simple interest on $6,000 for one year at 10%. (b) What is the difference between the simple interest and the answer in Problem 1?
10. (a) What is the simple interest on $100 for two years at 6% interest rate? (b) Compare the simple interest with the compound interest in Problem 2, and find the difference.
11. (a) What is the simple interest on $3,000 for six months at a simple interest rate of 12%? (b) Compare the simple interest with the compound interest in Problem 3, and find the difference.
12. (a) Find the simple interest on $2,000 for two months at 6%. (b) What is the difference between the simple interest and the answer in Problem 4?

## 11.3 FINDING THE COMPOUND AMOUNT BY FORMULA

To find the compound amount by formula, we shall use the following symbols:

Let $P$ = original principal
$i$ = interest rate per conversion period
$n$ = number of conversion periods
$S$ = compound amount, or the principal at the end of the $n$th period

The compound amount formula is:

$$S = P(1 + i)^n \qquad \text{(11–1)}[1]$$

**Example 1**     What is the compound amount at the end of nine months if $10,000 is borrowed at 4% compounded quarterly?

$P = 10,000$, $i = 1\%$ (per quarter), $n = 3$ (quarters)

---

[1] *Proof—Formula (11–1)*

In Example 1 of Section 11.2, let

the original principal $10,000 = P$, and
the interest rate per quarter (conversion period) $= i$.

The computation in Example 1 may be written symbolically as follows:

Original principal . . . . . . . . .     $P$
Add: Interest (1st quarter)  . .(+) $Pi$
———————
Principal (1st quarter end)  . .     $P(1 + i)$
Add: Interest (2d quarter) . . .(+) $P(1 + i)i$
———————
Principal (2d quarter end) . . .     $P(1 + i)(1 + i) = P(1 + i)^2$
Add: Interest (3d quarter) . . .            $(+)P(1 + i)^2i$
———————
Principal (3d quarter, end)  . .            $P(1 + i)^2(1 + i) = P(1 + i)^3$

When this idea is extended, the compound amount at the end of the $n$th period may be expressed as:

$$S = P(1 + i)^n$$

Substituting these values in the compound amount formula:

$$S = P(1 + i)^n = 10,000(1 + 1\%)^3$$
$$= 10,000(1.01)(1.01)(1.01)$$
$$= 10,000(1.030301)$$
$$= \$10,303.01$$

The answer may be compared with the answer in Example 1 of the preceding section.

When the value of $n$ in formula (11–1) becomes large, considerable time is required in calculating the value of the factor $(1 + i)^n$. For convenience, the most common values of $(1 + i)^n$ are tabulated in Tables 5 and 5A in the Appendix. In Table 5, the numbers of the conversion periods are whole numbers; that is, $n$ is a round number, such as 1, 2, 3, and so on. In Table 5A, the numbers of the conversion periods are fractional numbers; that is, $n$ is a fraction, such as $\frac{1}{2}, \frac{1}{3}, \frac{1}{4}$, and is generally represented by $1/m$. Each of the values (entries) in the tables is the compound amount when the principal is 1.

Symbolically, let $s =$ the compound amount $S$ when the principal is 1. Then, the formula becomes:

$$s = S = P(1 + i)^n = 1(1 + i)^n, \text{ or } s = (1 + i)^n.$$

The unit value of each entry may best be represented by a dollar, although it may be represented by any other unit. Thus, each entry in the tables becomes the compound amount in dollars when the principal is \$1. The factor $(1 + i)^n$ is also frequently referred to as the *accumulation factor* in computing a compound amount.

The methods of computing a compound amount by using the compound amount formula and the tables are illustrated below.

# A. Use of Table 5

When Table 5 is used, formula (11–1) may be written as follows:

Compound amount *(S)* = Principal *(P)* × An entry in Table 5.

(The entry is at the interest rate $i$ per conversion period for $n$ conversion periods.)

Tables 5 through 11 (the compound interest and annuity tables) provide 8 decimal places for each entry. It is obvious that it would be a waste of time if all 8 places were employed in multiplying a multiplicand of a small value. In most financial problems, the answers are required to contain dollars and cents. In order to avoid unnecessary multiplication and at the same time to obtain a result close enough to the exact value, a simple rule is used in this text:

*If an answer is to be computed to the nearest cent, the minimum number of decimal places to be multiplied is equal to the number of digits in the multiplicand, including dollars and cents.*

For example, in finding a compound amount if the principal is $250.10 which has three dollar-digits (250) and two cent-digits (.10), an entry in Table 5 containing five decimal places is employed in multiplication.

Hereafter, unless otherwise specified, the words "interest" and "amount" mean compound interest and compound amount respectively, and the interest rate expressed by % means the nominal annual rate.

**Example 2**    Find the amount of $1,500 invested at 6% compounded semiannually and due at the end of $8\frac{1}{2}$ years.

The principal ($P$) is $1,500.00, which has six digits.

The interest rate ($i$) per conversion period (six months) is $6\%/2 = 3\%$.

The number of conversion periods ($n$) is $8\frac{1}{2} \times 2 = 17$ (semiannual periods).

The value of the factor $(1 + i)^n = (1 + 3\%)^{17}$ is found to be 1.65284763 in the 3% column opposite $n = 17$ in Table 5.

Since the principal in dollars and cents has 6 digits, only 6 decimal places of the factor are needed in multiplication. Thus, the factor 1.65284763 is rounded to 1.652848.

The compounded amount $(S) = 1,500(1 + 3\%)^{17}$
$$= 1,500(1.652848)$$
$$= \$2,479.272, \text{ round to } \$2,479.27$$

***Note:***    The multiplication $1,500(1 + 3\%)^{17}$ may also be performed by using logarithms. The mantissa for log 1,500 is given in Table 2 and the value of log $(1 + 3\%)^{17}$ is given in Table 12. Detailed computation is presented in Example 1 of Section 12.2.

**Example 3**    A note having a face value of $1,000 and bearing interest at 8% compounded quarterly will mature in $10\frac{1}{2}$ years. What is the maturity value?

$P = 1,000$, $i = 8\%/4 = 2\%$ (per quarter), and $n = 10\frac{1}{2} \times 4 = 42$ (quarters)

The value of the factor $(1 + 2\%)^{42}$ is found to be 2.29724447 in Table 5.

Thus, the compound amount (or the maturity value) is

$S = P(1 + i)^n = 1,000(1 + 2\%)^{42}$
$$= 1,000(2.297244) = \$2,297.244, \text{ rounded to } \$2,297.24.$$

# B. The Number of Conversion Periods (*n*) is Greater than the Highest Number in Table 5

When the number of conversion periods is greater than that given in Table 5, the number of conversion periods may be divided into several smaller numbers which are listed in the table. The product of the corresponding entries of the smaller numbers is the desired accumulation factor. For example,

$$(1+4\%)^{239} = (1+4\%)^{100}(1+4\%)^{100}(1+4\%)^{39}$$
$$(1+3\%)^{126} = (1+3\%)^{100}(1+3\%)^{26}$$

Although the values on the left sides of the equations are not listed in the table, the values of the expanded factors on the right sides of the equations are included in the table. Thus, the entries in the table may be used in computing the accumulation factor $(1 + i)^n$ when the value of $n$ is greater than the highest number in the table.

**Example 4**  Find the compound amount when the principal is $1,200, the interest rate is $3\frac{1}{2}\%$ compounded annually, and the term is 125 years.

$P = 1,200$, $i = 3\frac{1}{2}\%$ (annual), $n = 125$ (years)

The factor $(1 + i)^n = (1 + 3\frac{1}{2}\%)^{125} = (1 + 3\frac{1}{2}\%)^{100}(1 + 3\frac{1}{2}\%)^{25}$.

According to Table 5, $(1 + 3\frac{1}{2}\%)^{100} = 31.19140798$ and $(1 + 3\frac{1}{2}\%)^{25} = 2.36324498$.

Thus, $(1 + 3\frac{1}{2}\%)^{125} = 31.19140798 \times 2.36324498 = 73.712938$.

$S = 1,200(1 + 3\frac{1}{2}\%)^{125} = 1,200(73.712938) = \$88,455.53$

*Note:*  The above computation may also be performed by using logarithms. See Example 2 of Section 12.2.

## EXERCISE 11–2

### Reference: Sections 11.3 A and B

**A.** *Find the compound amount in each of the following problems:*

|  | Principal (P) | Interest Rate (i) | Time (n) |
|---|---|---|---|
| 1. | $1,200 | 4% compounded quarterly | 10 years |
| 2. | 500 | 12% compounded monthly | $1\frac{1}{2}$ years |
| 3. | 650 | 10% compounded annually | 25 years |
| 4. | 4,200 | 5% compounded semiannually | 9 years |
| 5. | 3,500 | $6\frac{1}{2}\%$ compounded monthly | 20 years |
| 6. | 200 | 8% compounded quarterly | 30 years |
| 7. | 800 | 7% compounded semiannually | 6 years |
| 8. | 2,000 | $5\frac{1}{2}\%$ compounded annually | 15 years |
| 9. | 1,000 | 6% compounded every 2 months | 1 year |
| 10. | 5,000 | 9% compounded every 4 months | 2 years |

**B.** *Statement Problems:*

**11.** Accumulate $2,500 for eight years at 7% compounded quarterly. How much is the interest?

**12.** Carl Johnson deposits $550 in the First National Bank which pays $5\frac{1}{2}\%$ compounded semiannually. What amount will he have at the end of 11 years?

13. What will the amount be after one year if $1,000 is invested at 6% compounded (a) monthly? (b) quarterly? (c) semiannually? (d) annually?
14. What will the amount be after ten years if $500 is invested at 7% compounded (a) monthly? (b) quarterly? (c) semiannually? (d) annually?
15. Find the amount and the interest on $1,000 at 6% compounded semiannually for (a) 10 years, (b) 20 years, (c) 30 years.
16. Accumulate $600 at 8% compounded quarterly for (a) nine months, (b) five years, (c) ten years. What are the amount and the interest in each case?
17. A note having a face value of $1,650 and bearing interest at 8% compounded monthly will mature in three years. What is the maturity value?
18. Find the maturity value of a five-year note with a face value of $2,500 and interest at 9% compounded quarterly.
19. Find the difference between investments (a) and (b): (a) $1,500 is invested for five years at 8% compounded monthly; (b) $1,500 is invested for five years at 8% simple interest.
20. James Moore deposited $10,000 in the Home Savings Bank, which pays 6% compounded quarterly. At the same time he deposited another $10,000 in the Bank of Commerce, which pays $6\frac{1}{2}$% compounded annually. Compare the interest received from the two banks at the end of ten years. (a) Which bank pays more interest? (b) What is the difference?

# C. The Interest Rate Changes During Compound Accumulation

If the interest rate changes during compound accumulation, the compound amount is the product of the principal and the several accumulation factors which are at different interest rates for respective given periods.

**Example 5**    If the principal is $500 and the interest rate is 6% compounded semiannually for the first five years and 8% compounded quarterly for the next six years, what is the compound amount at the end of the 11th year?

The values for computing the amount at the end of the first five years are:

$P = 500$, $i = 6\%/2 = 3\%$ (per six months), $n = 5 \times 2 = 10$ (semiannual periods).

$S = 500(1 + 3\%)^{10} = 500(1.34392) = \$671.96$

The values for computing the amount at the end of the 11th year for the remaining six-year period are: $P = \$671.96$ (the new principal at the end of the fifth year), $i = 8\%/4 = 2\%$ (per quarter), $n = 6 \times 4 = 24$ (quarters).

Thus, the compound amount at the end of the 11th year is:

$S = 671.96(1 + 2\%)^{24} = 671.96(1.60844) = \$1,080.81$, or
$S = 500(1 + 3\%)^{10}(1 + 2\%)^{24} = 500(1.34392)(1.60844) = \$1,080.81$

The example is diagrammed as follows:

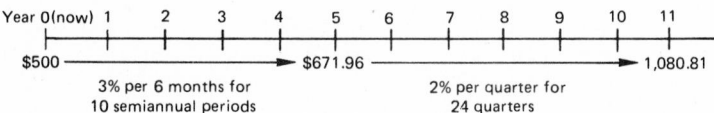

# D. The Interest Rate Per Conversion Period ($i$) Is Not Given in the Table

When the interest rate is not given in the table, the interpolation method may be used to obtain an approximate entry which is accurate enough for most purposes.

**Example 6**   Find the compound amount if $1,000 is invested at $4\frac{1}{4}\%$ compounded semiannually for five years.

$P = 1,000$, $i = 4\frac{1}{4}\%/2 = 2\frac{1}{8}\%$ (per six months), $n = 5 \times 2 = 10$ (semiannual periods)

There is no $2\frac{1}{8}\%$ column in Table 5. However, the rate which is just above and that which is just below the rate $2\frac{1}{8}\%$ may be found in the table, and the accumulation factor for $2\frac{1}{8}\%$ may be obtained through interpolation. When the interpolation method is used, it is assumed that the differences between the value of $(1 + i)^n$ are proportional to the differences between the values of $i$ in the table.

The factor $(1 + 2\frac{1}{8}\%)^{10}$ is obtained by the interpolation method as follows:

$$
\begin{array}{lccl}
 & i & (1+i)^{10} & \\
 & 2\frac{1}{4}\% & 1.24920343 & (1) \\
 & 2\frac{1}{8}\% & x & (2) \\
 & 2\% & 1.21899442 & (3) \\
(2)-(3) & \dfrac{\frac{1}{8}\%}{\frac{1}{4}\%}\begin{smallmatrix}1\\2\end{smallmatrix} = & \dfrac{x-1.21899442}{0.03020901} & (4) \\
(1)-(3) & & & (5)
\end{array}
$$

The differences on line (4) are obtained by subtracting the values on line (3) from the corresponding values on line (2), or

$\frac{1}{8}\% = 2\frac{1}{8}\% - 2\%$,   and   $x - 1.21899442$ (= unknown)

The differences on line (5) are obtained in a similar manner, or

$\frac{1}{4}\% = 2\frac{1}{4}\% - 2\%$,   and   $0.03020901 = 1.24920343 - 1.21899442$

The differences on lines (4) and (5) give the proportion which indicates that $\frac{1}{8}\%$ is to $(x - 1.21899442)$ as $\frac{1}{4}\%$ is to $0.03020901$. The proportion is also expressed in equation form on these two lines.

Solve for $x$ in the equation. First, the fraction at the left side of the equation is simplified by multiplying both numerator and denominator by 800, or

$$\frac{\frac{1}{8}\% \times 800}{\frac{1}{4}\% \times 800} = \frac{1}{2}, \text{ and } \frac{1}{2} = \frac{x - 1.21899442}{0.03020901}.$$

Then, $x - 1.21899442 = 0.03020901 \cdot \frac{1}{2}$,
$$x = 1.21899442 + 0.015104505 = 1.234098925, \quad \text{or}$$

$$(1 + 2\tfrac{1}{8}\%)^{10} = 1.234098925$$

Thus, $S = 1,000(1 + 2\tfrac{1}{8}\%)^{10} = 1,000(1.234099) = \$1,234.10$

***Note:***
1. In the above arrangement, the larger values are placed on the top line in order to facilitate subtraction.
2. The order of the subtraction, either first by subtracting line (3) from line (2) or first by subtracting line (3) from line (1), does not affect the answer. The value of $x$ in the proportion

$$\frac{\tfrac{1}{8}\%}{\tfrac{1}{4}\%} = \frac{x - 1.21899442}{0.03020901} \quad \text{is the same as in the reversed-term proportion}$$

$$\frac{\tfrac{1}{4}\%}{\tfrac{1}{8}\%} = \frac{0.03020901}{x - 1.21899442}.$$

However, the former proportion does simplify the operation in solving for $x$.
3. According to the rule of the number of decimal places in a multiplier, only 6 decimal places are required in multiplying the 6-digit number 1,000.00. Thus, the result in the above interpolation would be a satisfactory one if the value of $(1 + i)^n$ included only 7 decimal places. The one extra place provides for safety in rounding to the 6-place requirement.
4. The value of $(1 + 2\tfrac{1}{8}\%)^{10}$ may also be obtained by using logarithms or the binomial theorem. (See Problems 11 and 12 of Exercise 12–1, page 359, for instruction.) The value obtained by using the binomial theorem is the most accurate and is 1.234015729. The value obtained by using logarithms (7-place table) is 1.234015625 (see Example 3, Section 12.2), which is very close to the value obtained by using the binomial theorem. Notice that the first seven digits 1.234015 are the same by both methods; the eighth digits, 7 and 6 respectively by the two methods, are very close to each other.

# EXERCISE 11–3

## Reference: Sections 11.3 C and D

**A.** *Statement Problems:*

1. A man invested $200 for ten years. The interest rate is 8% compounded annually for the first six years and 10% compounded semiannually for the next four years. What is the amount at the end of ten years?
2. Helen invested $300 for eight years. The interest rate is 7% compounded quarterly for the first five years and 5% compounded monthly for the next three years. What is the amount at the end of eight years?
3. Accumulate $600 for 15 years if the interest rate is 8% compounded semiannually for the first ten years and 9% compounded monthly for the remaining five years. Find the amount at the end of 15 years.

4. Accumulate $500 for 18 years if the interest rate is 5% compounded quarterly for the first six years and 6% compounded annually for the remaining 12 years. Find the amount at the end of 18 years.

5. Find the amount at the end of seven years if $400 is invested at 6% compounded monthly for the first two years and at $6\frac{1}{2}$% compounded annually for the last five years.

6. Find the amount at the end of 12 years if $1,000 is invested at 4% compounded semiannually for the first five years and at 6% compounded quarterly for the last seven years.

**B.** *Find the compound amount in each of the following problems. (Use the interpolation method to find each accumulation factor.)*

|  | Principal (P) | Interest Rate (i) | Time (n) |
|---|---|---|---|
| 7. | $1,000 | $5\frac{1}{4}$% compounded quarterly | 3 years |
| 8. | 1,500 | $7\frac{3}{4}$% compounded annually | 20 years |
| 9. | 900 | $4\frac{1}{2}$% compounded monthly | 7 months |
| 10. | 850 | $8\frac{1}{2}$% compounded semiannually | 12 years |
| 11. | 2,200 | $6\frac{1}{4}$% compounded quarterly | 6 years |
| 12. | 2,400 | $8\frac{1}{4}$% compounded monthly | 10 months |

# E. The Conversion Periods Include a Fractional Part

When the conversion periods include a fractional part, either of the following two methods may be used in computing the compound amount:

**Method A**     Use the formula $S = P(1 + i)^n$, where $n$ is a whole number representing the total number of whole conversion periods. (Use Table 5.) The computed value, $S$, is further computed by the simple interest method for the remaining fractional period.

**★Method B**     Use the formula $S = P(1 + i)^n$, where $n$ is a mixed number which equals the entire time. (Use Tables 5 and 5A.)

Theoretically speaking, Method B is more reasonable than the other because the compound method is used throughout. However, Method A is widely employed in practice because its computation is less complicated than that of Method B.

**Example 7**     Find the compound amount and the compound interest when $1,000 is invested for three years and two months at 6% compounded semiannually.

**Method A**     $P = 1,000$, $i = 6\%/2 = 3\%$ (per six months), $n = 3 \times 2 = 6$ (semiannual periods)

Thus, the compound amount at the end of the sixth conversion period is $S = 1,000(1 + 3\%)^6 = 1,000(1.194052) = \$1,194.05$

The simple interest for the remaining period (two months) is

$1,194.05 \times 6\% \times 2/12 = \$11.94$

The final compound amount is

$1,194.05 + 11.94 = \$1,205.99$

The compound interest $= 1,205.99 - 1,000.00 = \$205.99$

Method A is diagrammed as follows:

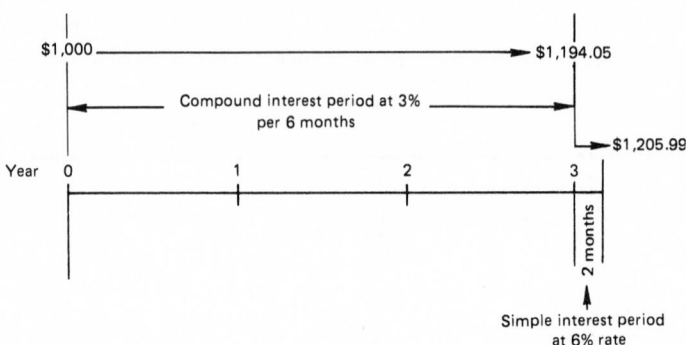

**★Method B**   $P = 1,000$, $i = 6\%/2 = 3\%$ (per six months), $n = 3\frac{2}{12} \times 2 = 6\frac{1}{3}$ (semiannual periods)

Thus,

$S = P(1 + i)^n = 1,000(1 + 3\%)^{6\frac{1}{3}} = 1,000(1 + 3\%)^6(1 + 3\%)^{\frac{1}{3}}$
$= 1,000(1.194052)(1.009902)$
$= \$1,205.88$ (Tables 5 and 5A)

The compound interest $= S - P = 1,205.88 - 1,000.00 = \$205.88$

Notice that the interest obtained in Method A is greater than that calculated in Method B. When the investment time is a fraction of the conversion period, use of the compound interest method always gives less interest than the simple interest method.

*Note:*   The multiplication $1,000(1 + 3\%)^6(1 + 3\%)^{\frac{1}{3}}$ may be performed by using logarithms. See Example 4 of Section 12.2.

## EXERCISE 11–4

### Reference: Section 11.3 E

**A.** *Find the compound amount in each of the following problems. Use Method A in Problems 1–6 and ★Method B in Problems 7–10.*

| | Principal (P) | Interest Rate (i) | Time (n) |
|---|---|---|---|
| **1.** | $ 500 | 6% compounded monthly | $10\frac{1}{2}$ months |
| **2.** | 800 | 7% compounded quarterly | 6 years, 2 months |
| **3.** | 2,400 | 5% compounded semiannually | 15 years, 4 months |
| **4.** | 3,600 | 10% compounded annually | 20 years, 5 months |

| Principal (P) | Interest Rate (i) | Time (n) |
|---|---|---|
| **5.** 1,700 | 8% compounded quarterly | 4 years, 2 months |
| **6.** 1,200 | 8% compounded monthly | 2 years, $\frac{1}{2}$ month |
| **7.** 3,000 | 6% compounded quarterly | 3 years, 1 month |
| **8.** 2,000 | 5% compounded monthly | $8\frac{1}{2}$ months |
| **9.** 1,500 | 7% compounded annually | 12 years, 4 months |
| **10.** 1,800 | 9% compounded semiannually | 5 years, 3 months |

**B.** *Statement Problems:*

**11.** What are the amount and the interest if $16,000 is borrowed at 6% compounded semiannually for nine years and 11 months? Use Method A.

**12.** What are the amount and the interest if $10,000 is borrowed at $5\frac{1}{2}$% compounded annually for ten years and eight months? Use Method A.

★**13.** Find the amount and the interest if $5,000 is invested at 9% compounded monthly for five years and $7\frac{1}{3}$ months. Use Method B.

★**14.** Find the amount and the interest if $2,500 is invested at 10% compounded quarterly for seven years and four months. Use Method B.

# 11.4 FINDING THE PRESENT VALUE AND COMPOUND DISCOUNT

As stated in the previous chapter, there are numerous occasions in business when it becomes necessary to discount an amount which is due on a future date. "To discount a given compound amount due in the future" means to find its present value on the date of discount. The difference between the value of the compound amount and its present value is called *compound discount.* Therefore, the compound discount on the compound amount is the same as the compound interest on the present value.

For instance, in Example 2, page 332, the amount of $1,500 invested at 6% compounded semiannually and due at the end of $8\frac{1}{2}$ years is $2,479.27. The compound interest is $2,479.27 − $1,500 = $979.27. This example may be stated in a different way. The present value of $2,479.27 due at the end of $8\frac{1}{2}$ years at 6% compounded semiannually is $1,500, and the compound discount is $979.27. In other words, $1,500 is equivalent to $2,479.27 after $8\frac{1}{2}$ years according to the compound interest rate. The amount is found by applying the formula $S = P(1 + i)^n$. From the relationship, the present value *(P)* is obtained as follows:

$$P = S(1 + i)^{-n} \quad \textbf{(11–2)}, \quad \text{or} \quad P = \frac{S}{(1 + i)^n} \quad \textbf{(11–2A)}$$

For convenience, the most common values of $(1 + i)^{-n}$ are tabulated in Table 6 of the Appendix. The values (entries) in the table may best be considered as the present values in dollars when the compound amount is $1, although each entry may be considered as the value in a unit other than a dollar.

Let $p$ = the present value $P$ when the compound amount is 1. Then, the formula becomes:

$$p = P = S(1 + i)^{-n} = 1(1 + i)^{-n}, \quad \text{or} \quad p = (1 + i)^{-n}.$$

The factor $(1 + i)^{-n}$ is frequently referred to as the *discount factor* in discounting a compound amount. The methods of finding the present value of a given amount that is due on a future date are presented below.

## A. Use of Table 6

When Table 6 is used, formula (11–2) may be expressed as follows:

Present value *(P)* = Compound amount *(S)* × An entry in Table 6.

(The entry is at the interest rate $i$ per conversion period and for $n$ conversion periods.)

**Example 1**   Find the present value of $2,479.27 due at the end of $8\frac{1}{2}$ years if money is worth 6% compounded semiannually.

The amount *(S)* = $2,479.27, the interest rate per semiannual period *(i)* = 6%/2 = 3%, and the number of conversion periods *(n)* = $8\frac{1}{2}$ × 2 = 17 (semiannual periods). The discount factor $(1 + i)^{-n} = (1 + 3\%)^{-17} = .60501645$ (Table 6).

Substituting these values in formula (11–2)

$$P = S(1 + i)^{-n} = 2{,}479.27(1 + 3\%)^{-17} = 2{,}479.27(.605016) = \$1{,}500$$

**Note:**   The multiplication $2{,}479.27(1 + 3\%)^{-17}$ may also be performed by using logarithms. The mantissa for log 2,479.27 is obtained from Table 2 and the value of log $(1 + 3\%)^{-17}$ is given in Table 12. Detailed computation is presented in Example 5 of Section 12.2.

**Example 2**   If $1,000 is due five years from now and money is worth 4% compounded quarterly, find its present value and the compound discount.

The given amount *(S)* = $1,000, $i$ = 4%/4 = 1% (per quarter), $n$ = 5 × 4 = 20 (quarters), and the factor $(1 + 1\%)^{-20} = .81954447$ (Table 6).

Present value $P$     = $1{,}000(1 + 1\%)^{-20}$
                      = $1{,}000(.819544) = \$819.54$

Compound discount = Compound amount − Present value
                  = 1{,}000 − 819.54
                  = \$180.46

The value of $P$ may be obtained by using formula (11–2A), but division is involved:

$$P = \frac{S}{(1 + i)^n} = \frac{1{,}000}{(1 + 1\%)^{20}} = \frac{1{,}000}{1.22019} = \$819.54 \qquad \text{(Table 5)}$$

The solution may also be stated as follows:

If $819.54 is invested now at 4% compounded quarterly for five years, the compound amount at the end of the fifth year is $1,000.

*Check:* $S = P(1 + i)^n = 819.54(1 + 1\%)^{20} = 819.54(1.22019)$
$= \$999.99$, or rounded to $1,000

The example is diagrammed as follows:

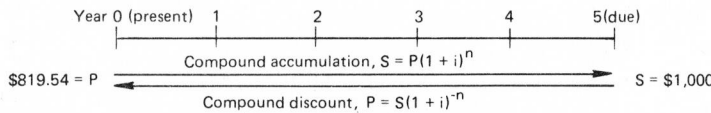

**Note:** The compound amount *(S)* is always larger than the present value *(P)*. Here the present value *(P)* may also be thought of as the principal of the investment.

## EXERCISE 11–5

### Reference: Section 11.4 A

**A.** *Find the present value in each of the following problems:*

| | Amount (S) | Interest Rate (i) | Time (n) |
|---|---|---|---|
| **1.** | $2,000 | 10% compounded quarterly | 5 years |
| **2.** | 600 | 5% compounded monthly | 2 years |
| **3.** | 400 | 6% compounded annually | 10 years |
| **4.** | 3,500 | 9% compounded semiannually | 7 years |
| **5.** | 1,500 | 8% compounded monthly | 4 years |
| **6.** | 800 | 7% compounded quarterly | 6 years |
| **7.** | 4,000 | 6% compounded semiannually | 20 years |
| **8.** | 700 | $9\frac{1}{2}\%$ compounded annually | 15 years |

**B.** *Statement Problems:*

**9.** Find the present value of $1,400 due at the end of nine years if money is worth (a) 5% compounded quarterly, (b) 7% compounded semiannually. How much is the compound discount in each case?

**10.** Find the present value of $2,500 due at the end of three years if money is worth (a) 6% compounded monthly, (b) 7% compounded annually. How much is the compounded discount in each case?

**11.** Jane Harrison has $1,500 at the end of three years in her savings account. The interest rate is 4% compounded monthly. How much did she deposit in the account three years ago?

12. How much money does R. T. White need if she can invest the money at 5% compounded quarterly for six years and receive $5,000 at the end of the period?

13. If $3,600 is due seven years from now and money is worth 5% compounded annually, find the present value and the compound discount.

14. Find the present value and the compound discount if $1,800 is due ten years from now and money is worth 12% compounded semiannually.

15. What principal will accumulate to $3,200 in four years at 4% compounded quarterly?

16. What principal will accumulate to $4,300 in 12 years at 6% compounded annually?

17. A man paid a two-year debt with $1,690.74. The interest charged was at 6% compounded monthly. What was the principal?

18. A man borrowed some money for five years. When the debt was due, he paid $5,200 for the money borrowed and the interest charged. The interest rate was 7% compounded quarterly. How much did he borrow?

## B. Compound Discount on Notes

If a note is non-interest-bearing, the present value of its face value is the proceeds. Here, the word "proceeds" represents the value received by the seller of the note, which is discounted at a compound interest rate. The method of finding the present value of a note is the same as that explained above. However, the word "present" usually is referred to here as the date of discount. Example 2 on page 340 may be stated in the following manner:

> A non-interest-bearing note of $1,000 is due five years from now. If the note is now discounted at 4% compounded quarterly, what are the proceeds and the compound discount? The answers: proceeds = $819.54, and compound discount = $180.46.

If a note is interest bearing, the proceeds is the present value on the date of discount computed from the maturity value of the note. The maturity value includes the face value of the note and the interest. Thus, two steps are required in finding the proceeds:

**Step (1)**     Find the compound amount of the face value of the note according to the rate and the time stipulated on the note. The compound amount is the maturity value. (Use the formula $S = P(1 + i)^n$.)

**Step (2)**     Find the present value (on the date of discount) of the maturity value, according to the rate and the time of discount. (Use the formula $P = S(1 + i)^{-n}$.)

**Example 3**     A note of $1,000 dated January 1, 1977, at 6% compounded quarterly for ten years, was discounted on January 1, 1981. What are the proceeds and the compounded discount if the note was discounted at 8% compounded semiannually?

**Step (1)**  Find the maturity value on January 1, 1987, according to the rate and the time stipulated on the note. $P =$ \$1,000 (face value), $i = 6\%/4 = 1\frac{1}{2}\%$ (per quarter), $n = 10 \times 4 = 40$ (quarters).

Maturity value $(S) = P(1 + i)^n = 1,000(1 + 1\frac{1}{2}\%)^{40}$
$$= 1,000(1.814018) = \$1,814.02$$

**Step (2)**  Find the present value (as of January 1, 1981, the date of discount, or six years before the maturity date).

$S =$ \$1,814.02, $i = 8\%/2 = 4\%$ (per semiannual period), $n = 6 \times 2 = 12$ (semiannual periods).

Proceeds (or present value $P$) $= S(1 + i)^{-n} = 1,814.02(1 + 4\%)^{-12}$
$$= 1,814.02(.624597) = \$1,133.03$$

Compound discount $= 1,814.02 - 1,133.03 = \$680.99$

The example is diagrammed as follows:

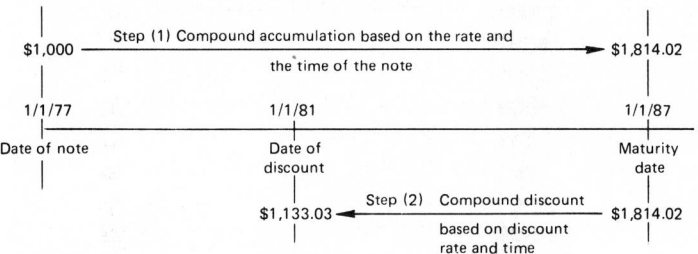

## C. The Discount Time Includes a Fraction of a Conversion Period

When the discount time includes a fraction of a conversion period, the proceeds may be computed by either of the following methods:

**Method A**  Use the formula $P = S(1 + i)^{-n}$, where $n$ is a whole number representing the total number of *whole* conversion periods plus 1. (Use Table 6.) The computed value $P$ is then accumulated by the simple interest method for the extra fractional period included in $n$ to obtain the proceeds.

**★Method B**  Use the formula $P = S(1 + i)^{-n}$, where $n$ is a mixed number which equals the entire discount time. (Use Tables 6 and 5A.)

Theoretically speaking, Method B is more reasonable than the other because the compound discount method is used throughout. However, Method A is widely employed in practice because its computation is less complicated than that of Method B.

**Example 4**    A non-interest-bearing note of $1,000 is discounted at 6% compounded semiannually for three years and two months. Find the proceeds and the compound discount.

**Method A**    $S = 1,000$
$i = 6\%/2 = 3\%$ (per semiannual period)
$n = 6 + 1 = 7$ (semiannual periods)

$P = S(1 + i)^{-n} = 1,000(1 + 3\%)^{-7} = 1,000(.813092)$
$\phantom{P} = \$813.09$

By the simple interest method, accumulate $P$ for the extra fractional period of four months (7 semiannual periods, or $3\frac{1}{2}$ years, minus three years and two months) at 6% as follows:

Simple interest $= 813.09 \times 6\% \times 4/12 = \$16.26$

The proceeds are: $813.09 + 16.26 = \$829.35$

Compound discount $= 1,000 - 829.35 = \$170.65$

Method A is diagrammed as follows:

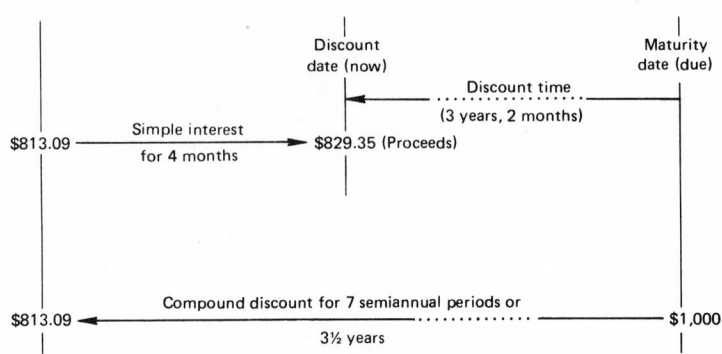

**★Method B**    $S = 1,000$
$i = 6\%/2 = 3\%$ (per semiannual period)
$n = 3\frac{2}{12} \times 2 = 6\frac{1}{3}$ (semiannual periods)

$P = S(1 + i)^{-n} = 1,000(1 + 3\%)^{-6\frac{1}{3}} = 1,000(1 + 3\%)^{-6}(1 + 3\%)^{-\frac{1}{3}}$

$\phantom{P} = 1,000 \times \dfrac{(1 + 3\%)^{-6}}{(1 + 3\%)^{\frac{1}{3}}}$    (Table 6)
(Table 5A)

$\phantom{P} = 1,000 \times \dfrac{.837484}{1.009902} = \$829.27$

Compound discount $= 1,000.00 - 829.27 = \$170.73$

**Note:**    The proceeds in Method A are larger than those in Method B. Such a condition is always true when the discount time includes a fraction of the conversion period.

## EXERCISE 11–6

### Reference: Sections 11.4 B and C

**A.** *Find (a) the proceeds, and (b) the compound discount in each of the following problems:*

| | Date of Note | Face Value | Compound Interest Rate of Note | Term of Note | Date of Discount | Discount Rate |
|---|---|---|---|---|---|---|
| **1.** | 7/1/80 | $1,000 | none | 4 years | 7/1/81 | 12%, monthly |
| **2.** | 8/1/80 | 6,000 | none | 12 years | 2/1/83 | 6%, quarterly |
| **3.** | 5/1/81 | 2,500 | none | 7 years | 5/1/84 | 8%, annually |
| **4.** | 4/1/81 | 3,000 | none | 5½ years | 10/1/84 | 11%, semi-annually |
| **5.** | 1/2/82 | 1,500 | 5%, semi-annually | 10 years | 1/2/85 | 4%, quarterly |
| **6.** | 2/1/82 | 1,200 | 9%, monthly | 5 years | 2/1/83 | 6%, annually |
| **7.** | 3/1/83 | 2,400 | 4%, quarterly | 6 years | 3/1/86 | 5%, semi-annually |
| **8.** | 5/1/83 | 8,000 | 6%, annually | 8 years | 5/1/88 | 7%, monthly |

**B.** *Statement Problems:*

**9.** A non-interest-bearing note of $1,800 is discounted at 5% compounded monthly for 7½ years. Find the proceeds.

**10.** A non-interest-bearing note of $5,500 is discounted at 7% compounded quarterly five years before it is due. Find the proceeds.

**11.** A note of $4,500 dated June 1, 1980, at 5% compounded quarterly for 6½ years, is discounted on October 1, 1982. Find the proceeds if the note is discounted at 4% compounded monthly.

**12.** A note of $400 dated May 1, 1980, at 5% compounded monthly for four years, is discounted on February 1, 1983. Find the proceeds if the note is discounted at 6% compounded quarterly.

**13.** B. C. Power received a seven-year, 5½% compounded annually, $5,000 note dated April 1, 1980. Power discounted the note at 6% compounded semiannually on February 1, 1981. Find the proceeds. Use Method A.

**14.** F. W. Bondson has a 4½-year note of $3,600 at 7% compounded monthly. The maturity date is February 1, 1983. If the note is discounted on January 1, 1981, at 5% compounded annually, how much will Bondson receive? Use Method A.

**15.** A nine-year note bearing interest at 4% compounded semiannually is discounted at 5% compounded quarterly. The face value of the note is $7,200, and the discount period is five years and two months. Find the proceeds. Use Method A.

**16.** Jack H. Kelly received a non-interest-bearing note for $4,200. He discounted the note at 10% compounded semiannually three years and

two months before it was due. How much proceeds did he receive? Use
Method A.

★**17.** Mary Dolton signs a note for $7,000 due in $3\frac{1}{2}$ years to a bank that charges
$5\frac{1}{2}\%$ compounded annually. What should Dolton receive as the proceeds
from the bank? Use Method B.

★**18.** John Edwards has a note that will pay him $2,000 at the end of $5\frac{1}{2}$ years.
He sells the note three years and one month before it is due at 7% com-
pounded quarterly. How much proceeds does he receive from the sale?
Use Method B.

# 11.5 FINDING THE INTEREST RATE

When finding the interest rate, Table 5 in the Appendix may be used as
explained in Section A.

## A. Use of Table 5

Solve $(1 + i)^n$ from the formula $S = P(1 + i)^n$. Thus,

$$(1 + i)^n = \frac{S}{P} \tag{11-3}$$

Formula (11–3) may be expressed as follows:

$$\text{An entry in Table 5} = \frac{\text{Compound amount}}{\text{Principal}}$$

Formula (11–3) contains four values. If the values of $S$, $P$, and $n$ are known,
an entry which is equal to $\frac{S}{P}$ may be found in the $n$ row of Table 5. The
value of the interest rate *(i)* is thus found in the column containing the entry.
If the exact entry cannot be found in the table, the interpolation method may
be used to find an approximate value of $i$.

**Example 1**     If $1,000 will accumulate to $5,054.47 in 17 years, what is the interest
rate compounded annually?

$P = 1,000$, $S = 5,054.47$, $n = 17$ (years)

Substituting these values in formula (11–3):

$$(1 + i)^{17} = \frac{5,054.47}{1,000} = 5.05447$$

In the $n = 17$ row of Table 5, the entry 5.05447 is found in the 10%
column. Thus, $i = 10\%$.

**Example 2**     At what nominal interest rate compounded semiannually for ten years
will $300 accumulate to $890?

$P = 300$, $S = 890$, $n = 10 \times 2 = 20$ (semiannual periods)

Substituting these values in formula (11–3):

$$(1 + i)^{20} = \frac{890}{300} = 2.9667$$

There is no entry 2.9667 in the row where $n = 20$ in Table 5. However, an entry which is just above and one which is just below the value of 2.9667 may be found in the table and the interest rate may be obtained through interpolation. When the interpolation method is used, it is assumed that the differences between the values of $i$ are proportional to the differences between the values of $(1 + i)^n$ in the table. The findings are arranged for interpolation as follows:

|         | $i$           | $(1 + i)^{20}$ |     |
|---------|---------------|----------------|-----|
|         | 6%            | 3.2071         | (1) |
|         | $x$           | 2.9667         | (2) |
|         | $5\frac{1}{2}\%$ | 2.9178      | (3) |

$$\frac{(2) - (3)}{(1) - (3)} \qquad \frac{x - 5\frac{1}{2}\%}{\frac{1}{2}\%} = \frac{0.0489}{0.2893} \qquad \begin{matrix}(4)\\(5)\end{matrix}$$

Solve for $x$ from the proportion formed by the differences on lines (4) and (5):

$$x - 5\frac{1}{2}\% = \frac{1}{2}\% \left(\frac{0.0489}{0.2893}\right) = \frac{1}{200} \cdot \frac{489}{2893} = .000845$$

$x = 5\frac{1}{2}\% + .000845 = .055 + .000845 = .055845$, or
$i = .055845$ (interest rate per semiannual period)

The nominal interest rate is

$.055845 \times 2 = .111690$
$\qquad\qquad = 11.169\%$, or rounded to 11.17%

**Note:**
1. The values of $(1 + i)^n$ include four decimal places in the above interpolation. This practice may be followed in solving the problems in the following exercises. In most cases, the accuracy of the result of an interpolation will not be any greater if the values include more than four decimal places.
2. The time unit of $n$ should always agree with the time unit of $i$ in computing compound interest problems. For instance, in the above example, $n$ represents the number of *semiannual* periods and $i$ represents the interest rate per *semiannual* period.
3. The $i$ value may also be solved by using logarithms as presented in Example 6 of Section 12.2.

# B. Effective Annual Interest Rate

The effective annual interest rate is commonly abbreviated as the *effective rate*. If the principal is $1, the value of the compound interest for a one-year period is the effective rate. In general, the effective rate is the ratio of the compound interest earned for a one-year period to the principal, as shown below:

$$\text{Effective rate} = \frac{\text{Compound interest for a one-year period}}{\text{Principal}}$$

In other words, an effective rate is an interest rate compounded annually.

**Example 3**      If \$1 is invested at 6% compounded quarterly for one year, what is the effective rate?

$P = 1$, $i = 6\%/4 = 1\frac{1}{2}\%$ (per quarter), $n = 4$ (quarters)

The compound amount is computed as follows:

$S = P(1 + i)^n = 1(1 + 1\frac{1}{2}\%)^4 = 1(1.06136355) = 1.06136355$

The compound interest is

$1.06136355 - 1 = .06136355$

The effective rate is .06136355, which may be rounded to 6.14%

Thus, 6.14% compounded annually is equivalent to an interest rate of 6% compounded quarterly.

Normally, the effective rate is greater than the nominal rate (stated annual rate). In Example 3, the effective rate is greater than the nominal rate by .14% (or 6.14% − 6%).

To obtain a formula for the effective rate, the following assumptions are made:

Let $j =$ nominal rate
     $m =$ number of conversion periods for *one* year
     $i = j/m$ (per conversion period)
     $f =$ effective rate

These values are then substituted in the compound amount formula (11–1). Thus, in a one-year period:

According to the nominal rate, $S = P(1 + j/m)^m$.
According to the effective rate, $S = P(1 + f)$.

The right sides of the two equations above are equated as follows:

$P(1 + f) = P(1 + j/m)^m$,    or    $1 + f = (1 + j/m)^m$

$$f = \left(1 + \frac{j}{m}\right)^m - 1 \qquad\qquad\qquad \textbf{(11–4)}$$

or,      $f = (1 + i)^m - 1$

**Example 4**      Find the effective rate if money is worth 6% compounded quarterly on the investment market.

$j = 6\%$, $m = 4$. Substituting the values in formula (11–4):

$$f = \left(1 + \frac{6\%}{4}\right)^4 - 1 = (1 + 1\frac{1}{2}\%)^4 - 1 = 1.06136355 - 1$$

$$= .06136355, \text{ or } 6.14\%$$

**Note:**   The above effective rate, 6.14%, is computed from formula (11–4) without mentioning the values of $S$ and $P$. The answer may be compared with that in Example 3.

The effective rate is frequently used as a device to compare one interest rate with another rate compounded at different time intervals. It is especially useful to those who invest or borrow money from various sources. By comparing the effective rates of the various sources, a person may select the one having the lowest effective rate for borrowing and the one having the highest effective rate for investing.

**Example 5**   Bank A offers its depositors an interest rate of 6% compounded monthly, while Bank B gives its depositors an interest rate of $6\frac{1}{2}\%$ compounded semiannually. Which of the two banks makes the better offer?

The effective rate based on the interest rate of Bank A is:

$f = (1 + 6\%/12)^{12} - 1 = (1 + \frac{1}{2}\%)^{12} - 1$
$= 1.0617 - 1 = .0617$, or 6.17%

The effective rate based on the interest rate of Bank B is:

$f = (1 + 6\frac{1}{2}\%/2)^2 - 1 = (1 + 3\frac{1}{4}\%)^2 - 1$
$= 1.0661 - 1 = .0661$, or 6.61%

The effective rate of Bank B is greater than that of Bank A by .44% (or 6.61% − 6.17%); that is, Bank B offers a better interest rate to its depositors.

**Note:**   1. If there is only one conversion period in *one* year ($m = 1$), the value of $f$ in formula (11–4) becomes:

$f = (1 + j/1)^1 - 1 = j$

Also, when $m = 1$,   $i = j/m = j/1 = j$,   and $f = j = i$

The relationships may be stated as follows:

If there is only *one* conversion period in *one* year, the effective rate equals the nominal rate, which in turn equals the interest rate per conversion period.

2. If the number of conversion periods per year *(m)* is increased while the value of the nominal rate *(j)* remains constant, the value of the effective rate *(f)* also is increased. For example, the effective rates for the nominal rate 6% compounded annually, semiannually, quarterly, monthly, semimonthly, weekly, and daily are shown below. The values of $f$ are computed by substituting the respective values of $m$ in formula (11–4) as illustrated in Example 4 above.

| | Annually | Semi-annually | Quarterly | Monthly | Semi-monthly | Weekly | Daily |
|---|---|---|---|---|---|---|---|
| $m =$ | 1 | 2 | 4 | 12 | 24 | 52 | 365 |
| $f =$ | 6% | 6.09% | 6.13636% | 6.16778% | 6.17570% | 6.17998% | 6.18313% |

The table indicates that the effective rate *(f)* increases as the number of conversion periods *(m)* increases. However, the increases of the rate are rather moderate.

## EXERCISE 11–7

**Reference: Section 11.5**

**A.** *Find the interest rate per conversion period in each of the following problems:*

| | Principal | Amount | Term | Interest Rate Compounded |
|---|---|---|---|---|
| 1. | $1,000 | $1,233 | $3\frac{1}{2}$ years | monthly |
| 2. | 2,500 | 3,220 | $4\frac{1}{4}$ years | quarterly |
| 3. | 4,000 | 7,690 | $9\frac{1}{2}$ years | semiannually |
| 4. | 3,000 | 5,406 | 11 years | annually |
| 5. | 2,500 | 2,960 | 4 years | quarterly |
| 6. | 5,000 | 7,800 | 6 years | semiannually |
| 7. | 200 | 700 | 30 years | annually |
| 8. | 3,600 | 5,600 | 7 years | monthly |

**B.** *Statement Problems:*

9. At what nominal interest rate compounded quarterly for $5\frac{1}{2}$ years will $1,200 accumulate to the amount of $1,700?

10. If $2,800 amounts to $4,200 in eight years with interest compounded semiannually, what is the nominal interest rate?

11. What is the effective rate if $1 is invested for one year at 4% compounded (a) annually? (b) semiannually? (c) quarterly? (d) monthly?

12. What is the effective rate if money is worth 5% compounded (a) annually? (b) semiannually? (c) quarterly? (d) monthly?

13. Harry invested his money at 3% compounded monthly, while Betty invested her money at $3\frac{1}{2}$% compounded semiannually. Who receives the better interest rate?

14. Which is the higher interest rate in the following cases: (a) 7% compounded quarterly, (b) $7\frac{1}{4}$% compounded annually?

## 11.6 FINDING THE NUMBER OF CONVERSION PERIODS

In formula (11–3), $(1 + i)^n = S/P$, if the values of S, P, and i are known, an entry which is equal to the value of *S/P* may be found in the *i* column in Table 5. The value of *n*, the number of conversion periods, is thus found in the row containing the entry. If the value of *S/P* cannot be found in the table, the interpolation method may be used for finding the value of $n$. However, most long-term investors are not interested in a fraction of a conversion period. Therefore, it is generally unnecessary to carry out the interpolation.

**Example 1**    How long will it take $1,000 to accumulate to the amount of $1,105 at 4% compounded semiannually?

$S = 1,105$, $P = 1,000$, $i = 4\%/2 = 2\%$ (per six months)

Substituting the values in formula (11–3):

$$(1 + i)^n = \frac{S}{P}$$

$$(1 + 2\%)^n = \frac{1,105}{1,000} = 1.105$$

$n = 6$ semiannual periods, or three years (answer)

In the 2% column in Table 5, the value 1.105 is between the entries 1.10408080 (where $n = 5$) and 1.12616242 (where $n = 6$). Since the nearest value to 1.105 is 1.10408080, the required time is slightly over 5 conversion periods, or $2\frac{1}{2}$ years. The finding may be written:

$5 < n < 6$; that is, $n$ is greater than 5 but is smaller than 6.

However, the sixth conversion period is necessary for the principal to accumulate to at least $1,105. For simplicity in this text, the larger value of $n$ is hereafter regarded as the answer to this type of problem.

*Check:*    $1,000(1 + 2\%)^5 = 1,000(1.104081) = \$1,104.08$, which is $.92 less than the required amount.

$1,000(1 + 2\%)^6 = 1,000(1.126162) = \$1,126.16$, which is $21.16 more than the required amount.

*Note:*    The $n$ value may also be solved by using logarithms as presented in Example 7 of Section 12.2.

## EXERCISE 11–8

### Reference: Section 11.6

**A.** *Find the number of conversion periods in each of the following problems:*

|    | Principal | Amount    | Interest Rate      | Compounded   |
|----|-----------|-----------|--------------------|--------------|
| 1. | $6,000    | $ 7,931   | 8%                 | monthly      |
| 2. | 3,000     | 5,100     | 5%                 | quarterly    |
| 3. | 8,000     | 10,500    | 6%                 | semiannually |
| 4. | 4,500     | 7,800     | $5\frac{1}{2}\%$   | annually     |
| 5. | 5,000     | 5,700     | 4%                 | quarterly    |
| 6. | 7,500     | 12,000    | 7%                 | semiannually |
| 7. | 4,000     | 9,000     | 9%                 | annually     |
| 8. | 7,200     | 11,200    | 6%                 | monthly      |

**B.** *Statement Problems:*

9. How long will it take $1,000 to accumulate to the amount of $1,100 at 12% compounded monthly?

10. How much time is required for $1,500 to yield $1,000 interest if the interest rate is 5% compounded quarterly?

11. How many years are needed for $4,000 to yield $1,375.66 interest if the interest rate is 6% compounded semiannually?

12. How long will it take $3,000 to amount to $8,753.27 at a $5\frac{1}{2}\%$ effective rate?

13. On January 1, 1980, Judy Horton borrowed $1,200 and agreed to repay it with $465.07 interest. If the interest is at 6% compounded quarterly, what amount must she repay and on what date?

14. On July 1, 1980, Albert Todd borrowed $2,800 at 5% compounded semiannually. He repaid $4,156.61 on the due date. Find the due date.

# 11.7 SUMMARY OF COMPOUND INTEREST FORMULAS

| Application | Formula | Formula Number | Reference Page |
|---|---|---|---|
| Finding the compound amount | $S = P(1 + i)^n$ | (11–1) | 330 |
| Finding the present value | $P = S(1 + i)^{-n}$ | (11–2) | 339 |
| | or | | |
| | $P = \dfrac{S}{(1 + i)^n}$ | (11–2A) | 339 |
| Finding the interest rate ($i$) and the number of conversion periods ($n$) | $(1 + i)^n = \dfrac{S}{P}$ | (11–3) | 346 |
| Finding the effective rate | $f = \left(1 + \dfrac{j}{m}\right)^m - 1$ | (11–4) | 348 |

## EXERCISE 11–9

**Review of Chapter 11**

1. What are the compound amount and the compound interest at the end of ten years if $4,000 is borrowed at 5% compounded quarterly?

2. Find the compound amount and the compound interest at the end of six years if $5,000 is invested at 6% compounded monthly.

3. (a) What is the simple interest on $1,000 for five years at 12%? (b) What is the compound interest on $1,000 for five years at 12% compounded monthly?

4. What is the interest on $2,500 for $4\frac{1}{2}$ years at (a) $4\frac{1}{2}$% simple interest? (b) $4\frac{1}{2}$% compounded quarterly?

5. A note having a face value of $2,500 will mature in six years. The interest charged is 6% compounded monthly. Find the maturity value.

6. Find the compound amount if $3,000 is invested at 5% compounded monthly for 20 years.

7. The principal is $600 and the interest rate is 8% compounded monthly for the first seven years and 10% compounded semiannually for the next three years. Find the compound amount at the end of the tenth year.

8. What is the amount at the end of nine years if $1,000 is invested at 4% compounded quarterly for the first five years and at $5\frac{1}{2}$% compounded semiannually for the next four years?

9. Find the amount if $2,000 is invested at $5\frac{1}{4}$% compounded quarterly for seven years.

10. What is the amount if $4,000 is borrowed at $6\frac{1}{4}$% compounded monthly for ten years?

11. What are the amount and the interest if $5,000 is invested for five years and two months at 7% compounded annually?

12. Find the amount and the interest if $300 is borrowed for ten years and one month at 5% compounded quarterly.

13. (a) Find the present value if $650 is due at the end of $5\frac{1}{2}$ years and money is worth 4% compounded quarterly. (b) What is the compound discount?

14. (a) What is the present value if $820 is due at the end of four years and money is worth 6% compounded monthly? (b) What is the compound discount?

15. A note of $500, dated April 1, 1977, plus 5% interest compounded quarterly was due in eight years. It was discounted at $5\frac{1}{2}$% compounded monthly on April 1, 1980. Find the proceeds and compound discount.

16. Carl had a note that would pay him $400 plus 5% interest compounded quarterly at the end of six years. He sold the note two years before it was due at 6% compounded monthly. How much proceeds did he receive?

17. A non-interest-bearing note of $800 is discounted at 5% compounded quarterly for five years and two months. Find the proceeds and the compound discount.

18. Tina received a note that would pay her $700 on the due date. She discounted the note at 4% compounded semiannually four years and one month before it was due. Find the proceeds and the compound discount.

19. If $900 will accumulate to $1,500 in ten years, what is the interest rate compounded quarterly?

20. What is the nominal interest rate compounded monthly that will enable $1,000 to amount to $1,800 in eight years?

21. What is the effective rate if $1 is invested for one year at 5% compounded (a) annually? (b) semiannually? (c) quarterly? (d) monthly?
22. What is the effective rate if money is worth 8% compounded monthly?
23. Alan invested his money at $5\frac{1}{2}$% compounded quarterly and Paula invested her money at 6% compounded annually. Which one of the two rates is higher?
24. Which is the higher rate: 4% compounded monthly or $4\frac{1}{2}$% compounded semiannually?
25. How long will it take $200 to accumulate to the amount of $300 at 12% compounded monthly?
26. How much time is needed for $400 to yield $136 interest if the interest rate is 10% compounded semiannually?

# Chapter 12

# *Compound Interest—
# Additional Problems

## 12.1 GENERAL STATEMENT

The additional problems concerning compound interest included in this chapter are: (1) applications of logarithms, (2) equivalent values, (3) equated date, (4) equivalent rates, and (5) continuously compounded interest.

Tables 2, 3, 12, 13, and 16 are provided for convenience in computing the examples and problems in Chapters 11 to 20 by the use of logarithms. Logarithms can be used to compute compound interest and annuity (Chapters 13 to 20) problems under three different conditions:

1. *The available compound interest tables, such as Tables 5 through 11 in this book, do not provide enough information.* Example 3 of Section 12.2 is used to illustrate a problem under this condition. The example illustrates the fact that instead of using the interpolation method as discussed in Chapter 11, we may use the logarithmic method to obtain a more accurate calculation for various interest rates.

2. *The compound interest tables are not available.* Under this condition the logarithmic method is frequently useful since logarithmic tables, such as Table 2 with six-place mantissas, are printed in many mathematical, statistical, and other scientific books which can easily be obtained. Examples 6 and 7 are used to illustrate the method by using Table 2 only in the computations.

3. *Logarithms can be used to simplify the operations of multiplication, division, raising to powers, and extracting roots.* The logarithmic method is not always the best way to find the answers in multiplication and division. In some cases, the conventional method is simpler. The student should reason, based on knowledge of logarithms, to decide which one of the two methods is the most convenient way for solving a given problem. In general, the decision of choosing the method is not too difficult to

make if a student is familiar with logarithmic operations. For instance, it is obvious that the conventional method should be employed in finding the answer for multiplying 2.35678 by 1,000 since the multiplication process can be completed simply by moving the decimal point three places to the right, or

$$2.35678 \times 1,000 = 2,356.78.$$

However, in finding the answer for expression

$$S = 1,200(1 + 3\tfrac{1}{2}\%)^{100}(1 + 3\tfrac{1}{2}\%)^{25},$$

the logarithmic method is the better one. (See Example 2.)

Note that the results of the mathematical operations by using logarithms are approximations. However, if the interpolation method is properly applied to the tables of logarithms, the results usually are very close to the actual answers.

In finding equivalent values and equated date, the equation of value must be used. An understanding of the concept of the equation of value is important in derivations and applications of formulas regarding interest problems. The equation of value involving simple interest problems has been presented in Chapter 9. The equation of value involving compound interest problems is discussed in this chapter.

The subjects of equivalent rates and continuously compounded interest are closely related to the subject of effective annual interest rate. It is suggested to review the material in Section 11.5 B before studying the two subjects.

# 12.2 APPLICATIONS OF LOGARITHMS IN COMPOUND INTEREST PROBLEMS

The logarithmic method may be used to solve any unknown value if any three of the four values in formula (11–1), $S = P(1 + i)^n$, are known. To obtain a more accurate answer, the use of seven-place mantissa tables, if applicable, is preferred to that of six-place tables.

**Example 1**   Find the value of $S$ when $S = 1,500(1 + 3\%)^{17}$.

By applying logarithms,

$$
\begin{array}{ll}
\log 1,500 & = 3.176\ 0910 \text{ (Table 2)} \\
(+) \log (1 + 3\%)^{17} & = 0.218\ 2328 \text{ (Table 12)} \\
\hline
\log S & = 3.394\ 3238
\end{array}
$$

Find antilog 3.394 3238 by the interpolation method from Table 2. The number of significant digits ($x$ below) is determined by adding 4 to the value of characteristic, or $4 + 3 = 7$ digits. This number will assure enough decimal places so that the answer may be rounded to the nearest cent.

| Number | Mantissa | | |
|---|---|---|---|
| 2480 000 | 394 4520 | (1) | |
| $x$ | 394 3238 | (2) | $x = 2479\ 000 + \dfrac{468}{1750}(1{,}000)$ |
| 2479 000 | 394 2770 | (3) | $= 2479\ 267$ |
| $\dfrac{x - 2479\ 000}{1\ 000} = $ | $\dfrac{468}{1750}$ | $\dfrac{(2) - (3)}{(1) - (3)}$ | $S = 2{,}479.267$, or rounded to 2,479.27. |

The answer $2,479.27 may be compared with that of Example 2 in Section 11.3, page 332.

**Example 2**    Find the value of $S$ when $S = 1{,}200(1 + 3\frac{1}{2}\%)^{100}(1 + 3\frac{1}{2}\%)^{25}$

$$\begin{aligned}
\log 1{,}200 &= 3.079\ 1810 \text{ (Table 2)}\\
\log (1 + 3\tfrac{1}{2}\%)^{100} &= 1.494\ 0350 \text{ (Table 12)}\\
(+)\ \log (1 + 3\tfrac{1}{2}\%)^{25} &= 0.373\ 5087 \text{ (Table 12)}\\
\hline
\log S &= 4.946\ 7247
\end{aligned}$$

Find antilog 4.9467247 by the interpolation method from Table 2. The rule stated in Example 1 requires $4 + 4 = 8$ significant digits since the characteristic is 4. However, we shall use only 7 digits as the maximum number since the accuracy of the answer would not increase if 8 digits were used in the interpolation. (See the note on page 336.)

| Number | Mantissa | | |
|---|---|---|---|
| 8846 000 | 946 7470 | (1) | |
| $x$ | 946 7247 | (2) | $x = 8845\ 000 + \dfrac{267}{490}(1{,}000)$ |
| 8845 000 | 946 6980 | (3) | $= 8845\ 545$ |
| $\dfrac{x - 8845\ 000}{1\ 000} = $ | $\dfrac{267}{490}$ | $\dfrac{(2) - (3)}{(1) - (3)}$ | $S = 88{,}455.45$ |

The answer $88,455.45 may be compared with that of Example 4 in Section 11.3, page 333.

**Example 3**    Find the value of $S$ when $S = 1{,}000(1 + 2\frac{1}{8}\%)^{10}$.

$$\begin{aligned}
\log 1{,}000 &= 3.0000000 \text{ (Table 3)}\\
(+)\ \log (1 + 2\tfrac{1}{8}\%)^{10} = 10 \times \log 1.02125 &= 0.0913205 \text{ (Table 3, by interpolation)}\\
\hline
\log S &= 3.0913205
\end{aligned}$$

Find the antilog by interpolation from Table 2.

$S = 1{,}234.015625$, or rounded to 1,234.02.

The answer $1,234.02 may be compared with that of Example 6 in Section 11.3, pages 335 and 336 (See Note 4).

**Example 4**     Find the value of $S$ when $S = 1,000(1 + 3\%)^6(1 + 3\%)^{\frac{1}{3}}$.

$$\log 1,000 \qquad = 3.000\ 0000\ \text{(Table 3)}$$
$$\log (1 + 3\%)^6 = 0.077\ 0233\ \text{(Table 12)}$$
$$(+)\ \log (1 + 3\%)^{\frac{1}{3}} = 0.004\ 2791\ \text{(Table 13)}$$
$$\log S = 3.081\ 3024$$

Find the antilog by interpolation from Table 2.

$S = \$1,205.876$, or round to $\$1,205.88$.

The answer $\$1,205.88$ may be compared with that of Example 7 in Section 11.3, pages 337 and 338.

**Example 5**     Find the value of $P$ when $P = 2,479.27(1 + 3\%)^{-17}$.

$$\log 2,479.27 \quad = \quad 3.394\ 3243 \qquad \text{(Table 2, by interpolation)}$$
$$(+)\ \log (1 + 3\%)^{-17} = \quad 9.781\ 7672 - 10\ \text{(Table 12)}$$
$$\log P = 13.176\ 0915 - 10$$
$$= 3.176\ 0915$$

Find the antilog by interpolation from Table 2. $P = 1,500.00$.

The answer $\$1,500$ may be compared with that of Example 1 in Section 11.4, page 340.

**Example 6**     Find the value of $i$ when $S = 890$, $P = 300$, and $n = 20$.

Substituting the known values in formula (11–3), $(1+i)^n = \dfrac{S}{P}$:

$$(1 + i)^{20} = \frac{890}{300}$$

By applying logarithms,

$$\log (1 + i)^{20} = \log \left(\frac{890}{300}\right)$$

$$20 \times \log (1 + i) = \log 890 - \log 300$$

$$\log 890 = 2.949390$$
$$(-)\ \log 300 = 2.477121 \quad \text{(Table 2)}$$
$$20 \times \log (1 + i) = 0.472269$$

$$\log (1 + i) = \frac{0.472269}{20} = 0.023613$$

Find the antilog, $(1 + i) = 1.055857$ (by interpolation)
$$i = .055857, \quad \text{or} \quad 5.5857\%$$

The answer may be compared with that of Example 2 in Section 11.5, pages 346 and 347.

**Example 7**     Find the value of $n$ when $S = 1,105$, $P = 1,000$, and $i = 2\%$.

Substituting the known values in formula (11–3):

$$(1 + 2\%)^n = \frac{S}{P} = \frac{1,105}{1,000}$$

By applying logarithms,

$$\log(1 + 2\%)^n = \log\left(\frac{1,105}{1,000}\right)$$

$$n \times \log 1.02 = \log 1,105 - \log 1,000$$

$$n = \frac{\log 1,105 - \log 1,000}{\log 1.02} = \frac{3.043362 - 3}{.0086002} = 5.042 \quad \text{(Table 2)}$$

The answer may be compared with that of Example 1 in Section 11.6, page 351.

## EXERCISE 12–1

**Reference: Section 12.2**

**A.** *Use the logarithmic method to find the unknown value in each of the following problems:*

| | S | P | i | n |
|---|---|---|---|---|
| **1.** | $  ? | $4,000 | 3% | 10 |
| **2.** | 250 | ? | $1\frac{1}{4}\%$ | 42 |
| **3.** | 1,140 | 1,000 | ? | 40 |
| **4.** | 2,930 | 2,500 | 1% | ? |
| **5.** | 640 | ? | 4% | 30 |
| **6.** | ? | 300 | $5\frac{1}{2}\%$ | 20 |
| **7.** | 5,470 | 3,600 | $\frac{1}{2}\%$ | ? |
| **8.** | 4,160 | 2,800 | ? | 16 |
| **9.** | ? | 5,000 | $3\frac{1}{2}\%$ | 12 |
| **10.** | 1,665 | ? | $1\frac{1}{2}\%$ | 22 |

**B.** *Statement Problems:*

**11.** Compute $(1 + 7\frac{1}{4}\%)^3$ by the following methods: (a) binomial theorem (see page 84), (b) interpolation (from Table 5), and (c) logarithmic (carry your answer to seven decimal places). Which method gives the most accurate answer? the next accurate? the least accurate?

**12.** Compute $(1 + 4\frac{1}{4}\%)^4$ by the methods indicated in Problem 11. Which method gives the most accurate answer? the next accurate? the least accurate?

## 12.3 EQUIVALENT VALUES INVOLVING COMPOUND INTEREST

It was stated in Chapter 9 that a single obligation or a set of obligations may be replaced by another single obligation or set of obligations due at different times. In order to satisfy both the creditors and the debtors, the values of the new obligations should be equivalent to the values of the original ones. An *equation of value* is usually arranged in order to obtain the required equivalent values. The equation gives the equivalent values of the original obligations and the new obligations on a *comparison date,* sometimes called the *focal date,* at the agreed or present investment market interest rate. The answer for a required equivalent value may vary slightly in simple interest problems depending on the selection of the comparison date. However, in compound interest problems the selection of the comparison date does not affect the answer.

The formula $S = P(1 + i)^n$ is an equation of value since the value of $S$ is equivalent to the value of $P$ after $n$ periods with a compound interest rate $i$ per period. Thus, if $P = \$1$, $i = 6\%$ compounded annually, $n = 3$ (years), then $S = 1(1 + 6\%)^3 = \$1.19$. The illustration may be stated as follows: If money is worth 6% compounded annually (the value on the present investment market), \$1 now is equivalent to \$1.19 in three years.

Likewise, the formula $P = S(1 + i)^{-n}$ is an equation of value since the value of $P$ is equivalent to the value of $S$ for $n$ periods *before* it is due when the interest rate $i$ per period is involved. Thus, if $S = \$1$, $i = 6\%$ compounded annually, and $n = 3$ (years), then $P = 1(1 + 6\%)^{-3} = \$.84$. Therefore, \$1 due in three years at 6% compounded annually is equivalent to \$.84 now.

Note that a sum of money has different values at different times if interest is involved, and the amount due in the future is normally larger than its equivalent value at the present time. A person may borrow \$1 now and repay \$1.19 after three years. On the other hand, a creditor may agree to discharge a debt of \$1 which is due in three years by having the debtor pay only \$.84 now. The values in the two transactions are equivalent to each other under the compound interest method. The following examples illustrate further problems in equivalent values involving compound interest.

**Example 1**   A debt of \$200 is due at the end of four years. If money is worth 6% compounded quarterly, what is the value of the debt when it is paid (a) at the end of one year? (b) at the end of six years?

According to the problem, \$200 is the maturity value or the amount due at the end of four years. The interest rate, which is agreed upon by both lender and borrower to settle the debt, is 6% compounded quarterly.

(a) If the debt of \$200 is paid at the end of one year, which is three years (or 12 quarters) before the due date, the required equivalent value is less than \$200. Thus, the compound discount formula $P = S(1 + i)^{-n}$ is used to compute the required value. In other words, the value is obtained by discounting the maturity value (or the amount on the due date) by the compound discount method for the advanced time of three years.

$S = 200$, $i = 6\%/4 = 1\frac{1}{2}\%$ (per quarter), $n = 12$ (quarters)

Substituting the values in the compound discount formula:

$P = 200(1 + 1\frac{1}{2}\%)^{-12} = 200(0.83639) = \$167.28$

If the debt is paid at the end of the first year, the payment is \$167.28.

(b) If the debt of $200 is paid at the end of six years, which is two years (or eight quarters) after the due date, the required equivalent value is more than $200. Thus, the compound amount formula $S = P(1 + i)^n$ is used to compute the required value. In other words, the value is obtained by accumulating the amount on the due date for the extended time of two years.

$P = 200$, $i = 1\frac{1}{2}\%$ (per quarter), $n = 8$ (quarters)

Substituting the values in the compound amount formula:

$S = 200(1 + 1\frac{1}{2}\%)^8 = 200(1.12649) = \$225.30$

When the debt is paid at the end of the sixth year, the payment is $225.30.

The example may be diagrammed as follows:

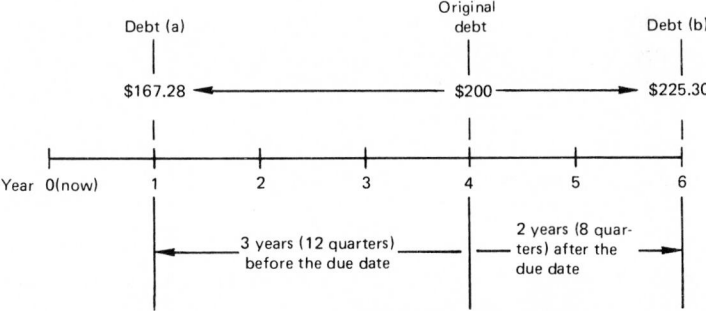

**Example 2**    A man owes (a) $300 due in three years and (b) $400 due in eight years. He and his creditor have agreed to settle the debts by two equal payments in five and six years respectively. Find the size of each payment if money is worth 6% compounded semiannually.

Let $x$ be each payment and the comparison date be six years from now. The values on the comparison date are computed below.

(1) The value of the old debt of $300 becomes $358.22 on the comparison date and is computed as follows:

$P = 300$, $i = 6\%/2 = 3\%$, $n = (6 - 3) \times 2 = 6$ (semiannual periods, from the due date to the comparison date)

Substituting the values in the formula $S = P(1 + i)^n$:

$S = 300(1 + 3\%)^6$
$= 300(1.19405) = \$358.22$

(2) The value of the old debt of $400 becomes $355.40 on the comparison date and is computed as follows:

$S = 400$, $i = 3\%$, $n = (8 - 6) \times 2 = 4$ (semiannual periods from the comparison date to the due date)

Substituting the values in the formula $P = S(1 + i)^{-n}$:

$$P = 400(1 + 3\%)^{-4}$$
$$= 400(.88849) = \$355.40$$

(3) The value of the new debt, which is the first payment due in five years, becomes $x(1.03)^2$ on the comparison date and is computed as follows:

$P = x$, $i = 3\%$, $n = (6 - 5) \times 2 = 2$ (semiannual periods from the due date to the comparison date)

Substituting the values in the formula $S = P(1 + i)^n$:

$$S = x(1 + 3\%)^2 = x(1.03)^2$$

(4) The value of the second payment due in six years does not change and is $x$ since the comparison date is also in six years.

The values in Example 2 are diagrammed in the following manner:

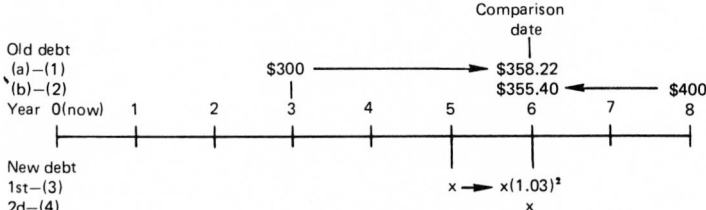

The equation of value based on the comparison date is given below:

New Debts       Old Debts

$$x + x(1.03)^2 = 355.40 + 358.22. \quad \text{Solve for } x,$$
$$x + x(1.0609) = 713.62$$
$$2.0609x = 713.62$$
$$x = \$346.27$$

**Example 3**    A man owes (a) $700 due in three years and (b) $1,000 due in eight years. His creditor has agreed for him to pay the debts with a payment of $800 in one year and the remainder in five years. If money is worth 4% compounded annually, what size must the second payment be?

Let $x$ be the second payment, which is to be made on the comparison date, or five years hence. The following diagram indicates the equivalent values on the comparison date of the given values.

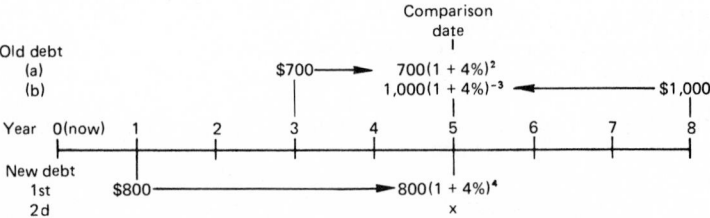

The equation of value based on the comparison date follows:

New Debts | Old Debts

$$\overbrace{x + 800(1 + 4\%)^4} = \overbrace{1,000(1 + 4\%)^{-3} + 700(1 + 4\%)^2},$$
$$x = 1,000(0.888996) + 700(1.0816) - 800(1.16986)$$
$$= 888.996 + 757.120 - 935.888$$
$$= \$710.23$$

**Example 4**   A man owes (a) \$500 due in two years, and (b) \$1,000 with interest at 4% compounded quarterly due in three years. If money is worth 6% compounded semiannually, what single payment seven years hence will be equivalent to the two original obligations?

Let $x$ be the unknown single payment and the comparison date be seven years hence. Since (b) is an interest-bearing debt, the maturity value based on a 4% interest rate compounded quarterly for three years (or 12 quarters) should be computed first. The maturity value is then accumulated at 6% compounded semiannually for four years (or eight semiannual periods) from the due date to the comparison date.

The maturity value at the end of three years is

$$\$1,000(1 + 4\%/4)^{12} = 1,000(1 + 1\%)^{12} = 1,000(1.126825) = \$1,126.83$$

and its value on the comparison date becomes

$$\$1,126.83(1 + 6\%/2)^8 = 1,126.83(1 + 3\%)^8 = \$1,427.43$$

The entire problem is diagrammed in the following manner:

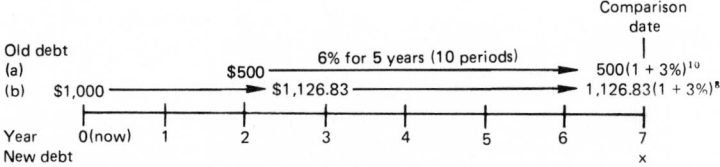

The equation of value based on the comparison date is written below:

New Debt | Old Debts

$$\overbrace{x = 1,126.83(1 + 3\%)^8} + 500(1 + 3\%)^{10}$$
$$= 1,126.83(1.26677) + 500(1.34392)$$
$$= 1,427.43 + 671.96$$
$$= \$2,099.39$$

# EXERCISE 12–2

### Reference: Section 12.3

**A.** *Find the value of the new obligations in each of the following problems:*

|  | Original Debts | Interest Rate, Compounded | New Debts and Comparison Date |
|---|---|---|---|
| **1.** | \$300 due in 2 years | 5%, quarterly | All in 6 years |
| **2.** | \$650 due in 3 years | 6%, monthly | All in 5 years |

|  | *Original Debts* | *Interest Rate, Compounded* | *New Debts and Comparison Date* |
|---|---|---|---|
| **3.** | (a) $5,000 due in 4 years | 6%, quarterly | Two equal payments: one in 6 years, the other in 9 years. Comparison date: 9 years hence. |
|  | (b) $2,000 due in 12 years |  |  |
| **4.** | (a) $2,400 due in 3 years | 4%, annually | Two equal payments: one in 7 years, the other in 16 years. Comparison date: 7 years hence. |
|  | (b) $4,700 due in 14 years |  |  |
| **5.** | (a) $1,000 due in 5 years | 7%, semiannually | $600 in 1 year, the remainder in 8 years. |
|  | (b) $1,600 due in 10 years |  |  |
| **6.** | (a) $3,400 due in 4 years | 5%, monthly | $3,000 in 5 years, the remainder in 7 years. |
|  | (b) $4,500 due in 9 years |  |  |
| **7.** | (a) $1,800 due in 6 years | 4%, annually | All in 18 years |
|  | (b) $2,500 due in 11 years |  |  |
| **8.** | (a) $1,500 due in 7 years | 5%, semiannually | All in 8 years |
|  | (b) $4,000 due in 10 years |  |  |

**B.** *Statement Problems:*

9. A debt of $4,200 is due in seven years. If money is worth 6% compounded monthly, what is the value of the debt if it is paid: (a) five years hence, (b) seven years hence, (c) ten years hence?

10. A debt of $5,200 is due in eight years. If money is worth 5% compounded quarterly, what is the value of the debt if it is paid: (a) at the end of four years, (b) at the end of eight years, (c) at the end of 11 years?

11. A man owes (a) $2,800 due in three years, and (b) $3,600 due in ten years. He and his creditor agree to settle the obligations by two equal payments, one in five years and the other in 15 years. Find the size of each payment if money is worth 4% compounded semiannually and the comparison date is 15 years hence.

12. Find the size of each payment in Problem 11 if the comparison date is five years hence.

13. A man owes (a) $2,000 due in four years and (b) $1,700 due in six years. His creditor has agreed for him to pay the debts with a payment of $1,500 in three years and the remainder in eight years. If money is worth 7% compounded quarterly, what size must the second payment be?

14. Refer to Problem 13. If the remainder of the debt is to be paid in five years, what is the size of the second payment?

15. A lady owes (a) $300 due in one year and (b) $700 due in four years plus interest at 6% compounded semiannually. If money is worth 5% compounded monthly, what single payment three years from now will be equivalent to the two debts?

16. Refer to Problem 15. What single payment made six years from now will be equivalent to the two debts?

## 12.4 EQUATED DATE

The equated date is generally defined as the date on which a single payment equal to the sum of a set of obligations is made to discharge the obligations. Nevertheless, the idea may be extended to a situation where the single payment is not equal to the sum of a set of old obligations.

The basic principle for computing an equated date is the same as the one used in Section 12.3. However, as shown in the following examples, the amount of the payment for discharging the old debts in an equation of value is known, but the equated date is unknown.

**Example 1**    John borrowed some money from Mary as follows: (a) $100 due in one year, (b) $300 due in two years, and (c) $400 due in two and one-half years. If money is worth 4% compounded semiannually, when can John discharge all of his debts by a single payment of $800?

Let "now" be the comparison date. The problem may be diagrammed as follows:

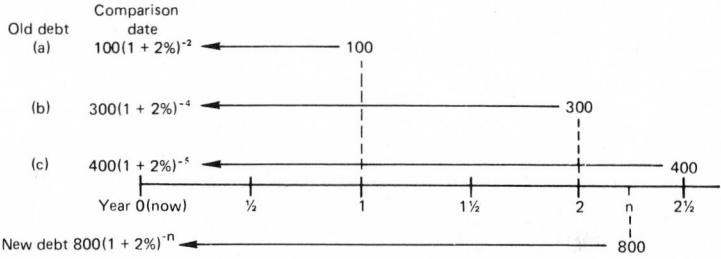

From the above diagram, the following equation of value may be written:

$$800(1 + 2\%)^{-n} = 100(1 + 2\%)^{-2} + 300(1 + 2\%)^{-4} + 400(1 + 2\%)^{-5}$$
$$= 100(.96117) + 300(.92385) + 400(.90573)$$
$$= 96.117 + 277.155 + 362.292$$
$$= 735.564$$

$$(1 + 2\%)^{-n} = \frac{735.564}{800} = .9195$$

The $n$ value is interpolated from Table 6 as follows: (Write the larger numbers, which are in the column of values all known, on the top lines.)

| | $n$ | $(1 + 2\%)^{-n}$ | |
|---|---|---|---|
| | 4 | .9238 | (1) |
| | $x$ | .9195 | (2) |
| | 5 | .9057 | (3) |
| $(2) - (3)$ | $\dfrac{x - 5}{-1}$ | $\dfrac{.0138}{.0181}$ | (4) |
| $(1) - (3)$ | | | (5) |

Solve for $x$ from the proportion formed by the differences on lines (4) and (5):

$$x - 5 = (-1)\left(\frac{.0138}{.0181}\right) = (-1)\left(\frac{138}{181}\right) = -.7624$$

$$x = 5 - .7624 = 4.2376$$

Thus, $n = 4.2376$ (semiannual periods), or two years and 43 days (.2376 × 180 days = 43 days)

**Note:**   The value of $n$ may be obtained by the use of logarithms as follows:

$$(1 + 2\%)^{-n} = .9195, \qquad - n \log 1.02 = \log .9195$$

$$- n = \frac{\log .9195}{\log 1.02} = \frac{9.963552 - 10}{0.0086} = \frac{-.036448}{0.0086} = -4.2381$$

$n = 4.2381$. This answer is more accurate than that obtained by the interpolation method.

**Example 2**   Refer to Example 1. If the single payment is \$810, when can John discharge all of his debts?

Again let "now" be the comparison date. Then,

$810(1 + 2\%)^{-n} = 735.564$.   (Notice that the right side of the equation of value is identical to that of Example 1.)

$$(1 + 2\%)^{-n} = \frac{735.564}{810} = .9081$$

By interpolation from Table 6,

$n = 4.8674$ (semiannual periods), or two years and 156 days
(.8674 × 180 days = 156 days)

**Example 3**   Refer to Example 1. If the debt of \$400 due in $2\frac{1}{2}$ years is charged with interest at 3% compounded quarterly, when can John discharge his entire debt by a single payment of \$800?

Let "now" be the comparison date. The maturity value of the \$400 debt at the end of $2\frac{1}{2}$ years will be:

$400(1 + \frac{3}{4}\%)^{10}$

Thus, the equation of value is

$$800(1 + 2\%)^{-n} = 100(1 + 2\%)^{-2} + 300(1 + 2\%)^{-4}$$
$$+ 400(1 + \tfrac{3}{4}\%)^{10}(1 + 2\%)^{-5}$$
$$= 96.117 + 277.155 + 400(1.07758)(.90573)$$
$$= 96.117 + 277.155 + 390.399$$
$$= 763.671$$

$$(1 + 2\%)^{-n} = \frac{763.671}{800} = .9546$$

By interpolation from Table 6,

$n = 2.3492$ (semiannual periods), or one year and 63 days
(.3492 × 180 days = 63 days)

## EXERCISE 12–3

**Reference: Section 12.4**

**A.** *Find the equated date in each of the following problems:*

|  | Original Debts | Interest Rate, Compounded | Single Payment Used to Discharge the Original Debts |
|---|---|---|---|
| **1.** | (a) $5,000 due in 4 years | 6%, quarterly | $7,000 |
|  | (b) $2,000 due in 12 years |  |  |
| **2.** | (a) $2,400 due in 3 years | 4%, annually | 7,100 |
|  | (b) $4,700 due in 14 years |  |  |
| **3.** | (a) $1,000 due in 5 years | 7%, semiannually | 2,600 |
|  | (b) $1,600 due in 10 years |  |  |
| **4.** | (a) $2,000 due in 2 years | 9%, monthly | 2,500 |
|  | (b) $500 due in $3\frac{1}{2}$ years |  |  |
| **5.** | (a) $180 due in 6 years | 4%, annually | 530 |
|  | (b) $200 due in 4 years |  |  |
|  | (c) $150 due in 8 years |  |  |
| **6.** | (a) $150 due in 7 years | 5%, semiannually | 750 |
|  | (b) $200 due in 8 years |  |  |
|  | (c) $400 due in 10 years |  |  |

**B.** *Statement Problems:*

**7.** When will the two debts in Problem 1 be discharged if the single payment is (a) $6,800? (b) $7,200?

**8.** When will the two debts in Problem 2 be discharged if the single payment is (a) $6,700? (b) $7,400?

**9.** Find the date on which the two debts in Problem 3 can be settled by a single payment of $2,500.

**10.** Find the date on which the two debts in Problem 4 can be settled by a single payment of $2,700.

**11.** Larry owes Steve (a) $200 due in two years, (b) $300 with interest at 3% compounded semiannually due in three years, and (c) $700 with interest at 4% compounded quarterly due in four years. If money now is worth $5\frac{1}{2}\%$ (effective rate), when will a single amount of $1,200 repay the three debts?

**12.** Patricia owes Christina (a) $400 due in four years, (b) $500 with interest at 4% compounded monthly due in five years, and (c) $800 with interest at 5% compounded annually due in seven years. If money now is worth 6% compounded semiannually, when will a single amount of $1,700 repay the three debts?

**13.** Refer to Problem 11. If Larry pays Steve $500 now, when should he pay another $700 to settle the entire debt?

**14.** Refer to Problem 12. If Patricia pays Christina $900 now, when should she pay another $800 to settle the entire debt?

## 12.5 EQUIVALENT RATES

If a principal invested at various interest rates will accumulate to the same compound amount in a certain period of time, the rates are said to be equivalent to each other. The various interest rates are thus called *equivalent rates*. Equivalent rates may be obtained by the use of the effective rate method based on a one-year period as illustrated in the following examples.

**Example 1**   At what nominal rate compounded quarterly will a principal yield an interest which is equivalent to an effective rate of 7%?

$m = 4$ (quarters), $f = 7\%$

Substituting the values in formula (11–4):

$7\% = (1 + j/4)^4 - 1$, $(1 + j/4)^4 = 1 + 7\%$

Extracting the fourth root of each side of the above equation; then

$(1 + j/4) = (1 + 7\%)^{\frac{1}{4}} = 1.01706$                    (Table 5A)

Thus, $j/4 = 1.01706 - 1 = .01706$
    $j = .01706 \times 4 = .06824$, or the nominal rate is 6.824%, which is rounded to 6.82%.

The nominal rate 6.82% compounded quarterly is equivalent to an effective rate of 7%.

**Note:**   A more accurate answer for Example 1 may be obtained from Table 11. Table 11 gives the values of $j_m$ (nominal rate $j$ compounded $m$ times a year) and their equivalent values of $f$ (effective rate). The formula for the value of $j_m$ may be derived from the effective rate formula (11–4) as follows:

$$\left(1 + \frac{j}{m}\right)^m = 1 + f$$

Extracting the $m$th root of each side of the above equation, then

$1 + \dfrac{j}{m} = (1 + f)^{1/m}$, and

$j = m[(1 + f)^{1/m} - 1]$

When $f = 7\%$, and $m = 4$, the value shown in Table 11 is

$j = .06823410$, or 6.82341%.

**Example 2**   At what nominal rate compounded monthly will a principal accumulate to the same amount as at 8% compounded quarterly?

Let the unknown nominal rate be $j$; then $i = j/12$ (per month). The effective rate in the first case is:

$f = (1 + j/12)^{12} - 1$

In the latter case, $i = 8\%/4 = 2\%$ (per quarter). The effective rate is

$f = (1 + 2\%)^4 - 1$

Since the accumulated amount in the first case is the same as the amount in the latter case, the effective rates must be the same in both cases. Thus,

$(1 + j/12)^{12} - 1 = (1 + 2\%)^4 - 1$, or
$(1 + j/12)^{12} = (1 + 2\%)^4$

Extracting the 12th root on each side of the above equation; then

$$(1 + j/12) = (1 + 2\%)^{\frac{4}{12}} = (1 + 2\%)^{\frac{1}{3}} = 1.006623 \qquad \text{(Table 5A)}$$

$j/12 = 1.006623 - 1 = .006623$

$j = .006623 \times 12 = .079476$, or rounded to 7.95%

It may be stated that 7.95% compounded monthly is equivalent to 8% compounded quarterly. The statement holds true for any principal and for any number of periods of investment.

From Example 2, note that the nominal rate of 7.95% is computed from the equation

$$(1 + j/12) = (1 + 2\%)^{\frac{1}{3}},$$

which does not contain the values of *S* and *P*. Furthermore, both sides of the equation are the accumulation factors for a one-month period, which is also the conversion period of the unknown nominal rate. Thus, computation of equivalent rate problems may be simplified by using an equation which contains only the accumulation factors of a length equal to *one conversion period* for the unknown nominal rate.

**Example 3**    If a principal *P*, invested at 6% compounded quarterly for three years, will accumulate to the compound amount *S*, at what nominal rate compounded semiannually will the principal accumulate to the same amount in the same period?

Let the unknown nominal rate be *j*, then $i = j/2$ (per semiannual period). The accumulation factor for one conversion period (six months) is $(1 + j/2)$.

In the first case, $i = 6\%/4 = 1\frac{1}{2}\%$ (per quarter). The accumulation factor for a six-month period (the conversion period for the unknown rate *j*) or two quarters is $(1 + 1\frac{1}{2}\%)^2$. The equation may be written as follows:

$(1 + j/2) = (1 + 1\frac{1}{2}\%)^2$

Since $(1 + 1\frac{1}{2}\%)^2 = 1.030225$ \qquad (Table 5)

$1 + j/2 = 1.030225$

$j/2 = 1.030225 - 1$

$j = .030225 \times 2 = .06045$, or 6.05%

Thus, a principal *P* invested at 6% compounded quarterly will accumulate to the same amount as invested at 6.05% compounded semiannually during a period of three years. The values of *P*, *S*, and *n* (three years) need not be included in the computation.

## 12.6 CONTINUOUSLY COMPOUNDED INTEREST

Although compound interest is usually computed at regularly stated intervals such as annually, semiannually, quarterly, or monthly, it may be computed more frequently such as every minute, every second, or continuously. Continuous compounding is not commonly used in the actual investment market. However, its concept is theoretically important in analyzing financial problems.

To compute an interest at a nominal rate compounded continuously, first find the equivalent effective rate, then compute the compound interest based on the effective rate. The formula for finding the effective rate of the nominal rate $j$ compounded continuously can be derived from formula (11–4), which is

$$f = \left(1 + \frac{j}{m}\right)^m - 1,$$

where $f$ = effective rate,
$j$ = nominal rate, and
$m$ = number of conversion periods for one year

The derivation is presented below:

Let $k = \dfrac{m}{j}$, and $\dfrac{1}{k} = \dfrac{j}{m}$. Then, the term

$$\left(1 + \frac{j}{m}\right)^m = \left[\left(1 + \frac{j}{m}\right)^{\frac{m}{j}}\right]^j = \left[\left(1 + \frac{1}{k}\right)^k\right]^j$$

The values of $\left(1 + \dfrac{1}{k}\right)^k$ can be computed as follows:

| *When k is* | *the value of* $\left(1 + \dfrac{1}{k}\right)^k$ *is* |
|:---:|:---:|
| 1 | $\left(1 + \dfrac{1}{1}\right)^1 = 2$ |
| 2 | $\left(1 + \dfrac{1}{2}\right)^2 = (1.5)^2 = 2.25$ |
| 10 | $\left(1 + \dfrac{1}{10}\right)^{10} = (1.1)^{10} = 2.594$ |
| 100 | $\left(1 + \dfrac{1}{100}\right)^{100} = (1.01)^{100} = 2.705$ |
| 1,000 | $\left(1 + \dfrac{1}{1,000}\right)^{1,000} = (1.001)^{1,000} = 2.716$ |
| 10,000 | $\left(1 + \dfrac{1}{10,000}\right)^{10,000} = (1,0001)^{10,000} = 2.7164$ |
| . . . . . . | . . . . . . . . . .     (Use Tables 2 and 3.) |

When $k$ approaches an infinitely large value ($k \to \infty$), the limit of $(1 + 1/k)^k$, usually denoted by the letter $e$, is an irrational number and is 2.71828 approximately. It is written

$$e = \lim_{k \to \infty}\left(1 + \frac{1}{k}\right)^k = 2.71828 \text{ approximately.}$$

(An irrational number is the number which cannot be written as a fraction with numerator and denominator being integers—it is a never-ending decimal.)

When $j$ is compounded continuously, $m$ becomes infinitely large; the value of $k = m/j$ also becomes infinitely large, and the term $(1 + j/m)^m$ equals $e^j$, or

$$\left(1 + \frac{j}{m}\right)^m = \left[\left(1 + \frac{1}{k}\right)^k\right]^j = e^j$$

When $e^j$ is substituted into formula (11–4), the effective rate of the nominal rate $j$ compounded continuously is

$$f = e^j - 1 \qquad\qquad\qquad\qquad \textbf{(12–1)}$$

The value of $e^j$ can be approximated by using logarithms as illustrated in Example 1(a) or by a table as illustrated in other examples below. Table 12–1 shows the values of $e^j$ for selected values of $j$ computed to eight decimal places. The value of $e^j$ for other values of $j$ may also be obtained from the table after applying the laws of exponents as illustrated in Example 2.

**Example 1**   Find the effective rate if money is worth 6% compounded continuously. Here $j = 6\% = .06$

(a) Use logarithms:

$e^j = 2.71828^{.06}$

$\log e^j = \log (2.71828^{.06}) = .06(\log 2.71828)$
$\qquad = .06(0.434294) = 0.026058.$

$e^j = 1.061837$ (By interpolation from Table 2.)

Substituting $e^j$ value in formula (12–1),

$f = 1.061837 - 1 = 0.061837$, or $6.1837\%$

(b) Use Table 12–1:

$e^j = 1.06183655$ at $j = .06$ or 6%.
$f = 1.06183655 - 1 = 0.06183655$ or $6.183655\%$.

The value of $f$ is more accurate when we use Table 12–1.

**Table 12–1** **VALUES OF $e^j$ FOR SELECTED VALUES OF $j$**

| $j$ | $e^j$ | $j$ | $e^j$ | $j$ | $e^j$ |
|------|-------------|------|-------------|------|-------------|
| .000 | 1.0000 0000 |      |             |      |             |
| .001 | 1.0010 0050 | .01  | 1.0100 5017 | .1   | 1.1051 7092 |
| .002 | 1.0020 0200 | .02  | 1.0202 0134 | .2   | 1.2214 0276 |
| .003 | 1.0030 0450 | .03  | 1.0304 5453 | .3   | 1.3498 5881 |
| .004 | 1.0040 0801 | .04  | 1.0408 1077 | .4   | 1.4918 2470 |
|      |             |      |             |      |             |
| .005 | 1.0050 1252 | .05  | 1.0512 7110 | .5   | 1.6487 2127 |
| .006 | 1.0060 1804 | .06  | 1.0618 3655 | .6   | 1.8221 1880 |
| .007 | 1.0070 2456 | .07  | 1.0725 0818 | .7   | 2.0137 5271 |
| .008 | 1.0080 3209 | .08  | 1.0832 8707 | .8   | 2.2255 4093 |
| .009 | 1.0090 4062 | .09  | 1.0941 7428 | .9   | 2.4596 0311 |
|      |             |      |             | 1.0  | 2.7182 8183 |

**Example 2** Find the effective rate if money is worth $7\frac{1}{2}\%$ compounded continuously.

Here $j = 7\frac{1}{2}\% = .075$.

$e^j = e^{.075} = e^{.07}(e^{.005}) = 1.07250818(1.00501252)$
    $= 1.07788415$. (Table 12–1)

Substituting $e^j$ value in formula (12–1),

$f = 1.07788415 - 1 = 0.07788415$, or $7.788415\%$.

By substituting the effective rate for continuous compounding $f$ (formula 12–1) for $i$ in the compound amount formula $S$, we have

$$S = P(1 + i)^n = P(1 + f)^n = P(1 + [e^j - 1])^n$$
$$= P(e^j)^n = P(e^{jn})$$

Thus, the formula for finding the compound amount *(S)* of the principal *(P)* at the nominal rate $j$ compounded continuously for $n$ years is

$$S = P(e^{jn}) \hspace{3cm} \text{(12–2)}$$

**Example 3** Find the compound amount and the compound interest when $10,000 is invested at 5% compounded continuously for (a) one year, and (b) two years.

$P = \$10,000$, $j = 5\% = .05$. Use formula (12–2).

(a) $n = 1$ year, and $jn = .05(1) = .05$.

$S = 10,000(e^{.05}) = 10,000(1.05127110)$
  $= \$10,512.71$. (Compound amount)

Compound interest $= 10,512.71 - 10,000.00$
                   $= \$512.71$.

(b) $n = 2$ years, and $jn = .05(2) = .10$.

$$S = 10,000(e^{.1}) = 10,000(1.10517092)$$
$$= \$11,051.71 \text{ (Compound amount)}$$

$$\text{Compound interest} = 11,051.71 - 10,000$$
$$= \$1,051.71.$$

## EXERCISE 12–4

### Reference: Sections 12.5 and 12.6

1. At what nominal rate compounded semiannually will a principal yield interest which is equivalent to an effective rate of $6\frac{1}{2}\%$?
2. What nominal rate compounded monthly is equivalent to an effective rate of 4%?
3. At what nominal rate compounded semiannually will a principal yield interest which is equivalent to 4% compounded monthly?
4. What nominal rate compounded quarterly is equivalent to 5% compounded monthly?
5. Find the nominal rate compounded quarterly which is equivalent to 7% compounded semiannually.
6. Find the nominal rate compounded monthly which is equivalent to 6% compounded semiannually.
7. Find the effective rate if money is worth (a) 5%, and (b) 20% compounded continuously.
8. Find the effective rate if money is worth (a) 8%, and (b) 50% compounded continuously.
9. What is the effective rate if money is invested at $4\frac{1}{2}\%$ compounded continuously?
10. What is the effective rate if money is invested at $6\frac{1}{2}\%$ compounded continuously?
11. Find the compound amount and the compound interest if $1,000 is invested at 4% compounded continuously for (a) one year, and (b) two years.
12. Find the compound amount and the compound interest if $1,000 is invested at 3% compounded continuously for (a) one year, and (b) three years.

## EXERCISE 12–5

### Review of Chapter 12

1. Use the logarithmic method to find each of the following unknown values:

(a) $S = 2,000 (1 + 5\%)^{18}$
(b) $P = 500/(1 + 6\%)^6$
(c) $(1 + i)^{25} = 1,400/370$
(d) $(1 + 4\%)^n = 1,980/920$

2. Use the logarithmic method to find each of the following unknown values:

    (a) $S = 4{,}500 \, (1 + 6\%)^{32}$     (c) $(1 + i)^{30} = 1{,}620/590$

    (b) $P = 750/(1 + 3\%)^{40}$       (d) $(1 + 5\%)^{n} = 4{,}200/1{,}180$

3. A debt of \$500 is due at the end of six years. If money is worth 5% compounded monthly, what is the value of the debt when it is paid at the end of (a) two years? (b) nine years?

4. A debt of \$800 is due in three years. If interest is 6% compounded quarterly, what is the value of the debt when it is paid at the end of (a) one year? (b) $5\frac{1}{2}$ years?

5. Bob owes John \$300 due in four years and \$800 due in ten years. Assume that the two debts are to be discharged by 2 equal payments in three years and eight years respectively. What is the size of each payment if money is worth 4% compounded quarterly? Let eight years from now be the comparison date.

6. Compute Problem 5 by letting three years hence be the comparison date.

7. Carl owes Dean \$900 due in two years and \$1,500 due in seven years. Assume that the two debts are to be discharged by a payment of \$700 in three years and the remainder in six years. What is the size of the second payment if money is worth 6% compounded semiannually?

8. Refer to Problem 7. (a) If the two debts are to be discharged by 2 equal payments in three years and five years respectively, what is the size of each payment? (b) What single payment would discharge the two debts ten years hence?

9. Mary owes Jack \$400 due in one year and \$950 with interest at 5% compounded monthly due in eight years. If money is worth 7% compounded annually, what is the single payment ten years from now that will discharge the two debts?

10. Refer to Problem 9. If the two debts are to be discharged by a payment of \$500 in two years and the remainder in five years, what is the size of the second payment?

11. Susan borrowed some money from Janet as follows: \$50 due in one year, \$200 due in three years, and \$300 due in five years. If money is worth 6% compounded monthly, when can Susan discharge all her debts by a single payment of \$550?

12. Dorothy promised to pay Bob the following amounts: \$100 due in two years, \$400 due in five years, and \$500 plus interest at 4% compounded semiannually due in six years. If money is worth 6% compounded quarterly, when can Dorothy repay her debts by a single payment of \$1,000?

13. What nominal rate compounded quarterly is equivalent to a 5% effective rate?

14. Find the nominal rate compounded semiannually that is equivalent to an effective rate of $4\frac{1}{2}\%$.

15. What nominal rate compounded monthly is equivalent to 7% compounded semiannually?

**16.** Find the nominal rate compounded semiannually that is equivalent to 5% compounded quarterly.

**17.** Find the effective rate if money is invested at (a) 7% and (b) $5\frac{1}{2}$% compounded continuously.

**18.** What is the effective rate if money is invested at (a) 4% and (b) $8\frac{1}{2}$% compounded continuously.

**19.** Find the compound amount and the compound interest if $10,000 is invested at 10% compounded continuously for (a) one year, and (b) two years.

**20.** Find the compound amount and the compound interest if $10,000 is invested at 20% compounded continuously for (a) one year, and (b) four years.

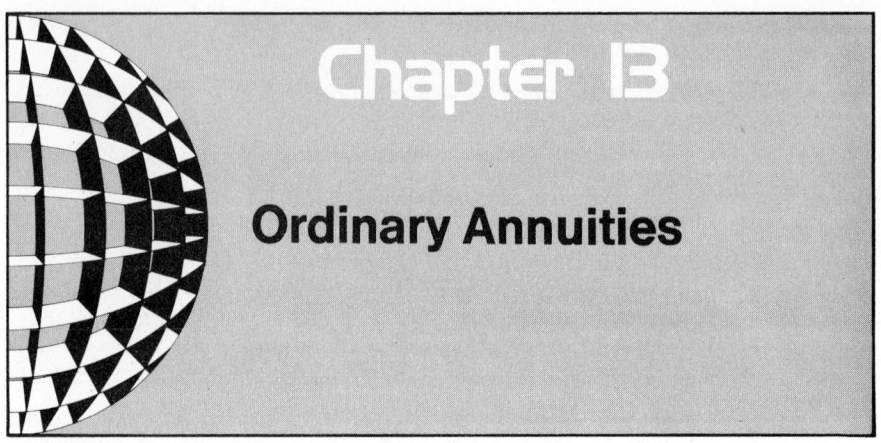

# Chapter 13

# Ordinary Annuities

There are numerous types of annuity problem. Financing the huge social security system, for example, is a type of annuity problem. Additional examples of annuities are periodic savings; rental payments; purchases of cars, houses, or home appliances on installment payment plans; life insurance premiums; and interest payments on bonds. From the above examples, we can see that the subject of annuities affects business firms as well as practically every family in the United States.

## 13.1 INTRODUCTION TO ANNUITIES

Generally speaking, an *annuity* is a series of periodic payments, usually made in equal amounts. The payments are computed by the compound interest method and are made at equal intervals of time, such as annually, semiannually, quarterly, or monthly. The word annuity originally referred only to annual payments, but it now applies to payment intervals of any length of time.

The period of time between two successive payment dates is called the *payment interval.* The time between the beginning of the first payment interval and the end of the last payment interval is called the *term* of the annuity.

## A. Annuities Classified by Term

According to their terms, annuities may be classified into three groups:

1. *Annuity Certain.* The term of an annuity certain begins and ends on definite dates, such as a five-year term from January 1, 1980, to January 1, 1985.
2. *Perpetuity.* The term of a perpetuity begins on a definite date but never ends, such as a principal which remains forever untouched, drawing interest. The length of the term is infinite.

3. *Contingent Annuity.* The term of a contingent annuity begins on a definite date but the ending date is not fixed in advance. Instead the ending date depends upon some condition happening in the future, such as life insurance premiums being paid only so long as the insured is living, the length of time therefore being uncertain.

## B. Annuities Classified by Dates of Payment

According to the dates of payment, annuities may be classified into three groups:

1. *Ordinary Annuity.* Periodic payments are made at the *end* of each payment interval. For example, if the term of an annuity is one year, which begins on January 1, and the payment interval is one quarter, the first payment should be made three months later, or on April 1, the end of the first quarter; the second payment should be made on July 1, the end of the second quarter; and so on.

2. *Annuity Due.* Periodic payments are made at the *beginning* of each payment interval. For instance, in the above example the first payment is made on January 1, the beginning of the first quarter; the second payment is made on April 1, the beginning of the second quarter; and so on.

3. *Deferred Annuity.* Periodic payments are made at the *end* of each payment interval. However, the term of the annuity does not begin until *after* a designated period of time. For example, a man borrows $100 on April 15, 1980, and agrees to repay the loan by making a series of three equal annual payments, but the first payment is not due until two years from the date of the loan.

## C. Annuities Classified by Length of Payment Interval and Interest Conversion Period

According to the *length* of payment interval and interest conversion period, annuities may be divided into two groups:

1. *Simple Annuity.* The payment interval coincides with the interest conversion period. In other words, the payment date is the interest computing date. For example, when the payment interval is one month, the interest is compounded monthly. When each of the payments of an annuity is made at the end of each month, the interest is also computed and compounded at the end of each month.

2. *Complex Annuity (General Annuity).* The payment interval does not coincide with the interest conversion period. For example, the payment interval is one month, and the interest is compounded quarterly; or the payment interval is one quarter, and the interest is compounded monthly. The formulas for a complex annuity may also be used for solving simple

annuity problems. Thus, the complex annuity is considered as a general case of annuity and is also called a *general annuity.*

Hereafter, unless otherwise specified, the word *annuity* means an *ordinary annuity,* which is also an *annuity certain.* Only ordinary annuities of the simple annuity type are discussed in this chapter. Other types of annuities are presented in Chapter 14.

## 13.2 AMOUNT OF AN ANNUITY

The *amount* of an annuity is the final value at the end of the term of the annuity. The amount includes all of the periodic payments and the compound interest.

## A. Computation in General

The amount of an annuity is obtained by totaling the compound amounts of the individual periodic payments. Each of the compound amounts is computed by the formula $S = P(1 + i)^n$.

**Example 1**   What is the amount of an annuity if the size of each payment is $100, payable at the end of each quarter for one year at an interest rate of 4% compounded quarterly?

The first payment is made at the end of the first quarter, which is three quarters before the end of the term of the annuity. Thus, interest is accumulated on the first payment for three interest periods; on the second payment, for two interest periods; and on the third payment, for one interest period. The fourth payment is not entitled to interest since it is paid at the end of the term.

The entire computation is diagrammed as follows:

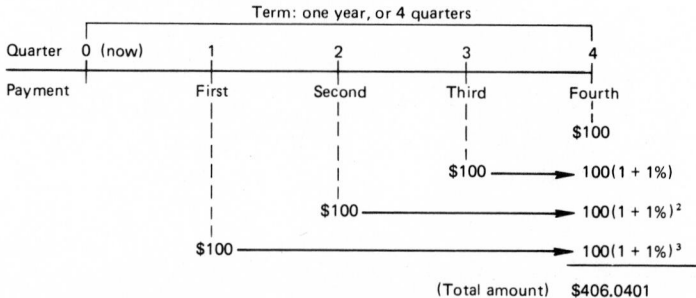

The amount of the annuity, $406.0401, which is the final value at the end of the fourth quarter, is computed as follows: (Use Table 5)

$$100 \qquad\qquad = 100(1)$$
$$100(1 + 1\%) \ = 100(1.01)$$
$$100(1 + 1\%)^2 = 100(1.0201)$$
$$100(1 + 1\%)^3 = 100(1.030301)$$

(Total amount)   $100(4.060401) = \$406.0401$, or $\$406.04$

The total of the compound interest on the four payments is

$$\$406.04 - (100 \times 4) = \$6.04$$

The preceding example may be applied in the following case:

> A man deposits $100 in a bank at the end of each quarter for one year. If the money earns interest at 4% compounded quarterly, how much does he have in his account at the end of the year after the last payment is made? Answer: He has $406.04.

## EXERCISE 13–1

### Reference: Section 13.2 A

**A.** *Using the method employed in Example 1, find the amount of each annuity and the total interest on the payments in each of the following cases. (Assume that each payment is made at the end of each payment interval.)*

|  | Each Payment | Payment Interval | Term | Compound Interest Rate |
|---|---|---|---|---|
| **1.** | $1,000 | 1 month | 4 months | 6%, monthly |
| **2.** | 200 | 1 quarter | 9 months | 4%, quarterly |
| **3.** | 500 | 6 months | 1 year | 5%, semiannually |
| **4.** | 700 | 1 year | 2 years | 10%, annually |
| **5.** | 3,000 | 1 quarter | 1 year | 8%, quarterly |
| **6.** | 600 | 6 months | $1\frac{1}{2}$ years | 6%, semiannually |

**B.** *Statement Problems:*

7. What is the amount of an annuity if the size of each payment is $2,000, payable at the end of each year for three years at an interest rate of 9% compounded annually?

8. Find the amount of an annuity if the size of each payment is $80, payable at the end of each month for four months at an interest rate of 12% compounded monthly.

## B. Computation by Formula (13–1)

Let $R$ = size of each regular payment (or periodic rent)
   $i$ = interest rate per conversion period
   $n$ = number of payments during the term of an annuity (It is also

the number of payment intervals, or the number of conversion periods.)

$S_n =$ the amount of an ordinary annuity

## The formula[1] for the amount of an ordinary annuity is:

---

[1] *Proof—Formula (13–1), the amount of an ordinary annuity*

In Example 1, since $R = \$100$, $i = 1\%$, and $n = 4$ (quarterly payments), a diagram may be drawn with symbols as shown below.

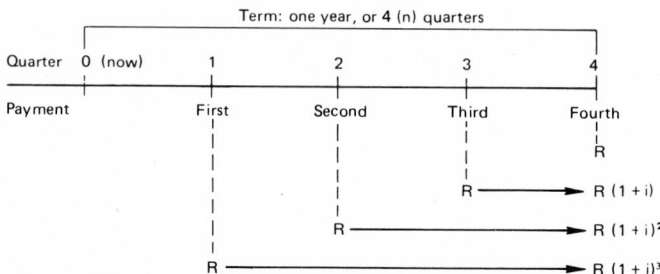

Notice that the number of interest conversion periods for the first payment is 3, which is 1 less than 4, or $(n - 1)$; the number for the second payment is 2, which is 2 less than 4, or $(n - 2)$; and so on. On the other hand, the number of interest conversion periods for the last payment, the fourth or $n$th payment, is zero; the number for the next to the last, the third or $(n - 1)$th payment, is 1; the number for the second or $(n - 2)$th payment is 2; and so on. Extend this idea and let $n =$ any number of payments. The following results may be obtained:

| | |
|---|---|
| The compound amount of the 1st payment | $= R(1 + i)^{n-1}$ |
| The compound amount of the 2d payment | $= R(1 + i)^{n-2}$ |
| . . . . . . . . . . . . . . . . . . . . . . . . . | $= \ldots \ldots$ |
| The compound amount of the $(n - 2)$th payment | $= R(1 + i)^2$ |
| The compound amount of the $(n - 1)$th payment | $= R(1 + i)$ |
| The compound amount of the $n$th (the last) payment | $= R$ |

There are $n$ compound amounts.

Let $S_n =$ the sum of $n$ compound amounts, (or the amount of the annuity).

Thus, $S_n = R + R(1 + i) + R(1 + i)^2 + \ldots \ldots \ldots + R(1 + i)^{n-2} + R(1 + i)^{n-1}$     Step (1)

Multiply both sides of the equation in Step (1) by $(1 + i)$.

Then, $S_n(1 + i) = R(1 + i) + R(1 + i)^2 + R(1 + i)^3 + \ldots \ldots$
$+ R(1 + i)^{n-1} + R(1 + i)^n$     Step (2)

Subtract the equation in Step (2) from the equation in Step (1).

Then,

$S_n - S_n(1 + i) = R - R(1 + i)^n.$ Factor,            Step (3)
$S_n[1 - (1 + i)] = R[1 - (1 + i)^n], S_n(-i) = R[1 - (1 + i)^n]$

$$S_n = \frac{R[1 - (1 + i)^n]}{-i} = \frac{R[i - (1 + i)^n]}{-i} \cdot \frac{-1}{-1}$$

$$S_n = R \cdot \frac{(1 + i)^n - 1}{i}$$

**Note:** The right side of the equation in Step (1) is a geometric progression and may also be solved by the geometric progression formula in Chapter 3, page 81.

$$S_n = R \cdot \frac{(1+i)^n - 1}{i} \qquad \text{(13-1)}$$

Formula (13–1) is obtained by using the method employed in Example 1, pages 378 and 379. When formula (13–1) is used, the answer to Example 1 may be computed as follows:

$R = \$100$ (per quarter), $i = 4\%/4 = 1\%$ (per quarter), and $n = 4$ (quarterly payments)

Substituting the values in formula (13–1):

$$S_n = S_4 = 100 \cdot \frac{(1 + 1\%)^4 - 1}{1\%} = 100 \cdot \frac{1.04060401 - 1}{.01}$$

$$= 100 \cdot \frac{.04060401}{.01} = 100(4.060401) = \$406.0401, \text{ or } \$406.04$$

The value of $(1 + 1\%)^4$ is obtained from Table 5. The answer here is the same as that obtained in Example 1.

For convenience, the value of $\dfrac{(1+i)^n - 1}{i}$ is usually represented by the symbol $s_{\overline{n}|i}$ (which is read $s$ angle $n$ at $i$). The values of $s_{\overline{n}|i}$ for various interest rates *(i)* and numbers of payments *(n)* are provided in Table 7. The unit value of each entry in the table is best represented by one dollar, although it may be represented by any other unit. Therefore, each entry in the table becomes the amount of the annuity in dollars when each payment is $1, or when $R = \$1$.

When Table 7 is employed, the computation of the amount of an annuity is simplified. In general, formula (13–1) is written in the following form:

$$S_n = R s_{\overline{n}|i} \qquad \text{(13-1), or}$$

$$\begin{pmatrix} \text{Amount of an} \\ \text{ordinary annuity } S_n \end{pmatrix} = \begin{pmatrix} \text{Size of each} \\ \text{payment } R \end{pmatrix} \times \begin{pmatrix} \text{An entry} \\ \text{in Table 7} \end{pmatrix}$$

(The entry is at the interest rate *i* per conversion period for *n* conversion periods or payments.)

Example 1 may now be computed in the following manner:

$$S_n = R s_{\overline{n}|i} = 100 s_{\overline{4}|1\%} = 100(4.060401) = \$406.0401, \text{ or } \$406.04$$

The answer is the same as that found in Example 1.

**Example 2**  Find the amount of an annuity of $150 payable at the end of each year for 15 years, if the interest rate is 5% compounded annually.

$R = \$150$ (per year), $i = 5\%$ (per year), and $n = 15$ (annual payments)

Substituting the values in formula (13–1):

$$S_n = 150s_{\overline{15}|5\%} = 150(21.57856) = \$3{,}236.78$$

**Note:**     The multiplication $150s_{\overline{15}|5\%}$ may also be performed by using logarithms:

$$
\begin{aligned}
\log 150 \ \ &= 2.176\,0910 \ \text{(Table 2)} \\
(+) \log s_{\overline{15}|5\%} &= 1.334\,0226 \ \text{(Table 12)} \\
\hline
\log S_n &= 3.510\,1136
\end{aligned}
$$

Find the antilog by interpolation from Table 2.

$S_n = \$3{,}236.781$, or rounded to \$3,236.78.

**Example 3**     If \$20 is deposited at the end of each month for three years in a fund which earns 6% interest compounded monthly, what will be the final value at the end of the three-year term? What is the total interest?

$R = \$20$ (per month), $i = 6\%/12 = \frac{1}{2}\%$ (per month), $n = 3 \times 12 = 36$ (monthly payments)

Substituting the values in formula (13–1):

Final value $= S_n = Rs_{\overline{n}|i} = 20s_{\overline{36}|1/2\%} = 20(39.3361) = \$786.72$

Total deposits $= 20 \times 36 = \$720$
Total interest $= 786.72 - 720 = \$66.72$

**Example 4**     In Example 3, how much will the amount be two years after the last deposit is made?

The final value at the end of the three years now becomes the principal which is accumulated for two years.

Substituting $P = \$786.72$, $i = \frac{1}{2}\%$, $n = 2 \times 12 = 24$ (months) in the formula $S = P(1 + i)^n$:

$S = 786.72(1 + \frac{1}{2}\%)^{24} = 786.72(1.12715978) = \$886.76$

# EXERCISE 13–2

**Reference: Section 13.2 B**

**A.** *Find the amount of the ordinary annuity in each of the following problems:*

| Payment (R) | Payment Interval | Term | Compound Interest Rate |
|---|---|---|---|
| 1. $1,000 | 1 month | 2 years | 6%, monthly |
| 2. 1,250 | 1 quarter | 10 years | 5%, quarterly |
| 3. 880 | 6 months | $8\frac{1}{2}$ years | 7%, semiannually |
| 4. 1,000 | 1 year | 30 years | 10%, annually |
| 5. 400 | 1 quarter | 15 years, 6 months | 6%, quarterly |
| 6. 500 | 1 month | 4 years, 3 months | 4%, monthly |
| 7. 300 | 1 year | 20 years | $5\frac{1}{2}\%$, annually |
| 8. 800 | 6 months | 12 years | 8%, semiannually |

**B.** *Statement Problems:*

9. What is the amount of an annuity if the size of each payment is $250, payable at the end of each quarter for five years at an interest rate of 4% compounded quarterly?

10. Ana Perez deposits $450 in a bank at the end of each month for three years and nine months. If the money earns interest at 5% compounded monthly, how much money does she have in her account at the end of the period?

11. Find the amount of an annuity of $56 payable at the end of every six months for $4\frac{1}{2}$ years, if the interest rate is 6% compounded semiannually.

12. Find the amount of an annuity of $80 payable at the end of each year for 25 years, if money is worth 7% compounded annually.

13. Frieda Grant deposits $45 monthly at an interest rate of 12% compounded monthly. How much will she have in her account at the end of two years and four months?

14. At the end of each quarter, a company placed $1,500 in a sinking fund. The fund was invested at 7% compounded quarterly. (a) What will be the final value at the end of five years? (b) What will be the total interest?

15. At the end of each month during a three-year period, a business manager of a hospital invested one sixth of his monthly salary of $900. How much will the amount be four years after the last investment is made if the interest rate is 4% compounded monthly?

16. Bill Morton deposited $50 every six months in a fund earning interest at 5% compounded semiannually. The first deposit was made when he was 20 years of age and the last deposit was made when he was 25. If he leaves the fund intact, how much will he have in the fund when he is 28?

## 13.3 PRESENT VALUE OF AN ANNUITY

The present value of an annuity is the value at the beginning of the term of the annuity. The methods for computing the present value are based on either of the following two different interpretations of the value:

1. It is the sum of the present values of the periodic payments of an annuity.
2. It is the single principal which, at a given compound interest rate, will accumulate to the amount of an annuity by the end of the term of the annuity.

## A. Computation in General

**Example 1**     What is the present value of an annuity if the size of each payment is $100 payable at the end of each quarter for one year and the interest rate is 4% compounded quarterly?

**Method A**    When the present value of an annuity is considered as the *sum of the present values* of the periodic payments, each of the present values *(P)* is computed by the compound discount formula $P = S(1 + i)^{-n}$. In the present case, $S$ is the payment, or $S = \$100$.

The first payment is made at the end of the first quarter, which is one quarter after the beginning of the term of the annuity. Thus, the present value of the first payment is obtained by discounting the payment for one quarter, or one interest period. The present value of the second payment is obtained by discounting the payment for two periods, and so on.

The computation is diagrammed as follows:

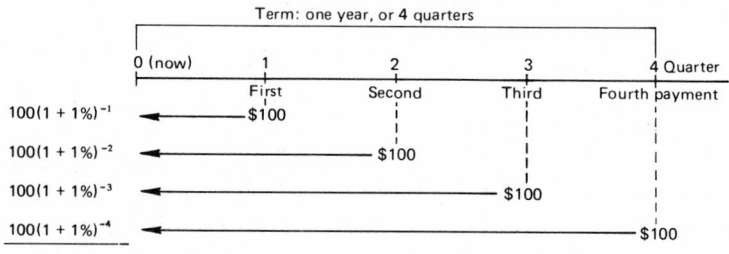

$390.20 (Present value of the annuity)

The present value of the annuity, $390.20, is computed by using Table 6 as follows:

$100(1 + 1\%)^{-1} = 100(0.99009901)$
$100(1 + 1\%)^{-2} = 100(0.98029605)$
$100(1 + 1\%)^{-3} = 100(0.97059015)$
$100(1 + 1\%)^{-4} = \underline{100(0.96098034)}$
$\qquad\qquad\qquad 100(3.90196555) = \$390.196555$, or $390.20

**Method B**    When the present value of an annuity is considered as the *single principal* of the amount of the annuity, the principal *(P)* is obtained by the compound discount formula $P = S(1 + i)^{-n}$. In the present case, $S$ is equal to the amount of the annuity, $S_n$. The computation is as follows: (Also, see Example 1, pages 378 and 379.)

**Step (1)**    To obtain the value of $S_n$, use formula (13–1):

$R = 100$, $i = 4\%/4 = 1\%$, $n = 4$

$S_n = Rs_{\overline{n}|i} = 100s_{\overline{4}|1\%} = 100(4.060401)$
$\qquad = \$406.0401$                                        (Table 7)

**Step (2)**    The single principal $P = 406.0401(1 + 1\%)^{-4}$
$\qquad = 406.0401(0.96098034) = \$390.19655$, or $390.20
$\qquad\qquad\qquad\qquad\qquad\qquad\qquad\qquad\qquad\qquad$ (Table 6)

The sum of compound discounts on the four payments is:

$(100 \times 4) - \$390.20 = \$9.80$

The computation in the above example may also be applied in solving problems such as the following:

> A man would like to borrow money from a bank which charges interest at 4% compounded quarterly. If he agrees to pay $100 at the end of each quarter for one year, how much money should he receive from the bank at the time of borrowing? Answer: He should receive $390.20.

## EXERCISE 13–3

**Reference: Section 13.3 A**

**A.** *Find the present value of the annuity in each of the following problems. Use the methods presented in Example 1, pages 383 and 384. Use Method A for Problems 1–4, and Method B for Problems 5–8.*

|  | Payment | Payment Interval | Term | Compound Interest Rate |
|---|---|---|---|---|
| **1.** | $2,000 | 1 month | 4 months | 6%, monthly |
| **2.** | 1,000 | 1 quarter | 9 months | 4%, quarterly |
| **3.** | 200 | 6 months | 1 year | 5%, semiannually |
| **4.** | 700 | 1 year | 2 years | 10%, annually |
| **5.** | 600 | 1 quarter | 1 year | 8%, quarterly |
| **6.** | 3,000 | 6 months | 1½ years | 6%, semiannually |

**B.** *Statement Problems:*

**7.** What is the present value of an annuity if the size of each payment is $2,000 payable at the end of each year for three years and the interest rate is 9% compounded annually?

**8.** Find the present value of an annuity if the size of each payment is $800 payable at the end of each month for four months at an interest rate of 12% compounded monthly.

# B. Computation by Formula (13–2)

Let $R$ = size of each regular payment (or periodic rent)
    $i$ = interest rate per conversion period
    $n$ = number of payments during the term of an annuity (It is also the number of payment intervals, or the number of conversion periods.)
    $A_n$ = the present value of an ordinary annuity

The formula[2] for the present value of an ordinary annuity is:

$$A_n = R \cdot \frac{1 - (1+i)^{-n}}{i} \qquad\qquad (13\text{–}2)$$

Formula (13–2) is obtained by using the methods employed in Example 1, pages 383 and 384. When formula (13–2) is used, the answer to Example 1 may be computed as follows:

> $R = \$100$ (per quarter), $i = 4\%/4 = 1\%$ (per quarter), and $n = 4$ (quarterly payments)

Substituting the values in formula (13–2):

$$A_n = A_4 = 100 \cdot \frac{1 - (1 + 1\%)^{-4}}{1\%} = 100 \cdot \frac{1 - 0.96098034}{.01}$$

$$= 100 \cdot \frac{0.03901966}{.01} = 100(3.901966) = \$390.1966, \text{ or } \$390.20$$

The value of $(1 + 1\%)^{-4}$ is found in Table 6. The answer here is the same as that obtained in Example 1.

For convenience, the value of $\dfrac{1 - (1+i)^{-n}}{i}$ is usually represented by the symbol $a_{\overline{n}|i}$ (which is read $a$ angle $n$ at $i$). The values of $a_{\overline{n}|i}$ for various interest

---

[2] *Proof—Formula (13–2), the present value of an annuity*

The following diagram shows that the present value of an annuity of $R$ payable at the end of each period for four periods at interest rate $i$ per period is $A_4$, and the amount of the annuity is $S_4$.

Here, $A_4 = R(1 + i)^{-4} + R(1 + i)^{-3} + R(1 + i)^{-2} + R(1 + i)^{-1}$.

Multiply both sides of the equation by $(1 + i)^4$:

$$A_4(1 + i)^4 = R + R(1 + i) + R(1 + i)^2 + R(1 + i)^3 = S_4$$

Extend this idea by letting $n$ = number of periods. Then,

$$A_n(1 + i)^n = S_n$$

$$A_n = S_n(1 + i)^{-n} = R \cdot \frac{(1 + i)^n - 1}{i} \cdot (1 + i)^{-n}$$

$$A_n = R \cdot \frac{1 - (1 + i)^{-n}}{i} = Ra_{\overline{n}|i}$$

The proof also indicates that:

1. The present value of an annuity is the sum of the present values of the periodic payments.
2. The present value of an annuity is the single principal of the amount of the annuity.

rates *(i)* and numbers of payments *(n)* are provided in Table 8. The unit value of each entry in the table is best represented by one dollar, although it may be represented by any other unit. Therefore, each entry in the table becomes the present value of an annuity in dollars when each payment is $1, or when $R = \$1$.

When Table 8 is employed, the computation of the present value of an annuity is simplified. In general, formula (13–2) is written in the following form:

$$A_n = Ra_{\overline{n}|i}$$                                        **(13–2)**, or

$$\left(\begin{array}{c}\text{Present value of an}\\ \text{ordinary annuity } A_n\end{array}\right) = \left(\begin{array}{c}\text{Size of each}\\ \text{payment } R\end{array}\right) \times \left(\begin{array}{c}\text{An entry in}\\ \text{Table 8}\end{array}\right)$$

(The entry is at the interest rate *i* per conversion period for *n* conversion periods or payments.)

Example 1 may now be computed in the following manner:

$$A_n = Ra_{\overline{n}|i} = 100a_{\overline{4}|1\%} = 100(3.90196555) = \$390.196555, \text{ or } \$390.20$$

**Example 2**    If a man wishes to receive $20 at the end of each month for three years from a bank which pays interest at 6% compounded monthly, how much must he deposit in the bank now?

The monthly payment by the bank is $20, or $R = \$20$; $i = 6\%/12 = \frac{1}{2}\%$ (per month), $n = 3 \times 12 = 36$ (monthly payments)

Substituting the above values in formula (13–2):

$$A_n = Ra_{\overline{n}|i} = 20a_{\overline{36}|1/2\%} = 20(32.871) = \$657.42$$

The present value of the annuity is $657.42. Thus, the man must deposit $657.42 in the bank now. The sum of the compound interest paid by the bank on the 36 payments is computed as follows:

Payments $= 20 \times 36 = \$720$
Compound interest $= 720 - 657.42 = \$62.58$

**Note:**      The multiplication $20a_{\overline{36}|1/2\%}$ may also be performed by using logarithms:

$$\begin{array}{ll}\log 20 & = 1.301\ 0300\ \text{(Table 2)}\\ (+) \log a_{\overline{36}|1/2\%} & = 1.516\ 8131\ \text{(Table 12)}\\ \hline \log A_n & = 2.817\ 8431\end{array}$$

Find the antilog by interpolation from Table 2. $A_n = \$657.42$.

**Example 3**    What is the cash value of a car that can be bought for $200 down and $82 a month for 30 months if money is worth 8% compounded monthly?

Since a down payment has been made, the first of the regular payments should be made at the end of the month following the date of purchase. Thus, this is an ordinary annuity problem.

$R = \$82$ (per month), $i = 8\%/12 = \frac{2}{3}\%$ (per month), $n = 30$ (months or payments)

Substituting the above values in formula (13–2):

$A_n = 82a_{\overline{30}|2/3\%} = 82(27.1088) = \$2,222.92$

The cash value of the car $= 200 + 2,222.92 = \$2,422.92$

**Example 4**     Find the present value of an annuity of $150 payable at the end of each year for 15 years if the interest rate is 5% compounded annually.

$R = \$150$ (per year), $i = 5\%$ (per year), $n = 15$ (yearly payments)

Substituting the values in formula (13–2):

$A_n = 150a_{\overline{15}|5\%} = 150(10.37966) = \$1,556.95$

**Note:**     The relationship of magnitude among the present value, the sum of actual payments, and the amount of an annuity may be expressed as follows:

Present value $<$ Actual payments $<$ Amount

Using the data given in Example 4, the above expression may be illustrated in the following manner:

Present value $= \$1,556.95$; Actual payments $= 150 \times 15 = \$2,250$;
Amount $= 150s_{\overline{15}|5\%} = 150(21.57856) = \$3,236.78$

$\$1,556.95 < \$2,250 < \$3,236.78$

## EXERCISE 13–4

**Reference: Section 13.3 B**

**A.** *Find the present value of the ordinary annuity in each of the following problems:*

| Payment (R) | Payment Interval | Term | Compound Interest Rate |
|---|---|---|---|
| **1.** $1,000 | 1 month | 2 years | 6%, monthly |
| **2.** 1,250 | 1 quarter | 10 years | 5%, quarterly |
| **3.** 880 | 6 months | $8\frac{1}{2}$ years | 7%, semiannually |
| **4.** 1,200 | 1 year | 30 years | 10%, annually |
| **5.** 800 | 1 quarter | 15 years, 6 months | 6%, quarterly |
| **6.** 400 | 1 month | 4 years, 3 months | 4%, monthly |
| **7.** 500 | 1 year | 20 years | $5\frac{1}{2}\%$, annually |
| **8.** 600 | 6 months | 12 years | 8%, semiannually |

**B.** *Statement Problems:*

**9.** What is the present value of an annuity if the size of each payment is $200 payable at the end of each quarter for eight years at an interest rate of 7% compounded quarterly?

**10.** A man wishes to withdraw $350 at the end of every six months for ten years. If the money earns interest at 5% compounded semiannually, how much must he deposit now?

11. Find the present value of an annuity of $70 payable at the end of each month for four and one-half years if the interest is at 5% compounded monthly.
12. Find the present value of an annuity of $95 payable at the end of each year for 15 years if money is worth $4\frac{1}{2}$% compounded annually.
13. K. G. Griffin purchased a refrigerator and made a down payment of $50. She agreed to pay $30 per month thereafter for one year. If the interest was at 7% compounded monthly, what was the cash price of the refrigerator?
14. Fred Johnson wants to buy a television set. Store A offered him a payment plan of $70 down and $50 per quarter thereafter for six payments. Store B offered him a payment plan of $80 down and $25 per quarter thereafter for 12 payments. Which store offered him the better plan? Why? Assume that the interest rate charged by both stores is 8% compounded quarterly.
15. A house sold for $1,000 cash and $60 per month for ten years. Find the equivalent cash price if interest was at 5% compounded monthly.
16. Clare Griffith borrowed some money from her employer and agreed to repay the loan by paying $150 at the end of every six months for three years. If money was worth 5% compounded semiannually, how much did she receive from her employer?

## 13.4 ADDITIONAL PROBLEMS IN COMPUTING AMOUNT AND PRESENT VALUE OF AN ANNUITY

## A. The Interest Rate ($i$) Is Not Given in the Tables

If an interest rate $(i)$ is not given in the tables, the values of $s_{\overline{n}|i}$ and $a_{\overline{n}|i}$ may be found by either of the following two methods: (a) the interpolation method, or (b) the use of logarithms.

The interpolation method was used in Chapter 11, page 335, to obtain an *approximate* entry from the compound amount table. However, if the method is used in interpolating an entry from the annuity tables, the answer is even less accurate than that obtained from the compound interest tables. Therefore, the use of logarithms is preferred in finding the values.

**Example 1**   Find (a) the amount and (b) the present value of an annuity of $200 payable at the end of each year for 20 years, if money is worth 5.2% compounded annually.

$R = $200$ (per year), $i = 5.2\%$ (per year), $n = 20$ (years)

**Method A**   *Interpolation*

(a) Finding the amount.

$$S_n = Rs_{\overline{n}|i} = 200s_{\overline{20}|5.2\%}$$

The following interpolation is made according to the values obtained from Table 7:

$$
\begin{array}{ccc}
& i & s_{\overline{20}|i} \\
& 5\tfrac{1}{2}\% = 5.5\% & 34.868318 \;(1) \\
& 5.2\% & x \qquad (2) \\
& 5.0\% & 33.065954 \;(3) \\
(2)-(3) & .2\% & x-33.065954 \;(4) \\
(1)-(3) & .5\% & 1.802364 \;(5)
\end{array}
$$

The values of $s_{\overline{20}|i}$ include six decimal places. The one extra place provides for safety in rounding to the five-place requirement.

Solve for $x$ from the proportion formed by the differences on lines (4) and (5).

$$
x-33.065954 = 1.802364\left(\frac{.2\%}{.5\%}\right) = 1.802364\left(\frac{2}{5}\right) = 0.720946
$$

$$
x = 33.065954 + 0.720946 = 33.786900, \text{ or } s_{\overline{20}|5.2\%} = 33.786900
$$

$$
S_n = 200(33.7869) = \$6{,}757.38
$$

(b) Finding the present value.

$$
A_n = Ra_{\overline{n}|i} = 200a_{\overline{20}|5.2\%}
$$

The following interpolation is made according to the values obtained from Table 8: (Write the larger numbers, which are in the column of values all known, on the top lines.)

$$
\begin{array}{ccc}
& i & a_{\overline{20}|i} \\
& 5\tfrac{1}{2}\% = 5.5\% & 11.950382 \;(1) \\
& 5.2\% & x \qquad (2) \\
& 5.0\% & 12.462210 \;(3) \\
(2)-(3) & .2\% & x-12.462210 \;(4) \\
(1)-(3) & .5\% & -.511828 \;(5)
\end{array}
$$

Solve for $x$ from the proportion formed by the differences on lines (4) and (5).

$$
x-12.462210 = (-.511828)(\tfrac{2}{5}) = -.2047312
$$

$$
x = 12.462210 - .2047312 = 12.2574788, \text{ or } a_{\overline{20}|5.2\%} = 12.2574788
$$

$$
A_n = 200(12.25748) = \$2{,}451.50
$$

**★Method B**   *Using Logarithms*

(a) Finding the amount.

$$
S_n = R \cdot \frac{(1+i)^n - 1}{i}
$$

$$
= 200 \cdot \frac{(1+5.2\%)^{20} - 1}{5.2\%}
$$

Compute $(1+5.2\%)^{20}$ by logarithms:

$$
\log (1+5.2\%)^{20} = 20 \cdot \log 1.052
$$
$$
= 20(0.0220157) = 0.440314
$$

Find the antilog (to six significant digits).

Thus, $(1 + 5.2\%)^{20} = 2.75622$

$$S_n = 200 \cdot \frac{2.75622 - 1}{.052} = 200(33.77346) = \$6,754.69$$

(b) Finding the present value.

$$A_n = R \cdot \frac{1 - (1 + i)^{-n}}{i}$$

$$= 200 \cdot \frac{1 - (1 + 5.2\%)^{-20}}{5.2\%}$$

Compute $(1 + 5.2\%)^{-20}$ by logarithms:

$$\log (1 + 5.2\%)^{-20} = (-20) \log 1.052 = (-20)(0.0220157)$$
$$= -0.440314 = 9.559686 - 10$$

Find the antilog (to six significant digits).

Thus, $(1 + 5.2\%)^{-20} = 0.362816$

$$A_n = 200 \cdot \frac{1 - 0.362816}{.052} = 200(12.25354) = \$2,450.71$$

*Note:*  The values of $(1 + 5.2\%)^{20}$ and $(1 + 5.2\%)^{-20}$ may also be obtained by using the binomial theorem as discussed in Chapter 3, page 84. Also, see Problems 11 and 12, Exercise 12–1, for the accuracy of the different methods in finding the value of $(1 + i)^n$.

# B. The Number of Payments (*n*) Is Greater Than the Highest Number in the Tables

If the number of payments *(n)* is greater than the highest number in the tables, the values of $s_{\overline{n}|i}$ and $a_{\overline{n}|i}$ may be found as explained below.

**Example 2**  What is the amount of an annuity of $100 payable at the end of each month for 25 years if money is worth 6% compounded monthly?

$R = \$100$ (per month), $i = 6\%/12 = \frac{1}{2}\%$ (per month), $n = 25 \times 12 = 300$ (monthly payments). The value of *n* is greater than the highest number given for the interest rate $\frac{1}{2}\%$ in both Tables 5 and 7. In such cases, either of two methods may be used to solve the problem:

**Method A**  Use formulas $S_n = Rs_{\overline{n}|i}$ and $S = P(1 + i)^n$

In this method the annuity is divided into two equal parts of 150 payments each. The total amount of the first 150 payments on the 150th payment date is computed as follows:

$S_n = S_{150} = Rs_{\overline{150}|1/2\%} = 100(222.6095) = 22,260.95$                    (Table 7)

The amount of the partial annuity is further accumulated to the end of the term of the annuity by using the compound amount formula for 150 periods as shown below:

$$S = 22,260.95(1 + \tfrac{1}{2}\%)^{150} = 22,260.95(2.1130475) = \$47,038.44$$

The amount of the second 150 payments (151st to 300th payment inclusive) at the end of the term of the annuity is also $22,260.95. The total amount of the annuity is:

$$47,038.44 + 22,260.95 = \$69,299.39$$

Method A is diagrammed as follows:

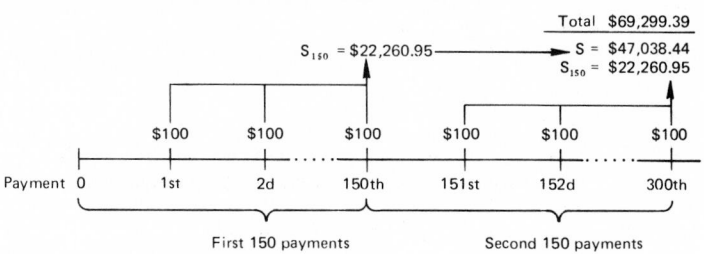

**★Method B**    Use formula $S_n = R \cdot \dfrac{(1 + i)^n - 1}{i}$

$n = 300$, the total number of monthly payments

$$S_n = S_{300} = 100 \cdot \frac{(1 + \tfrac{1}{2}\%)^{300} - 1}{\tfrac{1}{2}\%}$$

$$= 100 \cdot \frac{(1 + \tfrac{1}{2}\%)^{150}(1 + \tfrac{1}{2}\%)^{150} - 1}{\tfrac{1}{2}\%}$$

$$= 100 \cdot \frac{(2.1130475)(2.1130475) - 1}{.005}$$

$$= 100 \cdot \frac{4.4649697 - 1}{.005}$$

$$= \$69,299.39$$

(The value of $(1 + \tfrac{1}{2}\%)^{150}$ is found in Table 5.)

**Note:**    The value of $(1 + \tfrac{1}{2}\%)^{300}$ may also be obtained by using logarithms as follows:

$$\log (1 + \tfrac{1}{2}\%)^{300} = 300(\log 1.005) = 300(.0021661) = .64983$$

Thus, $(1 + \tfrac{1}{2}\%)^{300} = 4.46509$               (Table 3)

**Example 3**    What is the present value of an annuity of $100 payable at the end of each month for 25 years if money is worth 6% compounded monthly?

$R = \$100$ (per month), $i = 6\%/12 = \tfrac{1}{2}\%$ (per month), $n = 25 \times 12 = 300$ (monthly payments).

The value of $n$ is greater than the highest number given for an interest rate of $\frac{1}{2}\%$ in both Tables 6 and 8. In such cases, either of two methods may be used to solve the problem:

**Method A**  Use formulas $A_n = Ra_{\overline{n}|i}$ and $P = S(1 + i)^{-n}$

In this method the annuity is divided into two equal parts of 150 payments each. The present value of the first 150 payments is computed as follows:

$A_{150} = Ra_{\overline{150}|1/2\%} = 100(105.34998) = \$10,534.998$, or $\$10,535$

The present value of the second 150 payments (151st to 300th payment inclusive) is computed by using two steps:

**Step (1)**  Find the value of the 150 payments at the beginning of the 151st payment interval. The value should also be $\$10,535$.

**Step (2)**  Discount the value found in Step (1) at compound interest for 150 periods:

$P = 10,535(1 + \frac{1}{2}\%)^{-150} = 10,535(0.4732501) = \$4,985.69$

The total present value of the annuity is:

$10,535 + 4,985.69 = \$15,520.69$

Method A is diagrammed as follows:

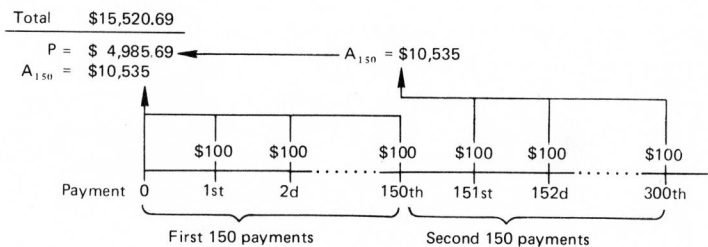

**★Method B**  Use formula $A_n = R \cdot \dfrac{1 - (1 + i)^{-n}}{i}$

$n = 300$, the total number of monthly payments

$$A_n = A_{300} = 100 \cdot \frac{1 - (1 + \frac{1}{2}\%)^{-300}}{\frac{1}{2}\%}$$

$$= 100 \cdot \frac{1 - (1 + \frac{1}{2}\%)^{-150}(1 + \frac{1}{2}\%)^{-150}}{\frac{1}{2}\%}$$

$$= 100 \cdot \frac{1 - (0.47325012)(0.47325012)}{.005}$$

$$= 100 \cdot \frac{1 - 0.22396568}{.005} = \frac{77.603432}{.005} = \$15,520.69$$

(The value of $(1 + \frac{1}{2}\%)^{-150}$ is found in Table 6.)

**Note:**    The value of $(1 + \frac{1}{2}\%)^{-300}$ may also be obtained by using logarithms as follows:

$$\log (1 + \tfrac{1}{2}\%)^{-300} = (-300) \log 1.005 = (-300)(.0021661) = -.64983$$
$$= 9.35017 - 10 \qquad\qquad\text{(Table 3)}$$

Thus, $(1 + \frac{1}{2}\%)^{-300} = 0.22396$

## EXERCISE 13-5

### Reference: Section 13.4

*Statement Problems:*

1. What are the amount and the present value of an annuity of $300 payable at the end of each year for five years if money is worth 4.3% compounded annually?
2. What are the amount and the present value of an annuity if the size of each payment is $160 payable at the end of every six months for ten years at an interest rate of 6.8% compounded semiannually?
3. Find the amount and the present value of an annuity of $200 payable at the end of each quarter for eight years if the interest rate is 6.4% compounded quarterly.
4. Find the amount and the present value of an annuity of $250 payable at the end of each month for three years if money is worth 7.2% compounded monthly.
5. What is the amount of an annuity of $500 payable at the end of each month for 30 years if money is worth 7% compounded monthly?
6. Find the amount of an annuity of $300 payable at the end of each quarter for 35 years if interest is 4% compounded quarterly.
7. What is the present value of the annuity in Problem 5?
8. Find the present value of the annuity in Problem 6.
9. What are the amount and the present value of an annuity of $200 payable at the end of every six months for 60 years if the interest rate is 5% compounded semiannually?
10. Find the amount and the present value of an annuity of $100 payable at the end of each year for 120 years if the interest rate is 6% compounded annually.

## 13.5 FINDING THE SIZE OF EACH PERIODIC PAYMENT ( *R* )

Frequently the size of each periodic payment must be determined when the amount or the present value of an annuity is known. In this type of problem the interest rate and the term of the annuity are usually given.

## A. The Present Value Is Known

To find the size of each periodic payment when the present value is known, use the formula $A_n = Ra_{\overline{n}|i}$ in either of the following two forms:

$$R = \frac{A_n}{a_{\overline{n}|i}} \text{ (Use Table 8).} \quad \text{Or,} \quad R = A_n \left( \frac{1}{a_{\overline{n}|i}} \right) \text{ (Use Table 9)}$$

Certain values of $\dfrac{1}{a_{\overline{n}|i}}$ are tabulated in Table 9. Each value in the table is the size of the payment when the present value of an annuity is $1.

**Example 1**    The present value of an annuity for ten years is $10,000. Find the size of the quarterly payment if the interest rate is 8% compounded quarterly.

$A_n = \$10,000$, $i = 8\%/4 = 2\%$ (per quarter), $n = 10 \times 4 = 40$ (quarterly payments)

Substituting the values in the formula above:

$$R = 10,000 \left( \frac{1}{a_{\overline{40}|2\%}} \right) = 10,000(0.0365558)$$

$$= \$365.558, \text{ or } \$365.56 \qquad\qquad\qquad \text{(Table 9)}$$

Or, using Table 8, the problem can be solved as follows:

$$R = \frac{10,000}{a_{\overline{40}|2\%}} = \frac{10,000}{27.35548} = \$365.56$$

**Note:**    Since the operations in division are more complicated than those in multiplication, the use of Table 9 is preferred in finding the size of each periodic payment.

**Example 2**    A man purchased a house for $96,000. He made a down payment of $16,000 and agreed to make equal payments at the end of each month for 20 years. If the interest is 6% compounded monthly, what is the size of the monthly payment?

$A_n = 96,000 - 16,000 = \$80,000$, $i = 6\%/12 = \frac{1}{2}\%$ (per month), $n = 20 \times 12 = 240$ (monthly payments)

Substituting the values in the above formula:

$$R = 80,000 \left( \frac{1}{a_{\overline{240}|1/2\%}} \right) = 80,000(0.0071643) = \$573.144, \text{ or } \$573.15$$

**Note:**    1. Finance companies usually round such a figure to the next higher value, $573.15.

2. The multiplication $80,000 \left( \dfrac{1}{a_{\overline{240}|1/2\%}} \right)$ may also be performed by using logarithms:

$$\log 80{,}000 = 4.903\ 0900 \qquad \text{(Table 2)}$$

$$(+) \log \frac{1}{a_{\overline{240}|1/2\%}} = 7.855\ 1744 - 10\ \text{(Table 12)}$$

$$\log R = 12.758\ 2644 - 10$$
$$= 2.758\ 2644$$

Find the antilog by interpolation from Table 2. $R = \$573.145$ or rounded to $\$573.15$.

## B. The Amount Is Known

To find the size of each periodic payment when the amount is known, use the formula $S_n = Rs_{\overline{n}|i}$ in either of the following two forms:

$$R = \frac{S_n}{s_{\overline{n}|i}} \ \text{(Use Table 7). Or, } R = S_n \cdot \frac{1}{s_{\overline{n}|i}} = S_n \left( \frac{1}{a_{\overline{n}|i}} - i \right) \text{(Use Table 9)}[3]$$

**Example 3**    The amount of an annuity for ten years is $10,000. Find the size of the quarterly payment if the interest rate is 8% compounded quarterly.

$S_n = \$10{,}000$, $i = 8\%/4 = 2\%$ (per quarter), $n = 10 \times 4 = 40$ (quarterly payments)

Substituting the values in the above formula and using Table 9,

$$R = 10{,}000 \left( \frac{1}{a_{\overline{40}|2\%}} - 2\% \right) = 10{,}000(0.0365558 - .02)$$

$$= 10{,}000(0.0165558) = \$165.558, \text{ or } \$165.56$$

Or, if Table 7 is used:

$$R = \frac{10{,}000}{s_{\overline{40}|2\%}} = \frac{10{,}000}{60.40198} = \$165.56$$

**Note:**    It is more convenient to use Table 9 than Table 7 in finding the value of $R$ since division may be avoided when the former table is used.

---

[3] *Proof—for* $\dfrac{1}{a_{\overline{n}|i}} - i = \dfrac{1}{s_{\overline{n}|i}}$

Since $a_{\overline{n}|i} = \dfrac{1 - (1+i)^{-n}}{i}$, the reciprocals of both sides of the equation must also be equal.

Then,

$$\frac{1}{a_{\overline{n}|i}} = \frac{i}{1-(1+i)^{-n}}$$

Thus,

$$\frac{1}{a_{\overline{n}|i}} - i = \frac{i}{1-(1+i)^{-n}} - i = \frac{i - i[1-(1+i)^{-n}]}{1-(1+i)^{-n}} = \frac{i(1+i)^{-n}}{1-(1+i)^{-n}}$$

$$= \frac{i(1+i)^{-n}}{1-(1+i)^{-n}} \cdot \frac{(1+i)^{n}}{(1+i)^{n}} = \frac{i}{(1+i)^{n}-1} = \frac{1}{\dfrac{(1+i)^{n}-1}{i}} = \frac{1}{s_{\overline{n}|i}}$$

**Example 4**   A man desires to have a $12,000 fund at the end of 20 years. If his savings can be invested at 6% compounded monthly, how much must he invest at the end of each month for 20 years?

$S_n = 12{,}000$, $i = 6\%/12 = \frac{1}{2}\%$ (per month), $n = 20 \times 12 = 240$ (months)

Substituting the values in the above formula and using Table 9,

$$R = 12{,}000\left(\frac{1}{a_{\overline{240}|1/2\%}} - \tfrac{1}{2}\%\right) = 12{,}000(.0071643 - .005)$$

$$= 12{,}000(.0021643) = \$25.9716, \text{ or } \$25.97 \text{ (per month)}$$

## EXERCISE 13–6

### Reference: Section 13.5

**A.** *Find the size of the payment in each of the following ordinary annuities:*

| | Amount (Sₙ) | Present Value (Aₙ) | Payment Interval | Term | Compound Interest Rate |
|---|---|---|---|---|---|
| **1.** | $ 3,000 | | 1 year | 5 years | 6%, annually |
| **2.** | | $ 4,000 | 6 months | 8 years | 8%, semiannually |
| **3.** | | 50,000 | 1 month | 7 years, 1 month | 6%, monthly |
| **4.** | 20,000 | | 1 quarter | 10 years, 6 months | 7%, quarterly |
| **5.** | | 6,000 | 1 quarter | 3 years | 4%, quarterly |
| **6.** | 10,000 | | 1 month | 4 years, 3 months | 5%, monthly |
| **7.** | 500 | | 6 months | 2½ years | 12%, semiannually |
| **8.** | | 800 | 1 year | 6 years | 4½%, annually |

**B.** *Statement Problems:*

**9.** The amount of an annuity for nine years is $5,000. What is the size of the annual payment if the interest rate is 5% compounded annually?

**10.** The present value of an annuity for 12 years is $4,200. Find the size of the semiannual payment if the interest rate is 7% compounded semiannually.

**11.** Bill Sanders bought a truck for $2,800. He made a down payment of $500 and agreed to pay the balance in 24 equal monthly payments. If the interest charged was 8% compounded monthly, how much should Sanders pay each month?

**12.** Doris Hicks bought a machine for $560. She paid $50 down and agreed to pay the balance plus interest at 6% compounded quarterly in equal quarterly payments for three years. What is the quarterly payment?

**13.** A debt of $2,500 was repaid in ten equal quarterly payments. If the rate of interest was 7% compounded quarterly, what was the size of each payment?

14. A man wishes to have a $5,000 fund at the end of five years. If his money can be invested at 4% compounded monthly, how much must he invest at the end of each month during the period?

15. A store manager plans to exchange his old car at the end of four years for a newer one worth $4,000. The trade-in value of the old car at that time is estimated to be $400. If money can be invested at 6% compounded quarterly, how much must the manager invest at the end of each quarter in order to make the exchange?

16. Ed Merrick wishes to provide a college education fund for his daughter who is now eight years old. If the fund can earn 6% interest compounded semiannually and is to be used when she reaches 18 years of age, what must be the size of each semiannual deposit in order to provide a fund of $10,000? Assume that Merrick wishes to make the first deposit six months from now and the last deposit on his daughter's eighteenth birthday.

## 13.6 FINDING THE INTEREST RATE PER CONVERSION PERIOD ( $i$ ) AND THE NOMINAL (ANNUAL) INTEREST RATE

Sometimes an investor or borrower desires to know the interest rate of an annuity. In this type of problem, the size of each periodic payment, the term, and the amount or the present value of the annuity are usually given.

## A. The Amount Is Known

To find the interest rate when the amount is known, use the formula $S_n = Rs_{\overline{n}|i}$.

**Example 1**   At what nominal rate compounded quarterly will an annuity of $150 payable at the end of each quarter amount to $6,600 in eight years?

$S_n = \$6,600$, $R = \$150$ (per quarter), $n = 8 \times 4 = 32$ (quarterly payments), $i = ?$ (per quarter)

Substituting the values in the formula above:

$$6{,}600 = 150s_{\overline{32}|i}, \quad s_{\overline{32}|i} = \frac{6{,}600}{150} = 44$$

Follow the line for $n = 32$ in Table 7 to find the value of 44 or the two values closest to 44. It is found that the first value greater than 44 is 44.22702961, which is located in the 2% column, and the first value smaller than 44 is 43.30793563, which is located in the $1\frac{7}{8}$% column.

Therefore, the desired value of $i$ is greater than $1\frac{7}{8}\%$ and is smaller than 2%, or

$$1\frac{7}{8}\% < i < 2\%$$

When a more accurate value of $i$ is needed, the interpolation method may be employed as follows:

| | $i$ | $s_{\overline{32}|i}$ | |
|---|---|---|---|
| | 2% | 44.2270 | (1) |
| | $x$ | 44.0000 | (2) |
| | $1\frac{7}{8}\%$ | 43.3079 | (3) |
| (2) − (3) | $x - 1\frac{7}{8}\%$ | .6921 | (4) |
| (1) − (3) | $\frac{1}{8}\%$ | .9191 | (5) |

Solve for $x$ from the proportion formed by the differences on lines (4) and (5).

$$x - 1\frac{7}{8}\% = \frac{1}{8}\%\left(\frac{.6921}{.9191}\right) = \frac{1}{800}\cdot\frac{6921}{9191} = .00094$$

$$x = 1\frac{7}{8}\% + .00094 = .01875 + .00094 = .01969$$

The desired value of $i$ is .01969, or 1.969% per quarter.

The nominal interest rate = $.01969 \times 4 = .07876$, or 7.88%.

**Example 2**    T. R. Ford signed a ten-month non-interest-bearing note for $5,000. He was offered the privilege of discharging the obligation by making 10 equal monthly payments of $488 payable at the end of each month. If he can invest his money at $5\frac{1}{2}\%$ compounded monthly, should he accept the offer?

$S_n$ = $5,000, $R$ = $488 (per month), $n$ = 10 (monthly payments), $i$ = ?

Substituting the values in the formula:

$$5,000 = 488 s_{\overline{10}|i}$$

$$s_{\overline{10}|i} = \frac{5,000}{488} = 10.2459$$

Follow the line for $n$ = 10 in Table 7 to find the value of 10.2459 or the two values closest to it. The first value greater than 10.2459 is 10.2473, which is located in the $\frac{13}{24}\%$ column, and the first value smaller than 10.2459 is 10.2280, which is located in the $\frac{1}{2}\%$ column. Thus, the desired value of $i$ is between $\frac{1}{2}\%$ and $\frac{13}{24}\%$, or

$$\frac{1}{2}\% < i < \frac{13}{24}\%$$

The nominal rate = $i \times 12$, which must be greater than ($\frac{1}{2}\% \times 12$) or 6%, but smaller than ($\frac{13}{24}\% \times 12$) or $6\frac{1}{2}\%$. Since Ford can invest his money at only $5\frac{1}{2}\%$ compounded monthly, he should accept the offer to discharge his obligation by making the monthly payment. In this type of problem, use of the interpolation method is not required.

# B. The Present Value Is Known

To find the interest rate when the present value is known, use the formula $A_n = Ra_{\overline{n}|i}$

**Example 3**    The present value of an annuity of $200 payable at the end of every six months for 10 years is $3,000. What is the nominal rate compounded semiannually?

$A_n = \$3,000$, $R = \$200$ (per six months), $n = 10 \times 2 = 20$ (semiannual periods or payments), $i = ?$ (per semiannual period)

Substituting the values in the above formula:

$$3,000 = 200a_{\overline{20}|i}, \qquad a_{\overline{20}|i} = \frac{3,000}{200} = 15$$

Follow the line for $n = 20$ in Table 8 to find the value of 15 or the two values closest to it. The first value greater than 15 is 15.22725213, which is located in the $2\frac{3}{4}\%$ column, and the first value smaller than 15 is 14.87747486, which is located in the 3% column. Thus, the desired value of $i$ is

$$2\frac{3}{4}\% < i < 3\%$$

When a more accurate value of $i$ is needed, the interpolation method may be employed as follows: (Write the larger numbers, which are in the column of values all known, on the top lines.)

|  | $i$ | $a_{\overline{20}|i}$ |  |
|---|---|---|---|
|  | $2\frac{3}{4}\%$ | 15.2273 | (1) |
|  | $x$ | 15.0000 | (2) |
|  | $3\%$ | 14.8775 | (3) |
| $(2)-(3)$ | $x-3\%$ | .1225 | (4) |
| $(1)-(3)$ | $-\frac{1}{4}\%$ | .3498 | (5) |

The terms $\dfrac{x-3\%}{-\frac{1}{4}\%} = \dfrac{.1225}{.3498}$

Solve for $x$ from the proportion formed by the differences on lines (4) and (5).

$$x - 3\% = (-\tfrac{1}{4}\%)\left(\frac{.1225}{.3498}\right) = -\left(\frac{1}{400}\right)\left(\frac{1225}{3498}\right) = -.0009$$

$$x = 3\% - .0009 = .03 - .0009 = .0291$$

The desired value of $i$ is .0291, or 2.91% per semiannual period. The nominal interest rate $= .0291 \times 2 = .0582$, or 5.82%.

**Example 4**    T. R. Rosen bought a car and paid $400 down plus $120 at the end of each month for three years. The cash price of the car was $4,012.90. What rate of interest did he pay?

$A_n = 4,012.90 - 400 = \$3,612.90$, $R = \$120$ (per month),
$n = 3 \times 12 = 36$ (payments or months), $i = ?$ (per month)

Substituting the values in the formula:

$$3{,}612.90 = 120a_{\overline{36}|i}$$

$$a_{\overline{36}|i} = \frac{3{,}612.90}{120} = 30.1075$$

Follow the line for $n = 36$ in Table 8 to find the value of 30.1075 or the two values closest to it. Since 30.1075 appears in the 1% column, no interpolation is needed. The desired value of $i$ is 1%. The nominal interest rate is

$$i \times 12 = 1\% \times 12 = 12\%$$

## EXERCISE 13–7

### Reference: Section 13.6

**A.** *Find the interest rate per conversion period (i) and the nominal interest rate in each of the following problems. (Omit interpolation for Problems 1–6, use the interpolation method to find the answers for Problems 7–14.)*

| | Amount $(S_n)$ | Present Value $(A_n)$ | Payment | Term | Interest Conversion Period |
|---|---|---|---|---|---|
| 1. | $2,680 | | $200 annually | 10 years | 1 year |
| 2. | | $6,850 | 500 semiannually | 10 years | 6 months |
| 3. | | 8,502 | 260 monthly | 3 years | 1 month |
| 4. | 926 | | 50 quarterly | 4 years | 1 quarter |
| 5. | | 6,642 | 270 quarterly | 7 years | 1 quarter |
| 6. | 2,520 | | 100 monthly | 2 years | 1 month |
| 7. | 700 | | 65 semiannually | 5 years | 6 months |
| 8. | | 530 | 80 annually | 8 years | 1 year |

*do not interpolate*

**B.** *Statement Problems:*

9. At what nominal interest rate compounded semiannually will an annuity of $220 payable at the end of every six months amount to $2,530 in five years?

10. A man deposited $80 each month in a financial association. He received $1,000 immediately after the 12th deposit was made. If the nominal interest rate was compounded monthly, what was the rate?

11. The present value of an annuity of $50 payable at the end of each quarter for $9\frac{1}{2}$ years is $1,380. What is the nominal interest rate compounded quarterly?

12. Mary borrowed $600 from her employer and agreed to repay it in 10 equal monthly payments of $65. The first payment is to be made at the end of one month after the borrowing. The monthly payment plan results in the interest rate being compounded monthly. What is the nominal interest rate?

13. Janet Davis signed a six-year non-interest-bearing note for $520. She is allowed to discharge the debt by making six equal annual payments of $75 payable at the end of each year. If she can invest her money at 5% compounded annually, should she invest the money instead of paying the debt? Why?

14. The cash price of a washing machine is $370. If it can be bought by paying $25 down and $20 at the end of each month for $1\frac{1}{2}$ years, what is the nominal interest rate compounded monthly?

## 13.7 FINDING THE TERM OF AN ANNUITY ($n$)

Before the term of an annuity can be found, the size of the periodic payment, the interest rate per conversion period, and the amount or the present value of the annuity must be given.

## A. The Amount Is Known

To find the term of an annuity when the amount is known, use the formula $S_n = Rs_{\overline{n}|i}$.

**Example 1**     If $30 is deposited at the end of each month, how many months will be required for the deposits to amount to $1,220, if the interest rate is 6% compounded monthly?

$S_n = \$1,220$, $R = \$30$ (per month), $i = 6\%/12 = \frac{1}{2}\%$ (per month), $n = ?$ (monthly payments)

Substituting the values in the above formula:

$$1,220 = 30s_{\overline{n}|1/2\%}, \qquad s_{\overline{n}|1/2\%} = \frac{1,220}{30} = 40.6667$$

In the $\frac{1}{2}\%$ column of Table 7, find the two values closest to 40.6667. The findings are as follows:

When $n = 37$, the entry $= 40.53278549$.

When $n = 38$, the entry $= 41.73544942$.

Since 40.6667 is between the two entries above, the desired value of $n$ is greater than 37 but smaller than 38. Thus, the amount will be less than $1,220 immediately after the 37th deposit is made, but will be larger than $1,220 after the 38th deposit. This statement is supported by the following computation:

$$S_n = 30s_{\overline{37}|1/2\%} = 30(40.5328) = \$1,215.98$$

$$S_n = 30s_{\overline{38}|1/2\%} = 30(41.7354) = \$1,252.06$$

Thus, in order to provide the amount of $1,220, the 38th deposit is required. However, the size of the last deposit is less than the regular deposit of $30. The answer to this problem is therefore 38 deposits or 38 months, which is three years and two months. The interpolation method is not used in the present case, since in practice, payments of an annuity are made at equal payment intervals.

# B. The Present Value Is Known

To find the term of an annuity when the present value is known, use the formula $A_n = Ra_{\overline{n}|i}$.

**Example 2** A man borrows $4,000 and agrees to repay it by paying $200 at the end of each quarter. If the interest charged is 8% compounded quarterly, how long will he have to pay?

$A_n = \$4,000$, $R = \$200$ (per quarter), $i = 8\%/4 = 2\%$ (per quarter), $n = ?$ (quarters or payments)

Substituting the values in the above formula:

$$4,000 = 200a_{\overline{n}|2\%}, \qquad a_{\overline{n}|2\%} = \frac{4,000}{200} = 20$$

In the 2% column of Table 8, find the two values closest to 20. The findings are as follows:

When $n = 25$, the entry $= 19.52345647$.
When $n = 26$, the entry $= 20.12104376$.

Since 20 is between the two entries above, the desired value of $n$ is greater than 25 but smaller than 26. In other words, as computed below, the present value of 25 payments is smaller than $4,000, and the present value of 26 payments is larger than $4,000.

$A_{25} = 200a_{\overline{25}|2\%} = 200(19.52346) = \$3,904.69$
$A_{26} = 200a_{\overline{26}|2\%} = 200(20.12104) = \$4,024.21$

Thus, in order to repay $4,000 (the present value of the annuity), the 26th payment is required. However, the last payment will be less than the regular $200 payment (see Note 1 below). The answer to this problem is therefore 26 payments or 26 quarters, which are equal to six years and six months. Use of the interpolation method is unnecessary in problems such as this.

**Note:** 1. The exact size of the final payment is $159.49 in Example 2. (See Problem 1, page 451.) The method of finding the final payment and the use of the fractional part of $n$ value are discussed in Chapter 15, page 451.
2. In each of the two examples above, the greater value of $n$ (38 in Example 1 and 26 in Example 2) is used as the answer to the problem.

This practice should be followed in solving the problems in the following exercises in the text.

## EXERCISE 13–8

**Reference: Section 13.7**

**A.** *Find the term in each of the following ordinary annuities:*

| | Amount (S_n) | Present Value (A_n) | Payment | Compound Interest Rate |
|---|---|---|---|---|
| 1. | $2,500 | | $ 200 annually | $5\frac{1}{2}\%$, annually |
| 2. | | $ 3,879 | 450 semiannually | 4%, semiannually |
| 3. | | 6,000 | 300 monthly | 6%, monthly |
| 4. | 936 | | 60 quarterly | 7%, quarterly |
| 5. | | 4,092 | 120 quarterly | 5%, quarterly |
| 6. | 1,025 | | 50 monthly | 4%, monthly |
| 7. | 5,520 | | 300 semiannually | 7%, semiannually |
| 8. | | 18,400 | 2,000 annually | $8\frac{1}{2}\%$, annually |

**B.** *Statement Problems:*

9. If $150 was deposited at the end of every six months, how much time was required for the deposits to amount to $5,800 if the interest rate was 3% compounded semiannually?

10. The price of a small house was $10,000. The buyer made a down payment of $1,000 and agreed to pay $70 at the end of each month. If money was worth 5% compounded monthly, how long did it take the buyer to pay the balance and the interest?

11. A man borrowed $7,500 and agreed to repay it by paying $400 at the end of each year. If the interest rate was 4% compounded annually, how many payments was he required to make?

12. On January 1, 1980, Norma decided to deposit $250 in a savings account at the end of each quarter, with the first deposit to be made on April 1. The interest rate is 6% compounded quarterly. When will $3,800 be on deposit in Norma's account?

## 13.8 SUMMARY OF ORDINARY ANNUITY FORMULAS

| Application | Formula | Formula Number | Reference Page |
|---|---|---|---|
| Finding the amount | $S_n = R \cdot \dfrac{(1+i)^n - 1}{i} = Rs_{\overline{n}|i}$ | (13–1) | 381 |
| Finding the present value | $A_n = R \cdot \dfrac{1-(1+i)^{-n}}{i} = Ra_{\overline{n}|i}$ | (13–2) | 386 and 387 |

## EXERCISE 13–9

**Review of Chapter 13**

1. What is the amount of an annuity if the payment is $30 payable at the end of every six months for 20 years at 9% compounded semiannually?

2. Find the amount of an annuity of $75 payable at the end of each month for five years if the interest rate is 5% compounded monthly.

3. (a) If $40 is deposited at the end of each quarter for 10 years in a bank that pays 10% interest compounded quarterly, what will be the final value at the end of 10 years? (b) What is the total interest at the end of 12 years?

4. (a) If $90 is deposited at the end of each year for six years in a fund that earns 6% interest compounded annually, what will be the value of the fund at the end of nine years? (b) What is the total interest earned?

5. What is the present value of an annuity if the payment is $65 payable at the end of each month for eight years and the interest rate is 6% compounded monthly?

6. If Jerome Wilson wishes to receive $80 at the end of each quarter for seven years from a financial company that pays 4% interest compounded quarterly, how much must he deposit in the company now?

7. What was the cash price of a house bought for $750 down and $60 a month for 15 years, if the interest rate was 5% compounded monthly?

8. Find the present value of an annuity of $300 payable at the end of every six months for 30 years if the interest rate is $4\frac{1}{2}$% compounded semiannually.

9. What are the amount and the present value of an annuity of $25 payable at the end of each month for four years if the interest rate is 6% compounded monthly?

10. Find the amount and the present value of an annuity that will pay $40 each quarter for 35 quarters with the first payment to be made three months from now. Assume that the interest rate is 5% compounded quarterly.

11. What are the amount and the present value of an annuity of $50 payable at the end of each quarter for 20 years if money is worth $6\frac{1}{4}$% compounded quarterly?

12. Find the amount and the present value of an annuity of $150 payable at the end of every six months for five years if interest is $5\frac{1}{4}$% compounded semiannually.

13. What are the amount and the present value of an annuity of $40 payable at the end of each month for 30 years if the interest rate is 5% compounded monthly?

14. Find the amount and the present value of an annuity of $100 payable at the end of each quarter for 40 years if the interest rate is 6% compounded quarterly.

15. The present value of an annuity payable semiannually for 15 years is $7,500. What is the size of the semiannual payment if the interest rate is 4% compounded semiannually?

16. The price of a small building was $8,000. The buyer made a down payment of $3,000. The balance was to be paid in monthly installments for eight years. If the interest rate charged was 6% compounded monthly, how much did the buyer pay each month?

17. The amount of an annuity payable quarterly for 12 years is $8,500. What is the size of the quarterly payment if the interest rate is 5% compounded quarterly?

18. Shirley Roth wishes to have $4,000 at the end of five years. If her savings can be invested at 4% compounded monthly, how much must she save at the end of each month for five years?

19. At what nominal interest rate compounded monthly will an annuity of $120 payable at the end of each month amount to $10,000 in six years?

20. At what nominal interest rate compounded quarterly will an annuity of $70 payable at the end of each quarter amount to $8,000 in 25 years?

21. Judy Reese figures that she will have $2,790.80 in her savings account at the end of five years. She deposits $40 one month from now and $40 thereafter at the end of each month. At what nominal interest rate compounded monthly has she figured the interest?

22. Steven Kyle plans to invest $100 each month with the first investment to be made one month from now. He expects $3,993.01 at the end of three years. What must be the nominal interest rate compounded monthly?

23. At what nominal interest rate compounded semiannually will an annuity of $500 payable at the end of every six months for $6\frac{1}{2}$ years have a present value of $5,500?

24. The present value of an annuity of $350 payable at the end of each quarter for six years is $6,500. What is the nominal interest rate compounded quarterly?

25. Robert Oaks bought a used car for $300 down with monthly payments of $50 for 20 months. The cash price was $1,225.40. What was the nominal interest rate charged?

26. Jane Allen bought a color television set. The cash price was $423.32. Under the terms of her installment purchase, she made 24 monthly payments of $20 each, with the first payment beginning on the date of purchase. What was the nominal interest rate charged?

27. If $50 is deposited at the end of each quarter, how many quarterly deposits will be needed for the deposits to amount to $1,000 if the interest rate is 5% compounded quarterly?

28. Johnson plans to invest $150 each month starting one month from now. He wishes to have at least $4,500 as the final value. If he can earn 6% interest compounded monthly on his investment, how many monthly deposits are required for the final value?

29. A company is considering the purchase of a new machine that will increase operating efficiency and thus save $2,000 each year in labor costs. It is estimated that the machine will be used for ten years and it can then be

sold for $1,000. If money is worth 6%, how much can the company afford to pay for this machine?

**30.** A piece of land is available at a price of $5,000. Company G is considering its purchase for future plant expansion. If the land will not be needed for 20 years and the annual taxes will be 2% of the purchase price, what must the prospective price of the land be in 20 years to make it worthwhile for the company to buy the land now? Assume that money is worth 6%.

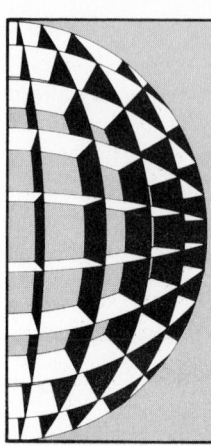

# Chapter 14

# Other Annuities Certain

## 14.1 ANNUITY DUE

An *annuity due* is an annuity for which the periodic payments are made at the *beginning* of each payment interval. The term of an annuity due begins on the date of the first payment and ends one payment interval after the last payment is made.

## A. Amount of an Annuity Due, $S_n$(due)

The *amount* of an annuity due is the value at the end of the term of the annuity. It includes all the periodic payments plus the compound interest. By a method similar to that used in finding the amount of an ordinary annuity, the amount of an annuity due may be found by totaling the individual compound amounts of the periodic payments (see Chapter 13, pages 378 and 379). Each of the compound amounts is computed by the formula $S = P(1 + i)^n$. However, a simpler method of finding the amount of an annuity due is to use the formula for finding the amount of an ordinary annuity, $S_n = Rs_{\overline{n}|i}$. When this formula is used, the amount of an annuity due may be found in either of two ways.

**Method A**  First, find the amount of the ordinary annuity of $(n + 1)$ payments. Then, subtract the additional payment from the amount obtained.

$S_n(\textbf{due}) = Rs_{\overline{n+1}|i} - R$, or

$S_n(\textbf{due}) = R(s_{\overline{n+1}|i} - 1)$  (14–1)

**Example 1**  What is the amount of an annuity due for one year if each payment is $100 payable at the beginning of each quarter and the interest rate is 4% compounded quarterly?

$R = \$100$ (per quarter), $i = 4\%/4 = 1\%$ (per quarter),
$n = 4$ (quarterly payments)

Substituting the values in formula (14–1):

$$S_4(\text{due}) = 100s_{\overline{4+1}|1\%} - 100 = 100s_{\overline{5}|1\%} - 100$$
$$= 100(5.10101) - 100 = \$410.10 \text{ (Table 7, } n = 5)$$

The example is diagrammed as follows:

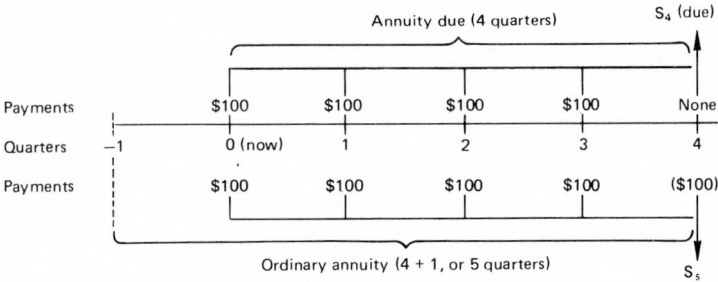

The diagram shows that if an additional payment ($100) is made at the end of the fourth quarter, the 5 (or 4 + 1) payments form an ordinary annuity. The amount of the ordinary annuity is $S_5$ (or $S_{4+1}$). The difference between the amount of the ordinary annuity of five payments and the amount of the annuity due of four payments is the additional payment ($100). Thus,

$$S_4(\text{due}) = S_{4+1} - 100 = 100s_{\overline{4+1}|1\%} - 100$$

Extending this idea, let

$n =$ number of payments (or number of interest conversion periods)
$R =$ size of each regular payment

Then,

$$S_n(\text{due}) = Rs_{\overline{n+1}|i} - R$$

**Example 2**    If $20 is deposited at the beginning of each month in a fund which earns interest at 6% compounded monthly, what is the final value at the end of three years?

$R = \$20$ (per month), $i = 6\%/12 = \frac{1}{2}\%$ (per month),
$n = 3 \times 12 = 36$ (months or payments)

Substituting the values in formula (14–1):

$$S_{36}(\text{due}) = 20s_{\overline{36+1}|1/2\%} - 20 = 20(40.5328 - 1) = \$790.66$$
$$\text{(Table 7: } n = 36 + 1 = 37)$$

**★Method B**    First, find the amount as if it were an ordinary annuity. Then, accumulate the amount obtained for one interest period.

$$S_n(\text{due}) = Rs_{\overline{n}|i} \cdot (1 + i) \tag{14–2}$$

Example 1 may be computed in the following manner when formula (14–2) is used:

$R = \$100$, $i = 1\%$, $n = 4$ (quarterly payments)

$S_n(\text{due}) = 100s_{\overline{4}|1\%} (1 + 1\%) = 100(4.060401)(1.01) = \$410.10$

The example is diagrammed as follows:

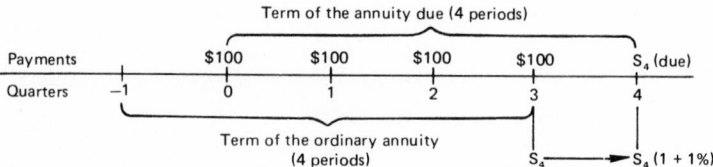

The diagram shows that the annuity due is first converted to an ordinary annuity. The amount of the ordinary annuity ($S_4$) is the value at the end of the third quarter. The required amount of the annuity due is the value at the end of the fourth quarter. Thus, $S_4$ is accumulated for one interest period, or

$S_4(\text{due}) = S_4(1 + i) = 100s_{\overline{4}|1\%} \cdot (1 + 1\%)$

Extending this idea, then,

$S_n(\text{due}) = S_n( + i) = Rs_{\overline{n}|i} \cdot (1 + i)$

Example 2 may be computed in the following manner when formula (14–2) is used:

$R = \$20$, $i = \frac{1}{2}\%$, $n = 36$

$S_{36}(\text{due}) = 20s_{\overline{36}|1/2\%} \cdot (1 + \frac{1}{2}\%) = 20(39.3361)(1.005) = \$790.66$

**Note:**   It is important to master the methods rather than to merely memorize the formulas. Method A is preferred in most cases since the computation is simpler than that in Method B.

# B. Present Value of an Annuity Due, $A_n(\text{due})$

The *present value* of an annuity due is the value at the beginning of the term of the annuity. By a method similar to that of finding the present value of an ordinary annuity, the present value of an annuity due may be found by totaling the individual present values of the periodic payments (see Chapter 13, page 383). Each of the present values is computed by the formula $P = S(1 + i)^{-n}$. However, a simpler method of finding the present value of an annuity due is to use the formula for finding the present value of an ordinary annuity, $A_n = Ra_{\overline{n}|i}$. When this formula is used, the present value may be found in either of two ways.

**Method A**   First, find the present value of the ordinary annuity of $(n - 1)$ payments. Then, add the excluded payment to the present value obtained.

$A_n(\text{due}) = Ra_{\overline{n-1}|i} + R,$ or

$A_n(\text{due}) = R(a_{\overline{n-1}|i} + 1)$                      (14–3)

**Example 3**   What is the present value of an annuity due if the size of each payment is \$100 payable at the beginning of each quarter for one year and the interest rate is 4% compounded quarterly?

$R = \$100$ (per quarter), $i = 4\%/4 = 1\%$ (per quarter), $n = 4$ (quarterly payments)

Substituting the values in formula (14–3):

$A_n(\text{due}) = 100a_{\overline{4-1}|1\%} + 100 = 100a_{\overline{3}|1\%} + 100$

$= 100(2.94099) + 100 = \$394.10$ (Table 8: $n = 4 - 1 = 3$)

The example is diagrammed as follows:

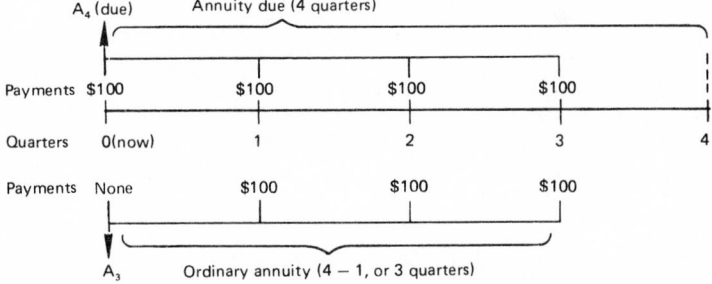

The diagram shows that if the \$100 payment at the beginning of the first quarter is excluded, the remaining three (or $4 - 1$) payments form an ordinary annuity. The present value of the ordinary annuity is $A_3$ (or $A_{4-1}$). The difference between the present value of the ordinary annuity of three payments and the present value of the annuity due of four payments is the excluded payment of \$100. Thus,

$A_4(\text{due}) = A_{4-1} + 100 = 100a_{\overline{4-1}|1\%} + 100$

Extending this idea, let

$n = $ number of payments (or number of interest conversion periods)
$R = $ size of each regular payment

Then,

$A_n(\text{due}) = Ra_{\overline{n-1}|i} + R$

**Example 4**   What is the selling price of a television set that can be bought for \$35 a month for 10 months beginning now, if money is worth 6% compounded monthly?

This is an annuity due problem since the first payment starts now, the beginning of the first payment interval.

$R = \$35$ (per month), $i = 6\%/12 = \frac{1}{2}\%$ (per month), $n = 10$ (months or payments)

Substituting the values in formula (14–3):

$A_n(\text{due}) = 35a_{\overline{10-1}|1/2\%} + 35 = 35(8.7791 + 1) = \$342.27$

$$\text{(Table 8: } n = 10 - 1 = 9)$$

**★Method B**     First, find the present value as if it were an ordinary annuity. Then, accumulate the present value obtained for one interest period.

$$A_n(\text{due}) = Ra_{\overline{n}|i} \cdot (1 + i) \tag{14–4}$$

Example 3 may be computed in the following manner when formula (14–4) is used:

$R = \$100$, $i = 1\%$, $n = 4$ (quarterly payments)

$$A_n(\text{due}) = 100a_{\overline{4}|1\%} \cdot (1 + 1\%) = 100(3.90197)(1.01) = \$394.10$$

The example is diagrammed as follows:

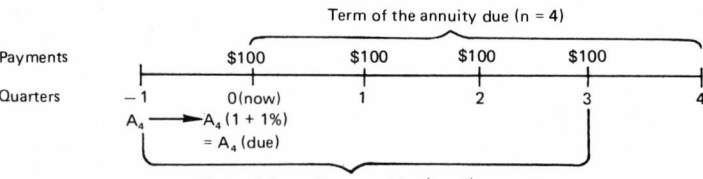

The diagram shows that the annuity due is first converted to an ordinary annuity. The present value of the ordinary annuity ($A_4$) is the value at the beginning of one quarter before the beginning of the first quarter. The required present value of the annuity due is the value at the beginning of the first quarter. Thus, $A_4$ is accumulated for one interest period, or

$$A_4(\text{due}) = A_4(1 + i) = 100a_{\overline{4}|1\%} \cdot (1 + 1\%)$$

Extending this idea, then,

$$A_n(\text{due}) = A_n \cdot (1 + i) = Ra_{\overline{n}|i} \cdot (1 + i)$$

Example 4 may be computed in the following manner when formula (14–4) is used:

$$A_{10}(\text{due}) = 35a_{\overline{10}|1/2\%} \cdot (1 + \frac{1}{2}\%) = 35(9.7304)(1.005) = \$342.27$$

# C. Relationship Between the Amount and the Present Value of an Annuity Due

The present value of an annuity due is also the single principal which, invested at a given compound interest rate, will accumulate to the amount of the annuity due by the end of the term. The relationship between the amount and the present value may be expressed by using the compound interest formula

$S = P(1 + i)^n$ and the compound discount formula $P = S(1 + i)^{-n}$. Here, $P$ is the present value, $A_n$(due); and $S$ is the amount of the annuity due, $S_n$(due). The formulas may be written in the following manner:

$$S_n(\text{due}) = A_n(\text{due})(1 + i)^n, \text{ and}$$

$$A_n(\text{due}) = S_n(\text{due})(1 + i)^{-n}$$

When the amount of an annuity due is known, for instance, the present value of the annuity due of Example 3 can be computed by using the $A_n$(due) formula, as shown below:

$$S_4(\text{due}) = \$410.10 \text{ (See Example 1)}, \ i = 1\%, \ n = 4$$

$$A_4(\text{due}) = S_4(\text{due})(1 + 1\%)^{-4} = 410.10(.96098) = \$394.10$$

## EXERCISE 14–1

### Reference: Sections 14.1 A, B, and C

**A.** *Find the amount and the present value of the annuity due in each of the following:*

|      | Payment (R) | Payment Interval | Term | Compound Interest Rate |
|------|-------------|------------------|------|------------------------|
| 1.   | $ 250       | 1 month          | 3 years | 5%, monthly |
| 2.   | 60          | 1 quarter        | 9 years | 6%, quarterly |
| 3.   | 120         | 6 months         | $4\frac{1}{2}$ years | 7%, semiannually |
| 4.   | 100         | 1 year           | 20 years | 10%, annually |
| 5.   | 500         | 1 quarter        | $12\frac{1}{2}$ years | 5%, quarterly |
| 6.   | 220         | 1 month          | $2\frac{1}{2}$ years | 4%, monthly |
| 7.   | 1,000       | 1 year           | 25 years | $5\frac{1}{2}\%$, annually |
| 8.   | 1,200       | 6 months         | 10 years | 8%, semiannually |

**B.** *Statement Problems:*

9. Find the amount of an annuity due of $700 payable at the beginning of each quarter for six years if the interest rate is 4% compounded quarterly.

10. What is the amount of an annuity due for two years and five months if each payment is $450 payable at the beginning of each month and the interest rate is 5% compounded monthly?

11. Find the present value of the annuity due in Problem 9.

12. What is the present value of the annuity due in Problem 10?

13. If $600 is deposited at the beginning of each month in a bank that pays 3% interest compounded monthly, what is the final value at the end of three years and four months?

14. On July 1, 1980, a man deposits $150 in a savings and loan association that pays 4% compounded quarterly. The man continues to deposit $150

every quarter thereafter. How much will be in his account on July 1, 1985, immediately before the deposit on this date is made?

15. What is the cash price of a freezer that can be bought for $50 a quarter for $2\frac{1}{2}$ years if the first payment is made now and the interest rate is 7% compounded quarterly?

16. A house was rented for $100 per month, each month's rent payable in advance. If money was worth 6% compounded monthly, what was the cash value of the rent for one year?

# D. Other Types of Problems in an Annuity Due

In formula (14–1), $S_n(\text{due}) = R(s_{\overline{n+1}|i} - 1)$, there are four quantities: $S_n(\text{due})$, $R$, $n$, and $i$. If any three of them are known, the one unknown may be determined by using the formula. Likewise, in formula (14–3), $A_n(\text{due}) = R(a_{\overline{n-1}|i} + 1)$, there are four quantities: $A_n(\text{due})$, $R$, $n$, and $i$. If any three of them are known, the one unknown may be determined by using the formula. The methods used in finding the values of $S_n(\text{due})$ and $A_n(\text{due})$ have already been discussed in this section. In the remaining portion of the section, the methods of finding the values of $R$, $i$, and $n$ are given.

## FINDING THE VALUE OF $R$ WHEN $S_n$(due) IS KNOWN

**Example 5**   A man wishes to receive $2,000 five years from now. How much must he invest at the beginning of each year if the first payment starts now and the interest is $4\frac{1}{2}$% compounded annually?

$S_n(\text{due}) = \$2,000$, $i = 4\frac{1}{2}\%$ (per year), $n = 5$ (years or payments), $R = ?$ (per year)

Substituting the values in the formula $S_n(\text{due}) = R(s_{\overline{n+1}|i} - 1)$:

$2,000 = R(s_{\overline{5+1}|4\ 1/2\%} - 1) = R(6.716892 - 1)$

$R = \dfrac{2,000}{5.716892} = \$349.84$ (Table 7, $n = 6$)

## FINDING THE VALUE OF $R$ WHEN $A_n$(due) IS KNOWN

**Example 6**   A washer which sells for $250 can be bought under terms of 20 equal monthly payments starting now. If money is worth 6% compounded monthly, what is the size of each payment?

$A_n(\text{due}) = \$250$, $i = 6\%/12 = \frac{1}{2}\%$ (per month), $n = 20$ (months or payments), $R = ?$ (per month)

Substituting the values in the formula $A_n(\text{due}) = R(a_{\overline{n-1}|i} + 1)$:

$$250 = R(a_{\overline{20}\rceil 1/2\%} + 1) = R(18.08236 + 1)$$

$$R = \frac{250}{19.08236} = \$13.10$$

## FINDING THE VALUE OF $i$ WHEN $S_n$(due) IS KNOWN

**Example 7**   At what nominal rate compounded annually will an annuity due of \$1,000, payable at the beginning of each year for four years, amount to \$4,500?

$S_n$(due) = \$4,500, $R$ = \$1,000 (per year), $n$ = 4 (years or payments), $i$ = ? (annual)

Substituting the values in the formula $S_n$(due) = $Rs_{\overline{n+1}\rceil i} - R$:

$$4,500 = 1,000s_{\overline{4+1}\rceil i} - 1,000$$

$$s_{\overline{5}\rceil i} = \frac{4,500 + 1,000}{1,000} = 5.5$$

In Table 7, $s_{\overline{5}\rceil 4\ 1/2\%} = 5.4707$, and $s_{\overline{5}\rceil 5\%} = 5.5256$

Thus, the value of $i$ is greater than $4\frac{1}{2}\%$ but smaller than 5%. It may be written:

$$4\tfrac{1}{2}\% < i < 5\%$$

## FINDING THE VALUE OF $i$ WHEN $A_n$(due) IS KNOWN

**Example 8**   What is the nominal rate compounded quarterly if the present value of an annuity of \$300 payable at the beginning of each quarter for six years is \$5,800?

$A_n$(due) = \$5,800, $R$ = \$300 (per quarter), $n$ = 6 × 4 = 24 (quarterly payments), $i$ = ? (per quarter)

Substituting the values in the formula $A_n$(due) = $Ra_{\overline{n-1}\rceil i} + R$:

$$5,800 = 300a_{\overline{24-1}\rceil i} + 300, \quad a_{\overline{23}\rceil i} = \frac{5,800 - 300}{300} = 18.3333$$

In Table 8, $a_{\overline{23}\rceil 1\ 7/8\%} = 18.5442$, and $a_{\overline{23}\rceil 2\%} = 18.2922$

Thus, the value of $i$ is greater than $1\frac{7}{8}\%$ but smaller than 2%. It may be written:

$$1\tfrac{7}{8}\% < i < 2\%$$

Since $1\frac{7}{8}\% \times 4 = 7\frac{1}{2}\%$, and $2\% \times 4 = 8\%$, the value of the nominal rate is between $7\frac{1}{2}\%$ and 8%. It may be written:

$$7\tfrac{1}{2}\% < \text{nominal rate} < 8\%$$

***Note:***   When a more accurate value of $i$, such as in $s_{\overline{5}\rceil i}$ of Example 7 and in $a_{\overline{23}\rceil i}$ of Example 8, is needed, the interpolation method explained in Chapter 13, page 399, may be used.

## FINDING THE VALUE OF $n$ WHEN $S_n$(due) IS KNOWN

**Example 9**  If $100 is deposited at the beginning of each month at an interest rate of 9% compounded monthly, how many months will be required for the deposits to amount to at least $7,600?

$S_n$(due) = $7,600, $R$ = $100 (per month), $i = 9\%/12 = \frac{3}{4}\%$ (per month), $n$ = ? (months or payments)

Substituting the values in the formula $S_n$(due) = $Rs_{\overline{n+1}|i} - R$:

$$7,600 = 100s_{\overline{n+1}|3/4\%} - 100$$

$$s_{\overline{n+1}|3/4\%} = \frac{7,600 + 100}{100} = 77$$

In the $\frac{3}{4}\%$ column of Table 7, find the two entries with values closest to 77.

The entries are as follows:

The entry for $s_{\overline{61}|3/4\%}$ is 76.9898.

The entry for $s_{\overline{62}|3/4\%}$ is 78.5672.

Since 77 is between the two entries above, the desired value of $(n + 1)$ is greater than 61 but smaller than 62. However, the amount in the example is at least $7,600. Therefore, 62, the larger number, is employed.

$n + 1 = 62$, $n = 62 - 1 = 61$ months, or 5 years 1 month

## FINDING THE VALUE OF $n$ WHEN $A_n$(due) IS KNOWN

**Example 10**  A man bought a $1,500 boat and agreed to pay for it in installments of $150 at the beginning of every six months, starting on the date of purchase. If the interest charged is 5% compounded semiannually, how long will it take the man to pay for the boat?

$A_n$(due) = $1,500, $R$ = $150 (per six months), $i = 5\%/2 = 2\frac{1}{2}\%$ (per six months), $n$ = ? (semiannual periods or payments)

Substituting the values in the formula $A_n$(due) = $Ra_{\overline{n-1}|i} + R$:

$$1,500 = 150a_{\overline{n-1}|2\ 1/2\%} + 150$$

$$a_{\overline{n-1}|2\ 1/2\%} = \frac{1,500 - 150}{150} = 9$$

In the $2\frac{1}{2}\%$ column of Table 8, find the two entries with values closest to 9. The entries are as follows:

The entry for $a_{\overline{10}|2\ 1/2\%}$ is 8.7521.

The entry for $a_{\overline{11}|2\ 1/2\%}$ is 9.5142.

Since 9 is between the two entries above, the desired value of $(n - 1)$ is greater than 10 but less than 11. The interpolation method is unnecessary in this case. In order to repay the entire debt, the greater number, 11, is considered as the value of $(n - 1)$. Thus,

$n - 1 = 11$, $n = 11 + 1 = 12$ semiannual periods or six years.

## EXERCISE 14–2

**Reference: Section 14.1 D**

**A.** *Find the unknown value in each annuity due: (Omit interpolation)*

|  | Amount | Present Value | Payment | Term (n) | Compound Interest Rate |
|---|---|---|---|---|---|
| 1. | $ 2,500 | | $100, monthly | 2 years | ?, monthly |
| 2. | 530 | | 60, semiannually | ? | 5%, semiannually |
| 3. | | $ 990 | 60, quarterly | 5 years | ?, quarterly |
| 4. | | 5,000 | ?, annually | 12 years | 4%, annually |
| 5. | | 3,800 | 250, semiannually | ? | 6%, semiannually |
| 6. | 12,500 | | 450, quarterly | 6 years | ?, quarterly |
| 7. | | 20,000 | ?, annually | 15 years | $8\frac{1}{2}$%, annually |
| 8. | | 1,800 | 30, monthly | ? | 5%, monthly |
| 9. | 6,000 | | ?, semiannually | $7\frac{1}{2}$ years | 4%, semiannually |
| 10. | 3,000 | | ?, quarterly | $4\frac{1}{2}$ years | 6%, quarterly |
| 11. | 3,200 | | 120, monthly | ? | 7%, monthly |
| 12. | | 2,400 | 340, annually | 9 years | ?, annually |

**B.** *Statement Problems:*

13. How much money must Heather invest at the beginning of each quarter if she wishes to receive $1,500 six years from now? Assume that the first payment starts now and the interest rate is 7% compounded quarterly.

14. H. K. Jackson wishes to have $500 on December 1 for Christmas shopping. Starting on January 1 of this year, she will make regular monthly investments which will earn 6% interest compounded monthly. However, she does not plan to invest on December 1. What must be the size of each monthly investment in order to accomplish this goal?

15. A house which sells for $10,000 can be purchased under terms requiring 120 monthly payments. Assume that the first payment begins now and the interest is 6% compounded monthly. What is the size of each monthly payment?

16. Jack Newton purchased a mobile home on March 1, 1980, and agreed to pay for it in equal quarterly payments. The first payment was made on the date of purchase. The last payment will be made on March 1, 1985. The cash price of the home was $4,000. If money is worth 5% compounded quarterly, how much should Newton pay each quarter?

17. At what nominal rate compounded semiannually will an annuity due of $500, payable at the beginning of every six months for ten years, amount to $12,772?

18. Alice Williams invested $200 at the beginning of each quarter for 20 quarters. At the end of the 20th quarter, she received $4,403.80, including principal and interest. If the interest rate was compounded quarterly, what was the interest rate?

19. What is the nominal rate compounded annually if the present value of an annuity due of $80, payable at the beginning of each year for eight years, is $530?

20. Betty Hunt bought a used car for $600 from her cousin on January 1, 1980. She agreed to pay for it by making payments of $60 each month until the last payment on November 1, 1980. The first payment was made on the date of purchase. If the interest was compounded monthly, what was the interest rate?

21. If $60 is deposited at the beginning of each month at 5% compounded monthly, how many months will be needed for the deposits to amount to at least $3,000?

22. Joe Kelly signed a note to his employer on March 1, 1980. The face value of $800 is to be paid in full when it is due. Assume that the note may be discharged by equal monthly payments of $50 each starting now and the interest is computed at 4% compounded monthly. When should the last payment be made?

23. Bill buys a $13,500 farm and agrees to pay $500 at the beginning of each quarter until he completes his payments. The first payment is due on the date of purchase. How long will it take him to pay for the farm if the interest rate is 4% compounded quarterly?

24. If the present value of an annuity due of $200 payable semiannually is $2,800 and interest is computed at 6% compounded semiannually, what is the number of payments?

## 14.2 DEFERRED ANNUITY

When the term of an annuity starts on a future date, the annuity is called a *deferred annuity*. The period between now and the beginning of the term of the annuity is called the *period of deferment*. The computation of a deferred annuity may be conveniently carried out if the ordinary annuity formulas are used. Hereafter, the name "deferred annuity" actually means "deferred ordinary annuity." It should be recalled that the first payment of an ordinary annuity is always made at the end of the first payment period. Thus, an annuity of $100 payable quarterly for six payments with the first payment to be made at the end of the *third* quarter is a deferred annuity. The period of deferment consists of *two* quarters, and the term of the ordinary annuity is six quarters, starting at the beginning of the third quarter and continuing to the end of the eighth quarter. (See diagram in Example 2, page 420.)

### A. The Amount of a Deferred Annuity

The *amount* of a deferred annuity is the final value at the end of the term of the annuity. The amount includes all the periodic payments plus the accumulated interest. Thus, the amount of the deferred annuity is the same as the amount of the ordinary annuity. Let $S_n$(defer.) = the amount of a deferred annuity. It follows that

$$S_n(\text{defer.}) = S_n = Rs_{\overline{n}|i} \tag{14-5}$$

**Example 1** Find the amount of an annuity of $100 payable at the end of each quarter for six payments. The interest rate is 6% compounded quarterly. The first payment is due at the end of nine months.

This example is identical to the diagram on page 420, which shows that there are no payments during the period of deferment. Therefore, in computing the amount of the annuity, the portion of deferment may be disregarded.

$R = \$100$ (per quarter), $i = 6\%/4, = 1\frac{1}{2}\%$ (per quarter), $n = 6$ (payments or quarters)

Substituting the above values in the formula $S_n(\text{defer.}) = Rs_{\overline{n}|i}$:

$S_6(\text{defer.}) = 100s_{\overline{6}|\ 1\ 1/2\%} = 100(6.22955) = \$622.96$

# B. The Present Value of a Deferred Annuity

The *present value* of a deferred annuity is the value at the beginning of the period of deferment, *not* at the beginning of the term of the ordinary annuity. Let $d =$ the number of the deferred payment intervals. The present value of a deferred annuity, denoted by $A_n$(defer.), may be found by either of the following two methods:

**Method A** First, consider that the payments were made during the period of deferment. Second, consider that there were two ordinary annuities: one consists of $d$ payments, while the other consists of $d + n$ payments. Third, subtract the present value of the annuity consisting of $d$ payments from the present value of the annuity consisting of $d + n$ payments. The remainder is the present value of the deferred annuity. These steps may be accomplished by the formula:

$$A_n(\text{defer.}) = A_{d+n} - A_d = Ra_{\overline{d+n}|i} - Ra_{\overline{d}|i}, \text{ or}$$

$$A_n(\text{defer.}) = R(a_{\overline{d+n}|i} - a_{\overline{d}|i}) \tag{14-6}$$

**Example 2** Find the present value of an annuity of $100 payable at the end of each quarter for six payments. The interest rate is 6% compounded quarterly. The first payment is due at the end of nine months.

$R = \$100$, $i = 6\%/4 = 1\frac{1}{2}\%$, $n = 6$, $d = 2$ (2 quarters or 6 months)

Substituting the above values in formula (14-6):

$$A_{d+n} = A_{2+6} = A_8 = Ra_{\overline{8}|\ 1\ 1/2\%} = 100a_{\overline{8}|\ 1\ 1/2\%}$$

$$A_d = A_2 = Ra_{\overline{2}|\ 1\ 1/2\%} = 100a_{\overline{2}|\ 1\ 1/2\%}$$

$A_6(\text{defer.}) = A_8 - A_2 = 100a_{\overline{8}|\,1\,1/2\%} - 100a_{\overline{2}|\,1\,1/2\%}$

$\qquad = 100(7.48592) - 100(1.95588) = 748.592 - 195.588 \text{ (Table 8)}$

$\qquad = \$553.004, \text{ or } \$553$

Method A is diagrammed below:

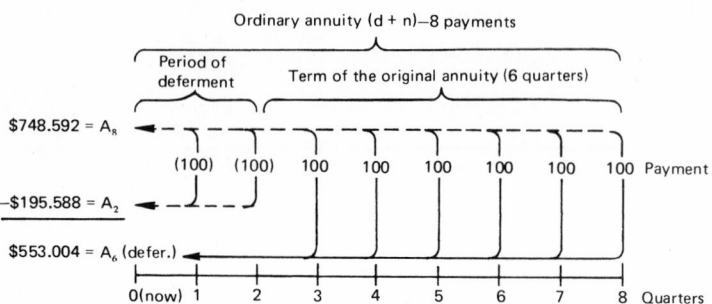

**Example 3**     Find the present value of an ordinary annuity of $500 each year for 15 years if the first payment is due at the end of five years and money is worth $5\frac{1}{2}\%$ compounded annually.

$R = \$500$ (per year), $i = 5\frac{1}{2}\%$ (per year), $n = 15$ (years or payments), $d = 4$ (The payment made at the end of the fifth year covers the payment interval from the end of the fourth year to the end of the fifth year. Thus, the period of deferment is four years, or four payments.)

Substituting the values in the formula $A_n(\text{defer.}) = R\,(a_{\overline{d+n}|\,i} - a_{\overline{d}|\,i})$:

$A_n(\text{defer.}) = 500(a_{\overline{4+15}|\,5\,1/2\%} - a_{\overline{4}|\,5\,1/2\%}) = 500(11.60765 - 3.50515)$

$\qquad = 500(8.1025) = \$4,051.25$ (Table 8)

**★Method B**     Discount the present value of the ordinary annuity for the period of deferment. This may be computed by use of the following formula:

$$A_n(\text{defer.}) = A_n(1+i)^{-d} = Ra_{\overline{n}|\,i} \cdot (1+i)^{-d} \qquad \textbf{(14–7)}$$

Example 2 may then be computed as follows:

$A_n = A_6 = 100a_{\overline{6}|\,1\,1/2\%} = 100(5.69719) = \$569.72$ (Table 8)

$A_n(\text{defer.}) = A_n(1+i)^{-d} = 569.72(1 + 1\frac{1}{2}\%)^{-2}$

$\qquad = 569.72(.97066) = \$553$ (Table 6)

Example 2 is diagrammed below to illustrate Method B.

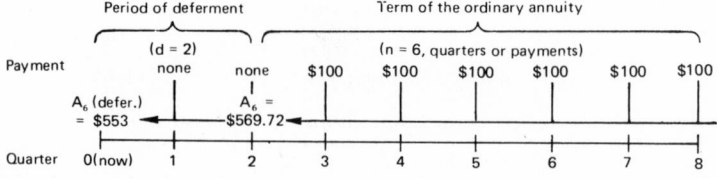

Method B may be used in computing Example 3 as follows:

Substituting the values in the formula

$$A_n(\text{defer.}) = Ra_{\overline{n}|\,i} \cdot (1 + i)^{-d}:$$

$$A_n(\text{defer.}) = 500a_{\overline{15}|\,5\ 1/2\%} \cdot (1 + 5\tfrac{1}{2}\%)^{-4}$$

$$= 500(10.03758)(0.807217) = \$4,051.25$$

**Note:** The use of Method A, rather than Method B, is recommended since only Table 8 is needed in Method A, while both Tables 6 and 8 are needed in Method B. Therefore, Method A will be used in the following discussion.

# C. Other Types of Deferred Annuity Problems

### FINDING THE PAYMENT OF A DEFERRED ANNUITY

**Example 4** A man borrows $10,000 at 5% compounded semiannually, and agrees to repay it in 14 equal semiannual payments. Find the size of each payment if the first payment is due at the end of $3\frac{1}{2}$ years.

$A_n(\text{defer.}) = \$10,000$, $i = 5\%/2 = 2\frac{1}{2}\%$ (per six months), $n = 14$ (payments or semiannual periods), $d = 3 \times 2 = 6$ (payments or semiannual periods), $R = ?$

Substituting the values in formula (14–6):

$$10,000 = R(a_{\overline{6+14}|\,2\ 1/2\%} - a_{\overline{6}|\,2\ 1/2\%}) = R(15.589162 - 5.508125)$$

$$= R(10.081037)$$

$$R = \frac{10,000}{10.081037} = \$991.96 \text{ (per six months)}$$

### FINDING THE TERM OF A DEFERRED ANNUITY

**Example 5** If $50 is deposited at the end of each month and the interest rate is 6% compounded monthly, how many months will be required for the deposits to equal a present value of $4,500? The first deposit is made at the end of six months.

$A_n(\text{defer.}) = \$4,500$, $R = \$50$ (per month), $i = 6\%/12 = \frac{1}{2}\%$ (per month), $d = 5$ (months or payments), $n = ?$ (months or payments)

Substituting the values in the formula $A_n(\text{defer.}) = Ra_{\overline{d+n}|\,i} - Ra_{\overline{d}|\,i}$:

$$4,500 = 50a_{\overline{5+n}|\,1/2\%} - 50a_{\overline{5}|\,1/2\%} = 50a_{\overline{5+n}|\,1/2\%} - 50(4.9259)$$

$$= 50a_{\overline{5+n}|\,1/2\%} - 246.295$$

$$a_{\overline{5+n}|\,1/2\%} = \frac{4,500 + 246.295}{50} = 94.9259$$

In the $\frac{1}{2}$% column of Table 8, find the first entry greater than 94.9259.

$a_{\overline{130}|1/2\%} = 95.4216$

Thus,

$5 + n = 130, \ n = 130 - 5 = 125$ (payments or months)

The first payment is due at the end of six months. There are 125 monthly payments.

# EXERCISE 14-3

## Reference: Section 14.2

**A.** *Find the unknown value of the deferred annuity in each of the following problems:*

| | Amount $S_n$(defer.) | Present Value $A_n$(defer.) | Payment (R) | Number of Payments (n) | Period of Deferment (d) | Compound Interest Rate |
|---|---|---|---|---|---|---|
| **1.** | ? | ? | $260, semi-annually | 15 | 5 | 7%, semi-annually |
| **2.** | | $ 750 | 80, monthly | ? | 4 | 4%, monthly |
| **3.** | | 2,000 | ?, annually | 10 | 3 | 10%, annually |
| **4.** | ? | ? | 500, quarterly | 7 | 10 | 6%, quarterly |
| **5.** | | 1,600 | 125, quarterly | ? | 7 | 5%, quarterly |
| **6.** | ? | ? | 400, annually | 18 | 8 | 9%, annually |
| **7.** | ? | ? | 600, monthly | 14 | 12 | 5%, monthly |
| **8.** | | 5,000 | ?, semi-annually | 20 | 6 | $4\frac{1}{2}$%, semi-annually |

**B.** *Statement Problems:*

9. Find the amount and the present value of an annuity of $150 payable at the end of every three months for 30 payments. The first payment is due at the end of seven years. The interest rate is 5% compounded quarterly.

10. Find the amount and the present value of 40 monthly payments of $75 each. The first payment is due in two years. The interest rate is 6% compounded monthly.

11. James Berman purchased a theater for $80,000 on January 2, 1980. He paid $10,000 cash and agreed to pay the balance plus interest at 4% compounded annually in 14 annual payments, with the first payment due on January 2, 1983. What is the size of each payment?

12. If $400 is to be paid at the end of every six months, the first payment is to be made at the end of three years, and the interest rate is 4% compounded

semiannually, how many payments will be needed to discharge a debt whose present value is $5,000?

**13.** A man borrowed $6,500 at 7% interest compounded quarterly and agreed to repay the loan in quarterly payments of $500 each. The first payment is due in two years. Find the number of payments.

**14.** A student borrowed $250 and agreed to repay the principal and the interest at 4% compounded monthly in 20 equal monthly payments. The first payment is due in $1\frac{1}{2}$ years. How large is each payment?

**15.** If money is worth $5\frac{1}{2}$% compounded annually, what single payment now is equivalent to 45 annual payments of $350 each with the first payment due in five years?

**16.** Carla Duncan purchases a farm on April 1, 1980. She agrees to pay for it in 30 semiannual payments of $600 each. If the first payment is to be made on October 1, 1981, and the interest rate is 6% compounded semiannually, what is the cash price of the farm?

# 14.3 COMPLEX (OR GENERAL) ANNUITY

When the length of the payment interval of an annuity is not the same as the length of the interest conversion period, the annuity is called a *complex annuity*. Thus, if each of the *payments* of an annuity is made *monthly* and the *interest* is compounded or converted *quarterly,* or if each of the *payments* is made *quarterly* and the *interest* is compounded *monthly,* the annuity is called a complex annuity. On the preceding pages, *n* represents the number of payments of an annuity, and also the number of interest periods of an annuity. In the remaining portion of this chapter in order to avoid confusion in a complex annuity problem, *n represents only the number of payments of an annuity.* The letter *c* will be used to represent the number of interest periods in one payment interval. Thus, the number of the total interest periods of a complex annuity is the product of *n* and *c,* or *nc.*

For example, assume that the payment of an annuity is made quarterly and the interest is compounded monthly. A one-year term of this annuity consists of four payments (or $n = 4$), each payment interval consists of three interest periods (or $c = 3$), and there are 12 interest periods ($nc = 4 \times 3 = 12$) during the year.

The diagram below shows the quarterly payment of an annuity with interest compounded monthly. In this illustration, # denotes the date for computing the interest.

| | | | R | | | R | | | R | | | R | |
|---|---|---|---|---|---|---|---|---|---|---|---|---|---|
| • | # | # | # | # | # | # | # | # | # | # | # | # | |
| 0(now) | 1 | 2 | 3 | 4 | 5 | 6 | 7 | 8 | 9 | 10 | 11 | 12 | Month |
| | | | 1 | | | 2 | | | 3 | | | 4 | Quarter |

If the payment of an annuity is made monthly and the interest is compounded quarterly, a one-year term of an annuity consists of 12 payments (or $n = 12$), each payment interval consists of $\frac{1}{3}$ interest periods (or $c = \frac{1}{3}$), and there are four interest periods (or $nc = 12 \times \frac{1}{3} = 4$) during the year. This type of payment is diagrammed as shown below.

| | # | | # | | # | | # | |
|---|---|---|---|---|---|---|---|---|
| · R R | R | R R | R | R R | R | R R | R |
| 0(now) 1 2 | 3 | 4 5 | 6 | 7 8 | 9 | 10 11 | 12 Month |
| | 1 | | 2 | | 3 | | 4 Quarter |

Additional illustrations of complex annuities are presented in the following table:

| Payment Interval | Interest Conversion Period | Term of Annuity | Total Number of Payments ($n$) | Number of Interest Periods in One Payment Interval ($c$) | Total Interest Periods ($n \times c$) |
|---|---|---|---|---|---|
| 1 quarter | 1 month | 2 years | 8 | 3 | 24 |
| 1 month | 1 quarter | 2 years | 24 | $\frac{1}{3}$ | 8 |
| 6 months | 1 month | 1 year | 2 | 6 | 12 |
| 1 year | 1 quarter | 1 year | 1 | 4 | 4 |
| 1 quarter | 6 months | 1 year | 4 | $\frac{1}{2}$ | 2 |
| 1 month | 1 year | 1 year | 12 | $\frac{1}{12}$ | 1 |
| 1 quarter | 1 quarter | 1 year | 4 | 1 | 4 |
| 1 month | 1 month | 1 year | 12 | 1 | 12 |

When $c = 1$, the number of payments ($n$) is the same as the number of interest periods ($nc = n(1) = n$). The formulas developed below may apply in any case including simple annuity problems. Therefore, complex annuity is also referred to simply as a general case in annuity problems or as a *general annuity*.

# A. The Amount and the Present Value of an Ordinary Complex Annuity

The terms which have been used in the previous sections and in Chapter 13 are also used here with the same meanings. Thus, the word *ordinary* is used to indicate that the periodic payment of a complex annuity is made at the end of each payment interval. The *amount* of a complex annuity $(S_{nc})$ is defined as the final value at the end of the term of the annuity. The *present value* of a complex annuity $(A_{nc})$ is the value at the beginning of the term of the annuity.

Basically, as discussed in the previous sections and in Chapter 13, the amount and the present value of an annuity may be found by using the following two compound interest formulas:

$$S = P(1 + i)^n \quad \text{and} \quad P = S(1 + i)^{-n}$$

However, the two principal annuity formulas below, which are derived from the two formulas above, offer a more convenient way to solve any type of *simple* annuity problems: (See Chapter 13, pages 379–381 and 385–387.)

$$S_n = Rs_{\overline{n}|i} = R \cdot \frac{(1 + i)^n - 1}{i} \tag{13–1}$$

$$A_n = Ra_{\overline{n}|i} = R \cdot \frac{1 - (1 + i)^{-n}}{i} \tag{13–2}$$

Two methods will be presented in which the complex annuities are first converted into simple annuities and then computed as ordinary simple annuities by applying the formulas cited above.

**Method A**  *By Use of the Formulas $S_n = Rs_{\overline{n}|i}$ and $A_n = Ra_{\overline{n}|i}$.* In applying these two formulas, each of the original periodic payments is first converted into a new periodic *equivalent payment,* which is assumed to be made at the end of each interest conversion period.

**Example 1**  Find the amount and the present value of an annuity of $100 payable at the end of each quarter for 10 years if the interest rate is 6% compounded monthly.

Each of the original quarterly payments of $100 is first converted into a new equivalent monthly payment, $E$. The original payment, $100, thus is the amount of an annuity of $E$ payable at the end of each month for three months at 6% compounded monthly. That is,

$S_n = \$100$ (in one quarter or 3 months),
$i = 6\%/12 = \frac{1}{2}\%$ (per month), and
$n = 3$ (payments of $\$E$ per month).

Substituting the values in formula $S_n = Es_{\overline{n}|i}$:

$$100 = Es_{\overline{3}|1/2\%}$$

Solve for $E$,

$$E = \frac{100}{s_{\overline{3}|1/2\%}} = 100\left(\frac{1}{a_{\overline{3}|1/2\%}} - \frac{1}{2}\%\right) = 100\left(.336672 - \frac{1}{2}\%\right)$$

$$= 100(.331672) = \$33.1672 \tag{Table 9}$$

The payment of $100 at the end of each quarter is equivalent to the payment of $33.1672 at the end of each *month*. Therefore, the amount of an annuity of $100 payable at the end of each quarter should equal the amount of an annuity of $33.1672 payable at the end of each month. Here the term is 10 years and the number of quarterly payments is 40 (or 10 × 4). Each payment interval consists of three interest periods.

The number of total monthly interest periods is 120 (or 40 × 3). The amount of an ordinary annuity of 120 payments of $E$ each month at 6% compounded monthly is computed as follows:

$$S_{120} = Es_{\overline{120}|1/2\%} = 33.1672(163.8793) = \$5,435.42$$

The present value of the ordinary annuity would be

$$A_{120} = Ea_{\overline{120}|1/2\%} = 33.1672(90.07345) = \$2,987.48$$

Example 1 is diagrammed as follows:

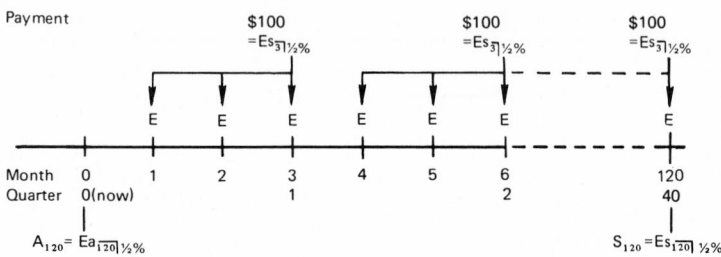

The above calculations may be expanded by letting

$R$ = size of actual periodic payment
$E$ = new equivalent payment at the end of each interest period
$i$ = given interest rate per conversion period
$c$ = number of interest periods in one payment interval, or
$\quad = \dfrac{\text{payment interval}}{\text{interest period}}$
$n$ = number of actual payments

Then, $R = Es_{\overline{c}|i}$, and

$$E = \frac{R}{s_{\overline{c}|i}}$$

The *formula for the amount of an ordinary complex annuity*, $S_{nc}$, may be obtained as follows:

$$S_{nc} = Es_{\overline{nc}|i} = \frac{R}{s_{\overline{c}|i}} \cdot s_{\overline{nc}|i}, \text{ or it may be written as}$$

$$S_{nc} = Rs_{\overline{nc}|i} \cdot \frac{1}{s_{\overline{c}|i}} \qquad\qquad \textbf{(14–8)}$$

The *formula for the present value of an ordinary complex annuity*, $A_{nc}$, may be obtained as follows:

$$A_{nc} = Ea_{\overline{nc}|i} = \frac{R}{s_{\overline{c}|i}} \cdot a_{\overline{nc}|i}, \text{ or it may be written as}$$

$$A_{nc} = Ra_{\overline{nc}|i} \cdot \frac{1}{s_{\overline{c}|i}} \qquad\qquad \textbf{(14–9)}$$

It should be observed that when $c = 1$ (interest interval = payment interval), the value of $\dfrac{1}{s_{\overline{c}|i}}$ becomes $\dfrac{1}{s_{\overline{1}|i}} = \dfrac{1}{1} = 1$. Thus,

$$S_{nc} = Rs_{\overline{n(1)}|i} \cdot \frac{1}{s_{\overline{1}|i}} = Rs_{\overline{n}|i}, \text{ and } A_{nc} = Ra_{\overline{n(1)}|i} \cdot \frac{1}{s_{\overline{1}|i}} = Ra_{\overline{n}|i}$$

These facts indicate that the complex annuity formulas are identical to the simple annuity formulas when the interest conversion period coincides with the payment interval.

**Note:** The values of $s_{\overline{nc}|i}$ and $s_{\overline{c}|i}$ may be found in Table 7. If $c$ is fractional, the value of $s_{\overline{c}|i}$ may be found in Table 7A, where $c = 1/m$. ($m =$ the number of payments in one given interest period.) The value of $\dfrac{1}{s_{\overline{c}|i}}$ may be found in Table 9 by the use of the formula $\dfrac{1}{s_{\overline{c}|i}} = \dfrac{1}{a_{\overline{c}|i}} - i$. However, if $c$ is fractional, its value may be found in Table 10, where $c = 1/m$. The value of $a_{\overline{nc}|i}$ may be found in Table 8.

When formulas (14–8 and 14–9) are applied, the computation for Example 1 may be summarized as follows:

$R = \$100$ (per quarter), $i = 6\%/12 = \frac{1}{2}\%$ (monthly), $n = 10 \times 4 = 40$ (quarterly payments), $c = 3$ (interest periods in one quarter, the payment interval) which is computed as follows:

$$c = \frac{\text{payment interval}}{\text{interest interval}} = \frac{1 \text{ quarter}}{1 \text{ month}} = \frac{3 \text{ months}}{1 \text{ month}} = 3$$

Substituting the above values in formulas 14–8 and 14–9 respectively:

$$S_{nc} = S_{40(3)} = 100s_{\overline{40\times3}|1/2\%} \cdot \frac{1}{s_{\overline{3}|1/2\%}}$$

$$= 100(163.87935)(.336672 - \tfrac{1}{2}\%)$$
$$= 100(163.87935)(.331672) = \$5,435.42 \qquad \text{(Tables 7 and 9)}$$

$$A_{nc} = A_{40(3)} = 100a_{\overline{40\times3}|1/2\%} \cdot \frac{1}{s_{\overline{3}|1/2\%}} = 100(90.07345)(.331672)$$

$$= \$2,987.48 \qquad \text{(Tables 8 and 9)}$$

The above results obtained for Example 1 may be checked by using the formula $S = P(1 + i)^n$: $P = A_{nc} = \$2,987.48$, $i = \frac{1}{2}\%$, $n = 120$

$$S = 2,987.48(1 + \tfrac{1}{2}\%)^{120} = 2,987.48(1.8193967) = \$5,435.42$$

Or, the results may be checked by using the formula $P = S(1 + i)^{-n}$:

$S = S_{nc} = \$5,435.42$
$P = 5,435.42(1 + \tfrac{1}{2}\%)^{-120} = 5,435.42(.5496327) = \$2,987.48$

**Example 2**  Find the amount and the present value of an annuity of $100 payable at the end of each month for six years if the interest rate is 4% compounded semiannually.

$R = \$100$ (monthly payment), $i = 4\%/2 = 2\%$ (per six months), $n = 6 \times 12 = 72$ (monthly payments), $c = \frac{1}{6}$ (interest conversion periods in one month, the payment interval, or

$$c = \frac{1 \text{ month}}{6 \text{ months}} = \frac{1}{6}.)$$

Substituting the values in formulas 14–8 and 14–9 respectively:

$$S_{nc} = S_{72(1/6)} = 100 s_{\overline{72(1/6)}|\,2\%} \cdot \frac{1}{s_{\overline{1/6}|\,2\%}}$$

$$= 100 s_{\overline{12}|\,2\%} \cdot 6.049807$$

$$= 100(13.41209)(6.049807) = 1{,}341.209(6.049807)$$

$$= \$8{,}114.06 \qquad\qquad\qquad \text{(Tables 7 and 10)}$$

$$A_{nc} = A_{72(1/6)} = 100 a_{\overline{72(1/6)}|\,2\%} \cdot \frac{1}{s_{\overline{1/6}|\,2\%}}$$

$$= 100 a_{\overline{12}|\,2\%} \cdot 6.049807$$

$$= 100(10.57534)(6.049807) = \$6{,}397.88 \qquad \text{(Tables 8 and 10)}$$

**Note:**  The above multiplications may also be performed by using logarithms. For example, $S_{nc}$ is computed as follows:

$$\log 100 \quad = 2.000\ 0000 \text{ (Table 3)}$$
$$\log s_{\overline{12}|\,2\%} = 1.127\ 4964 \text{ (Table 12)}$$

$$(+) \log \frac{1}{s_{\overline{1/6}|\,2\%}} = 0.781\ 7415 \text{ (Table 13)}$$
$$\overline{\log\ S_{nc} = 3.909\ 2379}$$

Find the antilog by interpolation from Table 2. $S_{nc} = \$8{,}114.057$, or rounded to $\$8{,}114.06$.

# EXERCISE 14–4

## Reference: Section 14.3 A

**A.** *Find the amount and the present value of the complex annuity in each of the following problems:*

| | Payment (R) | Payment Interval | Term | Interest Rate Compounded |
|---|---|---|---|---|
| **1.** | $ 250 | 1 month | $3\frac{1}{2}$ years | 6%, quarterly |
| **2.** | 140 | 1 quarter | 2 years | 5%, semiannually |
| **3.** | 70 | 6 months | 5 years | 12%, monthly |
| **4.** | 85 | 1 year | 10 years | 6%, quarterly |
| **5.** | 300 | 1 quarter | 12 years | $4\frac{1}{2}\%$, annually |
| **6.** | 460 | 1 month | $1\frac{1}{2}$ years | 7%, semiannually |
| **7.** | 1,000 | 1 year | 4 years | 5%, monthly |
| **8.** | 2,500 | 6 months | 20 years | $8\frac{1}{2}\%$, annually |

**B.** *Statement Problems:*

9. Find the amount and the present value of an annuity of $350 payable at the end of each month for three years if the interest rate is (a) 5% compounded annually, and (b) 5% compounded monthly.

10. What are the amount and the present value of an annuity of $500 payable at the end of each quarter for six years if the interest rate is (a) 4% compounded annually and (b) 4% compounded quarterly?

11. A man bought a store and agreed to pay $2,000 at the end of every six months for seven years. What is the equivalent cash price of the store if the interest rate is 5% compounded quarterly?

12. A company deposits $800 at the end of every nine months in a bank that pays 3% interest compounded monthly. Find the amount of the company's account at the end of $4\frac{1}{2}$ years.

13. What is the present value of the annuity in Problem 12?

14. What is the present value of a series of $350 payments made at the end of every four months for five years if the interest rate is 6% compounded monthly?

★**Method B**   *By Use of the Formulas*   $S_n = R \cdot \dfrac{(1+r)^n - 1}{r}$ *and*

$$A_n = R \cdot \frac{1 - (1+r)^{-n}}{r}.$$

In applying formulas (13–1) and (13–2), let $r =$ the interest rate per payment interval. Then convert the value of $r$ into the given interest rate $i$. This method is illustrated by the following solutions for Examples 1 and 2.

*Solution for Example 1, page 425:*

$R = \$100$ (quarterly payment), $n = 40$ (quarterly payments), $i = \frac{1}{2}\%$ (monthly rate), $c = 3$ (interest periods in one payment interval, or

$\dfrac{3 \text{ months}}{1 \text{ month}} = 3$), $r =$ interest rate per quarter

In one payment interval, one quarter or three months, the compound amount on $1 at rate $r$ per quarter is $1 + r$

and at rate $\frac{1}{2}\%$ per month is $(1+\frac{1}{2}\%)^3$.

The two amounts are equal. Thus,

$1 + r = (1+\frac{1}{2}\%)^3$ and $r = (1+\frac{1}{2}\%)^3 - 1$

Let $S_{40} =$ the amount of the annuity of 40 quarterly payments at the quarterly rate $r$.

Then,   $S_{40} = Rs_{\overline{40}|r} = 100 \cdot \dfrac{(1+r)^{40} - 1}{r} = 100 \cdot \dfrac{[(1+\frac{1}{2}\%)^3]^{40} - 1}{(1+\frac{1}{2}\%)^3 - 1}$

$= 100 \cdot \dfrac{(1+\frac{1}{2}\%)^{120} - 1}{\frac{1}{2}\%} \cdot \dfrac{\frac{1}{2}\%}{(1+\frac{1}{2}\%)^3 - 1}$

$$= 100s_{\overline{120}|1/2\%} \cdot \frac{\frac{1}{2}\%}{(1+\frac{1}{2}\%)^3 - 1} = 100s_{\overline{120}|1/2\%} \cdot \frac{1}{s_{\overline{3}|1/2\%}}$$

$$= 100(163.87935)(.331672) = \$5,435.42$$

Let $A_{40}$ = the present value of the annuity of 40 quarterly payments at the quarterly rate $r$.

Then, $A_{40} = Ra_{\overline{40}|r} = 100 \cdot \dfrac{1-(1+r)^{-40}}{r} = 100 \cdot \dfrac{1-[(1+\frac{1}{2}\%)^3]^{-40}}{(1+\frac{1}{2}\%)^3 - 1}$

$$= 100 \cdot \frac{1-(1+\frac{1}{2}\%)^{-120}}{(1+\frac{1}{2}\%)^3 - 1}$$

$$= 100 \cdot \frac{1-(1+\frac{1}{2}\%)^{-120}}{\frac{1}{2}\%} \cdot \frac{\frac{1}{2}\%}{(1+\frac{1}{2}\%)^3 - 1}$$

$$= 100a_{\overline{120}|1/2\%} \cdot \frac{1}{s_{\overline{3}|1/2\%}} = 100(90.07345)(.331672) = \$2,987.48$$

*Solution for Example 2, page 427:*

$R$ = \$100 (monthly payment), $n$ = 72 (monthly payments), $i$ = 2% (per 6 months), $c = \dfrac{1}{6}$ (interest conversion periods in one payment interval, or $\dfrac{1 \text{ month}}{6 \text{ months}} = \dfrac{1}{6}$), $r$ = interest rate per month

In one payment interval (one month), the compound amount of \$1 at rate $r$ per month is $1 + r$, and at 2% per six months is $(1 + 2\%)^{1/6}$.

Thus,

$$1 + r = (1 + 2\%)^{1/6} \text{ and } r = (1 + 2\%)^{1/6} - 1$$

$$S_{72} = Rs_{\overline{72}|r} = 100 \cdot \frac{(1+r)^{72} - 1}{r} = 100 \cdot \frac{[(1+2\%)^{1/6}]^{72} - 1}{(1+2\%)^{1/6} - 1}$$

$$= 100 \cdot \frac{(1+2\%)^{12} - 1}{(1+2\%)^{1/6} - 1}$$

$$= 100 \cdot \frac{(1+2\%)^{12} - 1}{2\%} \cdot \frac{2\%}{(1+2\%)^{1/6} - 1}$$

$$= 100s_{\overline{12}|2\%} \cdot \frac{1}{s_{\overline{1/6}|2\%}}$$

$$= 100(13.41209)(6.0498075) = \$8,114.06$$

Similarly,

$$A_{72} = Ra_{\overline{72}|r} = 100 \cdot \frac{1-(1+r)^{-72}}{r} = 100 \cdot \frac{1-[(1+2\%)^{1/6}]^{-72}}{(1+2\%)^{1/6} - 1}$$

$$= 100 \cdot \frac{1-(1+2\%)^{-12}}{(1+2\%)^{1/6} - 1}$$

$$= 100 \cdot \frac{1-(1+2\%)^{-12}}{2\%} \cdot \frac{2\%}{(1+2\%)^{1/6} - 1}$$

$$= 100a_{\overline{12}|2\%} \cdot \frac{1}{s_{\overline{176}|2\%}}$$

$$= 100(10.57534)(6.0498075) = \$6,397.88$$

**Note:**   The method used in the above illustration provides another way to prove formulas (14–8) and (14–9). The proofs are presented below.

$1 + r = (1 + i)^c$, and $r = (1 + i)^c - 1$

$$S_n = Rs_{\overline{n}|r} = R \cdot \frac{(1 + r)^n - 1}{r} = R \cdot \frac{[(1 + i)^c]^n - 1}{(1 - i)^c - 1}$$

$$= R \cdot \frac{(1 + i)^{nc} - 1}{i} \cdot \frac{i}{(1 + i)^c - 1}$$

$$= Rs_{\overline{nc}|i} \cdot \frac{i}{(1 + i)^c - 1}$$

$$= Rs_{\overline{nc}|i} \cdot \frac{1}{s_{\overline{c}|i}}$$

Here the value of $S_n$ is the same as the value of $S_{nc}$ obtained by Method A.

Thus,

$$S_{nc} = Rs_{\overline{nc}|i} \cdot \frac{1}{s_{\overline{c}|i}} \qquad\qquad (14\text{–}8)$$

Similarly,

$$A_n = Ra_{\overline{n}|r} = R \cdot \frac{1 - (1 + r)^{-n}}{r} = R \cdot \frac{1 - [(1 + i)^c]^{-n}}{(1 + i)^c - 1}$$

$$= R \cdot \frac{1 - (1 + i)^{-nc}}{i} \cdot \frac{i}{(1 + i)^c - 1}$$

$$= Ra_{\overline{nc}|i} \cdot \frac{i}{(1 + i)^c - 1} = Ra_{\overline{nc}|i} \cdot \frac{1}{s_{\overline{c}|i}}$$

Here the value of $A_n$ is the same as the value of $A_{nc}$ obtained by Method A.

Thus,

$$A_{nc} = Ra_{\overline{nc}|i} \cdot \frac{1}{s_{\overline{c}|i}} \qquad\qquad (14\text{–}9)$$

The value of the third factor, $\frac{i}{(1 + i)^c - 1}$, may be obtained by using Table 5 (when $c$ is a whole number) or Table 5A (when $c$ is a fraction). However, it is more convenient to find the value of $\frac{1}{s_{\overline{c}|i}}$ from Tables 9 and 10 as noted in Method A.

## ★EXERCISE 14–5

**Reference: Section 14.3 A**

*Compute Problems 1–8 of Exercise 14–4 by using Method B, as described on pages 429 to 431.*

## ★B. The Size of Payment of an Ordinary Complex Annuity

In finding the size of payment of an ordinary complex annuity, use formula (14–8) when the amount of the annuity is known, and formula (14–9) when the present value of the annuity is known.

**Example 3**   A man wishes to receive $20,000 five years from now. How much must he invest at the end of each year if the first payment starts one year from now and he can get 5% interest compounded semiannually?

$S_{nc} = \$20,000$, $i = 5\%/2 = 2\frac{1}{2}\%$ (per six months), $n = 5$ (annual payments), $c = 2$ (interest periods in one year), $R = ?$

Substituting the above values in formula (14–8):

$$20,000 = Rs_{\overline{5 \times 2}|2\,1/2\%} \cdot \frac{1}{s_{\overline{2}|2\,1/2\%}}$$

$$R = 20,000s_{\overline{2}|2\,1/2\%} \cdot \frac{1}{s_{\overline{10}|2\,1/2\%}}$$

$$= 20,000(2.0250000)(.11425876 - .025)$$

$$= \$3,614.98 \qquad\qquad \text{(Tables 7 and 9)}$$

**Example 4**   A lot which sells for $1,600 can be bought for $600 down with the balance payable in 24 equal monthly payments. If the interest rate is 6% compounded annually, what is the size of the monthly payment?

$A_{nc} = 1,600 - 600 = \$1,000$, $i = 6\%$ (per year), $c = 1/12$ (interest periods in one month), $n = 24$ (monthly payments), $R = ?$

Substituting the above values in formula (14–9):

$$1,000 = Ra_{\overline{24(1/12)}|6\%} \cdot \frac{1}{s_{\overline{1/12}|6\%}}$$

$$R = 1,000s_{\overline{1/12}|6\%} \cdot \frac{1}{a_{\overline{2}|6\%}}$$

$$= 1,000(.081126)(.545437)$$

$$= \$44.25 \qquad\qquad \text{(Tables 7A and 9)}$$

## ★C. The Amount and the Present Value of a Complex Annuity Due

An annuity due has been defined previously as an annuity with periodic payments made at the beginning of each payment interval. In the following diagram, $R$ represents the payment and $\#$ represents the date for computing interest. Assume that the term of the annuity is one year, the payments are made quarterly, and the interest is compounded monthly. Notice that when each payment, $R$, accumulates for three interest periods (or one payment interval, quarter), $R$ becomes $R(1 + i)^3$. In other words, the value of $R$ at the beginning of each payment interval is equivalent to the value of $R(1 + i)^3$ at the end of each payment interval. The values of $R(1 + i)^3$ form an ordinary complex annuity. The amount of the ordinary annuity according to formula (14–8) is:

$$S_{nc} = \frac{R(1+i)^3}{s_{\overline{3}|i}} \cdot s_{\overline{4 \times 3}|i}$$

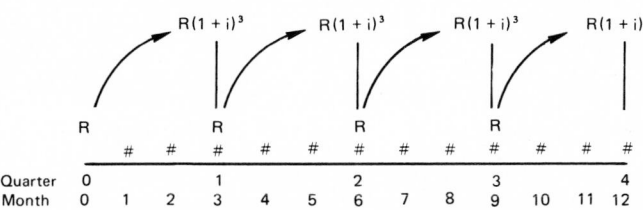

| Quarter | 0 | | | 1 | | | 2 | | | 3 | | | 4 |
| Month | 0 | 1 | 2 | 3 | 4 | 5 | 6 | 7 | 8 | 9 | 10 | 11 | 12 |

Similarly, let $c$ = the number of interest periods in one payment interval and $n$ = the number of payments. The amount of the complex annuity due, $S_{nc}$(due), therefore may be obtained from formula (14–8) by replacing $R$ by $R(1 + i)^c$ as follows:

$$S_{nc}(\text{due}) = \frac{R(1+i)^c}{s_{\overline{c}|i}} \cdot s_{\overline{nc}|i} = \frac{R}{s_{\overline{c}|i} \cdot (1+i)^{-c}} \cdot s_{\overline{nc}|i}$$

Since $s_{\overline{c}|i} \cdot (1+i)^{-c} = \dfrac{(1+i)^c - 1}{i}(1+i)^{-c} = \dfrac{1 - (1+i)^{-c}}{i} = a_{\overline{c}|i}$,

the above may be written

$$S_{nc}(\text{due}) = \frac{R}{a_{\overline{c}|i}} \cdot s_{\overline{nc}|i}, \quad \text{or}$$

$$S_{nc}(\text{due}) = Rs_{\overline{nc}|i} \cdot \frac{1}{a_{\overline{c}|i}} \tag{14–10}$$

The present value of the complex annuity due, $A_{nc}$(due), may be obtained from formula (14–9) by a method similar to that used in developing formula (14–10), and is written as follows:

$$A_{nc}(\text{due}) = \frac{R(1+i)^c}{s_{\overline{c}|i}} \cdot a_{\overline{nc}|i} = \frac{R}{a_{\overline{c}|i}} \cdot a_{\overline{nc}|i}, \quad \text{or}$$

$$A_{nc}\,(\text{due}) = Ra_{\overline{nc}|i} \cdot \frac{1}{a_{\overline{c}|i}} \qquad\qquad\qquad (14\text{--}11)$$

**Example 5**

If the interest rate is 6% compounded monthly, what is the amount and the present value of an annuity of $150 payable at the beginning of each quarter for one year?

$R = \$150$ (per quarter), $n = 4$ (quarterly payments), $i = 6\%/12 = \frac{1}{2}\%$ (per month), $c = 3$ (interest periods in one quarter)

Substituting the values in formulas (14–10) and (14–11) respectively:

$$S_{4(3)}(\text{due}) = 150 \cdot s_{\overline{4\times3}|1/2\%} \cdot \frac{1}{a_{\overline{3}|1/2\%}} = 150(12.33556)(.33667) = \$622.95$$

(Tables 7 and 9)

$$A_{4(3)}(\text{due}) = 150 \cdot a_{\overline{4\times3}|1/2\%} \cdot \frac{1}{a_{\overline{3}|1/2\%}} = 150(11.61893)(.33667) = \$586.76$$

(Tables 8 and 9)

**Example 6**

Find the amount and the present value of an annuity of $100 payable at the beginning of each month for two years. Assume that the interest rate is 4% compounded quarterly.

$R = \$100$ (per month), $n = 2 \times 12 = 24$ (monthly payments), $i = 4\%/4 = 1\%$ (per quarter), $c = \frac{1}{3}$ (interest periods in one month), and $nc = 24 \times \frac{1}{3} = 8$ (interest periods in two years).

$$S_{nc}(\text{due}) = S_{24(1/3)}\,(\text{due}) = 100 \cdot s_{\overline{8}|1\%} \cdot \frac{1}{a_{\overline{1/3}|1\%}}$$

$$= 100(8.285671)(3.009978 + .01) = \$2,502.25$$

(Tables 7 and 10)

$$A_{nc}(\text{due}) = A_{24(1/3)}(\text{due}) = 100 \cdot a_{\overline{8}|1\%} \cdot \frac{1}{a_{\overline{1/3}|1\%}}$$

$$= 100(7.651678)(3.009978 + .01) = \$2,310.79$$

(Tables 8 and 10)

Notice that $\dfrac{1}{a_{\overline{1/3}|1\%}} = \dfrac{1}{s_{\overline{1/3}|1\%}} + 1\% = 3.009978 + .01$      (Table 10)

**Note:**

The above multiplications may also be performed by using logarithms. For example, $S_{nc}(\text{due})$ is computed as follows:

|  |  |  |
|---|---|---|
| log 100 | = | 2.000 0000 (Table 3) |
| (+)log $s_{\overline{8}|1\%}$ | = | 0.918 3277 (Table 12) |

2.918 3277

(−)log $a_{\overline{1/3}|1\%}$  = −1 + 0.519 9962 (or 9.519 9962 − 10, Table 13)

    log $S_{nc}(\text{due})$ = +1 + 2.398 3315
                  = 3.3983315

Find the antilog by interpolation from Table 2. $S_{nc}$(due) = \$2,502.256, or rounded to \$2,502.26.

## ★D. The Amount and the Present Value of a Deferred Complex Annuity

The amount of a deferred complex annuity is the final value at the end of the term of the annuity. Therefore, the amount of a deferred complex annuity, $S_{nc}$(defer.), is the same as the amount of the ordinary complex annuity, or

$$S_{nc}(\textbf{defer.}) = S_{nc} = Rs_{\overline{nc}|i} \cdot \frac{1}{s_{\overline{c}|i}} \qquad (14\text{–}12)$$

The present value of a deferred complex annuity, $A_{nc}$(defer.), is the value at the beginning of the period of deferment and may be obtained by either of the two methods described below.

Let $d$ = the number of deferred payment intervals
$c$ = the number of interest periods per payment interval

The period of deferment should include $cd$ interest periods, and the term of the deferred annuity should include $nc$ interest periods.

**Method A**     First, consider that the payments were made during the period of defer-ment. Second, consider that there are two ordinary annuities; one consists of $d$ payments (or $cd$ interest periods), while the other consists of $d + n$ payments (or $cd + nc = c(d + n)$ interest periods). Third, subtract the present value of the annuity consisting of $d$ payments from the present value of the annuity consisting of $(d + n)$ payments. The remainder is the answer. This value may be obtained by formula as follows:

$$A_{nc}(\text{defer.}) = A_{cd+nc} - A_{cd} = \frac{R}{s_{\overline{c}|i}} \cdot a_{\overline{c(d+n)}|i} - \frac{R}{s_{\overline{c}|i}} a_{\overline{cd}|i}$$

or

$$A_{nc}(\textbf{defer.}) = \frac{R}{s_{\overline{c}|i}} (a_{\overline{c(d+n)}|i} - a_{\overline{cd}|i}) \qquad (14\text{–}13)$$

**Method B**     Discount the present value of the ordinary complex annuity for the period of deferment. This may be done by formula as shown below:

$$A_{nc}(\textbf{defer.}) = A_{nc}(1 + i)^{-cd} \qquad (14\text{–}14)$$

or

$$A_{nc}(\text{defer.}) = \frac{R}{s_{\overline{c}|i}} \cdot a_{\overline{nc}|i} \cdot (1 + i)^{-cd}$$

Methods A and B are diagrammed as follows: (Also see the diagrams on page 420.)

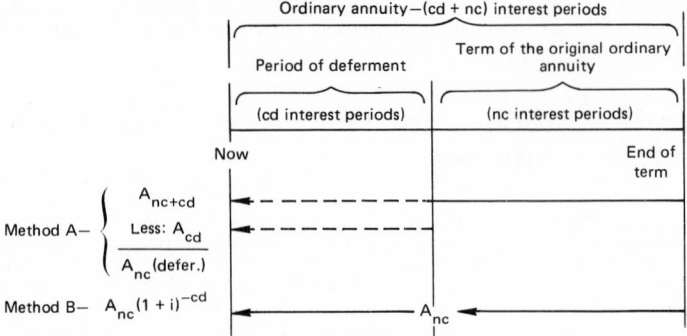

**Example 7**   Find the amount and the present value of an annuity of $150 payable quarterly for 20 payments if the first payment is due at the end of 15 months and money is worth 6% compounded semiannually.

$R = \$150$ (per quarter), $n = 20$ (quarterly payments), $i = 6\%/2 = 3\%$ (per six months), $c = \frac{1}{2}$ (interest periods in one quarter), $d = 4$ (quarters or 12 months, since the first payment covers the payment interval from the end of the 12th month to the end of the 15th month). Substituting the above values in formula (14–12):

$$S_{nc}(\text{defer.}) = 150 s_{\overline{20 \times 1/2}\,|3\%} \cdot \frac{1}{s_{\overline{1/2}\,|3\%}}$$

$$= 150(11.46388)(2.01489)$$
$$= \$3,464.77$$

Substituting the values in formula (14–13):

$$A_{nc}(\text{defer.}) = \frac{150}{s_{\overline{1/2}\,|3\%}} \cdot (a_{\overline{1/2(20+4)}\,|3\%} - a_{\overline{4 \times 1/2}\,|3\%})$$

$$= 150(2.01489)(9.954004 - 1.913470)$$

$$= 302.2335(8.040534)$$
$$= \$2,430.12$$

Substituting the values in formula (14–14):

$$A_{nc}(\text{defer.}) = \frac{150}{s_{\overline{1/2}\,|3\%}} \cdot a_{\overline{20 \times 1/2}\,|3\%} \cdot (1 + 3\%)^{-(4 \times 1/2)}$$

$$= 150(2.01489)(8.530203)(.942596)$$
$$= \$2,430.12$$

The present value may be checked by the use of the formula $P = S(1 + i)^{-n}$ as follows:

$S = \$3,464.77$, $i = 3\%$ (semiannually), $n = 12$ (semiannual periods or $20 + 4 = 24$ quarters)

$$A_{nc}(\text{defer.}) = P = 3,464.77(1 + 3\%)^{-12} = 3,464.77(0.70137988)$$
$$= \$2,430.12$$

## ★EXERCISE 14–6

### Reference: Sections 14.3 B, C, and D

**A.** *Find the payment of the ordinary complex annuity in each of the following problems:*

| | Amount ($S_{nc}$) | Present Value ($A_{nc}$) | Number of Payments (n) | Compound Interest Rate |
|---|---|---|---|---|
| **1.** | $1,000 | | 5 annual payments | 6%, semiannually |
| **2.** | 5,400 | | 12 semiannual payments | 9%, monthly |
| **3.** | | $3,500 | 24 monthly payments | 5%, quarterly |
| **4.** | | 4,800 | 28 quarterly payments | 8%, annually |
| **5.** | 360 | | 3 semiannual payments | 6%, monthly |
| **6.** | | 270 | 9 monthly payments | 10%, quarterly |

**B.** *Find the amount and the present value of the complex annuity due in each of the following problems:*

| | Payment (R) | Payment Interval | Term | Compound Interest Rate |
|---|---|---|---|---|
| **7.** | $2,500 | 1 month | $3\frac{1}{2}$ years | 6%, quarterly |
| **8.** | 120 | 1 quarter | 2 years | 5%, semiannually |
| **9.** | 80 | 6 months | 5 years | 12%, monthly |
| **10.** | 60 | 1 year | 8 years | 7%, quarterly |
| **11.** | 450 | 1 quarter | 15 years | $5\frac{1}{2}$%, annually |
| **12.** | 620 | 1 month | 2 years | 4%, semiannually |

**C.** *Find the amount and the present value of the deferred complex annuity in each of the following problems:*

| | Payment (R) | Number of Payments (n) | Number of Payment Intervals Deferred (d) | Compound Interest Rate |
|---|---|---|---|---|
| **13.** | $200, annually | 20 | 3 (years) | 4%, quarterly |
| **14.** | 460, monthly | 15 | 6 (months) | 6%, quarterly |
| **15.** | 75, semiannually | 18 | 9 ($4\frac{1}{2}$ years) | 7%, monthly |
| **16.** | 80, quarterly | 12 | 8 (quarters) | 5%, semiannually |
| **17.** | 350, quarterly | 36 | 4 (quarters) | 8%, annually |
| **18.** | 500, annually | 5 | 2 (years) | 6%, monthly |

**D.** *Statement Problems:*

**19.** The amount of an annuity at the end of ten years is $8,000, the payments are made at the end of each year, and the interest rate is 5% compounded semiannually. What is the size of each annual payment?

20. Don Emerson wishes to receive $6,000 four years from now. How much must he invest at the end of each quarter during the four-year period? Assume that he will make his first investment three months from now and he can earn $5\frac{1}{2}\%$ interest compounded annually.

21. The present value of an annuity for three years is $500, the payments are made at the end of every six months, and the interest rate is 6% compounded monthly. How large is each payment?

22. Anna Parker wishes to receive $2,000 in cash now. She agrees to repay it by making 15 equal monthly payments with the first payment to be made one month from now. The interest rate is 4% compounded quarterly. What is the size of each payment?

23. Find the amount and the present value of an annuity of $1,200 payable at the beginning of each year for six years with interest at 5% compounded monthly.

24. What are the amount and the present value of an annuity of $2,800 payable at the end of every six months for 18 years with interest at $8\frac{1}{2}\%$ compounded annually?

25. What are the amount and the present value of an annuity of $130 payable monthly for 30 payments, with the first payment at the end of 19 months from the present time with interest at 4% compounded semiannually?

26. Find the amount and the present value of an annuity of $180 payable semiannually, for eight payments, with the first payment in $5\frac{1}{2}$ years with interest at 5% compounded quarterly.

# 14.4 SUMMARY OF ANNUITY CERTAIN FORMULAS

*Symbols:*   $R =$ size of equal payments of an annuity
  $n =$ number of payments
  $i =$ interest rate per conversion period
  $c =$ number of interest periods in one payment interval, or
   $=$ payment interval/interest period
  $d =$ number of deferred payment intervals

| Application | | Formula | Formula Number | Reference Page |
|---|---|---|---|---|
| *Simple Annuity* | | | | |
| Annuity Due | Amount | $S_n(\text{due}) = Rs_{\overline{n+1}|i} - R,$ | (14–1) | 408 |
| | | or | | |
| | | $S_n(\text{due}) = Rs_{\overline{n}|i} \cdot (1 + i)$ | (14–2) | 409 |
| | Present Value | $A_n(\text{due}) = Ra_{\overline{n-1}|i} + R,$ | (14–3) | 411 |
| | | or | | |
| | | $A_n(\text{due}) = Ra_{\overline{n}|i} \cdot (1 + i)$ | (14–4) | 412 |

| Application | | Formula | Formula Number | Reference Page |
|---|---|---|---|---|
| *Simple Annuity* | | | | |
| Deferred Annuity | Amount | $S_n(\text{defer.}) = S_n = Rs_{\overline{n}|i}$ | (14–5) | 419 |
| | Present Value | $A_n(\text{defer.}) = Ra_{\overline{d+n}|i} - Ra_{\overline{d}|i},$ | (14–6) | 419 |
| | | or | | |
| | | $A_n(\text{defer.}) = Ra_{\overline{n}|i} \cdot (1+i)^{-d}$ | (14–7) | 420 |
| *Complex Annuity* | | | | |
| Ordinary Annuity | Amount | $S_{nc} = Rs_{\overline{nc}|i} \cdot \dfrac{1}{s_{\overline{c}|i}}$ | (14–8) | 426 and 431 |
| | Present Value | $A_{nc} = Ra_{\overline{nc}|i} \cdot \dfrac{1}{s_{\overline{c}|i}}$ | (14–9) | 426 and 431 |
| Annuity Due | Amount | $S_{nc}(\text{due}) = Rs_{\overline{nc}|i} \cdot \dfrac{1}{a_{\overline{c}|i}}$ | (14–10) | 433 |
| | Present Value | $A_{nc}(\text{due}) = Ra_{\overline{nc}|i} \cdot \dfrac{1}{a_{\overline{c}|i}}$ | (14–11) | 434 |
| Deferred Annuity | Amount | $S_{nc}(\text{defer.}) = S_{nc} = Rs_{\overline{nc}|i} \cdot \dfrac{1}{s_{\overline{c}|i}}$ | (14–12) | 435 |
| | Present Value | $A_{nc}(\text{defer.}) = \dfrac{R}{s_{\overline{c}|i}}(a_{\overline{c(d+n)}|i} - a_{\overline{cd}|i})$ | (14–13) | 435 |
| | | or | | |
| | | $A_{nc}(\text{defer.}) = A_{nc}(1+i)^{-cd}$ | (14–14) | 435 |

## EXERCISE 14–7

### Review of Chapters 13 and 14

1. What are the amount and the present value of an annuity of $140 payable at the beginning of each quarter for 30 quarters if the interest rate is 5% compounded quarterly?

2. What are the amount and the present value of an annuity of $60 payable at the beginning of every six months for 20 years if the interest rate is 4% compounded semiannually?

3. In Problem 1, if payments are payable at the end of each quarter, what are the amount and the present value?

4. Find the amount and the present value in Problem 2 if the payments of $60 each are payable at the end of every six months.

5. Refer to Problem 1. What are the amount and the present value if the payments of the annuity are payable at the end of each quarter and the interest rate is 5% compounded (a) monthly, (b) semiannually?

**6.** Refer to Problem 2. What are the amount and the present value if the payments are payable at the end of each semiannual period and the interest rate is 4% compounded (a) quarterly, (b) annually?

★**7.** Refer to Problem 1. What are the amount and the present value if the interest rate is 5% compounded (a) monthly, (b) semiannually.

★**8.** Refer to Problem 2. Find the amount and the present value if the interest rate is 4% compounded (a) quarterly, (b) annually.

**9.** Tom plans to deposit $30 now and $30 hereafter every month for a total of 36 deposits. If his deposits can earn 5% interest compounded monthly, what is the final value at the end of three years?

**10.** Assume that $80 is deposited now and hereafter for 26 additional quarterly deposits of $80 each. What is the final value if the interest rate is 6% compounded quarterly?

**11.** Refer to Problem 9. What is the present value of the annuity?

**12.** Refer to Problem 10. What is the present value of the annuity?

**13.** On April 1, 1980, Jane Taylor deposits $120 in a bank that pays 6% interest compounded quarterly. She plans to deposit the same amount every three months thereafter until the last deposit on April 1, 1984. How much money will be in her account on July 1, 1984?

**14.** A suite of living room furniture can be bought for $40 per month for 12 monthly payments with the first payment due now. If money is worth 7% compounded monthly, what is the cash price of the suite?

**15.** A house can be bought for $1,120 down plus $120 per month payable at the end of each month. The last monthly payment will be 14 years and 11 months from the date of purchase. The payment plan is computed at 6% interest compounded monthly. What is the cash price of the house?

**16.** Refer to Problem 15. If the house can be rented for $85 per month payable in advance each month and the house is expected to have a value of $12,000 at the end of 15 years, should someone who wishes to occupy the house for 15 years only, buy or rent the house? Assume that the money can be invested at (a) 6% compounded monthly, (b) 5% compounded monthly.

**17.** What are the amount and the present value of an annuity of $40 payable at the end of each month for five years if the interest rate is 6% compounded quarterly?

**18.** Find the amount and the present value of an annuity of $75 payable at the end of each year for 24 years if the interest rate is 6% compounded quarterly.

**19.** Johnson wishes to have $3,000 six years from now. How much must he invest each year if the first investment starts now and the interest is 5% compounded annually? He will not make an investment at the end of the six years.

**20.** Davy's father wishes to have $5,000 when Davy reaches 18 years of age. How much must the father invest now and each quarter thereafter at a 4% interest rate compounded quarterly? Davy is six years old now. His father does not wish to make an investment on Davy's 18th birthday.

★**21.** Laura wants to have $3,000 at the end of six years. Her investment can earn 5% interest compounded monthly. How much must she invest each year if the first investment starts (a) now? (b) at the end of one year?

★**22.** Compute Problem 20 assuming the interest rate is 4% compounded semiannually. Also, find the size of the quarterly investment if Davy's father makes the first investment three months from now and the last investment on Davy's 18th birthday. The interest rate is 4% compounded semiannually.

**23.** A washing machine can be bought for 18 equal monthly payments with the first payment due now. If the cash price is $400 and the interest rate is 6% compounded monthly, what is the size of each payment?

**24.** Mrs. Rogers purchased· a farm on May 1, 1980, and promised to pay for it in equal quarterly installments. The cash price of the farm is $7,000. The first payment was made on the purchase date and the last payment is to be made on May 1, 1985. What is the size of each quarterly payment if the interest rate is 4% compounded quarterly?

★**25.** What is the answer in Problem 23 if the interest rate is 6% compounded semiannually?

★**26.** What is the answer in Problem 24 if the interest rate is 4% compounded monthly?

**27.** At what nominal rate compounded quarterly will an annuity of $300 payable at the beginning of each quarter for eight years amount to $12,000?

**28.** What is the nominal rate compounded monthly if the amount of an annuity of $60 payable at the beginning of each month for three years is $2,500?

**29.** At what nominal rate compounded quarterly does an annuity of $80 payable at the beginning of each quarter for nine years have a present value of $2,300?

**30.** What is the nominal rate compounded semiannually if the present value of an annuity of $150 payable at the beginning of every six months for 10 years is $2,500?

**31.** If $80 is deposited at the beginning of each quarter at 6% compounded quarterly, how many payments will be required for the deposits to amount to at least $3,000?

**32.** On March 1, 1980, Bobson plans to invest $120 each month with the first investment starting then. She wishes to have at least $5,000 as the final value. If she can earn 6% interest compounded monthly on her investment, on what date will she have the final value?

**33.** Carlson purchased a $6,000 car and agreed to pay for it with monthly installments of $180 each, starting on the date of purchase. If the interest rate is 5% compounded monthly, how many monthly payments are required?

**34.** The present value of an annuity of $60 payable at the beginning of each quarter is $2,500. What is the number of payments of the annuity if the interest rate is 4% compounded quarterly?

**35.** What are the amount and the present value of an annuity of $120 payable at the end of every six months for 15 payments, with the first payment to be made two years from now? Assume that the interest rate is 5% compounded semiannually.

36. Find the amount and the present value of an annuity of $50 per quarter for 30 payments if the first payment is due four years from now and money is worth 8% compounded quarterly.

37. Smith borrows $8,000 at 6% interest compounded quarterly and agrees to repay it in 20 equal quarterly payments. What is the size of each payment if the first payment is due at the end of five years?

38. Thomas borrows $600 at 4% compounded monthly and agrees to repay it in 16 monthly payments. Find the size of each monthly payment if the first payment is due at the end of one year.

39. If $100 is deposited at the end of each quarter and the interest rate is 12% compounded quarterly, how many quarterly payments will be needed for the deposits to have a present value of $2,000? Assume that the first deposit is made at the end of two years.

40. If $25 is deposited at the end of ten months from now and $25 every month thereafter, how many monthly deposits will be required for a value which now is equivalent to $800? Assume that the interest rate is 5% compounded monthly.

41. Mrs. Smith deposited $1,000 on each of the following dates: 1/1/80, 4/1/80, 7/1/80, 10/1/80, 1/1/81. What is the single value on each of the following dates that is equivalent to the five deposits above? (a) 1/1/81? (b) 1/1/80? (c) 10/1/79? (d) 1/1/79? Assume that money is worth 4% compounded quarterly.

42. Let 1/1/81 be the comparison date. Find the value on the comparison date for each of the single values obtained in Problem 41.

# Part Four

## MATHEMATICS IN INVESTMENT — APPLICATIONS

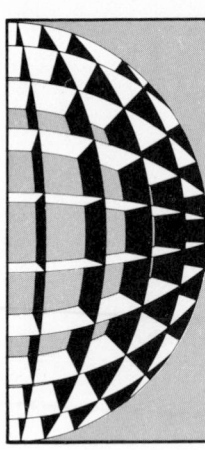

# Chapter 15

# Extinction of Debts

## 15.1 DEBT EXTINCTION BY AMORTIZATION

The word "debt" in this chapter refers to a long-term obligation. Long-term debts are normally in the form of long-term notes or bonds with a maturity date which is more than one year. Generally, notes are issued to a *single source* from which a loan is obtained, whereas bonds are issued to a *group* of creditors. Long-term debts usually involve large sums of money. A borrower may promise to discharge the debt either by making periodic partial payments under the *amortization* method or by establishing a *sinking fund* into which periodic deposits are made in order to pay a single sum on the date of maturity.

The amortization method broadly refers to the discharging of a debt by means of a set of regular or irregular and equal or unequal payments. The methods for irregular and unequal payments were presented in Chapter 9 (Section 9.4, Partial Payments: the Merchants' Rule and the United States Rule.) In this chapter only a debt discharged by a sequence of *equal* payments at *equal* intervals of time is considered. *The original principal of the debt, therefore, is the present value of an annuity of the equal payments.* In order to discharge a debt, each payment must be greater than the periodic interest, so that a part of the payment applies to the interest and the remainder applies to the principal until the principal becomes zero.

The following discussion first treats long-term debts other than bonds. Amortization of bonded debts is discussed later in this chapter.

## A. Finding the Size of the Periodic Payment

The size of the periodic payment for amortizing a debt may be found by using the method discussed in Section 13.5 of Chapter 13. The method shows how to find the size of each periodic payment of an ordinary annuity when the present value is known. In applying this method, consider the value of the debt as the present value of the annuity.

**Example 1** A man purchased a $75,000 house and made a $15,000 down payment. He agreed to pay the balance by making equal payments at the end of each month for 15 years. If the interest charged is 8% compounded monthly, what is the size of the monthly payment?

The unpaid balance is the present value, or $A_n = 75,000 - 15,000 = 60,000$, $i = 8\%/12 = \frac{2}{3}\%$ (per month), and $n = 15 \times 12 = 180$ (monthly payments)

Substituting the values in the formula $A_n = Ra_{\overline{n}|i}$:

$$60,000 = Ra_{\overline{180}|2/3\%}$$

$$R = \frac{60,000}{a_{\overline{180}|2/3\%}}$$

$R = 60,000(.0095565) = \$573.39$ $\qquad$ (Table 9)

# B. Finding the Outstanding Principal

Often both the creditor and the borrower must know the amount of the *outstanding principal* or the *unpaid balance* on a certain date. The information may be needed for various reasons: it may be necessary for accounting purposes; the creditor may want to sell the unpaid balance; or the creditor and the borrower may agree to settle the balance on an earlier date. The outstanding principal may be determined under two types of arrangements: (a) all periodic payments are equal, or (b) all periodic payments, except the final payment, are equal.

## (1) ALL PERIODIC PAYMENTS ARE EQUAL

When it is necessary for all the periodic payments to be the same size, the method given in Example 1 should be used to find the size of the payments. The outstanding principal on a certain date is the present value of an annuity formed by the remaining unpaid payments, as shown below:

**Example 2** Refer to Example 1. Find the outstanding principal after the man made the monthly payments for 10 years.

$R = \$573.39$ (per month), $i = 2/3\%$ (per month), $n$ (remaining payments) $= 180$ (total) $- 120$ (paid, or $10 \times 12$) $= 60$ (monthly payments).

Substituting the values in formula $A_n = Ra_{\overline{n}|i}$:

$A_n = 573.39 a_{\overline{60}|2/3\%} = 573.39(49.31843) = \$28,278.69$

The above computation is diagrammed as follows:

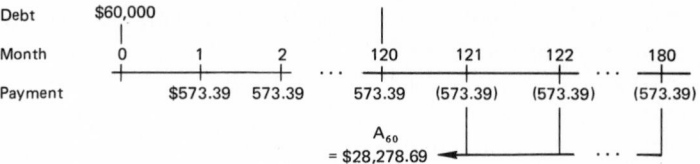

Instead of using the formula method as presented in Example 2, the outstanding principal on a certain date may be obtained by constructing an amortization schedule such as that shown in the following example.

**Example 3**   A debt of $4,000 is to be amortized by equal payments at the end of every six months for three years. If the interest charged is 6% compounded semiannually, find the outstanding principal after each payment is made.

**Step (1)**   Find the size of the periodic payment.

$A_n = \$4,000$, $i = 6\%/2 = 3\%$ (per six months), $n = 3 \times 2 = 6$ (semiannual periods)

$$4,000 = Ra_{\overline{6}|3\%}$$

$$R = \frac{4,000}{a_{\overline{6}|3\%}} = 4,000(.1845975) = \$738.39 \qquad \text{(Table 9)}$$

**Step (2)**   Find the outstanding principals by constructing the amortization schedule shown below.

## AMORTIZATION SCHEDULE
**(Example 3)**

| (1) <br> Period <br> (6-Month <br> Interval) | (2) <br> Outstanding <br> Principal at <br> Beginning of <br> Each Period <br> (2) − (5)* | (3) <br> Interest Due <br> at End <br> of Period <br> (2) × 3% | (4) <br> Equal <br> Payment at <br> End of Each <br> Period | (5) <br> Portion of <br> Principal Re- <br> duced by <br> Each Payment <br> (4) − (3) |
|---|---|---|---|---|
| 1 | $4,000.00 | $120.00 | $ 738.39 | $ 618.39 |
| 2 | 3,381.61 | 101.45 | 738.39 | 636.94 |
| 3 | 2,744.67 | 82.34 | 738.39 | 656.05 |
| 4 | 2,088.62 | 62.66 | 738.39 | 675.73 |
| 5 | 1,412.89 | 42.39 | 738.39 | 696.00 |
| 6 | 716.89 | 21.51 | 738.40 | 716.89 |
| Total | | $430.35 | $4,430.35 | $4,000.00 |

\* Of the previous period. For example, $3,381.61 = \$4,000 − \$618.39$.

Observe the amortization schedule of Example 3. Column (2) shows the outstanding principal after each payment is made. For example, the outstanding principal after the fourth payment is $1,412.89. The fourth payment is made at the end of the fourth period. Thus, $1,412.89 is also the principal at the beginning of the fifth period. The discharged portion of the original principal after the fourth payment is $2,587.11 (= $4,000 − $1,412.89, or = $618.39 + $636.94 + $656.05 + $675.73, see column (5) of the schedule).

Each outstanding principal shown in Column (2) may be checked by using the formula method, $A_n = Ra_{\overline{n}|i}$. For example, the outstanding principal after the fourth payment is made is the present value of an annuity formed by the two remaining unpaid payments.

> $A_n = ?$, $R = 738.39$, $i = 3\%$, $n = 2$ (the number of the remaining semiannual payments)

Substituting the values in the formula as follows:

$$A_n = 738.39a_{\overline{2}|3\%} = 738.39(1.91347) = \$1,412.89$$

The last figures in Columns (2) and (5) should be the same. The total for Column (5) should be equal to the original principal, $4,000. Theoretically speaking, all the payments should be equal. However, the schedule shows that the sixth payment is $738.40. The discrepancy of one cent results from rounding all computations to the nearest cent. For example, interest due at the end of the sixth period is computed as follows:

> $716.89 \times 3\% = \$21.5067$, which is rounded to $21.51

The size of the sixth payment therefore is $716.89 + 21.51 = $738.40. The final payment covers the outstanding principal at the beginning of the last payment interval and the interest due thereon.

Here, the interest for each period is computed by the simple interest method. It should be observed that *when a debtor makes each of the simple interest payments on the interest date, the simple interest method is actually a compound interest method.* Also, note that as the principal is gradually reduced, the periodic interest becomes smaller after each payment is made. Thus, a greater portion of each equal payment is used in reducing the principal.

## EXERCISE 15–1

### Reference: Sections 15.1 A and B1

**A.** *Find the size of the periodic payment and the outstanding principal at the indicated time in each of the following problems, without constructing an amortization schedule. Payments are assumed to be made at the end of each period.*

| | Debt | Number of Payments by Amortization | Compound Interest Rate | Required Outstanding Principal |
|---|---|---|---|---|
| **1.** | $ 5,000 | 18, monthly | 12%, monthly | after 10th payment |
| **2.** | 3,000 | 12, semiannual | 10%, semiannually | after 5th payment |

|  | Debt | Number of Payments by Amortization | Compound Interest Rate | Required Outstanding Principal |
|---|---|---|---|---|
| 3. | $ 4,000 | 4, quarterly | 4%, quarterly | after 3d payment |
| 4. | 6,000 | 8, annual | 5%, annually | after 1st payment |
| 5. | 8,000 | 20, semiannual | 7%, semiannually | after 7th payment |
| 6. | 20,000 | 45, monthly | 6%, monthly | after 18th payment |
| 7. | 200 | 5, annual | 8%, annually | after 2d payment |
| 8. | 500 | 10, quarterly | 7%, quarterly | after 6th payment |

**B.** *Statement Problems:*

9. A debt of $6,000 is to be amortized with four equal semiannual payments. If the interest rate is 6% compounded semiannually, what is the size of each payment? Construct an amortization schedule.

10. A loan of $2,000 is to be amortized with five equal annual payments. The interest rate is 4% compounded annually. Find the annual payment and construct an amortization schedule.

11. A man bought an $8,000 farm and made a $1,000 down payment. He agreed to pay the balance by making equal payments at the end of every three months for a period of two years. The interest charged was 8% compounded quarterly. Find the outstanding principal after the fourth payment by constructing a partial amortization schedule.

12. A $15,000 house was purchased with a down payment of $2,000 and monthly payments for 15 years. The interest rate was 6% compounded monthly. (a) Find the size of the monthly payment. (b) Construct a partial amortization schedule to find the outstanding principal after the third payment.

## (2) ALL PERIODIC PAYMENTS EXCEPT THE FINAL PAYMENT ARE EQUAL

Sometimes the size of each payment is not obtained by the method explained in Section A above. Instead, it is specified by the agreement between the creditor and the debtor, and a more convenient or rounded figure, such as $50 or $100, is decided upon as the size of each payment. The exact size of the final payment is not known. It may or may not equal the size of other payments. Under such a condition, when an amortization schedule is not constructed, the outstanding principal on a certain date is computed by a method different from that discussed above. The following example is used to illustrate the methods of computation for this type of problem.

**Example 4**    A debt of $6,000 is to be discharged by payments of $1,000 at the end of every three months. Interest charged is 4% compounded quarterly. Find (a) the number of payments, (b) the outstanding principal after each payment is made, (c) the interest included in each payment, (d) the principal included in each payment, and (e) the size of the final payment and the total of the payments.

**Method A**    *Constructing an Amortization Schedule.* After an amortization schedule has been constructed, the answers may be found in the respective columns as shown below:

## AMORTIZATION SCHEDULE
(Example 4)

| (1)<br>Period<br>(3-Month<br>Interval) | (2)<br>Outstanding<br>Principal at<br>Beginning of<br>Each Period<br>(2) − (5) | (3)<br>Interest<br>Due at<br>End of<br>Period<br>(2) × 1% | (4)<br>Payment at<br>End of<br>Each Period | (5)<br>Portion of<br>Principal<br>Reduced by<br>Each Payment<br>(4) − (3) |
|---|---|---|---|---|
| 1 | $6,000.00 | $ 60.00 | $1,000.00 | $  940.00 |
| 2 | 5,060.00 | 50.60 | 1,000.00 | 949.40 |
| 3 | 4,110.60 | 41.11 | 1,000.00 | 958.89 |
| 4 | 3,151.71 | 31.52 | 1,000.00 | 968.48 |
| 5 | 2,183.23 | 21.83 | 1,000.00 | 978.17 |
| 6 | 1,205.06 | 12.05 | 1,000.00 | 987.95 |
| 7 | 217.11    +  | 2.17   = | 219.28 | 217.11 |
| Total | | $219.28 | $6,219.28 | $6,000.00 |

**Method B**    *Without Constructing an Amortization Schedule.* When a schedule is not constructed, the answers in the schedule above may be obtained directly as follows:

*Column (1)*—The number of payments. Use the formula $a_{\overline{n}|i} = \dfrac{A_n}{R}$:

$A_n = \$6,000$, $R = \$1,000$ (per quarter), $i = 4\%/4 = 1\%$ (per quarter), $n = ?$ (quarters)

$$a_{\overline{n}|1\%} = \frac{6,000}{1,000} = 6.$$ From Table 8, we have:

| $n$ | $a_{\overline{n}|1\%}$ |
|---|---|
| 6 | 5.79547647 |
| ? | 6.00000000 |
| 7 | 6.72819453 |

Thus, $n$ must be between 6 and 7. However, the debt of $6,000 cannot be completely discharged by six payments of $1,000 each. The seventh payment is necessary, although the payment may be smaller than each of the first six payments.

*Column (2)*—The outstanding principal after each payment is made. Only the outstanding principal after the fifth payment (or at the beginning of the sixth payment interval) is computed here for the purpose of illustration.

**Step (1)**  Find the value of the original debt on the date of the fifth payment as if no payments were made previously. Use the formula $S = P(1 + i)^n$:

$P = 6{,}000$, $i = 1\%$, $n = 5$

$S = 6{,}000(1 + 1\%)^5 = 6{,}000(1.051010) = \$6{,}306.06$

**Step (2)**  Find the value of the five payments up to that date as if the payments were invested. Use the formula $S_n = R s_{\overline{n}|i}$:

$S_n = 1{,}000 s_{\overline{5}|1\%} = 1{,}000(5.10100) = \$5{,}101.00$

**Step (3)**  Find the difference between the results of Steps (1) and (2).

$\$6{,}306.06 - \$5{,}101.00 = \$1{,}205.06$

The above computation is diagrammed below:

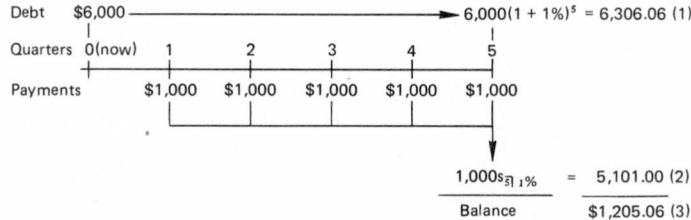

*Columns (3) and (5)*—The interest and the principal included in each payment. Only the sixth payment is computed here for illustration. Interest for the sixth payment period = Outstanding principal after the fifth payment is made multiplied by $1\% = 1{,}205.06(1\%)$ = \$12.05.

Principal included in the sixth payment = sixth payment − interest for the sixth payment period = $1{,}000 - 12.05 = \$987.95$.

*Column (4)*—The final payment of \$219.28 and the total payments of \$6,219.28. They may be obtained by any one of the following three methods without constructing a schedule:

**Method A**  Assume that the debtor paid \$1,000 (which is the same amount as the other payments) on the seventh payment date. The overpayment after the seventh payment is \$780.72 and is computed as follows: (See the method used for Column (2) above.)

$S_7 = 1{,}000 s_{\overline{7}|1\%} \qquad = 1{,}000(7.213535) = \$7{,}213.535$ (Amount of payments on the seventh payment date)

$S\ = 6{,}000(1 + 1\%)^7 = 6{,}000(1.0721354) = \$6{,}432.812$ (Amount of the debt on the seventh payment date)

Overpayment = $\overline{\$\ 780.723}$, rounded to \$780.72

The overpayment should be recovered. Thus,

the final payment = $1,000.00 − $780.72 = $219.28

The total of the seven payments is the sum of the six equal payments of $1,000 each and the final small payment, or

the total of the payments = 1,000(6) + 219.28 = $6,219.28

**★Method B**  Find the outstanding principal after the sixth payment (the last of the equal payments of $1,000) and then add the interest on the outstanding principal to obtain the final payment.

$S = 6,000(1 + 1\%)^6 = 6,000(1.0615202) = \$6,369.121$  (Amount of the debt)

$S_6 = 1,000s_{\overline{6}|1\%}\quad = 1,000(6.152015)\ =\ \underline{\$6,152.015}$  (Amount of payments)

$\$\ \ 217.106$, or $217.11 (Outstanding principal after the sixth payment)

(See the method used for Column (2) above.)

The interest for the seventh period = 217.11(1%) = $2.17.

The final payment = 217.11 + 2.17 = $219.28.

**★Method C**  First, find the total of the seven payments as follows:

By interpolation, the actual value of $n$ (number of payments) is 6.2192769. (See solution for Column (1) for $a_{\overline{n}|i}$ values.)

Total of payments = number of payments *(n)* × the size of each payment *(R)*
$$= 6.2192769(1,000) = \$6,219.2769,\ \text{or}\ \$6,219.28.$$

Then, subtract the sum of the six equal payments from the total:

The final payment = 6,219.28 − 1,000(6) = $219.28.

# EXERCISE 15–2

## Reference: Section 15.1 B2

**A.** *In each of the following problems, find (a) the number of payments, (b) the outstanding principal at the indicated time, (c) the interest and the principal included in the next payment after the indicated time in (b), and (d) the size of the final payment and the total of the cash payments. Do not construct an amortization schedule in finding your answers.*

| | Debt | Payment (Made at End of Each Period) | Compound Interest Rate | Required Outstanding Principal |
|---|---|---|---|---|
| **1.** | $ 4,000 | $200 every 3 months | 8%, quarterly | after 20th payment |
| **2.** | 6,000 | $600 every 3 months | 6%, quarterly | after 7th payment |
| **3.** | 5,000 | $1,000 every 6 months | 4%, semiannually | after 3d payment |

|  | Debt | Payment (Made at End of Each Period) | Compound Interest Rate | Required Out-standing Principal |
|---|---|---|---|---|
| **4.** | $    800 | $100 every year | 5%, annually | after 4th payment |
| **5.** | 1,400 | $50 every month | 12%, monthly | after 6th payment |
| **6.** | 25,000 | $2,000 every 6 months | 7%, semiannually | after 11th payment |

**B.** *Statement Problems:*

7. A debt of $8,000 is to be amortized with $2,500 being paid at the end of every six months. The interest rate is 6% compounded semiannually. Construct an amortization schedule.
8. A debt of $4,000 is to be amortized with $800 being paid at the end of each year. The interest rate is 4% compounded annually. Construct an amortization schedule.

## 15.2 AMORTIZATION BY THE ADD-ON INTEREST METHOD

The add-on interest method is frequently used by finance companies and banks in computing the equal periodic payments for amortizing a personal loan. In this method, interest charged is added on to the amount of the original loan. The length of borrowing time is usually limited to a range from a few months to about 18 months although a longer period may also be used for such loans. Under this method, the periodic payments are computed as follows:

1. Compute the interest *(I)* on the principal *(P)* by the simple interest method. Use the formula $I = Pin$, where $i =$ the *stated* annual interest rate and $n =$ the borrowing time expressed in the units of years.
2. Divide the sum of the simple interest and the principal $(S = P + I)$ by the number of payments to obtain the size of each payment.

The size of the periodic payment computed by the add-on interest method is usually larger than the size computed by the annuity formula $A_n = Ra_{\overline{n}|i}$. Thus, the annual interest rate charged by using the add-on interest method is actually larger than the stated rate. A moneylender should investigate carefully the actual interest rate charged to avoid a situation constituting usury under state laws.

**Example 1**    A man borrowed $1,200 from a bank and agreed to make 12 equal monthly payments, the first installment being payable one month from the date of borrowing. The bank computed the monthly payments by the "add-on interest method" at the advertised interest rate of 6% per year. Find (a) the size of each payment, and (b) the actual annual interest rate charged by the bank.

(a) Under the add-on interest method, the simple interest computed at 6% per year is immediately added to the principal in computing the monthly payments.

$I$ (interest) $= Pin = 1{,}200 \times 6\% \times 1 = \$72.$ ($n = 1$, year)
$S$ (amount) $= P + I = 1{,}200 + 72 = \$1{,}272.$
Size of payment $= 1{,}272 \div 12 = \$106$ (per month).

(b) Since the equal payments are paid in regular intervals, this loan payment plan constitutes an ordinary annuity problem.

$A_n = \$1{,}200$, $R = \$106$ (per month), $n = 12$ (monthly payments), $i = ?$ (per month).

Substituting the values in formula $A_n = Ra_{\overline{n}|i}$ as follows:

$$a_{\overline{n}|i} = \frac{A_n}{R} = \frac{1{,}200}{106} = 11.3208.$$

By interpolation from Table 8, the actual interest rate is found to be 10.92% compounded monthly. The interpolation is shown below: (Write the larger numbers, which are in the column of values all known, on the top lines.)

| | $i$ | $a_{\overline{12}|i}$ | |
|---|---|---|---|
| | $\frac{7}{8}\%$ | 11.3445 | (1) |
| | $x$ | 11.3208 | (2) |
| | $1\%$ | 11.2551 | (3) |

$$\frac{(2)-(3)}{(1)-(3)} \quad \frac{x-1\%}{-\frac{1}{8}\%} = \frac{.0657}{.0894}$$

$$x = 1\% + (-\tfrac{1}{8}\,\%)\left(\frac{.0657}{.0894}\right) = .01 - \left(\frac{1}{800}\right)\left(\frac{657}{894}\right) = .0091, \text{ or}$$

$i = .91\%$ per month.
The nominal rate $= i \times 12 = .91\% \times 12 = 10.92\%$ compounded monthly.

**Note:**  1. If the periodic payments are computed by the annuity formula, the size of each monthly payment is only $103.28, or

$$R = \frac{1{,}200}{a_{\overline{12}|1/2\%}} = 1{,}200(.086066) = \$103.28,$$

which is smaller than $106, the amount by the add-on interest method.
2. If the effective annual interest rate is desired, the formula $f = (1 + i)^m - 1$ as presented in Section 11.5 may be used. For the above example,

$$f = \left(1 + \frac{10.92\%}{12}\right)^{12} - 1 = (1 + .91\%)^{12} - 1$$

$$= 1.115 - 1 = .115 = 11.5\% \text{ (the effective rate)}$$

The factor $(1 + .94\%)^{12} = (1.0091)^{12}$ is computed by using logarithms:

$12(\log 1.0091) = 12(.0039342) = .0472104.$
Find the antilog, $(1.0091)^{12} = 1.115.$

3. If the stated annual interest rate and the payment interval are not changed, an amortization plan based on the add-on interest method with a *longer* period of repayment will give a *lower* actual interest rate charged. In the above example, the amortization plan of 1 year (or 12 monthly payments) gives the actual rate of .91% per month, or $i$ is larger than $\frac{7}{8}$%. However, with the same stated interest rate of 6% and monthly payment interval, the amortization plan of 8 years (or $8 \times 12 = 96$ monthly payments) will give a lower actual rate, or $i$ is smaller than $\frac{7}{8}$%. The 8-year plan is computed as follows:

$I = 1,200 \times 6\% \times 8 = \$576.$
$S = 1,200 + 576 = \$1,776.$
$R = 1,776 \div 96 = \$18.50$ per month.

$$a_{\overline{n}|i} = \frac{A_n}{R} = \frac{1,200}{18.50} = 64.8649.$$

From Table 8: $\frac{3}{4}\% < i < \frac{7}{8}\%$.   $(n = 96)$

# ★15.3 AMORTIZATION OF CALLABLE BONDS

A *bond* is a type of promissory note issued by corporations or government units for the purpose of borrowing money from a group of creditors, rather than from an individual. Most bonds are redeemable on their maturity date. However, some bonds are redeemable prior to the maturity date if the issuer calls for them. Bonds with such provisions are known as *callable bonds*.

When a company redeems, or retires, a bond, the principal is often reduced by a multiple of the face value that appears on the bond. Since bonds are usually issued in fixed denominations, such as $100, $500, and $1,000, equal periodic payments, which include the interest and the principal for bond retirement, very often are impossible to achieve. The following example is used to illustrate the method of equalizing each of the periodic payments, insofar as possible, in retiring a bonded debt.

**Example 1**     A company issued $200,000 of bonds at 4% interest payable semiannually. The face value of each bond is $1,000. The bonds are to be retired within a three-year period. Construct a schedule to equalize each semiannual payment, including interest payment and principal retirement.

There are six interest payment periods. The ideal size of the payment, interest and principal included, on each interest date is an equal figure, which may be computed by using the formula $A_n = Ra_{\overline{n}|i}$:

$A_n = \$200,000$, $n = 6$ (payments), $i = 4\%/2 = 2\%$ (per six months)

Substituting the values in the above formula:

$200,000 = Ra_{\overline{6}|2\%},$

$$R = 200,000\left(\frac{1}{a_{\overline{6}|2\%}}\right) = 200,000(.17852581) = \$35,705.16$$

When the ideal size of each payment is used as a guide (see Column (4)), the following schedule may be constructed:

## AMORTIZATION SCHEDULE FOR A CALLABLE BOND DEBT

| (1) Period (6-Month Interval) | (2) Outstanding Principal at Beginning of Each Period (2) − (5) | (3) Interest Due at End of Period (2) × 2% | (4) Ideal Payment on Principal $35,705.16 − (3) | (5) Bond Value Retired, Multiple of $1,000* Closest to (4) | (6) Total Periodic Payment (3) + (5) |
|---|---|---|---|---|---|
| 1 | $200,000 | $ 4,000 | $ 31,705.16 | $ 32,000 | $ 36,000 |
| 2 | 168,000 | 3,360 | 32,345.16 | 32,000 | 35,360 |
| 3 | 136,000 | 2,720 | 32,985.16 | 33,000 | 35,720 |
| 4 | 103,000 | 2,060 | 33,645.16 | 34,000 | 36,060 |
| 5 | 69,000 | 1,380 | 34,325.16 | 34,000 | 35,380 |
| 6 | 35,000 | 700 | 35,005.16 | 35,000 | 35,700 |
| Total | | $14,220 | $200,010.96 | $200,000 | $214,220 |

* The face value of each bond.

## EXERCISE 15–3

### Reference: Sections 15.2 and 15.3

1. Assume that a bank's stated nominal interest rate is 6%. Find the monthly payments that a bank requires on an $800 personal loan to be repaid in 16 equal monthly installments by (a) the add-on interest method and (b) the annuity formula method as presented in Section 15.1. Which one of the two methods gives higher monthly payments?

2. A man borrowed $1,500 from a finance company and agreed to repay the loan in 8 equal monthly payments, the first payment due in one month. Assume that the company's stated nominal interest rate is 5%. Find the monthly payments by (a) the add-on interest method and (b) the annuity formula method (see Section 15.1). Which one of the two methods requires higher payments?

3. Refer to Problem 1(a). What is the actual annual interest rate charged by the bank?

4. Refer to Problem 2(a). What is the actual annual interest rate charged by the finance company?

★5. A company issued $150,000 of bonds at 5% interest payable annually. The face value of each bond is $500. The bonds are to be retired within five years. Construct a schedule to equalize each annual payment, including interest payment and principal retirement.

★6. The J. P. Tylon Company issued $100,000 of bonds, each with a face value of $100. The bonds are to be retired within three years. Construct a schedule to equalize each semiannual payment, including 4% interest payable semiannually and principal retirement.

# 15.4 DEBT EXTINCTION BY SINKING FUND

In some cases, the principal of a long-term investment may be repaid on the maturity date, but the interest is paid periodically when it is due. Since a long-term debt is usually for a large amount, debtors often periodically deposit a sum of money in a fund, known as a *sinking fund,* in order to retire the principal on the maturity date. The periodic deposits need not be of equal amount nor be made at equal intervals of time. However, in this chapter, only examples of periodic deposits made at equal intervals and in equal amounts are considered. The deposits may be made either at the end of or at the beginning of each period. The deposits thus form an annuity problem, and *the amount of the annuity is the value of the principal of the debt on the maturity date.* The size of the periodic deposit can be obtained from the ordinary annuity formula $S_n = Rs_{\overline{n}|i}$ if the periodic deposit *(R)* is made at the end of each period.

Since the sinking fund is established for the purpose of paying the principal of the debt at maturity, the periodic interest on the debt should not be paid out of the fund. The interest rate on the debt may or may not equal the rate used for the sinking fund investment. The interest on the debt is called interest *expense,* whereas the interest from the sinking fund investment is called sinking fund interest *income.* It should be emphasized here that in the following discussion *the interest date is also regarded as the date for making the periodic deposit to the fund.* The debtor thus is making two payments on each payment date— one for interest on the debt and the other as a deposit in the fund.

**Example 1**   A $4,000 debt is to be repaid at the end of three years. Interest charged is 7% payable at the end of every six months. The debtor establishes a sinking fund which earns 6% interest compounded semiannually. (a) Find the interest payment on the debt for each six-month period. (b) Construct a sinking fund accumulation schedule.

(a) The semiannual interest payment for the debt is

$4,000(7\%)(\tfrac{1}{2}) = \$140$

(b) The sinking fund accumulation schedule is constructed as follows:

First, the size of each semiannual deposit in the sinking fund should be found. Here, we have the problem of finding the periodic payment of an ordinary annuity when the amount is known.

$S_n = \$4,000$, $i = 6\%/2 = 3\%$ (per six months),
$n = 3 \times 2 = 6$ (semiannual periods), $R = ?$ (per six months).

Thus,

$$R = S_n \cdot \frac{1}{s_{\overline{n}|i}} = 4,000 \cdot \frac{1}{s_{\overline{6}|3\%}} = 4,000(.1845975 - .03)$$

$$= 4,000(.1545975) = \$618.39 \qquad \text{(Table 9)}$$

## SINKING FUND ACCUMULATION SCHEDULE

| (1) <br><br> At End <br> of <br> Period <br> (6-Month <br> Interval) | (2) <br> Interest <br> Income <br> on <br> Sinking <br> Fund <br> $3\% \times (5)*$ | (3) <br><br><br> Periodic <br> Deposit <br> in Fund | (4) <br><br><br> Periodic <br> Increase <br> in Fund <br> $(2) + (3)$ | (5) <br> Sinking <br> Fund <br> Accumu- <br> lated <br> $(4) + (5)*$ | (6) <br><br><br><br> Book <br> Value <br> $4,000 - (5)$ |
|---|---|---|---|---|---|
| 1 | . . . | $ 618.39 | $ 618.39 | $ 618.39 | $3,381.61 |
| 2 | $ 18.55 | 618.39 | 636.94 | 1,255.33 | 2,744.67 |
| 3 | 37.66 | 618.39 | 656.05 | 1,911.38 | 2,088.62 |
| 4 | 57.34 | 618.39 | 675.73 | 2,587.11 | 1,412.89 |
| 5 | 77.61 | 618.39 | 696.00 | 3,283.11 | 716.89 |
| 6 | 98.49 | 618.40** | 716.89 | 4,000.00 | . . . |
| Total | $289.65 | $3,710.35 | $4,000.00 | | |

\* Of the previous period. For example, $18.55 = 618.39(3\%)$; and $37.66 = 1,255.33(3\%)$.
\*\* Correction for one cent discrepancy.

The information in the columns of the sinking fund schedule can be obtained directly as illustrated in the following example.

**Example 2**  Refer to Example 1. Find (a) the amount in the sinking fund at the end of the fourth period, (b) the sinking fund interest income for the fifth payment period, and (c) the book value of the debt at the end of the fourth period, without constructing a schedule.

(a) The amount in the sinking fund at the end of the fourth period.

It is the amount of an annuity of $618.39 payable semiannually at 6% compounded semiannually for four periods.

$R = 618.39, \ i = 3\%, \ n = 4$

$S_4 = 618.39 s_{\overline{4}|3\%} = 618.39(4.183627) = \$2,587.11$

(b) The sinking fund interest income for the fifth payment period.

The principal at the beginning of the fifth payment period is the amount in the sinking fund at the end of the fourth period, $2,587.11.

$I = 2,587.11(3\%) = \$77.61$

(c) The book value of the debt at the end of the fourth period.

The *book value* is the net obligation, which equals the original debt less the accumulated amount in the fund at that time.

$4,000 - 2,587.11 = \$1,412.89$

**Example 3**  Refer to Example 1. Assume that the debt bears 6% interest. What is the total cost to the debtor at the end of every six months?

The periodic (semiannual) interest for the debt is $4,000(6\%)(\frac{1}{2}) = \$120$

The periodic deposit in the sinking fund is the same as that in Example 1, $618.39, since the interest rate on the debt does not affect the interest rate of the sinking fund.

The total cost $= 618.39 + 120.00 = \$738.39$

Note that the cost is the same as the size of the periodic payment by the amortization method in Example 3, page 446.

In Example 1, the rate of interest is assumed to be unchanged throughout the three-year period. However, in practice, the interest rate on the sinking fund investment does sometimes change. When it changes, the periodic deposits are adjusted for the difference between the scheduled interest income and the actual interest income.

**Example 4**    In Example 1 assume that the interest rate on the sinking fund was 3% per six-month period during the first and second periods, $3\frac{1}{2}$% during the third and fourth periods, and $2\frac{1}{2}$% during the fifth and sixth periods. Construct a sinking fund accumulation schedule as a guide for the periodic deposits.

## ADJUSTED PERIODIC DEPOSITS SCHEDULE

| (1) At End of Period (6 Months) | (2) Scheduled Interest Income (See Example 1) | (3) Actual Interest Income (See Below) | (4) Interest Discrepancy (2) − (3) | (5) Adjusted Deposit Schedule $618.39 + (4) | (6) Periodic Increase in Fund (3) + (5) |
|---|---|---|---|---|---|
| 1 | . . . | . . . | . . . | $ 618.39 | $ 618.39 |
| 2 | $ 18.55 | $ 18.55 | . . . | 618.39 | 636.94 |
| 3 | 37.66 | 43.94 | −6.28 | 612.11 | 656.05 |
| 4 | 57.34 | 66.90 | −9.56 | 608.83 | 675.73 |
| 5 | 77.61 | 64.68 | 12.93 | 631.32 | 696.00 |
| 6 | 98.49 | 82.08 | 16.41 | 634.81* | 716.89 |
| Total | $289.65 | $276.15 | 13.50 | $3,723.85 | $4,000.00 |

\* Corrected for one cent discrepancy.

The interest in Column (3) is based on the following expression:

$$\text{Actual interest income} = \text{Sinking fund accumulated} \times \text{Interest rate}$$
$$\text{(See Column (5) of Example 1)}$$

Thus, the interest for each period is computed as follows:

First period $= 0(3\%) = 0.$
Second period $= 618.39(3\%) = \$18.55.$
Third period $= 1,255.33(3\frac{1}{2}\%) = \$43.94.$

Fourth period $= 1,911.38(3\frac{1}{2}\%) = \$66.90$.
Fifth period $= 2,587.11(2\frac{1}{2}\%) = \$64.68$.
Sixth period $= 3,283.11(2\frac{1}{2}\%) = \$82.08$.

Notice that the values in Column (6), periodic increase in fund, of the above schedule are the same as the values in Column (4) of the sinking fund accumulation schedule of Example 1. The sum of the periodic increases in the fund equals the sum of the actual interest income plus the sum of the adjusted (actual) deposits: $276.15 + 3,723.85 = \$4,000$.

## EXERCISE 15–4

**Reference: Section 15.4**

**A.** *In Problems 1–6, find (a) the interest payment on the debt for each interest period, (b) the size of deposits to the sinking fund, (c) the amount in the sinking fund at the end of nth period, (d) the book value of the debt at the end of nth period, and (e) the sinking fund interest income for the* $(n + 1)th$ *payment period. Do not construct a sinking fund accumulation schedule in finding your answers.*

| | Debt | Interest Rate on the Debt | Number of Deposits in Sinking Fund | Interest Rate on Sinking Fund | nth Period |
|---|---|---|---|---|---|
| 1. | $ 6,000 | 10%, quarterly | 20, quarterly | 6%, quarterly | 6th |
| 2. | 4,000 | 8%, annually | 15, annually | 4%, annually | 12th |
| 3. | 10,000 | 6%, semiannually | 8, semiannually | 5%, semiannually | 5th |
| 4. | 30,000 | 12%, monthly | 40, monthly | 5%, monthly | 34th |
| 5. | 450 | 7%, annually | 5, annually | 10%, annually | 3d |
| 6. | 800 | 6%, quarterly | 10, quarterly | 6%, quarterly | 7th |

**B.** *Statement Problems*

7. A $5,000 debt is to be repaid at the end of two years. The debtor establishes a sinking fund which earns 4% interest compounded semiannually. Construct a sinking fund accumulation schedule.
8. A man borrows $8,000 for five years. The interest rate on the loan is 5% payable at the end of each year. He makes annual deposits in a sinking fund earning 4% interest. Find the annual interest payment on the loan and construct a sinking fund accumulation schedule.
9. Refer to Problem 7. Assume that the interest rate on the sinking fund was 4% compounded semiannually during the first year and 6% compounded semiannually during the second year. Construct a sinking fund accumulation schedule as a guide for the periodic deposits.

10. Refer to Problem 8. Assume that the interest rate on the sinking fund was 4% during the first three years and 5% during the last two years. Construct a sinking fund accumulation schedule as a guide for the periodic deposits.

## EXERCISE 15–5

### Review of Chapter 15

1. T. R. Jennigan bought a $50,000 store and made a down payment of $20,000. The balance will be paid by equal quarterly payments for six years with the first payment due three months from the date of purchase. (a) Find the size of the quarterly payments if the interest rate is 6% compounded quarterly. (b) What is the outstanding principal after the tenth payment is made?

2. A debt of $6,000 is to be amortized by equal payments at the end of each month for five years. (a) If the interest charged is 5% compounded monthly, what is the size of each monthly payment? (b) What is the outstanding principal after the 35th payment is made?

3. Reynolds borrowed $3,000. He agreed to discharge the loan together with the interest by making four equal quarterly payments, with the first payment to be made three months from the date of borrowing. Assume that the interest charged is 4% compounded quarterly. Construct an amortization schedule.

4. A debt of $7,000 is to be amortized in five equal semiannual payments. Construct an amortization schedule assuming 6% interest compounded semiannually for the debt.

5. A loan of $10,000 is to be discharged by paying $2,000 at the end of each year. The interest rate is 5% compounded annually. Construct an amortization schedule.

6. A debt of $6,000 is to be amortized with payments of $1,500 at the end of every six months. The interest rate is 4% compounded semiannually. Construct an amortization schedule.

7. White bought a house for $15,000 and made a down payment of $3,000. The balance is to be amortized with payments of $100 at the end of each month. The interest rate is 6% compounded monthly. What is the outstanding principal after the 55th payment?

8. A debt of $30,000 is to be repaid by making a $1,500 payment at the end of each quarter. The interest rate is 8% compounded quarterly. What is the outstanding principal after the 12th payment?

9. In Problem 7, what are the interest and the principal included in the 56th monthly payment?

10. In Problem 8, find the interest and the principal included in the 13th quarterly payment.

11. Mrs. Booker borrowed $1,000 from a finance company. She agreed to repay the loan by making 10 equal monthly payments, the first installment being payable in one month from the date of borrowing. The company computed the monthly payments by the add-on interest method at 6% per year. Find (a) the size of each payment, and (b) the actual annual interest rate charged by the company.

12. Mrs. Adams borrowed $900 from a bank at the stated nominal interest rate of 4% per year. The bank requires that the loan must be repaid in 18 equal monthly installments based on the add-on interest method, the first payment being due in one month. What are (a) the size of each payment, and (b) the actual annual interest rate charged by the bank?

★13. Johnson & Co. issued $300,000 of bonds each with a face value of $1,000. The bonds are to be retired at the end of every year over a five-year period. Construct an amortization schedule to equalize each annual payment, including 10% interest payable annually and the retirement of the principal.

★14. T. H. White & Co. issued $400,000 of 4% bonds. The interest is payable semiannually and the face value of each bond is $500. The bonds are to be retired at the end of every six months over a two-year period. Construct an amortization schedule to equalize the semiannual payment, including the interest and the principal.

15. A debt of $5,000 is to be repaid at the end of $2\frac{1}{2}$ years under the sinking fund plan with the fund earning 4% interest compounded semiannually. The interest rate on the debt is 8% payable semiannually. (a) Find the value of each interest payment on the debt, and (b) construct a sinking fund schedule.

16. A $7,000 loan will be repaid at the end of four years by a sinking fund which earns 6% compounded annually. The interest on the loan is payable annually at 9%. (a) Find the interest payment on the loan for each year, and (b) construct a sinking fund schedule.

17. In Problem 15, assume that the debt bears 4% interest compounded semiannually. (a) What is the total of the interest payment and the sinking fund deposit that must be made by the debtor at the end of every six months? (b) If the debt is to be amortized by equal semiannual payments at 4% compounded semiannually, what is the size of each payment?

18. In Problem 16, assume that the interest on the loan is 6% payable annually. (a) What is the total payment, including the interest on the loan and the deposit in the sinking fund, made by the borrower at the end of every year? (b) If the loan is to be amortized by equal annual payments at 6% compounded annually, what is the size of each payment?

19. In Problem 15, assume that the interest rate on the sinking fund was 2% per six-month period during the first year, 3% per six-month period during the second year, and 4% for the last six months of the borrowing time. Construct a sinking fund accumulation schedule.

20. In Problem 16, assume that the interest rate on the sinking fund was 6% for the first year, 5% for the second year, and 7% for the remaining two years during the loan period. Construct a sinking fund accumulation schedule.

21. A $15,000 debt is to be discharged at the end of ten years by a sinking fund which is invested at 6% compounded quarterly. Find (a) the amount in the sinking fund and the book value of the debt at the end of six years, and (b) the sinking fund interest income for the first quarter of the seventh year.

22. Collins borrowed $5,000 and agreed to repay the principal at the end of three years but to pay interest periodically. She established a sinking fund which earns 7% compounded monthly. Find (a) the amount in the sinking fund and the book value of the debt at the end of two years, and (b) the sinking fund interest income for the first month of the third year.

# Chapter 16

# Investment in Bonds

## 16.1 STOCKS AND BONDS

Stocks and bonds are frequently purchased and sold by investors in an investment market to make profits. *Stock,* also called *capital stock,* represents ownership in a corporation and is divided into shares. Those who purchase a share of stock acquire not only a share of the ownership of the corporation but also the right to receive income in the form of dividends. Unlike stocks, *bonds* are generally issued by corporations or governmental units for the purpose of *borrowing* funds from a group of creditors. Those who purchase bonds expect the issuing party to repay the principal on a future date, as well as to provide a periodic income in the form of interest during the life of the investment.

The prices of both stocks and bonds fluctuate frequently on the investment market, although the price of bonds fluctuates within a much smaller range than that of stocks. An investor should have the ability to investigate the possibility of making a fair profit and the safety of such investments. An extensive study of stocks and bonds requires special volumes and is beyond the scope of this text. The following studies are limited to the mathematical operations peculiar to the investment in bonds.

Note that an investor who purchases or sells stocks through a broker usually has to pay a commission or brokerage fee for the broker's services. On the New York Stock Exchange, for example, the charges for the commissions and fees are based on the market value of each stock, but the rate is different for 100-share lots than for a lot consisting of less than 100 shares. The method of computing the charges is basically the same as the method of computing the commissions and fees for buying and selling merchandise presented in Section 8.4.

# 16.2 COMPUTING THE PURCHASE PRICE OF A BOND

Certain terms frequently used in computing various problems concerning the investment in bonds are explained below:

1. *Face value* or *par value*. The value stated on the bond, usually called the denomination, such as $1,000.
2. *Redemption value*. The value that the issuing party pays to the bondholder when the bond is surrendered. A bond is usually redeemed at the maturity date and is paid according to the face value, or is said to be redeemable at par. However, some bonds may be called prior to the date of maturity. The redemption values of some bonds may also be set above par to make the bonds more attractive.
3. *Bond rate* or *contract rate*. The interest rate stated on the bond. This rate is used as a basis for computing the interest payment.
4. *Yield rate* or *investor's rate*. The actual interest rate that is expected by the purchaser of the bond. The yield rate is usually the prevailing rate on the investment market when the bond is purchased and is often not equal to the bond rate.
5. *Interest dates*. The interest on most bonds is payable semiannually on the first day of the payable month. Sometimes the interest payment dates are indicated by the initial letters of the months. Thus, if the interest is payable semiannually on January 1 and July 1, the dates may be abbreviated as J-J; if on February 1 and August 1, the initials F-A may be used; etc.
6. *Purchase price* or *flat price*. The purchase price is computed at the yield rate. The purchase price is also the value quoted on the bond market plus accrued interest on the bond, if any. Thus, the quoted price is also called the "and interest" price.
7. *Bond abbreviations*. The name of the issuing party, the bond rate, and the redemption date of a bond are usually abbreviated in publications.

   Thus, *Gen Am Tran 4s 81* means that the bond was issued by General American Transportation Corp., it bears 4% interest payable semiannually and the date of maturity is 1981.

An investor may purchase bonds on the interest payment dates or between the interest payment dates. The methods of computing the purchase prices at different times are presented below.

## A. Purchase Price on Interest Date

An investor purchasing a bond acquires two items:

1. The redemption value which will be realized at a future date; that is, at the redemption or maturity date.

2. The periodic interest payment according to the interest rate contracted on the bond.

Therefore, the purchase price of a bond is the sum of the present values of the two items above. The first item, the redemption value, is computed by use of the compound discount formula $P = S(1 + i)^{-n}$; where $P$ is the present value of the redemption value, $S$ is the redemption value, $i$ is the yield rate (or investor's interest rate), and $n$ is the number of interest periods between the date of purchase and the date of redemption.

The second item, the periodic interest payment is computed by use of formula $A_n = Ra_{\overline{n}|i}$; where $A_n$ = the present value of all interest payments, $n$ and $i$ mean the same as $n$ and $i$ in the first item above, and $R$ = the periodic interest payment according to the bond contract.

*The interest conversion period for the yield rate (investor's rate) is assumed to coincide with the interest payment period for the bond. When the purchase is made on an interest date, the bond interest payment on that date is not included in the purchase price.* In summary,

$$\textbf{Purchase price} = P + A_n, \text{ or}$$
$$= S(1+i)^{-n} + Ra_{\overline{n}|i} \qquad \textbf{(16-1)}$$

**Example 1**    A \$1,000, 6% bond will be redeemed on March 1, 1996. Interest is payable semiannually on March 1 and September 1. Find the purchase price of the bond if the date of purchase is March 1, 1980, the yield rate is 5% compounded semiannually, and the bond is redeemable (a) at par, and (b) at 105%.

(a) The present value of the redemption value is computed as follows:

The redemption value is at par, \$1,000, which is due in 16 years (from March 1, 1980, to March 1, 1996).

$S = \$1,000$, $i = 5\%/2 = 2\frac{1}{2}\%$ (yield rate per six months)
$n = 16 \times 2 = 32$ (semiannual interest periods)

$P = 1,000(1 + 2\frac{1}{2}\%)^{-32}$
   $= 1,000(.453771)$
   $= \$453.77$

The present value of the interest payments is computed as follows:

The periodic interest payment according to the bond (or contract) rate is

$R = 1,000(6\%)(\frac{1}{2}) = \$30$ (per six months)

Thus, $A_n = 30a_{\overline{32}|2\ 1/2\%} = 30(21.8492) = \$655.48$

The purchase price is

$P + A_n = 453.77 + 655.48 = \$1,109.25$

The solution to Example 1 may be diagrammed as follows:

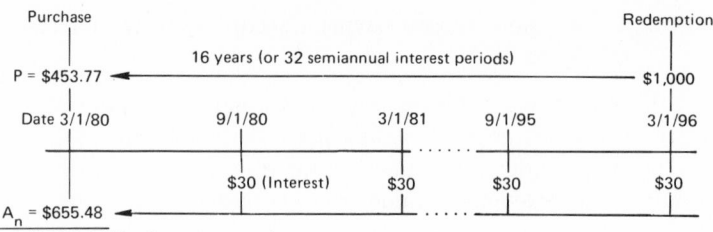

(b) The present value of the redemption value is computed as follows:

The redemption value is 105% of the face value, or $S = 1,000(105\%)$ = $1,050. The other values are the same as above.

$$P = 1,050(1 + 2\tfrac{1}{2}\%)^{-32} = 1,050(.453771) = \$476.46$$

The present value of the interest payments is also the same as above. Thus, the purchase price is

$$476.46 + 655.48 = \$1,131.94$$

**Example 2**　The investor's interest rate is 6% compounded semiannually. Find the purchase price of a $1,500 bond with 5% interest payable semiannually, and redeemable in six years (a) at par, and (b) at 98%.

(a) $S = \$1,500$ (at par), $i = 6\%/2 = 3\%$ (investor's rate per six months), $n = 6 \times 2 = 12$ (semiannual periods), $R = 1,500(5\%)(\tfrac{1}{2}) = \$37.50$

The purchase price $= 1,500(1 + 3\%)^{-12} + 37.50a_{\overline{12}|3\%}$
$= 1,500(.70138) + 37.50(9.954)$
$= 1,052.07 + 373.27 = \$1,425.34$

(b) $S = 1,500(98\%) = \$1,470$

The purchase price $= 1,470(1 + 3\%)^{-12} + 37.50a_{\overline{12}|3\%}$
$= 1,470(.70138) + 37.50(9.954)$
$= 1,031.03 + 373.27 = \$1,404.30$

# EXERCISE 16–1

### Reference: Section 16.2 A

**A.** *Find the purchase price of the bond in each of the following problems:*

| | Par Value | Redemption Value | Bond Rate | Bond Interest Dates | Time Before Redemption | Yield (Investor's) Rate, Compounded Semiannually |
|---|---|---|---|---|---|---|
| **1.** | $1,000 | at par | 6% | J—J | 5 years | 5% |
| **2.** | 1,000 | 110% | 4% | F—A | $4\tfrac{1}{2}$ years | 3% |
| **3.** | 2,000 | 95% | 5% | M—S | 6 years | 7% |
| **4.** | 4,000 | at par | 3% | A—O | 8 years | 6% |

| Par Value | Redemption Value | Bond Rate | Bond Interest Dates | Time Before Redemption | Yield (Investor's) Rate, Compounded Semiannually |
|---|---|---|---|---|---|
| 5. $ 600 | 105% | 7% | M—N | $7\frac{1}{2}$ years | 4% |
| 6. 5,000 | 98% | 6% | J—D | 10 years | 5% |
| 7. 6,000 | at par | 4% | A—O | 12 years | 6% |
| 8. 400 | at par | 5% | M—N | 7 years | 4% |

**B.** *Statement Problems:*

9. A $10,000, 5% bond will be redeemed on January 1, 1998. Interest is payable semiannually on January 1 and July 1. Find the purchase price of the bond if the date of purchase is July 1, 1980, the yield rate is 4% compounded semiannually, and the bond is redeemable (a) at par, and (b) at 108%.
10. Find the purchase price of a $1,000, 3% bond, if it is bought to yield 4% compounded semiannually. The bond interest is payable semiannually, and the bond is redeemable at par in (a) three years, (b) 15 years.
11. The investor's interest rate is 5% compounded semiannually. Find the purchase price of a $2,000 bond with 3% interest payable semiannually, and redeemable at par in (a) four years, and (b) 9 years.
12. An $8,000, 6% bond will be redeemed on April 1, 1988. Interest is payable semiannually on April 1 and October 1. Find the purchase price of the bond if the date of purchase is April 1, 1981, the yield rate is $5\frac{1}{2}$% compounded semiannually, and the bond is redeemable (a) at par, and (b) at 95%.

# B. Purchase Price Between Interest Dates

When a bond is purchased between interest dates, the purchase price on the interest date that immediately precedes the purchase date is first computed. The interest at the yield rate for the period between the interest date and the purchase date is then added to obtain the purchase price on the purchase date. *Hereafter, unless otherwise specified, the bond is assumed to be redeemable at par, the face value.* This assumption is made in order to simplify the computation and to meet most practical situations.

**Example 3**  Refer to Example 1(a). If the bond is bought on April 30, 1980, what is the purchase price of the bond?

The purchase price on the interest date, March 1, 1980, which immediately precedes the purchase date, is $1,109.25. See the solution for Example 1(a).

The interest at the yield rate for the period between the interest date (March 1, 1980) and the purchase date (April 30, 1980) is computed as follows:

The period is 60 days, yield rate is 5%, the principal for computing the interest is $1,109.25. Thus,

$I = 1,109.25(5\%)(60/360) = \$9.24$

The purchase price on April 30, 1980, is

$1,109.25 + 9.24 = \$1,118.49$

On the other hand, the purchase price is the bondholder's selling price. The price should include the incurred, yet not paid, bond interest, called *accrued interest*, for the period from March 1, 1980, to the purchase date (or for 60 days). The accrued interest at the bond rate is computed as follows:

$1,000(6\%)(60/360) = \$10$

The accrued interest is the seller's income since he or she owns the bond during the 60 days. Thus, the selling price of $1,118.49 may be considered to include two items: (1) the accrued interest at the bond rate, $10, and (2) the net price for the bond, $1,108.49 (or $1,118.49 − $10).

The purchase price (or the bondholder's selling price) of $1,118.49 is frequently referred to by a bond house as the *flat price,* and the net price of the bond, $1,108.49, without including the accrued interest, as the *quoted price.*

The above illustration is diagrammed as follows:

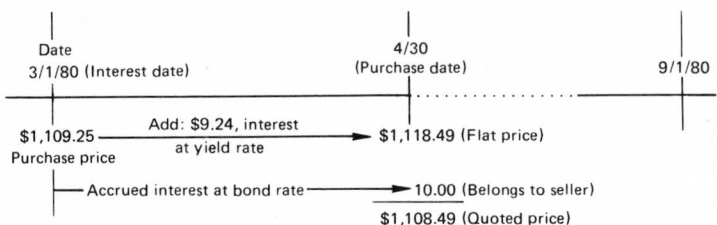

Thus, in general,

$$\frac{\textbf{Flat price}}{\textbf{(purchase price)}} = \textbf{Quoted price} + \textbf{Accrued interest on a bond}$$

However, if the bond is purchased on an interest date, there is no accrued interest. Thus,

**Flat price (purchase price on the interest date) = Quoted price**

**Example 4**     A $1,000, 3% bond, redeemable in six years and two months, interest payable semiannually, is bought to yield $3\frac{1}{2}\%$ compounded semiannually. What are (a) the purchase price, (b) the accrued interest on the bond, and (c) the quoted price?

(a) The interest date immediately preceding the purchase date is six years and six months (or 13 semiannual periods) before redemption. The purchase price on the interest date is computed as follows:

Yield rate $(i) = 3\frac{1}{2}\%/2 = 1\frac{3}{4}\%$ (per six months)
$R = 1,000 \times 3\% \times \frac{1}{2} = \$15$
$n = 6\frac{1}{2} \times 2 = 13$ (semiannual periods)

The purchase price $= 1,000(1 + 1\frac{3}{4}\%)^{-13} + 15a_{\overline{13}|1\ 3/4\%}$
$= 1,000(0.798091) + 15(11.5376)$
$= 798.091 + 173.064 = 971.155$, rounded to $\$971.16$

For the four months after the last interest date, the interest on the purchase price based on the yield rate is $971.16(3\frac{1}{2}\%)(\frac{4}{12}) = \$11.33$

The purchase price on the purchase date, six years and two months before redemption is $971.16 + 11.33 = \$982.49$

(b) According to the bond contract, the accrued interest for the four-month period is $1,000(3\%)(\frac{4}{12}) = \$10$

(c) The quoted price = the purchase price − the accrued interest on the bond $= 982.49 - 10 = \$972.49$

**Note:** Quoted prices are usually listed in bond tables. A sample bond table is given on page 482. The bond table values are computed by using the compound interest method throughout. However, the difference between the results obtained by using the simple interest method and the compound interest method is small. When the compound interest method is used, the answer to Example 4(a) is $\$982.45$, a 4¢ difference (or, $982.49 - 982.45$), and is computed as follows:

$S = 971.155(1 + 1\frac{3}{4}\%)^{2/3} = 971.155(1.00579963)^2 = \$982.45$, where $\frac{2}{3}$ represents four months, or $\frac{2}{3}$ of the semiannual interest period. (Table 5A)

**Example 5** On February 9, 1980, a man acquired $10,000 worth of $4\frac{1}{2}\%$ bonds, which were quoted on the market on that date at $92\frac{1}{4}\%$. Interest on the bonds was payable on May 1 and November 1. Find (a) the quoted price, (b) the accrued interest on the bonds, and (c) the purchase price (or flat price).

(a) The quoted price is at $92\frac{1}{4}\%$ of the face value. Thus,
the quoted price $= 10,000(92\frac{1}{4}\%)$
$= 10,000(.9225)$
$= \$9,225$

(b) The accrued interest on the bonds at the bond rate for the period from November 1, 1979, to February 9, 1980, or 100 days (during which time the seller owns the bonds), is computed as follows:

$10,000(4\frac{1}{2}\%)(\frac{100}{360}) = \$125$

(c) The purchase price = the quoted price + the accrued interest
$= 9,225 + 125 = \$9,350$

## EXERCISE 16–2

**Reference: Section 16.2 B**

**A.** *In each of the following problems, find (a) the purchase price, (b) the accrued interest on the bond, and (c) the quoted price:*

| Par Value | Bond Rate Payable Semiannually | Time Before Redemption | Yield Rate, Compounded Semiannually |
|---|---|---|---|
| 1. $ 4,000 | 6% | 5 years and 1 month | 5% |
| 2.   2,000 | 4% | 4 years and 9 months | 3% |
| 3.   5,000 | 5% | 6 years and 4 months | 7% |
| 4.   6,000 | 3% | 8 years and 2 months | 6% |
| 5.    900 | 4% | 7 years and 5 months | 3% |
| 6.    700 | 5% | 10 years and 4 months | 4% |
| 7. 10,000 | 3% | 12 years and 3 months | 5% |
| 8. 25,000 | 7% | 3 years and 5 months | 5% |

**B.** *Statement Problems:*

9. A $3,000, 5% bond, redeemable in five years and three months, interest payable semiannually, is bought to yield 6% compounded semiannually. What are (a) the purchase price, and (b) the quoted price?

10. A $3,500, 4% bond will be redeemed on May 1, 1990. Interest is payable semiannually on May 1 and November 1. Find the purchase price of the bond if the date of purchase is July 1, 1980, and the yield rate is 3% compounded semiannually.

11. A $7,000, 6% bond, interest payable semiannually on March 1 and September 1, redeemable on March 1, 1985, is bought to yield 4% compounded semiannually on November 15, 1981. Find the purchase price.

12. Refer to Problem 11. What would be the purchase price of the bond if the yield rate were 7% compounded semiannually?

13. On May 31, a man purchased a $2,500 bond. The interest rate on the bond was 3% payable semiannually on April 1 and October 1. The bond was quoted on the market at 80%. Find (a) the quoted price, (b) the accrued interest, and (c) the purchase price of the bond.

14. Refer to Problem 13. If the bond were quoted on the market on May 31 at 110%, what are the new answers to (a), (b), and (c)?

## 16.3 BOND PREMIUM AND DISCOUNT

## A. General Computation

In Example 1(a) of Section 16.2, it was found that a $1,000, 6% bond, interest payable semiannually, redeemable on March 1, 1996, was sold on March 1, 1980, for $1,109.25, to give the purchaser a yield rate of 5% compounded semiannually. The purchase price is $109.25 larger than the face value (which is now assumed to be equal to the redemption value) as shown below:

$$1,109.25 - 1,000 = \$109.25 \text{ (premium)}$$

When the purchase price of a bond is larger than its face value, the excess amount is called the *premium* on the bond. In the above example, the premium is $109.25. Premium on a bond is paid by the investor when the bond interest rate exceeds the yield rate. The premium can be recovered periodically through bond interest payments which are greater than the interest based on the yield rate. The excess income of the purchaser in the above example is computed as follows:

Periodic bond interest payment
= bond face value × bond interest rate per interest period
= $1,000(6\%)(\frac{1}{2}) = \$30$

Periodic bond interest based on yield rate (expected interest income of bond purchaser)
= bond face value × yield rate per interest period
= $1,000(5\%)(\frac{1}{2}) = \$25$

The excess income per interest period $= 30 - 25 = \$5$

There are 32 interest payments from March 1, 1980, to March 1, 1996, or 32 excess payments of $5 each. The present value of 32 semiannual payments of $5 each at 5% compounded semiannually (yield rate) is computed by use of formula

$$A_n = Ra_{\overline{n}|i}, \text{ where } R = \$5 \text{ (the excess income)}, \ i = 5\%/2 = 2\tfrac{1}{2}\%,$$
$$n = 32 \text{ (payments)}$$

The premium on the bond $= A_{32} = 5a_{\overline{32}|2\,1/2\%} = 5(21.849) = \$109.25$

Thus, *the premium on a bond is the present value of an annuity which is formed by the periodical excess income.*

When the bond face value and the premium are known, the purchase price may be obtained as follows:

Purchase price = Face value + Premium $= 1,000 + 109.25 = \$1,109.25$

On the other hand, it was found that a $1,500, 5% bond, interest payable semiannually, redeemable in six years, was sold at $1,425.34 to give the purchaser a yield rate of 6% compounded semiannually. (See Example 2 in Section 16.2.) When the purchase price is smaller than the face value, the difference is called the *discount* on the bond. A bond is purchased at a discount when the bond interest rate is smaller than the yield rate. The deficit interest for the above example is computed as follows:

Periodic bond interest payment
= bond face value × bond interest rate per interest period
= $1,500(5\%)(\frac{1}{2}) = \$37.50$

Periodic bond interest based on yield rate
= bond face value × yield rate per interest period
= $1,500(6\%)(\frac{1}{2}) = \$45.00$

The deficit per interest period $= 45.00 - 37.50 = \$7.50$

According to the face value, the investor will sustain a $7.50 loss each interest period for six yers, or a total of 12 losses of $7.50 each. The present value of the annuity which is formed by the periodic deficits is computed by use of the formula

$$A_n = Ra_{\overline{n}|i}, \text{ where } R = \$7.50 \text{ (the periodic deficit)}, i = 6\%/2 = 3\%$$
$$\text{(at yield rate)}, n = 6 \times 2 = 12 \text{ (losses)}$$

$$A_{12} = 7.50a_{\overline{12}|3\%} = 7.50(9.954) = \$74.655, \text{ rounded to } \$74.66$$

Thus, *the discount is the present value of an annuity which is formed by the periodic deficit income.* The discount must be subtracted from the face value to obtain the purchase price, as shown below:

$$\text{Purchase price} = \text{Face value} - \text{Discount} = 1,500 - 74.66 = \$1,425.34$$

In summary, let    $i =$ yield rate per interest period
$b =$ bond rate per interest period
$F =$ face value of bond

When $b$ is greater than $i$:

$$\textbf{Premium} = (Fb - Fi)a_{\overline{n}|i} = F(b - i)a_{\overline{n}|i} \qquad \textbf{(16–2)}$$

When $b$ is smaller than $i$:

$$\textbf{Discount} = (Fi - Fb)a_{\overline{n}|i} = F(i - b)a_{\overline{n}|i} \qquad \textbf{(16–3)}$$

When $b$ is equal to $i$, there is no premium or discount, and the purchase price = the face value.

**Example 1**    A $10,000, $3\frac{1}{2}\%$ bond, redeemable in 10 years, interest payable semiannually, is bought to yield 3% interest compounded semiannually. Find (a) the premium, and (b) the purchase price.

$b = 3\frac{1}{2}\%/2 = 1\frac{3}{4}\%$ (per six months), $i = 3\%/2 = 1\frac{1}{2}\%$ (per six months), $n = 10 \times 2 = 20$ (semiannual payments), $F = \$10,000$.

Since the bond rate is greater than the yield rate, there must be a premium.

(a)  Premium $= 10,000(1\frac{3}{4}\% - 1\frac{1}{2}\%)a_{\overline{20}|1\,1/2\%}$
$= 10,000(\frac{1}{4}\%)a_{\overline{20}|1\,1/2\%} = 25(17.1686) = \$429.22$

(b)  Purchase price $= 10,000 + 429.22 = \$10,429.22$

**Example 2**    A $10,000, $3\frac{1}{2}\%$ bond, redeemable in 10 years, interest payable semiannually, is bought to yield 8% interest compounded semiannually. Find (a) the discount, and (b) the purchase price.

$b = 3\frac{1}{2}\%/2 = 1\frac{3}{4}\%$, $i = 8\%/2 = 4\%$, $n = 10 \times 2 = 20$, $F = \$10,000$.

Since the bond rate is smaller than the yield rate, there must be a discount.

(a) Discount $= 10,000(4\% - 1\frac{3}{4}\%)a_{\overline{20}|4\%}$
$= 10,000(2\frac{1}{4}\%)a_{\overline{20}|4\%} = 225(13.5903) = \$3,057.82.$

(b) Purchase price $= 10,000 - 3,057.82 = \$6,942.18.$

**Example 3**    Refer to Example 2. If the bond is bought to yield $3\frac{1}{2}\%$ interest compounded semiannually, find (a) the premium or the discount, and (b) the purchase price.

(a) $b = 1\frac{3}{4}\%$ and $i = 1\frac{3}{4}\%$. Since the bond rate is equal to the yield rate, there is no premium or discount.

(b) The purchase price is the face value, $10,000.

**★Note:**    When the redemption value is not at par, the following expressions may be obtained by a method of reasoning similar to that in the illustrations above:

**Premium $= [(Face\ value \times b)$**
       $-\ (Redemption\ value \times i)]a_{\overline{n}|i}$    **(16–4)**

**Purchase price $=$ Redemption value $+$ premium**

The premium may be thought of as a positive figure, whereas the discount may be thought of as a negative premium. In other words, when the premium becomes a negative figure, it is a discount. Or,

**$-$ Premium $=$ Discount**

Example 1(b) of Section 16.2 may be computed as follows:

Premium $= [1,000(6\%)(\frac{1}{2}) - 1,050(5\%)(\frac{1}{2})]a_{\overline{32}|2\ 1/2\%}$
$= (30 - 26.25)a_{\overline{32}|2\ 1/2\%} = 3.75(21.8492) = \$81.9345,$ rounded
                                    to $81.93

Purchase price $= 1,050 + 81.93 = \$1,131.93$

(The 1¢ discrepancy from the answer \$1,131.94 is due to rounding.)

Example 2(b) of Section 16.2 may be computed as follows:

Premium $= [1,500(5\%)(\frac{1}{2}) - 1,470(6\%)(\frac{1}{2})]a_{\overline{12}|3\%}$
$= (37.50 - 44.10)a_{\overline{12}|3\%} = -6.60(9.954) = -65.6964,$ rounded
                                   to $-$65.70

Purchase price $= 1,470 + (-65.70) = \$1,404.30$

## EXERCISE 16–3

### Reference: Section 16.3 A

**A.** *Find (a) the premium or the discount, and (b) the purchase price in each of the following problems:*

| | Par Value | Bond Rate Payable Semiannually | Time Before Redemption | Yield Rate, Compounded Semiannually |
|---|---|---|---|---|
| 1. | $ 4,000 | 6% | 5 years | 5% |
| 2. | 2,000 | 4% | $4\frac{1}{2}$ years | 3% |

| | Par Value | Bond Rate Payable Semiannually | Time Before Redemption | Yield Rate, Compounded Semiannually |
|---|---|---|---|---|
| 3. | $ 5,000 | 5% | 6 years | 7% |
| 4. | 6,000 | 3% | 8 years | 6% |
| 5. | 900 | 4% | 7 years | 3% |
| 6. | 700 | 5% | 10 years | 4% |
| 7. | 10,000 | 3% | 12 years | 5% |
| 8. | 25,000 | 7% | 3 years | 5% |

**B.** *Statement Problems:*

9. A $3,000, 4% bond, redeemable in eight years, interest payable semiannually, is bought to yield 5% interest compounded semiannually. Find (a) the premium or the discount, and (b) the purchase price.
10. Refer to Problem 9. If the yield rate is 3% compounded semiannually, find the answers to (a) and (b).
11. Refer to Problem 9. If the yield rate is 4% compounded semiannually, find the answers to (a) and (b).
★12. Compute Problems 2, 3, 5, 6, of Exercise 16–1 by the method used in Section 16.3 A, page 473. (Formula 16–4)

# B. Amortization of Premium

An investor who purchases a bond at premium should be aware that the premium is not redeemable on the maturity date of the bond. The premium is recovered periodically through the interest receipts on the bond. Thus, the book value of the bond investment should be reduced accordingly in the investor's record, until the premium becomes zero on the maturity date. The process of reducing the book value of a bond investment to par by periodic deductions is called *amortization of the bond premium.*

**Example 4**     A $10,000, 6% bond, interest payable semiannually, redeemable in $3\frac{1}{2}$ years, is bought to yield 5% interest compounded semiannually. Find the purchase price and construct a schedule for amortization of the premium.

$b = 6\%/2 = 3\%$, $i = 5\%/2 = 2\frac{1}{2}\%$, $b$ is greater than $i$, and $n = 3\frac{1}{2} \times 2 = 7$ (semiannual payments)

Premium $= 10,000(3\% - 2\frac{1}{2}\%)a_{\overline{7}|\,2\,1/2\%} = 10,000(\frac{1}{2}\%)a_{\overline{7}|\,2\,1/2\%}$
$= 50(6.3494) = \$317.47$

Purchase price $= 10,000 + 317.47 = \$10,317.47$

The schedule on page 475 shows that the periodic premium amortization is the excess of the interest receipt from the bond over the investor's yield. Investors are willing to purchase a bond at a premium because they can recover the premium through the high periodic interest receipts from the bond.

*Note:* 1. The investor receives:  $ 2,100.00 (interest)
+10,000.00 (redemption value)
12,100.00
The investor paid:  −10,317.47 (purchase price)
The investor's net gain  $ 1,782.53 (see Column (3))

2. According to the purchase price and the yield rate, the excess income of the first period is $42.06. It is computed as follows:

The investor's expected interest for the first period is

10,317.47 × 2½% = $257.936, rounded to $257.94

However, the actual interest receipt for the first period from the bond is

10,000 × 3% = $300

The first period excess income is

300.00 − 257.94 = $42.06

3. The excess income is subtracted from the original purchase price to obtain the book value of the bond at the end of the first period.

10,317.47 − 42.06 = $10,275.41

## AMORTIZATION SCHEDULE FOR BOND PREMIUM

| (1)<br>At End of<br>Interest<br>Period | (2)<br>Interest Receipt<br>from Bond<br>$10,000 × 3% = $300 | (3)<br>Yield<br>(Investor's<br>Interest)<br>(5) × 2½% | (4)<br>Premium<br>Amorti-<br>zation<br>(2) − (3) | (5)<br>Book Value<br>of Bond<br>(5) − (4) |
|---|---|---|---|---|
| | | | | $10,317.47 |
| 1 | $ 300 | $ 257.94 | $ 42.06 | 10,275.41 |
| 2 | 300 | 256.89 | 43.11 | 10,232.30 |
| 3 | 300 | 255.81 | 44.19 | 10,188.11 |
| 4 | 300 | 254.70 | 45.30 | 10,142.81 |
| 5 | 300 | 253.57 | 46.43 | 10,096.38 |
| 6 | 300 | 252.41 | 47.59 | 10,048.79 |
| 7 | 300 | 251.21* | 48.79 | 10,000.00 |
| Total | $2,100 | $1,782.53 | $317.47 | |

* Correction for one cent discrepancy. The amount should be $251.22 (or 10,048.79 × 2½% = $251.21975).

# C. Accumulation of Discount

An investor who purchases a bond at discount should know that the entire face value of the bond is redeemable to the bondholder on the maturity date.

Investors receive a smaller periodic interest from the bond than they would receive if the interest rate on the bond were equal to the current market interest rate. However, the periodic deficits are recovered through receipt of the full redemption value. Each of the periodic deficits is added to the original purchase price listed in the investor's records. The book value increases periodically and will be equal to par on the maturity date. The process of increasing the book value of a bond investment to par by periodic additions is called *accumulation* of the bond discount.

**Example 5**  A $10,000, 6% bond, interest payable semiannually, redeemable in $3\frac{1}{2}$ years, is bought to yield 7% interest compounded semiannually. Find the purchase price, and construct a schedule for accumulation of the discount.

$i = 7\%/2 = 3\frac{1}{2}\%$, $b = 6\%/2 = 3\%$, $i$ is greater than $b$, $n = 3\frac{1}{2} \times 2 = 7$ (semiannual interest periods)

Discount $= 10,000(3\frac{1}{2}\% - 3\%)a_{\overline{7}|3\ 1/2\%}$
$\phantom{Discount } = 50(6.114544) = \$305.7272$, rounded to $305.73

Purchase price $= 10,000 - 305.73 = \$9,694.27$

## ACCUMULATION SCHEDULE FOR BOND DISCOUNT

| (1) At End of Interest Period | (2) Interest Receipt from bond $10,000 × 3% = \$300 | (3) Yield (Investor's Expected Interest) (5) × 3½% | (4) Discount Accumulation (3) − (2) | (5) Book Value of Bond (5) + (4) |
|---|---|---|---|---|
| | | | | $ 9,694.27 |
| 1 | $ 300 | $ 339.30 | $ 39.30 | 9,733.57 |
| 2 | 300 | 340.67 | 40.67 | 9,774.24 |
| 3 | 300 | 342.10 | 42.10 | 9,816.34 |
| 4 | 300 | 343.57 | 43.57 | 9,859.91 |
| 5 | 300 | 345.10 | 45.10 | 9,905.01 |
| 6 | 300 | 346.68 | 46.68 | 9,951.69 |
| 7 | 300 | 348.31 | 48.31 | 10,000.00 |
| Total | $2,100 | $2,405.73 | $305.73 | |

**Note:**  1. According to the purchase price and the yield rate, the deficit of the first period is $39.30. It is computed as follows:

The investor's expected interest for the first period is

$9,694.27 \times 3\frac{1}{2}\% = \$339.30$

However, the actual interest receipt for the first period from the bond is only

$10,000 \times 3\% = \$300$

The first period deficit is

$339.30 - 300.00 = \$39.30$

The deficit is added to the original purchase price to obtain the book value of the bond at the end of the first period.

$9,694.27 + 39.30 = \$9,733.57$

2. The book value of a bond on any interest date is the purchase price of the bond on that date. Thus, the book value may be checked by the method used in finding the purchase price. (See Section 16.2 A or 16.3 A.) For example, the book value at the end of the 5th period in Example 5 may be computed as follows:

$n = 2$, which represents the number of interest periods from the end of the 5th period to the redemption date.

Discount $= 10,000(3\frac{1}{2}\% - 3\%)a_{\overline{2}|3\ 1/2\%} = 50(1.8997) = \$94.99$

Book value (= Purchase price) $= 10,000 - 94.99 = \$9,905.01$

It can be determined from the above schedule that the periodic discount accumulation is the deficit of the interest receipt from the bond in relation to the investor's yield. Investors are willing to purchase a bond that offers smaller periodic interest payments than those offered on the prevailing investment market, because they know that the deficits may be accumulated to an amount equal to the discount and may be recovered through redemption of the bond on the maturity date.

# EXERCISE 16–4

## Reference: Sections 16.3 B and C

1. A $4,000 bond, interest at 5% payable semiannually, redeemable in $2\frac{1}{2}$ years, is purchased to yield 4% interest compounded semiannually. Find the purchase price, and construct a schedule for amortization of the premium.
2. A $3,000 bond, interest at 4% payable semiannually, redeemable in three years, is bought to yield 3% interest compounded semiannually. Find the purchase price, and construct a schedule for amortization of the premium.
3. Refer to Problem 1. If the yield rate is 7% compounded semiannually, find the purchase price and construct a schedule for accumulation of the discount.
4. Refer to Problem 2. If the yield rate is 5% compounded semiannually, find the purchase price and construct a schedule for accumulation of the discount.
5. An $8,000, 6% bond will be redeemed on April 1, 1989. Interest is payable semiannually on April 1 and October 1. The bond was bought on April 1, 1979, to yield an interest rate of $5\frac{1}{2}\%$ compounded semiannually. Find the book value of the bond on April 1, 1982. (A schedule is not required.)

**6.** Refer to Problem 5. If the yield rate were 10% compounded semiannually, what would be the book value of the bond on April 1, 1987? (A schedule is not required.)

# 16.4 APPROXIMATE YIELD RATE ON BOND INVESTMENT

When an investor purchases a bond on the market, the bond is usually listed at a quoted price. If the yield rate is not indicated, it should be determined by the investor so that it is possible to decide which one of several bonds is the best investment, or know if the interest payment is what was expected. This information may be found *approximately* by either Method A or Method B as discussed below.

## A. Average Investment Method

Under the *average investment method,* the yield rate is obtained by dividing the annual income by the average annual investment.

$$\text{Yield rate (approximate)} = \frac{\text{Annual income}}{\text{Average annual investment}}$$

Here,

$$\text{Average annual investment} = \frac{\text{Beginning investment} + \text{Ending investment}}{2}, \text{ or}$$

$$= \frac{\text{Quoted price} + \text{Face value}}{2}$$

Annual income = Annual interest receipts − Annual premium amortization, or
Annual income = Annual interest receipts + Annual discount accumulation.

The annual premium amortization and the annual discount accumulation are computed by the following respective expressions:

$$\text{Annual premium amortized} = \frac{\text{Total premium}}{\text{Number of years of the investment}}$$

$$\text{Annual discount accumulated} = \frac{\text{Total discount}}{\text{Number of years of the investment}}$$

**Example 1**     A $1,000, 4% bond, redeemable in five years, interest payable semiannually, is bought at the quoted price of $1,060. What is the nominal yield rate?

The annual income is computed first:

Annual interest receipts = 1,000(4%) = $40 (a gain)
Annual premium amortization = (1,060 − 1,000)/5 = $12 (a loss)

The annual income = 40 − 12 = $28 (net gain)

The average annual investment $= (1,060 + 1,000)/2 = \$1,030$

The nominal yield rate $= \dfrac{28}{1,030} = .02718$, or $2.718\%$

**Note:** The average annual investment may be computed as follows:

$(1,060 + 1,048 + 1,036 + 1,024 + 1,012 + 1,000)/6 = 6,180/6 = \$1,030$

The annual investments form an arithmetic progression, whose common difference is the annual premium amortization, \$12.

**Example 2** A \$1,000, 5% bond, redeemable in eight years, interest payable semiannually, is bought at the quoted price of \$970. What is the nominal yield rate?

The annual income is computed first.

Annual interest receipts $= 1,000(5\%) = \$50$ (a gain)
Annual discount accumulation $= (1,000 - 970)/8 = \$3.75$ (a gain)

The annual income $= 50 + 3.75 = \$53.75$ (net gain)

The average annual investment $= (970 + 1,000)/2 = \$985$

The nominal yield rate $= \dfrac{53.75}{985} = .05457$, or $5.457\%$

# ★B. Interpolation Method

The *interpolation method* is based on the available interest rates given in Table 8. By one or several trial operations (beginning with the bond interest rate), two purchase prices are found: One is greater than the quoted price and the other one is smaller than the quoted price. Then, through interpolation, the desired interest rate is found. The number of trial operations can be reduced if the average investment method, described above, is used before the interpolation process.

*Solution for Example 1 by interpolation method:*

Since the quoted price is at a premium, the yield rate must be smaller than the bond rate, 4%. According to the solution in Method A, the nominal yield rate is .02718. The interest rate per six months is .02718/$2 = .01359$. The two interest rates closest to .01359 in Table 8 are .01375, or $1\frac{3}{8}\%$, and .0125, or $1\frac{1}{4}\%$. The two rates are then tried to find the purchase prices closest to the quoted price of the bond:

$b = 4\%/2 = 2\%$ (per six months)

When $i = 1\frac{1}{4}\%$,
Purchase price $= 1,000 + 1,000(2\% - 1\frac{1}{4}\%)a_{\overline{16}|\,1\,1/4\%}$
$\qquad\qquad\quad = 1,000 + 1,000(.0075)(9.3455)$
$\qquad\qquad\quad = 1,000 + 70.09 = \$1,070.09$

When $i = 1\frac{3}{8}\%$,
Purchase price $= 1,000 + 1,000(2\% - 1\frac{3}{8}\%)a_{\overline{16}|\,1\,3/8\%}$
$\qquad\qquad\quad = 1,000 + 1,000(.00625)(9.2836)$
$\qquad\qquad\quad = 1,000 + 58.02 = \$1,058.02$

***Note:*** When the yield rate becomes greater, the purchase price becomes smaller. When the yield rate becomes smaller, the purchase price becomes greater.

The interpolation method is then carried out as follows: (The larger numbers, which are in the column of values all known, are written on the top lines.)

$$
\begin{array}{cccc}
 & i & \begin{array}{c}\textit{Purchase}\\\textit{Price}\end{array} & \\
 & 1\frac{1}{4}\% & 1{,}070.09 & (1)\\
 & x & 1{,}060.00 & (2)\\
 & 1\frac{3}{8}\% & 1{,}058.02 & (3)\\
\hline
(2)-(3)\quad & x-1\frac{3}{8}\% & 1.98 & (4)\\
(1)-(3)\quad & -\frac{1}{8}\% & 12.07 & (5)
\end{array}
$$

Solve for $x$ from the proportion formed by the differences on lines (4) and (5).

$$x - 1\frac{3}{8}\% = \left(-\frac{1}{8}\%\right)\left(\frac{1.98}{12.07}\right) = -\left(\frac{1}{800}\right)\left(\frac{198}{1{,}207}\right) = -.000205$$

$x = 1\frac{3}{8}\% - .000205 = .01375 - .000205 = .013545$, or
$\quad = 1.3545\%$ (per six months)

The nominal yield rate $= 1.3545\% \times 2 = 2.709\%$

*Solution for Example 2 by interpolation method:*

Since the quoted price is at a discount, the yield rate must be greater than the bond rate, 5%. However, according to the solution in Method A, the nominal yield rate is found to be approximately 5.457%. The interest rate per six months is 5.457%/2 = 2.7285%. The two interest rates closest to 2.7285% in Table 8 are $2\frac{1}{2}\%$ and $2\frac{3}{4}\%$. The two rates are tried to find the purchase prices closest to the quoted price of the bond:

$b = 5\%/2 = 2\frac{1}{2}\%$ (per six months)

When $i = 2\frac{1}{2}\%$,
Purchase price = quoted price = \$1,000; because $i = b$

When $i = 2\frac{3}{4}\%$,
Purchase price $= 1{,}000 - 1{,}000(2\frac{3}{4}\% - 2\frac{1}{2}\%)a_{\overline{16}|2\ 3/4\%}$
$\quad\quad = 1{,}000 - 1{,}000(\frac{1}{4}\%)(12.8046)$
$\quad\quad = 1{,}000 - 32.01 = \$967.99$

The interpolation method is then carried out as follows:

$$
\begin{array}{cccc}
 & i & \begin{array}{c}\textit{Purchase}\\\textit{Price}\end{array} & \\
 & 2\frac{1}{2}\% & 1{,}000.00 & (1)\\
 & x & 970.00 & (2)\\
 & 2\frac{3}{4}\% & 967.99 & (3)\\
\hline
(2)-(3)\quad & x-2\frac{3}{4}\% & 2.01 & (4)\\
(1)-(3)\quad & -\frac{1}{4}\% & 32.01 & (5)
\end{array}
$$

Solve for $x$ from the proportion formed by the differences on lines (4) and (5).

$$x - 2\frac{3}{4}\% = \left(-\frac{1}{4}\%\right)\left(\frac{2.01}{32.01}\right) = -\left(\frac{1}{400}\right)\left(\frac{201}{3,201}\right) = -.000157$$

$x = 2\frac{3}{4}\% - .000157 = .0275 - .000157 = .027343$ (per six months)

The nominal yield rate $= .027343 \times 2 = .054686$, rounded to 5.469%.

## EXERCISE 16–5

### Reference: Section 16.4

**A.** *Find the approximate nominal yield rate in each of the following problems. Use Method A for Problems 1–6.* ★*Use Method B for Problems 7 and 8.*

| | Par Value | Bond Rate Payable Semiannually | Time Before Redemption | Quoted Price |
|---|---|---|---|---|
| **1.** | $1,000 | 5% | 15 years | $1,240 |
| **2.** | 2,000 | 4% | 10 years | 2,300 |
| **3.** | 2,500 | $3\frac{1}{2}\%$ | 7 years | 2,360 |
| **4.** | 3,000 | 5% | 6 years | 2,820 |
| **5.** | 4,000 | $5\frac{1}{2}\%$ | 14 years | 4,350 |
| **6.** | 5,000 | $4\frac{1}{2}\%$ | 5 years | 4,780 |
| **7.** | 3,500 | 4% | 4 years | 3,380 |
| **8.** | 500 | 6% | 12 years | 560 |

**B.** *Statement Problems:*

**9.** A $1,000, 5% bond, interest payable semiannually, redeemable on August 1, 1988, is bought at the quoted price of $920 on August 1, 1980. What is the nominal yield rate? (Use Method A.)

**10.** A $2,000, $3\frac{1}{2}\%$ bond, is to be redeemed on September 1, 1990. Interest is payable semiannually on March 1 and September 1. If the bond is quoted at 96(%) on March 1, 1980, what is the nominal yield rate? (Use Method A.)

**11.** Refer to Problem 9. If the bond were bought at the quoted price of $1,080 on August 1, 1980, what would be the nominal yield rate compounded semiannually? (★Use Method B.)

**12.** Refer to Problem 10. If the bond were quoted at 104(%) on March 1, 1980, what would be the nominal yield rate compounded semiannually? (★Use Method B.)

## 16.5 BOND TABLES

For convenience, companies that buy and sell bonds commonly use prepared bond tables to compute the purchase price of a bond and the approximate yield rate. These tables include the most frequently used bond rates and yield rates, as well as the purchase prices on a variety of time lengths before the date of bond maturity. Some of the values of a $100 bond in such tables are given on this page.

# A. Finding the Purchase Price

**Example 1**    A $10,000, $3\frac{1}{2}$% bond, redeemable in 10 years, interest payable semiannually, is bought to yield 3% interest compounded semiannually. Find the purchase price.

## SELECTED "AND INTEREST" PRICES (QUOTED PRICES) OF A $100 BOND INTEREST PAYABLE SEMIANNUALLY

| Nominal Yield Rate in % | Nominal Bond Interest Rate | | | | | |
|---|---|---|---|---|---|---|
| | 3% | | | $3\frac{1}{2}$% | | |
| | Time Before Redemption | | | Time Before Redemption | | |
| | 6 Years | 6 Years, 1 Month | 6 Years, 2 Months | 9 Years | $9\frac{1}{2}$ Years | 10 Years |
| 3.00 | $100.000 | $99.998 | $99.998 | $103.918 | $104.107 | $104.292 |
| 3.05 | 99.728 | 99.723 | 99.718 | 103.518 | 103.687 | 103.853 |
| 3.10 | 99.456 | 99.448 | 99.440 | 103.121 | 103.270 | 103.417 |
| 3.15 | 99.186 | 99.174 | 99.163 | 102.724 | 102.854 | 102.982 |
| 3.20 | 98.916 | 98.901 | 98.886 | 102.330 | 102.441 | 102.550 |
| 3.25 | 98.647 | 98.628 | 98.610 | 101.937 | 102.029 | 102.120 |
| 3.30 | 98.379 | 98.357 | 98.336 | 101.546 | 101.620 | 101.692 |
| 3.35 | 98.112 | 98.086 | 98.062 | 101.157 | 101.212 | 101.266 |
| 3.40 | 97.845 | 97.817 | 97.789 | 100.770 | 100.806 | 100.842 |
| 3.45 | 97.580 | 97.548 | 97.517 | 100.384 | 100.402 | 100.420 |
| 3.50 | 97.315 | 97.280 | 97.245 | 100.000 | 100.000 | 100.000 |
| 3.55 | 97.051 | 97.013 | 96.975 | 99.618 | 99.600 | 99.582 |
| 3.60 | 96.788 | 96.746 | 96.705 | 99.237 | 99.201 | 99.166 |
| 3.65 | 96.526 | 96.481 | 96.437 | 99.858 | 98.805 | 98.753 |
| 3.70 | 96.264 | 96.216 | 96.169 | 98.481 | 98.410 | 98.341 |

Since the bond is bought on an interest date, the purchase price is the quoted price in the bond table. The entry in the above table for the bond rate $3\frac{1}{2}$%, 10 years before redemption, yield rate 3.00%, is $104.292. Since the value of the entry is for a $100 bond, the value of a $10,000 bond is

$$104.292\left(\frac{10,000}{100}\right) = 104.292(100) = \$10,429.20$$

**Note:**    This answer may be checked against that given in Example 1(b) in Section 16.3.

**Example 2** If a $1,000, 3% bond, redeemable in six years and two months, interest payable semiannually, is bought to yield $3\frac{1}{2}$% compounded semiannually, what is the (a) quoted price, (b) accrued interest on the bond, and (c) purchase price?

(a) According to the bond table above, the quoted price for the bond is

$$97.245\left(\frac{1,000}{100}\right) = \$972.45$$

(b) Since the bond is redeemable in six years and two months and interest is payable semiannually, the last interest payment date must be six years and six months before redemption. Thus, there is accrued interest for four months on the bond.

The accrued interest on the bond is

$$1,000(3\%)(4/12) = \$10$$

(c) The purchase price = the quoted price + the accrued interest
$$= 972.45 + 10 = \$982.45$$

*Note:* These answers may be checked against those given in Example 4 in Section 16.2 B, where the simple interest method is used in computing the interest for the fractional interest period.

# B. Finding the Approximate Yield Rate

**Example 3** A $100, $3\frac{1}{2}$% bond, redeemable in $9\frac{1}{2}$ years, interest payable semiannually, is quoted at $99.50. What is the approximate nominal yield rate?

The quoted price is between the two entries, 99.600 and 99.201, in the $9\frac{1}{2}$ years column of the $3\frac{1}{2}$% bond section of the bond table. Thus, the yield rate is between 3.55% and 3.60%. If a more accurate answer is desired, the interpolation method may be used, as shown below:

The larger numbers, which are in the column of values all known, are written on the top lines.

|  | Yield Rate | Quoted Price |  |
|---|---|---|---|
|  | 3.55% | 99.600 | (1) |
|  | $x$ | 99.500 | (2) |
|  | 3.60% | 99.201 | (3) |
| (2) − (3) | $\dfrac{x - 3.60\%}{-.05\%}$ | $\dfrac{0.299}{0.399}$ | (4) |
| (1) − (3) |  |  | (5) |

Solve for $x$ from the proportion formed by the differences on lines (4) and (5):

$$x - 3.60\% = \left(-.05\%\right)\left(\frac{0.299}{0.399}\right)$$

$$= -\left(.0005\right)\left(\frac{299}{399}\right) = -.000375,$$

$$x = .036 - .000375$$
$$= .035625, \text{ or } 3.56\%.$$

## EXERCISE 16–6

### Reference: Section 16.5

**A.** *Find the unknown value (?) of the bond in each of the following problems. The bond interest is payable semiannually: (Omit interpolation in Problems 7–10.)*

| | Bond Face Value | Time Before Redemption | Bond Interest Rate | Yield Rate (Compounded Semiannually) | Quoted Price |
|---|---|---|---|---|---|
| 1. | $1,000 | 9 years | 3½% | 3.20% | ? |
| 2. | 2,000 | 9½ years | 3½% | 3.25% | ? |
| 3. | 3,000 | 6 years | 3% | 3.45% | ? |
| 4. | 4,000 | 6 years, 1 month | 3% | 3.55% | ? |
| 5. | 500 | 6 years, 2 months | 3% | 3.65% | ? |
| 6. | 600 | 10 years | 3½% | 3.30% | ? |
| 7. | 100 | 9½ years | 3½% | ? | $102.26 |
| 8. | 100 | 10 years | 3½% | ? | 99.80 |
| 9. | 1,000 | 6 years | 3% | ? | 976.45 |
| 10. | 600 | 9 years | 3½% | ? | 617.40 |

**B.** *Statement Problems:*

11. A $2,000, 3% bond, redeemable in six years, interest payable semiannually, is purchased to yield 3.6% compounded semiannually. Find the purchase price.

12. A $3,000, 3½% bond, redeemable in 9½ years, interest payable semiannually, is bought to yield 3.2% compounded semiannually. Find the purchase price.

13. If a $4,000, 3% bond, redeemable in six years and one month, interest payable semiannually, is bought to yield 3.25% compounded semiannually, what are the (a) quoted price, (b) accrued interest on the bond, and (c) purchase price?

14. If a $2,500, 3% bond, redeemable in six years and two months, interest payable semiannually, is bought to yield 3.7% compounded semiannually, what are the (a) quoted price, (b) accrued interest on the bond, and (c) purchase price?

**15.** A $1,000, 3% bond, redeemable in six years, interest payable semiannually, is quoted at $972.50. What is the approximate nominal yield rate? (Use the interpolation method to find the answer.)

**16.** A $1,000, 3½% bond, redeemable in 10 years, interest payable semiannually, is quoted at $1,027. What is the approximate nominal yield rate? (Use the interpolation method to find the answer.)

# ★16.6 OTHER TYPES OF BONDS

## A. Annuity Bonds

An *annuity bond* is a contract in which the issuer promises to pay both the principal and the interest periodically until the entire debt is paid.

**Example 1**   An annuity bond of $5,000 is to be repaid in 10 equal semiannual payments, principal and interest included. The bond interest rate is 4% compounded semiannually. Assume that the yield rate is 5% compounded semiannually. Find the purchase price (a) now, and (b) after the sixth payment is made.

(a) First, the size of the 10 semiannual payments should be determined. The method to follow is the same as the one used in finding the size of the payments in an ordinary annuity problem when the present value ($5,000 in this example) is known. (See Section 13.5 A.)

$A_n = \$5,000$, $b = 4\%/2 = 2\%$ (*bond interest rate* per six months), and $n = 10$ (semiannual payments), $R = ?$ (per six months)

Substituting the values in the formula $A_n = Ra_{\overline{n}|b}$

$5,000 = Ra_{\overline{10}|2\%}$

$$R = \frac{5,000}{a_{\overline{10}|2\%}} = 5,000(.1113265) = \$556.63 \qquad \text{(Table 9)}$$

Second, find the present value of an annuity of $556.63 payable (to the purchaser) at the end of every six months, for 10 payments, at the *yield rate* of 5% compounded semiannually.

$A_n = ?$, $R = 556.53$, $i = 5\%/2 = 2\frac{1}{2}\%$ (*yield rate* per six months), and $n = 10$ (semiannual payments).

Substituting the above values in the formula $A_n = Ra_{\overline{n}|i}$:

$A_{10} = 556.63 a_{\overline{10}|2\ 1/2\%} = 556.63(8.75206)$
$\qquad = \$4,871.66$

(b) Since the bond is purchased after the sixth payment, the annuity is formed by the remaining four semiannual payments of $556.63 each. The present value of the annuity is computed as follows:

$n = 4$, $i = 2\frac{1}{2}\%$ (yield rate)

$A_4 = 556.63 a_{\overline{4}|2\ 1/2\%} = 556.63(3.76197) = \$2,094.03$

# B. Serial Bonds

When the bonds in an issue are redeemable periodically on a series of specified due dates, the bonds are called *serial bonds*. According to the different due dates, a serial bond may be thought of as several groups of bonds combined in one issue. Thus, the purchase price of a serial bond is obtained by totaling the purchase prices of the individual groups of bonds.

**Example 2**  A three-year, 4% bond for $15,000 provides that the bond is to be redeemed at the end of each year by payments of $5,000 each and that the interest is to be paid semiannually. If the bond is purchased now to yield 3% compounded semiannually, what is the purchase price?

$b = 4\%/2 = 2\%$, $i = 3\%/2 = 1\frac{1}{2}\%$ (per six months).

Since $b$ is greater than $i$, there must be a premium. The excess of the periodic bond interest payment over the semiannual yield for a $5,000 bond is

$$5,000(2\%) - 5,000(1\frac{1}{2}\%) = 5,000(2\% - 1\frac{1}{2}\%)$$
$$= 5,000(\tfrac{1}{2}\%)$$
$$= \$25 \text{ (per six months)}$$

Use the premium method, formula (16–2), as follows:

The purchase price for the $5,000 bond which is due in one year is

$$5,000 + 25a_{\overline{2}|1\ 1/2\%} = 5,000 + 25(1.9559)$$
$$= 5,000 + 48.90 = \$5,048.90$$

The purchase price for the $5,000 bond which is due in two years is

$$5,000 + 25a_{\overline{4}|1\ 1/2\%} = 5,000 + 25(3.8544)$$
$$= 5,000 + 96.36 = \$5,096.36$$

The purchase price for the $5,000 bond which is due in three years is

$$5,000 + 25a_{\overline{6}|1\ 1/2\%} = 5,000 + 25(5.6972)$$
$$= 5,000 + 142.43 = \$5,142.43$$

The total purchase price is

$$5,048.90 + 5,096.36 + 5,142.43 = \$15,287.69$$

# ★EXERCISE 16–7

## Reference: Section 16.6

1. A $3,000 annuity bond is to be repaid in eight equal semiannual payments, principal and interest included. The bond rate is $4\frac{1}{2}\%$ compounded semiannually. Find the purchase price (a) now, and (b) after the fifth payment is made. Assume that the yield rate is 6% compounded semiannually.

2. A $4,000 annuity bond is to be repaid by 12 equal semiannual payments, principal and interest included. The bond rate is 5% compounded semiannually. Assume that the yield rate is $6\frac{1}{2}\%$. Find the purchase price (a) now, and (b) after the ninth payment is made.

3. Refer to Problem 1. Assume that the yield rate is 3% compounded semiannually. What are the answers to (a) and (b)?

4. Refer to Problem 2. Assume that the yield rate is 4% compounded semiannually. What are the answers to (a) and (b)?

5. A 3% serial bond of $18,000, interest payable semiannually, is to be redeemed in three annual installments of $6,000 each. The bond is bought on the interest date, which is one year before the first redemption date. If the yield rate is 5% compounded semiannually, what is the purchase price?

6. A 5% bond for $16,000 is to be redeemed by a series of four annual payments of $4,000 each. The first redemption date is April 1, 1981. The bond interest is payable on April 1 and October 1 each year. If the bond is purchased to yield 4% compounded semiannually, what is the purchase price on April 1, 1980.

7. In Problem 5, if the bond is bought on the interest date, which is seven years before the first annual redemption date, what is the purchase price?

8. In Problem 6, if the first redemption date is October 1, 1989, what is the purchase price on April 1, 1980?

# 16.7 SUMMARY OF BOND INVESTMENT FORMULAS

*Symbols:*  $S =$ redemption value of bond
$R =$ periodic bond interest payment
$i =$ yield rate per interest period
$b =$ bond rate per interest payment period
$n =$ number of interest periods or payments
$F =$ face value of bond

| Application | Formula | Formula Number | Reference Page |
|---|---|---|---|
| Finding the purchase price of a bond on the interest date | Purchase price $= S(1 + i)^{-n} + Ra_{\overline{n}|i}$ | (16–1) | 465 |
| Finding the premium (or discount) | *When face value = redemption value,*<br>Premium $= F(b - i)a_{\overline{n}|i}$<br>Discount $= F(i - b)a_{\overline{n}|i}$ | (16–2)<br>(16–3) | 472<br>472 |
| | Purchase price = Face value + Premium, or<br>Purchase price = Face value − Discount | | |
| | *In general,*<br>Premium $= [(\text{Face value} \times b) -$<br>$(\text{Redemption value} \times i)]a_{\overline{n}|i}$ | (16–4) | 473 |
| | Purchase price = Redemption value<br>+ Premium | | |
| | Here, − Premium = Discount | | |

## EXERCISE 16–8

### Review of Chapter 16

1. A $1,000, 4% bond is bought five years before redemption to yield 5% compounded semiannually. The interest on the bond is payable semiannually. Find the purchase price if the bond is redeemable at (a) par, (b) 103(%), and (c) 97(%).

2. A $500, 6% bond is purchased on February 1, 1981, to yield 4% compounded semiannually. The interest on the bond is payable on February 1 and August 1 each year. Find the purchase price by assuming that the bond is redeemable on August 1, 1990, at (a) par, (b) 104(%), and (c) 96(%).

3. Refer to Problem 1(a). If the bond is bought four years and 10 months before redemption, what is (a) the purchase price? (b) the accrued interest on the bond? and (c) the quoted price?

4. Refer to Problem 2(a). Assuming that the bond is purchased on May 1, 1981, what is (a) the purchase price? (b) the accrued interest on the bond? and (c) the quoted price?

5. On April 30, 1980, a man purchased $2,000 of 4% bonds. Bonds were quoted on the market on that date at 96(%). Interest on the bonds was payable on March 1 and September 1. Find (a) the quoted price, (b) the accrued interest on the bonds, and (c) the purchase price.

6. A $5\frac{1}{2}$% bond of $5,000 was quoted on the market at $96\frac{1}{2}$(%) on April 21, 1981. Interest on the bond was payable semiannually on April 1 and October 1. Find (a) the quoted price, (b) the accrued interest on the bond, and (c) the purchase price.

7. A $7,000, 5% bond, redeemable in eight years, interest payable semiannually, is purchased to yield 4% interest compounded semiannually. Find (a) the premium and (b) the purchase price.

8. A $5,000, 3% bond, redeemable in 10 years, interest payable semiannually, is bought to yield $4\frac{1}{2}$% interest compounded semiannually. Find (a) the discount and (b) the purchase price.

9. Refer to Problem 7. What is the purchase price if the yield rate is (a) 6% compounded semiannually? (b) 5% compounded semiannually?

10. Refer to Problem 8. What is the purchase price if the yield rate is (a) $2\frac{1}{2}$% compounded semiannually? (b) 3% compounded semiannually?

11. A $6,000, 5% bond, interest payable semiannually, is bought two years before the redemption date to yield 6% compounded semiannually. (a) Find the purchase price. (b) Construct a schedule showing the periodic changes of the book value to par.

12. A $2,000, 6% bond, interest payable semiannually, redeemable in $2\frac{1}{2}$ years, is purchased to yield 4% compounded semiannually. (a) Find the purchase price. (b) Construct a schedule showing the periodic changes of the book value to par.

13. Work Problem 11, using a yield rate of 3% compounded semiannually.

**14.** Work Problem 12, using a yield rate of 8% compounded semiannually.

**15.** A $3,000, 6% bond, redeemable in seven years, interest payable semiannually, is bought at the quoted price of $3,420. What is the approximate nominal yield rate? (Use the average investment method.)

**16.** A $5,000, $4\frac{1}{2}$% bond, redeemable in 12 years, interest payable semiannually, is bought at the quoted price of $4,640. What is the approximate nominal yield rate? (Use the average investment method.)

★**17.** Work Problem 15, using a quoted price of $2,720. (Use the interpolation method.)

★**18.** Work Problem 16, using a quoted price of $5,240. (Use the interpolation method.)

**19.** An $8,000, $3\frac{1}{2}$% bond, redeemable in nine years, interest payable semiannually, is bought to yield $3\frac{1}{4}$% interest compounded semiannually. Find the purchase price by using the bond table.

**20.** A $10,000, 3% bond, redeemable in six years, interest payable semiannually, is bought to yield 3.55% interest compounded semiannually. Find the purchase price by using the bond table.

**21.** If a $10,000, 3% bond, redeemable in six years and two months, interest payable semiannually, is bought to yield 3.35% compounded semiannually, what is the purchase price? (Use the bond table.)

**22.** A $5,000, 3% bond, redeemable in six years and one month, interest payable semiannually, is bought to yield 3.65% compounded semiannually. What is the purchase price? (Use the bond table.)

**23.** A $2,000, $3\frac{1}{2}$% bond, redeemable in 10 years with interest payable semiannually, is quoted at $2,040. Find the approximate nominal yield rate by using the bond table.

**24.** A $100, 3% bond, redeemable in six years, interest payable semiannually, is quoted at $96.45. Find the approximate nominal yield rate by using the bond table.

★**25.** An annuity bond of $10,000 is to be retired in eight semiannual payments, including principal and interest. The bond interest rate is 5% and the yield rate is 6%, both compounded semiannually. What is the purchase price (a) now, and (b) after the fifth payment is made?

★**26.** A 3% annuity bond of $6,000 is to be repaid in 12 semiannual payments, principal and interest included. Assume that the yield rate is $2\frac{1}{2}$% compounded semiannually. Find the purchase price (a) now, and (b) after the eighth semiannual payment.

★**27.** A 5% bond of $21,000 is to be redeemed by three payments of $7,000 each at the end of every two years. The interest on the bond is payable semiannually. If the bond is purchased now to yield 6% compounded semiannually, what is the purchase price?

★**28.** A 4% bond of $12,000 is to be redeemed by a series of four annual payments of $3,000 each with the first payment on August 1, 1981. Interest on the bond is payable on February 1 and August 1 each year. If the bond is bought to yield 3% compounded semiannually, find the purchase price on August 1, 1980.

# Chapter 17

## Depreciation and Depletion

## 17.1 INTRODUCTION TO DEPRECIATION

The tangible assets of a business, excluding land, usually have limited useful lives. Buildings, machines, and various types of equipment, after being used for a number of years, eventually come to the end of their lives. They must be retired from the business regardless of efforts to maintain and repair them. At the time of retirement, the assets may have a small trade-in or scrap value, or may be worthless. In either case, there is a loss in the value of the property. This loss is called *depreciation expense,* or simply *depreciation.*

Depreciation expense should be periodically charged to business operating expenses or to the cost of goods manufactured during the useful life of the asset. The total of the periodic depreciation charges is limited to the cost of the property. Thus, the computation of the periodic depreciation is actually a process of allocating the cost of the property as an expense or a cost of goods manufactured to the proper business operating periods. The allocation is necessary in order to calculate the periodic net income from business operations. The placement of depreciation expense on an income statement is explained in Chapter 8.

An account, which generally bears the name *accumulated depreciation,* or *allowance for depreciation,* is often used by accountants to record the amount of accumulated depreciation. The difference between the original cost of an asset and its total amount in the accumulated depreciation account is its book value. The book value is not necessarily the same as the market value or the resale value. Rather, it indicates the unallocated cost of the asset.

Retirement of assets is caused by various factors, such as wear and tear, decay, damage, inadequacy, and obsolescence. These factors may operate gradually at one time and drastically at another time. Thus, the value of property may decrease more at one time than at another. However, the allocation of the cost of property is usually gradual and is done in a systematic and rational manner.

There are many methods of estimating the depreciation charges for each business operation period. The methods listed below are generally known and are illustrated in this chapter:

1. *Methods of Averages.* (Section 17.2)
   A. Straight line method
   B. Service hours method
   C. Product units method
2. *Reducing Charge Methods.* (Section 17.3)
   A. Diminishing rate on fixed depreciation—sum of the years-digits method
   B. Fixed rate on diminishing book value
3. *Compound Interest Methods.* (Section 17.4)
   A. Annuity
   B. Sinking fund
4. *Composite Rate Method.* (Section 17.5)

The following symbols are used in illustrating the depreciation methods listed above:

$$C = \text{original cost of an asset}$$
$$T = \text{estimated trade-in value or scrap value}$$
$$C - T = \text{total depreciation charges or expenses}$$
$$n = \text{useful life of the asset estimated in years, service-hours, or product-units}$$
$$r = \text{rate of depreciation expense per year, per service-hour, per product-unit, or per dollar}$$

## 17.2 DEPRECIATION—METHODS OF AVERAGES

## A. Straight Line Method

The *straight line method* is based on the assumption that the depreciation charges are equal for each year. In other words, the depreciable asset contributes its services equally to each year's operation. The formula for this method is

$$r = \frac{C - T}{n} \tag{17–1}$$

$r$ = depreciation expense per year, and $n$ = number of years

**Example 1**    A machine which was purchased for \$1,100 has an estimated useful life of five years and a trade-in value of \$120. Use the straight line method to find the depreciation charges for each year, and construct a depreciation schedule.

$C = 1,100$,  $T = 120$,  $n = 5$ (years)

Substituting the values in formula (17–1):

$$r = \frac{C - T}{n} = \frac{1,100 - 120}{5} = \frac{980}{5} = \$196 \text{ (per year)}$$

## DEPRECIATION SCHEDULE—STRAIGHT LINE METHOD
(Example 1)

| (1)<br><br><br><br>End of Year | (2)<br>Annual<br>Depreciation<br>Expense | (3)<br>Accumulated<br>Depreciation<br>from (2) | (4)<br>Book Value of<br>Machine<br>$1,100 − (3) |
|---|---|---|---|
| 0 | . . . | . . . | $1,100 |
| 1 | $196 | $196 | 904 |
| 2 | 196 | 392 | 708 |
| 3 | 196 | 588 | 512 |
| 4 | 196 | 784 | 316 |
| 5 | 196 | 980 | 120 |
| Total | $980 | | |

**Note:**     The annual depreciation expense is a constant amount, $196. If the above data are plotted on graph paper, the accumulated depreciation forms a straight line. Thus, this method is known as a "straight line" method.

# B. Service Hours Method

The *service hours method* relates depreciation to estimated productive capacity of the asset in terms of its hours of useful service. Under this method, first the depreciation rate per service hour *(r)* is found by using formula (17–1), $r = \dfrac{C - T}{n}$. For this method, $n$ = number of service hours. Next, the depreciation charges for a given year are determined by multiplying the actual number of service hours used in the year by $r$.

**Example 2**     Refer to Example 1. Assume that the useful life of the machine is estimated to be 20,000 service hours and the actual number of hours spent in production each year is as follows:

1st year: 5,000 service hours
2d year: 4,500 service hours
3d year: 4,200 service hours
4th year: 3,400 service hours
5th year: 2,900 service hours

Use the service hours method to find the depreciation charges for each year. Construct a depreciation schedule.

$C = 1,100$, $T = 120$, $n = 20,000$ (service hours)

Substituting the values in formula (17–1):

$$r = \frac{1,100 - 120}{20,000} = \$.049 \text{ (per service hour)}$$

The annual depreciation charges are computed as follows:

1st year: 5,000 × .049 = $245.00
2d year: 4,500 × .049 = $220.50
3d year: 4,200 × .049 = $205.80
4th year: 3,400 × .049 = $166.60
5th year: 2,900 × .049 = $142.10

**DEPRECIATION SCHEDULE—SERVICE HOURS METHOD**
(Example 2)

| (1)<br>End of Year | (2)<br>Annual<br>Depreciation<br>Expense | (3)<br>Accumulated<br>Depreciation | (4)<br>Book Value of<br>Machine<br>$1,100 − (3) |
|---|---|---|---|
| 0 | . . . | . . . | $1,100.00 |
| 1 | $245.00 | $245.00 | 855.00 |
| 2 | 220.50 | 465.50 | 634.50 |
| 3 | 205.80 | 671.30 | 428.70 |
| 4 | 166.60 | 837.90 | 262.10 |
| 5 | 142.10 | 980.00 | 120.00 |
| Total | $980.00 | | |

# C. Product Units Method

Under the *product units method,* depreciation is related to the estimated number of units that will be produced by each asset during its useful life. To determine the amount of depreciation, first, the depreciation rate per unit of product *(r)* is found by using formula (17–1), $r = \dfrac{C - T}{n}$. For this method, $n$ = number of product units. Then, the depreciation charges for a given period are determined by multiplying the number of units produced in the period by *r*.

**Example 3**    Refer to Example 1. Assume that the useful life of the machine is estimated to be 70,000 product units and the number of units produced each year is estimated as follows:

1st year—14,000 units
2d year—15,000 units
3d year—16,500 units
4th year—17,000 units
5th year— 7,500 units

Use the product units method to find the depreciation charges for each year. Construct a depreciation schedule.

$C = 1,100$, $T = 120$, $n = 70,000$ (units)

Substituting the values in formula (17–1):

$$r = \frac{1,100 - 120}{70,000} = \$.014 \text{ (per unit)}$$

The annual depreciation charges are computed as follows:

1st year: $14,000 \times .014 = \$196$
2d year: $15,000 \times .014 = \$210$
3d year: $16,500 \times .014 = \$231$
4th year: $17,000 \times .014 = \$238$
5th year: $\phantom{0}7,500 \times .014 = \$105$

## DEPRECIATION SCHEDULE—PRODUCT UNITS METHOD
(Example 3)

| (1)<br><br><br>End of Year | (2)<br>Annual<br>Depreciation<br>Expense | (3)<br><br>Accumulated<br>Depreciation | (4)<br>Book Value of<br>Machine<br>$1,100 − (3) |
|---|---|---|---|
| 0 | . . . | . . . | $1,100 |
| 1 | $196 | $196 | 904 |
| 2 | 210 | 406 | 694 |
| 3 | 231 | 637 | 463 |
| 4 | 238 | 875 | 225 |
| 5 | 105 | 980 | 120 |
| Total | $980 | | |

## EXERCISE 17–1

### Reference: Section 17.2

1. A building which was constructed for $50,000 has an estimated useful life of 20 years and a salvage value of $5,000. Use the straight line method to find the depreciation charges for each year.
2. A piece of equipment which was purchased for $800 has an estimated useful life of seven years and a scrap value of $30. Use the straight line method to compute the depreciation charges for each year.
3. The cost of a machine purchased by the Gordon Company is $2,650. It is estimated that the machine will have a $250 trade-in value at the end of its useful life, which is estimated at five years. Use the straight line method to find the depreciation charges for each year, and construct a depreciation schedule.
4. The Kent Company has a machine costing $5,400 with an estimated useful life of six years and a trade-in value of $300. Use the straight line method to find the depreciation charges for each year, and construct a depreciation schedule.

5. Refer to Problem 3. Assume that the useful life of the machine is estimated to be 30,000 service hours and that the actual number of hours spent in production for each year is as follows:

> 1st year: 5,500 hours     4th year: 5,800 hours
> 2d year: 7,400 hours     5th year: 5,100 hours
> 3d year: 6,200 hours

Use the service hours method to find the depreciation charges for each year. Construct a depreciation schedule.

6. Refer to Problem 3. Assume that the useful life of the machine is estimated to be 100,000 units of production, and that the number of units produced each year is estimated as follows:

> 1st year: 24,000 units     4th year: 18,000 units
> 2d year: 23,000 units     5th year: 16,000 units
> 3d year: 19,000 units

Use the product units method to find the depreciation charges for each year. Construct a depreciation schedule.

7. Refer to Problem 4. Assume that the useful life of the machine is estimated to be 17,000 service hours and the actual number of hours spent in production for the first year is 2,800 hours. Use the service hours method to compute the depreciation charges for the first year.

8. Refer to Problem 4. Assume that the useful life of the machine is estimated to be 50,000 units of production and the number of units produced during the first year is 8,500 units. Use the product units method to compute the depreciation charges for the first year.

## 17.3 DEPRECIATION—REDUCING CHARGE METHODS

Generally, the maintenance and repair expenses for new equipment are less than those for older equipment. Therefore, larger amounts of depreciation expense are often charged to the earlier years of the useful life of certain equipment than are charged to the later years. When this is done, the sum of the depreciation expenses and the maintenance and repair costs for each year during the useful life are equalized.

## A. Diminishing Rate on Fixed Depreciation—Sum of the Years-Digits Method

Under the *sum of the years-digits method,* the depreciation expense for the earlier years is greater than that of later years. The total depreciation is fixed and is the difference between the original cost and the trade-in or scrap value $(C - T)$. The rate of depreciation is expressed in a changing fraction which becomes smaller each year. In this changing fraction, the numerator is the number of remaining years of life. The denominator is the sum of the digits that represent the years of life.

**Example 1**    A machine which was purchased for $1,100 has an estimated useful life of five years and a trade-in value of $120. (The information is the same as that in Example 1 of Section 17.2, page 491.) Use the sum of the years-digits method to find the depreciation charges for each year and construct a depreciation schedule.

The sum [1] of the five years digits is

$$1 + 2 + 3 + 4 + 5 = 15$$

The total depreciation charge is $1,100 - 120 = \$980$. The annual depreciation charges are computed as follows:

1st year: $980 \times \frac{5}{15} = \$326.67$
2d year: $980 \times \frac{4}{15} = 261.33$
3d year: $980 \times \frac{3}{15} = 196.00$
4th year: $980 \times \frac{2}{15} = 130.67$
5th year: $980 \times \frac{1}{15} = \underline{\phantom{00}65.33}$
Total: $\phantom{000}\$980.00$

## DEPRECIATION SCHEDULE—SUM OF THE YEARS-DIGITS METHOD
(Example 1)

| (1)<br>End of Year | (2)<br>Annual<br>Depreciation<br>Expense | (3)<br>Accumulated<br>Depreciation | (4)<br>Book Value of<br>Machine<br>$1,100 − (3) |
|---|---|---|---|
| 0 | . . . | . . . | $1,100.00 |
| 1 | $326.67 | $326.67 | 773.33 |
| 2 | 261.33 | 588.00 | 512.00 |
| 3 | 196.00 | 784.00 | 316.00 |
| 4 | 130.67 | 914.67 | 185.33 |
| 5 | 65.33 | 980.00 | 120.00 |
| Total | $980.00 | | |

---

[1] The sum of the years-digits may be obtained by using the sum of the arithmetic progression formula given in Section 3.3 B:

$$S_n = \frac{n}{2}(a + L).$$

where $S_n$ is the sum, $n$ is the number of years in the life of the asset, $a$ is the first number in the series of numbers, and $L$ is the last number in the series. In Example 1, $n = 5$, $a = 1$, and $L = 5$.

The sum of the years-digits $= \frac{5}{2}(1 + 5) = 2.5 \times 6 = 15$

In Example 2, $n = 5$, $a = 8$, and $L = 12$.

The sum of the years-digits $= \frac{5}{2}(8 + 12) = 2.5 \times 20 = 50$

When the rates based on the sum of the years-digits method are considered too extreme, the rates may be modified by adding the same number to each of the numbers of the years.

**Example 2**　　Refer to Example 1. Find the annual depreciation charges by adding 7 to each of the numbers of the years.

The sum of the five years-digits becomes

$$(1 + 7) + (2 + 7) + (3 + 7) + (4 + 7) + (5 + 7)$$
$$= 8 + 9 + 10 + 11 + 12 = 50$$

Thus, the annual depreciation charges are as follows:

1st year: $980 \times \frac{12}{50} = \$235.20$
2d year: $980 \times \frac{11}{50} = 215.60$
3d year: $980 \times \frac{10}{50} = 196.00$
4th year: $980 \times \frac{9}{50} = 176.40$
5th year: $980 \times \frac{8}{50} = \underline{156.80}$
　　Total:　　　　　$\$980.00$

The difference between each successive year in Example 2 is $980 \times \frac{1}{50}$, or \$19.60; whereas, the difference between each successive year in Example 1 is $980 \times \frac{1}{15}$, or \$65.33. Thus, the rates in Example 2 are more moderate than those in Example 1.

# B. Fixed Rate on Diminishing Book Value

Under this method, the depreciation expense for earlier years is higher than that of later years. The depreciation expense for each year is obtained by multiplying the fixed (or constant) annual rate by the diminishing book value of an asset as of the beginning of each year. As shown below, there are two ways to compute the fixed annual depreciation rate.

### ACCORDING TO FEDERAL TAX REGULATIONS

This method was specifically mentioned in the Internal Revenue Code of 1954 as the *declining balance method*. The declining balance method provides a steadily declining depreciation charge over the estimated life of the asset. The annual rate of depreciation must not exceed twice the straight line rate for the depreciable asset. The maximum rate may be obtained as follows:

1. Find the annual depreciation rate by dividing 100% by the number of years of useful life of the property (straight line method).
2. Find the maximum annual depreciation rate by multiplying the annual depreciation rate obtained above by 2.

The scrap value or the trade-in value under this method is not deducted from the cost of the property prior to the rate application. As shown in the following example, the scrap value often is not equal to the original estimation when using this maximum rate.

**Example 3**    Refer to Example 1. Use the declining balance method to find the maximum depreciation charges for each year, and construct a depreciation schedule.

The annual depreciation rate based on the straight line method is

$100\%/5 = 20\%$ (per year)

The maximum annual depreciation rate is

$20\% \times 2 = 40\%$

The annual depreciation charges are computed in the following schedule:

## DEPRECIATION SCHEDULE—DECLINING BALANCE METHOD
(Example 3)

| (1)<br>End of Year | (2)<br>Annual<br>Depreciation<br>Expense<br>(4)* × 40% | (3)<br>Accumulated<br>Depreciation | (4)<br>Book Value of<br>Machine<br>$1,100 − (3) |
|---|---|---|---|
| 0 | . . . | . . . | $1,100.00 |
| 1 | $  440.00 | $  440.00 | 660.00 |
| 2 | 264.00 | 704.00 | 396.00 |
| 3 | 158.40 | 862.40 | 237.60 |
| 4 | 95.04 | 957.44 | 142.56 |
| 5 | 57.02 | 1,014.46 | 85.54 |
| Total | $1,014.46 | | |

* The diminishing book value as of the beginning of each year, which is also the value at the end of each preceding year. For example, the book value as of the beginning of the third year is $396, which is also the book value at the end of the second year. The depreciation charges for the third year are computed as follows:

$396 \times 40\% = \$158.40$.

Note that the book value at the end of fifth year is $85.54, which is not equal to the original estimated amount of $120.[2]

## ★ACCORDING TO THE FIXED RATE FORMULA

When the following fixed rate formula is used, the book value at the end of the life of the asset is equal to the scrap or trade-in value. The formula for the rate of annual depreciation charges *(r)* is as follows:

---

[2] The book value at the end of the fifth year can be checked by using the $n$th term formula of a geometric progression (see Section 3.3 C) as follows:

$L = ar^{(n-1)} = 1,100(1 - 40\%)^{6-1} = 1,100(.6)^5 = 1,100(.07776) = 85.536$ or $\$85.54$.

$$r = 1 - \sqrt[n]{\frac{T}{C}} \qquad\qquad \text{(17–2)}^{[3]}$$

**Example 4** Refer to Example 1. Use the fixed rate formula to find the depreciation charges for each year, and construct a depreciation schedule.

$C = 1,100, \ T = 120, \ n = 5$ (years)

Substituting the values in formula (17–2):

$$r = 1 - \sqrt[5]{\frac{120}{1,100}}$$

The value of $\sqrt[5]{\frac{120}{1,100}}$ may be obtained by using logarithms as follows:

---

[3] *Proof—Formula (17–2)*

    $C$ = the original cost
    $T$ = the trade-in value or scrap value
    $n$ = the number of years of useful life
    $r$ = the annual depreciation rate based on the original cost, or declining book value

The depreciation charges and the book value at the end of each year are as follows:

| | Depreciation Charges | Book Value |
|---|---|---|
| At the end of the 1st year: | $Cr$ | $C - Cr = C(1 - r)$ |
| At the end of the 2d year: | $Cr(1 - r)$ | $C(1 - r) - Cr(1 - r)$ <br> $= C(1 - r)(1 - r)$ <br> $= C(1 - r)^2$ |
| At the end of the 3d year: | $Cr(1 - r)^2$ | $C(1 - r)^2 - Cr(1 - r)^2$ <br> $= C(1 - r)^2(1 - r)$ <br> $= C(1 - r)^3$ |
| At the end of the $n$th year: | $Cr(1 - r)^{n-1}$ | $C(1 - r)^n$ |

Since the book value at the end of the $n$th year is also the trade-in or scrap value *(T)* then

    $C(1 - r)^n = T$

Divide both sides by $C$

    $(1 - r)^n = \dfrac{T}{C}$

Extract the $n$th root of each side

    $1 - r = \sqrt[n]{\dfrac{T}{C}}$

Then,

    $r = 1 - \sqrt[n]{\dfrac{T}{C}}$

$$\log \sqrt[5]{\frac{120}{1,100}} = (1/5) \log \left(\frac{120}{1,100}\right)$$

$$= (1/5)(\log 120 - \log 1,100)$$
$$= (1/5)(2.079181 - 3.041393)$$
$$= (1/5)(-.962212)$$
$$= -.1924424 = 9.8075576 - 10$$

Find the antilog,

$$\sqrt[5]{\frac{120}{1,100}} = 0.642033$$

$r = 1 - 0.642033 = 0.357967$, or $35.7967\%$

The annual depreciation charges are computed in the following schedule:

## DEPRECIATION SCHEDULE—BASED ON THE FIXED RATE FORMULA
**(Example 4)**

| (1)<br><br><br><br>End of Year | (2)<br>Annual<br>Depreciation<br>Expense<br>(4)* × .357967 | (3)<br><br><br>Accumulated<br>Depreciation | (4)<br><br>Book Value of<br>Machine<br>$1,100 − (3) |
|---|---|---|---|
| 0 | . . . | . . . | $1,100.00 |
| 1 | $393.76 | $393.76 | 706.24 |
| 2 | 252.81 | 646.57 | 453.43 |
| 3 | 162.31 | 808.88 | 291.12 |
| 4 | 104.21 | 913.09 | 186.91 |
| 5 | 66.91 | 980.00 | 120.00 |
| Total | $980.00 | | |

\* Of the preceding year. For example, $393.76 = 1,100.00 \times .357967$;
$252.81 = 706.24 \times .357967$.

## EXERCISE 17–2

### Reference: Section 17.3

1. A truck, which was bought for $3,350, has an estimated useful life of six years and a trade-in value of $200. Use the sum of the years-digits method to find the depreciation charges for each year, and construct a depreciation schedule.

2. The Johnson Steel Company has a machine costing $2,800 with an estimated useful life of five years and a scrap value of $100. Use the sum of the years-digits method to find the depreciation charges for each year, and construct a depreciation schedule.

3. Refer to Problem 1. Find the annual depreciation charges if 8 is added to each of the numbers of the six years.
4. Refer to Problem 2. What are the annual depreciation charges if 6 is added to each of the numbers of the five years?
5. Refer to Problem 1. Construct a depreciation schedule using the two fixed rate methods: (a) according to federal tax regulations and ★(b) according to the fixed rate formula.
6. Refer to Problem 2. Construct a depreciation schedule using the two fixed rate methods: (a) according to federal tax regulations, and ★(b) according to the fixed rate formula.

# ★17.4 DEPRECIATION—COMPOUND INTEREST METHODS

In the previous methods, no consideration is given to the interest on either the original cost or its diminishing book value. The following two methods are used in finding the depreciation charges when interest is involved. Both methods will give the same *net* annual depreciation charges.

## A. Annuity Method

The annuity method resembles the method of amortizing a debt. Under the annuity method, the periodic depreciation charges are equal and include not only a part of the cost of the asset but also the interest on the book value for each operating period. The periodic book value is assumed to be earning the same interest as the amount would earn if it were invested elsewhere.

Before computing the periodic depreciation charges, find the present value of the total depreciation charges. Let

$i =$ the interest rate per period (year), and
$n =$ the estimated number of years of the useful life of the asset

The present value of the trade-in value is $P = T(1 + i)^{-n}$, which is obtained by using the compound discount formula. The present value of the total depreciation charges is the difference between the original cost $(C)$ and the present value of the estimated trade-in or scrap value $(P)$. It may be expressed as follows:

$$\text{Present value of total depreciation charges} = C - P$$
$$= C - T(1 + i)^{-n}$$

The annual depreciation charges are required to be equal. Thus, the present value may be thought of as the present value of an annuity $(A_n)$ with payments consisting of equal depreciation charges, or

$$C - T(1 + i)^{-n} = A_n = Ra_{\overline{n}|i}$$

Here, $R$ represents the annual depreciation charges. Thus, the annual depreciation charges $(R)$ may be obtained as follows:

$$R = \frac{A_n}{a_{\overline{n}|i}} = \frac{C - T(1+i)^{-n}}{a_{\overline{n}|i}} \qquad \textbf{(17-3)}$$

**Example 1**    A machine which was purchased for $1,100 has an estimated useful life of five years and a trade-in value of $120. (The information is the same as that in Example 1 of Section 17.2, page 491.) Use the annuity method to find the depreciation charges for each year and construct a depreciation schedule. Assume that the effective interest rate is 6%.

$C = 1,100$, $T = 120$, $i = 6\%$, $n = 5$ (years)

The present value of the trade-in or scrap value is

$P = 120(1 + 6\%)^{-5} = 120(.74726) = \$89.67$

The present value of the total depreciation charges is

$A_n = C - P = 1,100 - 89.67 = \$1,010.33$

The annual depreciation charges are

$$R = \frac{A_n}{a_{\overline{n}|i}} = \frac{1,010.33}{a_{\overline{5}|6\%}} = 1,010.33 \times .237396 = \$239.85 \qquad \text{(Table 9)}$$

## DEPRECIATION SCHEDULE—ANNUITY METHOD
(Example 1)

| (1) End of Year | (2) Annual Depreciation Charges $(R)$ | (3) Interest Income (6) × 6% | (4) Net Depreciation Charges to Be Accumulated (2) − (3) | (5) Accumulated Depreciation from (4) | (6) Book Value $1,100 − (5) |
|---|---|---|---|---|---|
| 0 | . . . | . . . | . . . | . . . | $1,100.00 |
| 1 | $ 239.85 | $ 66.00 | $173.85 | $173.85 | 926.15 |
| 2 | 239.85 | 55.57 | 184.28 | 358.13 | 741.87 |
| 3 | 239.85 | 44.51 | 195.34 | 553.47 | 546.53 |
| 4 | 239.85 | 32.79 | 207.06 | 760.53 | 339.47 |
| 5 | 239.84* | 20.37 | 219.47 | 980.00 | 120.00 |
| Total | $1,199.24 | $219.24 | $980.00 | | |

*Corrected for one cent discrepancy.

An accountant using the annuity method in computing annual depreciation charges keeps two accounts:

1. Depreciation charges (or expense) (See Column (2))
2. Interest income (See Column (3))

Only the difference between the annual depreciation charges and the interest income is used in reducing the book value of the investment. For example, although the total depreciation charges for the operation of the asset during the first year are $239.85, the net loss is only $173.85 (or $239.85 − $66.00). Thus, the book value at the end of the first year is reduced by $173.85 to obtain a new book value of $926.15 (or $1,100 − $173.85).

# B. Sinking Fund Method

Under the sinking fund method, it is assumed that a sinking fund is established for the purpose of replacing an asset at the end of its useful life. The periodic depreciation charges are exactly the same as the periodic increases (including the periodic deposit and the interest) in the sinking fund. Thus, the depreciation charges for each year are not equal. However, the total of the depreciation charges is equal to the amount in the sinking fund $(S_n)$ at the end of the useful life of the asset. The size of each deposit $(R)$ made in the sinking fund can be obtained by using the annuity formula

$$S_n = Rs_{\overline{n}|i}, \quad \text{or} \quad R = \frac{S_n}{s_{\overline{n}|i}} = \frac{C - T}{s_{\overline{n}|i}} \tag{17-4}$$

**Example 2**  Assume that the effective interest rate is 6%. Use the data in Example 1 to find the annual depreciation charges by the sinking fund method. Construct a depreciation schedule.

$C = 1,100$, $T = 120$, $i = 6\%$, $n = 5$ (years)

The total depreciation at the end of the fifth year is

$C - T = 1,100 - 120 = \$980$

which should be equal to the final amount in the sinking fund. Thus,

$S_n = \$980$

Substituting the values in formula (17-4):

The annual deposit $R = \dfrac{980}{s_{\overline{5}|6\%}} = 980\left(\dfrac{1}{a_{\overline{5}|6\%}} - 6\%\right)$

$$= 980(0.2374 - .06) = \$173.85 \qquad \text{(Table 9)}$$

The annual depreciation charges are shown in column (4) in the following depreciation schedule:

## DEPRECIATION SCHEDULE—SINKING FUND METHOD
(Example 2)

| (1)<br>End of<br>Year | (2)<br><br>Periodic<br>Deposit<br>in Fund<br>(R) | (3)<br>Interest<br>Income<br>from<br>Sinking<br>Fund<br>(5) × 6% | (4)<br>Periodic<br>Increase<br>in Fund<br>=<br>Annual<br>Depreciation<br>Charges<br>(2) + (3) | (5)<br>Accumulated<br>Sinking Fund<br>=<br>Accumulated<br>Depreciation<br>from (4) | (6)<br><br><br><br>Book Value<br>$1,100<br>− (5) |
|---|---|---|---|---|---|
| 0 | . . . | . . . | . . . | . . . | $1,100.00 |
| 1 | $173.85 | . . . | $173.85 | $173.85 | 926.15 |
| 2 | 173.85 | $ 10.43 | 184.28 | 358.13 | 741.87 |
| 3 | 173.85 | 21.49 | 195.34 | 553.47 | 546.53 |
| 4 | 173.85 | 33.21 | 207.06 | 760.53 | 339.47 |
| 5 | 173.84* | 45.63 | 219.47 | 980.00 | 120.00 |
| Total | $869.24 | $110.76 | $980.00 | | |

*Corrected for one cent discrepancy.

Note that the values in Columns (4), (5), and (6) above are the same as the values in the same columns of the depreciation schedule in Example 1 by the annuity method. Also, the actual establishment of a sinking fund for replacement purposes is unnecessary. The depreciation schedule may be used as a standard or a guide for charging the periodic depreciation expense, regardless of whether or not a sinking fund has been established.

## ★EXERCISE 17–3

**Reference: Section 17.4**

1. A piece of equipment which was bought for $2,400 has an estimated useful life of four years and a scrap value of $300. Use the annuity method to find the annual depreciation charges, and construct a depreciation schedule. Assume that the effective interest rate is 5%.

2. The Boston Sales Company has a machine costing $5,000 with an estimated useful life of six years and a scrap value of $800. Use the annuity method to find the annual depreciation charges, and construct a depreciation schedule. Assume that the effective interest rate is 4%.

3. Refer to Problem 1. Use the sinking fund method to find the depreciation charges for each year, and construct a depreciation schedule.

4. Refer to Problem 2. Use the sinking fund method to find the depreciation charges for each year, and construct a depreciation schedule.

5. Find the book value at the end of the third year in Problem 1 without referring to a depreciation schedule.
6. Find the book value at the end of the fourth year in Problem 2 without referring to a depreciation schedule.

## ★17.5 DEPRECIATION—COMPOSITE RATE METHOD

The preceding methods of computing depreciation expense are based on a single piece of property. The *composite rate method* is used for computing the depreciation charges of a group of assets.

## A. Finding the Composite Rate

The *composite rate* is obtained by dividing the total annual depreciation charges by the total cost of the group of assets. The individual annual depreciation charges of each asset are obtained by the *straight line method.*

**Example 1** Find the composite rate of the group of assets in the table below:

| Asset | Original Cost | Scrap Value | Total Depreciation | Estimated Life | Annual Depreciation Charges |
|-------|-------|-------|-------|-------|-------|
| A | $10,000 | $1,000 | $ 9,000 | 10 years | $ 900 |
| B | 5,000 | 200 | 4,800 | 12 years | 400 |
| C | 4,500 | 275 | 4,225 | 5 years | 845 |
|  | $19,500 | $1,475 | $18,025 |  | $2,145 |

$$\text{Composite rate} = \frac{\text{Total annual depreciation charges}}{\text{Total cost}}$$

$$= \frac{2,145}{19,500} = .11, \text{ or } 11\%$$

The composite rate may be used to compute depreciation charges during the later years of a group of assets if there are no significant changes in the values and useful lives of the assets due to replacement, retirement, or addition. Thus, the work of computing the depreciation expense for each item of the group may be avoided. For example, if the total cost of the above group of assets in the next year were $19,600, which would be regarded as a minor change from the cost of this year, the depreciation charge for the next year would be computed as follows:

$$\$19,600 \times 11\% = \$2.156$$

# B. Finding the Composite Life

The *composite life* of a group of assets is the average life of the group. Composite life is a useful value to management. For example, in obtaining a loan by pledging a group of assets as security, the creditor generally wants to know the average life of the assets. In computing the composite life, the annual depreciation charges of the group of assets may be obtained by using (1) the composite rate as discussed above, or (2) the sinking fund method as discussed in Section 17.4 B.

When the composite rate is used, the depreciation charges are assumed to be *equal* for each year. The composite life is obtained by dividing the total depreciation charges by the total annual depreciation charges of the group of assets.

**Example 2**     Find the composite life of the group of assets in Example 1.

$$\text{Composite life} = \frac{\text{Total depreciation charges}}{\text{Total annual depreciation charges}}$$

$$= \frac{18,025}{2,145} = 8.4 \text{ years}$$

When the sinking fund method is used in computing the annual depreciation charges, the charges for each asset are *not equal* for each year. Thus, a fixed composite rate cannot be obtained. A sinking fund schedule is necessary in this case in order to compute the annual depreciation charges for the group of assets. However, the annual deposits in the fund for each asset are equal during the life of the asset. (See Example 2 of Section 17.4, pages 503 and 504.) The composite life by this method, therefore, is the time necessary for the total annual deposits at the given interest rate to accumulate to the total depreciation charges of the group of assets.

**Example 3**     Use the data in Example 1. Find the composite life of the group of assets based on the sinking fund method. Assume that the effective interest rate is 6%.

The size of the annual deposit for each asset in the fund is computed by using the formula $R = \dfrac{S_n}{s_{\overline{n}|i}}$: (Use Table 9.)

ASSET A: $R = 9,000/s_{\overline{10}|6\%} = 9,000(.135868 - .06) = \$\quad 682.81$
ASSET B: $R = 4,800/s_{\overline{12}|6\%} = 4,800(.119277 - .06) = \quad 284.53$
ASSET C: $R = 4,255/s_{\overline{5}|6\%} = 4,225(.237396 - .06) = \quad \underline{749.50}$
$\qquad\qquad\qquad\qquad\qquad$ Total annual deposit $= \$1,716.84$

The composite life, which is the time necessary for the total annual deposits of $1,716.84 to accumulate to the total depreciation charges of $18,025 at 6%, is computed by using the amount of the annuity formula as follows:

$S_n = \$18,025$, $R = \$1,716.84$ (per year), $i = 6\%$ (per year), $n = ?$ (years).

Substituting the values in the formula $S_n = Rs_{\overline{n}|i}$,

$$18,025 = 1,716.84s_{\overline{n}|6\%}$$

$$s_{\overline{n}|6\%} = \frac{18,025}{1,716.84} = 10.49894$$

In the 6% column of Table 7, the value 10.49894 is between 9.89747 ($n = 8$) and 11.49132 ($n = 9$). By interpolation, $n = 8.38$, the composite life in years.

## ★EXERCISE 17–4

### Reference: Section 17.5

**A.** *In each of the following problems, use the straight line method to find (a) the composite rate, and (b) the composite life:*

| Asset | Original Cost | Scrap Value | Estimated Life |
|---|---|---|---|
| 1. A | $ 5,000 | $200 | 8 years |
| B | 2,300 | 100 | 11 years |
| C | 800 | 60 | 20 years |
| 2. X | 6,400 | 100 | 15 years |
| Y | 4,500 | 300 | 7 years |
| Z | 3,600 | 400 | 16 years |
| 3. L | 12,000 | 800 | 10 years |
| M | 1,800 | 300 | 5 years |
| N | 550 | none | 5 years |
| 4. E | 620 | 20 | 12 years |
| F | 2,400 | 100 | 4 years |
| G | 300 | none | 6 years |

**B.** *Statement Problems:*

5. Refer to Problem 1. Use the sinking fund method to find the composite life. Assume that the effective interest rate is 5%.
6. Refer to Problem 2. Use the sinking fund method to find the composite life. Assume that the effective interest rate is 3%.

## ★17.6 DEPLETION

## A. Introduction

After a period of removal operations, some natural resources, such as minerals, oil, gas, and timber, are eventually exhausted in the areas of the deposits and cannot be replaced in the near future. Such natural resources are frequently called *wasting assets.* The reduction in the value of such a wasting asset resulting from exhaustion is called *depletion.*

# B. Method of Computing Depletion

In general, *total depletion* is the difference between the cost and the salvage value of the property. The *annual depletion deduction* is obtained by multiplying the number of units sold during the year by the depletion rate per unit. The depletion rate per unit is derived by dividing the total depletion by the number of units estimated to be in the reserve of the property.

**Example 1**     Jameson invested $200,000 in a coal mine. The mine is estimated to have a reserve of 264,000 tons of coal. The land can be salvaged for $2,000. Assume that during the first year $\frac{1}{5}$ of the reserve, or 52,800 tons of coal, was mined and sold. Find the total depletion and the depletion deduction for the first year of operation.

Total depletion = 200,000 − 2,000 = $198,000
Depletion rate per unit = 198,000 ÷ 264,000 = $0.75 (per ton)
Depletion deduction for the first year = 0.75 × 52,800 = $39,600

**Example 2**     Refer to Example 1. Assume that Jameson receeives $50,000 as his income before depletion at the end of the first year. What is his net income after depletion?

Net income = Income before depletion − Depletion
= 50,000 − 39,600 = $10,400

# C. Sinking Fund for Depletion

Investors generally expect to receive periodic interest on their investment, but may wish to withdraw their original contributions at the end of the terms of the investment rather than through periodic recovery. Thus, the owner of a wasting asset may deposit a portion of his or her annual receipt (income before depletion) at the end of each year in a sinking fund, which will eventually accumulate to an amount equal to the total depletion. Then, net annual income from the property is the difference between the income before depletion and the annual deposit in the sinking fund.

$$\begin{pmatrix}\text{Annual net income} \\ \text{from investment}\end{pmatrix} = \begin{pmatrix}\text{Income before} \\ \text{depletion}\end{pmatrix} - \begin{pmatrix}\text{Annual deposit in} \\ \text{sinking fund}\end{pmatrix}$$

The amounts of the annual deposits in the sinking fund are all equal and the size of each annual deposit can be obtained by using the formula

$$R = \frac{S_n}{s_{\overline{n}|i}}, \text{ where}$$

$R$ = annual deposit in the sinking fund
$S_n$ = total depletion (or cost − salvage value)
$n$ = number of interest periods (or deposits)
$i$ = interest rate per period for sinking fund

**Example 3**   Use the information given in Examples 1 and 2. Assume that annual sales and annual income before depletion are expected to be equal each year and the mine is estimated to be exhausted at the end of the five years. If Jameson wishes to withdraw his original investment ($200,000) at the end of the fifth year and he can invest a portion of his annual income in a sinking fund earning 6% effective interest, what are (a) the size of each annual deposit? (b) the net income from the investment for each year? and (c) the rate of the annual net income on the investment?

(a) Jameson's original investment, $200,000, may be recovered at the end of five years from two sources; the salvage value of the mine ($2,000), and the savings from the annual receipts in the sinking fund, which will accumulate to $198,000 in five years. Since the fund earns 6% interest annually, the annual deposit *(R)* should be:

$$R = \frac{S_n}{s_{\overline{n}|i}} = \frac{198,000}{s_{\overline{5}|6\%}} = \frac{198,000}{5.63709296} = \$35,124.49$$

Thus, if Jameson receives $50,000 income annually for five years, he should deposit $35,124.49 in the sinking fund each year in order to draw $198,000 at the end of the fifth year.

(b) The net income from the investment after the deposit in the sinking fund is the same for each year.

Annual net income = 50,000 − 35,124.49 = $14,875.51

(c) The rate of the annual net income on the investment is

$$\frac{14,875.51}{200,000} = .07437755, \text{ rounded to } 7.44\%$$

**Note:**   1. The accumulated sinking fund at the end of the operating period is the same as the total depletion. However, the periodic increase in the sinking fund is *not* intended to be a guide for the periodic depletion deduction from income. The periodic depletion deductions should be based on the actual quantities that are sold. In our example, the units sold each year are assumed to be equal during the five-year period. The depletion deduction for each year is a constant amount of $39,600 (see Example 1), but the periodic increases in the sinking fund are not the same each year (see the sinking fund schedule below). The periodic depletion deductions and the periodic increases in the sinking fund are separate transactions.

The sinking fund schedule is constructed as follows:

## SINKING FUND SCHEDULE
(Example 3(a))

| (1) | (2) | (3) | (4) | (5) | (6) |
|---|---|---|---|---|---|
| | | Sinking | | | |
| | Deposit | Fund | | Accumulated | To Be |
| | in | Interest | Periodic | Sinking | Recovered |
| End of | Sinking | Income | Increase | Fund | $200,000 |
| Year | Fund | (5) × 6% | (2) + (3) | from (4) | − (5) |
| 0 | . . . | . . . | . . . | . . . | $200,000.00 |
| 1 | $ 35,124.49 | . . . | $ 35,124.49 | $ 35,124.49 | 164,875.51 |
| 2 | 35,124.49 | $ 2,107.47 | 37,231.96 | 72,356.45 | 127,643.55 |
| 3 | 35,124.49 | 4,341.39 | 39,465.88 | 111,822.33 | 88,177.67 |
| 4 | 35,124.49 | 6,709.34 | 41,833.83 | 153,656.16 | 46,343.84 |
| 5 | 35,124.47* | 9,219.37 | 44,343.84 | 198,000.00 | 2,000.00 |
| Total | $175,622.43 | $22,377.57 | $198,000.00 | | |

*Corrected for two cent discrepancy.

2. In Example 3, since the units sold each year are assumed to be equal, the amount of $10,400 (see Example 2) is the annual net income (after depletion) from the mine operation during the five years. The amount of $14,875.51 is the average annual net income when the sinking fund interest income is included. The actual annual net income is not the same for each year during the five years and may be computed as follows: (See column (4).)

| (1) | (2) | (3) | (4) |
|---|---|---|---|
| | Income from | | Total |
| | Operation after | Interest Income | Net Income |
| End of Year | Depletion | from Sinking Fund | (2) + (3) |
| 1 | $10,400 | . . . | $10,400.00 |
| 2 | 10,400 | $ 2,107.47 | 12,507.47 |
| 3 | 10,400 | 4,341.39 | 14,741.39 |
| 4 | 10,400 | 6,709.34 | 17,109.34 |
| 5 | 10,400 | 9,219.37 | 19,619.37 |
| Total | $52,000 | $22,377.57 | $74,377.57 |

The average annual net income $= \dfrac{74,377.57}{5} = \$14,875.51$, which is the same as the answer in Solution (b).

In summary, let $D =$ annual income before depletion (or dividend)
$C =$ cost of original investment (or purchase price of the wasting asset)
$T =$ salvage value (or trade-in value)
$R =$ annual deposit to sinking fund
$I =$ annual net income after sinking fund deposit

$r =$ rate of the annual net income on the cost of the original investment, or $I/C$
$i =$ interest rate per period for sinking fund
$n =$ number of years of the life of depletion

Then,

$D = I + R$, or

$$D = Cr + \frac{C - T}{s_{\overline{n}|i}} \tag{17-5}$$

Here, $Cr = I$, since
$r = I/C$; and
$C - T = S_n$

If there is no salvage value $(T)$, the formula becomes

$$D = Cr + \frac{C}{s_{\overline{n}|i}} = C\left(r + \frac{1}{s_{\overline{n}|i}}\right) \tag{17-6}$$

Any quantity in the above formulas may be solved if the other quantities are known.

Example 3 may be computed by using formula (17–5) in the following manner:

$C = 200,000$, $T = 2,000$, $D = 50,000$, $n = 5$ (years), $i = 6\%$ (per year)
(a) $R = ?$, (b) $I = ?$, and (c) $r = ?$.

The computations are shown as follows:

(a) $R = \dfrac{C - T}{s_{\overline{n}|i}} = \dfrac{(200,000 - 2000)}{s_{\overline{5}|6\%}} = \dfrac{198,000}{s_{\overline{5}|6\%}} = \$35,124.49$

(b) $I = D - R = 50,000.00 - 35,124.49 = \$14,875.51$

(c) $r = \dfrac{I}{C} = \dfrac{14,875.51}{200,000} = .07437755$, rounded to 7.44%

**Example 4**   A timberland is estimated to yield an annual income before depletion of $30,000 for the next 30 years. At the end of that time, the land can be sold for $1,000. What is the purchase price of the timberland if the purchaser wants to secure a yield of 7% on his investment and if he can invest the sinking fund at 4%?

$D = 30,000$, $T = 1,000$, $r = 7\%$, $i = 4\%$, $n = 30$, $C = ?$

Substituting the values in formula (17–5):

$$D = Cr + \frac{C - T}{s_{\overline{n}|i}}$$

$$30,000 = C(7\%) + \frac{(C - 1,000)}{s_{\overline{30}|4\%}}$$

$$= .07\,C + (C - 1,000)(.0178301) \qquad \text{(Table 9)}$$
$$= .07\,C + .0178301\,C - (.0178301)(1,000)$$
$$= .0878301\,C - 17.8301$$
$$.0878301\,C = 30,000 + 17.8301 = 30,017.8301$$

$$C = \frac{30,017.8301}{.0878301} = \$341,771.56 \text{ (purchase price)}$$

**Example 5**   Refer to Example 4. Assume that the land at the end of the 30th year will be worthless. What is the purchase price of the timberland?

$T = 0$. Substituting the other values (in Example 4) in formula (17–6):

$$D = C\left(r + \frac{1}{s_{\overline{n}|\,i}}\right)$$

$$30,000 = C\left(7\% + \frac{1}{s_{\overline{30}|\,4\%}}\right) = C(.07 + .0178301) = .0878301C$$

$$C = \frac{30,000}{.0878301} = \$341,568.55 \text{ (purchase price)}$$

## ★EXERCISE 17–5

**Reference: Section 17.6**

1. Baxter bought a mine for \$30,000 and expected to operate it for four years. At the end of the period, the mine will be exhausted and the salvage property can be sold for \$2,000. Assume that the mine is estimated to have a reserve of 400,000 units and that during the first year of operation, $\frac{1}{4}$ of the reserve was mined and sold. The income before depletion is \$9,000 for this year. Find (a) the total depletion, (b) the depletion rate per unit, (c) the depletion deduction for the first year, and (d) the net income for the first year of operation.

2. A company purchased a piece of land containing oil wells for \$100,000. The total reserves of crude oil in the wells are estimated at 200,000 barrels and are expected to be removed in 10 years. The salvage land can be sold for \$4,000 at the end of the operation. Assume that during the first year of operation, $\frac{1}{10}$ of the reserve was removed and sold, and the income before depletion was \$14,000. Find (a) the total depletion, (b) the depletion rate per barrel, (c) the depletion deduction for the first year, and (d) the net income for the first year of operation.

3. Refer to Problem 1. Assume that the annual sales and income before depletion are equal for each year during the four years. Baxter wishes to keep his cost of investment intact until the end of the period, and he can invest part of the income in a sinking fund at 3%. Find (a) the size of each deposit in the sinking fund, (b) his net income for each year, and (c) the rate of the annual net income on his cost of investment.

4. Refer to Problem 2. Assume that the sales and income before depletion are equal every year during the 10 years. The company wants to have the cost of investment recovered when the wells become completely exhausted in 10 years so that the company may use the fund to purchase new wells. If the company can invest a part of its income in a sinking fund earning 4% effective interest, what are (a) the size of each annual deposit in the sinking fund? (b) the net annual income for each year? and (c) the rate of the annual net income on the cost of investment?

5. Refer to Problem 3. What are answers to (a), (b), and (c) if the salvage property would be worthless at the end of four years?

6. Refer to Problem 4. What are answers to (a), (b), and (c) if the salvage land would be worthless at the end of 10 years?

7. A piece of land with natural resources is estimated to yield an annual income before depletion of $6,000 for the next 15 years. At the end of that time, the land can be sold for $300. What should be the purchase price of the land if the purchaser wants a yield of 6% on her investment and she can invest the sinking fund at $4\frac{1}{2}$% effective interest?

8. A silver mine is estimated to yield an annual income before depletion of $25,000 for the next 20 years. The salvage land is expected to be worth $900 at the end of the period. If the purchaser wishes a yield of 8% on her investment and she can invest the sinking fund at 5% effective interest, what should be the purchase price of the mine?

9. Refer to Problem 7. If the land were worthless at the end of 15 years, what should be the purchase price?

10. Refer to Problem 8. Find the purchase price if the mine were worthless at the end of 20 years.


## 17.7 SUMMARY OF FORMULAS

| Application | Formula | Formula Number | Reference Page |
|---|---|---|---|
| *Depreciation*   *Common symbols:* <br> $C$ = original cost of asset, <br> $T$ = estimated trade-in or scrap value | | | |
| Methods of averages | $r = \dfrac{C - T}{n}$ | (17–1) | 491 |

$r$ = rate of depreciation expense per year, per service-hour, per product-unit, or per dollar
$n$ = useful life of the asset estimated in number of years, service-hours, or product-units

| | | | |
|---|---|---|---|
| Fixed-rate method | $r = 1 - \sqrt[n]{T/C}$ | (17–2) | 499 |

$r$ = rate of depreciation per year based on diminishing book value of asset
$n$ = number of years of the estimated life

Annuity method $$R = \frac{C - T(1+i)^{-n}}{a_{\overline{n}|i}}$$ (17–3)    502

$R =$ annual total depreciation expense
$i =$ interest rate per period (year)
$n =$ number of years of the estimated life
Net annual depreciation $= R -$ interest income

Sinking fund method $$R = \frac{C - T}{s_{\overline{n}|i}}$$ (17–4)    503

$R =$ annual deposit in sinking fund
$i$ and $n$ mean the same as in formula (17–3)
Net annual depreciation $= R +$ interest income

*Depletion*

Establishment of sinking
fund (with salvage value) $$D = Cr + \frac{C - T}{s_{\overline{n}|i}}$$ (17–5)    511

Establishment of sinking fund
(without salvage value) $$D = C\left(r + \frac{1}{s_{\overline{n}|i}}\right)$$ (17–6)    511

$D =$ annual income before depletion
$C =$ cost of original investment (or purchase price of the wasting asset)
$T =$ salvage value (or trade-in value)
$r =$ rate of annual net income on investment
$i =$ interest rate per period for sinking fund
$n =$ number of years of the life of depletion

# EXERCISE 17–6

## Review of Chapter 17

1. A garage which was constructed for $3,000 has an estimated scrap value of $300 at the end of five years. Use the following methods to find the depreciation charges for each year and construct depreciation schedules for methods (d) and (e):

   (a) Straight line method
   (b) Sum of the years-digits method
   (c) Fixed rate—1. Tax method
   ★2. Formula method (use percent rate including three decimals)
   ★(d) Annuity method (based on 6% effective interest)
   ★(e) Sinking fund method (based on 6% effective interest)

2. A typewriter which was bought for $320 has an estimated useful life of four years and a trade-in value of $20. Use the following methods to find the depreciation charges for each year and construct depreciation schedules for methods (d) and (e):

(a) Straight line method

(b) Sum of the years-digits method

(c) Fixed rate—1. Tax method

★2. Formula method

★(d) Annuity method (based on 4% effective interest)

★(e) Sinking fund method (based on 4% effective interest)

3. The cost of a bookbinding machine is $1,200. It is estimated that the machine will have a $200 trade-in value at the end of its useful life. Assume that the useful life of the machine is estimated to be 25,000 service-hours and the actual number of hours spent in production for the first year is 2,200, and for the second year, 2,000. Find the depreciation expense for each of the two years.

4. Refer to Problem 3. Assume that the useful life of the machine is estimated to be 300,000 copies of books, and the number of copies bound for the first year is 25,000 and for the second year, 24,000. What is the depreciation expense for each of the two years?

★5. Find the composite rate of the group of assets in the following table:

| Asset | Original Cost | Scrap Value | Estimated Life |
|---|---|---|---|
| Tables | $90,000 | $2,000 | 11 years |
| Chairs | 8,000 | 600 | 8 years |
| Cabinets | 5,000 | 500 | 15 years |

★6. Refer to Problem 5. Find the composite life of the group of assets by (a) the straight line method, and (b) the sinking fund method, based on 5% effective interest.

★7. Wanda Barker invested $500,000 in a zinc mine. The mine is estimated to have a reserve of 10,000 tons of zinc. The salvage land can be sold for $4,000. Assume that during the first year $\frac{1}{4}$ of the estimated reserve was mined and sold. Find (a) the total depletion and the depletion deduction for the first year of operation, and (b) the net income if Wanda receives $165,000 as the income before depletion at the end of the first year.

★8. A man invested $800,000 in land containing wasting assets. It is estimated to have a reserve of 5 million units. The salvage land can be sold for $2,500. Assume that during the first year, 600,000 units were mined and sold. (a) What are the total depletion and the depletion deduction for the first year of operation, and (b) What is the net income if the man receives $180,000 as the income before depletion at the end of the first year?

★9. Refer to Problem 7. Assume that the mine is estimated to be exhausted at the end of four years and that the sales and the income before depletion in each year are expected to be equal. If Wanda wishes to invest a portion of her annual income in a sinking fund which will earn 5% compounded annually so that she may recover her original investment at the end of the fourth year of operation, find (a) the size of each annual deposit in the fund, (b) the net income from the investment in the mine, and (c) the rate of the annual net income on the original investment.

★**10.** A $200,000 mine is scheduled for 15 years of operation. Assume that the operation for each year is the same, the income before depletion for each year is $30,000, and the salvage land of the mine can be sold for $2,000 at the end of operation. The owners wish to recover their original investment by means of a sinking fund earning 6% annually. Find (a) the annual deposit in the sinking fund, (b) the net income from the mine investment, and (c) the rate of the annual net income to the original mine investment.

★**11.** A copper mine is estimated to yield an annual income before depletion of $50,000 for 20 years. The salvage land can be sold for $1,500 at the end of 20 years. Find the purchase price of the mine if the purchaser wishes a 6% yield on his investment and he can invest the sinking fund at 5% compounded annually.

★**12.** Some land containing oil wells is estimated to yield an annual income before depletion of $600,000 for 10 years. The land can be sold for $2,000 at the end of the tenth year. What is the purchase price of the land if the investor wants a 5% yield on her investment and she can invest part of the annual income in a sinking fund earning 3% annually?

★**13.** Refer to Problem 11. If the land becomes worthless at the end of 20 years, what should the purchase price be?

★**14.** Refer to Problem 12. If the land becomes worthless at the end of 10 years, what should the purchase price of the land be?

# Chapter 18

## Perpetuity and Capitalization

## 18.1 PERPETUITY

When the term of an annuity begins on a definite date but never ends, the annuity is called a *perpetuity*. In other words, the payments of a perpetuity continue forever. Since there is no end to a perpetuity, it is impossible to determine its final value. However, as will be shown in the examples below, the present value of a perpetuity can be determined.

Perpetuities may be divided into two groups: (a) simple and (b) complex (general). Since a perpetuity is a type of annuity, the qualified words such as ordinary, due, deferred, simple, complex, and general, used previously in annuity problems are also used within this chapter.

## A. Simple Perpetuities

When the payments of a perpetuity are made at the *end* of each interest period, the perpetuity is called a *simple ordinary perpetuity*. It will be recalled that in the method used to find the simple interest on an investment, the simple interest *(I)* is obtained by using the formula $I = Pin$. When $n = 1$, and $i$ represents the rate per period, the formula becomes $I = Pi$. The formula indicates that if $P$ is invested now at the interest rate of $i$ per period, the periodic interest is the value of $Pi$. The interest may be drawn periodically as long as the principal *(P)* is invested. Thus, if $100 is invested now at the interest rate of 2% per quarter, the quarterly interest is $2 (or $100 \times 2\%$), which may be drawn by the investor at the end of each quarter as long as the $100 principal is left in the investment. The size of the investment is found by dividing both sides of the formula $I = Pi$ by $i$. Thus,

$$P = \frac{I}{i}$$

This idea is used in a similar manner in the case of simple perpetuities. Let $A_\infty$ denote the present value of a simple ordinary perpetuity. Then

$$A_\infty = P = \frac{I}{i}, \quad \text{or} \quad A_\infty = \frac{I}{i} \tag{18-1}$$

**Note:** The symbol "$\infty$" represents "infinity." $I$ is the periodic payment (or receipt, whichever the case may be) of the perpetuity made at the end of each period, and $i$ is the interest rate per period.

**Example 1** Find the present value of a simple perpetuity of $500 payable at the end of each quarter if the interest rate is 2% per quarter (or 8% compounded quarterly).

$I = 500$, $i = 2\%$

Substituting the values in formula (18–1):

$$A_\infty = \frac{I}{i} = \frac{500}{.02} = \$25,000$$

The answer indicates that if $25,000 is invested now at 2% per quarter, the investor can draw $500 at the end of each quarter forever; that is, if the principal remains intact and the interest rate does not change. In other words, $25,000 is the cash equivalent of a perpetuity of $500 payable at the end of each quarter when the given interest rate is involved.

**Example 2** Find the present value of a simple annuity of $500 payable at the end of each quarter for (a) 20 years, (b) 25 years, and (c) 50 years. The interest rate is 2% per quarter.

(a)  $R = 500$, $i = 2\%$, $n = 20 \times 4 = 80$ (quarters)
$A_{80} = 500 a_{\overline{80}|2\%} = 500(39.74451) = \$19,872.26$

(b)  $n = 25 \times 4 = 100$ (quarters)
$A_{100} = 500 a_{\overline{100}|2\%} = 500(43.09835) = \$21,549.18$

(c)  $n = 50 \times 4 = 200$ (quarters)

First, the annuity is divided into two parts with each part consisting of 100 quarterly payments. (See page 391.)

The present value of the first part consisting of 100 payments is $21,549.18 (See (b) above.)

The present value of the second part consisting of 100 payments is

$P = 21,549.18(1 + 2\%)^{-100} = 21,549.18(.138033) = \$2,974.50$

Then, the present value of the 200 payments is computed as follows:

$A_{200} = 21,549.18 + 2,974.50 = \$24,523.68$

These answers may be compared with that given in Example 1.

| n (Quarters) | Present Value |
|---|---|
| 80 | $19,872.26 |
| 100 | 21,549.18 |
| 200 | 24,523.68 |
| ∞ | 25,000.00 |

The comparison indicates that as the length of the term of an annuity increases, its present value gets closer to the present value of a perpetuity.

When the payments of a perpetuity are made at the *beginning* of each interest period, the perpetuity is called a *simple perpetuity due.*

**Example 3**   Find the present value of a simple perpetuity of $200 payable at the beginning of each month if the interest rate is 6% compounded monthly.

First, the present value of a simple perpetuity of $200 payable at the *end* of each month is computed as follows:

$I = 200$, $i = 6\%/12 = \frac{1}{2}\%$ (per month)

Substituting the values in formula (18–1):

$$A_\infty = \frac{I}{i} = \frac{200}{\frac{1}{2}\%} = \frac{200}{.005} = \$40,000$$

The present value of a simple perpetuity of $200 payable at the *beginning* of each month is

$40,000 + 200 = \$40,200$

Note that $200 is the first payment, whose present value is the value of the payment unchanged.

## B. Complex (General) Perpetuities

When each of the periodic payments of a perpetuity is made at the end of several interest periods, the perpetuity is called a *complex* (or *general*) *perpetuity.*

**Example 4**   A man invests $1,000 now at an interest rate of 4% compounded quarterly and wants to draw interest at the end of each year forever. How much interest will he receive annually?

The compound amount of $1,000 at the end of every fourth quarter (or every year) is

$1,000(1 + 1\%)^4 = 1,000(1.040604) = \$1,040.60$

The compound interest at the end of each year is

$1,040.60 - 1,000.00 = \$40.60$

Example 4 is a complex perpetuity problem and may be stated in the following manner:

If the present value of a perpetuity is \$1,000 and the interest rate is 4% compounded quarterly, the periodic payment at the end of every four interest periods (quarters) is \$40.60.

Similarly, let

$R =$ the size of the periodic payment (or periodic interest)
$i =$ interest rate per interest conversion period
$c =$ interest conversion periods per payment interval
$A_\infty =$ present value of a perpetuity, with payments of $R$ made at the end of every $c$ interest periods

The value of $R$ is computed as follows:

$$R = A_\infty(1+i)^c - A_\infty = A_\infty[(1+i)^c - 1]$$

Thus,

$$A_\infty = \frac{R}{(1+i)^c - 1}, \quad \text{or} \quad A_\infty = \frac{R}{i} \cdot \frac{1}{s_{\overline{c}|i}} \qquad \textbf{(18–2)}\ ^1$$

**Note:**　When $c = 1$, the value of $s_{\overline{c}|i} = 1$. Then $A_\infty = \dfrac{R}{i}$ and $R = I$.

Formula (18–2) becomes identical to formula (18–1).

Thus, formula (18–2) is a general formula for ordinary perpetuities.

The following diagram supports the above illustrations in Example 4 and formula (18–2).

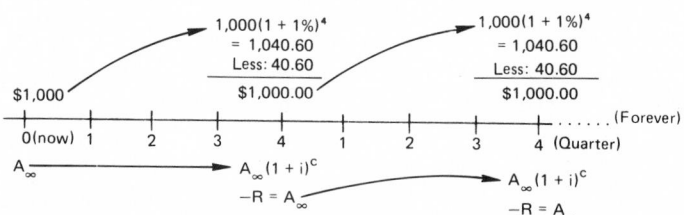

**Example 5**　Find the present value of a perpetuity of \$500 payable semiannually if money is worth 6% compounded monthly, and (a) the first payment is due six months hence, (b) the first payment is due now.

(a) $R = \$500$ (per six months), $i = 6\%/12 = \frac{1}{2}\%$ (monthly), $c = 6$ (interest periods in one payment interval). Substituting the values in formula (18–2):

---

$^1$ *Proof—Formula (18–2).*

$$A_\infty = \frac{R}{(1+i)^c - 1} = \frac{i}{i} \cdot \frac{R}{(1+i)^c - 1} = \frac{R}{i} \cdot \frac{i}{(1+i)^c - 1}$$

$$= \frac{R}{i} \cdot \frac{1}{s_{\overline{c}|i}}$$

$$A_\infty = \frac{R}{i} \cdot \frac{1}{s_{\overline{c}|i}} = \frac{500}{\frac{1}{2}\%} \cdot \frac{1}{s_{\overline{6}|1/2\%}} = \frac{500}{1/200}\left(\frac{1}{a_{\overline{6}|1/2\%}} - \frac{1}{2}\%\right)$$

$$= 100,000(.16959546 - .005) = \$16,459.55 \qquad \text{(Table 9)}$$

**Note:** The present value of the perpetuity may also be computed by using Table 5 as follows:

$$A_\infty = \frac{R}{(1+i)^c - 1} = \frac{500}{(1+\frac{1}{2}\%)^6 - 1} = \frac{500}{1.03037751 - 1}$$

$$= \$16,459.55$$

Either the method given in (a) or that presented above may be employed. However, in order to avoid long division, the former method is preferred.

(b) The present value of a complex perpetuity *due* is obtained by adding one payment to the answer in (a) as follows:

$$500 + 16,459.55 = \$16,959.55$$

Note that $500 is the first payment, whose present value is the value of the payment unchanged.

# EXERCISE 18–1

## Reference: Section 18.1

**A.** *Find the present value of the perpetuity in each of the following problems:*

| Payment | Interest Rate |
|---|---|
| **1.** $300 quarterly, at the end of each quarter | 3% per quarter |
| **2.** $450 semiannually, at the end of every six months | $4\frac{1}{2}\%$ per six months |
| **3.** $600 semiannually, at the end of every six months | 6% compounded monthly |
| **4.** $250 annually, at the end of each year | 5% compounded quarterly |
| **5.** $350 quarterly, at the beginning of each quarter | 2% per quarter |
| **6.** $700 monthly, at the beginning of each month | $\frac{1}{2}\%$ per month |
| **7.** $800 annually, at the beginning of each year | 4% compounded monthly |
| **8.** $100 semiannually, at the beginning of each six months | 5% compounded quarterly |

**B.** *Statement Problems:*

**9.** Find the present value of a simple perpetuity of $1,000 payable semiannually if the interest rate is 2% per six months and the first payment is due (a) six months from now, and (b) now.

10. What is the present value of a simple perpetuity of $1,200 payable quarterly if the interest rate is $1\frac{1}{2}\%$ per quarter and the first payment is due (a) three months from now, and (b) now?

11. Refer to Problem 9. If the interest rate is 4% compounded quarterly, find the answers to (a) and (b).

12. Refer to Problem 10. If the interest rate is 6% compounded monthly, find the answers to (a) and (b).

13. The alumni of a college want to provide a scholarship fund that will permanently give $1,000 at the end of each year. If the effective interest rate is 6%, how large must the fund be?

14. A foundation is to be established for the purpose of awarding $2,000 to an outstanding scientist at the end of each year. If money can be invested by the foundation at 5% compounded annually, how large should the fund be?

15. Find the answer to Problem 13 if the interest is 6% compounded monthly.

16. Find the answer to Problem 14 if the interest is 5% compounded semi-annually.

# 18.2 CAPITALIZATION

*Capitalization* is the process of converting an unlimited number of periodic payments into a single present value or cash equivalent. In other words, if the single sum were invested now at a given interest rate, the periodic interest would be payable forever. Thus, the single sum is the present value of a perpetuity which is formed by the periodic payments.

## A. Asset and Liability Valuations

Capitalization is a very useful method for evaluating assets and liabilities. Income-producing properties (tangible or intangible) and liabilities are often capitalized as standards for estimating their values.

**Example 1**    What is the cash equivalent of one acre of land if the land yields a net rental of $6 per year and money is worth (a) 5% effective interest rate, and (b) 5% compounded quarterly?

(a) $I = \$6$ (per year), $i = 5\%$ (per year)

Substituting the values in formula (18–1):

$$A_\infty = \frac{I}{i} = \frac{6}{5\%} = \frac{6}{.05} = \$120 \text{ (land value)}$$

(b) $R = \$6$ (per year), $i = 5\%/4 = 1\frac{1}{4}\%$ (per quarter), $c = 4$ (quarters in a yearly payment interval)

Substituting the values in formula (18–2):

$$A_\infty = \frac{R}{i} \cdot \frac{1}{s_{\overline{c}|i}} = \frac{6}{1\frac{1}{4}\%} \cdot \frac{1}{s_{\overline{4}|1\,1/4\%}} = 480(.257861 - .0125)$$

$$= 480(.245361) = \$117.77 \text{ (land value)}$$

**Example 2**  Capitalize an obligation of $120 payable at the end of each year forever if the effective interest rate is 6%.

$I = \$120$ (per year), $i = 6\%$ (per year)

$$A_\infty = \frac{120}{6\%} = \$2,000 \quad \text{(present value of the obligation)}$$

Thus, if a debtor who has $2,000 now may use the money to pay off his or her obligation.

# B. Capitalized Cost

An asset, such as a building, a machine, or a piece of equipment, often needs to be renewed or replaced periodically after it is constructed or bought. The cost of the asset may be capitalized so that a sufficient sum of money can be invested now and the accumulated interest will become available for an unlimited number of future renewals or replacements. The *capitalized cost* is generally defined as the sum of the original cost and the present value of the future renewals. The future renewals form a perpetuity.

Let $K =$ capitalized cost
   $F =$ first (or original) cost
   $i =$ interest rate per interest conversion period
   $c =$ number of interest periods in one renewal interval
   $R =$ each renewal cost if $c > 1$
   $I =$ each renewal cost if $c = 1$

The computations for capitalized cost *(K)* are as follows:

If the *interest period coincides with the renewal interval* (or $c = 1$), the value of $K$ is the sum of the first cost and the present value of the simple ordinary perpetuity, or

$$K = F + \frac{I}{i} \tag{18-3}$$

**Example 3**  The first cost of a new car is $3,000. Thereafter, the purchaser wants to trade his car for a new one every year. Assume that he has to pay $400 for each trade-in. If interest is 4%, find the capitalized cost for the car.

$F = \$3,000$, $I = \$400$ (per year), $i = 4\%$ (per year).

$$K = 3,000 + \frac{400}{4\%} = 3,000 + 10,000 = \$13,000$$

If the *number of interest periods in one renewal interval is more than 1 (or c > 1)*, the value of $K$ is the sum of the first cost and the present value of the complex ordinary perpetuity. In general,

$$K = F + \frac{R}{i} \cdot \frac{1}{s_{\overline{c}|i}} \qquad (18\text{-}4)$$

**Example 4**   The original cost of a warehouse was $30,000. The warehouse must be completely rebuilt every 25 years. If money can be invested at 6% compounded quarterly, what is the capitalized cost of the warehouse? Assume that the cost of each replacement will be $27,000.

$F = \$30,000$, $R = \$27,000$ (every 25 years), $i = 6\%/4 = 1\frac{1}{2}\%$ (per quarter), $c = 25 \times 4 = 100$ (quarters in a 25-year payment interval)

The capitalized cost of the warehouse is equal to the first cost added to the present value of the future replacement costs.

$$K = 30,000 + \frac{27,000}{1\frac{1}{2}\%} \cdot \frac{1}{s_{\overline{100}|1\,1/2\%}}$$

$$= 30,000 + \frac{27,000}{.015}(0.01937057 - 0.015)$$

$$= 30,000 + (1,800,000)(0.00437057)$$
$$= 30,000 + 7,867.026 = \$37,867.026, \text{ or } \$37,867.03$$

However, when the *cost of replacement (R) is the same as the first cost (F)* the value of $K$ may be computed by using the following formula:

$$K = \frac{R}{i} \cdot \frac{1}{a_{\overline{c}|i}} \qquad (18\text{-}5)\,[2]$$

**Example 5**   In Example 4, assume that the cost of replacement will be $30,000, the same as the original cost. What is the capitalized cost of the warehouse?

$F = \$30,000$, $R = F = \$30,000$, $i = 1\frac{1}{2}\%$, $c = 100$ (quarters)

$$K = \frac{30,000}{1\frac{1}{2}\%} \cdot \frac{1}{a_{\overline{100}|1\,1/2\%}}$$

$$= 2,000,000(0.01937057) = \$38,741.14$$

*Check:*   The present value of the investment is $38,741.14. After the original cost of $30,000 has been used, the remaining principal is $8,741.14. The

---

[2] *Proof—Formula (18–5)*

When $F = R$, formula (18–4) may be written as follows:

$$K = R + \frac{R}{i} \cdot \frac{1}{s_{\overline{c}|i}} = R\left(1 + \frac{1}{i} \cdot \frac{1}{s_{\overline{c}|i}}\right) = R\left[1 + \frac{1}{i}\left(\frac{1}{a_{\overline{c}|i}} - i\right)\right]$$

$$= R\left(1 + \frac{1}{ia_{\overline{c}|i}} - 1\right) = \frac{R}{i} \cdot \frac{1}{a_{\overline{c}|i}}$$

principal, $8,741.14, is invested at 6% compounded quarterly. At the end of 25 years, when the warehouse will be replaced for the first time, the compound amount will be as follows:

$$P = \$8,741.14, \quad i = \frac{6\%}{4} + 1\tfrac{1}{2}\% \text{ (per quarter)}, \quad n = 25 \times 4 = 100 \text{ (quarters)}$$

$$S = 8,741.14(1 + 1\tfrac{1}{2}\%)^{100} = 8,741.14(4.432046)$$
$$= \$38,741.1346, \text{ rounded to } \$38,741.14 \text{ to agree with the answer to Example 5.}$$

Therefore, another $30,000 is available for the first replacement. The remaining part is intact and becomes the new principal to be invested for the next 25 years.

**★Example 6**   Refer to Example 5. Assume that 20 years after the warehouse was built, there is a need for a major repair which will prolong the useful life for three years; that is, the warehouse will become useless and must be replaced at the end of 28 years. How much of the capitalized cost can the owner afford to pay for repair costs?

At the end of 20 years, the remaining capitalized cost, $8,741.14, will have accumulated to the following amount: ($n = 20 \times 4 = 80$ quarters)

$$S = 8,741.14(1 + 1\tfrac{1}{2}\%)^{80}$$
$$= 8,741.14(3.290663) = \$28,764.15$$

At the end of 28 years, the required capitalized cost is $38,741.14, the same as the cost when the first warehouse was constructed. The principal, which is required to accumulate to the amount of $38,741.14 from the end of the 20th to the end of the 28th year (eight years, or 32 quarters) is computed as follows:

$$P = 38,741.14(1 + 1\tfrac{1}{2}\%)^{-32}$$
$$= 38,741.14(.6209929) = \$24,057.97$$

After deducting the required principal, the remaining portion of the capitalized cost investment at the end of the 20th year may be used for the major repair, as shown below:

The repair cost $= 28,764.15 - 24,057.97 = \$4,706.18$

Example 6 is diagrammed as follows:

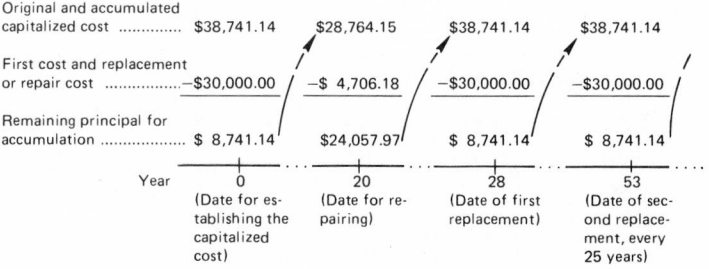

## EXERCISE 18–2

**Reference: Section 18.2**

1. What is the cash equivalent of a lot if the lot can be rented for $80 per year and money is worth (a) 4%, and (b) 6% compounded monthly?

2. Capitalize an obligation of $250 payable at the end of each quarter forever if interest is (a) 6% compounded quarterly, and (b) 4% compounded monthly.

3. The annual income from a piece of property is $20,000 a year. If someone wishes a return on an investment of 5% compounded semiannually, what should be the purchase price of the property?

4. The annual future earnings of a store are conservatively estimated at $10,000. (a) At what price will a person purchase the store if he or she wishes a return of 4% compounded quarterly on the investment? (b) Assume that the net assets of the store are valued at $225,000. What is the price of goodwill (the excess payment over the value of the net assets)?

5. A factory bought a machine for $2,400. The machine is to be exchanged every year. The net cost of each exchange is estimated to be $700. If interest is 7%, what is the capitalized cost of the machine?

6. A truck was purchased for $3,000. The truck will be traded in for a new one every year. Assume that it is necesary to pay $500 for each trade-in. If interest is 2½%, find the capitalized cost of the truck.

7. Refer to Problem 5. Compute the capitalized cost of the machine if the interest is 7% compounded quarterly.

8. Refer to Problem 6. Compute the capitalized cost of the truck if the interest is 2½% compounded semiannually.

9. The original cost of a library was $20,000. The library must be rebuilt every 20 years. If money can be invested at 4% compounded semiannually, what is the capitalized cost of the library? Assume that the cost of each replacement will be $18,000.

10. A building for the School of Business Administration in a college was constructed at a cost of $550,000. The building must be replaced every 40 years and the cost of each replacement is estimated to be $570,000. Compute the capitalized cost if the interest rate is 5%.

11. Refer to Problem 9. Assume that the cost of replacement will be $20,000, the same as the original cost. What is the capitalized cost of the library?

12. Refer to Problem 10. Compute the capitalized cost, assuming that the cost of each replacement is estimated at $550,000.

★13. Refer to Problem 11. Assume that 15 years after the library was built, there is a need for a major repair which will prolong the useful life for 4 years; that is, the library will become useless and must be replaced at the end of 24 years. How much of the capitalized cost can the owner afford to pay for repair costs?

★**14.** Refer to Problem 12. Assume that 30 years after the building was constructed, the building is demolished and must be rebuilt. How much can the college afford to spend for rebuilding from the capitalized cost investment if the new type of construction must be replaced thereafter at the same cost every 30 years?

# ★18.3 COMPARISON OF BUYING COSTS

The method for determining capitalized cost is also useful in selecting equipment (or service) from a number of different types or brands. If the various types of equipment give the same service, the buyer can choose the type with the lowest capitalized cost and thus save money. (See Example 1 below.) The method is also useful in figuring the replacement cost for a different grade or type of equipment (or service) from the same capitalized cost. (See Examples 2 and 3.)

**Example 1**   The cost of machine A is $200 and must be replaced every 10 years at the same cost. The cost of machine B is $190 and must be replaced every eight years at a cost of $180. If money is worth 5% compounded annually, which machine is a better buy?

The capitalized cost of machine A is:

$$K = \frac{200}{5\%} \cdot \frac{1}{a_{\overline{10}|5\%}} = 4{,}000(0.129505) = \$518.02$$

The capitalized cost of machine B is:

$$K = 190 + \frac{180}{5\%} \cdot \frac{1}{s_{\overline{8}|5\%}} = 190 + 3{,}600(0.154722 - .05)$$

$$= 190 + 377 = \$567$$

Since machine A has a lower capitalized cost, it is a better buy.

**Example 2**   A piece of equipment which now needs to be replaced was purchased for $150 with a guaranteed life of 10 years. If new equipment is guaranteed for a useful life of 12 years, how much can the buyer afford to pay with the same capitalized cost which is invested at 5%?

Since no replacement costs are stated for either piece of equipment, the replacement costs are considered the same as the original costs in computing the value of the capitalized costs of both items.

The capitalized cost of the old equipment is

$$K = \frac{150}{5\%} \cdot \frac{1}{a_{\overline{10}|5\%}}$$

Let $R$ = the cost of the new equipment.

The capitalized cost of the new equipment is

$$K = \frac{R}{5\%} \cdot \frac{1}{a_{\overline{12}|5\%}}$$

Equate the right sides of the two equations above since the capitalized cost is the same. Then, solve for $R$ as follows:

$$\frac{R}{5\%} \cdot \frac{1}{a_{\overline{12}|5\%}} = \frac{150}{5\%} \cdot \frac{1}{a_{\overline{10}|5\%}}; \qquad \frac{R}{a_{\overline{12}|5\%}} = \frac{150}{a_{\overline{10}|5\%}}$$

$$R = \frac{150}{a_{\overline{10}|5\%}} \cdot a_{\overline{12}|5\%} = 150(.129505)(8.86325) = \$172.18$$

**Example 3**   Refer to Example 2. Assume that the cost of the new piece of equipment is the same as the cost of the old piece. If an attachment had been added to the new equipment to prolong the guaranteed life to 12 years, how much money can the buyer afford to pay for the additional attachment from the same capitalized cost?

$R =$ the entire cost of the replacement, or
$R =$ the cost of the new equipment + the cost of the attachment
   $= \$172.18$.

Since the cost of the new equipment is the same as that of the old, or $150, the cost of the attachment $= 172.18 - 150 = \$22.18$.

# ★EXERCISE 18–3

## Reference: Section 18.3

1. The cost of one type of garage is $800. It has to be replaced every eight years at the same cost. The cost of another type of garage is $1,000. It has to be replaced every 10 years at the same cost. If money is worth 4% compounded annually, which type of garage is less expensive?

2. A typewriter worth $250 has to be replaced every five years. Another typewriter worth $210 has to be replaced every four years. If money is worth 5%, which typewriter is the better buy?

3. Refer to Problem 1. If the $1,000 garage must be replaced every 10 years at a cost of $900, which type of garage is less expensive?

4. Refer to Problem 2. If the typewriter worth $210 can be replaced every four years at a net cost of $200, which typewriter is the better buy?

5. A machine which now needs to be replaced was purchased for $1,000 with a guaranteed life of 15 years. If a new machine is guaranteed for a useful life of 18 years, how much can the buyer afford to pay with the same capitalized cost which is invested at 5%?

6. A house which was painted three years ago for $70 now needs to be repainted. If a better type of paint is used, it will last four years. How much can the owner afford to pay for the better paint with the same capitalized cost which is invested at $3\frac{1}{2}\%$?

7. Refer to Problem 5. Assume that the price of the new machine is the same as that of the old machine. However, the purchaser wishes to buy a special service so that the new machine will last 20 years. How much can the purchaser afford to pay for the service from the same capitalized cost?

8. Refer to Problem 6. (a) If a type of paint that will last five years is used for the repainting job, how much can the owner afford to pay? (b) What is the difference between the prices of the three-year paint and the five-year paint?

# 18.4 SUMMARY OF FORMULAS

*Symbols:*     $A_\infty$ = present value of an ordinary perpetuity
        $I$ = periodic payment (or renewal cost) if $c = 1$
        $R$ = periodic payment (or renewal cost) if $c > 1$
        $K$ = capitalized cost
        $F$ = first cost from the capitalized cost
        $i$ = interest rate per interest period
        $c$ = number of interest conversion periods in one payment (or renewal) interval.

| Application | Formula | Formula Number | Refer-ence Page |
|---|---|---|---|
| Simple ordinary perpetuity | $A_\infty = \dfrac{I}{i}$ | (18–1) | 518 |
| Complex (ordinary) perpetuity | $A_\infty = \dfrac{R}{i} \cdot \dfrac{1}{s_{\overline{c}\rvert i}}$ | (18–2) | 520 |
| Capitalized cost | When $c = 1$, $$K = F + \frac{I}{i}$$ | (18–3) | 523 |
| | When $c > 1$, $$K = F + \frac{R}{i} \cdot \frac{1}{s_{\overline{c}\rvert i}}$$ | (18–4) | 524 |
| | When $F = R$, $$K = \frac{R}{i} \cdot \frac{1}{a_{\overline{c}\rvert i}}$$ | (18–5) | 524 |

# EXERCISE 18–4

## Review of Chapter 18

1. Find the present value of a perpetuity of $100 payable at the end of each month if the interest rate is 6% compounded monthly.

2. What is the present value of a perpetuity of $2,500 payable at the end of each quarter if the interest rate is 5% compounded quarterly?

3. Refer to Problem 1. If the first payment of the perpetuity is due now, what is the present value?

4. Refer to Problem 2. If the first payment of the perpetuity is due now, what is the present value?

5. Find the present value of a perpetuity of $50 payable at the end of each quarter if the interest rate is 6% compounded monthly.

6. What is the present value of a perpetuity of $200 payable at the end of each year if money is worth 4% compounded semiannually?

7. Refer to Problem 5. What is the present value of the perpetuity if the first payment is due now?

8. Refer to Problem 6. Find the present value of the perpetuity, assuming that the first payment is due now.

9. What is the cash equivalent of a piece of property if the income from it for every six months is $500 and money is worth (a) 6% compounded semiannually? and (b) 4% compounded quarterly?

10. Capitalize a debt of $100 payable at the end of each year forever if interest is (a) 4% compounded annually, and (b) 5% compounded monthly.

11. A highway bridge is constructed at a cost of $100,000. The bridge must be rebuilt every 30 years. If money can be invested at 5% compounded semiannually, find the capitalized cost of the bridge. Assume that the cost of each rebuilding will be $90,000.

12. The original cost of a bus station is estimated at $50,000. Thereafter, it should be reconstructed every 15 years, and the reconstruction cost is estimated to be $30,000 each time. If money can be invested at 4% compounded monthly, what is the capitalized cost of the station?

13. Refer to Problem 11. Assume that the cost of each rebuilding is $100,000. What is the capitalized cost?

14. Refer to Problem 12. Assume that the remodeling cost is estimated at $50,000 each time. Find the capitalization cost.

★15. Refer to Problem 13. Assume that 22 years after the bridge was constructed, a major repair is needed and the bridge will have a useful life of another 15 years after the repair. At the end of the life of the bridge, it is to be rebuilt and will be rebuilt thereafter every 30 years. How much of the capitalized cost is available for the repair?

★16. Refer to Problem 14. Assume that 12 years after the station was built, a major repair is necessary. It is estimated that eight years after the repair, the station will then be in need of reconstruction and thereafter every 15 years. How much of the capitalized cost can be spent for the repair?

★17. The cost of television set X is $400, and it must be replaced every eight years at a cost of $390. The cost of television set Y is $360, and it must be replaced every six years at the same cost. If money is worth 6% compounded semiannually, which of the two sets is the cheaper one?

★**18.** The cost of washing machine G is $300, and it must be replaced every 10 years at a cost of $280. The cost of washing machine F is $350, and it must be replaced every 12 years at a cost of $315. If money is worth 7% compounded annually, which machine is comparatively lower in cost?

★**19.** A machine which now needs to be replaced was bought for $800 with a guaranteed life of six years. If a new machine is guaranteed for a useful life of eight years, how much can the buyer afford to pay with the same capitalized cost which earns $5\frac{1}{2}$% interest compounded quarterly?

★**20.** A truck was purchased five years ago for $3,500. The capitalized cost of the truck was established for replacement every 5 years at the same cost and invested at 6% compounded quarterly. If a new truck has an estimated useful life of six years, how much can the owner afford to pay for the new truck from the capitalized cost?

★**21.** Refer to Problem 19. Assume that the cost of the new machine which has a useful life of eight years is also $800, the same as the cost of the old one. How much can the buyer afford to pay from the capitalized cost for an attachment to the new machine?

★**22.** Refer to Problem 20. Assume that the cost of the new truck with a useful life of six years is $3,500, the same as the cost of the old truck. How much can the owner afford to pay from the capitalized cost for an extra piece of equipment?

# Chapter 19

# Life Annuities

## 19.1   INTRODUCTION

Over the years the life insurance business has come to be one of the most important industries in the nation. According to a report made by the American Council of Life Insurance, the insurance companies of the United States had assets worth $771 million in 1890, but this amount had increased to more than $352 billion in 1978.[1] Most of these dollars are earmarked to meet the life insurance companies' future obligations to policyholders. One such obligation is the life annuity, which will be discussed in this chapter.

The basic idea of a *life annuity* is simple. People generally find it rather difficult to save enough money during their working years to support themselves in their old age. Furthermore, individuals themselves would not need their savings should they die before reaching retirement age. With a life annuity, each person within an age group contributes an equal amount of money to an agent, such as an insurance company, for the purpose of sharing in the total amount at a future date, provided that person is still alive. Survivors can later enjoy an amount larger than their original contributions since some of the contributors will not be alive then and interest is paid by the insurance company for use of the contributions. Since no one knows if he or she will be alive on a particular future date and the annuity is payable depending on a future occurrence, a life annuity is a type of contingent annuity.

The basic idea of *life insurance* is the same as that of life annuity. Both life insurance and life annuity contracts are designed for protection against the contingency of future life. However, a life annuity is provided for the purchaser of the annuity (the *annuitant*) to use the money in old age, whereas the purchaser of life insurance (the *insured*) is not usually the one who receives the benefits provided by the life insurance contract (the *policy*). A life annuity is payable to the annuitant by the insurance company if the annuitant is still *alive* on an indicated date, according to the annuity contract. Life insurance

---

[1] *Life Insurance Fact Book* (Washington: American Council of Life Insurance, 1978), p. 69.

is payable to the beneficiary of the insured if the insured *dies* within the indicated time stated in the insurance policy. Thus, the life annuity is not a life insurance contract. However, since the mathematics of a life annuity, or actuarial calculation, is based on a concept similar to that used in life insurance, life annuities have always been considered as part of the life insurance business and are among the oldest types of insurance contracts.

The cost, which is used to provide funds for the payment of the benefit according to a life annuity or an insurance contract, is called the *net premium*. In addition to the net premium, other amounts of money that are charged by an insurance company are called *loading costs,* which include the profit element and the operating expenses of the company, such as salaries, rent, and depreciation. The sum of the net premium and the loading costs is called the *gross premium.* Since both the operating expenses and the profit rates differ among insurance companies, for the sake of simplicity, *only the net premium is computed in this and the following chapter.*

The fundamental relationship between the net premium and the future benefits under any type of annuity contract or insurance policy may be expressed *on the purchase date* as follows:

$$\text{Present value of net premium} = \text{Present value of future benefit(s)}$$

The net premium may be paid in a single amount, called the *net single premium,* on the purchase date. It may also be paid in equal annual payments, called the *net annual premiums.* Net single premiums are generally paid for annuity contracts, while net annual premiums are usually paid for life insurance policies. However, a knowledge of the net single premium is necessary in computing a set of net annual premiums for an insurance policy.

Insurance companies usually invest their collected premiums in various fields to earn interest. *Unless otherwise specified, net premiums are computed at a nominal interest rate of $2\frac{1}{2}\%$ in all problems in this text.*

Generally, the age of a purchaser on his or her last birthday is taken in computing the purchase price of an insurance contract, but a pro rata allowance is sometimes made for each month that has elapsed since the last birthday. In simplifying the computation in this and the following chapter, it is assumed that *all annuity contracts and insurance policies are made on the purchaser's birthday.* Thus, the expression "a person aged 25" means that the person reaches his 25th birthday on the purchase date.

## 19.2 MORTALITY TABLES

The computation of life annuity and life insurance net premiums is primarily based on a mortality table. A *mortality table* is a statistical table showing the death rate of people of every age group. Although nobody can predict how long a certain individual will live or when that individual will die, studies of the mortality of people based on years of experience enable insurance companies to make a reasonably accurate prediction of the death rate of any particular age group. A large representative group of people, usually policyholders, is included in each study. The number of people living and dying in each age group is recorded and the findings are tabulated. For example, the American Experience Table was calculated from the mortality experience of the Mutual Life Insurance Company of New York. With the development of actuarial science, medical discoveries, and a higher standard of living which prolongs the life of individuals, new mortality tables have been constructed to replace the old ones and are available to meet the current needs of the life insurance business. The best-known mortality tables used in recent years by life insurance companies are as follows:

> American Experience Table of Mortality—First published as a part of New York law in 1868. Covered experience, 1843–58.
> American Men Ultimate Mortality Table—Published in 1918. Covered experience, 1900–15.
> The 1937 Standard Annuity Mortality Table—Published in 1938. Based primarily on experience, 1932–36.
> Commissioners 1941 Standard Ordinary Table of Mortality—Based on experience, 1930–40.
> Commissioners 1958 Standard Ordinary Table of Mortality—Based on experience, 1950–54.
> Annuity Table for 1971—(Male)—Based on experience, 1960–67.
> United States Total Population Mortality Table—Based on experience, 1969–71.

The basic principle involved in the computation of life annuity and life insurance problems is not affected by the use of a particular mortality table. For the sake of simplicity, only the Commissioners 1958 Standard Ordinary Table of Mortality, commonly referred to as the 1958 CSO Table (Table 14 in the Appendix), will be used in this text. From the CSO Table, the symbols that are used frequently in this chapter are $l_x$ and $d_x$.[2] The number of people living at age $x$ is represented by $l_x$, and the number of people who will die between the ages $x$ and $x + 1$ is represented by $d_x$. The table is based on a study of 10 million people starting at the age of 0. Thus, the expression $l_{30} = 9,480,358$ means that there are 9,480,358 persons alive at the age of 30 out of a group of 10 million people. A total of 20,193 persons from the group will die between the ages of 30 and 31. The number of deaths at that age is written as

$$d_{30} = 20,193.$$ Thus, the number of people living at age 31 is
$$l_{31} = l_{30} - d_{30} = 9,480,358 - 20,193 = 9,460,165$$

The death rate for people aged 30 (or written as $q_{30}$) is as follows:

---

[2] The symbols used in the 1958 CSO Table, along with the other symbols used in this and the following chapters, except a few additional symbols, are based on the statement of the "International Actuarial Notation," printed in *Transactions of the Actuarial Society of America,* Volume XLVIII, 1947, pp. 166–176.

$$q_{30} = \frac{d_{30}}{l_{30}} = \frac{20{,}193}{9{,}480{,}358} = .00213 \text{ (per person)}$$

The value of $q_{30}$ can be obtained directly from the deaths per 1,000 column of the 1958 CSO Table (Table 14). The table shows that the death rate per 1,000 at age 30 is 2.13. Thus,

$$q_{30} = \frac{2.13}{1{,}000} = .00213$$

## EXERCISE 19–1

**Reference: Section 19.2**

**A.** *Find the number of people in each of the following expressions:*

1. (a) $l_5$    (b) $l_{23}$    (c) $l_{32}$    (d) $l_{46}$    (e) $l_{78}$    (f) $l_{99}$
2. (a) $l_{15}$    (b) $l_{26}$    (c) $l_{41}$    (d) $l_{52}$    (e) $l_{69}$    (f) $l_{88}$
3. (a) $d_5$    (b) $d_{23}$    (c) $d_{32}$    (d) $d_{47}$    (e) $d_{68}$    (f) $d_{99}$
4. (a) $d_{15}$    (b) $d_{26}$    (c) $d_{41}$    (d) $d_{56}$    (e) $d_{72}$    (f) $d_{85}$

**B.** *Statement Problems:*

5. Find the death rate per thousand for persons aged (a) 8, (b) 20, (c) 56, (d) 70.
6. Find the death rate per thousand for persons aged (a) 10, (b) 25, (c) 61, (d) 86.
7. From a group of 50,000 now age 18, how many will probably (a) be alive at age 50, and (b) die after reaching age 50 but before reaching age 51?
8. From a group of 80,000 now age 25 how many are predicted (a) to be alive at age 65, and (b) to die after reaching age 65 but before reaching age 66?

## 19.3 PURE ENDOWMENT CONTRACTS

A *pure endowment* contract provides that the face value of the contract be paid if the purchaser of the pure endowment survives to the end of the contract term. However, no payment is made to him or her if the purchaser dies during the period. Although pure endowment contracts are rarely issued by an insurance company, a study of this type of contract is a good starting point to learn the value of a mortality table.

**Example 1**    A person is 30 years of age and wishes to purchase a pure endowment policy that will pay $1,000 when age 65 is reached. Find the net single premium of the policy.

According to the 1958 CSO Mortality Table (Table 14) there are 9,480,358 persons alive at age 30 and 6,800,531 persons alive at age 65. If each one of the group of 9,480,358 persons, aged 30, wants to buy a pure endowment of $1 which will be payable at age 65 if that person is still living then, the required payments to be made by a life insurance company, at age 65, will be $6,800,531.

Assume that the insurance company can invest its money at an interest rate of $2\frac{1}{2}\%$ compounded annually. The present value of the required payments is obtained by the compound discount formula $P = S(1 + i)^{-n}$ as follows:

$S = 6,800,531$, $i = 2\frac{1}{2}\%$, $n = 35$ (there are 35 years between age 30 and age 65). Thus,

$$P = 6,800,531(1 + 2\frac{1}{2}\%)^{-35} = 6,800,531(.42137107) = \$2,865,547.02$$
(Table 6)

The above illustration is diagrammed as follows:

**Based on a $1 Pure Endowment Contract**

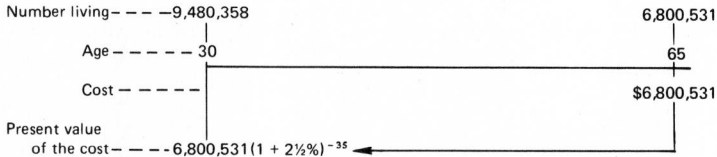

The present value (at age 30) is divided among the group of 9,480,358 persons. The net single premium for each person aged 30 is

$$\frac{2,865,547.02}{9,480,358} = \$0.30226$$

For a $1,000 pure endowment policy, the net single premium is

$$0.30226 \times 1,000 = \$302.26$$

A simpler way to compute the net single premium of a pure endowment policy is to apply the following formula:

$$_nE_x = \frac{D_{x+n}}{D_x} \qquad\qquad \textbf{(19–1)} \,^3$$

---

[3] *Proof—Formula (19–1)*

Let $l_x$ represent the number of persons at age $x$. Each of them wants to buy a pure endowment policy of $1 payable at age $x + n$ if he or she is then alive. The diagram, which is similar to that of Example 1, may be arranged symbolically as follows:

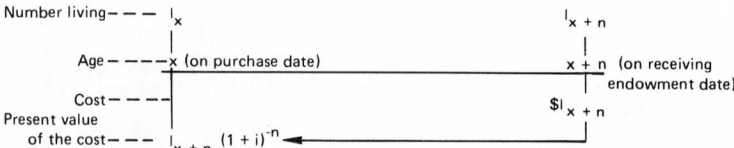

$_nE_x =$ the net single premium of a \$1, $n$ year, pure endowment contract issued at age $x$. The contract promises to pay the annuitant the endowment at the end of $n$ years or at age $x + n$ if the annuitant is then still alive.

$D_x$ and $D_{x+n}$ are symbols whose values are listed in Table 15 in the Appendix.

Example 1 may be computed in the following manner when formula (19–1) is used:

$$x = 30, \quad n = 35$$

The net single premium for a \$1 payment to each annuitant at age 65 is

$$_nE_x = {}_{35}E_{30} = \frac{D_{x+n}}{D_x} = \frac{D_{30+35}}{D_{30}} = \frac{D_{65}}{D_{30}} = \frac{1{,}366{,}128.5462}{4{,}519{,}691.3751} = .30226$$

For a \$1,000 payment, the net single premium $= .30226 \times 1{,}000$
$$= \$302.26$$

**Note:** The division $D_{65}/D_{30}$ may also be performed by using logarithms as follows:

$$
\begin{array}{llr}
\log D_{65} = 6.135\ 4916 = 16.135\ 4916 - 10 & & \text{(Table 16)} \\
(-)\ \log D_{30} \qquad\qquad\quad = \phantom{1}6.655\ 1088 & & \\
\hline
\log {}_nE_x = \phantom{1}9.480\ 3828 - 10 & &
\end{array}
$$

Find the antilog by interpolation from Table 2. $_nE_x = .30226$

---

[3] *Proof (continued)*

Let $_nE_x =$ the net single premium of a \$1, $n$ year, pure endowment contract for each annuitant at age $x$. The contract will pay \$1 to each annuitant at the end of $n$ years or at age $x + n$ if the annuitant is still living.

Then

$$_nE_x = \frac{l_{x+n}(1 + i)^{-n}}{l_x}$$

Let $v = (1 + i)^{-1}$, or $v^n = (1 + i)^{-n}$ (In Table 6, $v^n = p = (1 + i)^{-n}$)

Then,

$$_nE_x = \frac{v^n l_{x+n}}{l_x}. \qquad \text{Multiply both the numerator and the denominator by } v^x,$$

$$_nE_x = \frac{v^{x+n}l_{x+n}}{v^x l_x}, \qquad \text{or}$$

$$_nE_x = \frac{D_{x+n}}{D_x} \qquad\qquad\qquad\qquad\qquad\qquad\qquad\qquad (19\text{--}1)$$

$D_x$ represents the value of $v^x l_x$ for convenience in writing.

The values of $D_{65}$ and $D_{30}$ are obtained by using Table 6 as follows: (See Example 1)

$$D_{65} = v^{65} l_{65} = (1 + 2\tfrac{1}{2}\%)^{-65}(6{,}800{,}531) = .20088557(6{,}800{,}531) = 1{,}366{,}128.5462$$
$$D_{30} = v^{30} l_{30} = (1 + 2\tfrac{1}{2}\%)^{-30}(9{,}480{,}358) = .47674269(9{,}480{,}358) = 4{,}519{,}691.3751$$

For convenience, the values of $D_x$ are tabulated in Table 15. Note that the values in Table 15 are computed at an interest rate of $2\tfrac{1}{2}\%$ compounded annually.

**Example 2**     Find the net single premium of a $2,000 pure endowment policy payable in 10 years to a person now aged 18.

$x = 18$, $n = 10$

$$_nE_x = {}_{10}E_{18} = \frac{D_{18+10}}{D_{18}} = \frac{D_{28}}{D_{18}} = \frac{4,768,076.98}{6,218,174.46} = .7667969 \qquad \text{(Table 15)}$$

For a $2,000 pure endowment policy, the net single payment is

$0.7667969 \times 2,000 = \$1,533.59$

**Note:**     *In order to simplify mathematical operations, round the decimals of the values in the commutation columns (Table 15) when computing the problems in the exercises in this chapter.* Examples:

$D_{65} = 1,366,128.5462$, rounded to $1,366,129$

$N_{96} = 11,610.1087$, rounded to $11,610$

# EXERCISE 19–2

**Reference: Section 19.3**

**A.** *Find the net single premium of the pure endowment contract in each of the following problems:*

| | Contract Amount | Age on Purchase Date | Age on Payment Date |
|---|---|---|---|
| 1. | $2,000 | 25 | 30 |
| 2. | 2,000 | 20 | 28 |
| 3. | 1,000 | 35 | 45 |
| 4. | 1,000 | 40 | 65 |
| 5. | 4,000 | 30 | 55 |
| 6. | 4,000 | 45 | 70 |
| 7. | 5,000 | 24 | 32 |
| 8. | 5,000 | 50 | 80 |

**B.** *Statement Problems:*

9. Find the net single premium of a pure endowment contract of $1,000 payable in 15 years to a person now aged 22.
10. What is the net single premium of a 25-year pure endowment contract of $3,000 to a person now aged 34?
11. What is the net single premium of a pure endowment contract of $1,000 payable in 15 years to a person now aged 42?
12. Find the net single premium of a 25-year pure endowment contract of $3,000 to a person now aged 54.
13. How much should a person aged 36 pay an insurance company in order to receive $1,500 at age 60, if then living?

14. How much should a life insurance company collect from a person aged 28 if the company will·pay $5,000 to the person at age 40 if he or she is then alive?

15. A person aged 26 pays $300 to a life insurance company for a 30-year pure endowment contract. How much will that person receive at age 56 if then alive?

16. A mother paid $800 for a pure endowment contract for her son now aged four. The endowment will be payable to her son if and when he reaches age 20. How much will the son receive if he is then alive?

## 19.4 WHOLE LIFE ANNUITIES

Life annuities are generally classified into two major groups: *whole* life annuities and *temporary* life annuities.

A *whole life annuity* is a contract under which an insurance company will pay the annuitant a given sum periodically for life, ceasing with the last payment preceding the annuitant's death. The purchase price of a whole life annuity depends on the *age* of the annuitant and the *time* of the first payment made to the annuitant.

When the first annual payment is made one year after the date of purchase, the annuity is called an *ordinary whole life annuity,* or an *immediate whole life annuity.* When the first annual payment is made at the time of purchase, it is called a *whole life annuity due.* If the first payment begins after a period of more than one year has elapsed, it is called a *deferred whole life annuity.* The purchase price for each type of whole life annuity is computed below.

## A. Ordinary Whole Life Annuity (Immediate Whole Life Annuity)

**Example 1**  Find the net single premium of an ordinary whole life annuity of $1 payable at the end of each year for a person aged 95 years. The first payment will be made one year later (or when the age of 96 is reached). Assume that the 1958 CSO Table is used and the interest rate is $2\frac{1}{2}\%$.

The net single premium is $1.25. The findings from the 1958 CSO Table (Table 14) and the computation are diagrammed below:

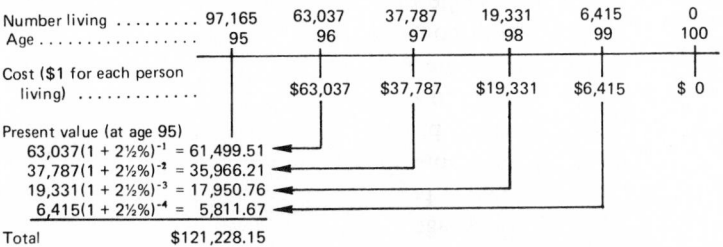

```
Number living ........ 97,165   63,037   37,787   19,331   6,415    0
Age ................    95       96       97       98       99     100

Cost ($1 for each person
   living) ...........          $63,037  $37,787  $19,331  $6,415  $ 0

Present value (at age 95)
   63,037(1 + 2½%)⁻¹ = 61,499.51
   37,787(1 + 2½%)⁻² = 35,966.21
   19,331(1 + 2½%)⁻³ = 17,950.76
    6,415(1 + 2½%)⁻⁴ =  5,811.67
Total               $121,228.15
```

The term "cost" applies to the costs of both the insurance company and the group of annuitants. In other words, the cost to an insurance company is equal to the cost to the group of annuitants. When only the net single premium is computed, the insurance company may be thought of as an agent who collects premiums on the purchase date and pays benefits during later years. The total cost to an insurance company on the purchase date should be divided by the number of annuitants living at that time. Thus, the net single premium for each annuitant is

$$\frac{121,228.15}{97,165} = \$1.24765, \text{ or } \$1.25$$

In general,    let $a_x$ = the net single premium, or the present value, of an ordinary whole life annuity of $1 payable at the end of each year for a person whose age now is $x$ years.

Then        $$a_x = \frac{N_{x+1}}{D_x}$$                **(19–2)** [4]

---

[4] *Proof—Formula (19–2)*

The steps necessary in finding the value of $a_x$ are the same as those used in Example 1 and are shown symbolically as follows:

Total present value of the costs $= l_{x+1}(1 + i)^{-1} + l_{x+2}(1 + i)^{-2} + l_{x+3}(1 + i)^{-3} + \cdots \cdots$
$$+ l_{99}(1 + i)^{-(99 - x)}$$

Let $v = (1 + i)^{-1}$

The present value $= vl_{x+1} + v^2 l_{x+2} + v^3 l_{x+3} + \cdots \cdots \cdots + v^{99 - x} l_{99}$

Let $a_x$ = the net single premium, or the present value of an ordinary whole life annuity of $1 payable at the end of each year for a person whose age now is $x$ years

$$a_x = \frac{\text{Total present value of the costs}}{\text{Number of annuitants at age } x \text{ on the purchase date}}$$

$$a_x = \frac{vl_{x+1} + v^2 l_{x+2} + v^3 l_{x+3} + \cdots \cdots \cdots \cdots + v^{99-x} l_{99}}{l_x}$$

Multiply both the numerator and the denominator by $v^x$. Then

$$a_x = \frac{v^{x+1} l_{x+1} + v^{x+2} l_{x+2} + v^{x+3} l_{x+3} + \cdots \cdots \cdots \cdots + v^{99} l_{99}}{v^x l_x}$$

Let $R =$ the annual payment to the annuitant

$A =$ the net single premium for an ordinary whole life annuity that pays $R$ per year for life

Then
$$A = Ra_x = R \cdot \frac{N_{x+1}}{D_x} \tag{19–3}$$

The values of $N_x$ and $D_x$, based on an interest rate of $2\frac{1}{2}\%$ compounded annually, are listed in Table 15.

Example 1 may be computed as follows when formula (19–3) is used:

$R = \$1,\ x = 95$

$$A = 1 \cdot \frac{N_{95+1}}{D_{95}} = \frac{N_{96}}{D_{95}} = \frac{11{,}610.1087}{9{,}305.5630} = 1.24765, \text{ or } \$1.25$$

**Note:**   The division $N_{96}/D_{95}$ may also be performed by using logarithms:

$$
\begin{array}{ll}
\log N_{96} = 4.064\ 8363 & \text{(Table 16)} \\
(-)\log D_{95} = 3.968\ 7427 & \\
\hline
\log a_{95} = \quad .096\ 0936 &
\end{array}
$$

Find the antilog by interpolation from Table 2.
$a_{95} = 1.24765$.

**Example 2**   A person, aged 35, wishes to purchase an ordinary whole life annuity which will pay $1,000 at the age of 36 and the same amount at the end of each year thereafter for life. Find the net single premium of the annuity.

Since the first payment is to be made one year after the date of purchase, the contract is an ordinary whole life annuity. The interest rate is assumed to be $2\frac{1}{2}\%$.

$x = 35,\ R = \$1,000$

Substituting the above values in formula (19–3):

$$A = R \cdot \frac{N_{x+1}}{D_x} = R \cdot \frac{N_{35+1}}{D_{35}} = 1{,}000 \cdot \frac{N_{36}}{D_{35}}$$

$$= 1{,}000 \cdot \frac{89{,}956{,}987.56}{3{,}949{,}851.09} = \$22{,}774.78 \tag{Table 15}$$

---

[4] *Proof (continued)*

According to Section 19.3 (footnote 3), $D_x = v^x l_x$. Thus,

$$a_x = \frac{D_{x+1} + D_{x+2} + D_{x+3} + \cdots \cdots + D_{99}}{D_x}$$

Let $N_x = D_x + D_{x+1} + D_{x+2} + \cdots \cdots \cdots \cdots + D_{99}$.   Then,

$N_{x+1} = D_{x+1} + D_{x+2} + \cdots \cdots \cdots \cdots \cdots + D_{99}$   and

$$a_x = \frac{N_{x+1}}{D_x} \tag{19–2}$$

**Example 3**     A person, aged 25, has $50,000. If the money is used to purchase an ordinary whole life annuity with the first payment payable one year from the purchase date, what is the size of each annual payment?

The net single premium of the annuity is known, $50,000 = A$, $x = 25$, $R = ?$

Substituting the above values in formula (19–3):

$$50,000 = R \cdot \frac{N_{25+1}}{D_{25}} = R \cdot \frac{N_{26}}{D_{25}}$$

$$R = 50,000 \cdot \frac{D_{25}}{N_{26}} = 50,000 \cdot \frac{5,165,007.95}{134,674,488.96} = \$1,917.59 \text{ (per year)}$$

# EXERCISE 19–3

## Reference: Section 19.4 A

1. A person, aged 20, wishes to purchase an ordinary whole life annuity which will pay $1,000 at age 21 and the same amount at the end of each year thereafter. What is the net single premium of the annuity?

2. A person, aged 32, wants to buy an annuity that will pay $2,500 annually for life with the first payment to be made one year after the purchase date. What is the purchase price (the net single premium)?

3. Find the net single premium for an ordinary whole life annuity of $2,500 per year for a person now aged 60.

4. What is the net single premium for an ordinary whole life annuity of $1,000 per year for a person now aged 30?

5. Find the net single premium for an ordinary whole life annuity of $2,000 payable at the end of each year for a person now aged 45.

6. Compute the net single premium for an ordinary whole life annuity of $3,000 per year if the annuity is bought by a person now aged 40.

7. What is the net single premium for an ordinary whole life annuity of $4,000 per year for a person now aged 50?

8. Find the net single premium for an ordinary whole life annuity of $5,000 payable at the end of each year for a person now aged 55.

9. If the net single premium of an ordinary whole life annuity for a person now aged 30 is $20,000, what is the size of each annual payment?

10. Refer to Problem 9. What is the size of each annual payment if the annuity is purchased by a person aged 22?

11. A person aged 27 has $120,000. If the money is used to buy an ordinary whole life annuity with the first payment to be made one year from the purchase date, what is the size of each annual payment?

12. A person aged 48 paid $70,000 for an ordinary whole life annuity with the first payment to be made in one year. Find the size of the annual payment.

## B. Whole Life Annuity Due

The first payment of an ordinary whole life annuity is made one year after the date of purchase, whereas the first payment of a whole life annuity *due* is made at the *time of purchase*. Thus, if the annual payment is $1, the net single premium of a whole life annuity due on the purchase date is *$1 more* than the net single premium of an ordinary whole life annuity.

Let $\ddot{a}_x$ = the net single premium, or the present value, of a whole life annuity due of $1 payable now and each year hereafter for life for a person now aged $x$ years

Then $\quad \ddot{a}_x = 1 + a_x$, or

$$\ddot{a}_x = \frac{N_x}{D_x} \qquad\qquad \textbf{(19–4)}\ ^5$$

Let $A$(due) = the net single premium or the present value of a whole life annuity due which will pay $R$ per year for life

$$A\textbf{(due)} = R\ddot{a}_x = R \cdot \frac{N_x}{D_x} \qquad\qquad \textbf{(19–5)}$$

**Example 4**  A person, aged 35, wishes to purchase a whole life annuity which will pay $1,000 now and the same amount at the end of each year thereafter for life. Find the net single premium of the annuity.

$x = 35$, $R = \$1,000$. Since the first payment is made now, this is a whole life annuity due problem. The net single premium is

$$A\text{(due)} = R\ddot{a}_x = 1,000 \cdot \frac{N_{35}}{D_{35}} = 1,000 \cdot \frac{93,906,838.64}{3,949,851.09}$$

$$= \$23,774.78$$

***Note:***  Example 4 is identical to Example 2 except that the first payment in Example 4 is made at the time of purchase. Since the annuitant receives $1,000 at the time of purchase, the cost is also $1,000 higher than the cost in Example 2. Thus, the difference between the two purchase prices in Examples 4 and 2 is $1,000, or $23,774.78 − $22,774.78.

**Example 5**  A person aged 25 owes a life insurance company $50,000. If the company allows that person to discharge the obligation by annual payments payable for life, with the first payment due now, what is the size of the annual payment?

---

[5] *Proof—Formula (19–4)*

$$\ddot{a}_x = 1 + a_x = 1 + \frac{N_{x+1}}{D_x} = \frac{D_x + N_{x+1}}{D_x} = \frac{D_x + (D_{x+1} + D_{x+2} + \cdots D_{99})}{D_x}$$

$$= \frac{N_x}{D_x} \qquad\qquad \textbf{(19–4)}$$

The above result may also be obtained by a method similar to that used in obtaining the ordinary whole life annuity formula (19–2).

The present value of the annuity $A$(due) is known.

$A$(due) = \$50,000, $x$ = 25, $R$ = ? (annual payment)

Substituting the values in formula (19–5):

$$A(\text{due}) = R\ddot{a}_x = R \cdot \frac{N_x}{D_x} = R \cdot \frac{N_{25}}{D_{25}}$$

Thus

$$50,000 = R \cdot \frac{N_{25}}{D_{25}}$$

$$R = 50,000 \cdot \frac{D_{25}}{N_{25}} = 50,000 \cdot \frac{5,165,007.95}{139,839,496.91} = \$1,846.76$$

**Note:**   The concept of finding the annual payments of a whole life annuity due is important in finding the *annual* premiums payable for life for a life insurance policy. (See Section 20.2 B.)

# ★C. Deferred Whole Life Annuity

The first payment of a deferred whole life annuity begins after a period of more than one year has elapsed from the date of purchase. The period of deferment may be expressed in two ways:

1. It is the period from the date of purchase to the date of the first payment. The payments thus form a whole life annuity *due* with the term beginning on the date of the first payment.
2. It is the period from the date of purchase to the date which is one year prior to the date of the first payment. The payments thus form an *ordinary* whole life annuity.

For convenience in this chapter, the period of deferment is expressed from the date of purchase to the date of the first payment (item No. 1 above). For example, if a person aged 60 buys a whole life annuity with the first payment to be made at 65 years of age, the period of deferment is considered to be five years. The annuity is a deferred whole life annuity *due,* with the term beginning at age 65.

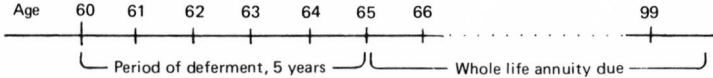

Let $k$ = the period of deferment in years

$_k|\ddot{a}_x$ = the net single premium, or the present value, of a deferred annuity of \$1 per year for life, with the first payment at the end of the deferment period, $k$ years, for a person now aged $x$ years

Then, $$_k|\ddot{a}_x = \frac{N_{x+k}}{D_x}$$ **(19–6)** [6]

Let $A(\text{defer}) =$ the net single premium, or the present value, of a whole life annuity which will pay $R$ per year after $k$ years

Then, $$A(\textbf{defer.}) = R \cdot {}_k|\ddot{a}_x = R \cdot \frac{N_{x+k}}{D_x}$$ **(19–7)**

**Example 6**   A person, aged 25, wishes to purchase a whole life annuity that will pay \$3,000 a year for life. The first payment is due at age 65. Find the net single premium of the annuity.

The period of deferment $k = 65 - 25 = 40$ (years), $x = 25$, $R = \$3,000$

Substituting the values in formula (19–7):

$$A(\text{defer.}) = 3,000 \cdot \frac{N_{25+40}}{D_{25}} = 3,000 \cdot \frac{N_{65}}{D_{25}}$$

$$= 3,000 \cdot \frac{15,077,832.60}{5,165,007.95} = \$8,757.68$$

**Example 7**   A 14-year-old boy inherited \$50,000. If he uses the money to purchase a whole life annuity with the first payment due at age 25, what will be the size of each payment?

$A(\text{defer.}) = \$50,000$, $x = 14$, $k = 25 - 14 = 11$ (years),

$x + k = 14 + 11 = 25$, $R = ?$ (per year)

---

[6] *Proof—Formula (19–6)*

The value of $_k|\ddot{a}_x$ is obtained as follows:

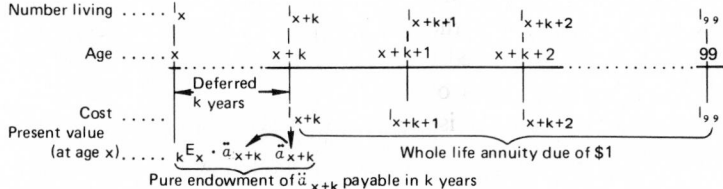

The following result is obtained from the above diagram:

$$_k|\ddot{a}_x = {}_kE_x \cdot \ddot{a}_{x+k} = \frac{D_{x+k}}{D_x} \cdot \frac{N_{x+k}}{D_{x+k}} = \frac{N_{x+k}}{D_x}$$

(19–6) (See Formulas (19–1) and (19–4))

***Note:***   Formula (19–6) may also be proved by using a method similar to that used in proving formula (19–2).

Substituting the values in formula (19–7):

$$50,000 = R \cdot \frac{N_{25}}{D_{14}}$$

$$R = 50,000 \cdot \frac{D_{14}}{N_{25}} = 50,000 \cdot \frac{6,905,108.16}{139,839,496.91} = \$2,468.94$$

## EXERCISE 19–4

**Reference: Sections 19.4 B and C**

1. Refer to Problem 1 of Exercise 19–3. What is the net single premium if the annuity pays $1,000 annually starting at age 20?
2. Refer to Problem 2 of Exercise 19–3. If the first payment is made on the purchase date, what is the purchase price?
3. A person, aged 45, wishes to buy a whole life annuity which will pay $1,000 now and the same amount at the end of each year thereafter for life. What is the net single premium of the annuity?
4. Find the net single premium of a whole life annuity of $2,000 per year for someone aged 30. Assume that the first $2,000 is payable to the annuitant on the purchase date.
5. What is the net single premium of a whole life annuity due of $3,000 per year for a person aged 18?
6. What is the net single premium of a whole life annuity due of $4,000 per year for a person aged 70?
7. If the net single premium of a whole life annuity due is $20,000, what is the size of the annual payment for a person now aged 30?
8. Refer to Problem 7. If the person is 22 years old now, what is the size of the annual payment?
9. A person, aged 55, purchases a life insurance policy. The net single premium (purchase price) of the policy is $2,000. If the insurance company allows the premium to be paid by equal annual payments for life, with the first payment due now (on the purchase date), find the size of the annual payment.
10. A person, who is the beneficiary of a $10,000 insurance policy, decides to use the money to purchase a whole life annuity with the first payment due now. If the person is 26 years old, what will be the size of each annual payment?
★11. Find the net single premium of a whole life annuity of $1,000 per year for a person now aged 36 if the first payment is to be made 10 years from now.
★12. A person, aged 42, wishes to buy a whole life annuity of $500 payable at the beginning of each year. The first payment is due at age 55. What is the net single premium of the annuity?

★**13.** Refer to Problem 3. What is the net single premium of the annuity if the first payment is to be made at age 50?

★**14.** Refer to Problem 4. What is the net single premium of the annuity if the first payment is to be made at age 38?

★**15.** Refer to Problem 10. If the first payment is to be made at age 40, what will be the size of each annual payment?

★**16.** A young man, aged 20, has $15,000. If he wishes to use the money to buy a whole life annuity with the first payment to be made at age 35, what is the size of each payment?

## 19.5 TEMPORARY LIFE ANNUITIES

When the payments of a life annuity cease at the end of a certain number of years, even though the annuitant is still living, the annuity is called a *temporary life annuity.* Like whole life annuities, temporary life annuities may be classified as ordinary, due, and deferred, depending upon the date of the first payment.

## A. Ordinary Temporary Life Annuity (Immediate Temporary Life Annuity)

The first annual payment of an *ordinary temporary life annuity* is made one year after the date of purchase. Thus, if a person now aged $x$ purchases an ordinary temporary life annuity, the first annual payment will be made to him at $x + 1$ years of age.

Let $n =$ the number of payments

$a_{x:\overline{n}|} =$ the net single premium, or the present value, at age $x$ of an ordinary temporary life annuity of $1 payable each year for $n$ annual payments

Then
$$a_{x:\overline{n}|} = \frac{N_{x+1} - N_{x+n+1}}{D_x} \qquad (19\text{–}8)\ [7]$$

---

[7] *Proof—Formula (19–8)*

The value of $a_{x:\overline{n}|}$ is obtained as follows:

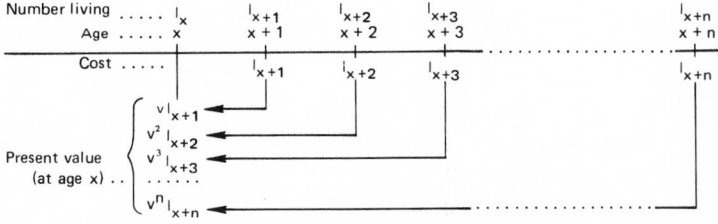

*(Continued on next page)*

Let $A$(tem.) = net single premium, or present value, of an ordinary temporary life annuity that will pay $R$ per year

Then,     $$A\textbf{(tem.)} = Ra_{x:\,\overline{n}|} = R \cdot \frac{N_{x+1} - N_{x+n+1}}{D_x} \qquad \textbf{(19–9)}$$

**Example 1**     What is the net single premium of a five-year ordinary temporary life
annuity of \$2,000 per year for a person aged 20 if the first payment is
to be made at age 21?

$x = 20, \; n = 5, \; R = \$2,000$

$$A(\text{tem.}) = Ra_{x:\,\overline{n}|} = 2{,}000 \cdot \frac{N_{20+1} - N_{20+5+1}}{D_{20}} = 2{,}000 \cdot \frac{N_{21} - N_{26}}{D_{20}}$$

$$= 2{,}000 \cdot \frac{161{,}928{,}780.91 - 134{,}674{,}488.96}{5{,}898{,}264.97}$$

$$= 2{,}000 \cdot \frac{27{,}254{,}291.95}{5{,}898{,}264.97} = \$9{,}241.46$$

# B. Temporary Life Annuity Due

The first payment of a *temporary life annuity due* is made on the date of
purchase. If the periodic payment is \$1, the present value of the first payment
is also \$1. The remaining payments form an ordinary temporary life annuity.
Let $n$ = the number of payments. The number of the remaining payments is
$n - 1$, and the present value of the remaining payments of \$1 each is $a_{x:\,\overline{n-1}|}$.

Let $\ddot{a}_{x:\,\overline{n}|}$ = the net single premium, or the present value, at age $x$, of a
temporary life annuity *due* of \$1 payable each year for $n$
annual payments

---

[7] *Proof (continued)*

The net single premium to each annuitant at the present time (age $x$) is

$$a_{x:\,\overline{n}|} = \frac{v l_{x+1} + v^2 l_{x+2} + v^3 l_{x+3} + \cdots \cdots \cdots + v^n l_{x+n}}{l_x}$$

Multiply both the numerator and the denominator by $v^x$, and substitute commutation symbols:

$$a_{x:\,\overline{n}|} = \frac{D_{x+1} + D_{x+2} + D_{x+3} + \cdots \cdots \cdots + D_{x+n}}{D_x}$$

Since $N_{x+1} = D_{x+1} + D_{x+2} + D_{x+3} + \cdots \cdots \cdots + D_{x+n} + D_{x+n+1} + \cdots \cdots + D_{99}$, and
$N_{x+n+1} = \qquad\qquad\qquad\qquad\qquad\qquad\qquad\qquad\quad D_{x+n+1} + \cdots \cdots + D_{99}$,

the difference between $N_{x+1}$ and $N_{x+n+1}$ equals the numerator in the fraction on the right
side in the above equation. Thus, the equation may be written in the following simple manner:

$$a_{x:\,\overline{n}|} = \frac{N_{x+1} - N_{x+n+1}}{D_x} \qquad (19–8)$$

Then,

$$\ddot{a}_{x:\overline{n}|} = 1 + a_{x:\overline{n-1}|}, \text{ or}$$

$$\ddot{a}_{x:\overline{n}|} = \frac{N_x - N_{x+n}}{D_x} \qquad\qquad \textbf{(19–10)} \; [8]$$

The net single premium of a temporary life annuity due of $R$ per year for $n$ payments is

$$A(\text{tem. due}) = R\ddot{a}_{x:\overline{n}|} = R \cdot \frac{N_x - N_{x+n}}{D_x} \qquad\qquad \textbf{(19–11)}$$

**Example 2**   What is the net single premium for a six-year temporary life annuity of \$2,000 per year for a person aged 20 if the first payment is due now?

$x = 20, \; n = 6, \; R = \$2,000$

$$A(\text{tem. due}) = 2,000 \cdot \frac{N_{20} - N_{20+6}}{D_{20}} = 2,000 \cdot \frac{N_{20} - N_{26}}{D_{20}}$$

$$= 2,000 \cdot \frac{167,827,045.88 - 134,674,488.96}{5,898,264.97}$$

$$= \frac{2,000(33,152,556.92)}{5,898,264.97} = \$11,241.46$$

**Note:**   The difference between the answers in Example 1 and Example 2 is \$2,000, which is the value of the first payment on the date of purchase.

**Example 3**   The purchase price (or the net single premium) of a life insurance policy issued to a person aged 25 is \$339.65. That person will pay the premium by making equal annual payments for 20 years or for life, whichever is the shorter of the two periods. If the first payment is due now (the purchase date), what is the size of the annual payment?

$A(\text{tem. due}) = \$339.65, \; x = 25, \; n = 20, \; R = ?$

Substituting the above values in formula (19–11):

$$339.65 = R \cdot \frac{N_{25} - N_{25+20}}{D_{25}}$$

$$R = 339.65 \cdot \frac{D_{25}}{N_{25} - N_{45}}$$

---

[8] *Proof—Formula (19–10)*

$$\ddot{a}_{x:\overline{n}|} = 1 + a_{x:\overline{n-1}|} = 1 + \frac{N_{x+1} - N_{x+(n-1)+1}}{D_x} = \frac{D_x + N_{x+1} - N_{x+n}}{D_x}$$

Since $D_x + N_{x+1} = N_x$ (see Section 19.4 B), then $\ddot{a}_{x:\overline{n}|} = \dfrac{N_x - N_{x+n}}{D_x}$ $\qquad$ (19–10)

$$= 339.65 \cdot \frac{5,165,007.95}{139,839,496.91 - 58,927,803.08}$$

$$= \$21.68 \text{ (annual payment)}$$

**Note:**     The concept of finding the annual payments of a temporary life annuity due is important in finding the annual premiums payable for a limited number of payments for a life insurance policy. (See Example 3, Section 20.2 B.)

# ★C. Deferred Temporary Life Annuity

The first annual payment of a *deferred temporary life annuity* is made after a period of $k$ (more than 1) years, or at age $x + k$ of the annuitant, if then still living. The $n$ annual payments form a temporary life annuity *due*.

Let $_k|\ddot{a}_{x:\overline{n}|}$ = the net single premium, or the present value, at age $x$, of a deferred temporary life annuity due of \$1 per year for $n$ annual payments with the first payment at the end of $k$ years, or at age $x + k$

Then,

$$_k|\ddot{a}_{x:\overline{n}|} = \frac{N_{x+k} - N_{x+k+n}}{D_x} \tag{19--12}[9]$$

The net single premium of a deferred temporary life annuity of $R$ per year is

$$A(\text{tem. defer.}) = R \cdot \frac{N_{x+k} - N_{x+k+n}}{D_x} \tag{19--13}$$

**Example 4**     What is the net single premium for an eight-year temporary life annuity of \$1,000 per year for a person aged 25 if the first payment is due at age 45?

$$x = 25, \ k = 45 - 25 = 20, \ n = 8, \ R = \$1,000$$

$$A(\text{tem.defer.}) = 1,000 \cdot \frac{N_{25+20} - N_{25+20+8}}{D_{25}} = 1,000 \cdot \frac{N_{45} - N_{53}}{D_{25}}$$

---

[9] *Proof—Formula (19–12)*

The value of $_k|\ddot{a}_{x:\overline{n}|}$ may be obtained by a method similar to the proof for formula (19–6) in Section 19.4 C as follows:

$$_k|\ddot{a}_{x:\overline{n}|} = {_kE_x} \cdot \ddot{a}_{x+k:\overline{n}|} = \frac{D_{x+k}}{D_x} \cdot \frac{N_{x+k} - N_{x+k+n}}{D_{x+k}} = \frac{N_{x+k} - N_{x+k+n}}{D_x} \tag{19--12}$$

**Note:**     The value of $\ddot{a}_{x+k:\overline{n}|}$ is the net single premium of a temporary life annuity due of \$1 payable for $n$ annual payments for a person now aged $x + k$. The value of $_k|\ddot{a}_{x:\overline{n}|}$ is equal to the present value (age $x$) of the pure endowment of $\ddot{a}_{x+k:\overline{n}|}$ payable in $k$ years. (See formulas (19–1) and (19–10).)

$$= 1,000 \cdot \frac{58,927,803.08 - 37,504,037.97}{5,165,007.95}$$

$$= \$4,147.87$$

## EXERCISE 19–5

### Reference: Section 19.5

1. What is the net single premium of a 10-year ordinary temporary life annuity of $1,000 per year for a person aged 30 if the first payment is to be made at age 31?

2. Find the net single premium of an ordinary temporary life annuity of 15 payments of $1,500 each, for a person aged 45 if the first payment is to be made one year after the purchase date.

3. How much would a person aged 40 have to pay for a 20-year ordinary temporary life annuity of $2,000 each year if the first payment is to be made at age 41?

4. What is the net single premium of a five-year ordinary temporary life annuity of $1,200 per year for a person aged 24 if the first payment is to be made at age 25?

5. A person aged 42 has $8,000. If the money is used to buy a 10-year ordinary temporary life annuity, what is the size of the annual payment to that individual?

6. A person aged 20 owes a life insurance company $1,500. The company allows the debt to be paid by 18 equal annual payments or for life, whichever period is the shorter. If the first payment is due at age 21, what is the size of the annual payment?

7. Find the cost of an ordinary temporary life annuity of $1,000 per year for 15 payments for a person aged 40 if the first payment is due now.

8. What is the net single premium of a 10-year ordinary temporary life annuity of $3,000 per year for a person aged 35 if the first payment is made on the date of purchase?

9. Refer to Problem 1. What is the net single premium if the first payment of the life annuity is made at age 30?

10. Refer to Problem 2. What is the net single premium if the first payment of the life annuity is made at age 45?

11. Refer to Problem 5. If that person buys a 10-year temporary life annuity due, what is the size of the annual payment?

12. Refer to Problem 6. If the first of the 18 annual payments is due at age 20, find the size of the annual payment.

★13. Find the net single premium for a 20-year temporary life annuity of $500 per year for a person aged 28 if the first payment is due at age 40.

★14. What is the net single premium for a 15-year temporary life annuity of $2,000 per year for a person now aged 32 if the first payment is to be made at age 50.

★**15.** Refer to Problem 5. If a 10-year temporary life annuity is bought with the first payment to be made to the individual at age 50, what is the size of the annual payment?

★**16.** A person aged 20 paid $1,500 to buy a 12-year temporary life annuity with the first payment to be made to him at age 36. What will be the size of each annual payment?

## 19.6 SUMMARY OF LIFE ANNUITY FORMULAS

*Symbols:*      $a$ = net single premium (present value) of a life annuity of $1 per year
$A$ = net single premium (present value) of a life annuity of $R$ per year
$x$ = age of the annuitant on the purchase date
$D_x = v^x l_x$
$N_x = D_x + D_{x+1} + D_{x+2} + \cdots \cdots \cdots \cdots + D_{99}$

$D_x$ and $N_x$ are commutation symbols. Values of the two symbols at the interest rate $2\frac{1}{2}\%$ are tabulated in Table 15. Logarithms of the values of $D_x$ and $N_x$ are tabulated in Table 16 (computed from Table 15).

| Application | Formula | Formula Number | Reference Page |
|---|---|---|---|
| Pure Endowment | $_nE_x = \dfrac{D_{x+n}}{D_x}$ | (19–1) | 536 |

$n$ = number of years from purchase date to payment date
$E$ = net single premium of a $1 pure endowment contract

*Whole Life Annuities*

| | | | |
|---|---|---|---|
| Ordinary (Immediate)— First Payment at Age $x + 1$: | $a_x = \dfrac{N_{x+1}}{D_x}$ | (19–2) | 540 |
| | $A = Ra_x = R \cdot \dfrac{N_{x+1}}{D_x}$ | (19–3) | 541 |
| Due—First Payment at Age $x$: | $\ddot{a}_x = 1 + a_x$, or $\ddot{a}_x = \dfrac{N_x}{D_x}$ | (19–4) | 543 |
| | $A(\text{due}) = R\ddot{a}_x = R \cdot \dfrac{N_x}{D_x}$ | (19–5) | 543 |
| Deferred—First Payment at Age $x + k$ ($k$ = Number of Years of Deferment) | $_k\vert\ddot{a}_x = \dfrac{N_{x+k}}{D_x}$ | (19–6) | 545 |
| | $A(\text{defer.}) = R \cdot {_k\vert\ddot{a}_x} = R \cdot \dfrac{N_{x+k}}{D_x}$ | (19–7) | 545 |

In general, for whole life annuities:

$$\frac{\text{Net single premium (present value)}}{\text{of an annuity of \$1 per year}} = \frac{N_{\text{age on first payment date}}}{D_{\text{age on purchase date}}}$$

| Application | Formula | Formula Number | Reference Page |
|---|---|---|---|

*Temporary Life Annuities*

$$n = \text{number of payments}$$

Ordinary (Immediate)— First Payment at Age $x+1$, for $n$ Payments, and Last Payment at Age $x+n$:

$$a_{x:\overline{n}|} = \frac{N_{x+1} - N_{x+n+1}}{D_x} \qquad (19\text{--}8) \qquad 547$$

$$A(\text{tem.}) = Ra_{x:\overline{n}|}$$

$$= R \cdot \frac{N_{x+1} - N_{x+n+1}}{D_x} \qquad (19\text{--}9) \qquad 548$$

Due—First Payment at Age $x$, for $n$ Payments, Last Payment at Age $x+n-1$:

$$\ddot{a}_{x:\overline{n}|} = 1 + a_{x:\overline{n-1}|}, \text{ or}$$

$$\ddot{a}_{x:\overline{n}|} = \frac{N_x - N_{x+n}}{D_x} \qquad (19\text{--}10) \qquad 549$$

$$A(\text{tem. due}) = R\ddot{a}_{x:\overline{n}|}$$

$$= R \cdot \frac{N_x - N_{x+n}}{D_x} \qquad (19\text{--}11) \qquad 549$$

Deferred—First Payment at Age $x+k$, Last Payment at Age $x+k+n-1$, for a Total of $n$ Payments:

$$_k|\ddot{a}_{x:\overline{n}|} = \frac{N_{x+k} - N_{x+k+n}}{D_x} \qquad (19\text{--}12) \qquad 550$$

$$A(\text{tem. defer.}) = R \cdot \frac{N_{x+k} - N_{x+k+n}}{D_x} \qquad (19\text{--}13) \qquad 550$$

In general, for temporary life annuities:

$$\text{Net single premium (present value)} \atop \text{of an annuity of \$1 per year} = \frac{N_{\text{age on first payment date}} - N_{\text{age on first payment date}} + \text{number of payments}}{D_{\text{age on purchase date}}}$$

## EXERCISE 19–6

### Review of Chapter 19

1. Define: (a) $l_7$, (b) $l_{54}$, (c) $d_{29}$, (d) $d_{62}$, (e) $q_{35}$, (f) $q_{46}$.
2. Define: (a) $l_{12}$, (b) $l_9$, (c) $d_{40}$, (d) $d_{53}$, (e) $q_{28}$, (f) $q_{25}$.
3. Find the net single premium of a \$2,500 pure endowment contract payable in 16 years to a person now aged 20.
4. What is the net single premium of a \$4,000 pure endowment contract payable in 24 years to a person now aged 43?
5. A life insurance company collected \$500 for a 20-year pure endowment contract from a person aged 26. How much will that person receive at age 46 if then alive?
6. A person aged 36 pays \$200 for a 15-year pure endowment contract. How much will that person receive from the insurance company if alive at the end of the 15-year period?

7. A person aged 24 wishes to buy a whole life annuity of $3,000 per year. What is the net single premium if the first payment of the annuity is made at (a) age 24, and (b) age 25?

8. A whole life annuity of $1,000 per year is bought by a person aged 38. What is the net single premium if the first payment of the annuity is made at (a) age 39? and (b) age 38?

★9. Refer to Problem 7. What is the net single premium if the first payment of the annuity is made at age 30?

★10. Refer to Problem 8. Find the net single premium if the first payment of the annuity is made at age 50.

11. A person aged 20 paid $10,000 to a life insurance company for a whole life annuity. What is the size of each annual payment if that person receives the first payment at (a) age 20, and (b) age 21?

12. A person aged 31 owes a life insurance company $1,000. The company allows the debt to be paid by annual payments payable for life. What is the size of the annual payment if the first payment is due at (a) age 32, and (b) age 31?

★13. Refer to Problem 11. What is the size of the annual payment if the first payment is made at age 33?

★14. Refer to Problem 12. Find the size of the annual payment if the first payment is due at age 40.

15. A person aged 29 wishes to buy a 12-year temporary life annuity of $1,000 per year. What is the net single premium if the first payment is made to that person at (a) age 30, and (b) age 29?

16. What is the net single premium of a 24-year life annuity of $600 per year for a person aged 46 if the first payment is made at (a) age 46, and (b) age 47?

★17. Refer to Problem 15. Find the net single premium if the first payment is made at age 37.

★18. Refer to Problem 16. What is the net single premium if the first payment is made at age 58?

19. A person aged 28 paid $4,000 to a life insurance company for a 10-year temporary life annuity. What is the size of each annual payment if the first payment is made at (a) age 28, and (b) age 29?

20. The purchase price of a life insurance policy issued to a person aged 40 is $700. The company allows the premium to be paid by 15 annual payments or by an annual payment for life, whichever period is shorter. What is the size of the annual payment if the first payment is due at (a) age 41, and (b) age 40?

★21. Refer to Problem 19. What is the size of the annual payment if the first payment is made at age 35?

★22. Refer to Problem 20. Find the size of the annual payment if the first payment is due at age 48.

## Chapter 20

# Life Insurance

## 20.1 BASIC TYPES OF LIFE INSURANCE

Life insurance companies have made available many types of life insurance contracts (policies) to meet individual needs. However, there are only three basic types of life insurance contracts: (1) whole life insurance, (2) term insurance, and (3) endowment insurance. Every life insurance contract is one of these three kinds or is a combination of them. The protection offered by any type of life insurance contract may also be deferred to a future date. Thus, in addition to the three basic types of insurance, a discussion of deferred life insurance is included in this chapter.

## 20.2 WHOLE LIFE INSURANCE

A *whole life insurance* contract provides that the insurance company will pay the face value of the policy to the beneficiary upon the death of the insured, regardless of when the death occurs. The premium for a whole life insurance policy, or simply called a whole life policy, may be paid by a single amount or in periodic payments. When a premium is payable periodically, there are two plans under which the premium may be paid. Under the *straight life* plan, premiums are payable until death, while under the *limited payment life* plan, premiums are payable for a specified number of years. *Net premiums are computed at a nominal interest rate of $2\frac{1}{2}\%$ in all of the life insurance problems in this chapter.*

# A. Finding the Net Single Premium

The following example is used to illustrate the method of finding the net single premium for a whole life policy.

**Example 1**   A $1,000 whole life policy is issued to a man aged 40. Find the net single premium.

First, find the net single premium for a $1 whole life policy. The cost of the $1 policy and its present value (at age 40) are diagrammed numerically and symbolically as shown below:

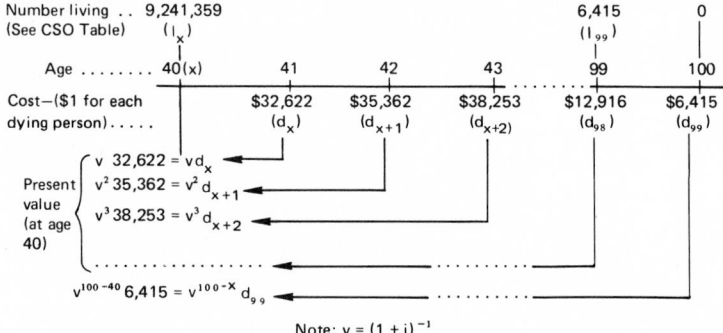

Note: v = (1 + i)⁻¹

The cost each year depends on the number of persons who die that year. According to the 1958 CSO table, 32,622 persons will die between ages 40 and 41. For simplicity in this chapter, *the cost is computed with the assumption that all death benefits are paid at the end of the year of death.* Therefore, $32,622 is required for the death benefits one year after the policies are issued (at the end of age 40 or the beginning of age 41).

The present value of the total cost is distributed among the people who are living at age 40. The cost of each policy, or the net single premium to each person at age 40, is denoted by $A_{40}$ and is computed as follows:

$$A_{40} = \frac{v(32{,}622) + v^2(35{,}362) + v^3(38{,}253) + \cdots\cdots + v^{100-40}(6{,}415)}{9{,}241{,}359}$$

The expression above may be calculated by using Table 6 (where $v^n = (1 + i)^{-n}$). However, the calculation is quite laborious, but can be simplified by using the following formula and the commutation columns in Table 15.

Let $A_x$ = the net single premium (or present value) of a $1 whole life insurance policy, issued at age $x$.

**Note:**   The symbol $A$ has a subscript, such as $A_x$, when it is used to represent the net single premium of a $1 life insurance policy. When the symbol $A$ has no subscript, it represents the net single premium of a life annuity of $R$ per payment, such as $A$ and $A$(due). (See Chapter 19).

Then, the following formula can be obtained by a method similar to that followed in the above illustration:

$$A_x = \frac{M_x}{D_x}$$
         **(20–1)** [1]

The values of $M_x$ and $D_x$ are listed in Table 15 (at a $2\frac{1}{2}\%$ interest rate).

The value of $A_{40}$ may be computed by using the above formula as follows:

$$A_{40} = \frac{M_{40}}{D_{40}} = \frac{1,607,743.17}{3,441,765.06} = .467128$$

For a \$1,000 whole life policy, the net single premium is

$.467128 \times 1,000 = \$467.13$

**Note:**    The division $M_{40}/D_{40}$ may also be performed by using logarithms:

$$
\begin{array}{lll}
\log M_{40} = 6.206\,2167 & = 16.206\,2167 - 10 & \\
(-) \log D_{40} & = \phantom{1}6.536\,7812 & \text{(Table 16)} \\
\hline
\log A_{40} & = \phantom{1}9.669\,4355 - 10 &
\end{array}
$$

Find the antilog by interpolation from Table 2.

$A_{40} = .4671274.$

# B. Finding the Net Annual Premium

## STRAIGHT LIFE (ALSO CALLED ORDINARY LIFE)

Under the straight life plan, premiums are payable periodically until death.

Let $P_x =$ the net annual premium which is payable to the insurance company for a \$1 policy each year for life, beginning at age $x$.

---

[1] *Proof—Formula (20–1)*

The value of $A_x$ is obtained as follows: (See the diagram in Example 1.)

$$A_x = \frac{vd_x + v^2 d_{x+1} + v^3 d_{x+2} + \cdots\cdots\cdots\cdots + v^{100-x} d_{99}}{l_x}$$

Multiply both the numerator and the denominator by $v^x$. Then,

$$A_x = \frac{v^{x+1} d_x + v^{x+2} d_{x+1} + v^{x+3} d_{x+2} + \cdots\cdots\cdots\cdots + v^{100} d_{99}}{v^x l_x}.$$

Let the commutation symbol $C_x = v^{x+1} d_x$. The above equation may be written

$$A_x = \frac{C_x + C_{x+1} + C_{x+2} + \cdots\cdots\cdots\cdots\cdots + C_{99}}{D_x}$$

Let the commutation symbol $M_x = C_x + C_{x+1} + C_{x+2} + \cdots\cdots\cdots\cdots + C_{99}$

The above equation may be further simplified as follows: $A_x = \dfrac{M_x}{D_x}$        (20–1)

The following formula can be obtained:

$$P_x = \frac{M_x}{N_x} \qquad\qquad\qquad \textbf{(20–2)} \, ^2$$

**Example 2**   Refer to Example 1. If the man wishes to pay the net premium annually, with the first annual premium payable at the date of purchase (at age 40), what should be the size of the net annual premium?

$x = 40$. Substituting the $x$ value in formula (20–2) as follows:

$$P_{40} = \frac{M_{40}}{N_{40}} = \frac{1,607,743.17}{75,194,899.17} = \$.021381$$

The annual premium for a $1,000 policy is

.021381 × 1,000 = $21.381, or $21.38

## LIMITED PAYMENT LIFE

Under the limited payment life plan, premiums are payable periodically for a specified number of years. A whole life policy with a limited number of payments provides protection during the lifetime of the insured, but the premiums are payable for only a specified number of years. Some examples are the 20-payment life, 30-payment life, and life paid up at age 65.

Let $_nP_x$ = the net annual premium, beginning at age $x$, for an $n$ payment life policy of $1.

The following formula can be obtained:

$$_nP_x = \frac{M_x}{N_x - N_{x+n}} \qquad\qquad\qquad \textbf{(20–3)} \, ^3$$

---

[2] *Proof—Formula (20–2)*

The insurance company collects only the annual premiums from the insured who is living. Thus, the annual premiums $(P_x)$ form a *whole life annuity due*. The present value of the annual premiums can be obtained by using formula (19–5),

$A(\text{due}) = R\ddot{a}_x$, or
$A(\text{due}) = P_x\ddot{a}_x$

The present value must be equal to the net single premium $A_x$, or $A(\text{due}) = A_x$. Substituting the value in the above equation. Then,

$$A_x = P_x\ddot{a}_x, \; P_x = A_x \div \ddot{a}_x = \frac{M_x}{D_x} \div \frac{N_x}{D_x} = \frac{M_x}{D_x} \cdot \frac{D_x}{N_x} = \frac{M_x}{N_x}, \text{ or } P_x = \frac{M_x}{N_x} \qquad (20\text{–}2)$$

**Note:**    This is identical to the type of problem of finding the unknown annual payment when the present value of a whole life annuity due is known. (See Example 5, pages 543 and 544.)

[3] *Proof—Formula (20–3)*

The $n$ annual premiums $(_nP_x)$ form a *temporary life annuity due*. The present value of the annual premiums can be obtained by using formula (19–11).

**Example 3**     A $1,000 whole life policy is issued to a man aged 25. Find the: (a) net single premium, (b) net annual premium if the policy is a straight life policy, and (c) net annual premium if the policy is a 20-payment life policy.

(a) $x = 25$

Substituting the value in formula (20–1):

$$A_{25} = \frac{M_{25}}{D_{25}} = \frac{1,754,288.51}{5,165,007.95} = \$.339649$$

The net single premium for a $1,000 policy is

.339649 × 1,000 = $339.649, or $339.65

(b) $x = 25$

Substituting the value in formula (20–2):

$$P_{25} = \frac{M_{25}}{N_{25}} = \frac{1,754,288.51}{139,839,496.91} = \$.0125450145$$

The net annual premium for the $1,000 policy is

.012545 × 1,000 = $12.545, or $12.55

(c) $n = 20$, $x = 25$

Substituting these values in formula (20–3):

$$_{20}P_{25} = \frac{M_{25}}{N_{25} - N_{25+20}} = \frac{M_{25}}{N_{25} - N_{45}}$$

$$= \frac{1,754,288.51}{139,839,496.91 - 58,927,803.08} = \$.02168152$$

---

[3] *Proof (continued)*

$A(\text{tem. due}) = R\ddot{a}_{x:\overline{n}|}$, or
$A(\text{tem. due}) = {_nP_x} \cdot \ddot{a}_{x:\overline{n}|}$

The present value must be equal to the net single premium $A_x$, or $A(\text{tem. due}) = A_x$. Substituting the value in the above equation, then, $A_x = {_nP_x}\ddot{a}_{x:\overline{n}|}$.

Since

$$A_x = \frac{M_x}{D_x} \text{ and } \ddot{a}_{x:\overline{n}|} = \frac{N_x - N_{x+n}}{D_x}$$

then

$$\frac{M_x}{D_x} = {_nP_x} \cdot \frac{N_x - N_{x+n}}{D_x}$$

Solve for ${_nP_x}$:

$$_nP_x = \frac{M_x}{D_x} \cdot \frac{D_x}{N_x - N_{x+n}}$$

$$_nP_x = \frac{M_x}{N_x - N_{x+n}} \tag{20–3}$$

The net annual premium for the $1,000 policy for 20 payments is
.02168 × 1,000 = $21.68 (Also see Example 3, Section 19.5.)

**Note:**   *In order to simplify mathematical operations, round the decimals of the
values in the commutation columns (Table 15) when computing the
problems in the exercises in this chapter.* Examples:

$C_{20} = 10,300.1828$, rounded to 10,300
$M_{25} = 1,754,288.5116$, rounded to 1,754,289

# EXERCISE 20–1

## Reference: Section 20.2

**A.** *For each of the following whole life policies, find (a) the net single premium,
and (b) the net annual premium:*

| | Face Value of Policy | Age of Insured on Purchase Date | Payment Plan |
|---|---|---|---|
| 1. | $2,000 | 26 | straight life |
| 2. | 2,000 | 28 | 5-payment life |
| 3. | 2,000 | 34 | 10-payment life |
| 4. | 2,000 | 42 | straight life |
| 5. | 1,000 | 50 | straight life |
| 6. | 1,000 | 55 | 15-payment life |
| 7. | 1,000 | 65 | 20-payment life |
| 8. | 1,000 | 75 | straight life |

**B.** *Statement Problems:*

**9.** Find the net single premium of a whole life policy of $1,000 issued to
someone aged (a) 10, (b) 30, (c) 60, and (d) 85.

**10.** Find the net single premium of a whole life policy of $1,000 issued to
someone aged (a) 4, (b) 24, (c) 44, and (d) 64.

**11.** A $1,000, whole life policy is issued to a person aged 35. Find the net
single premium.

**12.** What is the net single premium of a $2,000 whole life policy issued to a
person aged 45?

**13.** Refer to Problem 11. If the policy is a straight life policy, what is the net
annual premium?

**14.** Refer to Problem 12. Find the net annual premium if the policy is a straight
life policy.

**15.** Refer to Problem 11. If the policy is a 15-payment life policy, what is the
net annual premium?

**16.** Refer to Problem 12. Find the net annual premium if the policy is a 10-
payment life policy.

## 20.3 TERM INSURANCE

A *term insurance* policy provides that the insurance company will pay the face value of the policy to the beneficiary upon the death of the insured, if the insured dies during the term covered in the policy. The insurance company has no obligation for payment if the insured outlives the term. For example, if a five-year term policy is issued to someone aged 20, the insurance company is liable for payment of the policy if the insured dies within the five-year period, from the date of issuance until age 25.

## A. Finding the Net Single Premium

Let $n$ = the term in years, and
$A^1_{x:\overline{n}|}$ = the net single premium for a $1, $n$ year term policy issued to a person aged $x$.

The following formula can then be obtained:

$$A^1_{x:\overline{n}|} = \frac{M_x - M_{x+n}}{D_x} \qquad\qquad \textbf{(20–4)} \, [4]$$

---

[4] *Proof—Formula (20–4)*

The cost of a $1, $n$ year term policy and its net single premium (present value at age $x$) are diagrammed and derived as follows:

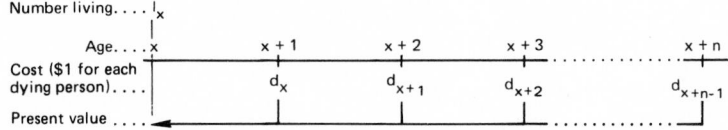

The present value of the cost at age $x$ is divided by the number of persons living at age $x$ as follows:

$$A^1_{x:\overline{n}|} = \frac{vd_x + v^2 d_{x+1} + v^3 d_{x+2} + \cdots\cdots\cdots\cdots\cdots\cdots + v^n d_{x+n-1}}{l_x}$$

Multiply both the numerator and the denominator by $v^x$, and substitute the commutation symbols. Then

$$A^1_{x:\overline{n}|} = \frac{C_x + C_{x+1} + C_{x+2} + \cdots\cdots\cdots\cdots\cdots\cdots + C_{x+n-1}}{D_x}$$

Since $\qquad M_x = C_x + C_{x+1} + C_{x+2} + \cdots\cdots\cdots C_{x+n-1} + C_{x+n} + \cdots\cdots C_{99},$
and $\qquad M_{x+n} = \qquad\qquad\qquad\qquad\qquad\qquad\qquad\qquad C_{x+n} + \cdots\cdots C_{99},$

the difference between $M_x$ and $M_{x+n}$ equals the numerator in the above equation. Thus, the equation may be written in the following manner:

$$A^1_{x:\overline{n}|} = \frac{M_x - M_{x+n}}{D_x} \qquad\qquad (20\text{–}4)$$

# B. Finding the Net Annual Premium

Let $P^1_{x:\overline{n}|} =$ the net annual premium for an $n$ year term policy of \$1 issued at age $x$.

The following formula can be obtained:

$$P^1_{x:\overline{n}|} = \frac{M_x - M_{x+n}}{N_x - N_{x+n}}$$ (20–5) [5]

In formula (20–5), the assumption is made that the number of years in the term of the policy is the same as the number of the annual premium payments. If the term $(n)$ is larger than the number of payments $(y)$, the letter $y$ should replace the letter $n$ in the denominator of the fraction: or

$$_yP^1_{x:\overline{n}|} = \frac{M_x - M_{x+n}}{N_x - N_{x+y}}$$ (20–6) [6]

**Example 1** A \$1,000, five-year term policy is issued to a man aged 20. Find (a) the net single premium, and (b) the net annual premium.

$x = 20,\ n = 5,\ x + n = 25$

(a) Substituting the values in formula (20–4):

---

[5] *Proof—Formula (20–5)*

The $n$ annual premiums ($P^1_{x:\overline{n}|}$) form a temporary life annuity due. The present value of the annual premiums can be obtained by using formula (19–11),

$A(\text{tem. due}) = R\ddot{a}_{x:\overline{n}|}$, or

$A(\text{tem. due}) = P^1_{x:\overline{n}|}\ddot{a}_{x:\overline{n}|} = P^1_{x:\overline{n}|} \cdot \dfrac{N_x - N_{x+n}}{D_x}$ (See Section 19.5 B.)

The present value must be equal to the net single premium $A^1_{x:\overline{n}|}$, or

$A(\text{tem. due}) = A^1_{x:\overline{n}|} = \dfrac{M_x - M_{x+n}}{D_x}$.

Substituting the value in the above equation:

$$P^1_{x:\overline{n}|} \cdot \frac{N_x - N_{x+n}}{D_x} = \frac{M_x - M_{x+n}}{D_x}$$

$$P^1_{x:\overline{n}|} = \frac{M_x - M_{x+n}}{N_x - N_{x+n}}$$ (20–5)

[6] *Proof—Formula (20–6)*

Here the $y$ annual premiums ($_yP^1_{x:\overline{n}|}$) form a temporary life annuity due. Thus,

$$A(\text{tem. due}) = {_yP^1_{x:\overline{n}|}} \cdot \frac{N_x - N_{x+y}}{D_x} = \frac{M_x - M_{x+n}}{D_x}$$

$$_yP^1_{x:\overline{n}|} = \frac{M_x - M_{x+n}}{N_x - N_{x+y}}$$ (20–6)

The net single premium $= 1,000 A^1_{x:\overline{n}|} = 1,000 \cdot \dfrac{M_{20} - M_{25}}{D_{20}}$

$$= 1,000 \cdot \frac{1,804,922.42 - 1,754,288.51}{5,898,264.97}$$

$$= 1,000 \cdot \frac{50,633.91}{5,898,264.97} = 1,000(.0085845)$$

$$= \$8.5845, \text{ or } \$8.58$$

(b) Since the number of annual premium payments is not indicated in the problem, the number of years in the term of the policy is assumed to be the same as the number of payments.

Substituting the $x$ and $n$ values in formula (20–5):

The net annual premium $= 1,000 P^1_{x:\overline{n}|} = 1,000 \cdot \dfrac{M_{20} - M_{25}}{N_{20} - N_{25}}$

$$= 1,000 \cdot \frac{1,804,922.42 - 1,754,288.51}{167,827,045.88 - 139,839,496.91}$$

$$= 1,000 \cdot \frac{50,633.91}{27,987,548.97}$$

$$= 1,000(.0018091584)$$
$$= \$1.8091584, \text{ or } \$1.81$$

**Example 2** Refer to Example 1. Assume that the net premium is payable in three equal annual payments. Find the net annual premium.

$x = 20$, $n = 5$ (years, the term of the policy), $y = 3$ (annual payments), $x + n = 25$, and $x + y = 23$

Substituting the values in formula (20–6):

The net annual premium $= 1,000 {}_y P^1_{x:\overline{n}|} = 1,000 \cdot \dfrac{M_{20} - M_{25}}{N_{20} - N_{23}}$

$$= 1,000 \cdot \frac{50,633.91}{167,827,045.88 - 150,590,926.74}$$

$$= 1,000(.002937663)$$
$$= \$2.94$$

# EXERCISE 20–2

## Reference: Section 20.3

**A.** *For each of the following term insurance policies, find (a) the net single premium, and (b) the net annual premium:*

| Face Value of Policy | Age of Insured on Purchase Date | Term of Policy | Payment Plan |
|---|---|---|---|
| **1.** $1,000 | 30 | 5 years | 5 payments |
| **2.** 1,000 | 25 | 10 years | 10 payments |

| Face Value of Policy | Age of Insured on Purchase Date | Term of Policy | Payment Plan |
|---|---|---|---|
| 3. $2,000 | 35 | 15 years | 15 payments |
| 4. 2,000 | 40 | 20 years | 20 payments |
| 5. 3,000 | 26 | 12 years | 12 payments |
| 6. 3,000 | 38 | 16 years | 16 payments |
| 7. 4,000 | 45 | 10 years | 6 payments |
| 8. 4,000 | 22 | 18 years | 10 payments |

**B.** *Statement Problems:*

9. Find the net single premium and the net annual premium for a 10-year, $5,000 term policy issued to someone aged (a) 18, (b) 28, and (c) 50.
10. Find the net single premium and the net annual premium for a 20-year, $10,000 term policy issued to someone aged (a) 16, (b) 36, and (c) 56.
11. A $1,000, 25-year term policy is issued to a person aged 24. Find (a) the net single premium, and (b) the net annual premium.
12. A $2,000, 30-year term policy is issued to a person aged 32. Find (a) the net single premium, and (b) the net annual premium.
13. Refer to Problem 11. If the policy specifies that the net premium is payable in 20 equal annual payments, find the size of the net annual premium.
14. Refer to Problem 12. If the policy specifies that the net premium is payable in 15 equal annual payments, what is the size of the net annual premium?

## 20.4 ENDOWMENT INSURANCE

An *endowment insurance* policy combines the features of a pure endowment and a term insurance policy. The provisions of the combination are that (a) if the insured is living at the end of the term of the policy, the face value of the policy will be payable to the policyholder; and (b) if the insured dies during the term of the policy, the face value of the policy will be payable to the designated beneficiary. Thus, an *n* year endowment insurance policy may be treated as a combined policy consisting of an *n* year pure endowment and an *n* year term insurance policy.

## A. Finding the Net Single Premium

Let $A_{x:\overline{n}|}$ = the net single premium of an *n* year endowment insurance policy of $1, issued at age *x*.

Then, the value of $A_{x:\overline{n}|}$ is the sum of the net single premium of a $1, *n* year pure endowment policy and the net single premium of a $1, *n* year term insurance policy, which may be written as follows:

$$A_{x:\overline{n}|} = {}_n E_x + A^1_{x:\overline{n}|} = \frac{D_{x+n}}{D_x} + \frac{M_x - M_{x+n}}{D_x}, \text{ or}$$

$$A_{x:\overline{n}|} = \frac{M_x - M_{x+n} + D_{x+n}}{D_x} \qquad (20\text{-}7)$$

## B. Finding the Net Annual Premium

Let $P_{x:\overline{n}|}$ = the net annual premium of an $n$ year endowment insurance policy of \$1, issued at age $x$.

Then, the following formula may be obtained:

$$P_{x:\overline{n}|} = \frac{M_x - M_{x+n} + D_{x+n}}{N_x - N_{x+n}} \qquad (20\text{-}8)\ ^{[7]}$$

In formula (20–8), the assumption is made that the number of years in the term of the policy is the same as the number of the annual premium payments. If the term *(n)* is larger than the number of payments *(y)*, the letter *y* should replace the letter *n* in the denominator of the fraction, or

$$_yP_{x:\overline{n}|} = \frac{M_x - M_{x+n} + D_{x+n}}{N_x - N_{x+y}} \qquad (20\text{-}9)\ ^{[8]}$$

**Example 1** $\quad$ A \$1,000, 20-year endowment insurance policy was bought by someone aged 40. Find (a) the net single premium, and (b) the net annual premium.

$$x = 40,\ n = 20,\ x + n = 60$$

---

[7] *Proof—Formula (20–8)*

The $n$ annual premiums ($P_{x:\overline{n}|}$) form a temporary life annuity due. The present value of the annual premiums can be obtained by using formula (19–11),

$$A(\text{tem. due}) = R\ddot{a}_{x:\overline{n}|},\ \text{or}$$

$$A(\text{tem. due}) = P_{x:\overline{n}|} \cdot \ddot{a}_{x:\overline{n}|} = P_{x:\overline{n}|} \cdot \frac{N_x - N_{x+n}}{D_x}$$

The present value must be equal to the net single premium $A_{x:\overline{n}|}$, or

$$A(\text{tem. due}) = A_{x:\overline{n}|} = \frac{M_x - M_{x+n} + D_{x+n}}{D_x}\ (\text{See Formula } (20\text{-}7))$$

Thus,

$$P_{x:\overline{n}|} \cdot \frac{N_x - N_{x+n}}{D_x} = \frac{M_x - M_{x+n} + D_{x+n}}{D_x}$$

$$P_{x:\overline{n}|} = \frac{M_x - M_{x+n} + D_{x+n}}{N_x - N_{x+n}} \qquad (20\text{-}8)$$

[8] *Proof—Formula (20–9)*

Here, the $y$ annual premiums ($_yP_{x:\overline{n}|}$) form a temporary life annuity due. Thus,

$$A(\text{tem. due}) = {}_yP_{x:\overline{n}|} \cdot \frac{N_x - N_{x+y}}{D_x} = \frac{M_x - M_{x+n} + D_{x+n}}{D_x}$$

$$_yP_{x:\overline{n}|} = \frac{M_x - M_{x+n} + D_{x+n}}{N_x - N_{x+y}} \qquad (20\text{-}9)$$

(a) The net single premium is computed by using formula (20–7) as follows:

$$A_{x:\overline{n}|} = A_{40:\overline{20}|} = \frac{M_{40} - M_{60} + D_{60}}{D_{40}}$$

$$= \frac{1,607,743.17 - 1,187,445.15 + 1,749,787.72}{3,441,765.06}$$

$$= \frac{2,170,085.74}{3,441,765.06} = \$.630515$$

The net single premium of the 20-year endowment insurance of $1,000 is

$.630515 \times 1,000 = \$630.515$, or $630.52

(b) Since the number of annual premium payments is not indicated in the problem, the number of years in the term of the policy is assumed to be the same as the number of payments.

Substituting the $x$ and $n$ values in formula (20–8):

$$\text{Net annual premium} = 1,000\, P_{40:\overline{20}|} = 1,000 \cdot \frac{M_{40} - M_{60} + D_{60}}{N_{40} - N_{60}}$$

$$= 1,000 \cdot \frac{2,170,085.74}{75,194,899.17 - 23,056,044.97}$$

$$= 1,000(.04162) = \$41.62$$

**Example 2**     Refer to Example 1. Assume that the net single premium is payable in 15 equal annual payments. Find the size of the annual premium payment.

$x = 40$, $n = 20$, $y = 15$, $x + n = 60$, and $x + y = 55$

Substituting the values in formula (20–9):

$$\text{Net annual premium} = 1,000\,_{15}P_{40:\overline{20}|} = 1,000 \cdot \frac{M_{40} - M_{60} + D_{60}}{N_{40} - N_{55}}$$

$$= \frac{1,000(2,170,085.74)}{75,194,899.17 - 32,978,578.86} = \$51.40$$

# EXERCISE 20–3

## Reference: Section 20.4

**A.** *For each of the following endowment insurance policies, find (a) the net single premium, and (b) the net annual premium:*

| Face Value of Policy | Age of Insured on Purchase Date | Term of Policy | Payment Plan |
|---|---|---|---|
| **1.** $1,000 | 30 | 5 years | 5 payments |
| **2.** 1,000 | 25 | 10 years | 10 payments |

| Face Value of Policy | Age of Insured on Purchase Date | Term of Policy | Payment Plan |
|---|---|---|---|
| 3. $2,000 | 35 | 15 years | 15 payments |
| 4. 2,000 | 45 | 20 years | 20 payments |
| 5. 3,000 | 22 | 25 years | 25 payments |
| 6. 3,000 | 32 | 18 years | 18 payments |
| 7. 4,000 | 50 | 20 years | 15 payments |
| 8. 5,000 | 20 | 10 years | 8 payments |

**B.** *Statement Problems:*

9. A $1,000, 30-year endowment insurance policy was purchased by someone aged 28. Find (a) the net single premium, and (b) the net annual premium.

10. A $1,500, 45-year endowment insurance policy was bought by someone aged 20. Find (a) the net single premium, and (b) the net annual premium.

11. Refer to Problem 9. If the policy were purchased by a person aged 35, what would be the answers to (a) and (b)?

12. Refer to Problem 10. If the policy were purchased by a person aged 25, what would be the answers to (a) and (b)?

13. Refer to Problem 9. Assuming that the net single premium is payable in 25 equal annual payments, what is the size of the net annual premium?

14. Refer to Problem 10. What should be the size of the net annual premium if the premium of the policy were payable in 30 equal annual payments?

# ★20.5 DEFERRED LIFE INSURANCE

Life insurance may be deferred for a specified period of time. When the insurance is deferred for $k$ years, the insurance protection does not begin at the time the policy is issued, but only after $k$ years have passed. Thus, a 10-year deferred whole life insurance policy issued to someone aged 20 does not provide insurance protection until the age of 30. However, insurance premiums are paid beginning at the age of 20, or on the purchase date. An insurance company seldom sells a deferred insurance policy. More often, the company sells a combined insurance policy which includes a deferred provision.

The net single premium for a insurance policy may be derived by the same reasoning as in the preceding sections. However, the following methods involve less computation.

## A. Deferred Whole Life Insurance

Let $_k|A_x =$ The net single premium for a whole life insurance policy of $1 deferred $k$ years issued at age $x$.

Then, the value of $_k|A_x$ *equals* the net single premium for a $1 whole life insurance policy *minus* the net single premium for a $1, $k$ year term insurance policy.

Thus,

$$_k|A_x = A_x - A^1_{x:\overline{k}|} = \frac{M_x}{D_x} - \frac{M_x - M_{x+k}}{D_x}, \text{ or}$$

$$_k|A_x = \frac{M_{x+k}}{D_x} \tag{20-10}$$

# B. Deferred Term Insurance

Let $_k|A^1_{x:\overline{n}|}$ = The net single premium for an $n$ year term insurance policy of \$1 deferred $k$ years issued at age $x$.

Then, the value of $_k|A^1_{x:\overline{n}|}$ *equals* the net single premium for a \$1, $k + n$ term insurance policy *minus* the net single premium for a \$1, $k$ year term insurance policy. Thus,

$$_k|A^1_{x:\overline{n}|} = A^1_{x:\overline{k+n}|} - A^1_{x:\overline{k}|}$$

$$= \frac{M_x - M_{x+k+n}}{D_x} - \frac{M_x - M_{x+k}}{D_x}, \text{ or}$$

$$_k|A^1_{x:\overline{n}|} = \frac{M_{x+k} - M_{x+k+n}}{D_x} \tag{20-11}$$

# C. Deferred Endowment Insurance

Let $_k|A_{x:\overline{n}|}$ = The net single premium for an $n$ year endowment insurance policy of \$1 deferred $k$ years issued at age $x$.

Then, the value of $_k|A_{x:\overline{n}|}$ *equals* the net single premium for a $k + n$ year pure endowment policy of \$1 *plus* the net single premium for an $n$ year term insurance policy of \$1 deferred $k$ years. Thus,

$$_k|A_{x:\overline{n}|} = _{k+n}E_x + _k|A^1_{x:\overline{n}|} = \frac{D_{x+k+n}}{D_x} + \frac{M_{x+k} - M_{x+k+n}}{D_x}, \text{ or}$$

$$_k|A_{x:\overline{n}|} = \frac{M_{x+k} - M_{x+k+n} + D_{x+k+n}}{D_x} \tag{20-12}$$

**Example 1**   A policy issued to someone aged 20 provides the following: (a) \$1,000, if the insured dies in 30 years, (b) \$3,000, if the insured dies after 30 years. Find the net annual premium for life.

The policy actually combines two types of insurance: (a) 30-year term insurance of \$1,000, and (b) whole life insurance of \$3,000 deferred for 30 years.

The net single premium for type (a) is $1,000A^1_{20:\overline{30}|}$. (Formula (20–4) )
The net single premium for type (b) is $3,000 \cdot _{30}|A_{20}$. (Formula (20–10) )

Let $P =$ the annual premium of the policy payable for life.

The annual premiums $(P)$ form a whole life annuity due. The present value of the annuity is $P\ddot{a}_x$ or $P\ddot{a}_{20}$. (Formula (19–5))

The present value of the annuity must be equal to the two net single premiums, or

$$P\ddot{a}_{20} = 1{,}000 A^{1}_{20\,:\,\overline{30|}} + 3{,}000 \cdot {}_{30|}A_{20}$$

$$P \cdot \frac{N_{20}}{D_{20}} = 1{,}000 \cdot \frac{M_{20} - M_{20+30}}{D_{20}} + 3{,}000 \cdot \frac{M_{20+30}}{D_{20}}$$

$$P = \frac{D_{20}}{N_{20}} \cdot \frac{1{,}000(M_{20} - M_{50}) + 3{,}000 M_{50}}{D_{20}} = \frac{1{,}000 M_{20} + 2{,}000 M_{50}}{N_{20}}$$

$$= \frac{1{,}000(1{,}804{,}922.42) + 2{,}000(1{,}454{,}100.51)}{167{,}827{,}045.88} = \$28.08$$

**Example 2**   A policy, issued to a boy aged 10, promises to pay (a) \$1,000 if he dies before reaching age 25, (b) \$2,000 if he dies after reaching 25 but before 37, and (c) \$5,000 if he dies after reaching 37 but before 65, or if he is alive at 65. Find the net annual premium if the policy is a 20-payment policy.

The policy consists of the following types of insurance benefits: (a) a 15-year term insurance of \$1,000, (b) a 12-year term insurance of \$2,000, deferred 15 years—from age 10 to age 25, and (c) a 28-year endowment insurance of \$5,000, deferred 27 years—from age 10 to age 37.

As of the purchase date:

The net single premium for type (a) is $1{,}000 A^{1}_{10\,:\,\overline{15|}}$. (Formula (20–4))

The net single premium for type (b) is $2{,}000 \cdot {}_{15|}A^{1}_{10\,:\,\overline{12|}}$. (Formula (20–11))

The net single premium for type (c) is $5{,}000 \cdot {}_{27|}A_{10\,:\,\overline{28|}}$. (Formula (20–12))

The 20 annual premiums $(P)$ form a temporary life annuity due. The present value of the annuity is $P\ddot{a}_{x\,:\,\overline{n|}}$ or $P\ddot{a}_{10\,:\,\overline{20|}}$. (Formula (19–11))

The present value of the annuity must be equal to the three net single premiums, or

$$P\ddot{a}_{10\,:\,\overline{20|}} = 1{,}000 A^{1}_{10\,:\,\overline{15|}} + 2{,}000 \cdot {}_{15|}A^{1}_{10\,:\,\overline{12|}} + 5{,}000 \cdot {}_{27|}A_{10\,:\,\overline{28|}}$$

$$P \cdot \frac{N_{10} - N_{30}}{D_{10}} = 1{,}000 \cdot \frac{M_{10} - M_{25}}{D_{10}} + 2{,}000 \cdot \frac{M_{25} - M_{37}}{D_{10}} +$$

$$5{,}000 \cdot \frac{M_{37} - M_{65} + D_{65}}{D_{10}}$$

$$P(N_{10} - N_{30}) = 1{,}000(M_{10} - M_{25}) + 2{,}000(M_{25} - M_{37}) + 5{,}000(M_{37} - M_{65} + D_{65})$$

$$P = \frac{1{,}000 M_{10} + 1{,}000 M_{25} + 3{,}000 M_{37} - 5{,}000 M_{65} + 5{,}000 D_{65}}{N_{10} - N_{30}}$$

$$= \$86.19$$

## ★EXERCISE 20-4

**Reference: Section 20.5**

1. Find the net single premium for a whole life insurance policy of $1,000 deferred 15 years, issued to someone now aged 25.
2. Find the net single premium for a whole life insurance policy of $1,500 deferred 22 years, issued to someone now aged 18.
3. What is the net single premium for a five-year term insurance policy of $1,000 deferred three years, issued to a person who is 30 years of age?
4. What is the net single premium for a 12-year term insurance policy of $2,000 deferred eight years, issued to a person who is 40 years of age?
5. Find the net single premium for a 20-year endowment insurance policy of $3,000 deferred 10 years, issued to someone who is 20 years of age.
6. What is the net single premium for a 30-year endowment insurance policy of $2,500 deferred 20 years, issued to someone now aged 35?
7. A policy issued to a person aged 25 provides the following: (a) $2,000 if the insured dies within 20 years, (b) $5,000 if the insured dies after 20 years. Find the net annual premium for life.
8. A policy issued to a person aged 30 provides the following: (a) $2,500 if the insured dies within 10 years, (b) $3,500 if the insured dies after 10 years. Find the net annual premium for life.
9. A policy issued to a child at age eight promises to pay: (a) $1,000 if the insured dies before age 20, (b) $3,000 if death occurs after age 20 but before 25, and (c) $6,000 if death occurs after age 25 but before 50, or if the insured is living at age 50. Find the net annual premium if the policy is a 30-payment policy.
10. A policy issued to a woman aged 22 provides that the insurance company will pay: (a) $2,000 if she dies before age 40, (b) $4,000 if she dies after reaching age 40 but before 65, and (c) $1,000 if she dies after reaching age 65 but before 80, or if she is alive at age 80. What is the net annual premium if the policy is a 40-payment policy?
11. Refer to Problem 9. If item (c) reads: "$6,000 if the insured dies after reaching age 25," what is the net annual premium?
12. Refer to Problem 10. Find the net annual premium if item (c) reads: "$1,000 if she dies after reaching age 65."

## 20.6 NATURAL PREMIUM AND LEVEL PREMIUM

The net single premium of a one-year term insurance policy is called the *natural premium*. According to the 1958 CSO Table, the death rate decreases from birth until age 10 and increases after the age of 10. Thus, if a person, age 10, purchases a one-year term policy every year, the natural premium would increase from year to year. The natural premium for a particular age may be computed by using the following term insurance formula:

$$A^1_{x:\overline{n}|} = \frac{M_x - M_{x+n}}{D_x}. \qquad \text{Here } n = 1. \text{ Thus,}$$

$$A^1_{x:\overline{1}|} = \frac{M_x - M_{x+1}}{D_x} = \frac{C_x}{D_x}, \text{ or it may be written}$$

$$c_x = \frac{C_x}{D_x} \qquad\qquad\qquad\qquad \textbf{(20–13)}\ [9]$$

The values of $C_x$ based on $2\frac{1}{2}\%$ interest are given in Table 15.

The value of $c_x$ is called the natural premium at age $x$, or the net single premium for a \$1, one-year term policy issued at age $x$.

**Example 1**   Find the net single premium for a \$1,000, one-year term policy if the policy is issued at age (a) 20, (b) 21, (c) 22, (d) 23, and (e) 24.

Since the policy is a one-year term policy, the natural premium formula is used to compute the value of the net single premium for each age as follows:

(a) $x = 20$

Substituting the value in formula (20–13):

the natural premium for a \$1 policy is:

$$c_x = \frac{C_x}{D_x} = \frac{C_{20}}{D_{20}} = \frac{10,300.18}{5,898,264.97} = .0017463$$

The natural premium (or the net single premium) for a \$1,000 policy is

$$.0017463 \times 1,000 = \$1.7463, \text{ or } \$1.75$$

(b)  $x = 21$

$$c_{21} = \frac{C_{21}}{D_{21}} = .0017853$$

Total net single premium $= .0017853 \times 1,000 = \$1.7853$, or \$1.79

(c)  $x = 22$

$$c_{22} = \frac{C_{22}}{D_{22}} = .0018146$$

Total net single premium $= .0018146 \times 1,000 = \$1.8146$, or \$1.81

(d)  $x = 23$

$$c_{23} = \frac{C_{23}}{D_{23}} = .0018439$$

---

[9] *Proof—Formula (20–13)*

$$M_x = C_x + C_{x+1} + C_{x+2} + \cdots\cdots\cdots\cdots\cdots C_{99}$$
$$M_{x+1} = \qquad\quad C_{x+1} + C_{x+2} + \cdots\cdots\cdots\cdots\cdots C_{99}$$

$$\overline{M_x - M_{x+1} = C_x}$$

Also see the proof for formula (20–1) for the value of $C_x$.

Total net single premium = .0018439 × 1,000 = $1.8439, or $1.84

(e)   $x = 24$

$$c_{24} = \frac{C_{24}}{D_{24}} = .0018634$$

Total net single premium = .0018634 × 1,000 = $1.8634, or $1.86

**Note:**  The division $C_x/D_x$ may also be performed by using logarithms. The division in (a), for example, is computed:

$$\begin{array}{ll} \log C_{20} = 4.012\ 8449 = 14.012\ 8449 - 10 & \\ (-)\ \log D_{20} \qquad\qquad\quad = \ \ 6.770\ 7243 & \text{(Table 16)} \\ \hline \qquad\qquad \log c_{20} = \ \ 7.242\ 1206 - 10 & \end{array}$$

Find the antilog by interpolation from Table 2.

$c_{20} = .0017463.$

The natural premium represents the net cost of the death claim. The premium is collected by the insurance company at the beginning of each age and is invested at $2\frac{1}{2}\%$. The total amount at the end of each age should be enough to pay the death claim. The answer to (a) in Example 1 may be checked as follows:

At age 20, there are $l_{20}$ or 9,664,994 persons living. The total premium collected from the group at the beginning of age 20 is

1.7463 × 9,664,994 = $16,877,979.02

The interest on the total premium for one year at $2\frac{1}{2}\%$ is

16,877,979.02 × $2\frac{1}{2}\%$ = $421,949.48

The total amount at the end of age 20 is

16,877,979.02 + 421,949.48 = $17,299,928.50

There are $d_{20}$ or 17,300 persons dying during the period from the beginning of age 20 to the end of age 20. The death claim against the total amount for each death is

$$\frac{17,299,928.50}{17,300} = \$999.996, \text{ or } \$1,000 \text{ (policy value)}$$

The answers in Example 1 indicate that the net cost of the death benefits (net single premium) to the insurance company for a $1,000, one-year term policy is $1.75 if the policyholder is 20 years old, $1.79 if the policyholder is 21 years old, $1.81 if the policyholder is 22 years old, etc. The natural premium increases from year to year as the policyholder grows older. However, an insurance company usually sells policies having a term of more than one year and collects equal annual premiums for each policy. Since the net annual premium is a fixed amount for every year during the policy term, it is called a *level premium*.

**Example 2**  A $1,000, five-year term policy is issued to a person aged 20. (a) Find the natural premium for each age during the term of the policy. (b)

Find the level premium (net annual premium). (c) Construct a chart of the natural premiums and the level premium.

(a) The natural premium for each age is as follows:

| | |
|---|---|
| Age 20: | $1.7463 |
| Age 21: | $1.7853 |
| Age 22: | $1.8146 |
| Age 23: | $1.8439 |
| Age 24: | $1.8634 (See Example 1) |

(b) The level premium is

$$1,000 P_{20:\overline{5}|}^1 = 1,000 \cdot \frac{M_{20} - M_{25}}{N_{20} - N_{25}} = \$1.8092 \quad \begin{matrix} \text{(See Example 1(b),} \\ \text{Section 20.3, page 563.)} \end{matrix}$$

(c) Chart (See below.)

## LEVEL PREMIUM FOR A FIVE-YEAR TERM POLICY ISSUED AT AGE 20 AND NATURAL PREMIUMS FOR AGES 20 THROUGH 24 (POLICY FACE VALUE: $1,000)

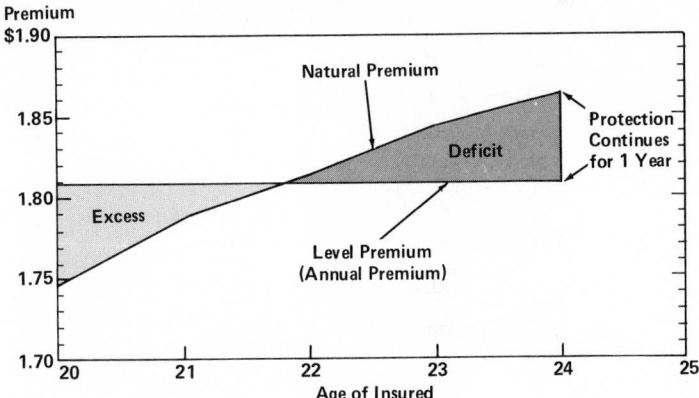

**Source:** Example 2(a) and (b).

The answers in Example 2 are also tabulated in the following schedule:

## COMPARISON OF LEVEL PREMIUM AND NATURAL PREMIUM

| (1) | (2) | (3) Excess (or Deficit) of Level Premium over Natural Premium, |
|---|---|---|
| Age | Natural Premium | $1.8092 − (2) |
| 20 | $1.7463 | $0.0629 |
| 21 | 1.7853 | 0.0239 |
| 22 | 1.8146 | −0.0054 |
| 23 | 1.8439 | −0.0347 |
| 24 | 1.8634 | −0.0542 |

In Example 2, during the first year the insurance company collects $.06 (or $1.8092 − $1.7463) more than the net cost of the insurance. (See column (3) in the above schedule.) The company usually deposits the excess premium, $.06, in a *reserve fund,* which is invested to earn interest to meet future needs. (See Section 20.7.) On the other hand, when the policyholder reaches age 24, the insurance company collects $.05 (or $1.8092 − $1.8634) less than the net cost to the company. The company usually makes up the deficit premium from the reserve fund.

In general, for every insurance policy, the level premium is greater than the natural premium (the net cost to the company) in the earlier policy years. On the other hand, in the later policy years the level premium is less than the natural premium. If the policyholder wishes to cancel the contract before the entire amount of the reserve fund has been used, it is possible to recover a *cash surrender value,* which is paid by the life insurance company when the policyholder surrenders the policy to the company.

The following example illustrates the relationship between the natural premiums and the level premium for a straight whole life policy.

**Example 3**    Find the natural premiums for a $1,000 policy if the policy is issued at the ages indicated in column (1) of the schedule below. Also find the net annual premium (the level premium) for a $1,000 straight whole life policy issued to a person aged 50. Compare the natural premiums with the level premium and show the excess or deficit premiums.

The natural premiums for the required ages are computed by using formula (20–13) and are arranged respectively in column (2) of the schedule below.

## LEVEL PREMIUM FOR A $1,000, STRAIGHT WHOLE LIFE POLICY ISSUED AT AGE 50 AND NATURAL PREMIUMS FOR VARIOUS AGES

| (1)<br><br>Age<br>$(x)$ | (2)<br><br>Natural Premium<br>$1,000 \cdot \dfrac{C_x}{D_x}$ | (3)<br>Excess (or Deficit) of<br>Level Premium over<br>Natural Premium<br>$\$32.38 - (2)$ |
|---|---|---|
| 50 | $ 8.12 | $ 24.26 |
| 55 | 12.68 | 19.70 |
| 60 | 19.84 | 12.54 |
| 65 | 30.98 | 1.40 |
| 70 | 48.58 | − 16.20 |
| 75 | 71.58 | − 39.20 |
| 80 | 107.30 | − 74.92 |
| 85 | 157.21 | −124.83 |
| 90 | 222.58 | −190.20 |
| 95 | 342.67 | −310.29 |
| 99 | 975.61 | −943.23 |

The net annual premium (the level premium) is

$$1,000\,P_{50} = 1,000 \cdot \frac{M_{50}}{N_{50}} = \$32.38$$

The comparison between the natural premiums and the level premium is shown in column (3) of the schedule.

Example 3 is diagrammed in the following chart, which covers a portion of the information presented in the schedule above:

**LEVEL PREMIUM FOR A $1,000 STRAIGHT WHOLE LIFE POLICY FOR A PERSON AGED 50 AND NATURAL PREMIUMS FOR VARIOUS AGES**

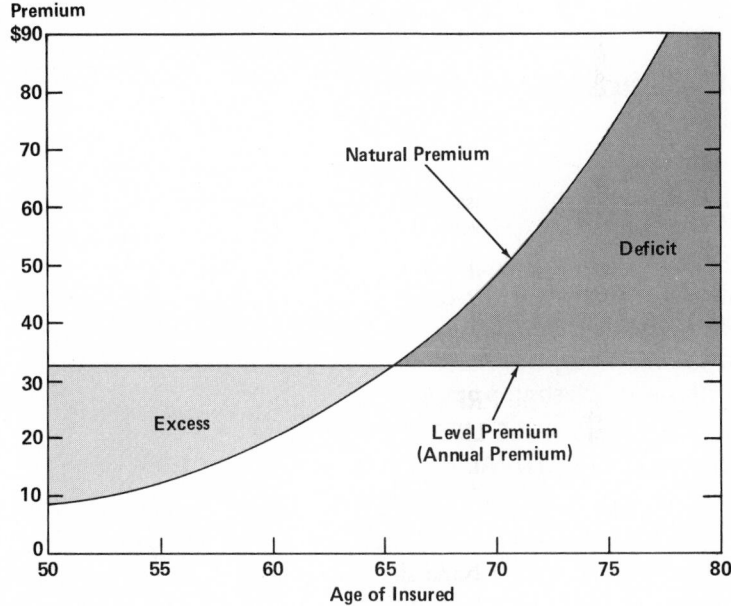

Source: Example 3.

## EXERCISE 20–5

### Reference: Section 20.6

1. Find the net single premium for a $1,000, one-year term policy, if the policy is issued at age (a) 8, (b) 9, (c) 10, (d) 11, and (e) 12.
2. Find the net single premium for a $2,000, one-year term policy, if the policy is issued at age (a) 30, (b) 31, (c) 32, (d) 33, and (e) 34.

3. Refer to the checking method described on page 572. Use this method to check whether the natural premium obtained in Problem 1(a) is sufficient to pay the net cost of the death claim.

4. Refer to the checking method described on page 572. Use this method to check whether the natural premium obtained in Problem 2(a) is sufficient to pay the net cost of the death claim.

5. A $1,000, five-year term policy is issued to someone aged 25. Construct a chart of the natural premiums and the level premium for the policy.

6. A $1,000, five-year term policy is issued to someone aged 40. Construct a chart of the natural premiums and the level premium for the policy.


# ★20.7 TERMINAL RESERVES


## A. General Computation

*Terminal reserve* is the value accumulated from the excess premiums and the interest on the premiums. It represents the value of an insurance policy at the end of any policy year; the premium then due is not included. For example, the fourth terminal reserve for an insurance policy is the value of the policy at the end of the fourth year after the policy is issued, but it does not include the net annual premium for the fifth year. The value of the terminal reserve at the end of a particular policy year may be obtained in various ways. Two methods are illustrated below.


### RETROSPECTIVE METHOD

The *retrospective method* is based on the premiums collected in the *past* and the death benefits paid in the *past*. Premiums are collected by the insurance company at the *beginning* of each policy year and are invested at a given interest rate for accumulation. The death benefits are paid from this accumulated sum. It is assumed here, as in the previous discussion, that the death benefits are paid at the *end* of the year of death. The remaining part (premiums and interest less death benefit payments) is the terminal reserve, which is divided by the number of surviving policyholders in the 1958 CSO Table to determine the terminal reserve per policyholder for the year.

**Example 1**    The CSO Table shows that $l_{20} = 9,664,994$. Assume that each of the 9,664,994 persons aged 20 is issued a $1,000, five-year term insurance policy and the annual premiums are invested at $2\frac{1}{2}\%$. Find the terminal reserve per surviving policyholder at the end of each policy year.

The terminal reserves are computed in the following table:

| (1) | (2) | (3) | (4) | (5) | (6) | (7) | (8) |
|---|---|---|---|---|---|---|---|
| | | | | One Year's | | | |
| | Surviving Policy-holders at | Premiums Paid at Beginning of Year | Reserve Fund at Beginning | Interest for the Reserve Fund | Death Claims at End of Year | Reserve Fund at End of | Terminal Reserve per |
| Policy Year | Beginning of Year | (2) × 1.8091584* | of Year (3) + (7)** | (4) × $2\frac{1}{2}$% | $1,000 Each (of $d_x$) | Year (4) + (5) − (6) | Survivor (7) ÷ (2)*** |
| 1 | 9,664,994 | $17,485,505 | $17,485,505 | $437,138 | $17,300,000 | $622,643 | $.064538 |
| 2 | 9,647,694 | 17,454,207 | 18,076,850 | 451,921 | 17,655,000 | 873,771 | .090734 |
| 3 | 9,630,039 | 17,422,266 | 18,296,037 | 457,401 | 17,912,000 | 841,438 | .087539 |
| 4 | 9,612,127 | 17,389,860 | 18,231,298 | 455,782 | 18,167,000 | 520,080 | .054209 |
| 5 | 9,593,960 | 17,356,993 | 17,877,073 | 446,927 | 18,324,000 | –0– | –0– |

* Net annual premium. See Section 20.6, Example 2(b).
** Of the preceding year. For example, $18,076,850 = 17,454,207 + 622,643.
*** Of the succeeding year. For example, $.064538 = 622,643 ÷ 9,647,694.

The method above may be used to compute the terminal reserves for any type of insurance. As shown below, the procedure used in this method may also be expressed symbolically to obtain a formula. The formula can then be used to find the terminal reserve per surviving policyholder at the end of any given policy year without constructing a table.

Let $P$ = the net annual premium (or level premium) for a policy of $1
   $t$ = the number of years the policy is in force; at the end of the $t$th policy year, the terminal reserve is desired
   $V$ = $t$th terminal reserve per surviving policyholder for a $1 policy
   $V' = V \times$ Policy value = the total $t$th terminal reserve per surviving policyholder

If the $t$th terminal reserve is on a date which is before or on the date of the last payment of the $n$ annual premiums, the formula for the value of $V$ is as follows:

$$V = \frac{P(N_x - N_{x+t}) - (M_x - M_{x+t})}{D_{x+t}}, \text{ where } t \leq n \qquad \textbf{(20–14)} \, ^{10}$$

---

[10] *Proof—Formula (20–14)*

The number of years that the policy has been in force *(t)* is smaller than or equal to the number of annual premium payments *(n)* (or, $t \leq n$).

Let age $x + t$ be the comparison date and $i$ be the interest rate compounded annually. The accumulated values of the *past* annual premiums and the *past* death benefits at age $x + t$ are diagrammed respectively as follows:

*(continues on following page)*

If the $t$th terminal reserve is on a date which is after the last payment of the $n$ annual premiums (this may occur in a limited payment life insurance policy as in Example 5(b) below), the formula for the value of $V$ is as follows:

---

[10] *Proof (continued)*

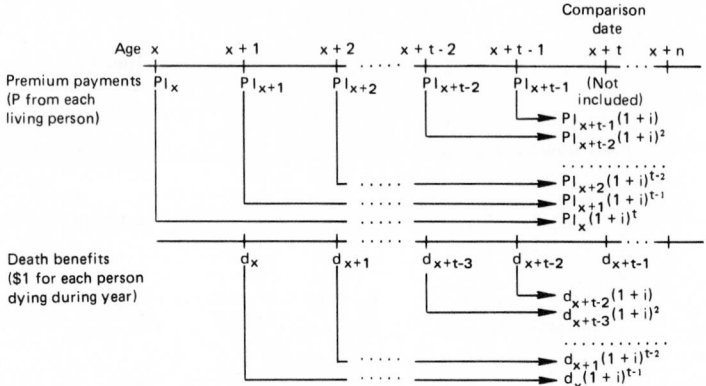

At the end of the $t$th policy year, the comparison date, the total accumulated annual premiums (not considering the payments of the death benefits) are:

$$Pl_x(1+i)^t + Pl_{x+1}(1+i)^{t-1} + \cdots \cdots \cdots + Pl_{x+t-1}(1+i) \qquad \text{(I)}$$

The total accumulated annual death benefits (if they had been withheld and invested by the insurance company) at the end of the $t$th policy year are:

$$d_x(1+i)^{t-1} + d_{x+1}(1+i)^{t-2} + \cdots \cdots \cdots \cdots + d_{x+t-1} \qquad \text{(II)}$$

The total accumulated annual death benefits are subtracted from the total accumulated annual premiums to obtain the total terminal reserve at the end of the $t$th policy year. The total terminal reserve is divided by the $l_{x+t}$ policyholders who are living at age $x + t$. The result is the terminal reserve per surviving policyholder and is as follows:

$$V = \frac{(\text{I}) - (\text{II})}{l_{x+t}}, \text{ or}$$

$$V = \frac{P[l_x(1+i)^t + l_{x+1}(1+i)^{t-1} + \cdots + l_{x+t-1}(1+i)] - [d_x(1+i)^{t-1} + d_{x+1}(1+i)^{t-2} + \cdots + d_{x+t-1}]}{l_{x+t}}$$

Substitute $v$ for $(1+i)^{-1}$, or $v^{-1} = (1+i)$.

$$V = \frac{P[l_x v^{-t} + l_{x+1} v^{-(t-1)} + \cdots + l_{x+t-1} v^{-1}] - [d_x v^{-(t-1)} + d_{x+1} v^{-(t-2)} + \cdots + d_{x+t-1}]}{l_{x+t}}$$

Multiply both the numerator and the denominator of the fraction by $v^{x+t}$.

$$V = \frac{P(v^x l_x + v^{x+1} l_{x+1} + \cdots + v^{x+t-1} l_{x+t-1}) - (v^{x+1} d_x + v^{x+2} d_{x+1} + \cdots + v^{x+t} d_{x+t-1})}{v^{x+t} l_{x+t}}$$

Substitute the appropriate commutation symbols:

$$V = \frac{P(D_x + D_{x+1} + \cdots + D_{x+t-1}) - (C_x + C_{x+1} + \cdots + C_{x+t-1})}{D_{x+t}}$$

$$V = \frac{P(N_x - N_{x+t}) - (M_x - M_{x+t})}{D_{x+t}}, \text{ where } t \leq n \qquad (20\text{-}14)$$

$$V = \frac{P(N_x - N_{x+n}) - (M_x - M_{x+t})}{D_{x+t}}, \text{ where } t > n \qquad \text{(20–15)} [11]$$

**Example 2**   What is the third terminal reserve for a $1,000, five-year term policy issued to a person aged 20?

$P = .0018091584$ (for a $1 policy, see Section 20.6, Example 2(b)), $x = 20$, $n = 5$, $t = 3$, $x + t = 23$

Since $t$ is smaller ($<$) than $n$, the above values are substituted in formula (20–14) as follows:

$$V = \frac{.0018091584(N_{20} - N_{23}) - (M_{20} - M_{23})}{D_{23}} = .000087539$$

The third terminal reserve for a $1,000 policy is

$$V' = 1,000\,V = 1,000(.000087539) = \$.087539$$

The answer may be compared with that given in column (8) of the table in Example 1 of this section.

---

[11] *Proof—Formula (20–15)*

The number of years that the policy has been in force *(t)* is larger than the number of annual premium payments *(n)* (or, $t > n$).

If the *t*th terminal reserve is on a date after the last payment of the *n* annual premiums is made, the total accumulated annual premiums at the end of the *t*th policy year (the comparison date) would be

$$Pl_x(1 + i)^t + Pl_{x+1}(1 + i)^{t-1} + \cdots + Pl_{x+n-2}(1 + i)^{t-(n-2)} + Pl_{x+n-1}(1 + i)^{t-(n-1)}$$
$$= P(l_x v^{-t} + l_{x+1} v^{-(t-1)} + \cdots + l_{x+n-2} v^{-[t-(n-2)]} + l_{x+n-1} v^{-[t-(n-1)]})$$
$$= P(l_x v^{-t} + l_{x+1} v^{-t+1} + \cdots + l_{x+n-2} v^{-t+n-2} + l_{x+n-1} v^{-t+n-1}) \qquad \text{(IA)}$$

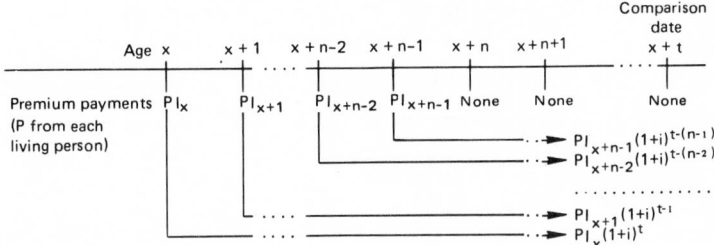

The total accumulated annual death benefits is the same as shown in the diagram for the proof of formula (20–14), or (II). The terminal reserve per surviving policyholder thus is as follows:

$$V = \frac{\text{(IA)} - \text{(II)}}{l_{x+t}}.$$

Multiply both the numerator and the denominator of the fraction by $v^{x+t}$, and substitute the appropriate commutation symbols as done in proving formula (20–14). Then,

$$V = \frac{P(N_x - N_{x+n}) - (M_x - M_{x+t})}{D_{x+t}}, \text{ where } t > n \qquad \text{(20–15)}$$

**Example 3**　Find the seventh terminal reserve for a 10-year endowment policy of $1,000 issued to a man aged 20.

$x = 20$, $n = 10$, $t = 7$, $x + t = 27$, $t$ is smaller than $n$.

The net annual premium of a 10-year endowment policy of $1 issued to a man aged 20 is:

$$P = P_{20:\overline{10|}} = \frac{M_{20} - M_{30} + D_{30}}{N_{20} - N_{30}} = .087980555 \text{ (Formula (20–8))}$$

Substituting the above values in formula (20–14):

$$V = \frac{.087980555(N_{20} - N_{27}) - (M_{20} - M_{27})}{D_{27}} = .67169$$

The seventh terminal reserve for the $1,000 policy is

$$V' = 1,000\,V = 1,000(.67169) = \$671.69$$

**Example 4**　Find the tenth terminal reserve for a $1,000 straight whole life policy issued to a person aged 25.

$P = .0125450145$ (for a $1 policy, see Example 3(b), Section 20.2), $x = 25$, $t = 10$, $x + t = 35$. $t$ is smaller than the number of payments $(n)$ since the premiums are payable until the death of the insured.

Substituting the values in formula (20–14):

$$V = \frac{.0125450145(N_{25} - N_{35}) - (M_{25} - M_{35})}{D_{35}} = .12187$$

The tenth terminal reserve for the $1,000 policy is

$$V' = 1,000\,V = 1,000(.12187) = \$121.87$$

**Example 5**　A $1,000 whole life policy is issued to a person aged 25. If the policy is a 20-payment life policy, find the (a) 15th and (b) 30th terminal reserves.

The net annual premium for a policy of $1 is $.02168152 (see Section 20.2, Example 3(c)), or $P = .02168152$.

(a) $x = 25$, $n = 20$, and $t = 15$, which is smaller than the value of $n$. $x + t = 25 + 15 = 40$. The 15th terminal reserve is computed by using formula (20–14) as follows:

$$V = \frac{P(N_x - N_{x+t}) - (M_x - M_{x+t})}{D_{x+t}}$$

$$= \frac{.02168152(N_{25} - N_{40}) - (M_{25} - M_{40})}{D_{40}} = .36465$$

The terminal reserve for a $1,000 policy is

$$V' = 1,000\,V = 1,000(.36465) = \$364.65$$

(b) $x = 25$, $n = 20$, and $t = 30$, which is greater $(>)$ than the value of $n$. $x + n = 25 + 20 = 45$, $x + t = 25 + 30 = 55$.

Substituting the values in formula (20–15):

$$V = \frac{P(N_x - N_{x+n}) - (M_x - M_{x+t})}{D_{x+t}}$$

$$= \frac{.02168152(N_{25} - N_{45}) - (M_{25} - M_{55})}{D_{55}} = .62455$$

The terminal reserve for a $1,000 policy is

$$V' = 1,000\,V = 1,000(.62455) = \$624.55$$

## ★EXERCISE 20–6

**Reference: Section 20.7 A**

1. A 15-year term insurance policy of $1,000 was issued to a person aged 25. Find (a) the 5th, and (b) the 15th terminal reserves.
2. What are (a) the 8th and (b) the 12th terminal reserves for a 20-year term insurance policy of $2,000 issued to a person aged 30?
3. Find (a) the 6th and (b) the 25th terminal reserve for a 25-year endowment policy of $1,000 issued to someone aged 22.
4. A 15-year endowment policy of $2,000 was issued to someone aged 35. Find (a) the 4th and (b) the 10th terminal reserves.
5. What are (a) the 12th and (b) the 50th terminal reserve for a $1,000 straight life policy issued to a person aged 30?
6. A $1,000 straight life policy was issued to a person aged 20. Find (a) the 15th and (b) the 65th terminal reserves.
7. A $1,000 whole life policy is issued to someone aged 26. If the policy is a 25-payment life policy, find (a) the 10th and (b) the 34th terminal reserves.
8. A $1,000 whole life policy is issued to someone aged 30. If the policy is a 15-payment life policy, find (a) the 5th and (b) the 25th terminal reserves.

### PROSPECTIVE METHOD

The *prospective method* is based on the annual premiums to be collected in the *future* and the annual death benefits to be paid in the *future*.

Let age $x + t$ be the comparison date. Values at age $x + t$ may be written as follows:

$$\begin{bmatrix} t\text{th terminal} \\ \text{reserve } (V') \end{bmatrix} = \begin{bmatrix} \text{Present value} \\ \text{(at age } x + t) \text{ of} \\ \text{future death} \\ \text{benefits} \end{bmatrix} - \begin{bmatrix} \text{Present value (at} \\ \text{age } x + t) \text{ of fu-} \\ \text{ture net annual} \\ \text{premiums} \end{bmatrix} \quad \textbf{(20–16)}$$

At age $x + t$, the present value of the future death benefits is the net single premium for the benefits. The present value (at age $x + t$) of the future net annual premiums is the present value of a life annuity due formed by the future annual premiums.

**Example 6**     Find the third terminal reserve for a $1,000, five-year term policy issued to a person aged 20.

$x = 20$, $t = 3$, $x + t = 20 + 3 = 23$. The future or remaining term from age $x + t$, or 23, is $(5 - 3) = 2$ (years).

At age 23, the future death benefits of the policy are equal to a two-year term insurance policy of $1,000. The present value, or the net single premium, of the two-year policy is

$1,000\,A^1_{23:\overline{2}|}$

The net annual premium of the five-year term policy is computed as follows:

$1,000\,P^1_{20:\overline{5}|} = 1.8091584$ (See Section 20.6, Example 2(b).)

At age 23, the two future annual premium payments of $1.8091584 per year form a two-year life annuity due. The present value of the annuity is

$A(\text{tem. due}) = 1.8091584\,\ddot{a}_{23:\overline{2}|}$ (Formula (19–11))

Thus,

$$V' = 1,000\,A^1_{23:\overline{2}|} - 1.8091584\,\ddot{a}_{23:\overline{2}|}$$

$$= 1,000 \cdot \frac{M_{23} - M_{23+2}}{D_{23}} - 1.8091584 \cdot \frac{N_{23} - N_{23+2}}{D_{23}}$$

$$= \$.087539$$

The answer above may be compared with that given in Section 20.7, Example 2.

Example 6 is diagrammed below:

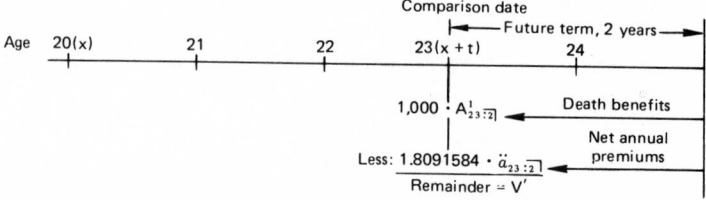

**Example 7**     Find the seventh terminal reserve for a 10-year endowment policy of $1,000 issued to a person aged 20.

$x = 20$, $t = 7$, $x + t = 20 + 7 = 27$. The future (remaining term) $= 10 - 7 = 3$ (years).

The future death benefits of the policy at age 27 are equivalent to a three-year endowment insurance policy of $1,000 for a person aged 27. The present value, or net single premium, of the three-year policy is

$$1,000\,A_{27:\overline{3}|}$$

The net annual premium of the 10-year endowment policy is

$$1,000\,P_{20:\overline{10}|} = 1,000(.087980555) = \$87.980555 \quad \text{(See Section 20.7, Example 3.)}$$

The future net annual premiums at age 27 form a three-year temporary life annuity due of $87.980555 per year. The present value of the annuity at age 27 is

$$87.980555\,\ddot{a}_{27:\overline{3}|}$$

Thus,

$$V' = 1,000\,A_{27:\overline{3}|} - 87.980555\,\ddot{a}_{27:\overline{3}|}$$

$$= 1,000 \cdot \frac{M_{27} - M_{27+3} + D_{27+3}}{D_{27}} - 87.980555 \cdot \frac{N_{27} - N_{30}}{D_{27}}$$

$$= \$671.69$$

The answer above may be compared with that given in Section 20.7, Example 3.

**Example 8**   Find the tenth terminal reserve for a $1,000 straight whole life policy issued to a person aged 25.

$x = 25$, $t = 10$, $x + t = 35$, the future (remaining term) = age 35 to 99 (the end of the CSO Table).

The future death benefits of the policy at age 35 are equivalent to a whole life policy of $1,000 for a person aged 35. The net single premium (present value) of the new whole life policy is

$$1,000\,A_{35}$$

The net annual premium of the original whole life policy is

$$1,000\,P_{25} = \$12.545 \quad \text{(See Example 3(b), Section 20.2)}$$

The future net annual premiums at age 35 form a whole life annuity due of $12.545 per year. The present value of this annuity is

$$12.545\,\ddot{a}_{35}$$

Thus,

$$V' = 1,000\,A_{35} - 12.545\,\ddot{a}_{35} = 1,000 \cdot \frac{M_{35}}{D_{35}} - 12.545\,\frac{N_{35}}{D_{35}}$$

$$= \$121.87$$

The answer above may be compared with that given in Example 4.

**Example 9**    Find the 30th terminal reserve for a $1,000, 20-payment life policy issued to a person aged 25.

$x = 25$, $t = 30$, $x + t = 55$, the future (remaining term of the life policy) = age 55 to 99 (the end of the CSO Table).

The future death benefits of the policy at age 55 are equivalent to a whole life policy of $1,000 for age 55. The net single premium of the policy for a person aged 55 is

$$1,000\,A_{55} = 1,000 \cdot \frac{M_{55}}{D_{55}} = \$624.55$$

There are no future net annual premiums at age 55 since the original policy is paid up in 20 annual premium payments. Thus,

$$V' = 624.55 - 0 = \$624.55$$

The answer above may be compared with that given in Example 5(b).

## ★EXERCISE 20–7

### Reference: Section 20.7 A

*Use the prospective method to compute the following problems:*

1. A life insurance policy was issued to a person aged 30. The value of future death benefits at age 40 is $467.13. Find the tenth terminal reserve by assuming that the net annual premium is $14.80 payable for life.
2. A life insurance policy was issued to a person aged 20. The value of future death benefits at the end of the 18th policy year is $895.72. If the net annual premium is $21.51 payable for life, what is the 18th terminal reserve?
3. Compute Problems 1, 3, 5, and 7 in Exercise 20–6.
4. Compute Problems 2, 4, 6, and 8 in Exercise 20–6.

## B. Uses of Terminal Reserve

The value of an insurance policy in any policy year is based on the terminal reserve. A policyholder may use the reserve for any one of the following purposes:

1. The policyholder may surrender the policy to the insurance company and receive the cash value of the reserve.
2. A policyholder who has no intention of surrendering the policy may borrow money on the reserve at a low interest rate from the insurance company, the reserve being regarded as security for the loan.

3. The policyholder may also use the reserve as a single premium payment to extend the original policy for a period of time, or to convert the original policy to a reduced amount of paid-up insurance. In fact, if a person stops paying the annual premium and fails to do anything about the policy, the company usually continues to keep the policy in force for an extended period of time based on the amount of the terminal reserve.

**Example 10**   The annual premium payment on a $1,000 straight whole life policy issued to a person aged 25 is discontinued at age 35. The policyholder wishes to use the reserve as the premium payment. Find (a) the extended term of the policy with the original face value ($1,000), and (b) the new policy face value for the same type of policy (whole life policy).

First, find the tenth terminal reserve of the original policy. In Example 4 of this section, the tenth terminal reserve for a $1,000 straight life policy issued to a person aged 25 is $121.87.

(a) The net single premium on a $1,000, $n$ year term policy issued at age 35 is now equal to the tenth terminal reserve, or

$$1,000\,A^1_{35:\overline{n}|} = 121.87 \qquad A^1_{35:\overline{n}|} = \frac{121.87}{1,000} = .12187$$

Thus,

$$A^1_{35:\overline{n}|} = \frac{M_{35} - M_{35+n}}{D_{35}} = .12187$$

$$\frac{1,659,440.36 - M_{35+n}}{3,949,851.09} = .12187$$

$$M_{35+n} = 1,178,072.01$$

The following nearest values are obtained from Table 15:

$$M_{60} = 1,187,445.15$$
$$M_{35+n} = 1,178,072.01$$
$$M_{61} = 1,152,722.42$$

When the interpolation method is used, the value of 1,178,072.01 is found to be $M_{60.26994}$, as follows:

| $x$ (age) | $M_x$ | |
|---|---|---|
| 60 | 1,187,445.15 | (1) |
| $35 + n$ | 1,178,072.01 | (2) |
| 61 | 1,152,722.42 | (3) |

$$\frac{(2)-(3)}{(1)-(3)} \qquad \frac{(35+n)-61}{-1} = \frac{25,349.59 \quad (4)}{34,722.73 \quad (5)}$$

Solve for $n$ from the proportion formed by the differences on lines (4) and (5):

$$(35 + n) - 61 = (-1) \cdot \frac{25,349.59}{34,722.73}$$

$$35 + n = -.73006 + 61 = 60.26994$$

$$n = 60.26994 - 35$$

$$= 25.26994, \text{ or } 25 \text{ years and } 99 \text{ days}$$
$$(.26994 \times 365 \text{ (days a year)} = 99 \text{ days})$$

(b) The net single premium of a $1 whole life policy at age 35 is

$$A_{35} = \frac{M_{35}}{D_{35}} = \$.420127$$

The face value of the new whole life policy at age 35 is

$$\frac{121.87}{.420127} = \$290.08$$

## ★EXERCISE 20–8

### Reference: Section 20.7 B

1. A 15-year term insurance policy of $1,000 was issued to a person at age 25. The policyholder stopped making annual premium payments at age 30. (a) What is the term of the new policy if the policyholder wishes to use the reserve to buy a term insurance policy with the same face value? (b) What is the amount of the new policy if the policyholder wishes to use the reserve to buy a 10-year term insurance policy? (Also see Problem 1, Exercise 20–6.)

2. Refer to Problem 1. Assume that the policyholder stopped making annual premium payments at age 32. What is the answer to (a)? What is the answer to (b) if the policyholder now wishes to use the reserve to buy a five-year term insurance policy?

3. A person now aged 28 is unable to maintain the annual premium payments on a $1,000, 25-year endowment insurance policy, which was issued at age 22. If the policyholder wishes to use the reserve as the premium payment, find (a) the term of the new policy for a term insurance policy with a face value of $1,000, and (b) the face value of the new policy for a 15-year endowment insurance policy. (Also see Problem 3, Exercise 20–6.)

4. Refer to Problem 3. If the policyholder is now 35 and is unable to maintain the annual premium payments, what is the answer to (a)? What is the answer to (b) for a 10-year endowment insurance policy?

5. A straight life policy of $1,000 issued to someone aged 30 is discontinued at age 42. (a) Find the term of the new policy if the policyholder wishes

to use the reserve to purchase an extended insurance policy of the same face value. (b) Find the amount of the new policy if the policyholder wishes to keep the same type of policy, the whole life policy. (Also see Problem 5, Exercise 20–6.)

6. Refer to Problem 5. Find the answers to (a) and (b) if the policy is discontinued at age 50.

## 20.8 SUMMARY OF LIFE INSURANCE FORMULAS

*Symbols:*   $A =$ the net single premium (or present value) of a \$1 life insurance policy (See note for symbol $A$ on page 556)

$P =$ the net annual premium of a \$1 life insurance policy

$V =$ terminal reserve for $t$th policy year of a \$1 life insurance policy

$V' =$ total terminal reserve for $t$th policy year of a life insurance policy

$x =$ age of the insured on the date the policy is issued

$n =$ number of net annual premium payments, also number of years in the length of a term or an endowment insurance policy

$y =$ number of net annual premium payments for a term insurance or an endowment insurance policy; $y$ is used only when the number of premium payments $(y)$ does not equal the number of years in the length of a policy $(n)$, or $y \neq n$

$k =$ number of years that a life policy is deferred

$D_x = v^x l_x$

$N_x = D_x + D_{x+1} + D_{x+2} + \cdots\cdots\cdots\cdots + D_{99}$

$C_x = v^{x+1} d_x$

$M_x = C_x + C_{x+1} + C_{x+2} + \cdots\cdots\cdots\cdots + C_{99}$

| Application | Formula | Formula Number | Reference page |
|---|---|---|---|
| *Whole Life Insurance* | | | |
| Net Single Premium | $A_x = \dfrac{M_x}{D_x}$ | (20–1) | 557 |
| Net Annual Premium | $P_x = \dfrac{M_x}{N_x}$ | (20–2) | 558 |
|  | $_n P_x = \dfrac{M_x}{N_x - N_{x+n}}$ | (20–3) | 558 |
| *Term Insurance* | | | |
| Net Single Premium | $A^1_{x:\overline{n}|} = \dfrac{M_x - M_{x+n}}{D_x}$ | (20–4) | 561 |
| Net Annual Premium | $P^1_{x:\overline{n}|} = \dfrac{M_x - M_{x+n}}{N_x - N_{x+n}}$ | (20–5) | 562 |
|  | $_y P^1_{x:\overline{n}|} = \dfrac{M_x - M_{x+n}}{N_x - N_{x+y}}$ | (20–6) | 562 |

| Application | Formula | Formula Number | Reference page |
|---|---|---|---|
| *Endowment Insurance* | | | |
| Net Single Premium | $A_{x\,:\,\overline{n}|} = \dfrac{M_x - M_{x+n} + D_{x+n}}{D_x}$ | (20–7) | 565 |
| Net Annual Premium | $P_{x\,:\,\overline{n}|} = \dfrac{M_x - M_{x+n} + D_{x+n}}{N_x - N_{x+n}}$ | (20–8) | 565 |
| | $_yP_{x:\overline{n}|} = \dfrac{M_x - M_{x+n} + D_{x+n}}{N_x - N_{x+y}}$ | (20–9) | 565 |
| *Deferred Life Insurance* | | | |
| Deferred Whole Life Insurance | $_k|A_x = \dfrac{M_{x+k}}{D_x}$ | (20–10) | 568 |
| Deferred Term Insurance | $_k|A^1_{x\,:\,\overline{n}|} = \dfrac{M_{x+k} - M_{x+k+n}}{D_x}$ | (20–11) | 568 |
| Deferred Endowment Insurance | $_k|A_{x:\overline{n}|} = \dfrac{M_{x+k} - M_{x+k+n} + D_{x+k+n}}{D_x}$ | (20–12) | 568 |
| *Natural Premium* | $A^1_{x\,:\,\overline{1}|} = c_x = \dfrac{C_x}{D_x}$ | (20–13) | 571 |

*In general,* (either the insurance protection beginning on the date the policy is issued or deferred for a number of years) the above formulas may be summarized in the following manner:

The *net single premium* of
a $1 whole life or term insurance policy is:

$$A = \frac{M_{\text{age when insurance protection begins}} - M_{\text{age when insurance protection ends}}}{D_{\text{age on the policy date}}}$$

a $1 endowment insurance policy is:

$$A = \frac{M_{\substack{\text{age when insurance} \\ \text{protection begins}}} - M_{\substack{\text{age when insurance} \\ \text{protection ends}}} + D_{\substack{\text{age when insurance} \\ \text{protection ends}}}}{D_{\text{age on the policy date}}}$$

The *net annual premium* of
a $1 whole life or term insurance policy is:

$$P = \frac{M_{\text{age when insurance protection begins}} - M_{\text{age when insurance protection ends}}}{N_{\text{age on the policy date}} - N_{\text{age when annual premium payment ends}}},$$

a $1 endowment insurance policy is:

|  |  | Formula | Refer-<br>ence |
| Application | Formula | Number | page |

$$P = \frac{M_{\text{age when insurance protection begins}} - M_{\text{age when insurance protection ends}} + D_{\text{age when insurance protection ends}}}{N_{\text{age on the policy date}} - N_{\text{age when annual premium payment ends}}}$$

The value of $M$, $D$, and $N$ for the age larger than the highest age (99) given in Table 15 is zero. Thus, the first and third general formulas above are also valid for whole life insurance policies.

*Terminal Reserves*

| Retrospective<br>Method | $V = \dfrac{P(N_x - N_{x+t}) - (M_x - M_{x+t})}{D_{x+t}}, \; (t \le n)$ | (20–14) | 577 |

$$V = \frac{P(N_x - N_{x+n}) - (M_x - M_{x+t})}{D_{x+t}}, \; (t > n) \qquad (20\text{–}15) \qquad 579$$

Prospective Method

$$\begin{bmatrix} t\text{th terminal} \\ \text{reserve } (V') \end{bmatrix} = \begin{bmatrix} \text{Present value (at} \\ \text{age } x + t) \text{ of fu-} \\ \text{ture death bene-} \\ \text{fits} \end{bmatrix} - \begin{bmatrix} \text{Present value (at} \\ \text{age } x + t) \text{ of fu-} \\ \text{ture net annual} \\ \text{premiums} \end{bmatrix} \qquad (20\text{–}16) \qquad 581$$

# EXERCISE 20–9

## Review of Chapter 20

1. A $1,000 whole life policy is issued to a person aged 32. Find (a) the net single premium, (b) the net annual premium if the policy is a straight life policy, and (c) the net annual premium if the policy is a 25-payment life policy.
2. A $1,000 whole life policy is issued to a person at age 20. What are (a) the net single premium, (b) the net annual premium if the policy is a straight life policy, and (c) the net annual premium if the policy is a 30-payment life policy?
3. Refer to Problem 1. If the policy is issued to someone at age 22, what are the answers to (a), (b), and (c)?
4. Refer to Problem 2. If the policy is issued to a child at age 10, what are the answers to (a), (b), and (c)?
5. A $1,000, 15-year term policy is issued to someone aged 30. Find (a) the net single premium, (b) the net annual premium if the policy is a 15-payment policy, and (c) the net annual premium if the policy is a 10-payment policy.
6. A $1,000, 20-year term policy is issued to someone aged 24. Find (a) the net single premium, (b) the net annual premium if the policy is a 20-payment policy, and (c) the net annual premium if the policy is a 15-payment policy.

7. Refer to Problem 5. Assuming that the policy is issued at age 40, what are the answers to (a), (b), and (c)?

8. Refer to Problem 6. Assuming that the policy is issued at age 14, what are the answers to (a), (b), and (c)?

9. A $1,000, 40-year endowment insurance policy was bought by a person aged 25. Find (a) the net single premium, (b) the net annual premium if the policy is a 40-payment policy, and (c) the net annual premium if the policy is a 35-payment policy.

10. A $1,000, 25-year endowment insurance policy was issued to a person at age 30. Find (a) the net single premium, (b) the net annual premium if the policy is a 25-payment policy, and (c) the net annual premium if the policy is a five-payment policy.

11. Refer to Problem 9. If the policy is bought by a person at age 18, what are the answers to (a), (b), and (c)?

12. Refer to Problem 10. If the policy is issued to a person aged 35, what are the answers to (a), (b), and (c)?

★13. A policy issued to a man at age 22 promises that the insurance company will pay $1,000 if the insured dies before reaching age 40, $2,000 if he dies after reaching 40 but before 50, $3,000 if he dies after reaching 50 but before 65 or if he is alive at 65, and $1,000 if he dies after 65. Find the net annual premiums if (a) the premium of the policy is payable annually for life, and (b) the premium is payable in 15 equal annual payments.

★14. Refer to Problem 13. Assume that the policy is issued to a boy at age 12. (a) What is the annual premium if the premium of the policy is payable annually for life? (b) What is the annual premium if the premium of the policy is payable in 25 equal annual payments?

15. A $1,000, 10-year term policy is issued to a woman aged 30. (a) What is the level premium? (b) What are the natural premiums for ages 30, 33, 36, and 39?

16. A $1,000, 15-year term policy is issued to a woman at age 50. (a) What is the level premium? (b) Find the natural premiums for ages 50, 55, 60, and 64.

★17. Find the 15th terminal reserve for a $1,000 policy issued at age 22. Assume that the policy is (a) a 25-year term insurance policy, (b) a 20-year endowment insurance policy, (c) a straight life policy, and (d) a 40-payment life policy.

★18. Find the 10th terminal reserve for a $1,000 policy issued at age 28. Assume that the policy is (a) a 30-year term insurance policy, (b) a 25-year endowment insurance policy, (c) a straight life policy, and (d) a 30-payment life policy.

★19. Refer to Problem 17. Suppose that the insured stops paying the annual premium at age 37 but wishes to buy a new term insurance policy of $1,000. What is the term of the new policy if the insured buys the policy with the reserve obtained from assumption (a), (b), (c), and (d)?

★**20.** Refer to Problem 18. Suppose that the insured is unable to maintain the annual premium payment at age 38, but wants to buy a new term insurance policy of $1,000. What is the term of the new policy if the insured buys the policy with the 10th terminal reserve obtained from assumption (a), (b), (c), and (d)?

★**21.** Refer to Problem 17. Suppose that the insured stops paying the annual premium at age 37 but wishes to buy a new policy of reduced face value. What is the face value of the new policy if the reserve obtained from assumption (a) is used to buy a 10-year term insurance policy? assumption (b) is used to buy a five-year endowment insurance policy? assumption (c) is used to buy a whole life insurance policy? and assumption (d) is used to buy a whole life insurance policy?

★**22.** Refer to Problem 18. Suppose that the insured is unable to maintain the annual premium payment at age 38, but wants to buy a new policy of reduced face value. What is the face value of the new policy if the reserve obtained from assumption (a) is used to buy a 20-year term insurance policy? assumption (b) is used to buy a 15-year endowment insurance policy? assumption (c) is used to buy a whole life insurance policy? and assumption (d) is used to buy a whole life insurance policy?

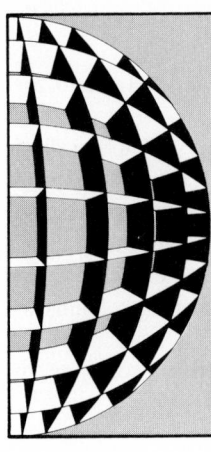

# Appendix A

# Tables

The tables included in this book are designed primarily for the text, *Mathematics for Management and Finance*. However, the coverage in the tables is complete enough for most practical business problems involving logarithms, compound interest, annuity, and life insurance. The special features of the tables are summarized below.

The tables of logarithms include six-place and seven-place mantissas (Tables 2 and 3). The difference between any two adjacent mantissas may be easily found by using the guide printed in the column headed $D$. The value in the $D$ column on each line is the *greatest* difference between adjacent mantissas on the line.

The compound interest and annuity tables (Tables 5 through 11) include the most commonly used periodic interest rates on the investment market today. The rates are:

$\frac{1}{4}\%$, $\frac{1}{3}\%$, $\frac{5}{12}\%$, $\frac{11}{24}\%$, $\frac{1}{2}\%$, $\frac{13}{24}\%$, $\frac{7}{12}\%$, $\frac{5}{8}\%$, $\frac{2}{3}\%$, $\frac{3}{4}\%$, $\frac{7}{8}\%$, $1\%$ (from 1 to 240 periods);

$1\frac{1}{8}\%$, $1\frac{1}{4}\%$, $1\frac{3}{8}\%$, $1\frac{1}{2}\%$, $1\frac{5}{8}\%$, $1\frac{3}{4}\%$, $1\frac{7}{8}\%$, $2\%$, $2\frac{1}{4}\%$, $2\frac{1}{2}\%$, $2\frac{3}{4}\%$, $3\%$, $3\frac{1}{4}\%$, $3\frac{1}{2}\%$, $3\frac{3}{4}\%$, $4\%$, $4\frac{1}{2}\%$, $5\%$, $5\frac{1}{2}\%$, $6\%$, $6\frac{1}{2}\%$, $7\%$, $7\frac{1}{2}\%$, $8\%$, $8\frac{1}{2}\%$, $9\%$, $9\frac{1}{2}\%$, $10\%$ (from 1 to 100 periods).

The selection of the above periodic rates is based on the nominal annual rates from $2\frac{1}{2}\%$ to $10\%$, at an interval of $\frac{1}{2}\%$, compounded (or converted) monthly, quarterly, semiannually, and annually. Table 4 summarizes the periodic rates and thus serves as a convenient guide to the use of Tables 5 through 11. Table 4 also presents the periodic rates converted to decimal fractions. Tables 12 and 13 (logarithms of values in Tables 5 through 10) are constructed for convenience in computing the examples and problems in Chapters 11 to 20 by the use of logarithms.

The values in Tables 5 through 13 have been computed and compiled by the author and have been checked with various sources, especially the tables in the third edition of this book. The author is grateful to Dale H. Shao for his help in obtaining the values by computer.

The insurance mortality table (Table 14—the Commissioners 1958 Standard Ordinary Mortality Table) and its Commutation Columns at $2\frac{1}{2}\%$ interest rate (Table 15) are the latest issues. The author wishes to express his appreciation to the Society of Actuaries for permission to reprint the two insurance tables. Table 16 provides logarithms of the values in Table 15. This table is computed solely by the author for figuring the answers in the examples and problems in Chapters 19 and 20 by the use of logarithms.

For a list of the titles of the tables included in the Appendix, see page vii in the Contents.

350   1,5,6,9,11

351   1,2,6,10

329.  2,6,8,10
333   12,4,6,20
336   1,7,11,12
341   1,4,7,11,17
345   1,4,5,7,10,12

# TABLE 1　　　　　THE NUMBER OF EACH DAY OF THE YEAR

| Day of Month | Jan. | Feb. | Mar. | Apr. | May | June | July | Aug. | Sept. | Oct. | Nov. | Dec. | Day of Month |
|---|---|---|---|---|---|---|---|---|---|---|---|---|---|
| 1 | 1 | 32 | 60 | 91 | 121 | 152 | 182 | 213 | 244 | 274 | 305 | 335 | 1 |
| 2 | 2 | 33 | 61 | 92 | 122 | 153 | 183 | 214 | 245 | 275 | 306 | 336 | 2 |
| 3 | 3 | 34 | 62 | 93 | 123 | 154 | 184 | 215 | 246 | 276 | 307 | 337 | 3 |
| 4 | 4 | 35 | 63 | 94 | 124 | 155 | 185 | 216 | 247 | 277 | 308 | 338 | 4 |
| 5 | 5 | 36 | 64 | 95 | 125 | 156 | 186 | 217 | 248 | 278 | 309 | 339 | 5 |
| 6 | 6 | 37 | 65 | 96 | 126 | 157 | 187 | 218 | 249 | 279 | 310 | 340 | 6 |
| 7 | 7 | 38 | 66 | 97 | 127 | 158 | 188 | 219 | 250 | 280 | 311 | 341 | 7 |
| 8 | 8 | 39 | 67 | 98 | 128 | 159 | 189 | 220 | 251 | 281 | 312 | 342 | 8 |
| 9 | 9 | 40 | 68 | 99 | 129 | 160 | 190 | 221 | 252 | 282 | 313 | 343 | 9 |
| 10 | 10 | 41 | 69 | 100 | 130 | 161 | 191 | 222 | 253 | 283 | 314 | 344 | 10 |
| 11 | 11 | 42 | 70 | 101 | 131 | 162 | 192 | 223 | 254 | 284 | 315 | 345 | 11 |
| 12 | 12 | 43 | 71 | 102 | 132 | 163 | 193 | 224 | 255 | 235 | 316 | 346 | 12 |
| 13 | 13 | 44 | 72 | 103 | 133 | 164 | 194 | 225 | 256 | 286 | 317 | 347 | 13 |
| 14 | 14 | 45 | 73 | 104 | 134 | 165 | 195 | 226 | 257 | 287 | 318 | 348 | 14 |
| 15 | 15 | 46 | 74 | 105 | 135 | 166 | 196 | 227 | 258 | 288 | 319 | 349 | 15 |
| 16 | 16 | 47 | 75 | 106 | 136 | 167 | 197 | 228 | 259 | 289 | 320 | 350 | 16 |
| 17 | 17 | 48 | 76 | 107 | 137 | 168 | 198 | 229 | 260 | 290 | 321 | 351 | 17 |
| 18 | 18 | 49 | 77 | 108 | 138 | 169 | 199 | 230 | 261 | 291 | 322 | 352 | 18 |
| 19 | 19 | 50 | 78 | 109 | 139 | 170 | 200 | 231 | 262 | 292 | 323 | 353 | 19 |
| 20 | 20 | 51 | 79 | 110 | 140 | 171 | 201 | 232 | 263 | 293 | 324 | 354 | 20 |
| 21 | 21 | 52 | 80 | 111 | 141 | 172 | 202 | 233 | 264 | 294 | 325 | 355 | 21 |
| 22 | 22 | 53 | 81 | 112 | 142 | 173 | 203 | 234 | 265 | 295 | 326 | 356 | 22 |
| 23 | 23 | 54 | 82 | 113 | 143 | 174 | 204 | 235 | 266 | 296 | 327 | 357 | 23 |
| 24 | 24 | 55 | 83 | 114 | 144 | 175 | 205 | 236 | 267 | 297 | 328 | 358 | 24 |
| 25 | 25 | 56 | 84 | 115 | 145 | 176 | 206 | 237 | 268 | 298 | 329 | 359 | 25 |
| 26 | 26 | 57 | 85 | 116 | 146 | 177 | 207 | 238 | 269 | 299 | 330 | 360 | 26 |
| 27 | 27 | 58 | 86 | 117 | 147 | 178 | 208 | 239 | 270 | 300 | 331 | 361 | 27 |
| 28 | 28 | 59 | 87 | 118 | 148 | 179 | 209 | 240 | 271 | 301 | 332 | 362 | 28 |
| 29 | 29 | * | 88 | 119 | 149 | 180 | 210 | 241 | 272 | 302 | 333 | 363 | 29 |
| 30 | 30 | | 89 | 120 | 150 | 181 | 211 | 242 | 273 | 303 | 334 | 364 | 30 |
| 31 | 31 | | 90 | | 151 | | 212 | 243 | | 304 | | 365 | 31 |

*For leap years, February has 29 days, and the number of each day from March 1 is one greater than the number given in the table.

## TABLE 2

**LOGARITHMS OF NUMBERS 1,000–1,499**
Six-Place Mantissas

| N | 0 | 1 | 2 | 3 | 4 | 5 | 6 | 7 | 8 | 9 | D# |
|---|---|---|---|---|---|---|---|---|---|---|----|
| 100 | 00 0000 | 0434 | 0868 | 1301 | 1734 | 2166 | 2598 | 3029 | 3461 | 3891 | 434 |
| 01 | 4321 | 4751 | 5181 | 5609 | 6038 | 6466 | 6894 | 7321 | 7748 | 8174 | 430 |
| 02 | 00 8600 | 9026 | 9451 | 9876 | *0300 | *0724 | *1147 | *1570 | *1993 | *2415 | 426 |
| 03 | 01 2837 | 3259 | 3680 | 4100 | 4521 | 4940 | 5360 | 5779 | 6197 | 6616 | 422 |
| 04 | 01 7033 | 7451 | 7868 | 8284 | 8700 | 9116 | 9532 | 9947 | *0361 | *0775 | 418 |
| 05 | 02 1189 | 1603 | 2016 | 2428 | 2841 | 3252 | 3664 | 4075 | 4486 | 4896 | 414 |
| 06 | 5306 | 5715 | 6125 | 6533 | 6942 | 7350 | 7757 | 8164 | 8571 | 8978 | 410 |
| 07 | 02 9384 | 9789 | *0195 | *0600 | *1004 | *1408 | *1812 | *2216 | *2619 | *3021 | 406 |
| 08 | 03 3424 | 3826 | 4227 | 4628 | 5029 | 5430 | 5830 | 6230 | 6629 | 7028 | 402 |
| 09 | 03 7426 | 7825 | 8223 | 8620 | 9017 | 9414 | 9811 | *0207 | *0602 | *0998 | 399 |
| 110 | 04 1393 | 1787 | 2182 | 2576 | 2969 | 3362 | 3755 | 4148 | 4540 | 4932 | 395 |
| 11 | 5323 | 5714 | 6105 | 6495 | 6885 | 7275 | 7664 | 8053 | 8442 | 8830 | 391 |
| 12 | 04 9218 | 9606 | 9993 | *0380 | *0766 | *1153 | *1538 | *1924 | *2309 | *2694 | 388 |
| 13 | 05 3078 | 3463 | 3846 | 4230 | 4613 | 4996 | 5378 | 5760 | 6142 | 6524 | 385 |
| 14 | 05 6905 | 7286 | 7666 | 8046 | 8426 | 8805 | 9185 | 9563 | 9942 | *0320 | 381 |
| 15 | 06 0698 | 1075 | 1452 | 1829 | 2206 | 2582 | 2958 | 3333 | 3709 | 4083 | 377 |
| 16 | 4458 | 4832 | 5206 | 5580 | 5953 | 6326 | 6699 | 7071 | 7443 | 7815 | 374 |
| 17 | 06 8186 | 8557 | 8928 | 9298 | 9668 | *0038 | *0407 | *0776 | *1145 | *1514 | 371 |
| 18 | 07 1882 | 2250 | 2617 | 2985 | 3352 | 3718 | 4085 | 4451 | 4816 | 5182 | 368 |
| 19 | 5547 | 5912 | 6276 | 6640 | 7004 | 7368 | 7731 | 8094 | 8457 | 8819 | 365 |
| 120 | 07 9181 | 9543 | 9904 | *0266 | *0626 | *0987 | 1347 | *1707 | *2067 | *2426 | 362 |
| 21 | 08. 2785 | 3144 | 3503 | 3861 | 4219 | 4576 | 4934 | 5291 | 5647 | 6004 | 359 |
| 22 | 6360 | 6716 | 7071 | 7426 | 7781 | 8136 | 8490 | 8845 | 9198 | 9552 | 356 |
| 23 | 08 9905 | *0258 | *0611 | *0963 | *1315 | *1667 | *2018 | *2370 | *2721 | *3071 | 353 |
| 24 | 09 3422 | 3772 | 4122 | 4471 | 4820 | 5169 | 5518 | 5866 | 6215 | 6562 | 350 |
| 25 | 09 6910 | 7257 | 7604 | 7951 | 8298 | 8644 | 8990 | 9335 | 9681 | *0026 | 347 |
| 26 | 10 0371 | 0715 | 1059 | 1403 | 1747 | 2091 | 2434 | 2777 | 3119 | 3462 | 344 |
| 27 | 3804 | 4146 | 4487 | 4828 | 5169 | 5510 | 5851 | 6191 | 6531 | 6871 | 342 |
| 28 | 10 7210 | 7549 | 7888 | 8227 | 8565 | 8903 | 9241 | 9579 | 9916 | *0253 | 339 |
| 29 | 11 0590 | 0926 | 1263 | 1599 | 1934 | 2270 | 2605 | 2940 | 3275 | 3609 | 337 |
| 130 | 3943 | 4277 | 4611 | 4944 | 5278 | 5611 | 5943 | 6276 | 6608 | 6940 | 334 |
| 31 | 11 7271 | 7603 | 7934 | 8265 | 8595 | 8926 | 9256 | 9586 | 9915 | *0245 | 332 |
| 32 | 12 0574 | 0903 | 1231 | 1560 | 1888 | 2216 | 2544 | 2871 | 3198 | 3525 | 329 |
| 33 | 3852 | 4178 | 4504 | 4830 | 5156 | 5481 | 5806 | 6131 | 6456 | 6781 | 326 |
| 34 | 12 7105 | 7429 | 7753 | 8076 | 8399 | 8722 | 9045 | 9368 | 9690 | *0012 | 324 |
| 35 | 13 0334 | 0655 | 0977 | 1298 | 1619 | 1939 | 2260 | 2580 | 2900 | 3219 | 322 |
| 36 | 3539 | 3858 | 4177 | 4496 | 4814 | 5133 | 5451 | 5769 | 6086 | 6403 | 319 |
| 37 | 6721 | 7037 | 7354 | 7671 | 7987 | 8303 | 8618 | 8934 | 9249 | 9564 | 317 |
| 38 | 13 9879 | *0194 | *0508 | *0822 | *1136 | *1450 | *1763 | *2076 | *2389 | *2702 | 315 |
| 39 | 14 3015 | 3327 | 3639 | 3851 | 4263 | 4574 | 4885 | 5196 | 5507 | 5818 | 312 |
| 140 | 6128 | 6438 | 6748 | 7058 | 7367 | 7676 | 7985 | 8294 | 8603 | 8911 | 310 |
| 41 | 14 9219 | 9527 | 9835 | *0142 | *0449 | *0756 | *1063 | *1370 | *1676 | *1982 | 308 |
| 42 | 15 2288 | 2594 | 2900 | 3205 | 3510 | 3815 | 4120 | 4424 | 4728 | 5032 | 306 |
| 43 | 5336 | 5640 | 5943 | 6246 | 6549 | 6852 | 7154 | 7457 | 7759 | 8061 | 304 |
| 44 | 15 8362 | 8664 | 8965 | 9266 | 9567 | 9868 | *0168 | *0469 | *0769 | *1068 | 302 |
| 45 | 16 1368 | 1667 | 1967 | 2266 | 2564 | 2863 | 3161 | 3460 | 3758 | 4055 | 300 |
| 46 | 4353 | 4650 | 4947 | 5244 | 5541 | 5838 | 6134 | 6430 | 6726 | 7022 | 297 |
| 47 | 16 7317 | 7613 | 7908 | 8203 | 8497 | 8792 | 9086 | 9380 | 9674 | 9968 | 296 |
| 48 | 17 0262 | 0555 | 0848 | 1141 | 1434 | 1726 | 2019 | 2311 | 2603 | 2895 | 293 |
| 49 | 3186 | 3478 | 3769 | 4060 | 4351 | 4641 | 4932 | 5222 | 5512 | 5802 | 292 |
| N | 0 | 1 | 2 | 3 | 4 | 5 | 6 | 7 | 8 | 9 | D |

* Prefix first two places on next line.
  *Example:* The mantissa for number (N) 1072 is *03* 0195.
# The *highest difference* between adjacent mantissas on the *individual line*. It is also the *lowest difference* between adjacent mantissas on the *preceding line* in many cases.

# TABLE 2

Table
2

| N | 0 | 1 | 2 | 3 | 4 | 5 | 6 | 7 | 8 | 9 | D |
|---|---|---|---|---|---|---|---|---|---|---|---|
| **150** | 17 6091 | 6381 | 6670 | 6959 | 7248 | 7536 | 7825 | 8113 | 8401 | 8689 | 290 |
| 51 | 17 8977 | 9264 | 9552 | 9839 | *0126 | *0413 | *0699 | *0986 | *1272 | *1558 | 288 |
| 52 | 18 1844 | 2129 | 2415 | 2700 | 2985 | 3270 | 3555 | 3839 | 4123 | 4407 | 286 |
| 53 | 4691 | 4975 | 5259 | 5542 | 5825 | 6108 | 6391 | 6674 | 6956 | 7239 | 284 |
| 54 | 18 7521 | 7803 | 8084 | 8366 | 8647 | 8928 | 9209 | 9490 | 9771 | *0051 | 282 |
| **55** | 19 0332 | 0612 | 0892 | 1171 | 1451 | 1730 | 2010 | 2289 | 2567 | 2846 | 280 |
| 56 | 3125 | 3403 | 3681 | 3959 | 4237 | 4514 | 4792 | 5069 | 5346 | 5623 | 278 |
| 57 | 5900 | 6176 | 6453 | 6729 | 7005 | 7281 | 7556 | 7832 | 8107 | 8382 | 277 |
| 58 | 19 8657 | 8932 | 9206 | 9481 | 9755 | *0029 | *0303 | *0577 | *0850 | *1124 | 275 |
| 59 | 20 1397 | 1670 | 1943 | 2216 | 2488 | 2761 | 3033 | 3305 | 3577 | 3848 | 273 |
| **160** | 4120 | 4391 | 4663 | 4934 | 5204 | 5475 | 5746 | 6016 | 6286 | 6556 | 272 |
| 61 | 6826 | 7096 | 7365 | 7634 | 7904 | 8173 | 8441 | 8710 | 8979 | 9247 | 270 |
| 62 | 20 9515 | 9783 | *0051 | *0319 | *0586 | *0853 | *1121 | *1388 | *1654 | *1921 | 268 |
| 63 | 21 2188 | 2454 | 2720 | 2986 | 3252 | 3518 | 3783 | 4049 | 4314 | 4579 | 266 |
| 64 | 4844 | 5109 | 5373 | 5638 | 5902 | 6166 | 6430 | 6694 | 6957 | 7221 | 265 |
| **65** | 21 7484 | 7747 | 8010 | 8273 | 8536 | 8798 | 9060 | 9323 | 9585 | 9846 | 263 |
| 66 | 22 0108 | 0370 | 0631 | 0892 | 1153 | 1414 | 1675 | 1936 | 2196 | 2456 | 262 |
| 67 | 2716 | 2976 | 3236 | 3496 | 3755 | 4015 | 4274 | 4533 | 4792 | 5051 | 260 |
| 68 | 5309 | 5568 | 5826 | 6084 | 6342 | 6600 | 6858 | 7115 | 7372 | 7630 | 259 |
| 69 | 22 7887 | 8144 | 8400 | 8657 | 8913 | 9170 | 9426 | 9682 | 9938 | *0193 | 257 |
| **170** | 23 0449 | 0704 | 0960 | 1215 | 1470 | 1724 | 1979 | 2234 | 2488 | 2742 | 256 |
| 71 | 2996 | 3250 | 3504 | 3757 | 4011 | 4264 | 4517 | 4770 | 5023 | 5276 | 254 |
| 72 | 5528 | 5781 | 6033 | 6285 | 6537 | 6789 | 7041 | 7292 | 7544 | 7795 | 253 |
| 73 | 23 8046 | 8297 | 8548 | 8799 | 9049 | 9299 | 9550 | 9800 | *0050 | *0300 | 251 |
| 74 | 24 0549 | 0799 | 1048 | 1297 | 1546 | 1795 | 2044 | 2293 | 2541 | 2790 | 250 |
| **75** | 3038 | 3286 | 3534 | 3782 | 4030 | 4277 | 4525 | 4772 | 5019 | 5266 | 248 |
| 76 | 5513 | 5759 | 6006 | 6252 | 6499 | 6745 | 6991 | 7237 | 7482 | 7728 | 247 |
| 77 | 24 7973 | 8219 | 8464 | 8709 | 8954 | 9198 | 9443 | 9687 | 9932 | *0176 | 246 |
| 78 | 25 0420 | 0664 | 0908 | 1151 | 1395 | 1638 | 1881 | 2125 | 2368 | 2610 | 244 |
| 79 | 2853 | 3096 | 3338 | 3580 | 3822 | 4064 | 4306 | 4548 | 4790 | 5031 | 243 |
| **180** | 5273 | 5514 | 5755 | 5996 | 6237 | 6477 | 6718 | 6958 | 7198 | 7439 | 241 |
| 81 | 25 7679 | 7918 | 8158 | 8398 | 8637 | 8877 | 9116 | 9355 | 9594 | 9833 | 240 |
| 82 | 26 0071 | 0310 | 0548 | 0787 | 1025 | 1263 | 1501 | 1739 | 1976 | 2214 | 239 |
| 83 | 2451 | 2688 | 2925 | 3162 | 3399 | 3636 | 3873 | 4109 | 4346 | 4582 | 237 |
| 84 | 4818 | 5054 | 5290 | 5525 | 5761 | 5996 | 6232 | 6467 | 6702 | 6937 | 236 |
| **85** | 7172 | 7406 | 7641 | 7875 | 8110 | 8344 | 8578 | 8812 | 9046 | 9279 | 235 |
| 86 | 26 9513 | 9746 | 9980 | *0213 | *0446 | *0679 | *0912 | *1144 | *1377 | *1609 | 234 |
| 87 | 27 1842 | 2074 | 2306 | 2538 | 2770 | 3001 | 3233 | 3464 | 3696 | 3927 | 232 |
| 88 | 4158 | 4389 | 4620 | 4850 | 5081 | 5311 | 5542 | 5772 | 6002 | 6232 | 231 |
| 89 | 6462 | 6692 | 6921 | 7151 | 7380 | 7609 | 7838 | 8067 | 8296 | 8525 | 230 |
| **190** | 27 8754 | 8982 | 9211 | 9439 | 9667 | 9895 | *0123 | *0351 | *0578 | *0806 | 229 |
| 91 | 28 1033 | 1261 | 1488 | 1715 | 1942 | 2169 | 2396 | 2622 | 2849 | 3075 | 228 |
| 92 | 3301 | 3527 | 3753 | 3979 | 4205 | 4431 | 4656 | 4882 | 5107 | 5332 | 226 |
| 93 | 5557 | 5782 | 6007 | 6232 | 6456 | 6681 | 6905 | 7130 | 7354 | 7578 | 225 |
| 94 | 28 7802 | 8026 | 8249 | 8473 | 8696 | 8920 | 9143 | 9366 | 9589 | 9812 | 224 |
| **95** | 29 0035 | 0257 | 0480 | 0702 | 0925 | 1147 | 1369 | 1591 | 1813 | 2034 | 223 |
| 96 | 2256 | 2478 | 2699 | 2920 | 3141 | 3363 | 3584 | 3804 | 4025 | 4246 | 222 |
| 97 | 4466 | 4687 | 4907 | 5127 | 5347 | 5567 | 5787 | 6007 | 6226 | 6446 | 221 |
| 98 | 6665 | 6884 | 7104 | 7323 | 7542 | 7761 | 7979 | 8198 | 8416 | 8635 | 220 |
| 99 | 29 8853 | 9071 | 9289 | 9507 | 9725 | 9943 | *0161 | *0378 | *0595 | *0813 | 218 |
| N | 0 | 1 | 2 | 3 | 4 | 5 | 6 | 7 | 8 | 9 | D |

## TABLE 2

**LOGARITHMS OF NUMBERS 2,000–2,499**
Six-Place Mantissas

| N | 0 | 1 | 2 | 3 | 4 | 5 | 6 | 7 | 8 | 9 | D |
|---|---|---|---|---|---|---|---|---|---|---|---|
| 200 | 30 1030 | 1247 | 1464 | 1681 | 1898 | 2114 | 2331 | 2547 | 2764 | 2980 | 217 |
| 01 | 3196 | 3412 | 3628 | 3844 | 4059 | 4275 | 4491 | 4706 | 4921 | 5136 | 216 |
| 02 | 5351 | 5566 | 5781 | 5996 | 6211 | 6425 | 6639 | 6854 | 7068 | 7282 | 215 |
| 03 | 7496 | 7710 | 7924 | 8137 | 8351 | 8564 | 8778 | 8991 | 9204 | 9417 | 214 |
| 04 | 30 9630 | 9843 | *0056 | *0268 | *0481 | *0693 | *0906 | *1118 | *1330 | *1542 | 213 |
| 05 | 31 1754 | 1966 | 2177 | 2389 | 2600 | 2812 | 3023 | 3234 | 3445 | 3656 | 212 |
| 06 | 3867 | 4078 | 4289 | 4499 | 4710 | 4920 | 5130 | 5340 | 5551 | 5760 | 211 |
| 07 | 5970 | 6180 | 6390 | 6599 | 6809 | 7018 | 7227 | 7436 | 7646 | 7854 | 210 |
| 08 | 31 8063 | 8272 | 8481 | 8689 | 8898 | 9106 | 9314 | 9522 | 9730 | 9938 | 209 |
| 09 | 32 0146 | 0354 | 0562 | 0769 | 0977 | 1184 | 1391 | 1598 | 1805 | 2012 | 208 |
| 210 | 2219 | 2426 | 2633 | 2839 | 3046 | 3252 | 3458 | 3665 | 3871 | 4077 | 207 |
| 11 | 4282 | 4488 | 4694 | 4899 | 5105 | 5310 | 5516 | 5721 | 5926 | 6131 | 206 |
| 12 | 6336 | 6541 | 6745 | 6950 | 7155 | 7359 | 7563 | 7767 | 7972 | 8176 | 205 |
| 13 | 32 8380 | 8583 | 8787 | 8991 | 9194 | 9398 | 9601 | 9805 | *0008 | *0211 | 204 |
| 14 | 33 0414 | 0617 | 0819 | 1022 | 1225 | 1427 | 1630 | 1832 | 2034 | 2236 | 203 |
| 15 | 2438 | 2640 | 2842 | 3044 | 3246 | 3447 | 3649 | 3850 | 4051 | 4253 | 202 |
| 16 | 4454 | 4655 | 4856 | 5057 | 5257 | 5458 | 5658 | 5859 | 6059 | 6260 | 201 |
| 17 | 6460 | 6660 | 6860 | 7060 | 7260 | 7459 | 7659 | 7858 | 8058 | 8257 | 200 |
| 18 | 33 8456 | 8656 | 8855 | 9054 | 9253 | 9451 | 9650 | 9849 | *0047 | *0246 | 200 |
| 19 | 34 0444 | 0642 | 0841 | 1039 | 1237 | 1435 | 1632 | 1830 | 2028 | 2225 | 199 |
| 220 | 2423 | 2620 | 2817 | 3014 | 3212 | 3409 | 3606 | 3802 | 3999 | 4196 | 198 |
| 21 | 4392 | 4589 | 4785 | 4981 | 5178 | 5374 | 5570 | 5766 | 5962 | 6157 | 197 |
| 22 | 6353 | 6549 | 6744 | 6939 | 7135 | 7330 | 7525 | 7720 | 7915 | 8110 | 196 |
| 23 | 34 8305 | 8500 | 8694 | 8889 | 9083 | 9278 | 9472 | 9666 | 9860 | *0054 | 195 |
| 24 | 35 0248 | 0442 | 0636 | 0829 | 1023 | 1216 | 1410 | 1603 | 1796 | 1989 | 194 |
| 25 | 2183 | 2375 | 2568 | 2761 | 2954 | 3147 | 3339 | 3532 | 3724 | 3916 | 193 |
| 26 | 4108 | 4301 | 4493 | 4685 | 4876 | 5068 | 5260 | 5452 | 5643 | 5834 | 192 |
| 27 | 6026 | 6217 | 6408 | 6599 | 6790 | 6981 | 7172 | 7363 | 7554 | 7744 | 191 |
| 28 | 7935 | 8125 | 8316 | 8506 | 8696 | 8886 | 9076 | 9266 | 9456 | 9646 | 191 |
| 29 | 35 9835 | *0025 | *0215 | *0404 | *0593 | *0783 | *0972 | *1161 | *1350 | *1539 | 190 |
| 230 | 36 1728 | 1917 | 2105 | 2294 | 2482 | 2671 | 2859 | 3048 | 3236 | 3424 | 189 |
| 31 | 3612 | 3800 | 3988 | 4176 | 4363 | 4551 | 4739 | 4926 | 5113 | 5301 | 188 |
| 32 | 5488 | 5675 | 5862 | 6049 | 6236 | 6423 | 6610 | 6796 | 6983 | 7169 | 187 |
| 33 | 7356 | 7542 | 7729 | 7915 | 8101 | 8287 | 8473 | 8659 | 8845 | 9030 | 187 |
| 34 | 36 9216 | 9401 | 9587 | 9772 | 9958 | *0143 | *0328 | *0513 | *0698 | *0883 | 186 |
| 35 | 37 1068 | 1253 | 1437 | 1622 | 1806 | 1991 | 2175 | 2360 | 2544 | 2728 | 185 |
| 36 | 2912 | 3096 | 3280 | 3464 | 3647 | 3831 | 4015 | 4198 | 4382 | 4565 | 184 |
| 37 | 4748 | 4932 | 5115 | 5298 | 5481 | 5664 | 5846 | 6029 | 6212 | 6394 | 184 |
| 38 | 6577 | 6759 | 6942 | 7124 | 7306 | 7488 | 7670 | 7852 | 8034 | 8216 | 183 |
| 39 | 37 8398 | 8580 | 8761 | 8943 | 9124 | 9306 | 9487 | 9668 | 9849 | *0030 | 182 |
| 240 | 38 0211 | 0392 | 0573 | 0754 | 0934 | 1115 | 1296 | 1476 | 1656 | 1837 | 181 |
| 41 | 2017 | 2197 | 2377 | 2557 | 2737 | 2917 | 3097 | 3277 | 3456 | 3636 | 180 |
| 42 | 3815 | 3995 | 4174 | 4353 | 4533 | 4712 | 4891 | 5070 | 5249 | 5428 | 180 |
| 43 | 5606 | 5785 | 5964 | 6142 | 6321 | 6499 | 6677 | 6856 | 7034 | 7212 | 179 |
| 44 | 7390 | 7568 | 7746 | 7923 | 8101 | 8279 | 8456 | 8634 | 8811 | 8989 | 178 |
| 45 | 38 9166 | 9343 | 9520 | 9698 | 9875 | *0051 | *0228 | *0405 | *0582 | *0759 | 178 |
| 46 | 39 0935 | 1112 | 1288 | 1464 | 1641 | 1817 | 1993 | 2169 | 2345 | 2521 | 177 |
| 47 | 2697 | 2873 | 3048 | 3224 | 3400 | 3575 | 3751 | 3926 | 4101 | 4277 | 176 |
| 48 | 4452 | 4627 | 4802 | 4977 | 5152 | 5326 | 5501 | 5676 | 5850 | 6025 | 175 |
| 49 | 6199 | 6374 | 6548 | 6722 | 6896 | 7071 | 7245 | 7419 | 7592 | 7766 | 175 |
| N | 0 | 1 | 2 | 3 | 4 | 5 | 6 | 7 | 8 | 9 | D |

**LOGARITHMS OF NUMBERS 2,500–2,999**

# TABLE 2

Six-Place Mantissas

Table 2

| N | 0 | 1 | 2 | 3 | 4 | 5 | 6 | 7 | 8 | 9 | D |
|---|---|---|---|---|---|---|---|---|---|---|---|
| 250 | 39 7940 | 8114 | 8287 | 8461 | 8634 | 8808 | 8981 | 9154 | 9328 | 9501 | 174 |
| 51 | 39 9674 | 9847 | *0020 | *0192 | *0365 | *0538 | *0711 | *0883 | *1056 | *1228 | 173 |
| 52 | 40 1401 | 1573 | 1745 | 1917 | 2089 | 2261 | 2433 | 2605 | 2777 | 2949 | 172 |
| 53 | 3121 | 3292 | 3464 | 3635 | 3807 | 3978 | 4149 | 4320 | 4492 | 4663 | 172 |
| 54 | 4834 | 5005 | 5176 | 5346 | 5517 | 5688 | 5858 | 6029 | 6199 | 6370 | 171 |
| 55 | 6540 | 6710 | 6881 | 7051 | 7221 | 7391 | 7561 | 7731 | 7901 | 8070 | 171 |
| 56 | 8240 | 8410 | 8579 | 8749 | 8918 | 9087 | 9257 | 9426 | 9595 | 9764 | 170 |
| 57 | 40 9933 | *0102 | *0271 | *0440 | *0609 | *0777 | *0946 | *1114 | *1283 | *1451 | 169 |
| 58 | 41 1620 | 1788 | 1956 | 2124 | 2293 | 2461 | 2629 | 2796 | 2964 | 3132 | 169 |
| 59 | 3300 | 3467 | 3635 | 3803 | 3970 | 4137 | 4305 | 4472 | 4639 | 4806 | 168 |
| 260 | 4973 | 5140 | 5307 | 5474 | 5641 | 5808 | 5974 | 6141 | 6308 | 6474 | 167 |
| 61 | 6641 | 6807 | 6973 | 7139 | 7306 | 7472 | 7638 | 7804 | 7970 | 8135 | 167 |
| 62 | 8301 | 8467 | 8633 | 8798 | 8964 | 9129 | 9295 | 9460 | 9625 | 9791 | 166 |
| 63 | 41 9956 | *0121 | *0286 | *0451 | *0616 | *0781 | *0945 | *1110 | *1275 | *1439 | 165 |
| 64 | 42 1604 | 1768 | 1933 | 2097 | 2261 | 2426 | 2590 | 2754 | 2918 | 3082 | 165 |
| 65 | 3246 | 3410 | 3574 | 3737 | 3901 | 4065 | 4228 | 4392 | 4555 | 4718 | 164 |
| 66 | 4882 | 5045 | 5208 | 5371 | 5534 | 5697 | 5860 | 6023 | 6186 | 6349 | 163 |
| 67 | 6511 | 6674 | 6836 | 6999 | 7161 | 7324 | 7486 | 7648 | 7811 | 7973 | 163 |
| 68 | 8135 | 8297 | 8459 | 8621 | 8783 | 8944 | 9106 | 9268 | 9429 | 9591 | 162 |
| 69 | 42 9752 | 9914 | *0075 | *0236 | *0398 | *0559 | *0720 | *0881 | *1042 | *1203 | 162 |
| 270 | 43 1364 | 1525 | 1685 | 1846 | 2007 | 2167 | 2328 | 2488 | 2649 | 2809 | 161 |
| 71 | 2969 | 3130 | 3290 | 3450 | 3610 | 3770 | 3930 | 4090 | 4249 | 4409 | 161 |
| 72 | 4569 | 4729 | 4888 | 5048 | 5207 | 5367 | 5526 | 5685 | 5844 | 6004 | 160 |
| 73 | 6163 | 6322 | 6481 | 6640 | 6799 | 6957 | 7116 | 7275 | 7433 | 7592 | 159 |
| 74 | 7751 | 7909 | 8067 | 8226 | 8384 | 8542 | 8701 | 8859 | 9017 | 9175 | 159 |
| 75 | 43 9333 | 9491 | 9648 | 9806 | 9964 | *0122 | *0279 | *0437 | *0594 | *0752 | 158 |
| 76 | 44 0909 | 1066 | 1224 | 1381 | 1538 | 1695 | 1852 | 2009 | 2166 | 2323 | 158 |
| 77 | 2480 | 2637 | 2793 | 2950 | 3106 | 3263 | 3419 | 3576 | 3732 | 3889 | 157 |
| 78 | 4045 | 4201 | 4357 | 4513 | 4669 | 4825 | 4981 | 5137 | 5293 | 5449 | 156 |
| 79 | 5604 | 5760 | 5915 | 6071 | 6226 | 6382 | 6537 | 6692 | 6848 | 7003 | 156 |
| 280 | 7158 | 7313 | 7468 | 7623 | 7778 | 7933 | 8088 | 8242 | 8397 | 8552 | 155 |
| 81 | 44 8706 | 8861 | 9015 | 9170 | 9324 | 9478 | 9633 | 9787 | 9941 | *0095 | 155 |
| 82 | 45 0249 | 0403 | 0557 | 0711 | 0865 | 1018 | 1172 | 1326 | 1479 | 1633 | 154 |
| 83 | 1786 | 1940 | 2093 | 2247 | 2400 | 2553 | 2706 | 2859 | 3012 | 3165 | 154 |
| 84 | 3318 | 3471 | 3624 | 3777 | 3930 | 4082 | 4235 | 4387 | 4540 | 4692 | 153 |
| 85 | 4845 | 4997 | 5150 | 5302 | 5454 | 5606 | 5758 | 5910 | 6062 | 6214 | 153 |
| 86 | 6366 | 6518 | 6670 | 6821 | 6973 | 7125 | 7276 | 7428 | 7579 | 7731 | 152 |
| 87 | 7882 | 8033 | 8184 | 8336 | 8487 | 8638 | 8789 | 8940 | 9091 | 9242 | 152 |
| 88 | 45 9392 | 9543 | 9694 | 9845 | 9995 | *0146 | *0296 | *0447 | *0597 | *0748 | 151 |
| 89 | 46 0898 | 1048 | 1198 | 1348 | 1499 | 1649 | 1799 | 1948 | 2098 | 2248 | 151 |
| 290 | 2398 | 2548 | 2697 | 2847 | 2997 | 3146 | 3296 | 3445 | 3594 | 3744 | 150 |
| 91 | 3893 | 4042 | 4191 | 4340 | 4490 | 4639 | 4788 | 4936 | 5085 | 5234 | 149 |
| 92 | 5383 | 5532 | 5680 | 5829 | 5977 | 6126 | 6274 | 6423 | 6571 | 6719 | 149 |
| 93 | 6868 | 7016 | 7164 | 7312 | 7460 | 7608 | 7756 | 7904 | 8052 | 8200 | 148 |
| 94 | 8347 | 8495 | 8643 | 8790 | 8938 | 9085 | 9233 | 9380 | 9527 | 9675 | 148 |
| 95 | 46 9822 | 9969 | *0116 | *0263 | *0410 | *0557 | *0704 | *0851 | *0998 | *1145 | 147 |
| 96 | 47 1292 | 1438 | 1585 | 1732 | 1878 | 2025 | 2171 | 2318 | 2464 | 2610 | 147 |
| 97 | 2756 | 2903 | 3049 | 3195 | 3341 | 3487 | 3633 | 3779 | 3925 | 4071 | 147 |
| 98 | 4216 | 4362 | 4508 | 4653 | 4799 | 4944 | 5090 | 5235 | 5381 | 5526 | 146 |
| 99 | 5671 | 5816 | 5962 | 6107 | 6252 | 6397 | 6542 | 6687 | 6832 | 6976 | 146 |
| N | 0 | 1 | 2 | 3 | 4 | 5 | 6 | 7 | 8 | 9 | D |

## TABLE 2

| N | 0 | 1 | 2 | 3 | 4 | 5 | 6 | 7 | 8 | 9 | D |
|---|---|---|---|---|---|---|---|---|---|---|---|
| 300 | 47 7121 | 7266 | 7411 | 7555 | 7700 | 7844 | 7989 | 8133 | 8278 | 8422 | 145 |
| 01 | 47 8566 | 8711 | 8855 | 8999 | 9143 | 9287 | 9431 | 9575 | 9719 | 9863 | 145 |
| 02 | 48 0007 | 0151 | 0294 | 0438 | 0582 | 0725 | 0869 | 1012 | 1156 | 1299 | 144 |
| 03 | 1443 | 1586 | 1729 | 1872 | 2016 | 2159 | 2302 | 2445 | 2588 | 2731 | 144 |
| 04 | 2874 | 3016 | 3159 | 3302 | 3445 | 3587 | 3730 | 3872 | 4015 | 4157 | 143 |
| 05 | 4300 | 4442 | 4585 | 4727 | 4869 | 5011 | 5153 | 5295 | 5437 | 5579 | 143 |
| 06 | 5721 | 5863 | 6005 | 6147 | 6289 | 6430 | 6572 | 6714 | 6855 | 6997 | 142 |
| 07 | 7138 | 7280 | 7421 | 7563 | 7704 | 7845 | 7986 | 8127 | 8269 | 8410 | 142 |
| 08 | 8551 | 8692 | 8833 | 8974 | 9114 | 9255 | 9396 | 9537 | 9677 | 9818 | 141 |
| 09 | 48 9958 | *0099 | *0239 | *0380 | *0520 | *0661 | *0801 | *0941 | *1081 | *1222 | 141 |
| 310 | 49 1362 | 1502 | 1642 | 1782 | 1922 | 2062 | 2201 | 2341 | 2481 | 2621 | 140 |
| 11 | 2760 | 2900 | 3040 | 3179 | 3319 | 3458 | 3597 | 3737 | 3876 | 4015 | 140 |
| 12 | 4155 | 4294 | 4433 | 4572 | 4711 | 4850 | 4989 | 5128 | 5267 | 5406 | 139 |
| 13 | 5544 | 5683 | 5822 | 5960 | 6099 | 6238 | 6376 | 6515 | 6653 | 6791 | 139 |
| 14 | 6930 | 7068 | 7206 | 7344 | 7483 | 7621 | 7759 | 7897 | 8035 | 8173 | 139 |
| 15 | 8311 | 8448 | 8586 | 8724 | 8862 | 8999 | 9137 | 9275 | 9412 | 9550 | 138 |
| 16 | 49 9687 | 9824 | 9962 | *0099 | *0236 | *0374 | *0511 | *0648 | *0785 | *0922 | 138 |
| 17 | 50 1059 | 1196 | 1333 | 1470 | 1607 | 1744 | 1880 | 2017 | 2154 | 2291 | 137 |
| 18 | 2427 | 2564 | 2700 | 2837 | 2973 | 3109 | 3246 | 3382 | 3518 | 3655 | 137 |
| 19 | 3791 | 3927 | 4063 | 4199 | 4335 | 4471 | 4607 | 4743 | 4878 | 5014 | 136 |
| 320 | 5150 | 5286 | 5421 | 5557 | 5693 | 5828 | 5964 | 6099 | 6234 | 6370 | 136 |
| 21 | 6505 | 6640 | 6776 | 6911 | 7046 | 7181 | 7316 | 7451 | 7586 | 7721 | 136 |
| 22 | 7856 | 7991 | 8126 | 8260 | 8395 | 8530 | 8664 | 8799 | 8934 | 9068 | 135 |
| 23 | 50 9203 | 9337 | 9471 | 9606 | 9740 | 9874 | *0009 | *0143 | *0277 | *0411 | 135 |
| 24 | 51 0545 | 0679 | 0813 | 0947 | 1081 | 1215 | 1349 | 1482 | 1616 | 1750 | 134 |
| 25 | 1883 | 2017 | 2151 | 2284 | 2418 | 2551 | 2684 | 2818 | 2951 | 3084 | 134 |
| 26 | 3218 | 3351 | 3484 | 3617 | 3750 | 3883 | 4016 | 4149 | 4282 | 4415 | 133 |
| 27 | 4548 | 4681 | 4813 | 4946 | 5079 | 5211 | 5344 | 5476 | 5609 | 5741 | 133 |
| 28 | 5874 | 6006 | 6139 | 6271 | 6403 | 6535 | 6668 | 6800 | 6932 | 7064 | 133 |
| 29 | 7196 | 7328 | 7460 | 7592 | 7724 | 7855 | 7987 | 8119 | 8251 | 8382 | 132 |
| 330 | 8514 | 8646 | 8777 | 8909 | 9040 | 9171 | 9303 | 9434 | 9566 | 9697 | 132 |
| 31 | 51 9828 | 9959 | *0090 | *0221 | *0353 | *0484 | *0615 | *0745 | *0876 | *1007 | 132 |
| 32 | 52 1138 | 1269 | 1400 | 1530 | 1661 | 1792 | 1922 | 2053 | 2183 | 2314 | 131 |
| 33 | 2444 | 2575 | 2705 | 2835 | 2966 | 3096 | 3226 | 3356 | 3486 | 3616 | 131 |
| 34 | 3746 | 3876 | 4006 | 4136 | 4266 | 4396 | 4526 | 4656 | 4785 | 4915 | 130 |
| 35 | 5045 | 5174 | 5304 | 5434 | 5563 | 5693 | 5822 | 5951 | 6081 | 6210 | 130 |
| 36 | 6339 | 6469 | 6598 | 6727 | 6856 | 6985 | 7114 | 7243 | 7372 | 7501 | 130 |
| 37 | 7630 | 7759 | 7888 | 8016 | 8145 | 8274 | 8402 | 8531 | 8660 | 8788 | 129 |
| 38 | 52 8917 | 9045 | 9174 | 9302 | 9430 | 9559 | 9687 | 9815 | 9943 | *0072 | 129 |
| 39 | 53 0200 | 0328 | 0456 | 0584 | 0712 | 0840 | 0968 | 1096 | 1223 | 1351 | 128 |
| 340 | 1479 | 1607 | 1734 | 1862 | 1990 | 2117 | 2245 | 2372 | 2500 | 2627 | 128 |
| 41 | 2754 | 2882 | 3009 | 3136 | 3264 | 3391 | 3518 | 3645 | 3772 | 3899 | 128 |
| 42 | 4026 | 4153 | 4280 | 4407 | 4534 | 4661 | 4787 | 4914 | 5041 | 5167 | 127 |
| 43 | 5294 | 5421 | 5547 | 5674 | 5800 | 5927 | 6053 | 6180 | 6306 | 6432 | 127 |
| 44 | 6558 | 6685 | 6811 | 6937 | 7063 | 7189 | 7315 | 7441 | 7567 | 7693 | 127 |
| 45 | 7819 | 7945 | 8071 | 8197 | 8322 | 8448 | 8574 | 8699 | 8825 | 8951 | 126 |
| 46 | 53 9076 | 9202 | 9327 | 9452 | 9578 | 9703 | 9829 | 9954 | *0079 | *0204 | 126 |
| 47 | 54 0329 | 0455 | 0580 | 0705 | 0830 | 0955 | 1080 | 1205 | 1330 | 1454 | 126 |
| 48 | 1579 | 1704 | 1829 | 1953 | 2078 | 2203 | 2327 | 2452 | 2576 | 2701 | 125 |
| 49 | 2825 | 2950 | 3074 | 3199 | 3323 | 3447 | 3571 | 3696 | 3820 | 3944 | 125 |
| N | 0 | 1 | 2 | 3 | 4 | 5 | 6 | 7 | 8 | 9 | D |

## TABLE 2

Table
2

| N | 0 | 1 | 2 | 3 | 4 | 5 | 6 | 7 | 8 | 9 | D |
|---|---|---|---|---|---|---|---|---|---|---|---|
| 350 | 54 4068 | 4192 | 4316 | 4440 | 4564 | 4688 | 4812 | 4936 | 5060 | 5183 | 124 |
| 51 | 5307 | 5431 | 5555 | 5678 | 5802 | 5925 | 6049 | 6172 | 6296 | 6419 | 124 |
| 52 | 6543 | 6666 | 6789 | 6913 | 7036 | 7159 | 7282 | 7405 | 7529 | 7652 | 124 |
| 53 | 7775 | 7898 | 8021 | 8144 | 8267 | 8389 | 8512 | 8635 | 8758 | 8881 | 123 |
| 54 | 54 9003 | 9126 | 9249 | 9371 | 9494 | 9616 | 9739 | 9861 | 9984 | *0106 | 123 |
| 55 | 55 0228 | 0351 | 0473 | 0595 | 0717 | 0840 | 0962 | 1084 | 1206 | 1328 | 123 |
| 56 | 1450 | 1572 | 1694 | 1816 | 1938 | 2060 | 2181 | 2303 | 2425 | 2547 | 122 |
| 57 | 2668 | 2790 | 2911 | 3033 | 3155 | 3276 | 3398 | 3519 | 3640 | 3762 | 122 |
| 58 | 3883 | 4004 | 4126 | 4247 | 4368 | 4489 | 4610 | 4731 | 4852 | 4973 | 122 |
| 59 | 5094 | 5215 | 5336 | 5457 | 5578 | 5699 | 5820 | 5940 | 6061 | 6182 | 121 |
| 360 | 6303 | 6423 | 6544 | 6664 | 6785 | 6905 | 7026 | 7146 | 7267 | 7387 | 121 |
| 61 | 7507 | 7627 | 7748 | 7868 | 7988 | 8108 | 8228 | 8349 | 8469 | 8589 | 121 |
| 62 | 8709 | 8829 | 8948 | 9068 | 9188 | 9308 | 9428 | 9548 | 9667 | 9787 | 120 |
| 63 | 55 9907 | *0026 | *0146 | *0265 | *0385 | *0504 | *0624 | *0743 | *0863 | *0982 | 120 |
| 64 | 56 1101 | 1221 | 1340 | 1459 | 1578 | 1698 | 1817 | 1936 | 2055 | 2174 | 120 |
| 65 | 2293 | 2412 | 2531 | 2650 | 2769 | 2887 | 3006 | 3125 | 3244 | 3362 | 119 |
| 66 | 3481 | 3600 | 3718 | 3837 | 3955 | 4074 | 4192 | 4311 | 4429 | 4548 | 119 |
| 67 | 4666 | 4784 | 4903 | 5021 | 5139 | 5257 | 5376 | 5494 | 5612 | 5730 | 119 |
| 68 | 5848 | 5966 | 6084 | 6202 | 6320 | 6437 | 6555 | 6673 | 6791 | 6909 | 118 |
| 69 | 7026 | 7144 | 7262 | 7379 | 7497 | 7614 | 7732 | 7849 | 7967 | 8084 | 118 |
| 370 | 8202 | 8319 | 8436 | 8554 | 8671 | 8788 | 8905 | 9023 | 9140 | 9257 | 118 |
| 71 | 56 9374 | 9491 | 9608 | 9725 | 9842 | 9959 | *0076 | *0193 | *0309 | *0426 | 117 |
| 72 | 57 0543 | 0660 | 0776 | 0893 | 1010 | 1126 | 1243 | 1359 | 1476 | 1592 | 117 |
| 73 | 1709 | 1825 | 1942 | 2058 | 2174 | 2291 | 2407 | 2523 | 2639 | 2755 | 117 |
| 74 | 2872 | 2988 | 3104 | 3220 | 3336 | 3452 | 3568 | 3684 | 3800 | 3915 | 116 |
| 75 | 4031 | 4147 | 4263 | 4379 | 4494 | 4610 | 4726 | 4841 | 4957 | 5072 | 116 |
| 76 | 5188 | 5303 | 5419 | 5534 | 5650 | 5765 | 5880 | 5996 | 6111 | 6226 | 116 |
| 77 | 6341 | 6457 | 6572 | 6687 | 6802 | 6917 | 7032 | 7147 | 7262 | 7377 | 116 |
| 78 | 7492 | 7607 | 7722 | 7836 | 7951 | 8066 | 8181 | 8295 | 8410 | 8525 | 115 |
| 79 | 8639 | 8754 | 8868 | 8983 | 9097 | 9212 | 9326 | 9441 | 9555 | 9669 | 115 |
| 380 | 57 9784 | 9898 | *0012 | *0126 | *0241 | *0355 | *0469 | *0583 | *0697 | *0811 | 115 |
| 81 | 58 0925 | 1039 | 1153 | 1267 | 1381 | 1495 | 1608 | 1722 | 1836 | 1950 | 114 |
| 82 | 2063 | 2177 | 2291 | 2404 | 2518 | 2631 | 2745 | 2858 | 2972 | 3085 | 114 |
| 83 | 3199 | 3312 | 3426 | 3539 | 3652 | 3765 | 3879 | 3992 | 4105 | 4218 | 114 |
| 84 | 4331 | 4444 | 4557 | 4670 | 4783 | 4896 | 5009 | 5122 | 5235 | 5348 | 113 |
| 85 | 5461 | 5574 | 5686 | 5799 | 5912 | 6024 | 6137 | 6250 | 6362 | 6475 | 113 |
| 86 | 6587 | 6700 | 6812 | 6925 | 7037 | 7149 | 7262 | 7374 | 7486 | 7599 | 113 |
| 87 | 7711 | 7823 | 7935 | 8047 | 8160 | 8272 | 8384 | 8496 | 8608 | 8720 | 113 |
| 88 | 8832 | 8944 | 9056 | 9167 | 9279 | 9391 | 9503 | 9615 | 9726 | 9838 | 112 |
| 89 | 58 9950 | *0061 | *0173 | *0284 | *0396 | *0507 | *0619 | *0730 | *0842 | *0953 | 112 |
| 390 | 59 1065 | 1176 | 1287 | 1399 | 1510 | 1621 | 1732 | 1843 | 1955 | 2066 | 112 |
| 91 | 2177 | 2288 | 2399 | 2510 | 2621 | 2732 | 2843 | 2954 | 3064 | 3175 | 111 |
| 92 | 3286 | 3397 | 3508 | 3618 | 3729 | 3840 | 3950 | 4061 | 4171 | 4282 | 111 |
| 93 | 4393 | 4503 | 4614 | 4724 | 4834 | 4945 | 5055 | 5165 | 5276 | 5386 | 111 |
| 94 | 5496 | 5606 | 5717 | 5827 | 5937 | 6047 | 6157 | 6267 | 6377 | 6487 | 111 |
| 95 | 6597 | 6707 | 6817 | 6927 | 7037 | 7146 | 7256 | 7366 | 7476 | 7586 | 110 |
| 96 | 7695 | 7805 | 7914 | 8024 | 8134 | 8243 | 8353 | 8462 | 8572 | 8681 | 110 |
| 97 | 8791 | 8900 | 9009 | 9119 | 9228 | 9337 | 9446 | 9556 | 9665 | 9774 | 110 |
| 98 | 59 9883 | 9992 | *0101 | *0210 | *0319 | *0428 | *0537 | *0646 | *0755 | *0864 | 109 |
| 99 | 60 0973 | 1082 | 1191 | 1299 | 1408 | 1517 | 1625 | 1734 | 1843 | 1951 | 109 |
| N | 0 | 1 | 2 | 3 | 4 | 5 | 6 | 7 | 8 | 9 | D |

## TABLE 2

| N | 0 | 1 | 2 | 3 | 4 | 5 | 6 | 7 | 8 | 9 | D |
|---|---|---|---|---|---|---|---|---|---|---|---|
| 400 | 60 2060 | 2169 | 2277 | 2386 | 2494 | 2603 | 2711 | 2819 | 2928 | 3036 | 109 |
| 01 | 3144 | 3253 | 3361 | 3469 | 3577 | 3686 | 3794 | 3902 | 4010 | 4118 | 109 |
| 02 | 4226 | 4334 | 4442 | 4550 | 4658 | 4766 | 4874 | 4982 | 5089 | 5197 | 108 |
| 03 | 5305 | 5413 | 5521 | 5628 | 5736 | 5844 | 5951 | 6059 | 6166 | 6274 | 108 |
| 04 | 6381 | 6489 | 6596 | 6704 | 6811 | 6919 | 7026 | 7133 | 7241 | 7348 | 108 |
| 05 | 7455 | 7562 | 7669 | 7777 | 7884 | 7991 | 8098 | 8205 | 8312 | 8419 | 108 |
| 06 | 8526 | 8633 | 8740 | 8847 | 8954 | 9061 | 9167 | 9274 | 9381 | 9488 | 107 |
| 07 | 60 9594 | 9701 | 9808 | 9914 | *0021 | *0128 | *0234 | *0341 | *0447 | *0554 | 107 |
| 08 | 61 0660 | 0767 | 0873 | 0979 | 1086 | 1192 | 1298 | 1405 | 1511 | 1617 | 107 |
| 09 | 1723 | 1829 | 1936 | 2042 | 2148 | 2254 | 2360 | 2466 | 2572 | 2678 | 107 |
| 410 | 2784 | 2890 | 2996 | 3102 | 3207 | 3313 | 3419 | 3525 | 3630 | 3736 | 106 |
| 11 | 3842 | 3947 | 4053 | 4159 | 4264 | 4370 | 4475 | 4581 | 4686 | 4792 | 106 |
| 12 | 4897 | 5003 | 5108 | 5213 | 5319 | 5424 | 5529 | 5634 | 5740 | 5845 | 106 |
| 13 | 5950 | 6055 | 6160 | 6265 | 6370 | 6476 | 6581 | 6686 | 6790 | 6895 | 106 |
| 14 | 7000 | 7105 | 7210 | 7315 | 7420 | 7525 | 7629 | 7734 | 7839 | 7943 | 105 |
| 15 | 8048 | 8153 | 8257 | 8362 | 8466 | 8571 | 8676 | 8780 | 8884 | 8989 | 105 |
| 16 | 61 9093 | 9198 | 9302 | 9406 | 9511 | 9615 | 9719 | 9824 | 9928 | *0032 | 105 |
| 17 | 62 0136 | 0240 | 0344 | 0448 | 0552 | 0656 | 0760 | 0864 | 0968 | 1072 | 104 |
| 18 | 1176 | 1280 | 1384 | 1488 | 1592 | 1695 | 1799 | 1903 | 2007 | 2110 | 104 |
| 19 | 2214 | 2318 | 2421 | 2525 | 2628 | 2732 | 2835 | 2939 | 3042 | 3146 | 104 |
| 420 | 3249 | 3353 | 3456 | 3559 | 3663 | 3766 | 3869 | 3973 | 4076 | 4179 | 104 |
| 21 | 4282 | 4385 | 4488 | 4591 | 4695 | 4798 | 4901 | 5004 | 5107 | 5210 | 104 |
| 22 | 5312 | 5415 | 5518 | 5621 | 5724 | 5827 | 5929 | 6032 | 6135 | 6238 | 103 |
| 23 | 6340 | 6443 | 6546 | 6648 | 6751 | 6853 | 6956 | 7058 | 7161 | 7263 | 103 |
| 24 | 7366 | 7468 | 7571 | 7673 | 7775 | 7878 | 7980 | 8082 | 8185 | 8287 | 103 |
| 25 | 8389 | 8491 | 8593 | 8695 | 8797 | 8900 | 9002 | 9104 | 9206 | 9308 | 103 |
| 26 | 62 9410 | 9512 | 9613 | 9715 | 9817 | 9919 | *0021 | *0123 | *0224 | *0326 | 102 |
| 27 | 63 0428 | 0530 | 0631 | 0733 | 0835 | 0936 | 1038 | 1139 | 1241 | 1342 | 102 |
| 28 | 1444 | 1545 | 1647 | 1748 | 1849 | 1951 | 2052 | 2153 | 2255 | 2356 | 102 |
| 29 | 2457 | 2559 | 2660 | 2761 | 2862 | 2963 | 3064 | 3165 | 3266 | 3367 | 102 |
| 430 | 3468 | 3569 | 3670 | 3771 | 3872 | 3973 | 4074 | 4175 | 4276 | 4376 | 101 |
| 31 | 4477 | 4578 | 4679 | 4779 | 4880 | 4981 | 5081 | 5182 | 5283 | 5383 | 101 |
| 32 | 5484 | 5584 | 5685 | 5785 | 5886 | 5986 | 6087 | 6187 | 6287 | 6388 | 101 |
| 33 | 6488 | 6588 | 6688 | 6789 | 6889 | 6989 | 7089 | 7189 | 7290 | 7390 | 101 |
| 34 | 7490 | 7590 | 7690 | 7790 | 7890 | 7990 | 8090 | 8190 | 8290 | 8389 | 100 |
| 35 | 8489 | 8589 | 8689 | 8789 | 8888 | 8988 | 9088 | 9188 | 9287 | 9387 | 100 |
| 36 | 63 9486 | 9586 | 9686 | 9785 | 9885 | 9984 | *0084 | *0183 | *0283 | *0382 | 100 |
| 37 | 64 0481 | 0581 | 0680 | 0779 | 0879 | 0978 | 1077 | 1177 | 1276 | 1375 | 100 |
| 38 | 1474 | 1573 | 1672 | 1771 | 1871 | 1970 | 2069 | 2168 | 2267 | 2366 | 100 |
| 39 | 2465 | 2563 | 2662 | 2761 | 2860 | 2959 | 3058 | 3156 | 3255 | 3354 | 99 |
| 440 | 3453 | 3551 | 3650 | 3749 | 3847 | 3946 | 4044 | 4143 | 4242 | 4340 | 99 |
| 41 | 4439 | 4537 | 4636 | 4734 | 4832 | 4931 | 5029 | 5127 | 5226 | 5324 | 99 |
| 42 | 5422 | 5521 | 5619 | 5717 | 5815 | 5913 | 6011 | 6110 | 6208 | 6306 | 99 |
| 43 | 6404 | 6502 | 6600 | 6698 | 6796 | 6894 | 6992 | 7089 | 7187 | 7285 | 98 |
| 44 | 7383 | 7481 | 7579 | 7676 | 7774 | 7872 | 7969 | 8067 | 8165 | 8262 | 98 |
| 45 | 8360 | 8458 | 8555 | 8653 | 8750 | 8848 | 8945 | 9043 | 9140 | 9237 | 98 |
| 46 | 64 9335 | 9432 | 9530 | 9627 | 9724 | 9821 | 9919 | *0016 | *0113 | *0210 | 98 |
| 47 | 65 0308 | 0405 | 0502 | 0599 | 0696 | 0793 | 0890 | 0987 | 1084 | 1181 | 97 |
| 48 | 1278 | 1375 | 1472 | 1569 | 1666 | 1762 | 1859 | 1956 | 2053 | 2150 | 97 |
| 49 | 2246 | 2343 | 2440 | 2536 | 2633 | 2730 | 2826 | 2923 | 3019 | 3116 | 97 |
| N | 0 | 1 | 2 | 3 | 4 | 5 | 6 | 7 | 8 | 9 | D |

# TABLE 2

| N | 0 | 1 | 2 | 3 | 4 | 5 | 6 | 7 | 8 | 9 | D |
|---|---|---|---|---|---|---|---|---|---|---|---|
| 450 | 65 3213 | 3309 | 3405 | 3502 | 3598 | 3695 | 3791 | 3888 | 3984 | 4080 | 97 |
| 51 | 4177 | 4273 | 4369 | 4465 | 4562 | 4658 | 4754 | 4850 | 4946 | 5042 | 97 |
| 52 | 5138 | 5235 | 5331 | 5427 | 5523 | 5619 | 5715 | 5810 | 5906 | 6002 | 97 |
| 53 | 6098 | 6194 | 6290 | 6386 | 6482 | 6577 | 6673 | 6769 | 6864 | 6960 | 96 |
| 54 | 7056 | 7152 | 7247 | 7343 | 7438 | 7534 | 7629 | 7725 | 7820 | 7916 | 96 |
| 55 | 8011 | 8107 | 8202 | 8298 | 8393 | 8488 | 8584 | 8679 | 8774 | 8870 | 96 |
| 56 | 8965 | 9060 | 9155 | 9250 | 9346 | 9441 | 9536 | 9631 | 9726 | 9821 | 96 |
| 57 | 65 9916 | *0011 | *0106 | *0201 | *0296 | *0391 | *0486 | *0581 | *0676 | *0771 | 95 |
| 58 | 66 0865 | 0960 | 1055 | 1150 | 1245 | 1339 | 1434 | 1529 | 1623 | 1718 | 95 |
| 59 | 1813 | 1907 | 2002 | 2096 | 2191 | 2286 | 2380 | 2475 | 2569 | 2663 | 95 |
| 460 | 2758 | 2852 | 2947 | 3041 | 3135 | 3230 | 3324 | 3418 | 3512 | 3607 | 95 |
| 61 | 3701 | 3795 | 3889 | 3983 | 4078 | 4172 | 4266 | 4360 | 4454 | 4548 | 95 |
| 62 | 4642 | 4736 | 4830 | 4924 | 5018 | 5112 | 5206 | 5299 | 5393 | 5487 | 94 |
| 63 | 5581 | 5675 | 5769 | 5862 | 5956 | 6050 | 6143 | 6237 | 6331 | 6424 | 94 |
| 64 | 6518 | 6612 | 6705 | 6799 | 6892 | 6986 | 7079 | 7173 | 7266 | 7360 | 94 |
| 65 | 7453 | 7546 | 7640 | 7733 | 7826 | 7920 | 8013 | 8106 | 8199 | 8293 | 94 |
| 66 | 8386 | 8479 | 8572 | 8665 | 8759 | 8852 | 8945 | 9038 | 9131 | 9224 | 94 |
| 67 | 66 9317 | 9410 | 9503 | 9596 | 9689 | 9782 | 9875 | 9967 | *0060 | *0153 | 93 |
| 68 | 67 0246 | 0339 | 0431 | 0524 | 0617 | 0710 | 0802 | 0895 | 0988 | 1080 | 93 |
| 69 | 1173 | 1265 | 1358 | 1451 | 1543 | 1636 | 1728 | 1821 | 1913 | 2005 | 93 |
| 470 | 2098 | 2190 | 2283 | 2375 | 2467 | 2560 | 2652 | 2744 | 2836 | 2929 | 93 |
| 71 | 3021 | 3113 | 3205 | 3297 | 3390 | 3482 | 3574 | 3666 | 3758 | 3850 | 93 |
| 72 | 3942 | 4034 | 4126 | 4218 | 4310 | 4402 | 4494 | 4586 | 4677 | 4769 | 92 |
| 73 | 4861 | 4953 | 5045 | 5137 | 5228 | 5320 | 5412 | 5503 | 5595 | 5687 | 92 |
| 74 | 5778 | 5870 | 5962 | 6053 | 6145 | 6236 | 6328 | 6419 | 6511 | 6602 | 92 |
| 75 | 6694 | 6785 | 6876 | 6968 | 7059 | 7151 | 7242 | 7333 | 7424 | 7516 | 92 |
| 76 | 7607 | 7698 | 7789 | 7881 | 7972 | 8063 | 8154 | 8245 | 8336 | 8427 | 92 |
| 77 | 8518 | 8609 | 8700 | 8791 | 8882 | 8973 | 9064 | 9155 | 9246 | 9337 | 91 |
| 78 | 67 9428 | 9519 | 9610 | 9700 | 9791 | 9882 | 9973 | *0063 | *0154 | *0245 | 91 |
| 79 | 68 0336 | 0426 | 0517 | 0607 | 0698 | 0789 | 0879 | 0970 | 1060 | 1151 | 91 |
| 480 | 1241 | 1332 | 1422 | 1513 | 1603 | 1693 | 1784 | 1874 | 1964 | 2055 | 91 |
| 81 | 2145 | 2235 | 2326 | 2416 | 2506 | 2596 | 2686 | 2777 | 2867 | 2957 | 91 |
| 82 | 3047 | 3137 | 3227 | 3317 | 3407 | 3497 | 3587 | 3677 | 3767 | 3857 | 90 |
| 83 | 3947 | 4037 | 4127 | 4217 | 4307 | 4396 | 4486 | 4576 | 4666 | 4756 | 90 |
| 84 | 4845 | 4935 | 5025 | 5114 | 5204 | 5294 | 5383 | 5473 | 5563 | 5652 | 90 |
| 85 | 5742 | 5831 | 5921 | 6010 | 6100 | 6189 | 6279 | 6368 | 6458 | 6547 | 90 |
| 86 | 6636 | 6726 | 6815 | 6904 | 6994 | 7083 | 7172 | 7261 | 7351 | 7440 | 90 |
| 87 | 7529 | 7618 | 7707 | 7796 | 7886 | 7975 | 8064 | 8153 | 8242 | 8331 | 90 |
| 88 | 8420 | 8509 | 8598 | 8687 | 8776 | 8865 | 8953 | 9042 | 9131 | 9220 | 89 |
| 89 | 68 9309 | 9398 | 9486 | 9575 | 9664 | 9753 | 9841 | 9930 | *0019 | *0107 | 89 |
| 490 | 69 0196 | 0285 | 0373 | 0462 | 0550 | 0639 | 0728 | 0816 | 0905 | 0993 | 89 |
| 91 | 1081 | 1170 | 1258 | 1347 | 1435 | 1524 | 1612 | 1700 | 1789 | 1877 | 89 |
| 92 | 1965 | 2053 | 2142 | 2230 | 2318 | 2406 | 2494 | 2583 | 2671 | 2759 | 89 |
| 93 | 2847 | 2935 | 3023 | 3111 | 3199 | 3287 | 3375 | 3463 | 3551 | 3639 | 88 |
| 94 | 3727 | 3815 | 3903 | 3991 | 4078 | 4166 | 4254 | 4342 | 4430 | 4517 | 88 |
| 95 | 4605 | 4693 | 4781 | 4868 | 4956 | 5044 | 5131 | 5219 | 5307 | 5394 | 88 |
| 96 | 5482 | 5569 | 5657 | 5744 | 5832 | 5919 | 6007 | 6094 | 6182 | 6269 | 88 |
| 97 | 6356 | 6444 | 6531 | 6618 | 6706 | 6793 | 6880 | 6968 | 7055 | 7142 | 88 |
| 98 | 7229 | 7317 | 7404 | 7491 | 7578 | 7665 | 7752 | 7839 | 7926 | 8014 | 88 |
| 99 | 8101 | 8188 | 8275 | 8362 | 8449 | 8535 | 8622 | 8709 | 8796 | 8883 | 87 |
| N | 0 | 1 | 2 | 3 | 4 | 5 | 6 | 7 | 8 | 9 | D |

**LOGARITHMS OF NUMBERS 5,000–5,499**

## TABLE 2

Six-Place Mantissas

| N | 0 | 1 | 2 | 3 | 4 | 5 | 6 | 7 | 8 | 9 | D |
|---|---|---|---|---|---|---|---|---|---|---|---|
| 500 | 69 8970 | 9057 | 9144 | 9231 | 9317 | 9404 | 9491 | 9578 | 9664 | 9751 | 87 |
| 01 | 69 9838 | 9924 | *0011 | *0098 | *0184 | *0271 | *0358 | *0444 | *0531 | *0617 | 87 |
| 02 | 70 0704 | 0790 | 0877 | 0963 | 1050 | 1136 | 1222 | 1309 | 1395 | 1482 | 87 |
| 03 | 1568 | 1654 | 1741 | 1827 | 1913 | 1999 | 2086 | 2172 | 2258 | 2344 | 87 |
| 04 | 2431 | 2517 | 2603 | 2689 | 2775 | 2861 | 2947 | 3033 | 3119 | 3205 | 86 |
| 05 | 3291 | 3377 | 3463 | 3549 | 3635 | 3721 | 3807 | 3893 | 3979 | 4065 | 86 |
| 06 | 4151 | 4236 | 4322 | 4408 | 4494 | 4579 | 4665 | 4751 | 4837 | 4922 | 86 |
| 07 | 5008 | 5094 | 5179 | 5265 | 5350 | 5436 | 5522 | 5607 | 5693 | 5778 | 86 |
| 08 | 5864 | 5949 | 6035 | 6120 | 6206 | 6291 | 6376 | 6462 | 6547 | 6632 | 86 |
| 09 | 6718 | 6803 | 6888 | 6974 | 7059 | 7144 | 7229 | 7315 | 7400 | 7485 | 86 |
| 510 | 7570 | 7655 | 7740 | 7826 | 7911 | 7996 | 8081 | 8166 | 8251 | 8336 | 86 |
| 11 | 8421 | 8506 | 8591 | 8676 | 8761 | 8846 | 8931 | 9015 | 9100 | 9185 | 85 |
| 12 | 70 9270 | 9355 | 9440 | 9524 | 9609 | 9694 | 9779 | 9863 | 9948 | *0033 | 85 |
| 13 | 71 0117 | 0202 | 0287 | 0371 | 0456 | 0540 | 0625 | 0710 | 0794 | 0879 | 85 |
| 14 | 0963 | 1048 | 1132 | 1217 | 1301 | 1385 | 1470 | 1554 | 1639 | 1723 | 85 |
| 15 | 1807 | 1892 | 1976 | 2060 | 2144 | 2229 | 2313 | 2397 | 2481 | 2566 | 85 |
| 16 | 2650 | 2734 | 2818 | 2902 | 2986 | 3070 | 3154 | 3238 | 3323 | 3407 | 85 |
| 17 | 3491 | 3575 | 3659 | 3742 | 3826 | 3910 | 3994 | 4078 | 4162 | 4246 | 84 |
| 18 | 4330 | 4414 | 4497 | 4581 | 4665 | 4749 | 4833 | 4916 | 5000 | 5084 | 84 |
| 19 | 5167 | 5251 | 5335 | 5418 | 5502 | 5586 | 5669 | 5753 | 5836 | 5920 | 84 |
| 520 | 6003 | 6087 | 6170 | 6254 | 6337 | 6421 | 6504 | 6588 | 6671 | 6754 | 84 |
| 21 | 6838 | 6921 | 7004 | 7088 | 7171 | 7254 | 7338 | 7421 | 7504 | 7587 | 84 |
| 22 | 7671 | 7754 | 7837 | 7920 | 8003 | 8086 | 8169 | 8253 | 8336 | 8419 | 84 |
| 23 | 8502 | 8585 | 8668 | 8751 | 8834 | 8917 | 9000 | 9083 | 9165 | 9248 | 83 |
| 24 | 71 9331 | 9414 | 9497 | 9580 | 9663 | 9745 | 9828 | 9911 | 9994 | *0077 | 83 |
| 25 | 72 0159 | 0242 | 0325 | 0407 | 0490 | 0573 | 0655 | 0738 | 0821 | 0903 | 83 |
| 26 | 0986 | 1068 | 1151 | 1233 | 1316 | 1398 | 1481 | 1563 | 1646 | 1728 | 83 |
| 27 | 1811 | 1893 | 1975 | 2058 | 2140 | 2222 | 2305 | 2387 | 2469 | 2552 | 83 |
| 28 | 2634 | 2716 | 2798 | 2881 | 2963 | 3045 | 3127 | 3209 | 3291 | 3374 | 83 |
| 29 | 3456 | 3538 | 3620 | 3702 | 3784 | 3866 | 3948 | 4030 | 4112 | 4194 | 82 |
| 530 | 4276 | 4358 | 4440 | 4522 | 4604 | 4685 | 4767 | 4849 | 4931 | 5013 | 82 |
| 31 | 5095 | 5176 | 5258 | 5340 | 5422 | 5503 | 5585 | 5667 | 5748 | 5830 | 82 |
| 32 | 5912 | 5993 | 6075 | 6156 | 6238 | 6320 | 6401 | 6483 | 6564 | 6646 | 82 |
| 33 | 6727 | 6809 | 6890 | 6972 | 7053 | 7134 | 7216 | 7297 | 7379 | 7460 | 82 |
| 34 | 7541 | 7623 | 7704 | 7785 | 7866 | 7948 | 8029 | 8110 | 8191 | 8273 | 82 |
| 35 | 8354 | 8435 | 8516 | 8597 | 8678 | 8759 | 8841 | 8922 | 9003 | 9084 | 82 |
| 36 | 9165 | 9246 | 9327 | 9408 | 9489 | 9570 | 9651 | 9732 | 9813 | 9893 | 81 |
| 37 | 72 9974 | *0055 | *0136 | *0217 | *0298 | *0378 | *0459 | *0540 | *0621 | *0702 | 81 |
| 38 | 73 0782 | 0863 | 0944 | 1024 | 1105 | 1186 | 1266 | 1347 | 1428 | 1508 | 81 |
| 39 | 1589 | 1669 | 1750 | 1830 | 1911 | 1991 | 2072 | 2152 | 2233 | 2313 | 81 |
| 540 | 2394 | 2474 | 2555 | 2635 | 2715 | 2796 | 2876 | 2956 | 3037 | 3117 | 81 |
| 41 | 3197 | 3278 | 3358 | 3438 | 3518 | 3598 | 3679 | 3759 | 3839 | 3919 | 81 |
| 42 | 3999 | 4079 | 4160 | 4240 | 4320 | 4400 | 4480 | 4560 | 4640 | 4720 | 81 |
| 43 | 4800 | 4880 | 4960 | 5040 | 5120 | 5200 | 5279 | 5359 | 5439 | 5519 | 80 |
| 44 | 5599 | 5679 | 5759 | 5838 | 5918 | 5998 | 6078 | 6157 | 6237 | 6317 | 80 |
| 45 | 6397 | 6476 | 6556 | 6635 | 6715 | 6795 | 6874 | 6954 | 7034 | 7113 | 80 |
| 46 | 7193 | 7272 | 7352 | 7431 | 7511 | 7590 | 7670 | 7749 | 7829 | 7908 | 80 |
| 47 | 7987 | 8067 | 8146 | 8225 | 8305 | 8384 | 8463 | 8543 | 8622 | 8701 | 80 |
| 48 | 8781 | 8860 | 8939 | 9018 | 9097 | 9177 | 9256 | 9335 | 9414 | 9493 | 80 |
| 49 | 73 9572 | 9651 | 9731 | 9810 | 9889 | 9968 | *0047 | *0126 | *0205 | *0284 | 80 |
| N | 0 | 1 | 2 | 3 | 4 | 5 | 6 | 7 | 8 | 9 | D |

# TABLE 2

| N | 0 | 1 | 2 | 3 | 4 | 5 | 6 | 7 | 8 | 9 | D |
|-----|---------|------|------|------|------|------|------|------|------|------|-----|
| 550 | 74 0363 | 0442 | 0521 | 0600 | 0678 | 0757 | 0836 | 0915 | 0994 | 1073 | 79 |
| 51 | 1152 | 1230 | 1309 | 1388 | 1467 | 1546 | 1624 | 1703 | 1782 | 1860 | 79 |
| 52 | 1939 | 2018 | 2096 | 2175 | 2254 | 2332 | 2411 | 2489 | 2568 | 2647 | 79 |
| 53 | 2725 | 2804 | 2882 | 2961 | 3039 | 3118 | 3196 | 3275 | 3353 | 3431 | 79 |
| 54 | 3510 | 3588 | 3667 | 3745 | 3823 | 3902 | 3980 | 4058 | 4136 | 4215 | 79 |
| 55 | 4293 | 4371 | 4449 | 4528 | 4606 | 4684 | 4762 | 4840 | 4919 | 4997 | 79 |
| 56 | 5075 | 5153 | 5231 | 5309 | 5387 | 5465 | 5543 | 5621 | 5699 | 5777 | 78 |
| 57 | 5855 | 5933 | 6011 | 6089 | 6167 | 6245 | 6323 | 6401 | 6479 | 6556 | 78 |
| 58 | 6634 | 6712 | 6790 | 6868 | 6945 | 7023 | 7101 | 7179 | 7256 | 7334 | 78 |
| 59 | 7412 | 7489 | 7567 | 7645 | 7722 | 7800 | 7878 | 7955 | 8033 | 8110 | 78 |
| 560 | 8188 | 8266 | 8343 | 8421 | 8498 | 8576 | 8653 | 8731 | 8808 | 8885 | 78 |
| 61 | 8963 | 9040 | 9118 | 9195 | 9272 | 9350 | 9427 | 9504 | 9582 | 9659 | 78 |
| 62 | 74 9736 | 9814 | 9891 | 9968 | *0045 | *0123 | *0200 | *0277 | *0354 | *0431 | 78 |
| 63 | 75 0508 | 0586 | 0663 | 0740 | 0817 | 0894 | 0971 | 1048 | 1125 | 1202 | 78 |
| 64 | 1279 | 1356 | 1433 | 1510 | 1587 | 1664 | 1741 | 1818 | 1895 | 1972 | 77 |
| 65 | 2048 | 2125 | 2202 | 2279 | 2356 | 2433 | 2509 | 2586 | 2663 | 2740 | 77 |
| 66 | 2816 | 2893 | 2970 | 3047 | 3123 | 3200 | 3277 | 3353 | 3430 | 3506 | 77 |
| 67 | 3583 | 3660 | 3736 | 3813 | 3889 | 3966 | 4042 | 4119 | 4195 | 4272 | 77 |
| 68 | 4348 | 4425 | 4501 | 4578 | 4654 | 4730 | 4807 | 4883 | 4960 | 5036 | 77 |
| 69 | 5112 | 5189 | 5265 | 5341 | 5417 | 5494 | 5570 | 5646 | 5722 | 5799 | 77 |
| 570 | 5875 | 5951 | 6027 | 6103 | 6180 | 6256 | 6332 | 6408 | 6484 | 6560 | 77 |
| 71 | 6636 | 6712 | 6788 | 6864 | 6940 | 7016 | 7092 | 7168 | 7244 | 7320 | 76 |
| 72 | 7396 | 7472 | 7548 | 7624 | 7700 | 7775 | 7851 | 7927 | 8003 | 8079 | 76 |
| 73 | 8155 | 8230 | 8306 | 8382 | 8458 | 8533 | 8609 | 8685 | 8761 | 8836 | 76 |
| 74 | 8912 | 8988 | 9063 | 9139 | 9214 | 9290 | 9366 | 9441 | 9517 | 9592 | 76 |
| 75 | 75 9668 | 9743 | 9819 | 9894 | 9970 | *0045 | *0121 | *0196 | *0272 | *0347 | 76 |
| 76 | 76 0422 | 0498 | 0573 | 0649 | 0724 | 0799 | 0875 | 0950 | 1025 | 1101 | 76 |
| 77 | 1176 | 1251 | 1326 | 1402 | 1477 | 1552 | 1627 | 1702 | 1778 | 1853 | 76 |
| 78 | 1928 | 2003 | 2078 | 2153 | 2228 | 2303 | 2378 | 2453 | 2529 | 2604 | 76 |
| 79 | 2679 | 2754 | 2829 | 2904 | 2978 | 3053 | 3128 | 3203 | 3278 | 3353 | 75 |
| 580 | 3428 | 3503 | 3578 | 3653 | 3727 | 3802 | 3877 | 3952 | 4027 | 4101 | 75 |
| 81 | 4176 | 4251 | 4326 | 4400 | 4475 | 4550 | 4624 | 4699 | 4774 | 4848 | 75 |
| 82 | 4923 | 4998 | 5072 | 5147 | 5221 | 5296 | 5370 | 5445 | 5520 | 5594 | 75 |
| 83 | 5669 | 5743 | 5818 | 5892 | 5966 | 6041 | 6115 | 6190 | 6264 | 6338 | 75 |
| 84 | 6413 | 6487 | 6562 | 6636 | 6710 | 6785 | 6859 | 6933 | 7007 | 7082 | 75 |
| 85 | 7156 | 7230 | 7304 | 7379 | 7453 | 7527 | 7601 | 7675 | 7749 | 7823 | 75 |
| 86 | 7898 | 7972 | 8046 | 8120 | 8194 | 8268 | 8342 | 8416 | 8490 | 8564 | 74 |
| 87 | 8638 | 8712 | 8786 | 8860 | 8934 | 9008 | 9082 | 9156 | 9230 | 9303 | 74 |
| 88 | 76 9377 | 9451 | 9525 | 9599 | 9673 | 9746 | 9820 | 9894 | 9968 | *0042 | 74 |
| 89 | 77 0115 | 0189 | 0263 | 0336 | 0410 | 0484 | 0557 | 0631 | 0705 | 0778 | 74 |
| 590 | 0852 | 0926 | 0999 | 1073 | 1146 | 1220 | 1293 | 1367 | 1440 | 1514 | 74 |
| 91 | 1587 | 1661 | 1734 | 1808 | 1881 | 1955 | 2028 | 2102 | 2175 | 2248 | 74 |
| 92 | 2322 | 2395 | 2468 | 2542 | 2615 | 2688 | 2762 | 2835 | 2908 | 2981 | 74 |
| 93 | 3055 | 3128 | 3201 | 3274 | 3348 | 3421 | 3494 | 3567 | 3640 | 3713 | 74 |
| 94 | 3786 | 3860 | 3933 | 4006 | 4079 | 4152 | 4225 | 4298 | 4371 | 4444 | 74 |
| 95 | 4517 | 4590 | 4663 | 4736 | 4809 | 4882 | 4955 | 5028 | 5100 | 5173 | 73 |
| 96 | 5246 | 5319 | 5392 | 5465 | 5538 | 5610 | 5683 | 5756 | 5829 | 5902 | 73 |
| 97 | 5974 | 6047 | 6120 | 6193 | 6265 | 6338 | 6411 | 6483 | 6556 | 6629 | 73 |
| 98 | 6701 | 6774 | 6846 | 6919 | 6992 | 7064 | 7137 | 7209 | 7282 | 7354 | 73 |
| 99 | 7427 | 7499 | 7572 | 7644 | 7717 | 7789 | 7862 | 7934 | 8006 | 8079 | 73 |
| N | 0 | 1 | 2 | 3 | 4 | 5 | 6 | 7 | 8 | 9 | D |

## LOGARITHMS OF NUMBERS 6,000–6,499

# TABLE 2

Six-Place Mantissas

| N | 0 | 1 | 2 | 3 | 4 | 5 | 6 | 7 | 8 | 9 | D |
|---|---|---|---|---|---|---|---|---|---|---|---|
| 600 | 77 8151 | 8224 | 8296 | 8368 | 8441 | 8513 | 8585 | 8658 | 8730 | 8802 | 73 |
| 01 | 8874 | 8947 | 9019 | 9091 | 9163 | 9236 | 9308 | 9380 | 9452 | 9524 | 73 |
| 02 | 77 9596 | 9669 | 9741 | 9813 | 9885 | 9957 | *0029 | *0101 | *0173 | *0245 | 73 |
| 03 | 78 0317 | 0389 | 0461 | 0533 | 0605 | 0677 | 0749 | 0821 | 0893 | 0965 | 72 |
| 04 | 1037 | 1109 | 1181 | 1253 | 1324 | 1396 | 1468 | 1540 | 1612 | 1684 | 72 |
| 05 | 1755 | 1827 | 1899 | 1971 | 2042 | 2114 | 2186 | 2258 | 2329 | 2401 | 72 |
| 06 | 2473 | 2544 | 2616 | 2688 | 2759 | 2831 | 2902 | 2974 | 3046 | 3117 | 72 |
| 07 | 3189 | 3260 | 3332 | 3403 | 3475 | 3546 | 3618 | 3689 | 3761 | 3832 | 72 |
| 08 | 3904 | 3975 | 4046 | 4118 | 4189 | 4261 | 4332 | 4403 | 4475 | 4546 | 72 |
| 09 | 4617 | 4689 | 4760 | 4831 | 4902 | 4974 | 5045 | 5116 | 5187 | 5259 | 72 |
| 610 | 5330 | 5401 | 5472 | 5543 | 5615 | 5686 | 5757 | 5828 | 5899 | 5970 | 72 |
| 11 | 6041 | 6112 | 6183 | 6254 | 6325 | 6396 | 6467 | 6538 | 6609 | 6680 | 71 |
| 12 | 6751 | 6822 | 6893 | 6964 | 7035 | 7106 | 7177 | 7248 | 7319 | 7390 | 71 |
| 13 | 7460 | 7531 | 7602 | 7673 | 7744 | 7815 | 7885 | 7956 | 8027 | 8098 | 71 |
| 14 | 8168 | 8239 | 8310 | 8381 | 8451 | 8522 | 8593 | 8663 | 8734 | 8804 | 71 |
| 15 | 8875 | 8946 | 9016 | 9087 | 9157 | 9228 | 9299 | 9369 | 9440 | 9510 | 71 |
| 16 | 78 9581 | 9651 | 9722 | 9792 | 9863 | 9933 | *0004 | *0074 | *0144 | *0215 | 71 |
| 17 | 79 0285 | 0356 | 0426 | 0496 | 0567 | 0637 | 0707 | 0778 | 0848 | 0918 | 71 |
| 18 | 0988 | 1059 | 1129 | 1199 | 1269 | 1340 | 1410 | 1480 | 1550 | 1620 | 71 |
| 19 | 1691 | 1761 | 1831 | 1901 | 1971 | 2041 | 2111 | 2181 | 2252 | 2322 | 71 |
| 620 | 2392 | 2462 | 2532 | 2602 | 2672 | 2742 | 2812 | 2882 | 2952 | 3022 | 70 |
| 21 | 3092 | 3162 | 3231 | 3301 | 3371 | 3441 | 3511 | 3581 | 3651 | 3721 | 70 |
| 22 | 3790 | 3860 | 3930 | 4000 | 4070 | 4139 | 4209 | 4279 | 4349 | 4418 | 70 |
| 23 | 4488 | 4558 | 4627 | 4697 | 4767 | 4836 | 4906 | 4976 | 5045 | 5115 | 70 |
| 24 | 5185 | 5254 | 5324 | 5393 | 5463 | 5532 | 5602 | 5672 | 5741 | 5811 | 70 |
| 25 | 5880 | 5949 | 6019 | 6088 | 6158 | 6227 | 6297 | 6366 | 6436 | 6505 | 70 |
| 26 | 6574 | 6644 | 6713 | 6782 | 6852 | 6921 | 6990 | 7060 | 7129 | 7198 | 70 |
| 27 | 7268 | 7337 | 7406 | 7475 | 7545 | 7614 | 7683 | 7752 | 7821 | 7890 | 70 |
| 28 | 7960 | 8029 | 8098 | 8167 | 8236 | 8305 | 8374 | 8443 | 8513 | 8582 | 70 |
| 29 | 8651 | 8720 | 8789 | 8858 | 8927 | 8996 | 9065 | 9134 | 9203 | 9272 | 69 |
| 630 | 79 9341 | 9409 | 9478 | 9547 | 9616 | 9685 | 9754 | 9823 | 9892 | 9961 | 69 |
| 31 | 80 0029 | 0098 | 0167 | 0236 | 0305 | 0373 | 0442 | 0511 | 0580 | 0648 | 69 |
| 32 | 0717 | 0786 | 0854 | 0923 | 0992 | 1061 | 1129 | 1198 | 1266 | 1335 | 69 |
| 33 | 1404 | 1472 | 1541 | 1609 | 1678 | 1747 | 1815 | 1884 | 1952 | 2021 | 69 |
| 34 | 2089 | 2158 | 2226 | 2295 | 2363 | 2432 | 2500 | 2568 | 2637 | 2705 | 69 |
| 35 | 2774 | 2842 | 2910 | 2979 | 3047 | 3116 | 3184 | 3252 | 3321 | 3389 | 69 |
| 36 | 3457 | 3525 | 3594 | 3662 | 3730 | 3798 | 3867 | 3935 | 4003 | 4071 | 69 |
| 37 | 4139 | 4208 | 4276 | 4344 | 4412 | 4480 | 4548 | 4616 | 4685 | 4753 | 69 |
| 38 | 4821 | 4889 | 4957 | 5025 | 5093 | 5161 | 5229 | 5297 | 5365 | 5433 | 68 |
| 39 | 5501 | 5569 | 5637 | 5705 | 5773 | 5841 | 5908 | 5976 | 6044 | 6112 | 68 |
| 640 | 6180 | 6248 | 6316 | 6384 | 6451 | 6519 | 6587 | 6655 | 6723 | 6790 | 68 |
| 41 | 6858 | 6926 | 6994 | 7061 | 7129 | 7197 | 7264 | 7332 | 7400 | 7467 | 68 |
| 42 | 7535 | 7603 | 7670 | 7738 | 7806 | 7873 | 7941 | 8008 | 8076 | 8143 | 68 |
| 43 | 8211 | 8279 | 8346 | 8414 | 8481 | 8549 | 8616 | 8684 | 8751 | 8818 | 68 |
| 44 | 8886 | 8953 | 9021 | 9088 | 9156 | 9223 | 9290 | 9358 | 9425 | 9492 | 68 |
| 45 | 80 9560 | 9627 | 9694 | 9762 | 9829 | 9896 | 9964 | *0031 | *0098 | *0165 | 68 |
| 46 | 81 0233 | 0300 | 0367 | 0434 | 0501 | 0569 | 0636 | 0703 | 0770 | 0837 | 68 |
| 47 | 0904 | 0971 | 1039 | 1106 | 1173 | 1240 | 1307 | 1374 | 1441 | 1508 | 68 |
| 48 | 1575 | 1642 | 1709 | 1776 | 1843 | 1910 | 1977 | 2044 | 2111 | 2178 | 67 |
| 49 | 2245 | 2312 | 2379 | 2445 | 2512 | 2579 | 2646 | 2713 | 2780 | 2847 | 67 |
| N | 0 | 1 | 2 | 3 | 4 | 5 | 6 | 7 | 8 | 9 | D |

## LOGARITHMS OF NUMBERS 6,500–6,999

# TABLE 2

Six-Place Mantissas

Table 2

| N | 0 | 1 | 2 | 3 | 4 | 5 | 6 | 7 | 8 | 9 | D |
|---|---|---|---|---|---|---|---|---|---|---|---|
| **650** | 81 2913 | 2980 | 3047 | 3114 | 3181 | 3247 | 3314 | 3381 | 3448 | 3514 | 67 |
| 51 | 3581 | 3648 | 3714 | 3781 | 3848 | 3914 | 3981 | 4048 | 4114 | 4181 | 67 |
| 52 | 4248 | 4314 | 4381 | 4447 | 4514 | 4581 | 4647 | 4714 | 4780 | 4847 | 67 |
| 53 | 4913 | 4980 | 5046 | 5113 | 5179 | 5246 | 5312 | 5378 | 5445 | 5511 | 67 |
| 54 | 5578 | 5644 | 5711 | 5777 | 5843 | 5910 | 5976 | 6042 | 6109 | 6175 | 67 |
| **55** | 6241 | 6308 | 6374 | 6440 | 6506 | 6573 | 6639 | 6705 | 6771 | 6838 | 67 |
| 56 | 6904 | 6970 | 7036 | 7102 | 7169 | 7235 | 7301 | 7367 | 7433 | 7499 | 67 |
| 57 | 7565 | 7631 | 7698 | 7764 | 7830 | 7896 | 7962 | 8028 | 8094 | 8160 | 67 |
| 58 | 8226 | 8292 | 8358 | 8424 | 8490 | 8556 | 8622 | 8688 | 8754 | 8820 | 66 |
| 59 | 8885 | 8951 | 9017 | 9083 | 9149 | 9215 | 9281 | 9346 | 9412 | 9478 | 66 |
| **660** | 81 9544 | 9610 | 9676 | 9741 | 9807 | 9873 | 9939 | *0004 | *0070 | *0136 | 66 |
| 61 | 82 0201 | 0267 | 0333 | 0399 | 0464 | 0530 | 0595 | 0661 | 0727 | 0792 | 66 |
| 62 | 0858 | 0924 | 0989 | 1055 | 1120 | 1186 | 1251 | 1317 | 1382 | 1448 | 66 |
| 63 | 1514 | 1579 | 1645 | 1710 | 1775 | 1841 | 1906 | 1972 | 2037 | 2103 | 66 |
| 64 | 2168 | 2233 | 2299 | 2364 | 2430 | 2495 | 2560 | 2626 | 2691 | 2756 | 66 |
| **65** | 2822 | 2887 | 2952 | 3018 | 3083 | 3148 | 3213 | 3279 | 3344 | 3409 | 66 |
| 66 | 3474 | 3539 | 3605 | 3670 | 3735 | 3800 | 3865 | 3930 | 3996 | 4061 | 66 |
| 67 | 4126 | 4191 | 4256 | 4321 | 4386 | 4451 | 4516 | 4581 | 4646 | 4711 | 65 |
| 68 | 4776 | 4841 | 4906 | 4971 | 5036 | 5101 | 5166 | 5231 | 5296 | 5361 | 65 |
| 69 | 5426 | 5491 | 5556 | 5621 | 5686 | 5751 | 5815 | 5880 | 5945 | 6010 | 65 |
| **670** | 6075 | 6140 | 6204 | 6269 | 6334 | 6399 | 6464 | 6528 | 6593 | 6658 | 65 |
| 71 | 6723 | 6787 | 6852 | 6917 | 6981 | 7046 | 7111 | 7175 | 7240 | 7305 | 65 |
| 72 | 7369 | 7434 | 7499 | 7563 | 7628 | 7692 | 7757 | 7821 | 7886 | 7951 | 65 |
| 73 | 8015 | 8080 | 8144 | 8209 | 8273 | 8338 | 8402 | 8467 | 8531 | 8595 | 65 |
| 74 | 8660 | 8724 | 8789 | 8853 | 8918 | 8982 | 9046 | 9111 | 9175 | 9239 | 65 |
| **75** | 9304 | 9368 | 9432 | 9497 | 9561 | 9625 | 9690 | 9754 | 9818 | 9882 | 65 |
| 76 | 82 9947 | *0011 | *0075 | *0139 | *0204 | *0268 | *0332 | *0396 | *0460 | *0525 | 65 |
| 77 | 83 0589 | 0653 | 0717 | 0781 | 0845 | 0909 | 0973 | 1037 | 1102 | 1166 | 65 |
| 78 | 1230 | 1294 | 1358 | 1422 | 1486 | 1550 | 1614 | 1678 | 1742 | 1806 | 64 |
| 79 | 1870 | 1934 | 1998 | 2062 | 2126 | 2189 | 2253 | 2317 | 2381 | 2445 | 64 |
| **680** | 2509 | 2573 | 2637 | 2700 | 2764 | 2828 | 2892 | 2956 | 3020 | 3083 | 64 |
| 81 | 3147 | 3211 | 3275 | 3338 | 3402 | 3466 | 3530 | 3593 | 3657 | 3721 | 64 |
| 82 | 3784 | 3848 | 3912 | 3975 | 4039 | 4103 | 4166 | 4230 | 4294 | 4357 | 64 |
| 83 | 4421 | 4484 | 4548 | 4611 | 4675 | 4739 | 4802 | 4866 | 4929 | 4993 | 64 |
| 84 | 5056 | 5120 | 5183 | 5247 | 5310 | 5373 | 5437 | 5500 | 5564 | 5627 | 64 |
| **85** | 5691 | 5754 | 5817 | 5881 | 5944 | 6007 | 6071 | 6134 | 6197 | 6261 | 64 |
| 86 | 6324 | 6387 | 6451 | 6514 | 6577 | 6641 | 6704 | 6767 | 6830 | 6894 | 64 |
| 87 | 6957 | 7020 | 7083 | 7146 | 7210 | 7273 | 7336 | 7399 | 7462 | 7525 | 64 |
| 88 | 7588 | 7652 | 7715 | 7778 | 7841 | 7904 | 7967 | 8030 | 8093 | 8156 | 64 |
| 89 | 8219 | 8282 | 8345 | 8408 | 8471 | 8534 | 8597 | 8660 | 8723 | 8786 | 63 |
| **690** | 8849 | 8912 | 8975 | 9038 | 9101 | 9164 | 9227 | 9289 | 9352 | 9415 | 63 |
| 91 | 83 9478 | 9541 | 9604 | 9667 | 9729 | 9792 | 9855 | 9918 | 9981 | *0043 | 63 |
| 92 | 84 0106 | 0169 | 0232 | 0294 | 0357 | 0420 | 0482 | 0545 | 0608 | 0671 | 63 |
| 93 | 0733 | 0796 | 0859 | 0921 | 0984 | 1046 | 1109 | 1172 | 1234 | 1297 | 63 |
| 94 | 1359 | 1422 | 1485 | 1547 | 1610 | 1672 | 1735 | 1797 | 1860 | 1922 | 63 |
| **95** | 1985 | 2047 | 2110 | 2172 | 2235 | 2297 | 2360 | 2422 | 2484 | 2547 | 63 |
| 96 | 2609 | 2672 | 2734 | 2796 | 2859 | 2921 | 2983 | 3046 | 3108 | 3170 | 63 |
| 97 | 3233 | 3295 | 3357 | 3420 | 3482 | 3544 | 3606 | 3669 | 3731 | 3793 | 63 |
| 98 | 3855 | 3918 | 3980 | 4042 | 4104 | 4166 | 4229 | 4291 | 4353 | 4415 | 63 |
| 99 | 4477 | 4539 | 4601 | 4664 | 4726 | 4788 | 4850 | 4912 | 4974 | 5036 | 63 |
| N | 0 | 1 | 2 | 3 | 4 | 5 | 6 | 7 | 8 | 9 | D |

# TABLE 2

| N | 0 | 1 | 2 | 3 | 4 | 5 | 6 | 7 | 8 | 9 | D |
|---|---|---|---|---|---|---|---|---|---|---|---|
| 700 | 84 5098 | 5160 | 5222 | 5284 | 5346 | 5408 | 5470 | 5532 | 5594 | 5656 | 62 |
| 01 | 5718 | 5780 | 5842 | 5904 | 5966 | 6028 | 6090 | 6151 | 6213 | 6275 | 62 |
| 02 | 6337 | 6399 | 6461 | 6523 | 6585 | 6646 | 6708 | 6770 | 6832 | 6894 | 62 |
| 03 | 6955 | 7017 | 7079 | 7141 | 7202 | 7264 | 7326 | 7388 | 7449 | 7511 | 62 |
| 04 | 7573 | 7634 | 7696 | 7758 | 7819 | 7881 | 7943 | 8004 | 8066 | 8128 | 62 |
| 05 | 8189 | 8251 | 8312 | 8374 | 8435 | 8497 | 8559 | 8620 | 8682 | 8743 | 62 |
| 06 | 8805 | 8866 | 8928 | 8989 | 9051 | 9112 | 9174 | 9235 | 9297 | 9358 | 62 |
| 07 | 84 9419 | 9481 | 9542 | 9604 | 9665 | 9726 | 9788 | 9849 | 9911 | 9972 | 62 |
| 08 | 85 0033 | 0095 | 0156 | 0217 | 0279 | 0340 | 0401 | 0462 | 0524 | 0585 | 62 |
| 09 | 0646 | 0707 | 0769 | 0830 | 0891 | 0952 | 1014 | 1075 | 1136 | 1197 | 62 |
| 710 | 1258 | 1320 | 1381 | 1442 | 1503 | 1564 | 1625 | 1686 | 1747 | 1809 | 62 |
| 11 | 1870 | 1931 | 1992 | 2053 | 2114 | 2175 | 2236 | 2297 | 2358 | 2419 | 61 |
| 12 | 2480 | 2541 | 2602 | 2663 | 2724 | 2785 | 2846 | 2907 | 2968 | 3029 | 61 |
| 13 | 3090 | 3150 | 3211 | 3272 | 3333 | 3394 | 3455 | 3516 | 3577 | 3637 | 61 |
| 14 | 3698 | 3759 | 3820 | 3881 | 3941 | 4002 | 4063 | 4124 | 4185 | 4245 | 61 |
| 15 | 4306 | 4367 | 4428 | 4488 | 4549 | 4610 | 4670 | 4731 | 4792 | 4852 | 61 |
| 16 | 4913 | 4974 | 5034 | 5095 | 5156 | 5216 | 5277 | 5337 | 5398 | 5459 | 61 |
| 17 | 5519 | 5580 | 5640 | 5701 | 5761 | 5822 | 5882 | 5943 | 6003 | 6064 | 61 |
| 18 | 6124 | 6185 | 6245 | 6306 | 6366 | 6427 | 6487 | 6548 | 6608 | 6668 | 61 |
| 19 | 6729 | 6789 | 6850 | 6910 | 6970 | 7031 | 7091 | 7152 | 7212 | 7272 | 61 |
| 720 | 7332 | 7393 | 7453 | 7513 | 7574 | 7634 | 7694 | 7755 | 7815 | 7875 | 61 |
| 21 | 7935 | 7995 | 8056 | 8116 | 8176 | 8236 | 8297 | 8357 | 8417 | 8477 | 61 |
| 22 | 8537 | 8597 | 8657 | 8718 | 8778 | 8838 | 8898 | 8958 | 9018 | 9078 | 61 |
| 23 | 9138 | 9198 | 9258 | 9318 | 9379 | 9439 | 9499 | 9559 | 9619 | 9679 | 61 |
| 24 | 85 9739 | 9799 | 9859 | 9918 | 9978 | *0038 | *0098 | *0158 | *0218 | *0278 | 60 |
| 25 | 86 0338 | 0398 | 0458 | 0518 | 0578 | 0637 | 0697 | 0757 | 0817 | 0877 | 60 |
| 26 | 0937 | 0996 | 1056 | 1116 | 1176 | 1236 | 1295 | 1355 | 1415 | 1475 | 60 |
| 27 | 1534 | 1594 | 1654 | 1714 | 1773 | 1833 | 1893 | 1952 | 2012 | 2072 | 60 |
| 28 | 2131 | 2191 | 2251 | 2310 | 2370 | 2430 | 2489 | 2549 | 2608 | 2668 | 60 |
| 29 | 2728 | 2787 | 2847 | 2906 | 2966 | 3025 | 3085 | 3144 | 3204 | 3263 | 60 |
| 730 | 3323 | 3382 | 3442 | 3501 | 3561 | 3620 | 3680 | 3739 | 3799 | 3858 | 60 |
| 31 | 3917 | 3977 | 4036 | 4096 | 4155 | 4214 | 4274 | 4333 | 4392 | 4452 | 60 |
| 32 | 4511 | 4570 | 4630 | 4689 | 4748 | 4808 | 4867 | 4926 | 4985 | 5045 | 60 |
| 33 | 5104 | 5163 | 5222 | 5282 | 5341 | 5400 | 5459 | 5519 | 5578 | 5637 | 60 |
| 34 | 5696 | 5755 | 5814 | 5874 | 5933 | 5992 | 6051 | 6110 | 6169 | 6228 | 60 |
| 35 | 6287 | 6346 | 6405 | 6465 | 6524 | 6583 | 6642 | 6701 | 6760 | 6819 | 60 |
| 36 | 6878 | 6937 | 6996 | 7055 | 7114 | 7173 | 7232 | 7291 | 7350 | 7409 | 59 |
| 37 | 7467 | 7526 | 7585 | 7644 | 7703 | 7762 | 7821 | 7880 | 7939 | 7998 | 59 |
| 38 | 8056 | 8115 | 8174 | 8233 | 8292 | 8350 | 8409 | 8468 | 8527 | 8586 | 59 |
| 39 | 8644 | 8703 | 8762 | 8821 | 8879 | 8938 | 8997 | 9056 | 9114 | 9173 | 59 |
| 740 | 9232 | 9290 | 9349 | 9408 | 9466 | 9525 | 9584 | 9642 | 9701 | 9760 | 59 |
| 41 | 86 9818 | 9877 | 9935 | 9994 | *0053 | *0111 | *0170 | *0228 | *0287 | *0345 | 59 |
| 42 | 87 0404 | 0462 | 0521 | 0579 | 0638 | 0696 | 0755 | 0813 | 0872 | 0930 | 59 |
| 43 | 0989 | 1047 | 1106 | 1164 | 1223 | 1281 | 1339 | 1398 | 1456 | 1515 | 59 |
| 44 | 1573 | 1631 | 1690 | 1748 | 1806 | 1865 | 1923 | 1981 | 2040 | 2098 | 59 |
| 45 | 2156 | 2215 | 2273 | 2331 | 2389 | 2448 | 2506 | 2564 | 2622 | 2681 | 59 |
| 46 | 2739 | 2797 | 2855 | 2913 | 2972 | 3030 | 3088 | 3146 | 3204 | 3262 | 59 |
| 47 | 3321 | 3379 | 3437 | 3495 | 3553 | 3611 | 3669 | 3727 | 3785 | 3844 | 59 |
| 48 | 3902 | 3960 | 4018 | 4076 | 4134 | 4192 | 4250 | 4308 | 4366 | 4424 | 58 |
| 49 | 4482 | 4540 | 4598 | 4656 | 4714 | 4772 | 4830 | 4888 | 4945 | 5003 | 58 |
| N | 0 | 1 | 2 | 3 | 4 | 5 | 6 | 7 | 8 | 9 | D |

# TABLE 2

| N | 0 | 1 | 2 | 3 | 4 | 5 | 6 | 7 | 8 | 9 | D |
|---|---|---|---|---|---|---|---|---|---|---|---|
| 750 | 87 5061 | 5119 | 5177 | 5235 | 5293 | 5351 | 5409 | 5466 | 5524 | 5582 | 58 |
| 51 | 5640 | 5698 | 5756 | 5813 | 5871 | 5929 | 5987 | 6045 | 6102 | 6160 | 58 |
| 52 | 6218 | 6276 | 6333 | 6391 | 6449 | 6507 | 6564 | 6622 | 6680 | 6737 | 58 |
| 53 | 6795 | 6853 | 6910 | 6968 | 7026 | 7083 | 7141 | 7199 | 7256 | 7314 | 58 |
| 54 | 7371 | 7429 | 7487 | 7544 | 7602 | 7659 | 7717 | 7774 | 7832 | 7889 | 58 |
| 55 | 7947 | 8004 | 8062 | 8119 | 8177 | 8234 | 8292 | 8349 | 8407 | 8464 | 58 |
| 56 | 8522 | 8579 | 8637 | 8694 | 8752 | 8809 | 8866 | 8924 | 8981 | 9039 | 58 |
| 57 | 9096 | 9153 | 9211 | 9268 | 9325 | 9383 | 9440 | 9497 | 9555 | 9612 | 58 |
| 58 | 87 9669 | 9726 | 9784 | 9841 | 9898 | 9956 | *0013 | *0070 | *0127 | *0185 | 58 |
| 59 | 88 0242 | 0299 | 0356 | 0413 | 0471 | 0528 | 0585 | 0642 | 0699 | 0756 | 58 |
| 760 | 0814 | 0871 | 0928 | 0985 | 1042 | 1099 | 1156 | 1213 | 1271 | 1328 | 58 |
| 61 | 1385 | 1442 | 1499 | 1556 | 1613 | 1670 | 1727 | 1784 | 1841 | 1898 | 57 |
| 62 | 1955 | 2012 | 2069 | 2126 | 2183 | 2240 | 2297 | 2354 | 2411 | 2468 | 57 |
| 63 | 2525 | 2581 | 2638 | 2695 | 2752 | 2809 | 2866 | 2923 | 2980 | 3037 | 57 |
| 64 | 3093 | 3150 | 3207 | 3264 | 3321 | 3377 | 3434 | 3491 | 3548 | 3605 | 57 |
| 65 | 3661 | 3718 | 3775 | 3832 | 3888 | 3945 | 4002 | 4059 | 4115 | 4172 | 57 |
| 66 | 4229 | 4285 | 4342 | 4399 | 4455 | 4512 | 4569 | 4625 | 4682 | 4739 | 57 |
| 67 | 4795 | 4852 | 4909 | 4965 | 5022 | 5078 | 5135 | 5192 | 5248 | 5305 | 57 |
| 68 | 5361 | 5418 | 5474 | 5531 | 5587 | 5644 | 5700 | 5757 | 5813 | 5870 | 57 |
| 69 | 5926 | 5983 | 6039 | 6096 | 6152 | 6209 | 6265 | 6321 | 6378 | 6434 | 57 |
| 770 | 6491 | 6547 | 6604 | 6660 | 6716 | 6773 | 6829 | 6885 | 6942 | 6998 | 57 |
| 71 | 7054 | 7111 | 7167 | 7223 | 7280 | 7336 | 7392 | 7449 | 7505 | 7561 | 57 |
| 72 | 7617 | 7674 | 7730 | 7786 | 7842 | 7898 | 7955 | 8011 | 8067 | 8123 | 57 |
| 73 | 8179 | 8236 | 8292 | 8348 | 8404 | 8460 | 8516 | 8573 | 8629 | 8685 | 57 |
| 74 | 8741 | 8797 | 8853 | 8909 | 8965 | 9021 | 9077 | 9134 | 9190 | 9246 | 57 |
| 75 | 9302 | 9358 | 9414 | 9470 | 9526 | 9582 | 9638 | 9694 | 9750 | 9806 | 56 |
| 76 | 88 9862 | 9918 | 9974 | *0030 | *0086 | *0141 | *0197 | *0253 | *0309 | *0365 | 56 |
| 77 | 89 0421 | 0477 | 0533 | 0589 | 0645 | 0700 | 0756 | 0812 | 0868 | 0924 | 56 |
| 78 | 0980 | 1035 | 1091 | 1147 | 1203 | 1259 | 1314 | 1370 | 1426 | 1482 | 56 |
| 79 | 1537 | 1593 | 1649 | 1705 | 1760 | 1816 | 1872 | 1928 | 1983 | 2039 | 56 |
| 780 | 2095 | 2150 | 2206 | 2262 | 2317 | 2373 | 2429 | 2484 | 2540 | 2595 | 56 |
| 81 | 2651 | 2707 | 2762 | 2818 | 2873 | 2929 | 2985 | 3040 | 3096 | 3151 | 56 |
| 82 | 3207 | 3262 | 3318 | 3373 | 3429 | 3484 | 3540 | 3595 | 3651 | 3706 | 56 |
| 83 | 3762 | 3817 | 3873 | 3928 | 3984 | 4039 | 4094 | 4150 | 4205 | 4261 | 56 |
| 84 | 4316 | 4371 | 4427 | 4482 | 4538 | 4593 | 4648 | 4704 | 4759 | 4814 | 56 |
| 85 | 4870 | 4925 | 4980 | 5036 | 5091 | 5146 | 5201 | 5257 | 5312 | 5367 | 56 |
| 86 | 5423 | 5478 | 5533 | 5588 | 5644 | 5699 | 5754 | 5809 | 5864 | 5920 | 56 |
| 87 | 5975 | 6030 | 6085 | 6140 | 6195 | 6251 | 6306 | 6361 | 6416 | 6471 | 56 |
| 88 | 6526 | 6581 | 6636 | 6692 | 6747 | 6802 | 6857 | 6912 | 6967 | 7022 | 56 |
| 89 | 7077 | 7132 | 7187 | 7242 | 7297 | 7352 | 7407 | 7462 | 7517 | 7572 | 55 |
| 790 | 7627 | 7682 | 7737 | 7792 | 7847 | 7902 | 7957 | 8012 | 8067 | 8122 | 55 |
| 91 | 8176 | 8231 | 8286 | 8341 | 8396 | 8451 | 8506 | 8561 | 8615 | 8670 | 55 |
| 92 | 8725 | 8780 | 8835 | 8890 | 8944 | 8999 | 9054 | 9109 | 9164 | 9218 | 55 |
| 93 | 9273 | 9328 | 9383 | 9437 | 9492 | 9547 | 9602 | 9656 | 9711 | 9766 | 55 |
| 94 | 89 9821 | 9875 | 9930 | 9985 | *0039 | *0094 | *0149 | *0203 | *0258 | *0312 | 55 |
| 95 | 90 0367 | 0422 | 0476 | 0531 | 0586 | 0640 | 0695 | 0749 | 0804 | 0859 | 55 |
| 96 | 0913 | 0968 | 1022 | 1077 | 1131 | 1186 | 1240 | 1295 | 1349 | 1404 | 55 |
| 97 | 1458 | 1513 | 1567 | 1622 | 1676 | 1731 | 1785 | 1840 | 1894 | 1948 | 55 |
| 98 | 2003 | 2057 | 2112 | 2166 | 2221 | 2275 | 2329 | 2384 | 2438 | 2492 | 55 |
| 99 | 2547 | 2601 | 2655 | 2710 | 2764 | 2818 | 2873 | 2927 | 2981 | 3036 | 55 |
| N | 0 | 1 | 2 | 3 | 4 | 5 | 6 | 7 | 8 | 9 | D |

## LOGARITHMS OF NUMBERS 8,000–8,499

# TABLE 2

### Six-Place Mantissas

| N | 0 | 1 | 2 | 3 | 4 | 5 | 6 | 7 | 8 | 9 | D |
|---|---|---|---|---|---|---|---|---|---|---|---|
| 800 | 90 3090 | 3144 | 3199 | 3253 | 3307 | 3361 | 3416 | 3470 | 3524 | 3578 | 55 |
| 01 | 3633 | 3687 | 3741 | 3795 | 3849 | 3904 | 3958 | 4012 | 4066 | 4120 | 55 |
| 02 | 4174 | 4229 | 4283 | 4337 | 4391 | 4445 | 4499 | 4553 | 4607 | 4661 | 55 |
| 03 | 4716 | 4770 | 4824 | 4878 | 4932 | 4986 | 5040 | 5094 | 5148 | 5202 | 54 |
| 04 | 5256 | 5310 | 5364 | 5418 | 5472 | 5526 | 5580 | 5634 | 5688 | 5742 | 54 |
| 05 | 5796 | 5850 | 5904 | 5958 | 6012 | 6066 | 6119 | 6173 | 6227 | 6281 | 54 |
| 06 | 6335 | 6389 | 6443 | 6497 | 6551 | 6604 | 6658 | 6712 | 6766 | 6820 | 54 |
| 07 | 6874 | 6927 | 6981 | 7035 | 7089 | 7143 | 7196 | 7250 | 7304 | 7358 | 54 |
| 08 | 7411 | 7465 | 7519 | 7573 | 7626 | 7680 | 7734 | 7787 | 7841 | 7895 | 54 |
| 09 | 7949 | 8002 | 8056 | 8110 | 8163 | 8217 | 8270 | 8324 | 8378 | 8431 | 54 |
| 810 | 8485 | 8539 | 8592 | 8646 | 8699 | 8753 | 8807 | 8860 | 8914 | 8967 | 54 |
| 11 | 9021 | 9074 | 9128 | 9181 | 9235 | 9289 | 9342 | 9396 | 9449 | 9503 | 54 |
| 12 | 90 9556 | 9610 | 9663 | 9716 | 9770 | 9823 | 9877 | 9930 | 9984 | *0037 | 54 |
| 13 | 91 0091 | 0144 | 0197 | 0251 | 0304 | 0358 | 0411 | 0464 | 0518 | 0571 | 54 |
| 14 | 0624 | 0678 | 0731 | 0784 | 0838 | 0891 | 0944 | 0998 | 1051 | 1104 | 54 |
| 15 | 1158 | 1211 | 1264 | 1317 | 1371 | 1424 | 1477 | 1530 | 1584 | 1637 | 54 |
| 16 | 1690 | 1743 | 1797 | 1850 | 1903 | 1956 | 2009 | 2063 | 2116 | 2169 | 54 |
| 17 | 2222 | 2275 | 2328 | 2381 | 2435 | 2488 | 2541 | 2594 | 2647 | 2700 | 54 |
| 18 | 2753 | 2806 | 2859 | 2913 | 2966 | 3019 | 3072 | 3125 | 3178 | 3231 | 54 |
| 19 | 3284 | 3337 | 3390 | 3443 | 3496 | 3549 | 3602 | 3655 | 3708 | 3761 | 53 |
| 820 | 3814 | 3867 | 3920 | 3973 | 4026 | 4079 | 4132 | 4184 | 4237 | 4290 | 53 |
| 21 | 4343 | 4396 | 4449 | 4502 | 4555 | 4608 | 4660 | 4713 | 4766 | 4819 | 53 |
| 22 | 4872 | 4925 | 4977 | 5030 | 5083 | 5136 | 5189 | 5241 | 5294 | 5347 | 53 |
| 23 | 5400 | 5453 | 5505 | 5558 | 5611 | 5664 | 5716 | 5769 | 5822 | 5875 | 53 |
| 24 | 5927 | 5980 | 6033 | 6085 | 6138 | 6191 | 6243 | 6296 | 6349 | 6401 | 53 |
| 25 | 6454 | 6507 | 6559 | 6612 | 6664 | 6717 | 6770 | 6822 | 6875 | 6927 | 53 |
| 26 | 6980 | 7033 | 7085 | 7138 | 7190 | 7243 | 7295 | 7348 | 7400 | 7453 | 53 |
| 27 | 7506 | 7558 | 7611 | 7663 | 7716 | 7768 | 7820 | 7873 | 7925 | 7978 | 53 |
| 28 | 8030 | 8083 | 8135 | 8188 | 8240 | 8293 | 8345 | 8397 | 8450 | 8502 | 53 |
| 29 | 8555 | 8607 | 8659 | 8712 | 8764 | 8816 | 8869 | 8921 | 8973 | 9026 | 53 |
| 830 | 9078 | 9130 | 9183 | 9235 | 9287 | 9340 | 9392 | 9444 | 9496 | 9549 | 53 |
| 31 | 91 9601 | 9653 | 9706 | 9758 | 9810 | 9862 | 9914 | 9967 | *0019 | *0071 | 53 |
| 32 | 92 0123 | 0176 | 0228 | 0280 | 0332 | 0384 | 0436 | 0489 | 0541 | 0593 | 53 |
| 33 | 0645 | 0697 | 0749 | 0801 | 0853 | 0906 | 0958 | 1010 | 1062 | 1114 | 53 |
| 34 | 1166 | 1218 | 1270 | 1322 | 1374 | 1426 | 1478 | 1530 | 1582 | 1634 | 52 |
| 35 | 1686 | 1738 | 1790 | 1842 | 1894 | 1946 | 1998 | 2050 | 2102 | 2154 | 52 |
| 36 | 2206 | 2258 | 2310 | 2362 | 2414 | 2466 | 2518 | 2570 | 2622 | 2674 | 52 |
| 37 | 2725 | 2777 | 2829 | 2881 | 2933 | 2985 | 3037 | 3089 | 3140 | 3192 | 52 |
| 38 | 3244 | 3296 | 3348 | 3399 | 3451 | 3503 | 3555 | 3607 | 3658 | 3710 | 52 |
| 39 | 3762 | 3814 | 3865 | 3917 | 3969 | 4021 | 4072 | 4124 | 4176 | 4228 | 52 |
| 840 | 4279 | 4331 | 4383 | 4434 | 4486 | 4538 | 4589 | 4641 | 4693 | 4744 | 52 |
| 41 | 4796 | 4848 | 4899 | 4951 | 5003 | 5054 | 5106 | 5157 | 5209 | 5261 | 52 |
| 42 | 5312 | 5364 | 5415 | 5467 | 5518 | 5570 | 5621 | 5673 | 5725 | 5776 | 52 |
| 43 | 5828 | 5879 | 5931 | 5982 | 6034 | 6085 | 6137 | 6188 | 6240 | 6291 | 52 |
| 44 | 6342 | 6394 | 6445 | 6497 | 6548 | 6600 | 6651 | 6702 | 6754 | 6805 | 52 |
| 45 | 6857 | 6908 | 6959 | 7011 | 7062 | 7114 | 7165 | 7216 | 7268 | 7319 | 52 |
| 46 | 7370 | 7422 | 7473 | 7524 | 7576 | 7627 | 7678 | 7730 | 7781 | 7832 | 52 |
| 47 | 7883 | 7935 | 7986 | 8037 | 8088 | 8140 | 8191 | 8242 | 8293 | 8345 | 52 |
| 48 | 8396 | 8447 | 8498 | 8549 | 8601 | 8652 | 8703 | 8754 | 8805 | 8857 | 52 |
| 49 | 8908 | 8959 | 9010 | 9061 | 9112 | 9163 | 9215 | 9266 | 9317 | 9368 | 52 |
| N | 0 | 1 | 2 | 3 | 4 | 5 | 6 | 7 | 8 | 9 | D |

# TABLE 2

Table
2

| N | 0 | 1 | 2 | 3 | 4 | 5 | 6 | 7 | 8 | 9 | D |
|---|---|---|---|---|---|---|---|---|---|---|---|
| 850 | 92 9419 | 9470 | 9521 | 9572 | 9623 | 9674 | 9725 | 9776 | 9827 | 9879 | 52 |
| 51 | 92 9930 | 9981 | *0032 | *0083 | *0134 | *0185 | *0236 | *0287 | *0338 | *0389 | 51 |
| 52 | 93 0440 | 0491 | 0542 | 0592 | 0643 | 0694 | 0745 | 0796 | 0847 | 0898 | 51 |
| 53 | 0949 | 1000 | 1051 | 1102 | 1153 | 1204 | 1254 | 1305 | 1356 | 1407 | 51 |
| 54 | 1458 | 1509 | 1560 | 1610 | 1661 | 1712 | 1763 | 1814 | 1865 | 1915 | 51 |
| 55 | 1966 | 2017 | 2068 | 2118 | 2169 | 2220 | 2271 | 2322 | 2372 | 2423 | 51 |
| 56 | 2474 | 2524 | 2575 | 2626 | 2677 | 2727 | 2778 | 2829 | 2879 | 2930 | 51 |
| 57 | 2981 | 3031 | 3082 | 3133 | 3183 | 3234 | 3285 | 3335 | 3386 | 3437 | 51 |
| 58 | 3487 | 3538 | 3589 | 3639 | 3690 | 3740 | 3791 | 3841 | 3892 | 3943 | 51 |
| 59 | 3993 | 4044 | 4094 | 4145 | 4195 | 4246 | 4296 | 4347 | 4397 | 4448 | 51 |
| 860 | 4498 | 4549 | 4599 | 4650 | 4700 | 4751 | 4801 | 4852 | 4902 | 4953 | 51 |
| 61 | 5003 | 5054 | 5104 | 5154 | 5205 | 5255 | 5306 | 5356 | 5406 | 5457 | 51 |
| 62 | 5507 | 5558 | 5608 | 5658 | 5709 | 5759 | 5809 | 5860 | 5910 | 5960 | 51 |
| 63 | 6011 | 6061 | 6111 | 6162 | 6212 | 6262 | 6313 | 6363 | 6413 | 6463 | 51 |
| 64 | 6514 | 6564 | 6614 | 6665 | 6715 | 6765 | 6815 | 6865 | 6916 | 6966 | 51 |
| 65 | 7016 | 7066 | 7117 | 7167 | 7217 | 7267 | 7317 | 7367 | 7418 | 7468 | 51 |
| 66 | 7518 | 7568 | 7618 | 7668 | 7718 | 7769 | 7819 | 7869 | 7919 | 7969 | 51 |
| 67 | 8019 | 8069 | 8119 | 8169 | 8219 | 8269 | 8320 | 8370 | 8420 | 8470 | 51 |
| 68 | 8520 | 8570 | 8620 | 8670 | 8720 | 8770 | 8820 | 8870 | 8920 | 8970 | 50 |
| 69 | 9020 | 9070 | 9120 | 9170 | 9220 | 9270 | 9320 | 9369 | 9419 | 9469 | 50 |
| 870 | 93 9519 | 9569 | 9619 | 9669 | 9719 | 9769 | 9819 | 9869 | 9918 | 9968 | 50 |
| 71 | 94 0018 | 0068 | 0118 | 0168 | 0218 | 0267 | 0317 | 0367 | 0417 | 0467 | 50 |
| 72 | 0516 | 0566 | 0616 | 0666 | 0716 | 0765 | 0815 | 0865 | 0915 | 0964 | 50 |
| 73 | 1014 | 1064 | 1114 | 1163 | 1213 | 1263 | 1313 | 1362 | 1412 | 1462 | 50 |
| 74 | 1511 | 1561 | 1611 | 1660 | 1710 | 1760 | 1809 | 1859 | 1909 | 1958 | 50 |
| 75 | 2008 | 2058 | 2107 | 2157 | 2207 | 2256 | 2306 | 2355 | 2405 | 2455 | 50 |
| 76 | 2504 | 2554 | 2603 | 2653 | 2702 | 2752 | 2801 | 2851 | 2901 | 2950 | 50 |
| 77 | 3000 | 3049 | 3099 | 3148 | 3198 | 3247 | 3297 | 3346 | 3396 | 3445 | 50 |
| 78 | 3495 | 3544 | 3593 | 3643 | 3692 | 3742 | 3791 | 3841 | 3890 | 3939 | 50 |
| 79 | 3989 | 4038 | 4088 | 4137 | 4186 | 4236 | 4285 | 4335 | 4384 | 4433 | 50 |
| 880 | 4483 | 4532 | 4581 | 4631 | 4680 | 4729 | 4779 | 4828 | 4877 | 4927 | 50 |
| 81 | 4976 | 5025 | 5074 | 5124 | 5173 | 5222 | 5272 | 5321 | 5370 | 5419 | 50 |
| 82 | 5469 | 5518 | 5567 | 5616 | 5665 | 5715 | 5764 | 5813 | 5862 | 5912 | 50 |
| 83 | 5961 | 6010 | 6059 | 6108 | 6157 | 6207 | 6256 | 6305 | 6354 | 6403 | 50 |
| 84 | 6452 | 6501 | 6551 | 6600 | 6649 | 6698 | 6747 | 6796 | 6845 | 6894 | 50 |
| 85 | 6943 | 6992 | 7041 | 7090 | 7140 | 7189 | 7238 | 7287 | 7336 | 7385 | 50 |
| 86 | 7434 | 7483 | 7532 | 7581 | 7630 | 7679 | 7728 | 7777 | 7826 | 7875 | 49 |
| 87 | 7924 | 7973 | 8022 | 8070 | 8119 | 8168 | 8217 | 8266 | 8315 | 8364 | 49 |
| 88 | 8413 | 8462 | 8511 | 8560 | 8609 | 8657 | 8706 | 8755 | 8804 | 8853 | 49 |
| 89 | 8902 | 8951 | 8999 | 9048 | 9097 | 9146 | 9195 | 9244 | 9292 | 9341 | 49 |
| 890 | 9390 | 9439 | 9488 | 9536 | 9585 | 9634 | 9683 | 9731 | 9780 | 9829 | 49 |
| 91 | 94 9878 | 9926 | 9975 | *0024 | *0073 | *0121 | *0170 | *0219 | *0267 | *0316 | 49 |
| 92 | 95 0365 | 0414 | 0462 | 0511 | 0560 | 0608 | 0657 | 0706 | 0754 | 0803 | 49 |
| 93 | 0851 | 0900 | 0949 | 0997 | 1046 | 1095 | 1143 | 1192 | 1240 | 1289 | 49 |
| 94 | 1338 | 1386 | 1435 | 1483 | 1532 | 1580 | 1629 | 1677 | 1726 | 1775 | 49 |
| 95 | 1823 | 1872 | 1920 | 1969 | 2017 | 2066 | 2114 | 2163 | 2211 | 2260 | 49 |
| 96 | 2308 | 2356 | 2405 | 2453 | 2502 | 2550 | 2599 | 2647 | 2696 | 2744 | 49 |
| 97 | 2792 | 2841 | 2889 | 2938 | 2986 | 3034 | 3083 | 3131 | 3180 | 3228 | 49 |
| 98 | 3276 | 3325 | 3373 | 3421 | 3470 | 3518 | 3566 | 3615 | 3663 | 3711 | 49 |
| 99 | 3760 | 3808 | 3856 | 3905 | 3953 | 4001 | 4049 | 4098 | 4146 | 4194 | 49 |
| N | 0 | 1 | 2 | 3 | 4 | 5 | 6 | 7 | 8 | 9 | D |

| N | 0 | 1 | 2 | 3 | 4 | 5 | 6 | 7 | 8 | 9 | D |
|---|---|---|---|---|---|---|---|---|---|---|---|
| 900 | 95 4243 | 4291 | 4339 | 4387 | 4435 | 4484 | 4532 | 4580 | 4628 | 4677 | 49 |
| 01 | 4725 | 4773 | 4821 | 4869 | 4918 | 4966 | 5014 | 5062 | 5110 | 5158 | 49 |
| 02 | 5207 | 5255 | 5303 | 5351 | 5399 | 5447 | 5495 | 5543 | 5592 | 5640 | 49 |
| 03 | 5688 | 5736 | 5784 | 5832 | 5880 | 5928 | 5976 | 6024 | 6072 | 6120 | 48 |
| 04 | 6168 | 6216 | 6265 | 6313 | 6361 | 6409 | 6457 | 6505 | 6553 | 6601 | 48 |
| 05 | 6649 | 6697 | 6745 | 6793 | 6840 | 6888 | 6936 | 6984 | 7032 | 7080 | 48 |
| 06 | 7128 | 7176 | 7224 | 7272 | 7320 | 7368 | 7416 | 7464 | 7512 | 7559 | 48 |
| 07 | 7607 | 7655 | 7703 | 7751 | 7799 | 7847 | 7894 | 7942 | 7990 | 8038 | 48 |
| 08 | 8086 | 8134 | 8181 | 8229 | 8277 | 8325 | 8373 | 8421 | 8468 | 8516 | 48 |
| 09 | 8564 | 8612 | 8659 | 8707 | 8755 | 8803 | 8850 | 8898 | 8946 | 8994 | 48 |
| 910 | 9041 | 9089 | 9137 | 9185 | 9232 | 9280 | 9328 | 9375 | 9423 | 9471 | 48 |
| 11 | 9518 | 9566 | 9614 | 9661 | 9709 | 9757 | 9804 | 9852 | 9900 | 9947 | 48 |
| 12 | 95 9995 | *0042 | *0090 | *0138 | *0185 | *0233 | *0280 | *0328 | *0376 | *0423 | 48 |
| 13 | 96 0471 | 0518 | 0566 | 0613 | 0661 | 0709 | 0756 | 0804 | 0851 | 0899 | 48 |
| 14 | 0946 | 0994 | 1041 | 1089 | 1136 | 1184 | 1231 | 1279 | 1326 | 1374 | 48 |
| 15 | 1421 | 1469 | 1516 | 1563 | 1611 | 1658 | 1706 | 1753 | 1801 | 1848 | 48 |
| 16 | 1895 | 1943 | 1990 | 2038 | 2085 | 2132 | 2180 | 2227 | 2275 | 2322 | 48 |
| 17 | 2369 | 2417 | 2464 | 2511 | 2559 | 2606 | 2653 | 2701 | 2748 | 2795 | 48 |
| 18 | 2843 | 2890 | 2937 | 2985 | 3032 | 3079 | 3126 | 3174 | 3221 | 3268 | 48 |
| 19 | 3316 | 3363 | 3410 | 3457 | 3504 | 3552 | 3599 | 3646 | 3693 | 3741 | 48 |
| 920 | 3788 | 3835 | 3882 | 3929 | 3977 | 4024 | 4071 | 4118 | 4165 | 4212 | 48 |
| 21 | 4260 | 4307 | 4354 | 4401 | 4448 | 4495 | 4542 | 4590 | 4637 | 4684 | 48 |
| 22 | 4731 | 4778 | 4825 | 4872 | 4919 | 4966 | 5013 | 5061 | 5108 | 5155 | 48 |
| 23 | 5202 | 5249 | 5296 | 5343 | 5390 | 5437 | 5484 | 5531 | 5578 | 5625 | 47 |
| 24 | 5672 | 5719 | 5766 | 5813 | 5860 | 5907 | 5954 | 6001 | 6048 | 6095 | 47 |
| 25 | 6142 | 6189 | 6236 | 6283 | 6329 | 6376 | 6423 | 6470 | 6517 | 6564 | 47 |
| 26 | 6611 | 6658 | 6705 | 6752 | 6799 | 6845 | 6892 | 6939 | 6986 | 7033 | 47 |
| 27 | 7080 | 7127 | 7173 | 7220 | 7267 | 7314 | 7361 | 7408 | 7454 | 7501 | 47 |
| 28 | 7548 | 7595 | 7642 | 7688 | 7735 | 7782 | 7829 | 7875 | 7922 | 7969 | 47 |
| 29 | 8016 | 8062 | 8109 | 8156 | 8203 | 8249 | 8296 | 8343 | 8390 | 8436 | 47 |
| 930 | 8483 | 8530 | 8576 | 8623 | 8670 | 8716 | 8763 | 8810 | 8856 | 8903 | 47 |
| 31 | 8950 | 8996 | 9043 | 9090 | 9136 | 9183 | 9229 | 9276 | 9323 | 9369 | 47 |
| 32 | 9416 | 9463 | 9509 | 9556 | 9602 | 9649 | 9695 | 9742 | 9789 | 9835 | 47 |
| 33 | 96 9882 | 9928 | 9975 | *0021 | *0068 | *0114 | *0161 | *0207 | *0254 | *0300 | 47 |
| 34 | 97 0347 | 0393 | 0440 | 0486 | 0533 | 0579 | 0626 | 0672 | 0719 | 0765 | 47 |
| 35 | 0812 | 0858 | 0904 | 0951 | 0997 | 1044 | 1090 | 1137 | 1183 | 1229 | 47 |
| 36 | 1276 | 1322 | 1369 | 1415 | 1461 | 1508 | 1554 | 1601 | 1647 | 1693 | 47 |
| 37 | 1740 | 1786 | 1832 | 1879 | 1925 | 1971 | 2018 | 2064 | 2110 | 2157 | 47 |
| 38 | 2203 | 2249 | 2295 | 2342 | 2388 | 2434 | 2481 | 2527 | 2573 | 2619 | 47 |
| 39 | 2666 | 2712 | 2758 | 2804 | 2851 | 2897 | 2943 | 2989 | 3035 | 3082 | 47 |
| 940 | 3128 | 3174 | 3220 | 3266 | 3313 | 3359 | 3405 | 3451 | 3497 | 3543 | 47 |
| 41 | 3590 | 3636 | 3682 | 3728 | 3774 | 3820 | 3866 | 3913 | 3959 | 4005 | 47 |
| 42 | 4051 | 4097 | 4143 | 4189 | 4235 | 4281 | 4327 | 4374 | 4420 | 4466 | 47 |
| 43 | 4512 | 4558 | 4604 | 4650 | 4696 | 4742 | 4788 | 4834 | 4880 | 4926 | 46 |
| 44 | 4972 | 5018 | 5064 | 5110 | 5156 | 5202 | 5248 | 5294 | 5340 | 5386 | 46 |
| 45 | 5432 | 5478 | 5524 | 5570 | 5616 | 5662 | 5707 | 5753 | 5799 | 5845 | 46 |
| 46 | 5891 | 5937 | 5983 | 6029 | 6075 | 6121 | 6167 | 6212 | 6258 | 6304 | 46 |
| 47 | 6350 | 6396 | 6442 | 6488 | 6533 | 6579 | 6625 | 6671 | 6717 | 6763 | 46 |
| 48 | 6808 | 6854 | 6900 | 6946 | 6992 | 7037 | 7083 | 7129 | 7175 | 7220 | 46 |
| 49 | 7266 | 7312 | 7358 | 7403 | 7449 | 7495 | 7541 | 7586 | 7632 | 7678 | 46 |
| N | 0 | 1 | 2 | 3 | 4 | 5 | 6 | 7 | 8 | 9 | D |

# TABLE 2

Table
2

| N | 0 | 1 | 2 | 3 | 4 | 5 | 6 | 7 | 8 | 9 | D |
|---|---|---|---|---|---|---|---|---|---|---|---|
| 950 | 97 7724 | 7769 | 7815 | 7861 | 7906 | 7952 | 7998 | 8043 | 8089 | 8135 | 46 |
| 51 | 8181 | 8226 | 8272 | 8317 | 8363 | 8409 | 8454 | 8500 | 8546 | 8591 | 46 |
| 52 | 8637 | 8683 | 8728 | 8774 | 8819 | 8865 | 8911 | 8956 | 9002 | 9047 | 46 |
| 53 | 9093 | 9138 | 9184 | 9230 | 9275 | 9321 | 9366 | 9412 | 9457 | 9503 | 46 |
| 54 | 97 9548 | 9594 | 9639 | 9685 | 9730 | 9776 | 9821 | 9867 | 9912 | 9958 | 46 |
| 55 | 98 0003 | 0049 | 0094 | 0140 | 0185 | 0231 | 0276 | 0322 | 0367 | 0412 | 46 |
| 56 | 0458 | 0503 | 0549 | 0594 | 0640 | 0685 | 0730 | 0776 | 0821 | 0867 | 46 |
| 57 | 0912 | 0957 | 1003 | 1048 | 1093 | 1139 | 1184 | 1229 | 1275 | 1320 | 46 |
| 58 | 1366 | 1411 | 1456 | 1501 | 1547 | 1592 | 1637 | 1683 | 1728 | 1773 | 46 |
| 59 | 1819 | 1864 | 1909 | 1954 | 2000 | 2045 | 2090 | 2135 | 2181 | 2226 | 46 |
| 960 | 2271 | 2316 | 2362 | 2407 | 2452 | 2497 | 2543 | 2588 | 2633 | 2678 | 46 |
| 61 | 2723 | 2769 | 2814 | 2859 | 2904 | 2949 | 2994 | 3040 | 3085 | 3130 | 46 |
| 62 | 3175 | 3220 | 3265 | 3310 | 3356 | 3401 | 3446 | 3491 | 3536 | 3581 | 46 |
| 63 | 3626 | 3671 | 3716 | 3762 | 3807 | 3852 | 3897 | 3942 | 3987 | 4032 | 46 |
| 64 | 4077 | 4122 | 4167 | 4212 | 4257 | 4302 | 4347 | 4392 | 4437 | 4482 | 45 |
| 65 | 4527 | 4572 | 4617 | 4662 | 4707 | 4752 | 4797 | 4842 | 4887 | 4932 | 45 |
| 66 | 4977 | 5022 | 5067 | 5112 | 5157 | 5202 | 5247 | 5292 | 5337 | 5382 | 45 |
| 67 | 5426 | 5471 | 5516 | 5561 | 5606 | 5651 | 5696 | 5741 | 5786 | 5830 | 45 |
| 68 | 5875 | 5920 | 5965 | 6010 | 6055 | 6100 | 6144 | 6189 | 6234 | 6279 | 45 |
| 69 | 6324 | 6369 | 6413 | 6458 | 6503 | 6548 | 6593 | 6637 | 6682 | 6727 | 45 |
| 970 | 6772 | 6817 | 6861 | 6906 | 6951 | 6996 | 7040 | 7085 | 7130 | 7175 | 45 |
| 71 | 7219 | 7264 | 7309 | 7353 | 7398 | 7443 | 7488 | 7532 | 7577 | 7622 | 45 |
| 72 | 7666 | 7711 | 7756 | 7800 | 7845 | 7890 | 7934 | 7979 | 8024 | 8068 | 45 |
| 73 | 8113 | 8157 | 8202 | 8247 | 8291 | 8336 | 8381 | 8425 | 8470 | 8514 | 45 |
| 74 | 8559 | 8604 | 8648 | 8693 | 8737 | 8782 | 8826 | 8871 | 8916 | 8960 | 45 |
| 75 | 9005 | 9049 | 9094 | 9138 | 9183 | 9227 | 9272 | 9316 | 9361 | 9405 | 45 |
| 76 | 9450 | 9494 | 9539 | 9583 | 9628 | 9672 | 9717 | 9761 | 9806 | 9850 | 45 |
| 77 | 98 9895 | 9939 | 9983 | *0028 | *0072 | *0117 | *0161 | *0206 | *0250 | *0294 | 45 |
| 78 | 99 0339 | 0383 | 0428 | 0472 | 0516 | 0561 | 0605 | 0650 | 0694 | 0738 | 45 |
| 79 | 0783 | 0827 | 0871 | 0916 | 0960 | 1004 | 1049 | 1093 | 1137 | 1182 | 45 |
| 980 | 1226 | 1270 | 1315 | 1359 | 1403 | 1448 | 1492 | 1536 | 1580 | 1625 | 45 |
| 81 | 1669 | 1713 | 1758 | 1802 | 1846 | 1890 | 1935 | 1979 | 2023 | 2067 | 45 |
| 82 | 2111 | 2156 | 2200 | 2244 | 2288 | 2333 | 2377 | 2421 | 2465 | 2509 | 45 |
| 83 | 2554 | 2598 | 2642 | 2686 | 2730 | 2774 | 2819 | 2863 | 2907 | 2951 | 45 |
| 84 | 2995 | 3039 | 3083 | 3127 | 3172 | 3216 | 3260 | 3304 | 3348 | 3392 | 45 |
| 85 | 3436 | 3480 | 3524 | 3568 | 3613 | 3657 | 3701 | 3745 | 3789 | 3833 | 45 |
| 86 | 3877 | 3921 | 3965 | 4009 | 4053 | 4097 | 4141 | 4185 | 4229 | 4273 | 44 |
| 87 | 4317 | 4361 | 4405 | 4449 | 4493 | 4537 | 4581 | 4625 | 4669 | 4713 | 44 |
| 88 | 4757 | 4801 | 4845 | 4889 | 4933 | 4977 | 5021 | 5065 | 5108 | 5152 | 44 |
| 89 | 5196 | 5240 | 5284 | 5328 | 5372 | 5416 | 5460 | 5504 | 5547 | 5591 | 44 |
| 990 | 5635 | 5679 | 5723 | 5767 | 5811 | 5854 | 5898 | 5942 | 5986 | 6030 | 44 |
| 91 | 6074 | 6117 | 6161 | 6205 | 6249 | 6293 | 6337 | 6380 | 6424 | 6468 | 44 |
| 92 | 6512 | 6555 | 6599 | 6643 | 6687 | 6731 | 6774 | 6818 | 6862 | 6906 | 44 |
| 93 | 6949 | 6993 | 7037 | 7080 | 7124 | 7168 | 7212 | 7255 | 7299 | 7343 | 44 |
| 94 | 7386 | 7430 | 7474 | 7517 | 7561 | 7605 | 7648 | 7692 | 7736 | 7779 | 44 |
| 95 | 7823 | 7867 | 7910 | 7954 | 7998 | 8041 | 8085 | 8129 | 8172 | 8216 | 44 |
| 96 | 8259 | 8303 | 8347 | 8390 | 8434 | 8477 | 8521 | 8564 | 8608 | 8652 | 44 |
| 97 | 8695 | 8739 | 8782 | 8826 | 8869 | 8913 | 8956 | 9000 | 9043 | 9087 | 44 |
| 98 | 9131 | 9174 | 9218 | 9261 | 9305 | 9348 | 9392 | 9435 | 9479 | 9522 | 44 |
| 99 | 99 9565 | 9609 | 9652 | 9696 | 9739 | 9783 | 9826 | 9870 | 9913 | 9957 | 44 |
| N | 0 | 1 | 2 | 3 | 4 | 5 | 6 | 7 | 8 | 9 | D |

## LOGARITHMS OF NUMBERS 10,000–10,499

# TABLE 3

### Seven-Place Mantissas

| N | 0 | 1 | 2 | 3 | 4 | 5 | 6 | 7 | 8 | 9 | D# |
|---|---|---|---|---|---|---|---|---|---|---|----|
| 1000 | 000 0000 | 0434 | 0869 | 1303 | 1737 | 2171 | 2605 | 3039 | 3473 | 3907 | 435 |
| 1001 | 4341 | 4775 | 5208 | 5642 | 6076 | 6510 | 6943 | 7377 | 7810 | 8244 | 434 |
| 1002 | 8677 | 9111 | 9544 | 9977 | *0411 | *0844 | *1277 | *1710 | *2143 | *2576 | 434 |
| 1003 | 001 3009 | 3442 | 3875 | 4308 | 4741 | 5174 | 5607 | 6039 | 6472 | 6905 | 433 |
| 1004 | 7337 | 7770 | 8202 | 8635 | 9067 | 9499 | 9932 | *0364 | *0796 | *1228 | 433 |
| 1005 | 002 1661 | 2093 | 2525 | 2957 | 3389 | 3821 | 4253 | 4685 | 5116 | 5548 | 432 |
| 1006 | 5980 | 6411 | 6843 | 7275 | 7706 | 8138 | 8569 | 9001 | 9432 | 9863 | 432 |
| 1007 | 003 0295 | 0726 | 1157 | 1588 | 2019 | 2451 | 2882 | 3313 | 3744 | 4174 | 432 |
| 1008 | 4605 | 5036 | 5467 | 5898 | 6328 | 6759 | 7190 | 7620 | 8051 | 8481 | 431 |
| 1009 | 8912 | 9342 | 9772 | *0203 | *0633 | *1063 | *1493 | *1924 | *2354 | *2784 | 431 |
| 1010 | 004 3214 | 3644 | 4074 | 4504 | 4933 | 5363 | 5793 | 6223 | 6652 | 7082 | 430 |
| 1011 | 7512 | 7941 | 8371 | 8800 | 9229 | 9659 | *0088 | *0517 | *0947 | *1376 | 430 |
| 1012 | 005 1805 | 2234 | 2663 | 3092 | 3521 | 3950 | 4379 | 4808 | 5237 | 5666 | 429 |
| 1013 | 6094 | 6523 | 6952 | 7380 | 7809 | 8238 | 8666 | 9094 | 9523 | 9951 | 429 |
| 1014 | 006 0380 | 0808 | 1236 | 1664 | 2092 | 2521 | 2949 | 3377 | 3805 | 4233 | 429 |
| 1015 | 4660 | 5088 | 5516 | 5944 | 6372 | 6799 | 7227 | 7655 | 8082 | 8510 | 428 |
| 1016 | 8937 | 9365 | 9792 | *0219 | *0647 | *1074 | *1501 | *1928 | *2355 | *2782 | 428 |
| 1017 | 007 3210 | 3637 | 4064 | 4490 | 4917 | 5344 | 5771 | 6198 | 6624 | 7051 | 427 |
| 1018 | 7478 | 7904 | 8331 | 8757 | 9184 | 9610 | *0037 | *0463 | *0889 | *1316 | 427 |
| 1019 | 008 1742 | 2168 | 2594 | 3020 | 3446 | 3872 | 4298 | 4724 | 5150 | 5576 | 426 |
| 1020 | 6002 | 6427 | 6853 | 7279 | 7704 | 8130 | 8556 | 8981 | 9407 | 9832 | 426 |
| 1021 | 009 0257 | 0683 | 1108 | 1533 | 1959 | 2384 | 2809 | 3234 | 3659 | 4084 | 426 |
| 1022 | 4509 | 4934 | 5359 | 5784 | 6208 | 6633 | 7058 | 7483 | 7907 | 8332 | 425 |
| 1023 | 8756 | 9181 | 9605 | *0030 | *0454 | *0878 | *1303 | *1727 | *2151 | *2575 | 425 |
| 1024 | 010 3000 | 3424 | 3848 | 4272 | 4696 | 5120 | 5544 | 5967 | 6391 | 6815 | 424 |
| 1025 | 7239 | 7662 | 8086 | 8510 | 8933 | 9357 | 9780 | *0204 | *0627 | *1050 | 424 |
| 1026 | 011 1474 | 1897 | 2320 | 2743 | 3166 | 3590 | 4013 | 4436 | 4859 | 5282 | 424 |
| 1027 | 5704 | 6127 | 6550 | 6973 | 7396 | 7818 | 8241 | 8664 | 9086 | 9509 | 423 |
| 1028 | 9931 | *0354 | *0776 | *1198 | *1621 | *2043 | *2465 | *2887 | *3310 | *3732 | 423 |
| 1029 | 012 4154 | 4576 | 4998 | 5420 | 5842 | 6264 | 6685 | 7107 | 7529 | 7951 | 422 |
| 1030 | 8372 | 8794 | 9215 | 9637 | *0059 | *0480 | *0901 | *1323 | *1744 | *2165 | 422 |
| 1031 | 013 2587 | 3008 | 3429 | 3850 | 4271 | 4692 | 5113 | 5534 | 5955 | 6376 | 421 |
| 1032 | 6797 | 7218 | 7639 | 8059 | 8480 | 8901 | 9321 | 9742 | *0162 | *0583 | 421 |
| 1033 | 014 1003 | 1424 | 1844 | 2264 | 2685 | 3105 | 3525 | 3945 | 4365 | 4785 | 421 |
| 1034 | 5205 | 5625 | 6045 | 6465 | 6885 | 7305 | 7725 | 8144 | 8564 | 8984 | 420 |
| 1035 | 9403 | 9823 | *0243 | *0662 | *1082 | *1501 | *1920 | *2340 | *2759 | *3178 | 420 |
| 1036 | 015 3598 | 4017 | 4436 | 4855 | 5274 | 5693 | 6112 | 6531 | 6950 | 7369 | 419 |
| 1037 | 7788 | 8206 | 8625 | 9044 | 9462 | 9881 | *0300 | *0718 | *1137 | *1555 | 419 |
| 1038 | 016 1974 | 2392 | 2810 | 3229 | 3647 | 4065 | 4483 | 4901 | 5319 | 5737 | 419 |
| 1039 | 6155 | 6573 | 6991 | 7409 | 7827 | 8245 | 8663 | 9080 | 9498 | 9916 | 418 |
| 1040 | 017 0333 | 0751 | 1168 | 1586 | 2003 | 2421 | 2838 | 3256 | 3673 | 4090 | 418 |
| 1041 | 4507 | 4924 | 5342 | 5759 | 6176 | 6593 | 7010 | 7427 | 7844 | 8260 | 418 |
| 1042 | 8677 | 9094 | 9511 | 9927 | *0344 | *0761 | *1177 | *1594 | *2010 | *2427 | 417 |
| 1043 | 018 2843 | 3259 | 3676 | 4092 | 4508 | 4925 | 5341 | 5757 | 6173 | 6589 | 417 |
| 1044 | 7005 | 7421 | 7837 | 8253 | 8669 | 9084 | 9500 | 9916 | *0332 | *0747 | 416 |
| 1045 | 019 1163 | 1578 | 1994 | 2410 | 2825 | 3240 | 3656 | 4071 | 4486 | 4902 | 416 |
| 1046 | 5317 | 5732 | 6147 | 6562 | 6977 | 7392 | 7807 | 8222 | 8637 | 9052 | 415 |
| 1047 | 9467 | 9882 | *0296 | *0711 | *1126 | *1540 | *1955 | *2369 | *2784 | *3198 | 415 |
| 1048 | 020 3613 | 4027 | 4442 | 4856 | 5270 | 5684 | 6099 | 6513 | 6927 | 7341 | 415 |
| 1049 | 7755 | 8169 | 8583 | 8997 | 9411 | 9824 | *0238 | *0652 | *1066 | *1479 | 414 |
| N | 0 | 1 | 2 | 3 | 4 | 5 | 6 | 7 | 8 | 9 | D |

\* Prefix first three places on next line.
  *Example:* The mantissa for number (N) 10024 is *001* 0411.

\# The *highest difference* between adjacent mantissas on the *individual line*. It is also the *lowest difference* between adjacent mantissas on the *preceding line* in many cases.

## TABLE 3

| N | 0 | 1 | 2 | 3 | 4 | 5 | 6 | 7 | 8 | 9 | D |
|---|---|---|---|---|---|---|---|---|---|---|---|
| 1050 | 021 1893 | 2307 | 2720 | 3134 | 3547 | 3961 | 4374 | 4787 | 5201 | 5614 | 414 |
| 1051 | 6027 | 6440 | 6854 | 7267 | 7680 | 8093 | 8506 | 8919 | 9332 | 9745 | 414 |
| 1052 | 022 0157 | 0570 | 0983 | 1396 | 1808 | 2221 | 2634 | 3046 | 3459 | 3871 | 413 |
| 1053 | 4284 | 4696 | 5109 | 5521 | 5933 | 6345 | 6758 | 7170 | 7582 | 7994 | 413 |
| 1054 | 8406 | 8818 | 9230 | 9642 | *0054 | *0466 | *0878 | *1289 | *1701 | *2113 | 412 |
| 1055 | 023 2525 | 2936 | 3348 | 3759 | 4171 | 4582 | 4994 | 5405 | 5817 | 6228 | 412 |
| 1056 | 6639 | 7050 | 7462 | 7873 | 8284 | 8695 | 9106 | 9517 | 9928 | *0339 | 412 |
| 1057 | 024 0750 | 1161 | 1572 | 1982 | 2393 | 2804 | 3214 | 3625 | 4036 | 4446 | 411 |
| 1058 | 4857 | 5267 | 5678 | 6088 | 6498 | 6909 | 7319 | 7729 | 8139 | 8549 | 411 |
| 1059 | 8960 | 9370 | 9780 | *0190 | *0600 | *1010 | *1419 | *1829 | *2239 | *2649 | 410 |
| 1060 | 025 3059 | 3468 | 3878 | 4288 | 4697 | 5107 | 5516 | 5926 | 6335 | 6744 | 410 |
| 1061 | 7154 | 7563 | 7972 | 8382 | 8791 | 9200 | 9609 | *0018 | *0427 | *0836 | 410 |
| 1062 | 026 1245 | 1654 | 2063 | 2472 | 2881 | 3289 | 3698 | 4107 | 4515 | 4924 | 409 |
| 1063 | 5333 | 5741 | 6150 | 6558 | 6967 | 7375 | 7783 | 8192 | 8600 | 9008 | 409 |
| 1064 | 9416 | 9824 | *0233 | *0641 | *1049 | *1457 | *1865 | *2273 | *2680 | *3088 | 409 |
| 1065 | 027 3496 | 3904 | 4312 | 4719 | 5127 | 5535 | 5942 | 6350 | 6757 | 7165 | 408 |
| 1066 | 7572 | 7979 | 8387 | 8794 | 9201 | 9609 | *0016 | *0423 | *0830 | *1237 | 408 |
| 1067 | 028 1644 | 2051 | 2458 | 2865 | 3272 | 3679 | 4086 | 4492 | 4899 | 5306 | 408 |
| 1068 | 5713 | 6119 | 6526 | 6932 | 7339 | 7745 | 8152 | 8558 | 8964 | 9371 | 407 |
| 1069 | 9777 | *0183 | *0590 | *0996 | *1402 | *1808 | *2214 | *2620 | *3026 | *3432 | 407 |
| 1070 | 029 3838 | 4244 | 4649 | 5055 | 5461 | 5867 | 6272 | 6678 | 7084 | 7489 | 406 |
| 1071 | 7895 | 8300 | 8706 | 9111 | 9516 | 9922 | *0327 | *0732 | *1138 | *1543 | 406 |
| 1072 | 030 1948 | 2353 | 2758 | 3163 | 3568 | 3973 | 4378 | 4783 | 5188 | 5592 | 405 |
| 1073 | 5997 | 6402 | 6807 | 7211 | 7616 | 8020 | 8425 | 8830 | 9234 | 9638 | 405 |
| 1074 | 031 0043 | 0447 | 0851 | 1256 | 1660 | 2064 | 2468 | 2872 | 3277 | 3681 | 405 |
| 1075 | 4085 | 4489 | 4893 | 5296 | 5700 | 6104 | 6508 | 6912 | 7315 | 7719 | 404 |
| 1076 | 8123 | 8526 | 8930 | 9333 | 9737 | *0140 | *0544 | *0947 | *1350 | *1754 | 404 |
| 1077 | 032 2157 | 2560 | 2963 | 3367 | 3770 | 4173 | 4576 | 4979 | 5382 | 5785 | 404 |
| 1078 | 6188 | 6590 | 6993 | 7396 | 7799 | 8201 | 8604 | 9007 | 9409 | 9812 | 403 |
| 1079 | 033 0214 | 0617 | 1019 | 1422 | 1824 | 2226 | 2629 | 3031 | 3433 | 3835 | 403 |
| 1080 | 4238 | 4640 | 5042 | 5444 | 5846 | 6248 | 6650 | 7052 | 7453 | 7855 | 402 |
| 1081 | 8257 | 8659 | 9060 | 9462 | 9864 | *0265 | *0667 | *1068 | *1470 | *1871 | 402 |
| 1082 | 034 2273 | 2674 | 3075 | 3477 | 3878 | 4279 | 4680 | 5081 | 5482 | 5884 | 402 |
| 1083 | 6285 | 6686 | 7087 | 7487 | 7888 | 8289 | 8690 | 9091 | 9491 | 9892 | 401 |
| 1084 | 035 0293 | 0693 | 1094 | 1495 | 1895 | 2296 | 2696 | 3096 | 3497 | 3897 | 401 |
| 1085 | 4297 | 4698 | 5098 | 5498 | 5898 | 6298 | 6698 | 7098 | 7498 | 7898 | 401 |
| 1086 | 8298 | 8698 | 9098 | 9498 | 9898 | *0297 | *0697 | *1097 | *1496 | *1896 | 400 |
| 1087 | 036 2295 | 2695 | 3094 | 3494 | 3893 | 4293 | 4692 | 5091 | 5491 | 5890 | 400 |
| 1088 | 6289 | 6688 | 7087 | 7486 | 7885 | 8284 | 8683 | 9082 | 9481 | 9880 | 399 |
| 1089 | 037 0279 | 0678 | 1076 | 1475 | 1874 | 2272 | 2671 | 3070 | 3468 | 3867 | 399 |
| 1090 | 4265 | 4663 | 5062 | 5460 | 5858 | 6257 | 6655 | 7053 | 7451 | 7849 | 399 |
| 1091 | 8248 | 8646 | 9044 | 9442 | 9839 | *0237 | *0635 | *1033 | *1431 | *1829 | 398 |
| 1092 | 038 2226 | 2624 | 3022 | 3419 | 3817 | 4214 | 4612 | 5009 | 5407 | 5804 | 398 |
| 1093 | 6202 | 6599 | 6996 | 7393 | 7791 | 8188 | 8585 | 8982 | 9379 | 9776 | 398 |
| 1094 | 039 0173 | 0570 | 0967 | 1364 | 1761 | 2158 | 2554 | 2951 | 3348 | 3745 | 397 |
| 1095 | 4141 | 4538 | 4934 | 5331 | 5727 | 6124 | 6520 | 6917 | 7313 | 7709 | 397 |
| 1096 | 8106 | 8502 | 8898 | 9294 | 9690 | *0086 | *0482 | *0878 | *1274 | *1670 | 396 |
| 1097 | 040 2066 | 2462 | 2858 | 3254 | 3650 | 4045 | 4441 | 4837 | 5232 | 5628 | 396 |
| 1098 | 6023 | 6419 | 6814 | 7210 | 7605 | 8001 | 8396 | 8791 | 9187 | 9582 | 396 |
| 1099 | 9977 | *0372 | *0767 | *1162 | *1557 | *1952 | *2347 | *2742 | *3137 | *3532 | 395 |
| 1100 | 041 3927 | 4322 | 4716 | 5111 | 5506 | 5900 | 6295 | 6690 | 7084 | 7479 | 395 |
| N | 0 | 1 | 2 | 3 | 4 | 5 | 6 | 7 | 8 | 9 | D |

Table
3

# TABLE 4

## INTEREST RATE PER CONVERSION PERIOD
### For Nominal Rates from $2\frac{1}{2}$% to 10%

| Nominal Rate (Annual) | Interest Rate Per Period If Nominal Rate Is Compounded | | |
|---|---|---|---|
| | Monthly | Quarterly | Semiannually |
| $2\frac{1}{2}$% (= .025) | $*\frac{5}{24}$% (= .002083̇) | $\frac{5}{8}$% (= .00625) | $1\frac{1}{4}$% (= .0125) |
| 3% (= .03) | $\frac{1}{4}$% (= .0025) | $\frac{3}{4}$% (= .0075) | $1\frac{1}{2}$% (= .015) |
| $3\frac{1}{2}$% (= .035) | $*\frac{7}{24}$% (= .002916̇) | $\frac{7}{8}$% (= .00875) | $1\frac{3}{4}$% (= .0175) |
| 4% (= .04) | $\frac{1}{3}$% (= .003̇) | 1% (= .01) | 2% (= .02) |
| $4\frac{1}{2}$% (= .045) | $*\frac{3}{8}$% (= .00375) | $1\frac{1}{8}$% (= .01125) | $2\frac{1}{4}$% (= .0225) |
| 5% (= .05) | $\frac{5}{12}$% (= .00416̇) | $1\frac{1}{4}$% (= .0125) | $2\frac{1}{2}$% (= .025) |
| $5\frac{1}{2}$% (= .055) | $\frac{11}{24}$% (= .004583̇) | $1\frac{3}{8}$% (= .01375) | $2\frac{3}{4}$% (= .0275) |
| 6% (= .06) | $\frac{1}{2}$% (= .005) | $1\frac{1}{2}$% (= .015) | 3% (= .03) |
| $6\frac{1}{2}$% (= .065) | $\frac{13}{24}$% (= .005416̇) | $1\frac{5}{8}$% (= .01625) | $3\frac{1}{4}$% (= .0325) |
| 7% (= .07) | $\frac{7}{12}$% (= .00583̇) | $1\frac{3}{4}$% (= .0175) | $3\frac{1}{2}$% (= .035) |
| $7\frac{1}{2}$% (= .075) | $\frac{5}{8}$% (= .00625) | $1\frac{7}{8}$% (= .01875) | $3\frac{3}{4}$% (= .0375) |
| 8% (= .08) | $\frac{2}{3}$% (= .006̇) | 2% (= .02) | 4% (= .04) |
| $8\frac{1}{2}$% (= .085) | $*\frac{17}{24}$% (= .007083̇) | $*2\frac{1}{8}$% (= .02125) | $*4\frac{1}{4}$% (= .0425) |
| 9% (= .09) | $\frac{3}{4}$% (= .0075) | $2\frac{1}{4}$% (= .0225) | $4\frac{1}{2}$% (= .045) |
| $9\frac{1}{2}$% (= .095) | $*\frac{19}{24}$% (= .007916̇) | $*2\frac{3}{8}$% (= .02375) | $*4\frac{3}{4}$% (= .0475) |
| 10% (= .10) | $*\frac{5}{6}$% (= .0083̇) | $2\frac{1}{2}$% (= .025) | 5% (= .05) |

* These rates are not included in the Compound Interest and Annuity Tables (5 through 11). However, approximate values for these rates can be obtained by interpolation from the values in the tables.

# TABLE 5

$$s = (1 + i)^n$$

| $n$ | $\frac{1}{4}\%$ | $\frac{1}{3}\%$ | $\frac{5}{12}\%$ | $\frac{11}{24}\%$ | $n$ |
|---|---|---|---|---|---|
| 1 | 1.0025 0000 | 1.0033 3333 | 1.0041 6667 | 1.0045 8333 | 1 |
| 2 | 1.0050 0625 | 1.0066 7778 | 1.0083 5069 | 1.0091 8767 | 2 |
| 3 | 1.0075 1877 | 1.0100 3337 | 1.0125 5216 | 1.0138 1312 | 3 |
| 4 | 1.0100 3756 | 1.0134 0015 | 1.0167 7112 | 1.0184 5976 | 4 |
| 5 | 1.0125 6266 | 1.0167 7815 | 1.0210 0767 | 1.0231 2770 | 5 |
| 6 | 1.0150 9406 | 1.0201 6741 | 1.0252 6187 | 1.0278 1704 | 6 |
| 7 | 1.0176 3180 | 1.0235 6797 | 1.0295 3379 | 1.0325 2786 | 7 |
| 8 | 1.0201 7588 | 1.0269 7986 | 1.0338 2352 | 1.0372 6028 | 8 |
| 9 | 1.0227 2632 | 1.0304 0313 | 1.0381 3111 | 1.0420 1439 | 9 |
| 10 | 1.0252 8313 | 1.0338 3780 | 1.0424 5666 | 1.0467 9029 | 10 |
| 11 | 1.0278 4634 | 1.0372 8393 | 1.0468 0023 | 1.0515 8808 | 11 |
| 12 | 1.0304 1596 | 1.0407 4154 | 1.0511 6190 | 1.0564 0786 | 12 |
| 13 | 1.0329 9200 | 1.0442 1068 | 1.0555 4174 | 1.0612 4973 | 13 |
| 14 | 1.0355 7448 | 1.0476 9138 | 1.0599 3983 | 1.0661 1379 | 14 |
| 15 | 1.0381 6341 | 1.0511 8369 | 1.0643 5625 | 1.0710 0015 | 15 |
| 16 | 1.0407 5882 | 1.0546 8763 | 1.0687 9106 | 1.0759 0890 | 16 |
| 17 | 1.0433 6072 | 1.0582 0326 | 1.0732 4436 | 1.0808 4015 | 17 |
| 18 | 1.0459 6912 | 1.0617 3060 | 1.0777 1621 | 1.0857 9400 | 18 |
| 19 | 1.0485 8404 | 1.0652 6971 | 1.0822 0670 | 1.0907 7055 | 19 |
| 20 | 1.0512 0550 | 1.0688 2060 | 1.0867 1589 | 1.0957 6992 | 20 |
| 21 | 1.0538 3352 | 1.0723 8334 | 1.0912 4387 | 1.1007 9220 | 21 |
| 22 | 1.0564 6810 | 1.0759 5795 | 1.0957 9072 | 1.1058 3749 | 22 |
| 23 | 1.0591 0927 | 1.0795 4448 | 1.1003 5652 | 1.1109 0592 | 23 |
| 24 | 1.0617 5704 | 1.0831 4296 | 1.1049 4134 | 1.1159 9757 | 24 |
| 25 | 1.0644 1144 | 1.0867 5344 | 1.1095 4526 | 1.1211 1256 | 25 |
| 26 | 1.0670 7247 | 1.0903 7595 | 1.1141 6836 | 1.1262 5099 | 26 |
| 27 | 1.0697 4015 | 1.0940 1053 | 1.1188 1073 | 1.1314 1297 | 27 |
| 28 | 1.0724 1450 | 1.0976 5724 | 1.1234 7244 | 1.1365 9862 | 28 |
| 29 | 1.0750 9553 | 1.1013 1609 | 1.1281 5358 | 1.1418 0803 | 29 |
| 30 | 1.0777 8327 | 1.1049 8715 | 1.1328 5422 | 1.1470 4131 | 30 |
| 31 | 1.0804 7773 | 1.1086 7044 | 1.1375 7444 | 1.1522 9859 | 31 |
| 32 | 1.0831 7892 | 1.1123 6601 | 1.1423 1434 | 1.1575 7995 | 32 |
| 33 | 1.0858 8687 | 1.1160 7389 | 1.1470 7398 | 1.1628 8553 | 33 |
| 34 | 1.0886 0159 | 1.1197 9414 | 1.1518 5346 | 1.1682 1542 | 34 |
| 35 | 1.0913 2309 | 1.1235 2679 | 1.1566 5284 | 1.1735 6974 | 35 |
| 36 | 1.0940 5140 | 1.1272 7187 | 1.1614 7223 | 1.1789 4860 | 36 |
| 37 | 1.0967 8653 | 1.1310 2945 | 1.1663 1170 | 1.1843 5212 | 37 |
| 38 | 1.0995 2850 | 1.1347 9955 | 1.1711 7133 | 1.1897 8040 | 38 |
| 39 | 1.1022 7732 | 1.1385 8221 | 1.1760 5121 | 1.1952 3356 | 39 |
| 40 | 1.1050 3301 | 1.1423 7748 | 1.1809 5142 | 1.2007 1171 | 40 |
| 41 | 1.1077 9559 | 1.1461 8541 | 1.1858 7206 | 1.2062 1497 | 41 |
| 42 | 1.1105 6508 | 1.1500 0603 | 1.1908 1319 | 1.2117 4346 | 42 |
| 43 | 1.1133 4149 | 1.1538 3938 | 1.1957 7491 | 1.2172 9728 | 43 |
| 44 | 1.1161 2485 | 1.1576 8551 | 1.2007 5731 | 1.2228 7656 | 44 |
| 45 | 1.1189 1516 | 1.1615 4446 | 1.2057 6046 | 1.2284 8141 | 45 |
| 46 | 1.1217 1245 | 1.1654 1628 | 1.2107 8446 | 1.2341 1195 | 46 |
| 47 | 1.1245 1673 | 1.1693 0100 | 1.2158 2940 | 1.2397 6830 | 47 |
| 48 | 1.1273 2802 | 1.1731 9867 | 1.2208 9536 | 1.2454 5057 | 48 |
| 49 | 1.1301 4634 | 1.1771 0933 | 1.2259 8242 | 1.2511 5889 | 49 |
| 50 | 1.1329 7171 | 1.1810 3303 | 1.2310 9068 | 1.2568 9336 | 50 |
| 51 | 1.1358 0414 | 1.1849 6981 | 1.2362 2022 | 1.2626 5413 | 51 |
| 52 | 1.1386 4365 | 1.1889 1971 | 1.2413 7114 | 1.2684 4129 | 52 |
| 53 | 1.1414 9026 | 1.1928 8277 | 1.2465 4352 | 1.2742 5498 | 53 |
| 54 | 1.1443 4398 | 1.1968 5905 | 1.2517 3745 | 1.2800 9531 | 54 |
| 55 | 1.1472 0484 | 1.2008 4858 | 1.2569 5302 | 1.2859 6242 | 55 |
| 56 | 1.1500 7285 | 1.2048 5141 | 1.2621 9033 | 1.2918 5641 | 56 |
| 57 | 1.1529 4804 | 1.2088 6758 | 1.2674 4946 | 1.2977 7742 | 57 |
| 58 | 1.1558 3041 | 1.2128 9714 | 1.2727 3050 | 1.3037 2557 | 58 |
| 59 | 1.1587 1998 | 1.2169 4013 | 1.2780 3354 | 1.3097 0098 | 59 |
| 60 | 1.1616 1678 | 1.2209 9659 | 1.2833 5868 | 1.3157 0377 | 60 |

Table
5

# TABLE 5

$$s = (1 + i)^n$$

| n | $\frac{1}{4}\%$ | $\frac{1}{3}\%$ | $\frac{5}{12}\%$ | $\frac{11}{24}\%$ | n |
|---|---|---|---|---|---|
| 61 | 1.1645 2082 | 1.2250 6658 | 1.2887 0601 | 1.3217 3408 | 61 |
| 62 | 1.1674 3213 | 1.2291 5014 | 1.2940 7561 | 1.3277 9203 | 62 |
| 63 | 1.1703 5071 | 1.2332 4730 | 1.2994 6760 | 1.3338 7774 | 63 |
| 64 | 1.1732 7658 | 1.2373 5813 | 1.3048 8204 | 1.3399 9135 | 64 |
| 65 | 1.1762 0977 | 1.2414 8266 | 1.3101 1905 | 1.3461 3298 | 65 |
| 66 | 1.1791 5030 | 1.2456 2093 | 1.3157 7872 | 1.3523 0275 | 66 |
| 67 | 1.1820 9817 | 1.2497 7300 | 1.3212 6113 | 1.3585 0081 | 67 |
| 68 | 1.1850 5342 | 1.2539 3891 | 1.3267 6638 | 1.3647 2727 | 68 |
| 69 | 1.1880 1605 | 1.2581 1871 | 1.3322 9458 | 1.3709 8227 | 69 |
| 70 | 1.1909 8609 | 1.2623 1244 | 1.3378 4580 | 1.3772 6594 | 70 |
| 71 | 1.1939 6356 | 1.2665 2015 | 1.3434 2016 | 1.3835 7841 | 71 |
| 72 | 1.1969 4847 | 1.2707 4188 | 1.3490 1774 | 1.3899 1981 | 72 |
| 73 | 1.1999 4084 | 1.2749 7769 | 1.3546 3865 | 1.3962 9027 | 73 |
| 74 | 1.2029 4069 | 1.2792 2761 | 1.3602 8298 | 1.4026 8994 | 74 |
| 75 | 1.2059 4804 | 1.2834 9170 | 1.3659 5082 | 1.4091 1893 | 75 |
| 76 | 1.2089 6291 | 1.2877 7001 | 1.3716 4229 | 1.4155 7739 | 76 |
| 77 | 1.2119 8532 | 1.2920 6258 | 1.3773 5746 | 1.4220 6546 | 77 |
| 78 | 1.2150 1528 | 1.2963 6945 | 1.3830 9645 | 1.4285 8326 | 78 |
| 79 | 1.2180 5282 | 1.3006 9068 | 1.3888 5935 | 1.4351 3093 | 79 |
| 80 | 1.2210 9795 | 1.3050 2632 | 1.3946 4627 | 1.4417 0861 | 80 |
| 81 | 1.2241 5070 | 1.3093 7641 | 1.4004 5729 | 1.4483 1645 | 81 |
| 82 | 1.2272 1108 | 1.3137 4099 | 1.4062 9253 | 1.4549 5456 | 82 |
| 83 | 1.2302 7910 | 1.3181 2013 | 1.4121 5209 | 1.4616 2310 | 83 |
| 84 | 1.2333 5480 | 1.3225 1386 | 1.4180 3605 | 1.4683 2221 | 84 |
| 85 | 1.2364 3819 | 1.3269 2224 | 1.4239 4454 | 1.4750 5202 | 85 |
| 86 | 1.2395 2928 | 1.3313 4532 | 1.4298 7764 | 1.4818 1267 | 86 |
| 87 | 1.2426 2811 | 1.3357 8314 | 1.4358 3546 | 1.4886 0432 | 87 |
| 88 | 1.2457 3468 | 1.3402 3575 | 1.4418 1811 | 1.4954 2709 | 88 |
| 89 | 1.2488 4901 | 1.3447 0320 | 1.4478 2568 | 1.5022 8113 | 89 |
| 90 | 1.2519 7114 | 1.3491 8554 | 1.4538 5829 | 1.5091 6658 | 90 |
| 91 | 1.2551 0106 | 1.3536 8283 | 1.4599 1603 | 1.5160 8360 | 91 |
| 92 | 1.2582 3882 | 1.3581 9510 | 1.4659 9902 | 1.5230 3231 | 92 |
| 93 | 1.2613 8441 | 1.3627 2242 | 1.4721 0735 | 1.5300 1288 | 93 |
| 94 | 1.2645 3787 | 1.3672 6483 | 1.4782 4113 | 1.5370 2544 | 94 |
| 95 | 1.2676 9922 | 1.3718 2238 | 1.4844 0047 | 1.5440 7014 | 95 |
| 96 | 1.2708 6847 | 1.3763 9512 | 1.4905 8547 | 1.5514 4712 | 96 |
| 97 | 1.2740 4564 | 1.3809 8310 | 1.4967 9624 | 1.5582 5655 | 97 |
| 98 | 1.2772 3075 | 1.3855 8638 | 1.5030 3289 | 1.5653 9856 | 98 |
| 99 | 1.2804 2383 | 1.3902 0500 | 1.5092 9553 | 1.5725 7330 | 99 |
| 100 | 1.2836 2489 | 1.3948 3902 | 1.5155 8426 | 1.5797 8093 | 100 |
| 101 | 1.2868 3395 | 1.3994 8848 | 1.5218 9919 | 1.5870 2159 | 101 |
| 102 | 1.2900 5104 | 1.4041 5344 | 1.5282 4044 | 1.5942 9544 | 102 |
| 103 | 1.2932 7616 | 1.4088 3395 | 1.5346 0811 | 1.6016 0263 | 103 |
| 104 | 1.2965 0935 | 1.4135 3007 | 1.5410 0231 | 1.6089 4331 | 104 |
| 105 | 1.2997 5063 | 1.4182 4183 | 1.5474 2315 | 1.6163 1763 | 105 |
| 106 | 1.3030 0000 | 1.4229 6931 | 1.5538 7075 | 1.6237 2575 | 106 |
| 107 | 1.3062 5750 | 1.4277 1254 | 1.5603 4521 | 1.6311 6783 | 107 |
| 108 | 1.3095 2315 | 1.4324 7158 | 1.5668 4665 | 1.6386 4401 | 108 |
| 109 | 1.3127 9696 | 1.4372 4649 | 1.5733 7518 | 1.6461 5447 | 109 |
| 110 | 1.3160 7895 | 1.4420 3731 | 1.5799 3091 | 1.6536 9934 | 110 |
| 111 | 1.3193 6915 | 1.4468 4410 | 1.5865 1395 | 1.6612 7880 | 111 |
| 112 | 1.3226 6757 | 1.4516 6691 | 1.5931 2443 | 1.6688 9299 | 112 |
| 113 | 1.3259 7424 | 1.4565 0580 | 1.5997 6245 | 1.6765 4208 | 113 |
| 114 | 1.3292 8917 | 1.4613 6082 | 1.6064 2812 | 1.6842 2623 | 114 |
| 115 | 1.3326 1240 | 1.4662 3202 | 1.6131 2157 | 1.6919 4560 | 115 |
| 116 | 1.3359 4393 | 1.4711 1946 | 1.6198 4291 | 1.6997 0036 | 116 |
| 117 | 1.3392 8379 | 1.4760 2320 | 1.6265 9226 | 1.7074 9065 | 117 |
| 118 | 1.3426 3200 | 1.4809 4327 | 1.6333 6973 | 1.7153 1665 | 118 |
| 119 | 1.3459 8858 | 1.4858 7975 | 1.6401 7543 | 1.7231 7852 | 119 |
| 120 | 1.3493 5355 | 1.4908 3268 | 1.6470 0950 | 1.7310 7642 | 120 |

**TABLE  5**

$$s = (1 + i)^n$$

| n | $\frac{1}{4}\%$ | $\frac{1}{3}\%$ | $\frac{5}{12}\%$ | $\frac{11}{24}\%$ | n |
|---|---|---|---|---|---|
| 121 | 1.3527 2693 | 1.4958 0212 | 1.6538 7204 | 1.7390 1052 | 121 |
| 122 | 1.3561 0875 | 1.5007 8813 | 1.6607 6317 | 1.7469 8098 | 122 |
| 123 | 1.3594 9902 | 1.5057 9076 | 1.6676 8302 | 1.7549 8798 | 123 |
| 124 | 1.3628 9777 | 1.5108 1006 | 1.6746 3170 | 1.7630 3167 | 124 |
| 125 | 1.3663 0501 | 1.5158 4609 | 1.6816 0933 | 1.7711 1224 | 125 |
| 126 | 1.3697 2077 | 1.5208 9892 | 1.6886 1603 | 1.7792 2983 | 126 |
| 127 | 1.3731 4508 | 1.5259 6858 | 1.6956 5193 | 1.7873 8464 | 127 |
| 128 | 1.3765 7794 | 1.5310 5514 | 1.7027 1715 | 1.7955 7682 | 128 |
| 129 | 1.3800 1938 | 1.5361 5866 | 1.7098 1181 | 1.8038 0654 | 129 |
| 130 | 1.3834 6943 | 1.5412 7919 | 1.7169 3602 | 1.8120 7399 | 130 |
| 131 | 1.3869 2811 | 1.5464 1678 | 1.7240 8992 | 1.8203 7933 | 131 |
| 132 | 1.3903 9543 | 1.5515 7151 | 1.7312 7363 | 1.8287 2273 | 132 |
| 133 | 1.3938 7142 | 1.5567 4341 | 1.7384 8727 | 1.8371 0438 | 133 |
| 134 | 1.3973 5609 | 1.5619 3256 | 1.7457 3097 | 1.8455 2444 | 134 |
| 135 | 1.4008 4948 | 1.5671 3900 | 1.7530 0485 | 1.8539 8310 | 135 |
| 136 | 1.4043 5161 | 1.5723 6279 | 1.7603 0903 | 1.8624 8052 | 136 |
| 137 | 1.4078 6249 | 1.5776 0400 | 1.7676 4365 | 1.8710 1689 | 137 |
| 138 | 1.4113 8214 | 1.5828 6268 | 1.7750 0884 | 1.8795 9238 | 138 |
| 139 | 1.4149 1060 | 1.5881 3889 | 1.7824 0471 | 1.8882 0718 | 139 |
| 140 | 1.4184 4787 | 1.5934 3269 | 1.7898 3139 | 1.8968 6146 | 140 |
| 141 | 1.4219 9399 | 1.5987 4413 | 1.7972 8902 | 1.9055 5541 | 141 |
| 142 | 1.4255 4898 | 1.6040 7328 | 1.8047 7773 | 1.9142 8921 | 142 |
| 143 | 1.4291 1285 | 1.6094 2019 | 1.8122 9763 | 1.9230 6303 | 143 |
| 144 | 1.4326 8563 | 1.6147 8492 | 1.8198 4887 | 1.9318 7707 | 144 |
| 145 | 1.4362 6735 | 1.6201 6754 | 1.8274 3158 | 1.9407 3151 | 145 |
| 146 | 1.4398 5802 | 1.6255 6810 | 1.8350 4588 | 1.9496 2653 | 146 |
| 147 | 1.4434 5766 | 1.6309 8666 | 1.8426 9190 | 1.9585 6231 | 147 |
| 148 | 1.4470 6631 | 1.6364 2328 | 1.8503 6978 | 1.9675 3906 | 148 |
| 149 | 1.4506 8397 | 1.6418 7802 | 1.8580 7966 | 1.9765 5695 | 149 |
| 150 | 1.4543 1068 | 1.6473 5095 | 1.8658 2166 | 1.9856 1617 | 150 |
| 151 | 1.4579 4646 | 1.6528 4212 | 1.8735 9591 | 1.9947 1691 | 151 |
| 152 | 1.4615 9132 | 1.6583 5160 | 1.8814 0256 | 2.0038 5936 | 152 |
| 153 | 1.4652 4530 | 1.6638 7943 | 1.8892 4174 | 2.0130 4371 | 153 |
| 154 | 1.4689 0842 | 1.6694 2570 | 1.8971 1358 | 2.0222 7016 | 154 |
| 155 | 1.4725 8069 | 1.6749 9045 | 1.9050 1822 | 2.0315 3890 | 155 |
| 156 | 1.4762 6214 | 1.6805 7375 | 1.9129 5580 | 2.0408 5012 | 156 |
| 157 | 1.4799 5279 | 1.6861 7566 | 1.9209 2645 | 2.0502 0402 | 157 |
| 158 | 1.4836 5268 | 1.6917 9625 | 1.9289 3031 | 2.0596 0079 | 158 |
| 159 | 1.4873 6181 | 1.6974 3557 | 1.9369 6752 | 2.0690 4062 | 159 |
| 160 | 1.4910 8021 | 1.7030 9369 | 1.9450 3821 | 2.0785 2373 | 160 |
| 161 | 1.4948 0791 | 1.7087 7067 | 1.9531 4254 | 2.0880 5029 | 161 |
| 162 | 1.4985 4493 | 1.7144 6657 | 1.9612 8063 | 2.0976 2053 | 162 |
| 163 | 1.5022 9129 | 1.7201 8146 | 1.9694 5264 | 2.1072 3462 | 163 |
| 164 | 1.5060 4702 | 1.7259 1540 | 1.9776 5869 | 2.1168 9278 | 164 |
| 165 | 1.5098 1214 | 1.7316 6845 | 1.9858 9893 | 2.1265 9520 | 165 |
| 166 | 1.5135 8667 | 1.7374 4068 | 1.9941 7351 | 2.1363 4210 | 166 |
| 167 | 1.5173 7064 | 1.7432 3215 | 2.0024 8257 | 2.1461 3367 | 167 |
| 168 | 1.5211 6406 | 1.7490 4292 | 2.0108 2625 | 2.1559 7011 | 168 |
| 169 | 1.5249 6697 | 1.7548 7306 | 2.0192 0469 | 2.1658 5164 | 169 |
| 170 | 1.5287 7939 | 1.7607 2264 | 2.0276 1804 | 2.1757 7846 | 170 |
| 171 | 1.5326 0134 | 1.7665 9172 | 2.0360 6645 | 2.1857 5078 | 171 |
| 172 | 1.5364 3284 | 1.7724 8035 | 2.0445 5006 | 2.1957 6880 | 172 |
| 173 | 1.5402 7393 | 1.7783 8862 | 2.0530 6902 | 2.2058 3274 | 173 |
| 174 | 1.5441 2461 | 1.7843 1658 | 2.0616 2347 | 2.2159 4281 | 174 |
| 175 | 1.5479 8492 | 1.7902 6431 | 2.0702 1357 | 2.2260 9922 | 175 |
| 176 | 1.5518 5488 | 1.7962 3185 | 2.0788 3946 | 2.2363 0217 | 176 |
| 177 | 1.5557 3452 | 1.8022 1929 | 2.0875 0129 | 2.2465 5189 | 177 |
| 178 | 1.5596 2386 | 1.8082 2669 | 2.0961 9921 | 2.2568 4858 | 178 |
| 179 | 1.5635 2292 | 1.8142 5411 | 2.1049 3338 | 2.2671 9247 | 179 |
| 180 | 1.5674 3172 | 1.8203 0163 | 2.1137 0393 | 2.2775 8377 | 180 |

Table
5

**TABLE 5**

$$s = (1 + i)^n$$

| n | $\frac{1}{4}\%$ | $\frac{1}{3}\%$ | $\frac{5}{12}\%$ | $\frac{11}{24}\%$ | n |
|---|---|---|---|---|---|
| 181 | 1.5713 5030 | 1.8263 6930 | 2.1225 1103 | 2.2880 2270 | 181 |
| 182 | 1.5752 7868 | 1.8324 5720 | 2.1313 5483 | 2.2985 0947 | 182 |
| 183 | 1.5792 1688 | 1.8385 6539 | 2.1402 3547 | 2.3090 4430 | 183 |
| 184 | 1.5831 6492 | 1.8446 9394 | 2.1491 5312 | 2.3196 2742 | 184 |
| 185 | 1.5871 2283 | 1.8508 4292 | 2.1581 0793 | 2.3302 5905 | 185 |
| 186 | 1.5910 9064 | 1.8570 1240 | 2.1671 0004 | 2.3409 3940 | 186 |
| 187 | 1.5950 6836 | 1.8632 0244 | 2.1761 2963 | 2.3516 6871 | 187 |
| 188 | 1.5990 5604 | 1.8694 1311 | 2.1851 9683 | 2.3624 4719 | 188 |
| 189 | 1.6030 5368 | 1.8756 4449 | 2.1943 0182 | 2.3732 7507 | 189 |
| 190 | 1.6070 6131 | 1.8818 9664 | 2.2034 4474 | 2.3841 5258 | 190 |
| 191 | 1.6110 7896 | 1.8881 6963 | 2.2126 2576 | 2.3950 7995 | 191 |
| 192 | 1.6151 0666 | 1.8944 6352 | 2.2218 4504 | 2.4060 5740 | 192 |
| 193 | 1.6191 4443 | 1.9007 7840 | 2.2311 0272 | 2.4170 8516 | 193 |
| 194 | 1.6231 9229 | 1.9071 1433 | 2.2403 9899 | 2.4281 6347 | 194 |
| 195 | 1.6272 5027 | 1.9134 7138 | 2.2497 3398 | 2.4392 9255 | 195 |
| 196 | 1.6313 1839 | 1.9198 4962 | 2.2591 0787 | 2.4504 7264 | 196 |
| 197 | 1.6353 9669 | 1.9262 4912 | 2.2685 2082 | 2.4617 0398 | 197 |
| 198 | 1.6394 8518 | 1.9326 6995 | 2.2779 7299 | 2.4729 8679 | 198 |
| 199 | 1.6435 8390 | 1.9391 1218 | 2.2874 6455 | 2.4843 2131 | 199 |
| 200 | 1.6476 9285 | 1.9455 7589 | 2.2969 9565 | 2.4957 0778 | 200 |
| 201 | 1.6518 1209 | 1.9520 6114 | 2.3065 6646 | 2.5071 4644 | 201 |
| 202 | 1.6559 4162 | 1.9585 6801 | 2.3161 7716 | 2.5186 3753 | 202 |
| 203 | 1.6600 8147 | 1.9650 9657 | 2.3258 2790 | 2.5301 8129 | 203 |
| 204 | 1.6642 3168 | 1.9716 4689 | 2.3355 1885 | 2.5417 7795 | 204 |
| 205 | 1.6683 9225 | 1.9782 1905 | 2.3452 5017 | 2.5534 2777 | 205 |
| 206 | 1.6725 6323 | 1.9848 1311 | 2.3550 2205 | 2.5651 3098 | 206 |
| 207 | 1.6767 4464 | 1.9914 2915 | 2.3648 3464 | 2.5768 8783 | 207 |
| 208 | 1.6809 3650 | 1.9980 6725 | 2.3746 8812 | 2.5886 9856 | 208 |
| 209 | 1.6851 3885 | 2.0047 2748 | 2.3845 8265 | 2.6005 6343 | 209 |
| 210 | 1.6893 5169 | 2.0114 0990 | 2.3945 1841 | 2.6124 8268 | 210 |
| 211 | 1.6935 7507 | 2.0181 1460 | 2.4044 9557 | 2.6244 5656 | 211 |
| 212 | 1.6978 0901 | 2.0248 4165 | 2.4145 1431 | 2.6364 8532 | 212 |
| 213 | 1.7020 5353 | 2.0315 9112 | 2.4245 7478 | 2.6485 6921 | 213 |
| 214 | 1.7063 0867 | 2.0383 6309 | 2.4346 7718 | 2.6607 0848 | 214 |
| 215 | 1.7105 7444 | 2.0451 5764 | 2.4448 2167 | 2.6729 0340 | 215 |
| 216 | 1.7148 5087 | 2.0519 7483 | 2.4550 0842 | 2.6851 5421 | 216 |
| 217 | 1.7191 3800 | 2.0588 1474 | 2.4652 3762 | 2.6974 6116 | 217 |
| 218 | 1.7234 3585 | 2.0656 7746 | 2.4755 0945 | 2.7098 2453 | 218 |
| 219 | 1.7277 4444 | 2.0725 6305 | 2.4858 2407 | 2.7222 4456 | 219 |
| 220 | 1.7320 6380 | 2.0794 7159 | 2.4961 8167 | 2.7347 2151 | 220 |
| 221 | 1.7363 9396 | 2.0864 0317 | 2.5065 8243 | 2.7472 5565 | 221 |
| 222 | 1.7407 3494 | 2.0933 5784 | 2.5170 2652 | 2.7598 4724 | 222 |
| 223 | 1.7450 8678 | 2.1003 3570 | 2.5275 1413 | 2.7724 9654 | 223 |
| 224 | 1.7494 4950 | 2.1073 3682 | 2.5380 4544 | 2.7852 0381 | 224 |
| 225 | 1.7538 2312 | 2.1143 6128 | 2.5486 2063 | 2.7979 6933 | 225 |
| 226 | 1.7582 0768 | 2.1214 0915 | 2.5592 3988 | 2.8107 9336 | 226 |
| 227 | 1.7626 0320 | 2.1284 8051 | 2.5699 0338 | 2.8236 7616 | 227 |
| 228 | 1.7670 0970 | 2.1355 7545 | 2.5806 1131 | 2.8366 1801 | 228 |
| 229 | 1.7714 2723 | 2.1426 9403 | 2.5913 6386 | 2.8496 1918 | 229 |
| 230 | 1.7758 5580 | 2.1498 3635 | 2.6021 6121 | 2.8626 7993 | 230 |
| 231 | 1.7802 9544 | 2.1570 0247 | 2.6130 0355 | 2.8758 0055 | 231 |
| 232 | 1.7847 4617 | 2.1641 9248 | 2.6238 9106 | 2.8889 8130 | 232 |
| 233 | 1.7892 0804 | 2.1714 0645 | 2.6348 2394 | 2.9022 2246 | 233 |
| 234 | 1.7936 8106 | 2.1786 4447 | 2.6458 0238 | 2.9155 2432 | 234 |
| 235 | 1.7981 6526 | 2.1859 0662 | 2.6568 2655 | 2.9288 8714 | 235 |
| 236 | 1.8026 6068 | 2.1931 9298 | 2.6678 9666 | 2.9423 1120 | 236 |
| 237 | 1.8071 6733 | 2.2005 0362 | 2.6790 1290 | 2.9557 9679 | 237 |
| 238 | 1.8116 8525 | 2.2078 3863 | 2.6901 7545 | 2.9693 4420 | 238 |
| 239 | 1.8162 1446 | 2.2151 9809 | 2.7013 8452 | 2.9829 5369 | 239 |
| 240 | 1.8207 5500 | 2.2225 8209 | 2.7126 4029 | 2.9966 2556 | 240 |

**TABLE  5**

$$s=(1+i)^n$$

| n | $\frac{1}{2}\%$ | $\frac{13}{24}\%$ | $\frac{7}{12}\%$ | $\frac{5}{8}\%$ | n |
|---|---|---|---|---|---|
| 1 | 1.0050 0000 | 1.0054 1667 | 1.0058 3333 | 1.0062 5000 | 1 |
| 2 | 1.0100 2500 | 1.0108 6267 | 1.0117 0069 | 1.0125 3906 | 2 |
| 3 | 1.0150 7513 | 1.0163 3818 | 1.0176 0228 | 1.0188 6743 | 3 |
| 4 | 1.0201 5050 | 1.0218 4334 | 1.0235 3830 | 1.0252 3535 | 4 |
| 5 | 1.0252 5125 | 1.0273 7833 | 1.0295 0894 | 1.0316 4307 | 5 |
| 6 | 1.0303 7751 | 1.0329 4330 | 1.0355 1440 | 1.0380 9084 | 6 |
| 7 | 1.0355 2940 | 1.0385 3841 | 1.0415 5490 | 1.0445 7891 | 7 |
| 8 | 1.0407 0704 | 1.0441 6382 | 1.0476 3064 | 1.0511 0753 | 8 |
| 9 | 1.0459 1058 | 1.0498 1971 | 1.0537 4182 | 1.0576 7695 | 9 |
| 10 | 1.0511 4013 | 1.0555 0623 | 1.0598 8865 | 1.0642 8743 | 10 |
| 11 | 1.0563 9583 | 1.0612 2356 | 1.0660 7133 | 1.0709 3923 | 11 |
| 12 | 1.0616 7781 | 1.0669 7185 | 1.0722 9008 | 1.0776 3260 | 12 |
| 13 | 1.0669 8620 | 1.0727 5128 | 1.0785 4511 | 1.0843 6780 | 13 |
| 14 | 1.0723 2113 | 1.0785 6202 | 1.0848 3662 | 1.0911 4510 | 14 |
| 15 | 1.0776 8274 | 1.0844 0423 | 1.0911 6483 | 1.0979 6476 | 15 |
| 16 | 1.0830 7115 | 1.0902 7809 | 1.0975 2996 | 1.1048 2704 | 16 |
| 17 | 1.0884 8651 | 1.0961 8376 | 1.1039 3222 | 1.1117 3221 | 17 |
| 18 | 1.0939 2894 | 1.1021 2142 | 1.1103 7182 | 1.1186 8053 | 18 |
| 19 | 1.0993 9858 | 1.1080 9125 | 1.1168 4899 | 1.1256 7229 | 19 |
| 20 | 1.1048 9558 | 1.1140 9341 | 1.1233 6395 | 1.1327 0774 | 20 |
| 21 | 1.1104 2006 | 1.1201 2808 | 1.1299 1690 | 1.1397 8716 | 21 |
| 22 | 1.1159 7216 | 1.1261 9544 | 1.1365 0808 | 1.1469 1083 | 22 |
| 23 | 1.1215 5202 | 1.1322 9566 | 1.1431 3771 | 1.1540 7902 | 23 |
| 24 | 1.1271 5978 | 1.1384 2893 | 1.1498 0602 | 1.1612 9202 | 24 |
| 25 | 1.1327 9558 | 1.1445 9542 | 1.1565 1322 | 1.1685 5009 | 25 |
| 26 | 1.1384 5955 | 1.1507 9531 | 1.1632 5955 | 1.1758 5353 | 26 |
| 27 | 1.1441 5185 | 1.1570 2879 | 1.1700 4523 | 1.1832 0262 | 27 |
| 28 | 1.1498 7261 | 1.1632 9603 | 1.1768 7049 | 1.1905 9763 | 28 |
| 29 | 1.1556 2197 | 1.1695 9722 | 1.1837 3557 | 1.1980 3887 | 29 |
| 30 | 1.1614 0008 | 1.1759 3253 | 1.1906 4069 | 1.2055 2661 | 30 |
| 31 | 1.1672 0708 | 1.1823 0217 | 1.1975 8610 | 1.2130 6115 | 31 |
| 32 | 1.1730 4312 | 1.1887 0631 | 1.2045 7202 | 1.2206 4278 | 32 |
| 33 | 1.1789 0833 | 1.1951 4513 | 1.2115 9869 | 1.2282 7180 | 33 |
| 34 | 1.1848 0288 | 1.2016 1883 | 1.2186 6634 | 1.2359 4850 | 34 |
| 35 | 1.1907 2689 | 1.2081 2760 | 1.2257 7523 | 1.2436 7318 | 35 |
| 36 | 1.1966 8052 | 1.2146 7163 | 1.2329 2559 | 1.2514 4614 | 36 |
| 37 | 1.2026 6393 | 1.2212 5110 | 1.2401 1765 | 1.2592 6767 | 37 |
| 38 | 1.2086 7725 | 1.2278 6621 | 1.2473 5167 | 1.2671 3810 | 38 |
| 39 | 1.2147 2063 | 1.2345 1715 | 1.2546 2789 | 1.2750 5771 | 39 |
| 40 | 1.2207 9424 | 1.2412 0412 | 1.2619 4655 | 1.2830 2682 | 40 |
| 41 | 1.2268 9821 | 1.2479 2731 | 1.2693 0791 | 1.2910 4574 | 41 |
| 42 | 1.2330 3270 | 1.2546 8691 | 1.2767 1220 | 1.2991 1477 | 42 |
| 43 | 1.2391 9786 | 1.2614 8313 | 1.2841 5969 | 1.3072 3424 | 43 |
| 44 | 1.2453 9385 | 1.2683 1617 | 1.2916 5062 | 1.3154 0446 | 44 |
| 45 | 1.2516 2082 | 1.2751 8621 | 1.2991 8525 | 1.3236 2573 | 45 |
| 46 | 1.2578 7892 | 1.2820 9347 | 1.3067 6383 | 1.3318 9839 | 46 |
| 47 | 1.2641 6832 | 1.2890 3815 | 1.3143 8662 | 1.3402 2276 | 47 |
| 48 | 1.2704 8916 | 1.2960 2044 | 1.3220 5388 | 1.3485 9915 | 48 |
| 49 | 1.2768 4161 | 1.3030 4055 | 1.3297 6586 | 1.3570 2790 | 49 |
| 50 | 1.2832 2581 | 1.3100 9868 | 1.3375 2283 | 1.3655 0932 | 50 |
| 51 | 1.2896 4194 | 1.3171 9505 | 1.3453 2504 | 1.3740 4375 | 51 |
| 52 | 1.2960 9015 | 1.3243 2986 | 1.3531 7277 | 1.3826 3153 | 52 |
| 53 | 1.3025 7060 | 1.3315 0331 | 1.3610 6628 | 1.3912 7297 | 53 |
| 54 | 1.3090 8346 | 1.3387 1562 | 1.3690 0583 | 1.3999 6843 | 54 |
| 55 | 1.3156 2887 | 1.3459 6700 | 1.3769 9170 | 1.4087 1823 | 55 |
| 56 | 1.3222 0702 | 1.3532 5765 | 1.3850 2415 | 1.4175 2272 | 56 |
| 57 | 1.3288 1805 | 1.3605 8780 | 1.3931 0346 | 1.4263 8224 | 57 |
| 58 | 1.3354 6214 | 1.3679 5765 | 1.4012 2990 | 1.4352 9713 | 58 |
| 59 | 1.3421 3946 | 1.3753 6742 | 1.4094 0374 | 1.4442 6773 | 59 |
| 60 | 1.3488 5015 | 1.3828 1732 | 1.4176 2526 | 1.4532 9441 | 60 |

## TABLE 5

$$s = (1 + i)^n$$

| n | $\frac{1}{2}$ % | $\frac{13}{24}$ % | $\frac{7}{12}$ % | $\frac{5}{8}$ % | n |
|---|---|---|---|---|---|
| 61 | 1.3555 9440 | 1.3903 0758 | 1.4258 9474 | 1.4623 7750 | 61 |
| 62 | 1.3623 7238 | 1.3978 3842 | 1.4342 1246 | 1.4715 1736 | 62 |
| 63 | 1.3691 8424 | 1.4054 1004 | 1.4425 7870 | 1.4807 1434 | 63 |
| 64 | 1.3760 3016 | 1.4130 2268 | 1.4509 9374 | 1.4899 6881 | 64 |
| 65 | 1.3829 1031 | 1.4206 7655 | 1.4594 5787 | 1.4992 8111 | 65 |
| 66 | 1.3898 2486 | 1.4283 7188 | 1.4679 7138 | 1.5086 5162 | 66 |
| 67 | 1.3967 7399 | 1.4361 0890 | 1.4765 3454 | 1.5180 8069 | 67 |
| 68 | 1.4037 5785 | 1.4438 8782 | 1.4851 4766 | 1.5275 6869 | 68 |
| 69 | 1.4107 7664 | 1.4517 0888 | 1.4938 1102 | 1.5371 1600 | 69 |
| 70 | 1.4178 3053 | 1.4595 7230 | 1.5025 2492 | 1.5467 2297 | 70 |
| 71 | 1.4249 1968 | 1.4674 7832 | 1.5112 8965 | 1.5563 8999 | 71 |
| 72 | 1.4320 4428 | 1.4754 2716 | 1.5201 0550 | 1.5661 1743 | 72 |
| 73 | 1.4392 0450 | 1.4834 1906 | 1.5289 7279 | 1.5759 0566 | 73 |
| 74 | 1.4464 0052 | 1.4914 5425 | 1.5378 9179 | 1.5857 5507 | 74 |
| 75 | 1.4536 3252 | 1.4995 3296 | 1.5468 6283 | 1.5956 6604 | 75 |
| 76 | 1.4609 0069 | 1.5076 5543 | 1.5558 8620 | 1.6056 3896 | 76 |
| 77 | 1.4682 0519 | 1.5158 2189 | 1.5649 6220 | 1.6156 7420 | 77 |
| 78 | 1.4755 4622 | 1.5240 3259 | 1.5740 9115 | 1.6257 7216 | 78 |
| 79 | 1.4829 2395 | 1.5322 8777 | 1.5832 7334 | 1.6359 3324 | 79 |
| 80 | 1.4903 3857 | 1.5405 8766 | 1.5925 0910 | 1.6461 5782 | 80 |
| 81 | 1.4977 9026 | 1.5489 3251 | 1.6017 9874 | 1.6564 4631 | 81 |
| 82 | 1.5052 7921 | 1.5573 2256 | 1.6111 4257 | 1.6667 9910 | 82 |
| 83 | 1.5128 0561 | 1.5657 5806 | 1.6205 4090 | 1.6772 1659 | 83 |
| 84 | 1.5203 6964 | 1.5742 3925 | 1.6299 9405 | 1.6876 9920 | 84 |
| 85 | 1.5279 7148 | 1.5827 6638 | 1.6395 0235 | 1.6982 4732 | 85 |
| 86 | 1.5356 1134 | 1.5913 3970 | 1.6490 6612 | 1.7088 6136 | 86 |
| 87 | 1.5432 8940 | 1.5999 5945 | 1.6586 8567 | 1.7195 4175 | 87 |
| 88 | 1.5510 0585 | 1.6086 2590 | 1.6683 6134 | 1.7302 8888 | 88 |
| 89 | 1.5587 6087 | 1.6173 3929 | 1.6780 9344 | 1.7411 0319 | 89 |
| 90 | 1.5665 5468 | 1.6260 9988 | 1.6878 8232 | 1.7519 8508 | 90 |
| 91 | 1.5743 8745 | 1.6349 0792 | 1.6977 2830 | 1.7629 3499 | 91 |
| 92 | 1.5822 5939 | 1.6437 6367 | 1.7076 3172 | 1.7739 5333 | 92 |
| 93 | 1.5901 7069 | 1.6526 6739 | 1.7175 9290 | 1.7850 4054 | 93 |
| 94 | 1.5981 2154 | 1.6616 1934 | 1.7276 1219 | 1.7961 9704 | 94 |
| 95 | 1.6061 1215 | 1.6706 1978 | 1.7376 8993 | 1.8074 2328 | 95 |
| 96 | 1.6141 4271 | 1.6796 6897 | 1.7478 2646 | 1.8187 1967 | 96 |
| 97 | 1.6222 1342 | 1.6887 6718 | 1.7580 2211 | 1.8300 8667 | 97 |
| 98 | 1.6303 2449 | 1.6979 1466 | 1.7682 7724 | 1.8415 2471 | 98 |
| 99 | 1.6384 7611 | 1.7071 1170 | 1.7785 9219 | 1.8530 3424 | 99 |
| 100 | 1.6466 6849 | 1.7163 5856 | 1.7889 6731 | 1.8646 1570 | 100 |
| 101 | 1.6549 0183 | 1.7256 5550 | 1.7994 0295 | 1.8762 6955 | 101 |
| 102 | 1.6631 7634 | 1.7350 0280 | 1.8098 9947 | 1.8879 9624 | 102 |
| 103 | 1.6714 9223 | 1.7444 0073 | 1.8204 5722 | 1.8997 9621 | 103 |
| 104 | 1.6798 4969 | 1.7538 4957 | 1.8310 7655 | 1.9116 6994 | 104 |
| 105 | 1.6882 4894 | 1.7633 4959 | 1.8417 5783 | 1.9236 1788 | 105 |
| 106 | 1.6966 9018 | 1.7729 0107 | 1.8525 0142 | 1.9356 4049 | 106 |
| 107 | 1.7051 7363 | 1.7825 0428 | 1.8633 0768 | 1.9477 3824 | 107 |
| 108 | 1.7136 9950 | 1.7921 5951 | 1.8741 7697 | 1.9599 1161 | 108 |
| 109 | 1.7222 6800 | 1.8018 6704 | 1.8851 0967 | 1.9721 6105 | 109 |
| 110 | 1.7308 7934 | 1.8116 2715 | 1.8961 0614 | 1.9844 8706 | 110 |
| 111 | 1.7395 3373 | 1.8214 4013 | 1.9071 6676 | 1.9968 9010 | 111 |
| 112 | 1.7482 3140 | 1.8313 0627 | 1.9182 9190 | 2.0093 7067 | 112 |
| 113 | 1.7569 7256 | 1.8412 2584 | 1.9294 8194 | 2.0219 2923 | 113 |
| 114 | 1.7657 5742 | 1.8511 9915 | 1.9407 3725 | 2.0345 6629 | 114 |
| 115 | 1.7745 8621 | 1.8612 2648 | 1.9520 5822 | 2.0472 8233 | 115 |
| 116 | 1.7834 5914 | 1.8713 0812 | 1.9634 4522 | 2.0600 7785 | 116 |
| 117 | 1.7923 7644 | 1.8814 4438 | 1.9748 9865 | 2.0729 5333 | 117 |
| 118 | 1.8013 3832 | 1.8916 3553 | 1.9864 1890 | 2.0859 0929 | 118 |
| 119 | 1.8103 4501 | 1.9018 8189 | 1.9980 0634 | 2.0989 4622 | 119 |
| 120 | 1.8193 9673 | 1.9121 8375 | 2.0096 6138 | 2.1120 6464 | 120 |

**TABLE 5**

$$s = (1 + i)^n$$

| n | $\frac{1}{2}$ % | $\frac{13}{24}$ % | $\frac{7}{12}$ % | $\frac{5}{8}$ % | n |
|---|---|---|---|---|---|
| 121 | 1.8284 9372 | 1.9225 4141 | 2.0213 8440 | 2.1252 6504 | 121 |
| 122 | 1.8376 3619 | 1.9329 5518 | 2.0331 7581 | 2.1385 4795 | 122 |
| 123 | 1.8468 2437 | 1.9434 2535 | 2.0450 3600 | 2.1519 1387 | 123 |
| 124 | 1.8560 5849 | 1.9539 5224 | 2.0569 6538 | 2.1653 6333 | 124 |
| 125 | 1.8653 3878 | 1.9645 3615 | 2.0689 6434 | 2.1788 9685 | 125 |
| 126 | 1.8746 6548 | 1.9751 7739 | 2.0810 3330 | 2.1925 1496 | 126 |
| 127 | 1.8840 3880 | 1.9858 7626 | 2.0931 7266 | 2.2062 1818 | 127 |
| 128 | 1.8934 5900 | 1.9966 3309 | 2.1053 8284 | 2.2200 0704 | 128 |
| 129 | 1.9029 2629 | 2.0074 4819 | 2.1176 6424 | 2.2338 8209 | 129 |
| 130 | 1.9124 4092 | 2.0183 2187 | 2.1300 1728 | 2.2478 4385 | 130 |
| 131 | 1.9220 0313 | 2.0292 5444 | 2.1424 4238 | 2.2618 9287 | 131 |
| 132 | 1.9316 1314 | 2.0402 4624 | 2.1549 3996 | 2.2760 2970 | 132 |
| 133 | 1.9412 7121 | 2.0512 9757 | 2.1675 1044 | 2.2902 5489 | 133 |
| 134 | 1.9509 7757 | 2.0624 0877 | 2.1801 5425 | 2.3045 6898 | 134 |
| 135 | 1.9607 3245 | 2.0735 8015 | 2.1928 7182 | 2.3189 7254 | 135 |
| 136 | 1.9705 3612 | 2.0848 1204 | 2.2056 6357 | 2.3334 6612 | 136 |
| 137 | 1.9803 8880 | 2.0961 0477 | 2.2185 2994 | 2.3480 5028 | 137 |
| 138 | 1.9902 9074 | 2.1074 5867 | 2.2314 7137 | 2.3627 2559 | 138 |
| 139 | 2.0002 4219 | 2.1188 7408 | 2.2444 8828 | 2.3774 9263 | 139 |
| 140 | 2.0102 4340 | 2.1303 5131 | 2.2575 8113 | 2.3923 5196 | 140 |
| 141 | 2.0202 9462 | 2.1418 9071 | 2.2707 5036 | 2.4073 0416 | 141 |
| 142 | 2.0303 9609 | 2.1534 9262 | 2.2839 9640 | 2.4223 4981 | 142 |
| 143 | 2.0405 4808 | 2.1651 5737 | 2.2973 1971 | 2.4374 8950 | 143 |
| 144 | 2.0507 5082 | 2.1768 8531 | 2.3107 2074 | 2.4527 2380 | 144 |
| 145 | 2.0610 0457 | 2.1886 7677 | 2.3241 9995 | 2.4680 5333 | 145 |
| 146 | 2.0713 0959 | 2.2005 3210 | 2.3377 5778 | 2.4834 7866 | 146 |
| 147 | 2.0816 6614 | 2.2124 5165 | 2.3513 9470 | 2.4990 0040 | 147 |
| 148 | 2.0920 7447 | 2.2244 3577 | 2.3651 1117 | 2.5146 1916 | 148 |
| 149 | 2.1025 3484 | 2.2364 8479 | 2.3789 0765 | 2.5303 3553 | 149 |
| 150 | 2.1130 4752 | 2.2485 9908 | 2.3927 8461 | 2.5461 5012 | 150 |
| 151 | 2.1236 1276 | 2.2607 7900 | 2.4067 4252 | 2.5620 6356 | 151 |
| 152 | 2.1342 3082 | 2.2730 2488 | 2.4207 8186 | 2.5780 7646 | 152 |
| 153 | 2.1449 0197 | 2.2853 3710 | 2.4349 0308 | 2.5941 8944 | 153 |
| 154 | 2.1556 2648 | 2.2977 1601 | 2.4491 0668 | 2.6104 0312 | 154 |
| 155 | 2.1664 0462 | 2.3101 6197 | 2.4633 9314 | 2.6267 1814 | 155 |
| 156 | 2.1772 3664 | 2.3226 7535 | 2.4777 6293 | 2.6431 3513 | 156 |
| 157 | 2.1881 2282 | 2.3352 5651 | 2.4922 1655 | 2.6596 5472 | 157 |
| 158 | 2.1990 6344 | 2.3479 0581 | 2.5067 5448 | 2.6762 7756 | 158 |
| 159 | 2.2100 5875 | 2.3606 2364 | 2.5213 7722 | 2.6930 0430 | 159 |
| 160 | 2.2211 0905 | 2.3734 1035 | 2.5360 8525 | 2.7098 3558 | 160 |
| 161 | 2.2322 1459 | 2.3862 6632 | 2.5508 7908 | 2.7267 7205 | 161 |
| 162 | 2.2433 7566 | 2.3991 9193 | 2.5657 5921 | 2.7438 1437 | 162 |
| 163 | 2.2545 9254 | 2.4121 8755 | 2.5807 2614 | 2.7609 6321 | 163 |
| 164 | 2.2658 6551 | 2.4252 5357 | 2.5957 8037 | 2.7782 1923 | 164 |
| 165 | 2.2771 9483 | 2.4383 9036 | 2.6109 2242 | 2.7955 8310 | 165 |
| 166 | 2.2885 8081 | 2.4515 9831 | 2.6261 5280 | 2.8130 5550 | 166 |
| 167 | 2.3000 2371 | 2.4648 7780 | 2.6414 7203 | 2.8306 3710 | 167 |
| 168 | 2.3115 2383 | 2.4782 2922 | 2.6568 8062 | 2.8483 2858 | 168 |
| 169 | 2.3230 8145 | 2.4916 5296 | 2.6723 7909 | 2.8661 3063 | 169 |
| 170 | 2.3346 9686 | 2.5051 4941 | 2.6879 6796 | 2.8840 4395 | 170 |
| 171 | 2.3463 7034 | 2.5187 1897 | 2.7036 4778 | 2.9020 6922 | 171 |
| 172 | 2.3581 0219 | 2.5323 6203 | 2.7194 1906 | 2.9202 0715 | 172 |
| 173 | 2.3698 9270 | 2.5460 7900 | 2.7352 8233 | 2.9384 5845 | 173 |
| 174 | 2.3817 4217 | 2.5598 7026 | 2.7512 3815 | 2.9568 2381 | 174 |
| 175 | 2.3936 5088 | 2.5737 3622 | 2.7672 8704 | 2.9753 0396 | 175 |
| 176 | 2.4056 1913 | 2.5876 7729 | 2.7834 2954 | 2.9938 9961 | 176 |
| 177 | 2.4176 4723 | 2.6016 9388 | 2.7996 6622 | 3.0126 1149 | 177 |
| 178 | 2.4297 3546 | 2.6157 8639 | 2.8159 9760 | 3.0314 4031 | 178 |
| 179 | 2.4418 8414 | 2.6299 5523 | 2.8324 2426 | 3.0503 8681 | 179 |
| 180 | 2.4540 9356 | 2.6442 0082 | 2.8489 4673 | 3.0694 5173 | 180 |

Table
5

# TABLE 5

$$s = (1 + i)^n$$

| n | $\frac{1}{2}$ % | $\frac{13}{24}$ % | $\frac{7}{12}$ % | $\frac{5}{8}$ % | n |
|---|---|---|---|---|---|
| 181 | 2.4663 6403 | 2.6585 2357 | 2.8655 6559 | 3.0886 3580 | 181 |
| 182 | 2.4786 9585 | 2.6729 2391 | 2.8822 8139 | 3.1079 3977 | 182 |
| 183 | 2.4910 8933 | 2.6874 0225 | 2.8990 9469 | 3.1272 6440 | 183 |
| 184 | 2.5035 4478 | 2.7019 5901 | 2.9160 0608 | 3.1469 1043 | 184 |
| 185 | 2.5160 6250 | 2.7165 9462 | 2.9330 1612 | 3.1665 7862 | 185 |
| 186 | 2.5286 4281 | 2.7313 0951 | 2.9501 2538 | 3.1863 6973 | 186 |
| 187 | 2.5412 8603 | 2.7461 0410 | 2.9673 3444 | 3.2062 8454 | 187 |
| 188 | 2.5539 9246 | 2.7609 7883 | 2.9846 4389 | 3.2263 2382 | 188 |
| 189 | 2.5667 6242 | 2.7759 3413 | 3.0020 5431 | 3.2464 8834 | 189 |
| 190 | 2.5795 9623 | 2.7909 7044 | 3.0195 6630 | 3.2667 7890 | 190 |
| 191 | 2.5924 9421 | 2.8060 8820 | 3.0371 8043 | 3.2871 9627 | 191 |
| 192 | 2.6054 5668 | 2.8212 8785 | 3.0548 9732 | 3.3077 4124 | 192 |
| 193 | 2.6184 8397 | 2.8365 6982 | 3.0727 1755 | 3.3284 1462 | 193 |
| 194 | 2.6315 7639 | 2.8519 3457 | 3.0906 4174 | 3.3492 1722 | 194 |
| 195 | 2.6447 3427 | 2.8673 8255 | 3.1086 7048 | 3.3701 4982 | 195 |
| 196 | 2.6579 5794 | 2.8829 1421 | 3.1268 0440 | 3.3912 1326 | 196 |
| 197 | 2.6712 4773 | 2.8985 2999 | 3.1450 4409 | 3.4124 0834 | 197 |
| 198 | 2.6846 0397 | 2.9142 3037 | 3.1633 9018 | 3.4337 3589 | 198 |
| 199 | 2.6980 2699 | 2.9300 1578 | 3.1818 4329 | 3.4551 9674 | 199 |
| 200 | 2.7115 1712 | 2.9458 8670 | 3.2004 0404 | 3.4767 9172 | 200 |
| 201 | 2.7250 7471 | 2.9618 4358 | 3.2190 7306 | 3.4985 2167 | 201 |
| 202 | 2.7387 0008 | 2.9778 8690 | 3.2378 3099 | 3.5203 8743 | 202 |
| 203 | 2.7523 9358 | 2.9940 1712 | 3.2567 3845 | 3.5423 8985 | 203 |
| 204 | 2.7661 5555 | 3.0102 3472 | 3.2757 3609 | 3.5645 2979 | 204 |
| 205 | 2.7799 8633 | 3.0265 4016 | 3.2948 4456 | 3.5868 0810 | 205 |
| 206 | 2.7938 8626 | 3.0429 3391 | 3.3140 6448 | 3.6092 2565 | 206 |
| 207 | 2.8078 5569 | 3.0594 1647 | 3.3333 9652 | 3.6317 8331 | 207 |
| 208 | 2.8218 9497 | 3.0759 8831 | 3.3528 4134 | 3.6544 8196 | 208 |
| 209 | 2.8360 0444 | 3.0926 4992 | 3.3723 9958 | 3.6773 2247 | 209 |
| 210 | 2.8501 8447 | 3.1094 0177 | 3.3920 7191 | 3.7003 0574 | 210 |
| 211 | 2.8644 3539 | 3.1262 4436 | 3.4118 5900 | 3.7234 3265 | 211 |
| 212 | 2.8787 5757 | 3.1431 7819 | 3.4317 6151 | 3.7467 0410 | 212 |
| 213 | 2.8931 5135 | 3.1602 0373 | 3.4517 8012 | 3.7701 2100 | 213 |
| 214 | 2.9076 1711 | 3.1773 2151 | 3.4719 1550 | 3.7936 8426 | 214 |
| 215 | 2.9221 5520 | 3.1945 3200 | 3.4921 6834 | 3.8173 9478 | 215 |
| 216 | 2.9367 6597 | 3.2118 3571 | 3.5125 3932 | 3.8412 5350 | 216 |
| 217 | 2.9514 4980 | 3.2292 3315 | 3.5330 2913 | 3.8652 6134 | 217 |
| 218 | 2.9662 0705 | 3.2467 2483 | 3.5536 3847 | 3.8894 1922 | 218 |
| 219 | 2.9810 3809 | 3.2643 1126 | 3.5743 6803 | 3.9137 2809 | 219 |
| 220 | 2.9959 4328 | 3.2819 9295 | 3.5952 1851 | 3.9381 8889 | 220 |
| 221 | 3.0109 2299 | 3.2997 7041 | 3.6161 9062 | 3.9628 0257 | 221 |
| 222 | 3.0259 7761 | 3.3176 4416 | 3.6372 8506 | 3.9875 7009 | 222 |
| 223 | 3.0411 0750 | 3.3356 1474 | 3.6585 0256 | 4.0124 9240 | 223 |
| 224 | 3.0563 1303 | 3.3536 8265 | 3.6798 4382 | 4.0375 7048 | 224 |
| 225 | 3.0715 9460 | 3.3718 4843 | 3.7013 0958 | 4.0628 0529 | 225 |
| 226 | 3.0869 5257 | 3.3901 1261 | 3.7229 0055 | 4.0881 9783 | 226 |
| 227 | 3.1023 8733 | 3.4084 7572 | 3.7446 1747 | 4.1137 4906 | 227 |
| 228 | 3.1178 9927 | 3.4269 3830 | 3.7664 6107 | 4.1394 5999 | 228 |
| 229 | 3.1334 8877 | 3.4455 0088 | 3.7884 3210 | 4.1653 3162 | 229 |
| 230 | 3.1491 5621 | 3.4641 6401 | 3.8105 3128 | 4.1913 6494 | 230 |
| 231 | 3.1649 0199 | 3.4829 2823 | 3.8327 5938 | 4.2175 6097 | 231 |
| 232 | 3.1807 2650 | 3.5017 9409 | 3.8551 1715 | 4.2439 2073 | 232 |
| 233 | 3.1966 3013 | 3.5207 6214 | 3.8776 0533 | 4.2704 4523 | 233 |
| 234 | 3.2126 1329 | 3.5398 3294 | 3.9002 2469 | 4.2971 3552 | 234 |
| 235 | 3.2286 7635 | 3.5590 0703 | 3.9229 7600 | 4.3239 9261 | 235 |
| 236 | 3.2448 1973 | 3.5782 8499 | 3.9458 6003 | 4.3510 1757 | 236 |
| 237 | 3.2610 4383 | 3.5976 6737 | 3.9688 7755 | 4.3782 1143 | 237 |
| 238 | 3.2773 4905 | 3.6171 5473 | 3.9920 2933 | 4.4055 7525 | 238 |
| 239 | 3.2937 3580 | 3.6367 4765 | 4.0153 1617 | 4.4331 1009 | 239 |
| 240 | 3.3102 0448 | 3.6564 4670 | 4.0387 3885 | 4.4608 1703 | 240 |

**TABLE 5**

$$s = (1 + i)^n$$

| $n$ | $\frac{2}{3}\%$ | $\frac{3}{4}\%$ | $\frac{7}{8}\%$ | 1% | $n$ |
|---|---|---|---|---|---|
| 1 | 1.0066 6667 | 1.0075 0000 | 1.0087 5000 | 1.0100 0000 | 1 |
| 2 | 1.0133 7778 | 1.0150 5625 | 1.0175 7656 | 1.0201 0000 | 2 |
| 3 | 1.0201 3363 | 1.0226 6917 | 1.0264 8036 | 1.0303 0100 | 3 |
| 4 | 1.0269 3452 | 1.0303 3919 | 1.0354 6206 | 1.0406 0401 | 4 |
| 5 | 1.0337 8075 | 1.0380 6673 | 1.0445 2235 | 1.0510 1005 | 5 |
| 6 | 1.0406 7262 | 1.0458 5224 | 1.0536 6192 | 1.0615 2015 | 6 |
| 7 | 1.0476 1044 | 1.0536 9613 | 1.0628 8147 | 1.0721 3535 | 7 |
| 8 | 1.0545 9451 | 1.0615 9885 | 1.0721 8168 | 1.0828 5671 | 8 |
| 9 | 1.0616 2514 | 1.0695 6084 | 1.0815 6327 | 1.0936 8527 | 9 |
| 10 | 1.0687 0264 | 1.0775 8255 | 1.0910 2695 | 1.1046 2213 | 10 |
| 11 | 1.0758 2732 | 1.0856 6441 | 1.1005 7343 | 1.1156 6835 | 11 |
| 12 | 1.0829 9951 | 1.0938 0690 | 1.1102 0345 | 1.1268 2503 | 12 |
| 13 | 1.0902 1950 | 1.1020 1045 | 1.1199 1773 | 1.1380 9328 | 13 |
| 14 | 1.0974 8763 | 1.1102 7553 | 1.1297 1701 | 1.1494 7421 | 14 |
| 15 | 1.1048 0422 | 1.1186 0259 | 1.1396 0203 | 1.1609 6896 | 15 |
| 16 | 1.1121 6958 | 1.1269 9211 | 1.1495 7355 | 1.1725 7864 | 16 |
| 17 | 1.1195 8404 | 1.1354 4455 | 1.1596 3232 | 1.1843 0443 | 17 |
| 18 | 1.1270 4794 | 1.1439 6039 | 1.1697 7910 | 1.1961 4748 | 18 |
| 19 | 1.1345 6159 | 1.1525 4009 | 1.1800 1467 | 1.2081 0895 | 19 |
| 20 | 1.1421 2533 | 1.1611 8414 | 1.1903 3980 | 1.2201 9004 | 20 |
| 21 | 1.1497 3950 | 1.1698 9302 | 1.2007 5527 | 1.2323 9194 | 21 |
| 22 | 1.1574 0443 | 1.1786 6722 | 1.2112 6188 | 1.2447 1586 | 22 |
| 23 | 1.1651 2046 | 1.1875 0723 | 1.2218 6042 | 1.2571 6302 | 23 |
| 24 | 1.1728 8793 | 1.1964 1353 | 1.2325 5170 | 1.2697 3465 | 24 |
| 25 | 1.1807 0718 | 1.2053 8663 | 1.2433 3653 | 1.2824 3200 | 25 |
| 26 | 1.1885 7857 | 1.2144 2703 | 1.2542 1572 | 1.2952 5631 | 26 |
| 27 | 1.1965 0242 | 1.2235 3523 | 1.2651 9011 | 1.3082 0888 | 27 |
| 28 | 1.2044 7911 | 1.2327 1175 | 1.2762 6052 | 1.3212 9097 | 28 |
| 29 | 1.2125 0897 | 1.2419 5709 | 1.2874 2780 | 1.3345 0388 | 29 |
| 30 | 1.2205 9236 | 1.2512 7176 | 1.2986 9280 | 1.3478 4892 | 30 |
| 31 | 1.2287 2964 | 1.2606 5630 | 1.3100 5636 | 1.3613 2740 | 31 |
| 32 | 1.2369 2117 | 1.2701 1122 | 1.3215 1935 | 1.3749 4068 | 32 |
| 33 | 1.2451 6731 | 1.2796 3706 | 1.3330 8265 | 1.3886 9009 | 33 |
| 34 | 1.2534 6843 | 1.2892 3434 | 1.3447 4712 | 1.4025 7699 | 34 |
| 35 | 1.2618 2489 | 1.2989 0359 | 1.3565 1366 | 1.4166 0276 | 35 |
| 36 | 1.2702 3705 | 1.3086 4537 | 1.3683 8315 | 1.4307 6878 | 36 |
| 37 | 1.2787 0530 | 1.3184 6021 | 1.3803 5650 | 1.4450 7647 | 37 |
| 38 | 1.2872 3000 | 1.3283 4866 | 1.3924 3462 | 1.4595 2724 | 38 |
| 39 | 1.2958 1153 | 1.3383 1128 | 1.4046 1843 | 1.4741 2251 | 39 |
| 40 | 1.3044 5028 | 1.3483 4861 | 1.4169 0884 | 1.4888 6373 | 40 |
| 41 | 1.3131 4661 | 1.3584 6123 | 1.4293 0679 | 1.5037 5237 | 41 |
| 42 | 1.3219 0092 | 1.3686 4969 | 1.4418 1322 | 1.5187 8989 | 42 |
| 43 | 1.3307 1360 | 1.3789 1456 | 1.4544 2909 | 1.5339 7779 | 43 |
| 44 | 1.3395 8502 | 1.3892 5642 | 1.4671 5534 | 1.5493 1757 | 44 |
| 45 | 1.3485 1559 | 1.3996 7584 | 1.4799 9295 | 1.5648 1075 | 45 |
| 46 | 1.3575 0569 | 1.4101 7341 | 1.4929 4289 | 1.5804 5885 | 46 |
| 47 | 1.3665 5573 | 1.4207 4971 | 1.5060 0614 | 1.5962 6344 | 47 |
| 48 | 1.3756 6610 | 1.4314 0533 | 1.5191 8370 | 1.6122 2608 | 48 |
| 49 | 1.3848 3721 | 1.4421 4087 | 1.5324 7655 | 1.6283 4834 | 49 |
| 50 | 1.3940 6946 | 1.4529 5693 | 1.5458 8572 | 1.6446 3182 | 50 |
| 51 | 1.4033 6325 | 1.4638 5411 | 1.5594 1222 | 1.6610 7814 | 51 |
| 52 | 1.4127 1901 | 1.4748 3301 | 1.5730 5708 | 1.6776 8892 | 52 |
| 53 | 1.4221 3713 | 1.4858 9426 | 1.5868 2133 | 1.6944 6581 | 53 |
| 54 | 1.4316 1805 | 1.4970 3847 | 1.6007 0602 | 1.7114 1047 | 54 |
| 55 | 1.4411 6217 | 1.5082 6626 | 1.6147 1219 | 1.7285 2457 | 55 |
| 56 | 1.4507 6992 | 1.5195 7825 | 1.6288 4093 | 1.7458 0982 | 56 |
| 57 | 1.4604 4172 | 1.5309 7509 | 1.6430 9328 | 1.7632 6792 | 57 |
| 58 | 1.4701 7799 | 1.5424 5740 | 1.6574 7035 | 1.7809 0060 | 58 |
| 59 | 1.4799 7918 | 1.5540 2583 | 1.6719 7322 | 1.7987 0960 | 59 |
| 60 | 1.4898 4571 | 1.5656 8103 | 1.6866 0298 | 1.8166 9670 | 60 |

Table 5

# TABLE 5

$$s = (1 + i)^n$$

| $n$ | $\frac{2}{3}\%$ | $\frac{3}{4}\%$ | $\frac{7}{8}\%$ | 1% | $n$ |
|-----|-----|-----|-----|-----|-----|
| 61 | 1.4997 7801 | 1.5774 2363 | 1.7013 6076 | 1.8348 6367 | 61 |
| 62 | 1.5097 7653 | 1.5892 5431 | 1.7162 4766 | 1.8532 1230 | 62 |
| 63 | 1.5198 4171 | 1.6011 7372 | 1.7312 6483 | 1.8717 4443 | 63 |
| 64 | 1.5299 7399 | 1.6131 8252 | 1.7464 1340 | 1.8904 6187 | 64 |
| 65 | 1.5401 7381 | 1.6252 8139 | 1.7616 9452 | 1.9093 6649 | 65 |
| 66 | 1.5504 4164 | 1.6374 7100 | 1.7771 0934 | 1.9284 6015 | 66 |
| 67 | 1.5607 7792 | 1.6497 5203 | 1.7926 5905 | 1.9477 4475 | 67 |
| 68 | 1.5711 8310 | 1.6621 2517 | 1.8083 4482 | 1.9672 2220 | 68 |
| 69 | 1.5816 5766 | 1.6745 9111 | 1.8241 6783 | 1.9868 9442 | 69 |
| 70 | 1.5922 0204 | 1.6871 5055 | 1.8401 2930 | 2.0067 6337 | 70 |
| 71 | 1.6028 1672 | 1.6998 0418 | 1.8562 3043 | 2.0268 3100 | 71 |
| 72 | 1.6135 0217 | 1.7125 5271 | 1.8724 7245 | 2.0470 9931 | 72 |
| 73 | 1.6242 5885 | 1.7253 9685 | 1.8888 5658 | 2.0675 7031 | 73 |
| 74 | 1.6350 8724 | 1.7383 3733 | 1.9053 8408 | 2.0882 4601 | 74 |
| 75 | 1.6459 8782 | 1.7513 7486 | 1.9220 5619 | 2.1091 2847 | 75 |
| 76 | 1.6569 6107 | 1.7645 1017 | 1.9388 7418 | 2.1302 1975 | 76 |
| 77 | 1.6680 0748 | 1.7777 4400 | 1.9558 3933 | 2.1515 2195 | 77 |
| 78 | 1.6791 2753 | 1.7910 7708 | 1.9729 5292 | 2.1730 3717 | 78 |
| 79 | 1.6903 2172 | 1.8045 1015 | 1.9902 1626 | 2.1947 6754 | 79 |
| 80 | 1.7015 9053 | 1.8180 4398 | 2.0076 3066 | 2.2167 1522 | 80 |
| 81 | 1.7129 3446 | 1.8316 7931 | 2.0251 9742 | 2.2388 8237 | 81 |
| 82 | 1.7243 5403 | 1.8454 1691 | 2.0429 1790 | 2.2612 7119 | 82 |
| 83 | 1.7358 4972 | 1.8592 5753 | 2.0607 9343 | 2.2838 8390 | 83 |
| 84 | 1.7474 2205 | 1.8732 0196 | 2.0788 2537 | 2.3067 2274 | 84 |
| 85 | 1.7590 7153 | 1.8872 5098 | 2.0970 1510 | 2.3297 8997 | 85 |
| 86 | 1.7707 9868 | 1.9014 0536 | 2.1153 6398 | 2.3530 8787 | 86 |
| 87 | 1.7826 0400 | 1.9156 6590 | 2.1338 7341 | 2.3766 1875 | 87 |
| 88 | 1.7944 8803 | 1.9300 3339 | 2.1525 4481 | 2.4003 8494 | 88 |
| 89 | 1.8064 5128 | 1.9445 0865 | 2.1713 7957 | 2.4243 8879 | 89 |
| 90 | 1.8184 9429 | 1.9590 9246 | 2.1903 7914 | 2.4486 3267 | 90 |
| 91 | 1.8306 1758 | 1.9737 8565 | 2.2095 4496 | 2.4731 1900 | 91 |
| 92 | 1.8428 2170 | 1.9885 8905 | 2.2288 7848 | 2.4978 5019 | 92 |
| 93 | 1.8551 0718 | 2.0035 0346 | 2.2483 8117 | 2.5228 2869 | 93 |
| 94 | 1.8674 7456 | 2.0185 2974 | 2.2680 5450 | 2.5480 5698 | 94 |
| 95 | 1.8799 2439 | 2.0336 6871 | 2.2878 9998 | 2.5735 3755 | 95 |
| 96 | 1.8924 5722 | 2.0489 2123 | 2.3079 1910 | 2.5992 7293 | 96 |
| 97 | 1.9050 7360 | 2.0642 8814 | 2.3281 1340 | 2.6252 6565 | 97 |
| 98 | 1.9177 7409 | 2.0797 7030 | 2.3484 8439 | 2.6515 1831 | 98 |
| 99 | 1.9305 5925 | 2.0953 6858 | 2.3690 3363 | 2.6780 3349 | 99 |
| 100 | 1.9434 2965 | 2.1110 8384 | 2.3897 6267 | 2.7048 1383 | 100 |
| 101 | 1.9563 8585 | 2.1269 1697 | 2.4106 7309 | 2.7318 6197 | 101 |
| 102 | 1.9694 2842 | 2.1428 6885 | 2.4317 6648 | 2.7591 8059 | 102 |
| 103 | 1.9825 5794 | 2.1589 4036 | 2.4530 4444 | 2.7867 7239 | 103 |
| 104 | 1.9957 7499 | 2.1751 3242 | 2.4745 0858 | 2.8146 4012 | 104 |
| 105 | 2.0090 8016 | 2.1914 4591 | 2.4961 6053 | 2.8427 8652 | 105 |
| 106 | 2.0224 7403 | 2.2078 8175 | 2.5180 0193 | 2.8712 1438 | 106 |
| 107 | 2.0359 5719 | 2.2244 4087 | 2.5400 3445 | 2.8999 2653 | 107 |
| 108 | 2.0495 3024 | 2.2411 2417 | 2.5622 5975 | 2.9289 2579 | 108 |
| 109 | 2.0631 9377 | 2.2579 3260 | 2.5846 7953 | 2.9582 1505 | 109 |
| 110 | 2.0769 4840 | 2.2748 6710 | 2.6072 9547 | 2.9877 9720 | 110 |
| 111 | 2.0907 9472 | 2.2919 2860 | 2.6301 0931 | 3.0176 7517 | 111 |
| 112 | 2.1047 3335 | 2.3091 1807 | 2.6531 2276 | 3.0478 5192 | 112 |
| 113 | 2.1187 6491 | 2.3264 3645 | 2.6763 3759 | 3.0783 3044 | 113 |
| 114 | 2.1328 9000 | 2.3438 8472 | 2.6997 5554 | 3.1091 1375 | 114 |
| 115 | 2.1471 0927 | 2.3614 6386 | 2.7233 7840 | 3.1402 0489 | 115 |
| 116 | 2.1614 2333 | 2.3791 7484 | 2.7472 0796 | 3.1716 0693 | 116 |
| 117 | 2.1758 3282 | 2.3970 1865 | 2.7712 4603 | 3.2033 2300 | 117 |
| 118 | 2.1903 3837 | 2.4149 9629 | 2.7954 9444 | 3.2353 5623 | 118 |
| 119 | 2.2049 4063 | 2.4331 0876 | 2.8199 5501 | 3.2677 0980 | 119 |
| 120 | 2.2196 4023 | 2.4513 5708 | 2.8446 2962 | 3.3003 8689 | 120 |

# TABLE 5

$$s = (1 + i)^n$$

| $n$ | $\frac{2}{3}\%$ | $\frac{3}{4}\%$ | $\frac{7}{8}\%$ | 1% | $n$ |
|---|---|---|---|---|---|
| 121 | 2.2344 3784 | 2.4697 4226 | 2.8695 2013 | 3.3333 9076 | 121 |
| 122 | 2.2493 3409 | 2.4882 6532 | 2.8946 2843 | 3.3667 2467 | 122 |
| 123 | 2.2643 2965 | 2.5069 2731 | 2.9199 5643 | 3.4003 9192 | 123 |
| 124 | 2.2794 2518 | 2.5257 2927 | 2.9455 0605 | 3.4343 9584 | 124 |
| 125 | 2.2946 2135 | 2.5446 7224 | 2.9712 7922 | 3.4687 3980 | 125 |
| 126 | 2.3099 1882 | 2.5637 5728 | 2.9972 7792 | 3.5034 2719 | 126 |
| 127 | 2.3253 1828 | 2.5829 8546 | 3.0235 0410 | 3.5384 6147 | 127 |
| 128 | 2.3408 2040 | 2.6023 5785 | 3.0499 5976 | 3.5738 4608 | 128 |
| 129 | 2.3564 2587 | 2.6218 7553 | 3.0766 4691 | 3.6095 8454 | 129 |
| 130 | 2.3721 3538 | 2.6415 3960 | 3.1035 6757 | 3.6456 8039 | 130 |
| 131 | 2.3879 4962 | 2.6613 5115 | 3.1307 2378 | 3.6821 3719 | 131 |
| 132 | 2.4038 6928 | 2.6813 1128 | 3.1581 1762 | 3.7189 5856 | 132 |
| 133 | 2.4198 9507 | 2.7014 2112 | 3.1857 5115 | 3.7561 4815 | 133 |
| 134 | 2.4360 2771 | 2.7216 8177 | 3.2136 2647 | 3.7937 0963 | 134 |
| 135 | 2.4522 6789 | 2.7420 9439 | 3.2417 4570 | 3.8316 4673 | 135 |
| 136 | 2.4686 1635 | 2.7626 6009 | 3.2701 1098 | 3.8699 6319 | 136 |
| 137 | 2.4850 7379 | 2.7833 8005 | 3.2987 2445 | 3.9086 6282 | 137 |
| 138 | 2.5016 4095 | 2.8042 5540 | 3.3275 8829 | 3.9477 4945 | 138 |
| 139 | 2.5183 1855 | 2.8252 8731 | 3.3567 0468 | 3.9872 2695 | 139 |
| 140 | 2.5351 0734 | 2.8464 7697 | 3.3860 7585 | 4.0270 9922 | 140 |
| 141 | 2.5520 0806 | 2.8678 2554 | 3.4157 0401 | 4.0673 7021 | 141 |
| 142 | 2.5690 2145 | 2.8893 3424 | 3.4455 9142 | 4.1080 4391 | 142 |
| 143 | 2.5861 4826 | 2.9110 0424 | 3.4757 4035 | 4.1491 2435 | 143 |
| 144 | 2.6033 8924 | 2.9328 3677 | 3.5061 5308 | 4.1906 1559 | 144 |
| 145 | 2.6207 4517 | 2.9548 3305 | 3.5368 3192 | 4.2325 2175 | 145 |
| 146 | 2.6382 1681 | 2.9769 9430 | 3.5677 7919 | 4.2748 4697 | 146 |
| 147 | 2.6558 0492 | 2.9993 2175 | 3.5989 9726 | 4.3175 9544 | 147 |
| 148 | 2.6735 1028 | 3.0218 1667 | 3.6304 8849 | 4.3607 7139 | 148 |
| 149 | 2.6913 3369 | 3.0444 8029 | 3.6622 5526 | 4.4043 7911 | 149 |
| 150 | 2.7092 7591 | 3.0673 1389 | 3.6943 0000 | 4.4484 2290 | 150 |
| 151 | 2.7273 3775 | 3.0903 1875 | 3.7266 2512 | 4.4929 0713 | 151 |
| 152 | 2.7455 2000 | 3.1134 9614 | 3.7592 3309 | 4.5378 3620 | 152 |
| 153 | 2.7638 2347 | 3.1368 4736 | 3.7921 2638 | 4.5832 1456 | 153 |
| 154 | 2.7822 4896 | 3.1603 7372 | 3.8253 0749 | 4.6290 4670 | 154 |
| 155 | 2.8007 9729 | 3.1840 7652 | 3.8587 7893 | 4.6753 3717 | 155 |
| 156 | 2.8194 6927 | 3.2079 5709 | 3.8925 4324 | 4.7220 9054 | 156 |
| 157 | 2.8382 6573 | 3.2320 1677 | 3.9266 0300 | 4.7693 1145 | 157 |
| 158 | 2.8571 8750 | 3.2562 5690 | 3.9609 6077 | 4.8170 0456 | 158 |
| 159 | 2.8762 3542 | 3.2806 7882 | 3.9956 1918 | 4.8651 7461 | 159 |
| 160 | 2.8954 1032 | 3.3052 8391 | 4.0305 8085 | 4.9138 2635 | 160 |
| 161 | 2.9147 1306 | 3.3300 7354 | 4.0658 4843 | 4.9629 6462 | 161 |
| 162 | 2.9341 4448 | 3.3550 4910 | 4.1014 2460 | 5.0125 9426 | 162 |
| 163 | 2.9537 0544 | 3.3802 1196 | 4.1373 1207 | 5.0627 2021 | 163 |
| 164 | 2.9733 9681 | 3.4055 6355 | 4.1735 1355 | 5.1133 4741 | 164 |
| 165 | 2.9932 1945 | 3.4311 0528 | 4.2100 3179 | 5.1644 8088 | 165 |
| 166 | 3.0131 7425 | 3.4568 3857 | 4.2468 6957 | 5.2161 2569 | 166 |
| 167 | 3.0332 6208 | 3.4827 6486 | 4.2840 2968 | 5.2682 8695 | 167 |
| 168 | 3.0534 8383 | 3.5088 8560 | 4.3215 1494 | 5.3209 6982 | 168 |
| 169 | 3.0738 4038 | 3.5352 0224 | 4.3593 2819 | 5.3741 7952 | 169 |
| 170 | 3.0943 3265 | 3.5617 1625 | 4.3974 7232 | 5.4279 2131 | 170 |
| 171 | 3.1149 6154 | 3.5884 2913 | 4.4359 5020 | 5.4822 0052 | 171 |
| 172 | 3.1357 2795 | 3.6153 4234 | 4.4747 6476 | 5.5370 2253 | 172 |
| 173 | 3.1566 3280 | 3.6424 5741 | 4.5139 1896 | 5.5923 9275 | 173 |
| 174 | 3.1776 7702 | 3.6697 7584 | 4.5534 1575 | 5.6483 1668 | 174 |
| 175 | 3.1988 6153 | 3.6972 9916 | 4.5932 5813 | 5.7047 9985 | 175 |
| 176 | 3.2201 8728 | 3.7250 2891 | 4.6334 4914 | 5.7618 4785 | 176 |
| 177 | 3.2416 5519 | 3.7529 6662 | 4.6739 9182 | 5.8194 6633 | 177 |
| 178 | 3.2632 6623 | 3.7811 1387 | 4.7148 8925 | 5.8776 6099 | 178 |
| 179 | 3.2850 2134 | 3.8094 7223 | 4.7561 4453 | 5.9364 3760 | 179 |
| 180 | 3.3069 2148 | 3.8380 4327 | 4.7977 6080 | 5.9958 0198 | 180 |

# TABLE 5

$$s = (1 + i)^n$$

| $n$ | $\frac{2}{3}\%$ | $\frac{3}{4}\%$ | $\frac{7}{8}\%$ | 1% | $n$ |
|---|---|---|---|---|---|
| 181 | 3.3289 6762 | 3.8668 2859 | 4.8397 4120 | 6.0557 6000 | 181 |
| 182 | 3.3511 6074 | 3.8958 2981 | 4.8820 8894 | 6.1163 1760 | 182 |
| 183 | 3.3735 0181 | 3.9250 4853 | 4.9248 0722 | 6.1774 8077 | 183 |
| 184 | 3.3959 9182 | 3.9544 8639 | 4.9678 9928 | 6.2392 5558 | 184 |
| 185 | 3.4186 3177 | 3.9841 4504 | 5.0113 6840 | 6.3016 4813 | 185 |
| 186 | 3.4414 2265 | 4.0140 2613 | 5.0552 1787 | 6.3646 6462 | 186 |
| 187 | 3.4643 6546 | 4.0441 3133 | 5.0994 5103 | 6.4283 1126 | 187 |
| 188 | 3.4874 6123 | 4.0744 6231 | 5.1440 7123 | 6.4925 9437 | 188 |
| 189 | 3.5107 1097 | 4.1050 2078 | 5.1890 8185 | 6.5575 2032 | 189 |
| 190 | 3.5341 1571 | 4.1358 0843 | 5.2344 8632 | 6.6230 9552 | 190 |
| 191 | 3.5576 7649 | 4.1668 2700 | 5.2802 8807 | 6.6893 2648 | 191 |
| 192 | 3.5813 9433 | 4.1980 7820 | 5.3264 9059 | 6.7562 1974 | 192 |
| 193 | 3.6052 7029 | 4.2295 6379 | 5.3730 9738 | 6.8237 8194 | 193 |
| 194 | 3.6293 0543 | 4.2612 8551 | 5.4201 1199 | 6.8920 1976 | 194 |
| 195 | 3.6535 0080 | 4.2932 4516 | 5.4675 3797 | 6.9609 3996 | 195 |
| 196 | 3.6778 5747 | 4.3254 4449 | 5.5153 7892 | 7.0305 4936 | 196 |
| 197 | 3.7023 7652 | 4.3578 8533 | 5.5636 3849 | 7.1008 5485 | 197 |
| 198 | 3.7270 5903 | 4.3905 6947 | 5.6123 2033 | 7.1718 6340 | 198 |
| 199 | 3.7519 0609 | 4.4234 9874 | 5.6614 2813 | 7.2435 8203 | 199 |
| 200 | 3.7769 1880 | 4.4566 7498 | 5.7109 6562 | 7.3160 1785 | 200 |
| 201 | 3.8020 9825 | 4.4901 0004 | 5.7609 3657 | 7.3891 7803 | 201 |
| 202 | 3.8274 4558 | 4.5237 7579 | 5.8113 4477 | 7.4630 6981 | 202 |
| 203 | 3.8529 6188 | 4.5577 0411 | 5.8621 9404 | 7.5377 0051 | 203 |
| 204 | 3.8786 4829 | 4.5918 8689 | 5.9134 8823 | 7.6130 7751 | 204 |
| 205 | 3.9045 0595 | 4.6263 2604 | 5.9652 3125 | 7.6892 0829 | 205 |
| 206 | 3.9305 3599 | 4.6610 2349 | 6.0174 2703 | 7.7661 0037 | 206 |
| 207 | 3.9567 3956 | 4.6959 8116 | 6.0700 7951 | 7.8437 6138 | 207 |
| 208 | 3.9831 1782 | 4.7312 0102 | 6.1231 9271 | 7.9221 9899 | 208 |
| 209 | 4.0096 7194 | 4.7666 8503 | 6.1767 7065 | 8.0014 2098 | 209 |
| 210 | 4.0364 0309 | 4.8024 3517 | 6.2308 1739 | 8.0814 3519 | 210 |
| 211 | 4.0633 1244 | 4.8384 5343 | 6.2853 3704 | 8.1622 4954 | 211 |
| 212 | 4.0904 0119 | 4.8747 4183 | 6.3403 3374 | 8.2438 7204 | 212 |
| 213 | 4.1176 7053 | 4.9113 0240 | 6.3958 1166 | 8.3263 1076 | 213 |
| 214 | 4.1451 2167 | 4.9481 3717 | 6.4517 7501 | 8.4095 7386 | 214 |
| 215 | 4.1727 5582 | 4.9852 4819 | 6.5082 2804 | 8.4936 6960 | 215 |
| 216 | 4.2005 7419 | 5.0226 3756 | 6.5651 7504 | 8.5786 0630 | 216 |
| 217 | 4.2285 7802 | 5.0603 0734 | 6.6226 2032 | 8.6643 9236 | 217 |
| 218 | 4.2567 6854 | 5.0982 5964 | 6.6805 6825 | 8.7510 3629 | 218 |
| 219 | 4.2851 4699 | 5.1364 9659 | 6.7390 2322 | 8.8385 4665 | 219 |
| 220 | 4.3137 1464 | 5.1750 2031 | 6.7979 8968 | 8.9269 3211 | 220 |
| 221 | 4.3424 7274 | 5.2138 3297 | 6.8574 7208 | 9.0162 0144 | 221 |
| 222 | 4.3714 2255 | 5.2529 3671 | 6.9174 7497 | 9.1063 6345 | 222 |
| 223 | 4.4005 6537 | 5.2923 3374 | 6.9780 0287 | 9.1974 2708 | 223 |
| 224 | 4.4299 0247 | 5.3320 2624 | 7.0390 6040 | 9.2894 0136 | 224 |
| 225 | 4.4594 3516 | 5.3720 1644 | 7.1006 5217 | 9.3822 9537 | 225 |
| 226 | 4.4891 6473 | 5.4123 0656 | 7.1627 8288 | 9.4761 1832 | 226 |
| 227 | 4.5190 9249 | 5.4528 9886 | 7.2254 5723 | 9.5708 7951 | 227 |
| 228 | 4.5492 1977 | 5.4937 9560 | 7.2886 7998 | 9.6665 8830 | 228 |
| 229 | 4.5795 4791 | 5.5349 9907 | 7.3524 5593 | 9.7632 5418 | 229 |
| 230 | 4.6100 7822 | 5.5765 1156 | 7.4167 8992 | 9.8608 8673 | 230 |
| 231 | 4.6408 1208 | 5.6183 3540 | 7.4816 8683 | 9.9594 9559 | 231 |
| 232 | 4.6717 5083 | 5.6604 7291 | 7.5471 5159 | 10.0590 9055 | 232 |
| 233 | 4.7028 9583 | 5.7029 2646 | 7.6131 8917 | 10.1596 8145 | 233 |
| 234 | 4.7342 4847 | 5.7456 9841 | 7.6798 0458 | 10.2612 7827 | 234 |
| 235 | 4.7658 1013 | 5.7887 9115 | 7.7470 0287 | 10.3638 9105 | 235 |
| 236 | 4.7975 8219 | 5.8322 0708 | 7.8147 8914 | 10.4675 2996 | 236 |
| 237 | 4.8295 6608 | 5.8759 4863 | 7.8831 6855 | 10.5722 0526 | 237 |
| 238 | 4.8617 6318 | 5.9200 1825 | 7.9521 4627 | 10.6779 2731 | 238 |
| 239 | 4.8941 7494 | 5.9644 1839 | 8.0217 2755 | 10.7847 0659 | 239 |
| 240 | 4.9268 0277 | 6.0091 5152 | 8.0919 1767 | 10.8925 5365 | 240 |

## TABLE 5

$$s = (1 + i)^n$$

| $n$ | $1\frac{1}{8}\%$ | $1\frac{1}{4}\%$ | $1\frac{3}{8}\%$ | $1\frac{1}{2}\%$ | $n$ |
|---|---|---|---|---|---|
| 1 | 1.0112 5000 | 1.0125 0000 | 1.0137 5000 | 1.0150 0000 | 1 |
| 2 | 1.0226 2656 | 1.0251 5625 | 1.0276 8906 | 1.0302 2500 | 2 |
| 3 | 1.0341 3111 | 1.0379 7070 | 1.0418 1979 | 1.0456 7838 | 3 |
| 4 | 1.0457 6509 | 1.0509 4534 | 1.0561 4481 | 1.0613 6355 | 4 |
| 5 | 1.0575 2994 | 1.0640 8215 | 1.0706 6680 | 1.0772 8400 | 5 |
| 6 | 1.0694 2716 | 1.0773 8318 | 1.0853 8847 | 1.0934 4326 | 6 |
| 7 | 1.0814 5821 | 1.0908 5047 | 1.1003 1256 | 1.1098 4491 | 7 |
| 8 | 1.0936 2462 | 1.1044 8610 | 1.1154 4186 | 1.1264 9259 | 8 |
| 9 | 1.1059 2789 | 1.1182 9218 | 1.1307 7918 | 1.1433 8998 | 9 |
| 10 | 1.1183 6958 | 1.1322 7083 | 1.1463 2740 | 1.1605 4083 | 10 |
| 11 | 1.1309 5124 | 1.1464 2422 | 1.1620 8940 | 1.1779 4894 | 11 |
| 12 | 1.1436 7444 | 1.1607 5452 | 1.1780 6813 | 1.1956 1817 | 12 |
| 13 | 1.1565 4078 | 1.1752 6395 | 1.1942 6656 | 1.2135 5244 | 13 |
| 14 | 1.1695 5186 | 1.1899 5475 | 1.2106 8773 | 1.2317 5573 | 14 |
| 15 | 1.1827 0932 | 1.2048 2918 | 1.2273 3469 | 1.2502 3207 | 15 |
| 16 | 1.1960 1480 | 1.2198 8955 | 1.2442 1054 | 1.2689 8555 | 16 |
| 17 | 1.2094 6997 | 1.2351 3817 | 1.2613 1843 | 1.2880 2033 | 17 |
| 18 | 1.2230 7650 | 1.2505 7739 | 1.2786 6156 | 1.3073 4064 | 18 |
| 19 | 1.2368 3611 | 1.2662 0961 | 1.2962 4316 | 1.3269 5075 | 19 |
| 20 | 1.2507 5052 | 1.2820 3723 | 1.3140 6650 | 1.3468 5501 | 20 |
| 21 | 1.2648 2146 | 1.2980 6270 | 1.3321 3492 | 1.3670 5783 | 21 |
| 22 | 1.2790 5071 | 1.3142 8848 | 1.3504 5177 | 1.3875 6370 | 22 |
| 23 | 1.2934 4003 | 1.3307 1709 | 1.3690 2048 | 1.4083 7715 | 23 |
| 24 | 1.3079 9123 | 1.3473 5105 | 1.3878 4451 | 1.4295 0281 | 24 |
| 25 | 1.3227 0613 | 1.3641 9294 | 1.4069 2738 | 1.4509 4535 | 25 |
| 26 | 1.3375 8657 | 1.3812 4535 | 1.4262 7263 | 1.4727 0953 | 26 |
| 27 | 1.3526 3442 | 1.3985 1092 | 1.4458 8388 | 1.4948 0018 | 27 |
| 28 | 1.3678 5156 | 1.4159 9230 | 1.4657 6478 | 1.5172 2218 | 28 |
| 29 | 1.3832 3989 | 1.4336 9221 | 1.4859 1905 | 1.5399 8051 | 29 |
| 30 | 1.3988 0134 | 1.4516 1336 | 1.5063 5043 | 1.5630 8022 | 30 |
| 31 | 1.4145 3785 | 1.4697 5853 | 1.5270 6275 | 1.5865 2642 | 31 |
| 32 | 1.4304 5140 | 1.4881 3051 | 1.5480 5986 | 1.6103 2432 | 32 |
| 33 | 1.4465 4398 | 1.5067 3214 | 1.5693 4569 | 1.6344 7918 | 33 |
| 34 | 1.4628 1760 | 1.5255 6629 | 1.5909 2419 | 1.6589 9637 | 34 |
| 35 | 1.4792 7430 | 1.5446 3587 | 1.6127 9940 | 1.6838 8132 | 35 |
| 36 | 1.4959 1613 | 1.5639 4382 | 1.6349 7539 | 1.7091 3954 | 36 |
| 37 | 1.5127 4519 | 1.5834 9312 | 1.6574 5630 | 1.7347 7663 | 37 |
| 38 | 1.5297 6357 | 1.6032 8678 | 1.6802 4633 | 1.7607 9828 | 38 |
| 39 | 1.5469 7341 | 1.6233 2787 | 1.7033 4971 | 1.7872 1025 | 39 |
| 40 | 1.5643 7687 | 1.6436 1946 | 1.7267 7077 | 1.8140 1841 | 40 |
| 41 | 1.5819 7611 | 1.6641 6471 | 1.7505 1387 | 1.8412 2868 | 41 |
| 42 | 1.5997 7334 | 1.6849 6677 | 1.7745 8343 | 1.8688 4712 | 42 |
| 43 | 1.6177 7079 | 1.7060 2885 | 1.7989 8396 | 1.8968 7982 | 43 |
| 44 | 1.6359 7071 | 1.7273 5421 | 1.8237 1999 | 1.9253 3302 | 44 |
| 45 | 1.6543 7538 | 1.7489 4614 | 1.8487 9614 | 1.9542 1301 | 45 |
| 46 | 1.6729 8710 | 1.7708 0797 | 1.8742 1708 | 1.9835 2621 | 46 |
| 47 | 1.6918 0821 | 1.7929 4306 | 1.8999 8757 | 2.0132 7910 | 47 |
| 48 | 1.7108 4105 | 1.8153 5485 | 1.9261 1240 | 2.0434 7829 | 48 |
| 49 | 1.7300 8801 | 1.8380 4679 | 1.9525 9644 | 2.0741 3046 | 49 |
| 50 | 1.7495 5150 | 1.8610 2237 | 1.9794 4464 | 2.1052 4242 | 50 |

Table 5

**TABLE 5**

$$s = (1 + i)^n$$

| $n$ | $1\frac{1}{8}\%$ | $1\frac{1}{4}\%$ | $1\frac{3}{8}\%$ | $1\frac{1}{2}\%$ | $n$ |
|---|---|---|---|---|---|
| 51 | 1.7692 3395 | 1.8842 8515 | 2.0066 6201 | 2.1368 2106 | 51 |
| 52 | 1.7891 3784 | 1.9078 3872 | 2.0342 5361 | 2.1688 7337 | 52 |
| 53 | 1.8092 6564 | 1.9316 8670 | 2.0622 2460 | 2.2014 0647 | 53 |
| 54 | 1.8296 1988 | 1.9558 3279 | 2.0905 8019 | 2.2344 2757 | 54 |
| 55 | 1.8502 0310 | 1.9802 8070 | 2.1193 2566 | 2.2679 4398 | 55 |
| 56 | 1.8710 1788 | 2.0050 3420 | 2.1484 6639 | 2.3019 6314 | 56 |
| 57 | 1.8920 6684 | 2.0300 9713 | 2.1780 0780 | 2.3364 9259 | 57 |
| 58 | 1.9133 5259 | 2.0554 7335 | 2.2079 5541 | 2.3715 3998 | 58 |
| 59 | 1.9348 7780 | 2.0811 6676 | 2.2383 1480 | 2.4071 1308 | 59 |
| 60 | 1.9566 4518 | 2.1071 8135 | 2.2690 9163 | 2.4432 1978 | 60 |
| 61 | 1.9786 5744 | 2.1335 2111 | 2.3002 9164 | 2.4798 6807 | 61 |
| 62 | 2.0009 1733 | 2.1601 9013 | 2.3319 2065 | 2.5170 6609 | 62 |
| 63 | 2.0234 2765 | 2.1871 9250 | 2.3639 8456 | 2.5548 2208 | 63 |
| 64 | 2.0461 9121 | 2.2145 3241 | 2.3964 8934 | 2.5931 4442 | 64 |
| 65 | 2.0692 1087 | 2.2422 1407 | 2.4294 4107 | 2.6320 4158 | 65 |
| 66 | 2.0924 8949 | 2.2702 4174 | 2.4628 4589 | 2.6715 2221 | 66 |
| 67 | 2.1160 2999 | 2.2986 1976 | 2.4967 1002 | 2.7115 9504 | 67 |
| 68 | 2.1398 3533 | 2.3273 5251 | 2.5310 3978 | 2.7522 6896 | 68 |
| 69 | 2.1639 0848 | 2.3564 4442 | 2.5658 4158 | 2.7935 5300 | 69 |
| 70 | 2.1882 5245 | 2.3858 9997 | 2.6011 2190 | 2.8354 5629 | 70 |
| 71 | 2.2128 7029 | 2.4157 2372 | 2.6368 8732 | 2.8779 8814 | 71 |
| 72 | 2.2377 6508 | 2.4459 2027 | 2.6731 4453 | 2.9211 5796 | 72 |
| 73 | 2.2629 3994 | 2.4764 9427 | 2.7099 0026 | 2.9649 7533 | 73 |
| 74 | 2.2883 9801 | 2.5074 5045 | 2.7471 6139 | 3.0094 4996 | 74 |
| 75 | 2.3141 4249 | 2.5387 9358 | 2.7849 3486 | 3.0545 9171 | 75 |
| 76 | 2.3401 7659 | 2.5705 2850 | 2.8232 2771 | 3.1004 1059 | 76 |
| 77 | 2.3665 0358 | 2.6026 6011 | 2.8620 4710 | 3.1469 1674 | 77 |
| 78 | 2.3931 2675 | 2.6351 9336 | 2.9014 0024 | 3.1941 2050 | 78 |
| 79 | 2.4200 4942 | 2.6681 3327 | 2.9412 9450 | 3.2420 3230 | 79 |
| 80 | 2.4472 7498 | 2.7014 8494 | 2.9817 3730 | 3.2906 6279 | 80 |
| 81 | 2.4748 0682 | 2.7352 5350 | 3.0227 3618 | 3.3400 2273 | 81 |
| 82 | 2.5026 4840 | 2.7694 4417 | 3.0642 9881 | 3.3901 2307 | 82 |
| 83 | 2.5308 0319 | 2.8040 6222 | 3.1064 3291 | 3.4409 7492 | 83 |
| 84 | 2.5592 7473 | 2.8391 1300 | 3.1491 4637 | 3.4925 8954 | 84 |
| 85 | 2.5880 6657 | 2.8746 0191 | 3.1924 4713 | 3.5449 7838 | 85 |
| 86 | 2.6171 8232 | 2.9105 3444 | 3.2363 4328 | 3.5981 5306 | 86 |
| 87 | 2.6466 2562 | 2.9469 1612 | 3.2808 4300 | 3.6521 2535 | 87 |
| 88 | 2.6764 0016 | 2.9837 5257 | 3.3259 5459 | 3.7069 0723 | 88 |
| 89 | 2.7065 0966 | 3.0210 4948 | 3.3716 8646 | 3.7625 1084 | 89 |
| 90 | 2.7369 5789 | 3.0588 1260 | 3.4180 4715 | 3.8189 4851 | 90 |
| 91 | 2.7677 4867 | 3.0970 4775 | 3.4650 4530 | 3.8762 3273 | 91 |
| 92 | 2.7988 8584 | 3.1357 6085 | 3.5126 8967 | 3.9343 7622 | 92 |
| 93 | 2.8303 7331 | 3.1749 5786 | 3.5609 8916 | 3.9933 9187 | 93 |
| 94 | 2.8622 1501 | 3.2146 4483 | 3.6099 5276 | 4.0532 9275 | 94 |
| 95 | 2.8944 1492 | 3.2548 2789 | 3.6595 8961 | 4.1140 9214 | 95 |
| 96 | 2.9269 7709 | 3.2955 1324 | 3.7099 0897 | 4.1758 0352 | 96 |
| 97 | 2.9599 0559 | 3.3367 0716 | 3.7609 2021 | 4.2384 4057 | 97 |
| 98 | 2.9932 0452 | 3.3784 1600 | 3.8126 3287 | 4.3020 1718 | 98 |
| 99 | 3.0268 7807 | 3.4206 4620 | 3.8650 5657 | 4.3665 4744 | 99 |
| 100 | 3.0609 3045 | 3.4634 0427 | 3.9182 0110 | 4.4320 4565 | 100 |

# TABLE 5

$$s = (1 + i)^n$$

| n | $1\frac{5}{8}\%$ | $1\frac{3}{4}\%$ | $1\frac{7}{8}\%$ | 2% | n |
|---|---|---|---|---|---|
| 1 | 1.0162 5000 | 1.0175 0000 | 1.0187 5000 | 1.0200 0000 | 1 |
| 2 | 1.0327 6406 | 1.0353 0625 | 1.0378 5156 | 1.0404 0000 | 2 |
| 3 | 1.0495 4648 | 1.0534 2411 | 1.0573 1128 | 1.0612 0800 | 3 |
| 4 | 1.0666 0161 | 1.0718 5903 | 1.0771 3587 | 1.0824 3216 | 4 |
| 5 | 1.0839 3388 | 1.0906 1656 | 1.0973 3216 | 1.1040 8080 | 5 |
| 6 | 1.1015 4781 | 1.1097 0235 | 1.1179 0714 | 1.1261 6242 | 6 |
| 7 | 1.1194 4796 | 1.1291 2215 | 1.1388 6790 | 1.1486 8567 | 7 |
| 8 | 1.1376 3899 | 1.1488 8178 | 1.1602 2167 | 1.1716 5938 | 8 |
| 9 | 1.1561 2563 | 1.1689 8721 | 1.1819 7583 | 1.1950 9257 | 9 |
| 10 | 1.1749 1267 | 1.1894 4449 | 1.2041 3788 | 1.2189 9442 | 10 |
| 11 | 1.1940 0500 | 1.2102 5977 | 1.2267 1546 | 1.2433 7431 | 11 |
| 12 | 1.2134 0758 | 1.2314 3931 | 1.2497 1638 | 1.2682 4179 | 12 |
| 13 | 1.2331 2545 | 1.2529 8950 | 1.2731 4856 | 1.2936 0663 | 13 |
| 14 | 1.2531 6374 | 1.2749 1682 | 1.2970 2009 | 1.3194 7876 | 14 |
| 15 | 1.2735 2765 | 1.2972 2786 | 1.3213 3922 | 1.3458 6834 | 15 |
| 16 | 1.2942 2248 | 1.3199 2935 | 1.3461 1433 | 1.3727 8571 | 16 |
| 17 | 1.3152 5359 | 1.3430 2811 | 1.3713 5398 | 1.4002 4142 | 17 |
| 18 | 1.3366 2646 | 1.3665 3111 | 1.3970 6686 | 1.4282 4625 | 18 |
| 19 | 1.3583 4664 | 1.3904 4540 | 1.4232 6187 | 1.4568 1117 | 19 |
| 20 | 1.3804 1977 | 1.4147 7820 | 1.4499 4803 | 1.4859 4740 | 20 |
| 21 | 1.4028 5160 | 1.4395 3681 | 1.4771 3455 | 1.5156 6634 | 21 |
| 22 | 1.4256 4793 | 1.4647 2871 | 1.5048 3082 | 1.5459 7967 | 22 |
| 23 | 1.4488 1471 | 1.4903 6146 | 1.5330 4640 | 1.5768 9926 | 23 |
| 24 | 1.4723 5795 | 1.5164 4279 | 1.5617 9102 | 1.6084 3725 | 24 |
| 25 | 1.4962 8377 | 1.5429 8054 | 1.5910 7460 | 1.6406 0599 | 25 |
| 26 | 1.5205 9838 | 1.5699 8269 | 1.6209 0725 | 1.6734 1811 | 26 |
| 27 | 1.5453 0810 | 1.5974 5739 | 1.6512 9926 | 1.7068 8648 | 27 |
| 28 | 1.5704 1936 | 1.6254 1290 | 1.6822 6112 | 1.7410 2421 | 28 |
| 29 | 1.5959 3868 | 1.6538 5762 | 1.7138 0352 | 1.7758 4469 | 29 |
| 30 | 1.6218 7268 | 1.6828 0013 | 1.7459 3734 | 1.8113 6158 | 30 |
| 31 | 1.6482 2811 | 1.7122 4913 | 1.7786 7366 | 1.8475 8882 | 31 |
| 32 | 1.6750 1182 | 1.7422 1349 | 1.8120 2379 | 1.8845 4059 | 32 |
| 33 | 1.7022 3076 | 1.7727 0223 | 1.8459 9924 | 1.9222 3140 | 33 |
| 34 | 1.7298 9201 | 1.8037 2452 | 1.8806 1172 | 1.9606 7603 | 34 |
| 35 | 1.7580 0275 | 1.8352 8970 | 1.9158 7319 | 1.9998 8955 | 35 |
| 36 | 1.7865 7030 | 1.8674 0727 | 1.9517 9582 | 2.0398 8734 | 36 |
| 37 | 1.8156 0207 | 1.9000 8689 | 1.9883 9199 | 2.0806 8509 | 37 |
| 38 | 1.8451 0560 | 1.9333 3841 | 2.0256 7434 | 2.1222 9879 | 38 |
| 39 | 1.8750 8857 | 1.9671 7184 | 2.0636 5573 | 2.1647 4477 | 39 |
| 40 | 1.9055 5875 | 2.0015 9734 | 2.1023 4928 | 2.2080 3966 | 40 |
| 41 | 1.9365 2408 | 2.0366 2530 | 2.1417 6833 | 2.2522 0046 | 41 |
| 42 | 1.9679 9260 | 2.0722 6624 | 2.1819 2648 | 2.2972 4447 | 42 |
| 43 | 1.9999 7248 | 2.1085 3090 | 2.2228 3760 | 2.3431 8936 | 43 |
| 44 | 2.0324 7203 | 2.1454 3019 | 2.2645 1581 | 2.3900 5314 | 44 |
| 45 | 2.0654 9970 | 2.1829 7522 | 2.3069 7548 | 2.4378 5421 | 45 |
| 46 | 2.0990 6407 | 2.2211 7728 | 2.3502 3127 | 2.4866 1129 | 46 |
| 47 | 2.1331 7387 | 2.2600 4789 | 2.3942 9811 | 2.5363 4352 | 47 |
| 48 | 2.1678 3794 | 2.2995 9872 | 2.4391 9120 | 2.5870 7039 | 48 |
| 49 | 2.2030 6531 | 2.3398 4170 | 2.4849 2603 | 2.6388 1179 | 49 |
| 50 | 2.2388 6512 | 2.3807 8893 | 2.5315 1839 | 2.6915 8803 | 50 |

Table 5

# TABLE 5

$$s = (1 + i)^n$$

| n | $1\frac{5}{8}\%$ | $1\frac{3}{4}\%$ | $1\frac{7}{8}\%$ | $2\%$ | n |
|---|---|---|---|---|---|
| 51 | 2.2752 4668 | 2.4224 5274 | 2.5789 8436 | 2.7454 1979 | 51 |
| 52 | 2.3122 1944 | 2.4648 4566 | 2.6273 4032 | 2.8003 2819 | 52 |
| 53 | 2.3497 9300 | 2.5079 8046 | 2.6766 0295 | 2.8563 3475 | 53 |
| 54 | 2.3879 7714 | 2.5518 7012 | 2.7267 8926 | 2.9134 6144 | 54 |
| 55 | 2.4267 8177 | 2.5965 2785 | 2.7779 1656 | 2.9717 3067 | 55 |
| 56 | 2.4662 1697 | 2.6419 6708 | 2.8300 0249 | 3.0311 6529 | 56 |
| 57 | 2.5062 9300 | 2.6882 0151 | 2.8830 6504 | 3.0917 8859 | 57 |
| 58 | 2.5470 2026 | 2.7352 4503 | 2.9371 2251 | 3.1536 2436 | 58 |
| 59 | 2.5884 0934 | 2.7831 1182 | 2.9921 9355 | 3.2166 9685 | 59 |
| 60 | 2.6304 7099 | 2.8318 1628 | 3.0482 9718 | 3.2810 3079 | 60 |
| 61 | 2.6732 1614 | 2.8813 7306 | 3.1054 5276 | 3.3466 5140 | 61 |
| 62 | 2.7166 5590 | 2.9317 9709 | 3.1636 8000 | 3.4135 8443 | 62 |
| 63 | 2.7608 0156 | 2.9831 0354 | 3.2229 9900 | 3.4818 5612 | 63 |
| 64 | 2.8056 6459 | 3.0353 0785 | 3.2834 3023 | 3.5514 9324 | 64 |
| 65 | 2.8512 5664 | 3.0884 2574 | 3.3449 9454 | 3.6225 2311 | 65 |
| 66 | 2.8975 8956 | 3.1424 7319 | 3.4077 1319 | 3.6949 7357 | 66 |
| 67 | 2.9446 7539 | 3.1974 6647 | 3.4716 0781 | 3.7688 7304 | 67 |
| 68 | 2.9925 2636 | 3.2534 2213 | 3.5367 0046 | 3.8442 5050 | 68 |
| 69 | 3.0411 5492 | 3.3103 5702 | 3.6030 1359 | 3.9211 3551 | 69 |
| 70 | 3.0905 7368 | 3.3682 8827 | 3.6705 7010 | 3.9995 5822 | 70 |
| 71 | 3.1407 9551 | 3.4272 3331 | 3.7393 9329 | 4.0795 4939 | 71 |
| 72 | 3.1918 3343 | 3.4872 0990 | 3.8095 0691 | 4.1611 4038 | 72 |
| 73 | 3.2437 0073 | 3.5482 3607 | 3.8809 3517 | 4.2443 6318 | 73 |
| 74 | 3.2964 1086 | 3.6103 3020 | 3.9537 0270 | 4.3292 5045 | 74 |
| 75 | 3.3499 7754 | 3.6735 1098 | 4.0278 3463 | 4.4158 3546 | 75 |
| 76 | 3.4044 1467 | 3.7377 9742 | 4.1033 5653 | 4.5041 5216 | 76 |
| 77 | 3.4597 3641 | 3.8032 0888 | 4.1802 9446 | 4.5942 3521 | 77 |
| 78 | 3.5159 5713 | 3.8697 6503 | 4.2586 7498 | 4.6861 1991 | 78 |
| 79 | 3.5730 9143 | 3.9374 8592 | 4.3385 2514 | 4.7798 4231 | 79 |
| 80 | 3.6311 5417 | 4.0063 9192 | 4.4198 7248 | 4.8754 3916 | 80 |
| 81 | 3.6901 6042 | 4.0765 0378 | 4.5027 4509 | 4.9729 4794 | 81 |
| 82 | 3.7501 2553 | 4.1478 4260 | 4.5871 7156 | 5.0724 0690 | 82 |
| 83 | 3.8110 6507 | 4.2204 2984 | 4.6731 8103 | 5.1738 5504 | 83 |
| 84 | 3.8729 9488 | 4.2942 8737 | 4.7608 0317 | 5.2773 3214 | 84 |
| 85 | 3.9359 3104 | 4.3694 3740 | 4.8500 6823 | 5.3828 7878 | 85 |
| 86 | 3.9998 8992 | 4.4459 0255 | 4.9410 0701 | 5.4905 3636 | 86 |
| 87 | 4.0648 8813 | 4.5237 0584 | 5.0336 5089 | 5.6003 4708 | 87 |
| 88 | 4.1309 4257 | 4.6028 7070 | 5.1280 3185 | 5.7123 5402 | 88 |
| 89 | 4.1980 7038 | 4.6834 2093 | 5.2241 8245 | 5.8266 0110 | 89 |
| 90 | 4.2662 8903 | 4.7653 8080 | 5.3221 3587 | 5.9431 3313 | 90 |
| 91 | 4.3356 1622 | 4.8487 7496 | 5.4219 2591 | 6.0619 9579 | 91 |
| 92 | 4.4060 6999 | 4.9336 2853 | 5.5235 8703 | 6.1832 3570 | 92 |
| 93 | 4.4776 6863 | 5.0199 6703 | 5.6271 5428 | 6.3069 0042 | 93 |
| 94 | 4.5504 3074 | 5.1078 1645 | 5.7326 6343 | 6.4330 3843 | 94 |
| 95 | 4.6243 7524 | 5.1972 0324 | 5.8401 5086 | 6.5616 9920 | 95 |
| 96 | 4.6995 2134 | 5.2881 5429 | 5.9496 5369 | 6.6929 3318 | 96 |
| 97 | 4.7758 8856 | 5.3806 9699 | 6.0612 0970 | 6.8267 9184 | 97 |
| 98 | 4.8534 9675 | 5.4748 5919 | 6.1748 5738 | 6.9633 2768 | 98 |
| 99 | 4.9323 6607 | 5.5706 6923 | 6.2906 3596 | 7.1025 9423 | 99 |
| 100 | 5.0125 1702 | 5.6681 5594 | 6.4085 8538 | 7.2446 4612 | 100 |

# TABLE 5

$$s = (1 + i)^n$$

| n | $2\frac{1}{4}\%$ | $2\frac{1}{2}\%$ | $2\frac{3}{4}\%$ | 3% | n |
|---|---|---|---|---|---|
| 1 | 1.0225 0000 | 1.0250 0000 | 1.0275 0000 | 1.0300 0000 | 1 |
| 2 | 1.0455 0625 | 1.0506 2500 | 1.0557 5625 | 1.0609 0000 | 2 |
| 3 | 1.0690 3014 | 1.0768 9063 | 1.0847 8955 | 1.0927 2700 | 3 |
| 4 | 1.0930 8332 | 1.1038 1289 | 1.1146 2126 | 1.1255 0881 | 4 |
| 5 | 1.1176 7769 | 1.1314 0821 | 1.1452 7334 | 1.1592 7407 | 5 |
| 6 | 1.1428 2544 | 1.1596 9342 | 1.1767 6836 | 1.1940 5230 | 6 |
| 7 | 1.1685 3901 | 1.1886 8575 | 1.2091 2949 | 1.2298 7387 | 7 |
| 8 | 1.1948 3114 | 1.2184 0290 | 1.2423 8055 | 1.2667 7008 | 8 |
| 9 | 1.2217 1484 | 1.2488 6297 | 1.2765 4602 | 1.3047 7318 | 9 |
| 10 | 1.2492 0343 | 1.2800 8454 | 1.3116 5103 | 1.3439 1638 | 10 |
| 11 | 1.2773 1050 | 1.3120 8666 | 1.3477 2144 | 1.3842 3387 | 11 |
| 12 | 1.3060 4999 | 1.3448 8882 | 1.3847 8378 | 1.4257 6089 | 12 |
| 13 | 1.3354 3611 | 1.3785 1104 | 1.4228 6533 | 1.4685 3371 | 13 |
| 14 | 1.3654 8343 | 1.4129 7382 | 1.4619 9413 | 1.5125 8972 | 14 |
| 15 | 1.3962 0680 | 1.4482 9817 | 1.5021 9896 | 1.5579 6742 | 15 |
| 16 | 1.4276 2146 | 1.4845 0562 | 1.5435 0944 | 1.6047 0644 | 16 |
| 17 | 1.4597 4294 | 1.5216 1826 | 1.5859 5595 | 1.6528 4763 | 17 |
| 18 | 1.4925 8716 | 1.5596 5872 | 1.6295 6973 | 1.7024 3306 | 18 |
| 19 | 1.5261 7037 | 1.5986 5019 | 1.6743 8290 | 1.7535 0605 | 19 |
| 20 | 1.5605 0920 | 1.6386 1644 | 1.7204 2843 | 1.8061 1123 | 20 |
| 21 | 1.5956 2066 | 1.6795 8185 | 1.7677 4021 | 1.8602 9457 | 21 |
| 22 | 1.6315 2212 | 1.7215 7140 | 1.8163 5307 | 1.9161 0341 | 22 |
| 23 | 1.6682 3137 | 1.7646 1068 | 1.8663 0278 | 1.9735 8651 | 23 |
| 24 | 1.7057 6658 | 1.8087 2595 | 1.9176 2610 | 2.0327 9411 | 24 |
| 25 | 1.7441 4632 | 1.8539 4410 | 1.9703 6082 | 2.0937 7793 | 25 |
| 26 | 1.7833 8962 | 1.9002 9270 | 2.0245 4575 | 2.1565 9127 | 26 |
| 27 | 1.8235 1588 | 1.9478 0002 | 2.0802 2075 | 2.2212 8901 | 27 |
| 28 | 1.8645 4499 | 1.9964 9502 | 2.1374 2682 | 2.2879 2768 | 28 |
| 29 | 1.9064 9725 | 2.0464 0739 | 2.1962 0606 | 2.3565 6551 | 29 |
| 30 | 1.9493 9344 | 2.0975 6758 | 2.2566 0173 | 2.4272 6247 | 30 |
| 31 | 1.9932 5479 | 2.1500 0677 | 2.3186 5828 | 2.5000 8035 | 31 |
| 32 | 2.0381 0303 | 2.2037 5694 | 2.3824 2138 | 2.5750 8276 | 32 |
| 33 | 2.0839 6034 | 2.2588 5086 | 2.4479 3797 | 2.6523 3524 | 33 |
| 34 | 2.1308 4945 | 2.3153 2213 | 2.5152 5626 | 2.7319 0530 | 34 |
| 35 | 2.1787 9356 | 2.3732 0519 | 2.5844 2581 | 2.8138 6245 | 35 |
| 36 | 2.2278 1642 | 2.4325 3532 | 2.6554 9752 | 2.8982 7833 | 36 |
| 37 | 2.2779 4229 | 2.4933 4870 | 2.7285 2370 | 2.9852 2668 | 37 |
| 38 | 2.3291 9599 | 2.5556 8242 | 2.8035 5810 | 3.0747 8348 | 38 |
| 39 | 2.3816 0290 | 2.6195 7448 | 2.8806 5595 | 3.1670 2698 | 39 |
| 40 | 2.4351 8897 | 2.6850 6384 | 2.9598 7399 | 3.2620 3779 | 40 |
| 41 | 2.4899 8072 | 2.7521 9043 | 3.0412 7052 | 3.3598 9893 | 41 |
| 42 | 2.5460 0528 | 2.8209 9520 | 3.1249 0546 | 3.4606 9589 | 42 |
| 43 | 2.6032 9040 | 2.8915 2008 | 3.2108 4036 | 3.5645 1677 | 43 |
| 44 | 2.6618 6444 | 2.9638 0808 | 3.2991 3847 | 3.6714 5227 | 44 |
| 45 | 2.7217 5639 | 3.0379 0328 | 3.3898 6478 | 3.7815 9584 | 45 |
| 46 | 2.7829 9590 | 3.1138 5086 | 3.4830 8606 | 3.8950 4372 | 46 |
| 47 | 2.8456 1331 | 3.1916 9713 | 3.5788 7093 | 4.0118 9503 | 47 |
| 48 | 2.9096 3961 | 3.2714 8956 | 3.6772 8988 | 4.1322 5188 | 48 |
| 49 | 2.9751 0650 | 3.3532 7680 | 3.7784 1535 | 4.2562 1944 | 49 |
| 50 | 3.0420 4640 | 3.4371 0872 | 3.8823 2177 | 4.3839 0602 | 50 |

Table
5

# TABLE 5

$$s = (1 + i)^n$$

| n | $2\frac{1}{4}\%$ | $2\frac{1}{2}\%$ | $2\frac{3}{4}\%$ | 3% | n |
|---|---|---|---|---|---|
| 51 | 3.1104 9244 | 3.5230 3644 | 3.9890 8562 | 4.5154 2320 | 51 |
| 52 | 3.1804 7852 | 3.6111 1235 | 4.0987 8547 | 4.6508 8590 | 52 |
| 53 | 3.2520 3929 | 3.7013 9016 | 4.2115 0208 | 4.7904 1247 | 53 |
| 54 | 3.3252 1017 | 3.7939 2491 | 4.3273 1838 | 4.9341 2485 | 54 |
| 55 | 3.4000 2740 | 3.8887 7303 | 4.4463 1964 | 5.0821 4859 | 55 |
| 56 | 3.4765 2802 | 3.9859 9236 | 4.5685 9343 | 5.2346 1305 | 56 |
| 57 | 3.5547 4990 | 4.0856 4217 | 4.6942 2975 | 5.3916 5144 | 57 |
| 58 | 3.6347 3177 | 4.1877 8322 | 4.8233 2107 | 5.5534 0098 | 58 |
| 59 | 3.7165 1324 | 4.2924 7780 | 4.9559 6239 | 5.7200 0301 | 59 |
| 60 | 3.8001 3479 | 4.3997 8975 | 5.0922 5136 | 5.8916 0310 | 60 |
| 61 | 3.8856 3782 | 4.5097 8449 | 5.2322 8827 | 6.0683 5120 | 61 |
| 62 | 3.9730 6467 | 4.6225 2910 | 5.3761 7620 | 6.2504 0173 | 62 |
| 63 | 4.0624 5862 | 4.7380 9233 | 5.5240 2105 | 6.4379 1379 | 63 |
| 64 | 4.1538 6394 | 4.8565 4464 | 5.6759 3162 | 6.6310 5120 | 64 |
| 65 | 4.2473 2588 | 4.9779 5826 | 5.8320 1974 | 6.8299 8273 | 65 |
| 66 | 4.3428 9071 | 5.1024 0721 | 5.9924 0029 | 7.0348 8222 | 66 |
| 67 | 4.4406 0576 | 5.2299 6739 | 6.1571 9130 | 7.2459 2868 | 67 |
| 68 | 4.5405 1939 | 5.3607 1658 | 6.3265 1406 | 7.4633 0654 | 68 |
| 69 | 4.6426 8107 | 5.4947 3449 | 6.5004 9319 | 7.6872 0574 | 69 |
| 70 | 4.7471 4140 | 5.6321 0286 | 6.6792 5676 | 7.9178 2191 | 70 |
| 71 | 4.8539 5208 | 5.7729 0543 | 6.8629 3632 | 8.1553 5657 | 71 |
| 72 | 4.9631 6600 | 5.9172 2806 | 7.0516 6706 | 8.4000 1727 | 72 |
| 73 | 5.0748 3723 | 6.0651 5876 | 7.2455 8791 | 8.6520 1778 | 73 |
| 74 | 5.1890 2107 | 6.2167 8773 | 7.4448 4158 | 8.9115 7832 | 74 |
| 75 | 5.3057 7405 | 6.3722 0743 | 7.6495 7472 | 9.1789 2567 | 75 |
| 76 | 5.4251 5396 | 6.5315 1261 | 7.8599 3802 | 9.4542 9344 | 76 |
| 77 | 5.5472 1993 | 6.6948 0043 | 8.0760 8632 | 9.7379 2224 | 77 |
| 78 | 5.6720 3237 | 6.8621 7044 | 8.2981 7869 | 10.0300 5991 | 78 |
| 79 | 5.7996 5310 | 7.0337 2470 | 8.5263 7861 | 10.3309 6171 | 79 |
| 80 | 5.9301 4530 | 7.2095 6782 | 8.7608 5402 | 10.6408 9056 | 80 |
| 81 | 6.0635 7357 | 7.3898 0701 | 9.0017 7751 | 10.9601 1727 | 81 |
| 82 | 6.2000 0397 | 7.5745 5219 | 9.2493 2639 | 11.2889 2079 | 82 |
| 83 | 6.3395 0406 | 7.7639 1599 | 9.5036 8286 | 11.6275 8842 | 83 |
| 84 | 6.4821 4290 | 7.9580 1389 | 9.7650 3414 | 11.9764 1607 | 84 |
| 85 | 6.6279 9112 | 8.1569 6424 | 10.0335 7258 | 12.3357 0855 | 85 |
| 86 | 6.7771 2092 | 8.3608 8834 | 10.3094 9583 | 12.7057 7981 | 86 |
| 87 | 6.9296 0614 | 8.5699 1055 | 10.5930 0696 | 13.0869 5320 | 87 |
| 88 | 7.0855 2228 | 8.7841 5832 | 10.8843 1465 | 13.4795 6180 | 88 |
| 89 | 7.2449 4653 | 9.0037 6228 | 11.1836 3331 | 13.8839 4865 | 89 |
| 90 | 7.4079 5782 | 9.2288 5633 | 11.4911 8322 | 14.3004 6711 | 90 |
| 91 | 7.5746 3688 | 9.4595 7774 | 11.8071 9076 | 14.7294 8112 | 91 |
| 92 | 7.7450 6621 | 9.6960 6718 | 12.1318 8851 | 15.1713 6556 | 92 |
| 93 | 7.9193 3020 | 9.9384 6886 | 12.4655 1544 | 15.6265 0652 | 93 |
| 94 | 8.0975 1512 | 10.1869 3058 | 12.8083 1711 | 16.0953 0172 | 94 |
| 95 | 8.2797 0921 | 10.4416 0385 | 13.1605 4584 | 16.5781 6077 | 95 |
| 96 | 8.4660 0267 | 10.7026 4395 | 13.5224 6085 | 17.0755 0559 | 96 |
| 97 | 8.6564 8773 | 10.9702 1004 | 13.8943 2852 | 17.5877 7076 | 97 |
| 98 | 8.8512 5871 | 11.2444 6530 | 14.2764 2255 | 18.1154 0388 | 98 |
| 99 | 9.0504 1203 | 11.5255 7693 | 14.6690 2417 | 18.6588 6600 | 99 |
| 100 | 9.2540 4630 | 11.8137 1635 | 15.0724 2234 | 19.2186 3198 | 100 |

**TABLE  5**

$$s = (1 + i)^n$$

| n | $3\frac{1}{4}\%$ | $3\frac{1}{2}\%$ | $3\frac{3}{4}\%$ | 4% | n |
|---|---|---|---|---|---|
| 1 | 1.0325 0000 | 1.0350 0000 | 1.0375 0000 | 1.0400 0000 | 1 |
| 2 | 1.0660 5625 | 1.0712 2500 | 1.0764 0625 | 1.0816 0000 | 2 |
| 3 | 1.1007 0308 | 1.1087 1788 | 1.1167 7148 | 1.1248 6400 | 3 |
| 4 | 1.1364 7593 | 1.1475 2300 | 1.1586 5042 | 1.1698 5856 | 4 |
| 5 | 1.1734 1140 | 1.1876 8631 | 1.2020 9981 | 1.2166 5290 | 5 |
| 6 | 1.2115 4727 | 1.2292 5533 | 1.2471 7855 | 1.2653 1902 | 6 |
| 7 | 1.2509 2255 | 1.2722 7926 | 1.2939 4774 | 1.3159 3178 | 7 |
| 8 | 1.2915 7754 | 1.3168 0904 | 1.3424 7078 | 1.3685 6905 | 8 |
| 9 | 1.3335 5381 | 1.3628 9735 | 1.3928 1344 | 1.4233 1181 | 9 |
| 10 | 1.3768 9430 | 1.4105 9876 | 1.4450 4394 | 1.4802 4428 | 10 |
| 11 | 1.4216 4337 | 1.4599 6972 | 1.4992 3309 | 1.5394 5406 | 11 |
| 12 | 1.4678 4678 | 1.5110 6866 | 1.5554 5433 | 1.6010 3222 | 12 |
| 13 | 1.5155 5180 | 1.5639 5606 | 1.6137 8387 | 1.6650 7351 | 13 |
| 14 | 1.5648 0723 | 1.6186 9452 | 1.6743 0076 | 1.7316 7645 | 14 |
| 15 | 1.6156 6347 | 1.6753 4883 | 1.7370 8704 | 1.8009 4351 | 15 |
| 16 | 1.6681 7253 | 1.7339 8604 | 1.8022 2781 | 1.8729 8125 | 16 |
| 17 | 1.7223 8814 | 1.7946 7555 | 1.8698 1135 | 1.9479 0050 | 17 |
| 18 | 1.7783 6575 | 1.8574 8920 | 1.9399 2928 | 2.0258 1652 | 18 |
| 19 | 1.8361 6264 | 1.9225 0132 | 2.0126 7662 | 2.1068 4918 | 19 |
| 20 | 1.8958 3792 | 1.9897 8886 | 2.0881 5200 | 2.1911 2314 | 20 |
| 21 | 1.9574 5266 | 2.0594 3147 | 2.1664 5770 | 2.2787 6807 | 21 |
| 22 | 2.0210 6987 | 2.1315 1158 | 2.2476 9986 | 2.3699 1879 | 22 |
| 23 | 2.0867 5464 | 2.2061 1448 | 2.3319 8860 | 2.4647 1554 | 23 |
| 24 | 2.1545 7416 | 2.2833 2849 | 2.4194 3818 | 2.5633 0416 | 24 |
| 25 | 2.2245 9782 | 2.3632 4498 | 2.5101 6711 | 2.6658 3633 | 25 |
| 26 | 2.2968 9725 | 2.4459 5856 | 2.6042 9838 | 2.7724 6978 | 26 |
| 27 | 2.3715 4641 | 2.5315 6711 | 2.7019 5956 | 2.8833 6858 | 27 |
| 28 | 2.4486 2167 | 2.6201 7196 | 2.8032 8305 | 2.9987 0332 | 28 |
| 29 | 2.5282 0188 | 2.7118 7798 | 2.9084 0616 | 3.1186 5145 | 29 |
| 30 | 2.6103 6844 | 2.8067 9370 | 3.0174 7139 | 3.2433 9751 | 30 |
| 31 | 2.6952 0541 | 2.9050 3148 | 3.1306 2657 | 3.3731 3341 | 31 |
| 32 | 2.7827 9959 | 3.0067 0759 | 3.2480 2507 | 3.5080 5875 | 32 |
| 33 | 2.8732 4058 | 3.1119 4235 | 3.3698 2601 | 3.6483 8110 | 33 |
| 34 | 2.9666 2089 | 3.2208 6033 | 3.4961 9448 | 3.7943 1634 | 34 |
| 35 | 3.0630 3607 | 3.3335 9045 | 3.6273 0178 | 3.9460 8899 | 35 |
| 36 | 3.1625 8475 | 3.4502 6611 | 3.7633 2559 | 4.1039 3255 | 36 |
| 37 | 3.2653 6875 | 3.5710 2543 | 3.9044 5030 | 4.2680 8986 | 37 |
| 38 | 3.3714 9323 | 3.6960 1132 | 4.0508 6719 | 4.4388 1345 | 38 |
| 39 | 3.4810 6676 | 3.8253 7171 | 4.2027 7471 | 4.6163 6599 | 39 |
| 40 | 3.5942 0143 | 3.9592 5972 | 4.3603 7876 | 4.8010 2063 | 40 |
| 41 | 3.7110 1298 | 4.0978 3381 | 4.5238 9296 | 4.9930 6145 | 41 |
| 42 | 3.8316 2090 | 4.2412 5799 | 4.6935 3895 | 5.1927 8391 | 42 |
| 43 | 3.9561 4858 | 4.3897 0202 | 4.8695 4666 | 5.4004 9527 | 43 |
| 44 | 4.0847 2341 | 4.5433 4160 | 5.0521 5466 | 5.6165 1508 | 44 |
| 45 | 4.2174 7692 | 4.7023 5855 | 5.2416 1046 | 5.8411 7568 | 45 |
| 46 | 4.3545 4492 | 4.8669 4110 | 5.4381 7085 | 6.0748 2271 | 46 |
| 47 | 4.4960 6763 | 5.0372 8404 | 5.6421 0226 | 6.3178 1562 | 47 |
| 48 | 4.6421 8983 | 5.2135 8898 | 5.8536 8109 | 6.5705 2824 | 48 |
| 49 | 4.7930 6100 | 5.3960 6459 | 6.0731 9413 | 6.8333 4937 | 49 |
| 50 | 4.9488 3548 | 5.5849 2686 | 6.3009 3891 | 7.1066 8335 | 50 |

Table
5

# TABLE 5

$$s = (1 + i)^n$$

| $n$ | $3\frac{1}{4}\%$ | $3\frac{1}{2}\%$ | $3\frac{3}{4}\%$ | $4\%$ | $n$ |
|---|---|---|---|---|---|
| 51 | 5.1096 7263 | 5.7803 9930 | 6.5372 2412 | 7.3909 5068 | 51 |
| 52 | 5.2757 3700 | 5.9827 1327 | 6.7823 7003 | 7.6865 8871 | 52 |
| 53 | 5.4471 9845 | 6.1921 0824 | 7.0367 0890 | 7.9940 5226 | 53 |
| 54 | 5.6242 3240 | 6.4088 3202 | 7.3005 8549 | 8.3138 1435 | 54 |
| 55 | 5.8070 1995 | 6.6331 4114 | 7.5743 5744 | 8.6463 6692 | 55 |
| 56 | 5.9957 4810 | 6.8653 0108 | 7.8583 9585 | 8.9922 2160 | 56 |
| 57 | 6.1906 0991 | 7.1055 8662 | 8.1530 8569 | 9.3519 1046 | 57 |
| 58 | 6.3918 0473 | 7.3542 8215 | 8.4588 2640 | 9.7259 8688 | 58 |
| 59 | 6.5995 3839 | 7.6116 8203 | 8.7760 3239 | 10.1150 2635 | 59 |
| 60 | 6.8140 2339 | 7.8780 9090 | 9.1051 3361 | 10.5196 2741 | 60 |
| 61 | 7.0354 7915 | 8.1538 2408 | 9.4465 7612 | 10.9404 1250 | 61 |
| 62 | 7.2641 3222 | 8.4392 0793 | 9.8008 2272 | 11.3780 2900 | 62 |
| 63 | 7.5002 1651 | 8.7345 8020 | 10.1683 5358 | 11.8331 5016 | 63 |
| 64 | 7.7439 7355 | 9.0402 9051 | 10.5496 6684 | 12.3064 7617 | 64 |
| 65 | 7.9956 5269 | 9.3567 0068 | 10.9452 7934 | 12.7987 3522 | 65 |
| 66 | 8.2555 1140 | 9.6841 8520 | 11.3557 2732 | 13.3106 8463 | 66 |
| 67 | 8.5238 1552 | 10.0231 3168 | 11.7815 6709 | 13.8431 1201 | 67 |
| 68 | 8.8008 3953 | 10.3739 4129 | 12.2233 7586 | 14.3968 3649 | 68 |
| 69 | 9.0868 6681 | 10.7370 2924 | 12.6817 5245 | 14.9727 0995 | 69 |
| 70 | 9.3821 8999 | 11.1128 2526 | 13.1573 1817 | 15.5716 1835 | 70 |
| 71 | 9.6871 1116 | 11.5017 7414 | 13.6507 1760 | 16.1944 8308 | 71 |
| 72 | 10.0019 4227 | 11.9043 3624 | 14.1626 1951 | 16.8422 6241 | 72 |
| 73 | 10.3270 0540 | 12.3209 8801 | 14.6937 1774 | 17.5159 5290 | 73 |
| 74 | 10.6626 3307 | 12.7522 2259 | 15.2447 3216 | 18.2165 9102 | 74 |
| 75 | 11.0091 6865 | 13.1985 5038 | 15.8164 0961 | 18.9452 5466 | 75 |
| 76 | 11.3669 6663 | 13.6604 9964 | 16.4095 2497 | 19.7030 6485 | 76 |
| 77 | 11.7363 9304 | 14.1386 1713 | 17.0248 8216 | 20.4911 8744 | 77 |
| 78 | 12.1178 2582 | 14.6334 6873 | 17.6633 1524 | 21.3108 3494 | 78 |
| 79 | 12.5116 5516 | 15.1456 4014 | 18.3256 8956 | 22.1632 6834 | 79 |
| 80 | 12.9182 8395 | 15.6757 3754 | 19.0129 0292 | 23.0497 9907 | 80 |
| 81 | 13.3381 2818 | 16.2243 8835 | 19.7258 8678 | 23.9717 9103 | 81 |
| 82 | 13.7716 1734 | 16.7922 4195 | 20.4656 0754 | 24.9306 6267 | 82 |
| 83 | 14.2191 9491 | 17.3799 7041 | 21.2330 6782 | 25.9278 8918 | 83 |
| 84 | 14.6813 1874 | 17.9882 6938 | 22.0293 0786 | 26.9650 0475 | 84 |
| 85 | 15.1584 6160 | 18.6178 5881 | 22.8554 0691 | 28.0436 0494 | 85 |
| 86 | 15.6511 1160 | 19.2694 8387 | 23.7124 8467 | 29.1653 4914 | 86 |
| 87 | 16.1597 7273 | 19.9439 1580 | 24.6017 0284 | 30.3319 6310 | 87 |
| 88 | 16.6849 6534 | 20.6419 5285 | 25.5242 6670 | 31.5452 4163 | 88 |
| 89 | 17.2272 2672 | 21.3644 2120 | 26.4814 2670 | 32.8070 5129 | 89 |
| 90 | 17.7871 1159 | 22.1121 7595 | 27.4744 8020 | 34.1193 3334 | 90 |
| 91 | 18.3651 9271 | 22.8861 0210 | 28.5047 7321 | 35.4841 0668 | 91 |
| 92 | 18.9620 6147 | 23.6871 1568 | 29.5737 0220 | 36.9034 7094 | 92 |
| 93 | 19.5783 2847 | 24.5161 6473 | 30.6827 1603 | 38.3796 0978 | 93 |
| 94 | 20.2146 2415 | 25.3742 3049 | 31.8333 1789 | 39.9147 9417 | 94 |
| 95 | 20.8715 9943 | 26.2623 2856 | 33.0270 6731 | 41.5113 8594 | 95 |
| 96 | 21.5499 2641 | 27.1815 1006 | 34.2655 8233 | 43.1718 4138 | 96 |
| 97 | 22.2502 9902 | 28.1328 6291 | 35.5505 4167 | 44.8987 1503 | 97 |
| 98 | 22.9734 3374 | 29.1175 1311 | 36.8836 8698 | 46.6946 6363 | 98 |
| 99 | 23.7200 7034 | 30.1366 2607 | 38.2668 2524 | 48.5624 5018 | 99 |
| 100 | 24.4909 7262 | 31.1914 0798 | 39.7018 3119 | 50.5049 4818 | 100 |

**TABLE 5**

$$s = (1 + i)^n$$

| n | $4\frac{1}{2}\%$ | 5% | $5\frac{1}{2}\%$ | 6% | n |
|---|---|---|---|---|---|
| 1 | 1.0450 0000 | 1.0500 0000 | 1.0550 0000 | 1.0600 0000 | 1 |
| 2 | 1.0920 2500 | 1.1025 0000 | 1.1130 2500 | 1.1236 0000 | 2 |
| 3 | 1.1411 6613 | 1.1576 2500 | 1.1742 4138 | 1.1910 1600 | 3 |
| 4 | 1.1925 1860 | 1.2155 0625 | 1.2388 2465 | 1.2624 7696 | 4 |
| 5 | 1.2461 8194 | 1.2762 8156 | 1.3069 6001 | 1.3382 2558 | 5 |
| 6 | 1.3022 6012 | 1.3400 9564 | 1.3788 4281 | 1.4185 1911 | 6 |
| 7 | 1.3608 6183 | 1.4071 0042 | 1.4546 7916 | 1.5036 3026 | 7 |
| 8 | 1.4221 0061 | 1.4774 5544 | 1.5346 8652 | 1.5938 4807 | 8 |
| 9 | 1.4860 9514 | 1.5513 2822 | 1.6190 9427 | 1.6894 7896 | 9 |
| 10 | 1.5529 6942 | 1.6288 9463 | 1.7081 4446 | 1.7908 4770 | 10 |
| 11 | 1.6228 5305 | 1.7103 3936 | 1.8020 9240 | 1.8982 9856 | 11 |
| 12 | 1.6958 8143 | 1.7958 5633 | 1.9012 0749 | 2.0121 9647 | 12 |
| 13 | 1.7721 9610 | 1.8856 4914 | 2.0057 7390 | 2.1329 2826 | 13 |
| 14 | 1.8519 4492 | 1.9799 3160 | 2.1160 9146 | 2.2609 0396 | 14 |
| 15 | 1.9352 8244 | 2.0789 2818 | 2.2324 7649 | 2.3965 5819 | 15 |
| 16 | 2.0223 7015 | 2.1828 7459 | 2.3552 6270 | 2.5403 5168 | 16 |
| 17 | 2.1133 7681 | 2.2920 1832 | 2.4848 0215 | 2.6927 7279 | 17 |
| 18 | 2.2084 7877 | 2.4066 1923 | 2.6214 6627 | 2.8543 3915 | 18 |
| 19 | 2.3078 6031 | 2.5269 5020 | 2.7656 4691 | 3.0255 9950 | 19 |
| 20 | 2.4117 1402 | 2.6532 9771 | 2.9177 5749 | 3.2071 3547 | 20 |
| 21 | 2.5202 4116 | 2.7859 6259 | 3.0782 3415 | 3.3995 6360 | 21 |
| 22 | 2.6336 5201 | 2.9252 6072 | 3.2475 3703 | 3.6035 3742 | 22 |
| 23 | 2.7521 6635 | 3.0715 2376 | 3.4261 5157 | 3.8197 4966 | 23 |
| 24 | 2.8760 1383 | 3.2250 9994 | 3.6145 8990 | 4.0489 3464 | 24 |
| 25 | 3.0054 3446 | 3.3863 5494 | 3.8133 9235 | 4.2918 7072 | 25 |
| 26 | 3.1406 7901 | 3.5556 7269 | 4.0231 2893 | 4.5493 8296 | 26 |
| 27 | 3.2820 0956 | 3.7334 5632 | 4.2444 0102 | 4.8223 4594 | 27 |
| 28 | 3.4296 9999 | 3.9201 2914 | 4.4778 4307 | 5.1116 8670 | 28 |
| 29 | 3.5840 3649 | 4.1161 3560 | 4.7241 2444 | 5.4183 8790 | 29 |
| 30 | 3.7453 1813 | 4.3219 4238 | 4.9839 5129 | 5.7434 9117 | 30 |
| 31 | 3.9138 5745 | 4.5380 3949 | 5.2580 6861 | 6.0881 0064 | 31 |
| 32 | 4.0899 8104 | 4.7649 4147 | 5.5472 6238 | 6.4533 8668 | 32 |
| 33 | 4.2740 3018 | 5.0031 8854 | 5.8523 6181 | 6.8405 8988 | 33 |
| 34 | 4.4663 6154 | 5.2533 4797 | 6.1742 4171 | 7.2510 2528 | 34 |
| 35 | 4.6673 4781 | 5.5160 1537 | 6.5138 2501 | 7.6860 8679 | 35 |
| 36 | 4.8773 7846 | 5.7918 1614 | 6.8720 8538 | 8.1472 5200 | 36 |
| 37 | 5.0968 6049 | 6.0814 0694 | 7.2500 5008 | 8.6360 8712 | 37 |
| 38 | 5.3262 1921 | 6.3854 7729 | 7.6488 0283 | 9.1542 5235 | 38 |
| 39 | 5.5658 9908 | 6.7047 5115 | 8.0694 8699 | 9.7035 0749 | 39 |
| 40 | 5.8163 6454 | 7.0399 8871 | 8.5133 0877 | 10.2857 1794 | 40 |
| 41 | 6.0781 0094 | 7.3919 8815 | 8.9815 4076 | 10.9028 6101 | 41 |
| 42 | 6.3516 1548 | 7.7615 8756 | 9.4755 2550 | 11.5570 3267 | 42 |
| 43 | 6.6374 3818 | 8.1496 6693 | 9.9966 7940 | 12.2504 5463 | 43 |
| 44 | 6.9361 2290 | 8.5571 5028 | 10.5464 9677 | 12.9854 8191 | 44 |
| 45 | 7.2482 4843 | 8.9850 0779 | 11.1265 5409 | 13.7646 1083 | 45 |
| 46 | 7.5744 1961 | 9.4342 5818 | 11.7385 1456 | 14.5904 8748 | 46 |
| 47 | 7.9152 6849 | 9.9059 7109 | 12.3841 3287 | 15.4659 1673 | 47 |
| 48 | 8.2714 5557 | 10.4012 6965 | 13.0652 6017 | 16.3938 7173 | 48 |
| 49 | 8.6436 7107 | 10.9213 3313 | 13.7838 4948 | 17.3775 0403 | 49 |
| 50 | 9.0326 3627 | 11.4673 9979 | 14.5419 6120 | 18.4201 5428 | 50 |

Table
5

**TABLE 5**

$$s = (1 + i)^n$$

| $n$ | $4\frac{1}{2}\%$ | $5\%$ | $5\frac{1}{2}\%$ | $6\%$ | $n$ |
|---|---|---|---|---|---|
| 51 | 9.4391 0490 | 12.0407 6978 | 15.3417 6907 | 19.5253 6353 | 51 |
| 52 | 9.8638 6463 | 12.6428 0826 | 16.1855 6637 | 20.6968 8534 | 52 |
| 53 | 10.3077 3853 | 13.2749 4868 | 17.0757 7252 | 21.9386 9846 | 53 |
| 54 | 10.7715 8677 | 13.9386 9611 | 18.0149 4001 | 23.2550 2037 | 54 |
| 55 | 11.2563 0817 | 14.6356 3092 | 19.0057 6171 | 24.6503 2159 | 55 |
| 56 | 11.7628 4204 | 15.3674 1246 | 20.0510 7860 | 26.1293 4089 | 56 |
| 57 | 12.2921 6993 | 16.1357 8309 | 21.1538 8793 | 27.6971 0134 | 57 |
| 58 | 12.8453 1758 | 16.9425 7224 | 22.3173 5176 | 29.3589 2742 | 58 |
| 59 | 13.4233 5687 | 17.7897 0085 | 23.5448 0611 | 31.1204 6307 | 59 |
| 60 | 14.0274 0793 | 18.6791 8589 | 24.8397 7045 | 32.9876 9085 | 60 |
| 61 | 14.6586 4129 | 19.6131 4519 | 26.2059 5782 | 34.9669 5230 | 61 |
| 62 | 15.3182 8014 | 20.5938 0245 | 27.6472 8550 | 37.0649 6944 | 62 |
| 63 | 16.0076 0275 | 21.6234 9257 | 29.1678 8620 | 39.2888 6761 | 63 |
| 64 | 16.7279 4487 | 22.7046 6720 | 30.7721 1994 | 41.6461 9967 | 64 |
| 65 | 17.4807 0239 | 23.8399 0056 | 32.4645 8654 | 44.1449 7165 | 65 |
| 66 | 18.2673 3400 | 25.0318 9559 | 34.2501 3880 | 46.7936 6994 | 66 |
| 67 | 19.0893 6403 | 26.2834 9037 | 36.1338 9643 | 49.6012 9014 | 67 |
| 68 | 19.9483 8541 | 27.5976 6488 | 38.1212 6074 | 52.5773 6755 | 68 |
| 69 | 20.8460 6276 | 28.9775 4813 | 40.2179 3008 | 55.7320 0960 | 69 |
| 70 | 21.7841 3558 | 30.4264 2554 | 42.4299 1623 | 59.0759 3018 | 70 |
| 71 | 22.7644 2168 | 31.9477 4681 | 44.7635 6163 | 62.6204 8599 | 71 |
| 72 | 23.7888 2066 | 33.5451 3415 | 47.2255 5751 | 66.3777 1515 | 72 |
| 73 | 24.8593 1759 | 35.2223 9086 | 49.8229 6318 | 70.3603 7806 | 73 |
| 74 | 25.9779 8688 | 36.9835 1040 | 52.5632 2615 | 74.5820 0074 | 74 |
| 75 | 27.1469 9629 | 38.8326 8592 | 55.4542 0359 | 79.0569 2079 | 75 |
| 76 | 28.3686 1112 | 40.7743 2022 | 58.5041 8479 | 83.8003 3603 | 76 |
| 77 | 29.6451 9862 | 42.8130 3623 | 61.7219 1495 | 88.8283 5620 | 77 |
| 78 | 30.9792 3256 | 44.9536 8804 | 65.1166 2027 | 94.1580 5757 | 78 |
| 79 | 32.3732 9802 | 47.2013 7244 | 68.6980 3439 | 99.8075 4102 | 79 |
| 80 | 33.8300 9643 | 49.5614 4107 | 72.4764 2628 | 105.7959 9348 | 80 |
| 81 | 35.3524 5077 | 52.0395 1312 | 76.4626 2973 | 112.1437 5309 | 81 |
| 82 | 36.9433 1106 | 54.6414 8878 | 80.6680 7436 | 118.8723 7828 | 82 |
| 83 | 38.6057 6006 | 57.3735 6322 | 85.1048 1845 | 126.0047 2097 | 83 |
| 84 | 40.3430 1926 | 60.2422 4138 | 89.7855 8347 | 133.5650 0423 | 84 |
| 85 | 42.1584 5513 | 63.2543 5344 | 94.7237 9056 | 141.5789 0449 | 85 |
| 86 | 44.0555 8561 | 66.4170 7112 | 99.9335 9904 | 150.0736 3875 | 86 |
| 87 | 46.0380 8696 | 69.7379 2467 | 105.4299 4698 | 159.0780 5708 | 87 |
| 88 | 48.1098 0087 | 73.2248 2091 | 111.2285 9407 | 168.6227 4050 | 88 |
| 89 | 50.2747 4191 | 76.8860 6195 | 117.3461 6674 | 178.7401 0493 | 89 |
| 90 | 52.5371 0530 | 80.7303 6505 | 123.8002 0591 | 189.4645 1123 | 90 |
| 91 | 54.9012 7504 | 84.7668 8330 | 130.6092 1724 | 200.8323 8190 | 91 |
| 92 | 57.3718 3241 | 89.0052 2747 | 137.7927 2419 | 212.8823 2482 | 92 |
| 93 | 59.9535 6487 | 93.4554 8884 | 145.3713 2402 | 225.6552 6431 | 93 |
| 94 | 62.6514 7529 | 98.1282 6328 | 153.3667 4684 | 239.1945 8017 | 94 |
| 95 | 65.4707 9168 | 103.0346 7645 | 161.8019 1791 | 253.5462 5498 | 95 |
| 96 | 68.4169 7730 | 108.1864 1027 | 170.7010 2340 | 268.7590 3028 | 96 |
| 97 | 71.4957 4128 | 113.5957 3078 | 180.0895 7969 | 284.8845 7209 | 97 |
| 98 | 74.7130 4964 | 119.2755 1732 | 189.9945 0657 | 301.9776 4642 | 98 |
| 99 | 78.0751 3687 | 125.2392 9319 | 200.4442 0443 | 320.0963 0520 | 99 |
| 100 | 81.5885 1803 | 131.5012 5785 | 211.4686 3567 | 339.3020 8351 | 100 |

# TABLE 5

$$s = (1 + i)^n$$

| $n$ | $6\frac{1}{2}\%$ | $7\%$ | $7\frac{1}{2}\%$ | $8\%$ | $n$ |
|---|---|---|---|---|---|
| 1 | 1.0650 0000 | 1.0700 0000 | 1.0750 0000 | 1.0800 0000 | 1 |
| 2 | 1.1342 2500 | 1.1449 0000 | 1.1556 2500 | 1.1664 0000 | 2 |
| 3 | 1.2079 4963 | 1.2250 4300 | 1.2422 9688 | 1.2597 1200 | 3 |
| 4 | 1.2864 6635 | 1.3107 9601 | 1.3354 6914 | 1.3604 8896 | 4 |
| 5 | 1.3700 8666 | 1.4025 5173 | 1.4356 2933 | 1.4693 2808 | 5 |
| 6 | 1.4591 4230 | 1.5007 3035 | 1.5433 0153 | 1.5868 7432 | 6 |
| 7 | 1.5539 8655 | 1.6057 8148 | 1.6590 4914 | 1.7138 2427 | 7 |
| 8 | 1.6549 9567 | 1.7181 8618 | 1.7834 7783 | 1.8509 3021 | 8 |
| 9 | 1.7625 7039 | 1.8384 5921 | 1.9172 3866 | 1.9990 0463 | 9 |
| 10 | 1.8771 3747 | 1.9671 5136 | 2.0610 3156 | 2.1589 2500 | 10 |
| 11 | 1.9991 5140 | 2.1048 5195 | 2.2156 0893 | 2.3316 3900 | 11 |
| 12 | 2.1290 9624 | 2.2521 9159 | 2.3817 7960 | 2.5181 7012 | 12 |
| 13 | 2.2674 8750 | 2.4098 4500 | 2.5604 1307 | 2.7196 2373 | 13 |
| 14 | 2.4148 7418 | 2.5785 3415 | 2.7524 4405 | 2.9371 9362 | 14 |
| 15 | 2.5718 4101 | 2.7590 3154 | 2.9588 7735 | 3.1721 6911 | 15 |
| 16 | 2.7390 1067 | 2.9521 6375 | 3.1807 9315 | 3.4259 4264 | 16 |
| 17 | 2.9170 4637 | 3.1588 1521 | 3.4193 5264 | 3.7000 1805 | 17 |
| 18 | 3.1066 5438 | 3.3799 3228 | 3.6758 0409 | 3.9960 1950 | 18 |
| 19 | 3.3085 8691 | 3.6165 2754 | 3.9514 8940 | 4.3157 0106 | 19 |
| 20 | 3.5236 4506 | 3.8696 8446 | 4.2478 5110 | 4.6609 5714 | 20 |
| 21 | 3.7526 8199 | 4.1405 6237 | 4.5664 3993 | 5.0338 3372 | 21 |
| 22 | 3.9966 0632 | 4.4304 0174 | 4.9089 2293 | 5.4365 4041 | 22 |
| 23 | 4.2563 8573 | 4.7405 2986 | 5.2770 9215 | 5.8714 6365 | 23 |
| 24 | 4.5330 5081 | 5.0723 6695 | 5.6728 7406 | 6.3411 8074 | 24 |
| 25 | 4.8276 9911 | 5.4274 3264 | 6.0983 3961 | 6.8484 7520 | 25 |
| 26 | 5.1414 9955 | 5.8073 5292 | 6.5557 1508 | 7.3963 5321 | 26 |
| 27 | 5.4756 9702 | 6.2138 6763 | 7.0473 9371 | 7.9880 6147 | 27 |
| 28 | 5.8316 1733 | 6.6488 3836 | 7.5759 4824 | 8.6271 0639 | 28 |
| 29 | 6.2106 7245 | 7.1142 5705 | 8.1441 4436 | 9.3172 7490 | 29 |
| 30 | 6.6143 6616 | 7.6122 5504 | 8.7549 5519 | 10.0626 5689 | 30 |
| 31 | 7.0442 9996 | 8.1451 1290 | 9.4115 7683 | 10.8676 6944 | 31 |
| 32 | 7.5021 7946 | 8.7152 7080 | 10.1174 4509 | 11.7370 8300 | 32 |
| 33 | 7.9898 2113 | 9.3253 3975 | 10.8762 5347 | 12.6760 4964 | 33 |
| 34 | 8.5091 5950 | 9.9781 1354 | 11.6919 7248 | 13.6901 3361 | 34 |
| 35 | 9.0622 5487 | 10.6765 8148 | 12.5688 7042 | 14.7853 4429 | 35 |
| 36 | 9.6513 0143 | 11.4239 4219 | 13.5115 3570 | 15.9681 7184 | 36 |
| 37 | 10.2786 3603 | 12.2236 1814 | 14.5249 0088 | 17.2456 2558 | 37 |
| 38 | 10.9467 4737 | 13.0792 7141 | 15.6142 6844 | 18.6252 7563 | 38 |
| 39 | 11.6582 8595 | 13.9948 2041 | 16.7853 3858 | 20.1152 9768 | 39 |
| 40 | 12.4160 7453 | 14.9744 5784 | 18.0442 3897 | 21.7245 2150 | 40 |
| 41 | 13.2231 1938 | 16.0226 6989 | 19.3975 5689 | 23.4624 8322 | 41 |
| 42 | 14.0826 2214 | 17.1442 5678 | 20.8523 7366 | 25.3394 8187 | 42 |
| 43 | 14.9979 9258 | 18.3443 5475 | 22.4163 0168 | 27.3666 4042 | 43 |
| 44 | 15.9728 6209 | 19.6284 5959 | 24.0975 2431 | 29.5559 7166 | 44 |
| 45 | 17.0110 9813 | 21.0024 5176 | 25.9048 3863 | 31.9204 4939 | 45 |
| 46 | 18.1168 1951 | 22.4726 2338 | 27.8477 0153 | 34.4740 8534 | 46 |
| 47 | 19.2944 1278 | 24.0457 0702 | 29.9362 7915 | 37.2320 1217 | 47 |
| 48 | 20.5485 4961 | 25.7289 0651 | 32.1815 0008 | 40.2105 7314 | 48 |
| 49 | 21.8842 0533 | 27.5299 2997 | 34.5951 1259 | 43.4274 1899 | 49 |
| 50 | 23.3066 7868 | 29.4570 2506 | 37.1897 4603 | 46.9016 1251 | 50 |

Table
5

# TABLE 5

$$s=(1+i)^n$$

| $n$ | $6\frac{1}{2}\%$ | $7\%$ | $7\frac{1}{2}\%$ | $8\%$ | $n$ |
|---|---|---|---|---|---|
| 51 | 24.8216 1279 | 31.5190 1682 | 39.9789 7698 | 50.6537 4151 | 51 |
| 52 | 26.4350 1762 | 33.7253 4799 | 42.9774 0026 | 54.7060 4084 | 52 |
| 53 | 28.1532 9377 | 36.0861 2235 | 46.2007 0528 | 59.0825 2410 | 53 |
| 54 | 29.9832 5786 | 38.6121 5092 | 49.6657 5817 | 63.8091 2603 | 54 |
| 55 | 31.9321 6963 | 41.3150 0148 | 53.3906 9004 | 68.9138 5611 | 55 |
| 56 | 34.0077 6065 | 44.2070 5159 | 57.3949 9179 | 74.4269 6460 | 56 |
| 57 | 36.2182 6509 | 47.3015 4520 | 61.6996 1617 | 80.3811 2177 | 57 |
| 58 | 38.5724 5233 | 50.6126 5336 | 66.3270 8739 | 86.8116 1151 | 58 |
| 59 | 41.0796 6173 | 54.1555 3910 | 71.3016 1894 | 93.7565 4043 | 59 |
| 60 | 43.7498 3974 | 57.9464 2683 | 76.6492 4036 | 101.2570 6367 | 60 |
| 61 | 46.5935 7932 | 62.0026 7671 | 82.3979 3339 | 109.3576 2876 | 61 |
| 62 | 49.6221 6198 | 66.3428 6408 | 88.5777 7839 | 118.1062 3906 | 62 |
| 63 | 52.8476 0251 | 70.9868 6457 | 95.2211 1177 | 127.5547 3819 | 63 |
| 64 | 56.2826 9667 | 75.9559 4509 | 102.3626 9515 | 137.7591 1724 | 64 |
| 65 | 59.9410 7195 | 81.2728 6124 | 110.0398 9729 | 148.7798 4662 | 65 |
| 66 | 63.8372 4163 | 86.9619 6153 | 118.2928 8959 | 160.6822 3435 | 66 |
| 67 | 67.9866 6234 | 93.0492 9884 | 127.1648 5631 | 173.5368 1310 | 67 |
| 68 | 72.4057 9539 | 99.5627 4976 | 136.7022 2053 | 187.4197 5815 | 68 |
| 69 | 77.1121 7209 | 106.5321 4224 | 146.9548 8707 | 202.4133 3880 | 69 |
| 70 | 82.1244 6327 | 113.9893 9220 | 157.9756 0360 | 218.6064 0590 | 70 |
| 71 | 87.4625 5339 | 121.9686 4965 | 169.8247 4137 | 236.0949 1837 | 71 |
| 72 | 93.1476 1936 | 130.5064 5513 | 182.5615 9697 | 254.9825 1184 | 72 |
| 73 | 99.2022 1461 | 139.6419 0699 | 196.2537 1675 | 275.3811 1279 | 73 |
| 74 | 105.6503 5856 | 149.4168 4048 | 210.9727 4550 | 297.4116 0181 | 74 |
| 75 | 112.5176 3187 | 159.8760 1931 | 226.7957 0141 | 321.2045 2996 | 75 |
| 76 | 119.8312 7794 | 171.0673 4066 | 243.8053 7902 | 346.9008 9236 | 76 |
| 77 | 127.6203 1101 | 183.0420 5451 | 262.0907 8245 | 374.6529 6374 | 77 |
| 78 | 135.9156 3122 | 195.8549 9832 | 281.7475 9113 | 404.6252 0084 | 78 |
| 79 | 144.7501 4725 | 209.5648 4820 | 302.8786 6046 | 436.9952 1691 | 79 |
| 80 | 154.1589 0683 | 224.2343 8758 | 325.5945 6000 | 471.9548 3426 | 80 |
| 81 | 164.1792 3577 | 239.9307 9471 | 350.0141 5200 | 509.7112 2101 | 81 |
| 82 | 174.8508 8609 | 256.7259 5034 | 376.2652 1340 | 550.4881 1869 | 82 |
| 83 | 186.2161 9369 | 274.6967 6686 | 404.4851 0440 | 594.5271 6818 | 83 |
| 84 | 198.3202 4628 | 293.9255 4054 | 434.8214 8723 | 642.0893 4164 | 84 |
| 85 | 211.2110 6229 | 314.5003 2838 | 467.4330 9878 | 693.4564 8897 | 85 |
| 86 | 224.9397 8134 | 336.5153 5137 | 502.4905 8119 | 748.9330 0808 | 86 |
| 87 | 239.5608 6712 | 360.0714 2596 | 540.1773 7477 | 808.8476 4873 | 87 |
| 88 | 255.1323 2349 | 385.2764 2578 | 580.6906 7788 | 873.5554 6063 | 88 |
| 89 | 271.7159 2451 | 412.2457 7558 | 624.2424 7872 | 943.4398 9748 | 89 |
| 90 | 289.3774 5961 | 441.1029 7988 | 671.0606 6463 | 1018.9150 8928 | 90 |
| 91 | 308.1869 9448 | 471.9801 8847 | 721.3902 1447 | 1100.4282 9642 | 91 |
| 92 | 328.2191 4912 | 505.0188 0166 | 775.4944 8056 | 1188.4625 6013 | 92 |
| 93 | 349.5533 9382 | 540.3701 1778 | 833.6565 6660 | 1283.5395 6494 | 93 |
| 94 | 372.2743 6441 | 578.1960 2602 | 896.1808 0910 | 1386.2227 3014 | 94 |
| 95 | 396.4721 9810 | 618.6697 4784 | 963.3943 6978 | 1497.1205 4855 | 95 |
| 96 | 422.2428 9098 | 661.9766 3019 | 1035.6489 4751 | 1616.8901 9244 | 96 |
| 97 | 449.6886 7889 | 708.3149 9430 | 1113.3226 1858 | 1746.2414 0783 | 97 |
| 98 | 478.9184 4302 | 757.8970 4390 | 1196.8218 1497 | 1885.9407 2046 | 98 |
| 99 | 510.0481 4181 | 810.9498 3698 | 1286.5834 5109 | 2036.8159 7809 | 99 |
| 100 | 543.2012 7103 | 867.7163 2557 | 1383.0772 0993 | 2199.7612 5634 | 100 |

# TABLE  5

$$s = (1 + i)^n$$

| $n$ | $8\frac{1}{2}\%$ | 9% | $9\frac{1}{2}\%$ | 10% | $n$ |
|---|---|---|---|---|---|
| 1 | 1.0850 0000 | 1.0900 0000 | 1.0950 0000 | 1.1000 0000 | 1 |
| 2 | 1.1772 2500 | 1.1881 0000 | 1.1990 2500 | 1.2100 0000 | 2 |
| 3 | 1.2772 8913 | 1.2950 2900 | 1.3129 3238 | 1.3310 0000 | 3 |
| 4 | 1.3858 5870 | 1.4115 8161 | 1.4376 6095 | 1.4641 0000 | 4 |
| 5 | 1.5036 5669 | 1.5386 2395 | 1.5742 3874 | 1.6105 1000 | 5 |
| 6 | 1.6314 6751 | 1.6771 0011 | 1.7237 9142 | 1.7715 6100 | 6 |
| 7 | 1.7701 4225 | 1.8280 3912 | 1.8875 5161 | 1.9487 1710 | 7 |
| 8 | 1.9206 0434 | 1.9925 6264 | 2.0668 6901 | 2.1435 8881 | 8 |
| 9 | 2.0838 5571 | 2.1718 9328 | 2.2632 2156 | 2.3579 4769 | 9 |
| 10 | 2.2609 8344 | 2.3673 6367 | 2.4782 2761 | 2.5937 4246 | 10 |
| 11 | 2.4531 6703 | 2.5804 2641 | 2.7136 5924 | 2.8531 1671 | 11 |
| 12 | 2.6616 8623 | 2.8126 6478 | 2.9714 5686 | 3.1384 2838 | 12 |
| 13 | 2.8879 2956 | 3.0658 0461 | 3.2537 4527 | 3.4522 7121 | 13 |
| 14 | 3.1334 0357 | 3.3417 2703 | 3.5628 5107 | 3.7974 9834 | 14 |
| 15 | 3.3997 4288 | 3.6424 8246 | 3.9013 2192 | 4.1772 4817 | 15 |
| 16 | 3.6887 2102 | 3.9703 0588 | 4.2719 4750 | 4.5949 7299 | 16 |
| 17 | 4.0022 6231 | 4.3276 3341 | 4.6777 8251 | 5.0544 7029 | 17 |
| 18 | 4.3424 5461 | 4.7171 2042 | 5.1221 7185 | 5.5599 1731 | 18 |
| 19 | 4.7115 6325 | 5.1416 6125 | 5.6087 7818 | 6.1159 0904 | 19 |
| 20 | 5.1120 4612 | 5.6044 1077 | 6.1416 1210 | 6.7274 9995 | 20 |
| 21 | 5.5465 7005 | 6.1088 0774 | 6.7250 6525 | 7.4002 4994 | 21 |
| 22 | 6.0180 2850 | 6.6586 0043 | 7.3639 4645 | 8.1402 7494 | 22 |
| 23 | 6.5295 6092 | 7.2578 7447 | 8.0635 2137 | 8.9543 0243 | 23 |
| 24 | 7.0845 7360 | 7.9110 8317 | 8.8295 5590 | 9.8497 3268 | 24 |
| 25 | 7.6867 6236 | 8.6230 8066 | 9.6683 6371 | 10.8347 0594 | 25 |
| 26 | 8.3401 3716 | 9.3991 5792 | 10.5868 5826 | 11.9181 7654 | 26 |
| 27 | 9.0490 4881 | 10.2450 8213 | 11.5926 0979 | 13.1099 9419 | 27 |
| 28 | 9.8182 1796 | 11.1671 3952 | 12.6939 0772 | 14.4209 9361 | 28 |
| 29 | 10.6527 6649 | 12.1721 8208 | 13.8998 2896 | 15.8630 9297 | 29 |
| 30 | 11.5582 5164 | 13.2676 7847 | 15.2203 1271 | 17.4494 0227 | 30 |
| 31 | 12.5407 0303 | 14.4617 6953 | 16.6662 4241 | 19.1943 4250 | 31 |
| 32 | 13.6066 6279 | 15.7633 2879 | 18.2495 3544 | 21.1137 7675 | 32 |
| 33 | 14.7632 2913 | 17.1820 2838 | 19.9832 4131 | 23.2251 5442 | 33 |
| 34 | 16.0181 0360 | 18.7284 1093 | 21.8816 4924 | 25.5476 6986 | 34 |
| 35 | 17.3796 4241 | 20.4139 6792 | 23.9604 0591 | 28.1024 3685 | 35 |
| 36 | 18.8569 1201 | 22.2512 2503 | 26.2366 4448 | 30.9126 8053 | 36 |
| 37 | 20.4597 4953 | 24.2538 3528 | 28.7291 2570 | 34.0039 4859 | 37 |
| 38 | 22.1988 2824 | 26.4366 8046 | 31.4583 9264 | 37.4043 4344 | 38 |
| 39 | 24.0857 2865 | 28.8159 8170 | 34.4469 3994 | 41.1447 7779 | 39 |
| 40 | 26.1330 1558 | 31.4094 2005 | 37.7193 9924 | 45.2592 5557 | 40 |
| 41 | 28.3543 2190 | 34.2362 6786 | 41.3027 4216 | 49.7851 8113 | 41 |
| 42 | 30.7644 3927 | 37.3175 3197 | 45.2265 0267 | 54.7636 9924 | 42 |
| 43 | 33.3794 1660 | 40.6761 0984 | 49.5230 2042 | 60.2400 6916 | 43 |
| 44 | 36.2166 6702 | 44.3369 5973 | 54.2277 0736 | 66.2640 7608 | 44 |
| 45 | 39.2950 8371 | 48.3272 8610 | 59.3793 3956 | 72.8904 8369 | 45 |
| 46 | 42.6351 6583 | 52.6767 4185 | 65.0203 7682 | 80.1795 3205 | 46 |
| 47 | 46.2591 5492 | 57.4176 4862 | 71.1973 1262 | 88.1974 8526 | 47 |
| 48 | 50.1911 8309 | 62.5852 3700 | 77.9610 5732 | 97.0172 3378 | 48 |
| 49 | 54.4574 3365 | 68.2179 0833 | 85.3673 5777 | 106.7189 5716 | 49 |
| 50 | 59.0863 1551 | 74.3575 2008 | 93.4772 5675 | 117.3908 5288 | 50 |

Table
5

**TABLE 5**

$$s = (1 + i)^n$$

| $n$ | $8\frac{1}{2}\%$ | 9% | $9\frac{1}{2}\%$ | 10% | $n$ |
|---|---|---|---|---|---|
| 51 | 64.1086 5233 | 81.0496 9688 | 102.3575 9614 | 129.1299 3817 | 51 |
| 52 | 69.5578 8778 | 88.3441 6960 | 112.0815 6778 | 142.0429 3198 | 52 |
| 53 | 75.4703 0824 | 96.2951 4487 | 122.7293 1672 | 156.2472 2518 | 53 |
| 54 | 81.8852 8444 | 104.9617 0790 | 134.3886 0181 | 171.8719 4770 | 54 |
| 55 | 88.8455 3362 | 114.4082 6162 | 147.1555 1898 | 189.0591 4247 | 55 |
| 56 | 96.3974 0398 | 124.7050 0516 | 161.1352 9328 | 207.9650 5672 | 56 |
| 57 | 104.5911 8332 | 135.9284 5563 | 176.4431 4614 | 228.7615 6239 | 57 |
| 58 | 113.4814 3390 | 148.1620 1663 | 193.2052 4502 | 251.6377 1863 | 58 |
| 59 | 123.1273 5578 | 161.4965 9813 | 211.5597 4330 | 276.8014 9049 | 59 |
| 60 | 133.5931 8102 | 176.0312 9196 | 231.6579 1892 | 304.4816 3954 | 60 |
| 61 | 144.9486 0141 | 191.8741 0824 | 253.6654 2121 | 334.9298 0350 | 61 |
| 62 | 157.2692 3253 | 209.1427 7798 | 277.7636 3623 | 368.4227 8385 | 62 |
| 63 | 170.6371 1729 | 227.9656 2800 | 304.1511 8167 | 405.2650 6223 | 63 |
| 64 | 185.1412 7226 | 248.4825 3452 | 333.0455 4393 | 445.7915 6845 | 64 |
| 65 | 200.8782 8041 | 270.8459 6262 | 364.6848 7060 | 490.3707 2530 | 65 |
| 66 | 217.9529 3424 | 295.2220 9926 | 399.3299 3331 | 539.4077 9783 | 66 |
| 67 | 236.4789 3365 | 321.7920 8819 | 437.2662 7697 | 593.3485 7761 | 67 |
| 68 | 256.5796 4301 | 350.7533 7613 | 478.8065 7329 | 652.6834 3537 | 68 |
| 69 | 278.3889 1267 | 382.3211 7998 | 524.2931 9775 | 717.9517 7891 | 69 |
| 70 | 302.0519 7024 | 416.7300 8618 | 574.1010 5153 | 789.7469 5680 | 70 |
| 71 | 327.7263 8771 | 454.2357 9393 | 628.6406 5143 | 868.7216 5248 | 71 |
| 72 | 355.5831 3067 | 495.1170 1539 | 688.3615 1331 | 955.5938 1773 | 72 |
| 73 | 385.8076 9678 | 539.6775 4677 | 753.7558 5708 | 1051.1531 9950 | 73 |
| 74 | 418.6013 5100 | 588.2485 2598 | 825.3626 6350 | 1156.2685 1945 | 74 |
| 75 | 454.1824 6584 | 641.1908 9332 | 903.7721 1654 | 1271.8953 7140 | 75 |
| 76 | 492.7879 7543 | 698.8980 7372 | 989.6304 6761 | 1399.0849 0853 | 76 |
| 77 | 534.6749 5335 | 761.7989 0036 | 1083.6453 6203 | 1538.9933 9939 | 77 |
| 78 | 580.1223 2438 | 830.3608 0139 | 1186.5916 7142 | 1692.8927 3933 | 78 |
| 79 | 629.4327 2195 | 905.0932 7351 | 1299.3178 8021 | 1862.1820 1326 | 79 |
| 80 | 682.9345 0332 | 986.5516 6813 | 1422.7530 7883 | 2048.4002 1459 | 80 |
| 81 | 740.9839 3610 | 1075.3413 1826 | 1557.9146 2131 | 2253.2402 3604 | 81 |
| 82 | 803.9675 7067 | 1172.1220 3690 | 1705.9165 1034 | 2478.5642 5965 | 82 |
| 83 | 872.3048 1418 | 1277.6130 2022 | 1867.9785 7882 | 2726.4206 8561 | 83 |
| 84 | 946.4507 2338 | 1392.5981 9204 | 2045.4365 4381 | 2999.0627 5417 | 84 |
| 85 | 1026.8990 3487 | 1517.9320 2933 | 2239.7530 1547 | 3298.9690 2959 | 85 |
| 86 | 1114.1854 5283 | 1654.5459 1197 | 2452.5295 5194 | 3628.8659 3255 | 86 |
| 87 | 1208.8912 1633 | 1803.4550 4404 | 2685.5198 5938 | 3991.7525 2581 | 87 |
| 88 | 1311.6469 6971 | 1965.7659 9801 | 2940.6442 4602 | 4390.9277 7839 | 88 |
| 89 | 1423.1369 6214 | 2142.6849 3783 | 3220.0054 4939 | 4830.0205 5623 | 89 |
| 90 | 1544.1036 0392 | 2335.5265 8223 | 3525.9059 6708 | 5313.0226 1185 | 90 |
| 91 | 1675.3524 1025 | 2545.7239 7464 | 3860.8670 3395 | 5844.3248 7303 | 91 |
| 92 | 1817.7573 6512 | 2774.8391 3235 | 4227.6494 0218 | 6428.7573 6034 | 92 |
| 93 | 1972.2667 4116 | 3024.5746 5426 | 4629.2760 9538 | 7071.6330 9637 | 93 |
| 94 | 2139.9094 1416 | 3296.7863 7315 | 5069.0573 2445 | 7778.7964 0601 | 94 |
| 95 | 2321.8017 1436 | 3593.4971 4673 | 5550.6177 7027 | 8556.6760 4661 | 95 |
| 96 | 2519.1548 6008 | 3916.9118 8994 | 6077.9264 5844 | 9412.3436 5127 | 96 |
| 97 | 2733.2830 2319 | 4269.4339 6003 | 6655.3294 7199 | 10353.5780 1640 | 97 |
| 98 | 2965.6120 8016 | 4653.6830 1643 | 7287.5857 7183 | 11388.9358 1803 | 98 |
| 99 | 3217.6891 0698 | 5072.5144 8791 | 7979.9064 2016 | 12527.8293 9984 | 99 |
| 100 | 3491.1926 8107 | 5529.0407 9183 | 8737.9975 3007 | 13780.6123 3982 | 100 |

# TABLE 5A

$$s = (1+i)^{\frac{1}{m}}$$

| $m$ | $\frac{1}{4}$% | $\frac{1}{3}$% | $\frac{5}{12}$% | $\frac{11}{24}$% | $\frac{1}{2}$% | $m$ |
|---|---|---|---|---|---|---|
| 2 | 1.0012 4922 | 1.0016 6528 | 1.0020 8117 | 1.0022 8905 | 1.0024 9688 | 2 |
| 3 | 1.0008 3264 | 1.0011 0988 | 1.0013 8696 | 1.0015 2545 | 1.0016 6390 | 3 |
| 4 | 1.0006 2441 | 1.0008 3229 | 1.0010 4004 | 1.0011 4387 | 1.0012 4766 | 4 |
| 6 | 1.0004 1623 | 1.0005 5479 | 1.0006 9324 | 1.0007 6243 | 1.0008 3160 | 6 |
| 12 | 1.0002 0809 | 1.0002 7735 | 1.0003 4656 | 1.0003 8114 | 1.0004 1571 | 12 |

| $m$ | $\frac{13}{24}$% | $\frac{7}{12}$% | $\frac{5}{8}$% | $\frac{2}{3}$% | $\frac{3}{4}$% | $m$ |
|---|---|---|---|---|---|---|
| 2 | 1.0027 0468 | 1.0029 1243 | 1.0031 2013 | 1.0033 2780 | 1.0037 4299 | 2 |
| 3 | 1.0018 0231 | 1.0019 4068 | 1.0020 7901 | 1.0022 1730 | 1.0024 9378 | 3 |
| 4 | 1.0013 5142 | 1.0014 5515 | 1.0015 5885 | 1.0016 6252 | 1.0018 6975 | 4 |
| 6 | 1.0009 0075 | 1.0009 6987 | 1.0010 3896 | 1.0011 0804 | 1.0012 4611 | 6 |
| 12 | 1.0004 5027 | 1.0004 8482 | 1.0005 1935 | 1.0005 5387 | 1.0006 2286 | 12 |

| $m$ | $\frac{7}{8}$% | 1% | $1\frac{1}{8}$% | $1\frac{1}{4}$% | $1\frac{3}{8}$% | $m$ |
|---|---|---|---|---|---|---|
| 2 | 1.0043 6547 | 1.0049 8756 | 1.0056 0927 | 1.0062 3059 | 1.0068 5153 | 2 |
| 3 | 1.0029 0820 | 1.0033 2228 | 1.0037 3602 | 1.0041 4943 | 1.0045 6249 | 3 |
| 4 | 1.0021 8036 | 1.0024 9068 | 1.0028 0071 | 1.0031 1046 | 1.0034 1992 | 4 |
| 6 | 1.0014 5304 | 1.0016 5976 | 1.0018 6627 | 1.0020 7256 | 1.0022 7865 | 6 |
| 12 | 1.0007 2626 | 1.0008 2954 | 1.0009 3270 | 1.0010 3575 | 1.0011 3868 | 12 |

| $m$ | $1\frac{1}{2}$% | $1\frac{5}{8}$% | $1\frac{3}{4}$% | $1\frac{7}{8}$% | 2% | $m$ |
|---|---|---|---|---|---|---|
| 2 | 1.0074 7208 | 1.0080 9226 | 1.0087 1205 | 1.0093 3146 | 1.0099 5049 | 2 |
| 3 | 1.0049 7521 | 1.0053 8759 | 1.0057 9963 | 1.0062 1134 | 1.0066 2271 | 3 |
| 4 | 1.0037 2909 | 1.0040 3798 | 1.0043 4658 | 1.0046 5490 | 1.0049 6293 | 4 |
| 6 | 1.0024 8452 | 1.0026 9018 | 1.0028 9562 | 1.0031 0086 | 1.0033 0589 | 6 |
| 12 | 1.0012 4149 | 1.0013 4418 | 1.0014 4677 | 1.0015 4923 | 1.0016 5158 | 12 |

| $m$ | $2\frac{1}{4}$% | $2\frac{1}{2}$% | $2\frac{3}{4}$% | 3% | $3\frac{1}{4}$% | $m$ |
|---|---|---|---|---|---|---|
| 2 | 1.0111 8742 | 1.0124 2284 | 1.0136 5675 | 1.0148 8916 | 1.0161 2007 | 2 |
| 3 | 1.0074 4444 | 1.0082 6484 | 1.0090 8390 | 1.0099 0163 | 1.0107 1805 | 3 |
| 4 | 1.0055 7815 | 1.0061 9225 | 1.0068 0522 | 1.0074 1707 | 1.0080 2781 | 4 |
| 6 | 1.0037 1532 | 1.0041 2392 | 1.0045 3168 | 1.0049 3862 | 1.0053 4474 | 6 |
| 12 | 1.0018 5594 | 1.0020 5984 | 1.0022 6328 | 1.0024 6627 | 1.0026 6881 | 12 |

| $m$ | $3\frac{1}{2}$% | $3\frac{3}{4}$% | 4% | $4\frac{1}{2}$% | 5% | $m$ |
|---|---|---|---|---|---|---|
| 2 | 1.0173 4950 | 1.0185 7744 | 1.0198 0390 | 1.0222 5242 | 1.0246 9508 | 2 |
| 3 | 1.0115 3314 | 1.0123 4693 | 1.0131 5940 | 1.0147 8046 | 1.0163 9636 | 3 |
| 4 | 1.0086 3745 | 1.0092 4598 | 1.0098 5341 | 1.0110 6499 | 1.0122 7223 | 4 |
| 6 | 1.0057 5004 | 1.0061 5452 | 1.0065 5820 | 1.0073 6312 | 1.0081 6485 | 6 |
| 12 | 1.0028 7090 | 1.0030 7254 | 1.0032 7374 | 1.0036 7481 | 1.0040 7412 | 12 |

Table
5A

## TABLE 5A

For Fractional Interest Periods

$$s = (1 + i)^{\frac{1}{m}}$$

| $m$ | $5\frac{1}{2}\%$ | 6% | $6\frac{1}{2}\%$ | 7% | $7\frac{1}{2}\%$ | $m$ |
|---|---|---|---|---|---|---|
| 2 | 1.0271 3193 | 1.0295 6301 | 1.0319 8837 | 1.0344 0804 | 1.0368 2207 | 2 |
| 3 | 1.0180 0713 | 1.0196 1282 | 1.0212 1347 | 1.0228 0912 | 1.0243 9981 | 3 |
| 4 | 1.0134 7517 | 1.0146 7385 | 1.0158 6828 | 1.0170 5853 | 1.0182 4460 | 4 |
| 6 | 1.0089 6339 | 1.0097 5879 | 1.0105 5107 | 1.0113 4026 | 1.0121 2638 | 6 |
| 12 | 1.0044 7170 | 1.0048 6755 | 1.0052 6169 | 1.0056 5415 | 1.0060 4492 | 12 |

| $m$ | 8% | $8\frac{1}{2}\%$ | 9% | $9\frac{1}{2}\%$ | 10% | $m$ |
|---|---|---|---|---|---|---|
| 2 | 1.0392 3048 | 1.0416 3333 | 1.0440 3065 | 1.0464 2248 | 1.0488 0885 | 2 |
| 3 | 1.0259 8557 | 1.0275 6644 | 1.0291 4247 | 1.0307 1368 | 1.0322 8012 | 3 |
| 4 | 1.0194 2655 | 1.0206 0440 | 1.0217 7818 | 1.0229 4793 | 1.0241 1369 | 4 |
| 6 | 1.0129 0946 | 1.0136 8952 | 1.0144 6659 | 1.0152 4070 | 1.0160 1187 | 6 |
| 12 | 1.0064 3403 | 1.0068 2149 | 1.0072 0732 | 1.0075 9153 | 1.0079 7414 | 12 |

# TABLE 6

$$p = (1 + i)^{-n} \quad [OR, \; v^n = (1 + i)^{-n}]$$

| n | $\frac{1}{4}$% | $\frac{1}{3}$% | $\frac{5}{12}$% | $\frac{11}{24}$% | n |
|---|---|---|---|---|---|
| 1 | 0.9975 0623 | 0.9966 7774 | 0.9958 5062 | 0.9954 3758 | 1 |
| 2 | 0.9950 1869 | 0.9933 6652 | 0.9917 1846 | 0.9908 9597 | 2 |
| 3 | 0.9925 3734 | 0.9900 6630 | 0.9876 0345 | 0.9863 7509 | 3 |
| 4 | 0.9900 6219 | 0.9867 7704 | 0.9835 0551 | 0.9818 7483 | 4 |
| 5 | 0.9875 9321 | 0.9834 9871 | 0.9794 2457 | 0.9773 9510 | 5 |
| 6 | 0.9851 3038 | 0.9802 3127 | 0.9753 6057 | 0.9729 3581 | 6 |
| 7 | 0.9826 7370 | 0.9769 7469 | 0.9713 1343 | 0.9684 9687 | 7 |
| 8 | 0.9802 2314 | 0.9737 2893 | 0.9672 8308 | 0.9640 7817 | 8 |
| 9 | 0.9777 7869 | 0.9704 9395 | 0.9632 6946 | 0.9596 7964 | 9 |
| 10 | 0.9753 4034 | 0.9672 6972 | 0.9592 7249 | 0.9553 0118 | 10 |
| 11 | 0.9729 0807 | 0.9640 5620 | 0.9552 9211 | 0.9509 4269 | 11 |
| 12 | 0.9704 8187 | 0.9608 5335 | 0.9513 2824 | 0.9466 0409 | 12 |
| 13 | 0.9680 6171 | 0.9576 6115 | 0.9473 8082 | 0.9422 8528 | 13 |
| 14 | 0.9656 4759 | 0.9544 7955 | 0.9434 4978 | 0.9379 8618 | 14 |
| 15 | 0.9632 3949 | 0.9513 0852 | 0.9395 3505 | 0.9337 0669 | 15 |
| 16 | 0.9608 3740 | 0.9481 4803 | 0.9356 3657 | 0.9294 4672 | 16 |
| 17 | 0.9584 4130 | 0.9449 9803 | 0.9317 5426 | 0.9252 0620 | 17 |
| 18 | 0.9560 5117 | 0.9418 5851 | 0.9278 8806 | 0.9209 8502 | 18 |
| 19 | 0.9536 6700 | 0.9387 2941 | 0.9240 3790 | 0.9167 8309 | 19 |
| 20 | 0.9512 8878 | 0.9356 1071 | 0.9202 0372 | 0.9126 0034 | 20 |
| 21 | 0.9489 1649 | 0.9325 0236 | 0.9163 8544 | 0.9084 3667 | 21 |
| 22 | 0.9465 5011 | 0.9294 0435 | 0.9125 8301 | 0.9042 9200 | 22 |
| 23 | 0.9441 8964 | 0.9263 1663 | 0.9087 9636 | 0.9001 6624 | 23 |
| 24 | 0.9418 3505 | 0.9232 3916 | 0.9050 2542 | 0.8960 5930 | 24 |
| 25 | 0.9394 8634 | 0.9201 7192 | 0.9012 7013 | 0.8919 7110 | 25 |
| 26 | 0.9371 4348 | 0.9171 1487 | 0.8975 3042 | 0.8879 0155 | 26 |
| 27 | 0.9348 0646 | 0.9140 6798 | 0.8938 0623 | 0.8838 5057 | 27 |
| 28 | 0.9324 7527 | 0.9110 3121 | 0.8900 9749 | 0.8798 1807 | 28 |
| 29 | 0.9301 4990 | 0.9080 0453 | 0.8864 0414 | 0.8758 0397 | 29 |
| 30 | 0.9278 3032 | 0.9049 8790 | 0.8827 2611 | 0.8718 0818 | 30 |
| 31 | 0.9255 1653 | 0.9019 8130 | 0.8790 6335 | 0.8678 3062 | 31 |
| 32 | 0.9232 0851 | 0.8989 8468 | 0.8754 1578 | 0.8638 7121 | 32 |
| 33 | 0.9209 0624 | 0.8959 9802 | 0.8717 8335 | 0.8599 2987 | 33 |
| 34 | 0.9186 0972 | 0.8930 2128 | 0.8681 6599 | 0.8560 0651 | 34 |
| 35 | 0.9163 1892 | 0.8900 5444 | 0.8645 6365 | 0.8521 0104 | 35 |
| 36 | 0.9140 3384 | 0.8870 9745 | 0.8609 7624 | 0.8482 1340 | 36 |
| 37 | 0.9117 5445 | 0.8841 5028 | 0.8574 0373 | 0.8443 4349 | 37 |
| 38 | 0.9094 8075 | 0.8812 1290 | 0.8538 4604 | 0.8404 9124 | 38 |
| 39 | 0.9072 1272 | 0.8782 8528 | 0.8503 0311 | 0.8366 5656 | 39 |
| 40 | 0.9049 5034 | 0.8753 6739 | 0.8467 7488 | 0.8328 3938 | 40 |
| 41 | 0.9026 9361 | 0.8724 5920 | 0.8432 6129 | 0.8290 3962 | 41 |
| 42 | 0.9004 4250 | 0.8695 6066 | 0.8397 6228 | 0.8252 5719 | 42 |
| 43 | 0.8981 9701 | 0.8666 7175 | 0.8362 7779 | 0.8214 9202 | 43 |
| 44 | 0.8959 5712 | 0.8637 9245 | 0.8328 0776 | 0.8177 4402 | 44 |
| 45 | 0.8937 2281 | 0.8609 2270 | 0.8293 5212 | 0.8140 1313 | 45 |
| 46 | 0.8914 9407 | 0.8580 6249 | 0.8259 1083 | 0.8102 9926 | 46 |
| 47 | 0.8892 7090 | 0.8552 1179 | 0.8224 8381 | 0.8066 0233 | 47 |
| 48 | 0.8870 5326 | 0.8523 7055 | 0.8190 7102 | 0.8029 2227 | 48 |
| 49 | 0.8848 4116 | 0.8495 3876 | 0.8156 7238 | 0.7992 5900 | 49 |
| 50 | 0.8826 3457 | 0.8467 1637 | 0.8122 8785 | 0.7956 1244 | 50 |
| 51 | 0.8804 3349 | 0.8439 0336 | 0.8089 1736 | 0.7919 8252 | 51 |
| 52 | 0.8782 3790 | 0.8410 9969 | 0.8055 6086 | 0.7883 6916 | 52 |
| 53 | 0.8760 4778 | 0.8383 0534 | 0.8022 1828 | 0.7847 7229 | 53 |
| 54 | 0.8738 6312 | 0.8355 2027 | 0.7988 8957 | 0.7811 9183 | 54 |
| 55 | 0.8716 8391 | 0.8327 4446 | 0.7955 7468 | 0.7776 2770 | 55 |
| 56 | 0.8695 1013 | 0.8299 7787 | 0.7922 7354 | 0.7740 7984 | 56 |
| 57 | 0.8673 4178 | 0.8272 2047 | 0.7889 8610 | 0.7705 4816 | 57 |
| 58 | 0.8651 7883 | 0.8244 7222 | 0.7857 1230 | 0.7670 3259 | 58 |
| 59 | 0.8630 2128 | 0.8217 3311 | 0.7824 5208 | 0.7635 3306 | 59 |
| 60 | 0.8608 6911 | 0.8190 0310 | 0.7792 0539 | 0.7600 4950 | 60 |

Table
6

# TABLE 6

$$p=(1+i)^{-n} \quad [OR, \ v^n=(1+i)^{-n}]$$

| $n$ | $\frac{1}{4}\%$ | $\frac{1}{3}\%$ | $\frac{5}{12}\%$ | $\frac{11}{24}\%$ | $n$ |
|---|---|---|---|---|---|
| 61 | 0.8587 2230 | 0.8162 8216 | 0.7759 7217 | 0.7565 8184 | 61 |
| 62 | 0.8565 8085 | 0.8135 7026 | 0.7727 5237 | 0.7531 2999 | 62 |
| 63 | 0.8544 4474 | 0.8108 6737 | 0.7695 4593 | 0.7496 9389 | 63 |
| 64 | 0.8523 1395 | 0.8081 7346 | 0.7663 5279 | 0.7462 7347 | 64 |
| 65 | 0.8501 8848 | 0.8054 8850 | 0.7631 7291 | 0.7428 6866 | 65 |
| 66 | 0.8480 6831 | 0.8028 1246 | 0.7600 0621 | 0.7394 7938 | 66 |
| 67 | 0.8459 5343 | 0.8001 4531 | 0.7568 5266 | 0.7361 0556 | 67 |
| 68 | 0.8438 4382 | 0.7974 8702 | 0.7537 1219 | 0.7327 4714 | 68 |
| 69 | 0.8417 3947 | 0.7948 3756 | 0.7505 8476 | 0.7294 0404 | 69 |
| 70 | 0.8396 4037 | 0.7921 9690 | 0.7474 7030 | 0.7260 7619 | 70 |
| 71 | 0.8375 4650 | 0.7895 6502 | 0.7443 6876 | 0.7227 6352 | 71 |
| 72 | 0.8354 5786 | 0.7869 4188 | 0.7412 8009 | 0.7194 6597 | 72 |
| 73 | 0.8333 7442 | 0.7843 2745 | 0.7382 0424 | 0.7161 8346 | 73 |
| 74 | 0.8312 9618 | 0.7817 2171 | 0.7351 4115 | 0.7129 1593 | 74 |
| 75 | 0.8292 2312 | 0.7791 2463 | 0.7320 9078 | 0.7096 6331 | 75 |
| 76 | 0.8271 5523 | 0.7765 3618 | 0.7290 5306 | 0.7064 2552 | 76 |
| 77 | 0.8250 9250 | 0.7739 5632 | 0.7260 2794 | 0.7032 0251 | 77 |
| 78 | 0.8230 3491 | 0.7713 8504 | 0.7230 1537 | 0.6999 9420 | 78 |
| 79 | 0.8209 8246 | 0.7688 2230 | 0.7200 1531 | 0.6968 0053 | 79 |
| 80 | 0.8189 3512 | 0.7662 6807 | 0.7170 2770 | 0.6936 2144 | 80 |
| 81 | 0.8168 9289 | 0.7637 2233 | 0.7140 5248 | 0.6904 5684 | 81 |
| 82 | 0.8148 5575 | 0.7611 8505 | 0.7110 8960 | 0.6873 0669 | 82 |
| 83 | 0.8128 2369 | 0.7586 5619 | 0.7081 3902 | 0.6841 7090 | 83 |
| 84 | 0.8107 9670 | 0.7561 3574 | 0.7052 0069 | 0.6810 4943 | 84 |
| 85 | 0.8087 7476 | 0.7536 2366 | 0.7022 7454 | 0.6779 4219 | 85 |
| 86 | 0.8067 5787 | 0.7511 1993 | 0.6993 6054 | 0.6748 4913 | 86 |
| 87 | 0.8047 4600 | 0.7486 2451 | 0.6964 5863 | 0.6717 7019 | 87 |
| 88 | 0.8027 3915 | 0.7461 3739 | 0.6935 6876 | 0.6687 0529 | 88 |
| 89 | 0.8007 3731 | 0.7436 5853 | 0.6906 9088 | 0.6656 5437 | 89 |
| 90 | 0.7987 4046 | 0.7411 8790 | 0.6878 2495 | 0.6626 1738 | 90 |
| 91 | 0.7967 4859 | 0.7387 2548 | 0.6849 7090 | 0.6595 9424 | 91 |
| 92 | 0.7947 6168 | 0.7362 7125 | 0.6821 2870 | 0.6565 8489 | 92 |
| 93 | 0.7927 7973 | 0.7338 2516 | 0.6792 9829 | 0.6535 8927 | 93 |
| 94 | 0.7908 0273 | 0.7313 8720 | 0.6764 7962 | 0.6506 0732 | 94 |
| 95 | 0.7888 3065 | 0.7289 5735 | 0.6736 7265 | 0.6476 3898 | 95 |
| 96 | 0.7868 6349 | 0.7265 3556 | 0.6708 7733 | 0.6446 8417 | 96 |
| 97 | 0.7849 0124 | 0.7241 2182 | 0.6680 9361 | 0.6417 4285 | 97 |
| 98 | 0.7829 4388 | 0.7217 1610 | 0.6653 2143 | 0.6388 1495 | 98 |
| 99 | 0.7809 9140 | 0.7193 1837 | 0.6625 6076 | 0.6359 0041 | 99 |
| 100 | 0.7790 4379 | 0.7169 2861 | 0.6598 1155 | 0.6329 9916 | 100 |
| 101 | 0.7771 0104 | 0.7145 4679 | 0.6570 7374 | 0.6301 1115 | 101 |
| 102 | 0.7751 6313 | 0.7121 7288 | 0.6543 4730 | 0.6272 3632 | 102 |
| 103 | 0.7732 3006 | 0.7098 0686 | 0.6516 3216 | 0.6243 7460 | 103 |
| 104 | 0.7713 0180 | 0.7074 4869 | 0.6489 2829 | 0.6215 2594 | 104 |
| 105 | 0.7693 7836 | 0.7050 9837 | 0.6462 3565 | 0.6186 9028 | 105 |
| 106 | 0.7674 5971 | 0.7027 5585 | 0.6435 5417 | 0.6158 6755 | 106 |
| 107 | 0.7655 4584 | 0.7004 2111 | 0.6408 8382 | 0.6130 5770 | 107 |
| 108 | 0.7636 3675 | 0.6980 9413 | 0.6382 2455 | 0.6102 6067 | 108 |
| 109 | 0.7617 3242 | 0.6957 7488 | 0.6355 7632 | 0.6074 7641 | 109 |
| 110 | 0.7598 3284 | 0.6934 6334 | 0.6329 3907 | 0.6047 0484 | 110 |
| 111 | 0.7579 3799 | 0.6911 5947 | 0.6303 1277 | 0.6019 4592 | 111 |
| 112 | 0.7560 4787 | 0.6888 6326 | 0.6276 9736 | 0.5991 9959 | 112 |
| 113 | 0.7541 6247 | 0.6865 7468 | 0.6250 9281 | 0.5964 6579 | 113 |
| 114 | 0.7522 8176 | 0.6842 9370 | 0.6224 9906 | 0.5937 4446 | 114 |
| 115 | 0.7504 0575 | 0.6820 2030 | 0.6199 1608 | 0.5910 3555 | 115 |
| 116 | 0.7485 3441 | 0.6797 5445 | 0.6173 4381 | 0.5883 3900 | 116 |
| 117 | 0.7466 6774 | 0.6774 9613 | 0.6147 8222 | 0.5856 5474 | 117 |
| 118 | 0.7448 0573 | 0.6752 4531 | 0.6122 3126 | 0.5829 8274 | 118 |
| 119 | 0.7429 4836 | 0.6730 0197 | 0.6096 9088 | 0.5803 2293 | 119 |
| 120 | 0.7410 9562 | 0.6707 6608 | 0.6071 6104 | 0.5776 7525 | 120 |

**TABLE 6**

$$p = (1+i)^{-n} \quad [OR, \ v^n = (1+i)^{-n}]$$

| n | $\frac{1}{4}\%$ | $\frac{1}{3}\%$ | $\frac{5}{12}\%$ | $\frac{11}{24}\%$ | n |
|---|---|---|---|---|---|
| 121 | 0.7392 4750 | 0.6685 3763 | 0.6046 4170 | 0.5750 3965 | 121 |
| 122 | 0.7374 0399 | 0.6663 1657 | 0.6021 3281 | 0.5724 1608 | 122 |
| 123 | 0.7355 6508 | 0.6641 0289 | 0.5996 3434 | 0.5698 0447 | 123 |
| 124 | 0.7337 3075 | 0.6618 9657 | 0.5971 4623 | 0.5672 0478 | 124 |
| 125 | 0.7319 0100 | 0.6596 9758 | 0.5946 6844 | 0.5646 1696 | 125 |
| 126 | 0.7300 7581 | 0.6575 0589 | 0.5922 0094 | 0.5620 4094 | 126 |
| 127 | 0.7282 5517 | 0.6553 2149 | 0.5897 4367 | 0.5594 7667 | 127 |
| 128 | 0.7264 3907 | 0.6531 4434 | 0.5872 9660 | 0.5569 2410 | 128 |
| 129 | 0.7246 2750 | 0.6509 7443 | 0.5848 5969 | 0.5543 8318 | 129 |
| 130 | 0.7228 2045 | 0.6488 1172 | 0.5824 3288 | 0.5518 5385 | 130 |
| 131 | 0.7210 1791 | 0.6466 5620 | 0.5800 1615 | 0.5493 3606 | 131 |
| 132 | 0.7192 1986 | 0.6445 0784 | 0.5776 0944 | 0.5468 2975 | 132 |
| 133 | 0.7174 2629 | 0.6423 6662 | 0.5752 1273 | 0.5443 3488 | 133 |
| 134 | 0.7156 3720 | 0.6402 3251 | 0.5728 2595 | 0.5418 5140 | 134 |
| 135 | 0.7138 5257 | 0.6381 0549 | 0.5704 4908 | 0.5393 7924 | 135 |
| 136 | 0.7120 7239 | 0.6359 8554 | 0.5680 8207 | 0.5369 1837 | 136 |
| 137 | 0.7102 9664 | 0.6338 7263 | 0.5657 2488 | 0.5344 6872 | 137 |
| 138 | 0.7085 2533 | 0.6317 6674 | 0.5633 7748 | 0.5320 3025 | 138 |
| 139 | 0.7067 5843 | 0.6296 6785 | 0.5610 3981 | 0.5296 0290 | 139 |
| 140 | 0.7049 9595 | 0.6275 7593 | 0.5587 1185 | 0.5271 8663 | 140 |
| 141 | 0.7032 3785 | 0.6254 9096 | 0.5563 9354 | 0.5247 8138 | 141 |
| 142 | 0.7014 8414 | 0.6234 1292 | 0.5540 8485 | 0.5223 8711 | 142 |
| 143 | 0.6997 3480 | 0.6213 4178 | 0.5517 8574 | 0.5200 0376 | 143 |
| 144 | 0.6979 8983 | 0.6192 7752 | 0.5494 9618 | 0.5176 3128 | 144 |
| 145 | 0.6962 4921 | 0.6172 2012 | 0.5472 1611 | 0.5152 6963 | 145 |
| 146 | 0.6945 1292 | 0.6151 6955 | 0.5449 4550 | 0.5129 1875 | 146 |
| 147 | 0.6927 8097 | 0.6131 2580 | 0.5426 8432 | 0.5105 7860 | 147 |
| 148 | 0.6910 5334 | 0.6110 8884 | 0.5404 3252 | 0.5082 4912 | 148 |
| 149 | 0.6893 3001 | 0.6090 5864 | 0.5381 9006 | 0.5059 3028 | 149 |
| 150 | 0.6876 1098 | 0.6070 3519 | 0.5359 5690 | 0.5036 2201 | 150 |
| 151 | 0.6858 9624 | 0.6050 1846 | 0.5337 3302 | 0.5013 2427 | 151 |
| 152 | 0.6841 8578 | 0.6030 0843 | 0.5315 1836 | 0.4990 3702 | 152 |
| 153 | 0.6824 7958 | 0.6010 0508 | 0.5293 1289 | 0.4967 6020 | 153 |
| 154 | 0.6807 7764 | 0.5990 0839 | 0.5271 1657 | 0.4944 9377 | 154 |
| 155 | 0.6790 7994 | 0.5970 1833 | 0.5249 2936 | 0.4922 3768 | 155 |
| 156 | 0.6773 8647 | 0.5950 3488 | 0.5227 5123 | 0.4899 9189 | 156 |
| 157 | 0.6756 9723 | 0.5930 5802 | 0.5205 8214 | 0.4877 5634 | 157 |
| 158 | 0.6740 1220 | 0.5910 8773 | 0.5184 2205 | 0.4855 3099 | 158 |
| 159 | 0.6723 3137 | 0.5891 2398 | 0.5162 7092 | 0.4833 1579 | 159 |
| 160 | 0.6706 5473 | 0.5871 6676 | 0.5141 2872 | 0.4811 1070 | 160 |
| 161 | 0.6689 8228 | 0.5852 1604 | 0.5119 9540 | 0.4789 1567 | 161 |
| 162 | 0.6673 1399 | 0.5832 7180 | 0.5098 7094 | 0.4767 3065 | 162 |
| 163 | 0.6656 4987 | 0.5813 3402 | 0.5077 5529 | 0.4745 5561 | 163 |
| 164 | 0.6639 8989 | 0.5794 0268 | 0.5056 4842 | 0.4723 9048 | 164 |
| 165 | 0.6623 3406 | 0.5774 7775 | 0.5035 5030 | 0.4702 3524 | 165 |
| 166 | 0.6606 8235 | 0.5755 5922 | 0.5014 6088 | 0.4680 8983 | 166 |
| 167 | 0.6590 3476 | 0.5736 4706 | 0.4993 8013 | 0.4659 5420 | 167 |
| 168 | 0.6573 9129 | 0.5717 4126 | 0.4973 0801 | 0.4638 2832 | 168 |
| 169 | 0.6557 5191 | 0.5698 4179 | 0.4952 4449 | 0.4617 1214 | 169 |
| 170 | 0.6541 1661 | 0.5679 4862 | 0.4931 8954 | 0.4596 0562 | 170 |
| 171 | 0.6524 8540 | 0.5660 6175 | 0.4911 4311 | 0.4575 0870 | 171 |
| 172 | 0.6508 5826 | 0.5641 8115 | 0.4891 0517 | 0.4554 2135 | 172 |
| 173 | 0.6492 3517 | 0.5623 0679 | 0.4870 7569 | 0.4533 4353 | 173 |
| 174 | 0.6476 1613 | 0.5604 3866 | 0.4850 5462 | 0.4512 7518 | 174 |
| 175 | 0.6460 0112 | 0.5585 7674 | 0.4830 4195 | 0.4492 1628 | 175 |
| 176 | 0.6443 9015 | 0.5567 2100 | 0.4810 3763 | 0.4471 6676 | 176 |
| 177 | 0.6427 8319 | 0.5548 7143 | 0.4790 4162 | 0.4451 2660 | 177 |
| 178 | 0.6411 8024 | 0.5530 2801 | 0.4770 5390 | 0.4430 9574 | 178 |
| 179 | 0.6395 8129 | 0.5511 9070 | 0.4750 7442 | 0.4410 7415 | 179 |
| 180 | 0.6379 8632 | 0.5493 5950 | 0.4731 0316 | 0.4390 6179 | 180 |

**TABLE   6**

$$p = (1 + i)^{-n} \quad [OR, \; v^n = (1 + i)^{-n}]$$

| n | $\frac{1}{4}\%$ | $\frac{1}{3}\%$ | $\frac{5}{12}\%$ | $\frac{11}{24}\%$ | n |
|---|---|---|---|---|---|
| 181 | 0.6363 9533 | 0.5475 3439 | 0.4711 4007 | 0.4370 5860 | 181 |
| 182 | 0.6348 0831 | 0.5457 1534 | 0.4691 8513 | 0.4350 6456 | 182 |
| 183 | 0.6332 2525 | 0.5439 0233 | 0.4672 3831 | 0.4330 7961 | 183 |
| 184 | 0.6316 4613 | 0.5420 9535 | 0.4652 9956 | 0.4311 0372 | 184 |
| 185 | 0.6300 7096 | 0.5402 9437 | 0.4633 6886 | 0.4291 3684 | 185 |
| 186 | 0.6284 9971 | 0.5384 9937 | 0.4614 4616 | 0.4271 7893 | 186 |
| 187 | 0.6269 3238 | 0.5367 1033 | 0.4595 3145 | 0.4252 2996 | 187 |
| 188 | 0.6253 6895 | 0.5349 2724 | 0.4576 2468 | 0.4232 8989 | 188 |
| 189 | 0.6238 0943 | 0.5331 5008 | 0.4557 2582 | 0.4213 5866 | 189 |
| 190 | 0.6222 5380 | 0.5313 7881 | 0.4538 3484 | 0.4194 3624 | 190 |
| 191 | 0.6207 0204 | 0.5296 1343 | 0.4519 5171 | 0.4175 2260 | 191 |
| 192 | 0.6191 5416 | 0.5278 5392 | 0.4500 7639 | 0.4156 1768 | 192 |
| 193 | 0.6176 1013 | 0.5261 0025 | 0.4482 0886 | 0.4137 2146 | 193 |
| 194 | 0.6160 6996 | 0.5243 5241 | 0.4463 4907 | 0.4118 3389 | 194 |
| 195 | 0.6145 3362 | 0.5226 1038 | 0.4444 9700 | 0.4099 5493 | 195 |
| 196 | 0.6130 0112 | 0.5208 7413 | 0.4426 5261 | 0.4080 8454 | 196 |
| 197 | 0.6114 7244 | 0.5191 4365 | 0.4408 1588 | 0.4062 2269 | 197 |
| 198 | 0.6099 4757 | 0.5174 1892 | 0.4389 8677 | 0.4043 6933 | 198 |
| 199 | 0.6084 2650 | 0.5156 9992 | 0.4371 6525 | 0.4025 2442 | 199 |
| 200 | 0.6069 0923 | 0.5139 8663 | 0.4353 5128 | 0.4006 8794 | 200 |
| 201 | 0.6053 9574 | 0.5122 7904 | 0.4335 4484 | 0.3988 5983 | 201 |
| 202 | 0.6038 8602 | 0.5105 7711 | 0.4317 4590 | 0.3970 4006 | 202 |
| 203 | 0.6023 8007 | 0.5088 8084 | 0.4299 5443 | 0.3952 2860 | 203 |
| 204 | 0.6008 7788 | 0.5071 9021 | 0.4281 7038 | 0.3934 2540 | 204 |
| 205 | 0.5993 7943 | 0.5055 0519 | 0.4263 9374 | 0.3916 3042 | 205 |
| 206 | 0.5978 8472 | 0.5038 2577 | 0.4246 2447 | 0.3898 4364 | 206 |
| 207 | 0.5963 9373 | 0.5021 5193 | 0.4228 6255 | 0.3880 6501 | 207 |
| 208 | 0.5949 0647 | 0.5004 8365 | 0.4211 0793 | 0.3862 9449 | 208 |
| 209 | 0.5934 2291 | 0.4988 2092 | 0.4193 6059 | 0.3845 3205 | 209 |
| 210 | 0.5919 4305 | 0.4971 6371 | 0.4176 2051 | 0.3827 7766 | 210 |
| 211 | 0.5904 6689 | 0.4955 1200 | 0.4158 8764 | 0.3810 3126 | 211 |
| 212 | 0.5889 9440 | 0.4938 6578 | 0.4141 6197 | 0.3792 9284 | 212 |
| 213 | 0.5875 2559 | 0.4922 2503 | 0.4124 4345 | 0.3775 6234 | 213 |
| 214 | 0.5860 6044 | 0.4905 8973 | 0.4107 3207 | 0.3758 3975 | 214 |
| 215 | 0.5845 9894 | 0.4889 5986 | 0.4090 2779 | 0.3741 2501 | 215 |
| 216 | 0.5831 4109 | 0.4873 3541 | 0.4073 3058 | 0.3724 1809 | 216 |
| 217 | 0.5816 8687 | 0.4857 1636 | 0.4056 4041 | 0.3707 1896 | 217 |
| 218 | 0.5802 3628 | 0.4841 0268 | 0.4039 5725 | 0.3690 2758 | 218 |
| 219 | 0.5787 8930 | 0.4824 9437 | 0.4022 8108 | 0.3673 4393 | 219 |
| 220 | 0.5773 4594 | 0.4808 9140 | 0.4006 1187 | 0.3656 6795 | 220 |
| 221 | 0.5759 0617 | 0.4792 9375 | 0.3989 4958 | 0.3639 9962 | 221 |
| 222 | 0.5744 7000 | 0.4777 0141 | 0.3972 9418 | 0.3623 3890 | 222 |
| 223 | 0.5730 3741 | 0.4761 1437 | 0.3956 4566 | 0.3606 8575 | 223 |
| 224 | 0.5716 0838 | 0.4745 3259 | 0.3940 0398 | 0.3590 4015 | 224 |
| 225 | 0.5701 8293 | 0.4729 5607 | 0.3923 6911 | 0.3574 0206 | 225 |
| 226 | 0.5687 6102 | 0.4713 8479 | 0.3907 4102 | 0.3557 7144 | 226 |
| 227 | 0.5673 4267 | 0.4698 1872 | 0.3891 1969 | 0.3541 4826 | 227 |
| 228 | 0.5659 2785 | 0.4682 5786 | 0.3875 0508 | 0.3525 3249 | 228 |
| 229 | 0.5645 1656 | 0.4667 0219 | 0.3858 9718 | 0.3509 2408 | 229 |
| 230 | 0.5631 0879 | 0.4651 5169 | 0.3842 9594 | 0.3493 2302 | 230 |
| 231 | 0.5617 0452 | 0.4636 0633 | 0.3827 0136 | 0.3477 2926 | 231 |
| 232 | 0.5603 0376 | 0.4620 6611 | 0.3811 1338 | 0.3461 4277 | 232 |
| 233 | 0.5589 0650 | 0.4605 3101 | 0.3795 3200 | 0.3445 6352 | 233 |
| 234 | 0.5575 1272 | 0.4590 0100 | 0.3779 5718 | 0.3429 9148 | 234 |
| 235 | 0.5561 2241 | 0.4574 7608 | 0.3763 8889 | 0.3414 2661 | 235 |
| 236 | 0.5547 3557 | 0.4559 5623 | 0.3748 2711 | 0.3398 6888 | 236 |
| 237 | 0.5533 5219 | 0.4544 4142 | 0.3732 7181 | 0.3383 1825 | 237 |
| 238 | 0.5519 7226 | 0.4529 3165 | 0.3717 2297 | 0.3367 7470 | 238 |
| 239 | 0.5505 9577 | 0.4514 2690 | 0.3701 8055 | 0.3352 3819 | 239 |
| 240 | 0.5492 2271 | 0.4499 2714 | 0.3686 4453 | 0.3337 0869 | 240 |

**TABLE 6**

$$p = (1 + i)^{-n} \quad [OR, \ v^n = (1 + i)^{-n}]$$

| $n$ | $\frac{1}{2}\%$ | $\frac{13}{24}\%$ | $\frac{7}{12}\%$ | $\frac{5}{8}\%$ | $n$ |
|---|---|---|---|---|---|
| 1 | 0.9950 2488 | 0.9946 1252 | 0.9942 0050 | 0.9937 8882 | 1 |
| 2 | 0.9900 7450 | 0.9892 5406 | 0.9884 3463 | 0.9876 1622 | 2 |
| 3 | 0.9851 4876 | 0.9839 2447 | 0.9827 0220 | 0.9814 8196 | 3 |
| 4 | 0.9802 4752 | 0.9786 2359 | 0.9770 0301 | 0.9753 8580 | 4 |
| 5 | 0.9753 7067 | 0.9733 5127 | 0.9713 3688 | 0.9693 2750 | 5 |
| 6 | 0.9705 1808 | 0.9681 0735 | 0.9657 0361 | 0.9633 0683 | 6 |
| 7 | 0.9656 8963 | 0.9628 9169 | 0.9601 0301 | 0.9573 2356 | 7 |
| 8 | 0.9608 8520 | 0.9577 0413 | 0.9545 3489 | 0.9513 7745 | 8 |
| 9 | 0.9561 0468 | 0.9525 4451 | 0.9489 9906 | 0.9454 6827 | 9 |
| 10 | 0.9513 4794 | 0.9474 1269 | 0.9434 9534 | 0.9395 9580 | 10 |
| 11 | 0.9466 1487 | 0.9423 0852 | 0.9380 2354 | 0.9337 5980 | 11 |
| 12 | 0.9419 0534 | 0.9372 3185 | 0.9325 8347 | 0.9279 6005 | 12 |
| 13 | 0.9372 1924 | 0.9321 8253 | 0.9271 7495 | 0.9221 9632 | 13 |
| 14 | 0.9325 5646 | 0.9271 6041 | 0.9217 9779 | 0.9164 6840 | 14 |
| 15 | 0.9279 1688 | 0.9221 6534 | 0.9164 5182 | 0.9107 7604 | 15 |
| 16 | 0.9233 0037 | 0.9171 9719 | 0.9111 3686 | 0.9051 1905 | 16 |
| 17 | 0.9187 0684 | 0.9122 5581 | 0.9058 5272 | 0.8994 9719 | 17 |
| 18 | 0.9141 3616 | 0.9073 4104 | 0.9005 9922 | 0.8939 1025 | 18 |
| 19 | 0.9095 8822 | 0.9024 5276 | 0.8953 7619 | 0.8883 5802 | 19 |
| 20 | 0.9050 6290 | 0.8975 9081 | 0.8901 8346 | 0.8828 4027 | 20 |
| 21 | 0.9005 6010 | 0.8927 5505 | 0.8850 2084 | 0.8773 5679 | 21 |
| 22 | 0.8960 7971 | 0.8879 4535 | 0.8798 8815 | 0.8719 0736 | 22 |
| 23 | 0.8916 2160 | 0.8831 6156 | 0.8747 8524 | 0.8664 9179 | 23 |
| 24 | 0.8871 8567 | 0.8784 0354 | 0.8697 1192 | 0.8611 0985 | 24 |
| 25 | 0.8827 7181 | 0.8736 7115 | 0.8646 6802 | 0.8557 6135 | 25 |
| 26 | 0.8783 7991 | 0.8689 6426 | 0.8596 5338 | 0.8504 4606 | 26 |
| 27 | 0.8740 0986 | 0.8642 8273 | 0.8546 6782 | 0.8451 6378 | 27 |
| 28 | 0.8696 6155 | 0.8596 2642 | 0.8497 1117 | 0.8399 1432 | 28 |
| 29 | 0.8653 3488 | 0.8549 9520 | 0.8447 8327 | 0.8346 9746 | 29 |
| 30 | 0.8610 2973 | 0.8503 8892 | 0.8398 8394 | 0.8295 1300 | 30 |
| 31 | 0.8567 4600 | 0.8458 0747 | 0.8350 1303 | 0.8243 6075 | 31 |
| 32 | 0.8524 8358 | 0.8412 5069 | 0.8301 7037 | 0.8192 4050 | 32 |
| 33 | 0.8482 4237 | 0.8367 1847 | 0.8253 5580 | 0.8141 5205 | 33 |
| 34 | 0.8440 2226 | 0.8322 1066 | 0.8205 6914 | 0.8090 9520 | 34 |
| 35 | 0.8398 2314 | 0.8277 2714 | 0.8158 1025 | 0.8040 6976 | 35 |
| 36 | 0.8356 4492 | 0.8232 6777 | 0.8110 7896 | 0.7990 7554 | 36 |
| 37 | 0.8314 8748 | 0.8188 3243 | 0.8063 7510 | 0.7941 1234 | 37 |
| 38 | 0.8273 5073 | 0.8144 2098 | 0.8016 9853 | 0.7891 7997 | 38 |
| 39 | 0.8232 3455 | 0.8100 3330 | 0.7970 4907 | 0.7842 7823 | 39 |
| 40 | 0.8191 3886 | 0.8056 6926 | 0.7924 2659 | 0.7794 0693 | 40 |
| 41 | 0.8150 6354 | 0.8013 2873 | 0.7878 3091 | 0.7745 6590 | 41 |
| 42 | 0.8110 0850 | 0.7970 1158 | 0.7832 6188 | 0.7697 5493 | 42 |
| 43 | 0.8069 7363 | 0.7927 1769 | 0.7787 1935 | 0.7649 7384 | 43 |
| 44 | 0.8029 5884 | 0.7884 4694 | 0.7742 0316 | 0.7602 2245 | 44 |
| 45 | 0.7989 6402 | 0.7841 9919 | 0.7697 1317 | 0.7555 0057 | 45 |
| 46 | 0.7949 8907 | 0.7799 7433 | 0.7652 4922 | 0.7508 0802 | 46 |
| 47 | 0.7910 3390 | 0.7757 7223 | 0.7608 1115 | 0.7461 4462 | 47 |
| 48 | 0.7870 9841 | 0.7715 9277 | 0.7563 9883 | 0.7415 1018 | 48 |
| 49 | 0.7831 8250 | 0.7674 3583 | 0.7520 1209 | 0.7369 0453 | 49 |
| 50 | 0.7792 8607 | 0.7633 0128 | 0.7476 5079 | 0.7323 2748 | 50 |
| 51 | 0.7754 0902 | 0.7591 8901 | 0.7433 1479 | 0.7277 7886 | 51 |
| 52 | 0.7715 5127 | 0.7550 9889 | 0.7390 0393 | 0.7232 5850 | 52 |
| 53 | 0.7677 1270 | 0.7510 3080 | 0.7347 1808 | 0.7187 6621 | 53 |
| 54 | 0.7638 9324 | 0.7469 8464 | 0.7304 5708 | 0.7143 0182 | 54 |
| 55 | 0.7600 9277 | 0.7429 6027 | 0.7262 2079 | 0.7098 6516 | 55 |
| 56 | 0.7563 1122 | 0.7389 5758 | 0.7220 0907 | 0.7054 5606 | 56 |
| 57 | 0.7525 4847 | 0.7349 7646 | 0.7178 2178 | 0.7010 7435 | 57 |
| 58 | 0.7488 0445 | 0.7310 1678 | 0.7136 5877 | 0.6967 1985 | 58 |
| 59 | 0.7450 7906 | 0.7270 7844 | 0.7095 1990 | 0.6923 9240 | 59 |
| 60 | 0.7413 7220 | 0.7231 6132 | 0.7054 0504 | 0.6880 9182 | 60 |

Table
6

**PRESENT VALUE**
When Compound Amount Is 1

# TABLE 6

$$p = (1 + i)^{-n} \quad [OR,\ v^n = (1 + i)^{-n}]$$

| n | $\frac{1}{2}\%$ | $\frac{13}{24}\%$ | $\frac{7}{12}\%$ | $\frac{5}{8}\%$ | n |
|---|---|---|---|---|---|
| 61 | 0.7376 8378 | 0.7192 6530 | 0.7013 1404 | 0.6838 1796 | 61 |
| 62 | 0.7340 1371 | 0.7153 9027 | 0.6972 4677 | 0.6795 7065 | 62 |
| 63 | 0.7303 6190 | 0.7115 3611 | 0.6932 0308 | 0.6753 4971 | 63 |
| 64 | 0.7267 2826 | 0.7070 0272 | 0.6891 8285 | 0.6711 5499 | 64 |
| 65 | 0.7231 1269 | 0.7038 8999 | 0.6851 8593 | 0.6669 8633 | 65 |
| 66 | 0.7195 1512 | 0.7000 9779 | 0.6812 1219 | 0.6628 4355 | 66 |
| 67 | 0.7159 3544 | 0.6963 2602 | 0.6772 6150 | 0.6587 2651 | 67 |
| 68 | 0.7123 7357 | 0.6925 7458 | 0.6733 3372 | 0.6546 3504 | 68 |
| 69 | 0.7088 2943 | 0.6888 4334 | 0.6694 2872 | 0.6505 6899 | 69 |
| 70 | 0.7053 0291 | 0.6851 3221 | 0.6655 4637 | 0.6465 2819 | 70 |
| 71 | 0.7017 9394 | 0.6814 4107 | 0.6616 8653 | 0.6425 1248 | 71 |
| 72 | 0.6983 0243 | 0.6777 6982 | 0.6578 4908 | 0.6385 2172 | 72 |
| 73 | 0.6948 2829 | 0.6741 1834 | 0.6540 3388 | 0.6345 5575 | 73 |
| 74 | 0.6913 7143 | 0.6704 8654 | 0.6502 4081 | 0.6306 1441 | 74 |
| 75 | 0.6879 3177 | 0.6668 7431 | 0.6464 6973 | 0.6266 9755 | 75 |
| 76 | 0.6845 0923 | 0.6632 8153 | 0.6427 2053 | 0.6228 0501 | 76 |
| 77 | 0.6811 0371 | 0.6597 0811 | 0.6389 9307 | 0.6189 3666 | 77 |
| 78 | 0.6777 1513 | 0.6561 5395 | 0.6352 8723 | 0.6150 9233 | 78 |
| 79 | 0.6743 4342 | 0.6526 1893 | 0.6316 0288 | 0.6112 7189 | 79 |
| 80 | 0.6709 8847 | 0.6491 0295 | 0.6279 3990 | 0.6074 7517 | 80 |
| 81 | 0.6676 5022 | 0.6456 0592 | 0.6242 9816 | 0.6037 0203 | 81 |
| 82 | 0.6643 2858 | 0.6421 2773 | 0.6206 7754 | 0.5999 5233 | 82 |
| 83 | 0.6610 2346 | 0.6386 6827 | 0.6170 7792 | 0.5962 2592 | 83 |
| 84 | 0.6577 3479 | 0.6352 2746 | 0.6134 9917 | 0.5925 2265 | 84 |
| 85 | 0.6544 6248 | 0.6318 0518 | 0.6099 4118 | 0.5888 4239 | 85 |
| 86 | 0.6512 0644 | 0.6284 0134 | 0.6064 0382 | 0.5851 8498 | 86 |
| 87 | 0.6479 6661 | 0.6250 1584 | 0.6028 8698 | 0.5815 5029 | 87 |
| 88 | 0.6447 4290 | 0.6216 4858 | 0.5993 9054 | 0.5779 3818 | 88 |
| 89 | 0.6415 3522 | 0.6182 9945 | 0.5959 1437 | 0.5743 4850 | 89 |
| 90 | 0.6383 4350 | 0.6149 6837 | 0.5924 5836 | 0.5707 8112 | 90 |
| 91 | 0.6351 6766 | 0.6116 5524 | 0.5890 2240 | 0.5672 3489 | 91 |
| 92 | 0.6320 0763 | 0.6083 5996 | 0.5856 0636 | 0.5637 1269 | 92 |
| 93 | 0.6288 6331 | 0.6050 8243 | 0.5822 1014 | 0.5602 1137 | 93 |
| 94 | 0.6257 3464 | 0.6018 2256 | 0.5788 3361 | 0.5567 3179 | 94 |
| 95 | 0.6226 2153 | 0.5985 8025 | 0.5754 7666 | 0.5532 7383 | 95 |
| 96 | 0.6195 2391 | 0.5953 5541 | 0.5721 3918 | 0.5498 3735 | 96 |
| 97 | 0.6164 4170 | 0.5921 4794 | 0.5688 2106 | 0.5464 2221 | 97 |
| 98 | 0.6133 7483 | 0.5889 5775 | 0.5655 2218 | 0.5430 2828 | 98 |
| 99 | 0.6103 2321 | 0.5857 8475 | 0.5622 4243 | 0.5396 5544 | 99 |
| 100 | 0.6072 8678 | 0.5826 2884 | 0.5589 8171 | 0.5363 0354 | 100 |
| 101 | 0.6042 6545 | 0.5794 8994 | 0.5557 3989 | 0.5329 7246 | 101 |
| 102 | 0.6012 5915 | 0.5763 6795 | 0.5525 1688 | 0.5296 6207 | 102 |
| 103 | 0.5982 6781 | 0.5732 6277 | 0.5493 1255 | 0.5263 7225 | 103 |
| 104 | 0.5952 9136 | 0.5701 7433 | 0.5461 2681 | 0.5231 0285 | 104 |
| 105 | 0.5923 2971 | 0.5671 0252 | 0.5429 5955 | 0.5198 5377 | 105 |
| 106 | 0.5893 8279 | 0.5640 4727 | 0.5398 1065 | 0.5166 2486 | 106 |
| 107 | 0.5864 5054 | 0.5610 0847 | 0.5366 8002 | 0.5134 1601 | 107 |
| 108 | 0.5835 3288 | 0.5579 8605 | 0.5335 6754 | 0.5102 2709 | 108 |
| 109 | 0.5806 2973 | 0.5549 7991 | 0.5304 7312 | 0.5070 5798 | 109 |
| 110 | 0.5777 4102 | 0.5519 8996 | 0.5273 9664 | 0.5039 0855 | 110 |
| 111 | 0.5748 6669 | 0.5490 1612 | 0.5243 3800 | 0.5007 7868 | 111 |
| 112 | 0.5720 0666 | 0.5460 5831 | 0.5212 9710 | 0.4976 6826 | 112 |
| 113 | 0.5691 6085 | 0.5431 1643 | 0.5182 7383 | 0.4945 7715 | 113 |
| 114 | 0.5663 2921 | 0.5401 9039 | 0.5152 6810 | 0.4915 0524 | 114 |
| 115 | 0.5635 1165 | 0.5372 8013 | 0.5122 7980 | 0.4884 5242 | 115 |
| 116 | 0.5607 0811 | 0.5343 8554 | 0.5093 0884 | 0.4854 1855 | 116 |
| 117 | 0.5579 1852 | 0.5315 0655 | 0.5063 5510 | 0.4824 0353 | 117 |
| 118 | 0.5551 4280 | 0.5286 4306 | 0.5034 1849 | 0.4794 0723 | 118 |
| 119 | 0.5523 8090 | 0.5257 9501 | 0.5004 9891 | 0.4764 2955 | 119 |
| 120 | 0.5496 3273 | 0.5229 6229 | 0.4975 9627 | 0.4734 7036 | 120 |

**TABLE   6**

$$p = (1+i)^{-n} \quad [OR, \ v^n = (1+i)^{-n}]$$

| n | $\frac{1}{2}\%$ | $\frac{13}{24}\%$ | $\frac{7}{12}\%$ | $\frac{5}{8}\%$ | n |
|---|---|---|---|---|---|
| 121 | 0.5468 9824 | 0.5201 4484 | 0.4947 1046 | 0.4705 2955 | 121 |
| 122 | 0.5441 7736 | 0.5173 4257 | 0.4918 4138 | 0.4676 0700 | 122 |
| 123 | 0.5414 7001 | 0.5145 5539 | 0.4889 8895 | 0.4647 0261 | 123 |
| 124 | 0.5387 7612 | 0.5117 8324 | 0.4861 5305 | 0.4618 1626 | 124 |
| 125 | 0.5360 9565 | 0.5090 2601 | 0.4833 3361 | 0.4589 4784 | 125 |
| 126 | 0.5334 2850 | 0.5062 8364 | 0.4805 3051 | 0.4560 9723 | 126 |
| 127 | 0.5307 7463 | 0.5035 5605 | 0.4805 3051 | 0.4532 6433 | 127 |
| 128 | 0.5281 3396 | 0.5008 4315 | 0.4749 7300 | 0.4504 4902 | 128 |
| 129 | 0.5255 0643 | 0.4981 4486 | 0.4722 1839 | 0.4476 5120 | 129 |
| 130 | 0.5228 9197 | 0.4954 6111 | 0.4694 7976 | 0.4448 7076 | 130 |
| 131 | 0.5202 9052 | 0.4927 9182 | 0.4667 5701 | 0.4421 0759 | 131 |
| 132 | 0.5177 0201 | 0.4901 3692 | 0.4640 5005 | 0.4393 6158 | 132 |
| 133 | 0.5151 2637 | 0.4874 9631 | 0.4613 5879 | 0.4366 3262 | 133 |
| 134 | 0.5125 6356 | 0.4848 6993 | 0.4586 8314 | 0.4339 2062 | 134 |
| 135 | 0.5100 1349 | 0.4822 5770 | 0.4560 2301 | 0.4312 2546 | 135 |
| 136 | 0.5074 7611 | 0.4796 5955 | 0.4533 7830 | 0.4285 4704 | 136 |
| 137 | 0.5049 5135 | 0.4770 7539 | 0.4507 4893 | 0.4258 8526 | 137 |
| 138 | 0.5024 3916 | 0.4745 0515 | 0.4481 3481 | 0.4232 4001 | 138 |
| 139 | 0.4999 3946 | 0.4719 4876 | 0.4455 3585 | 0.4206 1119 | 139 |
| 140 | 0.4974 5220 | 0.4694 0615 | 0.4429 5197 | 0.4179 9870 | 140 |
| 141 | 0.4949 7731 | 0.4668 7723 | 0.4403 8306 | 0.4154 0243 | 141 |
| 142 | 0.4925 1474 | 0.4643 6193 | 0.4378 2906 | 0.4128 2229 | 142 |
| 143 | 0.4900 6442 | 0.4618 6019 | 0.4352 8987 | 0.4102 5818 | 143 |
| 144 | 0.4876 2628 | 0.4593 7193 | 0.4327 6541 | 0.4077 0999 | 144 |
| 145 | 0.4852 0028 | 0.4568 9707 | 0.4302 5558 | 0.4051 7763 | 145 |
| 146 | 0.4827 8635 | 0.4544 3554 | 0.4277 6031 | 0.4026 6100 | 146 |
| 147 | 0.4803 8443 | 0.4519 8728 | 0.4252 7952 | 0.4001 6000 | 147 |
| 148 | 0.4779 9446 | 0.4495 5220 | 0.4228 1311 | 0.3976 7453 | 148 |
| 149 | 0.4756 1637 | 0.4471 3025 | 0.4203 6100 | 0.3952 0451 | 149 |
| 150 | 0.4732 5012 | 0.4447 2134 | 0.4179 2312 | 0.3927 4982 | 150 |
| 151 | 0.4708 9565 | 0.4423 2541 | 0.4154 9937 | 0.3903 1038 | 151 |
| 152 | 0.4685 5288 | 0.4399 4239 | 0.4130 8968 | 0.3878 8609 | 152 |
| 153 | 0.4662 2177 | 0.4375 7221 | 0.4106 9396 | 0.3854 7686 | 153 |
| 154 | 0.4639 0226 | 0.4352 1479 | 0.4083 1214 | 0.3830 8259 | 154 |
| 155 | 0.4615 9429 | 0.4328 7008 | 0.4059 4414 | 0.3807 0320 | 155 |
| 156 | 0.4592 9780 | 0.4305 3800 | 0.4035 8986 | 0.3783 3858 | 156 |
| 157 | 0.4570 1274 | 0.4282 1848 | 0.4012 4924 | 0.3759 8865 | 157 |
| 158 | 0.4547 3904 | 0.4259 1146 | 0.3989 2220 | 0.3736 5332 | 158 |
| 159 | 0.4524 7666 | 0.4236 1687 | 0.3966 0864 | 0.3713 3249 | 159 |
| 160 | 0.4502 2553 | 0.4213 3464 | 0.3943 0851 | 0.3690 2608 | 160 |
| 161 | 0.4479 8560 | 0.4190 6471 | 0.3920 2172 | 0.3667 3399 | 161 |
| 162 | 0.4457 5682 | 0.4168 0700 | 0.3897 4819 | 0.3644 5614 | 162 |
| 163 | 0.4435 3912 | 0.4145 6146 | 0.3874 8784 | 0.3621 9244 | 163 |
| 164 | 0.4413 3246 | 0.4123 2802 | 0.3852 4060 | 0.3599 4280 | 164 |
| 165 | 0.4391 3678 | 0.4101 0661 | 0.3830 0640 | 0.3577 0713 | 165 |
| 166 | 0.4369 5202 | 0.4078 9717 | 0.3807 8515 | 0.3554 8534 | 166 |
| 167 | 0.4347 7813 | 0.4056 9963 | 0.3785 7679 | 0.3532 7736 | 167 |
| 168 | 0.4326 1505 | 0.4035 1393 | 0.3763 8123 | 0.3510 8309 | 168 |
| 169 | 0.4304 6274 | 0.4013 4000 | 0.3741 9841 | 0.3489 0245 | 169 |
| 170 | 0.4283 2113 | 0.3991 7779 | 0.3720 2824 | 0.3467 3535 | 170 |
| 171 | 0.4261 9018 | 0.3970 2722 | 0.3698 7066 | 0.3445 8172 | 171 |
| 172 | 0.4240 6983 | 0.3948 8825 | 0.3677 2560 | 0.3424 4146 | 172 |
| 173 | 0.4219 6003 | 0.3927 6079 | 0.3655 9297 | 0.3403 1449 | 173 |
| 174 | 0.4198 6073 | 0.3906 4480 | 0.3634 7272 | 0.3382 0074 | 174 |
| 175 | 0.4177 7187 | 0.3885 4021 | 0.3613 6475 | 0.3361 0011 | 175 |
| 176 | 0.4156 9340 | 0.3864 4695 | 0.3592 6902 | 0.3340 1254 | 176 |
| 177 | 0.4136 2528 | 0.3843 6497 | 0.3571 8544 | 0.3319 3792 | 177 |
| 178 | 0.4115 6744 | 0.3822 9421 | 0.3551 1394 | 0.3298 7620 | 178 |
| 179 | 0.4095 1984 | 0.3802 3461 | 0.3530 5445 | 0.3278 2728 | 179 |
| 180 | 0.4074 8243 | 0.3781 8610 | 0.3510 0691 | 0.3257 9108 | 180 |

Table
6

## TABLE 6

$$p = (1 + i)^{-n} \quad [OR, \; v^n = (1 + i)^{-n}]$$

| n | $\frac{1}{2}$ % | $\frac{13}{24}$ % | $\frac{7}{12}$ % | $\frac{5}{8}$ % | n |
|---|---|---|---|---|---|
| 181 | 0.4054 5515 | 0.3761 4863 | 0.3489 7125 | 0.3237 6754 | 181 |
| 182 | 0.4034 3796 | 0.3741 2214 | 0.3469 4739 | 0.3217 5656 | 182 |
| 183 | 0.4014 3081 | 0.3721 0656 | 0.3449 3527 | 0.3197 5807 | 183 |
| 184 | 0.3994 3364 | 0.3701 0184 | 0.3429 3481 | 0.3177 7199 | 184 |
| 185 | 0.3974 4641 | 0.3681 0792 | 0.3409 4596 | 0.3157 9825 | 185 |
| 186 | 0.3954 6906 | 0.3661 2475 | 0.3389 6864 | 0.3138 3677 | 186 |
| 187 | 0.3935 0155 | 0.3641 5225 | 0.3370 0279 | 0.3118 8748 | 187 |
| 188 | 0.3915 4383 | 0.3621 9039 | 0.3350 4835 | 0.3099 5029 | 188 |
| 189 | 0.3895 9586 | 0.3602 3909 | 0.3331 0523 | 0.3080 2513 | 189 |
| 190 | 0.3876 5757 | 0.3582 9831 | 0.3311 7339 | 0.3061 1193 | 190 |
| 191 | 0.3857 2892 | 0.3563 6799 | 0.3292 5275 | 0.3042 1062 | 191 |
| 192 | 0.3838 0987 | 0.3544 4806 | 0.3273 4324 | 0.3023 2111 | 192 |
| 193 | 0.3819 0037 | 0.3525 3848 | 0.3254 4482 | 0.3004 4334 | 193 |
| 194 | 0.3800 0037 | 0.3506 3918 | 0.3235 5740 | 0.2985 7723 | 194 |
| 195 | 0.3781 0982 | 0.3487 5012 | 0.3216 8093 | 0.2967 2271 | 195 |
| 196 | 0.3762 2868 | 0.3468 7123 | 0.3198 1534 | 0.2948 7972 | 196 |
| 197 | 0.3743 5689 | 0.3450 0247 | 0.3179 6057 | 0.2930 4816 | 197 |
| 198 | 0.3724 9442 | 0.3431 4377 | 0.3161 1655 | 0.2912 2799 | 198 |
| 199 | 0.3706 4121 | 0.3412 9509 | 0.3142 8323 | 0.2894 1912 | 199 |
| 200 | 0.3687 9723 | 0.3394 5637 | 0.3124 6055 | 0.2876 2149 | 200 |
| 201 | 0.3669 6242 | 0.3376 2755 | 0.3106 4843 | 0.2858 3502 | 201 |
| 202 | 0.3651 3673 | 0.3358 0859 | 0.3088 4683 | 0.2840 5964 | 202 |
| 203 | 0.3633 2013 | 0.3339 9943 | 0.3070 5567 | 0.2822 9530 | 203 |
| 204 | 0.3615 1257 | 0.3322 0001 | 0.3052 7490 | 0.2805 4191 | 204 |
| 205 | 0.3597 1400 | 0.3304 1029 | 0.3035 0445 | 0.2787 9941 | 205 |
| 206 | 0.3579 2438 | 0.3286 3021 | 0.3017 4428 | 0.2770 6774 | 206 |
| 207 | 0.3561 4366 | 0.3268 5972 | 0.2999 9431 | 0.2753 4682 | 207 |
| 208 | 0.3543 7180 | 0.3250 9876 | 0.2982 5450 | 0.2736 3660 | 208 |
| 209 | 0.3526 0876 | 0.3233 4730 | 0.2965 2477 | 0.2719 3699 | 209 |
| 210 | 0.3508 5448 | 0.3216 0527 | 0.2948 0507 | 0.2702 4794 | 210 |
| 211 | 0.3491 0894 | 0.3198 7263 | 0.2930 9535 | 0.2685 6938 | 211 |
| 212 | 0.3473 7208 | 0.3181 4932 | 0.2913 9554 | 0.2669 0125 | 212 |
| 213 | 0.3456 4386 | 0.3164 3529 | 0.2897 0559 | 0.2652 4348 | 213 |
| 214 | 0.3439 2424 | 0.3147 3050 | 0.2880 2544 | 0.2635 9600 | 214 |
| 215 | 0.3422 1317 | 0.3130 3490 | 0.2863 5504 | 0.2619 5876 | 215 |
| 216 | 0.3405 1062 | 0.3113 4843 | 0.2846 9432 | 0.2603 3169 | 216 |
| 217 | 0.3388 1654 | 0.3096 7104 | 0.2830 4324 | 0.2587 1472 | 217 |
| 218 | 0.3371 3088 | 0.3080 0270 | 0.2814 0173 | 0.2571 0780 | 218 |
| 219 | 0.3354 5361 | 0.3063 4334 | 0.2797 6974 | 0.2555 1085 | 219 |
| 220 | 0.3337 8469 | 0.3046 9292 | 0.2781 4721 | 0.2539 2383 | 220 |
| 221 | 0.3321 2407 | 0.3030 5139 | 0.2765 3410 | 0.2523 4666 | 221 |
| 222 | 0.3304 7171 | 0.3014 1870 | 0.2749 3033 | 0.2507 7929 | 222 |
| 223 | 0.3288 2757 | 0.2997 9481 | 0.2733 3588 | 0.2492 2166 | 223 |
| 224 | 0.3271 9162 | 0.2981 7967 | 0.2717 5066 | 0.2476 7370 | 224 |
| 225 | 0.3255 6380 | 0.2965 7324 | 0.2701 7464 | 0.2461 3535 | 225 |
| 226 | 0.3239 4408 | 0.2949 7545 | 0.2686 0777 | 0.2446 0656 | 226 |
| 227 | 0.3223 3241 | 0.2933 8628 | 0.2670 4997 | 0.2430 8726 | 227 |
| 228 | 0.3207 2877 | 0.2918 0566 | 0.2655 0122 | 0.2415 7740 | 228 |
| 229 | 0.3191 3310 | 0.2902 3356 | 0.2639 6144 | 0.2400 7692 | 229 |
| 230 | 0.3175 4538 | 0.2886 6994 | 0.2624 3060 | 0.2385 8576 | 230 |
| 231 | 0.3159 6555 | 0.2871 1473 | 0.2609 0863 | 0.2371 0386 | 231 |
| 232 | 0.3143 9358 | 0.2855 6790 | 0.2593 9549 | 0.2356 3117 | 232 |
| 233 | 0.3128 2944 | 0.2840 2941 | 0.2578 9112 | 0.2341 6762 | 233 |
| 234 | 0.3112 7307 | 0.2824 9921 | 0.2563 9548 | 0.2327 1316 | 234 |
| 235 | 0.3097 2445 | 0.2809 7725 | 0.2549 0852 | 0.2312 6774 | 235 |
| 236 | 0.3081 8353 | 0.2794 6349 | 0.2534 3018 | 0.2298 3129 | 236 |
| 237 | 0.3066 5028 | 0.2779 5788 | 0.2519 6041 | 0.2284 0377 | 237 |
| 238 | 0.3051 2466 | 0.2764 6039 | 0.2504 9916 | 0.2269 8511 | 238 |
| 239 | 0.3036 0662 | 0.2749 7096 | 0.2490 4639 | 0.2255 7527 | 239 |
| 240 | 0.3020 9614 | 0.2734 8956 | 0.2476 0205 | 0.2241 7418 | 240 |

**TABLE 6**

$$p = (1+i)^{-n} \quad [OR, \; v^n = (1+i)^{-n}]$$

| $n$ | $\frac{2}{3}\%$ | $\frac{3}{4}\%$ | $\frac{7}{8}\%$ | 1% | $n$ |
|---|---|---|---|---|---|
| 1 | 0.9933 7748 | 0.9925 5583 | 0.9913 2590 | 0.9900 9901 | 1 |
| 2 | 0.9867 9882 | 0.9851 6708 | 0.9827 2704 | 0.9802 9605 | 2 |
| 3 | 0.9802 6373 | 0.9778 3333 | 0.9742 0276 | 0.9705 9015 | 3 |
| 4 | 0.9737 7192 | 0.9705 5417 | 0.9657 5243 | 0.9609 8034 | 4 |
| 5 | 0.9673 2310 | 0.9633 2920 | 0.9573 7539 | 0.9514 6569 | 5 |
| 6 | 0.9609 1699 | 0.9561 5802 | 0.9490 7102 | 0.9420 4524 | 6 |
| 7 | 0.9545 5330 | 0.9490 4022 | 0.9408 3868 | 0.9327 1805 | 7 |
| 8 | 0.9482 3175 | 0.9419 7540 | 0.9326 7775 | 0.9234 8322 | 8 |
| 9 | 0.9419 5207 | 0.9349 6318 | 0.9245 8761 | 0.9143 3982 | 9 |
| 10 | 0.9357 1398 | 0.9280 0316 | 0.9165 6765 | 0.9052 8695 | 10 |
| 11 | 0.9295 1720 | 0.9210 9494 | 0.9086 1724 | 0.8963 2372 | 11 |
| 12 | 0.9233 6145 | 0.9142 3815 | 0.9007 3581 | 0.8874 4923 | 12 |
| 13 | 0.9172 4648 | 0.9074 3241 | 0.8929 2273 | 0.8786 6260 | 13 |
| 14 | 0.9111 7200 | 0.9006 7733 | 0.8851 7743 | 0.8699 6297 | 14 |
| 15 | 0.9051 3775 | 0.8939 7254 | 0.8774 9931 | 0.8613 4947 | 15 |
| 16 | 0.8991 4346 | 0.8873 1766 | 0.8698 8779 | 0.8528 2126 | 16 |
| 17 | 0.8931 8886 | 0.8807 1231 | 0.8623 4230 | 0.8443 7749 | 17 |
| 18 | 0.8872 7371 | 0.8741 5614 | 0.8548 6225 | 0.8360 1731 | 18 |
| 19 | 0.8813 9772 | 0.8676 4878 | 0.8474 4709 | 0.8277 3992 | 19 |
| 20 | 0.8755 6065 | 0.8611 8985 | 0.8400 9625 | 0.8195 4447 | 20 |
| 21 | 0.8697 6224 | 0.8547 7901 | 0.8328 0917 | 0.8114 3017 | 21 |
| 22 | 0.8640 0222 | 0.8484 1589 | 0.8255 8530 | 0.8033 9621 | 22 |
| 23 | 0.8582 8035 | 0.8421 0014 | 0.8184 2409 | 0.7954 4179 | 23 |
| 24 | 0.8525 9638 | 0.8358 3140 | 0.8113 2499 | 0.7875 6613 | 24 |
| 25 | 0.8469 5004 | 0.8296 0933 | 0.8042 8748 | 0.7797 6844 | 25 |
| 26 | 0.8413 4110 | 0.8234 3358 | 0.7973 1101 | 0.7720 4796 | 26 |
| 27 | 0.8357 6931 | 0.8173 0380 | 0.7903 9505 | 0.7644 0392 | 27 |
| 28 | 0.8302 3441 | 0.8112 1966 | 0.7835 3908 | 0.7568 3557 | 28 |
| 29 | 0.8247 3617 | 0.8051 8080 | 0.7767 4258 | 0.7493 4215 | 29 |
| 30 | 0.8192 7434 | 0.7991 8690 | 0.7700 0504 | 0.7419 2292 | 30 |
| 31 | 0.8138 4868 | 0.7932 3762 | 0.7633 2594 | 0.7345 7715 | 31 |
| 32 | 0.8084 5896 | 0.7873 3262 | 0.7567 0477 | 0.7273 0411 | 32 |
| 33 | 0.8031 0492 | 0.7814 7158 | 0.7501 4104 | 0.7201 0307 | 33 |
| 34 | 0.7977 8635 | 0.7756 5418 | 0.7436 3424 | 0.7129 7334 | 34 |
| 35 | 0.7925 0299 | 0.7698 8008 | 0.7371 8388 | 0.7059 1420 | 35 |
| 36 | 0.7872 5463 | 0.7641 4896 | 0.7307 8947 | 0.6989 2495 | 36 |
| 37 | 0.7820 4102 | 0.7584 6051 | 0.7244 5053 | 0.6920 0490 | 37 |
| 38 | 0.7768 6194 | 0.7528 1440 | 0.7181 6657 | 0.6851 5337 | 38 |
| 39 | 0.7717 1716 | 0.7472 1032 | 0.7119 3712 | 0.6783 6967 | 39 |
| 40 | 0.7666 0645 | 0.7416 4796 | 0.7057 6171 | 0.6716 5314 | 40 |
| 41 | 0.7615 2959 | 0.7361 2701 | 0.6996 3986 | 0.6650 0311 | 41 |
| 42 | 0.7564 8635 | 0.7306 4716 | 0.6935 7111 | 0.6584 1892 | 42 |
| 43 | 0.7514 7650 | 0.7252 0809 | 0.6875 5500 | 0.6518 9992 | 43 |
| 44 | 0.7464 9984 | 0.7198 0952 | 0.6815 9108 | 0.6454 4546 | 44 |
| 45 | 0.7415 5613 | 0.7144 5114 | 0.6756 7889 | 0.6390 5492 | 45 |
| 46 | 0.7366 4516 | 0.7091 3264 | 0.6698 1798 | 0.6327 2764 | 46 |
| 47 | 0.7317 6672 | 0.7038 5374 | 0.6640 0792 | 0.6264 6301 | 47 |
| 48 | 0.7269 2058 | 0.6986 1414 | 0.6582 4824 | 0.6202 6041 | 48 |
| 49 | 0.7221 0654 | 0.6934 1353 | 0.6525 3853 | 0.6141 1921 | 49 |
| 50 | 0.7173 2437 | 0.6882 5165 | 0.6468 7835 | 0.6080 3882 | 50 |
| 51 | 0.7125 7388 | 0.6831 2819 | 0.6412 6726 | 0.6020 1864 | 51 |
| 52 | 0.7078 5485 | 0.6780 4286 | 0.6357 0484 | 0.5960 5806 | 52 |
| 53 | 0.7031 6707 | 0.6729 9540 | 0.6301 9067 | 0.5901 5649 | 53 |
| 54 | 0.6985 1033 | 0.6679 8551 | 0.6247 2433 | 0.5843 1336 | 54 |
| 55 | 0.6938 8444 | 0.6630 1291 | 0.6193 0541 | 0.5785 2808 | 55 |
| 56 | 0.6892 8918 | 0.6580 7733 | 0.6139 3349 | 0.5728 0008 | 56 |
| 57 | 0.6847 2435 | 0.6531 7849 | 0.6086 0817 | 0.5671 2879 | 57 |
| 58 | 0.6801 8975 | 0.6483 1612 | 0.6033 2904 | 0.5615 1365 | 58 |
| 59 | 0.6756 8518 | 0.6434 8995 | 0.5980 9571 | 0.5559 5411 | 59 |
| 60 | 0.6712 1044 | 0.6386 9970 | 0.5929 0776 | 0.5504 4962 | 60 |

Table
6

# TABLE 6

$$p = (1+i)^{-n} \quad [OR, \quad v^n = (1+i)^{-n}]$$

| $n$ | $\frac{2}{3}\%$ | $\frac{3}{4}\%$ | $\frac{7}{8}\%$ | 1% | $n$ |
|---|---|---|---|---|---|
| 61 | 0.6667 6534 | 0.6339 4511 | 0.5877 6482 | 0.5449 9962 | 61 |
| 62 | 0.6623 4968 | 0.6292 2592 | 0.5826 6649 | 0.5396 0358 | 62 |
| 63 | 0.6579 6326 | 0.6245 4185 | 0.5776 1238 | 0.5342 6097 | 63 |
| 64 | 0.6536 0588 | 0.6198 9266 | 0.5726 0211 | 0.5289 7126 | 64 |
| 65 | 0.6492 7737 | 0.6152 7807 | 0.5676 3530 | 0.5237 3392 | 65 |
| 66 | 0.6449 7752 | 0.6106 9784 | 0.5627 1158 | 0.5185 4844 | 66 |
| 67 | 0.6407 0614 | 0.6061 5170 | 0.5578 3056 | 0.5134 1430 | 67 |
| 68 | 0.6364 6306 | 0.6016 3940 | 0.5529 9188 | 0.5083 3099 | 68 |
| 69 | 0.6322 4807 | 0.5971 6070 | 0.5481 9517 | 0.5032 9801 | 69 |
| 70 | 0.6280 6100 | 0.5927 1533 | 0.5434 4007 | 0.4983 1486 | 70 |
| 71 | 0.6239 0165 | 0.5883 0306 | 0.5387 2622 | 0.4933 8105 | 71 |
| 72 | 0.6197 6985 | 0.5839 2363 | 0.5340 5325 | 0.4884 9609 | 72 |
| 73 | 0.6156 6542 | 0.5795 7681 | 0.5294 2082 | 0.4836 5949 | 73 |
| 74 | 0.6115 8816 | 0.5752 6234 | 0.5248 2857 | 0.4788 7078 | 74 |
| 75 | 0.6075 3791 | 0.5709 7999 | 0.5202 7615 | 0.4741 2949 | 75 |
| 76 | 0.6035 1448 | 0.5667 2952 | 0.5157 6322 | 0.4694 3514 | 76 |
| 77 | 0.5995 1769 | 0.5625 1069 | 0.5112 8944 | 0.4647 8726 | 77 |
| 78 | 0.5955 4738 | 0.5583 2326 | 0.5068 5447 | 0.4601 8541 | 78 |
| 79 | 0.5916 0336 | 0.5541 6701 | 0.5024 5796 | 0.4556 2912 | 79 |
| 80 | 0.5876 8545 | 0.5500 4170 | 0.4980 9959 | 0.4511 1794 | 80 |
| 81 | 0.5837 9350 | 0.5459 4710 | 0.4937 7902 | 0.4466 5142 | 81 |
| 82 | 0.5799 2732 | 0.5418 8297 | 0.4894 9593 | 0.4422 2913 | 82 |
| 83 | 0.5760 8674 | 0.5378 4911 | 0.4852 4999 | 0.4378 5063 | 83 |
| 84 | 0.5722 7159 | 0.5338 4527 | 0.4810 4089 | 0.4335 1547 | 84 |
| 85 | 0.5684 8171 | 0.5298 7123 | 0.4768 6829 | 0.4292 2324 | 85 |
| 86 | 0.5647 1693 | 0.5259 2678 | 0.4727 3188 | 0.4249 7350 | 86 |
| 87 | 0.5609 7709 | 0.5220 1169 | 0.4686 3136 | 0.4207 6585 | 87 |
| 88 | 0.5572 6201 | 0.5181 2575 | 0.4645 6640 | 0.4165 9985 | 88 |
| 89 | 0.5535 7153 | 0.5142 6873 | 0.4605 3671 | 0.4124 7510 | 89 |
| 90 | 0.5499 0549 | 0.5104 4043 | 0.4565 4197 | 0.4083 9119 | 90 |
| 91 | 0.5462 6374 | 0.5066 4063 | 0.4525 8187 | 0.4043 4771 | 91 |
| 92 | 0.5426 4610 | 0.5028 6911 | 0.4486 5613 | 0.4003 4427 | 92 |
| 93 | 0.5390 5241 | 0.4991 2567 | 0.4447 6444 | 0.3963 8046 | 93 |
| 94 | 0.5354 8253 | 0.4954 1009 | 0.4409 0651 | 0.3924 5590 | 94 |
| 95 | 0.5319 3629 | 0.4917 2217 | 0.4370 8204 | 0.3885 7020 | 95 |
| 96 | 0.5284 1353 | 0.4880 6171 | 0.4332 9075 | 0.3847 2297 | 96 |
| 97 | 0.5249 1410 | 0.4844 2850 | 0.4295 3234 | 0.3809 1383 | 97 |
| 98 | 0.5214 3785 | 0.4808 2233 | 0.4258 0654 | 0.3771 4241 | 98 |
| 99 | 0.5179 8462 | 0.4772 4301 | 0.4221 1305 | 0.3734 0832 | 99 |
| 100 | 0.5145 5426 | 0.4736 9033 | 0.4184 5159 | 0.3697 1121 | 100 |
| 101 | 0.5111 4661 | 0.4701 6410 | 0.4148 2190 | 0.3660 5071 | 101 |
| 102 | 0.5077 6154 | 0.4666 6412 | 0.4112 2370 | 0.3624 2644 | 102 |
| 103 | 0.5043 9888 | 0.4631 9019 | 0.4076 5670 | 0.3588 3806 | 103 |
| 104 | 0.5010 5849 | 0.4597 4213 | 0.4041 2064 | 0.3552 8521 | 104 |
| 105 | 0.4977 4022 | 0.4563 1973 | 0.4006 1526 | 0.3517 6753 | 105 |
| 106 | 0.4944 4393 | 0.4529 2281 | 0.3971 4028 | 0.3482 8469 | 106 |
| 107 | 0.4911 6946 | 0.4495 5117 | 0.3936 9545 | 0.3448 3632 | 107 |
| 108 | 0.4879 1669 | 0.4462 0464 | 0.3902 8049 | 0.3414 2210 | 108 |
| 109 | 0.4846 8545 | 0.4428 8302 | 0.3868 9516 | 0.3380 4168 | 109 |
| 110 | 0.4814 7561 | 0.4395 8612 | 0.3835 3919 | 0.3346 9474 | 110 |
| 111 | 0.4782 8703 | 0.4363 1377 | 0.3802 1233 | 0.3313 8093 | 111 |
| 112 | 0.4751 1957 | 0.4330 6577 | 0.3769 1433 | 0.3280 9993 | 112 |
| 113 | 0.4719 7308 | 0.4298 4196 | 0.3736 4494 | 0.3248 5141 | 113 |
| 114 | 0.4688 4743 | 0.4266 4214 | 0.3704 0391 | 0.3216 3506 | 114 |
| 115 | 0.4657 4248 | 0.4234 6615 | 0.3671 9099 | 0.3184 5056 | 115 |
| 116 | 0.4626 5809 | 0.4203 1379 | 0.3640 0593 | 0.3152 9758 | 116 |
| 117 | 0.4595 9413 | 0.4171 8491 | 0.3608 4851 | 0.3121 7582 | 117 |
| 118 | 0.4565 5046 | 0.4140 7931 | 0.3577 1847 | 0.3090 8497 | 118 |
| 119 | 0.4535 2695 | 0.4109 9683 | 0.3546 1559 | 0.3060 2473 | 119 |
| 120 | 0.4505 2346 | 0.4079 3731 | 0.3515 3961 | 0.3029 9478 | 120 |

# TABLE 6

$$p = (1 + i)^{-n} \quad [OR, \; v^n = (1 + i)^{-n}]$$

| $n$ | $\frac{2}{3}\%$ | $\frac{3}{4}\%$ | $\frac{7}{8}\%$ | $1\%$ | $n$ |
|---|---|---|---|---|---|
| 121 | 0.4475 3986 | 0.4049 0055 | 0.3484 9032 | 0.2999 9483 | 121 |
| 122 | 0.4445 7602 | 0.4018 8640 | 0.3454 6748 | 0.2970 2459 | 122 |
| 123 | 0.4416 3181 | 0.3988 9469 | 0.3424 7086 | 0.2940 8375 | 123 |
| 124 | 0.4387 0710 | 0.3959 2525 | 0.3395 0024 | 0.2911 7203 | 124 |
| 125 | 0.4358 0175 | 0.3929 7792 | 0.3365 5538 | 0.2882 8914 | 125 |
| 126 | 0.4329 1565 | 0.3900 5252 | 0.3336 3606 | 0.2854 3479 | 126 |
| 127 | 0.4300 4866 | 0.3871 4891 | 0.3307 4207 | 0.2826 0870 | 127 |
| 128 | 0.4272 0065 | 0.3842 6691 | 0.3278 7318 | 0.2798 1060 | 128 |
| 129 | 0.4243 7151 | 0.3814 0636 | 0.3250 2917 | 0.2770 4019 | 129 |
| 130 | 0.4215 6110 | 0.3785 6711 | 0.3222 0984 | 0.2742 9722 | 130 |
| 131 | 0.4187 6930 | 0.3757 4899 | 0.3194 1496 | 0.2715 8141 | 131 |
| 132 | 0.4159 9600 | 0.3729 5185 | 0.3166 4432 | 0.2688 9248 | 132 |
| 133 | 0.4132 4106 | 0.3701 7553 | 0.3138 9771 | 0.2662 3018 | 133 |
| 134 | 0.4105 0436 | 0.3674 1988 | 0.3111 7493 | 0.2635 9424 | 134 |
| 135 | 0.4077 8579 | 0.3646 8475 | 0.3084 7577 | 0.2609 8439 | 135 |
| 136 | 0.4050 8522 | 0.3619 6997 | 0.3058 0002 | 0.2584 0039 | 136 |
| 137 | 0.4024 0254 | 0.3592 7541 | 0.3031 4748 | 0.2558 4197 | 137 |
| 138 | 0.3997 3762 | 0.3566 0090 | 0.3005 1795 | 0.2533 0888 | 138 |
| 139 | 0.3970 9035 | 0.3539 4630 | 0.2979 1122 | 0.2508 0087 | 139 |
| 140 | 0.3944 6061 | 0.3513 1147 | 0.2953 2711 | 0.2483 1770 | 140 |
| 141 | 0.3918 4829 | 0.3486 9625 | 0.2927 6541 | 0.2458 5911 | 141 |
| 142 | 0.3892 5327 | 0.3461 0049 | 0.2902 2594 | 0.2434 2486 | 142 |
| 143 | 0.3866 7543 | 0.3435 2406 | 0.2877 0849 | 0.2410 1471 | 143 |
| 144 | 0.3841 1467 | 0.3409 6681 | 0.2852 1288 | 0.2386 2843 | 144 |
| 145 | 0.3815 7086 | 0.3384 2860 | 0.2827 3891 | 0.2362 6577 | 145 |
| 146 | 0.3790 4390 | 0.3359 0928 | 0.2802 8640 | 0.2339 2650 | 146 |
| 147 | 0.3765 3368 | 0.3334 0871 | 0.2778 5517 | 0.2316 1040 | 147 |
| 148 | 0.3740 4008 | 0.3309 2676 | 0.2754 4503 | 0.2293 1723 | 148 |
| 149 | 0.3715 6299 | 0.3284 6329 | 0.2730 5579 | 0.2270 4676 | 149 |
| 150 | 0.3691 0231 | 0.3260 1815 | 0.2706 8728 | 0.2247 9877 | 150 |
| 151 | 0.3666 5792 | 0.3235 9122 | 0.2683 3931 | 0.2225 7304 | 151 |
| 152 | 0.3642 2973 | 0.3211 8235 | 0.2660 1170 | 0.2203 6935 | 152 |
| 153 | 0.3618 1761 | 0.3187 9141 | 0.2637 0429 | 0.2181 8747 | 153 |
| 154 | 0.3594 2147 | 0.3164 1828 | 0.2614 1689 | 0.2160 2720 | 154 |
| 155 | 0.3570 4119 | 0.3140 6280 | 0.2591 4934 | 0.2138 8832 | 155 |
| 156 | 0.3546 7668 | 0.3117 2487 | 0.2569 0145 | 0.2117 7061 | 156 |
| 157 | 0.3523 2783 | 0.3094 0434 | 0.2546 7306 | 0.2096 7387 | 157 |
| 158 | 0.3499 9453 | 0.3071 0108 | 0.2524 6400 | 0.2075 9789 | 158 |
| 159 | 0.3476 7669 | 0.3048 1496 | 0.2502 7410 | 0.2055 4247 | 159 |
| 160 | 0.3453 7419 | 0.3025 4587 | 0.2481 0320 | 0.2035 0739 | 160 |
| 161 | 0.3430 8695 | 0.3002 9367 | 0.2459 5113 | 0.2014 9247 | 161 |
| 162 | 0.3408 1485 | 0.2980 5823 | 0.2438 1772 | 0.1994 9750 | 162 |
| 163 | 0.3385 5779 | 0.2958 3944 | 0.2417 0282 | 0.1975 2227 | 163 |
| 164 | 0.3363 1569 | 0.2936 3716 | 0.2396 0627 | 0.1955 6661 | 164 |
| 165 | 0.3340 8843 | 0.2914 5127 | 0.2375 2790 | 0.1936 3030 | 165 |
| 166 | 0.3318 7593 | 0.2892 8166 | 0.2354 6756 | 0.1917 1317 | 166 |
| 167 | 0.3296 7807 | 0.2871 2820 | 0.2334 2509 | 0.1898 1502 | 167 |
| 168 | 0.3274 9478 | 0.2849 9077 | 0.2314 0033 | 0.1879 3566 | 168 |
| 169 | 0.3253 2594 | 0.2828 6925 | 0.2293 9314 | 0.1860 7492 | 169 |
| 170 | 0.3231 7146 | 0.2807 6352 | 0.2274 0336 | 0.1842 3259 | 170 |
| 171 | 0.3210 3125 | 0.2786 7347 | 0.2254 3084 | 0.1824 0850 | 171 |
| 172 | 0.3189 0522 | 0.2765 9898 | 0.2234 7543 | 0.1806 0248 | 172 |
| 173 | 0.3167 9326 | 0.2745 3993 | 0.2215 3699 | 0.1788 1434 | 173 |
| 174 | 0.3146 9529 | 0.2724 9621 | 0.2196 1535 | 0.1770 4390 | 174 |
| 175 | 0.3126 1122 | 0.2704 6770 | 0.2177 1039 | 0.1752 9099 | 175 |
| 176 | 0.3105 4095 | 0.2684 5429 | 0.2158 2194 | 0.1735 5543 | 176 |
| 177 | 0.3084 8438 | 0.2664 5587 | 0.2139 4988 | 0.1718 3706 | 177 |
| 178 | 0.3064 4144 | 0.2644 7233 | 0.2120 9406 | 0.1701 3571 | 178 |
| 179 | 0.3044 1203 | 0.2625 0355 | 0.2102 5433 | 0.1684 5119 | 179 |
| 180 | 0.3023 9605 | 0.2605 4943 | 0.2084 3057 | 0.1667 8336 | 180 |

Table
6

# TABLE 6

$$p = (1 + i)^{-n} \quad [OR, \; v^n = (1 + i)^{-n}]$$

| $n$ | $\frac{2}{3}\%$ | $\frac{3}{4}\%$ | $\frac{7}{8}\%$ | 1% | $n$ |
|---|---|---|---|---|---|
| 181 | 0.3003 9343 | 0.2586 0986 | 0.2066 2262 | 0.1651 3204 | 181 |
| 182 | 0.2984 0407 | 0.2566 8472 | 0.2048 3035 | 0.1634 9707 | 182 |
| 183 | 0.2964 2788 | 0.2547 7392 | 0.2030 5363 | 0.1618 7829 | 183 |
| 184 | 0.2944 6478 | 0.2528 7734 | 0.2012 9233 | 0.1602 7553 | 184 |
| 185 | 0.2925 1469 | 0.2509 9488 | 0.1995 4630 | 0.1586 8864 | 185 |
| 186 | 0.2905 7750 | 0.2491 2643 | 0.1978 1541 | 0.1571 1747 | 186 |
| 187 | 0.2886 5315 | 0.2472 7189 | 0.1960 9954 | 0.1555 6185 | 187 |
| 188 | 0.2867 4154 | 0.2454 3116 | 0.1943 9855 | 0.1540 2163 | 188 |
| 189 | 0.2848 4259 | 0.2436 0413 | 0.1927 1232 | 0.1524 9667 | 189 |
| 190 | 0.2829 5621 | 0.2417 9070 | 0.1910 4071 | 0.1509 8680 | 190 |
| 191 | 0.2810 8233 | 0.2399 9077 | 0.1893 8361 | 0.1494 9188 | 191 |
| 192 | 0.2792 2086 | 0.2382 0423 | 0.1877 4087 | 0.1480 1176 | 192 |
| 193 | 0.2773 7171 | 0.2364 3100 | 0.1861 1239 | 0.1465 4630 | 193 |
| 194 | 0.2755 3482 | 0.2346 7097 | 0.1844 9803 | 0.1450 9535 | 194 |
| 195 | 0.2737 1008 | 0.2329 2404 | 0.1828 9768 | 0.1436 5876 | 195 |
| 196 | 0.2718 9743 | 0.2311 9011 | 0.1813 1121 | 0.1422 3640 | 196 |
| 197 | 0.2700 9679 | 0.2294 6909 | 0.1797 3849 | 0.1408 2811 | 197 |
| 198 | 0.2683 0807 | 0.2277 6089 | 0.1781 7942 | 0.1394 3378 | 198 |
| 199 | 0.2665 3119 | 0.2260 6540 | 0.1766 3388 | 0.1380 5324 | 199 |
| 200 | 0.2647 6608 | 0.2243 8253 | 0.1751 0174 | 0.1366 8638 | 200 |
| 201 | 0.2630 1267 | 0.2227 1219 | 0.1735 8289 | 0.1353 3305 | 201 |
| 202 | 0.2612 7086 | 0.2210 5428 | 0.1720 7721 | 0.1339 9312 | 202 |
| 203 | 0.2595 4059 | 0.2194 0871 | 0.1705 8460 | 0.1326 6645 | 203 |
| 204 | 0.2578 2178 | 0.2177 7540 | 0.1691 0493 | 0.1313 5293 | 204 |
| 205 | 0.2561 1435 | 0.2161 5424 | 0.1676 3809 | 0.1300 5240 | 205 |
| 206 | 0.2544 1823 | 0.2145 4515 | 0.1661 8398 | 0.1287 6475 | 206 |
| 207 | 0.2527 3334 | 0.2129 4804 | 0.1647 4249 | 0.1274 8985 | 207 |
| 208 | 0.2510 5961 | 0.2113 6282 | 0.1633 1349 | 0.1262 2758 | 208 |
| 209 | 0.2493 9696 | 0.2097 8940 | 0.1618 9690 | 0.1249 7780 | 209 |
| 210 | 0.2477 4533 | 0.2082 2769 | 0.1604 9259 | 0.1237 4040 | 210 |
| 211 | 0.2461 0463 | 0.2066 7761 | 0.1591 0046 | 0.1225 1524 | 211 |
| 212 | 0.2444 7480 | 0.2051 3907 | 0.1577 2040 | 0.1213 0222 | 212 |
| 213 | 0.2428 5576 | 0.2036 1198 | 0.1563 5232 | 0.1201 0121 | 213 |
| 214 | 0.2412 4744 | 0.2020 9626 | 0.1549 9611 | 0.1189 1209 | 214 |
| 215 | 0.2396 4978 | 0.2005 9182 | 0.1536 5165 | 0.1177 3474 | 215 |
| 216 | 0.2380 6269 | 0.1990 9858 | 0.1523 1886 | 0.1165 6905 | 216 |
| 217 | 0.2364 8612 | 0.1976 1646 | 0.1509 9763 | 0.1154 1490 | 217 |
| 218 | 0.2349 1998 | 0.1961 4537 | 0.1496 8787 | 0.1142 7218 | 218 |
| 219 | 0.2333 6422 | 0.1946 8523 | 0.1483 8946 | 0.1131 4077 | 219 |
| 220 | 0.2318 1877 | 0.1932 3596 | 0.1471 0231 | 0.1120 2057 | 220 |
| 221 | 0.2302 8354 | 0.1917 9748 | 0.1458 2633 | 0.1109 1145 | 221 |
| 222 | 0.2287 5848 | 0.1903 6970 | 0.1445 6142 | 0.1098 1332 | 222 |
| 223 | 0.2272 4353 | 0.1889 5256 | 0.1433 0748 | 0.1087 2606 | 223 |
| 224 | 0.2257 3860 | 0.1875 4596 | 0.1420 6442 | 0.1076 4956 | 224 |
| 225 | 0.2242 4365 | 0.1861 4984 | 0.1408 3213 | 0.1065 8373 | 225 |
| 226 | 0.2227 5859 | 0.1847 6411 | 0.1396 1054 | 0.1055 2844 | 226 |
| 227 | 0.2212 8337 | 0.1833 8869 | 0.1383 9955 | 0.1044 8361 | 227 |
| 228 | 0.2198 1791 | 0.1820 2352 | 0.1371 9905 | 0.1034 4911 | 228 |
| 229 | 0.2183 6217 | 0.1806 6850 | 0.1360 0898 | 0.1024 2487 | 229 |
| 230 | 0.2169 1606 | 0.1793 2358 | 0.1348 2922 | 0.1014 1076 | 230 |
| 231 | 0.2154 7953 | 0.1779 8866 | 0.1336 5970 | 0.1004 0669 | 231 |
| 232 | 0.2140 5251 | 0.1766 6368 | 0.1325 0032 | 0.0994 1257 | 232 |
| 233 | 0.2126 3495 | 0.1753 4857 | 0.1313 5100 | 0.0984 2828 | 233 |
| 234 | 0.2112 2677 | 0.1740 4325 | 0.1302 1165 | 0.0974 5375 | 234 |
| 235 | 0.2098 2791 | 0.1727 4764 | 0.1290 8218 | 0.0964 8886 | 235 |
| 236 | 0.2084 3833 | 0.1714 6168 | 0.1279 6251 | 0.0955 3352 | 236 |
| 237 | 0.2070 5794 | 0.1701 8529 | 0.1268 5255 | 0.0945 8765 | 237 |
| 238 | 0.2056 8669 | 0.1689 1840 | 0.1257 5221 | 0.0936 5113 | 238 |
| 239 | 0.2043 2453 | 0.1676 6094 | 0.1246 6143 | 0.0927 2389 | 239 |
| 240 | 0.2029 7139 | 0.1664 1284 | 0.1235 8010 | 0.0918 0584 | 240 |

# TABLE 6

$$p = (1 + i)^{-n} \quad [OR, \; v^n = (1 + i)^{-n}]$$

| $n$ | $1\frac{1}{8}\%$ | $1\frac{1}{4}\%$ | $1\frac{3}{8}\%$ | $1\frac{1}{2}\%$ | $n$ |
|---|---|---|---|---|---|
| 1 | 0.9888 7515 | 0.9876 5432 | 0.9864 3650 | 0.9852 2167 | 1 |
| 2 | 0.9778 7407 | 0.9754 6106 | 0.9730 5696 | 0.9706 6175 | 2 |
| 3 | 0.9669 9537 | 0.9634 1833 | 0.9598 5890 | 0.9563 1699 | 3 |
| 4 | 0.9562 3770 | 0.9515 2428 | 0.9468 3986 | 0.9421 8423 | 4 |
| 5 | 0.9455 9970 | 0.9397 7706 | 0.9339 9739 | 0.9282 6033 | 5 |
| 6 | 0.9350 8005 | 0.9281 7488 | 0.9213 2912 | 0.9145 4219 | 6 |
| 7 | 0.9246 7743 | 0.9167 1593 | 0.9088 3267 | 0.9010 2679 | 7 |
| 8 | 0.9143 9054 | 0.9053 9845 | 0.8965 0571 | 0.8877 1112 | 8 |
| 9 | 0.9042 1808 | 0.8942 2069 | 0.8843 4596 | 0.8745 9224 | 9 |
| 10 | 0.8941 5880 | 0.8831 8093 | 0.8723 5113 | 0.8616 6723 | 10 |
| 11 | 0.8842 1142 | 0.8722 7746 | 0.8605 1899 | 0.8489 3323 | 11 |
| 12 | 0.8743 7470 | 0.8615 0860 | 0.8488 4734 | 0.8363 8742 | 12 |
| 13 | 0.8646 4742 | 0.8508 7269 | 0.8373 3400 | 0.8240 2702 | 13 |
| 14 | 0.8550 2835 | 0.8403 6809 | 0.8259 7682 | 0.8118 4928 | 14 |
| 15 | 0.8455 1629 | 0.8299 9318 | 0.8147 7368 | 0.7998 5150 | 15 |
| 16 | 0.8361 1005 | 0.8197 4635 | 0.8037 2250 | 0.7880 3104 | 16 |
| 17 | 0.8268 0846 | 0.8096 2602 | 0.7928 2120 | 0.7763 8526 | 17 |
| 18 | 0.8176 1034 | 0.7996 3064 | 0.7820 6777 | 0.7649 1159 | 18 |
| 19 | 0.8085 1455 | 0.7897 5866 | 0.7714 6020 | 0.7536 0747 | 19 |
| 20 | 0.7995 1995 | 0.7800 0855 | 0.7609 9649 | 0.7424 7042 | 20 |
| 21 | 0.7906 2542 | 0.7703 7881 | 0.7506 7472 | 0.7314 9795 | 21 |
| 22 | 0.7818 2983 | 0.7608 6796 | 0.7404 9294 | 0.7206 8763 | 22 |
| 23 | 0.7731 3210 | 0.7514 7453 | 0.7304 4926 | 0.7100 3708 | 23 |
| 24 | 0.7645 3112 | 0.7421 9707 | 0.7205 4181 | 0.6995 4392 | 24 |
| 25 | 0.7560 2583 | 0.7330 3414 | 0.7107 6874 | 0.6892 0583 | 25 |
| 26 | 0.7476 1516 | 0.7239 8434 | 0.7011 2823 | 0.6790 2052 | 26 |
| 27 | 0.7392 9806 | 0.7150 4626 | 0.6916 1847 | 0.6689 8574 | 27 |
| 28 | 0.7310 7348 | 0.7062 1853 | 0.6822 3771 | 0.6590 9925 | 28 |
| 29 | 0.7229 4040 | 0.6974 9978 | 0.6729 8417 | 0.6493 5887 | 29 |
| 30 | 0.7148 9780 | 0.6888 8867 | 0.6638 5615 | 0.6397 6243 | 30 |
| 31 | 0.7069 4467 | 0.6803 8387 | 0.6548 5194 | 0.6303 0781 | 31 |
| 32 | 0.6990 8002 | 0.6719 8407 | 0.6459 6985 | 0.6209 9292 | 32 |
| 33 | 0.6913 0287 | 0.6636 8797 | 0.6372 0824 | 0.6118 1568 | 33 |
| 34 | 0.6836 1223 | 0.6554 9429 | 0.6285 6546 | 0.6027 7407 | 34 |
| 35 | 0.6760 0715 | 0.6474 0177 | 0.6200 3991 | 0.5938 6608 | 35 |
| 36 | 0.6684 8667 | 0.6394 0916 | 0.6116 3000 | 0.5850 8974 | 36 |
| 37 | 0.6610 4986 | 0.6315 1522 | 0.6033 3416 | 0.5764 4309 | 37 |
| 38 | 0.6536 9578 | 0.6237 1873 | 0.5951 5083 | 0.5679 2423 | 38 |
| 39 | 0.6464 2352 | 0.6160 1850 | 0.5870 7850 | 0.5595 3126 | 39 |
| 40 | 0.6392 3216 | 0.6084 1334 | 0.5791 1566 | 0.5512 6232 | 40 |
| 41 | 0.6321 2080 | 0.6009 0206 | 0.5712 6083 | 0.5431 1559 | 41 |
| 42 | 0.6250 8855 | 0.5934 8352 | 0.5635 1253 | 0.5350 8925 | 42 |
| 43 | 0.6181 3454 | 0.5861 5656 | 0.5558 6933 | 0.5271 8153 | 43 |
| 44 | 0.6112 5789 | 0.5789 2006 | 0.5483 2979 | 0.5193 9067 | 44 |
| 45 | 0.6044 5774 | 0.5717 7290 | 0.5408 9252 | 0.5117 1494 | 45 |
| 46 | 0.5977 3324 | 0.5647 1397 | 0.5335 5612 | 0.5041 5265 | 46 |
| 47 | 0.5910 8355 | 0.5577 4219 | 0.5263 1923 | 0.4967 0212 | 47 |
| 48 | 0.5845 0784 | 0.5508 5649 | 0.5191 8050 | 0.4893 6170 | 48 |
| 49 | 0.5780 0528 | 0.5440 5579 | 0.5121 3860 | 0.4821 2975 | 49 |
| 50 | 0.5715 7506 | 0.5373 3905 | 0.5051 9220 | 0.4750 0468 | 50 |

**Table 6**

# TABLE 6

$$p = (1 + i)^{-n} \quad [OR, \; v^n = (1 + i)^{-n}]$$

| $n$ | $1\frac{1}{8}\%$ | $1\frac{1}{4}\%$ | $1\frac{3}{8}\%$ | $1\frac{1}{2}\%$ | $n$ |
|---|---|---|---|---|---|
| 51 | 0.5652 1637 | 0.5307 0524 | 0.4983 4003 | 0.4679 8491 | 51 |
| 52 | 0.5589 2843 | 0.5241 5332 | 0.4915 8079 | 0.4610 6887 | 52 |
| 53 | 0.5527 1044 | 0.5176 8229 | 0.4849 1323 | 0.4542 5505 | 53 |
| 54 | 0.5465 6162 | 0.5112 9115 | 0.4783 3611 | 0.4475 4192 | 54 |
| 55 | 0.5404 8120 | 0.5049 7892 | 0.4718 4820 | 0.4409 2800 | 55 |
| 56 | 0.5344 6843 | 0.4987 4461 | 0.4654 4829 | 0.4344 1182 | 56 |
| 57 | 0.5285 2256 | 0.4925 8727 | 0.4591 3518 | 0.4279 9194 | 57 |
| 58 | 0.5226 4282 | 0.4865 0594 | 0.4529 0770 | 0.4216 6694 | 58 |
| 59 | 0.5168 2850 | 0.4804 9970 | 0.4467 6468 | 0.4154 3541 | 59 |
| 60 | 0.5110 7887 | 0.4745 6760 | 0.4407 0499 | 0.4092 9597 | 60 |
| 61 | 0.5053 9319 | 0.4687 0874 | 0.4347 2749 | 0.4032 4726 | 61 |
| 62 | 0.4997 7077 | 0.4629 2222 | 0.4288 3106 | 0.3972 8794 | 62 |
| 63 | 0.4942 1090 | 0.4572 0713 | 0.4230 1461 | 0.3914 1669 | 63 |
| 64 | 0.4887 1288 | 0.4515 6259 | 0.4172 7705 | 0.3856 3221 | 64 |
| 65 | 0.4832 7602 | 0.4459 8775 | 0.4116 1731 | 0.3799 3321 | 65 |
| 66 | 0.4778 9965 | 0.4404 8173 | 0.4060 3434 | 0.3743 1843 | 66 |
| 67 | 0.4725 8309 | 0.4350 4368 | 0.4005 2709 | 0.3687 8663 | 67 |
| 68 | 0.4673 2568 | 0.4296 7277 | 0.3950 9454 | 0.3633 3658 | 68 |
| 69 | 0.4621 2675 | 0.4243 6817 | 0.3897 3568 | 0.3579 6708 | 69 |
| 70 | 0.4569 8566 | 0.4191 2905 | 0.3844 4949 | 0.3526 7692 | 70 |
| 71 | 0.4519 0177 | 0.4139 5462 | 0.3792 3501 | 0.3474 6495 | 71 |
| 72 | 0.4468 7443 | 0.4088 4407 | 0.3740 9126 | 0.3423 3000 | 72 |
| 73 | 0.4419 0302 | 0.4037 9661 | 0.3690 1727 | 0.3372 7093 | 73 |
| 74 | 0.4369 8692 | 0.3988 1147 | 0.3640 1210 | 0.3322 8663 | 74 |
| 75 | 0.4321 2551 | 0.3938 8787 | 0.3590 7483 | 0.3273 7599 | 75 |
| 76 | 0.4273 1818 | 0.3890 2506 | 0.3542 0451 | 0.3225 3793 | 76 |
| 77 | 0.4225 6433 | 0.3842 2228 | 0.3494 0026 | 0.3177 7136 | 77 |
| 78 | 0.4178 6337 | 0.3794 7880 | 0.3446 6117 | 0.3130 7523 | 78 |
| 79 | 0.4132 1470 | 0.3747 9387 | 0.3399 8636 | 0.3084 4850 | 79 |
| 80 | 0.4086 1775 | 0.3701 6679 | 0.3353 7495 | 0.3038 9015 | 80 |
| 81 | 0.4040 7194 | 0.3655 9683 | 0.3308 2609 | 0.2993 9916 | 81 |
| 82 | 0.3995 7670 | 0.3610 8329 | 0.3263 3893 | 0.2949 7454 | 82 |
| 83 | 0.3951 3148 | 0.3566 2547 | 0.3219 1263 | 0.2906 1531 | 83 |
| 84 | 0.3907 3570 | 0.3522 2268 | 0.3175 4637 | 0.2863 2050 | 84 |
| 85 | 0.3863 8882 | 0.3478 7426 | 0.3132 3933 | 0.2820 8917 | 85 |
| 86 | 0.3820 9031 | 0.3435 7951 | 0.3089 9071 | 0.2779 2036 | 86 |
| 87 | 0.3778 3961 | 0.3393 3779 | 0.3047 9971 | 0.2738 1316 | 87 |
| 88 | 0.3736 3621 | 0.3351 4843 | 0.3006 6556 | 0.2697 6666 | 88 |
| 89 | 0.3694 7956 | 0.3310 1080 | 0.2965 8748 | 0.2657 7997 | 89 |
| 90 | 0.3653 6916 | 0.3269 2425 | 0.2925 6472 | 0.2618 5218 | 90 |
| 91 | 0.3613 0448 | 0.3228 8814 | 0.2885 9652 | 0.2579 8245 | 91 |
| 92 | 0.3572 8503 | 0.3189 0187 | 0.2846 8214 | 0.2541 6990 | 92 |
| 93 | 0.3533 1029 | 0.3149 6481 | 0.2808 2085 | 0.2504 1369 | 93 |
| 94 | 0.3493 7976 | 0.3110 7636 | 0.2770 1194 | 0.2467 1300 | 94 |
| 95 | 0.3454 9297 | 0.3072 3591 | 0.2732 5468 | 0.2430 6699 | 95 |
| 96 | 0.3416 4941 | 0.3034 4287 | 0.2695 4839 | 0.2394 7487 | 96 |
| 97 | 0.3378 4861 | 0.2996 9666 | 0.2658 9237 | 0.2359 3583 | 97 |
| 98 | 0.3340 9010 | 0.2959 9670 | 0.2622 8594 | 0.2324 4909 | 98 |
| 99 | 0.3303 7340 | 0.2923 4242 | 0.2587 2843 | 0.2290 1389 | 99 |
| 100 | 0.3266 9805 | 0.2887 3326 | 0.2552 1916 | 0.2256 2944 | 100 |

# TABLE 6

$$p = (1 + i)^{-n} \quad [OR, \; v^n = (1 + i)^{-n}]$$

| $n$ | $1\frac{5}{8}\%$ | $1\frac{3}{4}\%$ | $1\frac{7}{8}\%$ | $2\%$ | $n$ |
|---|---|---|---|---|---|
| 1 | 0.9840 0984 | 0.9828 0098 | 0.9815 9509 | 0.9803 9216 | 1 |
| 2 | 0.9682 7537 | 0.9658 9777 | 0.9635 2892 | 0.9611 6878 | 2 |
| 3 | 0.9527 9249 | 0.9492 8528 | 0.9457 9526 | 0.9423 2233 | 3 |
| 4 | 0.9375 5718 | 0.9329 5851 | 0.9283 8799 | 0.9238 4543 | 4 |
| 5 | 0.9225 6549 | 0.9169 1254 | 0.9113 0109 | 0.9057 3081 | 5 |
| 6 | 0.9078 1352 | 0.9011 4254 | 0.8945 2868 | 0.8879 7138 | 6 |
| 7 | 0.8932 9744 | 0.8856 4378 | 0.8780 6496 | 0.8705 6018 | 7 |
| 8 | 0.8790 1347 | 0.8704 1157 | 0.8619 0426 | 0.8534 9037 | 8 |
| 9 | 0.8649 5791 | 0.8554 4135 | 0.8460 4099 | 0.8367 5527 | 9 |
| 10 | 0.8511 2709 | 0.8407 2860 | 0.8304 6968 | 0.8203 4830 | 10 |
| 11 | 0.8375 1743 | 0.8262 6889 | 0.8151 8496 | 0.8042 6304 | 11 |
| 12 | 0.8241 2539 | 0.8120 5788 | 0.8001 8156 | 0.7884 9318 | 12 |
| 13 | 0.8109 4750 | 0.7980 9128 | 0.7854 5429 | 0.7730 3253 | 13 |
| 14 | 0.7979 8032 | 0.7843 6490 | 0.7709 9808 | 0.7578 7502 | 14 |
| 15 | 0.7852 2048 | 0.7708 7459 | 0.7568 0793 | 0.7430 1473 | 15 |
| 16 | 0.7726 6468 | 0.7576 1631 | 0.7428 7895 | 0.7284 4581 | 16 |
| 17 | 0.7603 0965 | 0.7445 8605 | 0.7292 0633 | 0.7141 6256 | 17 |
| 18 | 0.7481 5218 | 0.7317 7990 | 0.7157 8536 | 0.7001 5938 | 18 |
| 19 | 0.7361 8911 | 0.7191 9401 | 0.7026 1139 | 0.6864 3076 | 19 |
| 20 | 0.7244 1732 | 0.7068 2458 | 0.6896 7989 | 0.6729 7133 | 20 |
| 21 | 0.7128 3378 | 0.6946 6789 | 0.6769 8640 | 0.6597 7582 | 21 |
| 22 | 0.7014 3545 | 0.6827 2028 | 0.6645 2653 | 0.6468 3904 | 22 |
| 23 | 0.6902 1938 | 0.6709 7817 | 0.6522 9598 | 0.6341 5592 | 23 |
| 24 | 0.6791 8267 | 0.6594 3800 | 0.6402 9053 | 0.6217 2149 | 24 |
| 25 | 0.6683 2243 | 0.6480 9632 | 0.6285 0604 | 0.6095 3087 | 25 |
| 26 | 0.6576 3584 | 0.6369 4970 | 0.6169 3845 | 0.5975 7928 | 26 |
| 27 | 0.6471 2014 | 0.6259 9479 | 0.6055 8375 | 0.5858 6204 | 27 |
| 28 | 0.6367 7259 | 0.6152 2829 | 0.5944 3804 | 0.5743 7455 | 28 |
| 29 | 0.6265 9049 | 0.6046 4697 | 0.5834 9746 | 0.5631 1231 | 29 |
| 30 | 0.6165 7121 | 0.5942 4764 | 0.5727 5824 | 0.5520 7089 | 30 |
| 31 | 0.6067 1214 | 0.5840 2716 | 0.5622 1668 | 0.5412 4597 | 31 |
| 32 | 0.5970 1071 | 0.5739 8247 | 0.5518 6913 | 0.5306 3330 | 32 |
| 33 | 0.5874 6442 | 0.5641 1053 | 0.5417 1203 | 0.5202 2873 | 33 |
| 34 | 0.5780 7077 | 0.5544 0839 | 0.5317 4187 | 0.5100 2817 | 34 |
| 35 | 0.5688 2732 | 0.5448 7311 | 0.5219 5521 | 0.5000 2761 | 35 |
| 36 | 0.5597 3168 | 0.5355 0183 | 0.5123 4867 | 0.4902 2315 | 36 |
| 37 | 0.5507 8148 | 0.5262 9172 | 0.5029 1894 | 0.4806 1093 | 37 |
| 38 | 0.5419 7440 | 0.5172 4002 | 0.4936 6277 | 0.4711 8719 | 38 |
| 39 | 0.5333 0814 | 0.5083 4400 | 0.4845 7695 | 0.4619 4822 | 39 |
| 40 | 0.5247 8046 | 0.4996 0098 | 0.4756 5836 | 0.4528 9042 | 40 |
| 41 | 0.5163 8914 | 0.4910 0834 | 0.4669 0391 | 0.4440 1021 | 41 |
| 42 | 0.5081 3199 | 0.4825 6348 | 0.4583 1058 | 0.4353 0413 | 42 |
| 43 | 0.5000 0688 | 0.4742 6386 | 0.4498 7542 | 0.4267 6875 | 43 |
| 44 | 0.4920 1169 | 0.4661 0699 | 0.4415 9550 | 0.4184 0074 | 44 |
| 45 | 0.4841 4434 | 0.4580 9040 | 0.4334 6798 | 0.4101 9680 | 45 |
| 46 | 0.4764 0280 | 0.4502 1170 | 0.4254 9004 | 0.4021 5373 | 46 |
| 47 | 0.4687 8504 | 0.4424 6850 | 0.4176 5894 | 0.3942 6836 | 47 |
| 48 | 0.4612 8909 | 0.4348 5848 | 0.4099 7196 | 0.3865 3761 | 48 |
| 49 | 0.4539 1301 | 0.4273 7934 | 0.4024 2647 | 0.3789 5844 | 49 |
| 50 | 0.4466 5487 | 0.4200 2883 | 0.3950 1984 | 0.3715 2788 | 50 |

Table
6

## TABLE 6

$$p=(1+i)^{-n} \quad [OR, \ v^{n}=(1+i)^{-n}]$$

| $n$ | $1\frac{5}{8}\%$ | $1\frac{3}{4}\%$ | $1\frac{7}{8}\%$ | $2\%$ | $n$ |
|---|---|---|---|---|---|
| 51 | 0.4395 1278 | 0.4128 0475 | 0.3877 4954 | 0.3642 4302 | 51 |
| 52 | 0.4324 8490 | 0.4057 0492 | 0.3806 1305 | 0.3571 0100 | 52 |
| 53 | 0.4255 6940 | 0.3987 2719 | 0.3736 0790 | 0.3500 9902 | 53 |
| 54 | 0.4187 6448 | 0.3918 6947 | 0.3667 3168 | 0.3432 3433 | 54 |
| 55 | 0.4120 6837 | 0.3851 2970 | 0.3599 8202 | 0.3365 0425 | 55 |
| 56 | 0.4054 7933 | 0.3785 0585 | 0.3533 5658 | 0.3299 0613 | 56 |
| 57 | 0.3989 9565 | 0.3719 9592 | 0.3468 5308 | 0.3234 3738 | 57 |
| 58 | 0.3926 1564 | 0.3655 9796 | 0.3404 6928 | 0.3170 9547 | 58 |
| 59 | 0.3863 3766 | 0.3593 1003 | 0.3342 0298 | 0.3108 7791 | 59 |
| 60 | 0.3801 6006 | 0.3531 3025 | 0.3280 5200 | 0.3047 8227 | 60 |
| 61 | 0.3740 8124 | 0.3470 5676 | 0.3220 1424 | 0.2988 0614 | 61 |
| 62 | 0.3680 9962 | 0.3410 8772 | 0.3160 8759 | 0.2929 4720 | 62 |
| 63 | 0.3622 1365 | 0.3352 2135 | 0.3102 7003 | 0.2872 0314 | 63 |
| 64 | 0.3564 2179 | 0.3294 5587 | 0.3045 5954 | 0.2815 7170 | 64 |
| 65 | 0.3507 2255 | 0.3237 8956 | 0.2989 5415 | 0.2760 5069 | 65 |
| 66 | 0.3451 1444 | 0.3182 2069 | 0.2934 5193 | 0.2706 3793 | 66 |
| 67 | 0.3395 9601 | 0.3127 4761 | 0.2880 5097 | 0.2653 3130 | 67 |
| 68 | 0.3341 6581 | 0.3073 6866 | 0.2827 4942 | 0.2601 2873 | 68 |
| 69 | 0.3288 2245 | 0.3020 8222 | 0.2775 4544 | 0.2550 2817 | 69 |
| 70 | 0.3235 6452 | 0.2968 8670 | 0.2724 3724 | 0.2500 2761 | 70 |
| 71 | 0.3183 9067 | 0.2917 8054 | 0.2674 2306 | 0.2451 2511 | 71 |
| 72 | 0.3132 9956 | 0.2867 6221 | 0.2625 0116 | 0.2403 1874 | 72 |
| 73 | 0.3082 8985 | 0.2818 3018 | 0.2576 6985 | 0.2356 0660 | 73 |
| 74 | 0.3033 6024 | 0.2769 8298 | 0.2529 2746 | 0.2309 8687 | 74 |
| 75 | 0.2985 0946 | 0.2722 1914 | 0.2482 7236 | 0.2264 5771 | 75 |
| 76 | 0.2937 3625 | 0.2675 3724 | 0.2437 0293 | 0.2220 1737 | 76 |
| 77 | 0.2890 3936 | 0.2629 3586 | 0.2392 1760 | 0.2176 6408 | 77 |
| 78 | 0.2844 1757 | 0.2584 1362 | 0.2348 1482 | 0.2133 9616 | 78 |
| 79 | 0.2798 6969 | 0.2539 6916 | 0.2304 9308 | 0.2092 1192 | 79 |
| 80 | 0.2753 9453 | 0.2496 0114 | 0.2262 5087 | 0.2051 0973 | 80 |
| 81 | 0.2709 9093 | 0.2453 0825 | 0.2220 8674 | 0.2010 8797 | 81 |
| 82 | 0.2666 5774 | 0.2410 8919 | 0.2179 9926 | 0.1971 4507 | 82 |
| 83 | 0.2623 9384 | 0.2369 4269 | 0.2139 8700 | 0.1932 7948 | 83 |
| 84 | 0.2581 9812 | 0.2328 6751 | 0.2100 4859 | 0.1894 8968 | 84 |
| 85 | 0.2540 6949 | 0.2288 6242 | 0.2061 8267 | 0.1857 7420 | 85 |
| 86 | 0.2500 0688 | 0.2249 2621 | 0.2023 8789 | 0.1821 3157 | 86 |
| 87 | 0.2460 0923 | 0.2210 5770 | 0.1986 6296 | 0.1785 6036 | 87 |
| 88 | 0.2420 7550 | 0.2172 5572 | 0.1950 0659 | 0.1750 5918 | 88 |
| 89 | 0.2382 0468 | 0.2135 1914 | 0.1914 1751 | 0.1716 2665 | 89 |
| 90 | 0.2343 9575 | 0.2098 4682 | 0.1878 9449 | 0.1682 6142 | 90 |
| 91 | 0.2306 4772 | 0.2062 3766 | 0.1844 3631 | 0.1649 6217 | 91 |
| 92 | 0.2269 5963 | 0.2026 9057 | 0.1810 4178 | 0.1617 2762 | 92 |
| 93 | 0.2233 3051 | 0.1992 0450 | 0.1777 0972 | 0.1585 5649 | 93 |
| 94 | 0.2197 5942 | 0.1957 7837 | 0.1744 3899 | 0.1554 4754 | 94 |
| 95 | 0.2162 4543 | 0.1924 1118 | 0.1712 2845 | 0.1523 9955 | 95 |
| 96 | 0.2127 8763 | 0.1891 0190 | 0.1680 7701 | 0.1494 1132 | 96 |
| 97 | 0.2093 8512 | 0.1858 4953 | 0.1649 8357 | 0.1464 8169 | 97 |
| 98 | 0.2060 3702 | 0.1826 5310 | 0.1619 4706 | 0.1436 0950 | 98 |
| 99 | 0.2027 4245 | 0.1795 1165 | 0.1589 6644 | 0.1407 9363 | 99 |
| 100 | 0.1995 0057 | 0.1764 2422 | 0.1560 4068 | 0.1380 3297 | 100 |

## TABLE 6

$$p=(1+i)^{-n} \quad [OR, \ v^n=(1+i)^{-n}]$$

| n | $2\frac{1}{4}\%$ | $2\frac{1}{2}\%$ | $2\frac{3}{4}\%$ | $3\%$ | n |
|---|---|---|---|---|---|
| 1 | 0.9779 9511 | 0.9756 0976 | 0.9732 3601 | 0.9708 7379 | 1 |
| 2 | 0.9564 7444 | 0.9518 1440 | 0.9471 8833 | 0.9425 9591 | 2 |
| 3 | 0.9354 2732 | 0.9285 9941 | 0.9218 3779 | 0.9151 4166 | 3 |
| 4 | 0.9148 4335 | 0.9059 5064 | 0.8971 6573 | 0.8884 8705 | 4 |
| 5 | 0.8947 1232 | 0.8838 5429 | 0.8731 5400 | 0.8626 0878 | 5 |
| 6 | 0.8750 2427 | 0.8622 9687 | 0.8497 8491 | 0.8374 8426 | 6 |
| 7 | 0.8557 6946 | 0.8412 6524 | 0.8270 4128 | 0.8130 9151 | 7 |
| 8 | 0.8369 3835 | 0.8207 4657 | 0.8049 0635 | 0.7894 0923 | 8 |
| 9 | 0.8185 2161 | 0.8007 2836 | 0.7833 6385 | 0.7664 1673 | 9 |
| 10 | 0.8005 1013 | 0.7811 9840 | 0.7623 9791 | 0.7440 9391 | 10 |
| 11 | 0.7828 9499 | 0.7621 4478 | 0.7419 9310 | 0.7224 2128 | 11 |
| 12 | 0.7656 6748 | 0.7435 5589 | 0.7221 3440 | 0.7013 7988 | 12 |
| 13 | 0.7488 1905 | 0.7254 2038 | 0.7028 0720 | 0.6809 5134 | 13 |
| 14 | 0.7323 4137 | 0.7077 2720 | 0.6839 9728 | 0.6611 1781 | 14 |
| 15 | 0.7162 2628 | 0.6904 6556 | 0.6656 9078 | 0.6418 6195 | 15 |
| 16 | 0.7004 6580 | 0.6736 2493 | 0.6478 7424 | 0.6231 6694 | 16 |
| 17 | 0.6850 5212 | 0.6571 9506 | 0.6305 3454 | 0.6050 1645 | 17 |
| 18 | 0.6699 7763 | 0.6411 6591 | 0.6136 5892 | 0.5873 9461 | 18 |
| 19 | 0.6552 3484 | 0.6255 2772 | 0.5972 3496 | 0.5702 8603 | 19 |
| 20 | 0.6408 1647 | 0.6102 7094 | 0.5812 5057 | 0.5536 7575 | 20 |
| 21 | 0.6267 1538 | 0.5953 8629 | 0.5656 9398 | 0.5375 4928 | 21 |
| 22 | 0.6129 2457 | 0.5808 6467 | 0.5505 5375 | 0.5218 9250 | 22 |
| 23 | 0.5994 3724 | 0.5666 9724 | 0.5358 1874 | 0.5066 9175 | 23 |
| 24 | 0.5862 4668 | 0.5528 7535 | 0.5214 7809 | 0.4919 3374 | 24 |
| 25 | 0.5733 4639 | 0.5393 9059 | 0.5075 2126 | 0.4776 0557 | 25 |
| 26 | 0.5607 2997 | 0.5262 3472 | 0.4939 3796 | 0.4636 9473 | 26 |
| 27 | 0.5483 9117 | 0.5133 9973 | 0.4807 1821 | 0.4501 8906 | 27 |
| 28 | 0.5363 2388 | 0.5008 7778 | 0.4678 5227 | 0.4370 7675 | 28 |
| 29 | 0.5245 2213 | 0.4886 6125 | 0.4553 3068 | 0.4243 4636 | 29 |
| 30 | 0.5129 8008 | 0.4767 4269 | 0.4431 4421 | 0.4119 8676 | 30 |
| 31 | 0.5016 9201 | 0.4651 1481 | 0.4312 8391 | 0.3999 8715 | 31 |
| 32 | 0.4906 5233 | 0.4537 7055 | 0.4197 4103 | 0.3883 3703 | 32 |
| 33 | 0.4798 5558 | 0.4427 0298 | 0.4085 0708 | 0.3770 2625 | 33 |
| 34 | 0.4692 9641 | 0.4319 0534 | 0.3975 7380 | 0.3660 4490 | 34 |
| 35 | 0.4589 6960 | 0.4213 7107 | 0.3869 3314 | 0.3553 8340 | 35 |
| 36 | 0.4488 7002 | 0.4110 9372 | 0.3765 7727 | 0.3450 3243 | 36 |
| 37 | 0.4389 9268 | 0.4010 6705 | 0.3664 9856 | 0.3349 8294 | 37 |
| 38 | 0.4293 3270 | 0.3912 8492 | 0.3566 8959 | 0.3252 2615 | 38 |
| 39 | 0.4198 8528 | 0.3817 4139 | 0.3471 4316 | 0.3157 5355 | 39 |
| 40 | 0.4106 4575 | 0.3724 3062 | 0.3378 5222 | 0.3065 5684 | 40 |
| 41 | 0.4016 0954 | 0.3633 4695 | 0.3288 0995 | 0.2976 2800 | 41 |
| 42 | 0.3927 7216 | 0.3544 8483 | 0.3200 0968 | 0.2889 5922 | 42 |
| 43 | 0.3841 2925 | 0.3458 3886 | 0.3114 4495 | 0.2805 4294 | 43 |
| 44 | 0.3756 7653 | 0.3374 0376 | 0.3031 0944 | 0.2723 7178 | 44 |
| 45 | 0.3674 0981 | 0.3291 7440 | 0.2949 9702 | 0.2644 3862 | 45 |
| 46 | 0.3593 2500 | 0.3211 4576 | 0.2871 0172 | 0.2567 3653 | 46 |
| 47 | 0.3514 1809 | 0.3133 1294 | 0.2794 1773 | 0.2492 5876 | 47 |
| 48 | 0.3436 8518 | 0.3056 7116 | 0.2719 3940 | 0.2419 9880 | 48 |
| 49 | 0.3361 2242 | 0.2982 1576 | 0.2646 6122 | 0.2349 5029 | 49 |
| 50 | 0.3287 2608 | 0.2909 4221 | 0.2575 7783 | 0.2281 0708 | 50 |

Table
6

## TABLE 6

$$p = (1 + i)^{-n} \quad [OR, \quad v^n = (1 + i)^{-n}]$$

| n | $2\frac{1}{4}\%$ | $2\frac{1}{2}\%$ | $2\frac{3}{4}\%$ | 3 % | n |
|---|---|---|---|---|---|
| 51 | 0.3214 9250 | 0.2838 4606 | 0.2506 8402 | 0.2214 6318 | 51 |
| 52 | 0.3144 1810 | 0.2769 2298 | 0.2439 7471 | 0.2150 1280 | 52 |
| 53 | 0.3074 9936 | 0.2701 6876 | 0.2374 4497 | 0.2087 5029 | 53 |
| 54 | 0.3007 3287 | 0.2635 7928 | 0.2310 9000 | 0.2026 7019 | 54 |
| 55 | 0.2941 1528 | 0.2571 5052 | 0.2249 0511 | 0.1967 6717 | 55 |
| 56 | 0.2876 4330 | 0.2508 7855 | 0.2188 8575 | 0.1910 3609 | 56 |
| 57 | 0.2813 1374 | 0.2447 5956 | 0.2130 2749 | 0.1854 7193 | 57 |
| 58 | 0.2751 2347 | 0.2387 8982 | 0.2073 2603 | 0.1800 6984 | 58 |
| 59 | 0.2690 6940 | 0.2329 6568 | 0.2017 7716 | 0.1748 2508 | 59 |
| 60 | 0.2631 4856 | 0.2272 8359 | 0.1963 7679 | 0.1697 3309 | 60 |
| 61 | 0.2573 5801 | 0.2217 4009 | 0.1911 2097 | 0.1647 8941 | 61 |
| 62 | 0.2516 9487 | 0.2163 3179 | 0.1860 0581 | 0.1599 8972 | 62 |
| 63 | 0.2461 5635 | 0.2110 5541 | 0.1810 2755 | 0.1553 2982 | 63 |
| 64 | 0.2407 3971 | 0.2059 0771 | 0.1761 8253 | 0.1508 0565 | 64 |
| 65 | 0.2354 4226 | 0.2008 8557 | 0.1714 6718 | 0.1464 1325 | 65 |
| 66 | 0.2302 6138 | 0.1959 8593 | 0.1668 7804 | 0.1421 4879 | 66 |
| 67 | 0.2251 9450 | 0.1912 0578 | 0.1624 1172 | 0.1380 0853 | 67 |
| 68 | 0.2202 3912 | 0.1865 4223 | 0.1580 6493 | 0.1339 8887 | 68 |
| 69 | 0.2153 9278 | 0.1819 9242 | 0.1538 3448 | 0.1300 8628 | 69 |
| 70 | 0.2106 5309 | 0.1775 5358 | 0.1497 1726 | 0.1262 9736 | 70 |
| 71 | 0.2060 1769 | 0.1732 2300 | 0.1457 1023 | 0.1226 1880 | 71 |
| 72 | 0.2014 8429 | 0.1689 9805 | 0.1418 1044 | 0.1190 4737 | 72 |
| 73 | 0.1970 5065 | 0.1648 7615 | 0.1380 1503 | 0.1155 7998 | 73 |
| 74 | 0.1927 1458 | 0.1608 5478 | 0.1343 2119 | 0.1122 1357 | 74 |
| 75 | 0.1884 7391 | 0.1569 3149 | 0.1307 2622 | 0.1089 4521 | 75 |
| 76 | 0.1843 2657 | 0.1531 0389 | 0.1272 2747 | 0.1057 7205 | 76 |
| 77 | 0.1802 7048 | 0.1493 6965 | 0.1238 2235 | 0.1026 9131 | 77 |
| 78 | 0.1763 0365 | 0.1457 2649 | 0.1205 0837 | 0.0997 0030 | 78 |
| 79 | 0.1724 2411 | 0.1421 7218 | 0.1172 8309 | 0.0967 9641 | 79 |
| 80 | 0.1686 2993 | 0.1387 0457 | 0.1141 4412 | 0.0939 7710 | 80 |
| 81 | 0.1649 1925 | 0.1353 2153 | 0.1110 8917 | 0.0912 3990 | 81 |
| 82 | 0.1612 9022 | 0.1320 2101 | 0.1081 1598 | 0.0885 8243 | 82 |
| 83 | 0.1577 4105 | 0.1288 0098 | 0.1052 2237 | 0.0860 0236 | 83 |
| 84 | 0.1542 6997 | 0.1256 5949 | 0.1024 0620 | 0.0834 9743 | 84 |
| 85 | 0.1508 7528 | 0.1225 9463 | 0.0996 6540 | 0.0810 6547 | 85 |
| 86 | 0.1475 5528 | 0.1196 0452 | 0.0969 9795 | 0.0787 0434 | 86 |
| 87 | 0.1443 0835 | 0.1166 8733 | 0.0944 0190 | 0.0764 1198 | 87 |
| 88 | 0.1411 3286 | 0.1138 4130 | 0.0918 7533 | 0.0741 8639 | 88 |
| 89 | 0.1380 2724 | 0.1110 6468 | 0.0894 1638 | 0.0720 2562 | 89 |
| 90 | 0.1349 8997 | 0.1083 5579 | 0.0870 2324 | 0.0699 2779 | 90 |
| 91 | 0.1320 1953 | 0.1057 1296 | 0.0846 9415 | 0.0678 9105 | 91 |
| 92 | 0.1291 1445 | 0.1031 3460 | 0.0824 2740 | 0.0659 1364 | 92 |
| 93 | 0.1262 7331 | 0.1006 1912 | 0.0802 2131 | 0.0639 9383 | 93 |
| 94 | 0.1234 9468 | 0.0981 6500 | 0.0780 7427 | 0.0621 2993 | 94 |
| 95 | 0.1207 7719 | 0.0957 7073 | 0.0759 8469 | 0.0603 2032 | 95 |
| 96 | 0.1181 1950 | 0.0934 3486 | 0.0739 5104 | 0.0585 6342 | 96 |
| 97 | 0.1155 2029 | 0.0911 5596 | 0.0719 7181 | 0.0568 5769 | 97 |
| 98 | 0.1129 7828 | 0.0889 3264 | 0.0700 4556 | 0.0552 0164 | 98 |
| 99 | 0.1104 9221 | 0.0867 6355 | 0.0681 7086 | 0.0535 9382 | 99 |
| 100 | 0.1080 6084 | 0.0846 4737 | 0.0663 4634 | 0.0520 3284 | 100 |

# TABLE 6

$$p = (1 + i)^{-n} \quad [OR, \ v^n = (1 + i)^{-n}]$$

| n | $3\frac{1}{4}\%$ | $3\frac{1}{2}\%$ | $3\frac{3}{4}\%$ | 4% | n |
|---|---|---|---|---|---|
| 1 | 0.9685 2300 | 0.9661 8357 | 0.9638 5542 | 0.9615 3846 | 1 |
| 2 | 0.9380 3681 | 0.9335 1070 | 0.9290 1727 | 0.9245 5621 | 2 |
| 3 | 0.9085 1022 | 0.9019 4271 | 0.8954 3834 | 0.8889 9636 | 3 |
| 4 | 0.8799 1305 | 0.8714 4223 | 0.8630 7310 | 0.8548 0419 | 4 |
| 5 | 0.8522 1603 | 0.8419 7317 | 0.8318 7768 | 0.8219 2711 | 5 |
| 6 | 0.8253 9083 | 0.8135 0064 | 0.8018 0981 | 0.7903 1453 | 6 |
| 7 | 0.7994 1000 | 0.7859 9096 | 0.7728 2874 | 0.7599 1781 | 7 |
| 8 | 0.7742 4698 | 0.7594 1156 | 0.7448 9517 | 0.7306 9020 | 8 |
| 9 | 0.7498 7601 | 0.7337 3097 | 0.7179 7125 | 0.7025 8674 | 9 |
| 10 | 0.7262 7216 | 0.7089 1881 | 0.6920 2048 | 0.6755 6417 | 10 |
| 11 | 0.7034 1129 | 0.6849 4571 | 0.6670 0769 | 0.6495 8093 | 11 |
| 12 | 0.6812 7002 | 0.6617 8330 | 0.6428 9898 | 0.6245 9705 | 12 |
| 13 | 0.6598 2568 | 0.6394 0415 | 0.6196 6167 | 0.6005 7409 | 13 |
| 14 | 0.6390 5635 | 0.6177 8179 | 0.5972 6426 | 0.5774 7508 | 14 |
| 15 | 0.6189 4078 | 0.5968 9062 | 0.5756 7639 | 0.5552 6450 | 15 |
| 16 | 0.5994 5838 | 0.5767 0591 | 0.5548 6881 | 0.5339 0818 | 16 |
| 17 | 0.5805 8923 | 0.5572 0378 | 0.5348 1331 | 0.5133 7325 | 17 |
| 18 | 0.5623 1402 | 0.5383 6114 | 0.5154 8271 | 0.4936 2812 | 18 |
| 19 | 0.5446 1407 | 0.5201 5569 | 0.4968 5080 | 0.4746 4242 | 19 |
| 20 | 0.5274 7125 | 0.5025 6588 | 0.4788 9234 | 0.4563 8695 | 20 |
| 21 | 0.5108 6804 | 0.4855 7090 | 0.4615 8298 | 0.4388 3360 | 21 |
| 22 | 0.4947 8745 | 0.4691 5063 | 0.4448 9926 | 0.4219 5539 | 22 |
| 23 | 0.4792 1302 | 0.4532 8563 | 0.4288 1856 | 0.4057 2633 | 23 |
| 24 | 0.4641 2884 | 0.4379 5713 | 0.4133 1910 | 0.3901 2147 | 24 |
| 25 | 0.4495 1945 | 0.4231 4699 | 0.3983 7985 | 0.3751 1680 | 25 |
| 26 | 0.4353 6993 | 0.4088 3767 | 0.3839 8058 | 0.3606 8923 | 26 |
| 27 | 0.4216 6579 | 0.3950 1224 | 0.3701 0176 | 0.3468 1657 | 27 |
| 28 | 0.4083 9302 | 0.3816 5434 | 0.3567 2459 | 0.3334 7747 | 28 |
| 29 | 0.3955 3803 | 0.3687 4816 | 0.3438 3093 | 0.3206 5141 | 29 |
| 30 | 0.3830 8768 | 0.3562 7841 | 0.3314 0331 | 0.3083 1867 | 30 |
| 31 | 0.3710 2923 | 0.3442 3035 | 0.3194 2487 | 0.2964 6026 | 31 |
| 32 | 0.3593 5035 | 0.3325 8971 | 0.3078 7940 | 0.2850 5794 | 32 |
| 33 | 0.3480 3908 | 0.3213 4271 | 0.2967 5123 | 0.2740 9417 | 33 |
| 34 | 0.3370 8385 | 0.3104 7605 | 0.2860 2528 | 0.2635 5209 | 34 |
| 35 | 0.3264 7346 | 0.2999 7686 | 0.2756 8702 | 0.2534 1547 | 35 |
| 36 | 0.3161 9706 | 0.2898 3272 | 0.2657 2242 | 0.2436 6872 | 36 |
| 37 | 0.3062 4413 | 0.2800 3161 | 0.2561 1800 | 0.2342 9685 | 37 |
| 38 | 0.2966 0448 | 0.2705 6194 | 0.2468 6072 | 0.2252 8543 | 38 |
| 39 | 0.2872 6826 | 0.2614 1250 | 0.2379 3805 | 0.2166 2061 | 39 |
| 40 | 0.2782 2592 | 0.2525 7247 | 0.2293 3788 | 0.2082 8904 | 40 |
| 41 | 0.2694 6820 | 0.2440 3137 | 0.2210 4855 | 0.2002 7793 | 41 |
| 42 | 0.2609 8615 | 0.2357 7910 | 0.2130 5885 | 0.1925 7493 | 42 |
| 43 | 0.2527 7109 | 0.2278 0590 | 0.2053 5793 | 0.1851 6820 | 43 |
| 44 | 0.2448 1462 | 0.2201 0231 | 0.1979 3535 | 0.1780 4635 | 44 |
| 45 | 0.2371 0859 | 0.2126 5924 | 0.1907 8106 | 0.1711 9841 | 45 |
| 46 | 0.2296 4512 | 0.2054 6787 | 0.1838 8536 | 0.1646 1386 | 46 |
| 47 | 0.2224 1658 | 0.1985 1968 | 0.1772 3890 | 0.1582 8256 | 47 |
| 48 | 0.2154 1558 | 0.1918 0645 | 0.1708 3268 | 0.1521 9476 | 48 |
| 49 | 0.2086 3494 | 0.1853 2024 | 0.1646 5800 | 0.1463 4112 | 49 |
| 50 | 0.2020 6774 | 0.1790 5337 | 0.1587 0651 | 0.1407 1262 | 50 |

Table
6

## TABLE 6

$$p = (1 + i)^{-n} \quad [OR, \; v^{n} = (1 + i)^{-n}]$$

| $n$ | $3\frac{1}{4}\%$ | $3\frac{1}{2}\%$ | $3\frac{3}{4}\%$ | $4\%$ | $n$ |
|---|---|---|---|---|---|
| 51 | 0.1957 0725 | 0.1729 9843 | 0.1529 7013 | 0.1353 0059 | 51 |
| 52 | 0.1895 4698 | 0.1671 4824 | 0.1474 4109 | 0.1300 9672 | 52 |
| 53 | 0.1835 8061 | 0.1614 9589 | 0.1421 1189 | 0.1250 9300 | 53 |
| 54 | 0.1778 0204 | 0.1560 3467 | 0.1369 7532 | 0.1202 8173 | 54 |
| 55 | 0.1722 0537 | 0.1507 5814 | 0.1320 2440 | 0.1156 5551 | 55 |
| 56 | 0.1667 8486 | 0.1456 6004 | 0.1272 5243 | 0.1112 0722 | 56 |
| 57 | 0.1615 3497 | 0.1407 3433 | 0.1226 5295 | 0.1069 3002 | 57 |
| 58 | 0.1564 5034 | 0.1359 7520 | 0.1182 1971 | 0.1028 1733 | 58 |
| 59 | 0.1515 2575 | 0.1313 7701 | 0.1139 4671 | 0.0988 6282 | 59 |
| 60 | 0.1467 5617 | 0.1269 3431 | 0.1098 2815 | 0.0950 6040 | 60 |
| 61 | 0.1421 3673 | 0.1226 4184 | 0.1058 5846 | 0.0914 0423 | 61 |
| 62 | 0.1376 6269 | 0.1184 9453 | 0.1020 3225 | 0.0878 8868 | 62 |
| 63 | 0.1333 2948 | 0.1144 8747 | 0.0983 4434 | 0.0845 0835 | 63 |
| 64 | 0.1291 3267 | 0.1106 1591 | 0.0947 8972 | 0.0812 5803 | 64 |
| 65 | 0.1250 6796 | 0.1068 7528 | 0.0913 6359 | 0.0781 3272 | 65 |
| 66 | 0.1211 3120 | 0.1032 6114 | 0.0880 6129 | 0.0751 2762 | 66 |
| 67 | 0.1173 1835 | 0.0997 6922 | 0.0848 7835 | 0.0722 3809 | 67 |
| 68 | 0.1136 2552 | 0.0963 9538 | 0.0818 1046 | 0.0694 5970 | 68 |
| 69 | 0.1100 4893 | 0.0931 3563 | 0.0788 5346 | 0.0667 8818 | 69 |
| 70 | 0.1065 8492 | 0.0899 8612 | 0.0760 0333 | 0.0642 1940 | 70 |
| 71 | 0.1032 2995 | 0.0869 4311 | 0.0732 5622 | 0.0617 4942 | 71 |
| 72 | 0.0999 8058 | 0.0840 0300 | 0.0706 0841 | 0.0593 7445 | 72 |
| 73 | 0.0968 3349 | 0.0811 6232 | 0.0680 5630 | 0.0570 9081 | 73 |
| 74 | 0.0937 8546 | 0.0784 1770 | 0.0655 9643 | 0.0548 9501 | 74 |
| 75 | 0.0908 3338 | 0.0757 6590 | 0.0632 2547 | 0.0527 8367 | 75 |
| 76 | 0.0879 7422 | 0.0732 0376 | 0.0609 4022 | 0.0507 5353 | 76 |
| 77 | 0.0852 0505 | 0.0707 2828 | 0.0587 3756 | 0.0488 0147 | 77 |
| 78 | 0.0825 2305 | 0.0683 3650 | 0.0566 1451 | 0.0469 2449 | 78 |
| 79 | 0.0799 2548 | 0.0660 2560 | 0.0545 6821 | 0.0451 1970 | 79 |
| 80 | 0.0774 0966 | 0.0637 9285 | 0.0525 9586 | 0.0433 8433 | 80 |
| 81 | 0.0749 7304 | 0.0616 3561 | 0.0506 9481 | 0.0417 1570 | 81 |
| 82 | 0.0726 1311 | 0.0595 5131 | 0.0488 6246 | 0.0401 1125 | 82 |
| 83 | 0.0703 2747 | 0.0575 3750 | 0.0470 9635 | 0.0385 6851 | 83 |
| 84 | 0.0681 1377 | 0.0555 9178 | 0.0453 9407 | 0.0370 8510 | 84 |
| 85 | 0.0659 6976 | 0.0537 1187 | 0.0437 5332 | 0.0356 5875 | 85 |
| 86 | 0.0638 9323 | 0.0518 9553 | 0.0421 7188 | 0.0342 8726 | 86 |
| 87 | 0.0618 8206 | 0.0501 4060 | 0.0406 4759 | 0.0329 6852 | 87 |
| 88 | 0.0599 3420 | 0.0484 4503 | 0.0391 7840 | 0.0317 0050 | 88 |
| 89 | 0.0580 4765 | 0.0468 0679 | 0.0377 6232 | 0.0304 8125 | 89 |
| 90 | 0.0562 2048 | 0.0452 2395 | 0.0363 9741 | 0.0293 0890 | 90 |
| 91 | 0.0544 5083 | 0.0436 9464 | 0.0350 8184 | 0.0281 8163 | 91 |
| 92 | 0.0527 3688 | 0.0422 1704 | 0.0338 1383 | 0.0270 9772 | 92 |
| 93 | 0.0510 7688 | 0.0407 8941 | 0.0325 9164 | 0.0260 5550 | 93 |
| 94 | 0.0494 6914 | 0.0394 1006 | 0.0314 1363 | 0.0250 5337 | 94 |
| 95 | 0.0479 1200 | 0.0380 7735 | 0.0302 7820 | 0.0240 8978 | 95 |
| 96 | 0.0464 0387 | 0.0367 8971 | 0.0291 8380 | 0.0231 6325 | 96 |
| 97 | 0.0449 4322 | 0.0355 4562 | 0.0281 2897 | 0.0222 7235 | 97 |
| 98 | 0.0435 2854 | 0.0343 4359 | 0.0271 1226 | 0.0214 1572 | 98 |
| 99 | 0.0421 5839 | 0.0331 8221 | 0.0261 3230 | 0.0205 9204 | 99 |
| 100 | 0.0408 3137 | 0.0320 6011 | 0.0251 8776 | 0.0198 0004 | 100 |

# TABLE 6

$$p = (1 + i)^{-n} \quad [OR, \; v^n = (1 + i)^{-n}]$$

| n | $4\frac{1}{2}$ % | 5 % | $5\frac{1}{2}$ % | 6 % | n |
|---|---|---|---|---|---|
| 1 | 0.9569 3780 | 0.9523 8095 | 0.9478 6730 | 0.9433 9623 | 1 |
| 2 | 0.9157 2995 | 0.9070 2948 | 0.8984 5242 | 0.8899 9644 | 2 |
| 3 | 0.8762 9660 | 0.8638 3760 | 0.8516 1366 | 0.8396 1928 | 3 |
| 4 | 0.8385 6134 | 0.8227 0247 | 0.8072 1674 | 0.7920 9366 | 4 |
| 5 | 0.8024 5105 | 0.7835 2617 | 0.7651 3435 | 0.7472 5817 | 5 |
| 6 | 0.7678 9574 | 0.7462 1540 | 0.7252 4583 | 0.7049 6054 | 6 |
| 7 | 0.7348 2846 | 0.7106 8133 | 0.6874 3681 | 0.6650 5711 | 7 |
| 8 | 0.7031 8513 | 0.6768 3936 | 0.6515 9887 | 0.6274 1237 | 8 |
| 9 | 0.6729 0443 | 0.6446 0892 | 0.6176 2926 | 0.5918 9846 | 9 |
| 10 | 0.6439 2768 | 0.6139 1325 | 0.5854 3058 | 0.5583 9478 | 10 |
| 11 | 0.6161 9874 | 0.5846 7929 | 0.5549 1050 | 0.5267 8753 | 11 |
| 12 | 0.5896 6386 | 0.5568 3742 | 0.5259 8152 | 0.4969 6936 | 12 |
| 13 | 0.5642 7164 | 0.5303 2135 | 0.4985 6068 | 0.4688 3902 | 13 |
| 14 | 0.5399 7286 | 0.5050 6795 | 0.4725 6937 | 0.4423 0096 | 14 |
| 15 | 0.5167 2044 | 0.4810 1710 | 0.4479 3305 | 0.4172 6506 | 15 |
| 16 | 0.4944 6932 | 0.4581 1152 | 0.4245 8109 | 0.3936 4628 | 16 |
| 17 | 0.4731 7639 | 0.4362 9669 | 0.4024 4653 | 0.3713 6442 | 17 |
| 18 | 0.4528 0037 | 0.4155 2065 | 0.3814 6590 | 0.3503 4379 | 18 |
| 19 | 0.4333 0179 | 0.3957 3396 | 0.3615 7906 | 0.3305 1301 | 19 |
| 20 | 0.4146 4286 | 0.3768 8948 | 0.3427 2896 | 0.3118 0473 | 20 |
| 21 | 0.3967 8743 | 0.3589 4236 | 0.3248 6158 | 0.2941 5540 | 21 |
| 22 | 0.3797 0089 | 0.3418 4987 | 0.3079 2566 | 0.2775 0510 | 22 |
| 23 | 0.3633 5013 | 0.3255 7131 | 0.2918 7267 | 0.2617 9726 | 23 |
| 24 | 0.3477 0347 | 0.3100 6791 | 0.2766 5656 | 0.2469 7855 | 24 |
| 25 | 0.3327 3060 | 0.2953 0277 | 0.2622 3370 | 0.2329 9863 | 25 |
| 26 | 0.3184 0248 | 0.2812 4074 | 0.2485 6275 | 0.2198 1003 | 26 |
| 27 | 0.3046 9137 | 0.2678 4832 | 0.2356 0450 | 0.2073 6795 | 27 |
| 28 | 0.2915 7069 | 0.2550 9364 | 0.2233 2181 | 0.1956 3014 | 28 |
| 29 | 0.2790 1502 | 0.2429 4632 | 0.2116 7944 | 0.1845 5674 | 29 |
| 30 | 0.2670 0002 | 0.2313 7745 | 0.2006 4402 | 0.1741 1013 | 30 |
| 31 | 0.2555 0241 | 0.2203 5947 | 0.1901 8390 | 0.1642 5484 | 31 |
| 32 | 0.2444 9991 | 0.2098 6617 | 0.1802 6910 | 0.1549 5740 | 32 |
| 33 | 0.2339 7121 | 0.1998 7254 | 0.1708 7119 | 0.1461 8622 | 33 |
| 34 | 0.2238 9589 | 0.1903 5480 | 0.1619 6321 | 0.1379 1153 | 34 |
| 35 | 0.2142 5444 | 0.1812 9029 | 0.1535 1963 | 0.1301 0522 | 35 |
| 36 | 0.2050 2817 | 0.1726 5741 | 0.1455 1624 | 0.1227 4077 | 36 |
| 37 | 0.1961 9921 | 0.1644 3563 | 0.1379 3008 | 0.1157 9318 | 37 |
| 38 | 0.1877 5044 | 0.1566 0536 | 0.1307 3941 | 0.1092 3885 | 38 |
| 39 | 0.1796 6549 | 0.1491 4797 | 0.1239 2362 | 0.1030 5552 | 39 |
| 40 | 0.1719 2870 | 0.1420 4568 | 0.1174 6314 | 0.0972 2219 | 40 |
| 41 | 0.1645 2507 | 0.1352 8160 | 0.1113 3947 | 0.0917 1904 | 41 |
| 42 | 0.1574 4026 | 0.1288 3962 | 0.1055 3504 | 0.0865 2740 | 42 |
| 43 | 0.1506 6054 | 0.1227 0440 | 0.1000 3322 | 0.0816 2962 | 43 |
| 44 | 0.1441 7276 | 0.1168 6133 | 0.0948 1822 | 0.0770 0908 | 44 |
| 45 | 0.1379 6437 | 0.1112 9651 | 0.0898 7509 | 0.0726 5007 | 45 |
| 46 | 0.1320 2332 | 0.1059 9668 | 0.0851 8965 | 0.0685 3781 | 46 |
| 47 | 0.1263 3810 | 0.1009 4921 | 0.0807 4849 | 0.0646 5831 | 47 |
| 48 | 0.1208 9771 | 0.0961 4211 | 0.0765 3885 | 0.0609 9840 | 48 |
| 49 | 0.1156 9158 | 0.0915 6391 | 0.0725 4867 | 0.0575 4566 | 49 |
| 50 | 0.1107 0965 | 0.0872 0373 | 0.0687 6652 | 0.0542 8836 | 50 |

Table
6

# TABLE 6

$$p = (1 + i)^{-n} \quad [OR, \; v^n = (1 + i)^{-n}]$$

| $n$ | $4\frac{1}{2}\%$ | $5\%$ | $5\frac{1}{2}\%$ | $6\%$ | $n$ |
|---|---|---|---|---|---|
| 51 | 0.1059 4225 | 0.0830 5117 | 0.0651 8153 | 0.0512 1544 | 51 |
| 52 | 0.1013 8014 | 0.0790 9635 | 0.0617 8344 | 0.0483 1645 | 52 |
| 53 | 0.0970 1449 | 0.0753 2986 | 0.0585 6250 | 0.0455 8156 | 53 |
| 54 | 0.0928 3683 | 0.0717 4272 | 0.0555 0948 | 0.0430 0147 | 54 |
| 55 | 0.0888 3907 | 0.0683 2640 | 0.0526 1562 | 0.0405 6742 | 55 |
| 56 | 0.0850 1347 | 0.0650 7276 | 0.0498 7263 | 0.0382 7115 | 56 |
| 57 | 0.0813 5260 | 0.0619 7406 | 0.0472 7263 | 0.0361 0486 | 57 |
| 58 | 0.0778 4938 | 0.0590 2291 | 0.0448 0818 | 0.0340 6119 | 58 |
| 59 | 0.0744 9701 | 0.0562 1230 | 0.0424 7221 | 0.0321 3320 | 59 |
| 60 | 0.0712 8901 | 0.0535 3552 | 0.0402 5802 | 0.0303 1434 | 60 |
| 61 | 0.0682 1915 | 0.0509 8621 | 0.0381 5926 | 0.0285 9843 | 61 |
| 62 | 0.0652 8148 | 0.0485 5830 | 0.0361 6992 | 0.0269 7965 | 62 |
| 63 | 0.0624 7032 | 0.0462 4600 | 0.0342 8428 | 0.0354 5250 | 63 |
| 64 | 0.0597 8021 | 0.0440 4381 | 0.0324 9695 | 0.0240 1179 | 64 |
| 65 | 0.0572 0594 | 0.0419 4648 | 0.0308 0279 | 0.0226 5264 | 65 |
| 66 | 0.0547 4253 | 0.0399 4903 | 0.0291 9696 | 0.0213 7041 | 66 |
| 67 | 0.0523 8519 | 0.0380 4670 | 0.0276 7485 | 0.0201 6077 | 67 |
| 68 | 0.0501 2937 | 0.0362 3495 | 0.0262 3208 | 0.0190 1959 | 68 |
| 69 | 0.0479 7069 | 0.0345 0948 | 0.0248 6453 | 0.0179 4301 | 69 |
| 70 | 0.0459 0497 | 0.0328 6617 | 0.0235 6828 | 0.0169 2737 | 70 |
| 71 | 0.0439 2820 | 0.0313 0111 | 0.0223 3960 | 0.0159 6921 | 71 |
| 72 | 0.0420 3655 | 0.0298 1058 | 0.0211 7498 | 0.0150 6530 | 72 |
| 73 | 0.0402 2637 | 0.0283 9103 | 0.0200 7107 | 0.0142 1254 | 73 |
| 74 | 0.0384 9413 | 0.0270 3908 | 0.0190 2471 | 0.0134 0806 | 74 |
| 75 | 0.0368 3649 | 0.0257 5150 | 0.0180 3290 | 0.0126 4911 | 75 |
| 76 | 0.0352 5023 | 0.0245 2524 | 0.0170 9279 | 0.0119 3313 | 76 |
| 77 | 0.0337 3228 | 0.0233 5737 | 0.0162 0170 | 0.0112 5767 | 77 |
| 78 | 0.0322 7969 | 0.0222 4512 | 0.0153 5706 | 0.0106 2044 | 78 |
| 79 | 0.0308 8965 | 0.0211 8582 | 0.0145 5646 | 0.0100 1928 | 79 |
| 80 | 0.0295 5948 | 0.0201 7698 | 0.0137 9759 | 0.0094 5215 | 80 |
| 81 | 0.0282 8658 | 0.0192 1617 | 0.0130 7828 | 0.0089 1713 | 81 |
| 82 | 0.0270 6850 | 0.0183 0111 | 0.0123 9648 | 0.0084 1238 | 82 |
| 83 | 0.0259 0287 | 0.0174 2963 | 0.0117 5022 | 0.0079 3621 | 83 |
| 84 | 0.0247 8744 | 0.0165 9965 | 0.0111 3765 | 0.0074 8699 | 84 |
| 85 | 0.0237 2003 | 0.0158 0919 | 0.0105 5701 | 0.0070 6320 | 85 |
| 86 | 0.0226 9860 | 0.0150 5637 | 0.0100 0664 | 0.0066 6340 | 86 |
| 87 | 0.0217 2115 | 0.0143 3940 | 0.0094 8497 | 0.0062 8622 | 87 |
| 88 | 0.0207 8579 | 0.0136 5657 | 0.0089 9049 | 0.0059 3040 | 88 |
| 89 | 0.0198 9070 | 0.0130 0626 | 0.0085 2180 | 0.0055 9472 | 89 |
| 90 | 0.0190 3417 | 0.0123 8691 | 0.0080 7753 | 0.0052 7803 | 90 |
| 91 | 0.0182 1451 | 0.0117 9706 | 0.0076 5643 | 0.0049 7928 | 91 |
| 92 | 0.0174 3016 | 0.0112 3530 | 0.0072 5728 | 0.0046 9743 | 92 |
| 93 | 0.0166 7958 | 0.0107 0028 | 0.0068 7894 | 0.0044 3154 | 93 |
| 94 | 0.0159 6132 | 0.0101 9074 | 0.0065 2032 | 0.0041 8070 | 94 |
| 95 | 0.0152 7399 | 0.0097 0547 | 0.0061 8040 | 0.0039 4405 | 95 |
| 96 | 0.0146 1626 | 0.0092 4331 | 0.0058 5820 | 0.0037 2081 | 96 |
| 97 | 0.0139 8685 | 0.0088 0315 | 0.0055 5279 | 0.0035 1019 | 97 |
| 98 | 0.0133 8454 | 0.0083 8395 | 0.0052 6331 | 0.0033 1150 | 98 |
| 99 | 0.0128 0817 | 0.0079 8471 | 0.0049 8892 | 0.0031 2406 | 99 |
| 100 | 0.0122 5663 | 0.0076 0449 | 0.0047 2883 | 0.0029 4723 | 100 |

**TABLE  6**

$$p = (1 + i)^{-n} \quad [OR, \quad v^n = (1 + i)^{-n}]$$

| n | $6\frac{1}{2}\%$ | 7 % | $7\frac{1}{2}\%$ | 8 % | n |
|---|---|---|---|---|---|
| 1 | 0.9389 6714 | 0.9345 7944 | 0.9302 3256 | 0.9259 2593 | 1 |
| 2 | 0.8816 5928 | 0.8734 3873 | 0.8653 3261 | 0.8573 3882 | 2 |
| 3 | 0.8278 4909 | 0.8162 9788 | 0.8049 6057 | 0.7938 3224 | 3 |
| 4 | 0.7773 2309 | 0.7628 9521 | 0.7488 0053 | 0.7350 2985 | 4 |
| 5 | 0.7298 8084 | 0.7129 8618 | 0.6965 5863 | 0.6805 8320 | 5 |
| 6 | 0.6853 3412 | 0.6663 4222 | 0.6479 6152 | 0.6301 6963 | 6 |
| 7 | 0.6435 0621 | 0.6227 4974 | 0.6027 5490 | 0.5834 9040 | 7 |
| 8 | 0.6042 3119 | 0.5820 0910 | 0.5607 0223 | 0.5402 6888 | 8 |
| 9 | 0.5673 5323 | 0.5439 3374 | 0.5215 8347 | 0.5002 4897 | 9 |
| 10 | 0.5327 2604 | 0.5083 4929 | 0.4851 9393 | 0.4631 9349 | 10 |
| 11 | 0.5002 1224 | 0.4750 9280 | 0.4513 4319 | 0.4288 8286 | 11 |
| 12 | 0.4696 8285 | 0.4440 1196 | 0.4198 5413 | 0.3971 1376 | 12 |
| 13 | 0.4410 1676 | 0.4149 6445 | 0.3905 6198 | 0.3676 9792 | 13 |
| 14 | 0.4141 0025 | 0.3878 1724 | 0.3633 1347 | 0.3404 6104 | 14 |
| 15 | 0.3888 2652 | 0.3624 4602 | 0.3379 6602 | 0.3152 4170 | 15 |
| 16 | 0.3650 9533 | 0.3387 3460 | 0.3143 8699 | 0.2918 9047 | 16 |
| 17 | 0.3428 1251 | 0.3165 7439 | 0.2924 5302 | 0.2702 6895 | 17 |
| 18 | 0.3218 8969 | 0.2958 6392 | 0.2720 4932 | 0.2502 4903 | 18 |
| 19 | 0.3022 4384 | 0.2765 0833 | 0.2530 6913 | 0.2317 1206 | 19 |
| 20 | 0.2837 9703 | 0.2584 1900 | 0.2354 1315 | 0.2145 4821 | 20 |
| 21 | 0.2664 7608 | 0.2415 1309 | 0.2189 8897 | 0.1986 5575 | 21 |
| 22 | 0.2502 1228 | 0.2257 1317 | 0.2037 1067 | 0.1839 4051 | 22 |
| 23 | 0.2349 4111 | 0.2109 4688 | 0.1894 9830 | 0.1703 1528 | 23 |
| 24 | 0.2206 0198 | 0.1971 4662 | 0.1762 7749 | 0.1576 9934 | 24 |
| 25 | 0.2071 3801 | 0.1842 4918 | 0.1639 7906 | 0.1460 1790 | 25 |
| 26 | 0.1944 9579 | 0.1721 9549 | 0.1525 3866 | 0.1352 0176 | 26 |
| 27 | 0.1826 2515 | 0.1609 3037 | 0.1418 9643 | 0.1251 8682 | 27 |
| 28 | 0.1714 7902 | 0.1504 0221 | 0.1319 9668 | 0.1159 1372 | 28 |
| 29 | 0.1610 1316 | 0.1405 6282 | 0.1227 8761 | 0.1073 2752 | 29 |
| 30 | 0.1511 8607 | 0.1313 6712 | 0.1142 2103 | 0.0993 7733 | 30 |
| 31 | 0.1419 5875 | 0.1227 7301 | 0.1062 5212 | 0.0920 1605 | 31 |
| 32 | 0.1332 9460 | 0.1147 4113 | 0.0988 3918 | 0.0852 0005 | 32 |
| 33 | 0.1251 5925 | 0.1072 3470 | 0.0919 4343 | 0.0788 8893 | 33 |
| 34 | 0.1175 2042 | 0.1002 1934 | 0.0855 2877 | 0.0730 4531 | 34 |
| 35 | 0.1103 4781 | 0.0936 6294 | 0.0795 6164 | 0.0676 3454 | 35 |
| 36 | 0.1036 1297 | 0.0875 3546 | 0.0740 1083 | 0.0626 2458 | 36 |
| 37 | 0.0972 8917 | 0.0818 0884 | 0.0688 4729 | 0.0579 8572 | 37 |
| 38 | 0.0913 5134 | 0.0764 5686 | 0.0640 4399 | 0.0536 9048 | 38 |
| 39 | 0.0857 7590 | 0.0714 5501 | 0.0595 7580 | 0.0497 1341 | 39 |
| 40 | 0.0805 4075 | 0.0667 8038 | 0.0554 1935 | 0.0460 3093 | 40 |
| 41 | 0.0756 2512 | 0.0624 1157 | 0.0515 5288 | 0.0426 2123 | 41 |
| 42 | 0.0710 0950 | 0.0583 2857 | 0.0479 5617 | 0.0394 6411 | 42 |
| 43 | 0.0666 7559 | 0.0545 1268 | 0.0446 1039 | 0.0365 4084 | 43 |
| 44 | 0.0626 0619 | 0.0509 4643 | 0.0414 9804 | 0.0338 3411 | 44 |
| 45 | 0.0587 8515 | 0.0476 1349 | 0.0386 0283 | 0.0313 2788 | 45 |
| 46 | 0.0551 9733 | 0.0444 9859 | 0.0359 0961 | 0.0290 0730 | 46 |
| 47 | 0.0518 2848 | 0.0415 8746 | 0.0334 0428 | 0.0268 5861 | 47 |
| 48 | 0.0486 6524 | 0.0388 6679 | 0.0310 7375 | 0.0248 6908 | 48 |
| 49 | 0.0456 9506 | 0.0363 2410 | 0.0289 0582 | 0.0230 2693 | 49 |
| 50 | 0.0429 0616 | 0.0339 4776 | 0.0268 8913 | 0.0213 2123 | 50 |

Table
6

## TABLE 6

$$p = (1 + i)^{-n} \quad [OR, \; v^n = (1 + i)^{-n}]$$

| $n$ | $6\frac{1}{2}\%$ | $7\%$ | $7\frac{1}{2}\%$ | $8\%$ | $n$ |
|---|---|---|---|---|---|
| 51 | 0.0402 8747 | 0.0317 2688 | 0.0250 1315 | 0.0197 4188 | 51 |
| 52 | 0.0378 2861 | 0.0296 5129 | 0.0232 6804 | 0.0182 7952 | 52 |
| 53 | 0.0355 1982 | 0.0277 1148 | 0.0216 4469 | 0.0169 2548 | 53 |
| 54 | 0.0333 5195 | 0.0258 9858 | 0.0201 3460 | 0.0156 7174 | 54 |
| 55 | 0.0313 1638 | 0.0242 0428 | 0.0187 2986 | 0.0145 1087 | 55 |
| 56 | 0.0294 0505 | 0.0226 2083 | 0.0174 2312 | 0.0134 3599 | 56 |
| 57 | 0.0276 1038 | 0.0211 4096 | 0.0162 0756 | 0.0124 4073 | 57 |
| 58 | 0.0259 2524 | 0.0197 5791 | 0.0150 7680 | 0.0115 1920 | 58 |
| 59 | 0.0243 4295 | 0.0184 6533 | 0.0140 2493 | 0.0106 6592 | 59 |
| 60 | 0.0228 5723 | 0.0172 5732 | 0.0130 4644 | 0.0098 7585 | 60 |
| 61 | 0.0214 6218 | 0.0161 2834 | 0.0121 3623 | 0.0091 4431 | 61 |
| 62 | 0.0201 5229 | 0.0150 7321 | 0.0112 8951 | 0.0084 6695 | 62 |
| 63 | 0.0189 2233 | 0.0140 8711 | 0.0105 0187 | 0.0078 3977 | 63 |
| 64 | 0.0177 6745 | 0.0131 6553 | 0.0097 6918 | 0.0072 5905 | 64 |
| 65 | 0.0166 8305 | 0.0123 0423 | 0.0090 8761 | 0.0067 2134 | 65 |
| 66 | 0.0156 6484 | 0.0114 9928 | 0.0084 5359 | 0.0062 2346 | 66 |
| 67 | 0.0147 0877 | 0.0107 4699 | 0.0078 6381 | 0.0057 6247 | 67 |
| 68 | 0.0138 1105 | 0.0100 4392 | 0.0073 1517 | 0.0053 3562 | 68 |
| 69 | 0.0129 6812 | 0.0093 8684 | 0.0068 0481 | 0.0049 4039 | 69 |
| 70 | 0.0121 7664 | 0.0087 7275 | 0.0063 3006 | 0.0045 7443 | 70 |
| 71 | 0.0114 3346 | 0.0081 9883 | 0.0058 8842 | 0.0042 3558 | 71 |
| 72 | 0.0107 3565 | 0.0076 6246 | 0.0054 7760 | 0.0039 2184 | 72 |
| 73 | 0.0100 8042 | 0.0071 6117 | 0.0050 9544 | 0.0036 3133 | 73 |
| 74 | 0.0094 6518 | 0.0066 9269 | 0.0047 3995 | 0.0033 6234 | 74 |
| 75 | 0.0088 8750 | 0.0062 5485 | 0.0044 0925 | 0.0031 1328 | 75 |
| 76 | 0.0083 4507 | 0.0058 4565 | 0.0041 0163 | 0.0028 8267 | 76 |
| 77 | 0.0078 3574 | 0.0054 6323 | 0.0038 1547 | 0.0026 6914 | 77 |
| 78 | 0.0073 5751 | 0.0051 0582 | 0.0035 4928 | 0.0024 7142 | 78 |
| 79 | 0.0069 0846 | 0.0047 7179 | 0.0033 0165 | 0.0022 8835 | 79 |
| 80 | 0.0064 8681 | 0.0044 5962 | 0.0030 7130 | 0.0021 1885 | 80 |
| 81 | 0.0060 9090 | 0.0041 6787 | 0.0028 5703 | 0.0019 6190 | 81 |
| 82 | 0.0057 1916 | 0.0038 9520 | 0.0026 5770 | 0.0018 1657 | 82 |
| 83 | 0.0053 7010 | 0.0036 4038 | 0.0024 7228 | 0.0016 8201 | 83 |
| 84 | 0.0050 4235 | 0.0034 0222 | 0.0022 9979 | 0.0015 5742 | 84 |
| 85 | 0.0047 3460 | 0.0031 7965 | 0.0021 3934 | 0.0014 4205 | 85 |
| 86 | 0.0044 4563 | 0.0029 7163 | 0.0019 9009 | 0.0013 3523 | 86 |
| 87 | 0.0041 7430 | 0.0027 7723 | 0.0018 5124 | 0.0012 3633 | 87 |
| 88 | 0.0039 1953 | 0.0025 9554 | 0.0017 2209 | 0.0011 4475 | 88 |
| 89 | 0.0036 8031 | 0.0024 2574 | 0.0016 0194 | 0.0010 5995 | 89 |
| 90 | 0.0034 5569 | 0.0022 6704 | 0.0014 9018 | 0.0009 8144 | 90 |
| 91 | 0.0032 4478 | 0.0021 1873 | 0.0013 8621 | 0.0009 0874 | 91 |
| 92 | 0.0030 4674 | 0.0019 8012 | 0.0012 8950 | 0.0008 4142 | 92 |
| 93 | 0.0028 6079 | 0.0018 5058 | 0.0011 9953 | 0.0007 7910 | 93 |
| 94 | 0.0026 8619 | 0.0017 2952 | 0.0011 1585 | 0.0007 2138 | 94 |
| 95 | 0.0025 2224 | 0.0016 1637 | 0.0010 3800 | 0.0006 6795 | 95 |
| 96 | 0.0023 6831 | 0.0015 1063 | 0.0009 6558 | 0.0006 1847 | 96 |
| 97 | 0.0022 2376 | 0.0014 1180 | 0.0008 9821 | 0.0005 7266 | 97 |
| 98 | 0.0020 8804 | 0.0013 1944 | 0.0008 3555 | 0.0005 3024 | 98 |
| 99 | 0.0019 6060 | 0.0012 3312 | 0.0007 7725 | 0.0004 9096 | 99 |
| 100 | 0.0018 4094 | 0.0011 5245 | 0.0007 2303 | 0.0004 5459 | 100 |

# TABLE 6

$$p = (1 + i)^{-n} \quad [OR, \; v^n = (1 + i)^{-n}]$$

| $n$ | $8\frac{1}{2}\%$ | 9% | $9\frac{1}{2}\%$ | 10% | $n$ |
|---|---|---|---|---|---|
| 1 | 0.9216 5899 | 0.9174 3119 | 0.9132 4201 | 0.9090 9091 | 1 |
| 2 | 0.8494 5529 | 0.8416 7999 | 0.8340 1097 | 0.8264 4628 | 2 |
| 3 | 0.7829 0810 | 0.7721 8348 | 0.7616 5385 | 0.7513 1480 | 3 |
| 4 | 0.7215 7428 | 0.7084 2521 | 0.6955 7429 | 0.6830 1346 | 4 |
| 5 | 0.6650 4542 | 0.6499 3139 | 0.6352 2767 | 0.6209 2132 | 5 |
| 6 | 0.6129 4509 | 0.5962 6733 | 0.5801 1659 | 0.5644 7393 | 6 |
| 7 | 0.5649 2635 | 0.5470 3424 | 0.5297 8684 | 0.5131 5812 | 7 |
| 8 | 0.5206 6945 | 0.5018 6628 | 0.4838 2360 | 0.4665 0738 | 8 |
| 9 | 0.4798 7968 | 0.4604 2778 | 0.4418 4803 | 0.4240 9762 | 9 |
| 10 | 0.4422 8542 | 0.4224 1081 | 0.4035 1419 | 0.3855 4329 | 10 |
| 11 | 0.4076 3633 | 0.3875 3285 | 0.3685 0611 | 0.3504 9390 | 11 |
| 12 | 0.3757 0168 | 0.3555 3473 | 0.3365 3526 | 0.3186 3082 | 12 |
| 13 | 0.3462 6883 | 0.3261 7865 | 0.3073 3813 | 0.2896 6438 | 13 |
| 14 | 0.3191 4178 | 0.2992 4647 | 0.2806 7410 | 0.2633 3125 | 14 |
| 15 | 0.2941 3989 | 0.2745 3804 | 0.2563 2337 | 0.2393 9205 | 15 |
| 16 | 0.2710 9667 | 0.2518 6976 | 0.2340 8527 | 0.2176 2914 | 16 |
| 17 | 0.2498 5869 | 0.2310 7318 | 0.2137 7651 | 0.1978 4467 | 17 |
| 18 | 0.2302 8450 | 0.2119 9374 | 0.1952 2969 | 0.1798 5879 | 18 |
| 19 | 0.2122 4378 | 0.1944 8967 | 0.1782 9195 | 0.1635 0799 | 19 |
| 20 | 0.1956 1639 | 0.1784 3089 | 0.1628 2370 | 0.1486 4363 | 20 |
| 21 | 0.1802 9160 | 0.1636 9806 | 0.1486 9744 | 0.1351 3057 | 21 |
| 22 | 0.1661 6738 | 0.1501 8171 | 0.1357 9675 | 0.1228 4597 | 22 |
| 23 | 0.1531 4965 | 0.1377 8139 | 0.1240 1530 | 0.1116 7816 | 23 |
| 24 | 0.1411 5176 | 0.1264 0494 | 0.1132 5598 | 0.1015 2560 | 24 |
| 25 | 0.1300 9378 | 0.1159 6784 | 0.1034 3012 | 0.0922 9600 | 25 |
| 26 | 0.1199 0210 | 0.1063 9251 | 0.0944 5673 | 0.0839 0545 | 26 |
| 27 | 0.1105 0885 | 0.0976 0781 | 0.0862 6185 | 0.0762 7768 | 27 |
| 28 | 0.1018 5148 | 0.0895 4845 | 0.0787 7795 | 0.0693 4335 | 28 |
| 29 | 0.0938 7233 | 0.0821 5454 | 0.0719 4333 | 0.0630 3941 | 29 |
| 30 | 0.0865 1828 | 0.0753 7114 | 0.0657 0167 | 0.0573 0855 | 30 |
| 31 | 0.0797 4035 | 0.0691 4783 | 0.0600 0153 | 0.0520 9868 | 31 |
| 32 | 0.0734 9341 | 0.0634 3838 | 0.0547 9592 | 0.0473 6244 | 32 |
| 33 | 0.0677 3586 | 0.0582 0035 | 0.0500 4193 | 0.0430 5676 | 33 |
| 34 | 0.0624 2936 | 0.0533 9481 | 0.0457 0039 | 0.0391 4251 | 34 |
| 35 | 0.0575 3858 | 0.0489 8607 | 0.0417 3552 | 0.0355 8410 | 35 |
| 36 | 0.0530 3095 | 0.0449 4135 | 0.0381 1463 | 0.0323 4918 | 36 |
| 37 | 0.0488 7645 | 0.0412 3059 | 0.0348 0788 | 0.0294 0835 | 37 |
| 38 | 0.0450 4742 | 0.0378 2623 | 0.0317 8802 | 0.0267 3486 | 38 |
| 39 | 0.0415 1836 | 0.0347 0296 | 0.0290 3015 | 0.0243 0442 | 39 |
| 40 | 0.0382 6577 | 0.0318 3758 | 0.0265 1156 | 0.0220 9493 | 40 |
| 41 | 0.0352 6799 | 0.0292 0879 | 0.0242 1147 | 0.0200 8630 | 41 |
| 42 | 0.0325 0506 | 0.0267 9706 | 0.0221 1093 | 0.0182 6027 | 42 |
| 43 | 0.0299 5858 | 0.0245 8446 | 0.0201 9263 | 0.0166 0025 | 43 |
| 44 | 0.0276 1160 | 0.0225 5455 | 0.0184 4076 | 0.0150 9113 | 44 |
| 45 | 0.0254 4848 | 0.0206 9224 | 0.0168 4087 | 0.0137 1921 | 45 |
| 46 | 0.0234 5482 | 0.0189 8371 | 0.0153 7979 | 0.0124 7201 | 46 |
| 47 | 0.0216 1734 | 0.0174 1625 | 0.0140 4547 | 0.0113 3819 | 47 |
| 48 | 0.0199 2382 | 0.0159 7821 | 0.0128 2692 | 0.0103 0745 | 48 |
| 49 | 0.0183 6297 | 0.0146 5891 | 0.0117 1408 | 0.0093 7041 | 49 |
| 50 | 0.0169 2439 | 0.0134 4854 | 0.0106 9779 | 0.0085 1855 | 50 |

Table
6

**TABLE 6**

$$p = (1+i)^{-n} \quad [OR, \; v^n = (1+i)^{-n}]$$

| $n$ | $8\frac{1}{2}\%$ | 9% | $9\frac{1}{2}\%$ | 10% | $n$ |
|---|---|---|---|---|---|
| 51 | 0.0155 9852 | 0.0123 3811 | 0.0097 6967 | 0.0077 4414 | 51 |
| 52 | 0.0143 7651 | 0.0113 1937 | 0.0089 2207 | 0.0070 4013 | 52 |
| 53 | 0.0132 5024 | 0.0103 8474 | 0.0081 4801 | 0.0064 0011 | 53 |
| 54 | 0.0122 1221 | 0.0095 2728 | 0.0074 4111 | 0.0058 1829 | 54 |
| 55 | 0.0112 5549 | 0.0087 4063 | 0.0067 9553 | 0.0052 8935 | 55 |
| 56 | 0.0103 7372 | 0.0080 1892 | 0.0062 0597 | 0.0048 0850 | 56 |
| 57 | 0.0095 6104 | 0.0073 5681 | 0.0056 6755 | 0.0043 7136 | 57 |
| 58 | 0.0088 1201 | 0.0067 4937 | 0.0051 7584 | 0.0039 7397 | 58 |
| 59 | 0.0081 2167 | 0.0061 9208 | 0.0047 2680 | 0.0036 1270 | 59 |
| 60 | 0.0074 8541 | 0.0056 8081 | 0.0043 1671 | 0.0032 8427 | 60 |
| 61 | 0.0068 9900 | 0.0052 1175 | 0.0039 4220 | 0.0029 8570 | 61 |
| 62 | 0.0063 5852 | 0.0047 8142 | 0.0036 0018 | 0.0027 1427 | 62 |
| 63 | 0.0058 6039 | 0.0043 8663 | 0.0032 8784 | 0.0024 6752 | 63 |
| 64 | 0.0054 0128 | 0.0040 2443 | 0.0030 0259 | 0.0022 4320 | 64 |
| 65 | 0.0049 7814 | 0.0036 9214 | 0.0027 4209 | 0.0020 3927 | 65 |
| 66 | 0.0045 8815 | 0.0033 8728 | 0.0025 0419 | 0.0018 5389 | 66 |
| 67 | 0.0042 2871 | 0.0031 0760 | 0.0022 8694 | 0.0016 8535 | 67 |
| 68 | 0.0038 9743 | 0.0028 5101 | 0.0020 8853 | 0.0015 3214 | 68 |
| 69 | 0.0035 9210 | 0.0026 1560 | 0.0019 0733 | 0.0013 9285 | 69 |
| 70 | 0.0033 1069 | 0.0023 9963 | 0.0017 4185 | 0.0012 6623 | 70 |
| 71 | 0.0030 5133 | 0.0022 0150 | 0.0015 9073 | 0.0011 5112 | 71 |
| 72 | 0.0028 1228 | 0.0020 1972 | 0.0014 5273 | 0.0010 4647 | 72 |
| 73 | 0.0025 9196 | 0.0018 5296 | 0.0013 2669 | 0.0009 5134 | 73 |
| 74 | 0.0023 8891 | 0.0016 9996 | 0.0012 1159 | 0.0008 6485 | 74 |
| 75 | 0.0022 0176 | 0.0015 5960 | 0.0011 0647 | 0.0007 8623 | 75 |
| 76 | 0.0020 2927 | 0.0014 3082 | 0.0010 1048 | 0.0007 1475 | 76 |
| 77 | 0.0018 7030 | 0.0013 1268 | 0.0009 2281 | 0.0006 4978 | 77 |
| 78 | 0.0017 2377 | 0.0012 0430 | 0.0008 4275 | 0.0005 9070 | 78 |
| 79 | 0.0015 8873 | 0.0011 0486 | 0.0007 6963 | 0.0005 3700 | 79 |
| 80 | 0.0014 6427 | 0.0010 1363 | 0.0007 0286 | 0.0004 8819 | 80 |
| 81 | 0.0013 4956 | 0.0009 2994 | 0.0006 4188 | 0.0004 4381 | 81 |
| 82 | 0.0012 4383 | 0.0008 5315 | 0.0005 8620 | 0.0004 0346 | 82 |
| 83 | 0.0011 4639 | 0.0007 8271 | 0.0005 3534 | 0.0003 6678 | 83 |
| 84 | 0.0010 5658 | 0.0007 1808 | 0.0004 8889 | 0.0003 3344 | 84 |
| 85 | 0.0009 7381 | 0.0006 5879 | 0.0004 4648 | 0.0003 0313 | 85 |
| 86 | 0.0008 9752 | 0.0006 0440 | 0.0004 0774 | 0.0002 7557 | 86 |
| 87 | 0.0008 2720 | 0.0005 5449 | 0.0003 7237 | 0.0002 5052 | 87 |
| 88 | 0.0007 6240 | 0.0005 0871 | 0.0003 4006 | 0.0002 2774 | 88 |
| 89 | 0.0007 0267 | 0.0004 6670 | 0.0003 1056 | 0.0002 0704 | 89 |
| 90 | 0.0006 4762 | 0.0004 2817 | 0.0002 8362 | 0.0001 8822 | 90 |
| 91 | 0.0005 9689 | 0.0003 9282 | 0.0002 5901 | 0.0001 7111 | 91 |
| 92 | 0.0005 5013 | 0.0003 6038 | 0.0002 3654 | 0.0001 5555 | 92 |
| 93 | 0.0005 0703 | 0.0003 3063 | 0.0002 1602 | 0.0001 4141 | 93 |
| 94 | 0.0004 6731 | 0.0003 0333 | 0.0001 9728 | 0.0001 2855 | 94 |
| 95 | 0.0004 3070 | 0.0002 7828 | 0.0001 8016 | 0.0001 1687 | 95 |
| 96 | 0.0003 9696 | 0.0002 5530 | 0.0001 6453 | 0.0001 0624 | 96 |
| 97 | 0.0003 6586 | 0.0002 3422 | 0.0001 5026 | 0.0000 9659 | 97 |
| 98 | 0.0003 3720 | 0.0002 1488 | 0.0001 3722 | 0.0000 8780 | 98 |
| 99 | 0.0003 1078 | 0.0001 9714 | 0.0001 2531 | 0.0000 7982 | 99 |
| 100 | 0.0002 8644 | 0.0001 8086 | 0.0001 1444 | 0.0000 7257 | 100 |

**TABLE 7**

$$s_{\overline{n}|i} = \frac{(1+i)^n - 1}{i}$$

| n | $\frac{1}{4}\%$ | $\frac{1}{3}\%$ | $\frac{5}{12}\%$ | $\frac{11}{24}\%$ | n |
|---|---|---|---|---|---|
| 1 | 1.0000 0000 | 1.0000 0000 | 1.0000 0000 | 1.0000 0000 | 1 |
| 2 | 2.0025 0000 | 2.0033 3333 | 2.0041 6667 | 2.0045 8333 | 2 |
| 3 | 3.0075 0625 | 3.0100 1111 | 3.0125 1736 | 3.0137 7101 | 3 |
| 4 | 4.0150 2502 | 4.0200 4448 | 4.0250 6952 | 4.0275 8412 | 4 |
| 5 | 5.0250 6258 | 5.0334 4463 | 5.0418 4064 | 5.0460 4388 | 5 |
| 6 | 6.0376 2523 | 6.0502 2278 | 6.0628 4831 | 6.0691 7159 | 6 |
| 7 | 7.0527 1930 | 7.0703 9019 | 7.0881 1018 | 7.0969 8862 | 7 |
| 8 | 8.0703 5110 | 8.0939 5816 | 8.1176 4397 | 8.1295 1649 | 8 |
| 9 | 9.0905 2697 | 9.1209 3802 | 9.1514 6749 | 9.1667 7677 | 9 |
| 10 | 10.1132 5329 | 10.1513 4114 | 10.1895 9860 | 10.2087 9116 | 10 |
| 11 | 11.1385 3642 | 11.1851 7895 | 11.2320 5526 | 11.2555 8146 | 11 |
| 12 | 12.1663 8277 | 12.2224 6288 | 12.2788 5549 | 12.3071 6954 | 12 |
| 13 | 13.1967 9872 | 13.2632 0442 | 13.3300 1739 | 13.3635 7740 | 13 |
| 14 | 14.2297 9072 | 14.3074 1510 | 14.3855 5913 | 14.4248 2713 | 14 |
| 15 | 15.2653 6520 | 15.3551 0648 | 15.4454 9896 | 15.4909 4092 | 15 |
| 16 | 16.3035 2861 | 16.4062 9017 | 16.5098 5520 | 16.5619 4107 | 16 |
| 17 | 17.3442 8743 | 17.4609 7781 | 17.5786 4627 | 17.6378 4996 | 17 |
| 18 | 18.3876 4815 | 18.5191 8107 | 18.6518 9063 | 18.7186 9011 | 18 |
| 19 | 19.4336 1727 | 19.5809 1167 | 19.7296 0684 | 19.8044 8410 | 19 |
| 20 | 20.4822 0131 | 20.6461 8137 | 20.8118 1353 | 20.8952 5466 | 20 |
| 21 | 21.5334 0682 | 21.7150 0198 | 21.8985 2942 | 21.9910 2457 | 21 |
| 22 | 22.5872 4033 | 22.7873 8532 | 22.9897 7330 | 23.0918 1677 | 22 |
| 23 | 23.6437 0843 | 23.8633 4327 | 24.0855 6402 | 24.1976 5426 | 23 |
| 24 | 24.7028 1770 | 24.9428 8775 | 25.1859 2053 | 25.3085 6018 | 24 |
| 25 | 25.7645 7475 | 26.0260 3071 | 26.2908 6187 | 26.4245 5775 | 25 |
| 26 | 26.8289 8619 | 27.1127 8414 | 27.4004 0713 | 27.5456 7030 | 26 |
| 27 | 27.8960 5865 | 28.2031 6009 | 28.5145 7549 | 28.6719 2129 | 27 |
| 28 | 28.9657 9880 | 29.2971 7062 | 29.6333 8622 | 29.8033 3426 | 28 |
| 29 | 30.0382 1330 | 30.3948 2786 | 30.7568 5866 | 30.9399 3288 | 29 |
| 30 | 31.1133 0883 | 31.4961 4395 | 31.8850 1224 | 32.0817 4090 | 30 |
| 31 | 32.1910 9210 | 32.6011 3110 | 33.0178 6646 | 33.2287 8222 | 31 |
| 32 | 33.2715 6983 | 33.7098 0154 | 34.1554 4090 | 34.3810 8080 | 32 |
| 33 | 34.3547 4876 | 34.8221 6754 | 35.2977 5524 | 35.5386 6076 | 33 |
| 34 | 35.4406 3563 | 35.9382 4143 | 36.4448 2922 | 36.7015 4628 | 34 |
| 35 | 36.5292 3722 | 37.0580 3557 | 37.5966 8268 | 37.8697 6171 | 35 |
| 36 | 37.6205 6031 | 38.1815 6236 | 38.7533 3552 | 39.0433 3145 | 36 |
| 37 | 38.7146 1171 | 39.3088 3423 | 39.9148 0775 | 40.2222 8005 | 37 |
| 38 | 39.8113 9824 | 40.4398 6368 | 41.0811 1945 | 41.4066 3217 | 38 |
| 39 | 40.9109 2673 | 41.5746 6322 | 42.2522 9078 | 42.5964 1256 | 39 |
| 40 | 42.0132 0405 | 42.7132 4543 | 43.4283 4199 | 43.7916 4612 | 40 |
| 41 | 43.1182 3706 | 43.8556 2292 | 44.6092 9342 | 44.9923 5783 | 41 |
| 42 | 44.2260 3265 | 45.0018 0833 | 45.7951 6547 | 46.1985 7281 | 42 |
| 43 | 45.3365 9774 | 46.1518 1436 | 46.9859 7866 | 47.4103 1626 | 43 |
| 44 | 46.4499 3923 | 47.3056 5374 | 48.1817 5357 | 48.6276 1355 | 44 |
| 45 | 47.5660 6408 | 48.4633 3925 | 49.3825 1088 | 49.8504 9011 | 45 |
| 46 | 48.6849 7924 | 49.6248 8371 | 50.5882 7134 | 51.0789 7152 | 46 |
| 47 | 49.8066 9169 | 50.7902 9999 | 51.7990 5581 | 52.3130 8347 | 47 |
| 48 | 50.9312 0842 | 51.9596 0099 | 53.0148 8521 | 53.5528 5177 | 48 |
| 49 | 52.0585 3644 | 53.1327 9966 | 54.2357 8056 | 54.7983 0234 | 49 |
| 50 | 53.1886 8278 | 54.3099 0899 | 55.4617 6298 | 56.0494 6123 | 50 |
| 51 | 54.3216 5449 | 55.4909 4202 | 56.6928 5366 | 57.3063 5459 | 51 |
| 52 | 55.4574 5862 | 56.6759 1183 | 57.9290 7388 | 58.5690 0872 | 52 |
| 53 | 56.5961 0227 | 57.8648 3154 | 59.1704 4502 | 59.8374 5001 | 53 |
| 54 | 57.7375 9252 | 59.0577 1431 | 60.4169 8854 | 61.1117 0499 | 54 |
| 55 | 58.8819 3650 | 60.2545 7336 | 61.6687 2600 | 62.3918 0030 | 55 |
| 56 | 60.0291 4135 | 61.4554 2194 | 62.9256 7902 | 63.6777 6272 | 56 |
| 57 | 61.1792 1420 | 62.6602 7334 | 64.1878 6935 | 64.9696 1913 | 57 |
| 58 | 62.3321 6223 | 63.8691 4092 | 65.4553 1881 | 66.2673 9655 | 58 |
| 59 | 63.4879 9264 | 65.0820 3806 | 66.7280 4930 | 67.5711 2212 | 59 |
| 60 | 64.6467 1262 | 66.2989 7818 | 68.0060 8284 | 68.8808 2310 | 60 |

# TABLE   7

$$s_{\overline{n}|i} = \frac{(1+i)^n - 1}{i}$$

| n | $\frac{1}{4}\%$ | $\frac{1}{3}\%$ | $\frac{5}{12}\%$ | $\frac{11}{24}\%$ | n |
|---|---|---|---|---|---|
| 61 | 65.8083 2940 | 67.5199 7478 | 69.2894 4152 | 70.1965 2687 | 61 |
| 62 | 66.9728 5023 | 68.7450 4136 | 70.5781 4753 | 71.5182 6095 | 62 |
| 63 | 68.1402 8235 | 69.9741 9150 | 71.8722 2314 | 72.8460 5298 | 63 |
| 64 | 69.3106 3306 | 71.2074 3880 | 73.1716 9074 | 74.1799 3073 | 64 |
| 65 | 70.4839 0964 | 72.4447 9693 | 74.4765 7278 | 75.5199 2207 | 65 |
| 66 | 71.6601 1942 | 73.6862 7959 | 75.7868 9183 | 76.8660 5505 | 66 |
| 67 | 72.8392 6971 | 74.9319 0052 | 77.1026 7055 | 78.2183 5780 | 67 |
| 68 | 74.0213 6789 | 76.1816 7352 | 78.4239 3168 | 79.5768 5861 | 68 |
| 69 | 75.2064 2131 | 77.4356 1243 | 79.7506 9806 | 80.9415 8588 | 69 |
| 70 | 76.3944 3736 | 78.6937 3114 | 81.0829 9264 | 82.3125 6815 | 70 |
| 71 | 77.5854 2345 | 79.9560 4358 | 82.4208 3844 | 83.6898 3408 | 71 |
| 72 | 78.7793 8701 | 81.2225 6372 | 83.7642 5860 | 85.0734 1249 | 72 |
| 73 | 79.9763 3548 | 82.4933 0560 | 85.1132 7634 | 86.4633 3230 | 73 |
| 74 | 81.1762 7632 | 83.7682 8329 | 86.4679 1499 | 87.8596 2257 | 74 |
| 75 | 82.3792 1701 | 85.0475 1090 | 87.8281 9797 | 89.2623 1251 | 75 |
| 76 | 83.5851 6505 | 86.3310 0260 | 89.1941 4880 | 90.6714 3144 | 76 |
| 77 | 84.7941 2797 | 87.6187 7261 | 90.5657 9108 | 92.0870 0883 | 77 |
| 78 | 86.0061 1329 | 88.9108 3519 | 91.9431 4855 | 93.5090 7429 | 78 |
| 79 | 87.2211 2857 | 90.2072 0464 | 93.3262 4500 | 94.9376 5755 | 79 |
| 80 | 88.4391 8139 | 91.5078 9532 | 94.7151 0435 | 96.3727 8848 | 80 |
| 81 | 89.6602 7934 | 92.8129 2164 | 96.1097 5062 | 97.8144 9709 | 81 |
| 82 | 90.8844 3004 | 94.1222 9804 | 97.5102 0792 | 99.2628 1354 | 82 |
| 83 | 92.1116 4112 | 95.4360 3904 | 98.9165 0045 | 100.7177 6810 | 83 |
| 84 | 93.3419 2022 | 96.7541 5917 | 100.3286 5253 | 102.1793 9120 | 84 |
| 85 | 94.5752 7502 | 98.0766 7303 | 101.7466 8859 | 103.6477 1341 | 85 |
| 86 | 95.8117 1321 | 99.4035 9527 | 103.1706 3312 | 105.1227 6543 | 86 |
| 87 | 97.0512 4249 | 100.7349 4059 | 104.6005 1076 | 106.6045 7811 | 87 |
| 88 | 98.2938 7060 | 102.0707 2373 | 106.0363 4622 | 108.0931 8242 | 88 |
| 89 | 99.5396 0527 | 103.4109 5947 | 107.4781 6433 | 109.5886 0951 | 89 |
| 90 | 100.7884 5429 | 104.7556 6267 | 108.9259 9002 | 111.0908 9064 | 90 |
| 91 | 102.0404 2542 | 106.1048 4821 | 110.3798 4831 | 112.6000 5722 | 91 |
| 92 | 103.2955 2649 | 107.4585 3104 | 111.8397 6434 | 114.1161 4081 | 92 |
| 93 | 104.5537 6530 | 108.8167 2614 | 113.3057 6336 | 115.6391 7313 | 93 |
| 94 | 105.8151 4972 | 110.1794 4856 | 114.7778 7071 | 117.1691 8600 | 94 |
| 95 | 107.0796 8759 | 111.5467 1339 | 116.2561 1184 | 118.7062 1144 | 95 |
| 96 | 108.3473 8681 | 112.9185 3577 | 117.7405 1230 | 120.2502 8157 | 96 |
| 97 | 109.6182 5528 | 114.2949 3089 | 119.2310 9777 | 121.8014 2870 | 97 |
| 98 | 110.8923 0091 | 115.6759 1399 | 120.7278 9401 | 123.3596 8525 | 98 |
| 99 | 112.1695 3167 | 117.0615 0037 | 122.2309 2690 | 124.9250 8380 | 99 |
| 100 | 113.4499 5550 | 118.4517 0537 | 123.7402 2243 | 126.4976 5711 | 100 |
| 101 | 114.7335 8038 | 119.8465 4439 | 125.2558 0669 | 128.0774 3803 | 101 |
| 102 | 116.0204 1434 | 121.2460 3287 | 126.7777 0589 | 129.6644 5962 | 102 |
| 103 | 117.3104 6537 | 122.6501 8632 | 128.3059 4633 | 131.2587 5506 | 103 |
| 104 | 118.6037 4153 | 124.0590 2027 | 129.8405 5444 | 132.8603 5769 | 104 |
| 105 | 119.9002 5089 | 125.4725 5034 | 131.3815 5675 | 134.4693 0100 | 105 |
| 106 | 121.2000 0152 | 126.8907 9217 | 132.9289 7990 | 136.0856 1863 | 106 |
| 107 | 122.5030 0152 | 128.3137 6148 | 134.4828 5065 | 137.7093 4438 | 107 |
| 108 | 123.8092 5902 | 129.7414 7402 | 136.0431 9586 | 139.3405 1221 | 108 |
| 109 | 125.1187 8217 | 131.1739 4560 | 137.6100 4251 | 140.9791 5622 | 109 |
| 110 | 126.4315 7913 | 132.6111 9208 | 139.1834 1769 | 142.6253 1069 | 110 |
| 111 | 127.7476 5807 | 134.0532 2939 | 140.7633 4859 | 144.2790 1003 | 111 |
| 112 | 129.0670 2722 | 135.5000 7349 | 142.3498 6255 | 145.9402 8882 | 112 |
| 113 | 130.3896 9479 | 136.9517 4040 | 143.9429 8697 | 147.6091 8182 | 113 |
| 114 | 131.7156 6902 | 138.4082 4620 | 145.5427 4942 | 149.2857 2390 | 114 |
| 115 | 133.0449 5820 | 139.8696 0702 | 147.1491 7754 | 150.9699 5013 | 115 |
| 116 | 134.3775 7059 | 141.3358 3904 | 148.7622 9911 | 152.6618 9574 | 116 |
| 117 | 135.7135 1452 | 142.8069 5851 | 150.3821 4203 | 154.3615 9609 | 117 |
| 118 | 137.0527 9830 | 144.2829 8170 | 152.0087 3424 | 156.0690 8674 | 118 |
| 119 | 138.3954 3030 | 145.7639 2498 | 153.6421 0401 | 157.7844 0339 | 119 |
| 120 | 139.7414 1888 | 147.2498 0473 | 155.2822 7945 | 159.5075 8191 | 120 |

**TABLE   7**

$$s_{\overline{n}|i} = \frac{(1+i)^n - 1}{i}$$

| n | $\frac{1}{4}\%$ | $\frac{1}{3}\%$ | $\frac{5}{12}\%$ | $\frac{11}{24}\%$ | n |
|---|---|---|---|---|---|
| 121 | 141.0907 7242 | 148.7406 3741 | 156.9292 8894 | 161.2386 5832 | 121 |
| 122 | 142.4434 9935 | 150.2364 3953 | 158.5831 6098 | 162.9776 6884 | 122 |
| 123 | 143.7996 0810 | 151.7372 2766 | 160.2439 2415 | 164.7246 4982 | 123 |
| 124 | 145.1591 0712 | 153.2430 1842 | 161.9116 0717 | 166.4796 3780 | 124 |
| 125 | 146.5220 0489 | 154.7538 2848 | 163.5862 3887 | 168.2426 6947 | 125 |
| 126 | 147.8883 0990 | 156.2696 7458 | 165.2678 4819 | 170.0137 8171 | 126 |
| 127 | 149.2580 3068 | 157.7905 7349 | 166.9564 6423 | 171.7930 1154 | 127 |
| 128 | 150.6311 7575 | 159.3165 4207 | 168.6521 1616 | 173.5803 9618 | 128 |
| 129 | 152.0077 5369 | 160.8475 9721 | 170.3548 3331 | 175.3759 7299 | 129 |
| 130 | 153.3877 7308 | 162.3837 5587 | 172.0646 4512 | 177.1797 7954 | 130 |
| 131 | 154.7712 4251 | 163.9250 3506 | 173.7815 8114 | 178.9918 5353 | 131 |
| 132 | 156.1581 7062 | 165.4714 5184 | 175.5056 7106 | 180.8122 3285 | 132 |
| 133 | 157.5485 6604 | 167.0230 2335 | 177.2369 4469 | 182.6409 5559 | 133 |
| 134 | 158.9424 3746 | 168.5797 6676 | 178.9754 3196 | 184.4780 5997 | 134 |
| 135 | 160.3397 9355 | 170.1416 9931 | 180.7211 6293 | 186.3235 8441 | 135 |
| 136 | 161.7406 4304 | 171.7088 3831 | 182.4741 6777 | 188.1775 6751 | 136 |
| 137 | 163.1449 9464 | 173.2812 0111 | 184.2344 7680 | 190.0400 4802 | 137 |
| 138 | 164.5528 5713 | 174.8588 0511 | 186.0021 2046 | 191.9110 6491 | 138 |
| 139 | 165.9642 3927 | 176.4416 6779 | 187.7771 2929 | 193.7906 5729 | 139 |
| 140 | 167.3791 4987 | 178.0298 0669 | 189.5595 3400 | 195.6788 6447 | 140 |
| 141 | 168.7975 9775 | 179.6232 3937 | 191.3493 6539 | 197.5757 2593 | 141 |
| 142 | 170.2195 9174 | 181.2219 8351 | 193.1466 5441 | 199.4812 8134 | 142 |
| 143 | 171.6451 4072 | 182.8260 5678 | 194.9514 3214 | 201.3955 7055 | 143 |
| 144 | 173.0742 5357 | 184.4354 7697 | 196.7637 2977 | 203.3186 3358 | 144 |
| 145 | 174.5069 3921 | 186.0502 6190 | 198.5835 7865 | 205.2505 1065 | 145 |
| 146 | 175.9432 0655 | 187.6704 2944 | 200.4110 1022 | 207.1912 4216 | 146 |
| 147 | 177.3830 6457 | 189.2959 9753 | 202.2460 5610 | 209.1408 6868 | 147 |
| 148 | 178.8265 2223 | 190.9269 8419 | 204.0887 4800 | 211.0994 3100 | 148 |
| 149 | 180.2735 8854 | 192.5634 0747 | 205.9391 1778 | 213.0669 7006 | 149 |
| 150 | 181.7242 7251 | 194.2052 8550 | 207.7971 9744 | 215.0435 2700 | 150 |
| 151 | 183.1785 8319 | 195.8526 3645 | 209.6630 1910 | 217.0291 4317 | 151 |
| 152 | 184.6365 2965 | 197.5054 7857 | 211.5366 1501 | 219.0238 6008 | 152 |
| 153 | 186.0981 2097 | 199.1638 3017 | 213.4180 1757 | 221.0277 1943 | 153 |
| 154 | 187.5633 6627 | 200.8277 0960 | 215.3072 5931 | 223.0407 6315 | 154 |
| 155 | 189.0322 7469 | 202.4971 3530 | 217.2043 7289 | 225.0630 3331 | 155 |
| 156 | 190.5048 5538 | 204.1721 2575 | 219.1093 9111 | 227.0945 7222 | 156 |
| 157 | 191.9811 1752 | 205.8526 9950 | 221.0223 4691 | 229.1354 2234 | 157 |
| 158 | 193.4610 7031 | 207.5388 7517 | 222.9432 7336 | 231.1856 2636 | 158 |
| 159 | 194.9447 2298 | 209.2306 7142 | 224.8722 0366 | 233.2452 2714 | 159 |
| 160 | 196.4320 8479 | 210.9281 0699 | 226.8091 7118 | 235.3142 6777 | 160 |
| 161 | 197.9231 6500 | 212.6312 0068 | 228.7542 0939 | 237.3927 9150 | 161 |
| 162 | 199.4179 7292 | 214.3399 7135 | 230.7073 5193 | 239.4808 4179 | 162 |
| 163 | 200.9165 1785 | 216.0544 3792 | 232.6686 3256 | 241.5784 6232 | 163 |
| 164 | 202.4188 0914 | 217.7746 1938 | 234.6380 8520 | 243.6856 9693 | 164 |
| 165 | 203.9248 5617 | 219.5005 3478 | 236.6157 4389 | 245.8025 8971 | 165 |
| 166 | 205.4346 6831 | 221.2322 0323 | 238.6016 4282 | 247.9291 8492 | 166 |
| 167 | 206.9482 5498 | 222.9696 4390 | 240.5958 1633 | 250.0655 2701 | 167 |
| 168 | 208.4656 2562 | 224.7128 7605 | 242.5982 9890 | 252.2116 6068 | 168 |
| 169 | 209.9867 8968 | 226.4619 1897 | 244.6091 2514 | 254.3676 3079 | 169 |
| 170 | 211.5117 5665 | 228.2167 9203 | 246.6283 2983 | 256.5334 8243 | 170 |
| 171 | 213.0405 3604 | 229.9775 1467 | 248.6559 4787 | 258.7092 6089 | 171 |
| 172 | 214.5731 3739 | 231.7441 0639 | 250.6920 1432 | 260.8950 1167 | 172 |
| 173 | 216.1095 7023 | 233.5165 8674 | 252.7365 6438 | 263.0907 8047 | 173 |
| 174 | 217.6498 4415 | 235.2949 7537 | 254.7896 3340 | 265.2966 1322 | 174 |
| 175 | 219.1939 6876 | 237.0792 9195 | 256.8512 5687 | 267.5125 5603 | 175 |
| 176 | 220.7419 5369 | 238.8695 5626 | 258.9214 7044 | 269.7386 5524 | 176 |
| 177 | 222.2938 0857 | 240.6657 8811 | 261.0003 0990 | 271.9749 5741 | 177 |
| 178 | 223.8495 4309 | 242.4680 0741 | 263.0878 1120 | 274.2215 0930 | 178 |
| 179 | 225.4091 6695 | 244.2762 3410 | 265.1840 1041 | 276.4783 5789 | 179 |
| 180 | 226.9726 8987 | 246.0904 8821 | 267.2889 4379 | 278.7455 5036 | 180 |

## TABLE 7

$$s_{\overline{n}|i} = \frac{(1+i)^n - 1}{i}$$

| $n$ | $\frac{1}{4}\%$ | $\frac{1}{3}\%$ | $\frac{5}{12}\%$ | $\frac{11}{24}\%$ | $n$ |
|---|---|---|---|---|---|
| 181 | 228.5401 2159 | 247.9107 8984 | 269.4026 4772 | 281.0231 3413 | 181 |
| 182 | 230.1114 7190 | 249.7371 5914 | 271.5251 5875 | 283.3111 5683 | 182 |
| 183 | 231.6867 5058 | 251.5696 1634 | 273.6565 1358 | 285.6096 6630 | 183 |
| 184 | 233.2659 6745 | 253.4081 8172 | 275.7967 4905 | 287.9187 1060 | 184 |
| 185 | 234.8491 3237 | 255.2528 7566 | 277.9459 0217 | 290.2383 3803 | 185 |
| 186 | 236.4362 5520 | 257.1037 1858 | 280.1040 1010 | 292.5685 9708 | 186 |
| 187 | 238.0273 4584 | 258.9607 3098 | 282.2711 1014 | 294.9095 3648 | 187 |
| 188 | 239.6224 1420 | 260.8239 3341 | 284.4472 3977 | 297.2612 0519 | 188 |
| 189 | 241.2214 7024 | 262.6933 4652 | 286.6324 3660 | 299.6236 5238 | 189 |
| 190 | 242.8245 2392 | 264.5689 9101 | 288.8267 3842 | 301.9969 2745 | 190 |
| 191 | 244.4315 8523 | 266.4508 8765 | 291.0301 8316 | 304.3810 8004 | 191 |
| 192 | 246.0426 6419 | 268.3390 5727 | 293.2428 0892 | 306.7761 5999 | 192 |
| 193 | 247.6577 7085 | 270.2335 2080 | 295.4646 5396 | 309.1822 1739 | 193 |
| 194 | 249.2769 1528 | 272.1342 9920 | 297.6957 5669 | 311.5993 0255 | 194 |
| 195 | 250.9001 0756 | 274.0414 1353 | 299.9361 5567 | 314.0274 6602 | 195 |
| 196 | 252.5273 5783 | 275.9548 8491 | 302.1858 8965 | 316.4667 5857 | 196 |
| 197 | 254.1586 7623 | 277.8747 3453 | 304.4449 9753 | 318.9172 3122 | 197 |
| 198 | 255.7940 7292 | 279.8009 8364 | 306.7135 1835 | 321.3789 3519 | 198 |
| 199 | 257.4335 5810 | 281.7336 5359 | 308.9914 9134 | 323.8519 2198 | 199 |
| 200 | 259.0771 4200 | 283.6727 6577 | 311.2789 5589 | 326.3362 4329 | 200 |
| 201 | 260.7248 3485 | 285.6183 4165 | 313.5759 5154 | 328.8319 5107 | 201 |
| 202 | 262.3766 4694 | 287.5704 0279 | 315.8825 1801 | 331.3390 9751 | 202 |
| 203 | 264.0325 8855 | 289.5289 7080 | 318.1986 9516 | 333.8577 3504 | 203 |
| 204 | 265.6926 7003 | 291.4940 6737 | 320.5245 2306 | 336.3879 1633 | 204 |
| 205 | 267.3569 0170 | 293.4657 1426 | 322.8600 4191 | 338.9296 9428 | 205 |
| 206 | 269.0252 9396 | 295.4439 3331 | 325.2052 9208 | 341.4831 2204 | 206 |
| 207 | 270.6978 5719 | 297.4287 4642 | 327.5603 1413 | 344.0482 5302 | 207 |
| 208 | 272.3746 0183 | 299.4201 7557 | 329.9251 4877 | 346.6251 4084 | 208 |
| 209 | 274.0555 3834 | 301.4182 4283 | 332.2998 3689 | 349.2138 3941 | 209 |
| 210 | 275.7406 7718 | 303.4229 7030 | 334.6844 1955 | 351.8144 0284 | 210 |
| 211 | 277.4300 2888 | 305.4343 8020 | 337.0789 3796 | 354.4268 8552 | 211 |
| 212 | 279.1236 0395 | 307.4524 9480 | 339.4834 3354 | 357.0513 4208 | 212 |
| 213 | 280.8214 1296 | 309.4773 3645 | 341.8979 4784 | 359.6878 2739 | 213 |
| 214 | 282.5234 6649 | 311.5089 2757 | 344.3225 2263 | 362.3363 9660 | 214 |
| 215 | 284.2297 7516 | 313.5472 9067 | 346.7571 9980 | 364.9971 0509 | 215 |
| 216 | 285.9403 4960 | 315.5924 4830 | 349.2020 2147 | 367.6700 0849 | 216 |
| 217 | 287.6552 0047 | 317.6444 2313 | 351.6570 2989 | 370.3551 6269 | 217 |
| 218 | 289.3743 3847 | 319.7032 3787 | 354.1222 6752 | 373.0526 2385 | 218 |
| 219 | 291.0977 7432 | 321.7689 1533 | 356.5977 7696 | 375.7624 4838 | 219 |
| 220 | 292.8255 1875 | 323.8414 7838 | 359.0836 0104 | 378.4846 9293 | 220 |
| 221 | 294.5575 8255 | 325.9209 4998 | 361.5797 8271 | 381.2194 1444 | 221 |
| 222 | 296.2939 7651 | 328.0073 5315 | 364.0863 6513 | 383.9666 7009 | 222 |
| 223 | 298.0347 1145 | 330.1007 1099 | 366.6033 9166 | 386.7265 1733 | 223 |
| 224 | 299.7797 9823 | 332.2010 4669 | 369.1309 0579 | 389.4990 1387 | 224 |
| 225 | 301.5292 4772 | 334.3083 8351 | 371.6689 5123 | 392.2842 1768 | 225 |
| 226 | 303.2830 7084 | 336.4227 4479 | 374.2175 7186 | 395.0821 8701 | 226 |
| 227 | 305.0412 7852 | 338.5441 5394 | 376.7768 1174 | 397.8929 8037 | 227 |
| 228 | 306.8038 8171 | 340.6726 3446 | 379.3467 1512 | 400.7166 5653 | 228 |
| 229 | 308.5708 9142 | 342.8082 0990 | 381.9273 2644 | 403.5532 7454 | 229 |
| 230 | 310.3423 1865 | 344.9509 0394 | 384.5186 9030 | 406.4028 9371 | 230 |
| 231 | 312.1181 7444 | 347.1007 4028 | 387.1208 5151 | 409.2655 7364 | 231 |
| 232 | 313.8984 6988 | 349.2577 4275 | 389.7338 5505 | 412.1413 7419 | 232 |
| 233 | 315.6832 1605 | 351.4219 3523 | 392.3577 4612 | 415.0303 5549 | 233 |
| 234 | 317.4724 2409 | 353.5933 4168 | 394.9925 7006 | 417.9325 7795 | 234 |
| 235 | 319.2661 0515 | 355.7719 8615 | 397.6383 7243 | 420.8481 0227 | 235 |
| 236 | 321.0642 7042 | 357.9578 9277 | 400.2951 9899 | 423.7769 8940 | 236 |
| 237 | 322.8669 3109 | 360.1510 8575 | 402.9630 9565 | 426.7193 0060 | 237 |
| 238 | 324.6740 9842 | 362.3515 8937 | 405.6421 0855 | 429.6750 9740 | 238 |
| 239 | 326.4857 8367 | 364.5594 2800 | 408.3322 8400 | 432.6444 4159 | 239 |
| 240 | 328.3019 9813 | 366.7746 2609 | 411.0336 6852 | 435.6273 9528 | 240 |

# TABLE 7

$$s_{\overline{n}|\,i} = \frac{(1+i)^n - 1}{i}$$

| n | $\frac{1}{2}\%$ | $\frac{13}{24}\%$ | $\frac{7}{12}\%$ | $\frac{5}{8}\%$ | n |
|---|---|---|---|---|---|
| 1 | 1.0000 0000 | 1.0000 0000 | 1.0000 0000 | 1.0000 0000 | 1 |
| 2 | 2.0050 0000 | 2.0054 1667 | 2.0058 3333 | 2.0062 5000 | 2 |
| 3 | 3.0150 2500 | 3.0162 7934 | 3.0175 3403 | 3.0187 8906 | 3 |
| 4 | 4.0301 0012 | 4.0326 1752 | 4.0351 3631 | 4.0376 5649 | 4 |
| 5 | 5.0502 5063 | 5.0544 6086 | 5.0586 7460 | 5.0628 9185 | 5 |
| 6 | 6.0755 0188 | 6.0818 3919 | 6.0881 8354 | 6.0945 3492 | 6 |
| 7 | 7.1058 7939 | 7.1147 8249 | 7.1236 9794 | 7.1326 2576 | 7 |
| 8 | 8.1414 0879 | 8.1533 2090 | 8.1652 5285 | 8.1772 0468 | 8 |
| 9 | 9.1821 1583 | 9.1974 8472 | 9.2128 8349 | 9.2283 1220 | 9 |
| 10 | 10.2280 2641 | 10.2473 0443 | 10.2666 2531 | 10.2859 8916 | 10 |
| 11 | 11.2791 6654 | 11.3028 1066 | 11.3265 1396 | 11.3502 7659 | 11 |
| 12 | 12.3355 6237 | 12.3640 3422 | 12.3925 8529 | 12.4212 1582 | 12 |
| 13 | 13.3972 4018 | 13.4310 0607 | 13.4648 7537 | 13.4988 4842 | 13 |
| 14 | 14.4642 2639 | 14.5037 5735 | 14.5434 2048 | 14.5832 1622 | 14 |
| 15 | 15.5365 4752 | 15.5823 1937 | 15.6282 5710 | 15.6743 6132 | 15 |
| 16 | 16.6142 3026 | 16.6667 2360 | 16.7194 2193 | 16.7723 2608 | 16 |
| 17 | 17.6973 0141 | 17.7570 0169 | 17.8169 5189 | 17.8771 5312 | 17 |
| 18 | 18.7857 8791 | 18.8531 8544 | 18.9208 8411 | 18.9888 8532 | 18 |
| 19 | 19.8797 1685 | 19.9553 0687 | 20.0312 5593 | 20.1075 6586 | 19 |
| 20 | 20.9791 1544 | 21.0633 9811 | 21.1481 0493 | 21.2332 3814 | 20 |
| 21 | 22.0840 1101 | 22.1774 9152 | 22.2714 6887 | 22.3659 4588 | 21 |
| 22 | 23.1944 3107 | 23.2976 1960 | 23.4013 8577 | 23.5057 3304 | 22 |
| 23 | 24.3104 0322 | 24.4238 1504 | 24.5378 9386 | 24.6526 4387 | 23 |
| 24 | 25.4319 5524 | 25.5561 1070 | 25.6810 3155 | 25.8067 2290 | 24 |
| 25 | 26.5591 1502 | 26.6945 3963 | 26.8308 3759 | 26.9680 1492 | 25 |
| 26 | 27.6919 1059 | 27.8391 3506 | 27.9873 5081 | 28.1365 6501 | 26 |
| 27 | 28.8303 7015 | 28.9899 3037 | 29.1506 1035 | 29.3124 1854 | 27 |
| 28 | 29.9745 2200 | 30.1469 5916 | 30.3206 5558 | 30.4956 2116 | 28 |
| 29 | 31.1243 9461 | 31.3102 5519 | 31.4975 2607 | 31.6862 1879 | 29 |
| 30 | 32.2800 1658 | 32.4798 5241 | 32.6812 6164 | 32.8842 5766 | 30 |
| 31 | 33.4414 1666 | 33.6557 8494 | 33.8719 0233 | 34.0897 8427 | 31 |
| 32 | 34.6086 2375 | 34.8380 8711 | 35.0694 8843 | 35.3028 4542 | 32 |
| 33 | 35.7816 6686 | 36.0267 9341 | 36.2740 6045 | 36.5234 8820 | 33 |
| 34 | 36.9605 7520 | 37.2219 3854 | 37.4856 5913 | 37.7517 6000 | 34 |
| 35 | 38.1453 7807 | 38.4235 5738 | 38.7043 2548 | 38.9877 0850 | 35 |
| 36 | 39.3361 0496 | 39.6316 8498 | 39.9301 0071 | 40.2313 8168 | 36 |
| 37 | 40.5327 8549 | 40.8463 5661 | 41.1630 2630 | 41.4828 2782 | 37 |
| 38 | 41.7354 4942 | 42.0676 0771 | 42.4031 4395 | 42.7420 9549 | 38 |
| 39 | 42.9441 2666 | 43.2954 7391 | 43.6504 9562 | 44.0092 3359 | 39 |
| 40 | 44.1588 4730 | 44.5299 9106 | 44.9051 2352 | 45.2842 9130 | 40 |
| 41 | 45.3796 4153 | 45.7711 9518 | 46.1670 7007 | 46.5673 1812 | 41 |
| 42 | 46.6065 3974 | 47.0191 2249 | 47.4363 7798 | 47.8583 6386 | 42 |
| 43 | 47.8395 7244 | 48.2738 0940 | 48.7130 9018 | 49.1574 7863 | 43 |
| 44 | 49.0787 7030 | 49.5352 9254 | 49.9972 4988 | 50.4647 1287 | 44 |
| 45 | 50.3241 6415 | 50.8036 0871 | 51.2889 0050 | 51.7801 1733 | 45 |
| 46 | 51.5757 8497 | 52.0787 9492 | 52.5880 8575 | 53.1037 4306 | 46 |
| 47 | 52.8336 6390 | 53.3608 8839 | 53.8948 4959 | 54.4356 4146 | 47 |
| 48 | 54.0978 3222 | 54.6499 2654 | 55.2092 3621 | 55.7758 6421 | 48 |
| 49 | 55.3683 2138 | 55.9459 4697 | 56.5312 9009 | 57.1244 6337 | 49 |
| 50 | 56.6451 6299 | 57.2489 8752 | 57.8610 5595 | 58.4814 9126 | 50 |
| 51 | 57.9283 8880 | 58.5590 8620 | 59.1985 7877 | 59.8470 0058 | 51 |
| 52 | 59.2180 3075 | 59.8762 8125 | 60.5439 0381 | 61.2210 4434 | 52 |
| 53 | 60.5141 2090 | 61.2006 1111 | 61.8970 7659 | 62.6036 7586 | 53 |
| 54 | 61.8166 9150 | 62.5321 1442 | 63.2581 4287 | 63.9949 4884 | 54 |
| 55 | 63.1257 7496 | 63.8708 3004 | 64.6271 4870 | 65.3949 1727 | 55 |
| 56 | 64.4414 0384 | 65.2167 9703 | 66.0041 4040 | 66.8036 3550 | 56 |
| 57 | 65.7636 1086 | 66.5700 5469 | 67.3891 6455 | 68.2211 5822 | 57 |
| 58 | 67.0924 2891 | 67.9306 4248 | 68.7822 6801 | 69.6475 4046 | 58 |
| 59 | 68.4278 9105 | 69.2986 0013 | 70.1834 9791 | 71.0828 3759 | 59 |
| 60 | 69.7700 3051 | 70.6739 6755 | 71.5929 0165 | 72.5271 0532 | 60 |

Table
7

# TABLE 7

$$s_{\overline{n}|i} = \frac{(1+i)^n - 1}{i}$$

| n | $\frac{1}{2}$% | $\frac{13}{24}$% | $\frac{7}{12}$% | $\frac{5}{8}$% | n |
|---|---|---|---|---|---|
| 61 | 71.1188 8066 | 72.0567 8487 | 73.0105 2691 | 73.9803 9973 | 61 |
| 62 | 72.4744 7507 | 73.4470 9245 | 74.4364 2165 | 75.4427 7723 | 62 |
| 63 | 73.8368 4744 | 74.8449 3087 | 75.8706 3411 | 76.9142 9459 | 63 |
| 64 | 75.2060 3168 | 76.2503 4091 | 77.3132 1281 | 78.3950 0893 | 64 |
| 65 | 76.5820 6184 | 77.6633 6359 | 78.7642 0655 | 79.8849 7774 | 65 |
| 66 | 77.9649 7215 | 79.0840 4015 | 80.2236 6442 | 81.3842 5885 | 66 |
| 67 | 79.3547 9701 | 80.5124 1203 | 81.6916 3580 | 82.8929 1046 | 67 |
| 68 | 80.7515 7099 | 81.9485 2093 | 83.1681 7034 | 84.4109 9115 | 68 |
| 69 | 82.1553 2885 | 83.3924 0875 | 84.6533 1800 | 85.9385 5985 | 69 |
| 70 | 83.5661 0549 | 84.8441 1763 | 86.1471 2902 | 87.4756 7585 | 70 |
| 71 | 84.9839 3602 | 86.3036 8994 | 87.6496 5394 | 89.0223 9882 | 71 |
| 72 | 86.4088 5570 | 87.7711 6826 | 89.1609 4359 | 90.5787 8882 | 72 |
| 73 | 87.8408 9998 | 89.2465 9542 | 90.6810 4909 | 92.1449 0625 | 73 |
| 74 | 89.2801 0448 | 90.7300 1448 | 92.2100 2188 | 93.7208 1191 | 74 |
| 75 | 90.7265 0500 | 92.2214 6872 | 93.7479 1367 | 95.3065 6698 | 75 |
| 76 | 92.1801 3752 | 93.7210 0168 | 95.2947 7650 | 96.9022 3303 | 76 |
| 77 | 93.6410 3821 | 95.2286 5710 | 96.8506 6270 | 98.5078 7198 | 77 |
| 78 | 95.1092 4340 | 96.7444 7900 | 98.4156 2490 | 100.1235 4618 | 78 |
| 79 | 96.5847 8962 | 98.2685 1159 | 99.9897 1604 | 101.7493 1835 | 79 |
| 80 | 98.0677 1357 | 99.8007 9936 | 101.5729 8939 | 103.3852 5159 | 80 |
| 81 | 99.5580 5214 | 101.3413 8702 | 103.1654 9849 | 105.0314 0941 | 81 |
| 82 | 101.0558 4240 | 102.8903 1954 | 104.7672 9723 | 106.6878 5572 | 82 |
| 83 | 102.5611 2161 | 104.4476 4210 | 106.3784 3980 | 108.3546 5482 | 83 |
| 84 | 104.0739 2722 | 106.0134 0016 | 107.9989 8070 | 110.0318 7141 | 84 |
| 85 | 105.5942 9685 | 107.5876 3941 | 109.6289 7475 | 111.7195 7061 | 85 |
| 86 | 107.1222 6834 | 109.1704 0579 | 111.2684 7710 | 113.4178 1792 | 86 |
| 87 | 108.6578 7968 | 110.7617 4549 | 112.9175 4322 | 115.1266 7928 | 87 |
| 88 | 110.2011 6908 | 112.3617 0495 | 114.5762 2889 | 116.8462 2103 | 88 |
| 89 | 111.7521 7492 | 113.9703 3085 | 116.2445 9022 | 118.5765 0991 | 89 |
| 90 | 113.3109 3580 | 115.5876 7014 | 117.9226 8367 | 120.3176 1310 | 90 |
| 91 | 114.8774 9048 | 117.2137 7002 | 119.6105 6599 | 122.0695 9818 | 91 |
| 92 | 116.4518 7793 | 118.8486 7794 | 121.3082 9429 | 123.8325 3317 | 92 |
| 93 | 118.0341 3732 | 120.4924 4161 | 123.0159 2601 | 125.6064 8650 | 93 |
| 94 | 119.6243 0800 | 122.1451 0901 | 124.7335 1891 | 127.3915 2704 | 94 |
| 95 | 121.2224 2954 | 123.8067 2835 | 126.4611 3110 | 129.1877 2408 | 95 |
| 96 | 122.8285 4169 | 125.4773 4812 | 128.1988 2103 | 130.9951 4736 | 96 |
| 97 | 124.4426 8440 | 127.1570 1709 | 129.9466 4749 | 132.8138 6703 | 97 |
| 98 | 126.0648 9782 | 128.8457 8427 | 131.7046 6960 | 134.6439 5370 | 98 |
| 99 | 127.6952 2231 | 130.5436 9893 | 133.4729 4684 | 136.4854 7841 | 99 |
| 100 | 129.3336 9842 | 132.2508 1064 | 135.2515 3903 | 138.3385 1265 | 100 |
| 101 | 130.9803 6692 | 133.9671 6919 | 137.0405 0634 | 140.2031 2836 | 101 |
| 102 | 132.6352 6875 | 135.6928 2469 | 138.8399 0929 | 142.0793 9791 | 102 |
| 103 | 134.2984 4509 | 137.4278 2750 | 140.6498 0877 | 143.9673 9414 | 103 |
| 104 | 135.9699 3732 | 139.1722 2823 | 142.4702 6598 | 145.8671 9036 | 104 |
| 105 | 137.6497 8701 | 140.9260 7780 | 144.3013 4253 | 147.7788 6030 | 105 |
| 106 | 139.3380 3594 | 142.6894 2738 | 146.1431 0037 | 149.7024 7817 | 106 |
| 107 | 141.0347 2612 | 144.4623 2845 | 147.9956 0178 | 151.6381 1866 | 107 |
| 108 | 142.7398 9975 | 146.2448 3273 | 149.8589 0946 | 153.5858 5690 | 108 |
| 109 | 144.4535 9925 | 148.0369 9224 | 151.7330 8643 | 155.5457 6851 | 109 |
| 110 | 146.1758 6725 | 149.8388 5928 | 153.6181 9610 | 157.5179 2956 | 110 |
| 111 | 147.9067 4658 | 151.6504 8644 | 155.5143 0225 | 159.5024 1662 | 111 |
| 112 | 149.6462 8032 | 153.4719 2657 | 157.4214 6901 | 161.4993 0673 | 112 |
| 113 | 151.3945 1172 | 155.3032 3284 | 159.3397 6091 | 163.5086 7739 | 113 |
| 114 | 153.1514 8428 | 157.1444 5868 | 161.2692 4285 | 165.5306 0663 | 114 |
| 115 | 154.9172 4170 | 158.9956 5783 | 163.2099 8010 | 167.5651 7292 | 115 |
| 116 | 156.6918 2791 | 160.8568 8431 | 165.1620 3832 | 169.6124 5525 | 116 |
| 117 | 158.4752 8704 | 162.7281 9244 | 167.1254 8354 | 171.6725 3310 | 117 |
| 118 | 160.2676 6348 | 164.6096 3681 | 169.1003 8220 | 173.7454 8643 | 118 |
| 119 | 162.0690 0180 | 166.5012 7235 | 171.0868 0109 | 175.8313 9572 | 119 |
| 120 | 163.8793 4681 | 168.4031 5424 | 173.0848 0743 | 177.9303 4194 | 120 |

**TABLE 7**

$$s_{\overline{n}|i} = \frac{(1+i)^n - 1}{i}$$

| n | $\frac{1}{2}\%$ | $\frac{13}{24}\%$ | $\frac{7}{12}\%$ | $\frac{5}{8}\%$ | n |
|---|---|---|---|---|---|
| 121 | 165.6987 4354 | 170.3153 3799 | 175.0944 6881 | 180.0424 0658 | 121 |
| 122 | 167.5272 3726 | 172.2378 7940 | 177.1158 5321 | 182.1676 7162 | 122 |
| 123 | 169.3648 7344 | 174.1708 3458 | 179.1490 2902 | 184.3062 1957 | 123 |
| 124 | 171.2116 9781 | 176.1142 5994 | 181.1940 6502 | 186.4581 3344 | 124 |
| 125 | 173.0677 5630 | 178.0682 1218 | 183.2510 3040 | 188.6234 9677 | 125 |
| 126 | 174.9330 9508 | 180.0327 4833 | 185.3199 9475 | 190.8023 9363 | 126 |
| 127 | 176.8077 6056 | 182.0079 2572 | 187.4010 2805 | 192.9949 0859 | 127 |
| 128 | 178.6917 9936 | 183.9938 0198 | 189.4942 0071 | 195.2011 2677 | 128 |
| 129 | 180.5852 5836 | 185.9904 3507 | 191.5995 8355 | 197.4211 3381 | 129 |
| 130 | 182.4881 8465 | 187.9978 8326 | 193.7172 4779 | 199.6550 1589 | 130 |
| 131 | 184.4006 2557 | 190.0162 0513 | 195.8472 6507 | 201.9028 5974 | 131 |
| 132 | 186.3226 2870 | 192.0454 5958 | 197.9897 0745 | 204.1647 5262 | 132 |
| 133 | 188.2542 4184 | 194.0857 0582 | 200.1446 4741 | 206.4407 8232 | 133 |
| 134 | 190.1955 1305 | 196.1370 0339 | 202.3121 5785 | 208.7310 3721 | 134 |
| 135 | 192.1464 9062 | 198.1994 1216 | 204.4923 1210 | 211.0356 0619 | 135 |
| 136 | 194.1072 2307 | 200.2729 9231 | 206.6851 8393 | 213.3545 7873 | 136 |
| 137 | 196.0777 5919 | 202.3578 0435 | 208.8908 4750 | 215.6880 4485 | 137 |
| 138 | 198.0581 4798 | 204.4539 0912 | 211.1093 7744 | 218.0360 9513 | 138 |
| 139 | 200.0484 3872 | 206.5613 6780 | 213.3408 4881 | 220.3988 2072 | 139 |
| 140 | 202.0486 8092 | 208.6802 4187 | 215.5853 3710 | 222.7763 1335 | 140 |
| 141 | 204.0589 2432 | 210.8105 9318 | 217.8429 1823 | 225.1686 6531 | 141 |
| 142 | 206.0792 1894 | 212.9524 8390 | 220.1136 6858 | 227.5759 6947 | 142 |
| 143 | 208.1096 1504 | 215.1059 7652 | 222.3976 6498 | 229.9983 1928 | 143 |
| 144 | 210.1501 6311 | 217.2711 3389 | 224.6949 8470 | 232.4358 0878 | 144 |
| 145 | 212.2009 1393 | 219.4480 1920 | 227.0057 0544 | 234.8885 3258 | 145 |
| 146 | 214.2619 1850 | 221.6366 9597 | 229.3299 0539 | 237.3565 8591 | 146 |
| 147 | 216.3332 2809 | 223.8372 2807 | 231.6676 6317 | 239.8400 6457 | 147 |
| 148 | 218.4148 9423 | 226.0496 7972 | 234.0190 5787 | 242.3390 6497 | 148 |
| 149 | 220.5069 6870 | 228.2741 1549 | 236.3841 6904 | 244.8536 8413 | 149 |
| 150 | 222.6095 0354 | 230.5106 0028 | 238.7630 7670 | 247.3840 1966 | 150 |
| 151 | 224.7225 5106 | 232.7591 9937 | 241.1558 6131 | 249.9301 6978 | 151 |
| 152 | 226.8461 6382 | 235.0199 7836 | 243.5626 0384 | 252.4922 3334 | 152 |
| 153 | 228.9803 9464 | 237.2930 0325 | 245.9833 8569 | 255.0703 0980 | 153 |
| 154 | 231.1252 9661 | 239.5783 4035 | 248.4182 8877 | 257.6644 9923 | 154 |
| 155 | 233.2809 2309 | 241.8760 5636 | 250.8673 9546 | 260.2749 0235 | 155 |
| 156 | 235.4473 2771 | 244.1862 1833 | 253.3307 8860 | 262.9016 2049 | 156 |
| 157 | 237.6245 6435 | 246.5088 9368 | 255.8085 5153 | 265.5447 5562 | 157 |
| 158 | 239.8126 8717 | 248.8441 5018 | 258.3007 6808 | 268.2044 1035 | 158 |
| 159 | 242.0117 5060 | 251.1920 5600 | 260.8075 2256 | 270.8806 8791 | 159 |
| 160 | 244.2218 0936 | 253.5526 7964 | 263.3288 9978 | 273.5736 9221 | 160 |
| 161 | 246.4429 1840 | 255.9260 8998 | 265.8649 8503 | 276.2835 2779 | 161 |
| 162 | 248.6751 3300 | 258.3123 5630 | 268.4158 6411 | 279.0102 9983 | 162 |
| 163 | 250.9185 0866 | 260.7115 4823 | 270.9816 2331 | 281.7541 1421 | 163 |
| 164 | 253.1731 0120 | 263.1237 3579 | 273.5623 4945 | 284.5150 7742 | 164 |
| 165 | 255.4389 6671 | 265.5489 8936 | 276.1581 2982 | 287.2932 9666 | 165 |
| 166 | 257.7161 6154 | 267.9873 7971 | 278.7690 5225 | 290.0888 7976 | 166 |
| 167 | 260.0047 4235 | 270.4389 7802 | 281.3952 0505 | 292.9019 3526 | 167 |
| 168 | 262.3047 6606 | 272.9038 5582 | 284.0366 7708 | 295.7325 7235 | 168 |
| 169 | 264.6162 8989 | 275.3820 8504 | 286.6935 5770 | 298.5809 0093 | 169 |
| 170 | 266.9393 7134 | 277.8737 3800 | 289.3659 3678 | 301.4470 3156 | 170 |
| 171 | 269.2740 6820 | 280.3788 8741 | 292.0539 0475 | 304.3310 7551 | 171 |
| 172 | 271.6204 3854 | 282.8976 0639 | 294.7575 5252 | 307.2331 4473 | 172 |
| 173 | 273.9785 4073 | 285.4299 6842 | 297.4769 7158 | 310.1533 5189 | 173 |
| 174 | 276.3484 3344 | 287.9760 4742 | 300.2122 5392 | 313.0918 1033 | 174 |
| 175 | 278.7301 7561 | 290.5359 1767 | 302.9634 9206 | 316.0486 3415 | 175 |
| 176 | 281.1238 2648 | 293.1096 5389 | 305.7307 7910 | 319.0239 3811 | 176 |
| 177 | 283.5294 4562 | 295.6973 3119 | 308.5142 0864 | 322.0178 3773 | 177 |
| 178 | 285.9470 9284 | 298.2990 2506 | 311.3138 7486 | 325.0304 4921 | 178 |
| 179 | 288.3768 2831 | 300.9148 1145 | 314.1298 7247 | 328.0618 8952 | 179 |
| 180 | 290.8187 1245 | 303.5447 6668 | 316.9622 9672 | 331.1122 7633 | 180 |

Table
7

**TABLE 7**

$$s_{\overline{n}|i} = \frac{(1+i)^n - 1}{i}$$

| n | $\frac{1}{2}$ % | $\frac{13}{24}$ % | $\frac{7}{12}$ % | $\frac{5}{8}$ % | n |
|---|---|---|---|---|---|
| 181 | 293.2728 0601 | 306.1889 6750 | 319.8112 4345 | 334.1817 2806 | 181 |
| 182 | 295.7391 7004 | 308.8474 9107 | 322.6768 0904 | 337.2703 6386 | 182 |
| 183 | 298.2178 6589 | 311.5204 1498 | 325.5590 9043 | 340.3783 0363 | 183 |
| 184 | 300.7089 5522 | 314.2078 1723 | 328.4581 8512 | 343.5056 6803 | 184 |
| 185 | 303.2125 0000 | 316.9097 7624 | 331.3741 9120 | 346.6525 7845 | 185 |
| 186 | 305.7285 6250 | 319.6263 7086 | 334.3072 0731 | 349.8191 5707 | 186 |
| 187 | 308.2572 0531 | 322.3576 8037 | 337.2573 3269 | 353.0055 2680 | 187 |
| 188 | 310.7984 9134 | 325.1037 8447 | 340.2246 6713 | 356.2118 1134 | 188 |
| 189 | 313.3524 8379 | 327.8647 6330 | 343.2093 1102 | 359.4381 3516 | 189 |
| 190 | 315.9192 4621 | 330.6406 9744 | 346.2113 6534 | 362.6846 2351 | 190 |
| 191 | 318.4988 4244 | 333.4316 6788 | 349.2309 3163 | 365.9514 0241 | 191 |
| 192 | 321.0913 3666 | 336.2377 5608 | 352.2681 1207 | 369.2385 9867 | 192 |
| 193 | 323.6967 9334 | 339.0590 4393 | 355.3230 0939 | 372.5463 3991 | 193 |
| 194 | 326.3152 7731 | 341.8956 1375 | 358.3957 2694 | 375.8747 5454 | 194 |
| 195 | 328.9468 5369 | 344.7475 4832 | 361.4863 6868 | 379.2239 7175 | 195 |
| 196 | 331.5915 8796 | 347.6149 3088 | 364.5950 3917 | 382.5941 2158 | 196 |
| 197 | 334.2495 4590 | 350.4978 4509 | 367.7218 4356 | 385.9853 3484 | 197 |
| 198 | 336.9207 9363 | 353.3963 7508 | 370.8668 8765 | 389.3977 4318 | 198 |
| 199 | 339.6053 9760 | 356.3106 0545 | 374.0302 7783 | 392.8314 7907 | 199 |
| 200 | 342.3034 2459 | 359.2406 2123 | 377.2121 2112 | 396.2866 7582 | 200 |
| 201 | 345.0149 4171 | 362.1865 0792 | 380.4125 2516 | 399.7634 6754 | 201 |
| 202 | 347.7400 1642 | 365.1483 5151 | 383.6315 9822 | 403.2619 8921 | 202 |
| 203 | 350.4787 1650 | 368.1262 3841 | 386.8694 4921 | 406.7823 7665 | 203 |
| 204 | 353.2311 1008 | 371.1202 5554 | 390.1261 8766 | 410.3247 6650 | 204 |
| 205 | 355.9972 6563 | 374.1304 9026 | 393.4019 2376 | 413.8892 9629 | 205 |
| 206 | 358.7772 5196 | 377.1570 3041 | 396.6967 6831 | 417.4761 0439 | 206 |
| 207 | 361.5711 3822 | 380.1999 6433 | 400.0108 3280 | 421.0853 3005 | 207 |
| 208 | 364.3789 9391 | 383.2593 8080 | 403.3442 2932 | 424.7171 1336 | 208 |
| 209 | 367.2008 8888 | 386.3353 6911 | 406.6970 7066 | 428.3715 9532 | 209 |
| 210 | 370.0368 9333 | 389.4280 1903 | 410.0694 7024 | 432.0489 1779 | 210 |
| 211 | 372.8870 7779 | 392.5374 2080 | 413.4615 4215 | 435.7492 2352 | 211 |
| 212 | 375.7515 1318 | 395.6636 6516 | 416.8734 0114 | 439.4726 5617 | 212 |
| 213 | 378.6302 7075 | 398.8068 4335 | 420.3051 6265 | 443.2193 6027 | 213 |
| 214 | 381.5234 2210 | 401.9670 4708 | 423.7569 4276 | 446.9894 8127 | 214 |
| 215 | 384.4310 3921 | 405.1443 6859 | 427.2288 5826 | 450.7831 6553 | 215 |
| 216 | 387.3531 9441 | 408.3389 0058 | 430.7210 2660 | 454.6005 6032 | 216 |
| 217 | 390.2899 6038 | 411.5507 3629 | 434.2335 6593 | 458.4418 1382 | 217 |
| 218 | 393.2414 1018 | 414.7799 6945 | 437.7665 9506 | 462.3070 7515 | 218 |
| 219 | 396.2076 1723 | 418.0266 9428 | 441.3202 3353 | 466.1964 9437 | 219 |
| 220 | 399.1886 5532 | 421.2910 0554 | 444.8946 0156 | 470.1102 2246 | 220 |
| 221 | 402.1845 9859 | 424.5729 9849 | 448.4898 2007 | 474.0484 1135 | 221 |
| 222 | 405.1955 2159 | 427.8727 6890 | 452.1060 1069 | 478.0112 1392 | 222 |
| 223 | 408.2214 9920 | 431.1904 1306 | 455.7432 9575 | 481.9987 8401 | 223 |
| 224 | 411.2626 0669 | 434.5260 2780 | 459.4017 9831 | 486.0112 7641 | 224 |
| 225 | 414.3189 1973 | 437.8797 1045 | 463.0816 4213 | 490.0488 4689 | 225 |
| 226 | 417.3905 1432 | 441.2515 5888 | 466.7829 5171 | 494.1116 5218 | 226 |
| 227 | 420.4774 6690 | 444.6416 7149 | 470.5058 5226 | 498.1998 5001 | 227 |
| 228 | 423.5798 5423 | 448.0501 4722 | 474.2504 6973 | 502.3135 9907 | 228 |
| 229 | 426.6977 5350 | 451.4770 8551 | 478.0169 3081 | 506.4530 5907 | 229 |
| 230 | 429.8312 4227 | 454.9225 8639 | 481.8053 6290 | 510.6183 9068 | 230 |
| 231 | 432.9803 9848 | 458.3867 5040 | 485.6158 9419 | 514.8097 5563 | 231 |
| 232 | 436.1453 0047 | 461.8696 7863 | 489.4486 5357 | 519.0273 1660 | 232 |
| 233 | 439.3260 2697 | 465.3714 7273 | 493.3037 7071 | 523.2712 3733 | 233 |
| 234 | 442.5226 5711 | 468.8922 3487 | 497.1813 7604 | 527.5416 8256 | 234 |
| 235 | 445.7352 7040 | 472.4320 6781 | 501.0816 0074 | 531.8388 1808 | 235 |
| 236 | 448.9639 4675 | 475.9910 7484 | 505.0045 7674 | 536.1628 1069 | 236 |
| 237 | 452.2087 6648 | 479.5693 5983 | 508.9504 3677 | 540.5138 2826 | 237 |
| 238 | 455.4698 1031 | 483.1670 2720 | 512.9193 1432 | 544.8920 3968 | 238 |
| 239 | 458.7471 5936 | 486.7841 8193 | 516.9113 4365 | 549.2976 1493 | 239 |
| 240 | 462.0408 9516 | 490.4209 2958 | 520.9266 5983 | 553.7307 2502 | 240 |

# TABLE 7

$$s_{\overline{n}|}i = \frac{(1+i)^n - 1}{i}$$

| $n$ | $\frac{2}{3}\%$ | $\frac{3}{4}\%$ | $\frac{7}{8}\%$ | 1% | $n$ |
|---|---|---|---|---|---|
| 1 | 1.0000 0000 | 1.0000 0000 | 1.0000 0000 | 1.0000 0000 | 1 |
| 2 | 2.0066 6667 | 2.0075 0000 | 2.0087 5000 | 2.0100 0000 | 2 |
| 3 | 3.0200 4444 | 3.0225 5625 | 3.0263 2656 | 3.0301 0000 | 3 |
| 4 | 4.0401 7807 | 4.0452 2542 | 4.0528 0692 | 4.0604 0100 | 4 |
| 5 | 5.0671 1259 | 5.0755 6461 | 5.0882 6898 | 5.1010 0501 | 5 |
| 6 | 6.1008 9335 | 6.1136 3135 | 6.1327 9133 | 6.1520 1506 | 6 |
| 7 | 7.1415 6597 | 7.1594 8358 | 7.1864 5326 | 7.2135 3521 | 7 |
| 8 | 8.1891 7641 | 8.2131 7971 | 8.2493 3472 | 8.2856 7056 | 8 |
| 9 | 9.2437 7092 | 9.2747 7856 | 9.3215 1640 | 9.3685 2727 | 9 |
| 10 | 10.3053 9606 | 10.3443 3940 | 10.4030 7967 | 10.4622 1254 | 10 |
| 11 | 11.3740 9870 | 11.4219 2194 | 11.4941 0662 | 11.5668 3467 | 11 |
| 12 | 12.4499 2602 | 12.5075 8636 | 12.5946 8005 | 12.6825 0301 | 12 |
| 13 | 13.5329 2553 | 13.6013 9325 | 13.7048 8350 | 13.8093 2804 | 13 |
| 14 | 14.6231 4503 | 14.7034 0370 | 14.8248 0123 | 14.9474 2132 | 14 |
| 15 | 15.7206 3267 | 15.8136 7923 | 15.9545 1824 | 16.0968 9554 | 15 |
| 16 | 16.8254 3688 | 16.9322 8183 | 17.0941 2028 | 17.2578 6449 | 16 |
| 17 | 17.9376 0646 | 18.0592 7394 | 18.2436 9383 | 18.4304 4314 | 17 |
| 18 | 19.0571 9051 | 19.1947 1849 | 19.4033 2615 | 19.6147 4757 | 18 |
| 19 | 20.1842 3844 | 20.3386 7888 | 20.5731 0526 | 20.8108 9504 | 19 |
| 20 | 21.3188 0003 | 21.4912 1897 | 21.7531 1993 | 22.0190 0399 | 20 |
| 21 | 22.4609 2537 | 22.6524 0312 | 22.9434 5973 | 23.2391 9403 | 21 |
| 22 | 23.6106 6487 | 23.8222 9614 | 24.1442 1500 | 24.4715 8598 | 22 |
| 23 | 24.7680 6930 | 25.0009 6336 | 25.3554 7688 | 25.7163 0183 | 23 |
| 24 | 25.9331 8976 | 26.1884 7059 | 26.5773 3730 | 26.9734 6485 | 24 |
| 25 | 27.1060 7769 | 27.3848 8412 | 27.8098 8900 | 28.2431 9950 | 25 |
| 26 | 28.2867 8488 | 28.5902 7075 | 29.0532 2553 | 29.5256 3150 | 26 |
| 27 | 29.4753 6344 | 29.8046 9778 | 30.3074 4126 | 30.8208 8781 | 27 |
| 28 | 30.6718 6587 | 31.0282 3301 | 31.5726 3137 | 32.1290 9669 | 28 |
| 29 | 31.8763 4497 | 32.2609 4476 | 32.8488 9189 | 33.4503 8766 | 29 |
| 30 | 33.0888 5394 | 33.5029 0184 | 34.1363 1970 | 34.7848 9153 | 30 |
| 31 | 34.3094 4630 | 34.7541 7361 | 35.4350 1249 | 36.1327 4045 | 31 |
| 32 | 35.5381 7594 | 36.0148 2991 | 36.7450 6885 | 37.4940 6785 | 32 |
| 33 | 36.7750 9711 | 37.2849 4113 | 38.0665 8820 | 38.8690 0853 | 33 |
| 34 | 38.0202 6443 | 38.5645 7819 | 39.3996 7085 | 40.2576 9862 | 34 |
| 35 | 39.2737 3286 | 39.8538 1253 | 40.7444 1797 | 41.6602 7560 | 35 |
| 36 | 40.5355 5774 | 41.1527 1612 | 41.1009 3163 | 43.0768 7836 | 36 |
| 37 | 41.8057 9479 | 42.4613 6149 | 43.4693 1478 | 44.5076 4714 | 37 |
| 38 | 43.0845 0009 | 43.7798 2170 | 44.8496 7128 | 45.9527 2361 | 38 |
| 39 | 44.3717 3009 | 45.1081 7037 | 46.2421 0591 | 47.4122 5085 | 39 |
| 40 | 45.6675 4163 | 46.4464 8164 | 47.6467 2434 | 48.8863 7336 | 40 |
| 41 | 46.9719 9191 | 47.7948 3026 | 49.0636 3317 | 50.3752 3709 | 41 |
| 42 | 48.2851 3852 | 49.1532 9148 | 50.4929 3996 | 51.8789 8946 | 42 |
| 43 | 49.6070 3944 | 50.5219 4117 | 51.9347 5319 | 53.3977 7936 | 43 |
| 44 | 50.9377 5304 | 51.9008 5573 | 53.3891 8228 | 54.9317 5715 | 44 |
| 45 | 52.2773 3806 | 53.2901 1215 | 54.8563 3762 | 56.4810 7472 | 45 |
| 46 | 53.6258 5365 | 54.6897 8799 | 56.3363 3058 | 58.0458 8547 | 46 |
| 47 | 54.9833 5934 | 56.0999 6140 | 57.8292 7347 | 59.6263 4432 | 47 |
| 48 | 56.3499 1507 | 57.5207 1111 | 59.3352 7961 | 61.2226 0777 | 48 |
| 49 | 57.7255 8117 | 58.9521 1644 | 60.8544 6331 | 62.8348 3385 | 49 |
| 50 | 59.1104 1837 | 60.3942 5732 | 62.3869 3986 | 64.4631 8218 | 50 |
| 51 | 60.5044 8783 | 61.8472 1424 | 63.9328 2559 | 66.1078 1401 | 51 |
| 52 | 61.9078 5108 | 63.3110 6835 | 65.4922 3781 | 67.7688 9215 | 52 |
| 53 | 63.3205 7009 | 64.7859 0136 | 67.0652 9489 | 69.4465 8107 | 53 |
| 54 | 64.7427 0722 | 66.2717 9562 | 68.6521 1622 | 71.1410 4688 | 54 |
| 55 | 66.1743 2527 | 67.7688 3409 | 70.2528 2224 | 72.8524 5735 | 55 |
| 56 | 67.6154 8744 | 69.2771 0035 | 71.8675 3443 | 74.5809 8192 | 56 |
| 57 | 69.0662 5736 | 70.7966 7860 | 73.4963 7536 | 76.3267 9174 | 57 |
| 58 | 70.5266 9907 | 72.3276 5369 | 75.1394 6864 | 78.0900 5966 | 58 |
| 59 | 71.9968 7706 | 73.8701 1109 | 76.7969 3900 | 79.8709 6025 | 59 |
| 60 | 73.4768 5625 | 75.4241 3693 | 78.4689 1221 | 81.6696 6986 | 60 |

Table
7

## TABLE 7

$$s_{\overline{n}|i} = \frac{(1+i)^n - 1}{i}$$

| $n$ | $\frac{2}{3}\%$ | $\frac{3}{4}\%$ | $\frac{7}{8}\%$ | 1% | $n$ |
|---|---|---|---|---|---|
| 61 | 74.9667 0195 | 76.9898 1795 | 80.1555 1519 | 83.4863 6656 | 61 |
| 62 | 76.4664 7997 | 78.5672 4159 | 81.8568 7595 | 85.3212 3022 | 62 |
| 63 | 77.9762 5650 | 80.1564 9590 | 83.5731 2362 | 87.1744 4252 | 63 |
| 64 | 79.4960 9821 | 81.7576 6962 | 85.3043 8845 | 89.0461 8695 | 64 |
| 65 | 81.0260 7220 | 83.3708 5214 | 87.0508 0185 | 90.9366 4882 | 65 |
| 66 | 82.5662 4601 | 84.9961 3353 | 88.8124 9636 | 92.8460 1531 | 66 |
| 67 | 84.1166 8765 | 86.6336 0453 | 90.5896 0571 | 94.7744 7546 | 67 |
| 68 | 85.6774 6557 | 88.2833 5657 | 92.3822 6476 | 96.7222 2021 | 68 |
| 69 | 87.2486 4867 | 89.9454 8174 | 94.1906 0957 | 98.6894 4242 | 69 |
| 70 | 88.8303 0633 | 91.6200 7285 | 96.0147 7741 | 100.6763 3684 | 70 |
| 71 | 90.4225 0837 | 93.3072 2340 | 97.8549 0671 | 102.6831 0021 | 71 |
| 72 | 92.0253 2510 | 95.0070 2758 | 99.7111 3714 | 104.7099 3121 | 72 |
| 73 | 93.6388 2726 | 96.7195 8028 | 101.5836 0959 | 106.7570 3052 | 73 |
| 74 | 95.2630 8611 | 98.4449 7714 | 103.4724 6618 | 108.8246 0083 | 74 |
| 75 | 96.8981 7335 | 100.1833 1446 | 105.3778 5025 | 110.9128 4684 | 75 |
| 76 | 98.5441 6118 | 101.9346 8932 | 107.2999 0644 | 113.0219 7530 | 76 |
| 77 | 100.2011 2225 | 103.6991 9949 | 109.2387 8063 | 115.1521 9506 | 77 |
| 78 | 101.8691 2973 | 105.4769 4349 | 111.1946 1996 | 117.3037 1701 | 78 |
| 79 | 103.5482 5726 | 107.2680 2056 | 113.1675 7288 | 119.4767 5418 | 79 |
| 80 | 105.2385 7898 | 109.0725 3072 | 115.1577 8914 | 121.6715 2172 | 80 |
| 81 | 106.9401 6950 | 110.8905 7470 | 117.1654 1980 | 123.8882 3694 | 81 |
| 82 | 108.6531 0397 | 112.7222 5401 | 119.1906 1722 | 126.1271 1931 | 82 |
| 83 | 110.3774 5799 | 114.5676 7091 | 121.2335 3512 | 128.3883 9050 | 83 |
| 84 | 112.1133 0771 | 116.4269 2845 | 123.2943 2856 | 130.6722 7440 | 84 |
| 85 | 113.8607 2977 | 118.3001 3041 | 125.3731 5393 | 132.9789 9715 | 85 |
| 86 | 115.6198 0130 | 120.1873 8139 | 127.4701 6903 | 135.3087 8712 | 86 |
| 87 | 117.3905 9997 | 122.0887 8675 | 129.5855 3301 | 137.6618 7499 | 87 |
| 88 | 119.1732 0397 | 124.0044 5265 | 131.7194 0642 | 140.0384 9374 | 88 |
| 89 | 120.9676 9200 | 125.9344 8604 | 133.8719 5123 | 142.4388 7868 | 89 |
| 90 | 122.7741 4328 | 127.8789 9469 | 136.0433 3080 | 144.8632 6746 | 90 |
| 91 | 124.5926 3757 | 129.8380 8715 | 138.2337 0994 | 147.3119 0014 | 91 |
| 92 | 126.4232 5515 | 131.8118 7280 | 140.4432 5491 | 149.7850 1914 | 92 |
| 93 | 128.2660 7685 | 133.8004 6185 | 142.6721 3339 | 152.2828 6933 | 93 |
| 94 | 130.1211 8403 | 135.8039 6531 | 144.9205 1455 | 154.8056 9803 | 94 |
| 95 | 131.9886 5859 | 137.8224 9505 | 147.1885 6906 | 157.3537 5501 | 95 |
| 96 | 133.8685 8298 | 139.8561 6377 | 149.4764 6903 | 159.9272 9256 | 96 |
| 97 | 135.7610 4020 | 141.9050 8499 | 151.7843 8814 | 162.5265 6548 | 97 |
| 98 | 137.6661 1380 | 143.9693 7313 | 154.1125 0153 | 165.1518 3114 | 98 |
| 99 | 139.5838 8790 | 146.0491 4343 | 156.4609 8592 | 167.8033 4945 | 99 |
| 100 | 141.5144 4715 | 148.1445 1201 | 158.8300 1955 | 170.4813 8294 | 100 |
| 101 | 143.4578 7680 | 150.2555 9585 | 161.2197 8222 | 173.1861 9677 | 101 |
| 102 | 145.4142 6264 | 152.3825 1281 | 163.6304 5532 | 175.9180 5874 | 102 |
| 103 | 147.3836 9106 | 154.5253 8166 | 166.0622 2180 | 178.6772 3933 | 103 |
| 104 | 149.3662 4900 | 156.6843 2202 | 168.5152 6624 | 181.4640 1172 | 104 |
| 105 | 151.3620 2399 | 158.8594 5444 | 170.9897 7482 | 184.2786 5184 | 105 |
| 106 | 153.3711 0415 | 161.0509 0035 | 173.4859 3535 | 187.1214 3836 | 106 |
| 107 | 155.3935 7818 | 163.2587 8210 | 176.0039 3728 | 189.9926 5274 | 107 |
| 108 | 157.4295 3537 | 165.4832 2296 | 178.5439 7174 | 192.8925 7927 | 108 |
| 109 | 159.4790 6560 | 167.7243 4714 | 181.1062 3149 | 195.8215 0506 | 109 |
| 110 | 161.5422 5937 | 169.9822 7974 | 183.6909 1101 | 198.7797 2011 | 110 |
| 111 | 163.6192 0777 | 172.2571 4684 | 186.2982 0648 | 201.7675 1731 | 111 |
| 112 | 165.7100 0249 | 174.5490 7544 | 188.9283 1579 | 204.7851 9248 | 112 |
| 113 | 167.8147 3584 | 176.8581 9351 | 191.5814 3855 | 207.8330 4441 | 113 |
| 114 | 169.9335 0074 | 179.1846 2996 | 194.2577 7614 | 210.9113 7485 | 114 |
| 115 | 172.0663 9075 | 181.5285 1468 | 196.9575 3168 | 214.0204 8860 | 115 |
| 116 | 174.2135 0002 | 183.8899 7854 | 199.6809 1009 | 217.1606 9349 | 116 |
| 117 | 176.3749 2335 | 186.2691 5338 | 202.4281 1805 | 220.3323 0042 | 117 |
| 118 | 178.5507 5618 | 188.6661 7203 | 205.1993 6408 | 223.5356 2343 | 118 |
| 119 | 180.7410 9455 | 191.0811 6832 | 207.9948 5852 | 226.7709 7966 | 119 |
| 120 | 182.9460 3518 | 193.5142 7708 | 210.8148 1353 | 230.0386 8946 | 120 |

**TABLE 7**

$$s_{\overline{n}|i} = \frac{(1+i)^n - 1}{i}$$

| $n$ | $\frac{2}{3}\%$ | $\frac{3}{4}\%$ | $\frac{7}{8}\%$ | 1% | $n$ |
|---|---|---|---|---|---|
| 121 | 185.1656 7542 | 195.9656 3416 | 213.6594 4315 | 233.3390 7635 | 121 |
| 122 | 187.4001 1325 | 198.4353 7642 | 216.5289 6328 | 236.6724 6712 | 122 |
| 123 | 189.6494 4734 | 200.9236 4174 | 219.4235 9170 | 240.0391 9179 | 123 |
| 124 | 191.9137 7699 | 203.4305 6905 | 222.3435 4813 | 243.4395 8370 | 124 |
| 125 | 194.1932 0217 | 205.9562 9832 | 225.2890 5418 | 246.8739 7954 | 125 |
| 126 | 196.4878 2352 | 208.5009 7056 | 228.2603 3340 | 250.3427 1934 | 126 |
| 127 | 198.7977 4234 | 211.0647 2784 | 231.2576 1132 | 253.8461 4653 | 127 |
| 128 | 201.1230 6062 | 213.6477 1330 | 234.2811 1542 | 257.3846 0800 | 128 |
| 129 | 203.4638 8103 | 216.2500 7115 | 237.3310 7518 | 260.9584 5408 | 129 |
| 130 | 205.8203 0690 | 218.8719 4668 | 240.4077 2209 | 264.5680 3862 | 130 |
| 131 | 208.1924 4228 | 221.5134 8628 | 243.5112 8965 | 268.2137 1900 | 131 |
| 132 | 210.5803 9190 | 224.1748 3743 | 246.6420 1344 | 271.8958 5619 | 132 |
| 133 | 212.9842 6117 | 226.8561 4871 | 249.8001 3106 | 275.6148 1475 | 133 |
| 134 | 215.4041 5625 | 229.5575 6982 | 252.9858 8220 | 279.3709 6290 | 134 |
| 135 | 217.8401 8396 | 232.2792 5160 | 256.1995 0867 | 283.1646 7253 | 135 |
| 136 | 220.2924 5185 | 235.0213 4598 | 259.4412 5437 | 286.9963 1926 | 136 |
| 137 | 222.7610 6820 | 237.7840 0608 | 262.7113 6535 | 290.8662 8245 | 137 |
| 138 | 225.2461 4198 | 240.5673 8612 | 266.0100 8980 | 294.7749 4527 | 138 |
| 139 | 227.7477 8293 | 243.3716 4152 | 269.3376 7808 | 298.7226 9473 | 139 |
| 140 | 230.2661 0148 | 246.1969 2883 | 272.6943 8276 | 302.7099 2167 | 140 |
| 141 | 232.8012 0883 | 249.0434 0580 | 276.0804 5861 | 306.7370 2089 | 141 |
| 142 | 235.3532 1689 | 251.9112 3134 | 279.4961 6263 | 310.8043 9110 | 142 |
| 143 | 237.9222 3833 | 254.8005 6558 | 282.9417 5405 | 314.9124 3501 | 143 |
| 144 | 240.5083 8659 | 257.7115 6982 | 286.4174 9440 | 319.0615 5936 | 144 |
| 145 | 243.1117 7583 | 260.6444 0659 | 289.9236 4747 | 323.2521 7495 | 145 |
| 146 | 245.7325 2100 | 263.5992 3964 | 293.4604 7939 | 327.4846 9670 | 146 |
| 147 | 248.3707 3781 | 266.5762 3394 | 297.0282 5858 | 331.7595 4367 | 147 |
| 148 | 251.0265 4273 | 269.5755 5569 | 300.6272 5585 | 336.0771 3911 | 148 |
| 149 | 253.7000 5301 | 272.5973 7236 | 304.2577 4433 | 340.4379 1050 | 149 |
| 150 | 256.3913 8670 | 275.6418 5265 | 307.9199 9960 | 344.8422 8960 | 150 |
| 151 | 259.1006 6261 | 278.7091 6655 | 311.6142 9959 | 349.2907 1250 | 151 |
| 152 | 261.8280 0036 | 281.7994 8530 | 315.3409 2472 | 353.7836 1962 | 152 |
| 153 | 264.5735 2036 | 284.9129 8144 | 319.1001 5781 | 358.3214 5582 | 153 |
| 154 | 267.3373 4383 | 288.0498 2880 | 322.8922 8419 | 362.9046 7038 | 154 |
| 155 | 270.1195 9279 | 291.2102 0251 | 326.7175 9167 | 367.5337 1708 | 155 |
| 156 | 272.9203 9008 | 294.3942 7903 | 330.5763 7060 | 372.2090 5425 | 156 |
| 157 | 275.7398 5935 | 297.6022 3613 | 334.4689 1384 | 376.9311 4480 | 157 |
| 158 | 278.5781 2507 | 300.8342 5290 | 338.3955 1684 | 381.7004 5624 | 158 |
| 159 | 281.4353 1257 | 304.0905 0979 | 342.3564 7761 | 386.5174 6081 | 159 |
| 160 | 284.3115 4799 | 307.3711 8862 | 346.3520 9679 | 391.3826 3541 | 160 |
| 161 | 287.2069 5831 | 310.6764 7253 | 350.3826 7764 | 396.2964 6177 | 161 |
| 162 | 290.1216 7137 | 314.0065 4608 | 354.4485 2607 | 401.2594 2639 | 162 |
| 163 | 293.0558 1584 | 317.3615 9517 | 358.5499 5067 | 406.2720 2065 | 163 |
| 164 | 296.0095 2128 | 320.7418 0714 | 362.6872 6274 | 411.3347 4086 | 164 |
| 165 | 298.9829 1809 | 324.1473 7069 | 366.8607 7629 | 416.4480 8826 | 165 |
| 166 | 301.9761 3754 | 327.5784 7597 | 371.0708 0808 | 421.6125 6915 | 166 |
| 167 | 304.9893 1179 | 331.0353 1454 | 375.3176 7765 | 426.8286 9484 | 167 |
| 168 | 308.0225 7387 | 334.5180 7940 | 379.6017 0733 | 432.0969 8179 | 168 |
| 169 | 311.0760 5770 | 338.0269 6499 | 383.9232 2227 | 437.4179 5161 | 169 |
| 170 | 314.1498 9808 | 341.5621 6723 | 388.2825 5046 | 442.7921 3112 | 170 |
| 171 | 317.2442 3074 | 345.1238 8349 | 392.6800 2278 | 448.2200 5243 | 171 |
| 172 | 320.3591 9228 | 348.7123 1261 | 397.1159 7298 | 453.7022 5296 | 172 |
| 173 | 323.4949 2022 | 352.3276 5496 | 401.5907 3774 | 459.2392 7549 | 173 |
| 174 | 326.6515 5303 | 355.9701 1237 | 406.1046 5670 | 464.8316 6824 | 174 |
| 175 | 329.8292 3005 | 359.6398 8821 | 410.6580 7245 | 470.4799 8492 | 175 |
| 176 | 333.0280 9158 | 363.3371 8737 | 415.2513 3058 | 476.1847 8477 | 176 |
| 177 | 336.2482 7886 | 367.0622 1628 | 419.8847 7972 | 481.9466 3262 | 177 |
| 178 | 339.4899 3405 | 370.8151 8290 | 424.5587 7154 | 487.7660 9895 | 178 |
| 179 | 342.7532 0028 | 374.5962 9677 | 429.2736 6080 | 493.6437 5994 | 179 |
| 180 | 346.0382 2161 | 378.4057 6900 | 434.0298 0533 | 499.5801 9754 | 180 |

Table
7

## TABLE 7

$$s_{\overline{n}|\,i} = \frac{(1+i)^n - 1}{i}$$

| $n$ | $\frac{2}{3}\%$ | $\frac{3}{4}\%$ | $\frac{7}{8}\%$ | 1% | $n$ |
|---|---|---|---|---|---|
| 181 | 349.3451 4309 | 382.2438 1226 | 438.8275 6612 | 505.5759 9951 | 181 |
| 182 | 352.6741 1071 | 386.1106 4086 | 443.6673 0733 | 511.6317 5951 | 182 |
| 183 | 356.0252 7145 | 390.0064 7066 | 448.5493 9627 | 517.7480 7710 | 183 |
| 184 | 359.3987 7326 | 393.9315 1919 | 453.4742 0348 | 523.9255 5787 | 184 |
| 185 | 362.7947 6508 | 397.8860 0559 | 458.4421 0276 | 530.1648 1345 | 185 |
| 186 | 366.2133 9685 | 401.8701 5063 | 463.4534 7116 | 536.4664 6159 | 186 |
| 187 | 369.6548 1949 | 405.8841 7676 | 468.5086 8904 | 542.8311 2620 | 187 |
| 188 | 373.1191 8496 | 409.9283 0808 | 473.6081 4007 | 549.2594 3746 | 188 |
| 189 | 376.6066 4619 | 414.0027 7039 | 478.7522 1129 | 555.7520 3184 | 189 |
| 190 | 380.1173 5716 | 418.1077 9117 | 483.9412 9314 | 562.3095 5216 | 190 |
| 191 | 383.6514 7288 | 422.2435 9961 | 489.1757 7946 | 568.9326 4768 | 191 |
| 192 | 387.2091 4936 | 426.4104 2660 | 494.4560 6753 | 575.6219 7415 | 192 |
| 193 | 390.7905 4369 | 430.6085 0480 | 499.7825 5812 | 582.3781 9390 | 193 |
| 194 | 394.3958 1398 | 434.8380 6859 | 505.1556 5550 | 589.2019 7584 | 194 |
| 195 | 398.0251 1941 | 439.0993 5410 | 510.5757 6749 | 596.0939 9559 | 195 |
| 196 | 401.6786 2021 | 443.3925 9926 | 516.0433 0545 | 603.0549 3555 | 196 |
| 197 | 405.3564 7767 | 447.7180 4375 | 521.5586 8437 | 610.0854 8490 | 197 |
| 198 | 409.0588 5419 | 452.0759 2908 | 527.1223 2286 | 617.1863 3975 | 198 |
| 199 | 412.7859 1322 | 456.4664 9855 | 532.7346 4319 | 624.3582 0315 | 199 |
| 200 | 416.5378 1931 | 460.8899 9729 | 538.3960 7131 | 631.6017 8518 | 200 |
| 201 | 420.3147 3810 | 465.3466 7227 | 544.1070 3694 | 638.9178 0303 | 201 |
| 202 | 424.1168 3636 | 469.8367 7231 | 549.8679 7351 | 646.3069 8107 | 202 |
| 203 | 427.9442 8193 | 474.3605 4810 | 555.6793 1828 | 653.7700 5088 | 203 |
| 204 | 431.7972 4381 | 478.9182 5221 | 561.5415 1232 | 661.3077 5138 | 204 |
| 205 | 435.6758 9210 | 483.5101 3911 | 567.4550 0055 | 668.9208 2890 | 205 |
| 206 | 439.5803 9805 | 488.1364 6515 | 573.4202 3180 | 676.6100 3719 | 206 |
| 207 | 443.5109 3404 | 492.7974 8864 | 579.4376 5883 | 684.3761 3756 | 207 |
| 208 | 447.4676 7360 | 497.4934 6980 | 585.5077 3835 | 692.2198 9893 | 208 |
| 209 | 451.4507 9142 | 502.2246 7083 | 591.6309 3106 | 700.1420 9792 | 209 |
| 210 | 455.4604 6337 | 506.9913 5586 | 597.8077 0170 | 708.1435 1890 | 210 |
| 211 | 459.4968 6646 | 511.7937 9103 | 604.0385 1909 | 716.2249 5409 | 211 |
| 212 | 463.5601 7890 | 516.6322 4446 | 610.3238 5614 | 724.3872 0363 | 212 |
| 213 | 467.6505 8009 | 521.5069 8629 | 616.6641 8988 | 732.6310 7567 | 213 |
| 214 | 471.7682 5062 | 526.4182 8869 | 623.0600 0154 | 740.9573 8643 | 214 |
| 215 | 475.9133 7230 | 531.3664 2585 | 629.5117 7655 | 749.3669 6029 | 215 |
| 216 | 480.0861 2811 | 536.3516 7405 | 636.0200 0460 | 757.8606 2989 | 216 |
| 217 | 484.2867 0230 | 541.3743 1160 | 642.5851 7964 | 766.4392 3619 | 217 |
| 218 | 488.5152 8031 | 546.4346 1894 | 649.2077 9996 | 775.1036 2855 | 218 |
| 219 | 492.7720 4885 | 551.5328 7858 | 655.8883 6821 | 783.8546 6484 | 219 |
| 220 | 497.0571 9584 | 556.6693 7517 | 662.6273 9143 | 792.6932 1149 | 220 |
| 221 | 501.3709 1048 | 561.8443 9549 | 669.4253 8110 | 801.6201 4360 | 221 |
| 222 | 505.7133 8322 | 567.0582 2845 | 676.2828 5319 | 810.6363 4504 | 222 |
| 223 | 510.0848 0577 | 572.3111 6517 | 683.2003 2815 | 819.7427 0849 | 223 |
| 224 | 514.4853 7114 | 577.6034 9890 | 690.1783 3103 | 828.9401 3557 | 224 |
| 225 | 518.9152 7362 | 582.9355 2515 | 697.2173 9142 | 838.2295 3693 | 225 |
| 226 | 523.3747 0878 | 588.3075 4158 | 704.3180 4360 | 847.6118 3230 | 226 |
| 227 | 527.8638 7350 | 593.7198 4815 | 711.4808 2648 | 857.0879 5062 | 227 |
| 228 | 532.3829 6599 | 599.1727 4701 | 718.7062 8371 | 866.6588 3013 | 228 |
| 229 | 536.9321 8576 | 604.6665 4261 | 725.9949 6369 | 876.3254 1843 | 229 |
| 230 | 541.5117 3367 | 610.2015 4168 | 733.3474 1963 | 886.0886 7261 | 230 |
| 231 | 546.1218 1189 | 615.7780 5324 | 740.7642 0955 | 895.9495 5934 | 231 |
| 232 | 550.7626 2397 | 621.3963 8864 | 748.2458 9638 | 905.9090 5493 | 232 |
| 233 | 555.4343 7480 | 627.0568 6156 | 755.7930 4797 | 915.9681 4548 | 233 |
| 234 | 560.1372 7063 | 632.7597 8802 | 763.4062 3714 | 926.1278 2694 | 234 |
| 235 | 564.8715 1910 | 638.5054 8643 | 771.0860 4172 | 936.3891 0520 | 235 |
| 236 | 569.6373 2923 | 644.2942 7758 | 778.8330 4458 | 946.7529 9626 | 236 |
| 237 | 574.4349 1142 | 650.1264 8466 | 786.6478 3372 | 957.2205 2622 | 237 |
| 238 | 579.2644 7750 | 656.0024 3329 | 794.5310 0227 | 967.7927 3148 | 238 |
| 239 | 584.1262 4068 | 661.9224 5154 | 802.4831 4854 | 978.4706 5880 | 239 |
| 240 | 589.0204 1562 | 667.8868 6993 | 810.5048 7609 | 989.2553 6539 | 240 |

**TABLE 7**

$$s_{\overline{n}|i} = \frac{(1+i)^n - 1}{i}$$

| n | $1\frac{1}{8}\%$ | $1\frac{1}{4}\%$ | $1\frac{3}{8}\%$ | $1\frac{1}{2}\%$ | n |
|---|---|---|---|---|---|
| 1 | 1.0000 0000 | 1.0000 0000 | 1.0000 0000 | 1.0000 0000 | 1 |
| 2 | 2.0112 5000 | 2.0125 0000 | 2.0137 5000 | 2.0150 0000 | 2 |
| 3 | 3.0338 7656 | 3.0376 5625 | 3.0414 3906 | 3.0452 2500 | 3 |
| 4 | 4.0680 0767 | 4.0756 2695 | 4.0832 5885 | 4.0909 0338 | 4 |
| 5 | 5.1137 7276 | 5.1265 7229 | 5.1394 0366 | 5.1522 6693 | 5 |
| 6 | 6.1713 0270 | 6.1906 5444 | 6.2100 7046 | 6.2295 5093 | 6 |
| 7 | 7.2407 2986 | 7.2680 3762 | 7.2954 5893 | 7.3229 9419 | 7 |
| 8 | 8.3221 8807 | 8.3588 8809 | 8.3957 7149 | 8.4328 3911 | 8 |
| 9 | 9.4158 1269 | 9.4633 7420 | 9.5112 1335 | 9.5593 3169 | 9 |
| 10 | 10.5217 4058 | 10.5816 6637 | 10.6419 9253 | 10.7027 2167 | 10 |
| 11 | 11.6401 1016 | 11.7139 3720 | 11.7883 1993 | 11.8632 6249 | 11 |
| 12 | 12.7710 6140 | 12.8603 6142 | 12.9504 0933 | 13.0412 1143 | 12 |
| 13 | 13.9147 3584 | 14.0211 1594 | 14.1284 7745 | 14.2368 2960 | 13 |
| 14 | 15.0712 7662 | 15.1963 7988 | 15.3227 4402 | 15.4503 8205 | 14 |
| 15 | 16.2408 2848 | 16.3863 3463 | 16.5334 3175 | 16.6821 3778 | 15 |
| 16 | 17.4235 3780 | 17.5911 6382 | 17.7607 6644 | 17.9323 6984 | 16 |
| 17 | 18.6195 5260 | 18.8110 5336 | 19.0049 7697 | 19.2013 5539 | 17 |
| 18 | 19.8290 2257 | 20.0461 9153 | 20.2662 9541 | 20.4893 7572 | 18 |
| 19 | 21.0520 9907 | 21.2967 6893 | 21.5449 5697 | 21.7967 1636 | 19 |
| 20 | 22.2889 3519 | 22.5629 7854 | 22.8412 0013 | 23.1236 6710 | 20 |
| 21 | 23.5396 8571 | 23.8450 1577 | 24.1552 6663 | 24.4705 2211 | 21 |
| 22 | 24.8045 0717 | 25.1430 7847 | 25.4874 0155 | 25.8375 7994 | 22 |
| 23 | 26.0835 5788 | 26.4573 6695 | 26.8378 5332 | 27.2251 4364 | 23 |
| 24 | 27.3769 9790 | 27.7880 8403 | 28.2068 7380 | 28.6335 2080 | 24 |
| 25 | 28.6849 8913 | 29.1354 3508 | 29.5947 1832 | 30.0630 2361 | 25 |
| 26 | 30.0076 9526 | 30.4996 2802 | 31.0016 4569 | 31.5139 6896 | 26 |
| 27 | 31.3452 8183 | 31.8808 7337 | 32.4279 1832 | 32.9866 7850 | 27 |
| 28 | 32.6979 1625 | 33.2793 8429 | 33.8738 0220 | 34.4814 7867 | 28 |
| 29 | 34.0657 6781 | 34.6953 7659 | 35.3395 6698 | 35.9987 0085 | 29 |
| 30 | 35.4490 0769 | 36.1290 6880 | 36.8254 8602 | 37.5386 8137 | 30 |
| 31 | 36.8478 0903 | 37.5806 8216 | 38.3318 3646 | 39.1017 6159 | 31 |
| 32 | 38.2623 4688 | 39.0504 4069 | 39.8588 9921 | 40.6882 8801 | 32 |
| 33 | 39.6927 9829 | 40.5385 7120 | 41.4069 5907 | 42.2986 1233 | 33 |
| 34 | 41.1393 4227 | 42.0453 0334 | 42.9763 0476 | 43.9330 9152 | 34 |
| 35 | 42.6021 5987 | 43.5708 6963 | 44.5672 2895 | 45.5920 8789 | 35 |
| 36 | 44.0814 3417 | 45.1155 0550 | 46.1800 2835 | 47.2759 6921 | 36 |
| 37 | 45.5773 5030 | 46.6794 4932 | 47.8150 0374 | 48.9851 0874 | 37 |
| 38 | 47.0900 9549 | 48.2629 4243 | 49.4724 6004 | 50.7198 8538 | 38 |
| 39 | 48.6198 5906 | 49.8662 2921 | 51.1527 0636 | 52.4806 8366 | 39 |
| 40 | 50.1668 3248 | 51.4895 5708 | 52.8560 5608 | 54.2678 9391 | 40 |
| 41 | 51.7312 0934 | 53.1331 7654 | 54.5828 2685 | 56.0819 1232 | 41 |
| 42 | 53.3131 8545 | 54.7973 4125 | 56.3333 4072 | 57.9231 4100 | 42 |
| 43 | 54.9129 5879 | 56.4823 0801 | 58.1079 2415 | 59.7919 8812 | 43 |
| 44 | 56.5307 2957 | 58.1883 3686 | 59.9069 0811 | 61.6888 6794 | 44 |
| 45 | 58.1667 0028 | 59.9156 9108 | 61.7306 2810 | 63.6142 0096 | 45 |
| 46 | 59.8210 7566 | 61.6646 3721 | 63.5794 2423 | 65.5684 1398 | 46 |
| 47 | 61.4940 6276 | 63.4354 4518 | 65.4536 4131 | 67.5519 4018 | 47 |
| 48 | 63.1858 7097 | 65.2283 8824 | 67.3536 2888 | 69.5652 1929 | 48 |
| 49 | 64.8967 1201 | 67.0437 4310 | 69.2797 4128 | 71.6086 9758 | 49 |
| 50 | 66.6268 0002 | 68.8817 8989 | 71.2323 3772 | 73.6828 2804 | 50 |

**Table 7**

## TABLE 7

$$s_{\overline{n}|i} = \frac{(1+i)^n - 1}{i}$$

| $n$ | $1\frac{1}{8}\%$ | $1\frac{1}{4}\%$ | $1\frac{3}{8}\%$ | $1\frac{1}{2}\%$ | $n$ |
|---|---|---|---|---|---|
| 51 | 68.3763 5152 | 70.7428 1226 | 73.2117 8237 | 75.7880 7046 | 51 |
| 52 | 70.1455 8548 | 72.6270 9741 | 75.2184 4437 | 77.9248 9152 | 52 |
| 53 | 71.9347 2332 | 74.5349 3613 | 77.2526 9798 | 80.0937 6489 | 53 |
| 54 | 73.7439 8895 | 76.4666 2283 | 79.3149 2258 | 82.2951 7136 | 54 |
| 55 | 75.5736 0883 | 78.4224 5562 | 81.4055 0277 | 84.5295 9893 | 55 |
| 56 | 77.4238 1193 | 80.4027 3631 | 83.5248 2843 | 86.7975 4292 | 56 |
| 57 | 79.2948 2981 | 82.4077 7052 | 85.6732 9482 | 89.0995 0606 | 57 |
| 58 | 81.1868 9665 | 84.4378 6765 | 87.8513 0262 | 91.4359 9865 | 58 |
| 59 | 83.1002 4923 | 86.4933 4099 | 90.0592 5804 | 93.8075 3863 | 59 |
| 60 | 85.0351 2704 | 88.5745 0776 | 92.2975 7283 | 96.2146 5171 | 60 |
| 61 | 86.9917 7222 | 90.6816 8910 | 94.5666 6446 | 98.6578 7149 | 61 |
| 62 | 88.9704 2966 | 92.8152 1022 | 96.8669 5610 | 101.1377 3956 | 62 |
| 63 | 90.9713 4699 | 94.9754 0034 | 99.1988 7674 | 103.6548 0565 | 63 |
| 64 | 92.9947 7464 | 97.1625 9285 | 101.5628 6130 | 106.2096 2774 | 64 |
| 65 | 95.0409 6586 | 99.3771 2526 | 103.9593 5064 | 108.8027 7216 | 65 |
| 66 | 97.1101 7672 | 101.6193 3933 | 106.3887 9171 | 111.4348 1374 | 66 |
| 67 | 99.2026 6621 | 103.8895 8107 | 108.8516 3760 | 114.1063 3594 | 67 |
| 68 | 101.3186 9621 | 106.1882 0083 | 111.3483 4761 | 116.8179 3098 | 68 |
| 69 | 103.4585 3154 | 108.5155 5334 | 113.8793 8739 | 119.5701 9995 | 69 |
| 70 | 105.6224 4002 | 110.8719 9776 | 116.4452 2897 | 122.3637 5295 | 70 |
| 71 | 107.8106 9247 | 113.2578 9773 | 119.0463 5087 | 125.1992 0924 | 71 |
| 72 | 110.0235 6276 | 115.6736 2145 | 121.6832 3819 | 128.0771 9738 | 72 |
| 73 | 112.2613 2784 | 118.1195 4172 | 124.3563 8272 | 130.9983 5534 | 73 |
| 74 | 114.5242 6778 | 120.5960 3599 | 127.0662 8298 | 133.9633 3067 | 74 |
| 75 | 116.8126 6579 | 123.1034 8644 | 129.8134 4437 | 136.9727 8063 | 75 |
| 76 | 119.1268 0828 | 125.6422 8002 | 132.5983 7923 | 140.0273 7234 | 76 |
| 77 | 121.4669 8487 | 128.2128 0852 | 135.4216 0695 | 143.1277 8292 | 77 |
| 78 | 123.8334 8845 | 130.8154 6863 | 138.2836 5404 | 146.2746 9967 | 78 |
| 79 | 126.2266 1520 | 133.4506 6199 | 141.1850 5429 | 149.4688 2016 | 79 |
| 80 | 128.6466 6462 | 136.1187 9526 | 144.1263 4878 | 152.7108 5247 | 80 |
| 81 | 131.0939 3960 | 138.8202 8020 | 147.1080 8608 | 156.0015 1525 | 81 |
| 82 | 133.5687 4642 | 141.5555 3370 | 150.1308 2226 | 159.3415 3798 | 82 |
| 83 | 136.0713 9481 | 144.3249 7787 | 153.1951 2107 | 162.7316 6105 | 83 |
| 84 | 138.6021 9801 | 147.1290 4010 | 156.3015 5398 | 166.1726 3597 | 84 |
| 85 | 141.1614 7273 | 149.9681 5310 | 159.4507 0035 | 169.6652 2551 | 85 |
| 86 | 143.7495 3930 | 152.8427 5501 | 162.6431 4748 | 173.2102 0389 | 86 |
| 87 | 146.3667 2162 | 155.7532 8945 | 165.8794 9076 | 176.8083 5695 | 87 |
| 88 | 149.0133 4724 | 158.7002 0557 | 169.1603 3375 | 180.4604 8230 | 88 |
| 89 | 151.6897 4739 | 161.6839 5814 | 172.4862 8834 | 184.1673 8954 | 89 |
| 90 | 154.3962 5705 | 164.7050 0762 | 175.8579 7481 | 187.9299 0038 | 90 |
| 91 | 157.1332 1494 | 167.7638 2021 | 179.2760 2196 | 191.7488 4889 | 91 |
| 92 | 159.9009 6361 | 170.8608 6796 | 182.7410 6726 | 195.6250 8162 | 92 |
| 93 | 162.6998 4945 | 173.9966 2881 | 186.2537 5694 | 199.5594 5784 | 93 |
| 94 | 165.5302 2276 | 177.1715 8667 | 189.8147 4610 | 203.5528 4971 | 94 |
| 95 | 168.3924 3776 | 180.3862 3151 | 193.4246 9886 | 207.6061 4246 | 95 |
| 96 | 171.2868 5269 | 183.6410 5940 | 197.0842 8847 | 211.7202 3459 | 96 |
| 97 | 174.2138 2978 | 186.9365 7264 | 200.7941 9743 | 215.8960 3811 | 97 |
| 98 | 177.1737 3537 | 190.2732 7980 | 204.5551 1765 | 220.1344 7868 | 98 |
| 99 | 180.1669 3989 | 193.6516 9580 | 208.3677 5051 | 224.4364 9586 | 99 |
| 100 | 183.1938 1796 | 197.0723 4200 | 212.2328 0708 | 228.8030 4330 | 100 |

# TABLE 7

$$s_{\overline{n}|i} = \frac{(1+i)^n - 1}{i}$$

| $n$ | $1\frac{5}{8}\%$ | $1\frac{3}{4}\%$ | $1\frac{7}{8}\%$ | $2\%$ | $n$ |
|---|---|---|---|---|---|
| 1 | 1.0000 0000 | 1.0000 0000 | 1.0000 0000 | 1.0000 0000 | 1 |
| 2 | 2.0162 5000 | 2.0175 0000 | 2.0187 5000 | 2.0200 0000 | 2 |
| 3 | 3.0490 1406 | 3.0528 0625 | 3.0566 0156 | 3.0604 0000 | 3 |
| 4 | 4.0985 6054 | 4.1062 3036 | 4.1139 1284 | 4.1216 0800 | 4 |
| 5 | 5.1651 6215 | 5.1780 8939 | 5.1910 4871 | 5.2040 4016 | 5 |
| 6 | 6.2490 9603 | 6.2687 0596 | 6.2883 8087 | 6.3081 2096 | 6 |
| 7 | 7.3506 4385 | 7.3784 0831 | 7.4062 8801 | 7.4342 8338 | 7 |
| 8 | 8.4700 9181 | 8.5075 3045 | 8.5451 5591 | 8.5829 6905 | 8 |
| 9 | 9.6077 3080 | 9.6564 1224 | 9.7053 7759 | 9.7546 2843 | 9 |
| 10 | 10.7638 5643 | 10.8253 9945 | 10.8873 5342 | 10.9497 2100 | 10 |
| 11 | 11.9387 6909 | 12.0148 4394 | 12.0914 9129 | 12.1687 1542 | 11 |
| 12 | 13.1327 7409 | 13.2251 0371 | 13.3182 0675 | 13.4120 8973 | 12 |
| 13 | 14.3461 8167 | 14.4565 4303 | 14.5679 2313 | 14.6803 3152 | 13 |
| 14 | 15.5793 0712 | 15.7095 3253 | 15.8410 7169 | 15.9739 3815 | 14 |
| 15 | 16.8324 7086 | 16.9844 4935 | 17.1380 9178 | 17.2934 1692 | 15 |
| 16 | 18.1059 9851 | 18.2816 7721 | 18.4594 3100 | 18.6392 8525 | 16 |
| 17 | 19.4002 2099 | 19.6016 0656 | 19.8055 4534 | 20.0120 7096 | 17 |
| 18 | 20.7154 7458 | 20.9446 3468 | 21.1768 9931 | 21.4123 1238 | 18 |
| 19 | 22.0521 0104 | 22.3111 6578 | 22.5739 6617 | 22.8405 5863 | 19 |
| 20 | 23.4104 4768 | 23.7016 1119 | 23.9972 2804 | 24.2973 6980 | 20 |
| 21 | 24.7908 6746 | 25.1163 8938 | 25.4471 7606 | 25.7833 1719 | 21 |
| 22 | 26.1937 1905 | 26.5559 2620 | 26.9243 1062 | 27.2989 8354 | 22 |
| 23 | 27.6193 6699 | 28.0206 5490 | 28.4291 4144 | 28.8449 6321 | 23 |
| 24 | 29.0681 8170 | 29.5110 1637 | 29.9621 8784 | 30.4218 6247 | 24 |
| 25 | 30.5405 3966 | 31.0274 5915 | 31.5239 7886 | 32.0302 9972 | 25 |
| 26 | 32.0368 2343 | 32.5704 3969 | 33.1150 5347 | 33.6709 0572 | 26 |
| 27 | 33.5574 2181 | 34.1404 2238 | 34.7359 6072 | 35.3443 2383 | 27 |
| 28 | 35.1027 2991 | 35.7378 7977 | 36.3872 5998 | 37.0512 1031 | 28 |
| 29 | 36.6731 4927 | 37.3632 9267 | 38.0695 2111 | 38.7922 3451 | 29 |
| 30 | 38.2690 8795 | 39.0171 5029 | 39.7833 2463 | 40.5680 7921 | 30 |
| 31 | 39.8909 6063 | 40.6999 5042 | 41.5292 6197 | 42.3794 4079 | 31 |
| 32 | 41.5391 8874 | 42.4121 9955 | 43.3079 3563 | 44.2270 2961 | 32 |
| 33 | 43.2142 0055 | 44.1544 1305 | 45.1199 5942 | 46.1115 7020 | 33 |
| 34 | 44.9164 3131 | 45.9271 1527 | 46.9659 5866 | 48.0338 0160 | 34 |
| 35 | 46.6463 2332 | 47.7308 3979 | 48.8465 7038 | 49.9944 7763 | 35 |
| 36 | 48.4043 2608 | 49.5661 2949 | 50.7624 4358 | 51.9943 6719 | 36 |
| 37 | 50.1908 9637 | 51.4335 3675 | 52.7142 3940 | 54.0342 5453 | 37 |
| 38 | 52.0064 9844 | 53.3336 2365 | 54.7026 3138 | 56.1149 3962 | 38 |
| 39 | 53.8516 0404 | 55.2669 6206 | 56.7283 0572 | 58.2372 3841 | 39 |
| 40 | 55.7266 9261 | 57.2341 3390 | 58.7919 6146 | 60.4019 8318 | 40 |
| 41 | 57.6322 5136 | 59.2357 3124 | 60.8943 1073 | 62.6100 2284 | 41 |
| 42 | 59.5687 7544 | 61.2723 5654 | 63.0360 7906 | 64.8622 2330 | 42 |
| 43 | 61.5367 6805 | 63.3446 2278 | 65.2180 0554 | 67.1594 6777 | 43 |
| 44 | 63.5367 4053 | 65.4531 5367 | 67.4408 4315 | 69.5026 5712 | 44 |
| 45 | 65.5692 1256 | 67.5985 8386 | 69.7053 5895 | 71.8927 1027 | 45 |
| 46 | 67.6347 1226 | 69.7815 5908 | 72.0123 3443 | 74.3305 6447 | 46 |
| 47 | 69.7337 7634 | 72.0027 3636 | 74.3625 6571 | 76.8171 7576 | 47 |
| 48 | 71.8669 5020 | 74.2627 8425 | 76.7568 6381 | 79.3535 1927 | 48 |
| 49 | 74.0347 8814 | 76.5623 8298 | 79.1960 5501 | 81.9405 8966 | 49 |
| 50 | 76.2378 5345 | 78.9022 2468 | 81.6809 8104 | 84.5794 0145 | 50 |

Table
7

**TABLE 7**

$$s_{\overline{n}|i} = \frac{(1+i)^n - 1}{i}$$

| $n$ | $1\frac{5}{8}\%$ | $1\frac{3}{4}\%$ | $1\frac{7}{8}\%$ | $2\%$ | $n$ |
|---|---|---|---|---|---|
| 51 | 78.4767 1857 | 81.2830 1361 | 84.2124 9943 | 87.2709 8948 | 51 |
| 52 | 80.7519 6525 | 83.7054 6635 | 86.7914 8380 | 90.0164 0927 | 52 |
| 53 | 83.0641 8468 | 86.1703 1201 | 89.4188 2412 | 92.8167 3746 | 53 |
| 54 | 85.4139 7768 | 88.6782 9247 | 92.0954 2707 | 95.6730 7221 | 54 |
| 55 | 87.8019 5482 | 91.2301 6259 | 94.8222 1633 | 98.5865 3365 | 55 |
| 56 | 90.2287 3659 | 93.8266 9043 | 97.6001 3289 | 101.5582 6432 | 56 |
| 57 | 92.6949 5356 | 96.4686 5752 | 100.4301 3538 | 104.5894 2961 | 57 |
| 58 | 95.2012 4655 | 99.1568 5902 | 103.3132 0042 | 107.6812 1820 | 58 |
| 59 | 97.7482 6681 | 101.8921 0405 | 106.2503 2292 | 110.8348 4257 | 59 |
| 60 | 100.3366 7614 | 104.6752 1588 | 109.2425 1648 | 114.0515 3942 | 60 |
| 61 | 102.9671 4713 | 107.5070 3215 | 112.2908 1366 | 117.3325 7021 | 61 |
| 62 | 105.6403 6327 | 110.3884 0522 | 115.3962 6642 | 120.6792 2161 | 62 |
| 63 | 108.3570 1918 | 113.3202 0231 | 118.5599 4641 | 124.0928 0604 | 63 |
| 64 | 111.1178 2074 | 116.3033 0585 | 121.7829 4541 | 127.5746 6216 | 64 |
| 65 | 113.9234 8532 | 119.3386 1370 | 125.0663 7564 | 131.1261 5541 | 65 |
| 66 | 116.7747 4196 | 122.4270 3944 | 128.4113 7018 | 134.7486 7852 | 66 |
| 67 | 119.6723 3152 | 125.5695 1263 | 131.8190 8337 | 138.4436 5209 | 67 |
| 68 | 122.6170 0690 | 128.7669 7910 | 135.2906 9118 | 142.2125 2513 | 68 |
| 69 | 125.6095 3327 | 132.0204 0124 | 138.8273 9164 | 146.0567 7563 | 69 |
| 70 | 128.6506 8818 | 135.3307 5826 | 142.4304 0524 | 149.9779 1114 | 70 |
| 71 | 131.7412 6186 | 138.6990 4653 | 146.1009 7533 | 153.9774 6937 | 71 |
| 72 | 134.8820 5737 | 142.1262 7984 | 149.8403 6862 | 158.0570 1875 | 72 |
| 73 | 138.0738 9080 | 145.6134 8974 | 153.6498 7553 | 162.2181 5913 | 73 |
| 74 | 141.3175 9153 | 149.1617 2581 | 157.5308 1070 | 166.4625 2231 | 74 |
| 75 | 144.6140 0239 | 152.7720 5601 | 161.4845 1340 | 170.7917 7276 | 75 |
| 76 | 147.9639 7993 | 156.4455 6699 | 165.5123 4803 | 175.2076 0821 | 76 |
| 77 | 151.3683 9460 | 160.1833 6441 | 169.6157 0455 | 179.7117 6038 | 77 |
| 78 | 154.8281 3102 | 163.9865 7329 | 173.7959 9901 | 184.3059 9558 | 78 |
| 79 | 158.3440 8814 | 167.8563 3832 | 178.0546 7399 | 188.9921 1549 | 79 |
| 80 | 161.9171 7958 | 171.7938 2424 | 182.3931 9913 | 193.7719 5780 | 80 |
| 81 | 165.5483 3374 | 175.8002 1617 | 186.8130 7162 | 198.6473 9696 | 81 |
| 82 | 169.2384 9417 | 179.8767 1995 | 191.3158 1671 | 203.6203 4490 | 82 |
| 83 | 172.9886 1970 | 184.0245 6255 | 195.9029 8827 | 208.6927 5180 | 83 |
| 84 | 176.7996 8477 | 188.2449 9239 | 200.5761 6930 | 213.8666 0683 | 84 |
| 85 | 180.6726 7965 | 192.5392 7976 | 205.3369 7248 | 219.1439 3897 | 85 |
| 86 | 184.6086 1069 | 196.9087 1716 | 210.1870 4071 | 224.5268 1775 | 86 |
| 87 | 188.6085 0061 | 201.3546 1971 | 215.1280 4772 | 230.0173 5411 | 87 |
| 88 | 192.6733 8875 | 205.8783 2555 | 220.1616 9862 | 235.6177 0119 | 88 |
| 89 | 196.8043 3132 | 210.4811 9625 | 225.2897 3047 | 241.3300 5521 | 89 |
| 90 | 201.0024 0170 | 215.1646 1718 | 230.5139 1291 | 247.1566 5632 | 90 |
| 91 | 205.2686 9073 | 219.9299 9798 | 235.8360 4878 | 253.0997 8944 | 91 |
| 92 | 209.6043 0695 | 224.7787 7295 | 241.2579 7469 | 259.1617 8523 | 92 |
| 93 | 214.0103 7694 | 229.7124 0148 | 246.7815 6172 | 265.3450 2094 | 93 |
| 94 | 218.4880 4557 | 234.7323 6850 | 252.4087 1600 | 271.6519 2135 | 94 |
| 95 | 223.0384 7631 | 239.8401 8495 | 258.1413 7943 | 278.0849 5978 | 95 |
| 96 | 227.6628 5155 | 245.0373 8819 | 263.9815 3029 | 284.6466 5898 | 96 |
| 97 | 232.3623 7288 | 250.3255 4248 | 269.9311 8398 | 291.3395 9216 | 97 |
| 98 | 237.1382 6144 | 255.7062 3947 | 275.9923 9368 | 298.1663 8400 | 98 |
| 99 | 241.9917 5819 | 261.1810 9866 | 282.1672 5107 | 305.1297 1168 | 99 |
| 100 | 246.9241 2426 | 266.7517 6789 | 288.4578 8702 | 312.2323 0591 | 100 |

**TABLE 7**

$$s_{\overline{n}|\,i} = \frac{(1+i)^n - 1}{i}$$

| $n$ | $2\frac{1}{4}\%$ | $2\frac{1}{2}\%$ | $2\frac{3}{4}\%$ | $3\%$ | $n$ |
|---|---|---|---|---|---|
| 1 | 1.0000 0000 | 1.0000 0000 | 1.0000 0000 | 1.0000 0000 | 1 |
| 2 | 2.0225 0000 | 2.0250 0000 | 2.0275 0000 | 2.0300 0000 | 2 |
| 3 | 3.0680 0625 | 3.0756 2500 | 3.0832 5625 | 3.0909 0000 | 3 |
| 4 | 4.1370 3639 | 4.1525 1562 | 4.1680 4580 | 4.1836 2700 | 4 |
| 5 | 5.2301 1971 | 5.2563 2852 | 5.2826 6706 | 5.3091 3581 | 5 |
| 6 | 6.3477 9740 | 6.3877 3673 | 6.4279 4040 | 6.4684 0988 | 6 |
| 7 | 7.4906 2284 | 7.5474 3015 | 7.6047 0876 | 7.6624 6218 | 7 |
| 8 | 8.6591 6186 | 8.7361 1590 | 8.8138 3825 | 8.8923 3605 | 8 |
| 9 | 9.8539 9300 | 9.9545 1880 | 10.0562 1880 | 10.1591 0613 | 9 |
| 10 | 11.0757 0784 | 11.2033 8177 | 11.3327 6482 | 11.4638 7931 | 10 |
| 11 | 12.3249 1127 | 12.4834 6631 | 12.6444 1585 | 12.8077 9569 | 11 |
| 12 | 13.6022 2177 | 13.7955 5297 | 13.9921 3729 | 14.1920 2956 | 12 |
| 13 | 14.9082 7176 | 15.1404 4179 | 15.3769 2107 | 15.6177 9045 | 13 |
| 14 | 16.2437 0788 | 16.5189 5284 | 16.7997 8639 | 17.0863 2416 | 14 |
| 15 | 17.6091 9130 | 17.9319 2666 | 18.2617 8052 | 18.5989 1389 | 15 |
| 16 | 19.0053 9811 | 19.3802 2483 | 19.7639 7948 | 20.1568 8130 | 16 |
| 17 | 20.4330 1957 | 20.8647 3045 | 21.3074 8892 | 21.7615 8774 | 17 |
| 18 | 21.8927 6251 | 22.3863 4871 | 22.8934 4487 | 23.4144 3537 | 18 |
| 19 | 23.3853 4966 | 23.9460 0743 | 24.5230 1460 | 25.1168 6844 | 19 |
| 20 | 24.9115 2003 | 25.5446 5761 | 26.1973 9750 | 26.8703 7449 | 20 |
| 21 | 26.4720 2923 | 27.1832 7405 | 27.9178 2593 | 28.6764 8572 | 21 |
| 22 | 28.0676 4989 | 28.8628 5590 | 29.6855 6615 | 30.5367 8030 | 22 |
| 23 | 29.6991 7201 | 30.5844 2730 | 31.5019 1921 | 32.4528 8370 | 23 |
| 24 | 31.3674 0338 | 32.3490 3798 | 33.3682 2199 | 34.4264 7022 | 24 |
| 25 | 33.0731 6996 | 34.1577 6393 | 35.2858 4810 | 36.4592 6432 | 25 |
| 26 | 34.8173 1628 | 36.0117 0803 | 37.2562 0892 | 38.5530 4225 | 26 |
| 27 | 36.6007 0590 | 37.9120 0073 | 39.2807 5467 | 40.7096 3352 | 27 |
| 28 | 38.4242 2178 | 39.8598 0075 | 41.3609 7542 | 42.9309 2252 | 28 |
| 29 | 40.2887 6677 | 41.8562 9577 | 43.4984 0224 | 45.2188 5020 | 29 |
| 30 | 42.1952 6402 | 43.9027 0316 | 45.6946 0830 | 47.5754 1571 | 30 |
| 31 | 44.1446 5746 | 46.0002 7074 | 47.9512 1003 | 50.0026 7818 | 31 |
| 32 | 46.1379 1226 | 48.1502 7751 | 50.2698 6831 | 52.5027 5852 | 32 |
| 33 | 48.1760 1528 | 50.3540 3445 | 52.6522 8969 | 55.0778 4128 | 33 |
| 34 | 50.2599 7563 | 52.6128 8531 | 55.1002 2765 | 57.7301 7652 | 34 |
| 35 | 52.3908 2508 | 54.9282 0744 | 57.6154 8391 | 60.4620 8181 | 35 |
| 36 | 54.5696 1864 | 57.3014 1263 | 60.1999 0972 | 63.2759 4427 | 36 |
| 37 | 56.7974 3506 | 59.7339 4794 | 62.8554 0724 | 66.1742 2259 | 37 |
| 38 | 59.0753 7735 | 62.2272 9664 | 65.5839 3094 | 69.1594 4927 | 38 |
| 39 | 61.4045 7334 | 64.7829 7906 | 68.3874 8904 | 72.2342 3275 | 39 |
| 40 | 63.7861 7624 | 67.4025 5354 | 71.2681 4499 | 75.4012 5973 | 40 |
| 41 | 66.2213 6521 | 70.0876 1737 | 74.2280 1898 | 78.6632 9753 | 41 |
| 42 | 68.7113 4592 | 72.8398 0781 | 77.2692 8950 | 82.0231 9645 | 42 |
| 43 | 71.2573 5121 | 75.6608 0300 | 80.3941 9496 | 85.4838 9234 | 43 |
| 44 | 73.8606 4161 | 78.5523 2308 | 83.6050 3532 | 89.0484 0911 | 44 |
| 45 | 76.5225 0605 | 81.5161 3116 | 86.9041 7379 | 92.7198 6139 | 45 |
| 46 | 79.2442 6243 | 84.5540 3443 | 90.2940 3857 | 96.5014 5723 | 46 |
| 47 | 82.0272 5834 | 87.6678 8530 | 93.7771 2463 | 100.3965 0095 | 47 |
| 48 | 84.8728 7165 | 90.8595 8243 | 97.3559 9556 | 104.4083 9598 | 48 |
| 49 | 87.7825 1126 | 94.1310 7199 | 101.0332 8544 | 108.5406 4785 | 49 |
| 50 | 90.7576 1776 | 97.4843 4879 | 104.8117 0079 | 112.7968 6729 | 50 |

Table
7

## TABLE 7

$$s_{\overline{n}|i} = \frac{(1+i)^n - 1}{i}$$

| n | $2\frac{1}{4}\%$ | $2\frac{1}{2}\%$ | $2\frac{3}{4}\%$ | $3\%$ | n |
|---|---|---|---|---|---|
| 51 | 93.7996 6416 | 100.9214 5751 | 108.6940 2256 | 117.1806 7331 | 51 |
| 52 | 96.9101 5661 | 104.4444 9395 | 112.6831 0818 | 121.6961 9651 | 52 |
| 53 | 100.0906 3513 | 108.0556 0629 | 116.7818 9365 | 126.3470 8240 | 53 |
| 54 | 103.3426 7442 | 111.7569 9645 | 120.9933 9573 | 131.1374 9488 | 54 |
| 55 | 106.6678 8460 | 115.5509 2136 | 125.3207 1411 | 136.0716 1972 | 55 |
| 56 | 110.0679 1200 | 119.4396 9440 | 129.7670 3375 | 141.1537 6831 | 56 |
| 57 | 113.5444 4002 | 123.4256 8676 | 134.3356 2718 | 146.3883 8136 | 57 |
| 58 | 117.0991 8992 | 127.5113 2893 | 139.0298 5692 | 151.7800 3280 | 58 |
| 59 | 120.7339 2169 | 131.6991 1215 | 143.8531 7799 | 157.3334 3379 | 59 |
| 60 | 124.4504 3493 | 135.9915 8995 | 148.8091 4038 | 163.0534 3680 | 60 |
| 61 | 128.2505 6972 | 140.3913 7970 | 153.9013 9174 | 168.9450 3991 | 61 |
| 62 | 132.1362 0754 | 144.9011 6419 | 159.1336 8002 | 175.0133 9110 | 62 |
| 63 | 136.1092 7221 | 149.5236 9330 | 164.5098 5622 | 181.2637 9284 | 63 |
| 64 | 140.1717 3083 | 154.2617 8563 | 170.0338 7726 | 187.7017 0662 | 64 |
| 65 | 144.3255 9477 | 159.1183 3027 | 175.7098 0889 | 194.3327 5782 | 65 |
| 66 | 148.5729 2066 | 164.0962 8853 | 181.5418 2863 | 201.1627 4055 | 66 |
| 67 | 152.9158 1137 | 169.1986 9574 | 187.5342 2892 | 208.1976 2277 | 67 |
| 68 | 157.3564 1713 | 174.4286 6314 | 193.6914 2022 | 215.4435 5145 | 68 |
| 69 | 161.8969 3651 | 179.7893 7971 | 200.0179 3427 | 222.9068 5800 | 69 |
| 70 | 166.5396 1758 | 185.2841 1421 | 206.5184 2746 | 230.5940 6374 | 70 |
| 71 | 171.2867 5898 | 190.9162 1706 | 213.1976 8422 | 238.5118 8565 | 71 |
| 72 | 176.1407 1106 | 196.6891 2249 | 220.0606 2054 | 246.6672 4222 | 72 |
| 73 | 181.1038 7705 | 202.6063 5055 | 227.1122 8760 | 255.0672 5949 | 73 |
| 74 | 186.1787 1429 | 208.6715 0931 | 234.3578 7551 | 263.7192 7727 | 74 |
| 75 | 191.3677 3536 | 214.8882 9705 | 241.8027 1709 | 272.6308 5559 | 75 |
| 76 | 196.6735 0941 | 221.2605 0447 | 249.4522 9181 | 281.8097 8126 | 76 |
| 77 | 202.0986 6337 | 227.7920 1709 | 257.3122 2983 | 291.2640 7469 | 77 |
| 78 | 207.6458 8329 | 234.4868 1751 | 265.3883 1615 | 301.0019 9693 | 78 |
| 79 | 213.3179 1567 | 241.3489 8795 | 273.6864 9485 | 311.0320 5684 | 79 |
| 80 | 219.1175 6877 | 248.3827 1265 | 282.2128 7345 | 321.3630 1855 | 80 |
| 81 | 225.0477 1407 | 255.5922 8047 | 290.9737 2747 | 332.0039 0910 | 81 |
| 82 | 231.1112 8763 | 262.9820 8748 | 299.9755 0498 | 342.9640 2638 | 82 |
| 83 | 237.3112 9160 | 270.5566 3966 | 309.2248 3137 | 354.2529 4717 | 83 |
| 84 | 243.6507 9567 | 278.3205 5566 | 318.7285 1423 | 365.8805 3558 | 84 |
| 85 | 250.1329 3857 | 286.2785 6955 | 328.4935 4837 | 377.8569 5165 | 85 |
| 86 | 256.7609 2969 | 294.4355 3379 | 338.5271 2095 | 390.1926 6020 | 86 |
| 87 | 263.5380 5060 | 302.7964 2213 | 348.8366 1678 | 402.8984 4001 | 87 |
| 88 | 270.4676 5674 | 311.3663 3268 | 359.4296 2374 | 415.9853 9321 | 88 |
| 89 | 277.5531 7902 | 320.1504 9100 | 370.3139 3839 | 429.4649 5500 | 89 |
| 90 | 284.7981 2555 | 329.1542 5328 | 381.4975 7170 | 443.3489 0365 | 90 |
| 91 | 292.2060 8337 | 338.3831 0961 | 392.9887 5492 | 457.6493 7076 | 91 |
| 92 | 299.7807 2025 | 347.8426 8735 | 404.7959 4568 | 472.3788 5189 | 92 |
| 93 | 307.5257 8645 | 357.5387 5453 | 416.9278 3418 | 387.5502 1744 | 93 |
| 94 | 315.4451 1665 | 367.4772 2339 | 429.3933 4962 | 503.1767 2397 | 94 |
| 95 | 323.5426 3177 | 377.6641 5398 | 442.2016 6674 | 519.2720 2568 | 95 |
| 96 | 331.8223 4099 | 388.1057 5783 | 455.3622 1257 | 535.8501 8645 | 96 |
| 97 | 340.2883 4366 | 398.8084 0177 | 468.8846 7342 | 552.9256 9205 | 97 |
| 98 | 348.9448 3139 | 409.7786 1182 | 482.7790 0194 | 570.5134 6281 | 98 |
| 99 | 357.7960 9010 | 421.0230 7711 | 497.0554 2449 | 588.6288 6669 | 99 |
| 100 | 366.8465 0213 | 432.5486 5404 | 511.7244 4867 | 607.2877 3270 | 100 |

**AMOUNT OF ANNUITY**
When Periodic Payment Is 1

## TABLE 7

$$s_{\overline{n}|i} = \frac{(1+i)^n - 1}{i}$$

| n | $3\frac{1}{4}\%$ | $3\frac{1}{2}\%$ | $3\frac{3}{4}\%$ | 4% | n |
|---|---|---|---|---|---|
| 1 | 1.0000 0000 | 1.0000 0000 | 1.0000 0000 | 1.0000 0000 | 1 |
| 2 | 2.0325 0000 | 2.0350 0000 | 2.0375 0000 | 2.0400 0000 | 2 |
| 3 | 3.0985 5625 | 3.1062 2500 | 3.1139 0625 | 3.1216 0000 | 3 |
| 4 | 4.1992 5933 | 4.2149 4288 | 4.2306 7773 | 4.2464 6400 | 4 |
| 5 | 5.3357 3526 | 5.3624 6588 | 5.3893 2815 | 5.4163 2256 | 5 |
| 6 | 6.5091 4665 | 6.5501 5218 | 6.5914 2796 | 6.6329 7546 | 6 |
| 7 | 7.7206 9392 | 7.7794 0751 | 7.8386 0650 | 7.8982 9448 | 7 |
| 8 | 8.9716 1647 | 9.0516 8677 | 9.1325 5425 | 9.2142 2626 | 8 |
| 9 | 10.2631 9401 | 10.3684 9581 | 10.4750 2503 | 10.5827 9531 | 9 |
| 10 | 11.5967 4781 | 11.7313 9316 | 11.8678 3847 | 12.0061 0712 | 10 |
| 11 | 12.9736 4212 | 13.1419 9192 | 13.3128 8241 | 13.4863 5141 | 11 |
| 12 | 14.3952 8548 | 14.6019 6164 | 14.8121 1550 | 15.0258 0546 | 12 |
| 13 | 15.8631 3226 | 16.1130 3030 | 16.3675 6983 | 16.6268 3768 | 13 |
| 14 | 17.3786 8406 | 17.6769 8636 | 17.9813 5370 | 18.2919 1119 | 14 |
| 15 | 18.9434 9129 | 19.2956 8088 | 19.6556 5447 | 20.0235 8764 | 15 |
| 16 | 20.5591 5476 | 20.9710 2971 | 21.3927 4151 | 21.8245 3114 | 16 |
| 17 | 22.2273 2729 | 22.7050 1575 | 23.1949 6932 | 23.6975 1239 | 17 |
| 18 | 23.9497 1543 | 24.4996 9130 | 25.0647 8067 | 25.6454 1288 | 18 |
| 19 | 25.7280 8118 | 26.3571 8050 | 27.0047 0994 | 27.6712 2940 | 19 |
| 20 | 27.5642 4382 | 28.2796 8181 | 29.0173 8656 | 29.7780 7858 | 20 |
| 21 | 29.4600 8174 | 30.2694 7068 | 31.1055 3856 | 31.9692 0172 | 21 |
| 22 | 31.4175 3440 | 32.3289 0215 | 33.2719 9626 | 34.2479 6979 | 22 |
| 23 | 33.4386 0426 | 34.4604 1373 | 35.5196 9612 | 36.6178 8858 | 23 |
| 24 | 35.5253 5890 | 36.6665 2821 | 37.8516 8472 | 39.0826 0412 | 24 |
| 25 | 37.6799 3307 | 38.9498 5669 | 40.2711 2290 | 41.6459 0829 | 25 |
| 26 | 39.9045 3089 | 41.3131 0168 | 42.7812 9001 | 44.3117 4462 | 26 |
| 27 | 42.2014 2815 | 43.7590 6024 | 45.3855 8838 | 47.0842 1440 | 27 |
| 28 | 44.5729 7456 | 46.2906 2734 | 48.0875 4994 | 49.9675 8298 | 28 |
| 29 | 47.0215 9623 | 48.9107 9930 | 50.8908 3099 | 52.9662 8630 | 29 |
| 30 | 49.5497 9811 | 51.6226 7728 | 53.7992 3715 | 56.0849 3775 | 30 |
| 31 | 52.1601 6655 | 54.4294 7098 | 56.8167 0855 | 59.3283 3526 | 31 |
| 32 | 54.8553 7196 | 57.3345 0247 | 59.9473 3512 | 62.7014 6867 | 32 |
| 33 | 57.6381 7155 | 60.3412 1005 | 63.1953 6019 | 66.2095 2742 | 33 |
| 34 | 60.5114 1213 | 63.4531 5240 | 66.5651 8619 | 69.8579 0851 | 34 |
| 35 | 63.4780 3302 | 66.6740 1274 | 70.0613 8067 | 73.6522 2486 | 35 |
| 36 | 66.5410 6909 | 70.0076 0318 | 73.6886 8245 | 77.5983 1385 | 36 |
| 37 | 69.7036 5384 | 73.4578 6930 | 77.4520 0804 | 81.7022 4640 | 37 |
| 38 | 72.9690 2259 | 77.0288 9472 | 81.3564 5834 | 85.9703 3626 | 38 |
| 39 | 76.3405 1582 | 80.7249 0604 | 85.4073 2553 | 90.4091 4971 | 39 |
| 40 | 79.8215 8259 | 84.5502 7775 | 89.6101 0024 | 95.0255 1570 | 40 |
| 41 | 83.4157 8402 | 88.5095 3747 | 93.9704 7900 | 99.8265 3633 | 41 |
| 42 | 87.1267 9700 | 92.6073 7128 | 98.4943 7196 | 104.8195 9778 | 42 |
| 43 | 90.9584 1791 | 96.8486 2928 | 103.1879 1091 | 110.0123 8169 | 43 |
| 44 | 94.9145 6649 | 101.2383 3130 | 108.0574 5757 | 115.4128 7696 | 44 |
| 45 | 98.9992 8990 | 105.7816 7290 | 113.1096 1223 | 121.0293 9204 | 45 |
| 46 | 103.2167 6682 | 110.4840 3145 | 118.3512 2269 | 126.8705 6772 | 46 |
| 47 | 107.5713 1174 | 115.3509 7255 | 123.7893 9354 | 132.9453 9043 | 47 |
| 48 | 112.0673 7937 | 120.3882 5659 | 129.4314 9579 | 139.2632 0604 | 48 |
| 49 | 116.7095 6920 | 125.6018 4557 | 135.2851 7689 | 145.8337 3429 | 49 |
| 50 | 121.5026 3020 | 130.9979 1016 | 141.3583 7102 | 152.6670 8366 | 50 |

Table
7

**TABLE 7**

$$s_{\overline{n}|i} = \frac{(1+i)^n - 1}{i}$$

| n | $3\frac{1}{4}$ % | $3\frac{1}{2}$ % | $3\frac{3}{4}$ % | 4 % | n |
|---|---|---|---|---|---|
| 51 | 126.4514 6568 | 136.5828 3702 | 147.6593 0993 | 159.7737 6700 | 51 |
| 52 | 131.5611 3832 | 142.3632 3631 | 154.1965 3405 | 167.1647 1768 | 52 |
| 53 | 136.8368 7531 | 148.3459 4958 | 160.9789 0408 | 174.8513 0639 | 53 |
| 54 | 142.2840 7367 | 154.5380 5782 | 168.0156 1298 | 182.8453 5865 | 54 |
| 55 | 147.9083 0616 | 160.9468 8984 | 175.3161 9847 | 191.1591 7299 | 55 |
| 56 | 153.7153 2611 | 167.5800 3099 | 182.8905 5591 | 199.8055 3991 | 56 |
| 57 | 159.7110 7421 | 174.4453 3207 | 190.7489 5176 | 208.7977 6151 | 57 |
| 58 | 165.9016 8412 | 181.5509 1869 | 198.9020 3745 | 218.1496 7197 | 58 |
| 59 | 172.2934 8885 | 188.9052 0085 | 207.3608 6386 | 227.8756 5885 | 59 |
| 60 | 178.8930 2724 | 196.5168 8288 | 216.1368 9625 | 237.9906 8520 | 60 |
| 61 | 185.7070 5063 | 204.3949 7378 | 225.2420 2986 | 248.5103 1261 | 61 |
| 62 | 192.7425 2977 | 212.5487 9786 | 234.6886 0598 | 259.4507 2511 | 62 |
| 63 | 200.0066 6199 | 220.9880 0579 | 244.4894 2870 | 270.8287 5412 | 63 |
| 64 | 207.5068 7850 | 229.7225 8599 | 254.6577 8228 | 282.6619 0428 | 64 |
| 65 | 215.2508 5205 | 238.7628 7650 | 265.2074 4912 | 294.9683 8045 | 65 |
| 66 | 223.2465 0475 | 248.1195 7718 | 276.1527 2846 | 307.7671 1567 | 66 |
| 67 | 231.5020 1615 | 257.8037 6238 | 287.5084 5578 | 321.0778 0030 | 67 |
| 68 | 240.0258 3168 | 267.8268 9406 | 299.2900 2287 | 334.9209 1231 | 68 |
| 69 | 248.8266 7120 | 278.2008 3535 | 311.5133 9872 | 349.3177 4880 | 69 |
| 70 | 257.9135 3802 | 288.9378 6459 | 324.1951 5118 | 364.2904 5876 | 70 |
| 71 | 267.2957 2800 | 300.0506 8985 | 337.3524 6935 | 379.8620 7711 | 71 |
| 72 | 276.9828 3916 | 311.5524 6400 | 351.0031 8695 | 396.0565 6019 | 72 |
| 73 | 286.9847 8144 | 323.4568 0024 | 365.1658 0646 | 412.8988 2260 | 73 |
| 74 | 297.3117 8683 | 335.7777 8824 | 379.8595 2420 | 430.4147 7550 | 74 |
| 75 | 307.9744 1991 | 348.5300 1083 | 395.1042 5636 | 448.6313 6652 | 75 |
| 76 | 318.9835 8855 | 361.7285 6121 | 410.9206 6597 | 467.5766 2118 | 76 |
| 77 | 330.3505 5518 | 375.3890 6085 | 427.3301 9094 | 487.2796 8603 | 77 |
| 78 | 342.0869 4822 | 389.5276 7798 | 444.3550 7310 | 507.7708 7347 | 78 |
| 79 | 354.2047 7404 | 404.1611 4671 | 462.0183 8835 | 529.0817 0841 | 79 |
| 80 | 366.7164 2920 | 419.3067 8685 | 480.3440 7791 | 551.2449 7675 | 80 |
| 81 | 379.6347 1315 | 434.9825 2439 | 499.3569 8083 | 574.2947 7582 | 81 |
| 82 | 392.9728 4132 | 451.2069 1274 | 519.0828 6761 | 598.2665 6685 | 82 |
| 83 | 406.7444 5867 | 467.9991 5469 | 539.5484 7515 | 623.1972 2952 | 83 |
| 84 | 420.9636 5357 | 485.3791 2510 | 560.7815 4296 | 649.1251 1870 | 84 |
| 85 | 435.6449 7232 | 503.3673 9448 | 582.8108 5083 | 676.0901 2345 | 85 |
| 86 | 450.8034 3392 | 521.9852 5329 | 605.6662 5773 | 704.1337 2839 | 86 |
| 87 | 466.4545 4552 | 541.2547 3715 | 629.3787 4240 | 733.2990 7753 | 87 |
| 88 | 482.6143 1825 | 561.1986 5295 | 653.9804 4524 | 763.6310 4063 | 88 |
| 89 | 499.2992 8359 | 581.8406 0581 | 679.5047 1193 | 795.1762 8225 | 89 |
| 90 | 516.5265 1031 | 603.2050 2701 | 705.9861 3863 | 827.9833 3354 | 90 |
| 91 | 534.3136 2189 | 625.3172 0295 | 733.4606 1883 | 862.1026 6688 | 91 |
| 92 | 552.6788 1460 | 648.2033 0506 | 761.9653 9204 | 897.5867 7356 | 92 |
| 93 | 571.6408 7608 | 671.8904 2074 | 791.5390 9424 | 934.4902 4450 | 93 |
| 94 | 591.2192 0455 | 696.4065 8546 | 822.2218 1027 | 972.8698 5428 | 94 |
| 95 | 611.4338 2870 | 721.7808 1595 | 854.0551 2816 | 1012.7846 4845 | 95 |
| 96 | 632.3054 2813 | 748.0431 4451 | 887.0821 9546 | 1054.2960 3439 | 96 |
| 97 | 653.8553 5455 | 775.2246 5457 | 921.3477 7779 | 1097.4678 7577 | 97 |
| 98 | 676.1056 5357 | 803.3575 1748 | 956.8983 1944 | 1142.3665 9080 | 98 |
| 99 | 699.0790 8731 | 832.4750 3059 | 993.7820 0644 | 1189.0612 5443 | 99 |
| 100 | 722.7991 5765 | 862.6116 5666 | 1032.0488 3168 | 1237.6237 0461 | 100 |

**TABLE   7**

$$s_{\overline{n}|i} = \frac{(1+i)^n - 1}{i}$$

| $n$ | $4\frac{1}{2}\%$ | $5\%$ | $5\frac{1}{2}\%$ | $6\%$ | $n$ |
|---|---|---|---|---|---|
| 1 | 1.0000 0000 | 1.0000 0000 | 1.0000 0000 | 1.0000 0000 | 1 |
| 2 | 2.0450 0000 | 2.0500 0000 | 2.0550 0000 | 2.0600 0000 | 2 |
| 3 | 3.1370 2500 | 3.1525 0000 | 3.1680 2500 | 3.1836 0000 | 3 |
| 4 | 4.2781 9112 | 4.3101 2500 | 4.3422 6638 | 4.3746 1600 | 4 |
| 5 | 5.4707 0973 | 5.5256 3125 | 5.5810 9103 | 5.6370 9296 | 5 |
| 6 | 6.7168 9166 | 6.8019 1281 | 6.8880 5103 | 6.9753 1854 | 6 |
| 7 | 8.0191 5179 | 8.1420 0845 | 8.2668 9384 | 8.3938 3765 | 7 |
| 8 | 9.3800 1362 | 9.5491 0888 | 9.7215 7300 | 9.8974 6791 | 8 |
| 9 | 10.8021 1423 | 11.0265 6432 | 11.2562 5951 | 11.4913 1598 | 9 |
| 10 | 12.2882 0937 | 12.5778 9254 | 12.8753 5379 | 13.1807 9494 | 10 |
| 11 | 13.8411 7879 | 14.2067 8716 | 14.5834 9825 | 14.9716 4264 | 11 |
| 12 | 15.4640 3184 | 15.9171 2652 | 16.3855 9065 | 16.8699 4120 | 12 |
| 13 | 17.1599 1327 | 17.7129 8285 | 18.2867 9814 | 18.8821 3767 | 13 |
| 14 | 18.9321 0937 | 19.5986 3199 | 20.2925 7203 | 21.0150 6593 | 14 |
| 15 | 20.7840 5429 | 21.5785 6359 | 22.4086 6350 | 23.2759 6988 | 15 |
| 16 | 22.7193 3673 | 23.6574 9177 | 24.6411 3999 | 25.6725 2808 | 16 |
| 17 | 24.7417 0689 | 25.8403 6636 | 26.9964 0269 | 28.2128 7976 | 17 |
| 18 | 26.8550 8370 | 28.1323 8467 | 29.4812 0483 | 30.9056 5255 | 18 |
| 19 | 29.0635 6246 | 30.5390 0391 | 32.1026 7110 | 33.7599 9170 | 19 |
| 20 | 31.3714 2277 | 33.0659 5410 | 34.8683 1801 | 36.7855 9120 | 20 |
| 21 | 33.7831 3680 | 35.7192 5181 | 37.7860 7550 | 39.9927 2668 | 21 |
| 22 | 36.3033 7796 | 38.5052 1440 | 40.8643 0965 | 43.3922 9028 | 22 |
| 23 | 38.9370 2996 | 41.4304 7512 | 44.1118 4669 | 46.9958 2769 | 23 |
| 24 | 41.6891 9631 | 44.5019 9887 | 47.5379 9825 | 50.8155 7735 | 24 |
| 25 | 44.5652 1015 | 47.7270 9882 | 51.1525 8816 | 54.8645 1200 | 25 |
| 26 | 47.5706 4460 | 51.1134 5376 | 54.9659 8051 | 59.1563 8272 | 26 |
| 27 | 50.7113 2361 | 54.6691 2645 | 58.9891 0943 | 63.7057 6568 | 27 |
| 28 | 53.9933 3317 | 58.4025 8277 | 63.2335 1045 | 68.5281 1162 | 28 |
| 29 | 57.4230 3316 | 62.3227 1191 | 67.7113 5353 | 73.6397 9832 | 29 |
| 30 | 61.0070 6966 | 66.4388 4750 | 72.4354 7797 | 79.0581 8622 | 30 |
| 31 | 64.7523 8779 | 70.7607 8988 | 77.4194 2926 | 84.8016 7739 | 31 |
| 32 | 68.6662 4524 | 75.2988 2937 | 82.6774 9787 | 90.8897 7803 | 32 |
| 33 | 72.7562 2628 | 80.0637 7084 | 88.2247 6025 | 97.3431 6471 | 33 |
| 34 | 77.0302 5646 | 85.0669 5938 | 94.0771 2207 | 104.1837 5460 | 34 |
| 35 | 81.4966 1800 | 90.3203 0735 | 100.2513 6378 | 111.4347 7987 | 35 |
| 36 | 86.1639 6581 | 95.8363 2272 | 106.7651 8879 | 119.1208 6666 | 36 |
| 37 | 91.0413 4427 | 101.6281 3886 | 113.6372 7417 | 127.2681 1866 | 37 |
| 38 | 96.1382 0476 | 107.7095 4580 | 120.8873 2425 | 135.9042 0578 | 38 |
| 39 | 101.4644 2398 | 114.0950 2309 | 128.5361 2708 | 145.0584 5813 | 39 |
| 40 | 107.0303 2306 | 120.7997 7424 | 136.6056 1407 | 154.7619 6562 | 40 |
| 41 | 112.8466 8760 | 127.8397 6295 | 145.1189 2285 | 165.0476 8356 | 41 |
| 42 | 118.9247 8854 | 135.2317 5110 | 154.1004 6360 | 175.9505 4457 | 42 |
| 43 | 125.2764 0402 | 142.9933 3866 | 163.5759 8910 | 187.5075 7724 | 43 |
| 44 | 131.9138 4220 | 151.1430 0559 | 173.5726 6850 | 199.7580 3188 | 44 |
| 45 | 138.8499 6510 | 159.7001 5587 | 184.1191 6527 | 212.7435 1379 | 45 |
| 46 | 146.0982 1353 | 168.6851 6366 | 195.2457 1936 | 226.5081 2462 | 46 |
| 47 | 153.6726 3314 | 178.1194 2185 | 206.9842 3392 | 241.0986 1210 | 47 |
| 48 | 161.5879 0163 | 188.0253 9294 | 219.3683 6679 | 256.5645 2882 | 48 |
| 49 | 169.8593 5720 | 198.4266 6259 | 232.4336 2696 | 272.9584 0055 | 49 |
| 50 | 178.5030 2828 | 209.3479 9572 | 246.2174 7645 | 290.3359 0458 | 50 |

Table
7

**TABLE   7**

$$s_{\overline{n}|\,i} = \frac{(1+i)^n - 1}{i}$$

| n | $4\frac{1}{2}\%$ | 5% | $5\frac{1}{2}\%$ | 6% | n |
|---|---|---|---|---|---|
| 51 | 187.5356 6455 | 220.8153 9550 | 260.7594 3765 | 308.7560 5886 | 51 |
| 52 | 196.9747 6946 | 232.8561 6528 | 276.1012 0672 | 328.2814 2239 | 52 |
| 53 | 206.8386 3408 | 245.4989 7354 | 292.2867 7309 | 348.9783 0773 | 53 |
| 54 | 217.1463 7262 | 258.7739 2222 | 309.3625 4561 | 370.9170 0620 | 54 |
| 55 | 227.9179 5938 | 272.7126 1833 | 327.3774 8562 | 394.1720 2657 | 55 |
| 56 | 239.1742 6756 | 287.3482 4924 | 346.3832 4733 | 418.8223 4816 | 56 |
| 57 | 250.9371 0960 | 302.7156 6171 | 366.4343 2593 | 444.9516 8905 | 57 |
| 58 | 263.2292 7953 | 318.8514 4479 | 387.5882 1386 | 472.6487 9040 | 58 |
| 59 | 276.0745 9711 | 335.7940 1703 | 409.9055 6562 | 502.0077 1782 | 59 |
| 60 | 289.4979 5398 | 353.5837 1788 | 433.4503 7173 | 533.1281 8089 | 60 |
| 61 | 303.5253 6190 | 372.2629 0378 | 458.2901 4217 | 566.1158 7174 | 61 |
| 62 | 318.1840 0319 | 391.8760 4897 | 484.4960 9999 | 601.0828 2405 | 62 |
| 63 | 333.5022 8333 | 412.4698 5141 | 512.1433 8549 | 638.1477 9349 | 63 |
| 64 | 349.5098 8608 | 434.0933 4398 | 541.3112 7170 | 677.4366 6110 | 64 |
| 65 | 366.2378 3096 | 456.7980 1118 | 572.0833 9164 | 719.0828 6076 | 65 |
| 66 | 383.7185 3335 | 480.6379 1174 | 604.5479 7818 | 763.2278 3241 | 66 |
| 67 | 401.9858 6735 | 505.6698 0733 | 638.7981 1698 | 810.0215 0236 | 67 |
| 68 | 421.0752 3138 | 531.9532 9770 | 674.9320 1341 | 859.6227 9250 | 68 |
| 69 | 441.0236 1679 | 559.5509 6258 | 713.0532 7415 | 912.2001 6005 | 69 |
| 70 | 461.8696 7955 | 588.5285 1071 | 753.2712 0423 | 967.9321 6965 | 70 |
| 71 | 483.6538 1513 | 618.9549 3625 | 795.7011 2046 | 1027.0080 9983 | 71 |
| 72 | 506.4182 3681 | 650.9026 8306 | 840.4646 8209 | 1089.6285 8582 | 72 |
| 73 | 530.2070 5747 | 684.4478 1721 | 887.6902 3960 | 1156.0063 0097 | 73 |
| 74 | 555.0663 7505 | 719.6702 0807 | 937.5132 0278 | 1226.3666 7902 | 74 |
| 75 | 581.0443 6193 | 756.6537 1848 | 990.0764 2893 | 1300.9486 7977 | 75 |
| 76 | 608.1913 5822 | 795.4864 0440 | 1045.5306 3252 | 1380.0056 0055 | 76 |
| 77 | 636.5599 6934 | 836.2607 2462 | 1104.0348 1731 | 1463.8059 3659 | 77 |
| 78 | 666.2051 6796 | 879.0737 6085 | 1165.7567 3226 | 1552.6342 9278 | 78 |
| 79 | 697.1844 0052 | 924.0274 4889 | 1230.8733 5254 | 1646.7923 5035 | 79 |
| 80 | 729.5576 9854 | 971.2288 2134 | 1299.5713 8693 | 1746.5998 9137 | 80 |
| 81 | 763.3877 9497 | 1020.7902 6240 | 1372.0478 1321 | 1852.3958 8485 | 81 |
| 82 | 798.7402 4575 | 1072.8297 7552 | 1448.5104 4294 | 1964.5396 3794 | 82 |
| 83 | 835.6835 5680 | 1127.4712 6430 | 1529.1785 1730 | 2083.4120 1622 | 83 |
| 84 | 874.2893 1686 | 1184.8448 2752 | 1614.2833 3575 | 2209.4167 3719 | 84 |
| 85 | 914.6323 3612 | 1245.0870 6889 | 1704.0689 1922 | 2342.9817 4142 | 85 |
| 86 | 956.7907 9125 | 1308.3414 2234 | 1798.7927 0977 | 2484.5606 4591 | 86 |
| 87 | 1000.8463 7685 | 1374.7584 9345 | 1898.7263 0881 | 2634.6342 8466 | 87 |
| 88 | 1046.8844 6381 | 1444.4964 1812 | 2004.1562 5579 | 2793.7123 4174 | 88 |
| 89 | 1094.9942 6468 | 1517.7212 3903 | 2115.3848 4986 | 2962.3350 8225 | 89 |
| 90 | 1145.2690 0659 | 1594.6073 0098 | 2232.7310 1660 | 3141.0751 8718 | 90 |
| 91 | 1197.8061 1189 | 1675.3376 6603 | 2356.5312 2252 | 3330.5396 9841 | 91 |
| 92 | 1252.7073 8692 | 1760.1045 4933 | 2487.1404 3976 | 3531.3720 8032 | 92 |
| 93 | 1310.0792 1933 | 1849.1097 7680 | 2624.9331 6394 | 3744.2544 0514 | 93 |
| 94 | 1370.0327 8420 | 1942.5652 6564 | 2770.3044 8796 | 3969.9096 6944 | 94 |
| 95 | 1432.6842 5949 | 2040.6935 2892 | 2923.6712 3480 | 4209.1042 4961 | 95 |
| 96 | 1498.1550 5117 | 2143.7282 0537 | 3085.4731 5271 | 4462.6505 0459 | 96 |
| 97 | 1566.5720 2847 | 2251.9146 1564 | 3256.1741 7611 | 4731.4095 3486 | 97 |
| 98 | 1638.0677 6976 | 2365.5103 4642 | 3436.2637 5580 | 5016.2941 0696 | 98 |
| 99 | 1712.7808 1939 | 2484.7858 6374 | 3626.2582 6237 | 5318.2717 5337 | 99 |
| 100 | 1790.8559 5627 | 2610.0251 5693 | 3826.7024 6680 | 5638.3680 5857 | 100 |

**TABLE 7**

$$s_{\overline{n}|i} = \frac{(1+i)^n - 1}{i}$$

| n | $6\frac{1}{2}\%$ | 7% | $7\frac{1}{2}\%$ | 8% | n |
|---|---|---|---|---|---|
| 1 | 1.0000 0000 | 1.0000 0000 | 1.0000 0000 | 1.0000 0000 | 1 |
| 2 | 2.0650 0000 | 2.0700 0000 | 2.0750 0000 | 2.0800 0000 | 2 |
| 3 | 3.1992 2500 | 3.2149 0000 | 3.2306 2500 | 3.2464 0000 | 3 |
| 4 | 4.4071 7462 | 4.4399 4300 | 4.4729 2188 | 4.5061 1200 | 4 |
| 5 | 5.6936 4098 | 5.7507 3901 | 5.8083 9102 | 5.8666 0096 | 5 |
| 6 | 7.0637 2764 | 7.1532 9074 | 7.2440 2034 | 7.3359 2904 | 6 |
| 7 | 8.5228 6994 | 8.6540 2109 | 8.7873 2187 | 8.9228 0336 | 7 |
| 8 | 10.0768 5648 | 10.2598 0257 | 10.4463 7101 | 10.6366 2763 | 8 |
| 9 | 11.7318 5215 | 11.9779 8875 | 12.2298 4883 | 12.4875 5784 | 9 |
| 10 | 13.4944 2254 | 13.8164 4796 | 14.1470 8750 | 14.4865 6247 | 10 |
| 11 | 15.3715 6001 | 15.7835 9932 | 16.2081 1906 | 16.6454 8746 | 11 |
| 12 | 17.3707 1141 | 17.8884 5127 | 18.4237 2799 | 18.9771 2646 | 12 |
| 13 | 19.4998 0765 | 20.1406 4286 | 20.8055 0759 | 21.4952 9658 | 13 |
| 14 | 21.7672 9515 | 22.5504 8786 | 23.3659 2066 | 24.2149 2030 | 14 |
| 15 | 24.1821 6933 | 25.1290 2201 | 26.1183 6470 | 27.1521 1393 | 15 |
| 16 | 26.7540 1034 | 27.8880 5355 | 29.0772 4206 | 30.3242 8304 | 16 |
| 17 | 29.4930 2101 | 30.8402 1730 | 32.2580 3521 | 33.7502 2568 | 17 |
| 18 | 32.4100 6738 | 33.9990 3251 | 35.6773 8785 | 37.4502 4374 | 18 |
| 19 | 35.5167 2176 | 37.3789 6479 | 39.3531 9194 | 41.4462 6324 | 19 |
| 20 | 38.8253 0867 | 40.9954 9232 | 43.3046 8134 | 45.7619 6430 | 20 |
| 21 | 42.3489 5373 | 44.8651 7678 | 47.5525 3244 | 50.4229 2144 | 21 |
| 22 | 46.1016 3573 | 49.0057 3916 | 52.1189 7237 | 55.4567 5516 | 22 |
| 23 | 50.0982 4205 | 53.4361 4090 | 57.0278 9530 | 60.8932 9557 | 23 |
| 24 | 54.3546 2778 | 58.1766 7076 | 62.3049 8744 | 66.7647 5922 | 24 |
| 25 | 58.8876 7859 | 63.2490 3772 | 67.9778 6150 | 73.1059 3995 | 25 |
| 26 | 63.7153 7769 | 68.6764 7036 | 74.0762 0112 | 79.9544 1515 | 26 |
| 27 | 68.8568 7724 | 74.4838 2328 | 80.6319 1620 | 87.3507 6836 | 27 |
| 28 | 74.3325 7427 | 80.6976 9091 | 87.6793 0991 | 95.3388 2983 | 28 |
| 29 | 80.1641 9159 | 87.3465 2927 | 95.2552 5816 | 103.9659 3622 | 29 |
| 30 | 86.3748 6405 | 94.4607 8632 | 103.3994 0252 | 113.2832 1111 | 30 |
| 31 | 92.9892 3021 | 102.0730 4137 | 112.1543 5771 | 123.3458 6800 | 31 |
| 32 | 100.0335 3017 | 110.2181 5426 | 121.5659 3454 | 134.2135 3744 | 32 |
| 33 | 107.5357 0963 | 118.9334 2506 | 131.6833 7963 | 145.9506 2044 | 33 |
| 34 | 115.5255 3076 | 128.2587 6481 | 142.5596 3310 | 158.6266 7007 | 34 |
| 35 | 124.0346 9026 | 138.2368 7835 | 154.2516 0558 | 172.3168 0368 | 35 |
| 36 | 133.0969 4513 | 148.9134 5984 | 166.8204 7600 | 187.1021 4797 | 36 |
| 37 | 142.7482 4656 | 160.3374 0202 | 180.3320 1170 | 203.0703 1981 | 37 |
| 38 | 153.0268 8259 | 172.5610 2017 | 194.8569 1258 | 220.3159 4540 | 38 |
| 39 | 163.9736 2996 | 185.6402 9158 | 210.4711 8102 | 238.9412 2103 | 39 |
| 40 | 175.6319 1590 | 199.6351 1199 | 227.2565 1960 | 259.0565 1871 | 40 |
| 41 | 188.0479 9044 | 214.6095 6983 | 245.3007 5857 | 280.7810 4021 | 41 |
| 42 | 201.2711 0981 | 230.6322 3972 | 264.6983 1546 | 304.2435 2342 | 42 |
| 43 | 215.3537 3195 | 247.7764 9650 | 285.5506 8912 | 329.5830 0530 | 43 |
| 44 | 230.3517 2453 | 266.1208 5125 | 307.9669 9080 | 356.9496 4572 | 44 |
| 45 | 246.3245 8662 | 285.7493 1084 | 332.0645 1511 | 386.5056 1738 | 45 |
| 46 | 263.3356 8475 | 306.7517 6260 | 357.9693 5375 | 418.4260 6677 | 46 |
| 47 | 281.4525 0426 | 329.2243 8598 | 385.8170 5528 | 452.9001 5211 | 47 |
| 48 | 300.7469 1704 | 353.2700 9300 | 415.7533 3442 | 490.1321 6428 | 48 |
| 49 | 321.2954 6665 | 378.9989 9951 | 447.9348 3451 | 530.3427 3742 | 49 |
| 50 | 343.1796 7198 | 406.5289 2947 | 482.5299 4709 | 573.7701 5642 | 50 |

Table 7

# TABLE 7

$$s_{\overline{n}|i} = \frac{(1+i)^n - 1}{i}$$

| $n$ | $6\frac{1}{2}\%$ | $7\%$ | $7\frac{1}{2}\%$ | $8\%$ | $n$ |
|---|---|---|---|---|---|
| 51 | 366.4863 5066 | 435.9859 5454 | 519.7196 9313 | 620.6717 6893 | 51 |
| 52 | 391.3079 6345 | 467.5049 7135 | 559.6986 7011 | 671.3255 1044 | 52 |
| 53 | 417.7429 8108 | 501.2303 1935 | 602.6760 7037 | 726.0315 5128 | 53 |
| 54 | 445.8962 7485 | 537.3164 4170 | 648.8767 7565 | 785.1140 7538 | 54 |
| 55 | 475.8795 3271 | 575.9285 9262 | 698.5425 3382 | 848.9232 0141 | 55 |
| 56 | 507.8117 0234 | 617.2435 9410 | 751.9332 2386 | 917.8370 5752 | 56 |
| 57 | 541.8194 6299 | 661.4506 4569 | 809.3282 1564 | 992.2640 2213 | 57 |
| 58 | 578.0377 2808 | 708.7521 9089 | 871.0278 3182 | 1072.6451 4390 | 58 |
| 59 | 616.6101 8041 | 759.3648 4425 | 937.3549 1920 | 1159.4567 5541 | 59 |
| 60 | 657.6898 4214 | 813.5203 8335 | 1008.6565 3814 | 1253.2132 9584 | 60 |
| 61 | 701.4396 8187 | 871.4668 1018 | 1085.3057 7851 | 1354.4703 5951 | 61 |
| 62 | 748.0332 6120 | 933.4694 8690 | 1167.7037 1189 | 1463.8279 8827 | 62 |
| 63 | 797.6554 2317 | 999.8123 5098 | 1256.2814 9029 | 1581.9342 2733 | 63 |
| 64 | 850.5030 2568 | 1070.7992 1555 | 1351.5026 0206 | 1709.4889 6552 | 64 |
| 65 | 906.7857 2235 | 1146.7551 6064 | 1453.8652 9721 | 1847.2480 8276 | 65 |
| 66 | 966.7267 9430 | 1228.0280 2188 | 1563.9051 9450 | 1996.0279 2938 | 66 |
| 67 | 1030.5640 3593 | 1314.9899 8341 | 1682.1980 8409 | 2156.7101 6373 | 67 |
| 68 | 1098.5506 9827 | 1408.0392 8225 | 1809.3629 4040 | 2330.2469 7683 | 68 |
| 69 | 1170.9564 9365 | 1507.6020 3201 | 1946.0651 6093 | 2517.6667 3497 | 69 |
| 70 | 1248.0686 6574 | 1614.1341 7425 | 2093.0200 4800 | 2720.0800 7377 | 70 |
| 71 | 1330.1931 2901 | 1728.1235 6645 | 2250.9965 5160 | 2938.6864 7967 | 71 |
| 72 | 1417.6556 8240 | 1850.0922 1610 | 2420.8212 9296 | 3174.7813 9805 | 72 |
| 73 | 1510.8033 0176 | 1980.5986 7123 | 2603.3828 8994 | 3429.7639 0989 | 73 |
| 74 | 1610.0055 1637 | 2120.2405 7821 | 2799.6366 0668 | 3705.1450 2268 | 74 |
| 75 | 1715.6558 7493 | 2269.6574 1869 | 3010.6093 5218 | 4002.5566 2449 | 75 |
| 76 | 1828.1735 0681 | 2429.5334 3800 | 3237.4050 5360 | 4323.7611 5445 | 76 |
| 77 | 1948.0047 8475 | 2600.6007 7866 | 3481.2104 3262 | 4670.6620 4681 | 77 |
| 78 | 2075.6250 9576 | 2783.6428 3316 | 3743.3012 1506 | 5045.3150 1056 | 78 |
| 79 | 2211.5407 2698 | 2979.4978 3148 | 4025.0488 0619 | 5449.9402 1140 | 79 |
| 80 | 2356.2908 7423 | 3189.0626 7969 | 4327.9274 6666 | 5886.9354 2831 | 80 |
| 81 | 2510.4497 8106 | 3413.2970 6727 | 4653.5220 2666 | 6358.8902 6258 | 81 |
| 82 | 2674.6290 1683 | 3653.2278 6198 | 5003.5361 7866 | 6868.6014 8358 | 82 |
| 83 | 2849.4799 0292 | 3909.9538 1231 | 5379.8013 9206 | 7419.0896 0227 | 83 |
| 84 | 3035.6960 9661 | 4184.6505 7918 | 5784.2864 9646 | 8013.6167 7045 | 84 |
| 85 | 3234.0163 4289 | 4478.5761 1972 | 6219.1079 8369 | 8655.7061 1209 | 85 |
| 86 | 3445.2274 0518 | 4793.0764 4810 | 6686.5410 8247 | 9349.1626 0105 | 86 |
| 87 | 3670.1671 8652 | 5129.5917 9946 | 7189.0316 6366 | 10098.0956 0914 | 87 |
| 88 | 3909.7280 5364 | 5489.6632 2543 | 7729.2090 3843 | 10906.9432 5787 | 88 |
| 89 | 4164.8603 7713 | 5874.9396 5121 | 8309.8997 1631 | 11780.4987 1850 | 89 |
| 90 | 4436.5763 0164 | 6287.1854 2679 | 8934.1421 9504 | 12723.9386 1598 | 90 |
| 91 | 4725.9537 6125 | 6728.2884 0667 | 9605.2028 5966 | 13742.8537 0526 | 91 |
| 92 | 5034.1407 5573 | 7200.2685 9513 | 10326.5930 7414 | 14843.2820 0168 | 92 |
| 93 | 5362.3599 0485 | 7705.2873 9679 | 11102.0875 5470 | 16031.7445 6181 | 93 |
| 94 | 5711.9132 9867 | 8245.6575 1457 | 11935.7441 2130 | 17315.2841 2676 | 94 |
| 95 | 6084.1876 6308 | 8823.8535 4059 | 12831.9249 3040 | 18701.5068 5690 | 95 |
| 96 | 6480.6598 6118 | 9442.5232 8843 | 13795.3193 0018 | 20198.6274 0545 | 96 |
| 97 | 6902.9027 5216 | 10104.4999 1862 | 14830.9682 4769 | 21815.5175 9788 | 97 |
| 98 | 7352.5914 3105 | 10812.8149 1292 | 15944.2908 6627 | 23561.7590 0572 | 98 |
| 99 | 7831.5098 7406 | 11570.7119 5683 | 17141.1126 8124 | 25447.6997 2617 | 99 |
| 100 | 8341.5580 1588 | 12381.6617 9381 | 18427.6961 3233 | 27484.5157 0427 | 100 |

# AMOUNT OF ANNUITY
When Periodic Payment Is 1

## TABLE 7

$$s_{\overline{n}|i} = \frac{(1+i)^n - 1}{i}$$

| $n$ | $8\frac{1}{2}\%$ | $9\%$ | $9\frac{1}{2}\%$ | $10\%$ | $n$ |
|---|---|---|---|---|---|
| 1 | 1.0000 0000 | 1.0000 0000 | 1.0000 0000 | 1.0000 0000 | 1 |
| 2 | 2.0850 0000 | 2.0900 0000 | 2.0950 0000 | 2.1000 0000 | 2 |
| 3 | 3.2622 2500 | 3.2781 0000 | 3.2940 2500 | 3.3100 0000 | 3 |
| 4 | 4.5395 1413 | 4.5731 2900 | 4.6069 5738 | 4.6410 0000 | 4 |
| 5 | 5.9253 7283 | 5.9847 1061 | 6.0446 1833 | 6.1051 0000 | 5 |
| 6 | 7.4290 2952 | 7.5233 3456 | 7.6188 5707 | 7.7156 1000 | 6 |
| 7 | 9.0604 9702 | 9.2004 3468 | 9.3426 4849 | 9.4871 7100 | 7 |
| 8 | 10.8306 3927 | 11.0284 7380 | 11.2302 0009 | 11.4358 8810 | 8 |
| 9 | 12.7512 4361 | 13.0210 3644 | 13.2970 6910 | 13.5794 7691 | 9 |
| 10 | 14.8350 9932 | 15.1929 2972 | 15.5602 9067 | 15.9374 2460 | 10 |
| 11 | 17.0960 8276 | 17.5602 9339 | 18.0385 1828 | 18.5311 6706 | 11 |
| 12 | 19.5492 4979 | 20.1407 1980 | 20.7521 7752 | 21.3842 8377 | 12 |
| 13 | 22.2109 3603 | 22.9533 8458 | 23.7236 3438 | 24.5227 1214 | 13 |
| 14 | 25.0988 6559 | 26.0191 8919 | 26.9773 7965 | 27.9749 8336 | 14 |
| 15 | 28.2322 6916 | 29.3609 1622 | 30.5402 3072 | 31.7724 8169 | 15 |
| 16 | 31.6320 1204 | 33.0033 9868 | 34.4415 5263 | 35.9497 2986 | 16 |
| 17 | 35.3207 3306 | 36.9737 0456 | 38.7135 0013 | 40.5447 0285 | 17 |
| 18 | 39.3229 9538 | 41.3013 3797 | 43.3912 8265 | 45.5991 7313 | 18 |
| 19 | 43.6654 4998 | 46.0184 5839 | 48.5134 5450 | 51.1590 9045 | 19 |
| 20 | 48.3770 1323 | 51.1601 1964 | 54.1222 3267 | 57.2749 9949 | 20 |
| 21 | 53.4890 5936 | 56.7645 3041 | 60.2638 4478 | 64.0024 9944 | 21 |
| 22 | 59.0356 2940 | 62.8733 3815 | 66.9889 1003 | 71.4027 4939 | 22 |
| 23 | 65.0536 5790 | 69.5319 3858 | 74.3528 5649 | 79.5430 2433 | 23 |
| 24 | 71.5832 1882 | 76.7898 1305 | 82.4163 7785 | 88.4973 2676 | 24 |
| 25 | 78.6677 9242 | 84.7008 9623 | 91.2459 3375 | 98.3470 5943 | 25 |
| 26 | 86.3545 5478 | 93.3239 7689 | 100.9142 9745 | 109.1817 6538 | 26 |
| 27 | 94.6946 9193 | 102.7231 3481 | 111.5011 5571 | 121.0999 4192 | 27 |
| 28 | 103.7437 4075 | 112.9682 1694 | 123.0937 6551 | 134.2099 3611 | 28 |
| 29 | 113.5619 5871 | 124.1353 5646 | 135.7876 7323 | 148.6309 2972 | 29 |
| 30 | 124.2147 2520 | 136.3075 3855 | 149.6875 0218 | 164.4940 2269 | 30 |
| 31 | 135.7729 7684 | 149.5752 1702 | 164.9078 1489 | 181.9434 2496 | 31 |
| 32 | 148.3136 7987 | 164.0369 8655 | 181.5740 5731 | 201.1377 6745 | 32 |
| 33 | 161.9203 4266 | 179.8003 1534 | 199.8235 9275 | 222.2515 4420 | 33 |
| 34 | 176.6835 7179 | 196.9823 4372 | 219.8068 3406 | 245.4766 9862 | 34 |
| 35 | 192.7016 7539 | 215.7107 5465 | 241.6884 8330 | 271.0243 6848 | 35 |
| 36 | 210.0813 1780 | 236.1247 2257 | 265.6488 8921 | 299.1268 0533 | 36 |
| 37 | 228.9382 2981 | 258.3759 4760 | 291.8855 3369 | 330.0394 8586 | 37 |
| 38 | 249.3979 7935 | 282.6297 8288 | 320.6146 5939 | 364.0434 3445 | 38 |
| 39 | 271.5968 0759 | 309.0664 6334 | 352.0730 5203 | 401.4477 7789 | 39 |
| 40 | 295.6825 3624 | 337.8824 4504 | 386.5199 9197 | 442.5925 5568 | 40 |
| 41 | 321.8155 5182 | 369.2918 6510 | 424.2393 9121 | 487.8518 1125 | 41 |
| 42 | 350.1698 7372 | 403.5281 3296 | 465.5421 3337 | 537.6369 9237 | 42 |
| 43 | 380.9343 1299 | 440.8456 6492 | 510.7686 3604 | 592.4006 9161 | 43 |
| 44 | 414.3137 2959 | 481.5217 7477 | 560.2916 5647 | 652.6407 6077 | 44 |
| 45 | 450.5303 9661 | 525.8587 3450 | 614.5193 6383 | 718.9048 3685 | 45 |
| 46 | 489.8254 8032 | 574.1860 2060 | 673.8987 0340 | 791.7953 2054 | 46 |
| 47 | 532.4606 4615 | 626.8627 6245 | 738.9190 8022 | 871.9748 5259 | 47 |
| 48 | 578.7198 0107 | 684.2804 1107 | 810.1163 9284 | 960.1723 3785 | 48 |
| 49 | 628.9109 8416 | 746.8656 4807 | 888.0774 5016 | 1057.1895 7163 | 49 |
| 50 | 683.3684 1782 | 815.0835 5640 | 973.4448 0793 | 1163.9085 2880 | 50 |

Table
7

**TABLE 7**

$$s_{\overline{n}|i} = \frac{(1+i)^n - 1}{i}$$

| $n$ | $8\frac{1}{2}\%$ | $9\%$ | $9\frac{1}{2}\%$ | $10\%$ | $n$ |
|---|---|---|---|---|---|
| 51 | 742.4547 3333 | 889.4410 7647 | 1066.9220 6468 | 1281.2993 8168 | 51 |
| 52 | 806.5633 8566 | 970.4907 7336 | 1169.2796 6082 | 1410.4293 1984 | 52 |
| 53 | 876.1212 7345 | 1058.8349 4296 | 1281.3612 2860 | 1552.4722 5183 | 53 |
| 54 | 951.5915 8169 | 1155.1300 8782 | 1404.0905 4532 | 1708.7194 7701 | 54 |
| 55 | 1033.4768 6613 | 1260.0917 9573 | 1538.4791 4713 | 1880.5914 2471 | 55 |
| 56 | 1122.3223 9975 | 1374.5000 5734 | 1685.6346 6610 | 2069.6505 6718 | 56 |
| 57 | 1218.7198 0373 | 1499.2050 6251 | 1846.7699 5938 | 2277.6156 2390 | 57 |
| 58 | 1323.3109 8705 | 1635.1335 1813 | 2023.2131 0552 | 2506.3771 8629 | 58 |
| 59 | 1436.7924 2095 | 1783.2955 3476 | 2216.4183 5055 | 2758.0149 0492 | 59 |
| 60 | 1559.9197 7673 | 1944.7921 3289 | 2427.9780 9385 | 3034.8163 9541 | 60 |
| 61 | 1693.5129 5775 | 2120.8234 2485 | 2659.6360 1277 | 3339.2980 3496 | 61 |
| 62 | 1838.4615 5916 | 2312.6975 3309 | 2913.3014 3398 | 3674.2278 3845 | 62 |
| 63 | 1995.7307 9169 | 2521.8403 1107 | 3191.0650 7021 | 4042.6506 2230 | 63 |
| 64 | 2166.3679 0898 | 2749.8059 3906 | 3495.2162 5188 | 4447.9156 8453 | 64 |
| 65 | 2351.5091 8125 | 2998.2884 7358 | 3828.2617 9580 | 4893.7072 5298 | 65 |
| 66 | 2552.3874 6165 | 3269.1344 3620 | 4192.9466 6641 | 5384.0779 7828 | 66 |
| 67 | 2770.3403 9589 | 3564.3565 3546 | 4592.2765 9971 | 5923.4857 7610 | 67 |
| 68 | 3006.8193 2954 | 3886.1486 2365 | 5029.5428 7669 | 6516.8343 5371 | 68 |
| 69 | 3263.3989 7255 | 4236.9019 9978 | 5508.3494 4997 | 7169.5177 8909 | 69 |
| 70 | 3541.7878 8522 | 4619.2231 7976 | 6032.6426 4772 | 7887.4695 6799 | 70 |
| 71 | 3843.8398 5546 | 5035.9532 6594 | 6606.7436 9925 | 8677.2165 2479 | 71 |
| 72 | 4171.5662 4318 | 5490.1890 5987 | 7235.3843 5068 | 9545.9381 7727 | 72 |
| 73 | 4527.1493 7385 | 5985.3060 7526 | 7923.7458 6400 | 10501.5319 9500 | 73 |
| 74 | 4912.9570 7063 | 6524.9836 2203 | 8677.5017 2108 | 11552.6851 9450 | 74 |
| 75 | 5331.5584 2163 | 7113.2321 4801 | 9502.8643 8458 | 12708.9537 1395 | 75 |
| 76 | 5785.7408 8747 | 7754.4230 4134 | 10406.6365 0111 | 13980.8490 8535 | 76 |
| 77 | 6278.5288 6290 | 8453.3211 1506 | 11396.2669 6872 | 15379.9339 9388 | 77 |
| 78 | 6813.2038 1625 | 9215.1200 1541 | 12479.9123 3075 | 16918.9273 9327 | 78 |
| 79 | 7393.3261 4063 | 10045.4808 1680 | 13666.5040 0217 | 18611.8201 3260 | 79 |
| 80 | 8022.7588 6259 | 10950.5740 9031 | 14965.8218 8238 | 20474.0021 4585 | 80 |
| 81 | 8705.6933 6591 | 11937.1257 5844 | 16388.5749 6120 | 22522.4023 6044 | 81 |
| 82 | 9446.6773 0201 | 13012.4670 7670 | 17946.4895 8251 | 24775.6425 9648 | 82 |
| 83 | 10250.6448 7268 | 14184.5891 1360 | 19652.4060 9285 | 27254.2068 5613 | 83 |
| 84 | 11122.9496 8686 | 15462.2021 3382 | 21520.3846 7168 | 29980.6275 4175 | 84 |
| 85 | 12069.4004 1024 | 16854.8003 2587 | 23565.8212 1548 | 32979.6902 9592 | 85 |
| 86 | 13096.2994 4511 | 18372.7323 5520 | 25805.5742 3096 | 36278.6593 2551 | 86 |
| 87 | 14210.4848 9794 | 20027.2782 6716 | 28258.1037 8290 | 39907.5252 5806 | 87 |
| 88 | 15419.3761 1427 | 21830.7333 1121 | 30943.6426 4227 | 43899.2777 8387 | 88 |
| 89 | 16731.0230 8398 | 23796.4993 0922 | 33884.2678 8829 | 48290.2055 6226 | 89 |
| 90 | 18154.1600 4612 | 25939.1842 4705 | 37104.2733 3767 | 53120.2261 1848 | 90 |
| 91 | 19698.2636 5004 | 28274.7108 2928 | 40630.1793 0475 | 58433.2487 3033 | 91 |
| 92 | 21373.6160 6029 | 30820.4348 0392 | 44491.0463 3870 | 64277.5736 0336 | 92 |
| 93 | 23191.3734 2542 | 33595.2739 3627 | 48718.6957 4088 | 70706.3309 6370 | 93 |
| 94 | 25163.6401 6658 | 36619.8485 9054 | 53347.9718 3627 | 77777.9640 6007 | 94 |
| 95 | 27303.5495 8074 | 39916.6349 6368 | 58417.0291 6071 | 85556.7604 6608 | 95 |
| 96 | 29625.3512 9510 | 43510.1321 1041 | 63967.6469 3098 | 94113.4365 1269 | 96 |
| 97 | 32144.5061 5518 | 47427.0440 0035 | 70045.5733 8942 | 103525.7801 6395 | 97 |
| 98 | 34877.7891 7837 | 51696.4779 6038 | 76700.9028 6142 | 113879.3581 8035 | 98 |
| 99 | 37843.4012 5853 | 56350.1609 7682 | 83988.4886 3325 | 125268.2939 9838 | 99 |
| 100 | 41061.0903 6551 | 61422.6754 6473 | 91968.3950 5341 | 137796.1233 9822 | 100 |

# TABLE 7A

$$s_{\overline{1/m}|\,i} = \frac{(1+i)^{\frac{1}{m}} - 1}{i}$$

| $m$ | $\frac{1}{4}\%$ | $\frac{1}{3}\%$ | $\frac{5}{12}\%$ | $\frac{11}{24}\%$ | $\frac{1}{2}\%$ | $m$ |
|---|---|---|---|---|---|---|
| 2 | .4996 8789 | .4995 8403 | .4994 8025 | .4994 2839 | .4993 7656 | 2 |
| 3 | .3330 5594 | .3329 6365 | .3328 7144 | .3328 2537 | .3327 7932 | 3 |
| 4 | .2497 6597 | .2496 8811 | .2496 1032 | .2495 7146 | .2495 3261 | 4 |
| 6 | .1664 9332 | .1664 3566 | .1663 7805 | .1663 4927 | .1663 2050 | 6 |
| 12 | .0832 3800 | .0832 0629 | .0831 7461 | .0831 5879 | .0831 4297 | 12 |

| $m$ | $\frac{13}{24}\%$ | $\frac{7}{12}\%$ | $\frac{5}{8}\%$ | $\frac{2}{3}\%$ | $\frac{3}{4}\%$ | $m$ |
|---|---|---|---|---|---|---|
| 2 | .4993 2474 | .4992 7295 | .4992 2118 | .4991 6943 | .4990 6600 | 2 |
| 3 | .3327 3329 | .3326 8728 | .3326 4129 | .3325 9532 | .3325 0345 | 3 |
| 4 | .2494 9379 | .2494 5498 | .2494 1619 | .2493 7742 | .2492 9994 | 4 |
| 6 | .1662 9175 | .1662 6301 | .1662 3429 | .1662 0558 | .1661 4821 | 6 |
| 12 | .0831 2716 | .0831 1136 | .0830 9557 | .0830 7978 | .0830 4824 | 12 |

| $m$ | $\frac{7}{8}\%$ | $1\%$ | $1\frac{1}{8}\%$ | $1\frac{1}{4}\%$ | $1\frac{3}{8}\%$ | $m$ |
|---|---|---|---|---|---|---|
| 2 | .4989 1101 | .4987 5621 | .4986 0161 | .4984 4719 | .4982 9297 | 2 |
| 3 | .3323 6581 | .3322 2835 | .3320 9109 | .3319 5401 | .3318 1712 | 3 |
| 4 | .2491 8385 | .2490 6793 | .2489 5218 | .2488 3660 | .2487 2118 | 4 |
| 6 | .1660 6226 | .1659 7644 | .1658 9075 | .1658 0518 | .1657 1975 | 6 |
| 12 | .0830 0099 | .0829 5381 | .0829 0671 | .0828 5968 | .0828 1273 | 12 |

| $m$ | $1\frac{1}{2}\%$ | $1\frac{5}{8}\%$ | $1\frac{3}{4}\%$ | $1\frac{7}{8}\%$ | $2\%$ | $m$ |
|---|---|---|---|---|---|---|
| 2 | .4981 3893 | .4979 8509 | .4978 3143 | .4976 7797 | .4975 2469 | 2 |
| 3 | .3316 8042 | .3315 4390 | .3314 0758 | .3312 7143 | .3311 3548 | 3 |
| 4 | .2486 0593 | .2484 9084 | .2483 7592 | .2482 6117 | .2481 4658 | 4 |
| 6 | .1656 3445 | .1655 4927 | .1654 6423 | .1653 7931 | .1652 9452 | 6 |
| 12 | .0827 6585 | .0827 1904 | .0826 7231 | .0826 2565 | .0825 7907 | 12 |

| $m$ | $2\frac{1}{4}\%$ | $2\frac{1}{2}\%$ | $2\frac{3}{4}\%$ | $3\%$ | $3\frac{1}{4}\%$ | $m$ |
|---|---|---|---|---|---|---|
| 2 | .4972 1870 | .4969 1346 | .4966 0897 | .4963 0522 | .4960 0220 | 2 |
| 3 | .3308 6412 | .3305 9350 | .3303 2362 | .3300 5447 | .3297 8604 | 3 |
| 4 | .2479 1789 | .2476 8985 | .2474 6247 | .2472 3573 | .2470 0963 | 4 |
| 6 | .1651 2531 | .1649 5662 | .1647 8843 | .1646 2073 | .1644 5354 | 6 |
| 12 | .0824 8611 | .0823 9345 | .0823 0108 | .0822 0899 | .0821 1719 | 12 |

| $m$ | $3\frac{1}{2}\%$ | $3\frac{3}{4}\%$ | $4\%$ | $4\frac{1}{2}\%$ | $5\%$ | $m$ |
|---|---|---|---|---|---|---|
| 2 | .4956 9993 | .4953 9838 | .4950 9757 | .4944 9811 | .4939 0153 | 2 |
| 3 | .3295 1834 | .3292 5136 | .3289 8510 | .3284 5470 | .3279 2714 | 3 |
| 4 | .2467 8417 | .2465 5935 | .2463 3516 | .2458 8868 | .2454 4469 | 4 |
| 6 | .1642 8684 | .1641 2064 | .1639 5492 | .1636 2496 | .1632 9692 | 6 |
| 12 | .0820 2568 | .0819 3445 | .0818 4349 | .0816 6243 | .0814 8248 | 12 |

Table
7A

# TABLE 7A

$$s_{\overline{1/m}|i} = \frac{(1+i)^{\frac{1}{m}} - 1}{i}$$

| $m$ | $5\frac{1}{2}\%$ | $6\%$ | $6\frac{1}{2}\%$ | $7\%$ | $7\frac{1}{2}\%$ | $m$ |
|---|---|---|---|---|---|---|
| 2 | .4933 0780 | .4927 1690 | .4921 2880 | .4915 4348 | .4909 6090 | 2 |
| 3 | .3274 0237 | .3268 8037 | .3263 6113 | .3258 4460 | .3253 3076 | 3 |
| 4 | .2450 0317 | .2445 6410 | .2441 2746 | .2436 9321 | .2432 6135 | 4 |
| 6 | .1629 7080 | .1626 4657 | .1623 2422 | .1620 0372 | .1616 8505 | 6 |
| 12 | .0813 0362 | .0811 2584 | .0809 4914 | .0807 7351 | .0805 9892 | 12 |

| $m$ | $8\%$ | $8\frac{1}{2}\%$ | $9\%$ | $9\frac{1}{2}\%$ | $10\%$ | $m$ |
|---|---|---|---|---|---|---|
| 2 | .4903 8106 | .4898 0392 | .4892 2945 | .4886 5765 | .4880 8848 | 2 |
| 3 | .3248 1960 | .3243 1108 | .3238 0518 | .3233 0188 | .3228 0115 | 3 |
| 4 | .2428 3184 | .2424 0466 | .2419 7979 | .2415 5721 | .2411 3689 | 4 |
| 6 | .1613 6821 | .1610 5317 | .1607 3991 | .1604 2842 | .1601 1868 | 6 |
| 12 | .0804 2538 | .0802 5286 | .0800 8137 | .0799 1089 | .0797 4140 | 12 |

**PRESENT VALUE OF ANNUITY**
When Periodic Payment Is 1

## TABLE 8

$$a_{\overline{n}|i} = \frac{1-(1+i)^{-n}}{i}$$

| n | $\frac{1}{4}$% | $\frac{1}{3}$% | $\frac{5}{12}$% | $\frac{11}{24}$% | n |
|---|---|---|---|---|---|
| 1 | 0.9975 0623 | 0.9966 7774 | 0.9958 5062 | 0.9954 3758 | 1 |
| 2 | 1.9925 2492 | 1.9900 4426 | 1.9875 6908 | 1.9863 3355 | 2 |
| 3 | 2.9850 6227 | 2.9801 1056 | 2.9751 7253 | 2.9727 0863 | 3 |
| 4 | 3.9751 2446 | 3.9668 8760 | 3.9586 7804 | 3.9545 8346 | 4 |
| 5 | 4.9627 1766 | 4.9503 8631 | 4.9381 0261 | 4.9319 7856 | 5 |
| 6 | 5.9478 4804 | 5.9306 1759 | 5.9134 6318 | 5.9049 1437 | 6 |
| 7 | 6.9305 2174 | 6.9075 9228 | 6.8847 7661 | 6.8734 1123 | 7 |
| 8 | 7.9107 4487 | 7.8813 2121 | 7.8520 5970 | 7.8374 8941 | 8 |
| 9 | 8.8885 2357 | 8.8518 1516 | 8.8153 2916 | 8.7971 6905 | 9 |
| 10 | 9.8638 6391 | 9.8190 8487 | 9.7746 0165 | 9.7524 7023 | 10 |
| 11 | 10.8367 7198 | 10.7831 4107 | 10.7298 9376 | 10.7034 1292 | 11 |
| 12 | 11.8072 5384 | 11.7439 9442 | 11.6812 2200 | 11.6500 1701 | 12 |
| 13 | 12.7753 1555 | 12.7016 5557 | 12.6286 0283 | 12.5923 0229 | 13 |
| 14 | 13.7409 6314 | 13.6561 3512 | 13.5720 5261 | 13.5302 8846 | 14 |
| 15 | 14.7042 0264 | 14.6074 4364 | 14.5115 8766 | 14.4639 9515 | 15 |
| 16 | 15.6650 4004 | 15.5555 9167 | 15.4472 2422 | 15.3934 4188 | 16 |
| 17 | 16.6234 8133 | 16.5005 8970 | 16.3789 7848 | 16.3186 4807 | 17 |
| 18 | 17.5795 3250 | 17.4424 4821 | 17.3068 6654 | 17.2396 3309 | 18 |
| 19 | 18.5331 9950 | 18.3811 7762 | 18.2309 0443 | 18.1564 1618 | 19 |
| 20 | 19.4844 8828 | 19.3167 8832 | 19.1511 0815 | 19.0690 1652 | 20 |
| 21 | 20.4334 0477 | 20.2492 9069 | 20.0674 9359 | 19.9774 5320 | 21 |
| 22 | 21.3799 5488 | 21.1786 9504 | 20.9800 7661 | 20.8817 4520 | 22 |
| 23 | 22.3241 4452 | 22.1050 1167 | 21.8888 7297 | 21.7819 1144 | 23 |
| 24 | 23.2659 7957 | 23.0282 5083 | 22.7938 9839 | 22.6779 7074 | 24 |
| 25 | 24.2054 6591 | 23.9484 2275 | 23.6951 6853 | 23.5699 4184 | 25 |
| 26 | 25.1426 0939 | 24.8655 3763 | 24.5926 9895 | 24.4578 4339 | 26 |
| 27 | 26.0774 1585 | 25.7796 0561 | 25.4865 0517 | 25.3416 9396 | 27 |
| 28 | 27.0098 9112 | 26.6906 3682 | 26.3766 0266 | 26.2215 1203 | 28 |
| 29 | 27.9400 4102 | 27.5986 4135 | 27.2630 0680 | 27.0973 1600 | 29 |
| 30 | 28.8678 7134 | 28.5036 2925 | 28.1457 3291 | 27.9691 2418 | 30 |
| 31 | 29.7933 8787 | 29.4056 1055 | 29.0247 9626 | 28.8369 5480 | 31 |
| 32 | 30.7165 9638 | 30.3045 9523 | 29.9002 1205 | 29.7008 2601 | 32 |
| 33 | 31.6375 0262 | 31.2005 9325 | 30.7719 9540 | 30.5607 5588 | 33 |
| 34 | 32.5561 1234 | 32.0936 1454 | 31.6401 6139 | 31.4167 6239 | 34 |
| 35 | 33.4724 3126 | 32.9836 6898 | 32.5047 2504 | 32.2688 6343 | 35 |
| 36 | 34.3864 6510 | 33.8707 6642 | 33.3657 0128 | 33.1170 7683 | 36 |
| 37 | 35.2982 1955 | 34.7549 1670 | 34.2231 0501 | 33.9614 2032 | 37 |
| 38 | 36.2077 0030 | 35.6361 2960 | 35.0769 5105 | 34.8019 1156 | 38 |
| 39 | 37.1149 1302 | 36.5144 1488 | 35.9272 5416 | 35.6385 6812 | 39 |
| 40 | 38.0198 6336 | 37.3897 8228 | 36.7740 2904 | 36.4714 0750 | 40 |
| 41 | 38.9225 5697 | 38.2622 4147 | 37.6172 9033 | 37.3004 4712 | 41 |
| 42 | 39.8229 9947 | 39.1318 0213 | 38.4570 5261 | 38.1257 0431 | 42 |
| 43 | 40.7211 9648 | 39.9984 7389 | 39.2933 3040 | 38.9471 9633 | 43 |
| 44 | 41.6171 5359 | 40.8622 6633 | 40.1261 3816 | 39.7649 4035 | 44 |
| 45 | 42.5108 7640 | 41.7231 8903 | 40.9554 9028 | 40.5789 5348 | 45 |
| 46 | 43.4023 7048 | 42.5812 5153 | 41.7814 0111 | 41.3892 5274 | 46 |
| 47 | 44.2916 4137 | 43.4364 6332 | 42.6038 8492 | 42.1958 5507 | 47 |
| 48 | 45.1786 9463 | 44.2888 3387 | 43.4229 5594 | 42.9987 7734 | 48 |
| 49 | 46.0635 3580 | 45.1383 7263 | 44.2386 2832 | 43.7980 3634 | 49 |
| 50 | 46.9461 7037 | 45.9850 8900 | 45.0509 1617 | 44.5936 4878 | 50 |
| 51 | 47.8266 0386 | 46.8289 9236 | 45.8598 3353 | 45.3856 3131 | 51 |
| 52 | 48.7048 4176 | 47.6700 9205 | 46.6653 9439 | 46.1740 0047 | 52 |
| 53 | 49.5808 8953 | 48.5083 9739 | 47.4676 1267 | 46.9587 7276 | 53 |
| 54 | 50.4547 5265 | 49.3439 1767 | 48.2665 0224 | 47.7399 6459 | 54 |
| 55 | 51.3264 3656 | 50.1766 6213 | 49.0620 7692 | 48.5175 9229 | 55 |
| 56 | 52.1959 4669 | 51.0066 3999 | 49.8543 5046 | 49.2916 7213 | 56 |
| 57 | 53.0632 8847 | 51.8338 6046 | 50.6433 3656 | 50.0622 2029 | 57 |
| 58 | 53.9284 6730 | 52.6583 3268 | 51.4290 4885 | 50.8292 5288 | 58 |
| 59 | 54.7914 8858 | 53.4800 6580 | 52.2115 0093 | 51.5927 8594 | 59 |
| 60 | 55.6523 5769 | 54.2990 6890 | 52.9907 0632 | 52.3528 3545 | 60 |

Table
8

# TABLE 8

$$a_{\overline{n}|i} = \frac{1 - (1 + i)^{-n}}{i}$$

| n | $\frac{1}{4}$ % | $\frac{1}{3}$ % | $\frac{5}{12}$ % | $\frac{11}{24}$ % | n |
|---|---|---|---|---|---|
| 61 | 56.5110 7999 | 55.1153 5106 | 53.7666 7850 | 53.1094 1728 | 61 |
| 62 | 57.3676 6083 | 55.9289 2133 | 54.5394 3087 | 53.8625 4727 | 62 |
| 63 | 58.2221 0557 | 56.7397 8870 | 55.3089 7680 | 54.6122 4117 | 63 |
| 64 | 59.0744 1952 | 57.5479 6216 | 56.0753 2959 | 55.3585 1464 | 64 |
| 65 | 59.9246 0800 | 58.3534 5065 | 56.8385 0250 | 56.1013 8330 | 65 |
| 66 | 60.7726 7631 | 59.1562 6311 | 57.5985 0871 | 56.8408 6268 | 66 |
| 67 | 61.6186 2974 | 59.9564 0842 | 58.3553 6137 | 57.5769 6825 | 67 |
| 68 | 62.4624 7355 | 60.7538 9543 | 59.1090 7357 | 58.3097 1538 | 68 |
| 69 | 63.3042 1302 | 61.5487 3299 | 59.8596 5832 | 59.0391 1942 | 69 |
| 70 | 64.1438 5339 | 62.3409 2989 | 60.6071 2862 | 59.7651 9561 | 70 |
| 71 | 64.9813 9989 | 63.1304 9491 | 61.3514 9738 | 60.4879 5913 | 71 |
| 72 | 65.8168 5774 | 63.9174 3678 | 62.0927 7748 | 61.2074 2510 | 72 |
| 73 | 66.6502 3216 | 64.7017 6424 | 62.8309 8172 | 61.9236 0856 | 73 |
| 74 | 67.4815 2834 | 65.4834 8595 | 63.5661 2287 | 62.6365 2449 | 74 |
| 75 | 68.3107 5146 | 66.2626 1058 | 64.2982 1365 | 63.3461 8779 | 75 |
| 76 | 69.1379 0670 | 67.0391 4676 | 65.0272 6670 | 64.0526 1331 | 76 |
| 77 | 69.9629 9920 | 67.8131 0308 | 65.7532 9464 | 64.7558 1582 | 77 |
| 78 | 70.7860 3411 | 68.5844 8812 | 66.4763 1002 | 65.4558 1003 | 78 |
| 79 | 71.6070 1657 | 69.3533 1042 | 67.1963 2533 | 66.1526 1056 | 79 |
| 80 | 72.4259 5169 | 70.1195 7849 | 67.9133 5303 | 66.8462 3200 | 80 |
| 81 | 73.2428 4458 | 70.8833 0082 | 68.6274 0550 | 67.5366 8884 | 81 |
| 82 | 74.0577 0033 | 71.6444 8587 | 69.3384 9511 | 68.2239 9553 | 82 |
| 83 | 74.8705 2402 | 72.4031 4206 | 70.0466 3413 | 68.9081 6643 | 83 |
| 84 | 75.6813 2072 | 73.1592 7780 | 70.7518 3482 | 69.5892 1586 | 84 |
| 85 | 76.4900 9548 | 73.9129 0146 | 71.4541 0936 | 70.2671 5805 | 85 |
| 86 | 77.2968 5335 | 74.6640 2139 | 72.1534 6991 | 70.9420 0719 | 86 |
| 87 | 78.1015 9935 | 75.4126 4591 | 72.8499 2854 | 71.6137 7737 | 87 |
| 88 | 78.9043 3850 | 76.1587 8330 | 73.5434 9730 | 72.2824 8266 | 88 |
| 89 | 79.7050 7581 | 76.9024 4182 | 74.2341 8818 | 72.9481 3703 | 89 |
| 90 | 80.5038 1627 | 77.6436 2972 | 74.9220 1313 | 73.6107 5441 | 90 |
| 91 | 81.3005 6486 | 78.3823 5521 | 75.6069 8403 | 74.2703 4864 | 91 |
| 92 | 82.0953 2654 | 79.1186 2645 | 76.2891 1272 | 74.9269 3353 | 92 |
| 93 | 82.8881 0628 | 79.8524 5161 | 76.9684 1101 | 75.5805 2280 | 93 |
| 94 | 83.6789 0900 | 80.5838 3882 | 77.6448 9063 | 76.2311 3012 | 94 |
| 95 | 84.4677 3966 | 81.3127 9616 | 78.3185 6329 | 76.8787 6910 | 95 |
| 96 | 85.2546 0315 | 82.0393 3172 | 78.9894 4062 | 77.5234 5327 | 96 |
| 97 | 86.0395 0439 | 82.7634 5355 | 79.6575 3422 | 78.1651 9612 | 97 |
| 98 | 86.8224 4827 | 83.4851 6965 | 80.3228 5566 | 78.8040 1107 | 98 |
| 99 | 87.6034 3967 | 84.2044 8802 | 80.9854 1642 | 79.4399 1148 | 99 |
| 100 | 88.3824 8346 | 84.9214 1663 | 81.6452 2797 | 80.0729 1064 | 100 |
| 101 | 89.1595 8450 | 85.6359 6342 | 82.3023 0172 | 80.7030 2179 | 101 |
| 102 | 89.9347 4763 | 86.3481 3630 | 82.9566 4901 | 81.3302 5810 | 102 |
| 103 | 90.7079 7768 | 87.0579 4315 | 83.6082 8117 | 81.9546 3270 | 103 |
| 104 | 91.4792 7948 | 87.7653 9185 | 84.2572 0947 | 82.5761 5864 | 104 |
| 105 | 92.2486 5784 | 88.4704 9021 | 84.9034 4511 | 83.1948 4892 | 105 |
| 106 | 93.0161 1755 | 89.1732 4606 | 85.5469 9928 | 83.8107 1647 | 106 |
| 107 | 93.7816 6339 | 89.8736 6717 | 86.1878 8310 | 84.4237 7417 | 107 |
| 108 | 94.5453 0014 | 90.5717 6130 | 86.8261 0765 | 85.0340 3484 | 108 |
| 109 | 95.3070 3256 | 91.2675 3618 | 87.4616 8397 | 85.6415 1125 | 109 |
| 110 | 96.0668 6539 | 91.9609 9951 | 88.0946 2304 | 86.2462 1609 | 110 |
| 111 | 96.8248 0338 | 92.6521 5898 | 88.7249 3581 | 86.8481 6202 | 111 |
| 112 | 97.5808 5126 | 93.3410 2224 | 89.3526 3317 | 87.4473 6161 | 112 |
| 113 | 98.3350 1372 | 94.0275 9692 | 89.9777 2598 | 88.0438 2740 | 113 |
| 114 | 99.0872 9548 | 94.7118 9062 | 90.6002 2504 | 88.6375 7186 | 114 |
| 115 | 99.8377 0123 | 95.3939 1092 | 91.2201 4112 | 89.2286 0741 | 115 |
| 116 | 100.5862 3564 | 96.0736 6536 | 91.8374 8493 | 89.8169 4641 | 116 |
| 117 | 101.3329 0338 | 96.7511 6149 | 92.4522 6715 | 90.4026 0115 | 117 |
| 118 | 102.0777 0911 | 97.4264 0680 | 93.0644 9841 | 90.9855 8389 | 118 |
| 119 | 102.8206 5747 | 98.0994 0877 | 93.6741 8929 | 91.5659 0682 | 119 |
| 120 | 103.5617 5308 | 98.7701 7486 | 94.2813 5033 | 92.1435 8207 | 120 |

**PRESENT VALUE OF ANNUITY**
When Periodic Payment Is 1

## TABLE 8

$$a_{\overline{n}|i} = \frac{1 - (1 + i)^{-n}}{i}$$

| n | $\frac{1}{4}$ % | $\frac{1}{3}$ % | $\frac{5}{12}$ % | $\frac{11}{24}$ % | n |
|---|---|---|---|---|---|
| 121 | 104.3010 0058 | 99.4387 1248 | 94.8859 9203 | 92.7186 2172 | 121 |
| 122 | 105.0384 0457 | 100.1050 2905 | 95.4881 2484 | 93.2910 3780 | 122 |
| 123 | 105.7739 6965 | 100.7691 3195 | 96.0877 5918 | 93.8608 4227 | 123 |
| 124 | 106.5077 0040 | 101.4310 2852 | 96.6849 0541 | 94.4280 4705 | 124 |
| 125 | 107.2396 0139 | 102.0907 2610 | 97.2795 7385 | 94.9926 6401 | 125 |
| 126 | 107.9696 7720 | 102.7482 3199 | 97.8717 7479 | 95.5547 0495 | 126 |
| 127 | 108.6979 3237 | 103.4035 5348 | 98.4615 1846 | 96.1141 8161 | 127 |
| 128 | 109.4243 7144 | 104.0566 9782 | 99.0488 1506 | 96.6711 0571 | 128 |
| 129 | 110.1489 9894 | 104.7076 7225 | 99.6336 7475 | 97.2254 8889 | 129 |
| 130 | 110.8718 1939 | 105.3564 8397 | 100.2161 0764 | 97.7773 4273 | 130 |
| 131 | 111.5928 3730 | 106.0031 4016 | 100.7961 2379 | 98.3266 7879 | 131 |
| 132 | 112.3120 5716 | 106.6476 4800 | 101.3737 3323 | 98.8735 0854 | 132 |
| 133 | 113.0294 8345 | 107.2900 1462 | 101.9489 4596 | 99.4178 4343 | 133 |
| 134 | 113.7451 2065 | 107.9302 4713 | 102.5217 7191 | 99.9596 9483 | 134 |
| 135 | 114.4589 7321 | 108.5683 5262 | 103.0922 2099 | 100.4990 7407 | 135 |
| 136 | 115.1710 4560 | 109.2043 3816 | 103.6603 0306 | 101.0359 9244 | 136 |
| 137 | 115.8813 4224 | 109.8382 1079 | 104.2260 2794 | 101.5704 6116 | 137 |
| 138 | 116.5898 6758 | 110.4699 7754 | 104.7894 0542 | 102.1024 9141 | 138 |
| 139 | 117.2966 2601 | 111.0996 4538 | 105.3504 4523 | 102.6320 9431 | 139 |
| 140 | 118.0016 2196 | 111.7272 2131 | 105.9091 5708 | 103.1592 8094 | 140 |
| 141 | 118.7048 5981 | 112.3527 1227 | 106.4655 5061 | 103.6840 6232 | 141 |
| 142 | 119.4063 4395 | 112.9761 2519 | 107.0196 3547 | 104.2064 4942 | 142 |
| 143 | 120.1060 7875 | 113.5974 6696 | 107.5714 2121 | 104.7264 5318 | 143 |
| 144 | 120.8040 6858 | 114.2167 4448 | 108.1209 1739 | 105.2440 8446 | 144 |
| 145 | 121.5003 1778 | 114.8339 6460 | 108.6681 3350 | 105.7593 5409 | 145 |
| 146 | 122.1948 3071 | 115.4491 3415 | 109.2130 7900 | 106.2722 7284 | 146 |
| 147 | 122.8876 1168 | 116.0622 5995 | 109.7557 6332 | 106.7828 5143 | 147 |
| 148 | 123.5786 6502 | 116.6733 4879 | 110.2961 9584 | 107.2911 0056 | 148 |
| 149 | 124.2679 9503 | 117.2824 0743 | 110.8343 8590 | 107.7970 3083 | 149 |
| 150 | 124.9556 0601 | 117.8894 4262 | 111.3703 4280 | 108.3006 5284 | 150 |
| 151 | 125.6415 0226 | 118.4944 6109 | 111.9040 7582 | 108.8019 7711 | 151 |
| 152 | 126.3256 8804 | 119.0974 6952 | 112.4355 9418 | 109.3010 1413 | 152 |
| 153 | 127.0081 6762 | 119.6984 7461 | 112.9649 0707 | 109.7977 7433 | 153 |
| 154 | 127.6889 4525 | 120.2974 8300 | 113.4920 2364 | 110.2922 6810 | 154 |
| 155 | 128.3680 2519 | 120.8945 0133 | 114.0169 5300 | 110.7845 0578 | 155 |
| 156 | 129.0454 1166 | 121.4895 3621 | 114.5397 0423 | 111.2744 9767 | 156 |
| 157 | 129.7211 0889 | 122.0825 9422 | 115.0602 8637 | 111.7622 5400 | 157 |
| 158 | 130.3951 2109 | 122.6736 8195 | 115.5787 0842 | 112.2477 8499 | 158 |
| 159 | 131.0674 5246 | 123.2628 0593 | 116.0949 7934 | 112.7311 0078 | 159 |
| 160 | 131.7381 0719 | 123.8499 7269 | 116.6091 0805 | 113.2122 1148 | 160 |
| 161 | 132.4070 8946 | 124.4351 8873 | 117.1211 0346 | 113.6911 2714 | 161 |
| 162 | 133.0744 0346 | 125.0184 6053 | 117.6309 7440 | 114.1678 5779 | 162 |
| 163 | 133.7400 5332 | 125.5997 9454 | 118.1387 2969 | 114.6424 1340 | 163 |
| 164 | 134.4040 4321 | 126.1791 9722 | 118.6443 7811 | 115.1148 0388 | 164 |
| 165 | 135.0663 7727 | 126.7566 7497 | 119.1479 2841 | 115.5850 3912 | 165 |
| 166 | 135.7270 5962 | 127.3322 3419 | 119.6493 8929 | 116.0531 2895 | 166 |
| 167 | 136.3860 9439 | 127.9058 8125 | 120.1487 6942 | 116.5190 8315 | 167 |
| 168 | 137.0434 8567 | 128.4776 2251 | 120.6460 7743 | 116.9829 1147 | 168 |
| 169 | 137.6992 3758 | 129.0474 6430 | 121.1413 2192 | 117.4446 2361 | 169 |
| 170 | 138.3533 5419 | 129.6154 1292 | 121.6345 1146 | 117.9042 2923 | 170 |
| 171 | 139.0058 3959 | 130.1814 7467 | 122.1256 5456 | 118.3617 3793 | 171 |
| 172 | 139.6566 9785 | 130.7456 5582 | 122.6147 5973 | 118.8171 5928 | 172 |
| 173 | 140.3059 3302 | 131.3079 6261 | 123.1018 3542 | 119.2705 0281 | 173 |
| 174 | 140.9535 4914 | 131.8684 0127 | 123.5868 9004 | 119.7217 7799 | 174 |
| 175 | 141.5995 5027 | 132.4269 7801 | 124.0699 3199 | 120.1709 9427 | 175 |
| 176 | 142,2439 4042 | 132.9837 9901 | 124.5509 6962 | 120.6181 6103 | 176 |
| 177 | 142.8867 2361 | 133.5385 7045 | 125.0300 1124 | 121.0632 8763 | 177 |
| 178 | 143.5279 0385 | 134.0915 9845 | 125.5070 6513 | 121.5063 8337 | 178 |
| 179 | 144.1674 8514 | 134.6427 8915 | 125.9821 3955 | 121.9474 5753 | 179 |
| 180 | 144.8054 7146 | 135.1921 4866 | 126.4552 4271 | 122.3865 1931 | 180 |

Table
8

**PRESENT VALUE OF ANNUITY**
When Periodic Payment Is 1

**TABLE 8**

$$a_{\overline{n}|i} = \frac{1-(1+i)^{-n}}{i}$$

| n | $\frac{1}{4}$% | $\frac{1}{3}$% | $\frac{5}{12}$% | $\frac{11}{24}$% | n |
|---|---|---|---|---|---|
| 181 | 145.4418 6679 | 135.7396 8305 | 126.9263 8278 | 122.8235 7792 | 181 |
| 182 | 146.0766 7510 | 136.2853 9839 | 127.3955 6791 | 123.2586 4247 | 182 |
| 183 | 146.7099 0035 | 136.8293 0072 | 127.8628 0622 | 123.6917 2208 | 183 |
| 184 | 147.3415 4649 | 137.3713 9606 | 128.3281 0578 | 124.1228 2579 | 184 |
| 185 | 147.9716 1744 | 137.9116 9043 | 128.7914 7463 | 124.5519 6263 | 185 |
| 186 | 148.6001 1715 | 138.4501 8980 | 129.2529 2080 | 124.9791 4157 | 186 |
| 187 | 149.2270 4952 | 138.9869 0013 | 129.7124 5225 | 125.4043 7153 | 187 |
| 188 | 149.8524 1848 | 139.5218 2737 | 130.1700 7693 | 125.8276 6141 | 188 |
| 189 | 150.4762 2791 | 140.0549 7745 | 130.6258 0275 | 126.2490 2007 | 189 |
| 190 | 151.0984 8170 | 140.5863 5626 | 131.0796 3759 | 126.6684 5631 | 190 |
| 191 | 151.7191 8375 | 141.1159 6969 | 131.5315 8930 | 127.0859 7891 | 191 |
| 192 | 152.3383 3790 | 141.6438 2362 | 131.9816 6570 | 127.5015 9659 | 192 |
| 193 | 152.9559 4803 | 142.1699 2387 | 132.4298 7455 | 127.9153 1805 | 193 |
| 194 | 153.5720 1799 | 142.6942 7628 | 132.8762 2362 | 128.3271 5194 | 194 |
| 195 | 154.1865 5161 | 143.2168 8666 | 133.3207 2062 | 128.7371 0687 | 195 |
| 196 | 154.7995 5272 | 143.7377 6079 | 133.7633 7323 | 129.1451 9141 | 196 |
| 197 | 155.4110 2516 | 144.2569 0444 | 134.2041 8911 | 129.5514 1409 | 197 |
| 198 | 156.0209 7273 | 144.7743 2336 | 134.6431 7587 | 129.9557 8342 | 198 |
| 199 | 156.6293 9923 | 145.2900 2329 | 135.0803 4112 | 130.3583 0784 | 199 |
| 200 | 157.2363 0846 | 145.8040 0992 | 135.5156 9240 | 130.7589 9577 | 200 |
| 201 | 157.8417 0420 | 146.3162 8896 | 135.9492 3725 | 131.1578 5560 | 201 |
| 202 | 158.4455 9022 | 146.8268 6607 | 136.3809 8315 | 131.5548 9567 | 202 |
| 203 | 159.0479 7030 | 147.3357 4691 | 136.8109 3758 | 131.9501 2426 | 203 |
| 204 | 159.6488 4818 | 147.8429 3712 | 137.2391 0796 | 132.3435 4966 | 204 |
| 205 | 160.2482 2761 | 148.3484 4232 | 137.6655 0170 | 132.7351 8008 | 205 |
| 206 | 160.8461 1233 | 148.8522 6809 | 138.0901 2618 | 133.1250 2373 | 206 |
| 207 | 161.4425 0606 | 149.3544 2002 | 138.5129 8872 | 133.5130 8874 | 207 |
| 208 | 162.0374 1253 | 149.8549 0368 | 138.9340 9665 | 133.8993 8323 | 208 |
| 209 | 162.6308 3544 | 150.3537 2459 | 139.3534 5725 | 134.2839 1528 | 209 |
| 210 | 163.2227 7850 | 150.8508 8830 | 139.7710 7776 | 134.6666 9294 | 210 |
| 211 | 163.8132 4538 | 151.3464 0030 | 140.1869 6540 | 135.0477 2421 | 211 |
| 212 | 164.4022 3978 | 151.8402 6608 | 140.6011 2737 | 135.4270 1704 | 212 |
| 213 | 164.9897 6537 | 152.3324 9111 | 141.0135 7083 | 135.8045 7939 | 213 |
| 214 | 165.5758 2581 | 152.8230 8084 | 141.4243 0290 | 136.1804 1913 | 214 |
| 215 | 166.1604 2474 | 153.3120 4070 | 141.8333 3069 | 136.5545 4414 | 215 |
| 216 | 166.7435 6583 | 153.7993 7612 | 142.2406 6127 | 136.9269 6223 | 216 |
| 217 | 167.3252 5270 | 154.2850 9247 | 142.6463 0167 | 137.2976 8119 | 217 |
| 218 | 167.9054 8898 | 154.7691 9516 | 143.0502 5893 | 137.6667 0878 | 218 |
| 219 | 168.4842 7828 | 155.2516 8953 | 143.4525 4001 | 138.0340 5270 | 219 |
| 220 | 169.0616 2422 | 155.7325 8092 | 143.8531 5188 | 138.3997 2065 | 220 |
| 221 | 169.6375 3039 | 156.2118 7467 | 144.2521 0146 | 138.7637 2026 | 221 |
| 222 | 170.2120 0039 | 156.6895 7609 | 144.6493 9564 | 139.1260 5916 | 222 |
| 223 | 170.7850 3780 | 157.1656 9045 | 145.0450 4130 | 139.4867 4491 | 223 |
| 224 | 171.3566 4618 | 157.6402 2304 | 145.4390 4528 | 139.8457 8506 | 224 |
| 225 | 171.9268 2911 | 158.1131 7911 | 145.8314 1439 | 140.2031 8712 | 225 |
| 226 | 172.4955 9013 | 158.5845 6390 | 146.2221 5541 | 140.5589 5856 | 226 |
| 227 | 173.0629 3280 | 159.0543 8262 | 146.6112 7509 | 140.9131 0682 | 227 |
| 228 | 173.6288 6065 | 159.5226 4049 | 146.9987 8018 | 141.2656 3931 | 228 |
| 229 | 174.1933 7721 | 159.9893 4268 | 147.3846 7735 | 141.6165 6339 | 229 |
| 230 | 174.7564 8599 | 160.4544 9436 | 147.7689 7330 | 141.9658 8641 | 230 |
| 231 | 175.3181 9052 | 160.9181 0070 | 148.1516 7465 | 142.3136 1568 | 231 |
| 232 | 175.8784 9428 | 161.3801 6681 | 148.5327 8804 | 142.6597 5845 | 232 |
| 233 | 176.4374 0078 | 161.8406 9781 | 148.9123 2004 | 143.0043 2197 | 233 |
| 234 | 176.9949 1350 | 162.2996 9882 | 149.2902 7722 | 143.3473 1345 | 234 |
| 235 | 177.5510 3591 | 162.7571 7490 | 149.6666 6611 | 143.6887 4006 | 235 |
| 236 | 178.1057 7148 | 163.2131 3113 | 150.0414 9322 | 144.0286 0894 | 236 |
| 237 | 178.6591 2367 | 163.6675 7256 | 150.4147 6503 | 144.3669 2719 | 237 |
| 238 | 179.2110 9593 | 164.1205 0421 | 150.7864 8800 | 144.7037 0189 | 238 |
| 239 | 179.7616 9170 | 164.5719 3110 | 151.1566 6855 | 145.0389 4008 | 239 |
| 240 | 180.3109 1441 | 165.0218 5824 | 151.5253 1307 | 145.3726 4877 | 240 |

**TABLE 8**

$$a_{\overline{n}|i} = \frac{1-(1+i)^{-n}}{i}$$

| n | $\frac{1}{2}\%$ | $\frac{13}{24}\%$ | $\frac{7}{12}\%$ | $\frac{5}{8}\%$ | n |
|---|---|---|---|---|---|
| 1 | 0.9950 2488 | 0.9946 1252 | 0.9942 0050 | 0.9937 8882 | 1 |
| 2 | 1.9850 9938 | 1.9838 6657 | 1.9826 3513 | 1.9814 0504 | 2 |
| 3 | 2.9702 4814 | 2.9677 9104 | 2.9653 3732 | 2.9628 8699 | 3 |
| 4 | 3.9504 9566 | 3.9464 1462 | 3.9423 4034 | 3.9382 7279 | 4 |
| 5 | 4.9258 6633 | 4.9197 6589 | 4.9136 7722 | 4.9076 0029 | 5 |
| 6 | 5.8963 8441 | 5.8878 7325 | 5.8793 8083 | 5.8709 0712 | 6 |
| 7 | 6.8620 7404 | 6.8507 6494 | 6.8394 8384 | 6.8282 3068 | 7 |
| 8 | 7.8229 5924 | 7.8084 6906 | 7.7940 1874 | 7.7796 0813 | 8 |
| 9 | 8.7790 6392 | 8.7610 1357 | 8.7430 1780 | 8.7250 7640 | 9 |
| 10 | 9.7304 1186 | 9.7084 2626 | 9.6865 1314 | 9.6646 7220 | 10 |
| 11 | 10.6770 2673 | 10.6507 3478 | 10.6245 3667 | 10.5984 3200 | 11 |
| 12 | 11.6189 3207 | 11.5879 6663 | 11.5571 2044 | 11.5263 9205 | 12 |
| 13 | 12.5561 5131 | 12.5201 4916 | 12.4842 9509 | 12.4485 8837 | 13 |
| 14 | 13.4887 0777 | 13.4473 0956 | 13.4060 9288 | 13.3650 5676 | 14 |
| 15 | 14.4166 2465 | 14.3694 7491 | 14.3225 4470 | 14.2758 3281 | 15 |
| 16 | 15.3399 2502 | 15.2866 7210 | 15.2336 8156 | 15.1809 5186 | 16 |
| 17 | 16.2586 3186 | 16.1989 2791 | 16.1395 3427 | 16.0804 4905 | 17 |
| 18 | 17.1727 6802 | 17.1062 6895 | 17.0401 3350 | 16.9743 5931 | 18 |
| 19 | 18.0823 5624 | 18.0087 2171 | 17.9355 0969 | 17.8627 1733 | 19 |
| 20 | 18.9874 1915 | 18.9063 1251 | 18.8256 9315 | 18.7455 5759 | 20 |
| 21 | 19.8879 7925 | 19.7990 6756 | 19.7107 1398 | 19.6229 1438 | 21 |
| 22 | 20.7840 5896 | 20.6870 1291 | 20.5906 0213 | 20.4948 2174 | 22 |
| 23 | 21.6756 8055 | 21.5701 7447 | 21.4653 8738 | 21.3613 1353 | 23 |
| 24 | 22.5628 6622 | 22.4485 7800 | 22.3350 9930 | 22.2224 2338 | 24 |
| 25 | 23.4456 3803 | 23.3222 4915 | 23.1997 6732 | 23.0781 8473 | 25 |
| 26 | 24.3240 1794 | 24.1912 1341 | 24.0594 2070 | 23.9286 3079 | 26 |
| 27 | 25.1980 2780 | 25.0554 9614 | 24.9140 8852 | 24.7737 9457 | 27 |
| 28 | 26.0676 8936 | 25.9151 2256 | 25.7637 9968 | 25.6137 0889 | 28 |
| 29 | 26.9330 2423 | 26.7701 1776 | 26.6085 8295 | 26.4484 0635 | 29 |
| 30 | 27.7940 5397 | 27.6205 0668 | 27.4484 6689 | 27.2779 1935 | 30 |
| 31 | 28.6507 9997 | 28.4663 1414 | 28.2834 7993 | 28.1022 8010 | 31 |
| 32 | 29.5032 8355 | 29.3075 6483 | 29.1136 5030 | 28.9215 2060 | 32 |
| 33 | 30.3515 2592 | 30.1442 8330 | 29.9390 0610 | 29.7356 7265 | 33 |
| 34 | 31.1955 4818 | 30.9764 9396 | 30.7595 7524 | 30.5447 6785 | 34 |
| 35 | 32.0353 7132 | 31.8042 2109 | 31.5753 8549 | 31.3488 3761 | 35 |
| 36 | 32.8710 1624 | 32.6274 8886 | 32.3864 6445 | 32.1479 1315 | 36 |
| 37 | 33.7025 0372 | 33.4463 2129 | 33.1928 3955 | 32.9420 2550 | 37 |
| 38 | 34.5298 5445 | 34.2607 4227 | 33.9945 3808 | 33.7312 0546 | 38 |
| 39 | 35.3530 8900 | 35.0707 7557 | 34.7915 8716 | 34.5154 8369 | 39 |
| 40 | 36.1722 2786 | 35.8764 4482 | 35.5840 1374 | 35.2948 9062 | 40 |
| 41 | 36.9872 9141 | 36.6777 7355 | 36.3718 4465 | 36.0694 5652 | 41 |
| 42 | 37.7982 9991 | 37.4747 8513 | 37.1551 0653 | 36.8392 1145 | 42 |
| 43 | 38.6052 7354 | 38.2675 0282 | 37.9338 2588 | 37.6041 8529 | 43 |
| 44 | 39.4082 3238 | 39.0559 4976 | 38.7080 2904 | 38.3644 0774 | 44 |
| 45 | 40.2071 9640 | 39.8401 4896 | 39.4777 4221 | 39.1199 0831 | 45 |
| 46 | 41.0021 8547 | 40.6201 2329 | 40.2429 9143 | 39.8707 1634 | 46 |
| 47 | 41.7932 1937 | 41.3958 9552 | 41.0038 0258 | 40.6168 6096 | 47 |
| 48 | 42.5803 1778 | 42.1674 8829 | 41.7602 0141 | 41.3583 7114 | 48 |
| 49 | 43.3635 0028 | 42.9349 2412 | 42.5122 1349 | 42.0952 7566 | 49 |
| 50 | 44.1427 8635 | 43.6982 2540 | 43.2598 6428 | 42.8276 0314 | 50 |
| 51 | 44.9181 9537 | 44.4574 1441 | 44.0031 7907 | 43.5553 8201 | 51 |
| 52 | 45.6897 4664 | 45.2125 1329 | 44.7421 8301 | 44.2786 4050 | 52 |
| 53 | 46.4574 5934 | 45.9635 4409 | 45.4769 0108 | 44.9974 0671 | 53 |
| 54 | 47.2213 5258 | 46.7105 2873 | 46.2073 5816 | 45.7117 0853 | 54 |
| 55 | 47.9814 4535 | 47.4534 8900 | 46.9335 7895 | 46.4215 7370 | 55 |
| 56 | 48.7377 5657 | 48.1924 4658 | 47.6555 8802 | 47.1270 2976 | 56 |
| 57 | 49.4903 0505 | 48.9274 2304 | 48.3734 0980 | 47.8281 0410 | 57 |
| 58 | 50.2391 0950 | 49.6584 3982 | 49.0870 6856 | 48.5248 2396 | 58 |
| 59 | 50.9841 8855 | 50.3855 1826 | 49.7965 8846 | 49.2172 1636 | 59 |
| 60 | 51.7255 6075 | 51.1086 7958 | 50.5019 9350 | 49.9053 0818 | 60 |

Table
8

## TABLE 8

$$a_{\overline{n}|i} = \frac{1 - (1 + i)^{-n}}{i}$$

| n | $\frac{1}{2}$ % | $\frac{13}{24}$ % | $\frac{7}{12}$ % | $\frac{5}{8}$ % | n |
|---|---|---|---|---|---|
| 61 | 52.4632 4453 | 51.8279 4488 | 51.2033 0754 | 50.5891 2614 | 61 |
| 62 | 53.1972 5824 | 52.5433 3515 | 51.9005 5431 | 51.2686 9679 | 62 |
| 63 | 53.9276 2014 | 53.2548 7126 | 52.5937 5739 | 51.9440 4650 | 63 |
| 64 | 54.6543 4839 | 53.9625 7399 | 53.2829 4024 | 52.6152 0149 | 64 |
| 65 | 55.3774 6109 | 54.6664 6398 | 53.9681 2617 | 53.2821 8781 | 65 |
| 66 | 56.0969 7621 | 55.3665 6177 | 54.6493 3836 | 53.9450 3137 | 66 |
| 67 | 56.8129 1165 | 56.0628 8779 | 55.3265 9986 | 54.6037 5788 | 67 |
| 68 | 57.5252 8522 | 56.7554 6237 | 55.9999 3358 | 55.2583 9293 | 68 |
| 69 | 58.2341 1465 | 57.4443 0571 | 56.6693 6230 | 55.9089 6191 | 69 |
| 70 | 58.9394 1756 | 58.1294 3792 | 57.3349 0867 | 56.5554 9010 | 70 |
| 71 | 59.6412 1151 | 58.8108 7900 | 57.9965 9520 | 57.1980 0259 | 71 |
| 72 | 60.3395 1394 | 59.4886 4882 | 58.6544 4427 | 57.8365 2431 | 72 |
| 73 | 61.0343 4222 | 60.1627 6716 | 59.3084 7815 | 58.4710 8006 | 73 |
| 74 | 61.7257 1366 | 60.8332 5370 | 59.9587 1896 | 59.1016 9447 | 74 |
| 75 | 62.4136 4543 | 61.5001 2801 | 60.6051 8869 | 59.7283 9202 | 75 |
| 76 | 63.0981 5466 | 62.1634 0954 | 61.2479 0922 | 60.3511 9704 | 76 |
| 77 | 63.7792 5836 | 62.8231 1765 | 61.8869 0229 | 60.9701 3370 | 77 |
| 78 | 64.4569 7350 | 63.4792 7160 | 62.5221 8952 | 61.5852 2604 | 78 |
| 79 | 65.1313 1691 | 64.1318 9053 | 63.1537 9239 | 62.1964 9793 | 79 |
| 80 | 65.8023 0538 | 64.7809 9348 | 63.7817 3229 | 62.8039 7309 | 80 |
| 81 | 66.4699 5561 | 65.4265 9940 | 64.4060 3044 | 63.4076 7512 | 81 |
| 82 | 67.1342 8419 | 66.0687 2713 | 65.0267 0798 | 64.0076 2745 | 82 |
| 83 | 67.7953 0765 | 66.7073 9540 | 65.6437 8590 | 64.6038 5337 | 83 |
| 84 | 68.4530 4244 | 67.3426 2286 | 66.2572 8507 | 65.1963 7602 | 84 |
| 85 | 69.1075 0491 | 67.9744 2804 | 66.8672 2625 | 65.7852 1840 | 85 |
| 86 | 69.7587 1135 | 68.6028 2938 | 67.4736 3007 | 66.3704 0338 | 86 |
| 87 | 70.4066 7796 | 69.2278 4522 | 68.0765 1706 | 66.9519 5367 | 87 |
| 88 | 71.0514 2086 | 69.8494 9380 | 68.6759 0759 | 67.5298 9185 | 88 |
| 89 | 71.6929 5608 | 70.4677 9325 | 69.2718 2197 | 68.1042 4035 | 89 |
| 90 | 72.3312 9958 | 71.0827 6162 | 69.8642 8033 | 68.6750 2146 | 90 |
| 91 | 72.9664 6725 | 71.6944 1687 | 70.4533 0273 | 69.2422 5735 | 91 |
| 92 | 73.5984 7487 | 72.3027 7682 | 71.0389 0910 | 69.8059 7004 | 92 |
| 93 | 74.2273 3818 | 72.9078 5925 | 71.6211 1923 | 70.3661 8141 | 93 |
| 94 | 74.8530 7282 | 73.5096 8181 | 72.1999 5284 | 70.9229 1320 | 94 |
| 95 | 75.4756 9434 | 74.1082 6206 | 72.7754 2950 | 71.4761 8703 | 95 |
| 96 | 76.0952 1825 | 74.7036 1746 | 73.3475 6869 | 72.0260 2438 | 96 |
| 97 | 76.7116 5995 | 75.2957 6540 | 73.9163 8975 | 72.5724 4659 | 97 |
| 98 | 77.3250 3478 | 75.8847 2315 | 74.4819 1193 | 73.1154 7487 | 98 |
| 99 | 77.9353 5799 | 76.4705 0790 | 75.0441 5436 | 73.6551 3030 | 99 |
| 100 | 78.5426 4477 | 77.0531 3674 | 75.6031 3606 | 74.1914 3384 | 100 |
| 101 | 79.1469 1021 | 77.6326 2668 | 76.1588 7596 | 74.7244 0630 | 101 |
| 102 | 79.7481 6937 | 78.2089 9463 | 76.7113 9283 | 75.2540 6838 | 102 |
| 103 | 80.3464 3718 | 78.7822 5740 | 77.2607 0538 | 75.7804 4062 | 103 |
| 104 | 80.9417 2854 | 79.3524 3173 | 77.8068 3219 | 76.3035 4348 | 104 |
| 105 | 81.5340 5825 | 79.9195 3425 | 78.3497 9174 | 76.8233 9724 | 105 |
| 106 | 82.1234 4104 | 80.4835 8152 | 78.8896 0240 | 77.3400 2210 | 106 |
| 107 | 82.7098 9158 | 81.0445 8999 | 79.4262 8241 | 77.8534 3812 | 107 |
| 108 | 83.2934 2446 | 81.6025 7603 | 79.9598 4996 | 78.3636 6521 | 108 |
| 109 | 83.8740 5419 | 82.1575 5594 | 80.4903 2307 | 78.8707 2319 | 109 |
| 110 | 84.4517 9522 | 82.7095 4590 | 81.0177 1971 | 79.3746 3174 | 110 |
| 111 | 85.0266 6191 | 83.2585 6202 | 81.5420 5770 | 79.8754 1043 | 111 |
| 112 | 85.5986 6856 | 83.8046 2033 | 82.0633 5480 | 80.3730 7868 | 112 |
| 113 | 86.1678 2942 | 84.3477 3675 | 82.5816 2863 | 80.8676 5583 | 113 |
| 114 | 86.7341 5862 | 84.8879 2715 | 83.0968 9674 | 81.3591 6108 | 114 |
| 115 | 87.2976 7027 | 85.4252 0728 | 83.6091 7654 | 81.8476 1349 | 115 |
| 116 | 87.8583 7838 | 85.9595 9281 | 84.1184 8537 | 82.3330 3204 | 116 |
| 117 | 88.4162 9690 | 86.4910 9936 | 84.6248 4047 | 82.8154 3557 | 117 |
| 118 | 88.9714 3970 | 87.0197 4242 | 85.1282 5896 | 83.2948 4280 | 118 |
| 119 | 89.5238 2059 | 87.5455 3743 | 85.6287 5787 | 83.7712 7235 | 119 |
| 120 | 90.0734 5333 | 88.0684 9972 | 86.1263 5414 | 84.2447 4271 | 120 |

**TABLE   8**

$$a_{\overline{n}|i} = \frac{1-(1+i)^{-n}}{i}$$

| n | $\frac{1}{2}\%$ | $\frac{13}{24}\%$ | $\frac{7}{12}\%$ | $\frac{5}{8}\%$ | n |
|---|---|---|---|---|---|
| 121 | 90.6203 5157 | 88.5886 4456 | 86.6210 6460 | 84.7152 7226 | 121 |
| 122 | 91.1645 2892 | 89.1059 8713 | 87.1129 0598 | 85.1828 7926 | 122 |
| 123 | 91.7059 9893 | 89.6205 4253 | 87.6018 9493 | 85.6475 8188 | 123 |
| 124 | 92.2447 7505 | 90.1323 2576 | 88.0880 4798 | 86.1093 9814 | 124 |
| 125 | 92.7808 7070 | 90.6413 5177 | 88.5713 8159 | 86.5683 4598 | 125 |
| 126 | 93.3142 9921 | 91.1476 3541 | 89.0519 1210 | 87.0244 4320 | 126 |
| 127 | 93.8450 7384 | 91.6511 9146 | 89.5296 5577 | 87.4777 0753 | 127 |
| 128 | 94.3732 0780 | 92.1520 3461 | 90.0046 2877 | 87.9281 5655 | 128 |
| 129 | 94.8987 1423 | 92.6501 7947 | 90.4768 4716 | 88.3758 0776 | 129 |
| 130 | 95.4216 0619 | 93.1456 4058 | 90.9463 2692 | 88.8206 7852 | 130 |
| 131 | 95.9418 9671 | 93.6384 3241 | 91.4130 8393 | 89.2627 8610 | 131 |
| 132 | 96.4595 9872 | 94.1285 6932 | 91.8771 3399 | 89.7021 4768 | 132 |
| 133 | 96.9747 2509 | 94.6160 6563 | 92.3384 9278 | 90.1387 8030 | 133 |
| 134 | 97.4872 8865 | 95.1009 3557 | 92.7971 7592 | 90.5727 0092 | 134 |
| 135 | 97.9973 0214 | 95.5831 9327 | 93.2531 9893 | 91.0039 2638 | 135 |
| 136 | 98.5047 7825 | 96.0628 5282 | 93.7065 7722 | 91.4324 7342 | 136 |
| 137 | 99.0097 2960 | 96.5399 2820 | 94.1573 2616 | 91.8583 5868 | 137 |
| 138 | 99.5121 6876 | 97.0144 3336 | 94.6054 6097 | 92.2815 9869 | 138 |
| 139 | 100.0121 0821 | 97.4863 8212 | 95.0509 9682 | 92.7022 0988 | 139 |
| 140 | 100.5095 6041 | 97.9557 8827 | 95.4939 4878 | 93.1202 0857 | 140 |
| 141 | 101.0045 3772 | 98.4226 6550 | 95.9343 3185 | 93.5356 1100 | 141 |
| 142 | 101.4970 5246 | 98.8870 2743 | 96.3721 6091 | 93.9484 3330 | 142 |
| 143 | 101.9871 1688 | 99.3488 8762 | 96.8074 5078 | 94.3586 9148 | 143 |
| 144 | 102.4747 4316 | 99.8082 5955 | 97.2402 1619 | 94.7664 0147 | 144 |
| 145 | 102.9599 4344 | 100.2651 5662 | 97.6704 7177 | 95.1715 7910 | 145 |
| 146 | 103.4427 2979 | 100.7195 9216 | 98.0982 3208 | 95.5742 4010 | 146 |
| 147 | 103.9231 1422 | 101.1715 7944 | 98.5235 1160 | 95.9744 0010 | 147 |
| 148 | 104.4011 0868 | 101.6211 3164 | 98.9463 2470 | 96.3720 7463 | 148 |
| 149 | 104.8767 2506 | 102.0682 6189 | 99.3666 8570 | 96.7672 7913 | 149 |
| 150 | 105.3499 7518 | 102.5129 8323 | 99.7846 0882 | 97.1600 2895 | 150 |
| 151 | 105.8208 7083 | 102.9553 0864 | 100.2001 0819 | 97.5503 3933 | 151 |
| 152 | 106.2894 2371 | 103.3952 5103 | 100.6131 9786 | 97.9382 2542 | 152 |
| 153 | 106.7556 4548 | 103.8328 2324 | 101.0238 9183 | 98.3237 0228 | 153 |
| 154 | 107.2195 4774 | 104.2680 3804 | 101.4322 0397 | 98.7067 8488 | 154 |
| 155 | 107.6811 4203 | 104.7009 0812 | 101.8381 4811 | 99.0874 8808 | 155 |
| 156 | 108.1404 3983 | 105.1314 4612 | 102.2417 3797 | 99.4658 2666 | 156 |
| 157 | 108.5974 5257 | 105.5596 6460 | 102.6429 8721 | 99.8418 1532 | 157 |
| 158 | 109.0521 9161 | 105.9855 7606 | 103.0419 0941 | 100.2154 6864 | 158 |
| 159 | 109.5046 6827 | 106.4091 9293 | 103.4385 1805 | 100.5868 0113 | 159 |
| 160 | 109.9548 9380 | 106.8305 2758 | 103.8328 2656 | 100.9558 2721 | 160 |
| 161 | 110.4028 7940 | 107.2495 9229 | 104.2248 4828 | 101.3225 6120 | 161 |
| 162 | 110.8486 3622 | 107.6663 9929 | 104.6145 9647 | 101.6870 1734 | 162 |
| 163 | 111.2921 7535 | 108.0809 6075 | 105.0020 8431 | 102.0492 0978 | 163 |
| 164 | 111.7335 0781 | 108.4932 8877 | 105.3873 2491 | 102.4091 5258 | 164 |
| 165 | 112.1726 4458 | 108.9033 9538 | 105.7703 3132 | 102.7668 5971 | 165 |
| 166 | 112.6095 9660 | 109.3112 9254 | 106.1511 1647 | 103.1223 4505 | 166 |
| 167 | 113.0443 7473 | 109.7169 9217 | 106.5296 9326 | 103.4756 2241 | 167 |
| 168 | 113.4769 8978 | 110.1205 0610 | 106.9060 7449 | 103.8267 0550 | 168 |
| 169 | 113.9074 5252 | 110.5218 4610 | 107.2802 7290 | 104.1756 0795 | 169 |
| 170 | 114.3357 7365 | 110.9210 2388 | 107.6523 0114 | 104.5223 4330 | 170 |
| 171 | 114.7619 6383 | 111.3180 5111 | 108.0221 7181 | 104.8669 2502 | 171 |
| 172 | 115.1860 3366 | 111.7129 3935 | 108.3898 9741 | 105.2093 6648 | 172 |
| 173 | 115.6079 9369 | 112.1057 0014 | 108.7554 9038 | 105.5496 8098 | 173 |
| 174 | 116.0278 5442 | 112.4963 4494 | 109.1189 6309 | 105.8878 8172 | 174 |
| 175 | 116.4456 2629 | 112.8848 8515 | 109.4803 2785 | 106.2239 8183 | 175 |
| 176 | 116.8613 1969 | 113.2713 3210 | 109.8395 9687 | 106.5579 9436 | 176 |
| 177 | 117.2749 4496 | 113.6556 9707 | 110.1967 8230 | 106.8899 3229 | 177 |
| 178 | 117.6865 1240 | 114.0379 9129 | 110.5518 9624 | 107.2198 0849 | 178 |
| 179 | 118.0960 3224 | 114.4182 2590 | 110.9049 5070 | 107.5476 3576 | 179 |
| 180 | 118.5035 1467 | 114.7964 1200 | 111.2559 5761 | 107.8734 2684 | 180 |

Table
8

# TABLE 8

$$a_{\overline{n}|i} = \frac{1 - (1 + i)^{-n}}{i}$$

| n | $\frac{1}{2}\%$ | $\frac{13}{24}\%$ | $\frac{7}{12}\%$ | $\frac{5}{8}\%$ | n |
|---|---|---|---|---|---|
| 181 | 118.9089 6982 | 115.1725 6063 | 111.6049 2886 | 108.1971 9438 | 181 |
| 182 | 119.3124 0778 | 115.5466 8276 | 111.9518 7625 | 108.5189 5094 | 182 |
| 183 | 119.7138 3859 | 115.9187 8932 | 112.2968 1151 | 108.8387 0900 | 183 |
| 184 | 120.1132 7223 | 116.2888 9116 | 112.6397 4633 | 109.1564 8100 | 184 |
| 185 | 120.5107 1863 | 116.6569 9908 | 112.9806 9229 | 109.4722 7925 | 185 |
| 186 | 120.9061 8769 | 117.0231 2383 | 113.3196 6093 | 109.7861 1603 | 186 |
| 187 | 121.2996 8925 | 117.3872 7608 | 113.6566 6373 | 110.0980 0351 | 187 |
| 188 | 121.6912 3308 | 117.7494 6647 | 113.9917 1207 | 110.4079 5379 | 188 |
| 189 | 122.0808 2894 | 118.1097 0557 | 114.3248 1731 | 110.7159 7893 | 189 |
| 190 | 122.4684 8651 | 118.4680 0388 | 114.6559 9069 | 111.0220 9086 | 190 |
| 191 | 122.8542 1543 | 118.8243 7186 | 114.9852 4344 | 111.3263 0147 | 191 |
| 192 | 123.2380 2530 | 119.1788 1992 | 115.3125 8668 | 111.6286 2258 | 192 |
| 193 | 123.6199 2567 | 119.5313 5840 | 115.6380 3150 | 111.9290 6592 | 193 |
| 194 | 123.9999 2604 | 119.8819 9758 | 115.9615 8890 | 112.2276 4315 | 194 |
| 195 | 124.3780 3586 | 120.2307 4769 | 116.2832 6982 | 112.5243 6586 | 195 |
| 196 | 124.7542 6454 | 120.5776 1893 | 116.6030 8516 | 112.8192 4558 | 196 |
| 197 | 125.1286 2143 | 120.9226 2139 | 116.9210 4573 | 113.1122 9374 | 197 |
| 198 | 125.5011 1585 | 121.2657 6516 | 117.2371 6228 | 113.4035 2173 | 198 |
| 199 | 125.8717 5707 | 121.6070 6026 | 117.5514 4552 | 113.6929 4085 | 199 |
| 200 | 126.2405 5430 | 121.9465 1662 | 117.8639 0606 | 113.9805 6234 | 200 |
| 201 | 126.6075 1671 | 122.2841 4418 | 118.1745 5450 | 114.2663 9735 | 201 |
| 202 | 126.9726 5345 | 122.6199 5277 | 118.4834 0132 | 114.5504 5700 | 202 |
| 203 | 127.3359 7358 | 122.9539 5219 | 118.7904 5699 | 114.8327 5230 | 203 |
| 204 | 127.6974 8615 | 123.2861 5220 | 119.0957 3189 | 115.1132 9421 | 204 |
| 205 | 128.0572 0015 | 123.6165 6249 | 119.3992 3634 | 115.3920 9362 | 205 |
| 206 | 128.4151 2452 | 123.9451 9269 | 119.7009 8062 | 115.6691 6136 | 206 |
| 207 | 128.7712 6818 | 124.2720 5241 | 120.0009 7493 | 115.9445 0819 | 207 |
| 208 | 129.1256 3998 | 124.5971 5117 | 120.2992 2943 | 116.2181 4478 | 208 |
| 209 | 129.4782 4874 | 124.9204 9847 | 120.5957 5420 | 116.4900 8177 | 209 |
| 210 | 129.8291 0322 | 125.2421 0374 | 120.8905 5927 | 116.7603 2971 | 210 |
| 211 | 130.1782 1216 | 125.5619 7637 | 121.1836 5461 | 117.0288 9909 | 211 |
| 212 | 130.5255 8424 | 125.8801 2569 | 121.4750 5016 | 117.2958 0034 | 212 |
| 213 | 130.8712 2810 | 126.1965 6099 | 121.7647 5575 | 117.5610 4382 | 213 |
| 214 | 131.2151 5234 | 126.5112 9149 | 122.0527 8119 | 117.8246 3982 | 214 |
| 215 | 131.5573 6551 | 126.8243 2639 | 122.3391 3623 | 118.0865 9858 | 215 |
| 216 | 131.8978 7613 | 127.1356 7482 | 122.6238 3055 | 118.3469 3026 | 216 |
| 217 | 132.2366 9267 | 127.4453 4586 | 122.9068 7379 | 118.6056 4498 | 217 |
| 218 | 132.5738 2355 | 127.7533 4856 | 123.1882 7551 | 118.8627 5278 | 218 |
| 219 | 132.9092 7716 | 128.0596 9189 | 123.4680 4525 | 119.1182 6363 | 219 |
| 220 | 133.2430 6186 | 128.3643 8481 | 123.7461 9246 | 119.3721 8746 | 220 |
| 221 | 133.5751 8593 | 128.6674 3619 | 124.0227 2655 | 119.6245 3412 | 221 |
| 222 | 133.9056 5764 | 128.9688 5490 | 124.2976 5689 | 119.8753 1341 | 222 |
| 223 | 134.2344 8521 | 129.2686 4971 | 124.5709 9276 | 120.1245 3507 | 223 |
| 224 | 134.5616 7683 | 129.5668 2939 | 124.8427 4343 | 120.3722 0876 | 224 |
| 225 | 134.8872 4062 | 129.8634 0262 | 125.1129 1807 | 120.6183 4411 | 225 |
| 226 | 135.2111 8470 | 130.1583 7807 | 125.3815 2584 | 120.8629 5067 | 226 |
| 227 | 135.5335 1712 | 130.4517 6435 | 125.6485 7581 | 121.1060 3793 | 227 |
| 228 | 135.8542 4589 | 130.7435 7001 | 125.9140 7703 | 121.3476 1534 | 228 |
| 229 | 136.1733 7899 | 131.0338 0358 | 126.1780 3847 | 121.5876 9226 | 229 |
| 230 | 136.4909 2437 | 131.3224 7351 | 126.4404 6907 | 121.8262 7802 | 230 |
| 231 | 136.8068 8992 | 131.6095 8824 | 126.7013 7770 | 122.0633 8188 | 231 |
| 232 | 137.1212 8350 | 131.8951 5615 | 126.9607 7319 | 122.2990 1305 | 232 |
| 233 | 137.4341 1294 | 132.1791 8556 | 127.2186 6431 | 122.5331 8067 | 233 |
| 234 | 137.7453 8601 | 132.4616 8476 | 127.4750 5980 | 122.7658 9384 | 234 |
| 235 | 138.0551 1045 | 132.7426 6201 | 127.7299 6832 | 122.9971 6158 | 235 |
| 236 | 138.3632 9398 | 133.0221 2550 | 127.9833 9849 | 123.2269 9287 | 236 |
| 237 | 138.6699 4426 | 133.3000 8338 | 128.2353 5909 | 123.4553 9664 | 237 |
| 238 | 138.9750 6892 | 133.5765 4377 | 128.4858 5806 | 123.6823 8176 | 238 |
| 239 | 139.2786 7554 | 133.8515 1473 | 128.7349 0445 | 123.9079 5703 | 239 |
| 240 | 139.5807 7168 | 134.1250 0429 | 128.9825 0650 | 124.1321 3121 | 240 |

**PRESENT VALUE OF ANNUITY**
When Periodic Payment Is 1

## TABLE 8

$$a_{\overline{n}|i} = \frac{1 - (1 + i)^{-n}}{i}$$

| $n$ | $\frac{2}{3}\%$ | $\frac{3}{4}\%$ | $\frac{7}{8}\%$ | 1% | $n$ |
|---|---|---|---|---|---|
| 1 | 0.9933 7748 | 0.9925 5583 | 0.9913 2590 | 0.9900 9901 | 1 |
| 2 | 1.9801 7631 | 1.9777 2291 | 1.9740 5294 | 1.9703 9506 | 2 |
| 3 | 2.9604 4004 | 2.9555 5624 | 2.9482 5570 | 2.9409 8521 | 3 |
| 4 | 3.9342 1196 | 3.9261 1041 | 3.9140 0813 | 3.9019 6555 | 4 |
| 5 | 4.9015 3506 | 4.8894 3961 | 4.8713 8352 | 4.8534 3124 | 5 |
| 6 | 5.8624 5205 | 5.8455 9763 | 5.8204 5454 | 5.7954 7647 | 6 |
| 7 | 6.8170 0535 | 6.7946 3785 | 6.7612 9323 | 6.7281 9453 | 7 |
| 8 | 7.7652 3710 | 7.7366 1325 | 7.6939 7098 | 7.6516 7775 | 8 |
| 9 | 8.7071 8917 | 8.6715 7642 | 8.6185 5859 | 8.5660 1758 | 9 |
| 10 | 9.6429 0315 | 9.5995 7958 | 9.5351 2624 | 9.4713 0453 | 10 |
| 11 | 10.5724 2035 | 10.5206 7452 | 10.4437 4348 | 10.3676 2825 | 11 |
| 12 | 11.4957 8180 | 11.4349 1267 | 11.3444 7929 | 11.2550 7747 | 12 |
| 13 | 12.4130 2828 | 12.3423 4508 | 12.2374 0202 | 12.1337 4007 | 13 |
| 14 | 13.3242 0028 | 13.2430 2242 | 13.1225 7945 | 13.0037 0304 | 14 |
| 15 | 14.2293 3802 | 14.1369 9495 | 14.0000 7876 | 13.8650 5252 | 15 |
| 16 | 15.1284 8148 | 15.0243 1261 | 14.8699 6656 | 14.7178 7378 | 16 |
| 17 | 16.0216 7035 | 15.9050 2492 | 15.7323 0885 | 15.5622 5127 | 17 |
| 18 | 16.9089 4405 | 16.7791 8107 | 16.5871 7111 | 16.3982 6858 | 18 |
| 19 | 17.7903 4177 | 17.6468 2984 | 17.4346 1820 | 17.2260 0850 | 19 |
| 20 | 18.6659 0242 | 18.5080 1969 | 18.2747 1445 | 18.0455 5297 | 20 |
| 21 | 19.5356 6466 | 19.3627 9870 | 19.1075 2361 | 18.8569 8313 | 21 |
| 22 | 20.3996 6688 | 20.2112 1459 | 19.9331 0891 | 19.6603 7934 | 22 |
| 23 | 21.2579 4723 | 21.0533 1473 | 20.7515 3300 | 20.4558 2113 | 23 |
| 24 | 22.1105 4361 | 21.8891 4614 | 21.5628 5799 | 21.2433 8726 | 24 |
| 25 | 22.9574 9365 | 22.7187 5547 | 22.3671 4547 | 22.0231 5570 | 25 |
| 26 | 23.7988 3475 | 23.5421 8905 | 23.1644 5647 | 22.7952 0366 | 26 |
| 27 | 24.6346 0406 | 24.3594 9286 | 23.9548 5152 | 23.5596 0759 | 27 |
| 28 | 25.4648 3847 | 25.1707 1251 | 24.7383 9060 | 24.3164 4316 | 28 |
| 29 | 26.2895 7464 | 25.9758 9331 | 25.5151 3319 | 25.0657 8530 | 29 |
| 30 | 27.1088 4898 | 26.7750 8021 | 26.2851 3823 | 25.8077 0822 | 30 |
| 31 | 27.9226 9766 | 27.5683 1783 | 27.0484 6417 | 26.5422 8537 | 31 |
| 32 | 28.7311 5662 | 28.3556 5045 | 27.8051 6894 | 27.2695 8947 | 32 |
| 33 | 29.5342 6154 | 29.1371 2203 | 28.5553 0998 | 27.9896 9255 | 33 |
| 34 | 30.3320 4789 | 29.9127 7621 | 29.2989 4422 | 28.7026 6589 | 34 |
| 35 | 31.1245 5088 | 30.6826 5629 | 30.0361 2809 | 29.4085 8009 | 35 |
| 36 | 31.9118 0551 | 31.4468 0525 | 30.7669 1757 | 30.1075 0504 | 36 |
| 37 | 32.6938 4653 | 32.2052 6576 | 31.4913 6810 | 30.7995 0994 | 37 |
| 38 | 33.4707 0848 | 32.9580 8016 | 32.2095 3467 | 31.4846 6330 | 38 |
| 39 | 34.2424 2564 | 33.7052 9048 | 32.9214 7179 | 32.1630 3298 | 39 |
| 40 | 35.0090 3209 | 34.4469 3844 | 33.6272 3350 | 32.8346 8611 | 40 |
| 41 | 35.7705 6168 | 35.1830 6545 | 34.3268 7335 | 33.4996 8922 | 41 |
| 42 | 36.5270 4803 | 35.9137 1260 | 35.0204 4446 | 34.1581 0814 | 42 |
| 43 | 37.2785 2453 | 36.6389 2070 | 35.7079 9947 | 34.8100 0806 | 43 |
| 44 | 38.0250 2437 | 37.3587 3022 | 36.3895 9055 | 35.4554 5352 | 44 |
| 45 | 38.7665 8050 | 38.0731 8136 | 37.0652 6944 | 36.0945 0844 | 45 |
| 46 | 39.5032 2566 | 38.7823 1401 | 37.7350 8743 | 36.7272 3608 | 46 |
| 47 | 40.2349 9238 | 39.4861 6775 | 38.3990 9535 | 37.3536 9909 | 47 |
| 48 | 40.9619 1296 | 40.1847 8189 | 39.0573 4359 | 37.9739 5949 | 48 |
| 49 | 41.6840 1949 | 40.8781 9542 | 39.7098 8212 | 38.5880 7871 | 49 |
| 50 | 42.4013 4387 | 41.5664 4707 | 40.3567 6047 | 39.1961 1753 | 50 |
| 51 | 43.1139 1775 | 42.2495 7525 | 40.9980 2772 | 39.7981 3617 | 51 |
| 52 | 43.8217 7260 | 42.9276 1812 | 41.6337 3256 | 40.3941 9423 | 52 |
| 53 | 44.5249 3967 | 43.6006 1351 | 42.2639 2324 | 40.9843 5072 | 53 |
| 54 | 45.2234 5000 | 44.2685 9902 | 42.8886 4757 | 41.5686 6408 | 54 |
| 55 | 45.9173 3444 | 44.9316 1193 | 43.5079 5298 | 42.1471 9216 | 55 |
| 56 | 46.6066 2362 | 45.5896 8926 | 44.1218 8647 | 42.7199 9224 | 56 |
| 57 | 47.2913 4796 | 46.2428 6776 | 44.7304 9465 | 43.2871 2102 | 57 |
| 58 | 47.9715 3771 | 46.8911 8388 | 45.3338 2369 | 43.8486 3468 | 58 |
| 59 | 48.6472 2289 | 47.5346 7382 | 45.9319 1939 | 44.4045 8879 | 59 |
| 60 | 49.3184 3334 | 48.1733 7352 | 46.5248 2716 | 44.9550 3841 | 60 |

Table
8

**TABLE 8**

$$a_{\overline{n}|i} = \frac{1-(1+i)^{-n}}{i}$$

| $n$ | $\frac{2}{3}\%$ | $\frac{3}{4}\%$ | $\frac{7}{8}\%$ | 1% | $n$ |
|---|---|---|---|---|---|
| 61 | 49.9851 9868 | 48.8073 1863 | 47.1125 9198 | 45.5000 3803 | 61 |
| 62 | 50.6475 4836 | 49.4365 4455 | 47.6952 5846 | 46.0396 4161 | 62 |
| 63 | 51.3055 1161 | 50.0610 8640 | 48.2728 7084 | 46.5739 0258 | 63 |
| 64 | 51.9591 1749 | 50.6809 7906 | 48.8454 7296 | 47.1028 7385 | 64 |
| 65 | 52.6083 9486 | 51.2962 5713 | 49.4131 0826 | 47.6266 0777 | 65 |
| 66 | 53.2533 7238 | 51.9069 5497 | 49.9758 1984 | 48.1451 5621 | 66 |
| 67 | 53.8940 7852 | 52.5131 0667 | 50.5336 5039 | 48.6585 7050 | 67 |
| 68 | 54.5305 4158 | 53.1147 4607 | 51.0866 4227 | 49.1669 0149 | 68 |
| 69 | 55.1627 8965 | 53.7119 0677 | 51.6348 3745 | 49.6701 9949 | 69 |
| 70 | 55.7908 5064 | 54.3046 2210 | 52.1782 7752 | 50.1685 1435 | 70 |
| 71 | 56.4147 5230 | 54.8929 2516 | 52.7170 0374 | 50.6618 9539 | 71 |
| 72 | 57.0345 2215 | 55.4768 4880 | 53.2510 5699 | 51.1503 9148 | 72 |
| 73 | 57.6501 8756 | 56.0564 2561 | 53.7804 7781 | 51.6340 5097 | 73 |
| 74 | 58.2617 7573 | 56.6316 8795 | 54.3053 0638 | 52.1129 2175 | 74 |
| 75 | 58.8693 1363 | 57.2026 6794 | 54.8255 8253 | 52.5870 5124 | 75 |
| 76 | 59.4728 2811 | 57.7693 9746 | 55.3413 4575 | 53.0564 8638 | 76 |
| 77 | 60.0723 4581 | 58.3319 0815 | 55.8526 3520 | 53.5212 7364 | 77 |
| 78 | 60.6678 9319 | 58.8902 3141 | 56.3594 8966 | 53.9814 5905 | 78 |
| 79 | 61.2594 9654 | 59.4443 9842 | 56.8619 4762 | 54.4370 8817 | 79 |
| 80 | 61.8471 8200 | 59.9944 4012 | 57.3600 4721 | 54.8882 0611 | 80 |
| 81 | 62.4309 7549 | 60.5403 8722 | 57.8538 2623 | 55.3348 5753 | 81 |
| 82 | 63.0109 0281 | 61.0822 7019 | 58.3433 2216 | 55.7770 8666 | 82 |
| 83 | 63.5869 8954 | 61.6201 1930 | 58.8285 7215 | 56.2149 3729 | 83 |
| 84 | 64.1592 6114 | 62.1539 6456 | 59.3096 1304 | 56.6484 5276 | 84 |
| 85 | 64.7277 4285 | 62.6838 3579 | 59.7864 8133 | 57.0776 7600 | 85 |
| 86 | 65.2924 5979 | 63.2097 6257 | 60.2592 1321 | 57.5026 4951 | 86 |
| 87 | 65.8534 3687 | 63.7317 7427 | 60.7278 4457 | 57.9234 1535 | 87 |
| 88 | 66.4106 9888 | 64.2499 0002 | 61.1924 1097 | 58.3400 1520 | 88 |
| 89 | 66.9642 7041 | 64.7641 6875 | 61.6529 4768 | 58.7524 9030 | 89 |
| 90 | 67.5141 7591 | 65.2746 0918 | 62.1094 8965 | 59.1608 8148 | 90 |
| 91 | 68.0604 3964 | 65.7812 4981 | 62.5620 7152 | 59.5652 2919 | 91 |
| 92 | 68.6030 8574 | 66.2841 1892 | 63.0107 2765 | 59.9655 7346 | 92 |
| 93 | 69.1421 3815 | 66.7832 4458 | 63.4554 9210 | 60.3619 5392 | 93 |
| 94 | 69.6776 2068 | 67.2786 5467 | 63.8963 9861 | 60.7544 0982 | 94 |
| 95 | 70.2095 5696 | 67.7703 7685 | 64.3334 8066 | 61.1429 8002 | 95 |
| 96 | 70.7379 7049 | 68.2584 3856 | 64.7667 7141 | 61.5277 0299 | 96 |
| 97 | 71.2628 8460 | 68.7428 6705 | 65.1963 0375 | 61.9086 1682 | 97 |
| 98 | 71.7843 2245 | 69.2236 8938 | 65.6221 1028 | 62.2857 5923 | 98 |
| 99 | 72.3023 0707 | 69.7009 3239 | 66.0442 2333 | 62.6591 6755 | 99 |
| 100 | 72.8168 6132 | 70.1746 2272 | 66.4626 7492 | 63.0288 7877 | 100 |
| 101 | 73.3280 0794 | 70.6447 8682 | 66.8774 9683 | 63.3949 2947 | 101 |
| 102 | 73.8357 6948 | 71.1114 5094 | 67.2887 2052 | 63.7573 5591 | 102 |
| 103 | 74.3401 6835 | 71.5746 4113 | 67.6963 7722 | 64.1161 9397 | 103 |
| 104 | 74.8412 2684 | 72.0343 8325 | 68.1004 9786 | 64.4714 7918 | 104 |
| 105 | 75.3389 6706 | 72.4907 0298 | 68.5011 1312 | 64.8232 4671 | 105 |
| 106 | 75.8334 1099 | 72.9436 2579 | 68.8982 5341 | 65.1715 3140 | 106 |
| 107 | 76.3245 8045 | 73.3931 7696 | 69.2919 4885 | 65.5163 6772 | 107 |
| 108 | 76.8124 9714 | 73.8393 8160 | 69.6822 2935 | 65.8577 8983 | 108 |
| 109 | 77.2971 8259 | 74.2822 6461 | 70.0691 2451 | 66.1958 3151 | 109 |
| 110 | 77.7786 5820 | 74.7218 5073 | 70.4526 6370 | 66.5305 2625 | 110 |
| 111 | 78.2569 4523 | 75.1581 6450 | 70.8328 7604 | 66.8619 0718 | 111 |
| 112 | 78.7320 6480 | 75.5912 3027 | 71.2097 9037 | 67.1900 0710 | 112 |
| 113 | 79.2040 3788 | 76.0210 7223 | 71.5834 3531 | 67.5148 5852 | 113 |
| 114 | 79.6728 8531 | 76.4477 1437 | 71.9538 3922 | 67.8364 9358 | 114 |
| 115 | 80.1386 2779 | 76.8711 8052 | 72.3210 3020 | 68.1549 4414 | 115 |
| 116 | 80.6012 8589 | 77.2914 9431 | 72.6850 3614 | 68.4702 4173 | 116 |
| 117 | 81.0608 8002 | 77.7086 7922 | 73.0458 8465 | 68.7824 1755 | 117 |
| 118 | 81.5174 3048 | 78.1227 5853 | 73.4036 0312 | 69.0915 0252 | 118 |
| 119 | 81.9709 5743 | 78.5337 5536 | 73.7582 1871 | 69.3975 2725 | 119 |
| 120 | 82.4214 8089 | 78.9416 9267 | 74.1097 5832 | 69.7005 2203 | 120 |

**PRESENT VALUE OF ANNUITY**
When Periodic Payment Is 1

# TABLE 8

$$a_{\overline{n}|i} = \frac{1 - (1 + i)^{-n}}{i}$$

| $n$ | $\frac{2}{3}\%$ | $\frac{3}{4}\%$ | $\frac{7}{8}\%$ | 1% | $n$ |
|---|---|---|---|---|---|
| 121 | 82.8690 2076 | 79.3465 9322 | 74.4582 4864 | 70.0005 1686 | 121 |
| 122 | 83.3135 9678 | 79.7484 7962 | 74.8037 1613 | 70.2975 4145 | 122 |
| 123 | 83.7552 2859 | 80.1473 7432 | 75.1461 8699 | 70.5916 2520 | 123 |
| 124 | 84.1939 3568 | 80.5432 9957 | 75.4856 8723 | 70.8827 9722 | 124 |
| 125 | 84.6297 3743 | 80.9362 7749 | 75.8222 4261 | 71.1710 8636 | 125 |
| 126 | 85.0626 5308 | 81.3263 3001 | 76.1558 7867 | 71.4565 2115 | 126 |
| 127 | 85.4927 0173 | 81.7134 7892 | 76.4866 2074 | 71.7391 2985 | 127 |
| 128 | 85.9199 0238 | 82.0977 4583 | 76.8144 9391 | 72.0189 4045 | 128 |
| 129 | 86.3442 7389 | 82.4791 5219 | 77.1395 2309 | 72.2959 8064 | 129 |
| 130 | 86.7658 3499 | 82.8577 1929 | 77.4617 3292 | 72.5702 7786 | 130 |
| 131 | 87.1846 0430 | 83.2334 6828 | 77.7811 4788 | 72.8418 5927 | 131 |
| 132 | 87.6006 0029 | 83.6064 2013 | 78.0977 9220 | 73.1107 5175 | 132 |
| 133 | 88.0138 4135 | 83.9765 9566 | 78.4116 8991 | 73.3769 8193 | 133 |
| 134 | 88.4243 4571 | 84.3440 1554 | 78.7228 6484 | 73.6405 7617 | 134 |
| 135 | 88.8321 3150 | 84.7087 0029 | 79.0313 4061 | 73.9015 6056 | 135 |
| 136 | 89.2372 1673 | 85.0706 7026 | 79.3371 4063 | 74.1599 6095 | 136 |
| 137 | 89.6396 1926 | 85.4299 4567 | 79.6402 8811 | 74.4158 0293 | 137 |
| 138 | 90.0393 5688 | 85.7865 4657 | 79.9408 0606 | 74.6691 1181 | 138 |
| 139 | 90.4364 4724 | 86.1404 9288 | 80.2387 1728 | 74.9199 1268 | 139 |
| 140 | 90.8309 0785 | 86.4918 0434 | 80.5340 4440 | 75.1682 3038 | 140 |
| 141 | 91.2227 5614 | 86.8405 0059 | 80.8268 0981 | 75.4140 8948 | 141 |
| 142 | 91.6120 0941 | 87.1866 0108 | 81.1170 3575 | 75.6575 1434 | 142 |
| 143 | 91.9986 8485 | 87.5301 2514 | 81.4047 4423 | 75.8985 2905 | 143 |
| 144 | 92.3827 9952 | 87.8710 9195 | 81.6899 5711 | 76.1371 5747 | 144 |
| 145 | 92.7643 7038 | 88.2095 2055 | 81.9726 9602 | 76.3734 2324 | 145 |
| 146 | 93.1434 1429 | 88.5454 2982 | 82.2529 8242 | 76.6073 4974 | 146 |
| 147 | 93.5199 4797 | 88.8788 3854 | 82.5308 3759 | 76.8389 6014 | 147 |
| 148 | 93.8939 8805 | 89.2097 6530 | 82.8062 8262 | 77.0682 7737 | 148 |
| 149 | 94.2655 5104 | 89.5382 2858 | 83.0793 3841 | 77.2953 2413 | 149 |
| 150 | 94.6346 5335 | 89.8642 4673 | 83.3500 2569 | 77.5201 2290 | 150 |
| 151 | 95.0013 1128 | 90.1878 3795 | 83.6183 6499 | 77.7426 9594 | 151 |
| 152 | 95.3655 4100 | 90.5090 2029 | 83.8843 7670 | 77.9630 6529 | 152 |
| 153 | 95.7273 5861 | 90.8278 1171 | 84.1480 8099 | 78.1812 5276 | 153 |
| 154 | 96.0867 8008 | 91.1442 2998 | 84.4094 9788 | 78.3972 7996 | 154 |
| 155 | 96.4438 2127 | 91.4582 9279 | 84.6686 4722 | 78.6111 6828 | 155 |
| 156 | 96.7984 9795 | 91.7700 1765 | 84.9255 4867 | 78.8229 3889 | 156 |
| 157 | 97.1508 2578 | 92.0794 2199 | 85.1802 2173 | 79.0326 1276 | 157 |
| 158 | 97.5008 2031 | 92.3865 2307 | 85.4326 8573 | 79.2402 1065 | 158 |
| 159 | 97.8484 9700 | 92.6913 3803 | 85.6829 5983 | 79.4457 5312 | 159 |
| 160 | 98.1938 7119 | 92.9938 8390 | 85.9310 6303 | 79.6492 6052 | 160 |
| 161 | 98.5369 5813 | 93.2941 7757 | 86.1770 1415 | 79.8507 5299 | 161 |
| 162 | 98.8777 7298 | 93.5922 3580 | 86.4208 3187 | 80.0502 5048 | 162 |
| 163 | 99.2163 3078 | 93.8880 7524 | 86.6625 3470 | 80.2477 7275 | 163 |
| 164 | 99.5526 4647 | 94.1817 1239 | 86.9021 4096 | 80.4433 3936 | 164 |
| 165 | 99.8867 3490 | 94.4731 6367 | 87.1396 6886 | 80.6369 6966 | 165 |
| 166 | 100.2186 1083 | 94.7624 4533 | 87.3751 3642 | 80.8286 8284 | 166 |
| 167 | 100.5482 8890 | 95.0495 7352 | 87.6085 6150 | 81.0184 9786 | 167 |
| 168 | 100.8757 8368 | 95.3345 6429 | 87.8399 6184 | 81.2064 3352 | 168 |
| 169 | 101.2011 0961 | 95.6174 3354 | 88.0693 5498 | 81.3925 0844 | 169 |
| 170 | 101.5242 8107 | 95.8981 9706 | 88.2967 5835 | 81.5767 4103 | 170 |
| 171 | 101.8453 1232 | 96.1768 7053 | 88.5221 8919 | 81.7591 4953 | 171 |
| 172 | 102.1642 1754 | 96.4534 6951 | 88.7456 6462 | 81.9397 5201 | 172 |
| 173 | 102.4810 1080 | 96.7280 0944 | 88.9672 0161 | 82.1185 6635 | 173 |
| 174 | 102.7957 0609 | 97.0005 0565 | 89.1868 1696 | 82.2956 1025 | 174 |
| 175 | 103.1083 1731 | 97.2709 7335 | 89.4045 2735 | 82.4709 0123 | 175 |
| 176 | 103.4188 5826 | 97.5394 2764 | 89.6203 4929 | 82.6444 5667 | 176 |
| 177 | 103.7273 4264 | 97.8058 8352 | 89.8342 9917 | 82.8162 9373 | 177 |
| 178 | 104.0337 8408 | 98.0703 5585 | 90.0463 9323 | 82.9864 2944 | 178 |
| 179 | 104.3381 9610 | 98.3328 5940 | 90.2566 4757 | 83.1548 8063 | 179 |
| 180 | 104.6405 9216 | 98.5934 0884 | 90.4650 7813 | 83.3216 6399 | 180 |

Table
8

# TABLE 8

$$a_{\overline{n}|i} = \frac{1 - (1 + i)^{-n}}{i}$$

| $n$ | $\frac{2}{3}\%$ | $\frac{3}{4}\%$ | $\frac{7}{8}\%$ | 1% | $n$ |
|---|---|---|---|---|---|
| 181 | 104.9409 8559 | 98.8520 1869 | 90.6717 0075 | 83.4867 9603 | 181 |
| 182 | 105.2393 8966 | 99.1087 0342 | 90.8765 3110 | 83.6502 9310 | 182 |
| 183 | 105.5358 1754 | 99.3634 7734 | 91.0795 8474 | 83.8121 7138 | 183 |
| 184 | 105.8302 8232 | 99.6163 5468 | 91.2808 7706 | 83.9724 4691 | 184 |
| 185 | 106.1227 9701 | 99.8673 4956 | 91.4804 2336 | 84.1311 3556 | 185 |
| 186 | 106.4133 7451 | 100.1164 7599 | 91.6782 3877 | 84.2882 5303 | 186 |
| 187 | 106.7020 2766 | 100.3637 4788 | 91.8743 3831 | 84.4438 1488 | 187 |
| 188 | 106.9887 6920 | 100.6091 7904 | 92.0687 3686 | 84.5978 3652 | 188 |
| 189 | 107.2736 1179 | 100.8527 8316 | 92.2614 4918 | 84.7503 3318 | 189 |
| 190 | 107.5565 6800 | 101.0945 7386 | 92.4524 8989 | 84.9013 1998 | 190 |
| 191 | 107.8376 5033 | 101.3345 6462 | 92.6418 7350 | 85.0508 1186 | 191 |
| 192 | 108.1168 7119 | 101.5727 6886 | 92.8296 1438 | 85.1988 2363 | 192 |
| 193 | 108.3942 4291 | 101.8091 9986 | 93.0157 2677 | 85.3453 6993 | 193 |
| 194 | 108.6697 7772 | 102.0438 7083 | 93.2002 2480 | 85.4904 6528 | 194 |
| 195 | 108.9434 8780 | 102.2767 9487 | 93.3831 2248 | 85.6341 2404 | 195 |
| 196 | 109.2153 8523 | 102.5079 8498 | 93.5644 3368 | 85.7763 6043 | 196 |
| 197 | 109.4854 8202 | 102.7374 5407 | 93.7441 7218 | 85.9171 8855 | 197 |
| 198 | 109.7537 9009 | 102.9652 1496 | 93.9223 5160 | 86.0566 2232 | 198 |
| 199 | 110.0203 2128 | 103.1912 8036 | 94.0989 8548 | 86.1946 7557 | 199 |
| 200 | 110.2850 8736 | 103.4156 6289 | 94.2740 8721 | 86.3313 6195 | 200 |
| 201 | 110.5481 0003 | 103.6383 7507 | 94.4476 7010 | 86.4666 9500 | 201 |
| 202 | 110.8093 7089 | 103.8594 2935 | 94.6197 4731 | 86.6006 8812 | 202 |
| 203 | 111.0689 1148 | 104.0788 3807 | 94.7903 3191 | 86.7333 5457 | 203 |
| 204 | 111.3267 3326 | 104.2966 1347 | 94.9594 3684 | 86.8647 0750 | 204 |
| 205 | 111.5828 4761 | 104.5127 6771 | 95.1270 7493 | 86.9947 5990 | 205 |
| 206 | 111.8372 6583 | 104.7273 1286 | 95.2932 5891 | 87.1235 2465 | 206 |
| 207 | 112.0899 9917 | 104.9402 6091 | 95.4580 0140 | 87.2510 1451 | 207 |
| 208 | 112.3410 5878 | 105.1516 2373 | 95.6213 1490 | 87.3772 4208 | 208 |
| 209 | 112.5904 5574 | 105.3614 1313 | 95.7832 1179 | 87.5022 1989 | 209 |
| 210 | 112.8382 0107 | 105.5696 4082 | 95.9437 0438 | 87.6259 6028 | 210 |
| 211 | 113.0843 0570 | 105.7763 1843 | 96.1028 0484 | 87.7484 7553 | 211 |
| 212 | 113.3287 8049 | 105.9814 5750 | 96.2605 2524 | 87.8697 7775 | 212 |
| 213 | 113.5716 3625 | 106.1850 6948 | 96.4168 7756 | 87.9898 7896 | 213 |
| 214 | 113.8128 8370 | 106.3871 6574 | 96.5718 7367 | 88.1087 9105 | 214 |
| 215 | 114.0525 3347 | 106.5877 5756 | 96.7255 2532 | 88.2265 2579 | 215 |
| 216 | 114.2905 9616 | 106.7868 5614 | 96.8778 4419 | 88.3430 9484 | 216 |
| 217 | 114.5270 8228 | 106.9844 7259 | 97.0288 4182 | 88.4585 0975 | 217 |
| 218 | 114.7620 0227 | 107.1806 1796 | 97.1785 2968 | 88.5727 8193 | 218 |
| 219 | 114.9953 6649 | 107.3753 0318 | 97.3269 1914 | 88.6859 2270 | 219 |
| 220 | 115.2271 8526 | 107.5685 3914 | 97.4740 2145 | 88.7979 4327 | 220 |
| 221 | 115.4574 6880 | 107.7603 3662 | 97.6198 4779 | 88.9088 5472 | 221 |
| 222 | 115.6862 2728 | 107.9507 0632 | 97.7644 0921 | 89.0186 6804 | 222 |
| 223 | 115.9134 7081 | 108.1396 5888 | 97.9077 1668 | 89.1273 9410 | 223 |
| 224 | 116.1392 0941 | 108.3272 0484 | 98.0497 8110 | 89.2350 4366 | 224 |
| 225 | 116.3634 5306 | 108.5133 5468 | 98.1906 1323 | 89.3416 2739 | 225 |
| 226 | 116.5862 1165 | 108.6981 1879 | 98.3302 2378 | 89.4471 5583 | 226 |
| 227 | 116.8074 9502 | 108.8815 0748 | 98.4686 2332 | 89.5516 3944 | 227 |
| 228 | 117.0273 1293 | 109.0635 3100 | 98.6058 2238 | 89.6550 8855 | 228 |
| 229 | 117.2456 7510 | 109.2441 9950 | 98.7418 3135 | 89.7575 1342 | 229 |
| 230 | 117.4625 9115 | 109.4235 2308 | 98.8766 6057 | 89.8589 2417 | 230 |
| 231 | 117.6780 7068 | 109.6015 1174 | 99.0103 2027 | 89.9593 3087 | 231 |
| 232 | 117.8921 2320 | 109.7781 7543 | 99.1428 2059 | 90.0587 4343 | 232 |
| 233 | 118.1047 5814 | 109.9535 2400 | 99.2741 7159 | 90.1571 7171 | 233 |
| 234 | 118.3159 8491 | 110.1275 6724 | 99.4043 8324 | 90.2546 2546 | 234 |
| 235 | 118.5258 1282 | 110.3003 1488 | 99.5334 6541 | 90.3511 1432 | 235 |
| 236 | 118.7342 5115 | 110.4717 7656 | 99.6614 2792 | 90.4466 4784 | 236 |
| 237 | 118.9413 0909 | 110.6419 6184 | 99.7882 8046 | 90.5412 3548 | 237 |
| 238 | 119.1469 9578 | 110.8108 8024 | 99.9140 3268 | 90.6348 8662 | 238 |
| 239 | 119.3513 2031 | 110.9785 4118 | 100.0386 9410 | 90.7276 1051 | 239 |
| 240 | 119.5542 9170 | 111.1449 5403 | 100.1622 7421 | 90.8194 1635 | 240 |

**PRESENT VALUE OF ANNUITY**
When Periodic Payment Is 1

**TABLE 8**

$$a_{\overline{n}|i} = \frac{1 - (1 + i)^{-n}}{i}$$

| n | $1\frac{1}{8}\%$ | $1\frac{1}{4}\%$ | $1\frac{3}{8}\%$ | $1\frac{1}{2}\%$ | n |
|---|---|---|---|---|---|
| 1 | 0.9888 7515 | 0.9876 5432 | 0.9864 3650 | 0.9852 2167 | 1 |
| 2 | 1.9667 4923 | 1.9631 1538 | 1.9594 9346 | 1.9558 8342 | 2 |
| 3 | 2.9337 4460 | 2.9265 3371 | 2.9193 5237 | 2.9122 0042 | 3 |
| 4 | 3.8899 8230 | 3.8780 5798 | 3.8661 9222 | 3.8543 8465 | 4 |
| 5 | 4.8355 8200 | 4.8178 3504 | 4.8001 8962 | 4.7826 4497 | 5 |
| 6 | 5.7706 6205 | 5.7460 0992 | 5.7215 1874 | 5.6971 8717 | 6 |
| 7 | 6.6953 3948 | 6.6627 2585 | 6.6303 5140 | 6.5982 1396 | 7 |
| 8 | 7.6097 3002 | 7.5681 2429 | 7.5268 5712 | 7.4859 2508 | 8 |
| 9 | 8.5139 4810 | 8.4623 4498 | 8.4112 0308 | 8.3605 1732 | 9 |
| 10 | 9.4081 0690 | 9.3455 2591 | 9.2835 5421 | 9.2221 8455 | 10 |
| 11 | 10.2923 1832 | 10.2178 0337 | 10.1440 7320 | 10.0711 1779 | 11 |
| 12 | 11.1666 9302 | 11.0793 1197 | 10.9929 2054 | 10.9075 0521 | 12 |
| 13 | 12.0313 4044 | 11.9301 8466 | 11.8302 5454 | 11.7315 3222 | 13 |
| 14 | 12.8863 6880 | 12.7705 5275 | 12.6562 3136 | 12.5433 8150 | 14 |
| 15 | 13.7318 8509 | 13.6005 4592 | 13.4710 0504 | 13.3432 3301 | 15 |
| 16 | 14.5679 9514 | 14.4202 9227 | 14.2747 2754 | 14.1312 6405 | 16 |
| 17 | 15.3948 0360 | 15.2299 1829 | 15.0675 4874 | 14.9076 4931 | 17 |
| 18 | 16.2124 1395 | 16.0295 4893 | 15.8496 1651 | 15.6725 6089 | 18 |
| 19 | 17.0209 2850 | 16.8193 0759 | 16.6210 7671 | 16.4261 6837 | 19 |
| 20 | 17.8204 4845 | 17.5993 1613 | 17.3820 7320 | 17.1686 3879 | 20 |
| 21 | 18.6110 7387 | 18.3696 9495 | 18.1327 4792 | 17.9001 3673 | 21 |
| 22 | 19.3929 0371 | 19.1305 6291 | 18.8732 4086 | 18.6208 2437 | 22 |
| 23 | 20.1660 3580 | 19.8820 3744 | 19.6036 9012 | 19.3308 6145 | 23 |
| 24 | 20.9305 6693 | 20.6242 3451 | 20.3242 3193 | 20.0304 0537 | 24 |
| 25 | 21.6865 9276 | 21.3572 6865 | 21.0350 0067 | 20.7196 1120 | 25 |
| 26 | 22.4342 0792 | 22.0812 5299 | 21.7361 2890 | 21.3986 3172 | 26 |
| 27 | 23.1735 0598 | 22.7962 9925 | 22.4277 4737 | 22.0676 1746 | 27 |
| 28 | 23.9045 7946 | 23.5025 1778 | 23.1099 8508 | 22.7267 1671 | 28 |
| 29 | 24.6275 1986 | 24.2000 1756 | 23.7829 6925 | 23.3760 7558 | 29 |
| 30 | 25.3424 1766 | 24.8889 0623 | 24.4468 2540 | 24.0158 3801 | 30 |
| 31 | 26.0493 6233 | 25.5692 9010 | 25.1016 7734 | 24.6461 4582 | 31 |
| 32 | 26.7484 4236 | 26.2412 7418 | 25.7476 4719 | 25.2671 3874 | 32 |
| 33 | 27.4397 4522 | 26.9049 6215 | 26.3848 5543 | 25.8789 5442 | 33 |
| 34 | 28.1233 5745 | 27.5604 5644 | 27.0134 2089 | 26.4817 2849 | 34 |
| 35 | 28.7993 6460 | 28.2078 5822 | 27.6334 6080 | 27.0755 9458 | 35 |
| 36 | 29.4678 5127 | 28.8472 6737 | 28.2450 9080 | 27.6606 8431 | 36 |
| 37 | 30.1289 0114 | 29.4787 8259 | 28.8484 2496 | 28.2371 2740 | 37 |
| 38 | 30.7825 9692 | 30.1025 0133 | 29.4435 7579 | 28.8050 5163 | 38 |
| 39 | 31.4290 2044 | 30.7185 1983 | 30.0306 5430 | 29.3645 8288 | 39 |
| 40 | 32.0682 5260 | 31.3269 3316 | 30.6097 6996 | 29.9158 4520 | 40 |
| 41 | 32.7903 7340 | 31.9278 3522 | 31.1810 3079 | 30.4589 6079 | 41 |
| 42 | 33.3254 6195 | 32.5213 1874 | 31.7445 4332 | 30.9940 5004 | 42 |
| 43 | 33.9435 9649 | 33.1074 7530 | 32.3004 1264 | 31.5212 3157 | 43 |
| 44 | 34.5548 5438 | 33.6863 9536 | 32.8487 4243 | 32.0406 2223 | 44 |
| 45 | 35.1593 1212 | 34.2581 6825 | 33.3896 3495 | 32.5523 3718 | 45 |
| 46 | 35.7570 4536 | 34.8228 8222 | 33.9231 9108 | 33.0564 8983 | 46 |
| 47 | 36.3481 2891 | 35.3806 2442 | 34.4495 1031 | 33.5531 9195 | 47 |
| 48 | 36.9326 3674 | 35.9314 8091 | 34.9686 9081 | 34.0425 5365 | 48 |
| 49 | 37.5106 4202 | 36.4755 3670 | 35.4808 2941 | 34.5246 8339 | 49 |
| 50 | 38.0822 1708 | 37.0128 7575 | 35.9860 2161 | 34.9996 8807 | 50 |

Table
8

## TABLE 8

$$a_{\overline{n}|i} = \frac{1 - (1 + i)^{-n}}{i}$$

| n | $1\frac{1}{8}\%$ | $1\frac{1}{4}\%$ | $1\frac{3}{8}\%$ | $1\frac{1}{2}\%$ | n |
|---|---|---|---|---|---|
| 51 | 38.6474 3345 | 37.5435 8099 | 36.4843 6164 | 35.4676 7298 | 51 |
| 52 | 39.2063 6188 | 38.0677 3431 | 36.9759 4243 | 35.9287 4185 | 52 |
| 53 | 39.7590 7232 | 38.5854 1660 | 37.4608 5566 | 36.3829 9690 | 53 |
| 54 | 40.3056 3394 | 39.0967 0776 | 37.9391 9178 | 36.8305 3882 | 54 |
| 55 | 40.8461 1514 | 39.6016 8667 | 38.4110 3998 | 37.2714 6681 | 55 |
| 56 | 41.3805 8358 | 40.1004 3128 | 38.8764 8826 | 37.7058 7863 | 56 |
| 57 | 41.9091 0613 | 40.5930 1855 | 39.3356 2344 | 38.1338 7058 | 57 |
| 58 | 42.4317 4896 | 41.0795 2449 | 39.7885 3114 | 38.5555 3751 | 58 |
| 59 | 42.9485 7746 | 41.5600 2419 | 40.2352 9582 | 38.9709 7292 | 59 |
| 60 | 43.4596 5633 | 42.0345 9179 | 40.6760 0081 | 39.3802 6889 | 60 |
| 61 | 43.9650 4952 | 42.5033 0054 | 41.1107 2829 | 39.7835 1614 | 61 |
| 62 | 44.4648 2029 | 42.9662 2275 | 41.5395 5935 | 40.1808 0408 | 62 |
| 63 | 44.9590 3119 | 43.4234 2988 | 41.9625 7396 | 40.5722 2077 | 63 |
| 64 | 45.4477 4407 | 43.8749 9247 | 42.3798 5101 | 40.9578 5298 | 64 |
| 65 | 45.9310 2009 | 44.3209 8022 | 42.7914 6832 | 41.3377 8618 | 65 |
| 66 | 46.4089 1975 | 44.7614 6195 | 43.1975 0266 | 41.7121 0461 | 66 |
| 67 | 46.8815 0284 | 45.1965 0563 | 43.5980 2975 | 42.0808 9125 | 67 |
| 68 | 47.3488 2852 | 45.6261 7840 | 43.9931 2429 | 42.4442 2783 | 68 |
| 69 | 47.8109 5527 | 46.0505 4656 | 44.3828 5997 | 42.8021 9490 | 69 |
| 70 | 48.2679 4094 | 46.4696 7562 | 44.7673 0946 | 43.1548 7183 | 70 |
| 71 | 48.7198 4270 | 46.8836 3024 | 45.1465 4448 | 43.5023 3678 | 71 |
| 72 | 49.1667 1714 | 47.2924 7431 | 45.5206 3573 | 43.8446 6677 | 72 |
| 73 | 49.6086 2016 | 47.6962 7093 | 45.8896 5300 | 44.1819 3771 | 73 |
| 74 | 50.0456 0708 | 48.0950 8240 | 46.2536 6511 | 44.5142 2434 | 74 |
| 75 | 50.4777 3259 | 48.4889 7027 | 46.6127 3994 | 44.8416 0034 | 75 |
| 76 | 50.9050 5077 | 48.8779 9533 | 46.9669 4445 | 45.1641 3826 | 76 |
| 77 | 51.3276 1510 | 49.2622 1761 | 47.3163 4471 | 45.4819 0962 | 77 |
| 78 | 51.7454 7847 | 49.6416 9640 | 47.6610 0588 | 45.7949 8485 | 78 |
| 79 | 52.1586 9317 | 50.0164 9027 | 48.0009 9224 | 46.1034 3335 | 79 |
| 80 | 52.5673 1092 | 50.3866 5706 | 48.3363 6719 | 46.4073 2349 | 80 |
| 81 | 52.9713 8286 | 50.7522 5389 | 48.6671 9328 | 46.7067 2265 | 81 |
| 82 | 53.3709 5957 | 51.1133 3717 | 48.9935 3221 | 47.0016 9720 | 82 |
| 83 | 53.7660 9104 | 51.4699 6264 | 49.3154 4484 | 47.2923 1251 | 83 |
| 84 | 54.1568 2674 | 51.8221 8532 | 49.6329 9122 | 47.5786 3301 | 84 |
| 85 | 54.5432 1557 | 52.1700 5958 | 49.9462 3055 | 47.8607 2218 | 85 |
| 86 | 54.9253 0588 | 52.5136 3909 | 50.2552 2125 | 48.1386 4254 | 86 |
| 87 | 55.3031 4549 | 52.8529 7688 | 50.5600 2096 | 48.4124 5571 | 87 |
| 88 | 55.6767 8169 | 53.1881 2531 | 50.8606 8653 | 48.6822 2237 | 88 |
| 89 | 56.0462 6126 | 53.5191 3611 | 51.1572 7401 | 48.9480 0234 | 89 |
| 90 | 56.4116 3041 | 53.8460 6036 | 51.4498 3873 | 49.2098 5452 | 90 |
| 91 | 56.7729 3490 | 54.1689 4850 | 51.7384 3524 | 49.4678 3696 | 91 |
| 92 | 57.1302 1992 | 54.4878 5037 | 52.0231 1738 | 49.7220 0686 | 92 |
| 93 | 57.4835 3021 | 54.8028 1518 | 52.3039 3823 | 49.9724 2055 | 93 |
| 94 | 57.8329 0997 | 55.1138 9154 | 52.5809 5016 | 50.2191 3355 | 94 |
| 95 | 58.1784 0294 | 55.4211 2744 | 52.8542 0484 | 50.4622 0054 | 95 |
| 96 | 58.5200 5235 | 55.7245 7031 | 53.1237 5324 | 50.7016 7541 | 96 |
| 97 | 58.8579 0096 | 56.0242 6698 | 53.3896 4561 | 50.9376 1124 | 97 |
| 98 | 59.1919 9106 | 56.3202 6368 | 53.6519 3155 | 51.1700 6034 | 98 |
| 99 | 59.5223 6446 | 56.6126 0610 | 53.9106 5998 | 51.3990 7422 | 99 |
| 100 | 59.8490 6251 | 56.9013 3936 | 54.1658 7914 | 51.6247 0367 | 100 |

**PRESENT VALUE OF ANNUITY**
When Periodic Payment Is 1

**TABLE 8**

$$a_{\overline{n}|i} = \frac{1 - (1 + i)^{-n}}{i}$$

| $n$ | $1\frac{5}{8}\%$ | $1\frac{3}{4}\%$ | $1\frac{7}{8}\%$ | $2\%$ | $n$ |
|---|---|---|---|---|---|
| 1 | 0.9840 0984 | 0.9828 0098 | 0.9815 9509 | 0.9803 9216 | 1 |
| 2 | 1.9522 8521 | 1.9486 9875 | 1.9451 2402 | 1.9415 6094 | 2 |
| 3 | 2.9050 7769 | 2.8979 8403 | 2.8909 1928 | 2.8838 8327 | 3 |
| 4 | 3.8426 3488 | 3.8309 4254 | 3.8193 0727 | 3.8077 2870 | 4 |
| 5 | 4.7652 0037 | 4.7478 5508 | 4.7306 0836 | 4.7134 5951 | 5 |
| 6 | 5.6730 1389 | 5.6489 9762 | 5.6251 3704 | 5.6014 3089 | 6 |
| 7 | 6.5663 1134 | 6.5346 4139 | 6.5032 0200 | 6.4719 9107 | 7 |
| 8 | 7.4453 2481 | 7.4050 5297 | 7.3651 0626 | 7.3254 8144 | 8 |
| 9 | 8.3102 8271 | 8.2604 9432 | 8.2111 4725 | 8.1622 3671 | 9 |
| 10 | 9.1614 0980 | 9.1012 2291 | 9.0416 1693 | 8.9825 8501 | 10 |
| | | | | | 11 |
| 11 | 9.9989 2724 | 9.9274 9181 | 9.8568 0190 | 9.7868 4805 | 11 |
| 12 | 10.8230 5263 | 10.7395 4969 | 10.6569 8346 | 10.5753 4122 | 12 |
| 13 | 11.6340 0013 | 11.5376 4097 | 11.4424 3775 | 11.3483 7375 | 13 |
| 14 | 12.4319 8045 | 12.3220 0587 | 12.2134 3583 | 12.1062 4877 | 14 |
| 15 | 13.2172 0093 | 13.0928 8046 | 12.9702 4376 | 12.8492 6350 | 15 |
| 16 | 13.9898 6562 | 13.8504 9677 | 13.7131 2271 | 13.5777 0931 | 16 |
| 17 | 14.7501 7527 | 14.5950 8282 | 14.4423 2904 | 14.2918 7188 | 17 |
| 18 | 15.4983 2745 | 15.3268 6272 | 15.1581 1439 | 14.9920 3125 | 18 |
| 19 | 16.2345 1655 | 16.0460 5673 | 15.8607 2578 | 15.6784 6201 | 19 |
| 20 | 16.9589 3388 | 16.7528 8130 | 16.5504 0568 | 16.3514 3334 | 20 |
| 21 | 17.6717 6765 | 17.4475 4919 | 17.2273 9208 | 17.0112 0916 | 21 |
| 22 | 18.3732 0310 | 18.1302 6948 | 17.8919 1860 | 17.6580 4820 | 22 |
| 23 | 19.0634 2249 | 18.8012 4764 | 18.5442 1458 | 18.2922 0412 | 23 |
| 24 | 19.7426 0515 | 19.4606 8565 | 19.1845 0511 | 18.9139 2560 | 24 |
| 25 | 20.4109 2758 | 20.1087 8196 | 19.8130 1115 | 19.5234 5647 | 25 |
| 26 | 21.0685 6342 | 20.7457 3166 | 20.4299 4960 | 20.1210 4376 | 26 |
| 27 | 21.7156 8357 | 21.3717 2644 | 21.0355 3334 | 20.7068 9780 | 27 |
| 28 | 22.3524 5615 | 21.9869 5474 | 21.6299 7138 | 21.2812 7236 | 28 |
| 29 | 22.9790 4665 | 22.5916 0171 | 22.2134 6884 | 21.8443 8466 | 29 |
| 30 | 23.5956 1786 | 23.1858 4934 | 22.7862 2708 | 22.3964 5555 | 30 |
| 31 | 24.2023 2999 | 23.7698 7650 | 23.3484 4376 | 22.9377 0152 | 31 |
| 32 | 24.7993 4071 | 24.3438 5897 | 23.9003 1290 | 23.4683 3482 | 32 |
| 33 | 25.3868 0512 | 24.9079 6951 | 24.4420 2493 | 23.9885 6355 | 33 |
| 34 | 25.9648 7589 | 25.4623 7789 | 24.9737 6680 | 24.4985 9172 | 34 |
| 35 | 26.5337 0321 | 26.0072 5100 | 25.4957 2201 | 24.9986 1933 | 35 |
| 36 | 27.0934 3490 | 26.5427 5283 | 26.0080 7069 | 25.4888 4248 | 36 |
| 37 | 27.6442 1638 | 27.0690 4455 | 26.5109 8963 | 25.9694 5341 | 37 |
| 38 | 28.1861 9078 | 27.5862 8457 | 27.0046 5240 | 26.4406 4060 | 38 |
| 39 | 28.7194 9892 | 28.0946 2857 | 27.4892 2931 | 26.9025 8883 | 39 |
| 40 | 29.2442 7938 | 28.5942 2955 | 27.9648 8770 | 27.3554 7924 | 40 |
| 41 | 29.7606 6852 | 29.0852 3789 | 28.4317 9161 | 27.7994 8945 | 41 |
| 42 | 30.2688 0051 | 29.5678 0135 | 28.8901 0220 | 28.2347 9358 | 42 |
| 43 | 30.7688 0739 | 30.0420 6522 | 29.3399 7762 | 28.6615 6233 | 43 |
| 44 | 31.2608 1908 | 30.5081 7221 | 29.7815 7312 | 29.0799 6307 | 44 |
| 45 | 31.7449 6342 | 30.9662 6261 | 30.2150 4110 | 29.4901 5987 | 45 |
| 46 | 32.2213 6622 | 31.4164 7431 | 30.6405 3114 | 29.8923 1360 | 46 |
| 47 | 32.6901 5127 | 31.8589 4281 | 31.0581 9008 | 30.2865 8196 | 47 |
| 48 | 33.1514 4036 | 32.2938 0129 | 31.4681 6204 | 30.6731 1957 | 48 |
| 49 | 33.6053 5337 | 32.7211 8063 | 31.8705 8850 | 31.0520 7801 | 49 |
| 50 | 34.0520 0823 | 33.1412 0946 | 32.2656 0835 | 31.4236 0589 | 50 |

Table
8

**TABLE   8**

$$a_{\overline{n}|i} = \frac{1-(1+i)^{-n}}{i}$$

| $n$ | $1\frac{5}{8}\%$ | $1\frac{3}{4}\%$ | $1\frac{7}{8}\%$ | 2% | $n$ |
|---|---|---|---|---|---|
| 51 | 34.4915 2102 | 33.5540 1421 | 32.6533 5789 | 31.7878 4892 | 51 |
| 52 | 34.9240 0592 | 33.9597 1913 | 33.0339 7093 | 32.1449 4992 | 52 |
| 53 | 35.3495 7532 | 34.3584 4632 | 33.4075 7883 | 32.4950 4894 | 53 |
| 54 | 35.7683 3980 | 34.7503 1579 | 33.7743 1051 | 32.8382 8327 | 54 |
| 55 | 36.1804 0817 | 35.1354 4550 | 34.1342 9252 | 33.1747 8752 | 55 |
| 56 | 36.5858 8750 | 35.5139 5135 | 34.4876 4910 | 33.5046 9365 | 56 |
| 57 | 36.9848 8314 | 35.8859 4727 | 34.8345 0219 | 33.8281 3103 | 57 |
| 58 | 37.3774 9879 | 36.2515 4523 | 35.1749 7147 | 34.1452 2650 | 58 |
| 59 | 37.7638 3645 | 36.6108 5526 | 35.5091 7445 | 34.4561 0441 | 59 |
| 60 | 38.1439 9650 | 36.9639 8552 | 35.8372 2645 | 34.7608 8668 | 60 |
| 61 | 38.5180 7774 | 37.3110 4228 | 36.1592 4069 | 35.0596 9282 | 61 |
| 62 | 38.8861 7736 | 37.6521 3000 | 36.4753 2828 | 35.3526 4002 | 62 |
| 63 | 39.2483 9100 | 37.9873 5135 | 36.7855 9832 | 35.6398 4316 | 63 |
| 64 | 39.6048 1280 | 38.3168 0723 | 37.0901 5786 | 35.9214 1486 | 64 |
| 65 | 39.9555 3535 | 38.6405 9678 | 37.3891 1201 | 36.1974 6555 | 65 |
| 66 | 40.3006 4979 | 38.9588 1748 | 37.6825 6393 | 36.4681 0348 | 66 |
| 67 | 40.6402 4579 | 39.2715 6509 | 37.9706 1490 | 36.7334 3478 | 67 |
| 68 | 40.9744 1161 | 39.5789 3375 | 38.2533 6432 | 36.9935 6351 | 68 |
| 69 | 41.3032 3405 | 39.8810 1597 | 38.5309 0976 | 37.2485 9168 | 69 |
| 70 | 41.6267 9858 | 40.1779 0267 | 38.8033 4701 | 37.4986 1929 | 70 |
| 71 | 41.9451 8925 | 40.4696 8321 | 39.0707 7007 | 37.7437 4441 | 71 |
| 72 | 42.2584 8881 | 40.7564 4542 | 39.3332 7123 | 37.9840 6314 | 72 |
| 73 | 42.5667 7865 | 41.0382 7560 | 39.5909 4109 | 38.2196 6975 | 73 |
| 74 | 42.8701 3890 | 41.3152 5857 | 39.8438 6855 | 38.4506 5662 | 74 |
| 75 | 43.1686 4836 | 41.5874 7771 | 40.0921 4091 | 38.6771 1433 | 75 |
| 76 | 43.4623 8461 | 41.8550 1495 | 40.3358 4384 | 38.8991 3170 | 76 |
| 77 | 43.7514 2397 | 42.1179 5081 | 40.5750 6144 | 39.1167 9578 | 77 |
| 78 | 44.0358 4155 | 42.3763 6443 | 40.8098 7626 | 39.3301 9194 | 78 |
| 79 | 44.3157 1124 | 42.6303 3359 | 41.0403 6933 | 39.5394 0386 | 79 |
| 80 | 44.5911 0577 | 42.8799 3474 | 41.2666 2020 | 39.7445 1359 | 80 |
| 81 | 44.8620 9670 | 43.1252 4298 | 41.4887 0695 | 39.9456 0156 | 81 |
| 82 | 45.1287 5444 | 43.3663 3217 | 41.7067 0621 | 40.1427 4663 | 82 |
| 83 | 45.3911 4828 | 43.6032 7486 | 41.9206 9321 | 40.3360 2611 | 83 |
| 84 | 45.6493 4640 | 43.8361 4237 | 42.1307 4180 | 40.5255 1579 | 84 |
| 85 | 45.9034 1589 | 44.0650 0479 | 42.3369 2447 | 40.7112 8999 | 85 |
| 86 | 46.1534 2277 | 44.2899 3099 | 42.5393 1236 | 40.8934 2156 | 86 |
| 87 | 46.3994 3200 | 44.5109 8869 | 42.7379 7532 | 41.0719 8192 | 87 |
| 88 | 46.6415 0750 | 44.7282 4441 | 42.9329 8191 | 41.2470 4110 | 88 |
| 89 | 46.8797 1218 | 44.9417 6355 | 43.1243 9942 | 41.4186 6774 | 89 |
| 90 | 47.1141 0793 | 45.1516 1037 | 43.3122 9391 | 41.5869 2916 | 90 |
| 91 | 47.3447 5565 | 45.3578 4803 | 43.4967 3022 | 41.7518 9133 | 91 |
| 92 | 47.5717 1528 | 45.5605 3860 | 43.6777 7199 | 41.9136 1895 | 92 |
| 93 | 47.7950 4578 | 45.7597 4310 | 43.8554 8171 | 42.0721 7545 | 93 |
| 94 | 48.0148 0520 | 45.9555 2147 | 44.0299 2070 | 42.2276 2299 | 94 |
| 95 | 48.2310 5062 | 46.1479 3265 | 44.2011 4915 | 42.3800 2254 | 95 |
| 96 | 48.4438 3825 | 46.3370 3455 | 44.3692 2616 | 42.5294 3386 | 96 |
| 97 | 48.6532 2337 | 46.5228 8408 | 44.5342 0973 | 42.6759 1555 | 97 |
| 98 | 48.8592 6039 | 46.7055 3718 | 44.6961 5679 | 42.8195 2505 | 98 |
| 99 | 49.0620 0285 | 46.8850 4882 | 44.8551 2323 | 42.9603 1867 | 99 |
| 100 | 49.2615 0342 | 47.0614 7304 | 45.0111 6391 | 43.0983 5164 | 100 |

**TABLE 8**

$$a_{\overline{n}|i} = \frac{1 - (1 + i)^{-n}}{i}$$

| $n$ | $2\frac{1}{4}\%$ | $2\frac{1}{2}\%$ | $2\frac{3}{4}\%$ | $3\%$ | $n$ |
|---|---|---|---|---|---|
| 1 | 0.9779 9511 | 0.9756 0976 | 0.9732 3601 | 0.9708 7379 | 1 |
| 2 | 1.9344 6955 | 1.9274 2415 | 1.9204 2434 | 1.9134 6970 | 2 |
| 3 | 2.8698 9687 | 2.8560 2356 | 2.8422 6213 | 2.8286 1135 | 3 |
| 4 | 3.7847 4021 | 3.7619 7421 | 3.7394 2787 | 3.7170 9840 | 4 |
| 5 | 4.6794 5253 | 4.6458 2850 | 4.6125 8186 | 4.5797 0719 | 5 |
| 6 | 5.5544 7680 | 5.5081 2536 | 5.4623 6678 | 5.4171 9144 | 6 |
| 7 | 6.4102 4626 | 6.3493 9060 | 6.2894 0806 | 6.2302 8296 | 7 |
| 8 | 7.2471 8461 | 7.1701 3717 | 7.0943 1441 | 7.0196 9219 | 8 |
| 9 | 8.0657 0622 | 7.9708 6553 | 7.8776 7826 | 7.7861 0892 | 9 |
| 10 | 8.8662 1635 | 8.7520 6393 | 8.6400 7616 | 8.5302 0284 | 10 |
| 11 | 9.6491 1134 | 9.5142 0871 | 9.3820 6926 | 9.2526 2411 | 11 |
| 12 | 10.4147 7882 | 10.2577 6460 | 10.1042 0366 | 9.9540 0399 | 12 |
| 13 | 11.1635 9787 | 10.9831 8497 | 10.8070 1086 | 10.6349 5533 | 13 |
| 14 | 11.8959 3924 | 11.6909 1217 | 11.4910 0814 | 11.2960 7314 | 14 |
| 15 | 12.6121 6551 | 12.3813 7773 | 12.1566 9892 | 11.9379 3509 | 15 |
| 16 | 13.3126 3131 | 13.0550 0266 | 12.8045 7315 | 12.5611 0203 | 16 |
| 17 | 13.9976 8343 | 13.7121 9772 | 13.4351 0769 | 13.1661 1847 | 17 |
| 18 | 14.6676 6106 | 14.3533 6363 | 14.0487 6661 | 13.7535 1308 | 18 |
| 19 | 15.3228 9590 | 14.9788 9134 | 14.6460 0157 | 14.3237 9911 | 19 |
| 20 | 15.9637 1237 | 15.5891 6229 | 15.2272 5213 | 14.8774 7486 | 20 |
| 21 | 16.5904 2775 | 16.1845 4857 | 15.7929 4612 | 15.4150 2414 | 21 |
| 22 | 17.2033 5232 | 16.7654 1324 | 16.3434 9987 | 15.9369 1664 | 22 |
| 23 | 17.8027 8955 | 17.3321 1048 | 16.8793 1861 | 16.4436 0839 | 23 |
| 24 | 18.3890 3624 | 17.8849 8583 | 17.4007 9670 | 16.9355 4212 | 24 |
| 25 | 18.9623 8263 | 18.4243 7642 | 17.9083 1795 | 17.4131 4769 | 25 |
| 26 | 19.5231 1260 | 18.9506 1114 | 18.4022 5592 | 17.8768 4242 | 26 |
| 27 | 20.0715 0376 | 19.4640 1087 | 18.8829 7413 | 18.3270 3147 | 27 |
| 28 | 20.6078 2764 | 19.9648 8866 | 19.3508 2640 | 18.7641 0823 | 28 |
| 29 | 21.1323 4977 | 20.4535 4991 | 19.8061 5708 | 19.1884 5459 | 29 |
| 30 | 21.6453 2985 | 20.9302 9259 | 20.2493 0130 | 19.6004 4135 | 30 |
| 31 | 22.1470 2186 | 21.3954 0741 | 20.6805 8520 | 20.0004 2849 | 31 |
| 32 | 22.6376 7419 | 21.8491 7796 | 21.1003 2623 | 20.3887 6553 | 32 |
| 33 | 23.1175 2977 | 22.2918 8094 | 21.5088 3332 | 20.7657 9178 | 33 |
| 34 | 23.5868 2618 | 22.7237 8628 | 21.9064 0712 | 21.1318 3668 | 34 |
| 35 | 24.0457 9577 | 23.1451 5734 | 22.2933 4026 | 21.4872 2007 | 35 |
| 36 | 24.4946 6579 | 23.5562 5107 | 22.6699 1753 | 21.8322 5250 | 36 |
| 37 | 24.9336 5848 | 23.9573 1812 | 23.0364 1609 | 22.1672 3544 | 37 |
| 38 | 25.3629 9118 | 24.3486 0304 | 23.3931 0568 | 22.4924 6159 | 38 |
| 39 | 25.7828 7646 | 24.7303 4443 | 23.7402 4884 | 22.8082 1513 | 39 |
| 40 | 26.1935 2221 | 25.1027 7505 | 24.0781 0106 | 23.1147 7197 | 40 |
| 41 | 26.5951 3174 | 25.4661 2200 | 24.4069 1101 | 23.4123 9998 | 41 |
| 42 | 26.9879 0390 | 25.8206 0683 | 24.7269 2069 | 23.7013 5920 | 42 |
| 43 | 27.3720 3316 | 26.1664 4569 | 25.0383 6563 | 23.9819 0213 | 43 |
| 44 | 27.7477 0969 | 26.5038 4945 | 25.3414 7507 | 24.2542 7392 | 44 |
| 45 | 28.1151 1950 | 26.8330 2386 | 25.6364 7209 | 24.5187 1254 | 45 |
| 46 | 28.4744 4450 | 27.1541 6962 | 25.9235 7381 | 24.7754 4907 | 46 |
| 47 | 28.8258 6259 | 27.4674 8255 | 26.2029 9154 | 25.0247 0783 | 47 |
| 48 | 29.1695 4777 | 27.7731 5371 | 26.4749 3094 | 25.2667 0664 | 48 |
| 49 | 29.5056 7019 | 28.0713 6947 | 26.7395 9215 | 25.5016 5693 | 49 |
| 50 | 29.8343 9627 | 28.3623 1168 | 26.9971 6998 | 25.7297 6401 | 50 |

Table
8

**TABLE 8**

$$a_{\overline{n}|i} = \frac{1 - (1 + i)^{-n}}{i}$$

| n | $2\frac{1}{4}\%$ | $2\frac{1}{2}\%$ | $2\frac{3}{4}\%$ | 3% | n |
|---|---|---|---|---|---|
| 51 | 30.1558 8877 | 28.6461 5774 | 27.2478 5400 | 25.9512 2719 | 51 |
| 52 | 30.4703 0687 | 28.9230 8072 | 27.4918 2871 | 26.1662 3999 | 52 |
| 53 | 30.7778 0623 | 29.1932 4948 | 27.7292 7368 | 26.3749 9028 | 53 |
| 54 | 31.0785 3910 | 29.4568 2876 | 27.9603 6368 | 26.5776 6047 | 54 |
| 55 | 31.3726 5438 | 29.7139 7928 | 28.1852 6879 | 26.7744 2764 | 55 |
| 56 | 31.6602 9768 | 29.9648 5784 | 28.4041 5454 | 26.9654 6373 | 56 |
| 57 | 31.9416 1142 | 30.2096 1740 | 28.6171 8203 | 27.1509 3566 | 57 |
| 58 | 32.2167 3489 | 30.4484 0722 | 28.8245 0806 | 27.3310 0549 | 58 |
| 59 | 32.4858 0429 | 30.6813 7290 | 29.0262 8522 | 27.5058 3058 | 59 |
| 60 | 32.7489 5285 | 30.9086 5649 | 29.2226 6201 | 27.6755 6367 | 60 |
| 61 | 33.0063 1086 | 31.1303 9657 | 29.4137 8298 | 27.8403 5307 | 61 |
| 62 | 33.2580 0573 | 31.3467 2836 | 29.5997 8879 | 28.0003 4279 | 62 |
| 63 | 33.5041 6208 | 31.5577 8377 | 29.7808 1634 | 28.1556 7261 | 63 |
| 64 | 33.7449 0179 | 31.7636 9148 | 29.9569 9887 | 28.3064 7826 | 64 |
| 65 | 33.9803 4405 | 31.9645 7705 | 30.1284 6605 | 28.4528 9152 | 65 |
| 66 | 34.2106 0543 | 32.1605 6298 | 30.2953 4409 | 28.5950 4031 | 66 |
| 67 | 34.4357 9993 | 32.3517 6876 | 30.4577 5581 | 28.7330 4884 | 67 |
| 68 | 34.6560 3905 | 32.5383 1099 | 30.6158 2074 | 28.8670 3771 | 68 |
| 69 | 34.8714 3183 | 32.7203 0340 | 30.7696 5522 | 28.9971 2399 | 69 |
| 70 | 35.0820 8492 | 32.8978 5698 | 30.9193 7247 | 29.1234 2135 | 70 |
| 71 | 35.2881 0261 | 33.0710 7998 | 31.0650 8270 | 29.2460 4015 | 71 |
| 72 | 35.4895 8691 | 33.2400 7803 | 31.2068 9314 | 29.3650 8752 | 72 |
| 73 | 35.6866 3756 | 33.4049 5417 | 31.3449 0816 | 29.4806 6750 | 73 |
| 74 | 35.8793 5214 | 33.5658 0895 | 31.4792 2936 | 29.5928 8107 | 74 |
| 75 | 36.0678 2605 | 33.7227 4044 | 31.6099 5558 | 29.7018 2628 | 75 |
| 76 | 36.2521 5262 | 33.8758 4433 | 31.7371 8304 | 29.8075 9833 | 76 |
| 77 | 36.4324 2310 | 34.0252 1398 | 31.8610 0540 | 29.9102 8964 | 77 |
| 78 | 36.6087 2675 | 34.1709 4047 | 31.9815 1377 | 30.0099 8994 | 78 |
| 79 | 36.7811 5085 | 34.3131 1265 | 32.0987 9685 | 30.1067 8635 | 79 |
| 80 | 36.9497 8079 | 34.4518 1722 | 32.2129 4098 | 30.2007 6345 | 80 |
| 81 | 37.1147 0004 | 34.5871 3875 | 32.3240 3015 | 30.2920 0335 | 81 |
| 82 | 37.2759 9026 | 34.7191 5976 | 32.4321 4613 | 30.3805 8577 | 82 |
| 83 | 37.4337 3130 | 34.8479 6074 | 32.5373 6850 | 30.4665 8813 | 83 |
| 84 | 37.5880 0127 | 34.9736 2023 | 32.6397 7469 | 30.5500 8556 | 84 |
| 85 | 37.7388 7655 | 35.0962 1486 | 32.7394 4009 | 30.6311 5103 | 85 |
| 86 | 37.8864 3183 | 35.2158 1938 | 32.8364 3804 | 30.7098 5537 | 86 |
| 87 | 38.0307 4018 | 35.3325 0671 | 32.9308 3994 | 30.7862 6735 | 87 |
| 88 | 38.1718 7304 | 35.4463 4801 | 33.0227 1527 | 30.8604 5374 | 88 |
| 89 | 38.3099 0028 | 35.5574 1269 | 33.1121 3165 | 30.9324 7936 | 89 |
| 90 | 38.4448 9025 | 35.6657 6848 | 33.1991 5489 | 31.0024 0714 | 90 |
| 91 | 38.5769 0978 | 35.7714 8144 | 33.2838 4905 | 31.0702 9820 | 91 |
| 92 | 38.7060 2423 | 35.8746 1604 | 33.3662 7644 | 31.1362 1184 | 92 |
| 93 | 38.8322 9754 | 35.9752 3516 | 33.4464 9776 | 31.2002 0567 | 93 |
| 94 | 38.9557 9221 | 36.0734 0016 | 33.5245 7202 | 31.2623 3560 | 94 |
| 95 | 39.0765 6940 | 36.1691 7089 | 33.6005 5671 | 31.3226 5592 | 95 |
| 96 | 39.1946 8890 | 36.2626 0574 | 33.6745 0775 | 31.3812 1934 | 96 |
| 97 | 39.3102 0920 | 36.3537 6170 | 33.7464 7956 | 31.4380 7703 | 97 |
| 98 | 39.4231 8748 | 36.4426 9434 | 33.8165 2512 | 31.4932 7867 | 98 |
| 99 | 39.5336 7968 | 36.5294 5790 | 33.8846 9598 | 31.5468 7250 | 99 |
| 100 | 39.6417 4052 | 36.6141 0526 | 33.9510 4232 | 31.5989 0534 | 100 |

# PRESENT VALUE OF ANNUITY
## When Periodic Payment Is 1

**TABLE 8**

$$a_{\overline{n}|i} = \frac{1 - (1 + i)^{-n}}{i}$$

| n | $3\frac{1}{4}\%$ | $3\frac{1}{2}\%$ | $3\frac{3}{4}\%$ | 4% | n |
|---|---|---|---|---|---|
| 1 | 0.9685 2300 | 0.9661 8357 | 0.9638 5542 | 0.9615 3846 | 1 |
| 2 | 1.9065 5981 | 1.8996 9428 | 1.8928 7270 | 1.8860 9467 | 2 |
| 3 | 2.8150 7003 | 2.8016 3698 | 2.7883 1103 | 2.7750 9103 | 3 |
| 4 | 3.6949 8308 | 3.6730 7921 | 3.6513 8413 | 3.6298 9522 | 4 |
| 5 | 4.5471 9911 | 4.5150 5238 | 4.4832 6181 | 4.4518 2233 | 5 |
| 6 | 5.3725 8994 | 5.3285 5302 | 5.2850 7162 | 5.2421 3686 | 6 |
| 7 | 6.1719 9994 | 6.1145 4398 | 6.0579 0036 | 6.0020 5467 | 7 |
| 8 | 6.9462 4692 | 6.8739 5554 | 6.8027 9553 | 6.7327 4488 | 8 |
| 9 | 7.6961 2292 | 7.6076 8651 | 7.5207 6677 | 7.4353 3161 | 9 |
| 10 | 8.4223 9508 | 8.3166 0532 | 8.2127 8725 | 8.1108 9578 | 10 |
| 11 | 9.1258 0637 | 9.0015 5104 | 8.8797 9494 | 8.7604 7671 | 11 |
| 12 | 9.8070 7639 | 9.6633 3433 | 9.5226 9392 | 9.3850 7376 | 12 |
| 13 | 10.4669 0207 | 10.3027 3849 | 10.1423 5558 | 9.9856 4785 | 13 |
| 14 | 11.1059 5842 | 10.9205 2028 | 10.7396 1984 | 10.5631 2293 | 14 |
| 15 | 11.7248 9920 | 11.5174 1090 | 11.3152 9623 | 11.1183 8743 | 15 |
| 16 | 12.3243 5758 | 12.0941 1681 | 11.8701 6504 | 11.6522 9561 | 16 |
| 17 | 12.9049 4681 | 12.6513 2059 | 12.4049 7835 | 12.1656 6885 | 17 |
| 18 | 13.4672 6083 | 13.1896 8173 | 12.9204 6106 | 12.6592 9697 | 18 |
| 19 | 14.0118 7490 | 13.7098 3742 | 13.4173 1187 | 13.1339 3940 | 19 |
| 20 | 14.5393 4615 | 14.2124 0330 | 13.8962 0421 | 13.5903 2634 | 20 |
| 21 | 15.0502 1419 | 14.6979 7420 | 14.3577 8719 | 14.0291 5995 | 21 |
| 22 | 15.5450 0163 | 15.1671 2484 | 14.8026 8645 | 14.4511 1533 | 22 |
| 23 | 16.0242 1466 | 15.6204 1047 | 15.2315 0501 | 14.8568 4167 | 23 |
| 24 | 16.4883 4349 | 16.0583 6760 | 15.6448 2411 | 15.2469 6314 | 24 |
| 25 | 16.9378 6295 | 16.4815 1459 | 16.0432 0396 | 15.6220 7994 | 25 |
| 26 | 17.3732 3288 | 16.8903 5226 | 16.4271 8454 | 15.9827 6918 | 26 |
| 27 | 17.7948 9867 | 17.2853 6451 | 16.7972 8630 | 16.3295 8575 | 27 |
| 28 | 18.2032 9169 | 17.6670 1885 | 17.1540 1089 | 16.6630 6322 | 28 |
| 29 | 18.5988 2973 | 18.0357 6700 | 17.4978 4183 | 16.9837 1463 | 29 |
| 30 | 18.9819 1741 | 18.3920 4541 | 17.8292 4513 | 17.2920 3330 | 30 |
| 31 | 19.3529 4664 | 18.7362 7576 | 18.1486 7001 | 17.5884 9356 | 31 |
| 32 | 19.7122 9699 | 19.0688 6547 | 18.4565 4941 | 17.8735 5150 | 32 |
| 33 | 20.0603 3607 | 19.3902 0818 | 18.7533 0063 | 18.1476 4567 | 33 |
| 34 | 20.3974 1992 | 19.7006 8423 | 19.0393 2591 | 18.4111 9776 | 34 |
| 35 | 20.7238 9339 | 20.0006 6110 | 19.3150 1293 | 18.6646 1323 | 35 |
| 36 | 21.0400 9045 | 20.2904 9381 | 19.5807 3535 | 18.9082 8195 | 36 |
| 37 | 21.3463 3457 | 20.5705 2542 | 19.8368 5335 | 19.1425 7880 | 37 |
| 38 | 21.6429 3905 | 20.8410 8736 | 20.0837 1407 | 19.3678 6423 | 38 |
| 39 | 21.9302 0732 | 21.1024 9987 | 20.3216 5212 | 19.5844 8484 | 39 |
| 40 | 22.2084 3324 | 21.3550 7234 | 20.5509 8999 | 19.7927 7388 | 40 |
| 41 | 22.4779 0144 | 21.5991 0371 | 20.7720 3855 | 19.9930 5181 | 41 |
| 42 | 22.7388 8759 | 21.8348 8281 | 20.9850 9739 | 20.1856 2674 | 42 |
| 43 | 22.9916 5869 | 22.0626 8870 | 21.1904 5532 | 20.3707 9494 | 43 |
| 44 | 23.2364 7330 | 22.2827 9102 | 21.3883 9067 | 20.5488 4129 | 44 |
| 45 | 23.4735 8189 | 22.4954 5026 | 21.5791 7173 | 20.7200 3970 | 45 |
| 46 | 23.7032 2701 | 22.7009 1813 | 21.7630 5709 | 20.8846 5356 | 46 |
| 47 | 23.9256 4360 | 22.8994 3780 | 21.9402 9599 | 21.0429 3612 | 47 |
| 48 | 24.1410 5917 | 23.0912 4425 | 22.1111 2866 | 21.1951 3088 | 48 |
| 49 | 24.3496 9412 | 23.2765 6450 | 22.2757 8666 | 21.3414 7200 | 49 |
| 50 | 24.5517 6185 | 23.4556 1787 | 22.4344 9317 | 21.4821 8462 | 50 |

Table 8

**TABLE 8**

$$a_{\overline{n}|i} = \frac{1 - (1 + i)^{-n}}{i}$$

| $n$ | $3\frac{1}{4}\%$ | $3\frac{1}{2}\%$ | $3\frac{3}{4}\%$ | $4\%$ | $n$ |
|---|---|---|---|---|---|
| 51 | 24.7474 6911 | 23.6286 1630 | 22.5874 6330 | 21.6174 8521 | 51 |
| 52 | 24.9370 1609 | 23.7957 6454 | 22.7349 0438 | 21.7475 8193 | 52 |
| 53 | 25.1205 9669 | 23.9572 6043 | 22.8770 1627 | 21.8726 7493 | 53 |
| 54 | 25.2983 9873 | 24.1132 9510 | 23.0139 9159 | 21.9929 5667 | 54 |
| 55 | 25.4706 0410 | 24.2640 5323 | 23.1460 1599 | 22.1086 1218 | 55 |
| 56 | 25.6373 8896 | 24.4097 1327 | 23.2732 6842 | 22.2198 1940 | 56 |
| 57 | 25.7989 2393 | 24.5504 4760 | 23.3959 2137 | 22.3267 4943 | 57 |
| 58 | 25.9553 7427 | 24.6864 2281 | 23.5141 4108 | 22.4295 6676 | 58 |
| 59 | 26.1069 0002 | 24.8177 9981 | 23.6280 8779 | 22.5284 2957 | 59 |
| 60 | 26.2536 5619 | 24.9447 3412 | 23.7379 1594 | 22.6234 8997 | 60 |
| 61 | 26.3957 9292 | 25.0673 7596 | 23.8437 7440 | 22.7148 9421 | 61 |
| 62 | 26.5334 5561 | 25.1858 7049 | 23.9458 0665 | 22.8027 8289 | 62 |
| 63 | 26.6667 8510 | 25.3003 5796 | 24.0441 5099 | 22.8872 9124 | 63 |
| 64 | 26.7959 1777 | 25.4109 7388 | 24.1389 4071 | 22.9685 4927 | 64 |
| 65 | 26.9209 8573 | 25.5178 4916 | 24.2303 0430 | 23.0466 8199 | 65 |
| 66 | 27.0421 1693 | 25.6211 1030 | 24.3183 6559 | 23.1218 0961 | 66 |
| 67 | 27.1594 3529 | 25.7208 7951 | 24.4032 4394 | 23.1940 4770 | 67 |
| 68 | 27.2730 6081 | 25.8172 7489 | 24.4850 5440 | 23.2635 0740 | 68 |
| 69 | 27.3831 0974 | 25.9104 1052 | 24.5639 0786 | 23.3302 9558 | 69 |
| 70 | 27.4896 9467 | 26.0003 9664 | 24.6399 1119 | 23.3945 1498 | 70 |
| 71 | 27.5929 2462 | 26.0873 3975 | 24.7131 6741 | 23.4562 6440 | 71 |
| 72 | 27.6929 0520 | 26.1713 4275 | 24.7837 7582 | 23.5156 3885 | 72 |
| 73 | 27.7897 3869 | 26.2525 0508 | 24.8518 3211 | 23.5727 2966 | 73 |
| 74 | 27.8835 2416 | 26.3309 2278 | 24.9174 2854 | 23.6276 2468 | 74 |
| 75 | 27.9743 5754 | 26.4066 8868 | 24.9806 5402 | 23.6804 0834 | 75 |
| 76 | 28.0623 3175 | 26.4798 9244 | 25.0415 9423 | 23.7311 6187 | 76 |
| 77 | 28.1475 3681 | 26.5506 2072 | 25.1003 3179 | 23.7799 6333 | 77 |
| 78 | 28.2300 5986 | 26.6189 5721 | 25.1569 4631 | 23.8268 8782 | 78 |
| 79 | 28.3099 8534 | 26.6849 8281 | 25.2115 1451 | 23.8720 0752 | 79 |
| 80 | 28.3873 9500 | 26.7487 7567 | 25.2641 1037 | 23.9153 9185 | 80 |
| 81 | 28.4623 6804 | 26.8104 1127 | 25.3148 0518 | 23.9571 0754 | 81 |
| 82 | 28.5349 8115 | 26.8699 6258 | 25.3636 6764 | 23.9972 1879 | 82 |
| 83 | 28.6053 0862 | 26.9275 0008 | 25.4107 6399 | 24.0357 8730 | 83 |
| 84 | 28.6734 2239 | 26.9830 9186 | 25.4561 5806 | 24.0728 7240 | 84 |
| 85 | 28.7393 9215 | 27.0368 0373 | 25.4999 1139 | 24.1085 3116 | 85 |
| 86 | 28.8032 8538 | 27.0886 9926 | 25.5420 8326 | 24.1428 1842 | 86 |
| 87 | 28.8651 6743 | 27.1388 3986 | 25.5827 3086 | 24.1757 8694 | 87 |
| 88 | 28.9251 0163 | 27.1872 8489 | 25.6219 0926 | 24.2074 8745 | 88 |
| 89 | 28.9831 4928 | 27.2340 9168 | 25.6596 7158 | 24.2379 6870 | 89 |
| 90 | 29.0393 6976 | 27.2793 1564 | 25.6960 6899 | 24.2672 7759 | 90 |
| 91 | 29.0938 2059 | 27.3230 1028 | 25.7311 5083 | 24.2954 5923 | 91 |
| 92 | 29.1465 5747 | 27.3652 2732 | 25.7649 6466 | 24.3225 5695 | 92 |
| 93 | 29.1976 3436 | 27.4060 1673 | 25.7975 5630 | 24.3486 1245 | 93 |
| 94 | 29.2471 0349 | 27.4454 2680 | 25.8289 6993 | 24.3736 6582 | 94 |
| 95 | 29.2950 1549 | 27.4835 0415 | 25.8592 4812 | 24.3977 5559 | 95 |
| 96 | 29.3414 1936 | 27.5202 9387 | 25.8884 3192 | 24.4209 1884 | 96 |
| 97 | 29.3863 6258 | 27.5558 3948 | 25.9165 6089 | 24.4431 9119 | 97 |
| 98 | 29.4298 9112 | 27.5901 8308 | 25.9436 7315 | 24.4646 0692 | 98 |
| 99 | 29.4720 4951 | 27.6233 6529 | 25.9698 0544 | 24.4851 9896 | 99 |
| 100 | 29.5128 8088 | 27.6554 2540 | 25.9949 9320 | 24.5049 9900 | 100 |

**TABLE    8**

$$a_{\overline{n}|i} = \frac{1 - (1 + i)^{-n}}{i}$$

| n | $4\frac{1}{2}\%$ | 5% | $5\frac{1}{2}\%$ | 6% | n |
|---|---|---|---|---|---|
| 1 | 0.9569 3780 | 0.9523 8095 | 0.9478 6730 | 0.9433 9623 | 1 |
| 2 | 1.8726 6775 | 1.8594 1043 | 1.8463 1971 | 1.8333 9267 | 2 |
| 3 | 2.7489 6435 | 2.7232 4803 | 2.6979 3338 | 2.6730 1195 | 3 |
| 4 | 3.5875 2570 | 3.5459 5050 | 3.5051 5012 | 3.4651 0561 | 4 |
| 5 | 4.3899 7674 | 4.3294 7667 | 4.2702 8448 | 4.2123 6379 | 5 |
| 6 | 5.1578 7248 | 5.0756 9207 | 4.9955 3031 | 4.9173 2433 | 6 |
| 7 | 5.8927 0094 | 5.7863 7340 | 5.6829 6712 | 5.5823 8144 | 7 |
| 8 | 6.5958 8607 | 6.4632 1276 | 6.3345 6599 | 6.2097 9381 | 8 |
| 9 | 7.2687 9050 | 7.1078 2168 | 6.9521 9525 | 6.8016 9227 | 9 |
| 10 | 7.9127 1818 | 7.7217 3493 | 7.5376 2583 | 7.3600 8705 | 10 |
| 11 | 8.5289 1692 | 8.3064 1422 | 8.0925 3633 | 7.8868 7458 | 11 |
| 12 | 9.1185 8078 | 8.8632 5164 | 8.6185 1785 | 8.3838 4394 | 12 |
| 13 | 9.6828 5242 | 9.3935 7299 | 9.1170 7853 | 8.8526 8296 | 13 |
| 14 | 10.2228 2528 | 9.8986 4094 | 9.5896 4790 | 9.2949 8393 | 14 |
| 15 | 10.7395 4573 | 10.3796 5804 | 10.0375 8094 | 9.7122 4899 | 15 |
| 16 | 11.2340 1505 | 10.8377 6956 | 10.4621 6203 | 10.1058 9527 | 16 |
| 17 | 11.7071 9143 | 11.2740 6625 | 10.8646 0856 | 10.4772 5969 | 17 |
| 18 | 12.1599 9180 | 11.6895 8690 | 11.2460 7447 | 10.8276 0348 | 18 |
| 19 | 12.5932 9359 | 12.0853 2086 | 11.6076 5352 | 11.1581 1649 | 19 |
| 20 | 13.0079 3645 | 12.4622 1034 | 11.9503 8248 | 11.4699 2122 | 20 |
| 21 | 13.4047 2388 | 12.8211 5271 | 12.2752 4406 | 11.7640 7662 | 21 |
| 22 | 13.7844 2476 | 13.1630 0258 | 12.5831 6973 | 12.0415 8172 | 22 |
| 23 | 14.1477 7489 | 13.4885 7388 | 12.8750 4239 | 12.3033 7898 | 23 |
| 24 | 14.4954 7837 | 13.7986 4179 | 13.1516 9895 | 12.5503 5753 | 24 |
| 25 | 14.8282 0896 | 14.0939 4457 | 13.4139 3266 | 12.7833 5616 | 25 |
| 26 | 15.1466 1145 | 14.3751 8530 | 13.6624 9541 | 13.0031 6619 | 26 |
| 27 | 15.4513 0282 | 14.6430 3362 | 13.8980 9991 | 13.2105 3414 | 27 |
| 28 | 15.7428 7351 | 14.8981 2726 | 14.1214 2172 | 13.4061 6428 | 28 |
| 29 | 16.0218 8853 | 15.1410 7358 | 14.3331 0116 | 13.5907 2102 | 29 |
| 30 | 16.2888 8854 | 15.3724 5103 | 14.5337 4517 | 13.7648 3115 | 30 |
| 31 | 16.5443 9095 | 15.5928 1050 | 14.7239 2907 | 13.9290 8599 | 31 |
| 32 | 16.7888 9086 | 15.8026 7667 | 14.9041 9817 | 14.0840 4339 | 32 |
| 33 | 17.0228 6207 | 16.0025 4921 | 15.0750 6936 | 14.2302 2961 | 33 |
| 34 | 17.2467 5796 | 16.1929 0401 | 15.2370 3257 | 14.3681 4114 | 34 |
| 35 | 17.4610 1240 | 16.3741 9429 | 15.3905 5220 | 14.4982 4636 | 35 |
| 36 | 17.6660 4058 | 16.5468 5171 | 15.5360 6843 | 14.6209 8713 | 36 |
| 37 | 17.8622 3979 | 16.7112 8734 | 15.6739 9851 | 14.7367 8031 | 37 |
| 38 | 18.0499 9023 | 16.8678 9271 | 15.8047 3793 | 14.8460 1916 | 38 |
| 39 | 18.2296 5572 | 17.0170 4067 | 15.9286 6154 | 14.9490 7468 | 39 |
| 40 | 18.4015 8442 | 17.1590 8635 | 16.0461 2469 | 15.0462 9687 | 40 |
| 41 | 18.5661 0949 | 17.2943 6796 | 16.1574 6416 | 15.1380 1592 | 41 |
| 42 | 18.7235 4975 | 17.4232 0758 | 16.2629 9920 | 15.2245 4332 | 42 |
| 43 | 18.8742 1029 | 17.5459 1198 | 16.3630 3242 | 15.3061 7294 | 43 |
| 44 | 19.0183 8305 | 17.6627 7331 | 16.4578 5063 | 15.3831 8202 | 44 |
| 45 | 19.1563 4742 | 17.7740 6982 | 16.5477 2572 | 15.4558 3209 | 45 |
| 46 | 19.2883 7074 | 17.8800 6650 | 16.6329 1537 | 15.5243 6990 | 46 |
| 47 | 19.4147 0884 | 17.9810 1571 | 16.7136 6386 | 15.5890 2821 | 47 |
| 48 | 19.5356 0654 | 18.0771 5782 | 16.7902 0271 | 15.6500 2661 | 48 |
| 49 | 19.6512 9813 | 18.1687 2173 | 16.8627 5139 | 15.7075 7227 | 49 |
| 50 | 19.7620 0778 | 18.2559 2546 | 16.9315 1790 | 15.7618 6064 | 50 |

Table
8

## TABLE 8

$$a_{\overline{n}|i} = \frac{1-(1+i)^{-n}}{i}$$

| n | $4\frac{1}{2}\%$ | 5% | $5\frac{1}{2}\%$ | 6% | n |
|---|---|---|---|---|---|
| 51 | 19.8679 5003 | 18.3389 7663 | 16.9966 9943 | 15.8130 7607 | 51 |
| 52 | 19.9693 3017 | 18.4180 7298 | 17.0584 8287 | 15.8613 9252 | 52 |
| 53 | 20.0663 4466 | 18.4934 0284 | 17.1170 4538 | 15.9069 7408 | 53 |
| 54 | 20.1591 8149 | 18.5651 4556 | 17.1725 5486 | 15.9499 7554 | 54 |
| 55 | 20.2480 2057 | 18.6334 7196 | 17.2251 7048 | 15.9905 4297 | 55 |
| 56 | 20.3330 3404 | 18.6985 4473 | 17.2750 4311 | 16.0288 1412 | 56 |
| 57 | 20.4143 8664 | 18.7605 1879 | 17.3223 1575 | 16.0649 1898 | 57 |
| 58 | 20.4922 3602 | 18.8195 4170 | 17.3671 2393 | 16.0989 8017 | 58 |
| 59 | 20.5667 3303 | 18.8757 5400 | 17.4095 9614 | 16.1311 1337 | 59 |
| 60 | 20.6380 2204 | 18.9292 8953 | 17.4498 5416 | 16.1614 2771 | 60 |
| 61 | 20.7062 4118 | 18.9802 7574 | 17.4880 1343 | 16.1900 2614 | 61 |
| 62 | 20.7715 2266 | 19.0288 3404 | 17.5241 8334 | 16.2170 0579 | 62 |
| 63 | 20.8339 9298 | 19.0750 8003 | 17.5584 6762 | 16.2424 5829 | 63 |
| 64 | 20.8937 7319 | 19.1191 2384 | 17.5909 6457 | 16.2664 7009 | 64 |
| 65 | 20.9509 7913 | 19.1610 7033 | 17.6217 6737 | 16.2891 2272 | 65 |
| 66 | 21.0057 2165 | 19.2010 1936 | 17.6509 6433 | 16.3104 9314 | 66 |
| 67 | 21.0581 0684 | 19.2390 6606 | 17.6786 3917 | 16.3306 5390 | 67 |
| 68 | 21.1082 3621 | 19.2753 0101 | 17.7048 7125 | 16.3496 7349 | 68 |
| 69 | 21.1562 0690 | 19.3098 1048 | 17.7297 3579 | 16.3676 1650 | 69 |
| 70 | 21.2021 1187 | 19.3426 7665 | 17.7533 0406 | 16.3845 4387 | 70 |
| 71 | 21.2460 4007 | 19.3739 7776 | 17.7756 4366 | 16.4005 1308 | 71 |
| 72 | 21.2880 7662 | 19.4037 8834 | 17.7968 1864 | 16.4155 7838 | 72 |
| 73 | 21.3283 0298 | 19.4321 7937 | 17.8168 8970 | 16.4297 9093 | 73 |
| 74 | 21.3667 9711 | 19.4592 1845 | 17.8359 1441 | 16.4431 9899 | 74 |
| 75 | 21.4036 3360 | 19.4849 6995 | 17.8539 4731 | 16.4558 4810 | 75 |
| 76 | 21.4388 8383 | 19.5094 9518 | 17.8710 4010 | 16.4677 8123 | 76 |
| 77 | 21.4726 1611 | 19.5328 5257 | 17.8872 4180 | 16.4790 3889 | 77 |
| 78 | 21.5048 9579 | 19.5550 9768 | 17.9025 9887 | 16.4896 5933 | 78 |
| 79 | 21.5357 8545 | 19.5762 8351 | 17.9171 5532 | 16.4996 7862 | 79 |
| 80 | 21.5653 4493 | 19.5964 6048 | 17.9309 5291 | 16.5091 3077 | 80 |
| 81 | 21.5936 3151 | 19.6156 7665 | 17.9440 3120 | 16.5180 4790 | 81 |
| 82 | 21.6207 0001 | 19.6339 7776 | 17.9564 2767 | 16.5264 6028 | 82 |
| 83 | 21.6466 0288 | 19.6514 0739 | 17.9681 7789 | 16.5343 9649 | 83 |
| 84 | 21.6713 9032 | 19.6680 0704 | 17.9793 1554 | 16.5418 8348 | 84 |
| 85 | 21.6951 1035 | 19.6838 1623 | 17.9898 7255 | 16.5489 4668 | 85 |
| 86 | 21.7178 0895 | 19.6988 7260 | 17.9998 7919 | 16.5556 1008 | 86 |
| 87 | 21.7395 3009 | 19.7132 1200 | 18.0093 6416 | 16.5618 9630 | 87 |
| 88 | 21.7603 1588 | 19.7268 6857 | 18.0183 5466 | 16.5678 2670 | 88 |
| 89 | 21.7802 0658 | 19.7398 7483 | 18.0268 7645 | 16.5734 2141 | 89 |
| 90 | 21.7992 4075 | 19.7522 6174 | 18.0349 5398 | 16.5786 9944 | 90 |
| 91 | 21.8174 5526 | 19.7640 5880 | 18.0426 1041 | 16.5836 7872 | 91 |
| 92 | 21.8348 8542 | 19.7752 9410 | 18.0498 6769 | 16.5883 7615 | 92 |
| 93 | 21.8515 6499 | 19.7859 9438 | 18.0567 4662 | 16.5928 0769 | 93 |
| 94 | 21.8675 2631 | 19.7961 8512 | 18.0632 6694 | 16.5969 8839 | 94 |
| 95 | 21.8828 0030 | 19.8058 9059 | 18.0694 4734 | 16.6009 3244 | 95 |
| 96 | 21.8974 1655 | 19.8151 3390 | 18.0753 0553 | 16.6046 5325 | 96 |
| 97 | 21.9114 0340 | 19.8239 3705 | 18.0808 5832 | 16.6081 6344 | 97 |
| 98 | 21.9247 8794 | 19.8323 2100 | 18.0861 2164 | 16.6114 7494 | 98 |
| 99 | 21.9375 9612 | 19.8403 0571 | 18.0911 1055 | 16.6145 9900 | 99 |
| 100 | 21.9498 5274 | 19.8479 1020 | 18.0958 3939 | 16.6175 4623 | 100 |

# TABLE 8

$$a_{\overline{n}|i} = \frac{1 - (1 + i)^{-n}}{i}$$

| n | $6\frac{1}{2}\%$ | 7% | $7\frac{1}{2}\%$ | 8% | n |
|---|---|---|---|---|---|
| 1 | 0.9389 6714 | 0.9345 7944 | 0.9302 3256 | 0.9259 2593 | 1 |
| 2 | 1.8206 2642 | 1.8080 1817 | 1.7955 6517 | 1.7832 6475 | 2 |
| 3 | 2.6484 7551 | 2.6243 1604 | 2.6005 2574 | 2.5770 9699 | 3 |
| 4 | 3.4257 9860 | 3.3872 1126 | 3.3493 2627 | 3.3121 2684 | 4 |
| 5 | 4.1556 7944 | 4.1001 9744 | 4.0458 8490 | 3.9927 1004 | 5 |
| 6 | 4.8410 1356 | 4.7665 3966 | 4.6938 4642 | 4.6228 7966 | 6 |
| 7 | 5.4845 1977 | 5.3892 8940 | 5.2966 0132 | 5.2063 7006 | 7 |
| 8 | 6.0887 5096 | 5.9712 9851 | 5.8573 0355 | 5.7466 3894 | 8 |
| 9 | 6.6561 0419 | 6.5152 3225 | 6.3788 8703 | 6.2468 8791 | 9 |
| 10 | 7.1888 3022 | 7.0235 8154 | 6.8640 8096 | 6.7100 8140 | 10 |
| 11 | 7.6890 4246 | 7.4986 7434 | 7.3154 2415 | 7.1389 6426 | 11 |
| 12 | 8.1587 2532 | 7.9426 8630 | 7.7352 7827 | 7.5360 7802 | 12 |
| 13 | 8.5997 4208 | 8.3576 5074 | 8.1258 4026 | 7.9037 7594 | 13 |
| 14 | 9.0138 4233 | 8.7454 6799 | 8.4891 5373 | 8.2442 3698 | 14 |
| 15 | 9.4026 6885 | 9.1079 1401 | 8.8271 1974 | 8.5594 7869 | 15 |
| 16 | 9.7677 6418 | 9.4466 4860 | 9.1415 0674 | 8.8513 6916 | 16 |
| 17 | 10.1105 7670 | 9.7632 2299 | 9.4339 5976 | 9.1216 3811 | 17 |
| 18 | 10.4324 6638 | 10.0590 8691 | 9.7060 0908 | 9.3718 8714 | 18 |
| 19 | 10.7347 1022 | 10.3355 9524 | 9.9590 7821 | 9.6035 9920 | 19 |
| 20 | 11.0185 0725 | 10.5940 1425 | 10.1944 9136 | 9.8181 4741 | 20 |
| 21 | 11.2849 8333 | 10.8355 2733 | 10.4134 8033 | 10.0168 0316 | 21 |
| 22 | 11.5351 9562 | 11.0612 4050 | 10.6171 9101 | 10.2007 4366 | 22 |
| 23 | 11.7701 3673 | 11.2721 8738 | 10.8066 8931 | 10.3710 5895 | 23 |
| 24 | 11.9907 3871 | 11.4693 3400 | 10.9829 6680 | 10.5287 5828 | 24 |
| 25 | 12.1978 7673 | 11.6535 8318 | 11.1469 4586 | 10.6747 7619 | 25 |
| 26 | 12.3923 7251 | 11.8257 7867 | 11.2994 8452 | 10.8099 7795 | 26 |
| 27 | 12.5749 9766 | 11.9867 0904 | 11.4413 8095 | 10.9351 6477 | 27 |
| 28 | 12.7464 7668 | 12.1371 1125 | 11.5733 7763 | 11.0510 7849 | 28 |
| 29 | 12.9074 8984 | 12.2776 7407 | 11.6961 6524 | 11.1584 0601 | 29 |
| 30 | 13.0586 7591 | 12.4090 4118 | 11.8103 8627 | 11.2577 8334 | 30 |
| 31 | 13.2006 3465 | 12.5318 1419 | 11.9166 3839 | 11.3497 9939 | 31 |
| 32 | 13.3339 2925 | 12.6465 5532 | 12.0154 7757 | 11.4349 9944 | 32 |
| 33 | 13.4590 8850 | 12.7537 9002 | 12.1074 2099 | 11.5138 8837 | 33 |
| 34 | 13.5766 0892 | 12.8540 0936 | 12.1929 4976 | 11.5869 3367 | 34 |
| 35 | 13.6869 5673 | 12.9476 7230 | 12.2725 1141 | 11.6545 6822 | 35 |
| 36 | 13.7905 6970 | 13.0352 0776 | 12.3465 2224 | 11.7171 9279 | 36 |
| 37 | 13.8878 5887 | 13.1170 1660 | 12.4153 6952 | 11.7751 7851 | 37 |
| 38 | 13.9792 1021 | 13.1934 7345 | 12.4794 1351 | 11.8288 6899 | 38 |
| 39 | 14.0649 8611 | 13.2649 2846 | 12.5389 8931 | 11.8785 8240 | 39 |
| 40 | 14.1455 2687 | 13.3317 0884 | 12.5944 0866 | 11.9246 1333 | 40 |
| 41 | 14.2211 5199 | 13.3941 2041 | 12.6459 6155 | 11.9672 3457 | 41 |
| 42 | 14.2921 6149 | 13.4524 4898 | 12.6939 1772 | 12.0066 9867 | 42 |
| 43 | 14.3588 3708 | 13.5069 6167 | 12.7385 2811 | 12.0432 3951 | 43 |
| 44 | 14.4214 4327 | 13.5579 0810 | 12.7800 2615 | 12.0770 7362 | 44 |
| 45 | 14.4802 2842 | 13.6055 2159 | 12.8186 2898 | 12.1084 0150 | 45 |
| 46 | 14.5354 2575 | 13.6500 2018 | 12.8545 3858 | 12.1374 0880 | 46 |
| 47 | 14.5872 5422 | 13.6916 0764 | 12.8879 4287 | 12.1642 6741 | 47 |
| 48 | 14.6359 1946 | 13.7304 7443 | 12.9190 1662 | 12.1891 3649 | 48 |
| 49 | 14.6816 1451 | 13.7667 9853 | 12.9479 2244 | 12.2121 6341 | 49 |
| 50 | 14.7245 2067 | 13.8007 4629 | 12.9748 1157 | 12.2334 8464 | 50 |

Table
8

**TABLE  8**

$$a_{\overline{n}|i} = \frac{1 - (1 + i)^{-n}}{i}$$

| $n$ | $6\frac{1}{2}\%$ | $7\%$ | $7\frac{1}{2}\%$ | $8\%$ | $n$ |
|---|---|---|---|---|---|
| 51 | 14.7648 0814 | 13.8324 7317 | 12.9998 2472 | 12.2532 2652 | 51 |
| 52 | 14.8026 3675 | 13.8621 2446 | 13.0230 9276 | 12.2715 0604 | 52 |
| 53 | 14.8381 5658 | 13.8898 3594 | 13.0447 3745 | 12.2884 3152 | 53 |
| 54 | 14.8715 0852 | 13.9157 3453 | 13.0648 7205 | 12.3041 0326 | 54 |
| 55 | 14.9028 2490 | 13.9399 3881 | 13.0836 0190 | 12.3186 1413 | 55 |
| 56 | 14.9322 2996 | 13.9625 5964 | 13.1010 2503 | 12.3320 5012 | 56 |
| 57 | 14.9598 4033 | 13.9837 0059 | 13.1172 3258 | 12.3444 9085 | 57 |
| 58 | 14.9857 6557 | 14.0034 5850 | 13.1323 0938 | 12.3560 1005 | 58 |
| 59 | 15.0101 0852 | 14.0219 2383 | 13.1463 3431 | 12.3666 7597 | 59 |
| 60 | 15.0329 6574 | 14.0391 8115 | 13.1593 8075 | 12.3765 5182 | 60 |
| 61 | 15.0544 2793 | 14.0553 0949 | 13.1715 1698 | 12.3856 9613 | 61 |
| 62 | 15.0745 8022 | 14.0703 8270 | 13.1828 0649 | 12.3941 6308 | 62 |
| 63 | 15.0935 0255 | 14.0844 6981 | 13.1933 0836 | 12.4020 0286 | 63 |
| 64 | 15.1112 7000 | 14.0976 3534 | 13.2030 7755 | 12.4092 6190 | 64 |
| 65 | 15.1279 5305 | 14.1099 3957 | 13.2121 6516 | 12.4159 8324 | 65 |
| 66 | 15.1436 1789 | 14.1214 3885 | 13.2206 1875 | 12.4222 0671 | 66 |
| 67 | 15.1583 2666 | 14.1321 8584 | 13.2284 8256 | 12.4279 6917 | 67 |
| 68 | 15.1721 3771 | 14.1422 2976 | 13.2357 9773 | 12.4333 0479 | 68 |
| 69 | 15.1851 0583 | 14.1516 1660 | 13.2426 0254 | 12.4382 4518 | 69 |
| 70 | 15.1972 8247 | 14.1603 8934 | 13.2489 3260 | 12.4428 1961 | 70 |
| 71 | 15.2087 1593 | 14.1685 8817 | 13.2548 2102 | 12.4470 5519 | 71 |
| 72 | 15.2194 5158 | 14.1762 5063 | 13.2602 9862 | 12.4509 7703 | 72 |
| 73 | 15.2295 3200 | 14.1834 1180 | 13.2653 9407 | 12.4546 0836 | 73 |
| 74 | 15.2389 9718 | 14.1901 0449 | 13.2701 3402 | 12.4579 7070 | 74 |
| 75 | 15.2478 8468 | 14.1963 5933 | 13.2745 4327 | 12.4610 8399 | 75 |
| 76 | 15.2562 2974 | 14.2022 0498 | 13.2786 4490 | 12.4639 6665 | 76 |
| 77 | 15.2640 6549 | 14.2076 6821 | 13.2824 6038 | 12.4666 3579 | 77 |
| 78 | 15.2714 2299 | 14.2127 7403 | 13.2860 0965 | 12.4691 0721 | 78 |
| 79 | 15.2783 3145 | 14.2175 4582 | 13.2893 1130 | 12.4713 9557 | 79 |
| 80 | 15.2848 1826 | 14.2220 0544 | 13.2923 8261 | 12.4735 1441 | 80 |
| 81 | 15.2909 0917 | 14.2261 7331 | 13.2952 3964 | 12.4754 7631 | 81 |
| 82 | 15.2966 2832 | 14.2300 6851 | 13.2978 9734 | 12.4772 9288 | 82 |
| 83 | 15.3019 9843 | 14.2337 0889 | 13.3003 6961 | 12.4789 7489 | 83 |
| 84 | 15.3070 4078 | 14.2371 1111 | 13.3026 6941 | 12.4805 3230 | 84 |
| 85 | 15.3117 7538 | 14.2402 9076 | 13.3048 0875 | 12.4819 7436 | 85 |
| 86 | 15.3162 2101 | 14.2432 6239 | 13.3067 9884 | 12.4833 0959 | 86 |
| 87 | 15.3203 9532 | 14.2460 3962 | 13.3086 5008 | 12.4845 4592 | 87 |
| 88 | 15.3243 1485 | 14.2486 3516 | 13.3103 7217 | 12.4856 9066 | 88 |
| 89 | 15.3279 9516 | 14.2510 6089 | 13.3119 7411 | 12.4867 5061 | 89 |
| 90 | 15.3314 5086 | 14.2533 2794 | 13.3134 6429 | 12.4877 3205 | 90 |
| 91 | 15.3346 9564 | 14.2554 4667 | 13.3148 5050 | 12.4886 4079 | 91 |
| 92 | 15.3377 4239 | 14.2574 2680 | 13.3161 4000 | 12.4894 8221 | 92 |
| 93 | 15.3406 0318 | 14.2592 7738 | 13.3173 3954 | 12.4902 6131 | 93 |
| 94 | 15.3432 8937 | 14.2610 0690 | 13.3184 5538 | 12.4909 8269 | 94 |
| 95 | 15.3458 1162 | 14.2626 2327 | 13.3194 9338 | 12.4916 5064 | 95 |
| 96 | 15.3481 7992 | 14.2641 3390 | 13.3204 5896 | 12.4922 6911 | 96 |
| 97 | 15.3504 0368 | 14.2655 4570 | 13.3213 5717 | 12.4928 4177 | 97 |
| 98 | 15.3524 9172 | 14.2668 6514 | 13.3221 9272 | 12.4933 7201 | 98 |
| 99 | 15.3544 5232 | 14.2680 9826 | 13.3229 6997 | 12.4938 6297 | 99 |
| 100 | 15.3562 9326 | 14.2692 5071 | 13.3236 9299 | 12.4943 1757 | 100 |

# TABLE 8

$$a_{\overline{n}|i} = \frac{1 - (1+i)^{-n}}{i}$$

| $n$ | $8\frac{1}{2}\%$ | 9% | $9\frac{1}{2}\%$ | 10% | $n$ |
|---|---|---|---|---|---|
| 1 | 0.9216 5899 | 0.9174 3119 | 0.9132 4201 | 0.9090 9091 | 1 |
| 2 | 1.7711 1427 | 1.7591 1119 | 1.7472 5298 | 1.7355 3719 | 2 |
| 3 | 2.5540 2237 | 2.5312 9467 | 2.5089 0683 | 2.4868 5199 | 3 |
| 4 | 3.2755 9666 | 3.2397 1988 | 3.2044 8112 | 3.1698 6545 | 4 |
| 5 | 3.9406 4208 | 3.8896 5126 | 3.8397 0879 | 3.7907 8677 | 5 |
| 6 | 4.5535 8717 | 4.4859 1859 | 4.4198 2538 | 4.3552 6070 | 6 |
| 7 | 5.1185 1352 | 5.0329 5284 | 4.9496 1222 | 4.8684 1882 | 7 |
| 8 | 5.6391 8297 | 5.5348 1911 | 5.4334 3581 | 5.3349 2620 | 8 |
| 9 | 6.1190 6264 | 5.9952 4689 | 5.8752 8385 | 5.7590 2382 | 9 |
| 10 | 6.5613 4806 | 6.4176 5770 | 6.2787 9803 | 6.1445 6711 | 10 |
| 11 | 6.9689 8439 | 6.8051 9055 | 6.6473 0414 | 6.4950 6101 | 11 |
| 12 | 7.3446 8607 | 7.1607 2528 | 6.9838 3940 | 6.8136 9182 | 12 |
| 13 | 7.6909 5490 | 7.4869 0392 | 7.2911 7753 | 7.1033 5620 | 13 |
| 14 | 8.0100 9668 | 7.7861 5039 | 7.5718 5163 | 7.3666 8746 | 14 |
| 15 | 8.3042 3658 | 8.0606 8843 | 7.8281 7500 | 7.6060 7951 | 15 |
| 16 | 8.5753 3325 | 8.3125 5819 | 8.0622 6028 | 7.8237 0864 | 16 |
| 17 | 8.8251 9194 | 8.5436 3137 | 8.2760 3678 | 8.0215 5331 | 17 |
| 18 | 9.0554 7644 | 8.7556 2511 | 8.4712 6647 | 8.2014 1210 | 18 |
| 19 | 9.2677 2022 | 8.9501 1478 | 8.6495 5842 | 8.3649 2009 | 19 |
| 20 | 9.4633 3661 | 9.1285 4567 | 8.8123 8212 | 8.5135 6372 | 20 |
| 21 | 9.6436 2821 | 9.2922 4373 | 8.9610 7956 | 8.6486 9429 | 21 |
| 22 | 9.8097 9558 | 9.4424 2544 | 9.0968 7631 | 8.7715 4026 | 22 |
| 23 | 9.9629 4524 | 9.5802 0683 | 9.2208 9161 | 8.8832 1842 | 23 |
| 24 | 10.1040 9700 | 9.7066 1177 | 9.3341 4759 | 8.9847 4402 | 24 |
| 25 | 10.2341 9078 | 9.8225 7960 | 9.4375 7770 | 9.0770 4002 | 25 |
| 26 | 10.3540 9288 | 9.9289 7211 | 9.5320 3443 | 9.1609 4547 | 26 |
| 27 | 10.4646 0174 | 10.0265 7992 | 9.6182 9629 | 9.2372 2316 | 27 |
| 28 | 10.5664 5321 | 10.1161 2837 | 9.6970 7423 | 9.3065 6651 | 28 |
| 29 | 10.6603 2554 | 10.1982 8291 | 9.7690 1757 | 9.3696 0591 | 29 |
| 30 | 10.7468 4382 | 10.2736 5404 | 9.8347 1924 | 9.4269 1447 | 30 |
| 31 | 10.8265 8416 | 10.3428 0187 | 9.8947 2076 | 9.4790 1315 | 31 |
| 32 | 10.9000 7757 | 10.4062 4025 | 9.9495 1668 | 9.5263 7559 | 32 |
| 33 | 10.9678 1343 | 10.4644 4060 | 9.9995 5861 | 9.5694 3236 | 33 |
| 34 | 11.0302 4279 | 10.5178 3541 | 10.0452 5901 | 9.6085 7487 | 34 |
| 35 | 11.0877 8137 | 10.5668 2148 | 10.0869 9453 | 9.6441 5897 | 35 |
| 36 | 11.1408 1233 | 10.6117 6282 | 10.1251 0916 | 9.6765 0816 | 36 |
| 37 | 11.1896 8878 | 10.6529 9342 | 10.1599 1704 | 9.7059 1651 | 37 |
| 38 | 11.2347 3620 | 10.6908 1965 | 10.1917 0506 | 9.7326 5137 | 38 |
| 39 | 11.2762 5457 | 10.7255 2261 | 10.2207 3521 | 9.7569 5579 | 39 |
| 40 | 11.3145 2034 | 10.7573 6020 | 10.2472 4677 | 9.7790 5072 | 40 |
| 41 | 11.3497 8833 | 10.7865 6899 | 10.2714 5824 | 9.7991 3702 | 41 |
| 42 | 11.3822 9339 | 10.8133 6604 | 10.2935 6917 | 9.8173 9729 | 42 |
| 43 | 11.4122 5197 | 10.8379 5050 | 10.3137 6180 | 9.8339 9753 | 43 |
| 44 | 11.4398 6357 | 10.8605 0504 | 10.3322 0255 | 9.8490 8867 | 44 |
| 45 | 11.4653 1205 | 10.8811 9729 | 10.3490 4343 | 9.8628 0788 | 45 |
| 46 | 11.4887 6686 | 10.9001 8100 | 10.3644 2322 | 9.8752 7989 | 46 |
| 47 | 11.5103 8420 | 10.9175 9725 | 10.3784 6870 | 9.8866 1808 | 47 |
| 48 | 11.5303 0802 | 10.9335 7546 | 10.3912 9561 | 9.8969 2553 | 48 |
| 49 | 11.5486 7099 | 10.9482 3436 | 10.4030 0969 | 9.9062 9594 | 49 |
| 50 | 11.5655 9538 | 10.9616 8290 | 10.4137 0748 | 9.9148 1449 | 50 |

Table 8

# TABLE 8

$$a_{\overline{n}|i} = \frac{1 - (1 + i)^{-n}}{i}$$

| $n$ | $8\frac{1}{2}\%$ | 9% | $9\frac{1}{2}\%$ | 10% | $n$ |
|---|---|---|---|---|---|
| 51 | 11.5811 9390 | 10.9740 2101 | 10.4234 7715 | 9.9225 5862 | 51 |
| 52 | 11.5955 7041 | 10.9853 4038 | 10.4323 9923 | 9.9295 9875 | 52 |
| 53 | 11.6088 2066 | 10.9957 2512 | 10.4405 4724 | 9.9359 9886 | 53 |
| 54 | 11.6210 3287 | 11.0052 5240 | 10.4479 8834 | 9.9418 1715 | 54 |
| 55 | 11.6322 8836 | 11.0139 9303 | 10.4547 8388 | 9.9471 0650 | 55 |
| 56 | 11.6426 6208 | 11.0220 1195 | 10.4609 8984 | 9.9519 1500 | 56 |
| 57 | 11.6522 2311 | 11.0293 6876 | 10.4666 5739 | 9.9562 8636 | 57 |
| 58 | 11.6610 3513 | 11.0361 1813 | 10.4718 3323 | 9.9602 6033 | 58 |
| 59 | 11.6691 5680 | 11.0423 1021 | 10.4765 6003 | 9.9638 7303 | 59 |
| 60 | 11.6766 4221 | 11.0479 9102 | 10.4808 7674 | 9.9671 5730 | 60 |
| 61 | 11.6835 4121 | 11.0532 0277 | 10.4848 1894 | 9.9701 4300 | 61 |
| 62 | 11.6898 9973 | 11.0579 8419 | 10.4884 1912 | 9.9728 5727 | 62 |
| 63 | 11.6957 6012 | 11.0623 7082 | 10.4917 0696 | 9.9753 2479 | 63 |
| 64 | 11.7011 6140 | 11.0663 9525 | 10.4947 0955 | 9.9775 6799 | 64 |
| 65 | 11.7061 3954 | 11.0700 8738 | 10.4974 5165 | 9.9796 0727 | 65 |
| 66 | 11.7107 2769 | 11.0734 7466 | 10.4999 5584 | 9.9814 6115 | 66 |
| 67 | 11.7149 5639 | 11.0765 8226 | 10.5022 4278 | 9.9831 4650 | 67 |
| 68 | 11.7188 5382 | 11.0794 3327 | 10.5043 3130 | 9.9846 7864 | 68 |
| 69 | 11.7224 4592 | 11.0820 4887 | 10.5062 3863 | 9.9860 7149 | 69 |
| 70 | 11.7257 5661 | 11.0844 4850 | 10.5079 8049 | 9.9873 3772 | 70 |
| 71 | 11.7288 0793 | 11.0866 5000 | 10.5095 7122 | 9.9884 8883 | 71 |
| 72 | 11.7316 2021 | 11.0886 6973 | 10.5110 2395 | 9.9895 3530 | 72 |
| 73 | 11.7342 1218 | 11.0905 2269 | 10.5123 5064 | 9.9904 8664 | 73 |
| 74 | 11.7366 0109 | 11.0922 2265 | 10.5135 6223 | 9.9913 5149 | 74 |
| 75 | 11.7388 0284 | 11.0937 8225 | 10.5146 6870 | 9.9921 3772 | 75 |
| 76 | 11.7408 3211 | 11.0952 1307 | 10.5156 7918 | 9.9928 5247 | 76 |
| 77 | 11.7427 0241 | 11.0965 2575 | 10.5166 0199 | 9.9935 0225 | 77 |
| 78 | 11.7444 2618 | 11.0977 3005 | 10.5174 4474 | 9.9940 9295 | 78 |
| 79 | 11.7460 1492 | 11.0988 3491 | 10.5182 1437 | 9.9946 2996 | 79 |
| 80 | 11.7474 7919 | 11.0998 4854 | 10.5189 1724 | 9.9951 1814 | 80 |
| 81 | 11.7488 2874 | 11.1007 7847 | 10.5195 5912 | 9.9955 6195 | 81 |
| 82 | 11.7500 7257 | 11.1016 3163 | 10.5201 4531 | 9.9959 6541 | 82 |
| 83 | 11.7512 1896 | 11.1024 1434 | 10.5206 8065 | 9.9963 3219 | 83 |
| 84 | 11.7522 7554 | 11.1031 3242 | 10.5211 6955 | 9.9966 6563 | 84 |
| 85 | 11.7532 4935 | 11.1037 9121 | 10.5216 1602 | 9.9969 6875 | 85 |
| 86 | 11.7541 4686 | 11.1043 9561 | 10.5220 2377 | 9.9972 4432 | 86 |
| 87 | 11.7549 7407 | 11.1049 5010 | 10.5223 9613 | 9.9974 9483 | 87 |
| 88 | 11.7557 3647 | 11.1054 5881 | 10.5227 3619 | 9.9977 2258 | 88 |
| 89 | 11.7564 3914 | 11.1059 2551 | 10.5230 4675 | 9.9979 2962 | 89 |
| 90 | 11.7570 8677 | 11.1063 5368 | 10.5233 3037 | 9.9981 1783 | 90 |
| 91 | 11.7576 8365 | 11.1067 4649 | 10.5235 8938 | 9.9982 8894 | 91 |
| 92 | 11.7582 3378 | 11.1071 0688 | 10.5238 2592 | 9.9984 4449 | 92 |
| 93 | 11.7587 4081 | 11.1074 3750 | 10.5240 4193 | 9.9985 8590 | 93 |
| 94 | 11.7592 0812 | 11.1077 4083 | 10.5242 3921 | 9.9987 1445 | 94 |
| 95 | 11.7596 3882 | 11.1080 1911 | 10.5244 1937 | 9.9988 3132 | 95 |
| 96 | 11.7600 3578 | 11.1082 7441 | 10.5245 8390 | 9.9989 3757 | 96 |
| 97 | 11.7604 0164 | 11.1085 0863 | 10.5247 3415 | 9.9990 3415 | 97 |
| 98 | 11.7607 3884 | 11.1087 2352 | 10.5248 7137 | 9.9991 2195 | 98 |
| 99 | 11.7610 4962 | 11.1089 2066 | 10.5249 9669 | 9.9992 0178 | 99 |
| 100 | 11.7613 3606 | 11.1091 0152 | 10.5251 1113 | 9.9992 7434 | 100 |

# TABLE 8A

$$a_{\overline{1/m}|i} = \frac{1 - (1+i)^{-\frac{1}{m}}}{i}$$

| $m$ | $\frac{1}{4}\%$ | $\frac{1}{3}\%$ | $\frac{5}{12}\%$ | $\frac{11}{24}\%$ | $\frac{1}{2}\%$ | $m$ |
|---|---|---|---|---|---|---|
| 2 | .4990 6445 | .4987 5346 | .4984 4291 | .4982 8779 | .4981 3278 | 2 |
| 3 | .3327 7886 | .3325 9451 | .3324 1040 | .3323 1843 | .3322 2653 | 3 |
| 4 | .2496 1011 | .2494 8047 | .2493 5099 | .2492 8631 | .2492 2167 | 4 |
| 6 | .1664 2405 | .1663 4337 | .1662 6279 | .1662 2270 | .1661 8230 | 6 |
| 12 | .0832 2068 | .0831 8322 | .0831 4580 | .0831 2710 | .0831 0842 | 12 |

| $m$ | $\frac{13}{24}\%$ | $\frac{7}{12}\%$ | $\frac{5}{8}\%$ | $\frac{2}{3}\%$ | $\frac{3}{4}\%$ | $m$ |
|---|---|---|---|---|---|---|
| 2 | .4979 7788 | .4978 2308 | .4976 6839 | .4975 1381 | .4972 0496 | 2 |
| 3 | .3321 3468 | .3320 4289 | .3319 5116 | .3318 5949 | .3316 7633 | 3 |
| 4 | .2491 5707 | .2490 9251 | .2490 2799 | .2489 6351 | .2488 3468 | 4 |
| 6 | .1661 4210 | .1661 0192 | .1660 6176 | .1660 2162 | .1659 4143 | 6 |
| 12 | .0830 8975 | .0830 7109 | .0830 5243 | .0830 3379 | .0829 9654 | 12 |

| $m$ | $\frac{7}{8}\%$ | $1\%$ | $1\frac{1}{8}\%$ | $1\frac{1}{4}\%$ | $1\frac{3}{8}\%$ | $m$ |
|---|---|---|---|---|---|---|
| 2 | .4967 4249 | .4962 8098 | .4958 2042 | .4953 6080 | .4949 0213 | 2 |
| 3 | .3314 0203 | .3311 2825 | .3308 5501 | .3305 8228 | .3303 1009 | 3 |
| 4 | .2486 4172 | .2484 4912 | .2482 5688 | .2480 6500 | .2478 7347 | 4 |
| 6 | .1658 2131 | .1657 0141 | .1655 8172 | .1654 6225 | .1653 4299 | 6 |
| 12 | .0829 4075 | .0828 8506 | .0828 2945 | .0827 7395 | .0827 1854 | 12 |

| $m$ | $1\frac{1}{2}\%$ | $1\frac{5}{8}\%$ | $1\frac{3}{4}\%$ | $1\frac{7}{8}\%$ | $2\%$ | $m$ |
|---|---|---|---|---|---|---|
| 2 | .4944 4440 | .4939 8761 | .4935 3176 | .4930 7684 | .4926 2285 | 2 |
| 3 | .3300 3841 | .3297 6725 | .3294 9662 | .3292 2650 | .3289 5689 | 3 |
| 4 | .2476 8230 | .2474 9148 | .2473 0101 | .2471 1089 | .2469 2113 | 4 |
| 6 | .1652 2395 | .1651 0511 | .1649 8649 | .1648 6807 | .1647 4987 | 6 |
| 12 | .0826 6322 | .0826 0800 | .0825 5287 | .0824 9784 | .0824 4290 | 12 |

| $m$ | $2\frac{1}{4}\%$ | $2\frac{1}{2}\%$ | $2\frac{3}{4}\%$ | $3\%$ | $3\frac{1}{4}\%$ | $m$ |
|---|---|---|---|---|---|---|
| 2 | .4917 1765 | .4908 1613 | .4899 1828 | .4890 2406 | .4881 3346 | 2 |
| 3 | .3284 1922 | .3278 8360 | .3273 5001 | .3268 1843 | .3262 8886 | 3 |
| 4 | .2465 4264 | .2461 6554 | .2457 8981 | .2454 1546 | .2450 4247 | 4 |
| 6 | .1645 1409 | .1642 7915 | .1640 4503 | .1638 1173 | .1635 7925 | 6 |
| 12 | .0823 3331 | .0822 2408 | .0821 1523 | .0820 0674 | .0818 9862 | 12 |

| $m$ | $3\frac{1}{2}\%$ | $3\frac{3}{4}\%$ | $4\%$ | $4\frac{1}{2}\%$ | $5\%$ | $m$ |
|---|---|---|---|---|---|---|
| 2 | .4872 4645 | .4863 6300 | .4854 8311 | .4837 3386 | .4819 9854 | 2 |
| 3 | .3257 6129 | .3252 3570 | .3247 1208 | .3236 7070 | .3226 3706 | 3 |
| 4 | .2446 7084 | .2443 0055 | .2439 3161 | .2431 9770 | .2424 6905 | 4 |
| 6 | .1633 4759 | .1631 1673 | .1628 8668 | .1624 2897 | .1619 7442 | 6 |
| 12 | .0817 9086 | .0816 8347 | .0815 7643 | .0813 6344 | .0811 5185 | 12 |

**Table 8A**

# TABLE 8A

$$a_{\overline{1/m}|\,i} = \frac{1-(1+i)^{-\frac{1}{m}}}{i}$$

| $m$ | $5\frac{1}{2}\%$ | 6% | $6\frac{1}{2}\%$ | 7% | $7\frac{1}{2}\%$ | $m$ |
|---|---|---|---|---|---|---|
| 2 | .4802 7696 | .4785 6896 | .4768 7437 | .4751 9301 | .4735 2474 | 2 |
| 3 | .3216 1108 | .3205 9265 | .3195 8169 | .3185 7811 | .3175 8183 | 3 |
| 4 | .2417 4561 | .2410 2731 | .2403 1409 | .2396 0589 | .2389 0266 | 4 |
| 6 | .1615 2300 | .1610 7468 | .1606 2940 | .1601 8715 | .1597 4789 | 6 |
| 12 | .0809 4167 | .0807 3287 | .0805 2544 | .0803 1937 | .0801 1463 | 12 |

| $m$ | 8% | $8\frac{1}{2}\%$ | 9% | $9\frac{1}{2}\%$ | 10% | $m$ |
|---|---|---|---|---|---|---|
| 2 | .4718 6939 | .4702 2681 | .4685 9683 | .4669 7931 | .4653 7411 | 2 |
| 3 | .3165 9276 | .3156 1082 | .3146 3592 | .3136 6799 | .3127 0694 | 3 |
| 4 | .2382 0435 | .2375 1089 | .2368 2223 | .2361 3832 | .2354 5910 | 4 |
| 6 | .1593 1159 | .1588 7820 | .1584 4771 | .1580 2008 | .1575 9528 | 6 |
| 12 | .0799 1123 | .0797 0913 | .0795 0833 | .0793 0881 | .0791 1057 | 12 |

# TABLE 9

$$\frac{1}{a_{\overline{n}|i}} = \frac{i}{1-(1+i)^{-n}} \qquad \text{Note: } \frac{1}{s_{\overline{n}|i}} = \frac{1}{a_{\overline{n}|i}} - i$$

| n | $\frac{1}{4}\%$ | $\frac{1}{3}\%$ | $\frac{5}{12}\%$ | $\frac{11}{24}\%$ | n |
|---|---|---|---|---|---|
| 1 | 1.0025 0000 | 1.0033 3333 | 1.0041 6667 | 1.0045 8333 | 1 |
| 2 | 0.5018 7578 | 0.5025 0139 | 0.5031 2717 | 0.5034 4012 | 2 |
| 3 | 0.3350 0139 | 0.3355 5802 | 0.3361 1496 | 0.3363 9355 | 3 |
| 4 | 0.2515 6445 | 0.2520 8680 | 0.2526 0958 | 0.2528 7113 | 4 |
| 5 | 0.2015 0250 | 0.2020 0444 | 0.2025 0693 | 0.2027 5838 | 5 |
| 6 | 0.1681 2803 | 0.1686 1650 | 0.1691 0564 | 0.1693 5047 | 6 |
| 7 | 0.1442 8928 | 0.1447 6824 | 0.1452 4800 | 0.1454 8817 | 7 |
| 8 | 0.1264 1035 | 0.1268 8228 | 0.1273 5512 | 0.1275 9188 | 8 |
| 9 | 0.1125 0462 | 0.1129 7118 | 0.1134 3876 | 0.1136 7293 | 9 |
| 10 | 0.1013 8015 | 0.1018 4248 | 0.1023 0596 | 0.1025 3812 | 10 |
| 11 | 0.0922 7840 | 0.0927 3736 | 0.0931 9757 | 0.0934 2814 | 11 |
| 12 | 0.0846 9370 | 0.0851 4990 | 0.0856 0748 | 0.0858 3678 | 12 |
| 13 | 0.0782 7595 | 0.0787 2989 | 0.0791 8532 | 0.0794 1360 | 13 |
| 14 | 0.0727 7510 | 0.0732 2716 | 0.0736 8082 | 0.0739 0825 | 14 |
| 15 | 0.0680 0777 | 0.0684 5825 | 0.0689 1045 | 0.0691 3719 | 15 |
| 16 | 0.0638 3642 | 0.0642 8557 | 0.0647 3655 | 0.0649 6273 | 16 |
| 17 | 0.0601 5587 | 0.0606 0389 | 0.0610 5387 | 0.0612 7959 | 17 |
| 18 | 0.0568 8433 | 0.0573 3140 | 0.0577 8053 | 0.0580 0587 | 18 |
| 19 | 0.0539 5722 | 0.0544 0348 | 0.0548 5191 | 0.0550 7695 | 19 |
| 20 | 0.0513 2288 | 0.0517 6844 | 0.0522 1630 | 0.0524 4109 | 20 |
| 21 | 0.0489 3947 | 0.0493 8445 | 0.0498 3183 | 0.0500 5643 | 21 |
| 22 | 0.0467 7278 | 0.0472 1726 | 0.0476 6427 | 0.0478 8872 | 22 |
| 23 | 0.0447 9455 | 0.0452 3861 | 0.0456 8531 | 0.0459 0965 | 23 |
| 24 | 0.0429 8121 | 0.0434 2492 | 0.0438 7139 | 0.0440 9566 | 24 |
| 25 | 0.0413 1298 | 0.0417 5640 | 0.0422 0270 | 0.0424 2692 | 25 |
| 26 | 0.0397 7312 | 0.0402 1630 | 0.0406 6247 | 0.0408 8668 | 26 |
| 27 | 0.0383 4736 | 0.0387 9035 | 0.0392 3645 | 0.0394 6066 | 27 |
| 28 | 0.0370 2347 | 0.0374 6632 | 0.0379 1239 | 0.0381 3663 | 28 |
| 29 | 0.0357 9093 | 0.0362 3367 | 0.0366 7974 | 0.0369 0402 | 29 |
| 30 | 0.0346 4059 | 0.0350 8325 | 0.0355 2936 | 0.0357 5371 | 30 |
| 31 | 0.0335 6449 | 0.0340 0712 | 0.0344 5330 | 0.0346 7773 | 31 |
| 32 | 0.0325 5569 | 0.0329 9830 | 0.0334 4458 | 0.0336 6910 | 32 |
| 33 | 0.0316 0806 | 0.0320 5067 | 0.0324 9708 | 0.0327 2170 | 33 |
| 34 | 0.0307 1620 | 0.0311 5885 | 0.0316 0540 | 0.0318 3014 | 34 |
| 35 | 0.0298 7533 | 0.0303 1803 | 0.0307 6476 | 0.0309 8963 | 35 |
| 36 | 0.0290 8121 | 0.0295 2399 | 0.0299 7090 | 0.0301 9590 | 36 |
| 37 | 0.0283 3004 | 0.0287 7291 | 0.0292 2003 | 0.0294 4518 | 37 |
| 38 | 0.0276 1843 | 0.0280 6141 | 0.0285 0875 | 0.0287 3405 | 38 |
| 39 | 0.0269 4335 | 0.0273 8644 | 0.0278 3402 | 0.0280 5949 | 39 |
| 40 | 0.0263 0204 | 0.0267 4527 | 0.0271 9310 | 0.0274 1874 | 40 |
| 41 | 0.0256 9204 | 0.0261 3543 | 0.0265 8352 | 0.0268 0933 | 41 |
| 42 | 0.0251 1112 | 0.0255 5466 | 0.0260 0303 | 0.0262 2902 | 42 |
| 43 | 0.0245 5724 | 0.0250 0095 | 0.0254 4961 | 0.0256 7579 | 43 |
| 44 | 0.0240 2855 | 0.0244 7246 | 0.0249 2141 | 0.0251 4778 | 44 |
| 45 | 0.0235 2339 | 0.0239 6749 | 0.0244 1675 | 0.0246 4332 | 45 |
| 46 | 0.0230 4022 | 0.0234 8451 | 0.0239 3409 | 0.0241 6086 | 46 |
| 47 | 0.0225 7762 | 0.0230 2213 | 0.0234 7204 | 0.0236 9901 | 47 |
| 48 | 0.0221 3433 | 0.0225 7905 | 0.0230 2929 | 0.0232 5648 | 48 |
| 49 | 0.0217 0915 | 0.0221 5410 | 0.0226 0468 | 0.0228 3207 | 49 |
| 50 | 0.0213 0099 | 0.0217 4618 | 0.0221 9711 | 0.0224 2472 | 50 |
| 51 | 0.0209 0886 | 0.0213 5429 | 0.0218 0557 | 0.0220 3341 | 51 |
| 52 | 0.0205 3184 | 0.0209 7751 | 0.0214 2916 | 0.0216 5721 | 52 |
| 53 | 0.0201 6906 | 0.0206 1499 | 0.0210 6700 | 0.0212 9528 | 53 |
| 54 | 0.0198 1974 | 0.0202 6592 | 0.0207 1830 | 0.0209 4681 | 54 |
| 55 | 0.0194 8314 | 0.0199 2958 | 0.0203 8234 | 0.0206 1108 | 55 |
| 56 | 0.0191 5858 | 0.0196 0529 | 0.0200 5843 | 0.0202 8740 | 56 |
| 57 | 0.0188 4542 | 0.0192 9241 | 0.0197 4593 | 0.0199 7514 | 57 |
| 58 | 0.0185 4308 | 0.0189 9035 | 0.0194 4426 | 0.0196 7371 | 58 |
| 59 | 0.0182 5101 | 0.0186 9856 | 0.0191 5287 | 0.0193 8255 | 59 |
| 60 | 0.0179 6869 | 0.0184 1652 | 0.0188 7123 | 0.0191 0116 | 60 |

# TABLE 9

$$\frac{1}{a_{\overline{n}|i}} = \frac{i}{1-(1+i)^{-n}} \qquad \text{Note: } \frac{1}{s_{\overline{n}|i}} = \frac{1}{a_{\overline{n}|i}} - i$$

| $n$ | $\frac{1}{4}\%$ | $\frac{1}{3}\%$ | $\frac{5}{12}\%$ | $\frac{11}{24}\%$ | $n$ |
|---|---|---|---|---|---|
| 61 | 0.0176 9564 | 0.0181 4377 | 0.0185 9888 | 0.0188 2905 | 61 |
| 62 | 0.0174 3142 | 0.0178 7984 | 0.0183 3536 | 0.0185 6578 | 62 |
| 63 | 0.0171 7561 | 0.0176 2432 | 0.0180 8025 | 0.0183 1091 | 63 |
| 64 | 0.0169 2780 | 0.0173 7681 | 0.0178 3315 | 0.0180 6407 | 64 |
| 65 | 0.0166 8764 | 0.0171 3695 | 0.0175 9371 | 0.0178 2487 | 65 |
| 66 | 0.0164 5476 | 0.0169 0438 | 0.0173 6156 | 0.0175 9298 | 66 |
| 67 | 0.0162 2886 | 0.0166 7878 | 0.0171 3639 | 0.0173 6806 | 67 |
| 68 | 0.0160 0961 | 0.0164 5985 | 0.0169 1788 | 0.0171 4980 | 68 |
| 69 | 0.0157 9674 | 0.0162 4729 | 0.0167 0574 | 0.0169 3792 | 69 |
| 70 | 0.0155 8996 | 0.0160 4083 | 0.0164 9971 | 0.0167 3215 | 70 |
| 71 | 0.0153 8902 | 0.0158 4021 | 0.0162 9952 | 0.0165 3222 | 71 |
| 72 | 0.0151 9368 | 0.0156 4518 | 0.0161 0493 | 0.0163 3789 | 72 |
| 73 | 0.0150 0370 | 0.0154 5553 | 0.0159 1572 | 0.0161 4893 | 73 |
| 74 | 0.0148 1887 | 0.0152 7103 | 0.0157 3165 | 0.0159 6513 | 74 |
| 75 | 0.0146 3898 | 0.0150 9147 | 0.0155 5253 | 0.0157 8627 | 75 |
| 76 | 0.0144 6385 | 0.0149 1666 | 0.0153 7816 | 0.0156 1217 | 76 |
| 77 | 0.0142 9327 | 0.0147 4641 | 0.0152 0836 | 0.0154 4263 | 77 |
| 78 | 0.0141 2708 | 0.0145 8056 | 0.0150 4295 | 0.0152 7748 | 78 |
| 79 | 0.0139 6511 | 0.0144 1892 | 0.0148 8177 | 0.0151 1656 | 79 |
| 80 | 0.0138 0721 | 0.0142 6135 | 0.0147 2464 | 0.0149 5971 | 80 |
| 81 | 0.0136 5321 | 0.0141 0770 | 0.0145 7144 | 0.0148 0677 | 81 |
| 82 | 0.0135 0298 | 0.0139 5781 | 0.0144 2200 | 0.0146 5760 | 82 |
| 83 | 0.0133 5639 | 0.0138 1156 | 0.0142 7620 | 0.0145 1207 | 83 |
| 84 | 0.0132 1330 | 0.0136 6881 | 0.0141 3391 | 0.0143 7004 | 84 |
| 85 | 0.0130 7359 | 0.0135 2944 | 0.0139 9500 | 0.0142 3140 | 85 |
| 86 | 0.0129 3714 | 0.0133 9333 | 0.0138 5935 | 0.0140 9602 | 86 |
| 87 | 0.0128 0384 | 0.0132 6038 | 0.0137 2685 | 0.0139 6379 | 87 |
| 88 | 0.0126 7357 | 0.0131 3046 | 0.0135 9740 | 0.0138 3461 | 88 |
| 89 | 0.0125 4625 | 0.0130 0349 | 0.0134 7088 | 0.0137 0837 | 89 |
| 90 | 0.0124 2177 | 0.0128 7936 | 0.0133 4721 | 0.0135 8497 | 90 |
| 91 | 0.0123 0004 | 0.0127 5797 | 0.0132 2629 | 0.0134 6432 | 91 |
| 92 | 0.0121 8096 | 0.0126 3925 | 0.0131 0803 | 0.0133 4634 | 92 |
| 93 | 0.0120 6446 | 0.0125 2310 | 0.0129 9234 | 0.0132 3092 | 93 |
| 94 | 0.0119 5044 | 0.0124 0944 | 0.0128 7915 | 0.0131 1800 | 94 |
| 95 | 0.0118 3884 | 0.0122 9819 | 0.0127 6836 | 0.0130 0749 | 95 |
| 96 | 0.0117 2957 | 0.0121 8928 | 0.0126 5992 | 0.0128 9932 | 96 |
| 97 | 0.0116 2257 | 0.0120 8263 | 0.0125 5374 | 0.0127 9342 | 97 |
| 98 | 0.0115 1776 | 0.0119 7818 | 0.0124 4976 | 0.0126 8971 | 98 |
| 99 | 0.0114 1508 | 0.0118 7585 | 0.0123 4790 | 0.0125 8813 | 99 |
| 100 | 0.0113 1446 | 0.0117 7559 | 0.0122 4811 | 0.0124 8862 | 100 |
| 101 | 0.0112 1584 | 0.0116 7734 | 0.0121 5033 | 0.0123 9111 | 101 |
| 102 | 0.0111 1917 | 0.0115 8103 | 0.0120 5449 | 0.0122 9555 | 102 |
| 103 | 0.0110 2439 | 0.0114 8660 | 0.0119 6054 | 0.0122 0187 | 103 |
| 104 | 0.0109 3144 | 0.0113 9401 | 0.0118 6842 | 0.0121 1003 | 104 |
| 105 | 0.0108 4027 | 0.0113 0320 | 0.0117 7809 | 0.0120 1998 | 105 |
| 106 | 0.0107 5082 | 0.0112 1413 | 0.0116 8948 | 0.0119 3165 | 106 |
| 107 | 0.0106 6307 | 0.0111 2673 | 0.0116 0256 | 0.0118 4500 | 107 |
| 108 | 0.0105 7694 | 0.0110 4097 | 0.0115 1727 | 0.0117 6000 | 108 |
| 109 | 0.0104 9241 | 0.0109 5680 | 0.0114 3358 | 0.0116 7658 | 109 |
| 110 | 0.0104 0942 | 0.0108 7418 | 0.0113 5143 | 0.0115 9471 | 110 |
| 111 | 0.0103 2793 | 0.0107 9306 | 0.0112 7079 | 0.0115 1435 | 111 |
| 112 | 0.0102 4791 | 0.0107 1340 | 0.0111 9161 | 0.0114 3545 | 112 |
| 113 | 0.0101 6932 | 0.0106 3518 | 0.0111 1386 | 0.0113 5798 | 113 |
| 114 | 0.0100 9211 | 0.0105 5834 | 0.0110 3750 | 0.0112 8190 | 114 |
| 115 | 0.0100 1626 | 0.0104 8285 | 0.0109 6249 | 0.0112 0717 | 115 |
| 116 | 0.0099 4172 | 0.0104 0868 | 0.0108 8880 | 0.0111 3376 | 116 |
| 117 | 0.0098 6846 | 0.0103 3579 | 0.0108 1639 | 0.0110 6163 | 117 |
| 118 | 0.0097 9646 | 0.0102 6416 | 0.0107 4524 | 0.0109 9075 | 118 |
| 119 | 0.0097 2567 | 0.0101 9374 | 0.0106 7530 | 0.0109 2110 | 119 |
| 120 | 0.0096 5607 | 0.0101 2451 | 0.0106 0655 | 0.0108 5263 | 120 |

**PERIODIC PAYMENT**

When Present Value of Annuity Is 1

# TABLE 9

$$\frac{1}{a_{\overline{n}|i}} = \frac{i}{1 - (1+i)^{-n}} \qquad \text{Note: } \frac{1}{s_{\overline{n}|i}} = \frac{1}{a_{\overline{n}|i}} - i$$

| n | $\frac{1}{4}\%$ | $\frac{1}{3}\%$ | $\frac{5}{12}\%$ | $\frac{11}{24}\%$ | n |
|---|---|---|---|---|---|
| 121 | 0.0095 8764 | 0.0100 5645 | 0.0105 3896 | 0.0107 8532 | 121 |
| 122 | 0.0095 2033 | 0.0099 8951 | 0.0104 7251 | 0.0107 1914 | 122 |
| 123 | 0.0094 5412 | 0.0099 2367 | 0.0104 0715 | 0.0106 5407 | 123 |
| 124 | 0.0093 8899 | 0.0098 5892 | 0.0103 4288 | 0.0105 9007 | 124 |
| 125 | 0.0093 2491 | 0.0097 9521 | 0.0102 7965 | 0.0105 2713 | 125 |
| 126 | 0.0092 6186 | 0.0097 3253 | 0.0102 1745 | 0.0104 6521 | 126 |
| 127 | 0.0091 9981 | 0.0096 7085 | 0.0101 5625 | 0.0104 0429 | 127 |
| 128 | 0.0091 3873 | 0.0096 1015 | 0.0100 9603 | 0.0103 4435 | 128 |
| 129 | 0.0090 7861 | 0.0095 5040 | 0.0100 3677 | 0.0102 8537 | 129 |
| 130 | 0.0090 1942 | 0.0094 9158 | 0.0099 7844 | 0.0102 2732 | 130 |
| 131 | 0.0089 6115 | 0.0094 3368 | 0.0099 2102 | 0.0101 7018 | 131 |
| 132 | 0.0089 0376 | 0.0093 7667 | 0.0098 6449 | 0.0101 1393 | 132 |
| 133 | 0.0088 4725 | 0.0093 2053 | 0.0098 0883 | 0.0100 5856 | 133 |
| 134 | 0.0087 9159 | 0.0092 6524 | 0.0097 5403 | 0.0100 0403 | 134 |
| 135 | 0.0087 3675 | 0.0092 1079 | 0.0097 0005 | 0.0099 5034 | 135 |
| 136 | 0.0086 8274 | 0.0091 5715 | 0.0096 4689 | 0.0098 9746 | 136 |
| 137 | 0.0086 2952 | 0.0091 0430 | 0.0095 9453 | 0.0098 4538 | 137 |
| 138 | 0.0085 7707 | 0.0090 5223 | 0.0095 4295 | 0.0097 9408 | 138 |
| 139 | 0.0085 2539 | 0.0090 0093 | 0.0094 9213 | 0.0097 4354 | 139 |
| 140 | 0.0084 7446 | 0.0089 5037 | 0.0094 4205 | 0.0096 9375 | 140 |
| 141 | 0.0084 2425 | 0.0089 0054 | 0.0093 9271 | 0.0096 4468 | 141 |
| 142 | 0.0083 7476 | 0.0088 5143 | 0.0093 4408 | 0.0095 9634 | 142 |
| 143 | 0.0083 2597 | 0.0088 0301 | 0.0092 9615 | 0.0095 4869 | 143 |
| 144 | 0.0082 7787 | 0.0087 5528 | 0.0092 4890 | 0.0095 0172 | 144 |
| 145 | 0.0082 3043 | 0.0087 0822 | 0.0092 0233 | 0.0094 5543 | 145 |
| 146 | 0.0081 8365 | 0.0086 6182 | 0.0091 5641 | 0.0094 0979 | 146 |
| 147 | 0.0081 3752 | 0.0086 1607 | 0.0091 1114 | 0.0093 6480 | 147 |
| 148 | 0.0080 9201 | 0.0085 7094 | 0.0090 6650 | 0.0093 2044 | 148 |
| 149 | 0.0080 4712 | 0.0085 2643 | 0.0090 2247 | 0.0092 7669 | 149 |
| 150 | 0.0080 0284 | 0.0084 8252 | 0.0089 7905 | 0.0092 3355 | 150 |
| 151 | 0.0079 5915 | 0.0084 3921 | 0.0089 3622 | 0.0091 9101 | 151 |
| 152 | 0.0079 1605 | 0.0083 9648 | 0.0088 9398 | 0.0091 4905 | 152 |
| 153 | 0.0078 7351 | 0.0083 5433 | 0.0088 5231 | 0.0091 0765 | 153 |
| 154 | 0.0078 3153 | 0.0083 1273 | 0.0088 1119 | 0.0090 6682 | 154 |
| 155 | 0.0077 9010 | 0.0082 7167 | 0.0087 7063 | 0.0090 2653 | 155 |
| 156 | 0.0077 4921 | 0.0082 3116 | 0.0087 3060 | 0.0089 8679 | 156 |
| 157 | 0.0077 0885 | 0.0081 9118 | 0.0086 9110 | 0.0089 4756 | 157 |
| 158 | 0.0076 6900 | 0.0081 5171 | 0.0086 5211 | 0.0089 0886 | 158 |
| 159 | 0.0076 2966 | 0.0081 1275 | 0.0086 1364 | 0.0088 7067 | 159 |
| 160 | 0.0075 9082 | 0.0080 7429 | 0.0085 7566 | 0.0088 3297 | 160 |
| 161 | 0.0075 5247 | 0.0080 3631 | 0.0085 3817 | 0.0087 9576 | 161 |
| 162 | 0.0075 1459 | 0.0079 9882 | 0.0085 0116 | 0.0087 5903 | 162 |
| 163 | 0.0074 7719 | 0.0079 6180 | 0.0084 6462 | 0.0087 2278 | 163 |
| 164 | 0.0074 4025 | 0.0079 2524 | 0.0084 2855 | 0.0086 8698 | 164 |
| 165 | 0.0074 0377 | 0.0078 8913 | 0.0083 9293 | 0.0086 5164 | 165 |
| 166 | 0.0073 6773 | 0.0078 5347 | 0.0083 5775 | 0.0086 1674 | 166 |
| 167 | 0.0073 3213 | 0.0078 1825 | 0.0083 2301 | 0.0085 8229 | 167 |
| 168 | 0.0072 9695 | 0.0077 8346 | 0.0082 8871 | 0.0085 4826 | 168 |
| 169 | 0.0072 6220 | 0.0077 4909 | 0.0082 5482 | 0.0085 1465 | 169 |
| 170 | 0.0072 2787 | 0.0077 1513 | 0.0082 2135 | 0.0084 8146 | 170 |
| 171 | 0.0071 9394 | 0.0076 8158 | 0.0081 8829 | 0.0084 4868 | 171 |
| 172 | 0.0071 6042 | 0.0076 4844 | 0.0081 5562 | 0.0084 1629 | 172 |
| 173 | 0.0071 2728 | 0.0076 1568 | 0.0081 2336 | 0.0083 8430 | 173 |
| 174 | 0.0070 9454 | 0.0075 8332 | 0.0080 9147 | 0.0083 5270 | 174 |
| 175 | 0.0070 6217 | 0.0075 5133 | 0.0080 5997 | 0.0083 2148 | 175 |
| 176 | 0.0070 3018 | 0.0075 1972 | 0.0080 2884 | 0.0082 9063 | 176 |
| 177 | 0.0069 9855 | 0.0074 8847 | 0.0079 9808 | 0.0082 6014 | 177 |
| 178 | 0.0069 6729 | 0.0074 5759 | 0.0079 6768 | 0.0082 3002 | 178 |
| 179 | 0.0069 3638 | 0.0074 2706 | 0.0079 3763 | 0.0082 0025 | 179 |
| 180 | 0.0069 0582 | 0.0073 9688 | 0.0079 0794 | 0.0081 7083 | 180 |

Table 9

**TABLE 9**

$$\frac{1}{a_{\overline{n}|i}} = \frac{i}{1-(1+i)^{-n}} \quad \text{Note:} \quad \frac{1}{s_{\overline{n}|i}} = \frac{1}{a_{\overline{n}|i}} - i$$

| n | $\frac{1}{4}$ % | $\frac{1}{3}$ % | $\frac{5}{12}$ % | $\frac{11}{24}$ % | n |
|---|---|---|---|---|---|
| 181 | 0.0068 7560 | 0.0073 6704 | 0.0078 7858 | 0.0081 4176 | 181 |
| 182 | 0.0068 4572 | 0.0073 3754 | 0.0078 4957 | 0.0081 1302 | 182 |
| 183 | 0.0068 1617 | 0.0073 0838 | 0.0078 2088 | 0.0080 8462 | 183 |
| 184 | 0.0067 8695 | 0.0072 7954 | 0.0077 9253 | 0.0080 5654 | 184 |
| 185 | 0.0067 5805 | 0.0072 5102 | 0.0077 6449 | 0.0080 2878 | 185 |
| 186 | 0.0067 2947 | 0.0072 2281 | 0.0077 3677 | 0.0080 0134 | 186 |
| 187 | 0.0067 0120 | 0.0071 9492 | 0.0077 0936 | 0.0079 7420 | 187 |
| 188 | 0.0066 7323 | 0.0071 6734 | 0.0076 8226 | 0.0079 4738 | 188 |
| 189 | 0.0066 4557 | 0.0071 4005 | 0.0076 5546 | 0.0079 2085 | 189 |
| 190 | 0.0066 1820 | 0.0071 1307 | 0.0076 2895 | 0.0078 9463 | 190 |
| 191 | 0.0065 9112 | 0.0070 8637 | 0.0076 0274 | 0.0078 6869 | 191 |
| 192 | 0.0065 6434 | 0.0070 5996 | 0.0075 7681 | 0.0078 4304 | 192 |
| 193 | 0.0065 3783 | 0.0070 3384 | 0.0075 5117 | 0.0078 1767 | 193 |
| 194 | 0.0065 1160 | 0.0070 0799 | 0.0075 2580 | 0.0077 9258 | 194 |
| 195 | 0.0064 8565 | 0.0069 8242 | 0.0075 0071 | 0.0077 6777 | 195 |
| 196 | 0.0064 5997 | 0.0069 5711 | 0.0074 7589 | 0.0077 4322 | 196 |
| 197 | 0.0064 3455 | 0.0069 3208 | 0.0074 5133 | 0.0077 1894 | 197 |
| 198 | 0.0064 0939 | 0.0069 0730 | 0.0074 2704 | 0.0076 9492 | 198 |
| 199 | 0.0063 8450 | 0.0068 8279 | 0.0074 0300 | 0.0076 7116 | 199 |
| 200 | 0.0063 5985 | 0.0068 5852 | 0.0073 7922 | 0.0076 4766 | 200 |
| 201 | 0.0063 3546 | 0.0068 3451 | 0.0073 5569 | 0.0076 2440 | 201 |
| 202 | 0.0063 1131 | 0.0068 1074 | 0.0073 3240 | 0.0076 0139 | 202 |
| 203 | 0.0062 8741 | 0.0067 8722 | 0.0073 0936 | 0.0075 7862 | 203 |
| 204 | 0.0062 6375 | 0.0067 6393 | 0.0072 8655 | 0.0075 5609 | 204 |
| 205 | 0.0062 4032 | 0.0067 4089 | 0.0072 6398 | 0.0075 3380 | 205 |
| 206 | 0.0062 1712 | 0.0067 1807 | 0.0072 4165 | 0.0075 1174 | 206 |
| 207 | 0.0061 9416 | 0.0066 9548 | 0.0072 1954 | 0.0074 8990 | 207 |
| 208 | 0.0061 7141 | 0.0066 7312 | 0.0071 9766 | 0.0074 6829 | 208 |
| 209 | 0.0061 4890 | 0.0066 5098 | 0.0071 7600 | 0.0074 4691 | 209 |
| 210 | 0.0061 2660 | 0.0066 2906 | 0.0071 5456 | 0.0074 2574 | 210 |
| 211 | 0.0061 0451 | 0.0066 0736 | 0.0071 3333 | 0.0074 0479 | 211 |
| 212 | 0.0060 8264 | 0.0065 8587 | 0.0071 1232 | 0.0073 8405 | 212 |
| 213 | 0.0060 6098 | 0.0065 6459 | 0.0070 9152 | 0.0073 6352 | 213 |
| 214 | 0.0060 3953 | 0.0065 4351 | 0.0070 7092 | 0.0073 4320 | 214 |
| 215 | 0.0060 1828 | 0.0065 2264 | 0.0070 5053 | 0.0073 2308 | 215 |
| 216 | 0.0059 9723 | 0.0065 0198 | 0.0070 3034 | 0.0073 0316 | 216 |
| 217 | 0.0059 7638 | 0.0064 8151 | 0.0070 1035 | 0.0072 8344 | 217 |
| 218 | 0.0059 5573 | 0.0064 6123 | 0.0069 9055 | 0.0072 6392 | 218 |
| 219 | 0.0059 3527 | 0.0064 4115 | 0.0069 7095 | 0.0072 4459 | 219 |
| 220 | 0.0059 1500 | 0.0064 2126 | 0.0069 5153 | 0.0072 2545 | 220 |
| 221 | 0.0058 9492 | 0.0064 0156 | 0.0069 3231 | 0.0072 0649 | 221 |
| 222 | 0.0058 7503 | 0.0063 8205 | 0.0069 1327 | 0.0071 8773 | 222 |
| 223 | 0.0058 5531 | 0.0063 6272 | 0.0068 9441 | 0.0071 6914 | 223 |
| 224 | 0.0058 3578 | 0.0063 4356 | 0.0068 7573 | 0.0071 5073 | 224 |
| 225 | 0.0058 1643 | 0.0063 2458 | 0.0068 5723 | 0.0071 3251 | 225 |
| 226 | 0.0057 9725 | 0.0063 0578 | 0.0068 3891 | 0.0071 1445 | 226 |
| 227 | 0.0057 7824 | 0.0062 8716 | 0.0068 2076 | 0.0070 9657 | 227 |
| 228 | 0.0057 5941 | 0.0062 6870 | 0.0068 0278 | 0.0070 7886 | 228 |
| 229 | 0.0057 4075 | 0.0062 5042 | 0.0067 8497 | 0.0070 6132 | 229 |
| 230 | 0.0057 2225 | 0.0062 3230 | 0.0067 6732 | 0.0070 4395 | 230 |
| 231 | 0.0057 0391 | 0.0062 1434 | 0.0067 4984 | 0.0070 2673 | 231 |
| 232 | 0.0056 8574 | 0.0061 9655 | 0.0067 3252 | 0.0070 0969 | 232 |
| 233 | 0.0056 6773 | 0.0061 7892 | 0.0067 1536 | 0.0069 9280 | 233 |
| 234 | 0.0056 4988 | 0.0061 6144 | 0.0066 9836 | 0.0069 7606 | 234 |
| 235 | 0.0056 3218 | 0.0061 4412 | 0.0066 8151 | 0.0069 5949 | 235 |
| 236 | 0.0056 1464 | 0.0061 2696 | 0.0066 6482 | 0.0069 4307 | 236 |
| 237 | 0.0055 9725 | 0.0061 0995 | 0.0066 4828 | 0.0069 2679 | 237 |
| 238 | 0.0055 8001 | 0.0060 9308 | 0.0066 3189 | 0.0069 1067 | 238 |
| 239 | 0.0055 6292 | 0.0060 7637 | 0.0066 1565 | 0.0068 9470 | 239 |
| 240 | 0.0055 4598 | 0.0060 5980 | 0.0065 9956 | 0.0068 7887 | 240 |

**TABLE 9**

$$\frac{1}{a_{\overline{n}|i}} = \frac{i}{1-(1+i)^{-n}} \qquad \text{Note: } \frac{1}{s_{\overline{n}|i}} = \frac{1}{a_{\overline{n}|i}} - i$$

| $n$ | $\frac{1}{2}\%$ | $\frac{13}{24}\%$ | $\frac{7}{12}\%$ | $\frac{5}{8}\%$ | $n$ |
|---|---|---|---|---|---|
| 1 | 1.0050 0000 | 1.0054 1667 | 1.0058 3333 | 1.0062 5000 | 1 |
| 2 | 0.5037 5312 | 0.5040 6616 | 0.5043 7924 | 0.5046 9237 | 2 |
| 3 | 0.3366 7221 | 0.3369 5095 | 0.3372 2976 | 0.3375 0865 | 3 |
| 4 | 0.2531 3279 | 0.2533 9457 | 0.2536 5644 | 0.2539 1842 | 4 |
| 5 | 0.2030 0997 | 0.2032 6170 | 0.2035 1357 | 0.2037 6558 | 5 |
| 6 | 0.1695 9546 | 0.1698 4061 | 0.1700 8594 | 0.1703 3143 | 6 |
| 7 | 0.1457 2843 | 0.1459 6910 | 0.1462 0986 | 0.1464 5082 | 7 |
| 8 | 0.1278 2886 | 0.1280 6608 | 0.1283 0351 | 0.1285 4118 | 8 |
| 9 | 0.1139 0736 | 0.1141 4204 | 0.1143 7698 | 0.1146 1218 | 9 |
| 10 | 0.1027 7057 | 0.1030 0331 | 0.1032 3632 | 0.1034 6963 | 10 |
| 11 | 0.0936 5903 | 0.0938 9024 | 0.0941 2175 | 0.0943 5358 | 11 |
| 12 | 0.0860 6643 | 0.0862 9642 | 0.0865 2675 | 0.0867 5742 | 12 |
| 13 | 0.0796 4224 | 0.0798 7125 | 0.0801 0064 | 0.0803 3039 | 13 |
| 14 | 0.0741 3609 | 0.0743 6432 | 0.0745 9295 | 0.0748 2198 | 14 |
| 15 | 0.0693 6436 | 0.0695 9197 | 0.0698 1999 | 0.0700 4845 | 15 |
| 16 | 0.0651 8937 | 0.0654 1646 | 0.0656 4401 | 0.0658 7202 | 16 |
| 17 | 0.0615 0579 | 0.0617 3248 | 0.0619 5966 | 0.0621 8732 | 17 |
| 18 | 0.0582 3173 | 0.0584 5810 | 0.0586 8499 | 0.0589 1239 | 18 |
| 19 | 0.0553 0253 | 0.0555 2865 | 0.0557 5532 | 0.0559 8252 | 19 |
| 20 | 0.0526 6645 | 0.0528 9239 | 0.0531 1889 | 0.0533 4597 | 20 |
| 21 | 0.0502 8163 | 0.0505 0743 | 0.0507 3383 | 0.0509 6083 | 21 |
| 22 | 0.0481 1380 | 0.0483 3951 | 0.0485 6585 | 0.0487 9281 | 22 |
| 23 | 0.0461 3465 | 0.0463 6031 | 0.0465 8663 | 0.0468 1360 | 23 |
| 24 | 0.0443 2061 | 0.0445 4625 | 0.0447 7258 | 0.0449 9959 | 24 |
| 25 | 0.0426 5186 | 0.0428 7751 | 0.0431 0388 | 0.0433 3096 | 25 |
| 26 | 0.0411 1163 | 0.0413 3732 | 0.0415 6376 | 0.0417 9094 | 26 |
| 27 | 0.0396 8565 | 0.0399 1140 | 0.0401 3793 | 0.0403 6523 | 27 |
| 28 | 0.0383 6167 | 0.0385 8751 | 0.0388 1415 | 0.0390 4159 | 28 |
| 29 | 0.0371 2914 | 0.0373 5508 | 0.0375 8186 | 0.0378 0946 | 29 |
| 30 | 0.0359 7892 | 0.0362 0498 | 0.0364 3191 | 0.0366 5969 | 30 |
| 31 | 0.0349 0304 | 0.0351 2924 | 0.0353 5633 | 0.0355 8430 | 31 |
| 32 | 0.0338 9453 | 0.0341 2088 | 0.0343 4815 | 0.0345 7633 | 32 |
| 33 | 0.0329 4727 | 0.0331 7379 | 0.0334 0124 | 0.0336 2964 | 33 |
| 34 | 0.0320 5586 | 0.0322 8254 | 0.0325 1020 | 0.0327 3883 | 34 |
| 35 | 0.0312 1550 | 0.0314 4237 | 0.0316 7024 | 0.0318 9911 | 35 |
| 36 | 0.0304 2194 | 0.0306 4900 | 0.0308 7710 | 0.0311 0622 | 36 |
| 37 | 0.0296 7139 | 0.0298 9865 | 0.0301 2698 | 0.0303 5636 | 37 |
| 38 | 0.0298 6045 | 0.0291 8793 | 0.0294 1649 | 0.0296 4614 | 38 |
| 39 | 0.0282 8607 | 0.0285 1377 | 0.0287 4258 | 0.0289 7250 | 39 |
| 40 | 0.0276 4552 | 0.0278 7344 | 0.0281 0251 | 0.0283 3271 | 40 |
| 41 | 0.0270 3631 | 0.0272 6447 | 0.0274 9379 | 0.0277 2429 | 41 |
| 42 | 0.0264 5622 | 0.0266 8461 | 0.0269 1420 | 0.0271 4499 | 42 |
| 43 | 0.0259 0320 | 0.0261 3183 | 0.0263 6170 | 0.0265 9278 | 43 |
| 44 | 0.0253 7541 | 0.0256 0429 | 0.0258 3443 | 0.0260 6583 | 44 |
| 45 | 0.0248 7117 | 0.0251 0031 | 0.0253 3073 | 0.0255 6243 | 45 |
| 46 | 0.0243 8894 | 0.0246 1834 | 0.0248 4905 | 0.0250 8106 | 46 |
| 47 | 0.0239 2733 | 0.0241 5698 | 0.0243 8798 | 0.0246 2032 | 47 |
| 48 | 0.0234 8503 | 0.0237 1495 | 0.0239 4624 | 0.0241 7890 | 48 |
| 49 | 0.0230 6087 | 0.0232 9106 | 0.0235 2265 | 0.0237 5563 | 49 |
| 50 | 0.0226 5376 | 0.0228 8422 | 0.0231 1612 | 0.0233 4943 | 50 |
| 51 | 0.0222 6269 | 0.0224 9344 | 0.0227 2563 | 0.0229 5928 | 51 |
| 52 | 0.0218 8675 | 0.0221 1777 | 0.0223 5027 | 0.0225 8425 | 52 |
| 53 | 0.0215 2507 | 0.0217 5637 | 0.0219 8919 | 0.0222 2350 | 53 |
| 54 | 0.0211 7686 | 0.0214 0845 | 0.0216 4157 | 0.0218 7623 | 54 |
| 55 | 0.0208 4139 | 0.0210 7327 | 0.0213 0671 | 0.0215 4171 | 55 |
| 56 | 0.0205 1797 | 0.0207 5014 | 0.0209 8390 | 0.0212 1925 | 56 |
| 57 | 0.0202 0598 | 0.0204 3844 | 0.0206 7251 | 0.0209 0821 | 57 |
| 58 | 0.0199 0481 | 0.0201 3756 | 0.0203 7196 | 0.0206 0801 | 58 |
| 59 | 0.0196 1392 | 0.0198 4697 | 0.0200 8170 | 0.0203 1809 | 59 |
| 60 | 0.0193 3280 | 0.0195 6615 | 0.0198 0120 | 0.0200 3795 | 60 |

Table
9

## TABLE 9

$$\frac{1}{a_{\overline{n}|i}} = \frac{i}{1-(1+i)^{-n}} \qquad \text{Note: } \frac{1}{s_{\overline{n}|i}} = \frac{1}{a_{\overline{n}|i}} - i$$

| $n$ | $\frac{1}{2}\%$ | $\frac{13}{24}\%$ | $\frac{7}{12}\%$ | $\frac{5}{8}\%$ | $n$ |
|---|---|---|---|---|---|
| 61 | 0.0190 6096 | 0.0192 9461 | 0.0195 2999 | 0.0197 6709 | 61 |
| 62 | 0.0187 9796 | 0.0190 3191 | 0.0192 6762 | 0.0195 0508 | 62 |
| 63 | 0.0185 4337 | 0.0187 7762 | 0.0190 1366 | 0.0192 5148 | 63 |
| 64 | 0.0182 9681 | 0.0185 3136 | 0.0187 6773 | 0.0190 0591 | 64 |
| 65 | 0.0180 5789 | 0.0182 9275 | 0.0185 2946 | 0.0187 6800 | 65 |
| 66 | 0.0178 2627 | 0.0180 6144 | 0.0182 9848 | 0.0185 3739 | 66 |
| 67 | 0.0176 0163 | 0.0178 3711 | 0.0180 7449 | 0.0183 1376 | 67 |
| 68 | 0.0173 8366 | 0.0176 1945 | 0.0178 5716 | 0.0180 9680 | 68 |
| 69 | 0.0171 7206 | 0.0174 0817 | 0.0176 4622 | 0.0178 8622 | 69 |
| 70 | 0.0169 6657 | 0.0172 0299 | 0.0174 4138 | 0.0176 8175 | 70 |
| 71 | 0.0167 6693 | 0.0170 0366 | 0.0172 4239 | 0.0174 8313 | 71 |
| 72 | 0.0165 7289 | 0.0168 0993 | 0.0170 4901 | 0.0172 9011 | 72 |
| 73 | 0.0163 8422 | 0.0166 2158 | 0.0168 6100 | 0.0171 0247 | 73 |
| 74 | 0.0162 0070 | 0.0164 3838 | 0.0166 7814 | 0.0169 1999 | 74 |
| 75 | 0.0160 2214 | 0.0162 6013 | 0.0165 0024 | 0.0167 4246 | 75 |
| 76 | 0.0158 4832 | 0.0160 8663 | 0.0163 2709 | 0.0165 6968 | 76 |
| 77 | 0.0156 7908 | 0.0159 1771 | 0.0161 5851 | 0.0164 0147 | 77 |
| 78 | 0.0155 1423 | 0.0157 5317 | 0.0159 9432 | 0.0162 3766 | 78 |
| 79 | 0.0153 5360 | 0.0155 9287 | 0.0158 3436 | 0.0160 7808 | 79 |
| 80 | 0.0151 9704 | 0.0154 3663 | 0.0156 7847 | 0.0159 2256 | 80 |
| 81 | 0.0150 4439 | 0.0152 8430 | 0.0155 2650 | 0.0157 7096 | 81 |
| 82 | 0.0148 9552 | 0.0151 3575 | 0.0153 7830 | 0.0156 2314 | 82 |
| 83 | 0.0147 5028 | 0.0149 9084 | 0.0152 3373 | 0.0154 7895 | 83 |
| 84 | 0.0146 0855 | 0.0148 4944 | 0.0150 9268 | 0.0153 3828 | 84 |
| 85 | 0.0144 7021 | 0.0147 1141 | 0.0149 5501 | 0.0152 0098 | 85 |
| 86 | 0.0143 3513 | 0.0145 7666 | 0.0148 2060 | 0.0150 6696 | 86 |
| 87 | 0.0142 0320 | 0.0144 4505 | 0.0146 8935 | 0.0149 3608 | 87 |
| 88 | 0.0140 7431 | 0.0143 1650 | 0.0145 6115 | 0.0148 0826 | 88 |
| 89 | 0.0139 4837 | 0.0141 9088 | 0.0144 3588 | 0.0146 8337 | 89 |
| 90 | 0.0138 2527 | 0.0140 6811 | 0.0143 1347 | 0.0145 6134 | 90 |
| 91 | 0.0137 0493 | 0.0139 4809 | 0.0141 9380 | 0.0144 4205 | 91 |
| 92 | 0.0135 8724 | 0.0138 3073 | 0.0140 7679 | 0.0143 2542 | 92 |
| 93 | 0.0134 7213 | 0.0137 1594 | 0.0139 6236 | 0.0142 1137 | 93 |
| 94 | 0.0133 5950 | 0.0136 0365 | 0.0138 5042 | 0.0140 9982 | 94 |
| 95 | 0.0132 4930 | 0.0134 9377 | 0.0137 4090 | 0.0139 9067 | 95 |
| 96 | 0.0131 4143 | 0.0133 8623 | 0.0136 3372 | 0.0138 8387 | 96 |
| 97 | 0.0130 3583 | 0.0132 8096 | 0.0135 2880 | 0.0137 7933 | 97 |
| 98 | 0.0129 3242 | 0.0131 7788 | 0.0134 2608 | 0.0136 7700 | 98 |
| 99 | 0.0128 3115 | 0.0130 7694 | 0.0133 2549 | 0.0135 7679 | 99 |
| 100 | 0.0127 3194 | 0.0129 7806 | 0.0132 2696 | 0.0134 7864 | 100 |
| 101 | 0.0126 3473 | 0.0128 8118 | 0.0131 3045 | 0.0133 8251 | 101 |
| 102 | 0.0125 3947 | 0.0127 8625 | 0.0130 3587 | 0.0132 8832 | 102 |
| 103 | 0.0124 4610 | 0.0126 9321 | 0.0129 4319 | 0.0131 9602 | 103 |
| 104 | 0.0123 5457 | 0.0126 0201 | 0.0128 5234 | 0.0131 0555 | 104 |
| 105 | 0.0122 6481 | 0.0125 1259 | 0.0127 6328 | 0.0130 1687 | 105 |
| 106 | 0.0121 7679 | 0.0124 2489 | 0.0126 7594 | 0.0129 2992 | 106 |
| 107 | 0.0120 9045 | 0.0123 3889 | 0.0125 9029 | 0.0128 4465 | 107 |
| 108 | 0.0120 0575 | 0.0122 5452 | 0.0125 0628 | 0.0127 6102 | 108 |
| 109 | 0.0119 2264 | 0.0121 7174 | 0.0124 2385 | 0.0126 7898 | 109 |
| 110 | 0.0118 4107 | 0.0120 9050 | 0.0123 4298 | 0.0125 9848 | 110 |
| 111 | 0.0117 6102 | 0.0120 1078 | 0.0122 6361 | 0.0125 1950 | 111 |
| 112 | 0.0116 8242 | 0.0119 3252 | 0.0121 8571 | 0.0124 4198 | 112 |
| 113 | 0.0116 0526 | 0.0118 5568 | 0.0121 0923 | 0.0123 6588 | 113 |
| 114 | 0.0115 2948 | 0.0117 8024 | 0.0120 3414 | 0.0122 9118 | 114 |
| 115 | 0.0114 5506 | 0.0117 0615 | 0.0119 6041 | 0.0122 1783 | 115 |
| 116 | 0.0113 8195 | 0.0116 3337 | 0.0118 8799 | 0:0121 4579 | 116 |
| 117 | 0.0113 1013 | 0.0115 6188 | 0.0118 1686 | 0.0120 7504 | 117 |
| 118 | 0.0112 3956 | 0.0114 9165 | 0.0117 4698 | 0.0120 0555 | 118 |
| 119 | 0.0111 7021 | 0.0114 2263 | 0.0116 7832 | 0.0119 3727 | 119 |
| 120 | 0.0111 0205 | 0.0113 5480 | 0.0116 1085 | 0.0118 7018 | 120 |

**TABLE 9**

$$\frac{1}{a_{\overline{n}|i}} = \frac{i}{1 - (1 + i)^{-n}} \quad \text{Note:} \ \frac{1}{s_{\overline{n}|i}} = \frac{1}{a_{\overline{n}|i}} - i$$

| n | $\frac{1}{2}\%$ | $\frac{13}{24}\%$ | $\frac{7}{12}\%$ | $\frac{5}{8}\%$ | n |
|---|---|---|---|---|---|
| 121 | 0.0110 3505 | 0.0112 8813 | 0.0115 4454 | 0.0118 0425 | 121 |
| 122 | 0.0109 6918 | 0.0112 2259 | 0.0114 7936 | 0.0117 3945 | 122 |
| 123 | 0.0109 0441 | 0.0111 5816 | 0.0114 1528 | 0.0116 7575 | 123 |
| 124 | 0.0108 4072 | 0.0110 9480 | 0.0113 5228 | 0.0116 1313 | 124 |
| 125 | 0.0107 7808 | 0.0110 3249 | 0.0112 9033 | 0.0115 5157 | 125 |
| 126 | 0.0107 1647 | 0.0109 7121 | 0.0112 2941 | 0.0114 9102 | 126 |
| 127 | 0.0106 5586 | 0.0109 1093 | 0.0111 6948 | 0.0114 3148 | 127 |
| 128 | 0.0105 9623 | 0.0108 5163 | 0.0111 1054 | 0.0113 7292 | 128 |
| 129 | 0.0105 3755 | 0.0107 9329 | 0.0110 5255 | 0.0113 1531 | 129 |
| 130 | 0.0104 7981 | 0.0107 3588 | 0.0109 9550 | 0.0112 5864 | 130 |
| 131 | 0.0104 2298 | 0.0106 7938 | 0.0109 3935 | 0.0112 0288 | 131 |
| 132 | 0.0103 6703 | 0.0106 2377 | 0.0108 8410 | 0.0111 4800 | 132 |
| 133 | 0.0103 1197 | 0.0105 6903 | 0.0108 2972 | 0.0110 9400 | 133 |
| 134 | 0.0102 5775 | 0.0105 1514 | 0.0107 7619 | 0.0110 4086 | 134 |
| 135 | 0.0102 0436 | 0.0104 6209 | 0.0107 2349 | 0.0109 8854 | 135 |
| 136 | 0.0101 5179 | 0.0104 0985 | 0.0106 7161 | 0.0109 3703 | 136 |
| 137 | 0.0101 0002 | 0.0103 5841 | 0.0106 2052 | 0.0108 8633 | 137 |
| 138 | 0.0100 4902 | 0.0103 0774 | 0.0105 7021 | 0.0108 3640 | 138 |
| 139 | 0.0099 9879 | 0.0102 5784 | 0.0105 2067 | 0.0107 8723 | 139 |
| 140 | 0.0099 4930 | 0.0102 0869 | 0.0104 7187 | 0.0107 3881 | 140 |
| 141 | 0.0099 0055 | 0.0101 6026 | 0.0104 2380 | 0.0106 9111 | 141 |
| 142 | 0.0098 5250 | 0.0101 1255 | 0.0103 7644 | 0.0106 4414 | 142 |
| 143 | 0.0098 0516 | 0.0100 6554 | 0.0103 2978 | 0.0105 9786 | 143 |
| 144 | 0.0097 5850 | 0.0100 1921 | 0.0102 8381 | 0.0105 5226 | 144 |
| 145 | 0.0097 1252 | 0.0099 7355 | 0.0102 3851 | 0.0105 0734 | 145 |
| 146 | 0.0096 6718 | 0.0099 2855 | 0.0101 9386 | 0.0104 6307 | 146 |
| 147 | 0.0096 2250 | 0.0098 8420 | 0.0101 4986 | 0.0104 1944 | 147 |
| 148 | 0.0095 7844 | 0.0098 4047 | 0.0101 0649 | 0.0103 7645 | 148 |
| 149 | 0.0095 3500 | 0.0097 9736 | 0.0100 6374 | 0.0103 3407 | 149 |
| 150 | 0.0094 9217 | 0.0097 5486 | 0.0100 2159 | 0.0102 9230 | 150 |
| 151 | 0.0094 4993 | 0.0097 1295 | 0.0099 8003 | 0.0102 5112 | 151 |
| 152 | 0.0094 0827 | 0.0096 7162 | 0.0099 3905 | 0.0102 1052 | 152 |
| 153 | 0.0093 6719 | 0.0096 3087 | 0.0098 9865 | 0.0101 7049 | 153 |
| 154 | 0.0093 2666 | 0.0095 9067 | 0.0098 5880 | 0.0101 3102 | 154 |
| 155 | 0.0092 8668 | 0.0095 5102 | 0.0098 1950 | 0.0100 9209 | 155 |
| 156 | 0.0092 4723 | 0.0095 1190 | 0.0097 8074 | 0.0100 5370 | 156 |
| 157 | 0.0092 0832 | 0.0094 7332 | 0.0097 4251 | 0.0100 1584 | 157 |
| 158 | 0.0091 6992 | 0.0094 3525 | 0.0097 0479 | 0.0099 7850 | 158 |
| 159 | 0.0091 3203 | 0.0093 9768 | 0.0096 6758 | 0.0099 4166 | 159 |
| 160 | 0.0090 9464 | 0.0093 6062 | 0.0096 3087 | 0.0099 0532 | 160 |
| 161 | 0.0090 5773 | 0.0093 2404 | 0.0095 9464 | 0.0098 6947 | 161 |
| 162 | 0.0090 2131 | 0.0092 8795 | 0.0095 5890 | 0.0098 3410 | 162 |
| 163 | 0.0089 8536 | 0.0092 5232 | 0.0095 2362 | 0.0097 9919 | 163 |
| 164 | 0.0089 4987 | 0.0092 1716 | 0.0094 8881 | 0.0097 6475 | 164 |
| 165 | 0.0089 1483 | 0.0091 8245 | 0.0094 5445 | 0.0097 3076 | 165 |
| 166 | 0.0088 8024 | 0.0091 4819 | 0.0094 2053 | 0.0096 9722 | 166 |
| 167 | 0.0088 4608 | 0.0091 1436 | 0.0093 8705 | 0.0096 6411 | 167 |
| 168 | 0.0088 1236 | 0.0090 8096 | 0.0093 5401 | 0.0096 3143 | 168 |
| 169 | 0.0087 7906 | 0.0090 4798 | 0.0093 2138 | 0.0095 9918 | 169 |
| 170 | 0.0087 4617 | 0.0090 1542 | 0.0092 8917 | 0.0095 6733 | 170 |
| 171 | 0.0087 1369 | 0.0089 8327 | 0.0092 5736 | 0.0095 3589 | 171 |
| 172 | 0.0086 8161 | 0.0089 5151 | 0.0092 2595 | 0.0095 0486 | 172 |
| 173 | 0.0086 4992 | 0.0089 2015 | 0.0091 9494 | 0.0094 7421 | 173 |
| 174 | 0.0086 1862 | 0.0088 8918 | 0.0091 6431 | 0.0094 4395 | 174 |
| 175 | 0.0085 8770 | 0.0088 5858 | 0.0091 3406 | 0.0094 1407 | 175 |
| 176 | 0.0085 5715 | 0.0088 2836 | 0.0091 0418 | 0.0093 8456 | 176 |
| 177 | 0.0085 2697 | 0.0087 9850 | 0.0090 7468 | 0.0093 5542 | 177 |
| 178 | 0.0084 9715 | 0.0087 6901 | 0.0090 4553 | 0.0093 2664 | 178 |
| 179 | 0.0084 6768 | 0.0087 3987 | 0.0090 1673 | 0.0092 9821 | 179 |
| 180 | 0.0084 3857 | 0.0087 1107 | 0.0089 8828 | 0.0092 7012 | 180 |

Table
9

# TABLE 9

$$\frac{1}{a_{\overline{n}|i}} = \frac{i}{1-(1+i)^{-n}} \qquad \text{Note:} \quad \frac{1}{s_{\overline{n}|i}} = \frac{1}{a_{\overline{n}|i}} - i$$

| $n$ | $\frac{1}{2}\%$ | $\frac{13}{24}\%$ | $\frac{7}{12}\%$ | $\frac{5}{8}\%$ | $n$ |
|---|---|---|---|---|---|
| 181 | 0.0084 0979 | 0.0086 8262 | 0.0089 6018 | 0.0092 4238 | 181 |
| 182 | 0.0083 8136 | 0.0086 5451 | 0.0089 3241 | 0.0092 1498 | 182 |
| 183 | 0.0083 5325 | 0.0086 2673 | 0.0089 0497 | 0.0091 8791 | 183 |
| 184 | 0.0083 2547 | 0.0085 9927 | 0.0088 7786 | 0.0091 6116 | 184 |
| 185 | 0.0082 9802 | 0.0085 7214 | 0.0088 5107 | 0.0091 3473 | 185 |
| 186 | 0.0082 7088 | 0.0085 4532 | 0.0088 2459 | 0.0091 0862 | 186 |
| 187 | 0.0082 4404 | 0.0085 1881 | 0.0087 9843 | 0.0090 8282 | 187 |
| 188 | 0.0082 1752 | 0.0084 9261 | 0.0087 7257 | 0.0090 5732 | 188 |
| 189 | 0.0081 9129 | 0.0084 6670 | 0.0087 4701 | 0.0090 3212 | 189 |
| 190 | 0.0081 6537 | 0.0084 4110 | 0.0087 2174 | 0.0090 0722 | 190 |
| 191 | 0.0081 3973 | 0.0084 1578 | 0.0086 9677 | 0.0089 8260 | 191 |
| 192 | 0.0081 1438 | 0.0083 9075 | 0.0086 7208 | 0.0089 5828 | 192 |
| 193 | 0.0080 8931 | 0.0083 6601 | 0.0086 4767 | 0.0089 3423 | 193 |
| 194 | 0.0080 6452 | 0.0083 4154 | 0.0086 2355 | 0.0089 1046 | 194 |
| 195 | 0.0080 4000 | 0.0083 1734 | 0.0085 9969 | 0.0088 8696 | 195 |
| 196 | 0.0080 1576 | 0.0082 9341 | 0.0085 7610 | 0.0088 6374 | 196 |
| 197 | 0.0079 9178 | 0.0082 6975 | 0.0085 5278 | 0.0088 4077 | 197 |
| 198 | 0.0079 6806 | 0.0082 4635 | 0.0085 2972 | 0.0088 1807 | 198 |
| 199 | 0.0079 4459 | 0.0082 2321 | 0.0085 0691 | 0.0087 9562 | 199 |
| 200 | 0.0079 2138 | 0.0082 0032 | 0.0084 8436 | 0.0087 7343 | 200 |
| 201 | 0.0078 9843 | 0.0081 7768 | 0.0084 6206 | 0.0087 5148 | 201 |
| 202 | 0.0078 7571 | 0.0081 5528 | 0.0084 4000 | 0.0087 2978 | 202 |
| 203 | 0.0078 5324 | 0.0081 3313 | 0.0084 1818 | 0.0087 0832 | 203 |
| 204 | 0.0078 3101 | 0.0081 1121 | 0.0083 9661 | 0.0086 8709 | 204 |
| 205 | 0.0078 0901 | 0.0080 8953 | 0.0083 7526 | 0.0086 6610 | 205 |
| 206 | 0.0077 8724 | 0.0080 6808 | 0.0083 5415 | 0.0086 4535 | 206 |
| 207 | 0.0077 6571 | 0.0080 4686 | 0.0083 3327 | 0.0086 2482 | 207 |
| 208 | 0.0077 4440 | 0.0080 2587 | 0.0083 1261 | 0.0086 0451 | 208 |
| 209 | 0.0077 2330 | 0.0080 0509 | 0.0082 9217 | 0.0085 8442 | 209 |
| 210 | 0.0077 0243 | 0.0079 8454 | 0.0082 7194 | 0.0085 6455 | 210 |
| 211 | 0.0076 8178 | 0.0079 6419 | 0.0082 5194 | 0.0085 4490 | 211 |
| 212 | 0.0076 6133 | 0.0079 4407 | 0.0082 3214 | 0.0085 2545 | 212 |
| 213 | 0.0076 4110 | 0.0079 2415 | 0.0082 1256 | 0.0085 0622 | 213 |
| 214 | 0.0076 2107 | 0.0079 0443 | 0.0081 9318 | 0.0084 8719 | 214 |
| 215 | 0.0076 0125 | 0.0078 8492 | 0.0081 7400 | 0.0084 6836 | 215 |
| 216 | 0.0075 8162 | 0.0078 6561 | 0.0081 5502 | 0.0084 4973 | 216 |
| 217 | 0.0075 6220 | 0.0078 4650 | 0.0081 3624 | 0.0084 3130 | 217 |
| 218 | 0.0075 4297 | 0.0078 2758 | 0.0081 1766 | 0.0084 1306 | 218 |
| 219 | 0.0075 2393 | 0.0078 0886 | 0.0080 9926 | 0.0083 9502 | 219 |
| 220 | 0.0075 0508 | 0.0077 9032 | 0.0080 8106 | 0.0083 7716 | 220 |
| 221 | 0.0074 8642 | 0.0077 7197 | 0.0080 6304 | 0.0083 5949 | 221 |
| 222 | 0.0074 6794 | 0.0077 5381 | 0.0080 4520 | 0.0083 4200 | 222 |
| 223 | 0.0074 4965 | 0.0077 3583 | 0.0080 2755 | 0.0083 2469 | 223 |
| 224 | 0.0074 3154 | 0.0077 1802 | 0.0080 1008 | 0.0083 0757 | 224 |
| 225 | 0.0074 1360 | 0.0077 0040 | 0.0079 9278 | 0.0082 9061 | 225 |
| 226 | 0.0073 9584 | 0.0076 8295 | 0.0079 7566 | 0.0082 7383 | 226 |
| 227 | 0.0073 7825 | 0.0076 6567 | 0.0079 5871 | 0.0082 5723 | 227 |
| 228 | 0.0073 6083 | 0.0076 4856 | 0.0079 4192 | 0.0082 4079 | 228 |
| 229 | 0.0073 4358 | 0.0076 3162 | 0.0079 2531 | 0.0082 2452 | 229 |
| 230 | 0.0073 2649 | 0.0076 1484 | 0.0079 0886 | 0.0082 0841 | 230 |
| 231 | 0.0073 0957 | 0.0075 9823 | 0.0078 9257 | 0.0081 9247 | 231 |
| 232 | 0.0072 9281 | 0.0075 8178 | 0.0078 7645 | 0.0081 7668 | 232 |
| 233 | 0.0072 7621 | 0.0075 6549 | 0.0078 6048 | 0.0081 6105 | 233 |
| 234 | 0.0072 5977 | 0.0075 4935 | 0.0078 4467 | 0.0081 4558 | 234 |
| 235 | 0.0072 4348 | 0.0075 3337 | 0.0078 2902 | 0.0081 3027 | 235 |
| 236 | 0.0072 2735 | 0.0075 1755 | 0.0078 1351 | 0.0081 1511 | 236 |
| 237 | 0.0072 1137 | 0.0075 0187 | 0.0077 9816 | 0.0081 0009 | 237 |
| 238 | 0.0071 9554 | 0.0074 8634 | 0.0077 8296 | 0.0080 8523 | 238 |
| 239 | 0.0071 7985 | 0.0074 7097 | 0.0077 6790 | 0.0080 7051 | 239 |
| 240 | 0.0071 6431 | 0.0074 5573 | 0.0077 5299 | 0.0080 5593 | 240 |

## TABLE 9

$$\frac{1}{a_{\overline{n}|i}} = \frac{i}{1 - (1 + i)^{-n}} \qquad \text{Note: } \frac{1}{s_{\overline{n}|i}} = \frac{1}{a_{\overline{n}|i}} - i$$

| $n$ | $\frac{2}{3}\%$ | $\frac{3}{4}\%$ | $\frac{7}{8}\%$ | 1% | $n$ |
|---|---|---|---|---|---|
| 1 | 1.0066 6667 | 1.0075 0000 | 1.0087 5000 | 1.0100 0000 | 1 |
| 2 | 0.5050 0554 | 0.5056 3200 | 0.5065 7203 | 0.5075 1244 | 2 |
| 3 | 0.3377 8762 | 0.3383 4579 | 0.3391 8361 | 0.3400 2211 | 3 |
| 4 | 0.2541 8051 | 0.2547 0501 | 0.2554 9257 | 0.2562 8109 | 4 |
| 5 | 0.2040 1772 | 0.2045 2242 | 0.2052 8049 | 0.2060 3980 | 5 |
| 6 | 0.1705 7709 | 0.1710 6891 | 0.1718 0789 | 0.1725 4837 | 6 |
| 7 | 0.1466 9198 | 0.1471 7488 | 0.1479 0070 | 0.1486 2828 | 7 |
| 8 | 0.1287 7907 | 0.1292 5552 | 0.1299 7190 | 0.1306 9029 | 8 |
| 9 | 0.1148 4763 | 0.1153 1929 | 0.1160 2868 | 0.1167 4036 | 9 |
| 10 | 0.1037 0321 | 0.1041 7123 | 0.1048 7538 | 0.1055 8208 | 10 |
| 11 | 0.0945 8572 | 0.0950 5094 | 0.0957 5111 | 0.0964 5408 | 11 |
| 12 | 0.0869 8843 | 0.0874 5148 | 0.0881 4860 | 0.0888 4879 | 12 |
| 13 | 0.0805 6052 | 0.0810 2188 | 0.0817 1669 | 0.0824 1482 | 13 |
| 14 | 0.0750 5141 | 0.0755 1146 | 0.0762 0453 | 0.0769 0117 | 14 |
| 15 | 0.0702 7734 | 0.0707 3639 | 0.0714 2817 | 0.0721 2378 | 15 |
| 16 | 0.0661 0049 | 0.0665 5879 | 0.0672 4965 | 0.0679 4460 | 16 |
| 17 | 0.0624 1546 | 0.0628 7321 | 0.0635 6346 | 0.0642 5806 | 17 |
| 18 | 0.0591 4030 | 0.0595 9766 | 0.0602 8756 | 0.0609 8205 | 18 |
| 19 | 0.0562 1027 | 0.0566 6740 | 0.0573 5715 | 0.0580 5175 | 19 |
| 20 | 0.0535 7362 | 0.0540 3063 | 0.0547 2042 | 0.0554 1531 | 20 |
| 21 | 0.0511 8843 | 0.0516 4543 | 0.0523 3541 | 0.0530 3075 | 21 |
| 22 | 0.0490 2041 | 0.0494 7748 | 0.0501 6779 | 0.0508 6372 | 22 |
| 23 | 0.0470 4123 | 0.0474 9846 | 0.0481 8921 | 0.0488 8584 | 23 |
| 24 | 0.0452 2729 | 0.0456 8474 | 0.0463 7604 | 0.0470 7347 | 24 |
| 25 | 0.0435 5876 | 0.0440 1650 | 0.0447 0843 | 0.0454 0675 | 25 |
| 26 | 0.0420 1886 | 0.0424 7693 | 0.0431 6959 | 0.0438 6888 | 26 |
| 27 | 0.0405 9331 | 0.0410 5176 | 0.0417 4520 | 0.0424 4553 | 27 |
| 28 | 0.0392 6983 | 0.0397 2871 | 0.0404 2392 | 0.0411 2444 | 28 |
| 29 | 0.0380 3789 | 0.0384 9723 | 0.0391 9243 | 0.0398 9502 | 29 |
| 30 | 0.0368 8832 | 0.0373 4816 | 0.0380 4431 | 0.0387 4811 | 30 |
| 31 | 0.0358 1316 | 0.0362 7352 | 0.0369 7068 | 0.0376 7573 | 31 |
| 32 | 0.0348 0542 | 0.0352 6634 | 0.0359 6454 | 0.0366 7089 | 32 |
| 33 | 0.0338 5898 | 0.0343 2048 | 0.0350 1976 | 0.0357 2744 | 33 |
| 34 | 0.0329 6843 | 0.0334 3053 | 0.0341 3092 | 0.0348 3997 | 34 |
| 35 | 0.0321 2898 | 0.0325 9170 | 0.0332 9324 | 0.0340 0368 | 35 |
| 36 | 0.0313 3637 | 0.0317 9973 | 0.0325 0244 | 0.0332 1431 | 36 |
| 37 | 0.0305 8680 | 0.0310 5082 | 0.0317 5473 | 0.0324 6805 | 37 |
| 38 | 0.0298 7687 | 0.0303 4157 | 0.0310 4671 | 0.0317 6150 | 38 |
| 39 | 0.0292 0354 | 0.0296 6893 | 0.0303 7531 | 0.0310 9160 | 39 |
| 40 | 0.0285 6406 | 0.0290 3016 | 0.0297 3780 | 0.0304 5560 | 40 |
| 41 | 0.0279 5595 | 0.0284 2276 | 0.0291 3169 | 0.0298 5102 | 41 |
| 42 | 0.0273 7697 | 0.0278 4452 | 0.0285 5475 | 0.0292 7563 | 42 |
| 43 | 0.0268 2510 | 0.0272 9338 | 0.0280 0493 | 0.0287 2737 | 43 |
| 44 | 0.0262 9847 | 0.0267 6751 | 0.0274 8039 | 0.0282 0441 | 44 |
| 45 | 0.0257 9541 | 0.0262 6521 | 0.0269 7943 | 0.0277 0505 | 45 |
| 46 | 0.0253 1439 | 0.0257 8495 | 0.0265 0053 | 0.0272 2775 | 46 |
| 47 | 0.0248 5399 | 0.0253 2532 | 0.0260 4228 | 0.0267 7111 | 47 |
| 48 | 0.0244 1292 | 0.0248 8504 | 0.0256 0338 | 0.0263 3384 | 48 |
| 49 | 0.0239 9001 | 0.0244 6292 | 0.0251 8265 | 0.0259 1474 | 49 |
| 50 | 0.0235 8416 | 0.0240 5787 | 0.0247 7900 | 0.0255 1273 | 50 |
| 51 | 0.0231 9437 | 0.0236 6888 | 0.0243 9142 | 0.0251 2680 | 51 |
| 52 | 0.0228 1971 | 0.0232 9503 | 0.0240 1898 | 0.0247 5603 | 52 |
| 53 | 0.0224 5932 | 0.0229 3546 | 0.0236 6084 | 0.0243 9956 | 53 |
| 54 | 0.0221 1242 | 0.0225 8938 | 0.0233 1619 | 0.0240 5658 | 54 |
| 55 | 0.0217 7827 | 0.0222 5605 | 0.0229 8430 | 0.0237 2637 | 55 |
| 56 | 0.0214 5618 | 0.0219 3478 | 0.0226 6449 | 0.0234 0824 | 56 |
| 57 | 0.0211 4552 | 0.0216 2496 | 0.0223 5611 | 0.0231 0156 | 57 |
| 58 | 0.0208 4569 | 0.0213 2597 | 0.0220 5858 | 0.0228 0573 | 58 |
| 59 | 0.0205 5616 | 0.0210 3727 | 0.0217 7135 | 0.0225 2020 | 59 |
| 60 | 0.0202 7639 | 0.0207 5836 | 0.0214 9390 | 0.0222 4445 | 60 |

Table
9

**TABLE  9**

$$\frac{1}{a_{\overline{n}|i}} = \frac{i}{1-(1+i)^{-n}} \qquad \text{Note: } \frac{1}{s_{\overline{n}|i}} = \frac{1}{a_{\overline{n}|i}} - i$$

| $n$ | $\frac{2}{3}\%$ | $\frac{3}{4}\%$ | $\frac{7}{8}\%$ | 1% | $n$ |
|---|---|---|---|---|---|
| 61 | 0.0200 0592 | 0.0204 8873 | 0.0212 2575 | 0.0219 7800 | 61 |
| 62 | 0.0197 4429 | 0.0202 2795 | 0.0209 6644 | 0.0217 2041 | 62 |
| 63 | 0.0194 9108 | 0.0199 7560 | 0.0207 1557 | 0.0214 7125 | 63 |
| 64 | 0.0192 4590 | 0.0197 3127 | 0.0204 7273 | 0.0212 3013 | 64 |
| 65 | 0.0190 0837 | 0.0194 9460 | 0.0202 3754 | 0.0209 9667 | 65 |
| 66 | 0.0187 7815 | 0.0192 6524 | 0.0200 0968 | 0.0207 7052 | 66 |
| 67 | 0.0185 5491 | 0.0190 4286 | 0.0197 8879 | 0.0205 5136 | 67 |
| 68 | 0.0183 3835 | 0.0188 2716 | 0.0195 7459 | 0.0203 3889 | 68 |
| 69 | 0.0181 2816 | 0.0186 1785 | 0.0193 6677 | 0.0201 3280 | 69 |
| 70 | 0.0179 2409 | 0.0184 1464 | 0.0191 6506 | 0.0199 3282 | 70 |
| 71 | 0.0177 2586 | 0.0182 1728 | 0.0189 6921 | 0.0197 3870 | 71 |
| 72 | 0.0175 3324 | 0.0180 2554 | 0.0187 7897 | 0.0195 5019 | 72 |
| 73 | 0.0173 4600 | 0.0178 3917 | 0.0185 9411 | 0.0193 6706 | 73 |
| 74 | 0.0171 6391 | 0.0176 5796 | 0.0184 1441 | 0.0191 8910 | 74 |
| 75 | 0.0169 8678 | 0.0174 8170 | 0.0182 3966 | 0.0190 1609 | 75 |
| 76 | 0.0168 1440 | 0.0173 1020 | 0.0180 6967 | 0.0188 4784 | 76 |
| 77 | 0.0166 4659 | 0.0171 4328 | 0.0179 0426 | 0.0186 8416 | 77 |
| 78 | 0.0164 8318 | 0.0169 8074 | 0.0177 4324 | 0.0185 2488 | 78 |
| 79 | 0.0163 2400 | 0.0168 2244 | 0.0175 8645 | 0.0183 6983 | 79 |
| 80 | 0.0161 6889 | 0.0166 6821 | 0.0174 3374 | 0.0182 1885 | 80 |
| 81 | 0.0160 1769 | 0.0165 1790 | 0.0172 8494 | 0.0180 7179 | 81 |
| 82 | 0.0158 7027 | 0.0163 7136 | 0.0171 3992 | 0.0179 2851 | 82 |
| 83 | 0.0157 2649 | 0.0162 2847 | 0.0169 9854 | 0.0177 8887 | 83 |
| 84 | 0.0155 8621 | 0.0160 8908 | 0.0168 6067 | 0.0176 5273 | 84 |
| 85 | 0.0154 4933 | 0.0159 5308 | 0.0167 2619 | 0.0175 1998 | 85 |
| 86 | 0.0153 1570 | 0.0158 2034 | 0.0165 9497 | 0.0173 9050 | 86 |
| 87 | 0.0151 8524 | 0.0156 9076 | 0.0164 6691 | 0.0172 6418 | 87 |
| 88 | 0.0150 5781 | 0.0155 6423 | 0.0163 4190 | 0.0171 4089 | 88 |
| 89 | 0.0149 3334 | 0.0154 4064 | 0.0162 1982 | 0.0170 2056 | 89 |
| 90 | 0.0148 1170 | 0.0153 1989 | 0.0161 0060 | 0.0169 0306 | 90 |
| 91 | 0.0146 9282 | 0.0152 0190 | 0.0159 8413 | 0.0167 8832 | 91 |
| 92 | 0.0145 7660 | 0.0150 8657 | 0.0158 7031 | 0.0166 7624 | 92 |
| 93 | 0.0144 6296 | 0.0149 7382 | 0.0157 5908 | 0.0165 6673 | 93 |
| 94 | 0.0143 5181 | 0.0148 6356 | 0.0156 5033 | 0.0164 5971 | 94 |
| 95 | 0.0142 4308 | 0.0147 5571 | 0.0155 4401 | 0.0163 5511 | 95 |
| 96 | 0.0141 3668 | 0.0146 5020 | 0.0154 4002 | 0.0162 5284 | 96 |
| 97 | 0.0140 3255 | 0.0145 4696 | 0.0153 3829 | 0.0161 5284 | 97 |
| 98 | 0.0139 3062 | 0.0144 4592 | 0.0152 3877 | 0.0160 5503 | 98 |
| 99 | 0.0138 3082 | 0.0143 4701 | 0.0151 4137 | 0.0159 5936 | 99 |
| 100 | 0.0137 3308 | 0.0142 5017 | 0.0150 4604 | 0.0158 6574 | 100 |
| 101 | 0.0136 3735 | 0.0141 5533 | 0.0149 5271 | 0.0157 7413 | 101 |
| 102 | 0.0135 4357 | 0.0140 6243 | 0.0148 6133 | 0.0156 8446 | 102 |
| 103 | 0.0134 5168 | 0.0139 7143 | 0.0147 7184 | 0.0155 9668 | 103 |
| 104 | 0.0133 6162 | 0.0138 8226 | 0.0146 8418 | 0.0155 1073 | 104 |
| 105 | 0.0132 7334 | 0.0137 9487 | 0.0145 9830 | 0.0154 2656 | 105 |
| 106 | 0.0131 8680 | 0.0137 0922 | 0.0145 1416 | 0.0153 4412 | 106 |
| 107 | 0.0131 0194 | 0.0136 2524 | 0.0144 3169 | 0.0152 6336 | 107 |
| 108 | 0.0130 1871 | 0.0135 4291 | 0.0143 5086 | 0.0151 8423 | 108 |
| 109 | 0.0129 3708 | 0.0134 6216 | 0.0142 7162 | 0.0151 0669 | 109 |
| 110 | 0.0128 5700 | 0.0133 8297 | 0.0141 9393 | 0.0150 3069 | 110 |
| 111 | 0.0127 7842 | 0.0133 0527 | 0.0141 1774 | 0.0149 5620 | 111 |
| 112 | 0.0127 0131 | 0.0132 2905 | 0.0140 4301 | 0.0148 8317 | 112 |
| 113 | 0.0126 2562 | 0.0131 5425 | 0.0139 6971 | 0.0148 1155 | 113 |
| 114 | 0.0125 5132 | 0.0130 8084 | 0.0138 9780 | 0.0147 4133 | 114 |
| 115 | 0.0124 7838 | 0.0130 0878 | 0.0138 2724 | 0.0146 7245 | 115 |
| 116 | 0.0124 0675 | 0.0129 3803 | 0.0137 5799 | 0.0146 0488 | 116 |
| 117 | 0.0123 3641 | 0.0128 6858 | 0.0136 9003 | 0.0145 3860 | 117 |
| 118 | 0.0122 6732 | 0.0128 0037 | 0.0136 2331 | 0.0144 7356 | 118 |
| 119 | 0.0121 9944 | 0.0127 3338 | 0.0135 5781 | 0.0144 0974 | 119 |
| 120 | 0.0121 3276 | 0.0126 6758 | 0.0134 9350 | 0.0143 4709 | 120 |

## TABLE 9

$$\frac{1}{a_{\overline{n}|i}} = \frac{i}{1-(1+i)^{-n}} \qquad \text{Note: } \frac{1}{s_{\overline{n}|i}} = \frac{1}{a_{\overline{n}|i}} - i$$

| $n$ | $\frac{2}{3}\%$ | $\frac{3}{4}\%$ | $\frac{7}{8}\%$ | 1% | $n$ |
|---|---|---|---|---|---|
| 121 | 0.0120 6724 | 0.0126 0294 | 0.0134 3035 | 0.0142 8561 | 121 |
| 122 | 0.0120 0284 | 0.0125 3942 | 0.0133 6832 | 0.0142 2525 | 122 |
| 123 | 0.0119 3955 | 0.0124 7702 | 0.0133 0740 | 0.0141 6599 | 123 |
| 124 | 0.0118 7734 | 0.0124 1568 | 0.0132 4754 | 0.0141 0780 | 124 |
| 125 | 0.0118 1618 | 0.0123 5540 | 0.0131 8874 | 0.0140 5065 | 125 |
| 126 | 0.0117 5604 | 0.0122 9614 | 0.0131 3096 | 0.0139 9452 | 126 |
| 127 | 0.0116 9690 | 0.0122 3788 | 0.0130 7418 | 0.0139 3939 | 127 |
| 128 | 0.0116 3875 | 0.0121 8060 | 0.0130 1838 | 0.0138 8524 | 128 |
| 129 | 0.0115 8154 | 0.0121 2428 | 0.0129 6352 | 0.0138 3203 | 129 |
| 130 | 0.0115 2527 | 0.0120 6888 | 0.0129 0960 | 0.0137 7975 | 130 |
| 131 | 0.0114 6992 | 0.0120 1440 | 0.0128 5659 | 0.0137 2837 | 131 |
| 132 | 0.0114 1545 | 0.0119 6080 | 0.0128 0446 | 0.0136 7788 | 132 |
| 133 | 0.0113 6185 | 0.0119 0808 | 0.0127 5320 | 0.0136 2825 | 133 |
| 134 | 0.0113 0910 | 0.0118 5621 | 0.0127 0279 | 0.0135 7947 | 134 |
| 135 | 0.0112 5719 | 0.0118 0516 | 0.0126 5321 | 0.0135 3151 | 135 |
| 136 | 0.0112 0609 | 0.0117 5493 | 0.0126 0444 | 0.0134 8437 | 136 |
| 137 | 0.0111 5578 | 0.0117 0550 | 0.0125 5646 | 0.0134 3801 | 137 |
| 138 | 0.0111 0625 | 0.0116 5684 | 0.0125 0926 | 0.0133 9242 | 138 |
| 139 | 0.0110 5749 | 0.0116 0894 | 0.0124 6281 | 0.0133 4759 | 139 |
| 140 | 0.0110 0947 | 0.0115 6179 | 0.0124 1711 | 0.0133 0349 | 140 |
| 141 | 0.0109 6218 | 0.0115 1536 | 0.0123 7213 | 0.0132 6012 | 141 |
| 142 | 0.0109 1560 | 0.0114 6965 | 0.0123 2787 | 0.0132 1746 | 142 |
| 143 | 0.0108 6972 | 0.0114 2464 | 0.0122 8430 | 0.0131 7549 | 143 |
| 144 | 0.0108 2453 | 0.0113 8031 | 0.0122 4141 | 0.0131 3419 | 144 |
| 145 | 0.0107 8000 | 0.0113 3664 | 0.0121 9918 | 0.0130 9356 | 145 |
| 146 | 0.0107 3613 | 0.0112 9364 | 0.0121 5761 | 0.0130 5358 | 146 |
| 147 | 0.0106 9291 | 0.0112 5127 | 0.0121 1668 | 0.0130 1423 | 147 |
| 148 | 0.0106 5031 | 0.0112 0954 | 0.0120 7638 | 0.0129 7551 | 148 |
| 149 | 0.0106 0833 | 0.0111 6841 | 0.0120 3669 | 0.0129 3739 | 149 |
| 150 | 0.0105 6695 | 0.0111 2790 | 0.0119 9760 | 0.0128 9988 | 150 |
| 151 | 0.0105 2617 | 0.0110 8797 | 0.0119 5910 | 0.0128 6294 | 151 |
| 152 | 0.0104 8597 | 0.0110 4862 | 0.0119 2117 | 0.0128 2659 | 152 |
| 153 | 0.0104 4633 | 0.0110 0984 | 0.0118 8381 | 0.0127 9079 | 153 |
| 154 | 0.0104 0726 | 0.0109 7162 | 0.0118 4701 | 0.0127 5554 | 154 |
| 155 | 0.0103 6873 | 0.0109 3395 | 0.0118 1075 | 0.0127 2084 | 155 |
| 156 | 0.0103 3074 | 0.0108 9681 | 0.0117 7502 | 0.0126 8666 | 156 |
| 157 | 0.0102 9327 | 0.0108 6019 | 0.0117 3981 | 0.0126 5300 | 157 |
| 158 | 0.0102 5632 | 0.0108 2409 | 0.0117 0512 | 0.0126 1986 | 158 |
| 159 | 0.0102 1988 | 0.0107 8849 | 0.0116 7093 | 0.0125 8721 | 159 |
| 160 | 0.0101 8394 | 0.0107 5340 | 0.0116 3724 | 0.0125 5504 | 160 |
| 161 | 0.0101 4848 | 0.0107 1878 | 0.0116 0402 | 0.0125 2336 | 161 |
| 162 | 0.0101 1350 | 0.0106 8465 | 0.0115 7128 | 0.0124 9215 | 162 |
| 163 | 0.0100 7899 | 0.0106 5098 | 0.0115 3901 | 0.0124 6141 | 163 |
| 164 | 0.0100 4494 | 0.0106 1777 | 0.0115 0720 | 0.0124 3111 | 164 |
| 165 | 0.0100 1134 | 0.0105 8502 | 0.0114 7583 | 0.0124 0126 | 165 |
| 166 | 0.0099 7819 | 0.0105 5270 | 0.0114 4490 | 0.0123 7185 | 166 |
| 167 | 0.0099 4547 | 0.0105 2083 | 0.0114 1441 | 0.0123 4286 | 167 |
| 168 | 0.0099 1318 | 0.0104 8938 | 0.0113 8434 | 0.0123 1430 | 168 |
| 169 | 0.0098 8131 | 0.0104 5834 | 0.0113 5469 | 0.0122 8614 | 169 |
| 170 | 0.0098 4986 | 0.0104 2772 | 0.0113 2544 | 0.0122 5840 | 170 |
| 171 | 0.0098 1881 | 0.0103 9751 | 0.0112 9660 | 0.0122 3105 | 171 |
| 172 | 0.0097 8816 | 0.0103 6769 | 0.0112 6816 | 0.0122 0409 | 172 |
| 173 | 0.0097 5791 | 0.0103 3827 | 0.0112 4010 | 0.0121 7751 | 173 |
| 174 | 0.0097 2803 | 0.0103 0922 | 0.0112 1242 | 0.0121 5132 | 174 |
| 175 | 0.0096 9854 | 0.0102 8056 | 0.0111 8512 | 0.0121 2549 | 175 |
| 176 | 0.0096 6942 | 0.0102 5226 | 0.0111 5818 | 0.0121 0003 | 176 |
| 177 | 0.0096 4066 | 0.0102 2433 | 0.0111 3161 | 0.0120 7492 | 177 |
| 178 | 0.0096 1226 | 0.0101 9676 | 0.0111 0539 | 0.0120 5016 | 178 |
| 179 | 0.0095 8422 | 0.0101 6954 | 0.0110 7952 | 0.0120 2575 | 179 |
| 180 | 0.0095 5652 | 0.0101 4267 | 0.0110 5399 | 0.0120 0168 | 180 |

Table 9

# TABLE 9

$$\frac{1}{a_{\overline{n}|i}} = \frac{i}{1-(1+i)^{-n}} \qquad \text{Note: } \frac{1}{s_{\overline{n}|i}} = \frac{1}{a_{\overline{n}|i}} - i$$

| $n$ | $\frac{2}{3}\%$ | $\frac{3}{4}\%$ | $\frac{7}{8}\%$ | 1% | $n$ |
|---|---|---|---|---|---|
| 181 | 0.0095 2917 | 0.0101 1613 | 0.0110 2880 | 0.0119 7794 | 181 |
| 182 | 0.0095 0215 | 0.0100 8993 | 0.0110 0394 | 0.0119 5453 | 182 |
| 183 | 0.0094 7546 | 0.0100 6406 | 0.0109 7941 | 0.0119 3144 | 183 |
| 184 | 0.0094 4909 | 0.0100 3851 | 0.0109 5520 | 0.0119 0867 | 184 |
| 185 | 0.0094 2305 | 0.0100 1328 | 0.0109 3130 | 0.0118 8621 | 185 |
| 186 | 0.0093 9732 | 0.0099 8837 | 0.0109 0771 | 0.0118 6405 | 186 |
| 187 | 0.0093 7189 | 0.0099 6376 | 0.0108 8443 | 0.0118 4219 | 187 |
| 188 | 0.0093 4678 | 0.0099 3945 | 0.0108 6145 | 0.0118 2063 | 188 |
| 189 | 0.0093 2196 | 0.0099 1544 | 0.0108 3876 | 0.0117 9936 | 189 |
| 190 | 0.0092 9743 | 0.0098 9173 | 0.0108 1637 | 0.0117 7838 | 190 |
| 191 | 0.0092 7320 | 0.0098 6830 | 0.0107 9425 | 0.0117 5768 | 191 |
| 192 | 0.0092 4925 | 0.0098 4516 | 0.0107 7242 | 0.0117 3725 | 192 |
| 193 | 0.0092 2558 | 0.0098 2230 | 0.0107 5087 | 0.0117 1710 | 193 |
| 194 | 0.0092 0219 | 0.0097 9971 | 0.0107 2959 | 0.0116 9721 | 194 |
| 195 | 0.0091 7907 | 0.0097 7739 | 0.0107 0857 | 0.0116 7759 | 195 |
| 196 | 0.0091 5622 | 0.0097 5534 | 0.0106 8782 | 0.0116 5822 | 196 |
| 197 | 0.0091 3363 | 0.0097 3355 | 0.0106 6733 | 0.0116 3911 | 197 |
| 198 | 0.0091 1130 | 0.0097 1202 | 0.0106 4709 | 0.0116 2026 | 198 |
| 199 | 0.0090 8923 | 0.0096 9074 | 0.0106 2711 | 0.0116 0164 | 199 |
| 200 | 0.0090 6741 | 0.0096 6972 | 0.0106 0737 | 0.0115 8328 | 200 |
| 201 | 0.0090 4584 | 0.0096 4894 | 0.0105 8787 | 0.0115 6515 | 201 |
| 202 | 0.0090 2451 | 0.0096 2840 | 0.0105 6862 | 0.0115 4725 | 202 |
| 203 | 0.0090 0342 | 0.0096 0810 | 0.0105 4960 | 0.0115 2959 | 203 |
| 204 | 0.0089 8257 | 0.0095 8804 | 0.0105 3081 | 0.0115 1216 | 204 |
| 205 | 0.0089 6195 | 0.0095 6821 | 0.0105 1225 | 0.0114 9495 | 205 |
| 206 | 0.0089 4156 | 0.0095 4861 | 0.0104 9392 | 0.0114 7796 | 206 |
| 207 | 0.0089 2140 | 0.0095 2923 | 0.0104 7581 | 0.0114 6118 | 207 |
| 208 | 0.0089 0146 | 0.0095 1008 | 0.0104 5792 | 0.0114 4463 | 208 |
| 209 | 0.0088 8175 | 0.0094 9114 | 0.0104 4024 | 0.0114 2828 | 209 |
| 210 | 0.0088 6225 | 0.0094 7242 | 0.0104 2278 | 0.0114 1214 | 210 |
| 211 | 0.0088 4296 | 0.0094 5391 | 0.0104 0552 | 0.0113 9621 | 211 |
| 212 | 0.0088 2388 | 0.0094 3561 | 0.0103 8847 | 0.0113 8048 | 212 |
| 213 | 0.0088 0512 | 0.0094 1752 | 0.0103 7163 | 0.0113 6494 | 213 |
| 214 | 0.0087 8635 | 0.0093 9963 | 0.0103 5498 | 0.0113 4961 | 214 |
| 215 | 0.0087 6789 | 0.0093 8194 | 0.0103 3853 | 0.0113 3446 | 215 |
| 216 | 0.0087 4963 | 0.0093 6445 | 0.0103 2228 | 0.0113 1950 | 216 |
| 217 | 0.0087 3156 | 0.0093 4715 | 0.0103 0621 | 0.0113 0473 | 217 |
| 218 | 0.0087 1369 | 0.0093 3005 | 0.0102 9034 | 0.0112 9015 | 218 |
| 219 | 0.0086 9600 | 0.0093 1313 | 0.0102 7465 | 0.0112 7575 | 219 |
| 220 | 0.0086 7851 | 0.0092 9640 | 0.0102 5914 | 0.0112 6152 | 220 |
| 221 | 0.0086 6120 | 0.0092 7985 | 0.0102 4382 | 0.0112 4747 | 221 |
| 222 | 0.0086 4407 | 0.0092 6349 | 0.0102 2867 | 0.0112 3360 | 222 |
| 223 | 0.0086 2713 | 0.0092 4730 | 0.0102 1370 | 0.0112 1990 | 223 |
| 224 | 0.0086 1036 | 0.0092 3129 | 0.0101 9890 | 0.0112 0636 | 224 |
| 225 | 0.0085 9376 | 0.0092 1546 | 0.0101 8427 | 0.0111 9299 | 225 |
| 226 | 0.0085 7734 | 0.0091 9979 | 0.0101 6981 | 0.0111 7979 | 226 |
| 227 | 0.0085 6109 | 0.0091 8430 | 0.0101 5552 | 0.0111 6674 | 227 |
| 228 | 0.0085 4501 | 0.0091 6897 | 0.0101 4139 | 0.0111 5386 | 228 |
| 229 | 0.0085 2910 | 0.0091 5380 | 0.0101 2742 | 0.0111 4113 | 229 |
| 230 | 0.0085 1335 | 0.0091 3880 | 0.0101 1361 | 0.0111 2856 | 230 |
| 231 | 0.0084 9776 | 0.0091 2396 | 0.0100 9996 | 0.0111 1613 | 231 |
| 232 | 0.0084 8233 | 0.0091 0928 | 0.0100 8646 | 0.0111 0386 | 232 |
| 233 | 0.0084 6706 | 0.0090 9475 | 0.0100 7311 | 0.0110 9174 | 233 |
| 234 | 0.0084 5194 | 0.0090 8038 | 0.0100 5992 | 0.0110 7976 | 234 |
| 235 | 0.0084 3698 | 0.0090 6616 | 0.0100 4687 | 0.0110 6793 | 235 |
| 236 | 0.0084 2217 | 0.0090 5209 | 0.0100 3397 | 0.0110 5624 | 236 |
| 237 | 0.0084 0751 | 0.0090 3816 | 0.0100 2122 | 0.0110 4469 | 237 |
| 238 | 0.0083 9299 | 0.0090 2438 | 0.0100 0860 | 0.0110 3328 | 238 |
| 239 | 0.0083 7863 | 0.0090 1075 | 0.0099 9613 | 0.0110 2200 | 239 |
| 240 | 0.0083 6440 | 0.0089 9726 | 0.0099 8380 | 0.0110 1086 | 240 |

**TABLE 9**

$$\frac{1}{a_{\overline{n}|i}} = \frac{i}{1-(1+i)^{-n}} \qquad \text{Note: } \frac{1}{s_{\overline{n}|i}} = \frac{1}{a_{\overline{n}|i}} - i$$

| n | $1\frac{1}{8}\%$ | $1\frac{1}{4}\%$ | $1\frac{3}{8}\%$ | $1\frac{1}{2}\%$ | n |
|---|---|---|---|---|---|
| 1 | 1.0112 5000 | 1.0125 0000 | 1.0137 5000 | 1.0150 0000 | 1 |
| 2 | 0.5084 5323 | 0.5093 9441 | 0.5103 3597 | 0.5112 7792 | 2 |
| 3 | 0.3408 6130 | 0.3417 0117 | 0.3425 4173 | 0.3433 8296 | 3 |
| 4 | 0.2570 7058 | 0.2578 6102 | 0.2586 5243 | 0.2594 4479 | 4 |
| 5 | 0.2068 0034 | 0.2075 6211 | 0.2083 2510 | 0.2090 8932 | 5 |
| 6 | 0.1732 9034 | 0.1740 3381 | 0.1747 7877 | 0.1755 2521 | 6 |
| 7 | 0.1493 5762 | 0.1500 8872 | 0.1508 2157 | 0.1515 5616 | 7 |
| 8 | 0.1314 1071 | 0.1321 3314 | 0.1328 5758 | 0.1335 8402 | 8 |
| 9 | 0.1174 5432 | 0.1181 7055 | 0.1188 8906 | 0.1196 0982 | 9 |
| 10 | 0.1062 9131 | 0.1070 0307 | 0.1077 1737 | 0.1084 3418 | 10 |
| 11 | 0.0971 5984 | 0.0978 6839 | 0.0985 7973 | 0.0992 9384 | 11 |
| 12 | 0.0895 5203 | 0.0902 5831 | 0.0909 6764 | 0.0916 7999 | 12 |
| 13 | 0.0831 1626 | 0.0838 2100 | 0.0845 2904 | 0.0852 4036 | 13 |
| 14 | 0.0776 0138 | 0.0783 0515 | 0.0790 1246 | 0.0797 2332 | 14 |
| 15 | 0.0728 2321 | 0.0735 2646 | 0.0742 3351 | 0.0749 4436 | 15 |
| 16 | 0.0686 4363 | 0.0693 4672 | 0.0700 5388 | 0.0707 6508 | 16 |
| 17 | 0.0649 5698 | 0.0656 6023 | 0.0663 6780 | 0.0670 7966 | 17 |
| 18 | 0.0616 8113 | 0.0623 8479 | 0.0630 9301 | 0.0638 0578 | 18 |
| 19 | 0.0587 5120 | 0.0594 5548 | 0.0601 6457 | 0.0608 7847 | 19 |
| 20 | 0.0561 1531 | 0.0568 2039 | 0.0575 3054 | 0.0582 4574 | 20 |
| 21 | 0.0537 3145 | 0.0544 3749 | 0.0551 4884 | 0.0558 6550 | 21 |
| 22 | 0.0515 6525 | 0.0522 7238 | 0.0529 8507 | 0.0537 0332 | 22 |
| 23 | 0.0495 8833 | 0.0502 9666 | 0.0510 1080 | 0.0517 3075 | 23 |
| 24 | 0.0477 7701 | 0.0484 8665 | 0.0492 0235 | 0.0499 2410 | 24 |
| 25 | 0.0461 1144 | 0.0468 2247 | 0.0475 3981 | 0.0482 6345 | 25 |
| 26 | 0.0445 7479 | 0.0452 8729 | 0.0460 0635 | 0.0467 3196 | 26 |
| 27 | 0.0431 5273 | 0.0438 6677 | 0.0445 8763 | 0.0453 1527 | 27 |
| 28 | 0.0418 3299 | 0.0425 4863 | 0.0432 7134 | 0.0440 0108 | 28 |
| 29 | 0.0406 0498 | 0.0413 2228 | 0.0420 4689 | 0.0427 7878 | 29 |
| 30 | 0.0394 5953 | 0.0401 7854 | 0.0409 0511 | 0.0416 3919 | 30 |
| 31 | 0.0383 8866 | 0.0391 0942 | 0.0398 3798 | 0.0405 7430 | 31 |
| 32 | 0.0373 8535 | 0.0381 0791 | 0.0388 3850 | 0.0395 7710 | 32 |
| 33 | 0.0364 4349 | 0.0371 6786 | 0.0379 0053 | 0.0386 4144 | 33 |
| 34 | 0.0355 5763 | 0.0362 8387 | 0.0370 1864 | 0.0377 6189 | 34 |
| 35 | 0.0347 2299 | 0.0354 5111 | 0.0361 8801 | 0.0369 3363 | 35 |
| 36 | 0.0339 3529 | 0.0346 6533 | 0.0354 0438 | 0.0361 5240 | 36 |
| 37 | 0.0331 9072 | 0.0339 2270 | 0.0346 6394 | 0.0354 1437 | 37 |
| 38 | 0.0324 8589 | 0.0332 1983 | 0.0339 6327 | 0.0347 1613 | 38 |
| 39 | 0.0318 1773 | 0.0325 5365 | 0.0332 9931 | 0.0340 5463 | 39 |
| 40 | 0.0311 8349 | 0.0319 2141 | 0.0326 6931 | 0.0334 2710 | 40 |
| 41 | 0.0305 8069 | 0.0313 2063 | 0.0320 7078 | 0.0328 3106 | 41 |
| 42 | 0.0300 0709 | 0.0307 4906 | 0.0315 0148 | 0.0322 6426 | 42 |
| 43 | 0.0294 6064 | 0.0302 0466 | 0.0309 5936 | 0.0317 2465 | 43 |
| 44 | 0.0289 3949 | 0.0296 8557 | 0.0304 4257 | 0.0312 1038 | 44 |
| 45 | 0.0284 4197 | 0.0291 9012 | 0.0299 4941 | 0.0307 1976 | 45 |
| 46 | 0.0279 6652 | 0.0287 1675 | 0.0294 7836 | 0.0302 5125 | 46 |
| 47 | 0.0275 1173 | 0.0282 6406 | 0.0290 2799 | 0.0298 0342 | 47 |
| 48 | 0.0270 7632 | 0.0278 3075 | 0.0285 9701 | 0.0293 7500 | 48 |
| 49 | 0.0266 5910 | 0.0274 1564 | 0.0281 8423 | 0.0289 6478 | 49 |
| 50 | 0.0262 5898 | 0.0270 1763 | 0.0277 8857 | 0.0285 7168 | 50 |

Table
9

**TABLE 9**

$$\frac{1}{a_{\overline{n}|i}} = \frac{i}{1-(1+i)^{-n}} \qquad \text{Note: } \frac{1}{s_{\overline{n}|i}} = \frac{1}{a_{\overline{n}|i}} - i$$

| $n$ | $1\frac{1}{8}\%$ | $1\frac{1}{4}\%$ | $1\frac{3}{8}\%$ | $1\frac{1}{2}\%$ | $n$ |
|---|---|---|---|---|---|
| 51 | 0.0258 7494 | 0.0266 3571 | 0.0274 0900 | 0.0281 9469 | 51 |
| 52 | 0.0255 0606 | 0.0262 6897 | 0.0270 4461 | 0.0278 3287 | 52 |
| 53 | 0.0251 5149 | 0.0259 1653 | 0.0266 9453 | 0.0274 8537 | 53 |
| 54 | 0.0248 1043 | 0.0255 7760 | 0.0263 5797 | 0.0271 5138 | 54 |
| 55 | 0.0244 8213 | 0.0252 5145 | 0.0260 3418 | 0.0268 3018 | 55 |
| 56 | 0.0241 6592 | 0.0249 3739 | 0.0257 2249 | 0.0265 2106 | 56 |
| 57 | 0.0238 6116 | 0.0246 3478 | 0.0254 2225 | 0.0262 2341 | 57 |
| 58 | 0.0235 6726 | 0.0243 4303 | 0.0251 3287 | 0.0259 3661 | 58 |
| 59 | 0.0232 8366 | 0.0240 6158 | 0.0248 5380 | 0.0256 6012 | 59 |
| 60 | 0.0230 0985 | 0.0237 8993 | 0.0245 8452 | 0.0253 9343 | 60 |
| 61 | 0.0227 4534 | 0.0235 2758 | 0.0243 2455 | 0.0251 3604 | 61 |
| 62 | 0.0224 8969 | 0.0232 7410 | 0.0240 7344 | 0.0248 8751 | 62 |
| 63 | 0.0222 4247 | 0.0230 2904 | 0.0238 3076 | 0.0246 4741 | 63 |
| 64 | 0.0220 0329 | 0.0227 9203 | 0.0235 9612 | 0.0244 1534 | 64 |
| 65 | 0.0217 7178 | 0.0225 6268 | 0.0233 6914 | 0.0241 9094 | 65 |
| 66 | 0.0215 4758 | 0.0223 4065 | 0.0231 4949 | 0.0239 7386 | 66 |
| 67 | 0.0213 3037 | 0.0221 2560 | 0.0229 3682 | 0.0237 6376 | 67 |
| 68 | 0.0211 1985 | 0.0219 1724 | 0.0227 3082 | 0.0235 6033 | 68 |
| 69 | 0.0209 1571 | 0.0217 1527 | 0.0225 3122 | 0.0233 6329 | 69 |
| 70 | 0.0207 1769 | 0.0215 1941 | 0.0223 3773 | 0.0231 7235 | 70 |
| 71 | 0.0205 2552 | 0.0213 2941 | 0.0221 5009 | 0.0229 8727 | 71 |
| 72 | 0.0203 3896 | 0.0211 4501 | 0.0219 6806 | 0.0228 0779 | 72 |
| 73 | 0.0201 5779 | 0.0209 6600 | 0.0217 9140 | 0.0226 3368 | 73 |
| 74 | 0.0199 8177 | 0.0207 9215 | 0.0216 1991 | 0.0224 6473 | 74 |
| 75 | 0.0198 1072 | 0.0206 2325 | 0.0214 5336 | 0.0223 0072 | 75 |
| 76 | 0.0196 4442 | 0.0204 5910 | 0.0212 9157 | 0.0221 4146 | 76 |
| 77 | 0.0194 8269 | 0.0202 9953 | 0.0211 3435 | 0.0219 8676 | 77 |
| 78 | 0.0193 2536 | 0.0201 4436 | 0.0209 8151 | 0.0218 3645 | 78 |
| 79 | 0.0191 7226 | 0.0199 9341 | 0.0208 3290 | 0.0216 9036 | 79 |
| 80 | 0.0190 2323 | 0.0198 4652 | 0.0206 8836 | 0.0215 4832 | 80 |
| 81 | 0.0188 7812 | 0.0197 0356 | 0.0205 4772 | 0.0214 1019 | 81 |
| 82 | 0.0187 3678 | 0.0195 6437 | 0.0204 1086 | 0.0212 7583 | 82 |
| 83 | 0.0185 9908 | 0.0194 2881 | 0.0202 7762 | 0.0211 4509 | 83 |
| 84 | 0.0184 6489 | 0.0192 9675 | 0.0201 4789 | 0.0210 1784 | 84 |
| 85 | 0.0183 3409 | 0.0191 6808 | 0.0200 2153 | 0.0208 9396 | 85 |
| 86 | 0.0182 0654 | 0.0190 4267 | 0.0198 9843 | 0.0207 7333 | 86 |
| 87 | 0.0180 8215 | 0.0189 2041 | 0.0197 7847 | 0.0206 5584 | 87 |
| 88 | 0.0179 6081 | 0.0188 0119 | 0.0196 6155 | 0.0205 4138 | 88 |
| 89 | 0.0178 4240 | 0.0186 8491 | 0.0195 4756 | 0.0204 2984 | 89 |
| 90 | 0.0177 2684 | 0.0185 7146 | 0.0194 3641 | 0.0203 2113 | 90 |
| 91 | 0.0176 1403 | 0.0184 6076 | 0.0193 2799 | 0.0202 1516 | 91 |
| 92 | 0.0175 0387 | 0.0183 5272 | 0.0192 2222 | 0.0201 1182 | 92 |
| 93 | 0.0173 9629 | 0.0182 4724 | 0.0191 1902 | 0.0200 1104 | 93 |
| 94 | 0.0172 9119 | 0.0181 4425 | 0.0190 1829 | 0.0199 1273 | 94 |
| 95 | 0.0171 8851 | 0.0180 4366 | 0.0189 1997 | 0.0198 1681 | 95 |
| 96 | 0.0170 8816 | 0.0179 4541 | 0.0188 2397 | 0.0197 2321 | 96 |
| 97 | 0.0169 9007 | 0.0178 4941 | 0.0187 3022 | 0.0196 3186 | 97 |
| 98 | 0.0168 9418 | 0.0177 5560 | 0.0186 3866 | 0.0195 4268 | 98 |
| 99 | 0.0168 0041 | 0.0176 6391 | 0.0185 4921 | 0.0194 5560 | 99 |
| 100 | 0.0167 0870 | 0.0175 7428 | 0.0184 6181 | 0.0193 7057 | 100 |

## TABLE 9

$$\frac{1}{a_{\overline{n}|i}} = \frac{i}{1-(1+i)^{-n}} \qquad \text{Note: } \frac{1}{s_{\overline{n}|i}} = \frac{1}{a_{\overline{n}|i}} - i$$

| n | $1\frac{5}{8}\%$ | $1\frac{3}{4}\%$ | $1\frac{7}{8}\%$ | 2% | n |
|---|---|---|---|---|---|
| 1 | 1.0162 5000 | 1.0175 0000 | 1.0187 5000 | 1.0200 0000 | 1 |
| 2 | 0.5122 2024 | 0.5131 6295 | 0.5141 0604 | 0.5150 4950 | 2 |
| 3 | 0.3442 2487 | 0.3450 6746 | 0.3459 1073 | 0.3467 5467 | 3 |
| 4 | 0.2602 3810 | 0.2610 3237 | 0.2618 2759 | 0.2626 2375 | 4 |
| 5 | 0.2098 5476 | 0.2106 2142 | 0.2113 8930 | 0.2121 5839 | 5 |
| 6 | 0.1762 7314 | 0.1770 2256 | 0.1777 7345 | 0.1785 2581 | 6 |
| 7 | 0.1522 9250 | 0.1530 3059 | 0.1537 7040 | 0.1545 1196 | 7 |
| 8 | 0.1343 1247 | 0.1350 4292 | 0.1357 7537 | 0.1365 0980 | 8 |
| 9 | 0.1203 3285 | 0.1210 5813 | 0.1217 8566 | 0.1225 1544 | 9 |
| 10 | 0.1091 5351 | 0.1098 7534 | 0.1105 9969 | 0.1113 2653 | 10 |
| 11 | 0.1000 1073 | 0.1007 3038 | 0.1014 5278 | 0.1021 7794 | 11 |
| 12 | 0.0923 9537 | 0.0931 1377 | 0.0938 3518 | 0.0945 5960 | 12 |
| 13 | 0.0859 5496 | 0.0866 7283 | 0.0873 9396 | 0.0881 1835 | 13 |
| 14 | 0.0804 3771 | 0.0811 5562 | 0.0818 7704 | 0.0826 0197 | 14 |
| 15 | 0.0756 5898 | 0.0763 7739 | 0.0770 9955 | 0.0778 2547 | 15 |
| 16 | 0.0714 8031 | 0.0721 9958 | 0.0729 2285 | 0.0736 5013 | 16 |
| 17 | 0.0677 9580 | 0.0685 1623 | 0.0692 4091 | 0.0699 6984 | 17 |
| 18 | 0.0645 2309 | 0.0652 4492 | 0.0659 7127 | 0.0667 0210 | 18 |
| 19 | 0.0615 9715 | 0.0623 2061 | 0.0630 4882 | 0.0637 8177 | 19 |
| 20 | 0.0589 6597 | 0.0596 9122 | 0.0604 2148 | 0.0611 5672 | 20 |
| 21 | 0.0565 8743 | 0.0573 1464 | 0.0580 4709 | 0.0587 8477 | 21 |
| 22 | 0.0544 2709 | 0.0551 5638 | 0.0558 9116 | 0.0566 3140 | 22 |
| 23 | 0.0524 5648 | 0.0531 8796 | 0.0539 2517 | 0.0546 6810 | 23 |
| 24 | 0.0506 5188 | 0.0513 8565 | 0.0521 2540 | 0.0528 7110 | 24 |
| 25 | 0.0489 9336 | 0.0497 2952 | 0.0504 7188 | 0.0512 2044 | 25 |
| 26 | 0.0474 6408 | 0.0482 0269 | 0.0489 4775 | 0.0496 9923 | 26 |
| 27 | 0.0460 4967 | 0.0467 9079 | 0.0475 3861 | 0.0482 9309 | 27 |
| 28 | 0.0447 3781 | 0.0454 8151 | 0.0462 3215 | 0.0469 8967 | 28 |
| 29 | 0.0435 1791 | 0.0442 6424 | 0.0450 1773 | 0.0457 7836 | 29 |
| 30 | 0.0423 8075 | 0.0431 2975 | 0.0438 8616 | 0.0446 4992 | 30 |
| 31 | 0.0413 1834 | 0.0420 7005 | 0.0428 2941 | 0.0435 9635 | 31 |
| 32 | 0.0403 2365 | 0.0410 7812 | 0.0418 4046 | 0.0426 1061 | 32 |
| 33 | 0.0393 9054 | 0.0401 4779 | 0.0409 1314 | 0.0416 8653 | 33 |
| 34 | 0.0385 1357 | 0.0392 7363 | 0.0400 4202 | 0.0408 1867 | 34 |
| 35 | 0.0376 8792 | 0.0384 5082 | 0.0392 2227 | 0.0400 0221 | 35 |
| 36 | 0.0369 0931 | 0.0376 7507 | 0.0384 4960 | 0.0392 3285 | 36 |
| 37 | 0.0361 7393 | 0.0369 4257 | 0.0377 2021 | 0.0385 0678 | 37 |
| 38 | 0.0354 7837 | 0.0362 4990 | 0.0370 3066 | 0.0378 2057 | 38 |
| 39 | 0.0348 1955 | 0.0355 9399 | 0.0363 7788 | 0.0371 7114 | 39 |
| 40 | 0.0341 9472 | 0.0349 7209 | 0.0357 5913 | 0.0365 5575 | 40 |
| 41 | 0.0336 0140 | 0.0343 8170 | 0.0351 7190 | 0.0359 7188 | 41 |
| 42 | 0.0330 3732 | 0.0338 2057 | 0.0346 1393 | 0.0354 1729 | 42 |
| 43 | 0.0325 0045 | 0.0332 8666 | 0.0340 8319 | 0.0348 8993 | 43 |
| 44 | 0.0319 8893 | 0.0327 7810 | 0.0335 7781 | 0.0343 8794 | 44 |
| 45 | 0.0315 0106 | 0.0322 9321 | 0.0330 9610 | 0.0339 0962 | 45 |
| 46 | 0.0310 3531 | 0.0318 3043 | 0.0326 3651 | 0.0334 5342 | 46 |
| 47 | 0.0305 9025 | 0.0313 8836 | 0.0321 9763 | 0.0330 1792 | 47 |
| 48 | 0.0301 6460 | 0.0309 6570 | 0.0317 7815 | 0.0326 0184 | 48 |
| 49 | 0.0297 5716 | 0.0305 6124 | 0.0313 7689 | 0.0322 0396 | 49 |
| 50 | 0.0293 6684 | 0.0301 7391 | 0.0309 9275 | 0.0318 2321 | 50 |

Table
9

# TABLE 9

$$\frac{1}{a_{\overline{n}|i}} = \frac{i}{1 - (1 + i)^{-n}} \qquad \text{Note: } \frac{1}{s_{\overline{n}|i}} = \frac{1}{a_{\overline{n}|i}} - i$$

| n | $1\frac{5}{8}\%$ | $1\frac{3}{4}\%$ | $1\frac{7}{8}\%$ | 2% | n |
|---|---|---|---|---|---|
| 51 | 0.0289 9263 | 0.0298 0269 | 0.0306 2472 | 0.0314 5856 | 51 |
| 52 | 0.0286 3360 | 0.0294 4665 | 0.0302 7187 | 0.0311 0909 | 52 |
| 53 | 0.0282 8888 | 0.0291 0492 | 0.0299 3333 | 0.0307 7392 | 53 |
| 54 | 0.0279 5769 | 0.0287 7672 | 0.0296 0830 | 0.0304 5226 | 54 |
| 55 | 0.0276 3927 | 0.0284 6129 | 0.0292 9605 | 0.0301 4337 | 55 |
| 56 | 0.0273 3294 | 0.0281 5795 | 0.0289 9589 | 0.0298 4656 | 56 |
| 57 | 0.0270 3807 | 0.0278 6606 | 0.0287 0717 | 0.0295 6120 | 57 |
| 58 | 0.0267 5406 | 0.0275 8503 | 0.0284 2931 | 0.0292 8667 | 58 |
| 59 | 0.0264 8036 | 0.0273 1430 | 0.0281 6174 | 0.0290 2243 | 59 |
| 60 | 0.0262 1645 | 0.0270 5336 | 0.0279 0395 | 0.0287 6797 | 60 |
| 61 | 0.0259 6184 | 0.0268 0172 | 0.0276 5545 | 0.0285 2278 | 61 |
| 62 | 0.0257 1608 | 0.0265 5892 | 0.0274 1579 | 0.0282 8643 | 62 |
| 63 | 0.0254 7875 | 0.0263 2455 | 0.0271 8455 | 0.0280 5848 | 63 |
| 64 | 0.0252 4946 | 0.0260 9821 | 0.0269 6133 | 0.0278 3855 | 64 |
| 65 | 0.0250 2782 | 0.0258 7952 | 0.0267 4575 | 0.0276 2624 | 65 |
| 66 | 0.0248 1350 | 0.0256 6813 | 0.0265 3747 | 0.0274 2122 | 66 |
| 67 | 0.0246 0615 | 0.0254 6372 | 0.0263 3616 | 0.0272 2316 | 67 |
| 68 | 0.0244 0548 | 0.0252 6597 | 0.0261 4149 | 0.0270 3173 | 68 |
| 69 | 0.0242 1118 | 0.0250 7459 | 0.0259 5319 | 0.0268 4665 | 69 |
| 70 | 0.0240 2299 | 0.0248 8930 | 0.0257 7097 | 0.0266 6765 | 70 |
| 71 | 0.0238 4064 | 0.0247 0985 | 0.0255 9458 | 0.0264 9446 | 71 |
| 72 | 0.0236 6388 | 0.0245 3600 | 0.0254 2377 | 0.0263 2683 | 72 |
| 73 | 0.0234 9250 | 0.0243 6750 | 0.0252 5830 | 0.0261 6454 | 73 |
| 74 | 0.0233 2626 | 0.0242 0413 | 0.0250 9796 | 0.0260 0736 | 74 |
| 75 | 0.0231 6496 | 0.0240 4570 | 0.0249 4254 | 0.0258 5508 | 75 |
| 76 | 0.0230 0840 | 0.0238 9200 | 0.0247 9185 | 0.0257 0751 | 76 |
| 77 | 0.0228 5640 | 0.0237 4285 | 0.0246 4568 | 0.0255 6447 | 77 |
| 78 | 0.0227 0877 | 0.0235 9806 | 0.0245 0387 | 0.0254 2576 | 78 |
| 79 | 0.0225 6536 | 0.0234 5748 | 0.0243 6625 | 0.0252 9123 | 79 |
| 80 | 0.0224 2600 | 0.0233 2093 | 0.0242 3266 | 0.0251 6071 | 80 |
| 81 | 0.0222 9053 | 0.0231 8828 | 0.0241 0294 | 0.0250 3405 | 81 |
| 82 | 0.0221 5882 | 0.0230 5936 | 0.0239 7696 | 0.0249 1110 | 82 |
| 83 | 0.0220 3073 | 0.0229 3406 | 0.0238 5457 | 0.0247 9173 | 83 |
| 84 | 0.0219 0612 | 0.0228 1223 | 0.0237 3564 | 0.0246 7581 | 84 |
| 85 | 0.0217 8487 | 0.0226 9375 | 0.0236 2004 | 0.0245 6321 | 85 |
| 86 | 0.0216 6687 | 0.0225 7850 | 0.0235 0767 | 0.0244 5381 | 86 |
| 87 | 0.0215 5199 | 0.0224 6636 | 0.0233 9839 | 0.0243 4750 | 87 |
| 88 | 0.0214 4013 | 0.0223 5724 | 0.0232 9212 | 0.0242 4416 | 88 |
| 89 | 0.0213 3119 | 0.0222 5102 | 0.0231 8873 | 0.0241 4370 | 89 |
| 90 | 0.0212 2506 | 0.0221 4760 | 0.0230 8813 | 0.0240 4602 | 90 |
| 91 | 0.0211 2166 | 0.0220 4690 | 0.0229 9023 | 0.0239 5101 | 91 |
| 92 | 0.0210 2089 | 0.0219 4882 | 0.0228 9494 | 0.0238 5859 | 92 |
| 93 | 0.0209 2267 | 0.0218 5327 | 0.0228 0217 | 0.0237 6868 | 93 |
| 94 | 0.0208 2691 | 0.0217 6017 | 0.0227 1183 | 0.0236 8118 | 94 |
| 95 | 0.0207 3353 | 0.0216 6944 | 0.0226 2385 | 0.0235 9602 | 95 |
| 96 | 0.0206 4246 | 0.0215 8101 | 0.0225 3814 | 0.0235 1313 | 96 |
| 97 | 0.0205 5362 | 0.0214 9480 | 0.0224 5465 | 0.0234 3242 | 97 |
| 98 | 0.0204 6695 | 0.0214 1074 | 0.0223 7329 | 0.0233 5383 | 98 |
| 99 | 0.0203 8237 | 0.0213 2876 | 0.0222 9400 | 0.0232 7729 | 99 |
| 100 | 0.0202 9983 | 0.0212 4880 | 0.0222 1671 | 0.0232 0274 | 100 |

# TABLE 9

$$\frac{1}{a_{\overline{n}|i}} = \frac{i}{1-(1+i)^{-n}} \qquad \text{Note: } \frac{1}{s_{\overline{n}|i}} = \frac{1}{a_{\overline{n}|i}} - i$$

| n | $2\frac{1}{4}\%$ | $2\frac{1}{2}\%$ | $2\frac{3}{4}\%$ | 3% | n |
|---|---|---|---|---|---|
| 1 | 1.0225 0000 | 1.0250 0000 | 1.0275 0000 | 1.0300 0000 | 1 |
| 2 | 0.5169 3758 | 0.5188 2716 | 0.5207 1825 | 0.5226 1084 | 2 |
| 3 | 0.3484 4458 | 0.3501 3717 | 0.3518 3243 | 0.3535 3036 | 3 |
| 4 | 0.2642 1893 | 0.2658 1788 | 0.2674 2059 | 0.2690 2705 | 4 |
| 5 | 0.2137 0021 | 0.2152 4686 | 0.2167 9832 | 0.2183 5457 | 5 |
| 6 | 0.1800 3496 | 0.1815 4997 | 0.1830 7083 | 0.1845 9750 | 6 |
| 7 | 0.1560 0025 | 0.1574 9543 | 0.1589 9748 | 0.1605 0635 | 7 |
| 8 | 0.1379 8462 | 0.1394 6735 | 0.1409 5795 | 0.1424 5639 | 8 |
| 9 | 0.1239 8170 | 0.1254 5689 | 0.1269 4095 | 0.1284 3386 | 9 |
| 10 | 0.1127 8768 | 0.1142 5876 | 0.1157 3972 | 0.1172 3051 | 10 |
| 11 | 0.1036 3649 | 0.1051 0596 | 0.1065 8629 | 0.1080 7745 | 11 |
| 12 | 0.0960 1740 | 0.0974 8713 | 0.0989 6871 | 0.1004 6209 | 12 |
| 13 | 0.0895 7686 | 0.0910 4827 | 0.0925 3252 | 0.0940 2954 | 13 |
| 14 | 0.0840 6230 | 0.0855 3652 | 0.0870 2457 | 0.0885 2634 | 14 |
| 15 | 0.0792 8852 | 0.0807 6646 | 0.0822 5917 | 0.0837 6658 | 15 |
| 16 | 0.0751 1663 | 0.0765 9899 | 0.0780 9710 | 0.0796 1085 | 16 |
| 17 | 0.0714 4039 | 0.0729 2777 | 0.0744 3186 | 0.0759 5253 | 17 |
| 18 | 0.0681 7720 | 0.0696 7008 | 0.0711 8063 | 0.0727 0870 | 18 |
| 19 | 0.0652 6182 | 0.0667 6062 | 0.0682 7802 | 0.0698 1388 | 19 |
| 20 | 0.0626 4207 | 0.0641 4713 | 0.0656 7173 | 0.0672 1571 | 20 |
| 21 | 0.0602 7572 | 0.0617 8733 | 0.0633 1941 | 0.0648 7178 | 21 |
| 22 | 0.0581 2821 | 0.0596 4661 | 0.0611 8640 | 0.0627 4739 | 22 |
| 23 | 0.0561 7097 | 0.0576 9638 | 0.0592 4410 | 0.0608 1390 | 23 |
| 24 | 0.0543 8023 | 0.0559 1282 | 0.0574 6863 | 0.0590 4742 | 24 |
| 25 | 0.0527 3599 | 0.0542 7592 | 0.0558 3997 | 0.0574 2787 | 25 |
| 26 | 0.0512 2134 | 0.0527 6875 | 0.0543 4116 | 0.0559 3829 | 26 |
| 27 | 0.0498 2188 | 0.0513 7687 | 0.0529 5776 | 0.0545 6421 | 27 |
| 28 | 0.0485 2525 | 0.0500 8793 | 0.0516 7738 | 0.0532 9323 | 28 |
| 29 | 0.0473 2081 | 0.0488 9127 | 0.0504 8935 | 0.0521 1467 | 29 |
| 30 | 0.0461 9934 | 0.0477 7764 | 0.0493 8442 | 0.0510 1926 | 30 |
| 31 | 0.0451 5280 | 0.0467 3900 | 0.0483 5453 | 0.0499 9893 | 31 |
| 32 | 0.0441 7415 | 0.0457 6831 | 0.0473 9263 | 0.0490 4662 | 32 |
| 33 | 0.0432 5722 | 0.0448 5938 | 0.0464 9253 | 0.0481 5612 | 33 |
| 34 | 0.0423 9655 | 0.0440 0675 | 0.0456 4875 | 0.0473 2196 | 34 |
| 35 | 0.0415 8731 | 0.0432 0558 | 0.0448 5645 | 0.0465 3929 | 35 |
| 36 | 0.0408 2522 | 0.0424 5158 | 0.0441 1132 | 0.0458 0379 | 36 |
| 37 | 0.0401 0643 | 0.0417 4090 | 0.0434 0953 | 0.0451 1162 | 37 |
| 38 | 0.0394 2753 | 0.0410 7012 | 0.0427 4764 | 0.0444 5934 | 38 |
| 39 | 0.0387 8543 | 0.0404 3615 | 0.0421 2256 | 0.0438 4385 | 39 |
| 40 | 0.0381 7738 | 0.0398 3623 | 0.0415 3151 | 0.0432 6238 | 40 |
| 41 | 0.0376 0087 | 0.0392 6786 | 0.0409 7200 | 0.0427 1241 | 41 |
| 42 | 0.0370 5364 | 0.0387 2876 | 0.0404 4175 | 0.0421 9167 | 42 |
| 43 | 0.0365 3364 | 0.0382 1688 | 0.0399 3871 | 0.0416 9811 | 43 |
| 44 | 0.0360 3901 | 0.0377 3037 | 0.0394 6100 | 0.0412 2985 | 44 |
| 45 | 0.0355 6805 | 0.0372 6751 | 0.0390 0693 | 0.0407 8518 | 45 |
| 46 | 0.0351 1921 | 0.0368 2676 | 0.0385 7493 | 0.0403 6254 | 46 |
| 47 | 0.0346 9107 | 0.0364 0669 | 0.0381 6358 | 0.0399 6051 | 47 |
| 48 | 0.0342 8233 | 0.0360 0599 | 0.0377 7158 | 0.0395 7777 | 48 |
| 49 | 0.0338 9179 | 0.0356 2348 | 0.0373 9773 | 0.0392 1314 | 49 |
| 50 | 0.0335 1836 | 0.0352 5806 | 0.0370 4092 | 0.0388 6549 | 50 |

Table
9

**TABLE 9**

$$\frac{1}{a_{\overline{n}|i}} = \frac{i}{1-(1+i)^{-n}} \qquad \text{Note: } \frac{1}{s_{\overline{n}|i}} = \frac{1}{a_{\overline{n}|i}} - i$$

| $n$ | $2\frac{1}{4}\%$ | $2\frac{1}{2}\%$ | $2\frac{3}{4}\%$ | $3\%$ | $n$ |
|---|---|---|---|---|---|
| 51 | 0.0331 6102 | 0.0349 0870 | 0.0367 0014 | 0.0385 3382 | 51 |
| 52 | 0.0328 1884 | 0.0345 7446 | 0.0363 7444 | 0.0382 1718 | 52 |
| 53 | 0.0324 9094 | 0.0342 5449 | 0.0360 6297 | 0.0379 1471 | 53 |
| 54 | 0.0321 7654 | 0.0339 4799 | 0.0357 6491 | 0.0376 2558 | 54 |
| 55 | 0.0318 7489 | 0.0336 5419 | 0.0354 7953 | 0.0373 4907 | 55 |
| 56 | 0.0315 8530 | 0.0333 7243 | 0.0352 0612 | 0.0370 8447 | 56 |
| 57 | 0.0313 0712 | 0.0331 0204 | 0.0349 4404 | 0.0368 3114 | 57 |
| 58 | 0.0310 3977 | 0.0328 4244 | 0.0346 9270 | 0.0365 8848 | 58 |
| 59 | 0.0307 8268 | 0.0325 9307 | 0.0344 5153 | 0.0363 5593 | 59 |
| 60 | 0.0305 3533 | 0.0323 5340 | 0.0342 2002 | 0.0361 3296 | 60 |
| 61 | 0.0302 9724 | 0.0321 2294 | 0.0339 9767 | 0.0359 1908 | 61 |
| 62 | 0.0300 6795 | 0.0319 0126 | 0.0337 8402 | 0.0357 1385 | 62 |
| 63 | 0.0298 4704 | 0.0316 8790 | 0.0335 7866 | 0.0355 1682 | 63 |
| 64 | 0.0296 3411 | 0.0314 8249 | 0.0333 8118 | 0.0353 2760 | 64 |
| 65 | 0.0294 2878 | 0.0312 8463 | 0.0331 9120 | 0.0351 4581 | 65 |
| 66 | 0.0292 3070 | 0.0310 9398 | 0.0330 0837 | 0.0349 7110 | 66 |
| 67 | 0.0290 3955 | 0.0309 1021 | 0.0328 3236 | 0.0348 0313 | 67 |
| 68 | 0.0288 5500 | 0.0307 3300 | 0.0326 6285 | 0.0346 4159 | 68 |
| 69 | 0.0286 7677 | 0.0305 6206 | 0.0324 9955 | 0.0344 8618 | 69 |
| 70 | 0.0285 0458 | 0.0303 9712 | 0.0323 4218 | 0.0343 3663 | 70 |
| 71 | 0.0283 3816 | 0.0302 3790 | 0.0321 9048 | 0.0341 9266 | 71 |
| 72 | 0.0281 7728 | 0.0300 8417 | 0.0320 4420 | 0.0340 5404 | 72 |
| 73 | 0.0280 2169 | 0.0299 3568 | 0.0319 0311 | 0.0339 2053 | 73 |
| 74 | 0.0278 7118 | 0.0297 9222 | 0.0317 6698 | 0.0337 9191 | 74 |
| 75 | 0.0277 2554 | 0.0296 5358 | 0.0316 3560 | 0.0336 6796 | 75 |
| 76 | 0.0275 8457 | 0.0295 1956 | 0.0315 0878 | 0.0335 4849 | 76 |
| 77 | 0.0274 4808 | 0.0293 8997 | 0.0313 8633 | 0.0334 3331 | 77 |
| 78 | 0.0273 1589 | 0.0292 6463 | 0.0312 6806 | 0.0333 2224 | 78 |
| 79 | 0.0271 8784 | 0.0291 4338 | 0.0311 5382 | 0.0332 1510 | 79 |
| 80 | 0.0270 6376 | 0.0290 2605 | 0.0310 4342 | 0.0331 1175 | 80 |
| 81 | 0.0269 4350 | 0.0289 1248 | 0.0309 3674 | 0.0330 1201 | 81 |
| 82 | 0.0268 2692 | 0.0288 0254 | 0.0308 3361 | 0.0329 1576 | 82 |
| 83 | 0.0267 1387 | 0.0286 9608 | 0.0307 3389 | 0.0328 2284 | 83 |
| 84 | 0.0266 0423 | 0.0285 9298 | 0.0306 3747 | 0.0327 3313 | 84 |
| 85 | 0.0264 9787 | 0.0284 9310 | 0.0305 4420 | 0.0326 4650 | 85 |
| 86 | 0.0263 9467 | 0.0283 9633 | 0.0304 5397 | 0.0325 6284 | 86 |
| 87 | 0.0262 9452 | 0.0283 0255 | 0.0303 6667 | 0.0324 8202 | 87 |
| 88 | 0.0261 9730 | 0.0282 1165 | 0.0302 8219 | 0.0324 0393 | 88 |
| 89 | 0.0261 0291 | 0.0281 2353 | 0.0302 0041 | 0.0323 2848 | 89 |
| 90 | 0.0260 1126 | 0.0280 3809 | 0.0301 2125 | 0.0322 5556 | 90 |
| 91 | 0.0259 2224 | 0.0279 5523 | 0.0300 4460 | 0.0321 8508 | 91 |
| 92 | 0.0258 3577 | 0.0278 7486 | 0.0299 7038 | 0.0321 1694 | 92 |
| 93 | 0.0257 5176 | 0.0277 9690 | 0.0298 9850 | 0.0320 5107 | 93 |
| 94 | 0.0256 7012 | 0.0277 2126 | 0.0298 2887 | 0.0319 8737 | 94 |
| 95 | 0.0255 9078 | 0.0276 4786 | 0.0297 6141 | 0.0319 2577 | 95 |
| 96 | 0.0255 1366 | 0.0275 7662 | 0.0296 9605 | 0.0318 6619 | 96 |
| 97 | 0.0254 3868 | 0.0275 0747 | 0.0296 3272 | 0.0318 0856 | 97 |
| 98 | 0.0253 6578 | 0.0274 4034 | 0.0295 7134 | 0.0317 5281 | 98 |
| 99 | 0.0252 9489 | 0.0273 7517 | 0.0295 1185 | 0.0316 9886 | 99 |
| 100 | 0.0252 2594 | 0.0273 1188 | 0.0294 5418 | 0.0316 4667 | 100 |

**TABLE 9**

$$\frac{1}{a_{\overline{n}|i}} = \frac{i}{1-(1+i)^{-n}} \qquad \text{Note: } \frac{1}{s_{\overline{n}|i}} = \frac{1}{a_{\overline{n}|i}} - i$$

| n | $3\frac{1}{4}\%$ | $3\frac{1}{2}\%$ | $3\frac{3}{4}\%$ | 4% | n |
|---|---|---|---|---|---|
| 1 | 1.0325 0000 | 1.0350 0000 | 1.0375 0000 | 1.0400 0000 | 1 |
| 2 | 0.5245 0492 | 0.5264 0049 | 0.5282 9755 | 0.5301 9608 | 2 |
| 3 | 0.3552 3095 | 0.3569 3418 | 0.3586 4005 | 0.3603 4854 | 3 |
| 4 | 0.2706 3723 | 0.2722 5114 | 0.2738 6875 | 0.2754 9005 | 4 |
| 5 | 0.2199 1560 | 0.2214 8137 | 0.2230 5189 | 0.2246 2711 | 5 |
| 6 | 0.1861 2997 | 0.1876 6821 | 0.1892 1219 | 0.1907 6190 | 6 |
| 7 | 0.1620 2204 | 0.1635 4449 | 0.1650 7370 | 0.1666 0961 | 7 |
| 8 | 0.1439 6263 | 0.1454 7665 | 0.1469 9839 | 0.1485 2783 | 8 |
| 9 | 0.1299 3555 | 0.1314 4601 | 0.1329 6517 | 0.1344 9299 | 9 |
| 10 | 0.1187 3107 | 0.1202 4137 | 0.1217 6134 | 0.1232 9094 | 10 |
| 11 | 0.1095 7936 | 0.1110 9197 | 0.1126 1521 | 0.1141 4904 | 11 |
| 12 | 0.1019 6719 | 0.1034 8395 | 0.1050 1230 | 0.1065 5217 | 12 |
| 13 | 0.0955 3925 | 0.0970 6157 | 0.0985 9642 | 0.1001 4373 | 13 |
| 14 | 0.0900 4176 | 0.0915 7073 | 0.0931 1317 | 0.0946 6897 | 14 |
| 15 | 0.0852 8858 | 0.0868 2507 | 0.0883 7595 | 0.0899 4110 | 15 |
| 16 | 0.0811 4013 | 0.0826 8483 | 0.0842 4483 | 0.0858 2000 | 16 |
| 17 | 0.0774 8966 | 0.0790 4313 | 0.0806 1280 | 0.0821 9852 | 17 |
| 18 | 0.0742 5415 | 0.0758 1684 | 0.0773 9662 | 0.0789 9333 | 18 |
| 19 | 0.0713 6804 | 0.0729 4033 | 0.0745 3058 | 0.0761 3862 | 19 |
| 20 | 0.0687 7888 | 0.0703 6108 | 0.0719 6210 | 0.0735 8175 | 20 |
| 21 | 0.0664 4424 | 0.0680 3659 | 0.0696 4862 | 0.0712 8011 | 21 |
| 22 | 0.0643 2936 | 0.0659 3207 | 0.0675 5531 | 0.0691 9881 | 22 |
| 23 | 0.0624 0555 | 0.0640 1880 | 0.0656 5339 | 0.0673 0906 | 23 |
| 24 | 0.0606 4891 | 0.0622 7283 | 0.0639 1890 | 0.0655 8683 | 24 |
| 25 | 0.0590 3933 | 0.0606 7404 | 0.0623 3169 | 0.0640 1196 | 25 |
| 26 | 0.0575 5981 | 0.0592 0540 | 0.0608 7470 | 0.0625 6738 | 26 |
| 27 | 0.0561 9588 | 0.0578 5241 | 0.0595 3343 | 0.0612 3854 | 27 |
| 28 | 0.0549 3512 | 0.0566 0265 | 0.0582 9540 | 0.0600 1298 | 28 |
| 29 | 0.0537 6682 | 0.0554 4538 | 0.0571 4991 | 0.0588 7993 | 29 |
| 30 | 0.0526 8172 | 0.0543 7133 | 0.0560 8762 | 0.0578 3010 | 30 |
| 31 | 0.0516 7172 | 0.0533 7240 | 0.0551 0046 | 0.0568 5535 | 31 |
| 32 | 0.0507 2976 | 0.0524 4150 | 0.0541 8131 | 0.0559 4859 | 32 |
| 33 | 0.0498 4961 | 0.0515 7242 | 0.0533 2395 | 0.0551 0357 | 33 |
| 34 | 0.0490 2581 | 0.0507 5966 | 0.0525 2287 | 0.0543 1477 | 34 |
| 35 | 0.0482 5348 | 0.0499 9835 | 0.0517 7320 | 0.0535 7732 | 35 |
| 36 | 0.0475 2831 | 0.0492 8416 | 0.0510 7001 | 0.0528 8688 | 36 |
| 37 | 0.0468 4645 | 0.0486 1325 | 0.0504 1122 | 0.0522 3957 | 37 |
| 38 | 0.0462 0445 | 0.0479 8214 | 0.0497 9159 | 0.0516 3192 | 38 |
| 39 | 0.0455 9920 | 0.0473 8775 | 0.0492 0860 | 0.0510 6083 | 39 |
| 40 | 0.0450 2794 | 0.0468 2728 | 0.0486 5946 | 0.0505 2349 | 40 |
| 41 | 0.0444 8814 | 0.0462 9822 | 0.0481 4164 | 0.0500 1738 | 41 |
| 42 | 0.0439 7753 | 0.0457 9828 | 0.0476 5286 | 0.0495 4020 | 42 |
| 43 | 0.0434 9403 | 0.0453 2539 | 0.0471 9106 | 0.0490 8989 | 43 |
| 44 | 0.0430 3579 | 0.0448 7768 | 0.0467 5434 | 0.0486 6454 | 44 |
| 45 | 0.0426 0108 | 0.0444 5343 | 0.0463 4098 | 0.0482 6246 | 45 |
| 46 | 0.0421 8835 | 0.0440 5108 | 0.0459 4943 | 0.0478 8205 | 46 |
| 47 | 0.0417 9616 | 0.0436 6919 | 0.0455 7824 | 0.0475 2189 | 47 |
| 48 | 0.0414 2320 | 0.0433 0646 | 0.0452 2609 | 0.0471 8065 | 48 |
| 49 | 0.0410 6828 | 0.0429 6167 | 0.0448 9179 | 0.0468 5712 | 49 |
| 50 | 0.0407 3027 | 0.0426 3371 | 0.0445 7422 | 0.0465 5020 | 50 |

Table
9

**TABLE 9**

$$\frac{1}{a_{\overline{n}|i}} = \frac{i}{1-(1+i)^{-n}} \qquad \text{Note: } \frac{1}{s_{\overline{n}|i}} = \frac{1}{a_{\overline{n}|i}} - i$$

| $n$ | $3\frac{1}{4}\%$ | $3\frac{1}{2}\%$ | $3\frac{3}{4}\%$ | $4\%$ | $n$ |
|---|---|---|---|---|---|
| 51 | 0.0404 0817 | 0.0423 2156 | 0.0442 7235 | 0.0462 5885 | 51 |
| 52 | 0.0401 0103 | 0.0420 2429 | 0.0439 8523 | 0.0459 8212 | 52 |
| 53 | 0.0398 0797 | 0.0417 4100 | 0.0437 1199 | 0.0457 1915 | 53 |
| 54 | 0.0395 2819 | 0.0414 7090 | 0.0434 5183 | 0.0454 6910 | 54 |
| 55 | 0.0392 6095 | 0.0412 1323 | 0.0432 0398 | 0.0452 3124 | 55 |
| 56 | 0.0390 0553 | 0.0409 6730 | 0.0429 6775 | 0.0450 0487 | 56 |
| 57 | 0.0387 6131 | 0.0407 3245 | 0.0427 4249 | 0.0447 8932 | 57 |
| 58 | 0.0385 2767 | 0.0405 0810 | 0.0425 2760 | 0.0445 8401 | 58 |
| 59 | 0.0383 0405 | 0.0402 9366 | 0.0423 2251 | 0.0443 8836 | 59 |
| 60 | 0.0380 8993 | 0.0400 8862 | 0.0421 2670 | 0.0442 0185 | 60 |
| 61 | 0.0378 8483 | 0.0398 9249 | 0.0419 3967 | 0.0440 2398 | 61 |
| 62 | 0.0376 8827 | 0.0397 0480 | 0.0417 6097 | 0.0438 5430 | 62 |
| 63 | 0.0374 9983 | 0.0395 2513 | 0.0415 9016 | 0.0436 9237 | 63 |
| 64 | 0.0373 1912 | 0.0393 5308 | 0.0414 2684 | 0.0435 3780 | 64 |
| 65 | 0.0371 4574 | 0.0391 8826 | 0.0412 7063 | 0.0433 9019 | 65 |
| 66 | 0.0369 7935 | 0.0390 3031 | 0.0411 2118 | 0.0432 4921 | 66 |
| 67 | 0.0368 1962 | 0.0388 7892 | 0.0409 7816 | 0.0431 1451 | 67 |
| 68 | 0.0366 6622 | 0.0387 3376 | 0.0408 4124 | 0.0429 8578 | 68 |
| 69 | 0.0365 1886 | 0.0385 9453 | 0.0407 1013 | 0.0428 6272 | 69 |
| 70 | 0.0363 7727 | 0.0384 6095 | 0.0405 8456 | 0.0427 4506 | 70 |
| 71 | 0.0362 4117 | 0.0383 3277 | 0.0404 6426 | 0.0426 3253 | 71 |
| 72 | 0.0361 1033 | 0.0382 0973 | 0.0403 4898 | 0.0425 2489 | 72 |
| 73 | 0.0359 8451 | 0.0380 9160 | 0.0402 3848 | 0.0424 2190 | 73 |
| 74 | 0.0358 6347 | 0.0379 7816 | 0.0401 3255 | 0.0423 2334 | 74 |
| 75 | 0.0357 4702 | 0.0378 6919 | 0.0400 3098 | 0.0422 2900 | 75 |
| 76 | 0.0356 3496 | 0.0377 6450 | 0.0399 3356 | 0.0421 3869 | 76 |
| 77 | 0.0355 2709 | 0.0376 6390 | 0.0398 4011 | 0.0420 5221 | 77 |
| 78 | 0.0354 2323 | 0.0375 6721 | 0.0397 5045 | 0.0419 6939 | 78 |
| 79 | 0.0353 2323 | 0.0374 7426 | 0.0396 6442 | 0.0418 9007 | 79 |
| 80 | 0.0352 2690 | 0.0373 8489 | 0.0395 8184 | 0.0418 1408 | 80 |
| 81 | 0.0351 3411 | 0.0372 9894 | 0.0395 0258 | 0.0417 4127 | 81 |
| 82 | 0.0350 4471 | 0.0372 1628 | 0.0394 2647 | 0.0416 7150 | 82 |
| 83 | 0.0349 5855 | 0.0371 3676 | 0.0393 5340 | 0.0416 0463 | 83 |
| 84 | 0.0348 7550 | 0.0370 6025 | 0.0392 8323 | 0.0415 4054 | 84 |
| 85 | 0.0347 9545 | 0.0369 8662 | 0.0392 1582 | 0.0414 7909 | 85 |
| 86 | 0.0347 1826 | 0.0369 1576 | 0.0391 5107 | 0.0414 2018 | 86 |
| 87 | 0.0346 4383 | 0.0368 4756 | 0.0390 8887 | 0.0413 6370 | 87 |
| 88 | 0.0345 7205 | 0.0367 8190 | 0.0390 2910 | 0.0413 0953 | 88 |
| 89 | 0.0345 0281 | 0.0367 1868 | 0.0389 7166 | 0.0412 5758 | 89 |
| 90 | 0.0344 3601 | 0.0366 5781 | 0.0389 1646 | 0.0412 0775 | 90 |
| 91 | 0.0343 7156 | 0.0365 9919 | 0.0388 6340 | 0.0411 5995 | 91 |
| 92 | 0.0343 0937 | 0.0365 4273 | 0.0388 1240 | 0.0411 1410 | 92 |
| 93 | 0.0342 4935 | 0.0364 8834 | 0.0387 6336 | 0.0410 7010 | 93 |
| 94 | 0.0341 9142 | 0.0364 3594 | 0.0387 1622 | 0.0410 2789 | 94 |
| 95 | 0.0341 3550 | 0.0363 8546 | 0.0386 7088 | 0.0409 8738 | 95 |
| 96 | 0.0340 8151 | 0.0363 3682 | 0.0386 2729 | 0.0409 4850 | 96 |
| 97 | 0.0340 2939 | 0.0362 8995 | 0.0385 8537 | 0.0409 1119 | 97 |
| 98 | 0.0339 7906 | 0.0362 4478 | 0.0385 4504 | 0.0408 7538 | 98 |
| 99 | 0.0339 3045 | 0.0362 0124 | 0.0385 0626 | 0.0408 4100 | 99 |
| 100 | 0.0338 8351 | 0.0361 5927 | 0.0384 6895 | 0.0408 0800 | 100 |

**TABLE   9**

$$\frac{1}{a_{\overline{n}|i}} = \frac{i}{1-(1+i)^{-n}} \qquad \text{Note: } \frac{1}{s_{\overline{n}|i}} = \frac{1}{a_{\overline{n}|i}} - i$$

| $n$ | $4\frac{1}{2}\%$ | $5\%$ | $5\frac{1}{2}\%$ | $6\%$ | $n$ |
|---|---|---|---|---|---|
| 1 | 1.0450 0000 | 1.0500 0000 | 1.0550 0000 | 1.0600 0000 | 1 |
| 2 | 0.5339 9756 | 0.5378 0488 | 0.5416 1800 | 0.5454 3689 | 2 |
| 3 | 0.3637 7336 | 0.3672 0856 | 0.3706 5407 | 0.3741 0981 | 3 |
| 4 | 0.2787 4365 | 0.2820 1183 | 0.2852 9449 | 0.2885 9149 | 4 |
| 5 | 0.2277 9164 | 0.2309 7480 | 0.2341 7644 | 0.2373 9640 | 5 |
| 6 | 0.1938 7839 | 0.1970 1747 | 0.2001 7895 | 0.2033 6263 | 6 |
| 7 | 0.1697 0147 | 0.1728 1982 | 0.1759 6442 | 0.1791 3502 | 7 |
| 8 | 0.1516 0965 | 0.1547 2181 | 0.1578 6401 | 0.1610 3594 | 8 |
| 9 | 0.1375 7447 | 0.1406 9008 | 0.1438 3946 | 0.1470 2224 | 9 |
| 10 | 0.1263 7882 | 0.1295 0458 | 0.1326 6777 | 0.1358 6796 | 10 |
| 11 | 0.1172 4818 | 0.1203 8889 | 0.1235 7065 | 0.1267 9294 | 11 |
| 12 | 0.1096 6619 | 0.1128 2541 | 0.1160 2923 | 0.1192 7703 | 12 |
| 13 | 0.1032 7535 | 0.1064 5577 | 0.1096 8426 | 0.1129 6011 | 13 |
| 14 | 0.0978 2032 | 0.1010 2397 | 0.1042 7912 | 0.1075 8491 | 14 |
| 15 | 0.0931 1381 | 0.0963 4229 | 0.0996 2560 | 0.1029 6276 | 15 |
| 16 | 0.0890 1537 | 0.0922 6991 | 0.0955 8254 | 0.0989 5214 | 16 |
| 17 | 0.0854 1758 | 0.0886 9914 | 0.0920 4197 | 0.0954 4480 | 17 |
| 18 | 0.0822 3690 | 0.0855 4622 | 0.0889 1992 | 0.0923 5654 | 18 |
| 19 | 0.0794 0734 | 0.0827 4501 | 0.0861 5006 | 0.0896 2086 | 19 |
| 20 | 0.0768 7614 | 0.0802 4259 | 0.0836 7933 | 0.0871 8456 | 20 |
| 21 | 0.0746 0057 | 0.0779 9611 | 0.0814 6478 | 0.0850 0455 | 21 |
| 22 | 0.0725 4565 | 0.0759 7051 | 0.0794 7123 | 0.0830 4557 | 22 |
| 23 | 0.0706 8249 | 0.0741 3682 | 0.0776 6965 | 0.0812 7848 | 23 |
| 24 | 0.0689 8703 | 0.0724 7090 | 0.0760 3580 | 0.0796 7900 | 24 |
| 25 | 0.0674 3903 | 0.0709 5246 | 0.0745 4935 | 0.0782 2672 | 25 |
| 26 | 0.0660 2137 | 0.0695 6432 | 0.0731 9307 | 0.0769 0435 | 26 |
| 27 | 0.0647 1946 | 0.0682 9186 | 0.0719 5228 | 0.0756 9717 | 27 |
| 28 | 0.0635 2081 | 0.0671 2253 | 0.0708 1440 | 0.0745 9255 | 28 |
| 29 | 0.0624 1461 | 0.0660 4551 | 0.0697 6857 | 0.0735 7961 | 29 |
| 30 | 0.0613 9154 | 0.0650 5144 | 0.0688 0539 | 0.0726 4891 | 30 |
| 31 | 0.0604 4345 | 0.0641 3212 | 0.0679 1665 | 0.0717 9222 | 31 |
| 32 | 0.0595 6320 | 0.0632 8042 | 0.0670 9519 | 0.0710 0234 | 32 |
| 33 | 0.0587 4453 | 0.0624 9004 | 0.0663 3469 | 0.0702 7294 | 33 |
| 34 | 0.0579 8191 | 0.0617 5545 | 0.0656 2958 | 0.0695 9843 | 34 |
| 35 | 0.0572 7045 | 0.0610 7171 | 0.0649 7493 | 0.0689 7386 | 35 |
| 36 | 0.0566 0578 | 0.0604 3446 | 0.0643 6635 | 0.0683 9483 | 36 |
| 37 | 0.0559 8402 | 0.0598 3979 | 0.0637 9993 | 0.0678 5743 | 37 |
| 38 | 0.0554 0169 | 0.0592 8423 | 0.0632 7217 | 0.0673 5812 | 38 |
| 39 | 0.0548 5567 | 0.0587 6462 | 0.0627 7991 | 0.0668 9377 | 39 |
| 40 | 0.0543 4315 | 0.0582 7816 | 0.0623 2034 | 0.0664 6154 | 40 |
| 41 | 0.0538 6158 | 0.0578 2229 | 0.0618 9090 | 0.0660 5886 | 41 |
| 42 | 0.0534 0868 | 0.0573 9471 | 0.0614 8927 | 0.0656 8342 | 42 |
| 43 | 0.0529 8235 | 0.0569 9333 | 0.0611 1337 | 0.0653 3312 | 43 |
| 44 | 0.0525 8071 | 0.0566 1625 | 0.0607 6128 | 0.0650 0606 | 44 |
| 45 | 0.0522 0202 | 0.0562 6173 | 0.0604 3127 | 0.0647 0050 | 45 |
| 46 | 0.0518 4471 | 0.0559 2820 | 0.0601 2175 | 0.0644 1485 | 46 |
| 47 | 0.0515 0734 | 0.0556 1421 | 0.0598 3129 | 0.0641 4768 | 47 |
| 48 | 0.0511 8858 | 0.0553 1843 | 0.0595 5854 | 0.0638 9765 | 48 |
| 49 | 0.0508 8722 | 0.0550 3965 | 0.0593 0230 | 0.0636 6356 | 49 |
| 50 | 0.0506 0215 | 0.0547 7674 | 0.0590 6145 | 0.0634 4429 | 50 |

Table
9

**TABLE 9**

$$\frac{1}{a_{\overline{n}|i}} = \frac{i}{1-(1+i)^{-n}} \qquad \text{Note: } \frac{1}{s_{\overline{n}|i}} = \frac{1}{a_{\overline{n}|i}} - i$$

| n | $4\frac{1}{2}$% | 5% | $5\frac{1}{2}$% | 6% | n |
|---|---|---|---|---|---|
| 51 | 0.0503 3232 | 0.0545 2867 | 0.0588 3495 | 0.0632 3880 | 51 |
| 52 | 0.0500 7679 | 0.0542 9450 | 0.0586 2186 | 0.0630 4617 | 52 |
| 53 | 0.0498 3469 | 0.0540 7334 | 0.0584 2130 | 0.0628 6551 | 53 |
| 54 | 0.0496 0519 | 0.0538 6438 | 0.0582 3245 | 0.0626 9602 | 54 |
| 55 | 0.0493 8754 | 0.0536 6686 | 0.0580 5458 | 0.0625 3696 | 55 |
| 56 | 0.0491 8105 | 0.0534 8010 | 0.0578 8698 | 0.0623 8765 | 56 |
| 57 | 0.0489 8506 | 0.0533 0343 | 0.0577 2900 | 0.0622 4744 | 57 |
| 58 | 0.0487 9897 | 0.0531 3626 | 0.0575 8006 | 0.0621 1574 | 58 |
| 59 | 0.0486 2221 | 0.0529 7802 | 0.0574 3959 | 0.0619 9200 | 59 |
| 60 | 0.0484 5426 | 0.0528 2818 | 0.0573 0707 | 0.0618 7572 | 60 |
| 61 | 0.0482 9462 | 0.0526 8627 | 0.0571 8202 | 0.0617 6642 | 61 |
| 62 | 0.0481 4284 | 0.0525 5183 | 0.0570 6400 | 0.0616 6366 | 62 |
| 63 | 0.0479 9848 | 0.0524 2442 | 0.0569 5258 | 0.0615 6704 | 63 |
| 64 | 0.0478 6115 | 0.0523 0365 | 0.0568 4737 | 0.0614 7615 | 64 |
| 65 | 0.0477 3047 | 0.0521 8915 | 0.0567 4800 | 0.0613 9066 | 65 |
| 66 | 0.0476 0608 | 0.0520 8057 | 0.0566 5413 | 0.0613 1022 | 66 |
| 67 | 0.0474 8765 | 0.0519 7757 | 0.0565 6544 | 0.0612 3454 | 67 |
| 68 | 0.0473 7487 | 0.0518 7986 | 0.0564 8163 | 0.0611 6330 | 68 |
| 69 | 0.0472 6745 | 0.0517 8715 | 0.0564 0242 | 0.0610 9625 | 69 |
| 70 | 0.0471 6511 | 0.0516 9915 | 0.0563 2754 | 0.0610 3313 | 70 |
| 71 | 0.0470 6759 | 0.0516 1563 | 0.0562 5675 | 0.0609 7370 | 71 |
| 72 | 0.0469 7465 | 0.0515 3633 | 0.0561 8982 | 0.0609 1774 | 72 |
| 73 | 0.0468 8606 | 0.0514 6103 | 0.0561 2652 | 0.0608 6505 | 73 |
| 74 | 0.0468 0159 | 0.0513 8953 | 0.0560 6665 | 0.0608 1542 | 74 |
| 75 | 0.0467 2104 | 0.0513 2161 | 0.0560 1002 | 0.0607 6867 | 75 |
| 76 | 0.0466 4422 | 0.0512 5709 | 0.0559 5645 | 0.0607 2463 | 76 |
| 77 | 0.0465 7094 | 0.0511 9580 | 0.0559 0577 | 0.0606 8315 | 77 |
| 78 | 0.0465 0104 | 0.0511 3756 | 0.0558 5781 | 0.0606 4407 | 78 |
| 79 | 0.0464 3434 | 0.0510 8222 | 0.0558 1243 | 0.0606 0724 | 79 |
| 80 | 0.0463 7069 | 0.0510 2962 | 0.0557 6948 | 0.0605 7254 | 80 |
| 81 | 0.0463 0995 | 0.0509 7963 | 0.0557 2884 | 0.0605 3984 | 81 |
| 82 | 0.0462 5197 | 0.0509 3211 | 0.0556 9036 | 0.0605 0903 | 82 |
| 83 | 0.0461 9663 | 0.0508 8694 | 0.0556 5395 | 0.0604 7998 | 83 |
| 84 | 0.0461 4379 | 0.0508 4399 | 0.0556 1947 | 0.0604 5261 | 84 |
| 85 | 0.0460 9334 | 0.0508 0316 | 0.0555 8683 | 0.0604 2681 | 85 |
| 86 | 0.0460 4516 | 0.0507 6433 | 0.0555 5593 | 0.0604 0249 | 86 |
| 87 | 0.0459 9915 | 0.0507 2740 | 0.0555 2667 | 0.0603 7956 | 87 |
| 88 | 0.0459 5522 | 0.0506 9228 | 0.0554 9896 | 0.0603 5795 | 88 |
| 89 | 0.0459 1325 | 0.0506 5888 | 0.0554 7273 | 0.0603 3757 | 89 |
| 90 | 0.0458 7316 | 0.0506 2711 | 0.0554 4788 | 0.0603 1836 | 90 |
| 91 | 0.0458 3486 | 0.0505 9689 | 0.0554 2435 | 0.0603 0025 | 91 |
| 92 | 0.0457 9827 | 0.0505 6815 | 0.0554 0207 | 0.0602 8318 | 92 |
| 93 | 0.0457 6331 | 0.0505 4080 | 0.0553 8096 | 0.0602 6708 | 93 |
| 94 | 0.0457 2991 | 0.0505 1478 | 0.0553 6097 | 0.0602 5190 | 94 |
| 95 | 0.0456 9799 | 0.0504 9003 | 0.0553 4204 | 0.0602 3758 | 95 |
| 96 | 0.0456 6749 | 0.0504 6648 | 0.0553 2410 | 0.0602 2408 | 96 |
| 97 | 0.0456 3834 | 0.0504 4407 | 0.0553 0711 | 0.0602 1135 | 97 |
| 98 | 0.0456 1048 | 0.0504 2274 | 0.0552 9101 | 0.0601 9935 | 98 |
| 99 | 0.0455 8385 | 0.0504 0245 | 0.0552 7577 | 0.0601 8803 | 99 |
| 100 | 0.0455 5839 | 0.0503 8314 | 0.0552 6132 | 0.0601 7736 | 100 |

# TABLE 9

$$\frac{1}{a_{\overline{n}|i}} = \frac{i}{1 - (1+i)^{-n}} \qquad \text{Note: } \frac{1}{s_{\overline{n}|i}} = \frac{1}{a_{\overline{n}|i}} - i$$

| n | $6\frac{1}{2}\%$ | 7% | $7\frac{1}{2}\%$ | 8% | n |
|---|---|---|---|---|---|
| 1 | 1.0650 0000 | 1.0700 0000 | 1.0750 0000 | 1.0800 0000 | 1 |
| 2 | 0.5492 6150 | 0.5530 9179 | 0.5569 2771 | 0.5607 6923 | 2 |
| 3 | 0.3775 7570 | 0.3810 5166 | 0.3845 3763 | 0.3880 3351 | 3 |
| 4 | 0.2919 0274 | 0.2952 2812 | 0.2985 6751 | 0.3019 2080 | 4 |
| 5 | 0.2406 3454 | 0.2438 9069 | 0.2471 6472 | 0.2504 5645 | 5 |
| 6 | 0.2065 6831 | 0.2097 9580 | 0.2130 4489 | 0.2163 1539 | 6 |
| 7 | 0.1823 3137 | 0.1855 5322 | 0.1888 0032 | 0.1920 7240 | 7 |
| 8 | 0.1642 3730 | 0.1674 6776 | 0.1707 2702 | 0.1740 1476 | 8 |
| 9 | 0.1502 3803 | 0.1534 8647 | 0.1567 6716 | 0.1600 7971 | 9 |
| 10 | 0.1391 0469 | 0.1423 7750 | 0.1456 8593 | 0.1490 2949 | 10 |
| 11 | 0.1300 5521 | 0.1333 5690 | 0.1366 9747 | 0.1400 7634 | 11 |
| 12 | 0.1225 6817 | 0.1259 0199 | 0.1292 7783 | 0.1326 9502 | 12 |
| 13 | 0.1162 8256 | 0.1196 5085 | 0.1230 6420 | 0.1265 2181 | 13 |
| 14 | 0.1109 4048 | 0.1143 4494 | 0.1177 9737 | 0.1212 9685 | 14 |
| 15 | 0.1063 5278 | 0.1097 9462 | 0.1132 8724 | 0.1168 2954 | 15 |
| 16 | 0.1023 7757 | 0.1058 5765 | 0.1093 9116 | 0.1129 7687 | 16 |
| 17 | 0.0989 0633 | 0.1024 2519 | 0.1060 0003 | 0.1096 2943 | 17 |
| 18 | 0.0958 5461 | 0.0994 1260 | 0.1030 2896 | 0.1067 0210 | 18 |
| 19 | 0.0931 5575 | 0.0967 5301 | 0.1004 1090 | 0.1041 2763 | 19 |
| 20 | 0.0907 5640 | 0.0943 9293 | 0.0980 9219 | 0.1018 5221 | 20 |
| 21 | 0.0886 1333 | 0.0922 8900 | 0.0960 2937 | 0.0998 3225 | 21 |
| 22 | 0.0866 9120 | 0.0904 0577 | 0.0941 8687 | 0.0980 3207 | 22 |
| 23 | 0.0849 6078 | 0.0887 1393 | 0.0925 3528 | 0.0964 2217 | 23 |
| 24 | 0.0833 9770 | 0.0871 8902 | 0.0910 5008 | 0.0949 7796 | 24 |
| 25 | 0.0819 8148 | 0.0858 1052 | 0.0897 1067 | 0.0936 7878 | 25 |
| 26 | 0.0806 9480 | 0.0845 6103 | 0.0884 9961 | 0.0925 0713 | 26 |
| 27 | 0.0795 2288 | 0.0834 2573 | 0.0874 0204 | 0.0914 4809 | 27 |
| 28 | 0.0784 5305 | 0.0823 9193 | 0.0864 0520 | 0.0904 8891 | 28 |
| 29 | 0.0774 7440 | 0.0814 4865 | 0.0854 9811 | 0.0896 1854 | 29 |
| 30 | 0.0765 7744 | 0.0805 8640 | 0.0846 7124 | 0.0888 2743 | 30 |
| 31 | 0.0757 5393 | 0.0797 9691 | 0.0839 1628 | 0.0881 0728 | 31 |
| 32 | 0.0749 9665 | 0.0790 7292 | 0.0832 2599 | 0.0874 5081 | 32 |
| 33 | 0.0742 9924 | 0.0784 0807 | 0.0825 9397 | 0.0868 5163 | 33 |
| 34 | 0.0736 5610 | 0.0777 9674 | 0.0820 1461 | 0.0863 0411 | 34 |
| 35 | 0.0730 6226 | 0.0772 3396 | 0.0814 8291 | 0.0858 0326 | 35 |
| 36 | 0.0725 1332 | 0.0767 1531 | 0.0809 9447 | 0.0853 4467 | 36 |
| 37 | 0.0720 0534 | 0.0762 3685 | 0.0805 4533 | 0.0849 2440 | 37 |
| 38 | 0.0715 3480 | 0.0757 9505 | 0.0801 3197 | 0.0845 3894 | 38 |
| 39 | 0.0710 9854 | 0.0753 8676 | 0.0797 5124 | 0.0841 8513 | 39 |
| 40 | 0.0706 9373 | 0.0750 0914 | 0.0794 0031 | 0.0838 6016 | 40 |
| 41 | 0.0703 1779 | 0.0746 5962 | 0.0790 7663 | 0.0835 6149 | 41 |
| 42 | 0.0699 6842 | 0.0743 3591 | 0.0787 7789 | 0.0832 8684 | 42 |
| 43 | 0.0696 4352 | 0.0740 3590 | 0.0785 0201 | 0.0830 3414 | 43 |
| 44 | 0.0693 4119 | 0.0737 5769 | 0.0782 4710 | 0.0828 0152 | 44 |
| 45 | 0.0690 5968 | 0.0734 9957 | 0.0780 1146 | 0.0825 8728 | 45 |
| 46 | 0.0687 9743 | 0.0732 5996 | 0.0777 9353 | 0.0823 8991 | 46 |
| 47 | 0.0685 5300 | 0.0730 3744 | 0.0775 9190 | 0.0822 0799 | 47 |
| 48 | 0.0683 2505 | 0.0728 3070 | 0.0774 0527 | 0.0820 4027 | 48 |
| 49 | 0.0681 1240 | 0.0726 3853 | 0.0772 3247 | 0.0818 8557 | 49 |
| 50 | 0.0679 1393 | 0.0724 5985 | 0.0770 7241 | 0.0817 4286 | 50 |

Table
9

**TABLE   9**

$$\frac{1}{a_{\overline{n}|i}} = \frac{i}{1-(1+i)^{-n}} \qquad \text{Note: } \frac{1}{s_{\overline{n}|i}} = \frac{1}{a_{\overline{n}|i}} - i$$

| n | $6\frac{1}{2}$% | 7% | $7\frac{1}{2}$% | 8% | n |
|---|---|---|---|---|---|
| 51 | 0.0677 2861 | 0.0722 9365 | 0.0769 2411 | 0.0816 1116 | 51 |
| 52 | 0.0675 5553 | 0.0721 3901 | 0.0767 8668 | 0.0814 8959 | 52 |
| 53 | 0.0673 9382 | 0.0719 9509 | 0.0766 5927 | 0.0813 7735 | 53 |
| 54 | 0.0672 4267 | 0.0718 6110 | 0.0765 4112 | 0.0812 7370 | 54 |
| 55 | 0.0671 0137 | 0.0717 3633 | 0.0764 3155 | 0.0811 7796 | 55 |
| 56 | 0.0669 6923 | 0.0716 2011 | 0.0763 2991 | 0.0810 8952 | 56 |
| 57 | 0.0668 4563 | 0.0715 1183 | 0.0762 3559 | 0.0810 0780 | 57 |
| 58 | 0.0667 2999 | 0.0714 1093 | 0.0761 4807 | 0.0809 3227 | 58 |
| 59 | 0.0666 2177 | 0.0713 1689 | 0.0760 6683 | 0.0808 6247 | 59 |
| 60 | 0.0665 2047 | 0.0712 2923 | 0.0759 9142 | 0.0807 9795 | 60 |
| 61 | 0.0664 2564 | 0.0711 4749 | 0.0759 2140 | 0.0807 3830 | 61 |
| 62 | 0.0663 3684 | 0.0710 7127 | 0.0758 5638 | 0.0806 8314 | 62 |
| 63 | 0.0662 5367 | 0.0710 0019 | 0.0757 9600 | 0.0806 3214 | 63 |
| 64 | 0.0661 7577 | 0.0709 3388 | 0.0757 3992 | 0.0805 8497 | 64 |
| 65 | 0.0661 0280 | 0.0708 7203 | 0.0756 8782 | 0.0805 4135 | 65 |
| 66 | 0.0660 3442 | 0.0708 1431 | 0.0756 3942 | 0.0805 0100 | 66 |
| 67 | 0.0659 7034 | 0.0707 6046 | 0.0755 9446 | 0.0804 6367 | 67 |
| 68 | 0.0659 1029 | 0.0707 1021 | 0.0755 5268 | 0.0804 2914 | 68 |
| 69 | 0.0658 5400 | 0.0706 6331 | 0.0755 1386 | 0.0803 9719 | 69 |
| 70 | 0.0658 0124 | 0.0706 1953 | 0.0754 7778 | 0.0803 6764 | 70 |
| 71 | 0.0657 5177 | 0.0705 7866 | 0.0754 4425 | 0.0803 4029 | 71 |
| 72 | 0.0657 0539 | 0.0705 4051 | 0.0754 1308 | 0.0803 1498 | 72 |
| 73 | 0.0656 6190 | 0.0705 0490 | 0.0753 8412 | 0.0802 9157 | 73 |
| 74 | 0.0656 2112 | 0.0704 7164 | 0.0753 5719 | 0.0802 6989 | 74 |
| 75 | 0.0655 8287 | 0.0704 4060 | 0.0753 3216 | 0.0802 4984 | 75 |
| 76 | 0.0655 4699 | 0.0704 1160 | 0.0753 0889 | 0.0802 3128 | 76 |
| 77 | 0.0655 1335 | 0.0703 8453 | 0.0752 8726 | 0.0802 1410 | 77 |
| 78 | 0.0654 8178 | 0.0703 5924 | 0.0752 6714 | 0.0801 9820 | 78 |
| 79 | 0.0654 5217 | 0.0703 3563 | 0.0752 4844 | 0.0801 8349 | 79 |
| 80 | 0.0654 2440 | 0.0703 1357 | 0.0752 3106 | 0.0801 6987 | 80 |
| 81 | 0.0653 9834 | 0.0702 9297 | 0.0752 1489 | 0.0801 5726 | 81 |
| 82 | 0.0653 7388 | 0.0702 7373 | 0.0751 9986 | 0.0801 4559 | 82 |
| 83 | 0.0653 5094 | 0.0702 5576 | 0.0751 8588 | 0.0801 3479 | 83 |
| 84 | 0.0653 2941 | 0.0702 3897 | 0.0751 7288 | 0.0801 2479 | 84 |
| 85 | 0.0653 0921 | 0.0702 2329 | 0.0751 6079 | 0.0801 1553 | 85 |
| 86 | 0.0652 9026 | 0.0702 0863 | 0.0751 4955 | 0.0801 0696 | 86 |
| 87 | 0.0652 7247 | 0.0701 9495 | 0.0751 3910 | 0.0800 9903 | 87 |
| 88 | 0.0652 5577 | 0.0701 8216 | 0.0751 2938 | 0.0800 9168 | 88 |
| 89 | 0.0652 4010 | 0.0701 7021 | 0.0751 2034 | 0.0800 8489 | 89 |
| 90 | 0.0652 2540 | 0.0701 5905 | 0.0751 1193 | 0.0800 7859 | 90 |
| 91 | 0.0652 1160 | 0.0701 4863 | 0.0751 0411 | 0.0800 7277 | 91 |
| 92 | 0.0651 9864 | 0.0701 3888 | 0.0750 9684 | 0.0800 6737 | 92 |
| 93 | 0.0651 8649 | 0.0701 2978 | 0.0750 9007 | 0.0800 6238 | 93 |
| 94 | 0.0651 7507 | 0.0701 2128 | 0.0750 8378 | 0.0800 5775 | 94 |
| 95 | 0.0651 6436 | 0.0701 1333 | 0.0750 7793 | 0.0800 5347 | 95 |
| 96 | 0.0651 5431 | 0.0701 0590 | 0.0750 7249 | 0.0800 4951 | 96 |
| 97 | 0.0651 4487 | 0.0700 9897 | 0.0750 6743 | 0.0800 4584 | 97 |
| 98 | 0.0651 3601 | 0.0700 9248 | 0.0750 6272 | 0.0800 4244 | 98 |
| 99 | 0.0651 2769 | 0.0700 8643 | 0.0750 5834 | 0.0800 3930 | 99 |
| 100 | 0.0651 1988 | 0.0700 8076 | 0.0750 5427 | 0.0800 3638 | 100 |

**PERIODIC PAYMENT**
When Present Value of Annuity Is 1

**TABLE 9**

$$\frac{1}{a_{\overline{n}|i}} = \frac{i}{1 - (1+i)^{-n}} \qquad \text{Note: } \frac{1}{s_{\overline{n}|i}} = \frac{1}{a_{\overline{n}|i}} - i$$

| $n$ | $8\frac{1}{2}\%$ | $9\%$ | $9\frac{1}{2}\%$ | $10\%$ | $n$ |
|---|---|---|---|---|---|
| 1 | 1.0850 0000 | 1.0900 0000 | 1.0950 0000 | 1.1000 0000 | 1 |
| 2 | 0.5646 1631 | 0.5684 6890 | 0.5723 2697 | 0.5761 9048 | 2 |
| 3 | 0.3915 3925 | 0.3950 5476 | 0.3985 7997 | 0.4021 1480 | 3 |
| 4 | 0.3052 8789 | 0.3086 6866 | 0.3120 6300 | 0.3154 7080 | 4 |
| 5 | 0.2537 6575 | 0.2570 9246 | 0.2604 3642 | 0.2637 9748 | 5 |
| 6 | 0.2196 0708 | 0.2229 1978 | 0.2262 5328 | 0.2296 0738 | 6 |
| 7 | 0.1953 6922 | 0.1986 9052 | 0.2020 3603 | 0.2054 0550 | 7 |
| 8 | 0.1773 3065 | 0.1806 7438 | 0.1840 4561 | 0.1874 4402 | 8 |
| 9 | 0.1634 2372 | 0.1667 9880 | 0.1702 0454 | 0.1736 4054 | 9 |
| 10 | 0.1524 0771 | 0.1558 2009 | 0.1592 6615 | 0.1627 4539 | 10 |
| 11 | 0.1434 9293 | 0.1469 4666 | 0.1504 3693 | 0.1539 6314 | 11 |
| 12 | 0.1361 5286 | 0.1396 5066 | 0.1431 8771 | 0.1467 6332 | 12 |
| 13 | 0.1300 2287 | 0.1335 6656 | 0.1371 5206 | 0.1407 7852 | 13 |
| 14 | 0.1248 4244 | 0.1284 3317 | 0.1320 6809 | 0.1357 4622 | 14 |
| 15 | 0.1204 2046 | 0.1240 5888 | 0.1277 4370 | 0.1314 7378 | 15 |
| 16 | 0.1166 1354 | 0.1202 9991 | 0.1240 3470 | 0.1278 1662 | 16 |
| 17 | 0.1133 1198 | 0.1170 4625 | 0.1208 3078 | 0.1246 6413 | 17 |
| 18 | 0.1104 3041 | 0.1142 1229 | 0.1180 4610 | 0.1219 3022 | 18 |
| 19 | 0.1079 0140 | 0.1117 3041 | 0.1156 1284 | 0.1195 4687 | 19 |
| 20 | 0.1056 7097 | 0.1095 4648 | 0.1134 7670 | 0.1174 5962 | 20 |
| 21 | 0.1036 9541 | 0.1076 1663 | 0.1115 9370 | 0.1156 2439 | 21 |
| 22 | 0.1019 3892 | 0.1059 0499 | 0.1099 2784 | 0.1140 0506 | 22 |
| 23 | 0.1003 7193 | 0.1043 8188 | 0.1084 4938 | 0.1125 7181 | 23 |
| 24 | 0.0989 6975 | 0.1030 2256 | 0.1071 3351 | 0.1112 9978 | 24 |
| 25 | 0.0977 1168 | 0.1018 0625 | 0.1059 5939 | 0.1101 6807 | 25 |
| 26 | 0.0965 8016 | 0.1007 1536 | 0.1049 0940 | 0.1091 5904 | 26 |
| 27 | 0.0955 6025 | 0.0997 3491 | 0.1039 6852 | 0.1082 5764 | 27 |
| 28 | 0.0946 3914 | 0.0988 5205 | 0.1031 2389 | 0.1074 5101 | 28 |
| 29 | 0.0938 0577 | 0.0980 5572 | 0.1023 6444 | 0.1067 2807 | 29 |
| 30 | 0.0930 5058 | 0.0973 3635 | 0.1016 8058 | 0.1060 7925 | 30 |
| 31 | 0.0923 6524 | 0.0966 8560 | 0.1010 6399 | 0.1054 9621 | 31 |
| 32 | 0.0917 4247 | 0.0960 9619 | 0.1005 0739 | 0.1049 7172 | 32 |
| 33 | 0.0911 7588 | 0.0955 6173 | 0.1000 0441 | 0.1044 9941 | 33 |
| 34 | 0.0906 5984 | 0.0950 7660 | 0.0995 4945 | 0.1040 7371 | 34 |
| 35 | 0.0901 8937 | 0.0946 3584 | 0.0991 3756 | 0.1036 8971 | 35 |
| 36 | 0.0897 6006 | 0.0942 3505 | 0.0987 6437 | 0.1033 4306 | 36 |
| 37 | 0.0893 6799 | 0.0938 7033 | 0.0984 2600 | 0.1030 2994 | 37 |
| 38 | 0.0890 0966 | 0.0935 3820 | 0.0981 1901 | 0.1027 4693 | 38 |
| 39 | 0.0886 8193 | 0.0932 3555 | 0.0978 4032 | 0.1024 9098 | 39 |
| 40 | 0.0883 8201 | 0.0929 5961 | 0.0975 8719 | 0.1022 5941 | 40 |
| 41 | 0.0881 0737 | 0.0927 0789 | 0.0973 5716 | 0.1020 4980 | 41 |
| 42 | 0.0878 5576 | 0.0924 7814 | 0.0971 4803 | 0.1018 5999 | 42 |
| 43 | 0.0876 2512 | 0.0922 6837 | 0.0969 5783 | 0.1016 8805 | 43 |
| 44 | 0.0874 1363 | 0.0920 7675 | 0.0967 8478 | 0.1015 3224 | 44 |
| 45 | 0.0872 1961 | 0.0919 0165 | 0.0966 2729 | 0.1013 9100 | 45 |
| 46 | 0.0870 4154 | 0.0917 4160 | 0.0964 8390 | 0.1012 6295 | 46 |
| 47 | 0.0868 7807 | 0.0915 9525 | 0.0963 5333 | 0.1011 4682 | 47 |
| 48 | 0.0867 2795 | 0.0914 6139 | 0.0962 3439 | 0.1010 4148 | 48 |
| 49 | 0.0865 9005 | 0.0913 3893 | 0.0961 2603 | 0.1009 4590 | 49 |
| 50 | 0.0864 6334 | 0.0912 2687 | 0.0960 2728 | 0.1008 5917 | 50 |

Table
9

# TABLE 9

$$\frac{1}{a_{\overline{n}|i}} = \frac{i}{1 - (1+i)^{-n}} \qquad \text{Note: } \frac{1}{s_{\overline{n}|i}} = \frac{1}{a_{\overline{n}|i}} - i$$

| $n$ | $8\frac{1}{2}\%$ | 9% | $9\frac{1}{2}\%$ | 10% | $n$ |
|---|---|---|---|---|---|
| 51 | 0.0863 4688 | 0.0911 2430 | 0.0959 3728 | 0.1007 8046 | 51 |
| 52 | 0.0862 3983 | 0.0910 3041 | 0.0958 5523 | 0.1007 0900 | 52 |
| 53 | 0.0861 4139 | 0.0909 4443 | 0.0957 8042 | 0.1006 4413 | 53 |
| 54 | 0.0860 5087 | 0.0908 6570 | 0.0957 1220 | 0.1005 8523 | 54 |
| 55 | 0.0859 6761 | 0.0907 9359 | 0.0956 4999 | 0.1005 3175 | 55 |
| 56 | 0.0858 9101 | 0.0907 2754 | 0.0955 9325 | 0.1004 8317 | 56 |
| 57 | 0.0858 2053 | 0.0906 6702 | 0.0955 4149 | 0.1004 3906 | 57 |
| 58 | 0.0857 5568 | 0.0906 1157 | 0.0954 9426 | 0.1003 9898 | 58 |
| 59 | 0.0856 9599 | 0.0905 6076 | 0.0954 5118 | 0.1003 6258 | 59 |
| 60 | 0.0856 4106 | 0.0905 1419 | 0.0954 1187 | 0.1003 2951 | 60 |
| 61 | 0.0855 9049 | 0.0904 7152 | 0.0953 7599 | 0.1002 9946 | 61 |
| 62 | 0.0855 4393 | 0.0904 3240 | 0.0953 4325 | 0.1002 7217 | 62 |
| 63 | 0.0855 0107 | 0.0903 9654 | 0.0953 1338 | 0.1002 4736 | 63 |
| 64 | 0.0854 6160 | 0.0903 6366 | 0.0952 8611 | 0.1002 2482 | 64 |
| 65 | 0.0854 2526 | 0.0903 3352 | 0.0952 6122 | 0.1002 0434 | 65 |
| 66 | 0.0853 9179 | 0.0903 0589 | 0.0952 3850 | 0.1001 8573 | 66 |
| 67 | 0.0853 6097 | 0.0902 8056 | 0.0952 1776 | 0.1001 6882 | 67 |
| 68 | 0.0853 3258 | 0.0902 5732 | 0.0951 9883 | 0.1001 5345 | 68 |
| 69 | 0.0853 0643 | 0.0903 3602 | 0.0951 8154 | 0.1001 3948 | 69 |
| 70 | 0.0852 8234 | 0.0902 1649 | 0.0951 6576 | 0.1001 2678 | 70 |
| 71 | 0.0852 6016 | 0.0901 9857 | 0.0951 5136 | 0.1001 1524 | 71 |
| 72 | 0.0852 3972 | 0.0901 8214 | 0.0951 3821 | 0.1001 0476 | 72 |
| 73 | 0.0852 2089 | 0.0901 6708 | 0.0951 2620 | 0.1000 9522 | 73 |
| 74 | 0.0852 0354 | 0.0901 5326 | 0.0951 1524 | 0.1000 8656 | 74 |
| 75 | 0.0851 8756 | 0.0901 4058 | 0.0951 0523 | 0.1000 7868 | 75 |
| 76 | 0.0851 7284 | 0.0901 2896 | 0.0950 9609 | 0.1000 7153 | 76 |
| 77 | 0.0851 5927 | 0.0901 1830 | 0.0950 8775 | 0.1000 6502 | 77 |
| 78 | 0.0851 4677 | 0.0901 0852 | 0.0950 8013 | 0.1000 5911 | 78 |
| 79 | 0.0851 3526 | 0.0900 9955 | 0.0950 7317 | 0.1000 5373 | 79 |
| 80 | 0.0851 2465 | 0.0900 9132 | 0.0950 6682 | 0.1000 4884 | 80 |
| 81 | 0.0851 1487 | 0.0900 8377 | 0.0950 6102 | 0.1000 4440 | 81 |
| 82 | 0.0851 0586 | 0.0900 7685 | 0.0950 5572 | 0.1000 4036 | 82 |
| 83 | 0.0850 9756 | 0.0900 7050 | 0.0950 5088 | 0.1000 3669 | 83 |
| 84 | 0.0850 8990 | 0.0900 6467 | 0.0950 4647 | 0.1000 3335 | 84 |
| 85 | 0.0850 8285 | 0.0900 5933 | 0.0950 4243 | 0.1000 3032 | 85 |
| 86 | 0.0850 7636 | 0.0900 5443 | 0.0950 3875 | 0.1000 2756 | 86 |
| 87 | 0.0850 7037 | 0.0900 4993 | 0.0950 3539 | 0.1000 2506 | 87 |
| 88 | 0.0850 6485 | 0.0900 4581 | 0.0950 3232 | 0.1000 2278 | 88 |
| 89 | 0.0850 5977 | 0.0900 4202 | 0.0950 2951 | 0.1000 2071 | 89 |
| 90 | 0.0850 5508 | 0.0900 3855 | 0.0950 2695 | 0.1000 1883 | 90 |
| 91 | 0.0850 5077 | 0.0900 3537 | 0.0950 2461 | 0.1000 1711 | 91 |
| 92 | 0.0850 4679 | 0.0900 3245 | 0.0950 2248 | 0.1000 1556 | 92 |
| 93 | 0.0850 4312 | 0.0900 2977 | 0.0950 2053 | 0.1000 1414 | 93 |
| 94 | 0.0850 3974 | 0.0900 2731 | 0.0950 1874 | 0.1000 1286 | 94 |
| 95 | 0.0850 3663 | 0.0900 2505 | 0.0950 1712 | 0.1000 1169 | 95 |
| 96 | 0.0850 3375 | 0.0900 2298 | 0.0950 1563 | 0.1000 1063 | 96 |
| 97 | 0.0850 3111 | 0.0900 2109 | 0.0950 1428 | 0.1000 0966 | 97 |
| 98 | 0.0850 2867 | 0.0900 1934 | 0.0950 1304 | 0.1000 0878 | 98 |
| 99 | 0.0850 2642 | 0.0900 1775 | 0.0950 1191 | 0.1000 0798 | 99 |
| 100 | 0.0850 2435 | 0.0900 1628 | 0.0950 1087 | 0.1000 0726 | 100 |

**TABLE   10**

$$\frac{1}{s_{\overline{1/m}|i}} = \frac{i}{(1+i)^{\frac{1}{m}}-1} \qquad \text{Note: } \frac{1}{a_{\overline{1/m}|i}} = \frac{1}{s_{\overline{1/m}|i}} + i$$

| m | $\frac{1}{4}$% | $\frac{1}{3}$% | $\frac{5}{12}$% | $\frac{11}{24}$% | $\frac{1}{2}$% | m |
|---|---|---|---|---|---|---|
| 2 | 2.0012 4922 | 2.0016 6528 | 2.0020 8117 | 2.0022 8905 | 2.0024 9688 | 2 |
| 3 | 3.0024 9861 | 3.0033 3087 | 3.0041 6282 | 3.0045 7868 | 3.0049 9446 | 3 |
| 4 | 4.0037 4805 | 4.0049 9653 | 4.0062 4459 | 4.0068 6845 | 4.0074 9221 | 4 |
| 6 | 6.0062 4697 | 6.0083 2794 | 6.0104 0824 | 6.0114 4815 | 6.0124 8788 | 6 |
| 12 | 12.0137 4380 | 12.0183 2232 | 12.0228 9946 | 12.0251 8752 | 12.0274 7524 | 12 |

| m | $\frac{13}{24}$% | $\frac{7}{12}$% | $\frac{5}{8}$% | $\frac{2}{3}$% | $\frac{3}{4}$% | m |
|---|---|---|---|---|---|---|
| 2 | 2.0027 0468 | 2.0029 1243 | 2.0031 2013 | 2.0033 2780 | 2.0037 4300 | 2 |
| 3 | 3.0054 1016 | 3.0058 2579 | 3.0062 4135 | 3.0066 5682 | 3.0074 8755 | 3 |
| 4 | 4.0081 1586 | 4.0087 3940 | 4.0093 6283 | 4.0099 8616 | 4.0112 3249 | 4 |
| 6 | 6.0135 2744 | 6.0145 6684 | 6.0156 0607 | 6.0166 4513 | 6.0187 2276 | 6 |
| 12 | 12.0297 6261 | 12.0320 4964 | 12.0343 3633 | 12.0366 2268 | 12.0411 9435 | 12 |

| m | $1\frac{1}{8}$% | 1% | $1\frac{1}{8}$% | $1\frac{1}{4}$% | $1\frac{3}{8}$% | m |
|---|---|---|---|---|---|---|
| 2 | 2.0043 6547 | 2.0049 8756 | 2.0056 0927 | 2.0062 3059 | 2.0068 5153 | 2 |
| 3 | 3.0087 3306 | 3.0099 7789 | 3.0112 2203 | 3.0124 6549 | 3.0137 0827 | 3 |
| 4 | 4.0131 0118 | 4.0149 6891 | 4.0168 3567 | 4.0187 0147 | 4.0205 6632 | 4 |
| 6 | 6.0218 3794 | 6.0249 5163 | 6.0280 6382 | 6.0311 7452 | 6.0342 8372 | 6 |
| 12 | 12.0480 4930 | 12.0549 0119 | 12.0617 5002 | 12.0685 9580 | 12.0754 3853 | 12 |

| m | $1\frac{1}{2}$% | $1\frac{5}{8}$% | $1\frac{3}{4}$% | $1\frac{7}{8}$% | 2% | m |
|---|---|---|---|---|---|---|
| 2 | 2.0074 7208 | 2.0080 9226 | 2.0087 1205 | 2.0093 3146 | 2.0099 5049 | 2 |
| 3 | 3.0149 5037 | 3.0161 9179 | 3.0174 3253 | 3.0186 7260 | 3.0199 1199 | 3 |
| 4 | 4.0224 3021 | 4.0242 9314 | 4.0261 5513 | 4.0280 1615 | 4.0298 7623 | 4 |
| 6 | 6.0373 9144 | 6.0404 9767 | 6.0436 0242 | 6.0467 0569 | 6.0498 0748 | 6 |
| 12 | 12.0822 7822 | 12.0891 1488 | 12.0959 4851 | 12.1027 7911 | 12.1096 0670 | 12 |

| m | $2\frac{1}{4}$% | $2\frac{1}{2}$% | $2\frac{3}{4}$% | 3% | $3\frac{1}{4}$% | m |
|---|---|---|---|---|---|---|
| 2 | 2.0111 8742 | 2.0124 2284 | 2.0136 5675 | 2.0148 8916 | 2.0161 2007 | 2 |
| 3 | 3.0223 8875 | 3.0248 6282 | 3.0273 3422 | 3.0298 0294 | 3.0322 6902 | 3 |
| 4 | 4.0335 9355 | 4.0373 0709 | 4.0410 1687 | 4.0447 2289 | 4.0484 2518 | 4 |
| 6 | 6.0560 0664 | 6.0621 9992 | 6.0683 8735 | 6.0745 6894 | 6.0807 4472 | 6 |
| 12 | 12.1232 5284 | 12.1368 8698 | 12.1505 0915 | 12.1641 1941 | 12.1777 1779 | 12 |

| m | $3\frac{1}{2}$% | $3\frac{3}{4}$% | 4% | $4\frac{1}{2}$% | 5% | m |
|---|---|---|---|---|---|---|
| 2 | 2.0173 4950 | 2.0185 7744 | 2.0198 0390 | 2.0222 5242 | 2.0246 9508 | 2 |
| 3 | 3.0347 3244 | 3.0371 9322 | 3.0396 5138 | 3.0445 5985 | 3.0494 5791 | 3 |
| 4 | 4.0521 2374 | 4.0558 1860 | 4.0595 0975 | 4.0668 8103 | 4.0742 3769 | 4 |
| 6 | 6.0869 1471 | 6.0930 7893 | 6.0992 3740 | 6.1115 3716 | 6.1238 1418 | 6 |
| 12 | 12.1913 0434 | 12.2048 7909 | 12.2184 4211 | 12.2455 3306 | 12.2725 7753 | 12 |

Table
10

## TABLE 10

$$\frac{1}{s_{\overline{1/m}|i}} = \frac{i}{(1+i)^{\frac{1}{m}} - 1} \qquad \text{Note: } \frac{1}{a_{\overline{1/m}|i}} = \frac{1}{s_{\overline{1/m}|i}} + i$$

| $m$ | $5\frac{1}{2}\%$ | 6% | $6\frac{1}{2}\%$ | 7% | $7\frac{1}{2}\%$ | $m$ |
|---|---|---|---|---|---|---|
| 2 | 2.0271 3193 | 2.0295 6301 | 2.0319 8837 | 2.0344 0804 | 2.0368 2207 | 2 |
| 3 | 3.0543 4565 | 3.0592 2313 | 3.0640 9043 | 3.0689 4762 | 3.0737 9477 | 3 |
| 4 | 4.0815 7981 | 4.0889 0752 | 4.0962 2091 | 4.1035 2009 | 4.1108 0514 | 4 |
| 6 | 6.1360 6860 | 6.1483 0059 | 6.1605 1031 | 6.1726 9791 | 6.1848 6355 | 6 |
| 12 | 12.2995 7585 | 12.3265 2834 | 12.3534 3533 | 12.3802 9715 | 12.4071 1409 | 12 |

| $m$ | 8% | $8\frac{1}{2}\%$ | 9% | $9\frac{1}{2}\%$ | 10% | $m$ |
|---|---|---|---|---|---|---|
| 2 | 2.0392 3048 | 2.0416 3333 | 2.0440 3065 | 2.0464 2248 | 2.0488 0885 | 2 |
| 3 | 3.0786 3195 | 3.0834 5923 | 3.0882 7668 | 3.0930 8437 | 3.0978 8235 | 3 |
| 4 | 4.1180 7618 | 4.1253 3329 | 4.1325 7657 | 4.1398 0612 | 4.1470 2204 | 4 |
| 6 | 6.1970 0737 | 6.2091 2954 | 6.2212 3021 | 6.2333 0950 | 6.2453 6759 | 6 |
| 12 | 12.4338 8648 | 12.4606 1463 | 12.4872 9883 | 12.5139 3939 | 12.5405 3661 | 12 |

**VALUES OF $j_m$** (Nominal Rate $j$ compounded $m$ times per year) **AND THEIR EQUIVALENT VALUES OF $f$** (Effective Rate)

## TABLE 11

$$j_m = m[(1 + i)^{\frac{1}{m}} - 1]$$

| $m$ | $*\frac{1}{4}\%$ | $\frac{1}{3}\%$ | $\frac{5}{12}\%$ | $\frac{11}{24}\%$ | $\frac{1}{2}\%$ | $m$ |
|---|---|---|---|---|---|---|
| 2 | .0024 9844 | .0033 3056 | .0041 6234 | .0045 7809 | .0049 9377 | 2 |
| 3 | .0024 9792 | .0033 2964 | .0041 6089 | .0045 7635 | .0049 9169 | 3 |
| 4 | .0024 9766 | .0033 2917 | .0041 6017 | .0045 7548 | .0049 9065 | 4 |
| 6 | .0024 9740 | .0033 2871 | .0041 5945 | .0045 7460 | .0049 8962 | 6 |
| 12 | .0024 9714 | .0033 2825 | .0041 5873 | .0045 7373 | .0049 8858 | 12 |

| $m$ | $\frac{13}{24}\%$ | $\frac{7}{12}\%$ | $\frac{5}{8}\%$ | $\frac{2}{3}\%$ | $\frac{3}{4}\%$ | $m$ |
|---|---|---|---|---|---|---|
| 2 | .0054 0935 | .0058 2485 | .0062 4026 | .0066 5559 | .0074 8599 | 2 |
| 3 | .0054 0692 | .0058 2203 | .0062 3702 | .0066 5191 | .0074 8133 | 3 |
| 4 | .0054 0570 | .0058 2062 | .0062 3540 | .0066 5006 | .0074 7900 | 4 |
| 6 | .0054 0448 | .0058 1921 | .0062 3379 | .0066 4822 | .0074 7667 | 6 |
| 12 | .0054 0327 | .0058 1780 | .0062 3217 | .0066 4638 | .0074 7434 | 12 |

| $m$ | $\frac{7}{8}\%$ | $1\%$ | $1\frac{1}{8}\%$ | $1\frac{1}{4}\%$ | $1\frac{3}{8}\%$ | $m$ |
|---|---|---|---|---|---|---|
| 2 | .0087 3094 | .0099 7512 | .0112 1854 | .0124 6118 | .0137 0306 | 2 |
| 3 | .0087 2460 | .0099 6685 | .0112 0807 | .0124 4828 | .0136 8746 | 3 |
| 4 | .0087 2143 | .0099 6272 | .0112 0285 | .0124 4183 | .0136 7966 | 4 |
| 6 | .0087 1827 | .0099 5859 | .0111 9763 | .0124 3539 | .0136 7188 | 6 |
| 12 | .0087 1510 | .0099 5446 | .0111 9241 | .0124 2895 | .0136 6410 | 12 |

| $m$ | $1\frac{1}{2}\%$ | $1\frac{5}{8}\%$ | $1\frac{3}{4}\%$ | $1\frac{7}{8}\%$ | $2\%$ | $m$ |
|---|---|---|---|---|---|---|
| 2 | .0149 4417 | .0161 8452 | .0174 2410 | .0186 6292 | .0199 0099 | 2 |
| 3 | .0149 2562 | .0161 6277 | .0173 9890 | .0186 3402 | .0198 6813 | 3 |
| 4 | .0149 1636 | .0161 7182 | .0173 8631 | .0186 1959 | .0198 5173 | 4 |
| 6 | .0149 0710 | .0161 4105 | .0173 7374 | .0186 0517 | .0198 3534 | 6 |
| 12 | .0148 9785 | .0161 3021 | .0173 6119 | .0185 9077 | .0198 1898 | 12 |

| $m$ | $2\frac{1}{4}\%$ | $2\frac{1}{2}\%$ | $2\frac{3}{4}\%$ | $3\%$ | $3\frac{1}{4}\%$ | $m$ |
|---|---|---|---|---|---|---|
| 2 | .0223 7484 | .0248 4567 | .0273 1349 | .0297 7831 | .0322 4014 | 2 |
| 3 | .0223 3333 | .0247 9451 | .0272 5170 | .0297 0490 | .0321 5414 | 3 |
| 4 | .0223 1261 | .0247 6899 | .0272 2087 | .0296 6829 | .0321 1125 | 4 |
| 6 | .0222 9192 | .0247 4349 | .0271 9009 | .0296 3173 | .0320 6844 | 6 |
| 12 | .0222 7125 | .0247 1804 | .0271 5936 | .0295 9524 | .0320 2571 | 12 |

| $m$ | $3\frac{1}{2}\%$ | $3\frac{3}{4}\%$ | $4\%$ | $4\frac{1}{2}\%$ | $5\%$ | $m$ |
|---|---|---|---|---|---|---|
| 2 | .0346 9899 | .0371 5488 | .0396 0781 | .0445 0483 | .0493 9015 | 2 |
| 3 | .0345 9943 | .0370 4078 | .0394 7821 | .0443 4138 | .0491 8907 | 3 |
| 4 | .0345 4978 | .0369 8390 | .0394 1363 | .0442 5996 | .0490 8894 | 4 |
| 6 | .0345 0024 | .0369 2714 | .0393 4918 | .0441 7874 | .0489 8908 | 6 |
| 12 | .0344 5078 | .0368 7050 | .0392 8488 | .0440 9771 | .0488 8949 | 12 |

\* Example: Nominal rate .249844% (or .00249844) compounded semiannually is equivalent to the effective rate $\frac{1}{4}\%$.

**Table 11**

## VALUES OF $j_m$ (Nominal Rate $j$ compounded $m$ times per year) AND THEIR EQUIVALENT VALUES OF $f$ (Effective Rate)

**TABLE 11**

$$j_m = m[(1+i)^{\frac{1}{m}} - 1]$$

| $m$ | $5\frac{1}{2}\%$ | $6\%$ | $6\frac{1}{2}\%$ | $7\%$ | $7\frac{1}{2}\%$ | $m$ |
|---|---|---|---|---|---|---|
| 2 | .0542 6386 | .0591 2603 | .0639 7674 | .0688 1609 | .0736 4414 | 2 |
| 3 | .0540 2139 | .0588 3847 | .0636 4042 | .0684 2737 | .0731 9942 | 3 |
| 4 | .0539 0070 | .0586 9538 | .0634 7314 | .0682 3410 | .0729 7840 | 4 |
| 6 | .0537 8036 | .0585 5277 | .0633 0644 | .0680 4156 | .0727 5827 | 6 |
| 12 | .0536 6039 | .0584 1061 | 0631 4033 | .0678 4974 | .0725 3903 | 12 |

| $m$ | $8\%$ | $8\frac{1}{2}\%$ | $9\%$ | $9\frac{1}{2}\%$ | $10\%$ | $m$ |
|---|---|---|---|---|---|---|
| 2 | .0784 6097 | .0832 6667 | .0880 6130 | .0928 4495 | .0976 1770 | 2 |
| 3 | .0779 5670 | .0826 9933 | .0874 2740 | .0921 4104 | .0968 4035 | 3 |
| 4 | .0777 0619 | .0824 1758 | .0871 1272 | .0917 9174 | .0964 5476 | 4 |
| 6 | .0774 5674 | .0821 3712 | .0867 9955 | .0914 4420 | .0960 7121 | 6 |
| 12 | .0772 0836 | .0818 5792 | .0864 8788 | .0910 9841 | .0956 8968 | 12 |

**LOGARITHMS OF VALUES IN TABLES 5, 6, 7, 8, and 9**
For Computing Examples and Problems in

**TABLE 12**
Chapters 11 Through 20

| $n$ | $\log (1 + i)^n$ (Table 5) | $\log (1 + i)^{-n}$ (Table 6) | $\log s_{\overline{n}|i}$ (Table 7) | $\log a_{\overline{n}|i}$ (Table 8) | $\log \dfrac{1}{a_{\overline{n}|i}}$ (Table 9) | $n$ |
|---|---|---|---|---|---|---|
| | | | $\frac{1}{4}\%$ | | | |
| 5 | 0.005 4219 | 9.994 5781-10 | 0.701 1415 | 0.695 7196 | 9.304 2804-10 | 5 |
| 6 | 0.006 5063 | 9.993 4937 | 0.780 8661 | 0.774 3599 | 9.225 6401 | 6 |
| 9 | 0.009 7594 | 9.990 2406 | 0.958 5891 | 0.948 8297 | 9.051 1703 | 9 |
| 24 | 0.026 0252 | 9.973 9748 | 1.392 7465 | 1.366 7213 | 8.633 2787 | 24 |
| 28 | 0.030 3627 | 9.969 6373 | 1.461 8855 | 1.431 5228 | 8.568 4772 | 28 |
| 30 | 0.032 5314 | 9.967 4686 | 1.492 9462 | 1.460 4148 | 8.539 5852 | 30 |
| 36 | 0.039 0377 | 9.960 9623 | 1.575 4252 | 1.536 3876 | 8.462 6124 | 36 |
| 41 | 0.044 4596 | 9.955 5404 | 1.634 6610 | 1.590 2013 | 8.409 7987 | 41 |
| 42 | 0.045 5440 | 9.954 4560 | 1.645 6780 | 1.600 1340 | 8.399 8660 | 42 |
| 48 | 0.052 0503 | 9.947 9497 | 1.706 9840 | 1.654 9337 | 8.345 0663 | 48 |
| 54 | 0.058 5566 | 9.941 4434 | 1.761 4586 | 1.702 9021 | 8.297 0979 | 54 |
| 60 | 0.065 0629 | 9.934 9371 | 1.810 5465 | 1.745 4836 | 8.254 5164 | 60 |
| 67 | 0.072 6535 | 9.927 3465 | 1.862 3656 | 1.789 7120 | 8.210 2880 | 67 |
| 84 | 0.091 0880 | 9.908 9120-10 | 1.970 0766 | 1.878 9887 | 8.121 0113-10 | 84 |
| | | | $\frac{1}{3}\%$ | | | |
| 3 | 0.004 3357 | 9.995 6643-10 | 0.478 5681 | 0.474 2324 | 9.525 7677-10 | 3 |
| 4 | 0.005 7810 | 9.994 2190 | 0.604 2309 | 0.598 4499 | 9.401 5501 | 4 |
| 6 | 0.008 6714 | 9.991 3285 | 0.781 7713 | 0.773 0999 | 9.226 9001 | 6 |
| 7 | 0.010 1167 | 9.989 8833 | 0.849 4434 | 0.839 3267 | 9.160 6733 | 7 |
| 11 | 0.015 8976 | 9.984 1024 | 1.048 6429 | 1.032 7453 | 8.967 2547 | 11 |
| 12 | 0.017 3429 | 9.982 6571 | 1.087 1587 | 1.069 8158 | 8.930 1842 | 12 |
| 17 | 0.024 5691 | 9.975 4309 | 1.242 0686 | 1.217 4995 | 8.782 5005 | 17 |
| 24 | 0.034 6858 | 9.965 3142 | 1.396 9468 | 1.362 2610 | 8.637 7391 | 24 |
| 27 | 0.039 0215 | 9.960 9785 | 1.450 2978 | 1.411 2763 | 8.588 7237 | 27 |
| 29 | 0.041 9120 | 9.958 0880 | 1.482 7997 | 1.440 8877 | 8.559 1123 | 29 |
| 31 | 0.044 8025 | 9.955 1975-10 | 1.513 2326 | 1.468 4302 | 8.531 5698-10 | 31 |
| 36 | 0.052 0287 | 9.947 9713-10 | 1.581 8537 | 1.529 8250 | 8.470 1750-10 | 36 |
| 37 | 0.053 4739 | 9.946 5261 | 1.594 4902 | 1.541 0162 | 8.458 9837 | 37 |
| 48 | 0.069 3716 | 9.930 6284 | 1.715 6658 | 1.646 2942 | 8.353 7057 | 48 |
| 50 | 0.072 2620 | 9.927 7380 | 1.734 8791 | 1.662 6170 | 8.337 3830 | 50 |
| 51 | 0.073 7073 | 9.926 2927 | 1.744 2221 | 1.670 5148 | 8.329 4852 | 51 |
| 60 | 0.086 7145 | 9.913 2855 | 1.821 5069 | 1.734 7924 | 8.265 2076 | 60 |
| 63 | 0.091 0502 | 9.908 9498 | 1.844 9379 | 1.753 8877 | 8.246 1123 | 63 |
| 72 | 0.104 0573 | 9.895 9427 | 1.909 6767 | 1.805 6194 | 8.194 3806 | 72 |
| 96 | 0.138 7431 | 9.861 2569 | 2.052 7653 | 1.914 0221 | 8.085 9778 | 96 |
| 144 | 0.208 1147 | 9.791 8853 | 2.265 8445 | 2.057 7298 | 7.942 2702 | 144 |
| 180 | 0.260 1434 | 9.739 8566-10 | 2.391 0949 | 2.130 9515 | 7.869 0485-10 | 180 |

**Table 12**

# TABLE 12 LOGARITHMS OF VALUES IN TABLES 5, 6, 7, 8, and 9

| $n$ | $\log (1 + i)^n$ | $\log (1 + i)^{-n}$ | $\log s_{\overline{n}|i}$ | $\log a_{\overline{n}|i}$ | $\log \dfrac{1}{a_{\overline{n}|i}}$ | $n$ |
|---|---|---|---|---|---|---|
| | | | $\frac{5}{12}\%$ | | | |
| 3 | 0.005 4174 | 9.994 5826-10 | 0.478 9296 | 0.473 5122 | 9.526 4878-10 | 3 |
| 7 | 0.012 6406 | 9.987 3594 | 0.850 5305 | 0.837 8899 | 9.162 1102 | 7 |
| 8 | 0.014 4464 | 9.985 5536 | 0.909 4300 | 0.894 9836 | 9.105 0164 | 8 |
| 9 | 0.016 2522 | 9.983 7478 | 0.961 4907 | 0.945 2385 | 9.054 7615 | 9 |
| 12 | 0.021 6696 | 9.978 3304 | 1.089 1579 | 1.067 4883 | 8.932 5117 | 12 |
| 14 | 0.025 2812 | 9.974 7188 | 1.157 9268 | 1.132 6455 | 8.867 3544 | 14 |
| 18 | 0.032 5044 | 9.967 4956 | 1.270 7229 | 1.238 2184 | 8.761 7816 | 18 |
| 24 | 0.043 3392 | 9.956 6608 | 1.401 1578 | 1.357 8186 | 8.642 1814 | 24 |
| 25 | 0.045 1450 | 9.954 8550-10 | 1.419 8048 | 1.374 6598 | 8.625 3402-10 | 25 |
| 26 | 0.046 9508 | 9.953 0492-10 | 1.437 7570 | 1.390 8062 | 8.609 1938-10 | 26 |
| 28 | 0.050 5624 | 9.949 4376 | 1.471 7813 | 1.421 2189 | 8.578 7812 | 28 |
| 30 | 0.054 1740 | 9.945 8260 | 1.503 5866 | 1.449 4226 | 8.550 5874 | 30 |
| 34 | 0.061 3972 | 9.938 6028 | 1.561 6359 | 1.500 2387 | 8.499 7613 | 34 |
| 35 | 0.063 2030 | 9.936 7970 | 1.575 1495 | 1.511 9465 | 8,488 0535 | 35 |
| 36 | 0.065 0088 | 9.934 9912 | 1.588 3091 | 1.523 3003 | 8.476 6998 | 36 |
| 37 | 0.066 8146 | 9.933 1854 | 1.601 1340 | 1.534 3194 | 8.465 6806 | 37 |
| 40 | 0.072 2320 | 9.927 7680 | 1.637 7732 | 1.565 5412 | 8.434 4588 | 40 |
| 45 | 0.081 2610 | 9.918 7390-10 | 1.693 5732 | 1.612 3121 | 8.387 6789-10 | 45 |
| 48 | 0.086 6784 | 9.913 3216-10 | 1.724 3979 | 1.637 7194 | 8.362 2806-10 | 48 |
| 51 | 0.092 0958 | 9.907 9042 | 1.753 5283 | 1.661 4325 | 8.338 5674 | 51 |
| 60 | 0.108 3481 | 9.891 6519 | 1.832 5477 | 1.724 1997 | 8.275 8003 | 60 |
| 72 | 0.130 0177 | 9.869 9823 | 1.923 0587 | 1.793 0411 | 8.206 9590 | 72 |
| 90 | 0.162 5221 | 9.837 4779 | 2.037 1315 | 1.874 6094 | 8.125 3905 | 90 |
| 96 | 0.173 3569 | 9.826 6431 | 2.070 9259 | 1.897 5690 | 8.102 4310 | 96 |
| 180 | 0.325 0442 | 9.674 9558 | 2.426 9810 | 2.101 9368 | 7.898 0632 | 180 |
| 181 | 0.326 8500 | 9.673 1500 | 2.430 4019 | 2.103 5519 | 7.896 4481 | 181 |
| 240 | 0.433 3922 | 9.566 6078-10 | 2.613 8774 | 2.180 4852 | 7.819 5148-10 | 240 |
| | | | $\frac{11}{24}\%$ | | | |
| 60 | 0.119 1581 | 9.880 8419-10 | 1.838 0983 | 1.718 9402 | 8.281 0598-10 | 60 |
| | | | $\frac{1}{2}\%$ | | | |
| 1 | 0.002 1661 | 9.997 8339-10 | 0.000 0000 | 9.997 8339-10 | 0.002 1661 | 1 |
| 2 | 0.004 3321 | 9.995 6679 | 0.302 1144 | 0.297 7823 | 9.702 2177-10 | 2 |
| 3 | 0.006 4982 | 9.993 5018 | 0.479 2910 | 0.472 7927 | 9.527 2073 | 3 |
| 4 | 0.008 6642 | 9.991 3358 | 0.605 3159 | 0.596 6517 | 9.403 3483 | 4 |
| 5 | 0.010 8303 | 9.989 1697 | 0.703 3130 | 0.692 4826 | 9.307 5174 | 5 |
| 6 | 0.012 9964 | 9.987 0036 | 0.783 5821 | 0.770 5858 | 9.229 4142 | 6 |
| 9 | 0.019 4946 | 9.980 5054-10 | 0.962 9427 | 0.943 4482 | 9.056 5518-10 | 9 |
| 10 | 0.021 6606 | 9.978 3394-10 | 1.009 7918 | 0.988 1312 | 9.011 8688-10 | 10 |
| 11 | 0.023 8267 | 9.976 1733 | 1.052 2770 | 1.028 4503 | 8.971 5497 | 11 |
| 12 | 0.025 9927 | 9.974 0073 | 1.091 1591 | 1.065 1663 | 8.934 8337 | 12 |
| 17 | 0.036 8230 | 9.963 1770 | 1.247 9071 | 1.211 0840 | 8.788 9160 | 17 |
| 18 | 0.038 9891 | 9.961 0109 | 1.273 8294 | 1.234 8403 | 8.765 1597 | 18 |
| 19 | 0.041 1552 | 9.958 8448-10 | 1.298 4102 | 1.257 2550 | 8.742 7450-10 | 19 |

# TABLE 12 LOGARITHMS OF VALUES IN TABLES 5, 6, 7, 8, and 9

| $n$ | $\log (1+i)^n$ | $\log (1+i)^{-n}$ | $\log s_{\overline{n}|i}$ | $\log a_{\overline{n}|i}$ | $\log \dfrac{1}{a_{\overline{n}|i}}$ | $n$ |
|---|---|---|---|---|---|---|
| | | | $\frac{1}{2}\%$ (Continued) | | | |
| 23 | 0.049 8194 | 9.950 1806-10 | 1.385 7922 | 1.335 9727 | 8.664 0273-10 | 23 |
| 24 | 0.051 9855 | 9.948 0145 | 1.405 3797 | 1.353 3942 | 8.646 6058 | 24 |
| 27 | 0.058 4837 | 9.941 5163 | 1.459 8502 | 1.401 3666 | 8.598 6334 | 27 |
| 36 | 0.077 9782 | 9.922 0218 | 1.594 7914 | 1.516 8131 | 8.483 1869 | 36 |
| 37 | 0.080 1443 | 9.919 8557 | 1.607 8064 | 1.527 6622 | 8.472 3378 | 37 |
| 38 | 0.082 3103 | 9.917 6897 | 1.620 5051 | 1.538 1948 | 8.461 8052 | 38 |
| 40 | 0.086 6425 | 9.913 3575 | 1.645 0177 | 1.558 3752 | 8.441 6248 | 40 |
| 45 | 0.097 4728 | 9.902 5272-10 | 1.701 7766 | 1.604 3038 | 8.395 6962-10 | 45 |
| 48 | 0.103 9710 | 9.896 0290-10 | 1.733 1799 | 1.629 2089 | 8.370 7911-10 | 48 |
| 55 | 0.119 1334 | 9.880 8666 | 1.800 2067 | 1.681 0733 | 8.318 9267 | 55 |
| 60 | 0.129 9637 | 9.870 0363 | 1.843 6689 | 1.713 7052 | 8.286 2948 | 60 |
| 63 | 0.136 4619 | 9.863 5381 | 1.868 2731 | 1.731 8113 | 8.268 1887 | 63 |
| 66 | 0.142 9601 | 9.857 0399 | 1.891 8995 | 1.748 9394 | 8.251 0606 | 66 |
| 72 | 0.155 9564 | 9.844 0436 | 1.936 5583 | 1.780 6018 | 8.219 3982 | 72 |
| 80 | 0.173 2849 | 9.826 7151 | 1.991 5260 | 1.818 2411 | 8.181 7589 | 80 |
| 84 | 0.181 9492 | 9.818 0508-10 | 2.017 3420 | 1.835 3928 | 8.164 6072-10 | 84 |
| 85 | 0.184 1152 | 9.815 8848-10 | 2.023 6405 | 1.839 5252 | 8.160 4748-10 | 85 |
| 96 | 0.207 9419 | 9.792 0581 | 2.089 2993 | 1.881 3573 | 8.118 6427 | 96 |
| 120 | 0.259 9274 | 9.740 0726 | 2.214 5243 | 1.954 5968 | 8.045 4032 | 120 |
| 130 | 0.281 5880 | 9.718 4120 | 2.261 2348 | 1.979 6467 | 8.020 3533 | 130 |
| 150 | 0.324 9093 | 9.675 0907 | 2.347 5437 | 2.022 6344 | 7.977 3656 | 150 |
| 179 | 0.387 7250 | 9.612 2750 | 2.459 9603 | 2.072 2353 | 7.927 7647 | 179 |
| 180 | 0.389 8911 | 9.610 1089 | 2.463 6224 | 2.073 7312 | 7.926 2688 | 180 |
| 181 | 0.392 0572 | 9.607 9428 | 2.467 2718 | 2.075 2146 | 7.924 7854 | 181 |
| 240 | 0.519 8548 | 9.480 1452-10 | 2.664 6804 | 2.144 8256 | 7.855 1744-10 | 240 |
| | | | $\frac{13}{24}\%$ | | | |
| 10 | 0.023 4608 | 9.976 5392-10 | 1.010 6096 | 0.987 1489 | 9.012 8511-10 | 10 |
| 120 | 0.281 5296 | 9.718 4704-10 | 2.226 3502 | 1.944 8206 | 8.055 1794-10 | 120 |
| | | | $\frac{7}{12}\%$ | | | |
| 6 | 0.015 1561 | 9.984 8439-10 | 0.784 4877 | 0.769 3316 | 9.230 6684-10 | 6 |
| 11 | 0.027 7863 | 9.972 2137 | 1.054 0963 | 1.026 3100 | 8.973 6900 | 11 |
| 36 | 0.090 9369 | 9.909 0631 | 1.601 3004 | 1.510 3635 | 8.489 6365 | 36 |
| 54 | 0.136 4053 | 9.863 5947 | 1.801 1165 | 1.664 7112 | 8.335 2888 | 54 |
| 108 | 0.272 8106 | 9.727 1894 | 2.175 6825 | 1.902 8720 | 8.097 1280 | 108 |
| 120 | 0.303 1229 | 9.696 8771 | 2.238 2590 | 1.935 1361 | 8.064 8639 | 120 |
| 160 | 0.404 1638 | 9.595 8362 | 2.420 4985 | 2.016 3347 | 7.983 6653 | 160 |
| 162 | 0.409 2159 | 9.590 7841 | 2.428 8082 | 2.019 5923 | 7.980 4077 | 162 |
| 180 | 0.454 6843 | 9.545 3157 | 2.501 0077 | 2.046 3233 | 7.953 6767 | 180 |
| 200 | 0.505 2048 | 9.494 7952-10 | 2.576 5856 | 2.071 3808 | 7.928 6192-10 | 200 |
| | | | $\frac{2}{3}\%$ | | | |
| 10 | 0.028 8569 | 9.971 1431-10 | 1.013 0647 | 0.984 2078 | 9.015 7922-10 | 10 |
| 24 | 0.069 2565 | 9.930 7435 | 1.413 8560 | 1.344 5994 | 8.655 4006 | 24 |
| 30 | 0.086 5706 | 9.913 4294-10 | 1.519 6817 | 1.433 1111 | 8.566 8889-10 | 30 |

## TABLE 12 LOGARITHMS OF VALUES IN TABLES 5, 6, 7, 8, and 9

| $n$ | $\log (1+i)^n$ | $\log (1+i)^{-n}$ | $\log s_{\overline{n}|i}$ | $\log a_{\overline{n}|i}$ | $\log \dfrac{1}{a_{\overline{n}|i}}$ | $n$ |
|---|---|---|---|---|---|---|
| | | | $\frac{3}{4}\%$ | | | |
| 10 | 0.032 4505 | 9.967 5495-10 | 1.014 7027 | 0.982 2522 | 9.017 7478-10 | 10 |
| 18 | 0.058 4110 | 9.941 5890 | 1.283 1817 | 1.224 7708 | 8.775 2292 | 18 |
| 20 | 0.064 9011 | 9.935 0989 | 1.332 2610 | 1.267 3600 | 8.732 6400 | 20 |
| 24 | 0.077 8813 | 9.922 1187 | 1.418 1101 | 1.340 2288 | 8.659 7712 | 24 |
| 32 | 0.103 8418 | 9.896 1582 | 1.556 4814 | 1.452 6396 | 8.547 3604 | 32 |
| 40 | 0.129 8022 | 9.870 1978 | 1.666 9528 | 1.537 1506 | 8.462 8494 | 40 |
| 61 | 0.197 9483 | 9.802 0517 | 1.886 4333 | 1.688 4849 | 8.311 5151 | 61 |
| 62 | 0.201 1934 | 9.798 8066-10 | 1.895 2415 | 1.694 0481 | 8.305 9519-10 | 62 |
| | | | $\frac{7}{8}\%$ | | | |
| 8 | 0.030 2684 | 9.969 7316-10 | 0.916 4189 | 0.886 1505 | 9.113 8495-10 | 8 |
| 40 | 0.151 3419 | 9.848 6581-10 | 1.678 0331 | 1.526 6911 | 8.473 3089-10 | 40 |
| | | | $1\%$ | | | |
| 1 | 0.004 3214 | 9.995 6786-10 | 0.000 0000 | 9.995 6786-10 | 0.004 3214 | 1 |
| 2 | 0.008 6427 | 9.991 3573 | 0.303 1961 | 0.294 5533 | 9.705 4467-10 | 2 |
| 3 | 0.012 9641 | 9.987 0359 | 0.481 4570 | 0.468 4928 | 9.531 5072 | 3 |
| 4 | 0.017 2855 | 9.982 7145 | 0.608 5689 | 0.591 2834 | 9.408 7166 | 4 |
| 5 | 0.021 6069 | 9.978 3931 | 0.707 6557 | 0.686 0488 | 9.313 9512 | 5 |
| 6 | 0.025 9282 | 9.974 0718 | 0.789 0173 | 0.763 0891 | 9.236 9109 | 6 |
| 7 | 0.030 2496 | 9.969 7504 | 0.858 1481 | 0.827 8985 | 9.172 1015 | 7 |
| 8 | 0.034 5710 | 9.965 4290 | 0.918 3277 | 0.883 7567 | 9.116 2433 | 8 |
| 10 | 0.043 2137 | 9.956 7863 | 1.019 6234 | 0.976 4098 | 9.023 5902 | 10 |
| 12 | 0.051 8565 | 9.948 1435-10 | 1.103 2049 | 1.051 3485 | 8.948 6515-10 | 12 |
| 15 | 0.064 8206 | 9.935 1794-10 | 1.206 7422 | 1.141 9215 | 8.858 0785-10 | 15 |
| 16 | 0.069 1420 | 9.930 8580 | 1.236 9870 | 1.167 8449 | 8.832 1551 | 16 |
| 19 | 0.082 1061 | 9.917 8939 | 1.318 2908 | 1.236 1846 | 8.763 8154 | 19 |
| 20 | 0.086 4275 | 9.913 5725 | 1.342 7976 | 1.256 3701 | 8.743 6299 | 20 |
| 21 | 0.090 7488 | 9.909 2512 | 1.366 2209 | 1.275 4721 | 8.724 5279 | 21 |
| 22 | 0.095 0702 | 9.904 9298 | 1.388 6622 | 1.293 5919 | 8.706 4081 | 22 |
| 23 | 0.099 3916 | 9.900 6084 | 1.410 2084 | 1.310 8168 | 8.689 1832 | 23 |
| 24 | 0.103 7130 | 9.896 2870 | 1.430 9367 | 1.327 2237 | 8.672 7763 | 24 |
| 25 | 0.108 0343 | 9.891 9657 | 1.450 9138 | 1.342 8796 | 8.657 1204 | 25 |
| 28 | 0.120 9985 | 9.879 0015-10 | 1.506 8985 | 1.385 8999 | 8.614 1001-10 | 28 |
| 29 | 0.125 3198 | 9.874 6802-10 | 1.524 4012 | 1.399 0814 | 8.600 9186-10 | 29 |
| 30 | 0.129 6412 | 9.870 3588 | 1.541 3906 | 1.411 7494 | 8.588 2506 | 30 |
| 36 | 0.155 5695 | 9.844 4305 | 1.634 2442 | 1.478 6748 | 8.521 3252 | 36 |
| 40 | 0.172 8550 | 9.827 1450 | 1.689 1878 | 1.516 3329 | 8.483 6671 | 40 |
| 45 | 0.194 4618 | 9.805 5382 | 1.751 9029 | 1.557 4411 | 8.442 5589 | 45 |
| 49 | 0.211 7473 | 9.788 2527 | 1.798 2004 | 1.586 4531 | 8.413 5469 | 49 |
| 70 | 0.302 4962 | 9.697 5038 | 2.002 9272 | 1.700 4311 | 8.299 5689 | 70 |
| 80 | 0.345 7099 | 9.654 2901 | 2.085 1888 | 1.739 4790 | 8.260 5210 | 80 |
| 84 | 0.362 9954 | 9.637 0046 | 2.116 1835 | 1.753 1880 | 8.246 8120 | 84 |
| 92 | 0.397 5664 | 9.602 4336 | 2.175 4683 | 1.777 9019 | 8.222 0981 | 92 |
| 100 | 0.432 1374 | 9.567 8626-10 | 2.231 6769 | 1.799 5395 | 8.200 4605-10 | 100 |

## TABLE 12 LOGARITHMS OF VALUES IN TABLES 5, 6, 7, 8, and 9

| $n$ | $\log (1+i)^n$ | $\log (1+i)^{-n}$ | $\log s_{\overline{n}|i}$ | $\log a_{\overline{n}|i}$ | $\log \dfrac{1}{a_{\overline{n}|i}}$ | $n$ |
|---|---|---|---|---|---|---|
| | | | $1\frac{1}{8}\%$ | | | |
| 18 | 0.087 4536 | 9.912 5464-10 | 1.297 3013 | 1.209 8477 | 8.790 1523-10 | 18 |
| | | | $1\frac{1}{4}\%$ | | | |
| 2 | 0.010 7901 | 9.989 2099-10 | 0.303 7359 | 0.292 9457 | 9.707 0543-10 | 2 |
| 4 | 0.021 5801 | 9.978 4199 | 0.610 1944 | 0.588 6142 | 9.411 3858 | 4 |
| 7 | 0.037 7652 | 9.962 2348 | 0.861 4171 | 0.823 6519 | 9.176 3481 | 7 |
| 8 | 0.043 1603 | 9.956 8397 | 0.922 1484 | 0.878 9882 | 9.121 0118 | 8 |
| 10 | 0.053 9503 | 9.946 0497 | 1.024 5542 | 0.970 6037 | 9.029 3963 | 10 |
| 12 | 0.064 7404 | 9.935 2596 | 1.109 2531 | 1.044 5127 | 8.955 4873 | 12 |
| 16 | 0.086 3205 | 9.913 6795 | 1.245 2944 | 1.158 9740 | 8.841 0260 | 16 |
| 20 | 0.107 9006 | 9.892 0994 | 1.353 3964 | 1.245 4959 | 8.754 5041 | 20 |
| 21 | 0.113 2957 | 9.886 7043-10 | 1.377 3976 | 1.264 1018 | 8.735 8982-10 | 21 |
| 22 | 0.118 6907 | 9.881 3093-10 | 1.400 4184 | 1.281 7277 | 8.718 2723-10 | 22 |
| 24 | 0.129 4808 | 9.870 5192 | 1.443 8585 | 1.314 3777 | 8.685 6223 | 24 |
| 26 | 0.140 2708 | 9.859 7292 | 1.484 2945 | 1.344 0236 | 8.655 9764 | 26 |
| 27 | 0.145 6659 | 9.854 3341 | 1.503 5301 | 1.357 8643 | 8.642 1357 | 27 |
| 28 | 0.151 0609 | 9.848 9391 | 1.522 1752 | 1.371 1144 | 8.628 8856 | 28 |
| 29 | 0.156 4559 | 9.843 5441 | 1.540 2716 | 1.383 8157 | 8.616 1843 | 29 |
| 30 | 0.161 8510 | 9.838 1490 | 1.557 8567 | 1.396 0056 | 8.603 9944 | 30 |
| 31 | 0.167 2460 | 9.832 7540 | 1.574 9646 | 1.407 7186 | 8.592 2814 | 31 |
| 32 | 0.172 6410 | 9.827 3590-10 | 1.591 6259 | 1.418 9848 | 8.581 0152-10 | 32 |
| 33 | 0.178 0361 | 9.821 9639-10 | 1.607 8683 | 1.429 8323 | 8.570 1677-10 | 33 |
| 35 | 0.188 8261 | 9.811 1739 | 1.639 1962 | 1.450 3701 | 8.549 6299 | 35 |
| 36 | 0.194 2211 | 9.805 7789 | 1.654 3258 | 1.460 1047 | 8.539 8953 | 36 |
| 40 | 0.215 8013 | 9.784 1987 | 1.711 7192 | 1.495 9178 | 8.504 0822 | 40 |
| 42 | 0.226 5913 | 9.773 4087 | 1.738 7594 | 1.512 1681 | 8.487 8319 | 42 |
| 48 | 0.258 9615 | 9.741 0385 | 1.814 4366 | 1.555 4751 | 8.444 5249 | 48 |
| 49 | 0.264 3566 | 9.735 6434 | 1.826 3582 | 1.562 0017 | 8.437 9983 | 49 |
| 51 | 0.275 1466 | 9.724 8534 | 1.849 6823 | 1.574 5356 | 8.425 4644 | 51 |
| 57 | 0.307 5168 | 9.692 4832-10 | 1.915 9681 | 1.608 4513 | 8.391 5487-10 | 57 |
| | | | $1\frac{3}{8}\%$ | | | |
| 10 | 0.059 3087 | 9.940 6913-10 | 1.027 0230 | 0.967 7142 | 9.032 2858-10 | 10 |
| 12 | 0.071 1704 | 9.928 8296 | 1.112 2835 | 1.041 1131 | 8.958 8869 | 12 |
| 24 | 0.142 3408 | 9.857 6592 | 1.450 3550 | 1.308 0142 | 8.691 9858 | 24 |
| 28 | 0.166 0643 | 9.833 9357 | 1.529 8640 | 1.363 7996 | 8.636 2004 | 28 |
| 32 | 0.189 7878 | 9.810 2122 | 1.600 5253 | 1.410 7375 | 8.589 2625 | 32 |
| 40 | 0.237 2347 | 9.762 7653-10 | 1.723 0948 | 1.485 8600 | 8.514 1400-10 | 40 |

Table
12

## TABLE 12 LOGARITHMS OF VALUES IN TABLES 5, 6, 7, 8, and 9

| $n$ | $\log (1 + i)^n$ | $\log (1 + i)^{-n}$ | $\log s_{\overline{n}|i}$ | $\log a_{\overline{n}|i}$ | $\log \dfrac{1}{a_{\overline{n}|i}}$ | $n$ |
|---|---|---|---|---|---|---|
| | | | $1\frac{1}{2}\%$ | | | |
| 2 | 0.012 9321 | 9.987 0679-10 | 0.304 2751 | 0.291 3429 | 9.708 6571-10 | 2 |
| 3 | 0.019 3981 | 9.980 6019 | 0.483 6194 | 0.464 2213 | 9.535 7787 | 3 |
| 4 | 0.025 8642 | 9.974 1358 | 0.611 8193 | 0.585 9551 | 9.414 0449 | 4 |
| 5 | 0.032 3302 | 9.967 6698 | 0.711 9983 | 0.679 6682 | 9.320 3318 | 5 |
| 6 | 0.038 7963 | 9.961 2037 | 0.794 4568 | 0.755 6605 | 9.244 3395 | 6 |
| 7 | 0.045 2623 | 9.954 7377 | 0.864 6887 | 0.819 4264 | 9.180 5736 | 7 |
| 8 | 0.051 7283 | 9.948 2717 | 0.925 9738 | 0.874 2455 | 9.125 7545 | 8 |
| 9 | 0.058 1944 | 9.941 8056-10 | 0.980 4275 | 0.922 2332 | 9.077 7668-10 | 9 |
| 10 | 0.064 6604 | 9.935 3396-10 | 1.029 4943 | 0.964 8338 | 9.035 1662-10 | 10 |
| 11 | 0.071 1265 | 9.928 8735 | 1.074 2041 | 1.003 0777 | 8.996 9223 | 11 |
| 12 | 0.077 5925 | 9.922 4075 | 1.115 3179 | 1.037 7254 | 8.962 2746 | 12 |
| 14 | 0.090 5246 | 9.909 4754 | 1.188 9392 | 1.098 4146 | 8.901 5854 | 14 |
| 15 | 0.096 9906 | 9.903 0094 | 1.222 2517 | 1.125 2611 | 8.874 7389 | 15 |
| 16 | 0.103 4567 | 9.896 5433 | 1.253 6377 | 1.150 1810 | 8.849 8190 | 16 |
| 17 | 0.109 9227 | 9.890 0773 | 1.283 3319 | 1.173 4092 | 8.826 5908 | 17 |
| 19 | 0.122 8548 | 9.877 1452-10 | 1.338 3910 | 1.215 5363 | 8.784 4637-10 | 19 |
| 20 | 0.129 3208 | 9.870 6792-10 | 1.364 0567 | 1.234 7359 | 8.765 2641-10 | 20 |
| 21 | 0.135 7869 | 9.864 2131 | 1.388 6432 | 1.252 8563 | 8.747 1437 | 21 |
| 22 | 0.142 2529 | 9.857 7471 | 1.412 2518 | 1.269 9989 | 8.730 0011 | 22 |
| 24 | 0.155 1850 | 9.844 8150 | 1.456 8748 | 1.301 6897 | 8.698 3103 | 24 |
| 26 | 0.168 1171 | 9.831 8829 | 1.498 5031 | 1.330 3860 | 8.669 6140 | 26 |
| 28 | 0.181 0492 | 9.818 9508 | 1.537 5859 | 1.356 5367 | 8.643 4633 | 28 |
| 32 | 0.206 9134 | 9.793 0866 | 1.609 4694 | 1.402 5561 | 8.597 4439 | 32 |
| 35 | 0.226 3115 | 9.773 6885-10 | 1.658 8895 | 1.432 5780 | 8.567 4220-10 | 35 |
| 37 | 0.239 2436 | 9.760 7564-10 | 1.690 0641 | 1.450 8205 | 8.549 1795-10 | 37 |
| 38 | 0.245 7096 | 9.754 2904 | 1.705 1782 | 1.459 4687 | 8.540 5313 | 38 |
| 39 | 0.252 1756 | 9.747 8244 | 1.719 9995 | 1.467 8238 | 8.532 1762 | 39 |
| 40 | 0.258 6417 | 9.741 3583 | 1.734 5430 | 1.475 9013 | 8.524 0987 | 40 |
| 48 | 0.310 3700 | 9.689 6300 | 1.842 3922 | 1.532 0221 | 8.467 9779 | 48 |
| 62 | 0.400 8946 | 9.599 1054 | 2.004 9130 | 1.604 0185 | 8.395 9815 | 62 |
| 80 | 0.517 2834 | 9.482 7166 | 2.183 8700 | 1.666 5865 | 8.333 4135 | 80 |
| 96 | 0.620 7401 | 9.379 2599 | 2.325 7623 | 1.705 0223 | 8.294 9777 | 96 |
| 100 | 0.646 6042 | 9.353 3958-10 | 2.359 4617 | 1.712 8575 | 8.287 1425-10 | 100 |
| | | | $1\frac{5}{8}\%$ | | | |
| 21 | 0.147 0117 | 9.852 9883-10 | 1.394 2917 | 1.247 2800 | 8.752 7200-10 | 21 |
| 24 | 0.168 0134 | 9.831 9866 | 1.463 4179 | 1.295 4044 | 8.704 5956 | 24 |
| 80 | 0.560 0447 | 9.439 9553-10 | 2.209 2929 | 1.649 2482 | 8.350 7518-10 | 80 |

# TABLE 12 LOGARITHMS OF VALUES IN TABLES 5, 6, 7, 8, and 9

| $n$ | $\log (1+i)^n$ | $\log (1+i)^{-n}$ | $\log s_{\overline{n}|i}$ | $\log a_{\overline{n}|i}$ | $\log \dfrac{1}{a_{\overline{n}|i}}$ | $n$ |
|---|---|---|---|---|---|---|
| | | | $1\frac{3}{4}\%$ | | | |
| 4 | 0.030 1377 | 9.969 8623-10 | 0.613 4433 | 0.583 3056 | 9.416 6944-10 | 4 |
| 7 | 0.052 7409 | 9.947 2591 | 0.867 9627 | 0.815 2218 | 9.184 7782 | 7 |
| 8 | 0.060 2753 | 9.939 7247 | 0.929 8036 | 0.869 5282 | 9.130 4718 | 8 |
| 9 | 0.067 8098 | 9.932 1902 | 0.984 8157 | 0.917 0060 | 9.082 9940 | 9 |
| 10 | 0.075 3442 | 9.924 6558 | 1.034 4439 | 0.959 0998 | 9.040 9002 | 10 |
| 12 | 0.090 4130 | 9.909 5870-10 | 1.121 3991 | 1.030 9861 | 8.969 0139-10 | 12 |
| 13 | 0.097 9474 | 9.902 0526-10 | 1.160 0644 | 1.062 1170 | 8.937 8830-10 | 13 |
| 16 | 0.120 5507 | 9.879 4493 | 1.262 0160 | 1.141 4654 | 8.858 5346 | 16 |
| 20 | 0.150 6884 | 9.849 3116 | 1.374 7779 | 1.224 0895 | 8.775 9105 | 20 |
| 24 | 0.180 8260 | 9.819 1740 | 1.469 9841 | 1.289 1582 | 8.710 8418 | 24 |
| 32 | 0.241 1014 | 9.758 8986 | 1.627 4908 | 1.386 3894 | 8.613 6106 | 32 |
| 40 | 0.301 3767 | 9.698 6233 | 1.757 6552 | 1.456 2784 | 8.543 7216 | 40 |
| 42 | 0.316 4456 | 9.683 5544-10 | 1.787 2646 | 1.470 8190 | 8.529 1810-10 | 42 |
| | | | $1\frac{7}{8}\%$ | | | |
| 16 | 0.129 0819 | 9.870 9181-10 | 1.266 2183 | 1.137 1364 | 8.862 8636-10 | 16 |
| 23 | 0.185 5553 | 9.814 4447 | 1.453 7638 | 1.268 2084 | 8.731 7916 | 23 |
| 24 | 0.193 6229 | 9.806 3771 | 1.476 5735 | 1.282 9506 | 8.717 0494 | 24 |
| 32 | 0.258 1639 | 9.741 8361-10 | 1.636 5675 | 1.378 4036 | 8.621 5964-10 | 32 |
| | | | $2\%$ | | | |
| 2 | 0.017 2003 | 9.982 7997-10 | 0.305 3514 | 0.288 1510 | 9.711 8490-10 | 2 |
| 3 | 0.025 8005 | 9.974 1995 | 0.485 7782 | 0.459 9777 | 9.540 0223 | 3 |
| 4 | 0.034 4007 | 9.965 5993 | 0.615 0666 | 0.580 6660 | 9.419 3340 | 4 |
| 5 | 0.043 0009 | 9.956 9991 | 0.716 3407 | 0.673 3398 | 9.326 6602 | 5 |
| 6 | 0.051 6010 | 9.948 3990 | 0.799 9000 | 0.748 2990 | 9.251 7010 | 6 |
| 7 | 0.060 2012 | 9.939 7988 | 0.871 2391 | 0.811 0379 | 9.188 9621 | 7 |
| 8 | 0.068 8014 | 9.931 1986 | 0.933 6376 | 0.864 8362 | 9.135 1638 | 8 |
| 9 | 0.077 4015 | 9.922 5985-10 | 0.989 2107 | 0.911 8092 | 9.088 1908-10 | 9 |
| 10 | 0.086 0017 | 9.913 9983-10 | 1.039 4030 | 0.953 4014 | 9.046 5986-10 | 10 |
| 12 | 0.103 2021 | 9.896 7979 | 1.127 4964 | 1.024 2944 | 8.975 7056 | 12 |
| 14 | 0.120 4024 | 9.879 5976 | 1.203 4120 | 1.083 0096 | 8.916 9904 | 14 |
| 15 | 0.129 0026 | 9.870 9974 | 1.237 8808 | 1.108 8782 | 8.891 1218 | 15 |
| 16 | 0.137 6027 | 9.862 3973 | 1.270 4292 | 1.132 8265 | 8.867 1735 | 16 |
| 17 | 0.146 2029 | 9.853 7971 | 1.301 2920 | 1.155 0891 | 8.844 9109 | 17 |
| 18 | 0.154 8031 | 9.845 1969 | 1.330 6635 | 1.175 8605 | 8.824 1395 | 18 |
| 19 | 0.163 4033 | 9.836 5967-10 | 1.358 7067 | 1.195 3035 | 8.804 6965-10 | 19 |
| 20 | 0.172 0034 | 9.827 9966-10 | 1.385 5593 | 1.213 5558 | 8.786 4442-10 | 20 |
| 21 | 0.180 6036 | 9.819 3964 | 1.411 3388 | 1.230 7352 | 8.769 2648 | 21 |
| 23 | 0.197 8040 | 9.802 1960 | 1.460 0699 | 1.262 2660 | 8.737 7340 | 23 |
| 24 | 0.206 4041 | 9.793 5959 | 1.483 1858 | 1.276 7817 | 8.723 2183 | 24 |
| 25 | 0.215 0043 | 9.784 9957 | 1.505 5610 | 1.290 5567 | 8.709 4433 | 25 |
| 26 | 0.223 6045 | 9.776 3955 | 1.527 2548 | 1.303 6504 | 8.696 3496 | 26 |
| 30 | 0.258 0052 | 9.741 9948-10 | 1.608 1844 | 1.350 1793 | 8.649 8207-10 | 30 |

**Table 12**

# TABLE 12 LOGARITHMS OF VALUES IN TABLES 5, 6, 7, 8, and 9

| $n$ | $\log (1+i)^n$ | $\log (1+i)^{-n}$ | $\log s_{\overline{n}|i}$ | $\log a_{\overline{n}|i}$ | $\log \dfrac{1}{a_{\overline{n}|i}}$ | $n$ |
|---|---|---|---|---|---|---|
| | | | 2% (Continued) | | | |
| 32 | 0.275 2055 | 9.724 7945-10 | 1.645 6878 | 1.370 4823 | 8.629 5177-10 | 32 |
| 35 | 0.301 0060 | 9.698 9940 | 1.698 9221 | 1.397 9160 | 8.602 0840 | 35 |
| 39 | 0.335 4067 | 9.664 5933 | 1.765 2008 | 1.429 7941 | 8.570 2059 | 39 |
| 40 | 0.344 0069 | 9.655 9931 | 1.781 0512 | 1.437 0443 | 8.562 9557 | 40 |
| 41 | 0.352 6070 | 9.647 3930 | 1.796 6439 | 1.444 0368 | 8.555 9632 | 41 |
| 42 | 0.361 2072 | 9.638 7928 | 1.811 9918 | 1.450 7846 | 8.549 2154 | 42 |
| 80 | 0.688 0137 | 9.311 9863 | 2.287 2909 | 1.599 2772 | 8.400 7229 | 80 |
| 100 | 0.860 0172 | 9.139 9828-10 | 2.494 4777 | 1.634 4606 | 8.365 5394-10 | 100 |
| | | | $2\frac{1}{4}\%$ | | | |
| 6 | 0.057 9799 | 9.942 0201-10 | 0.802 6230 | 0.744 6432 | 9.255 3568-10 | 6 |
| 8 | 0.077 3065 | 9.922 6935 | 0.937 4759 | 0.860 1693 | 9.139 8307 | 8 |
| 10 | 0.096 6332 | 9.903 3668 | 1.044 3715 | 0.947 7383 | 9.052 2617 | 10 |
| 20 | 0.193 2663 | 9.806 7337 | 1.396 4002 | 1.203 1339 | 8.796 8661 | 20 |
| 24 | 0.231 9196 | 9.768 0804 | 1.496 4786 | 1.264 5589 | 8.735 4411 | 24 |
| 26 | 0.251 2462 | 9.748 7538 | 1.541 7953 | 1.290 5491 | 8.709 4509 | 26 |
| 60 | 0.579 7990 | 9.420 2010-10 | 2.094 9962 | 1.515 1973 | 8.484 8027-10 | 60 |
| | | | $2\frac{1}{2}\%$ | | | |
| 1 | 0.010 7239 | 9.989 2761-10 | 0.000 0000 | 9.989 2761-10 | 0.010 7239 | 1 |
| 2 | 0.021 4477 | 9.978 5523 | 0.306 4250 | 0.284 9773 | 9.715 0227-10 | 2 |
| 3 | 0.032 1716 | 9.967 8284 | 0.487 9334 | 0.455 7618 | 9.544 2382 | 3 |
| 4 | 0.042 8955 | 9.957 1045 | 0.618 3112 | 0.575 4158 | 9.424 5842 | 4 |
| 5 | 0.053 6193 | 9.946 3807 | 0.720 6825 | 0.667 0632 | 9.332 9368 | 5 |
| 6 | 0.064 3432 | 9.935 6568 | 0.805 3470 | 0.741 0038 | 9.258 9962 | 6 |
| 7 | 0.075 0671 | 9.924 9329 | 0.877 7991 | 0.802 7321 | 9.197 2679 | 7 |
| 8 | 0.085 7909 | 9.914 2091-10 | 0.941 3184 | 0.855 5275 | 9.144 4725-10 | 8 |
| 10 | 0.107 2387 | 9.892 7613-10 | 1.049 3491 | 0.942 1105 | 9.057 8895-10 | 10 |
| 11 | 0.117 9625 | 9.882 0375 | 1.096 3352 | 0.978 3727 | 9.021 6273 | 11 |
| 12 | 0.128 6864 | 9.871 3136 | 1.139 7391 | 1.011 0528 | 8.988 9472 | 12 |
| 14 | 0.150 1341 | 9.849 8659 | 1.217 9825 | 1.067 8484 | 8.932 1516 | 14 |
| 15 | 0.160 8580 | 9.839 1420 | 1.253 6269 | 1.092 7690 | 8.907 2310 | 15 |
| 16 | 0.171 5818 | 9.828 4182 | 1.287 3588 | 1.115 7770 | 8.884 2230 | 16 |
| 18 | 0.193 0296 | 9.806 9704 | 1.349 9833 | 1.156 9537 | 8.843 0463 | 18 |
| 20 | 0.214 4773 | 9.785 5227-10 | 1.407 3001 | 1.192 8228 | 8.807 1772-10 | 20 |
| 24 | 0.257 3728 | 9.742 6272-10 | 1.509 8614 | 1.252 4886 | 8.747 5114-10 | 24 |
| 25 | 0.268 0966 | 9.731 9034 | 1.533 4894 | 1.265 3928 | 8.734 6072 | 25 |
| 30 | 0.321 7160 | 9.678 2840 | 1.642 4913 | 1.320 7753 | 8.679 2247 | 30 |
| 35 | 0.375 3353 | 9.624 6647 | 1.739 7954 | 1.364 4601 | 8.635 5399 | 35 |
| 44 | 0.471 8501 | 9.528 1499 | 1.895 1590 | 1.423 3089 | 8.576 6911 | 44 |
| 60 | 0.643 4319 | 9.356 5681 | 2.133 5121 | 1.490 0802 | 8.509 9198 | 60 |
| 65 | 0.697 0513 | 9.302 9487 | 2.201 7201 | 1.504 6689 | 8.495 3311 | 65 |
| 66 | 0.707 7751 | 9.292 2249-10 | 2.215 0987 | 1.507 3235 | 8.492 6765-10 | 66 |

# TABLE 12 LOGARITHMS OF VALUES IN TABLES 5, 6, 7, 8, and 9

| $n$ | $\log (1 + i)^n$ | $\log (1 + i)^{-n}$ | $\log s_{\overline{n}|i}$ | $\log a_{\overline{n}|i}$ | $\log \dfrac{1}{a_{\overline{n}|i}}$ | $n$ |
|---|---|---|---|---|---|---|
| | | | $2\frac{3}{4}\%$ | | | |
| 8 | 0.094 2546 | 9.905 7454-10 | 0.945 1651 | 0.850 9104 | 9.149 0896-10 | 8 |
| 10 | 0.117 8183 | 9.882 1817 | 1.054 3359 | 0.936 5176 | 9.063 4824 | 10 |
| 14 | 0.164 9456 | 9.835 0544 | 1.225 3038 | 1.060 3581 | 8.939 6419 | 14 |
| 16 | 0.188 5093 | 9.811 4907 | 1.295 8744 | 1.107 3651 | 8.892 6349 | 16 |
| 20 | 0.235 6366 | 9.764 3634-10 | 1.418 2582 | 1.182 6215 | 8.817 3785-10 | 20 |
| | | | $3\%$ | | | |
| 1 | 0.012 8372 | 9.987 1628-10 | 0.000 0000 | 9.987 1628-10 | 0.012 8372 | 1 |
| 2 | 0.025 6744 | 9.974 3256 | 0.307 4960 | 0.281 8216 | 9.718 1784-10 | 2 |
| 3 | 0.038 5117 | 9.961 4883 | 0.490 0850 | 0.451 5733 | 9.548 4267 | 3 |
| 4 | 0.051 3489 | 9.948 6511 | 0.621 5530 | 0.570 2040 | 9.429 7960 | 4 |
| 5 | 0.064 1861 | 9.935 8139 | 0.725 0238 | 0.660 8377 | 9.339 1623 | 5 |
| 6 | 0.077 0233 | 9.922 9767 | 0.810 7976 | 0.733 7742 | 9.266 2258 | 6 |
| 7 | 0.089 8606 | 9.910 1394 | 0.884 3683 | 0.794 5078 | 9.205 4922 | 7 |
| 8 | 0.102 6978 | 9.897 3022 | 0.949 0159 | 0.846 3181 | 9.153 6819 | 8 |
| 9 | 0.115 5350 | 9.884 4650 | 1.006 8555 | 0.891 3205 | 9.108 6795 | 9 |
| 10 | 0.128 3722 | 9.871 6278-10 | 1.059 3316 | 0.930 9593 | 9.069 0407-10 | 10 |
| 11 | 0.141 2095 | 9.858 7905-10 | 1.107 4744 | 0.966 2649 | 9.033 7351-10 | 11 |
| 12 | 0.154 0467 | 9.845 9533 | 1.152 0445 | 0.997 9978 | 9.002 0022 | 12 |
| 13 | 0.166 8839 | 9.833 1161 | 1.193 6196 | 1.026 7357 | 8.973 2643 | 13 |
| 14 | 0.179 7211 | 9.820 2789 | 1.232 6486 | 1.052 9275 | 8.947 0725 | 14 |
| 15 | 0.192 5584 | 9.807 4416 | 1.269 4876 | 1.076 9292 | 8.923 0708 | 15 |
| 16 | 0.205 3956 | 9.794 6044 | 1.304 4233 | 1.099 0277 | 8.900 9723 | 16 |
| 17 | 0.218 2328 | 9.781 7672 | 1.337 6906 | 1.119 4578 | 8.880 5422 | 17 |
| 18 | 0.231 0700 | 9.768 9300 | 1.369 4837 | 1.138 4136 | 8.861 5864 | 18 |
| 19 | 0.243 9073 | 9.756 0927 | 1.399 9655 | 1.156 0582 | 8.843 9418 | 19 |
| 20 | 0.256 7445 | 9.743 2555-10 | 1.429 2737 | 1.172 5293 | 8.827 4707-10 | 20 |
| 21 | 0.269 5817 | 9.730 4183-10 | 1.457 5259 | 1.187 9442 | 8.812 0558-10 | 21 |
| 24 | 0.308 0934 | 9.691 9066 | 1.536 8925 | 1.228 7991 | 8.771 2009 | 24 |
| 25 | 0.320 9306 | 9.679 0694 | 1.561 8079 | 1.240 8773 | 8.759 1227 | 25 |
| 26 | 0.333 7678 | 9.666 2322 | 1.586 0587 | 1.252 2908 | 8.747 7092 | 26 |
| 30 | 0.385 1167 | 9.614 8833 | 1.677 3826 | 1.292 2658 | 8.707 7342 | 30 |
| 32 | 0.410 7912 | 9.589 2088 | 1.720 1821 | 1.309 3909 | 8.690 6091 | 32 |
| 40 | 0.513 4890 | 9.486 5110 | 1.877 3786 | 1.363 8896 | 8.636 1104 | 40 |
| 60 | 0.770 2335 | 9.229 7665-10 | 2.212 3298 | 1.442 0963 | 8.557 9037-10 | 60 |
| | | | $3\frac{1}{4}\%$ | | | |
| 2 | 0.027 7801 | 9.972 2199-10 | 0.308 0306 | 0.280 2504 | 9.719 7496-10 | 2 |
| 3 | 0.041 6702 | 9.958 3298 | 0.491 1594 | 0.449 4892 | 9.550 5108 | 3 |
| 4 | 0.055 5602 | 9.944 4398 | 0.623 1727 | 0.567 6124 | 9.432 3876 | 4 |
| 10 | 0.138 9006 | 9.861 0994 | 1.064 3362 | 0.925 4356 | 9.074 5644 | 10 |
| 12 | 0.166 6807 | 9.833 3193 | 1.158 2203 | 0.991 5396 | 9.008 4604 | 12 |
| 20 | 0.277 8012 | 9.722 1988-10 | 1.440 3461 | 1.162 5448 | 8.837 4552-10 | 20 |

Table
12

# TABLE 12 LOGARITHMS OF VALUES IN TABLES 5, 6, 7, 8, and 9

| $n$ | $\log (1+i)^n$ | $\log (1+i)^{-n}$ | $\log s_{\overline{n}|i}$ | $\log a_{\overline{n}|i}$ | $\log \dfrac{1}{a_{\overline{n}|i}}$ | $n$ |
|---|---|---|---|---|---|---|
| | | | $3\frac{1}{2}\%$ | | | |
| 2 | 0.029 8807 | 9.970 1193-10 | 0.308 5644 | 0.278 6837 | 9.721 3163-10 | 2 |
| 3 | 0.044 8210 | 9.955 1790 | 0.492 2329 | 0.447 4118 | 9.552 5882 | 3 |
| 4 | 0.059 7614 | 9.940 2386 | 0.624 7917 | 0.565 0303 | 8.434 9697 | 4 |
| 5 | 0.074 7017 | 9.925 2983 | 0.729 3645 | 0.654 6628 | 9.345 3372 | 5 |
| 6 | 0.089 6421 | 9.910 3579 | 0.816 2513 | 0.726 6093 | 9.273 3907 | 6 |
| 7 | 0.104 5824 | 9.895 4176 | 0.890 9465 | 0.786 3640 | 9.213 6360 | 7 |
| 8 | 0.119 5228 | 9.880 4772 | 0.956 7296 | 0.837 2067 | 9.162 7933 | 8 |
| 10 | 0.149 4035 | 9.850 5965 | 1.069 3496 | 0.919 9461 | 9.080 0539 | 10 |
| 11 | 0.164 3438 | 9.835 6562-10 | 1.118 6612 | 0.954 3173 | 9.045 6827-10 | 11 |
| 12 | 0.179 2842 | 9.820 7158-10 | 1.164 4112 | 0.985 1270 | 9.014 8730-10 | 12 |
| 13 | 0.194 2245 | 9.805 7755 | 1.207 1772 | 1.012 9527 | 8.987 0473 | 13 |
| 14 | 0.209 1649 | 9.790 8351 | 1.247 4083 | 1.038 2433 | 8.961 7567 | 14 |
| 15 | 0.224 1052 | 9.775 8948 | 1.285 4601 | 1.061 3549 | 8.938 6451 | 15 |
| 17 | 0.253 9859 | 9.746 0141 | 1.356 1218 | 1.102 1359 | 8.897 8641 | 17 |
| 18 | 0.268 9263 | 9.731 0737 | 1.389 1606 | 1.120 2343 | 8.879 7657 | 18 |
| 20 | 0.298 8070 | 9.701 1930 | 1.451 4745 | 1.152 6675 | 8.847 3325 | 20 |
| 24 | 0.358 5684 | 9.641 4316 | 1.564 2698 | 1.205 7014 | 8.794 2986 | 24 |
| 25 | 0.373 5087 | 9.626 4913-10 | 1.590 5059 | 1.216 9971 | 8.783 0029-10 | 25 |
| | | | $3\frac{3}{4}\%$ | | | |
| 14 | 0.223 8335 | 9.776 1665-10 | 1.254 8224 | 1.030 9889 | 8.969 0111-10 | 14 |
| | | | $4\%$ | | | |
| 2 | 0.034 0667 | 9.965 9333-10 | 0.309 6302 | 0.275 5635 | 9.724 4365-10 | 2 |
| 3 | 0.051 1000 | 9.948 9000 | 0.494 3773 | 0.443 2772 | 9.556 7228 | 3 |
| 4 | 0.068 1334 | 9.931 8666 | 0.628 0274 | 0.559 8941 | 9.440 1059 | 4 |
| 5 | 0.085 1667 | 9.914 8333 | 0.733 7045 | 0.648 5378 | 9.351 4622 | 5 |
| 6 | 0.102 2000 | 9.897 8000 | 0.821 7084 | 0.719 5084 | 9.280 4916 | 6 |
| 7 | 0.119 2334 | 9.880 7666 | 0.897 5333 | 0.778 2999 | 9.221 7001 | 7 |
| 8 | 0.136 2667 | 9.863 7333 | 0.964 4588 | 0.828 1922 | 9.171 8078 | 8 |
| 9 | 0.153 3001 | 9.846 6999 | 1.024 6004 | 0.871 3003 | 9.128 6997 | 9 |
| 10 | 0.170 3334 | 9.829 6666 | 1.079 4022 | 0.909 0688 | 9.090 9312 | 10 |
| 12 | 0.204 4001 | 9.795 5999-10 | 1.176 8378 | 0.972 4377 | 9.027 5623-10 | 12 |
| 14 | 0.238 4668 | 9.761 5332-10 | 1.262 2591 | 1.023 7924 | 8.976 2076-10 | 14 |
| 15 | 0.255 5001 | 9.744 4999 | 1.301 5419 | 1.046 0418 | 8.953 9582 | 15 |
| 16 | 0.272 5334 | 9.727 4666 | 1.338 9450 | 1.066 4115 | 8.933 5885 | 16 |
| 17 | 0.289 5668 | 9.710 4332 | 1.374 7028 | 1.085 1360 | 8.914 8640 | 17 |
| 19 | 0.323 6334 | 9.676 3666 | 1.442 0285 | 1.118 3950 | 8.881 6050 | 19 |
| 20 | 0.340 6668 | 9.659 3332 | 1.473 8966 | 1.133 2299 | 8.866 7701 | 20 |
| 21 | 0.357 7001 | 9.642 2999 | 1.504 7318 | 1.147 0317 | 8.852 9683 | 21 |
| 24 | 0.408 8001 | 9.591 1999 | 1.591 9835 | 1.183 1833 | 8.816 8167 | 24 |
| 30 | 0.511 0002 | 9.488 9998 | 1.748 8462 | 1.237 8460 | 8.762 1540 | 30 |
| 31 | 0.528 0335 | 9.471 9665-10 | 1.773 2621 | 1.245 2287 | 8.754 7713-10 | 31 |

# TABLE 12 LOGARITHMS OF VALUES IN TABLES 5, 6, 7, 8, and 9

| $n$ | $\log (1 + i)^n$ | $\log (1 + i)^{-n}$ | $\log s_{\overline{n}|i}$ | $\log a_{\overline{n}|i}$ | $\log \dfrac{1}{a_{\overline{n}|i}}$ | $n$ |
|---|---|---|---|---|---|---|
| | | | $4\frac{1}{2}\%$ | | | |
| 5 | 0.095 5815 | 9.904 4185-10 | 0.738 0437 | 0.642 4622 | 9.357 5378-10 | 5 |
| 6 | 0.114 6977 | 9.885 3023 | 0.827 1684 | 0.712 4706 | 9.287 5294 | 6 |
| 12 | 0.229 3955 | 9.770 6045 | 1.189 3227 | 0.959 9273 | 9.040 0727 | 12 |
| 15 | 0.286 7444 | 9.713 2556 | 1.317 7302 | 1.030 9859 | 8.969 0141 | 15 |
| 24 | 0.458 7910 | 9.541 2090-10 | 1.620 0235 | 1.161 2325 | 8.838 7675-10 | 24 |
| | | | $5\%$ | | | |
| 3 | 0.063 5679 | 9.936 4321-10 | 0.498 6551 | 0.435 0872 | 9.564 9128-10 | 3 |
| 4 | 0.084 7572 | 9.915 2428 | 0.634 4898 | 0.549 7327 | 9.450 2673 | 4 |
| 5 | 0.105 9465 | 9.894 0535 | 0.742 3819 | 0.636 4354 | 9.363 5646 | 5 |
| 6 | 0.127 1358 | 9.872 8642 | 0.832 6310 | 0.705 4952 | 9.294 5048 | 6 |
| 7 | 0.148 3251 | 9.851 6749-10 | 0.910 7316 | 0.762 4065 | 9.237 5935 | 7 |
| 8 | 0.169 5144 | 9.830 4856-10 | 0.979 9628 | 0.810 4485 | 9.189 5515 | 8 |
| 9 | 0.190 7037 | 9.809 2963 | 1.042 4402 | 0.851 7365 | 9.148 2635 | 9 |
| 10 | 0.211 8930 | 9.788 1070 | 1.099 6079 | 0.887 7149 | 9.112 2851 | 10 |
| 11 | 0.233 0823 | 9.766 9177 | 1.152 4959 | 0.919 4136 | 9.080 5864 | 11 |
| 12 | 0.254 2716 | 9.745 7284-10 | 1.201 8647 | 0.947 5930 | 9.052 4070-10 | 12 |
| 15 | 0.317 8395 | 9.682 1605-10 | 1.334 0226 | 1.016 1831 | 8.983 8169-10 | 15 |
| 18 | 0.381 4074 | 9.618 5926 | 1.449 2065 | 1.067 7992 | 8.932 2008 | 18 |
| 20 | 0.423 7860 | 9.576 2140 | 1.519 3811 | 1.095 5950 | 8.904 4050 | 20 |
| 30 | 0.635 6790 | 9.364 3210 | 1.822 4221 | 1.186 7431 | 8.813 2569 | 30 |
| 40 | 0.847 5720 | 9.152 4280-10 | 2.082 0661 | 1.234 4942 | 8.765 5058 | 40 |
| | | | $5\frac{1}{2}\%$ | | | |
| 2 | 0.046 5049 | 9.953 4951-10 | 0.312 8118 | 0.266 3070 | 9.733 6930-10 | 2 |
| 3 | 0.069 7574 | 9.930 2426 | 0.500 7886 | 0.431 0312 | 9.568 9688 | 3 |
| 4 | 0.093 0098 | 9.906 9902 | 0.637 7164 | 0.544 7066 | 9.455 2934 | 4 |
| 7 | 0.162 7672 | 9.837 2328 | 0.917 3424 | 0.754 5752 | 9.245 4248 | 7 |
| 10 | 0.232 5246 | 9.767 4754-10 | 1.109 7592 | 0.877 2346 | 9.122 7654-10 | 10 |
| 15 | 0.348 7869 | 9.651 2131-10 | 1.350 4160 | 1.001 6291 | 8.998 3709-10 | 15 |
| 19 | 0.441 7967 | 9.558 2033 | 1.506 5412 | 1.064 7445 | 8.935 2555 | 19 |
| 20 | 0.465 0492 | 9.534 9508 | 1.542 4310 | 1.077 3818 | 8.922 6182 | 20 |
| 24 | 0.558 0590 | 9.441 9410 | 1.677 0409 | 1.118 9819 | 8.881 0181 | 24 |
| 26 | 0.604 5640 | 9.395 4360 | 1.740 0939 | 1.135 5300 | 8.864 4700 | 26 |
| 49 | 1.139 3705 | 8.860 6295-10 | 2.366 2990 | 1.226 9284 | 8.773 0716-10 | 49 |

Table 12

## TABLE 12 LOGARITHMS OF VALUES IN TABLES 5, 6, 7, 8, and 9

| $n$ | $\log (1+i)^n$ | $\log (1+i)^{-n}$ | $\log s_{\overline{n}\rvert i}$ | $\log a_{\overline{n}\rvert i}$ | $\log \dfrac{1}{a_{\overline{n}\rvert i}}$ | $n$ |
|---|---|---|---|---|---|---|
| | | | 6% | | | |
| 1 | 0.025 3059 | 9.974 6941 − 10 | 0.000 0000 | 9.974 6941 − 10 | 0.025 3059 | 1 |
| 2 | 0.050 6117 | 9.949 3883 | 0.313 8672 | 0.263 2555 | 9.736 7445 − 10 | 2 |
| 3 | 0.075 9176 | 9.924 0824 | 0.502 9185 | 0.427 0009 | 9.572 9991 | 3 |
| 4 | 0.101 2235 | 9.898 7765 | 0.640 9399 | 0.539 7165 | 9.460 2835 | 4 |
| 5 | 0.126 5293 | 9.873 4707 − 10 | 0.751 0552 | 0.624 5259 | 9.375 4741 − 10 | 5 |
| 6 | 0.151 8352 | 9.848 1648 − 10 | 0.843 5640 | 0.691 7288 | 9.308 2712 − 10 | 6 |
| 8 | 0.202 4469 | 9.797 5531 | 0.995 5241 | 0.793 0772 | 9.206 9228 | 8 |
| 10 | 0.253 0587 | 9.746 9413 | 1.119 9416 | 0.866 8829 | 9.133 1171 | 10 |
| 12 | 0.303 6704 | 9.696 3296 | 1.227 1136 | 0.923 4432 | 9.076 5568 | 12 |
| 15 | 0.379 5880 | 9.620 4120 − 10 | 1.366 9077 | 0.987 3198 | 9.012 6802 − 10 | 15 |
| 20 | 0.506 1173 | 9.493 8827 − 10 | 1.565 6778 | 1.059 5604 | 8.940 4396 − 10 | 20 |
| 32 | 0.809 7877 | 9.190 2123 | 1.958 5150 | 1.148 7273 | 8.851 2727 | 32 |
| 60 | 1.518 3519 | 8.481 6481 − 10 | 2.726 8316 | 1.208 4797 | 8.791 5203 − 10 | 60 |
| | | | 7% | | | |
| 2 | 0.058 7676 | 9.941 2324 − 10 | 0.315 9703 | 0.257 2028 | 9.742 7972 − 10 | 2 |
| 3 | 0.088 1513 | 9.911 8487 | 0.507 1675 | 0.419 0161 | 9.580 9839 | 3 |
| 4 | 0.117 5351 | 9.882 4649 | 0.647 3774 | 0.529 8423 | 9.470 1577 | 4 |
| 5 | 0.146 9189 | 9.853 0811 − 10 | 0.759 7236 | 0.612 8047 | 9.387 1953 − 10 | 5 |
| 9 | 0.264 4540 | 9.735 5460 − 10 | 1.078 3839 | 0.813 9299 | 9.186 0701 − 10 | 9 |
| 10 | 0.293 8378 | 9.706 1622 | 1.140 3964 | 0.846 5587 | 9.153 4413 | 10 |
| 12 | 0.352 6053 | 9.647 3947 | 1.252 5728 | 0.899 9674 | 9.100 0326 | 12 |
| 25 | 0.734 5944 | 9.265 4056 − 10 | 1.801 0539 | 1.066 4594 | 8.933 5406 − 10 | 25 |
| | | | 8% | | | |
| 4 | 0.133 6950 | 9.866 3050 − 10 | 0.653 8020 | 0.520 1069 | 9.479 8931 − 10 | 4 |
| | | | 9% | | | |
| 10 | 0.374 2650 | 9.625 7350 − 10 | 1.181 6418 | 0.807 3767 | 9.192 6231 − 10 | 10 |
| | | | 10% | | | |
| 20 | 0.827 8540 | 9.172 1460 − 10 | 1.757 9650 | 0.930 1117 | 9.069 8886 − 10 | 20 |

# LOGARITHMS OF VALUES IN TABLES 5A, 7A, 8A, and 10
### For Computing Examples and Problems in
## TABLE 13
### Chapters 11 Through 20

| $m$ | $\log (1 + i)^{\frac{1}{m}}$ (Table 5A) | $\log s_{\overline{1/m}\,i}$ (Table 7A) | $\log a_{\overline{1/m}\,i}$ (Table 8A) | $\log \dfrac{1}{s_{\overline{1/m}\,i}}$ (Table 10) | $m$ |
|---|---|---|---|---|---|
| | | | $\frac{1}{4}\%$ | | |
| 3 | 0.000 3615 | 9. 522 5172- 10 | 9. 522 1557- 10 | 0. 477 4828 | 3 |
| | | | $\frac{5}{12}\%$ | | |
| 2 | 0.000 9029 | 9. 698 5183- 10 | 9. 697 7025- 10 | 0. 301 4817 | 2 |
| | | | $1\%$ | | |
| 3 | 0.001 4404 | 9. 521 4367- 10 | 9. 519 9962- 10 | 0. 478 5633 | 3 |
| | | | $1\frac{1}{4}\%$ | | |
| 3 | 0.001 7983 | 9. 521 0780- 10 | 9. 519 2796- 10 | 0. 478 9220 | 3 |
| | | | $1\frac{1}{2}\%$ | | |
| 3 | 0.002 1554 | 9. 520 7199- 10 | 9. 518 5645- 10 | 0. 479 2801 | 3 |
| | | | $1\frac{3}{4}\%$ | | |
| 3 | 0.002 5114 | 9. 520 3624- 10 | 9. 517 8509- 10 | 0. 479 6376 | 3 |
| | | | $2\%$ | | |
| 2 | 0.004 3001 | 9. 696 8146- 10 | 9. 285 5145- 10 | 0. 303 1854 | 2 |
| 3 | 0.002 8667 | 9. 520 0057 | 9. 517 1390 | 0. 479 9943 | 3 |
| 4 | 0.002 1500 | 9. 394 7083 | 9. 392 5583 | 0. 605 2917 | 4 |
| 6 | 0.001 4334 | 9. 218 2585- 10 | 9. 216 8251- 10 | 0. 781 7415 | 6 |
| | | | $2\frac{1}{2}\%$ | | |
| 2 | 0.005 3619 | 9. 696 2807- 10 | 9. 690 9189- 10 | 0. 303 7193 | 2 |

Table
13

# TABLE 13

| $m$ | $\log (1+i)^{\frac{1}{m}}$ | $\log s_{\overline{1/m}\,i}$ | $\log a_{\overline{1/m}\,i}$ | $\log \dfrac{1}{s_{\overline{1/m}\,i}}$ | $m$ |
|---|---|---|---|---|---|
| | | | **3%** | | |
| 2 | 0.006 4187 | 9.695 7488 − 10 | 9.689 3302 − 10 | 0.304 2512 | 2 |
| 3 | 0.004 2791 | 9.518 5856 | 9.514 3065 | 0.481 4144 | 3 |
| 4 | 0.003 2026 | 9.393 1112 | 9.389 9020 | 0.606 8888 | 4 |
| 6 | 0.002 1395 | 9.216 4845 − 10 | 9.214 3450 − 10 | 0.783 5155 | 6 |
| | | | $3\frac{1}{2}\%$ | | |
| 2 | 0.007 4701 | 9.695 2188 − 10 | 9.687 7486 − 10 | 0.304 7812 | 2 |
| 6 | 0.002 4901 | 9.215 6028 − 10 | 9.213 1127 − 10 | 0.784 3972 | 6 |
| | | | **4%** | | |
| 2 | 0.008 5167 | 9.694 6908 − 10 | 9.686 1741 − 10 | 0.305 3092 | 2 |
| 4 | 0.004 2584 | 9.391 5264 − 10 | 9.387 2681 − 10 | 0.608 4736 | 4 |
| | | | $4\frac{1}{2}\%$ | | |
| 4 | 0.004 7791 | 9.390 7386 − 10 | 9.385 9595 − 10 | 0.609 2614 | 4 |
| | | | **5%** | | |
| 12 | 0.001 7658 | 8.911 0642 − 10 | 8.909 2984 − 10 | 1.088 9358 | 12 |
| | | | $5\frac{1}{2}\%$ | | |
| 2 | 0.011 6262 | 9.693 1180 − 10 | 9.681 4918 − 10 | 0.306 8820 | 2 |
| 4 | 0.005 8131 | 9.389 1717 − 10 | 9.383 3586 − 10 | 0.610 8283 | 4 |
| | | | **6%** | | |
| 12 | 0.002 1088 | 8.909 1592 − 10 | 8.907 0504 − 10 | 1.090 8408 | 12 |
| | | | **7%** | | |
| 3 | 0.009 7946 | 9.513 0105 − 10 | 9.503 2159 − 10 | 0.486 9895 | 3 |
| 6 | 0.004 8973 | 9.209 5250 − 10 | 9.204 6277 − 10 | 0.790 4750 | 6 |
| | | | **10%** | | |
| 4 | 0.010 3482 | 9.382 2634 − 10 | 9.371 9153 − 10 | 0.617 7363 | 4 |

# TABLE 14

**COMMISSIONERS 1958 STANDARD ORDINARY MORTALITY TABLE**

| Age, $x$ | Number Living $l_x$ | Number Dying $d_x$ | Deaths per 1,000 | Age, $x$ | Number Living $l_x$ | Number Dying $d_x$ | Deaths per 1,000 |
|---|---|---|---|---|---|---|---|
| 0 | 10,000,000 | 70,800 | 7.08 | 50 | 8,762,306 | 72,902 | 8.32 |
| 1 | 9,929,200 | 17,475 | 1.76 | 51 | 8,689,404 | 79,160 | 9.11 |
| 2 | 9,911,725 | 15,066 | 1.52 | 52 | 8,610,244 | 85,758 | 9.96 |
| 3 | 9,896,659 | 14,449 | 1.46 | 53 | 8,524,486 | 92,832 | 10.89 |
| 4 | 9,882,210 | 13,835 | 1.40 | 54 | 8,431,654 | 100,337 | 11.90 |
| 5 | 9,868,375 | 13,322 | 1.35 | 55 | 8,331,317 | 108,307 | 13.00 |
| 6 | 9,855,053 | 12,812 | 1.30 | 56 | 8,223,010 | 116,849 | 14,21 |
| 7 | 9,842,241 | 12,401 | 1.26 | 57 | 8,106,161 | 125,970 | 15.54 |
| 8 | 9,829,840 | 12,091 | 1.23 | 58 | 7,980,191 | 135,663 | 17.00 |
| 9 | 9,817,749 | 11,879 | 1.21 | 59 | 7,844,528 | 145,830 | 18.59 |
| 10 | 9,805,870 | 11,865 | 1.21 | 60 | 7,698,698 | 156,592 | 20.34 |
| 11 | 9,794,005 | 12,047 | 1.23 | 61 | 7,542,106 | 167,736 | 22.24 |
| 12 | 9,781,958 | 12,325 | 1.26 | 62 | 7,374,370 | 179,271 | 24.31 |
| 13 | 9,769,633 | 12,896 | 1.32 | 63 | 7,195,099 | 191,174 | 26.57 |
| 14 | 9,756,737 | 13,562 | 1.39 | 64 | 7,003,925 | 203,394 | 29.04 |
| 15 | 9,743,175 | 14,225 | 1.46 | 65 | 6,800,531 | 215,917 | 31.75 |
| 16 | 9,728,950 | 14,983 | 1.54 | 66 | 6,584,614 | 228,749 | 34.74 |
| 17 | 9,713,967 | 15,737 | 1.62 | 67 | 6,355,865 | 241,777 | 38.04 |
| 18 | 9,698,230 | 16,390 | 1.69 | 68 | 6,114,088 | 254,835 | 41.68 |
| 19 | 9,681,840 | 16,846 | 1.74 | 69 | 5,859,253 | 267,241 | 45.61 |
| 20 | 9,664,994 | 17,300 | 1.79 | 70 | 5,592,012 | 278,426 | 49.79 |
| 21 | 9,647,694 | 17,655 | 1.83 | 71 | 5,313,586 | 287,731 | 54.15 |
| 22 | 9,630,039 | 17,912 | 1.86 | 72 | 5,025,855 | 294,766 | 58.65 |
| 23 | 9,612,127 | 18,167 | 1.89 | 73 | 4,731,089 | 299,289 | 63.26 |
| 24 | 9,593,960 | 18,324 | 1.91 | 74 | 4,431,800 | 301,894 | 68.12 |
| 25 | 9,575,636 | 18,481 | 1.93 | 75 | 4,129,906 | 303,011 | 73.37 |
| 26 | 9,557,155 | 18,732 | 1.96 | 76 | 3,826,895 | 303,014 | 79.18 |
| 27 | 9,538,423 | 18,981 | 1.99 | 77 | 3,523,881 | 301,997 | 85.70 |
| 28 | 9,519,442 | 19,324 | 2.03 | 78 | 3,221,884 | 299,829 | 93.06 |
| 29 | 9,500,118 | 19,760 | 2.08 | 79 | 2,922,055 | 295,683 | 101.19 |
| 30 | 9,480,358 | 20,193 | 2.13 | 80 | 2,626,372 | 288,848 | 109.98 |
| 31 | 9,460,165 | 20,718 | 2.19 | 81 | 2,337,524 | 278,983 | 119.35 |
| 32 | 9,439,447 | 21,239 | 2.25 | 82 | 2,058,541 | 265,902 | 129.17 |
| 33 | 9,418,208 | 21,850 | 2.32 | 83 | 1,792,639 | 249,858 | 139.38 |
| 34 | 9,396,358 | 22,551 | 2.40 | 84 | 1,542,781 | 231,433 | 150.01 |
| 35 | 9,373,807 | 23,528 | 2.51 | 85 | 1,311,348 | 211,311 | 161.14 |
| 36 | 9,350,279 | 24,685 | 2.64 | 86 | 1,100,037 | 190,108 | 172.82 |
| 37 | 9,325,594 | 26,112 | 2.80 | 87 | 909,929 | 168,455 | 185.13 |
| 38 | 9,299,482 | 27,991 | 3.01 | 88 | 741,474 | 146,997 | 198.25 |
| 39 | 9,271,491 | 30,132 | 3.25 | 89 | 594,477 | 126,303 | 212.46 |
| 40 | 9,241,359 | 32,622 | 3.53 | 90 | 468,174 | 106,809 | 228.14 |
| 41 | 9,208,737 | 35,362 | 3.84 | 91 | 361,365 | 88,813 | 245.77 |
| 42 | 9,173,375 | 38,253 | 4.17 | 92 | 272,552 | 72,480 | 265.93 |
| 43 | 9,135,122 | 41,382 | 4.53 | 93 | 200,072 | 57,881 | 289.30 |
| 44 | 9,093,740 | 44,741 | 4.92 | 94 | 142,191 | 45,026 | 316.66 |
| 45 | 9,048,999 | 48,412 | 5.35 | 95 | 97,165 | 34,128 | 351.24 |
| 46 | 9,000,587 | 52,473 | 5.83 | 96 | 63,037 | 25,250 | 400.56 |
| 47 | 8,948,114 | 56,910 | 6.36 | 97 | 37,787 | 18,456 | 488.42 |
| 48 | 8,891,204 | 61,794 | 6.95 | 98 | 19,331 | 12,916 | 668.15 |
| 49 | 8,829,410 | 67,104 | 7.60 | 99 | 6,415 | 6,415 | 1,000.00 |

Table 14

| Age, $x$ | $D_x$ | $N_x$ | $C_x$ | $M_x$ |
|---|---|---|---|---|
| 0 | 10,000,000.0000 | 324,850,104.9680 | 69,073.1710 | 2,076,826.7172 |
| 1 | 9,687,024.4290 | 314,850,104.9680 | 16,632.9566 | 2,007,753.5462 |
| 2 | 9,434,122.5838 | 305,163,080.5390 | 13,990.2787 | 1,991,120.5896 |
| 3 | 9,190,031.7084 | 295,728,957.9552 | 13,090.0808 | 1,977,130.3109 |
| 4 | 8,952,794.4741 | 286,538,926.2468 | 12,228.1241 | 1,964,040.2301 |
| 5 | 8,722,205.5791 | 277,586,131.7727 | 11,487.5189 | 1,951,812.1060 |
| 6 | 8,497,981.3556 | 268,863,926.1936 | 10,778.2903 | 1,940,324.5871 |
| 7 | 8,279,935.2370 | 260,365,944.8380 | 10,178.0782 | 1,929,546.2968 |
| 8 | 8,067,807.4636 | 252,086,009.6010 | 9,681.6066 | 1,919,368.2186 |
| 9 | 7,861,350.0557 | 244,018,202.1374 | 9,279.8558 | 1,909,686.6120 |
| 10 | 7,660,329.9546 | 236,156,852.0817 | 9,042.8478 | 1,900,406.7562 |
| 11 | 7,464,449.7860 | 228,496,522.1271 | 8,957.6178 | 1,891,363.9084 |
| 12 | 7,273,432.4866 | 221,032,072.3411 | 8,940.8062 | 1,882,406.2906 |
| 13 | 7,087,090.8833 | 213,758,639.8545 | 9,126.8500 | 1,873,465.4844 |
| 14 | 6,905,108.1581 | 206,671,548.9712 | 9,364.0939 | 1,864,338.6344 |
| 15 | 6,727,326.7826 | 199,766,440.8131 | 9,582.3146 | 1,854,974.5405 |
| 16 | 6,553,663.2627 | 193,039,114.0305 | 9,846.7536 | 1,845,392.2259 |
| 17 | 6,383,971.1254 | 186,485,450.7678 | 10,090.0279 | 1,835,545.4723 |
| 18 | 6,218,174.4633 | 180,101,479.6424 | 10,252.3993 | 1,825,455.4444 |
| 19 | 6,056,259.3006 | 173,883,305.1791 | 10,280.6243 | 1,815,203.0451 |
| 20 | 5,898,264.9735 | 167,827,045.8785 | 10,300.1828 | 1,804,922.4208 |
| 21 | 5,744,104.7377 | 161,928,780.9050 | 10,255.1657 | 1,794,622.2380 |
| 22 | 5,593,749.4258 | 156,184,676.1673 | 10,150.6810 | 1,784,367.0723 |
| 23 | 5,447,165.8414 | 150,590,926.7415 | 10,044.0865 | 1,774,216.3913 |
| 24 | 5,304,263.9929 | 145,143,760.9001 | 9,883.7932 | 1,764,172.3048 |
| 25 | 5,165,007.9517 | 139,839,496.9072 | 9,725.3439 | 1,754,288.5116 |
| 26 | 5,029,306.7854 | 134,674,488.9555 | 9,617.0037 | 1,744,563.1677 |
| 27 | 4,897,023.7928 | 129,645,182.1701 | 9,507.1611 | 1,734,946.1640 |
| 28 | 4,768,076.9758 | 124,748,158.3773 | 9,442.8900 | 1,725,439.0029 |
| 29 | 4,642,339.5370 | 119,980,081.4015 | 9,420.4356 | 1,715,996.1129 |
| 30 | 4,519,691.3751 | 115,337,741.8645 | 9,392.0634 | 1,706,575.6773 |
| 31 | 4,400,062.8465 | 110,818,050.4894 | 9,401.2183 | 1,697,183.6139 |
| 32 | 4,283,343.0569 | 106,417,987.6429 | 9,402.5686 | 1,687,782.3956 |
| 33 | 4,169,468.7479 | 102,134,644.5860 | 9,437.1317 | 1,678,379.8270 |
| 34 | 4,058,337.1968 | 97,965,175.8381 | 9,502.3390 | 1,668,942.6953 |
| 35 | 3,949,851.0856 | 93,906,838.6413 | 9,672.2130 | 1,659,440.3563 |
| 36 | 3,843,840.9771 | 89,956,987.5557 | 9,900.3401 | 1,649,768.1433 |
| 37 | 3,740,188.4751 | 86,113,146.5786 | 10,217.2318 | 1,639,867.8032 |
| 38 | 3,638,747.0704 | 82,372,958.1035 | 10,685.3232 | 1,629,650.5714 |
| 39 | 3,539,311.8617 | 78,734,211.0331 | 11,222.0794 | 1,618,965.2482 |
| 40 | 3,441,765.0620 | 75,194,899.1714 | 11,853.1042 | 1,607,743.1688 |
| 41 | 3,345,966.5023 | 71,753,134.1094 | 12,535.2926 | 1,595,890.0646 |
| 42 | 3,251,822.2774 | 68,407,167.6071 | 13,229.3739 | 1,583,354.7720 |
| 43 | 3,159,280.1784 | 65,155,345.3297 | 13,962.4424 | 1,570,125.3981 |
| 44 | 3,068,262.0685 | 61,996,065.1513 | 14,727.5918 | 1,556,162.9557 |
| 45 | 2,978,698.8164 | 58,927,803.0828 | 15,547.3085 | 1,541,435.3639 |
| 46 | 2,890,500.3526 | 55,949,104.2664 | 16,440.4699 | 1,525,888.0554 |
| 47 | 2,803,559.9048 | 53,058,603.9138 | 17,395.7457 | 1,509,447.5855 |
| 48 | 2,717,784.6405 | 50,255,044.0090 | 18,427.9447 | 1,492,051.8398 |
| 49 | 2,633,069.2135 | 47,537,259.3685 | 19,523.3861 | 1,473,623.8951 |

## COMMUTATION COLUMNS—INTEREST AT $2\frac{1}{2}\%$

# TABLE 15

### Based on 1958 CSO Mortality Table

| Age, $x$ | $D_x$ | $N_x$ | $C_x$ | $M_x$ |
|---|---|---|---|---|
| 50 | 2,549,324.6723 | 44,904,190.1550 | 20,692.9455 | 1,454,100.5090 |
| 51 | 2,466,453.0891 | 42,354,865.4827 | 21,921.2231 | 1,433,407.5635 |
| 52 | 2,384,374.4270 | 39,888,412.3936 | 23,169.1325 | 1,411,486.3404 |
| 53 | 2,303,049.8123 | 37,504,037.9666 | 24,468.5917 | 1,388,317.2079 |
| 54 | 2,222,409.2905 | 35,200,988.1543 | 25,801.7117 | 1,363,848.6162 |
| 55 | 2,142,402.4988 | 32,978,578.8638 | 27,171.9031 | 1,338,046.9045 |
| 56 | 2,062,976.8254 | 30,836,176.3650 | 28,599.9098 | 1,310,875.0014 |
| 57 | 1,984,060.3996 | 28,773,199.5396 | 30,080.3536 | 1,282,275.0916 |
| 58 | 1,905,588.3725 | 26,789,139.1400 | 31,604.8230 | 1,252,194.7380 |
| 59 | 1,827,505.7998 | 24,883,550.7675 | 33,144.7659 | 1,220,589.9150 |
| 60 | 1,749,787.7198 | 23,056,044.9677 | 34,722.7242 | 1,187,445.1491 |
| 61 | 1,672,387.2632 | 21,306,257.2479 | 36,286.6291 | 1,152,722.4249 |
| 62 | 1,595,310.6622 | 19,633,869.9847 | 37,836.1144 | 1,116,435.7958 |
| 63 | 1,518,564.5694 | 18,038,559.3225 | 39,364.2006 | 1,078,599.6814 |
| 64 | 1,442,162.1578 | 16,519,994.7531 | 40,858.9196 | 1,039,235.4808 |
| 65 | 1,366,128.5462 | 15,077,832.5953 | 42,316.6940 | 998,376.5612 |
| 66 | 1,290,491.6985 | 13,711,704.0491 | 43,738.1310 | 956,059.8672 |
| 67 | 1,215,278.1249 | 12,421,212.3506 | 45,101.6207 | 912,321.7362 |
| 68 | 1,140,535.6099 | 11,205,934.2257 | 46,378.0358 | 867,220.1155 |
| 69 | 1,066,339.5743 | 10,065,398.6158 | 47,449.5963 | 820,842.0797 |
| 70 | 992,881.7500 | 8,999,059.0415 | 48,229.7870 | 773,392.4834 |
| 71 | 920,435.3077 | 8,006,177.2915 | 48,625.9779 | 725,162.6964 |
| 72 | 849,359.6946 | 7,085,741.9838 | 48,599.8832 | 676,536.7185 |
| 73 | 780,043.7396 | 6,236,382.2892 | 48,142.0663 | 627,936.8353 |
| 74 | 712,876.2140 | 5,456,338.5496 | 47,376.6752 | 579,794.7690 |
| 75 | 648,112.3021 | 4,743,462.3356 | 46,392.1628 | 532,418.0938 |
| 76 | 585,912.5111 | 4,095,350.0335 | 45,261.0951 | 486,025.9310 |
| 77 | 526,360.8716 | 3,509,437.5224 | 44,008.9628 | 440,764.8359 |
| 78 | 469,513.8465 | 2,983,076.6508 | 42,627.3426 | 396,755.8731 |
| 79 | 415,434,9294 | 2,513,562.8043 | 41,012.5834 | 354,128.5305 |
| 80 | 364,289.7989 | 2,098,127.8749 | 39,087.3533 | 313,115.9471 |
| 81 | 316,317.3241 | 1,733,838.0760 | 36,831.6174 | 274,028.5938 |
| 82 | 271,770.6619 | 1,417,520.7519 | 34,248.4382 | 237,196.9764 |
| 83 | 230,893.6600 | 1,145,750.0900 | 31,397.0289 | 202,948.5382 |
| 84 | 193,865.0736 | 914,856.4300 | 28,372.4430 | 171,551.5093 |
| 85 | 160,764.2229 | 720,991.3564 | 25,273.7507 | 143,179.0663 |
| 86 | 131,569.3974 | 560,227.1335 | 22,183.1949 | 117,905.3156 |
| 87 | 106,177.1855 | 428,657.7361 | 19,177.1362 | 95,722.1207 |
| 88 | 84,410.3641 | 322,480.5506 | 16,326.1748 | 76,544.9845 |
| 89 | 66,025.3978 | 238,070.1865 | 13,685.6613 | 60,218.8097 |
| 90 | 50,729.3636 | 172,044.7887 | 11,291.0955 | 46,533.1484 |
| 91 | 38,200.9638 | 121,315.4251 | 9,159.6932 | 35,242.0529 |
| 92 | 28,109.5415 | 83,114.4613 | 7,292.8738 | 26,082.3597 |
| 93 | 20,131.0686 | 55,004.9198 | 5,681.8884 | 18,789.4859 |
| 94 | 13,958.1795 | 34,873.8512 | 4,312.1729 | 13,107.5975 |
| 95 | 9,305.5630 | 20,915.6717 | 3,188.7449 | 8,795.4246 |
| 96 | 5,889.8533 | 11,610.1087 | 2,301.6880 | 5,606.6797 |
| 97 | 3,444.5103 | 5,720.2554 | 1,641.3408 | 3,304.9917 |
| 98 | 1,719.1569 | 2,275.7451 | 1,120.6380 | 1,663.6509 |
| 99 | 556.5882 | 556.5882 | 543.0129 | 543.0129 |

**Table 15**

# TABLE 16      LOGARITHMS OF VALUES IN TABLE 15

| Age x | $\log D_x$ | $\log N_x$ | $\log C_x$ | $\log M_x$ | Age x |
|---|---|---|---|---|---|
| 0 | 7.000 0000 | 8.511 6830 | 4.839 3094 | 6.317 4003 | 0 |
| 1 | 6.986 1904 | 8.498 1038 | 4.220 9695 | 6.302 7104 | 1 |
| 2 | 6.974 7016 | 8.484 5320 | 4.145 8264 | 6.299 0976 | 2 |
| 3 | 6.963 3170 | 8.470 8939 | 4.116 9423 | 6.296 0353 | 3 |
| 4 | 6.951 9586 | 8.457 1837 | 4.087 3598 | 6.293 1504 | 4 |
| 5 | 6.940 6263 | 8.443 3978 | 4.060 2262 | 6.290 4380 | 5 |
| 6 | 6.929 3157 | 8.429 5325 | 4.032 5499 | 6.287 8744 | 6 |
| 7 | 6.918 0269 | 8.415 5842 | 4.007 6657 | 6.285 4552 | 7 |
| 8 | 6.906 7555 | 8.401 5487 | 3.985 9474 | 6.283 1583 | 8 |
| 9 | 6.895 4972 | 8.387 4222 | 3.967 5412 | 6.280 9621 | 9 |
| 10 | 6.884 2475 | 8.373 2005 | 3.956 3052 | 6.278 8465 | 10 |
| 11 | 6.872 9978 | 8.358 8796 | 3.952 1926 | 6.276 7751 | 11 |
| 12 | 6.861 7394 | 8.344 4553 | 3.951 3767 | 6.274 7134 | 12 |
| 13 | 6.850 4680 | 8.329 9236 | 3.960 3209 | 6.272 6457 | 13 |
| 14 | 6.839 1705 | 8.315 2807 | 3.971 4657 | 6.270 5248 | 14 |
| 15 | 6.827 8425 | 8.300 5225 | 3.981 4705 | 6.268 3379 | 15 |
| 16 | 6.816 4841 | 8.285 6453 | 3.993 2931 | 6.265 0887 | 16 |
| 17 | 6.805 0909 | 8.270 6449 | 4.003 8924 | 6.263 7651 | 17 |
| 18 | 6.793 6629 | 8.255 5173 | 4.010 8255 | 6.261 3712 | 18 |
| 19 | 6.782 2045 | 8.240 2579 | 4.012 0195 | 6.258 9252 | 19 |
| 20 | 6.770 7243 | 8.224 8619 | 4.012 8449 | 6.256 4585 | 20 |
| 21 | 6.759 2224 | 8.209 3240 | 4.010 9427 | 6.253 9731 | 21 |
| 22 | 6.747 7030 | 8.193 6384 | 4.006 4951 | 6.251 4842 | 22 |
| 23 | 6.736 1706 | 8.177 7988 | 4.001 9104 | 6.249 0066 | 23 |
| 24 | 6.724 6251 | 8.161 7983 | 3.994 9236 | 6.246 5410 | 24 |
| 25 | 6.713 0710 | 8.145 6298 | 3.987 9050 | 6.244 1011 | 25 |
| 26 | 6.701 5081 | 8.129 2854 | 3.983 0398 | 6.241 6867 | 26 |
| 27 | 6.689 9322 | 8.112 7564 | 3.978 0508 | 6.239 2860 | 27 |
| 28 | 6.678 3433 | 8.096 0342 | 3.975 1049 | 6.236 8996 | 28 |
| 29 | 6.666 7369 | 8.079 1092 | 3.974 0710 | 6.234 5163 | 29 |
| 30 | 6.655 1088 | 8.061 9714 | 3.972 7610 | 6.232 1255 | 30 |
| 31 | 6.643 4589 | 8.044 6105 | 3.973 1841 | 6.229 7288 | 31 |
| 32 | 6.631 7828 | 8.027 0151 | 3.973 2465 | 6.227 3165 | 32 |
| 33 | 6.620 0807 | 8.009 1731 | 3.974 8401 | 6.224 8903 | 33 |
| 34 | 6.608 3481 | 7.991 0717 | 3.977 8305 | 6.222 4414 | 34 |
| 35 | 6.596 5807 | 7.972 6972 | 3.985 5259 | 6.219 9617 | 35 |
| 36 | 6.584 7654 | 7.954 0349 | 3.995 6501 | 6.217 4229 | 36 |
| 37 | 6.572 8935 | 7.935 0694 | 4.009 3333 | 6.214 8089 | 37 |
| 38 | 6.560 9519 | 7.915 7847 | 4.028 7877 | 6.212 0945 | 38 |
| 39 | 6.548 9188 | 7.896 1635 | 4.050 0734 | 6.209 2375 | 39 |
| 40 | 6.536 7812 | 7.876 1884 | 4.073 8321 | 6.206 2167 | 40 |
| 41 | 6.524 5216 | 7.855 8409 | 4.098 1345 | 6.203 0030 | 41 |
| 42 | 6.512 1268 | 7.835 1016 | 4.121 5393 | 6.199 5782 | 42 |
| 43 | 6.499 5882 | 7.813 9500 | 4.144 9614 | 6.195 9343 | 43 |
| 44 | 6.486 8925 | 7.792 3642 | 4.168 1318 | 6.192 0551 | 44 |
| 45 | 6.474 0266 | 7.770 3202 | 4.191 6552 | 6.187 9253 | 45 |
| 46 | 6.460 9731 | 7.747 7931 | 4.215 9142 | 6.183 5227 | 46 |
| 47 | 6.447 7099 | 7.724 7559 | 4.240 4430 | 6.178 8180 | 47 |
| 48 | 6.434 2150 | 7.701 1797 | 4.265 4769 | 6.173 7839 | 48 |
| 49 | 6.420 4623 | 7.677 0342 | 4.290 5552 | 6.168 3866 | 49 |

# TABLE 16 — LOGARITHMS OF VALUES IN TABLE 15

| Age x | log $D_x$ | log $N_x$ | log $C_x$ | log $M_x$ | Age x |
|---|---|---|---|---|---|
| 50 | 6.406 4251 | 7.652 2868 | 4.315 8224 | 6.162 5945 | 50 |
| 51 | 6.392 0728 | 7.626 9033 | 4.340 8648 | 6.156 3697 | 51 |
| 52 | 6.377 3744 | 7.600 8468 | 4.364 9098 | 6.149 6767 | 52 |
| 53 | 6.362 3033 | 7.574 0780 | 4.388 6090 | 6.142 4887 | 53 |
| 54 | 6.346 8240 | 7.546 5549 | 4.411 6485 | 6.134 7662 | 54 |
| 55 | 6.330 9011 | 7.518 2319 | 4.434 1200 | 6.126 4713 | 55 |
| 56 | 6.314 4943 | 7.489 0605 | 4.456 3646 | 6.117 5613 | 56 |
| 57 | 6.297 5549 | 7.458 9881 | 4.478 2829 | 6.107 9812 | 57 |
| 58 | 6.280 0291 | 7.427 9588 | 4.499 7534 | 6.097 6719 | 58 |
| 59 | 6.261 8588 | 7.395 9123 | 4.520 4149 | 6.086 5698 | 59 |
| 60 | 6.242 9854 | 7.362 7848 | 4.540 6138 | 6.074 6135 | 60 |
| 61 | 6.223 3369 | 7.328 5071 | 4.559 7466 | 6.061 7248 | 61 |
| 62 | 6.202 8453 | 7.293 0059 | 4.577 9065 | 6.047 8337 | 62 |
| 63 | 6.181 4333 | 7.256 2019 | 4.595 1014 | 6.032 8603 | 63 |
| 64 | 6.159 0141 | 7.218 0099 | 4.611 2868 | 6.016 7139 | 64 |
| 65 | 6.135 4916 | 7.178 3389 | 4.626 5117 | 5.999 2944 | 65 |
| 66 | 6.110 7552 | 7.137 0914 | 4.640 8602 | 5.980 4850 | 66 |
| 67 | 6.084 6757 | 7.094 1640 | 4.654 1922 | 5.960 1480 | 67 |
| 68 | 6.057 1089 | 7.049 4481 | 4.666 3123 | 5.938 1294 | 68 |
| 69 | 6.027 8955 | 7.002 8310 | 4.676 2325 | 5.914 2596 | 69 |
| 70 | 5.996 8976 | 6.954 1971 | 4.683 3154 | 5.888 4000 | 70 |
| 71 | 5.963 9933 | 6.903 4252 | 4.686 8683 | 5.860 4354 | 71 |
| 72 | 5.929 0916 | 6.850 3854 | 4.686 6352 | 5.830 2914 | 72 |
| 73 | 5.892 1190 | 6.794 9328 | 4.682 5247 | 5.797 9159 | 73 |
| 74 | 5.853 0141 | 6.736 9013 | 4.675 5646 | 5.763 2743 | 74 |
| 75 | 5.811 6502 | 6.676 0954 | 4.666 4446 | 5.726 2528 | 75 |
| 76 | 5.767 8328 | 6.612 2910 | 4.655 7250 | 5.686 6594 | 76 |
| 77 | 5.721 2836 | 6.545 2375 | 4.643 5411 | 5.644 2069 | 77 |
| 78 | 5.671 6484 | 6.474 6644 | 4.629 6883 | 5.598 5234 | 78 |
| 79 | 5.618 5030 | 6.400 2898 | 4.612 9171 | 5.549 1609 | 79 |
| 80 | 5.561 4470 | 6.321 8320 | 4.592 0362 | 5.495 7052 | 80 |
| 81 | 5.500 1230 | 6.239 0085 | 4.566 2208 | 5.437 7959 | 81 |
| 82 | 5.434 2026 | 6.151 5295 | 4.534 6408 | 5.375 1092 | 82 |
| 83 | 5.363 4120 | 6.059 0899 | 4.496 8886 | 5.307 3860 | 83 |
| 84 | 5.287 4996 | 5.961 3529 | 4.452 8968 | 5.234 3945 | 84 |
| 85 | 5.206 1624 | 5.857 9300 | 4.402 6697 | 5.155 8796 | 85 |
| 86 | 5.119 1549 | 5.748 3642 | 4.346 0241 | 5.071 5334 | 86 |
| 87 | 5.026 0312 | 5.632 1107 | 4.282 7838 | 4.981 0123 | 87 |
| 88 | 4.926 3958 | 5.508 5035 | 4.212 8844 | 4.883 9167 | 88 |
| 89 | 4.819 7110 | 5.376 7050 | 4.136 2658 | 4.779 7321 | 89 |
| 90 | 4.705 2594 | 5.235 6415 | 4.052 7361 | 4.667 7625 | 90 |
| 91 | 4.582 0743 | 5.083 9160 | 3.961 8809 | 4.547 0612 | 91 |
| 92 | 4.448 8537 | 4.919 6766 | 3.862 8987 | 4.416 3469 | 92 |
| 93 | 4.303 8668 | 4.740 4016 | 3.754 4927 | 4.273 9149 | 93 |
| 94 | 4.144 8288 | 4.542 4999 | 3.634 6962 | 4.117 5231 | 94 |
| 95 | 3.968 7427 | 4.320 4718 | 3.503 6198 | 3.944 2568 | 95 |
| 96 | 3.770 1044 | 4.064 8363 | 3.362 0464 | 3.748 7057 | 96 |
| 97 | 3.537 1275 | 3.434 6097 | 3.215 1988 | 3.519 1704 | 97 |
| 98 | 3.235 3155 | 3.357 1236 | 3.049 4653 | 3.221 0622 | 98 |
| 99 | 2.745 5340 | 2.745 5340 | 2.734 8101 | 2.734 8101 | 99 |

Table 16

# Appendix B

## Formulas

Formulas of some chapters are summarized at the end of the chapters. This list shows the applications, symbol representations, and locations of the summaries of the formulas.

# LIST OF BASIC FORMULAS

This list shows the *Basic Formulas* for computing the simple interest, compound interest, and annuity types of problems.

| Chapter | Application and Formulas | Formula Number | Page |
|---|---|---|---|
| 9 | Simple interest<br>$I = Pin$<br>$S = P + I = P(1 + in)$ | 9–1<br>9–4 | 272<br>279 |
| 10 | Bank discount<br>$I' = Sdn$<br>$P' = S(1 - dn)$ | 10–1<br>10–2 | 311<br>311 |
| 11 | Compound interest<br>$S = P(1 + i)^n$<br>$P = S(1 + i)^{-n}$<br>$f = \left(1 + \dfrac{j}{m}\right)^m - 1$ | 11–1<br>11–2<br><br>11–4 | 330<br>339<br><br>348 |
| 13 | Ordinary annuity<br>$S_n = R \cdot \dfrac{(1 + i)^n - 1}{i} = Rs_{\overline{n}\rvert i}$<br><br>$A_n = R \cdot \dfrac{1 - (1 + i)^{-n}}{i} = Ra_{\overline{n}\rvert i}$ | 13–1<br><br><br>13–2 | 381<br><br><br>386 & 387 |
| 14 | Complex ordinary annuity<br>$S_{nc} = Rs_{\overline{nc}\rvert i} \cdot \dfrac{1}{s_{\overline{c}\rvert i}}$<br><br>$A_{nc} = Ra_{\overline{nc}\rvert i} \cdot \dfrac{1}{s_{\overline{c}\rvert i}}$ | 14–8<br><br><br>14–9 | 426 & 431<br><br><br>426 & 431 |
| 18 | Simple perpetuity<br>$A_\infty = \dfrac{I}{i}$<br>Complex perpetuity<br>$A_\infty = \dfrac{R}{i} \cdot \dfrac{1}{s_{\overline{c}\rvert i}}$ | 18–1<br><br><br>18–2 | 518<br><br><br>520 |

# Answers to Odd-Numbered Problems

## Exercise 1–1, Page 8

1. $\frac{4}{3}$
3. $\frac{91}{8}$
5. $\frac{35}{12}$
7. $\frac{48}{5}$
9. $\frac{161}{6}$
11. $\frac{40,312}{325}$
13. $1\frac{1}{4}$
15. $1\frac{3}{8}$
17. $3\frac{3}{8}$

19. $8\frac{2}{5}$
21. $5\frac{1}{31}$
23. $37\frac{29}{124}$
25. g.c.d., 4; $\frac{1}{2}$
27. g.c.d., 5; $\frac{2}{3}$
29. g.c.d., 5; $\frac{3}{8}$
31. g.c.d., 121; $\frac{7}{11}$
33. g.c.d., 23; $\frac{3}{8}$
35. g.c.d., 22; $\frac{14}{17}$

37. $\frac{3}{8} = \frac{9}{24}$, $\frac{1}{3} = \frac{8}{24}$
39. $\frac{6}{14} = \frac{36}{84}$, $\frac{5}{12} = \frac{35}{84}$
41. $\frac{5}{6} = \frac{50}{60}$, $\frac{3}{4} = \frac{45}{60}$, $\frac{2}{5} = \frac{24}{60}$

43. $\frac{3}{5} = \frac{42}{70}$, $\frac{1}{2} = \frac{35}{70}$, $\frac{2}{7} = \frac{20}{70}$
45. $\frac{3}{4} = \frac{630}{840}$, $\frac{3}{5} = \frac{504}{840}$, $\frac{3}{6} = \frac{420}{840}$, $\frac{3}{7} = \frac{360}{840}$, $\frac{3}{8} = \frac{315}{840}$
*or*

$\frac{3}{4} = \frac{210}{280}$, $\frac{3}{5} = \frac{168}{280}$, $\frac{3}{2} = \frac{1}{2} = \frac{140}{280}$, $\frac{3}{6} = \frac{120}{280}$, $\frac{3}{7} = \frac{105}{280}$

47. $\frac{21}{32} = \frac{315}{480}$, $\frac{19}{30} = \frac{304}{480}$, $\frac{23}{40} = \frac{276}{480}$, $\frac{25}{48} = \frac{250}{480}$

## Exercise 1–2, Page 13

1. 308,990
3. 288,778.26
5. 219,628.91
7. $\frac{2}{3}$
9. 1
11. $8\frac{2}{3}$
13. $6\frac{5}{12}$
15. $2\frac{21}{40}$
17. $17\frac{1}{8}$
19. $\frac{19}{21}$

21. $1\frac{9}{16}$
23. $1\frac{17}{100}$
25. $11\frac{13}{30}$
27. $22\frac{19}{33}$
29. $67\frac{3}{20}$
31. 177,751
33. 538,353
35. 33,450.853
37. $\frac{1}{2}$
39. $\frac{7}{15}$

41. $\frac{1}{25}$
43. $\frac{3}{7}$
45. $2\frac{1}{3}$
47. $7\frac{2}{3}$
49. $7\frac{7}{9}$
51. $5\frac{74}{99}$
53. $2\frac{1}{4}$
55. $1\frac{5}{6}$
57. $\frac{3}{20}$
59. $7\frac{11}{45}$

61. 4,424
63. 14,742
65. 257,013,594
67. 1,562.94
69. 14,215.52
71. 33.9768
73. $\frac{1}{12}$
75. $\frac{7}{18}$
77. $\frac{1}{2}$

79. $\frac{25}{156}$
81. $\frac{49}{225}$
83. $3\frac{21}{44}$
85. $\frac{10}{171}$
87. $\frac{2}{9}$
89. $8\frac{1}{15}$
91. $152\frac{11}{14}$
93. $3,468\frac{9}{40}$
95. 845

## Exercise 1–3, Page 19

1. 15, 11
3. 6, 62
5. 34, 22
7. 10, 253
9. 16.68, 0
11. .443, .039
13. 18, 16.75
15. 70, .74
17. $5\frac{5}{6}$, 5.83

19. $38\frac{7}{12}$, 38.58
21. $12\frac{455}{641}$, 12.71
23. $24\frac{13,797}{23,106}$, 24.60
25. 12.75
27. 132.44
29. 0.58
31. 7,362.06
33. 1.37
35. 21.01

37. $\frac{7}{2}$
39. $\frac{5}{4}$
41. $\frac{18}{17}$
43. $\frac{110}{339}$
45. 3
47. $\frac{17}{36}$
49. $7\frac{14}{23}$
51. $\frac{7}{9}$
53. $\frac{3}{13}$

55. $3\frac{1}{3}$
57. $16\frac{2}{5}$
59. $6\frac{3}{8}$
61. $2\frac{2}{3}$
63. $1\frac{1}{2}$
65. $\frac{14}{45}$
67. $\frac{25}{8}$
69. $5\frac{9}{31}$

71. $\frac{1}{8}$
73. $1\frac{1}{2}$
75. $\frac{14}{15}$
77. $\frac{45}{32}$
79. $1\frac{1}{15}$
81. $8\frac{31}{41}$
83. $\frac{38}{51}$

## Exercise 1–4, Page 25

1. .75
3. .267
5. .923
7. .575
9. 3.077
11. 4.8
13. 3.35
15. 42.438
17. $\frac{1}{2}$
19. $\frac{11}{25}$
21. $\frac{19}{250}$

23. $1\frac{3}{4}$
25. $3\frac{1}{500}$
27. $11\frac{7}{200}$
29. $4\frac{71}{200}$
31. $2\frac{3.501}{4.000}$
33. 24
35. 16
37. 4,000
39. 1,800
41. 70
43. 132

45. 100
47. 350
49. 30
51. 44
53. 600
55. 200
57. 5
59. 6
61. 1,000
63. 900
65. 156

67. 1,320
69. 3.33
71. 1.65
73. 176
75. 900
77. 1.26
79. 7
81. 2,700
83. 156
85. $.1\dot{6}$
87. $.\dot{1}142857\dot{}$

89. $.38\dot{3}$
91. $.\dot{5}1\dot{8}$
93. $.8\dot{6}$
95. $.11\dot{3}$
97. $\frac{4}{9}$
99. $\frac{1}{9}$
101. $\frac{23}{99}$
103. $\frac{13}{300}$
105. $4\frac{7}{18}$
107. $1\frac{169}{370}$
109. $8\frac{21,047}{49,950}$

## Exercise 2–1, Page 32

1. $-9$
3. $-34$
5. $-38$
7. $-37$
9. 22
11. 31
13. 16
15. 11
17. $-11.23$

19. $-24.37$
21. 12.736
23. 23.057
25. $-23$
27. 7
29. $-27$
31. 2
33. $4a$
35. $-25c$

37. $-25et$
39. $-77f$
41. $57h$
43. $28w$
45. $2cd - 2c$
47. $9ab - a$
49. $10a + 10b + 3$
51. $7xy + 28x + 7y$
53. 14

55. 49
57. 2
59. $-28$
61. $-17.3678$
63. $-31.361$
65. 6.79
67. 14.83
69. $-32$
71. 23

73. $10xy$
75. $40ab$
77. $-5bc$
79. $-2b$
81. $-5a + 6d$
83. $12f$
85. $9h$
87. $a - b + 1$
89. $6a + 3ab - 76b - 14$

## Exercise 2–2, Page 36

1. 30
3. 60
5. 18
7. 35
9. $-24$
11. $-72$
13. $-14$

15. $-2,108$
17. 128
19. 78,125
21. $a^8$
23. $c^4$
25. 144
27. $(xy)^3$

29. $(mn)^a$
31. 15,625
33. $p^{10}$
35. $y^{ab}$
37. $b^{y/x}$
39. 64
41. $-27xy$

43. $20xy^2$
45. $24x^3y^2$
47. $-15p^5q^3$
49. $8a + 6$
51. $20c - 15$
53. $4ta + 4tb$
55. $-21be + 14b^2$

57. $a^2 - b^2$
59. $a^2 - 2ab + b^2$
61. $-4y^2 + 14y - 6$
63. $6t^5 - 6at^3 + 12t^2 - 12a$

## Exercise 2–3, Page 40

1. $-4$
3. $-4$
5. $-9$
7. $-27$
9. 21
11. 19
13. 24
15. $-9$

17. 11
19. $-10$
21. 4
23. $\frac{1}{36}$
25. $a^3$
27. $\frac{1}{x^4}$
29. 25

31. 64
33. $(a/b)^3$
35. $(ab/c)^4$
37. $26x$
39. $21a$
41. $\frac{7}{4a}$
43. $\frac{-3}{x^3}$

45. $\frac{2b^3}{3} - 6b$
47. $-4a^4 + \frac{1}{2}b^2$
49. $-9m^2 - 2mn^7 - 3$
51. $\frac{-9a^2}{4} + a - b$
53. $3x + 5$

55. $(3x^2 - 2x + 1) + \dfrac{37}{8x + 5}$
57. $(5x + 3) + \dfrac{-6x - 11}{5x^2 - 2x + 3}$
59. $4x + \dfrac{14x + 4}{7x^2 - 3}$

## Exercise 2–4, Page 42

1. 14
3. 7
5. 7
7. 1,152

9. 18
11. $-24$
13. 118
15. 39

17. 26
19. 65
21. 309
23. $-8$

25. $3x - 3$
27. $7x - 4$
29. $-42x + 9y$
31. $6x - 15y$

## Exercise 2–5, Page 46

**1.** $5(3a + b)$
**3.** $3(x + 2)$
**5.** $6(-3x + y - z)$
**7.** $(a + 2c)(3x - y)$
**9.** $(a - b)(x + y)$
**11.** $(14c - 2d)(2a + b)$

**13.** $(3x + y^2)(3x - y^2)$
**15.** $(5x - 4y)(5x + 4y)$
**17.** $(x^2 + 7)(x^2 - 7)$
**19.** $(x + 3)^2$
**21.** $(2x + 6)^2$ or $4(x + 3)^2$
**23.** $(6y - 5)^2$

**25.** $(3a + 4b)^2$
**27.** $(x + 2)(x + 1)$
**29.** $(y + 1)(2y + 3)$
**31.** $(a + 1)(2a - 3)$
**33.** $(x + 3)(7x - 1)$
**35.** $(3b + 4)(7b - 5)$

## Exercise 2–6, Page 49

**1.** $x = \frac{7}{3} = 2\frac{1}{3}$
**3.** $x = 3$
**5.** $x = 5$
**7.** $x = 3$
**9.** $x = 12$
**11.** $x = .11$
**13.** $x = 8a/4 = 2a$
**15.** $x = 2d$

**17.** $x = (5n - d)/3c$
**19.** $x = -7a/26$
**21.** $x = \$22$
**23.** $x = 22$ years
**25.** smaller amount $= \$81$
larger amount $= \$179$
**27.** $x = \frac{1,948}{2} = \$974$

**29.** $x = 20$ (dimes)
$12 + 20 = 32$ (quarters)
**31.** original number $= 64$
**33.** 2.5 (hours); 150 (miles)
**35.** $x = 90(\frac{4}{9}) = 40$
**37.** $x = \$120$
**39.** $x = 6$
**41.** 3 (quarters); 9 (dimes); 18 (half-dollars)

## Exercise 2–7, Page 54

**1.** $x = 10$
**3.** $x = 3$; $y = 4$
**5.** $x = 5$; $y = 1$
**7.** $x = 2$; $y = -3$
**9.** $x = 5$; $y = 6$
**11.** $x = -4$; $y = 2$
**13.** $x = 10$; $y = 5$
**15.** $x = -5$; $y = 12$
**17.** $x = \frac{1}{2}$; $y = \frac{1}{3}$
**19.** $x = 2$; $y = 3$
**21.** $x = -1$; $y = 2$

**23.** $x = -2$; $y = -3$
**25.** $x = 1$; $y = 3$
**27.** $x = -3$; $y = 2$
**29.** $x = 4$; $y = -1$
**31.** $x = 2$; $y = -5$
**33.** $x = 4$; $y = -3$
**35.** $x = 5$; $y = -2$
**37.** dependent
**39.** inconsistent
**41.** dependent

**43.** inconsistent
**45.** hat, $15.50
coat, $48.50
**47.** $x = \$7$; $y = \$5$
**49.** $x = 35$ tickets; $y = 5$ tickets
**51.** girl's age, 13
brother's age, 7
**53.** 98
**55.** $x = 35$ pounds at $2.70
$y = 15$ pounds at $3.00

## Exercise 2–8, Page 60

**1.** $\frac{2}{3}$
**3.** $\frac{1}{a - b}$
**5.** $\frac{1}{a + b}$
**7.** $\frac{1}{3x - y^2}$
**9.** $\frac{4}{x^2 - 7}$
**11.** $\frac{4}{x + 3}$
**13.** $\frac{19x}{20}$
**15.** $2\frac{1}{6}\left(\frac{1}{x}\right) = \frac{13}{6x}$

**17.** $\frac{2a + b}{a + b}$
**19.** $\frac{3(4x + 1)}{2(2x + 1)(3x + 1)}$
**21.** $\frac{x}{15}$
**23.** $\frac{-7}{12x}$
**25.** $\frac{c}{a + c}$
**27.** $\frac{21x - 8}{(5x - 6)(-3x + 1)}$
**29.** $\frac{3a^2 b^3 x}{4y^2}$

**31.** $\frac{4n^2}{3ym^2}$
**33.** $\frac{1}{xy(x + y)}$
**35.** $\frac{x(2x + 3)}{(2x - 1)(2x + 1)}$
**37.** $\frac{1}{2}$
**39.** $\frac{2x(6x^2 - y^2)}{(2x - y)(x - y)}$
**41.** $\frac{2x - 1}{5x - 2}$
**43.** $\frac{xy^2 + 2}{2 + x}$

**45.** $x = 48$
**47.** $x = 12$
**49.** 10
**51.** $-6$
**53.** $-9$
**55.** 7
**57.** $3\frac{1}{5}$
**59.** $\frac{a^2 - b^2}{b - c}$
**61.** 45 and 35
**63.** 35 hours
**65.** 120 toy guns
**67.** 10 gallons

## Exercise 2–9, Page 66

**1.** $x=6$, $y=2$  
**3.** $x=7$, $y=1$  
**5.** $x=2$, $y=-4$  
**7.** $x=1$, $y=3$  
**9.** $x=3$, $y=2$  
**11.** $x=-2$, $y=-3$

## Exercise 3–1, Page 74

**1.** $\sqrt[5]{m}$  
**3.** $\sqrt[3]{35}$  
**5.** $\sqrt[4]{x}$  
**7.** $\sqrt[3]{x^5}$  
**9.** $\sqrt[4]{127^3}$  
**11.** $\sqrt[5]{a^3}$  
**13.** $a^{3/5}$  
**15.** $19^{1/2}$  
**17.** $45^{3/2}$  
**19.** $x^{5/3}$  
**21.** $28^{1/3}$  
**23.** $b^{2/6} = b^{1/3}$  
**25.** $\sqrt{x^2 y^4}$  
**27.** $\sqrt{5^4 x} = \sqrt{625x}$  
**29.** $\sqrt[3]{c^3 d^2}$  
**31.** $\sqrt{46,875}$  
**33.** $\sqrt{162t}$  
**35.** $\sqrt{a^5 b}$  
**37.** $17\sqrt{2}$  
**39.** $12\sqrt{3} + 2\sqrt{3} - \sqrt{3} = 13\sqrt{3}$  
**41.** $5\sqrt{7}$  
**43.** $30\sqrt{6}$  
**45.** $24\sqrt{70}$  
**47.** 2  
**49.** $\sqrt{.625}$ or $\dfrac{\sqrt{10}}{4}$  
**51.** $\dfrac{\sqrt[6]{648}}{3}$  
**53.** 19  
**55.** 145  
**57.** 32  
**59.** 67.4  
**61.** 21.313 or 21.31  
**63.** 1.0119 or 1.012

## Exercise 3–2, Page 77

**1.** $x=-1\frac{1}{2}$  
  $x=1\frac{1}{2}$  
**3.** $x=-1\frac{1}{2}$  
  $x=1\frac{1}{2}$  
**5.** $x=\frac{2}{5}$  
  $x=-\frac{4}{3}$  
**7.** $x=\frac{1}{4}$  
  $x=1\frac{1}{2}$  
**9.** $y=-7$  
  $y=1\frac{1}{3}$  
**11.** $y=-1\frac{2}{3}$  
  $y=-\frac{1}{4}$  
**13.** $x=3$  
  $x=2$  
**15.** $x=\frac{1}{3}$  
  $x=4$  
**17.** $x=1\frac{1}{3}$  
  $x=\frac{1}{2}$  
**19.** $x=7$  
  $x=\frac{3}{4}$  
**21.** $x=1\frac{1}{6}$  
  $x=-\frac{2}{3}$  
**23.** $x=2\frac{1}{3}$  
  $x=-2\frac{1}{3}$  
**25.** $m=3$  
  $m=-\frac{2}{7}$  
**27.** $n=1\frac{1}{3}$  
  $n=\frac{3}{8}$  
**29.** $x=1\frac{1}{5}$  
  $x=\frac{3}{7}$  
**31.** $x=\frac{1}{3}$  
  $x=-2\frac{1}{4}$

## Exercise 3–3, Page 82

**1.** $L=22$  
  $S_n=91$  
**3.** $L=16$  
  $S_n=72$  
**5.** $L=3.4$  
  $S_n=16.2$  
**7.** $L=-16$  
  $S_n=-72$  
**9.** $a=13$  
  $S_n=7$  
**11.** $L=22$  
  $d=3$  
**13.** $a=\frac{1}{3}$  
  $L=1$  
**15.** $n=8$  
  $L=-16$  
**17.** $L=6,144$  
  $S_n=12,285$  
**19.** $L=729$  
  $S_n=1,093$  
**21.** $L=1,458$  
  $S_n=2,186$  
**23.** $L=.000018$  
  $S_n=18.181818$  
**25.** When $r=5$, $L=-75$  
  When $r=-6$, $L=-108$  
**27.** $n=6$  
  $L=243$  
**29.** When $r=2$, $S_n=62$  
  When $r=-2$, $S_n=22$  
**31.** $n=6$  
  $a=3$  
**33.** $4\frac{1}{2}$, 7, $9\frac{1}{2}$, 12  
**35.** 3, 5, 7, 9, 11, 13  
**37.** 4, 8, 16, 32  
**39.** 2, 4, 8, 16, 32, 64  
**41.** \$3,172  
**43.** \$395.81

## Exercise 3–4, Page 87

**1.** $x^6 + 6x^5 y + 15x^4 y^2 + 20x^3 y^3 + 15x^2 y^4 + 6xy^5 + y^6$  
**3.** $x^4 + 16x^3 y + 96x^2 y^2 + 256xy^3 + 256y^4$  
**5.** $1 + 7i + 21i^2 + 35i^3 + 35i^4 + 21i^5 + 7i^6 + i^7$  
**7.** $x^6 - 12x^5 y + 60x^4 y^2 - 160x^3 y^3 + 240x^2 y^4 - 192xy^5 + 64y^6$  
**9.** 1.061208  
**11.** 1.1040808  
**13.** 1.1322656  
**15.** 1.7058475  
**17.** .90572  
**19.** .67392  
**21.** 1.0032738  
**23.** 1.0170594

## Exercise 3–5, Page 93

**1.** $\log 4 = 0.602060$
**3.** $\log 0.00325 = 7.511883 - 10$
**5.** $\log 0.2759 = 9.440752 - 10$
**7.** $\log 136 = 2.133539$
**9.** $\log 0.010492 = 8.0208583 - 10$
**11.** $10^{1.025306} = 10.6$
**13.** $10^{3.389520} = 2,452$
**15.** $10^{1.763428} = 58$

**17.** $10^{8.802089 - 10} = .0634$
**19.** $10^{2.0179927} = 104.23$
**21.** $2.454845$
**23.** $0.582404$
**25.** $3.636287$
**27.** $6.596817 - 10$
**29.** $3.375481$

**31.** $1.0191994$
**33.** $N = 159.1$
**35.** $N = 2.79$
**37.** $N = 0.003985$
**39.** $N = 49,100$
**41.** $N = 1.454$
**43.** $N = 0.00002796$

## Exercise 3–6, Page 95

**1.** $7.511455 - 10$
**3.** $3.814481$
**5.** $8.424620 - 10$
**7.** $9.8955 - 10$

**9.** $2.586857$
**11.** $1.916791$
**13.** $N = 3.4377$
**15.** $N = 370.04$

**17.** $.0034377$
**19.** $28,003$
**21.** $2,903.31$
**23.** $.0104341$

## Exercise 3–7, Page 99

**1.** $1.06455$
**3.** $174,605$
**5.** $8.147$
**7.** $-3.097$
**9.** $0.1607$
**11.** $2,803$

**13.** $27$
**15.** $.0008809$
**17.** $1.495$
**19.** $7,783,000$
**21.** $2,025$

**23.** $-38,070$
**25.** $17$
**27.** $3.9$
**29.** $2.89$
**31.** $.8071$

## Exercise 3–8, Page 101

**1.** $1\frac{1}{4}\%$
**3.** $2\%$

**5.** $6\%$
**7.** $2\%$

**9.** $100$
**11.** $30$

## Exercise 4–1, Page 109

**1.** (a) Finite set
   (b) Infinite set
   (c) Empty set
   (d) Finite set
**3.** (a) $A = \{a, b, c, d, e, f, g, h\}$
       $A = \{x | x$ is a letter and $x$ represents each of the first eight letters of the alphabet$\}$
   (b) $A = \{2, 3, 4, 5, 6, 7, 8, 9\}$
       $A = \{x | x$ is an integer and $2 \leq x \leq 9\}$
**5.**

**7.** (a) $A \cup B' = \{7, 8, 9, 10, 11, 13, 14\}$
    (b) $A \cap B' = A = \{7, 8, 10, 11, 14\}$
    (c) $A' = \{5, 6, 9, 12, 13\}$
    (d) $B - A = B = \{5, 6, 12\}$

**9.** (a) $A \cup B = \{a, b, c, d, e, f, g, h, i\}$
    (b) $A \cap B = \{a, e\}$
    (c) $A' = \{b, d, f, j, k\}$
    (d) $A \cup A' = U = \{a, b, c, d, e, f, g, h, i, j, k\}$
    (e) $A - B = A \cap B' = \{c, g, h, i\}$

**11.** (a) $A \cup B = \{1, 2, 3, 4, 5, 6, 7\}$
    (b) $A - C = A \cap C' = \{1, 2, 3\}$
    (c) $A \cap B = \{3, 6\}$
    (d) $B \cap C = \{6, 7\}$
    (e) $A \cap B \cap C = \{6\}$
    (f) $(A \cap B) \cap C = \{5, 6, 7\}$
    (g) $A' \cap B' \cap C = \{8, 9, 10\}$
    (h) $A \cap B \cap C' = \{3\}$

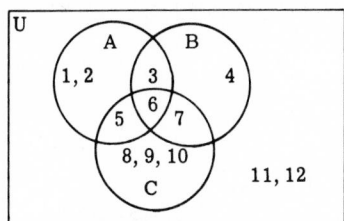

**13.** (a) $(A \cap B') \cup C$ ( //// )
    (b) $(A - B) - C$ ( \\\\\\ )
    (c) $(B - C) \cap A'$ ( ≡ )

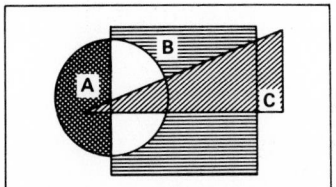

## Exercise 4–2, Page 116

**1.** (a) 6,720
    (b) 120
    (c) 120
    (d) 40,320
    (e) 1
    (f) 20
    (g) 1
    (h) 280,840

**3.** 16
**5.** 24
**7.** (a) 24
    (b) 12
**9.** 6
**11.** 360
**13.** 142,506

**15.** (a) 1
    (b) 4
    (c) 1
**17.** (a) 1,320
    (b) 495
**19.** (a) 120
    (b) 792

## Exercise 4–3, Page 125

**1.** (a) $\frac{6}{23}$
    (b) $\frac{17}{23}$
    (c) $\frac{17}{23}$
    (d) 1
    (e) 0
**3.** $\frac{55}{144}$
**5.** (a) $\frac{23}{35}$
    (b) $\frac{12}{35}$
    (c) $\frac{13}{35}$
    (d) $\frac{35}{35} = 1$
    (e) $\frac{18}{35}$

**7.** (a) $\frac{9}{64}$
    (b) $\frac{15}{64}$
    (c) $\frac{15}{32}$
    (d) $\frac{25}{64}$
    Yes. The probability
    of all possible ways is
    always equal to 1.
**9.** (a) $\frac{1}{8}$
    (b) $\frac{1}{4}$

**11.** (a) $\frac{343}{1,000}$
    (b) $\frac{441}{1,000}$
    (c) $\frac{189}{1,000}$
    (d) $\frac{27}{1,000}$
    Yes.
**13.** $\frac{125}{1,000} = .125$
    No, since the proba-
    bility is not close to .5
    (or $\frac{1}{2}$).
**15.** (a) .99821
    (b) .00179

## Exercise 5–1, Page 134

**1.** $[2, -3]$

**3.** $\begin{bmatrix} 7 \\ 12 \end{bmatrix}$

**5.** $[-2, 3]$

**7.** $\begin{bmatrix} -1 \\ 3 \\ -2 \end{bmatrix}$

**9.** $[30, 10]$

**11.** $\begin{bmatrix} 8 \\ 10 \end{bmatrix}$

**13.** $[24, 48, 54]$

**15.** $\begin{bmatrix} \frac{2}{5} \\ \frac{3}{5} \\ \frac{7}{5} \end{bmatrix}$

**17.** $32$

**19.** $97$

**21.** $\begin{bmatrix} 8 & 15 \\ 3 & 11 \end{bmatrix}$

**23.** $\begin{bmatrix} -4 & 1 \\ 1 & 2 \\ 5 & -2 \end{bmatrix}$

**25.** $\begin{bmatrix} 9 & 27 \\ 6 & 12 \end{bmatrix}$

**27.** $\begin{bmatrix} \frac{1}{4} & \frac{1}{2} \\ \frac{3}{4} & \frac{9}{4} \\ 2 & 1 \end{bmatrix}$

**29.** $\begin{bmatrix} 24 & 81 \\ 14 & 40 \end{bmatrix}$

**31.** $\begin{bmatrix} 21 & 63 & 81 \\ 12 & 32 & 38 \end{bmatrix}$

**33.** $\begin{bmatrix} 51 & 39 & 30 \\ 24 & 20 & 18 \end{bmatrix}$

**35.** $\begin{bmatrix} 46 & 74 \\ 80 & 79 \end{bmatrix}$

**37.** $\begin{bmatrix} 7 & 17 \\ 27 & 63 \\ 32 & 88 \end{bmatrix}$

**39.** $\begin{bmatrix} 70 & 68 \\ 22 & 41 \end{bmatrix}$

**41.** $\begin{bmatrix} 6 & 16 & 19 \\ 21 & 63 & 81 \\ 36 & 68 & 56 \end{bmatrix}$

**43.** $\begin{bmatrix} 12 & 10 & 9 \\ 51 & 39 & 30 \\ 36 & 44 & 60 \end{bmatrix}$

## Exercise 5–2, Page 138

**1.** (a) $10 - 21 = -11$
   (b) $2 \begin{vmatrix} 5 \end{vmatrix} - 3 \begin{vmatrix} 7 \end{vmatrix} = 10 - 21 = -11$

**3.** (a) $-14$
   (b) $-14$

**5.** (a) $240$
   (b) $240$

**7.** (a) $8 - 2 = 6$
   (b) $-2 + 8 = 6$

**9.** $10 - 21 = -11$

**11.** $168 - 60 + 132 = 240$

## Exercise 5–3, Page 143

**1.** $\begin{bmatrix} 1 & -3 \\ 4 & 7 \end{bmatrix} \cdot \begin{bmatrix} 1 & 0 \\ 0 & 1 \end{bmatrix} = \begin{bmatrix} 1 & -3 \\ 4 & 7 \end{bmatrix}$ and $\begin{bmatrix} 1 & 0 \\ 0 & 1 \end{bmatrix} \cdot \begin{bmatrix} 1 & -3 \\ 4 & 7 \end{bmatrix} = \begin{bmatrix} 1 & -3 \\ 4 & 7 \end{bmatrix}$

**3.** (a) & (b) No inverse

**5.** (a) $\begin{bmatrix} -\frac{7}{17} & \frac{5}{17} \\ \frac{9}{17} & -\frac{4}{17} \end{bmatrix}$

   (b) $-\frac{1}{17} \begin{bmatrix} 7 & -5 \\ -9 & 4 \end{bmatrix}$

**7.** $\frac{1}{240} \begin{bmatrix} 93 & 42 & -3 \\ -78 & -12 & 18 \\ -3 & -22 & 13 \end{bmatrix}$

## Exercise 5–4, Page 147

**1.** (a) and (b) $x = 6;\ y = 2$

**3.** (a) and (b) $x = 2;\ y = -3$

**5.** $x = 2;\ y = -3;\ z = 1$

**7.** $x = 1;\ y = -3;\ z = 2$

**Exercise 5–5, Page 153**

1. (a)
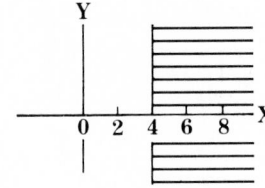
(b)

(c)
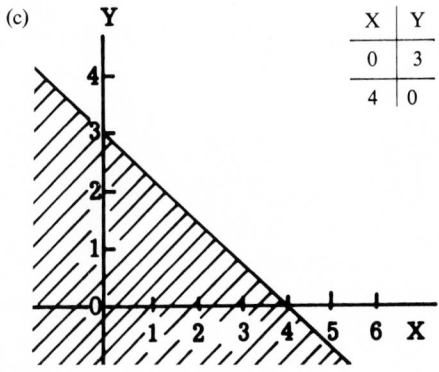

| X | Y |
|---|---|
| 0 | 3 |
| 4 | 0 |

(d)
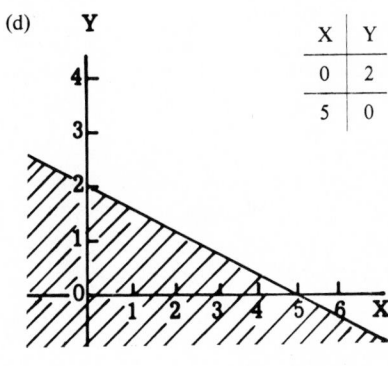

| X | Y |
|---|---|
| 0 | 2 |
| 5 | 0 |

3. (a) $X=0$; $Y=4$; $F=32$
   (b) $X=5$; $Y=2$; $F=23$
5. (a) $X=3$; $Y=6$; $F=66$
   (b) $X=6$; $Y=0$; $F=96$
7. 3 chairs and 2 tables. $35 profit.

**Exercise 5–6, page 159**

1. 7
3. 12
5. 23
7. 61
9. 125
11. 239
13. 1100
15. 11010
17. 101010
19. 110001

21. 1111101
23. 101010000
25. (a) 101, (b) 5
27. (a) 1001, (b) 9
29. (a) 11001, (b) 25
31. (a) 1000000, (b) 64
33. (a) 110, (b) 6
35. (a) 1001, (b) 9
37. (a) 101100, (b) 44
39. (a) 110, (b) 6

41. (a) 101010, (b) 42
43. (a) 1111000, (b) 120
45. (a) 11001000, (b) 200
47. (a) 101110100, (b) 372
49. (a) 11, (b) 3
51. (a) 100, (b) 4
53. (a) 101, (b) 5
55. (a) 1010, (b) 10
57. (a) 10100, (b) 20

**Exercise 6–1, Page 173**

**1.**          NATIONAL INCOME by Distributive Shares, 1976 and 1977
(Billions of Dollars)

| Item | 1976 | 1977 | Increase (+) or Decrease (−) |
|---|---|---|---|
| Compensation of employees ............ | 1,036.3 | 1,109.9 | +73.6 |
| Proprietors' income ................... | 88.0 | 95.1 | + 7.1 |
| Rental income of persons ............. | 23.3 | 24.5 | + 1.2 |
| Corporate profits and inventory valuation adjustment ............... | 128.1 | 125.4 | − 2.7 |
| Net interest ......................... | 88.4 | 95.3 | + 6.9 |
| Total ....................... | 1,364.1 | 1,450.2 | +86.1 |

Source: Department of Commerce, Survey of Current Business, July, 1977.

**3.** (a)          UNITS SHIPPED BY FOX DISTRIBUTORS, 1970–1979

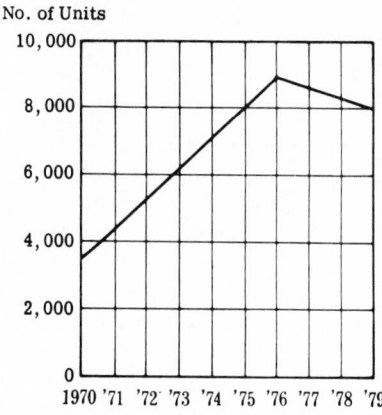

(b)          UNITS SHIPPED BY FOX DISTRIBUTORS, 1970–1979

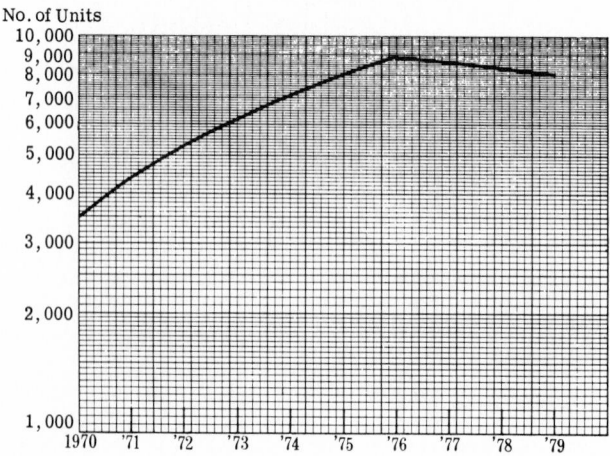

**5.**

**UNITS SHIPPED BY FOX DISTRIBUTORS, 1970–1979**

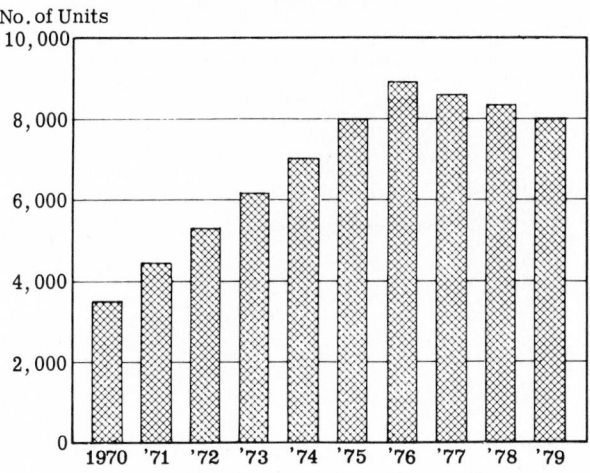

**7.**

**TYPES OF COMMON STOCKS OWNED BY BAGGE INVESTMENT COMPANY**

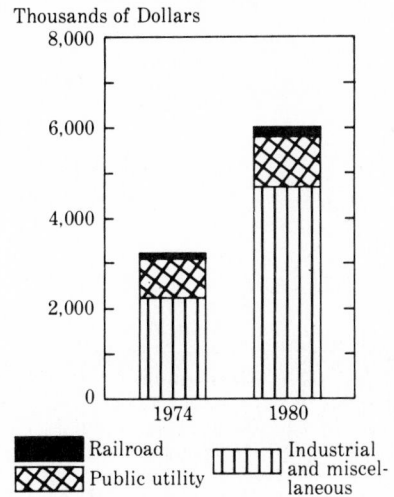

**9.**

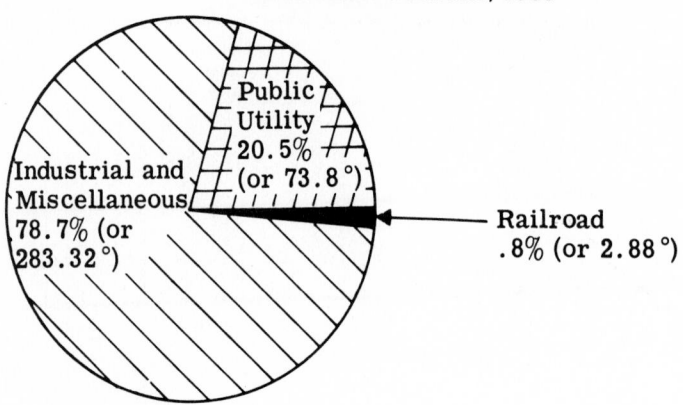

TYPES OF COMMON STOCKS OWNED BY BAGGE
INVESTMENT COMPANY, 1980

### Exercise 6–2, Page 179

**1.** (a) 6, (b) 5, (c) 4
Median

**3.** (a) 21, (b) 22

### Exercise 6–3, Page 184

**1.** (a) 17, (b) 5
**3.** $8.25

**5.** (a) 5, (b) 5.72

### Exercise 6–4, Page 188

**1.** (a) 10, (b) 2.86, (c) 3.38

**3.** (a) $2.13, (b) $2.74

### Exercise 7–1, Page 193

**1.** $\dfrac{25}{5} = \dfrac{5}{1}$

**2.** $\dfrac{13}{32}$

**5.** $\dfrac{104}{63}$

**7.** $\dfrac{245}{913}$

**9.** 20 miles/hour
**11.** $4/day

**13.** $A = 13 : 8$
$B = 4 : 3$
$A$'s ratio is higher
**15.** (a) $\frac{5}{8}$, (b) $\frac{1}{8}$, (c) $\frac{1}{4}$
**17.** 60 and 180
**19.** 108, 162, and 378
**21.** 120, 180, 300, and 420
**23.** 3,080, 800, and 3,808
**25.** $18,000, $12,000, $9,000, and $7,200

### Exercise 7–2, Page 196

**1.** $2\frac{1}{2}$
**3.** $4\frac{2}{3}$
**5.** 250
**7.** 30
**9.** 2

**11.** 6.4
**13.** $41\frac{1}{6}$
**15.** $\frac{1}{3}$
**17.** $96\frac{2}{3}$
**19.** $75

**21.** $77\frac{1}{2}$ feet
**23.** $108
**25.** $1\frac{2}{3}$ hours
**27.** 64

### Exercise 7–3, Page 202

1. (a) 85,200 millimeters, (b) 852 decimeters, (c) .852 hectometer
3. (a) 1,430 decigrams, (b) 14,300 centigrams, (c) .143 kilogram
5. (a) 3,580 grams, (b) 35,800 decigrams, (c) 358 decagrams
7. (a) 10,000 square centimeters, (b) .01 square decameter
9. (a) 50 deciliters, (b) .005 kiloliter
11. (a) 49.21 feet, (b) 16.40 yards
13. (a) 12.428 or 12.43 miles, (b) 21,873.28 yards, (c) 65,619.84 feet
15. (a) 771.60 grains, (b) 1.76 ounces
17. (a) 107,639 square feet, (b) 2.47105 or 2.47 acres
19. (a) 353.147 or 353.15 cubic feet, (b) 13.08 cubic yards
21. (a) 14.189 or 14.19 bushels, (b) 56.756 or 56.76 pecks, (c) 454.048 or 454.05 quarts
23. (a) 55.06 dry liters, (b) 220.24 dry liters, (c) 352.381 or 352.38 dry liters
25. 1,360.78 kilograms
27. 18.58 square meters
29. 10.6286 or 10.63 kilometers per liter

### Exercise 7–4, Page 205

1. .0039
3. .045
5. .14
7. 1.48
9. 45

11. $\frac{3}{50}$
13. $5\frac{1}{4}$
15. $\frac{3}{250}$
17. $\frac{3}{12,500}$
19. $\frac{21}{500,000}$

21. 29%
23. 2.2%
25. .26%
27. 7,200%
29. 146%

31. 2%
33. 371%
35. 92%
37. 1,647%
39. 55%

### Exercise 7–5, Page 207

1. 131.25
3. 18.39
5. 31.10
7. 35.5
9. 10.77
11. 15
13. 5.4375

15. 3
17. 73.44
19. 44.62
21. $191.25
23. (a) $7 (down payment), (b) 80% (of the price—unpaid balance)
25. $1,236 (saving)

### Exercise 7–6, Page 209

1. 25%
3. 200%
5. 14.1%
7. 130%
9. 40%

11. 8%
13. 16.7%
15. 30%
17. 25%

19. 30.6%
21. 36.5%
23. 25% (increase)
25. (a) 10% (loss), (b) $14.50 (loss)

### Exercise 7–7, Page 212

1. 400
3. 5,000
5. 7,000
7. 500
9. 80

11. 182.50
13. 200
15. 120
17. 215

19. 40
21. $2,500
23. $5
25. 180 (inches)

## Exercise 7–8, Page 217

1. $17.60
3. $7.92
5. $14.05
7. $80
9. $53.50
11. $324.50
13. $14

15. $218
17. $243.50
19. $14.40
21. $28.83
23. $120.34
25. $26.10
27. $118.75

29. (a) $28.60, (b) $10.01
31. $35
33. (a) $7.31, (b) $2.19
35. $56
37. (a) $22.49, (b) $27.49
39. $43.20

## Exercise 7–9, Page 219

1. (a) $15, (b) 25%, (c) $33\frac{1}{3}$%
3. (a) $9.15, (b) 24.56%, (c) 32.56%
5. (a) $2.08, (b) 28.57%, (c) 40%
7. (a) $23.10, (b) 26.19%, (c) 35.48%
9. (a) $42.30, (b) 32.92%, (c) 49.07%
11. (a) $275, (b) $250,
13. (a) $39, (b) $37.05
15. (a) $69.30, (b) $52.50

17. (a) $25.42, (b) $12.71
19. (a) $2,145.82, (b) $1,384.40
21. (a) $3,291.70, (b) $2,304.19
23. (a) $229.60, (b) 38.89%, (c) 28%
25. (a) 31.31%, (b) 23.85%
27. (a) $14,000, (b) $19,600
29. $3,000

## Exercise 7–10, Page 223

1. 18.03%
3. 31.03%
5. 31.03%
7. 39.39%
9. 44.44%
11. 60%
13. 16.28%

15. 56.25%
17. 127.27%
19. 300%
21. 900%
23. 11.11%
25. .2063, or 20.63%

27. $\frac{1}{3}$, or $33\frac{1}{3}$%
29. .105, or 10.5%
31. .189, or 18.9%
33. .735, or 73.5%
35. .2647, or 26.47%
37. .8182, or 81.82%

## Exercise 7–11, Page 224

1. 1,288 (bushels)
3. 78.1 (gallons)
5. 28.5 and 47.5
7. 98; 245; 343
9. $710 (Mesk); $994 (Dean)
11. (a) 1,200 decimeters, (b) 12,000 centimeters, (c) 12 decameters, (d) 120,000 millimeters
13. (a) 139.76 feet, (b) 1,677.14 inches, (c) 46.59 yards
15. 5; 10; 22.5; 31
17. 29.75
19. 460
21. $120
23. 150%
25. $360
27. $1,980 *(A)*, $3,168 *(B)*, $4,224 *(C)*
29. $200
31. $10
33. 1,100 TV sets
35. $30
37. $23.04
39. $60
41. $700
43. $.96

45. $45.50
47. $4.08
49. $5.50
51. $3
53. (a) 25%, (b) $33\frac{1}{3}$%
55. (a) $15, (b) $21
57. (a) $12, (b) $7.80
59. 25.93% of selling price
61. 20% of selling price
63. 45.5% of selling price
65. 61.29% of cost
67. 7.06% of cost
69. 56.7% of cost

### Exercise 8–1, Page 233

**1.** (a) $136.80, (b) $63.20, (c) 31.6%
**3.** (a) $100.41, (b) $49.59, (c) 33.06%
**5.** (a) $500, (b) $500, (c) .5 or 50%
**7.** (a) $6.48, (b) $23.52, (c) 78.4%

**9.** (a) $14.75, (b) $.45, (c) 2.96%
**11.** $6.29
**13.** $10.20
**15.** $2,513.70

### Exercise 8–2, Page 236

**1.** (a) $12.72, (b) $3.28
**3.** (a) $17.95, (b) $30.05
**5.** (a) $5.82, (b) $119.88
**7.** $55
**9.** $2,821.43
**11.** $720
**13.** 29.44%
**15.** 31.6%

**17.** 66.52%
**19.** (a) X Co. offered a lower price, (b) The difference is $.85.
**21.** $12.83
**23.** $800
**25.** $650
**27.** $270
**29.** (a) 25%, (b) 32.5%

### Exercise 8–3, Page 239

**1.** (a) $11, (b) $539
**3.** (a) $9.12, (b) $447.08
**5.** (a) $1.95, (b) $63.21
**7.** (a) none, (b) $24.30
**9.** (a) $.59, (b) $29.06

**11.** $1,550.36
**13.** (a) $824.50, (b) $833, (c) $850
**15.** (a) $567.75, (b) $579
**17.** (a) $4, (b) $138

### Exercise 8–4, Page 241

**1.** $1,271.40
**3.** $86.71
**5.** $9,209.38
**7.** $5.52

**9.** $180; $288; $249
**11.** $550
**13.** $2,200
**15.** $11,000

### Exercise 8–5, Page 245

**1.** $.01
**3.** $.03
**5.** $.06
**7.** $.12
**9.** $.20

**11.** $.10
**13.** (a) $.16, (b) $5.54
**15.** (a) $14, (b) $.42
**17.** (a) $3.20, (b) $482.00
**19.** (a) $8,300, (b) $8.25

### Exercise 8–6, Page 247

**1.** (a) 31.25 mills, (b) $6.25
**3.** (a) 20.41 mills, (b) $57.15
**5.** (a) 14.22 mills, (b) $12.80
**7.** (a) 25.55 mills, (b) $10.86

**9.** 18 mills
**11.** $114.30
**13.** (a) 13.89 mills, (b) $69.45

## Exercise 8–7, Page 255

**1.** (a) (1) $50.50, (2) $42.35
  (b) $607.15
  (c) (1) $42.35, (2) $.70, (3) $2.70
  (d) $745.75

(e) Federal income tax
  withheld ................ $ 50.50
  FICA tax ................ 84.70
  Employee's net ............ 607.15
  FUTA tax ................ .70
  State unempl. tax .......... 2.70
  Employer's total cost ...... $745.75

**3.** (a) (1) $48.70, (2) $27.23
  (b) $374.07
  (c) (1) $27.23, (2) None, (3) None
  (d) $477.23

(e) Federal income tax
  withheld ................ $ 48.70
  FICA tax ................ 54.46
  Employee's net ............ 374.07
  Employer's total cost ...... $477.23

**5.** (a) (1) $878.37, (2) $325.19
  (b) $4,171.44
  (c) (1) $325.19, (2) $37.63, (3) $145.13
  (d) $5,882.95

(e) Federal income tax
  withheld ................ $ 878.37
  FICA tax ................ 650.38
  Employee's net ............ 4,171.44
  FUTA tax ................ 37.63
  State unempl. tax .......... 145.13
  Employer's total cost ...... $5,882.95

**7.** (a) (1) $3,990, (2) $1,070.85
  (b) $16,389.15
  (c) (1) $1,070.85, (2) $42.00, (3) $162
  (d) $22,724.85

(e) Federal income tax
  withheld ................ $ 3,990.00
  FICA tax ................ 2,141.70
  Employee's net ............ 16,389.15
  FUTA tax ................ 42.00
  State unemployment tax ..... 162.00
  Employer's total cost ...... $22,724.85

**9.** (a) (1) $82.50, (2) $12.10
  (b) $855.40
  (c) (1) $12.10, (2) None, (3) None
  (d) $962.10

(e) Federal income tax
  withheld ................ $ 82.50
  FICA tax ................ 24.20
  Employee's net ............ 855.40
  Employer's total cost ...... $962.10

**11.** FICA tax: $50.82. Federal income tax withheld: $79.30
**13.** (a) $223.60, (b) $10.85, (c) $188.45
**15.** (a) $40,000, (b) $118,000

## Exercise 8–8, Page 270

**1.** (a) $881, (c) $822
**3.** (a) $3,727, (c) $3,430, (d) $4,607
**5.** (a) $1,194, (d) $1,476
**7.** (b) $2,392.50, (c) $2,597.50

**9.** (a) $2,064, (b) $14
**11.** (a) $4,204.20, (b) $204.20
**13.** $39,132

## Exercise 9–1, Page 275

**1.** $12.34
**3.** $32.40
**5.** $5.70
**7.** $6.30
**9.** $57.12

**11.** (a) 67 days, (b) 66 days
**13.** 157 days
**15.** (a) 39 days, (b) 39 days
**17.** (a) 390 days, (b) 384 days
**19.** (a) 114 days, (b) 113 days

## Exercise 9–2, Page 278

**1.** (a) $\frac{116}{360}$, (b) $\frac{116}{365}$
**3.** (a) $\frac{45}{360}$, (b) $\frac{45}{365}$
**5.** (a) $\frac{30}{360}$, (b) $\frac{30}{365}$
**7.** (a) (1) $63.60, (2) $63.60
   (b) $62.73
**9.** (a) (1) $527.50, (2) $527.50
   (b) $520.27
**11.** (a) (1) $24.66, (2) $24.66
   (b) $24.32

**13.** (a) (1) $8.52, (2) $8.52
   (b) $8.40
**15.** (a) (1) $17.60, (2) $17.60
   (b) $17.36
**17.** $.73
**19.** $5.11
**21.** $6.57
**23.** $.72
**25.** $2.88
**27.** $3.60

## Exercise 9–3, Page 282

**1.** Interest = $1.20
   Amount = $121.20
**3.** Amount = $4,556.25
   Time = 75 days
**5.** Interest = $19.20
   Time = 4 months
**7.** Interest = $7.60
   Interest rate = 4%
**9.** Amount = $2,720
   Time = 2 years
**11.** Amount = $3,979
   Interest rate = 5%
**13.** (a) $633.50, (b) $73,033.50

**15.** Interest = $41.67
   Amount = $1,041.67
**17.** Interest = $129.60
   Amount = $669.60
**19.** (a) $997.50, (b) November 7, 1980
**21.** 3%
**23.** 5%
**25.** 36.73%
**27.** 3 months
**29.** 30 days
**31.** $120 invested at 4%
   $300 invested at 6%

## Exercise 9–4, Page 287

**1.** $328.40
**3.** $5,500
**5.** $225
**7.** $3,400
**9.** $3,000

**11.** $1,580
**13.** $460
**15.** $2,200
**17.** (a) $877.19, (b) $122.81

**19.** (a) $1,607.14, (b) $192.86
**21.** $368.01
**23.** $504.90
**25.** $1,001.64

## Exercise 9–5, Page 292

**1.** (a) $208.66, (b) $208.71
**3.** (a) $363.20, (b) $363.21
**5.** (a) $426, (b) $426.30

**7.** (a) $1,248.34, (b) $1,248.72
**9.** (a) $879, (b) $884.56
**11.** $1,075

**13.** $1,076.01
**15.** $552.32
**17.** $551.61

## Exercise 9–6, Page 297

**1.** $2,030
**3.** $2,951.46
**5.** $7,546.67

**7.** $1,396.72 (each payment)
**9.** (a) $980.39, (b) $1,000, (c) $1,013.33
**11.** $1,517.20 (each payment)

**13.** $819.67 (each payment)
**15.** $4,197
**17.** $4,617.50

## Exercise 9–7, Page 304

**1.** 44 days
**3.** $3\frac{1}{3}$ months
**5.** $2\frac{1}{2}$ months
**7.** 125 days
**9.** 5 months

**11.** 9.22 months, or 9 months and 7 days
**13.** $5\frac{3}{10}$ months
**15.** $5\frac{1}{5}$ months
**17.** 30 days after June 30, or on July 30; $1,212

## Exercise 9–8, Page 306

1. (a) $200, (b) $12.50
3. (a) 105 days, (b) 104 days
5. (a) 513 days, (b) 506 days
7. $I = $20$
   $I_e = $19.73$
9. $I = $4.35$
   $I_e = $4.29$
11. $I = $16.50$
    $S = $456.50$
13. $644.70
15. (a) $12, (b) $612, (c) August 29, 1980
17. 3%
19. 4%
21. 3 months

23. (a) 30 days, (b) 20 days
25. $6,000
27. $5,000
29. $10
31. (a) $818.18, (b) $21.82
33. (a) $2,528.83, (b) $2,528.93
35. (a) $571.43, (b) $600, (c) $612
37. $753.47
39. $1,974.63
41. 94 days from now
43. 44 days
45. 3 months and 14 days
47. 111 days from April 10 or on July 30, 1980

## Exercise 10–1, Page 313

1. $2,800
   $237,200
3. $800, 6%
5. 45 days, $45

7. 6%, $8,887.50
9. $800, $42
11. $900, $39,100
13. $3,445.75

15. $653.27
17. 9%
19. 4 months

## Exercise 10–2, Page 319

1. (a) Feb. 5, 1980
   (b) $2,010
   (c) 20 days
   (d) $11.17
   (e) $1,998.83
3. (a) June 18, 1980
   (b) $1,800
   (c) 50 days
   (d) $15
   (e) $1,785

5. (a) Nov. 3, 1982
   (b) $4,247.25
   (c) 60 days
   (d) $35.39
   (e) $4,211.86
7. (a) Dec. 1, 1983
   (b) $2,537.50
   (c) 30 days
   (d) $14.80
   (e) $2,522.70

9. (a) Aug. 21, 1984
   (b) $1,674
   (c) 75 days
   (d) $31.39
   (e) $1,642.61
11. $7.50, $242.50
13. $4,500
15. $1.58, $378.42

17. (a) June 4
    (b) $2,430
    (c) 80 days
    (d) $21.60
    (e) $2,408.40
19. $36.05, $2,126.95
21. $50,000

## Exercise 10–3, Page 323

1. 8.80%
3. 6.84%
5. 5.83%
7. 10.34%

9. 8.28%
11. 12.37%
13. 4.96%

15. $2,450, 8.16%
17. $3,570, 5.04%
19. 9%, 5.08%

## Exercise 10–4, Page 325

1. (a) $6.30, (b) $623.70
3. (a) $672, (b) $673.08
5. $300
7. $13\frac{1}{3}$%
9. 144 days ($\frac{2}{5}$ years)

11. $600
13. $800.62
15. (a) $25, $1,975
    (b) $1,975.31, $24.69
    $.31 (difference)

17. 5.04%
19. 4.93%

## Exercise 11–1, Page 329

1. $6,615, $615
3. $3,182.70, $182.70

5. $1,157.63, $157.63
7. $10,303.01, $303.01

9. $600, $15
11. $180, $2.70

### Exercise 11–2, Page 333

| | |
|---|---|
| **1.** $1,786.64 | **13.** $1,061.68, $1,061.36, $1,060.90, $1,060 |
| **3.** $7,042.56 | **15.** (a) $1,806.11, $806.11 |
| **5.** $12,797.56 | (b) $3,262.04, $2,262.04 |
| **7.** $1,208.86 | (c) $5,891.60, $4,891.60 |
| **9.** $1,061.52 | **17.** $2,095.89 |
| **11.** $1,855.53 | **19.** $134.77 |

### Exercise 11–3, Page 336

| | | |
|---|---|---|
| **1.** $468.91 | **5.** $617.72 | **9.** $923.90 |
| **3.** $2,058.36 | **7.** $1,169.41 | **11.** $3,192.05 |

### Exercise 11–4, Page 338

| | | |
|---|---|---|
| **1.** $526.88 | **7.** $3,604.70 | **11.** $28,757.50, $12,757.50 |
| **3.** $5,118.60 | **9.** $3,455.34 | **13.** $8,269.33, $3,269.33 |
| **5.** $2,364.86 | | |

### Exercise 11–5, Page 341

| | | |
|---|---|---|
| **1.** $1,220.54 | **9.** (a) $895.17, $504.83 | **13.** $2,558.45, $1,041.55 |
| **3.** $223.36 | (b) $753.71, $646.29 | **15.** $2,729.03 |
| **5.** $1,090.38 | **11.** $1,330.65 | **17.** $1,500 |
| **7.** $1,226.23 | | |

### Exercise 11–6, Page 345

| | | |
|---|---|---|
| **1.** $698.92, $301.08 | **7.** $2,627.73, $419.63 | **13.** $5,051.89 |
| **3.** $1,837.58, $662.42 | **9.** $1,238.09 | **15.** $7,955.10 |
| **5.** $1,860.24, $597.68 | **11.** $5,262.85 | **17.** $5,803.83 |

### Exercise 11–7, Page 350

| | | |
|---|---|---|
| **1.** $\frac{1}{2}$% | **9.** 6.38% | **13.** H—3.04% |
| **3.** $3\frac{1}{2}$% | **11.** 4%, 4.04% | B—3.53% (better) |
| **5.** 1.06% | 4.06%, 4.07% | |
| **7.** 4.26% | | |

### Exercise 11–8, Page 351

| | | |
|---|---|---|
| **1.** 42 | **7.** 10 | **11.** 5 years |
| **3.** 10 | **9.** 10 months | **13.** $1,665.07, July 1, 1985 |
| **5.** 14 | | |

### Exercise 11–9, Page 352

1. $6,574.48, $2,574.48
3. $600, $816.70
5. $3,580.11
7. $1,405.03
9. $2,881.76
11. Method A—$7,094.58, $2,094.58
    Method B—$7,092.28, $2,092.28
13. $522.21, $127.79

15. $563.53, $178.54
17. Method A—$618.87, $181.13
    Method B—$618.86, $181.14
19. 5.14%
21. 5%, 5.06%, 5.09%, 5.12%
23. A—5.61%
    P—6% (higher)
25. 41 months (or 3 years and 5 months)

### Exercise 12–1, Page 359

1. $5,375.67
3. .328%
5. $197.32
7. 83.88

9. $7,555.35
11. (a) 1.2336498 (most accurate)
    (b) 1.2336699 (least accurate)
    (c) 1.2336506 (next accurate)

### Exercise 12–2, Page 363

1. $365.97
3. $3,829.01
5. $1,652.35
7. $6,171.69

9. (a) $3,726.18
   (b) $4,200
   (c) $5,026.06

11. $3,576.91
13. $2,470.79
15. $1,175.06

### Exercise 12–3, Page 367

1. 23.6952 (or 5 years and 333 days)
3. 15.7426 (or 7 years and 314 days)
5. 5.76266 (or 5 years and 275 days)
7. (a) 21.75 (or 5 years and 158 days)
   (b) 25.5882 (or 6 years and 143 days)

9. 14.6029 (or 7 years and 109 days)
11. 1.2672 (or 1 year and 96 days)
13. 2.2239 (or 2 years and 81 days)

### Exercise 12–4, Page 373

1. 6.4%
3. 4.03%
5. 6.94%

7. (a) 5.13%, (b) 22.14%
9. 4.60%

11. (a) $1,040.81, $40.81
    (b) $1,083.29, $83.29

### Exercise 12–5, Page 373

1. (a) 4,813.18, (b) 352.48
   (c) 5.47%, (d) 19.54
3. (a) $409.54, (b) $580.74
5. $491.20
7. $1,718.15
9. $2,356.63

11. 46.275 (or 3 years and 308 days)
13. 4.91%
15. 6.9%
17. (a) 7.25%, (b) 5.65%
19. (a) $11,051.71, $1,051.71
    (b) $12,214.03, $2,214.03

### Exercise 13–1, Page 379

1. $4,030.10, $30.10
3. $1,012.50, $12.50

5. $12,364.82, $364.82
7. $6,556.20

### Exercise 13–2, Page 382

**1.** $25,431.96
**3.** $19,980.42

**5.** $40,455.10
**7.** $10,460.50

**9.** $5,504.75
**11.** $568.91

**13.** $1,445.81
**15.** $6,719.18

### Exercise 13–3, Page 385

**1.** $7,900.99

**3.** $385.48

**5.** $2,284.63

**7.** $5,062.59

### Exercise 13–4, Page 388

**1.** $22,562.87
**3.** $11,133.16

**5.** $32,144.64
**7.** $5,975.19

**9.** $4,868.77
**11.** $3,378.66

**13.** $396.71
**15.** $6,656.88

### Exercise 13–5, Page 394

**1.** $1,634.69, $1,324.41 (Method A)
$1,634.64, $1,324.35 (Method B)

**3.** $8,273.80, $4,978.58 (Method A)
$8,273.90, $4,978.50 (Method B)

**5.** $609,985.50
**7.** $75,153.78
**9.** $146,865.21,
$7,586.74

### Exercise 13–6, Page 397

**1.** $532.19
**3.** $723.51

**5.** $533.09
**7.** $88.70

**9.** $453.45
**11.** $104.02

**13.** $274.69
**15.** $200.75

### Exercise 13–7, Page 401

**1.** $6\% < i < 6\frac{1}{2}\%$, nominal rate $= i$
**3.** $\frac{1}{2}\% < i < \frac{13}{24}\%$, nominal rate: between 6% and $6\frac{1}{2}\%$
**5.** $\frac{7}{8}\% < i < 1\%$, nominal rate: between $3\frac{1}{2}\%$ and 4%
**7.** $i = 1.636\%$, nominal rate $= 3.27\%$

**9.** $i = 3.068\%$, nominal rate $= 6.14\%$
**11.** $i = 1.747\%$, nominal rate $= 6.99\%$
**13.** No. 5.76% (rate on debt)

### Exercise 13–8, Page 404

**1.** 10 (years)
**3.** 22 (months)
**5.** 45 (quarters)

**7.** 15 (semiannual periods)
**9.** 31 (semiannual periods) or $15\frac{1}{2}$ (years)
**11.** 36 (years)

### Exercise 13–9, Page 405

**1.** $3,210.91
**3.** (a) $2,696.10, (b) $1,684.94
**5.** $4,946.19
**7.** $8,337.31
**9.** $1,352.45, $1,064.51

**11.** 7,865.70, $2,274.96
**13.** $33,290.34, $7,451.26
**15.** $334.88
**17.** $130.31
**19.** 4.83%

**21.** 6%
**23.** 4.95%
**25.** 9%
**27.** 18 (quarters), or $4\frac{1}{2}$ years
**29.** $15,278.57

### Exercise 14–1, Page 413

**1.** $9,728.70, $8,376.18
**3.** $1,287.77, $944.88
**5.** $34,871.41, $18,737.77

**7.** $53,965.98, $14,151.70
**9.** $19,070.24
**11.** $15,019.07

**13.** $25,270.94
**15.** $463.03

### Exercise 14–2, Page 417

1. 3%—4%
3. 8%—9%
5. 20 (semiannual periods or 10 years)
7. $2,219.73
9. $340.15
11. 25 (months or 2 years and 1 month)

13. $49.95
15. $110.47
17. $4\frac{1}{2}$%—$5\frac{1}{2}$%
19. $5\frac{1}{2}$%—6%
21. 46 (months or 3 years and 10 months)
23. 32 (quarters or 8 years)

### Exercise 14–3, Page 422

1. $5,016.88, $2,521.31
3. $433.23
5. 16

7. $8,631.34, $7,746.89
9. $5,419.36, $2,669.51
11. $7,167.58

13. 18
15. $4,675.16

### Exercise 14–4, Page 428

1. $11,645.53, $9,454.42
3. $929.27, $511.51
5. $18,867.11, $11,125.25
7. $4,317.58, $3,536.40

9. (a) $13,541.26, $11,697.45
   (b) $13,563.67, $11,678
11. $23,356.54
13. $4,440.20

### Exercise 14–5, Page 432

See answers to problems of Exercise 14–4.

### Exercise 14–6, Page 437

1. $177.08
3. $153.52
5. $116.43
7. $117,034.73
   $95,014.56
9. $1,127.36
   $620.55
11. $41,712.84
   $18,684.56

13. $5,993.08
   $2,399.29
15. $1,846.10
   $719.52
17. $17,998.65
   $8,336.86
19. $634.18
21. $92.41

23. $8,605.02
   $6,378.73
25. $4,092.85
   $3,493.21

### Exercise 14–7, Page 439

1. $5,121.30
   $3,528
3. $5,058.07
   $3,484.45
5. (a) $5,062.09
      $3,481.83
   (b) $5,052.13
      $3,488.32
7. (a) $5,125.63
      $3,525.54
   (b) $5,114.89
      $3,531.65

9. $1,167.44
11. $1,005.14
13. $2,338.73
15. $15,291.52
17. $2,788.67
   $2,070.50
19. $420.05
21. (a) $418.36
    (b) $439.76
23. $23.18
25. $23.16
27. 5%—$5\frac{1}{2}$%

29. 5%—$5\frac{1}{2}$%
31. 30
33. 36
35. $2,151.83
   $1,379.68
37. $618.31
39. 46
41. (a) $5,101.01
    (b) $4,901.97
    (c) $4,853.43
    (d) $4,710.69

## Exercise 15–1, Page 447

**1.** $304.91
  $2,333.07

**3.** $1,025.12
  $1,014.97

**5.** $562.89
  $5,799.31

**7.** $50.09
  $129.09

**9.** $R = $1,614.16

| (1) | (2)<br><br>(2) − (5) | (3)<br>(2) ×<br>3% | (4) | (5)<br><br>(4) − (3) |
|---|---|---|---|---|
| 1 | $6,000.00 | $180.00 | $1,614.16 | $1,434.16 |
| 2 | 4,565.84 | 136.98 | 1,614.16 | 1,477.18 |
| 3 | 3,088.66 | 92.66 | 1,614.16 | 1,521.50 |
| 4 | 1,567.16 | 47.01 | 1,614.17 | 1,567.16 |
| Total | | $456.65 | $6,456.65 | $6,000.00 |

**11.** $R = $955.57

| (1) | (2)<br><br>(2) − (5) | (3)<br>(2) ×<br>2% | (4) | (5)<br><br>(4) − (3) |
|---|---|---|---|---|
| 1 | $7,000.00 | $140.00 | $ 955.57 | $ 815.57 |
| 2 | 6,184.43 | 123.69 | 955.57 | 831.88 |
| 3 | 5,352.55 | 107.05 | 955.57 | 848.52 |
| 4 | 4,504.03 | 90.08 | 955.57 | 865.49 |
| 5 | 3,638.54 | . . . | . . . | . . . |
| Total | | $460.82 | $3,822.28 | $3,361.46 |

## Exercise 15–2, Page 451

**1.** (a) 26
  (b) $1,084.32
  (c) $21.69 (interest)
    $178.31 (principal)
  (d) $159.49
    $5,159.49

**3.** (a) 6
  (b) $2,245.64
  (c) $44.91
    $955.09
  (d) $322.69
    $5,322.69

**5.** (a) 34
  (b) $1,178.53
  (c) $11.79
    $38.21
  (d) $.72
    $1,650.72

**7.**

| (1) | (2)<br><br>(2) − (5) | (3)<br>(2) ×<br>3% | (4) | (5)<br><br>(4) − (3) |
|---|---|---|---|---|
| 1 | $8,000.00 | $240.00 | $2,500.00 | $2,260.00 |
| 2 | 5,740.00 | 172.20 | 2,500.00 | 2,327.80 |
| 3 | 3,412.20 | 102.37 | 2,500.00 | 2,397.63 |
| 4 | 1,014.57 | 30.44 | 1,045.01 | 1,014.57 |
| Total | | $545.01 | $8,545.01 | $8,000.00 |

## Exercise 15–3, Page 455

**1.** (a) $54.00 (higher monthly payment), (b) $52.15
**3.** 11.04% compounded monthly
**5.**

| (1) | (2) | (3) | (4) | (5) Multiple of $500, close to | (6) |
|---|---|---|---|---|---|
| | (2) − (5) | (2) × 5% | 34,646.22 − (3) | (4) | (3) + (5) |
| 1 | $150,000 | $ 7,500 | $27,146.22 | $ 27,000 | $ 34,500 |
| 2 | 123,000 | 6,150 | 28,496.22 | 28,500 | 34,650 |
| 3 | 94,500 | 4,725 | 29,921.22 | 30,000 | 34,725 |
| 4 | 64,500 | 3,225 | 31,421.22 | 31,500 | 34,725 |
| 5 | 33,000 | 1,650 | 32,996.22 | 33,000 | 34,650 |
| Total | | $23,250 | | $150,000 | $173,250 |

## Exercise 15–4, Page 459

**1.** (a) $150
   (b) $259.47
   (c) $1,616.38
   (d) $4,383.62
   (e) $24.25

**3.** (a) $300
   (b) $1,144.67
   (c) $6,016.76
   (d) $3,983.24
   (e) $150.42

**5.** (a) $31.50
   (b) $73.71
   (c) $243.98
   (d) $206.02
   (e) $24.40

**7.**

| (1) | (2) 2% × (5) | (3) | (4) (2) + (3) | (5) (4) + (5) | (6) Book Value $5,000 − (5) |
|---|---|---|---|---|---|
| 1 | . . . | $1,213.12 | $1,213.12 | $1,213.12 | $3,786.88 |
| 2 | $ 24.26 | 1,213.12 | 1,237.38 | 2,450.50 | 2,549.50 |
| 3 | 49.01 | 1,213.12 | 1,262.13 | 3,712.63 | 1,287.37 |
| 4 | 74.25 | 1,213.12 | 1,287.37 | 5,000.00 | . . . |
| Total | $147.52 | $4,852.48 | $5,000.00 | | |

**9.**

| (1) | (2) | (3) | (4) (2) − (3) | (5) 1,213.12 + (4) | (6) (3) + (5) |
|---|---|---|---|---|---|
| 1 | . . . | . . . | . . . | $1,213.12 | $1,213.12 |
| 2 | $24.26 | $ 24.26 | . . . | 1,213.12 | 1,237.38 |
| 3 | 49.01 | 73.52 | −$24.51 | 1,188.61 | 1,262.13 |
| 4 | 74.25 | 111.38 | − 37.13 | 1,175.99 | 1,287.37 |
| Total | | $209.16 | | $4,790.84 | $5,000.00 |

2,450.50 × 3% = 73.52
3,712.63 × 3% = 111.38

## Exercise 15–5, Page 460

**1.** $1,497.72, $18,786.47
**3.** $R = $768.84

| (1) | (2) | (3) (2) × 1% | (4) | (5) |
|---|---|---|---|---|
| 1 | $3,000.00 | $30.00 | $ 768.84 | $ 738.84 |
| 2 | 2,261.16 | 22.61 | 768.84 | 746.23 |
| 3 | 1,514.93 | 15.15 | 768.84 | 753.69 |
| 4 | 761.24 | 7.61 | 768.85 | 761.24 |
| | | $75.37 | $3,075.37 | $3,000.00 |

**5.**

| (1) | (2) | (3) (2) × 5% | (4) | (5) |
|---|---|---|---|---|
| 1 | $10,000.00 | $ 500.00 | $ 1,500.00 | $ 2,000.00 |
| 2 | 8,500.00 | 425.00 | 1,575.00 | 2,000.00 |
| 3 | 6,925.00 | 346.25 | 1,653.75 | 2,000.00 |
| 4 | 5,271.25 | 263.56 | 1,736.44 | 2,000.00 |
| 5 | 3,534.81 | 176.74 | 1,823.26 | 2,000.00 |
| 6 | 1,711.55 | 85.58 | 1,711.55 | 1,797.13 |
| | | $1,797.13 | $10,000.00 | $11,797.13 |

**7.** $9,474.97                **11.** (a) $105
**9.** $47.37, $52.63                    (b) 10.8% compounded monthly
**13.**

| (1) | (2) (2) − (5) | (3) (2) × 10% | (4) 79,139.24 − (3) | (5) | (6) (3) + (5) |
|---|---|---|---|---|---|
| 1 | $300,000 | $30,000 | $49,139.24 | $49,000 | $79,000 |
| 2 | 251,000 | 25,100 | 54,039.24 | 54,000 | 79,100 |
| 3 | 197,000 | 19,700 | 59,439.24 | 59,000 | 78,700 |
| 4 | 138,000 | 13,800 | 65,339.24 | 65,000 | 78,800 |
| 5 | 73,000 | 7,300 | 71,839.24 | 73,000 | 80,300 |
| Total | | $95,900 | | $300,000 | $395,900 |

**15.** (a) $200
(b)

| (1) | (2) (5) × 2% | (3) | (4) (2) + (3) | (5) | (6) Book Value $5,000 − (5) |
|---|---|---|---|---|---|
| 1 | . . . | $ 960.79 | $ 960.79 | $ 960.79 | $4,039.21 |
| 2 | $ 19.22 | 960.79 | 980.01 | 1,940.80 | 3,059.20 |
| 3 | 38.82 | 960.79 | 999.61 | 2,940.41 | 2,059.59 |
| 4 | 58.81 | 960.79 | 1,019.60 | 3,960.01 | 1,039.99 |
| 5 | 79.20 | 960.79 | 1,039.99 | 5,000.00 | . . . |
| | $196.05 | $4,803.95 | $5,000.00 | | |

**17.** (a) $1,060.79
(b) $1,060.79

**19.**

| (1) | (2) | (3) | (4)<br>(2) −<br>(3) | (5) | (6)<br>(3) +<br>(5) |
|---|---|---|---|---|---|
| 1 | . . . | . . . | . . . | $ 960.79 | $ 960.79 |
| 2 | $19.22 | $ 19.22 | . . . | 960.79 | 980.01 |
| 3 | 38.82 | 58.22 | −$19.40 | 941.39 | 999.61 |
| 4 | 58.81 | 88.21 | − 29.40 | 931.39 | 1,019.60 |
| 5 | 79.20 | 158.40 | − 79.20 | 881.59 | 1,039.99 |
|  |  | $324.05 |  | $4,675.95 | $5,000.00 |

**21.** (a) $7,914.59
$7,085.41
(b) $118.72

## Exercise 16–1, Page 466

**1.** $1,043.76
**3.** $1,740.56
**5.** $737.94

**7.** $4,983.86
**9.** (a) $11,249.94
(b) $11,649.96

**11.** (a) $1,856.59
(b) $1,712.93

## Exercise 16–2, Page 470

**1.** (a) $4,277.59
(b) $100
(c) $4,177.59
**3.** (a) $4,537.18
(b) $41.67
(c) $4,495.51

**5.** (a) $962.45
(b) $3
(c) $959.45
**7.** (a) $8,259.54
(b) $75
(c) $8,184.54

**9.** (a) $2,904.13
(b) $2,866.63
**11.** $7,515.15
**13.** (a) $2,000
(b) $12.50
(c) $2,012.50

## Exercise 16–3, Page 473

**1.** (a) $175.04 (premium), (b) $4,175.04
**3.** (a) $483.17 (discount), (b) $4,516.83
**5.** (a) $56.44 (premium), (b) $956.44

**7.** (a) $1,788.50 (discount), (b) $8,211.50
**9.** (a) $195.83 (discount), (b) $2,804.17
**11.** (a) 0, (b) $3,000

## Exercise 16–4, Page 477

**1.** $4,094.27

| (1) | (2)<br>4,000<br>× 2½% | (3)<br>(5) × 2% | (4)<br>(2) − (3) | (5)<br>(5) − (4) |
|---|---|---|---|---|
| 0 | . . . | . . . | . . . | $4,094.27 |
| 1 | $100 | $ 81.89 | $18.11 | 4,076.16 |
| 2 | 100 | 81.52 | 18.48 | 4,057.68 |
| 3 | 100 | 81.15 | 18.85 | 4,038.83 |
| 4 | 100 | 80.78 | 19.22 | 4,019.61 |
| 5 | 100 | 80.39 | 19.61 | 4,000.00 |
|  | $500 | $405.73 | $94.27 |  |

**3.** $3,819.40

| (1) | (2)<br>4,000<br>$\times 2\frac{1}{2}\%$ | (3)<br>(5) $\times 3\frac{1}{2}\%$ | (4)<br>(3) − (2) | (5)<br>(5) + (4) |
|---|---|---|---|---|
| 0 | . . . | . . . | . . . | $3,819.40 |
| 1 | $100 | $133.68 | $33.68 | 3,853.08 |
| 2 | 100 | 134.86 | 34.86 | 3,887.94 |
| 3 | 100 | 136.08 | 36.08 | 3,924.02 |
| 4 | 100 | 137.34 | 37.34 | 3,961.36 |
| 5 | 100 | 138.64 * | 38.64 | 4,000.00 |
| | $500 | $680.60 | $180.60 | |

* 138.65 —— 1¢ for correction.

**5.** $8,229.82

### Exercise 16–5, Page 481

**1.** 3.036%    **5.** 4.671%    **9.** 6.250%
**3.** 4.424%    **7.** 4.956%    **11.** 3.830%

### Exercise 16–6, Page 484

**1.** $1,023.30    **7.** 3.20% < ? < 3.25%    **13.** (a) $3,945.12    **15.** 3.51%
**3.** $2,927.40    **9.** 3.40% < ? < 3.45%    (b) $50
**5.** $482.19      **11.** $1,935.76           (c) $3,995.12

### Exercise 16–7, Page 486

**1.** (a) $2,905.87    **3.** (a) $3,098.87    **5.** $17,328.15
   (b) $1,170.93       (b) $1,205.53          **7.** $15,654.04

### Exercise 16–8, Page 488

**1.** (a) $956.24    **5.** (a) $1,920    **9.** (a) $6,560.36
   (b) $979.67        (b) $13.33          (b) $7,000
   (c) $932.80        (c) $1,933.33
**3.** (a) $964.21    **7.** (a) $475.22
   (b) $6.67          (b) $7,475.22
   (c) $957.54

**11.** (a) $5,888.49
   (b)

| (1) | (2)<br>6,000<br>$\times 2\frac{1}{2}\%$ | (3)<br>(5) $\times 3\%$ | (4)<br>(3) − (2) | (5)<br>(5) + (4) |
|---|---|---|---|---|
| 0 | . . . | . . . | . . . | $5,888.49 |
| 1 | $150 | $176.65 | $ 26.65 | 5,915.14 |
| 2 | 150 | 177.45 | 27.45 | 5,942.59 |
| 3 | 150 | 178.28 | 28.28 | 5,970.87 |
| 4 | 150 | 179.13 | 29.13 | 6,000.00 |
| | $600 | $711.51 | $111.51 | |

**13.** (a) $6,231.26
    (b)

| (1) | (2)<br>6,000<br>$\times 2\frac{1}{2}\%$ | (3)<br>(5)<br>$\times 1\frac{1}{2}\%$ | (4)<br><br>(2) − (3) | (5)<br><br>(5) − (4) |
|---|---|---|---|---|
| 0 | . . . | . . . | . . . | $6,231.26 |
| 1 | $150 | $ 93.47 | $ 56.53 | 6,174.73 |
| 2 | 150 | 92.62 | 57.38 | 6,117.35 |
| 3 | 150 | 91.76 | 58.24 | 6,059.11 |
| 4 | 150 | 90.89 | 59.11 | 6,000.00 |
| | $600 | $368.74 | $231.26 | |

**15.** 3.738%          **25.** (a) $9,790.15
**17.** 7.755%               (b) $3,944.98
**19.** $8,154.96     **27.** $20,275.82
**21.** $9,906.20
**23.** 3.264%

## Exercise 17–1, Page 494

**1.** $2,250
**3.** $480

| (1) | (2) | (3) | (4) |
|---|---|---|---|
| 0 | . . . | . . . | $2,650 |
| 1 | $ 480 | $ 480 | 2,170 |
| 2 | 480 | 960 | 1,690 |
| 3 | 480 | 1,440 | 1,210 |
| 4 | 480 | 1,920 | 730 |
| 5 | 480 | 2,400 | 250 |
| Total | $2,400 | | |

**5.** $440, $592, $496, $464, $408

| (1) | (2) | (3) | (4) |
|---|---|---|---|
| 0 | . . . | . . . | $2,650 |
| 1 | $ 440 | $ 440 | 2,210 |
| 2 | 592 | 1,032 | 1,618 |
| 3 | 496 | 1,528 | 1,122 |
| 4 | 464 | 1,992 | 658 |
| 5 | 408 | 2,400 | 250 |
| Total | $2,400 | | |

**7.** $840

## Exercise 17–2, Page 500

**1.** $900, $750, $600, $450, $300, $150

| (1) | (2) | (3) | (4) |
|---|---|---|---|
| 0 | . . . | . . . | $3,350 |
| 1 | $ 900 | $ 900 | 2,450 |
| 2 | 750 | 1,650 | 1,700 |
| 3 | 600 | 2,250 | 1,100 |
| 4 | 450 | 2,700 | 650 |
| 5 | 300 | 3,000 | 350 |
| 6 | 150 | 3,150 | 200 |
| | $3,150 | | |

**3.** $639.13, $593.48, $547.83, $502.17, $456.52, $410.87
**5.** (a) $33\frac{1}{3}\%$ or $\frac{1}{3}$ (rate)

| (1) | (2) $(4) \times \frac{1}{3}$ | (3) | (4) |
|---|---|---|---|
| 0 | . . . | . . . | $3,350.00 |
| 1 | $1,116.67 | $1,116.67 | 2,233.33 |
| 2 | 744.44 | 1,861.11 | 1,488.89 |
| 3 | 496.30 | 2,357.41 | 992.59 |
| 4 | 330.86 | 2,688.27 | 661.73 |
| 5 | 220.58 | 2,908.85 | 441.15 |
| 6 | 147.05 | 3,055.90 | 294.10 |
| | $3,055.90 | | |

(b) .374831 (rate)

| (1) | (2) $(4) \times .374831$ | (3) | (4) |
|---|---|---|---|
| 0 | . . . | . . . | $3,350.00 |
| 1 | $1,255.68 | $1,255.68 | 2,094.32 |
| 2 | 785.02 | 2,040.70 | 1,309.30 |
| 3 | 490.77 | 2,531.47 | 818.53 |
| 4 | 306.81 | 2,838.28 | 511.72 |
| 5 | 191.81 | 3,030.09 | 319.91 |
| 6 | 119.91 | 3,150.00 | 200.00 |
| | $3,150.00 | | |

### Exercise 17–3, Page 504

**1.** $607.23, $607.23, $607.23, $607.21

| (1) | (2) | (3)<br>(6) × 5% | (4)<br>(2) − (3) | (5) | (6)<br>2,400 − (5) |
|---|---|---|---|---|---|
| 0 | . . . | . . . | . . . | . . . | $2,400.00 |
| 1 | $  607.23 | $120.00 | $  487.23 | $  487.23 | 1,912.77 |
| 2 | 607.23 | 95.64 | 511.59 | 998.82 | 1,401.18 |
| 3 | 607.23 | 70.06 | 537.17 | 1,535.99 | 864.01 |
| 4 | 607.21 | 43.20 | 564.01 | 2,100.00 | 300.00 |
|  | $2,428.90 | $328.90 | $2,100.00 |  |  |

**3.** $487.23, $511.59, $537.17, $564.01

| (1) | (2) | (3)<br>(5) × 5% | (4)<br>(2) + (3) | (5) | (6)<br>2,400 − (5) |
|---|---|---|---|---|---|
| 0 | . . . | . . . | . . . | . . . | $2,400.00 |
| 1 | $  487.23 | . . . | $  487.23 | $  487.23 | 1,912.77 |
| 2 | 487.23 | $  24.36 | 511.59 | 998.82 | 1,401.18 |
| 3 | 487.23 | 49.94 | 537.17 | 1,535.99 | 864.01 |
| 4 | 487.21 | 76.80 | 564.01 | 2,100.00 | 300.00 |
|  | $1,948.90 | $151.10 | $2,100.00 |  |  |

**5.** $864.01

### Exercise 17–4, Page 507

**1.** (a) 10.33%, (b) 9.25 (years)      **3.** (a) 10.66%, (b) 8.66 (years)      **5.** 9.2303 (years)

### Exercise 17–5, Page 512

**1.** (a) $28,000      (d) $2,000      (c) 7.69%      (c) 6.1%
(b) $.07      **3.** (a) $6,692.76      **5.** (a) $7,170.81      **7.** $55,630.58
(c) $7,000      (b) $2,307.24      (b) $1,829.19      **9.** $55,497.07

### Exercise 17–6, Page 514

**1.** (a) $540
(b) $900, $720, $540, $360, $180
(c) —1 $1,200, $720, $432, $259.20, $155.52
    —2 $1,107.17, $698.55, $440.76, $278.09, $175.43
(d) $658.97

| (1) | (2) | (3)<br>(6) × 6% | (4)<br>(2) − (3) | (5)<br>from (4) | (6)<br>Book Value |
|---|---|---|---|---|---|
| 0 | . . . | . . . | . . . | . . . | $3,000.00 |
| 1 | $  658.97 | $180.00 | $  478.97 | $  478.97 | 2,521.03 |
| 2 | 658.97 | 151.26 | 507.71 | 986.68 | 2,013.32 |
| 3 | 658.97 | 120.80 | 538.17 | 1,524.85 | 1,475.15 |
| 4 | 658.97 | 88.51 | 570.46 | 2,095.31 | 904.69 |
| 5 | 658.97 | 54.28 | 604.69 | 2,700.00 | 300.00 |
|  | $3,294.85 | $594.85 | $2,700.00 |  |  |

(e) $478.97, $507.71, $538.17, $570.46, $604.69

| (1) | (2) | (3) (5) × 6% | (4) (2) + (3) | (5) from (4) | (6) Book Value |
|---|---|---|---|---|---|
| 0 | . . . | . . . | . . . | . . . | $3,000.00 |
| 1 | $ 478.97 | . . . | $ 478.97 | $ 478.97 | 2,521.03 |
| 2 | 478.97 | $ 28.74 | 507.71 | 986.68 | 2,013.32 |
| 3 | 478.97 | 59.20 | 538.17 | 1,524.85 | 1,475.15 |
| 4 | 478.97 | 91.49 | 570.46 | 2,095.31 | 904.69 |
| 5 | 478.97 | 125.72 | 604.69 | 2,700.00 | 300.00 |
| | $2,394.85 | $305.15 | $2,700.00 | | |

**3.** $88 (first year),
$80 (second year)
**5.** 8.96%
**7.** (a) $496,000, $124,000
(b) $41,000

**9.** (a) $115,077.87
(b) $49,922.13
(c) 9.98%
**11.** $554,564.76
**13.** $554,062.11

## Exercise 18–1, Page 521

**1.** $10,000
**3.** $19,751.46
**5.** $17,850
**7.** $20,435.98

**9.** (a) $50,000
(b) $51,000
**11.** (a) $49,751.24
(b) $50,751.24

**13.** $16,666.67
**15.** $16,213.29

## Exercise 18–2, Page 526

**1.** (a) $2,000
(b) $1,297.06
**3.** $395,061.73
**5.** $12,400
**7.** $12,141.29
**9.** $34,900.18
**11.** $36,555.75
**13.** $4,393.60

## Exercise 18–3, Page 528

**1.** $2,970.56 (first is less)
**3.** $2,874.05 (second is less)
**5.** $1,126.20
**7.** $200.64

## Exercise 18–4, Page 529

**1.** $20,000
**3.** $20,100
**5.** $3,316.72
**7.** $3,366.72

**9.** (a) $16,666.67
(b) $24,875.62
**11.** $126,472.24
**13.** $129,413.60

**15.** $25,479.28
**17.** $X$ ($K$ = $1,044.94)
**19.** $1,013.48
**21.** $213.48

## Exercise 19–1, Page 535

**1.** (a) 9,868,375
(b) 9,612,127
(c) 9,439,447
(d) 9,000,587
(e) 3,221,884
(f) 6,415

**3.** (a) 13,322
(b) 18,167
(c) 21,239
(d) 56,910
(e) 254,835
(f) 6,415

**5.** (a) 1.23
(b) 1.79
(c) 14.21
(d) 49.79
**7.** (a) 45,175
(b) 376

### Exercise 19–2, Page 538

**1.** $1,750.12    **7.** $4,037.64    **13.** $682.83
**3.** $754.13    **9.** $668.64    **15.** $731.37
**5.** $1,896.06    **11.** $610.14

### Exercise 19–3, Page 542

**1.** $27,453.63    **5.** $37,566.13    **9.** $815.70
**3.** $30,441.20    **7.** $66,456.60    **11.** $4,710.63

### Exercise 19–4, Page 546

**1.** $28,453.63    **7.** $783.73    **13.** $15,075.10
**3.** $19,783.07    **9.** $129.93    **15.** $668.84
**5.** $86,891.17    **11.** $14,555.52

### Exercise 19–5, Page 551

**1.** $8,643.27    **7.** $12,265.89    **13.** $5,467.49
**3.** $29,314.54    **9.** $8,881.77    **15.** $1,190.70
**5.** $940.81    **11.** $912.19

### Exercise 19–6, Page 553

**1.** (a) 9,842,241    **3.** $1,629.23    **11.** (a) $351.45    **17.** $8,309.58
    (b) 8,431,654    **5.** $869.97        (b) $364.25    **19.** (a) $450.08
    (c) 19,760    **7.** (a) $82,090.80    **13.** $577.50        (b) $462.41
    (d) 179,271        (b) $79,090.80    **15.** (a) $10,109.25    **21.** $545.25
    (e) .00251    **9.** $65,233.03        (b) $10,388.50
    (f) .00583

### Exercise 20–1, Page 560

**1.** (a) $693.76    **5.** (a) $570.39    **9.** (a) $248.08    **11.** $420.13
    (b) $25.91        (b) $32.38        (b) $377.59    **13.** $17.67
**3.** (a) $822.48    **7.** (a) $730.81        (c) $678.62    **15.** $33.86
    (b) $92.80        (b) $69.54        (d) $890.62

### Exercise 20–2, Page 563

**1.** (a) $10.43    **5.** (a) $68.55    **9.** (a) $80.42, $9.03    **11.** (a) $54.78
    (b) $2.20        (b) $6.59        (b) $100.45, $11.30        (b) $2.98
**3.** (a) $103.97    **7.** (a) $273.12        (c) $522.99, $61.02    **13.** $3.49
    (b) $8.38        (b) $49.09

### Exercise 20–3, Page 566

**1.** (a) $884.35
   (b) $186.51
**3.** (a) $1,394.82
   (b) $112.43

**5.** (a) $1,651.03
   (b) $89.55
**7.** (a) $2,625.94
   (b) $224.44

**9.** (a) $498.91
   (b) $24.28
**11.** (a) $513.23
   (b) $25.72

**13.** $27.27

### Exercise 20–4, Page 570

**1.** $311.28
**3.** $10.78

**5.** $1,425.06
**7.** $58.16

**9.** $102.31
**11.** $63.59

### Exercise 20–5, Page 575

**1.** (a) $1.20
   (b) $1.18
   (c) $1.18
   (d) $1.20
   (e) $1.23

**3.** Yes, natural premium equals cost of death claim.
**5.** Level $1,000 \, P^1_{25:\overline{5}|} = 1.94733$,
   $1,000 \, c_{25} = 1.88286$, $1,000 \, c_{26} = 1.91219$,
   $1,000 \, c_{27} = 1.94138$, $1,000 \, c_{28} = 1.98046$,
   $1,000 \, c_{29} = 2.02915$

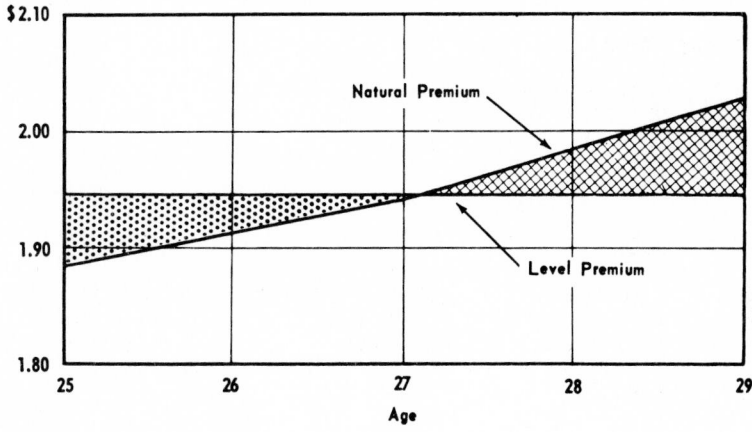

### Exercise 20–6, Page 581

**1.** (a) $1.73
   (b) 0
**3.** (a) $184.46
   (b) $1,000
**5.** (a) $175.65
   (b) $774.30
**7.** (a) $195.18
   (b) $678.62

### Exercise 20–7, Page 584

**1.** $143.78
**3.** See Exercise 20–6 for answers to Problems 1, 3, 5, and 7.

### Exercise 20–8, Page 586

**1.** (a) 304 days
   (b) $79.11
**3.** (a) 40 years and 168 days
   (b) $265.35
**5.** (a) 22 years and 242 days
   (b) $360.74

**Exercise 20–9, Page 589**

1. (a) $394.03
   (b) $15.86
   (c) $21.74
3. (a) $318.99
   (b) $11.42
   (c) $17.30
5. (a) $36.54
   (b) $2.93
   (c) $4.11
7. (a) $78.36
   (b) $6.39
   (c) $8.90
9. (a) $410.85
   (b) $17.01
   (c) $18.17
11. (a) $398.65
    (b) $16.17
    (c) $17.38

13. (a) $44.48
    (b) $99.15
15. (a) $2.46
    (b) $2.08, $2.26, $2.58, $3.17
17. (a) $11.31
    (b) $698.32
    (c) $175.41
    (d) $206.18
19. (a) 3 years and 313 days
    (b) a whole life policy of $1,000 and a cash value of $259.87
    (c) 28 years and 126 days
    (d) 30 years and 353 days
21. (a) $324.35
    (b) $789.48
    (c) $400.07
    (d) $470.25

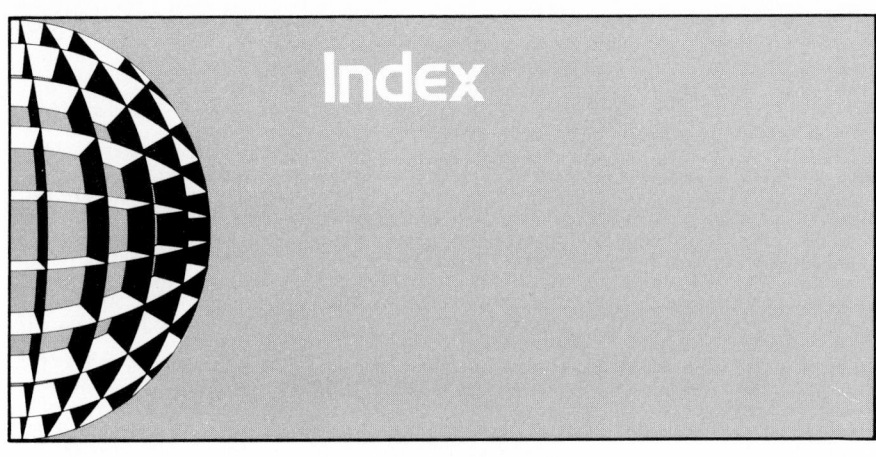

Index